Introduction to Business

Log on to the **Online Learning Center** *through*

glencoe.com!

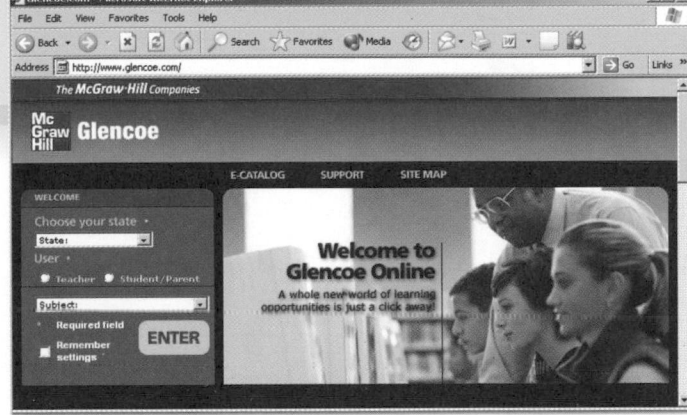

Integrated Academics

- Academic Applications:
  Math and English Language Arts
- Integrated Reading Strategies
- Science/Tech Trends
- Math Appendix
- Academic Vocabulary Glossary

New Student Edition Features

- Ask Standard & Poor's
- *BusinessWeek* Reader and Case Study
- Ethics in Business
- International Business
- Real World
- Real-World Business and Career Profile
- Unit Thematic Project
- Standardized Test Practice

Technology

- TeacherWorks™ Plus
- *ExamView®* Assessment Suite
- Vocabulary PuzzleMaker
- Presentation Plus!
- Interactive Student Edition
- Online Student Edition

Online Learning Center

- Curricula Correlations
- Answers to Section and Chapter Reviews
- Lesson Plans
- Performance Rubrics

GLENCOE
Introduction to
Business

Betty J. Brown
Ball State University

John E. Clow
National Council on Economic Education, New York, NY
Professor Emeritus, State University of New York, College at Oneonta

 **Glencoe**

New York, New York   Columbus, Ohio   Chicago, Illinois   Woodland Hills, California

Our Partners at McGraw-Hill

STANDARD &POOR'S

Standard & Poor's is the world's leading provider of independent investment research, indexes, and ratings. The investment data and analysis provided by *Standard and Poor's* are used around the world by financial decision-makers to help create growth and manage wealth. *Standard & Poor's* publishes the S&P 1200, the premier global equity performance benchmark; the S&P 500, the premier U.S. financial-market index; and credit ratings on more than 220,000 securities and funds worldwide.

BusinessWeek

BusinessWeek is the leading global resource for ground-breaking business news and news analysis that offers essential insight into the real world of business. *BusinessWeek* is the world's most widely read business magazine, with more than 8 million readers each week, including online and television viewers.

Notice: Information on featured companies, organizations, and their products and services is included for educational purposes only and does not present or imply endorsement of the *Introduction to Business* program.

 **Glencoe**

The *McGraw·Hill* Companies

Send all inquiries to:
Glencoe/McGraw-Hill
21600 Oxnard Street, Suite 500
Woodland Hills, CA 91367

ISBN: 978-0-07-874768-7   (Student Edition)
MHID: 0-07-874768-6   (Student Edition)
ISBN: 978-0-07-877694-6   (Teacher Wraparound Edition)
MHID: 0-07-877694-5   (Teacher Wraparound Edition)

1 2 3 4 5 6 7 8 9 079/043 11 10 09 08 07

Meet Our Authors

Dr. Betty J. Brown is a Professor of Business Information Systems Management and Coordinator of the Business and Marketing Education Program at Ball State University in Muncie, Indiana. She served on the faculty in business education and management at The University of Tennessee, Knoxville. In addition to teaching at the secondary and postsecondary levels, she has written articles and conducted workshops on the teaching of business and economic education. Dr. Brown has served as National President for Delta Pi Epsilon, national graduate honor society in business education, as Executive Director for the Policies Commission for Business and Economic Education, and is a recipient of the John Robert Gregg Award in business education.

Dr. John E. Clow is the Director of the Leatherstocking Center for Economic Education and Professor Emeritus of Business Education at the State University of New York, College at Oneonta. He has held professorial positions at a number of universities in Illinois and Iowa. He has been the Director of a number of national projects in personal finance and consumer economics for the National Council on Economic Education. He has held several college and university administrative positions, including president of Berkeley College in New York City. Dr. Clow has taught at the middle, high school, and college levels and has to his credit numerous speeches and publications in the areas of business and economic education.

Business and Career Education
Industry Advisory Board

Educational Reviewers

We wish to acknowledge the contributions of the following reviewers:

Teacher Wraparound Edition Table of Contents

CONNECT
students TO THE COMMUNITY,

Units

The thirty-five chapters in *Introduction to Business* are organized in eleven units, each with its own theme. Unit activities show you the "big picture," by providing activities and interviews that bring life to the world of business. The unit opener introduces two end-of-unit activities.

Real-World Business and Career Profile Preview

The unit opener introduces a real company that is profiled at the end of the unit. This preview includes a **Decision Making** question; something for students to think about as they begin the unit.

Unit 1

The Economy and You

peanutbutterlicious!

P.B. Loco café

Real-World Business and Career Profile | Preview

P.B.Loco produces and sells gourmet peanut butter in cafés and online. At the end of this unit, you will learn about the founders of P.B.Loco and how they achieved their success.

Decision Making Do you use a decision-making process every time you buy something?

Unit 1 **Thematic Project Preview**

Trends in the World of Business After completing the unit, you will research trends in the world of business to find out how they can affect business and workers.

Project Checklist As you read the chapters in this unit, use this checklist to prepare for the unit project.

✔ Think about how economic events affect workers you know.
✔ Consider how technology has evolved during your lifetime.
✔ Look for cultural diversity in your community.
✔ Notice how globalization affects business.

3

2

Thematic Project Preview

Each unit concludes with a thematic project based on a contemporary business issue. The thematic project is introduced here in the unit opener, along with a **Project Checklist**, to help students apply unit content to the thematic project activity.

real COMPANIES, and real CAREERS.

Real-World Business and Career Profile

This end-of-unit feature provides an interview with the owners of a successful and eclectic business. A follow-up critical thinking question prompts students to address real decisions business owners make every day.

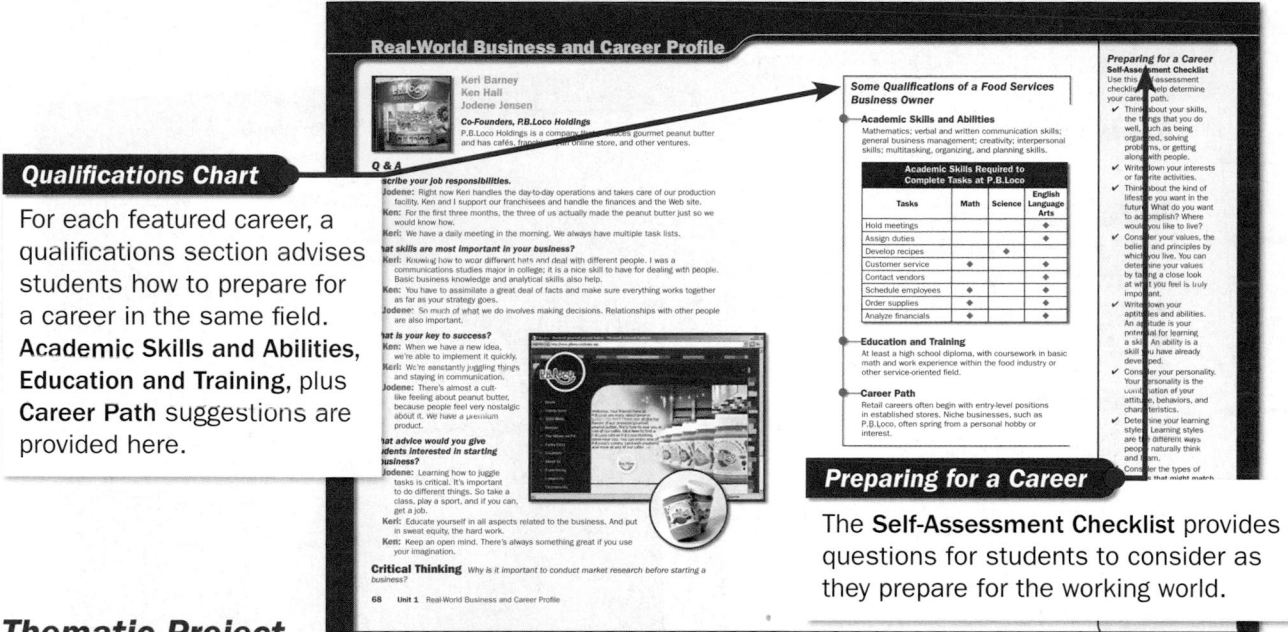

Qualifications Chart

For each featured career, a qualifications section advises students how to prepare for a career in the same field. **Academic Skills and Abilities, Education and Training,** plus **Career Path** suggestions are provided here.

Preparing for a Career

The **Self-Assessment Checklist** provides questions for students to consider as they prepare for the working world.

Thematic Project

Every unit concludes with a thematic project that explores an important issue in the dynamic world of business. Students will make decisions, conduct research, connect to their community, and develop a report.

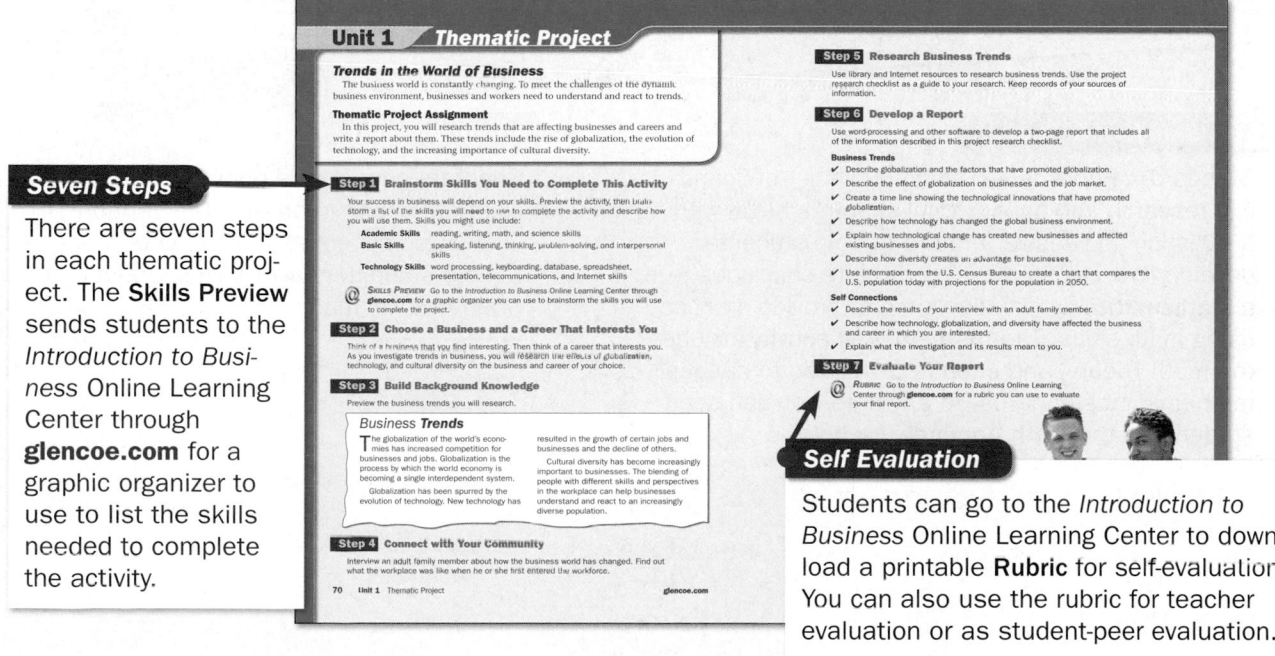

Seven Steps

There are seven steps in each thematic project. The **Skills Preview** sends students to the *Introduction to Business* Online Learning Center through **glencoe.com** for a graphic organizer to use to list the skills needed to complete the activity.

Self Evaluation

Students can go to the *Introduction to Business* Online Learning Center to download a printable **Rubric** for self-evaluation. You can also use the rubric for teacher evaluation or as student-peer evaluation.

Chapters

The chapters of *Introduction to Business* are organized around major business issues. They are divided logically into two sections and offer numerous learning strategies that will help your students get the most from their studies.

Chapter Objectives

Chapter Objectives by section preview the content students will learn.

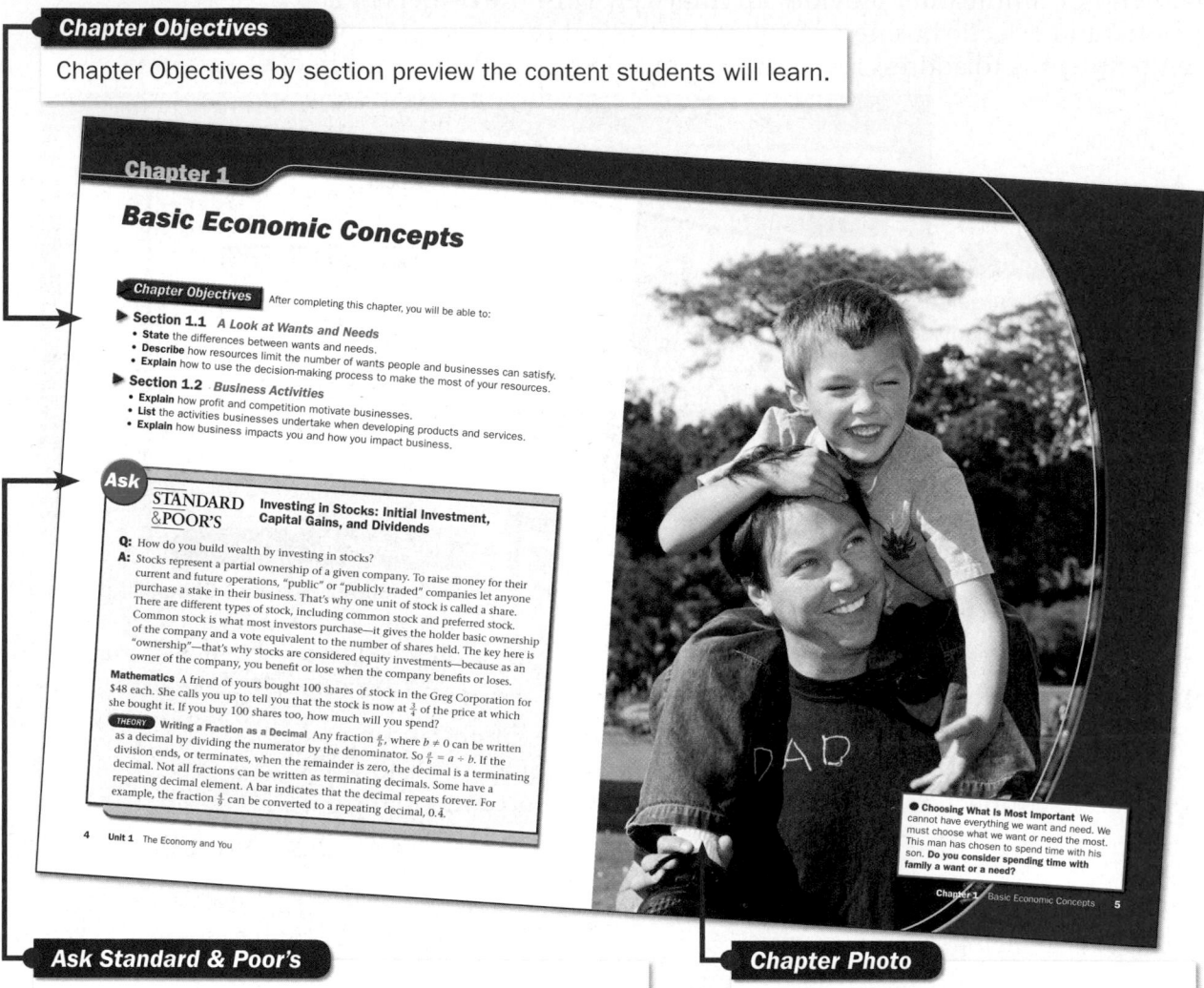

Ask Standard & Poor's

Standard & Poor's is a leading publisher of financial research and analysis. All chapters begin with a question-and-answer feature to help students develop financial literacy. The feature concludes with a **Mathematics** activity designed to provide practice using math skills. The mathematics activity includes the math **Theory**, and each is correlated to national mathematics standards. At any time, you can send students to the **Math Appendix** for help.

Chapter Photo

Chapters open with a photo to visually illustrate chapter content. The caption is followed by a question designed to help students start thinking about what they will read.

Chapter Review and Activities

The Chapter Review and Activities allow your students to practice their skills and reinforce understanding of key concepts in the chapter.

Review

Section Summaries, Vocabulary Review, and Review Key Concepts provide comprehension assessment.

Application Activities

Thinking, writing, technology, and ethics activities provide opportunities to assess skills and apply content to varied real-world situations.

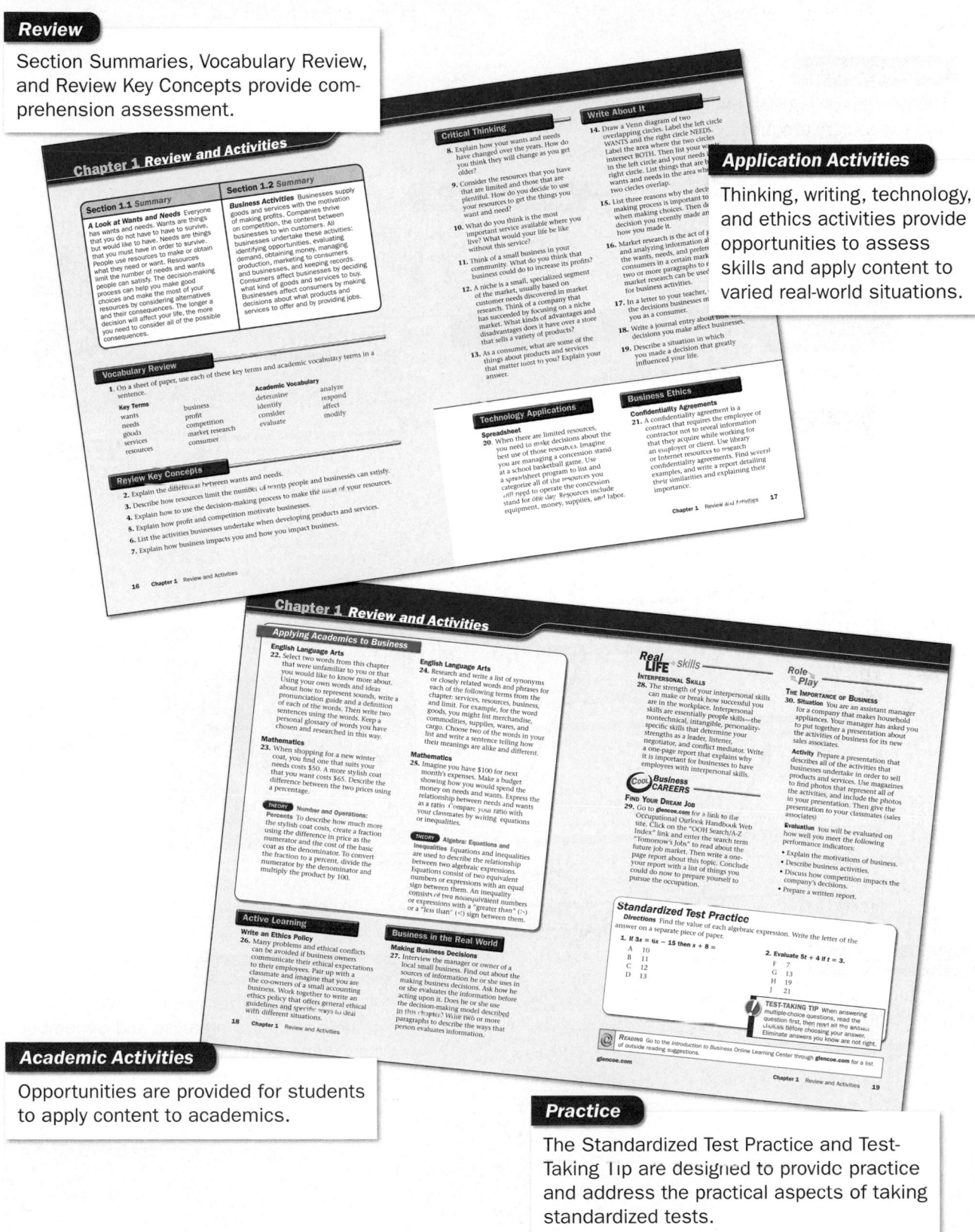

Academic Activities

Opportunities are provided for students to apply content to academics.

Practice

The Standardized Test Practice and Test-Taking Tip are designed to provide practice and address the practical aspects of taking standardized tests.

Student Edition Preview

Sections

Each chapter section begins with a Reading Guide to preview section content.

Reading Guide

The section objectives, main idea, key concepts, and vocabulary are previewed here.

Before You Read

A pre-reading question or statement will help students make a personal connection to content.

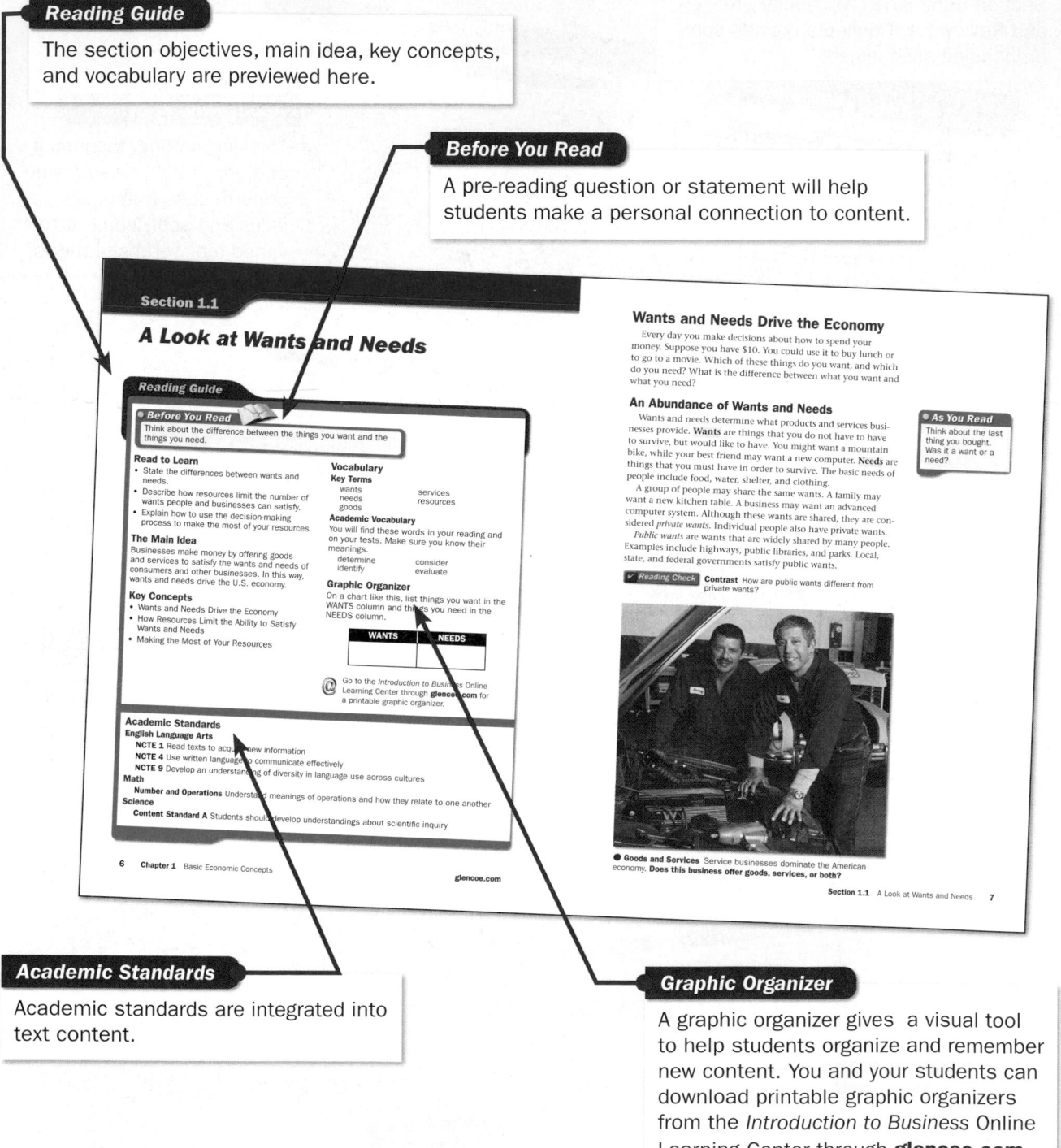

Section 1.1

A Look at Wants and Needs

Reading Guide

Before You Read
Think about the difference between the things you want and the things you need.

Read to Learn
- State the differences between wants and needs.
- Describe how resources limit the number of wants people and businesses can satisfy.
- Explain how to use the decision-making process to make the most of your resources.

The Main Idea
Businesses make money by offering goods and services to satisfy the wants and needs of consumers and other businesses. In this way, wants and needs drive the U.S. economy.

Key Concepts
- Wants and Needs Drive the Economy
- How Resources Limit the Ability to Satisfy Wants and Needs
- Making the Most of Your Resources

Vocabulary
Key Terms
wants
needs
goods
services
resources

Academic Vocabulary
You will find these words in your reading and on your tests. Make sure you know their meanings.
determine
identify
consider
evaluate

Graphic Organizer
On a chart like this, list things you want in the WANTS column and things you need in the NEEDS column.

WANTS	NEEDS

Go to the *Introduction to Business* Online Learning Center through **glencoe.com** for a printable graphic organizer.

Academic Standards
English Language Arts
NCTE 1 Read texts to acquire new information
NCTE 4 Use written language to communicate effectively
NCTE 9 Develop an understanding of diversity in language use across cultures
Math
Number and Operations Understand meanings of operations and how they relate to one another
Science
Content Standard A Students should develop understandings about scientific inquiry

6 **Chapter 1** Basic Economic Concepts

glencoe.com

Wants and Needs Drive the Economy

Every day you make decisions about how to spend your money. Suppose you have $10. You could use it to buy lunch or to go to a movie. Which of these things do you want, and which do you need? What is the difference between what you want and what you need?

An Abundance of Wants and Needs

Wants and needs determine what products and services businesses provide. **Wants** are things that you do not have to have to survive, but would like to have. You might want a mountain bike, while your best friend may want a new computer. **Needs** are things that you must have in order to survive. The basic needs of people include food, water, shelter, and clothing.

A group of people may share the same wants. A family may want a new kitchen table. A business may want an advanced computer system. Although these wants are shared, they are considered *private wants*. Individual people also have private wants.

Public wants are wants that are widely shared by many people. Examples include highways, public libraries, and parks. Local, state, and federal governments satisfy public wants.

✔ **Reading Check** **Contrast** How are public wants different from private wants?

As You Read
Think about the last thing you bought. Was it a want or a need?

● **Goods and Services** Service businesses dominate the American economy. **Does this business offer goods, services, or both?**

Section 1.1 A Look at Wants and Needs 7

Academic Standards

Academic standards are integrated into text content.

Graphic Organizer

A graphic organizer gives a visual tool to help students organize and remember new content. You and your students can download printable graphic organizers from the *Introduction to Business* Online Learning Center through **glencoe.com**.

Reading Strategies

Structured before, during, and after reading strategies are designed to enrich your students' reading skills.

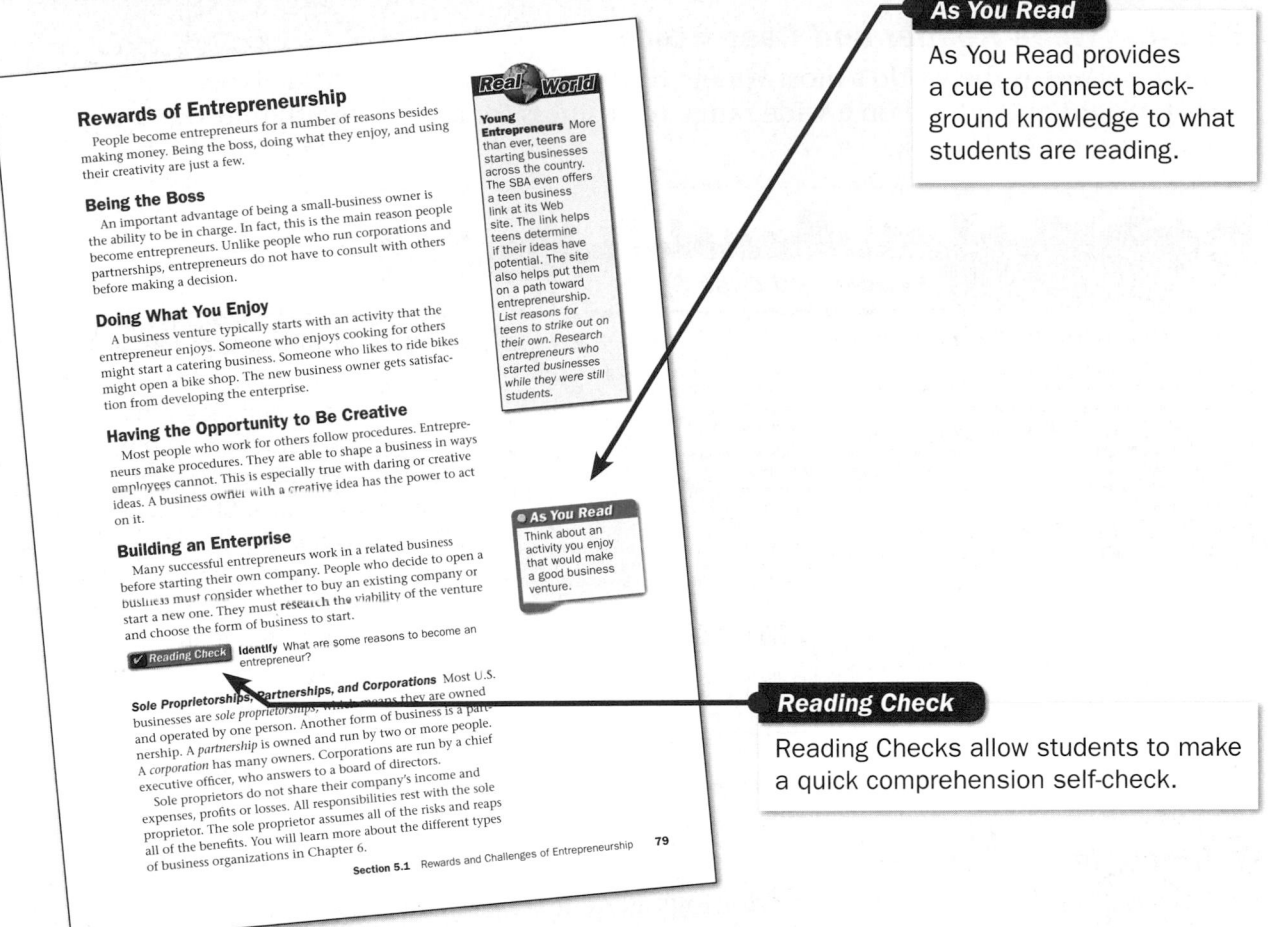

As You Read

As You Read

As You Read provides a cue to connect background knowledge to what students are reading.

Reading Check

Reading Checks allow students to make a quick comprehension self-check.

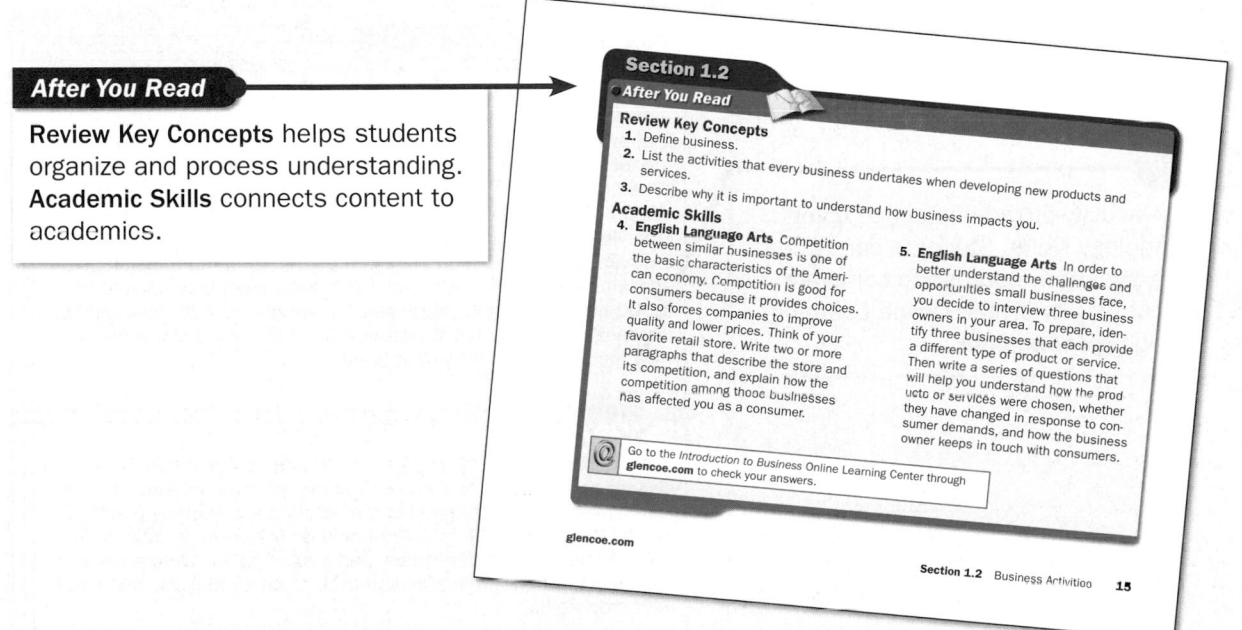

After You Read

Review Key Concepts helps students organize and process understanding. **Academic Skills** connects content to academics.

Features

The features in each chapter help students see the relevance between the classroom and the real world.

BusinessWeek Reader and Case Study

BusinessWeek is the world's most widely read business magazine. It delivers expert insight and advice on a wide range of business topics to more than 8 million readers each week.

BusinessWeek Reader and Case Study

From Adversity, Software Success

An idea for a new business can strike anywhere: In the shower, in the car, even in a dream. Mike Jetter got his in a cancer ward.

In 1994, the German programmer was stuck in a hospital room in Munich, following his second leukemia relapse and his second bone-marrow transplant. Given a 50% chance to live another year, Jetter needed a distraction badly.

At the time, so-called mind-mapping was all the rage in Europe. Hailed as a more creative way to think, it involves organizing ideas in a visual way, with big concepts written in a circle in the middle of a page, surrounded by smaller ideas that branch off from them. But with pencil and paper, you couldn't drag and drop, edit, or collaborate. So Jetter set out to write a computer program.

After his release from the hospital, he and his wife Bettina handed marketing for the product over to a German CD-ROM distributor,

assuming not much would come of it. Today the software has spawned a $30 million-a-year business called Mindjet, headquartered in San Francisco.

Now the Jetters are turning this desktop product into something companies can use broadly to help brainstorm, plan, collaborate, and organize a host of business activities.

 CASE STUDY Go to the *Introduction to Business* Online Learning Center through **glencoe.com** for the *BusinessWeek* Reader Case Study.

Active Learning

Team up with a classmate and work together to identify and research a successful company with a unique business concept. Write a brief presentation about the business. Give the presentation to your class.

Case Study and Active Learning

The *BusinessWeek* Reader is an excerpt from BusinessWeek magazine. You can send your students to the Online Learning Center through **glencoe.com** for a follow-up **Case Study** activity to print and complete. An **Active Learning** activity provides the opportunity for students to work on an extension activity individually or with a team.

Science/Tech TRENDS

Current trends in science and technology generate many business and career opportunities.

Science/Tech TRENDS

The Green Revolution

In 1798, Thomas Malthus, the great social scientist, showed that even as population increases geometrically (2, 4, 8, 16,...), the food supply increases arithmetically (1, 2, 3, 4,...). He predicted that hunger and conflict would be the result. In the 1960s, the Green Revolution promised to eliminate hunger by increasing crop yields. This was accomplished by using genetics to develop new varieties of grains and educating farmers in the technology of agriculture. Between 1960 and 1990, food production increased 1,000 percent, famine decreased 20 percent, caloric consumption increased 25 percent, and people around the world saw a rise in their incomes and standard of living.

Go to the *Introduction to Business* Online Learning Center through **glencoe.com** for links to Web sites where you can research how the technology of agriculture fueled the revolution in farming practices around the world. Look for information on irrigation strategies, the use of fertilizers and pesticides, and crop rotation. Write a few paragraphs about how farmers in countries, such as Mexico, increased their crop yields.

WebQuest

A WebQuest activity provides practice using related technology skills. Students can access links to Web sites they can use to complete the WebQuest activity on the Online Learning Center through **glencoe.com**.

Ethics in Business

Ethics in Business gives students the opportunity to form opinions and make decisions about ethical questions that arise in real life and in business.

?ETHICS in Business

A Conflict of Interest

- **Critical Reading** Life is full of important decisions. Think about the kinds of decisions that you make as you read the question below.

  You work as an event planner for a local company. You are in charge of hiring a caterer for the company's 10th anniversary celebration. You have bids from four caterers in town. One of the bids is from a caterer who is an old friend. His bid is higher than the three others.

- **Decision Making** Would your relationship with the caterer affect which company you would hire? Explain your answer.

Critical Reading

The feature begins with a **Critical Reading** statement to prepare students to evaluate the ethical situation. In **Decision Making**, students have the opportunity to answer a question about how they might handle the situation.

International Business

Here students will learn about cross-cultural business practices and concepts related to global trade.

International Business

Global Marketplace
More businesses that used to operate exclusively within the United States now market their products around the world. From farmers to fast-food franchisees to theme-park operators, businesspeople in every sector of the economy are considering entering the global marketplace. Even though companies may operate successfully in the U.S. market, an increasing number of them are thinking about "going international."

Examples of Language Across Cultures
  Q: In Italian, how do you say: "Hello, how are you?"
  A: Salve, come sta? (pronounced: Sălvā, kōmā stă?)

What are some other reasons a company might choose to enter a foreign market? What are some questions companies should ask before they enter a foreign market?

Language Across Cultures

Students are introduced to words and phrases in other languages, and asked a follow-up question.

Assessment

Introduction to Business features end-of-section and end-of-chapter review and activities. The varied assessments enable you and your students to evaluate understanding.

Section Assessment

Each section ends with review and academic questions.

After You Read

Assess comprehension with **Review Key Concepts** questions. Connect content to academics with the **Academic Skills** questions.

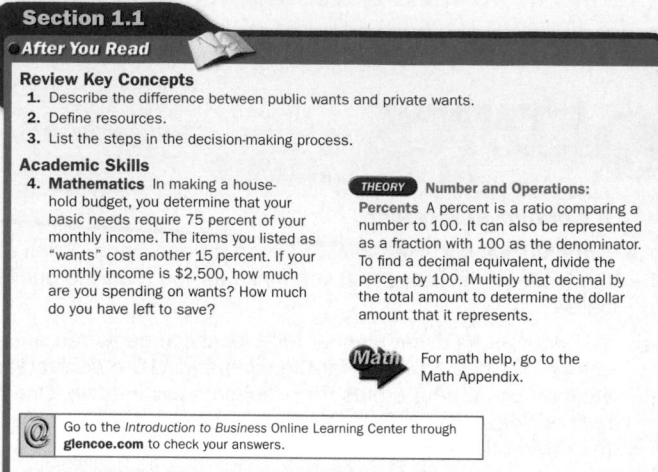

Section 1.1

After You Read

Review Key Concepts
1. Describe the difference between public wants and private wants.
2. Define resources.
3. List the steps in the decision-making process.

Academic Skills
4. **Mathematics** In making a household budget, you determine that your basic needs require 75 percent of your monthly income. The items you listed as "wants" cost another 15 percent. If your monthly income is $2,500, how much are you spending on wants? How much do you have left to save?

THEORY Number and Operations:
Percents A percent is a ratio comparing a number to 100. It can also be represented as a fraction with 100 as the denominator. To find a decimal equivalent, divide the percent by 100. Multiply that decimal by the total amount to determine the dollar amount that it represents.

Math For math help, go to the Math Appendix.

Go to the *Introduction to Business* Online Learning Center through **glencoe.com** to check your answers.

Chapter Review and Activities

The Chapter Review and Activities contains a varied review and activities.

Section Summaries

The summaries restate the main concepts of the section.

Critical Thinking

The Critical Thinking activities ask students to think more deeply to relate text to real situations.

Write About It

Here students will practice different types of writing.

Vocabulary Review

The vocabulary review includes **Key Terms** taught in section content. **Academic Vocabulary** helps students learn words that should be familiar to them from their reading and tests.

Review Key Concepts

Questions in the Review Key Concepts activity review student comprehension.

Technology Applications

Your students can practice technology skills and applications.

Business Ethics

Opportunities are provided for students to consider the ethical consequences of business decisions.

Chapter 1 Review and Activities

Section 1.1 Summary

A Look at Wants and Needs Everyone has wants and needs. Wants are things that you do not have to have to survive, but would like to have. Needs are things that you must have in order to survive. People use resources to make or obtain what they need or want. Resources limit the number of needs and wants people can satisfy. The decision-making process can help you make good choices and make the most of your resources by considering alternatives and their consequences. The longer a decision will affect your life, the more you need to consider all of the possible consequences.

Section 1.2 Summary

Business Activities Businesses supply goods and services with the motivation of making profits. Companies thrive on competition, the contest between businesses to win customers. All businesses undertake these activities: identifying opportunities, evaluating demand, obtaining money, managing production, marketing to consumers and businesses, and keeping records. Consumers affect businesses by deciding what kind of goods and services to buy. Businesses affect consumers by making decisions about what products and services to offer and by providing jobs.

Vocabulary Review

1. On a sheet of paper, use each of these key terms and academic vocabulary terms in a sentence.

Key Terms
wants
needs
goods
services
resources

business
profit
competition
market research
consumer

Academic Vocabulary
determine
identify
consider
evaluate

analyze
respond
affect
modify

Review Key Concepts

2. Explain the differences between wants and needs.
3. Describe how resources limit the number of wants people and businesses can satisfy.
4. Explain how to use the decision-making process to make the most of your resources.
5. Explain how profit and competition motivate businesses.
6. Identify the activities businesses undertake when developing products and services.
7. Explain how business impacts you and how you impact business.

Critical Thinking

8. Explain how your wants and needs have changed over the years. How do you think they will change as you get older?
9. Consider the resources that you have that are limited and those that are plentiful. How do you decide to use your resources to get the things you want and need?
10. What do you think is the most important service available where you live? What would your life be like without this service?
11. Think of a small business in your community. What do you think that business could do to increase its profits?
12. A niche is a small, specialized segment of the market, usually based on customer needs discovered in market research. Think of a company that has succeeded by focusing on a niche market. What kinds of advantages and disadvantages does it have over a store that sells a variety of products?
13. As a consumer, what are some of the decisions that products and services that matter most to you? Explain your answer.

Write About It

14. Draw a Venn diagram of two overlapping circles. Label the left circle WANTS and the right circle NEEDS. Label the area where the two circles intersect BOTH. Then list your wants in the left circle and your needs in the right circle. List things that are both wants and needs in the area where the two circles overlap.
15. List three reasons why the decision-making process is important to use when making choices. Then describe a decision you recently made and explain how you made it.
16. Market research is the act of gathering and analyzing information about the wants, needs, and preferences of consumers in a certain market. Write two or more paragraphs to explain how market research can be used as a basis for business activities.
17. In a letter to your teacher, explain how the decisions businesses make affect you as a consumer.
18. Write a journal entry about how the decisions you make affect businesses.
19. Describe a situation in which you made a decision that greatly influenced your life.

Technology Applications

Spreadsheet
20. When there are limited resources, you need to make decisions about the best use of those resources. Imagine you are managing a concession stand at a school basketball game. Use a spreadsheet program to list and categorize all of the resources you will need to operate the concession stand for one day. Resources include equipment, money, supplies, and labor.

Business Ethics

Confidentiality Agreements
21. A confidentiality agreement is a contract that requires the employee or contractor not to reveal information that they acquire while working for an employer or client. Use library or Internet resources to research confidentiality agreements. Find several examples, and write a report detailing their similarities and explaining their importance.

Chapter 1 Review and Activities

Chapter 1 Review and Activities **17**

Applying Academics

Four activities provide students with practice applying academic skills to business content.

Real-Life Skills

Activities designed to develop strong workplace and interpersonal skills.

Role Play

Role-play scenarios provide practice for competitive events. Performance evaluation information is provided.

Chapter 1 Review and Activities

Applying Academics to Business

English Language Arts
22. Select two words from this chapter that were unfamiliar to you or that you would like to know more about. Using your own words and ideas about how to represent sounds, write a pronunciation guide and a definition of each of the words. Then write two sentences using the words. Keep a personal glossary of words you have chosen and researched in this way.

Mathematics
23. When shopping for a new winter coat, you find one that suits your needs costs $50. A more stylish coat that you want costs $65. Describe the difference between the two prices using a percentage.

THEORY **Number and Operations: Percents** To describe how much more the stylish coat is, create a fraction using the difference in price as the numerator and the cost of the basic coat as the denominator. To convert the fraction to a percent, divide the numerator by the denominator and multiply the product by 100.

English Language Arts
24. Research and write a list of synonyms or closely related words and phrases for each of the following terms from the chapter: services, resources, business, and limit. For example, for the word goods, you might list merchandise, commodities, supplies, wares, and cargo. Choose two of the words in your list and write a sentence telling how their meanings are alike and different.

Mathematics
25. Imagine you have $100 for next month's expenses. Make a budget showing how you would spend the money on needs and wants. Express the relationship between needs and wants as a ratio. Compare your ratio with your classmates by writing equations or inequalities.

THEORY **Algebra: Equations and Inequalities** Equations and inequalities are used to describe the relationship between two algebraic expressions. Equations consist of two equivalent numbers or expressions with an equal sign between them. An inequality consists of two nonequivalent numbers or expressions with a "greater than" (>) or a "less than" (<) sign between them.

Active Learning

Write an Ethics Policy
26. Many problems and ethical conflicts can be avoided if business owners communicate their ethical expectations to their employees. Pair up with a classmate and imagine that you are the co-owners of a small accounting business. Work together to write an ethics policy that offers general ethical guidelines and specific ways to deal with different situations.

Business in the Real World

Making Business Decisions
27. Interview the manager or owner of a local small business. Find out about the sources of information he or she uses in making business decisions. Ask how he or she evaluates the information before acting upon it. Does he or she use the decision-making model described in this chapter? Write two or more paragraphs to describe the ways that person evaluates information.

18 Chapter 1 Review and Activities

Real LIFE skills

INTERPERSONAL SKILLS
28. The strength of your interpersonal skills can make or break how successful you are in the workplace. Interpersonal skills are essentially people skills—the nontechnical, intangible, personality-specific skills that determine your strengths as a leader, listener, negotiator, and conflict mediator. Write a one-page report that explains why it is important for businesses to have employees with interpersonal skills.

COOL Business CAREERS

FIND YOUR DREAM JOB
29. Go to glencoe.com for a link to the Occupational Outlook Handbook Web site. Click on the "OOH Search/A-Z Index" link and enter the search term "Tomorrow's Jobs" to read about the future job market. Then write a one-page report about this topic. Conclude your report with a list of things you could do now to prepare yourself to pursue the occupation.

Standardized Test Practice

Directions Find the value of each algebraic expression. Write the letter of the answer on a separate piece of paper.

1. If $3x = 6x - 15$ then $x + 8 =$
   - A 10
   - B 11
   - C 12
   - D 13

2. Evaluate $5t + 4$ if $t = 3$.
   - F 7
   - G 13
   - H 19
   - J 21

TEST-TAKING TIP When answering multiple-choice questions, read the question first, then read all the answer choices before choosing your answer. Eliminate answers you know are not correct.

READING Go to the Introduction to Business Online Learning Center through glencoe.com for a list of outside reading suggestions.

glencoe.com

Chapter 1 Review and Activities **19**

Role Play

THE IMPORTANCE OF BUSINESS
30. **Situation** You are an assistant manager for a company that makes household appliances. Your manager has asked you to put together a presentation about the activities of business for the new sales associates.

Activity Prepare a presentation that describes all of the activities that businesses undertake in order to sell products and services. Use magazines to find photos that represent all of the activities, and include the photos in your presentation. Then give the presentation to your classmates (sales associates).

Evaluation You will be evaluated on how well you meet the following performance indicators:
- Explain the motivations of business.
- Describe business activities.
- Discuss how competition impacts the company's decisions.
- Prepare a written report.

Active Learning

Here is an opportunity for students to "learn by doing," either on their own or as part of a team.

Business in the Real World

Activities to connect students to their local business community.

Cool Business Careers

Exploring careers can help your students set goals that can lead them to career success.

Standardized Test Practice

These activities provide an opportunity to sharpen students' test-taking skills. The activities also include a valuable **Test-Taking Tip**.

Choose *PROVEN* teaching solutions

Units

Units begin with well-organized, easy-to-reference pages preceding each unit of the student edition.

Overview

Chapter Objectives give you a preview of unit content.

Resources

A key is provided for coded teaching strategies, leveled instruction, and digital resources.

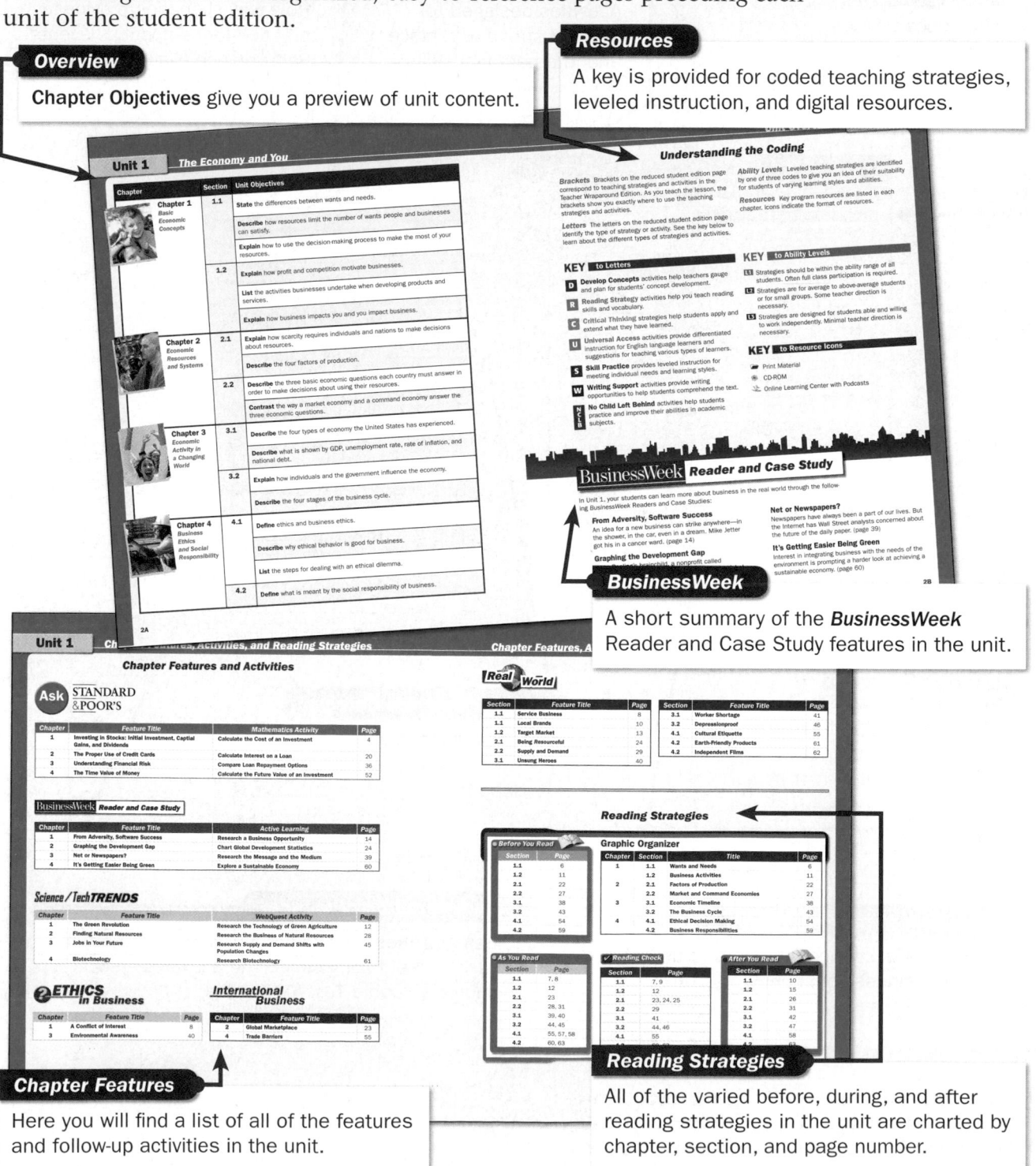

BusinessWeek

A short summary of the *BusinessWeek* Reader and Case Study features in the unit.

Chapter Features

Here you will find a list of all of the features and follow-up activities in the unit.

Reading Strategies

All of the varied before, during, and after reading strategies in the unit are charted by chapter, section, and page number.

for EFFECTIVE results.

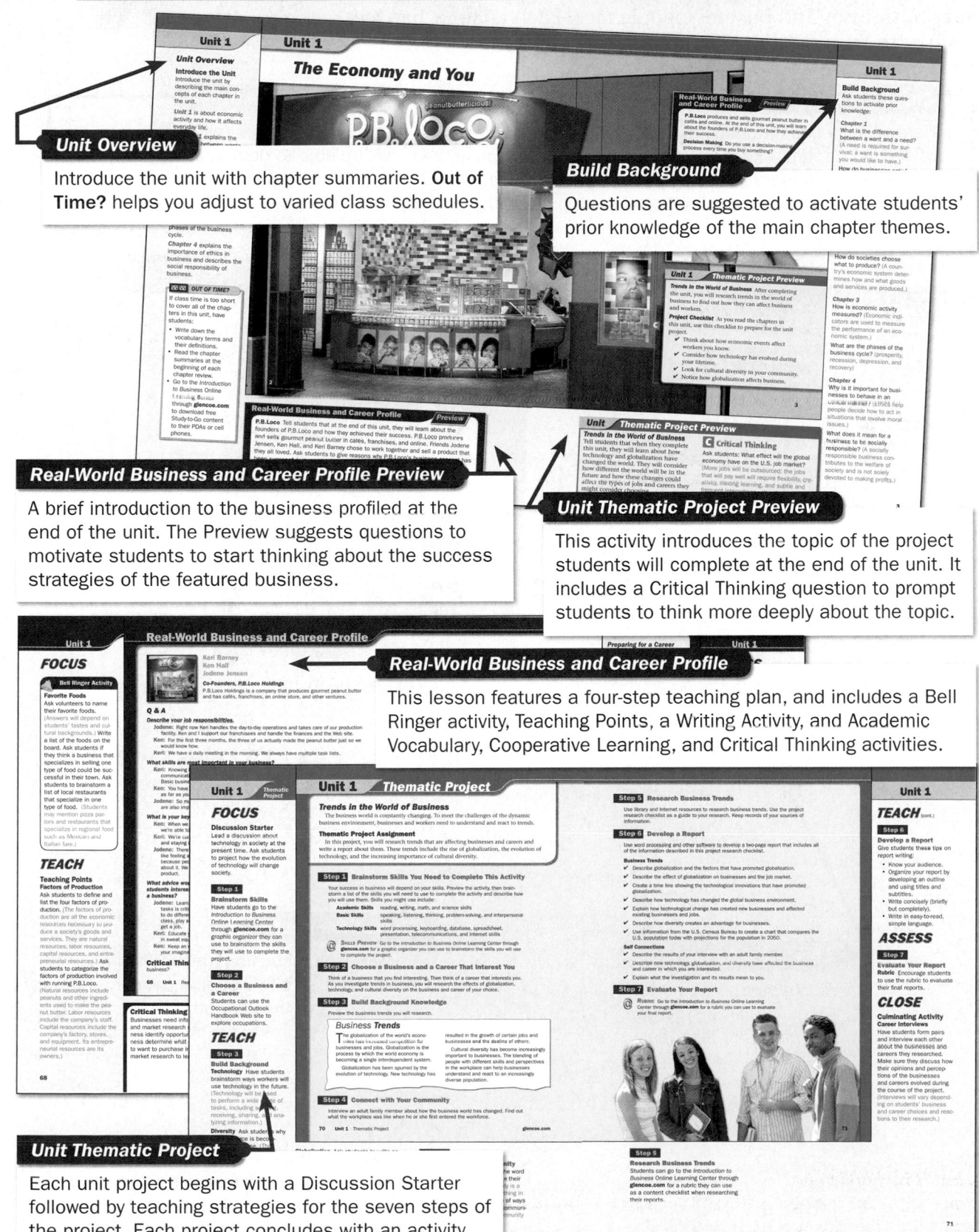

Unit Overview

Introduce the unit with chapter summaries. **Out of Time?** helps you adjust to varied class schedules.

Build Background

Questions are suggested to activate students' prior knowledge of the main chapter themes.

Real-World Business and Career Profile Preview

A brief introduction to the business profiled at the end of the unit. The Preview suggests questions to motivate students to start thinking about the success strategies of the featured business.

Unit Thematic Project Preview

This activity introduces the topic of the project students will complete at the end of the unit. It includes a Critical Thinking question to prompt students to think more deeply about the topic.

Real-World Business and Career Profile

This lesson features a four-step teaching plan, and includes a Bell Ringer activity, Teaching Points, a Writing Activity, and Academic Vocabulary, Cooperative Learning, and Critical Thinking activities.

Unit Thematic Project

Each unit project begins with a Discussion Starter followed by teaching strategies for the seven steps of the project. Each project concludes with an activity.

Chapters

Chapters in *Introduction to Business* are organized around the major issues businesses and businesspeople face. Each chapter has two sections, each with an individual lesson plan.

Chapter Overview

Here you will find **Introduce the Chapter**, a short summary of chapter content and main ideas, **Building Background**, with suggestions for accessing prior knowledge, and the answer to the **Ask Standard & Poor's** math problem and an extension activity.

Review the Objectives

Chapter Objectives tell how students will be able to demonstrate newly acquired knowledge.

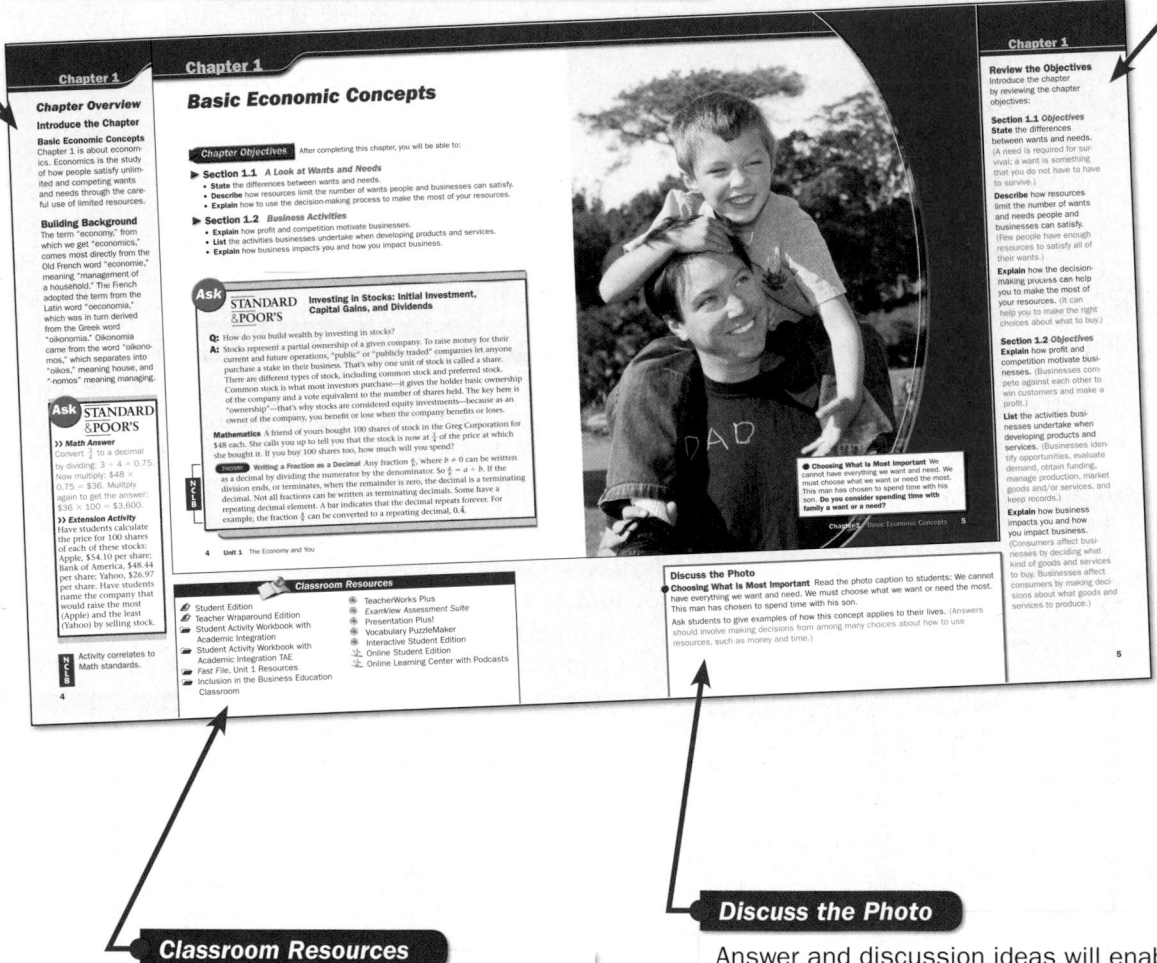

Classroom Resources

All chapter print and technology resources are listed here, to help you plan your lessons.

Discuss the Photo

Answer and discussion ideas will enable you to lead students to visually connect their own experiences to the chapter content. A follow-up question prompts further discussion.

Chapter Review and Activities

Answer Key

Answers and answer suggestions begin here. Extended answers are available on the *Introduction to Business* Online Learning Center Teacher site, which can be accessed through **glencoe.com**.

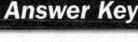

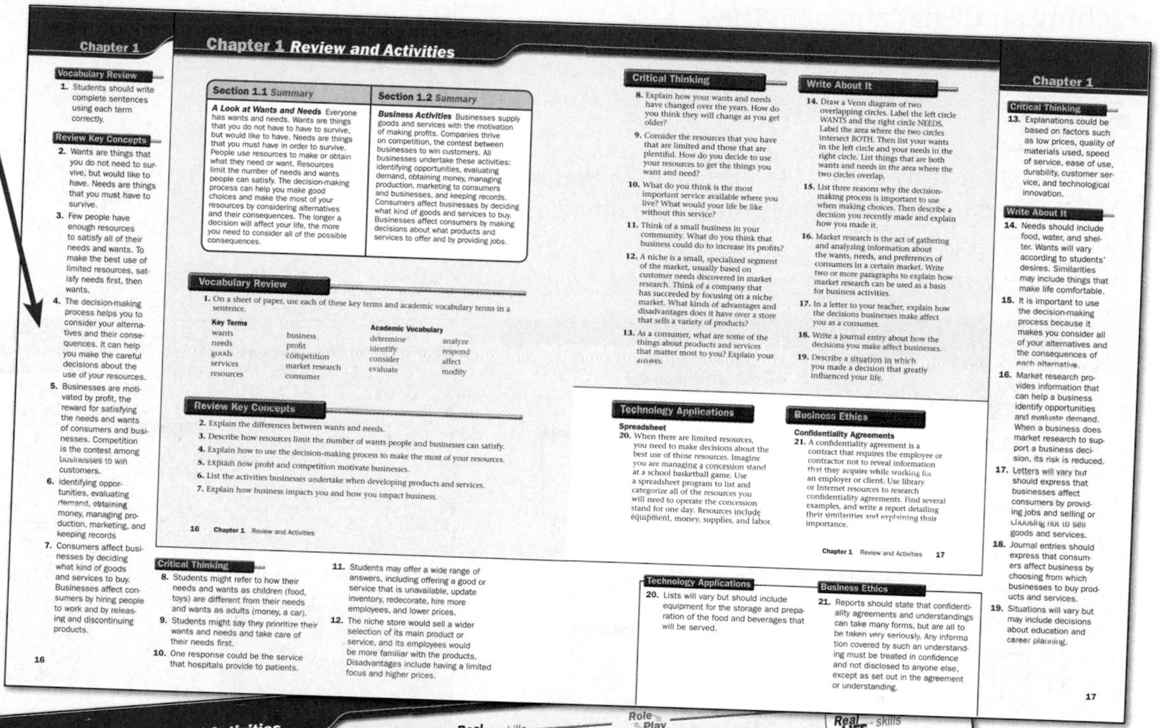

Chapter 1

Vocabulary Review
1. Students should write complete sentences using each term correctly.

Review Key Concepts
2. Wants are things that you do not need to survive, but would like to have. Needs are things that you must have to survive.
3. Few people have enough resources to satisfy all of their needs and wants. To make the best use of limited resources, satisfy needs first, then wants.
4. The decision-making process helps you to consider your alternatives and their consequences. It can help you make the careful decisions about the use of your resources.
5. Businesses are motivated by profit, the reward for satisfying the needs and wants of consumers and businesses. Competition is the contest among businesses to win customers.
6. Identifying opportunities, evaluating demand, obtaining money, managing production, marketing, and keeping records
7. Consumers affect businesses by deciding what kind of goods and services to buy. Businesses affect consumers by hiring people to work and by releasing and discontinuing products.

Chapter 1 Review and Activities

Section 1.1 Summary

A Look at Wants and Needs Everyone has wants and needs. Wants are things that you do not have to have to survive, but would like to have. Needs are things that you must have in order to survive. People use resources to make or obtain what they need or want. Resources limit the number of needs and wants people can satisfy. The decision-making process can help you make good choices and make the most of your resources by considering alternatives and their consequences. The longer a decision will affect your life, the more you need to consider all of the possible consequences.

Section 1.2 Summary

Business Activities Businesses supply goods and services with the motivation of making profits. Companies thrive on competition, the contest between businesses to win customers. All businesses undertake these activities: identifying opportunities, evaluating demand, obtaining money, managing production, marketing to consumers and businesses, and keeping records. Consumers affect businesses by deciding what kind of goods and services to buy. Businesses affect consumers by making decisions about what products and services to offer and by providing jobs.

Vocabulary Review

1. On a sheet of paper, use each of these key terms and academic vocabulary terms in a sentence.

Key Terms		Academic Vocabulary	
wants	business	determine	analyze
needs	profit	identify	respond
goods	competition	consider	affect
services	market research	evaluate	modify
resources	consumer		

Review Key Concepts

2. Explain the differences between wants and needs.
3. Describe how resources limit the number of wants people and businesses can satisfy.
4. Explain how to use the decision-making process to make the most of your resources.
5. Explain how profit and competition motivate businesses.
6. List the activities businesses undertake when developing products and services.
7. Explain how business impacts you and how you impact business.

16 Chapter 1 Review and Activities

Critical Thinking

8. Explain how your wants and needs have changed over the years. How do you think they will change as you get older?
9. Consider the resources that you have that are limited and those that are plentiful. How do you decide to use your resources to get the things you want and need?
10. What do you think is the most important service available where you live? What would your life be like without this service?
11. Think of a small business in your community. What do you think that business could do to increase its profits?
12. A niche is a small, specialized segment of the market, usually based on customer needs discovered in market research. Think of a company that has succeeded by focusing on a niche market. What kinds of advantages and disadvantages does it have over a store that sells a variety of products?
13. As a consumer, what are some of the things about products and services that matter most to you? Explain your answer.

Write About It

14. Draw a Venn diagram of two overlapping circles. Label the left circle WANTS and the right circle NEEDS. Label the area where the two circles intersect BOTH. Then list your wants in the left circle and your needs in the right circle. List things that are both wants and needs in the area where the two circles overlap.
15. List three reasons why the decision-making process is important to use when making choices. Then describe a decision you recently made and explain how you made it.
16. Market research is the act of gathering and analyzing information about the wants, needs, and preferences of consumers in a certain market. Write two or more paragraphs to explain how market research can be used as a basis for business activities.
17. In a letter to your teacher, explain how the decisions businesses make affect you as a consumer.
18. Write a journal entry about how the decisions you make affect businesses.
19. Describe a situation in which you made a decision that greatly influenced your life.

Technology Applications

Spreadsheet

20. When there are limited resources, you need to make decisions about the best use of those resources. Imagine you are managing a concession stand at a school basketball game. Use a spreadsheet program to list and categorize all of the resources you will need to operate the concession stand for one day. Resources include equipment, money, supplies, and labor.

Business Ethics

Confidentiality Agreements

21. A confidentiality agreement is a contract that requires the employee or contractor not to reveal information that they acquire while working for an employer or client. Use library or Internet resources to research confidentiality agreements. Find several examples, and write a report detailing their similarities and explaining their importance.

Chapter 1 Review and Activities 17

Critical Thinking
8. Students might refer to how their needs and wants as children (food, toys) are different from their needs and wants as adults (money, a car).
9. Students might say they prioritize their wants and needs and take care of their needs first.
10. One response could be the service that hospitals provide to patients.
11. Students may offer a wide range of answers, including offering a good or service that is unavailable, update inventory, redecorate, hire more employees, and lower prices.
12. The niche store would sell a wider selection of its main product or service, and its employees would be more familiar with the products. Disadvantages include having a limited focus and higher prices.

16

Technology Applications
20. Lists will vary but should include equipment for the storage and preparation of the food and beverages that will be served.

Business Ethics
21. Reports should state that confidentiality agreements and understandings can take many forms, but are all to be taken very seriously. Any information covered by such an understanding must be treated in confidence and not disclosed to anyone else, except as set out in the agreement or understanding.

Chapter 1

Critical Thinking
13. Explanations could be based on factors such as low prices, quality of materials used, speed of service, ease of use, durability, customer service, and technological innovation.

Write About It
14. Needs should include food, water, and shelter. Wants will vary according to students' desires. Similarities may include things that make life comfortable.
15. It is important to use the decision-making process because it makes you consider all of your alternatives and the consequences of each alternative.
16. Market research provides information that can help a business identify opportunities and evaluate demand. When a business does market research to support a business decision, its risk is reduced.
17. Letters will vary but should express that businesses affect consumers by providing jobs and selling or choosing not to sell goods and services.
18. Journal entries should express that consumers affect business by choosing from which businesses to buy products and services.
19. Situations will vary but may include decisions about education and career planning.

17

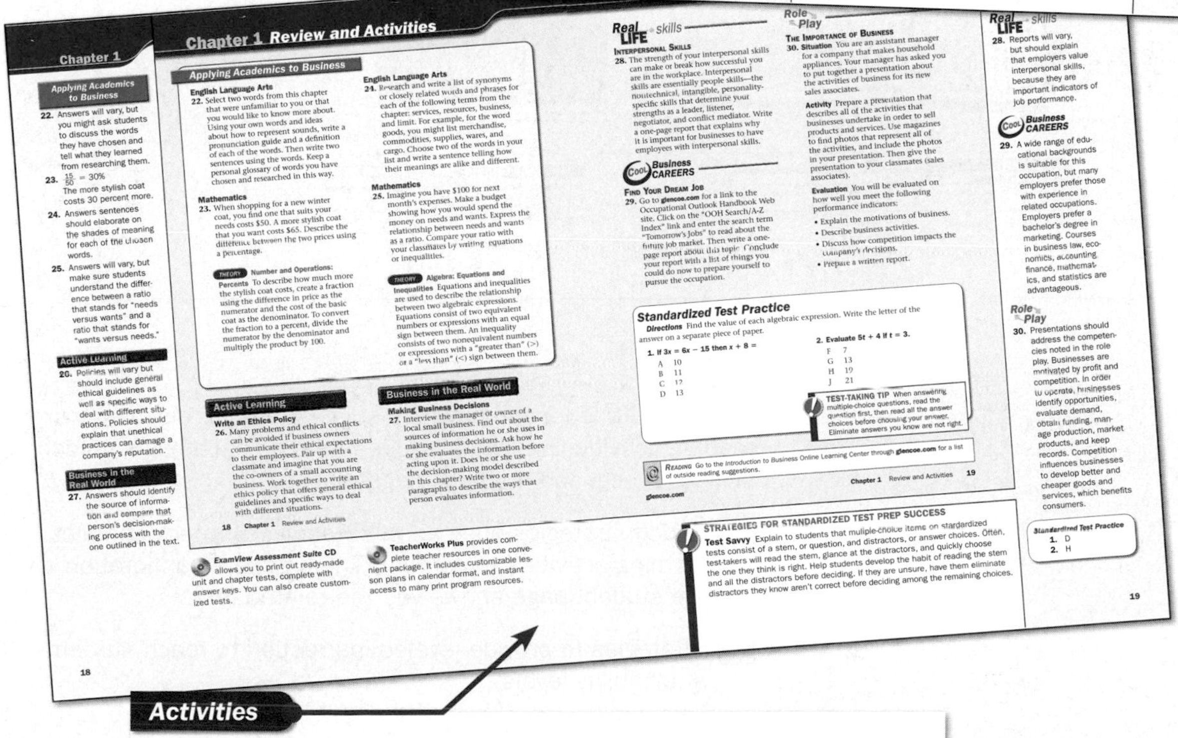

Chapter 1

Applying Academics to Business
22. Answers will vary, but you might ask students to discuss the words they have chosen and tell what they learned from researching them.
23. $\frac{15}{50}$ = 30%
The more stylish coat costs 30 percent more.
24. Answers sentences should elaborate on the shades of meaning for each of the chosen words.
25. Answers will vary, but make sure students understand the difference between a ratio that stands for "needs versus wants" and a ratio that stands for "wants versus needs."

Active Learning
26. Policies will vary but should include general ethical guidelines as well as specific ways to deal with different situations. Policies should explain that unethical practices can damage a company's reputation.

Business in the Real World
27. Answers should identify the source of information and compare that person's decision-making process with the one outlined in the text.

Chapter 1 Review and Activities

Applying Academics to Business

English Language Arts

22. Select two words from this chapter that were unfamiliar to you or that you would like to know more about. Using your own words and ideas about how to represent sounds, write a pronunciation guide and a definition of each of the words. Then write two sentences using the words. Keep a personal glossary of words you have chosen and researched in this way.

Mathematics

23. When shopping for a new winter coat, you find one that suits your needs cost $50. A more stylish coat that you want costs $65. Describe the difference between the two prices using a percentage.

Number and Operations: Percents To describe how much more the stylish coat costs, create a fraction using the difference in price as the numerator and the cost of the basic coat as the denominator. To convert the fraction to a percent, divide the numerator by the denominator and multiply the product by 100.

English Language Arts

24. Research and write a list of synonyms or closely related words and phrases for each of the following terms from the chapter: services, resources, business, goods, wants, and commodities, supplies, wares, and cargo. Choose two of the words in your list and write a sentence telling how their meanings are alike and different.

Mathematics

25. Imagine you have $100 for next month's expenses. Make a budget showing how you would spend the money on needs and wants. Express the relationship between needs and wants as a ratio. Compare your ratio with your classmates by writing equations or inequalities.

Algebra: Equations and Inequalities Equations and inequalities are used to describe the relationship between two algebraic expressions. Equations consist of two equivalent numbers or expressions with an equal sign between them. An inequality consists of two nonequivalent numbers or expressions with a "greater than" (>) or a "less than" (<) sign between them.

Active Learning

Write an Ethics Policy

26. Many problems and ethical conflicts can be avoided if business owners communicate their ethical expectations to their employees. Pair up with a classmate and imagine that you are the co-owners of a small accounting business. Work together to write an ethics policy that offers general ethical guidelines and specific ways to deal with different situations.

Business in the Real World

Making Business Decisions

27. Interview the manager or owner of a local small business. Find out about the sources of information he or she uses in making business decisions. Ask how he or she evaluates the information before acting upon it. Does he or she use the decision-making model described in this chapter? Write two or more paragraphs to describe the ways that person evaluates information.

18 Chapter 1 Review and Activities

Real LIFE skills

Interpersonal Skills

28. The strength of your interpersonal skills can make or break how successful you are in the workplace. Interpersonal skills are essentially people skills—the nontechnical, intangible, personality-specific skills that determine your strengths as a leader, listener, negotiator, and conflict mediator. Write a one-page report that explains why it is important for businesses to have employees with interpersonal skills.

Cool Business CAREERS

Find Your Dream Job

29. Go to **glencoe.com** for a link to the Occupational Outlook Handbook Web site. Click on the "OOH Search/A-Z Index" link and enter the search term "Tomorrow's Jobs" to read about the future job market. Then write a one-page report about this topic. Conclude your report with a list of things you could do now to prepare yourself to pursue the occupation.

Role Play

The Importance of Business

30. **Situation** You are an assistant manager for a company that makes household appliances. Your manager has asked you to put together a presentation about the activities of business for its new sales associates.

Activity Prepare a presentation that describes all of the activities that businesses undertake in order to sell products and services. Use magazines to find photos that represent all of the activities, and include the photos in your presentation. Then give the presentation to your classmates (sales associates).

Evaluation You will be evaluated on how well you meet the following performance indicators:
- Explain the motivations of business.
- Describe business activities.
- Discuss how competition impacts the company's decisions.
- Prepare a written report.

Standardized Test Practice

Directions Find the value of each algebraic expression. Write the letter of the answer on a separate piece of paper.

1. If $3x = 6x - 15$ then $x + 8 =$
A 10
B 11
C 12
D 13

2. Evaluate $5t + 4$ if $t = 3$.
F 7
G 13
H 19
J 21

TEST-TAKING TIP When answering multiple-choice questions, read the question first, then read all the answer choices before choosing your answer. Eliminate answers you know are not right.

Reading Go to the Introduction to Business Online Learning Center through **glencoe.com** for a list of outside reading suggestions.

Chapter 1 Review and Activities 19

ExamView Assessment Suite CD allows you to print out ready-made unit and chapter tests, complete with answer keys. You can also create customized tests.

TeacherWorks Plus provides complete teacher resources in one convenient package. It includes customizable lesson plans in calendar format, and instant access to many print program resources.

STRATEGIES FOR STANDARDIZED TEST PREP SUCCESS
Test Savvy Explain to students that multiple-choice items on standardized tests consist of a stem, or question, and distractors, or answer choices. Often, test-takers will read the stem, glance at the distractors, and quickly choose the one they think is right. Help students develop the habit of reading the stem and all the distractors before deciding. If they are unsure, have them eliminate distractors they know aren't correct before deciding among the remaining choices.

18

Real LIFE skills
28. Reports will vary, but should explain that employers value interpersonal skills, because they are important indicators of job performance.

Cool Business CAREERS
29. A wide range of educational backgrounds is suitable for this occupation, but many employers prefer those with experience in related occupations. Employers prefer a bachelor's degree in marketing. Courses in business law, economics, accounting, finance, mathematics, and statistics are advantageous.

Role Play
30. Presentations should address the competencies noted in the role play. Businesses are motivated by profit and competition. In order to operate, businesses identify opportunities, evaluate demand, obtain funding, manage production, market products, and keep records. Competition influences businesses to develop better and cheaper goods and services, which benefits consumers.

Standardized Test Practice
1. D
2. H

19

Activities

Academic and real world application answers are here, plus talking points on **STRATEGIES FOR STANDARDIZED TEST PREP SUCCESS.**

Sections

Each chapter has two sections. Each section has a six-part **Glencoe Classroom Management Plan**. Each lesson features teaching suggestions, background information, point-of-use teaching strategies, leveled activities for differentiated instruction, and answer keys. Bracketed letters on the reduced student edition pages correspond to teaching strategies in the Teacher Wraparound Edition, showing you exactly where to use the teaching strategies and activities.

FOCUS

A **Bell-Ringer Activity** begins the lesson, then **Preteaching** activities assure that all students have the same background and preparation.

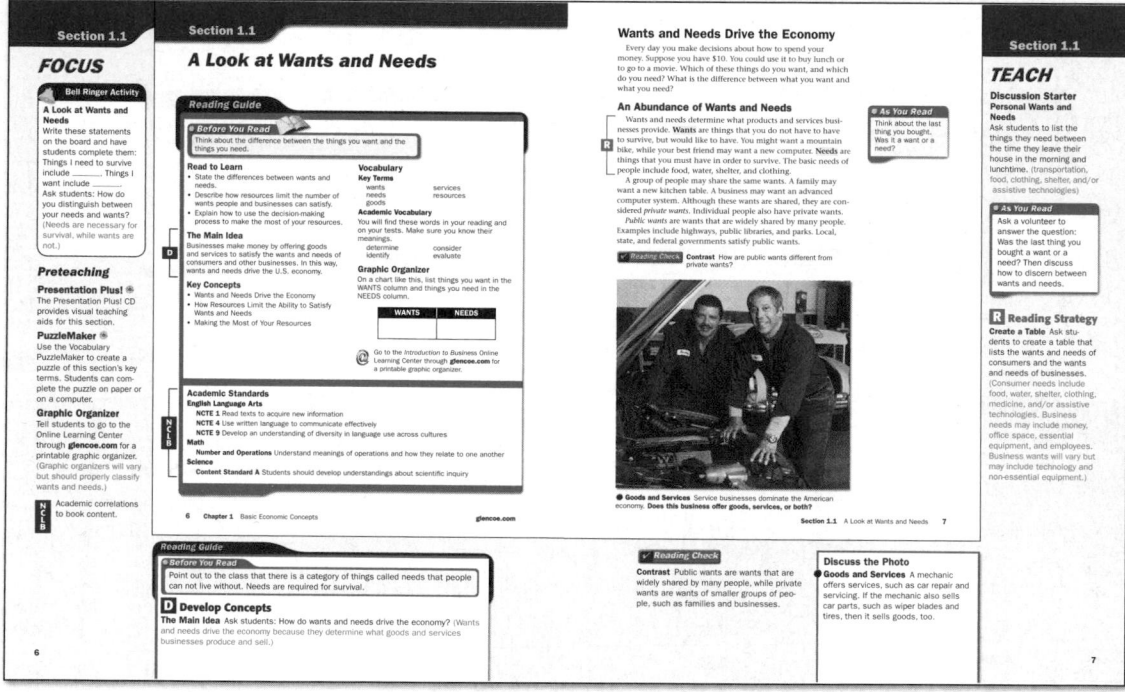

TEACH

This part of the lesson provides suggestions for discussion, reading activities, answers to questions on each page, guided skills practice, and resource suggestions.

R Coded strategies such as this Reading Strategy connect learning activities to content. The bracketed annotation on the student page shows you the related text.

S Strategies to provide leveled instruction to reach students at all ability levels.

ASSESS

Review opportunities enable you to evaluate your students' needs.

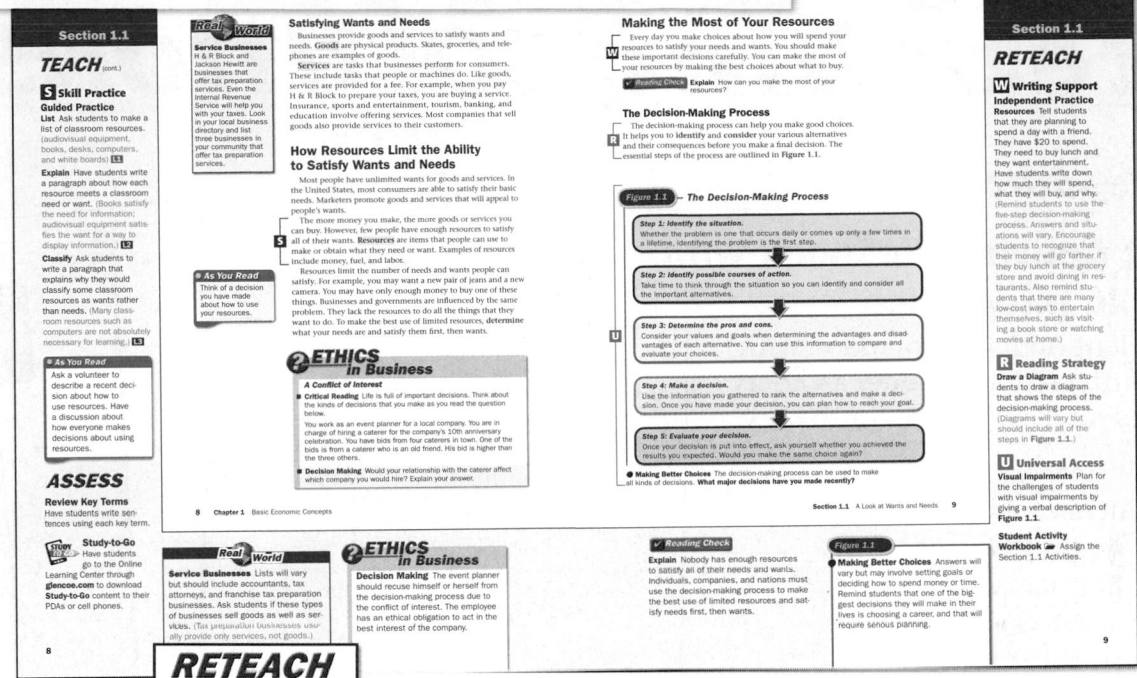

RETEACH

Independent writing practice, reading strategies, and enrichment activities are provided to reinforce lesson content. The variety of activities provided in RETEACH allows your students to assimilate knowledge using their varied learning styles.

W Activities for demonstrating understanding in writing are provided here.

U Strategies to reach all students in the classroom.

C Questions are designed to help students apply and extend what they learned.

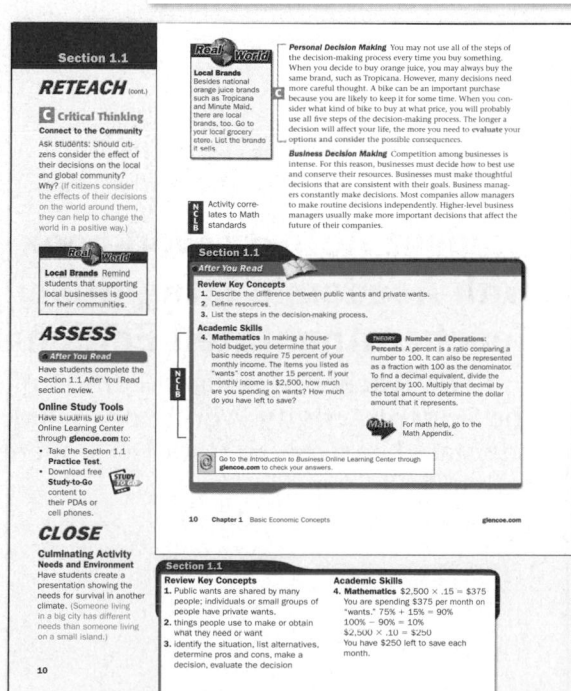

ASSESS

Re-evaluate student comprehension with varied assignments. Answers for the After You Read section review are provided.

CLOSE

Provides a Culminating Activity designed to use new knowledge in an independent assignment. The CLOSE activity helps students make the connection between what they read and its meaning and application to the real world.

EXPLORE *teaching* SOLUTIONS

Print Resources

Student Activity Workbook with Academic Integration

The Student Activity Workbook with Academic Integration includes a variety of activities for each chapter in the text.

- Note-Taking
- Academics
  - English Language Arts
  - Mathematics
  - Science
  - Social Studies
- Study Skills
- Test-Prep
- Test-Taking
- Content Vocabulary
- Academic Vocabulary

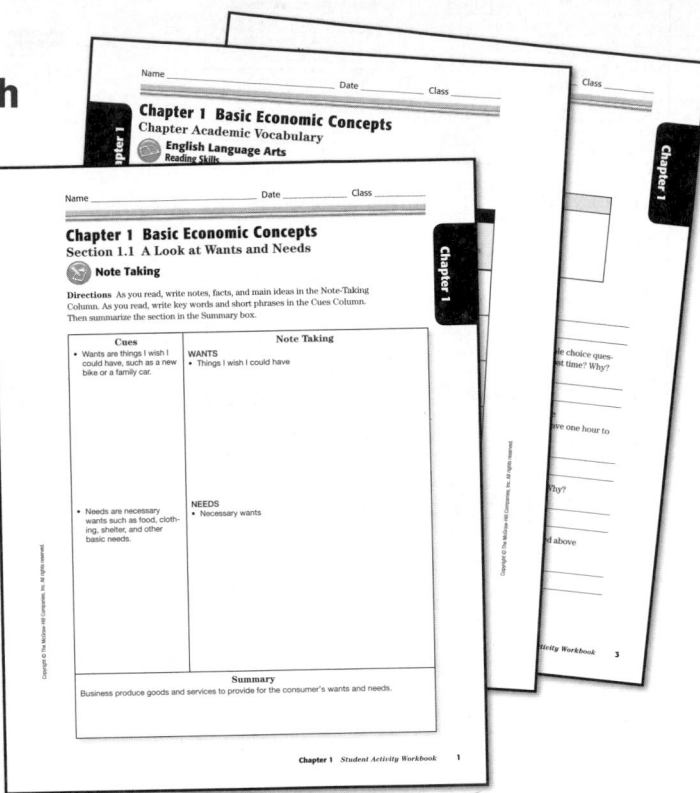

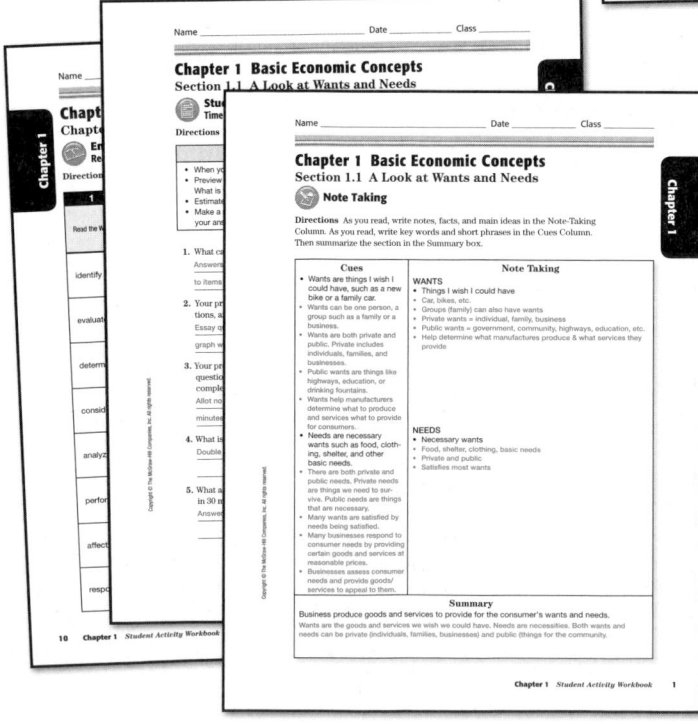

Student Activity Workbook with Academic Integration Teacher Annotated Edition

The Teacher Annotated Edition of the Student Activity Workbook includes annotated answers to all of the student activities.

for PLANNING and instructional SUPPORT.

Fast File Unit Resources

These booklets provide teaching materials and student activities to reinforce content.

Teacher Materials

- Lesson Plans
- Answer Keys
- Performance Rubrics

Student Materials

- Lesson Summaries with Key Terms and Academic Vocabulary
- Graphic Organizers
- Reading Activities
- Self-Checks
- *BusinessWeek* Reader Case Studies

Business Plan Project Workbook

The Business Plan Project Workbook teaches the essential elements of a business plan. It provides simple step-by-step directions for students to write their own business plans. A business plan template is available on the *Introduction to Business* Online Learning Center, which can be accessed through **glencoe.com**.

Business Plan Project Workbook Teacher Manual

The Business Plan Project Workbook Teacher Manual includes teaching suggestions for each section of the business plan, extension activities, and an answer key.

Technology Solutions

TeacherWorks™ Plus

TeacherWorks Plus gives you instant access to a variety of useful program resources in one easy-to-use CD. The software provides a calendar format for you to plan lessons, manage daily activities, access textbook materials, and utilize Internet resources. TeacherWorks Plus includes built-in lesson plans that can be customized to meet your individual classroom needs. It also includes links to printable program resources:

Printable Program Resources

Teacher Materials

- Lesson Plans
- Answer Keys
- Performance Rubrics

Student Materials

- Lesson Summaries with Key Terms and Academic Vocabulary
- Graphic Organizers
- Reading Activities
- Self Checks
- *BusinessWeek* Reader Case Studies
- Unit Thematic Project Academic Skills Preview Worksheets
- Unit Thematic Project Self-Assessment Rubrics
- Outside Reading Suggestions

Virtual Business

Virtual Business is a suite of business and marketing visual simulations that engage students in practical application. Topics covered include Marketing, Introduction to Business, Management, Supervision, Sports Marketing and Management, Retailing, and Entrepreneurship.

Virtual Business Retailing

Virtual Business Retailing is simulation of a convenience store that motivates students to want to learn more about business and marketing. Students control pricing, promotion, merchandising, market research, and more.

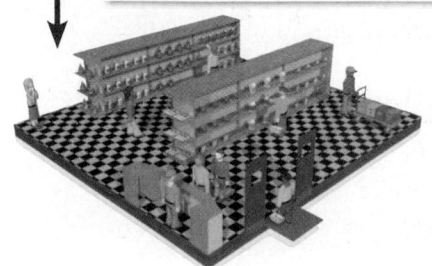

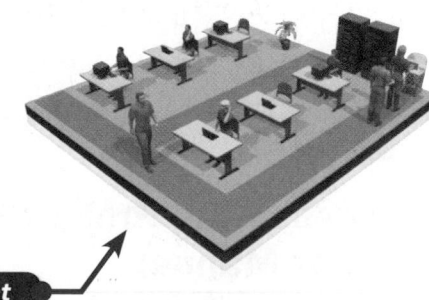

Virtual Business Management

Virtual Business Management is a simulation of a distribution business. Students locate and build a business, hire and supervise employees, deal with unions and strikes, and much more.

Interactive Student Edition

The Interactive Student Edition CD includes the complete text of the student edition, formatted like the hardbound book, in a pdf on CD, viewable through Adobe Acrobat Reader®. With Glencoe's Interactive Student Edition, you can search through a multitude of materials quickly, and click on the hotlinks to locate documents correlated to the Student Edition.

ExamView Assessment Suite

Streamline assessment from start to finish with the *ExamView Assessment Suite* CD. The *ExamView® Assessment Suite* (including the Test Generator and Test Manager) is a comprehensive solution for creating, administering, and scoring tests. It provides an accurate and exhaustive source of test items for a wide variety of examination styles. It contains thousands of test questions organized by chapter and unit. This easy-to-use software will help you to quickly create customized chapter, unit, midterm, or final assessments.

Use the ExamView Test Generator to:

- Create a paper test in fewer than five minutes.
- Print multiple versions of the same test.
- Enter your own questions.
- Develop tests using state and national standards.
- Prepare an online test, study guide, and worksheet.
- Upload tests to WebCT and Blackboard.

Use the ExamView Test Manager to:

- Create a class roster.
- Automatically score a paper test using a scanner.
- Administer and score an online test.
- Prepare a variety of useful class and student reports.

Technology Resources

Vocabulary PuzzleMaker

The Vocabulary Puzzlemaker CD is an easy-to-use program that lets you create crossword puzzles, word search puzzles, and jumble puzzles using content vocabulary or academic vocabulary. You can print the puzzles you create, or have students complete the puzzles on the computer.

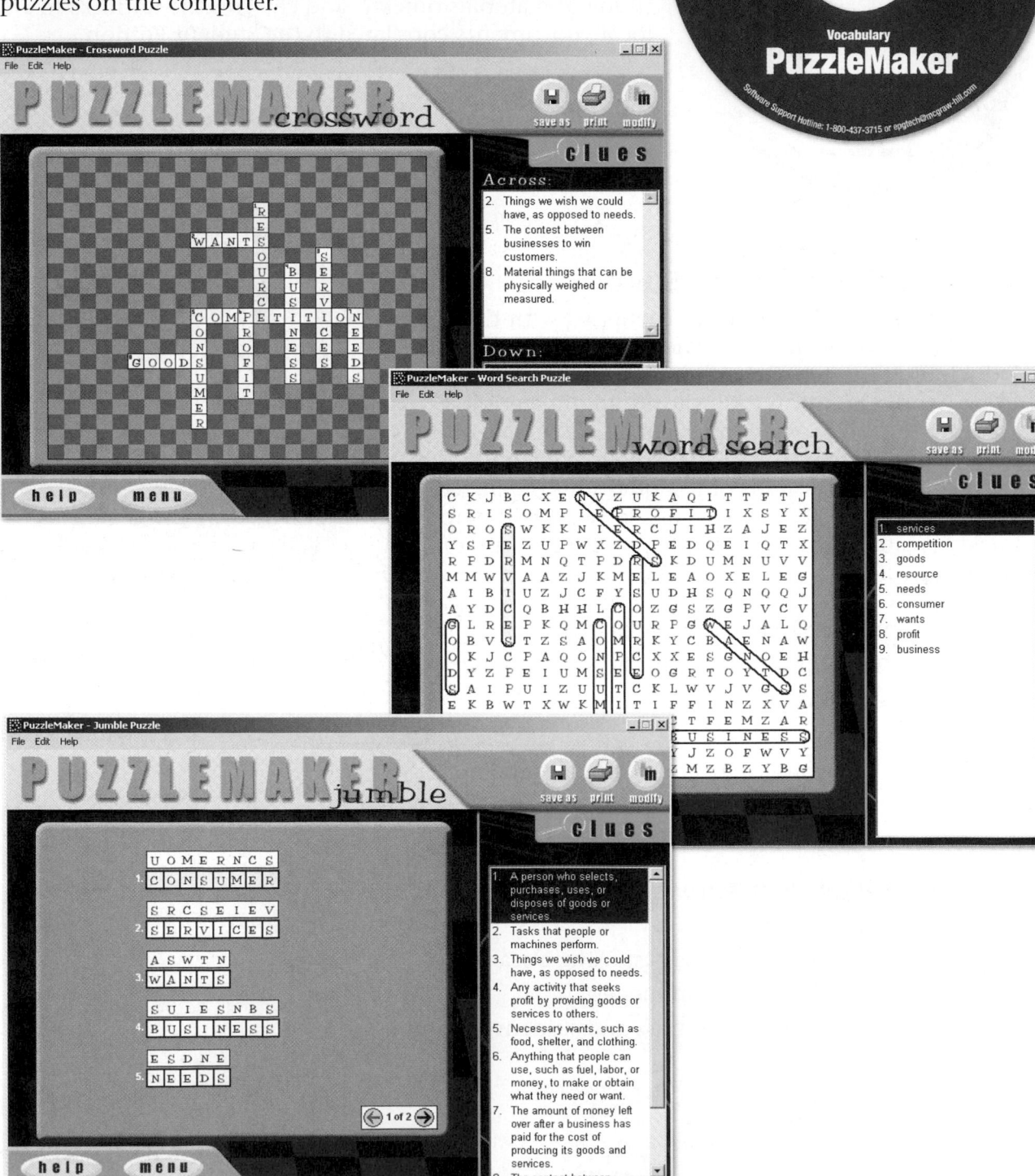

Presentation Plus!

The *Introduction to Business* Presentation Plus! CD provides visually motivating presentations that enable teachers to present dynamic lessons for every section in *Introduction to Business*. The PowerPoint® presentations, which can be edited and customized, include text highlights, graphic organizers, charts, graphs, and figures. It also includes chapter assessment presentations that can be used with TurningPoint® student response systems.

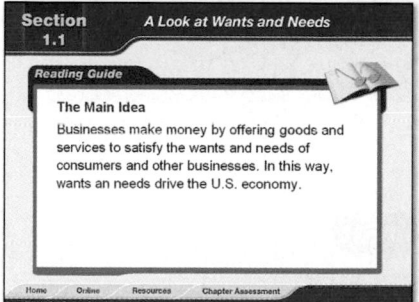

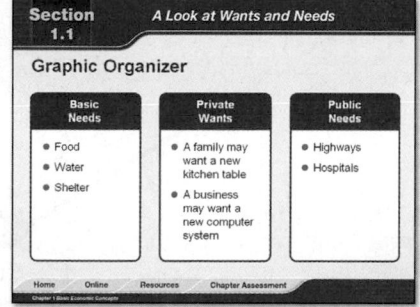

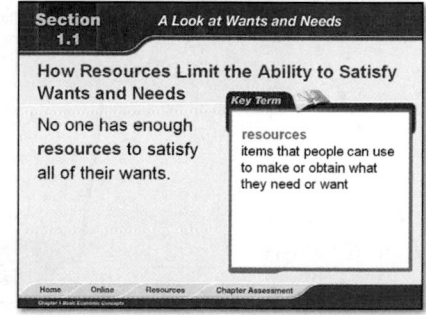

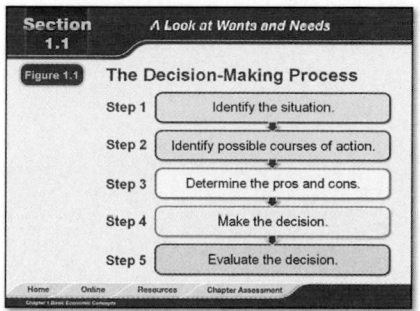

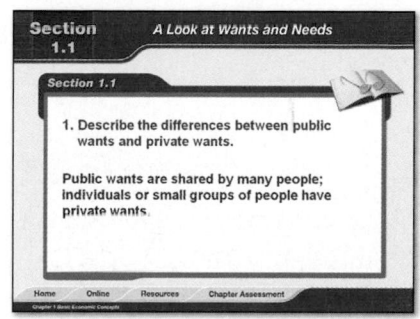

Technology Resources

How to Access the Online Learning Center

Follow these steps to access the textbook resources at the *Introduction to Business* Online Learning Center.

Step 1
Go to **glencoe.com**.

Step 2
Select your state from the pull-down menu.

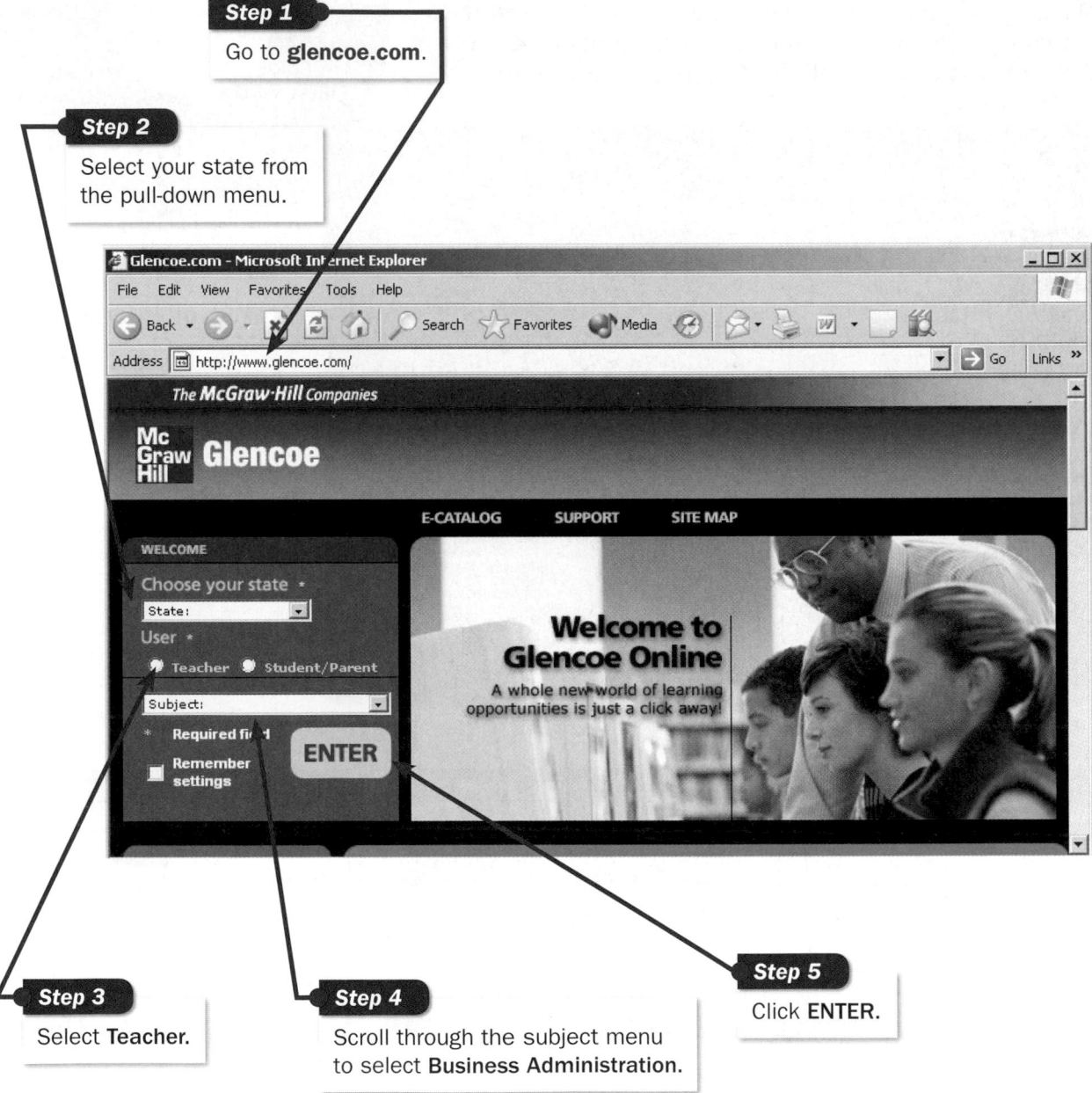

Step 3
Select **Teacher**.

Step 4
Scroll through the subject menu to select **Business Administration**.

Step 5
Click **ENTER**.

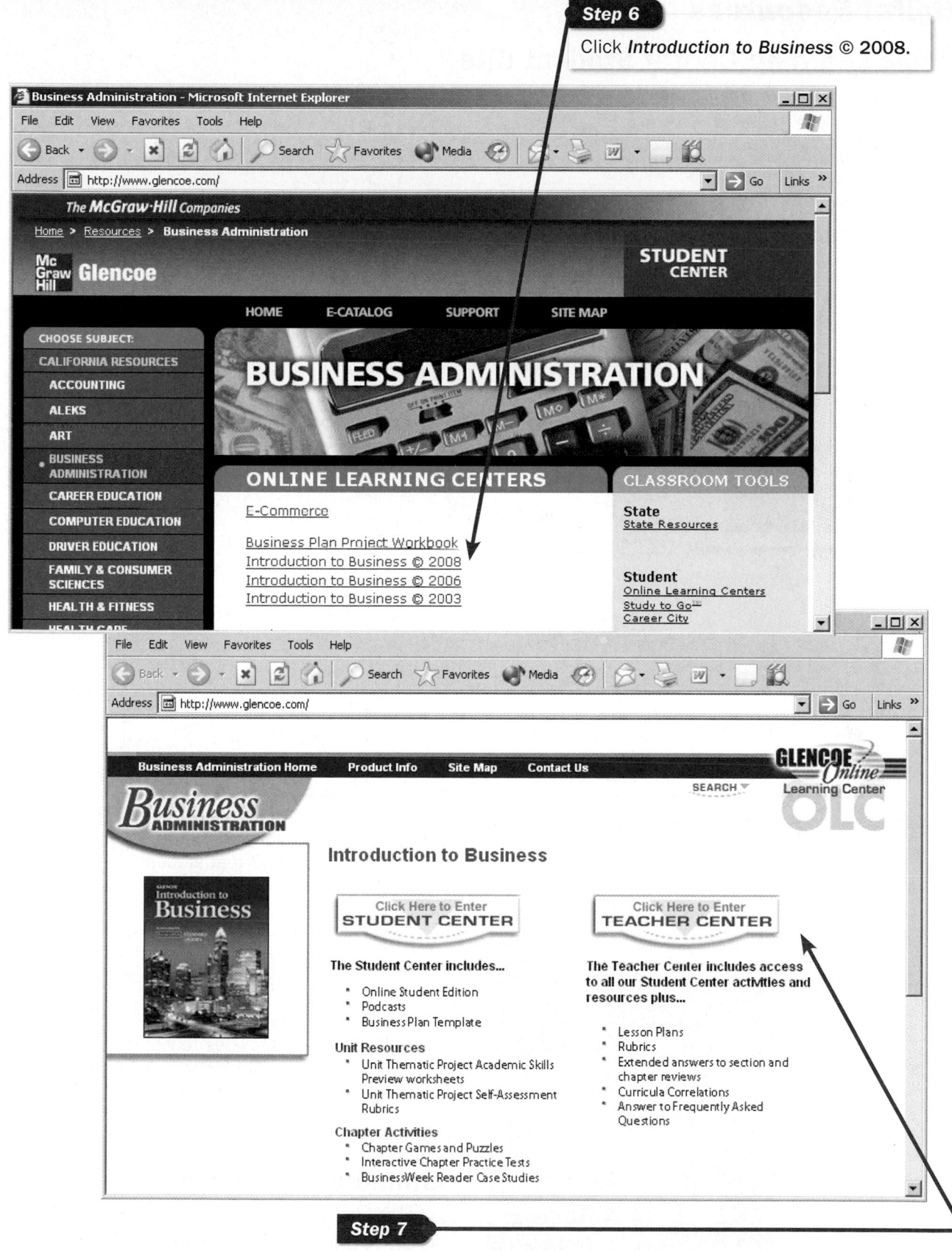

Step 6

Click *Introduction to Business* © 2008.

Step 7

Click **Teacher Center** to access a wide variety of classroom resources.

Digital Resources

Online Learning Center Student Site

The *Introduction to Business* Online Learning Center provides resources to enrich and enhance learning.

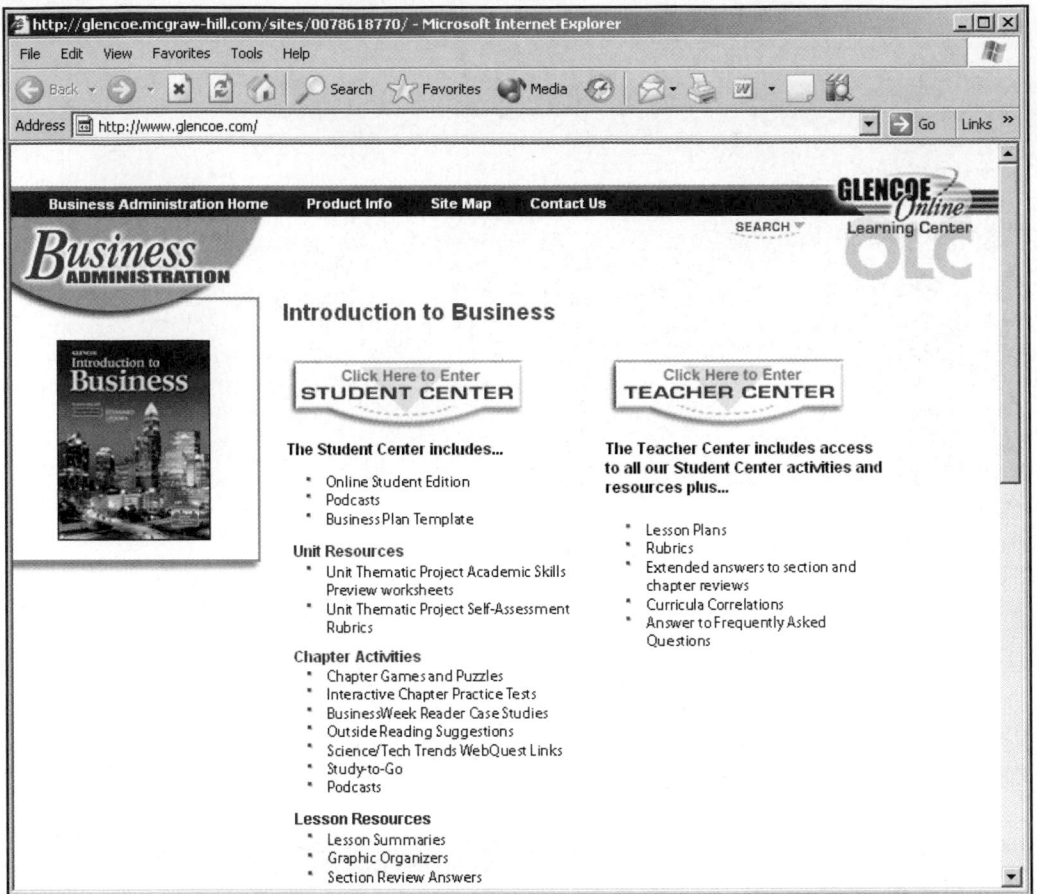

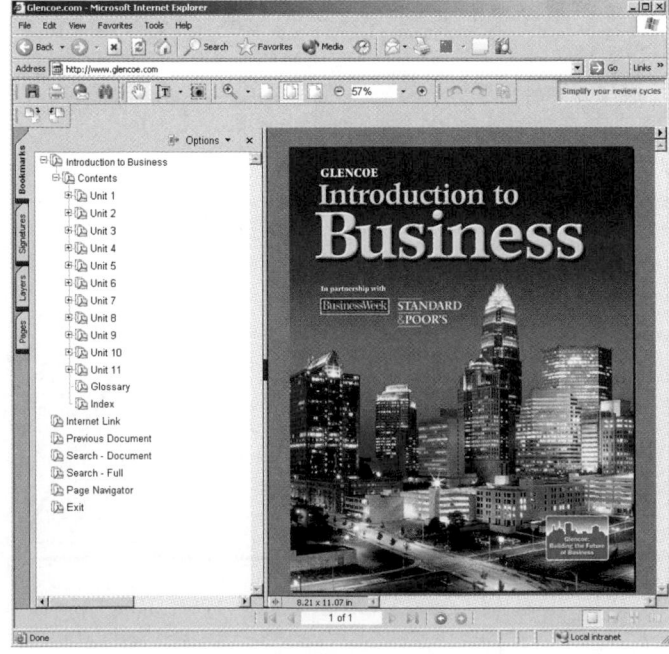

Glencoe's Study-to-Go is online content that students can download onto their PDAs, giving them a portable version of their textbook-related materials.

Glencoe's Teaching Today Web site provides teaching tips, free downloadable materials, in-depth articles, and a host of other features.

Online Student Edition

The Online Student Edition is an interactive version of the textbook. It offers the same content as the printed text, as well as multimedia-enhanced content.

Teach BUSINESS and ACADEMICS at the same time.

Scope and Sequence

These charts provide an overview of the academic standards covered in *Introduction to Business*.

National Council of Teachers of Mathematics Standards for Grades 9-12	
Number and Operation	
Understand numbers, ways of representing numbers, relationships among numbers, and number systems	pp. 10, 50, 58, 66, 184, 230, 246, 276, 284, 324, 332, 340, 388, 420, 456, 473, 496, 518, 526, 528, 562
Understand the meanings of operations and how they relate to one another	pp. 42, 90, 92, 178, 208, 230, 254, 270, 284, 298, 370, 418, 434, 448, 489, 502, 526, 616
Compute fluently and make reasonable estimates	pp. 18, 66, 90, 106, 107, 139, 154, 208, 231, 238, 260, 269, 292, 308, 326, 348, 354, 403, 418, 435, 456, 472, 473, 474, 488, 512, 527, 534, 542, 543, 602, 608, 617, 618, 624, 632, 633
Algebra	
Understand patterns, relations, and functions	pp. 10, 34, 36, 52, 74, 92, 122, 146, 162, 178, 192, 208, 238, 246, 254, 270, 284, 285, 310, 404, 410, 488, 534, 586, 592, 608, 618, 632
Represent and analyze mathematical situations and structures using algebraic symbols	pp. 4, 18, 52, 74, 106, 146, 154, 155, 222, 316, 362, 364, 380, 410, 458, 544, 632
Use mathematical models to represent and understand quantitative relationships	pp. 18, 162, 268, 276, 404, 464, 592
Analyze change in various contexts	pp. 24, 36, 74, 92, 124, 130, 138, 162, 208, 238, 292, 348, 354, 362, 388, 472, 488, 496, 518, 526, 542, 562, 578
Geometry	
Analyze characteristics of 2- and 3-dimensional geometric shapes and develop mathematical arguments about geometric relationships	pp. 138, 192, 230, 324, 340, 341, 394
Use visualization, spatial reasoning, and geometric modeling to solve problems	pp. 24, 34, 138, 166, 192, 340, 394
Measurement	
Understand measurable attributes of objects and the units, systems, and processes of measurement	pp. 24, 138, 168, 184, 192, 200, 230, 260, 276, 380, 480
Apply appropriate techniques, tools, and formulas to determine measurements	pp. 138, 177, 192, 324, 380, 394

continued on p. TM28

Scope and Sequence

continued from p. TM27

Data Analysis and Probability	
Formulate questions that can be addressed with data and collect, organize, and display relevant data to answer them.	pp. 36, 50, 98, 140, 176, 216, 362, 426, 510, 642, 578, 616
Select and use appropriate statistical methods to analyze data	pp. 194, 268, 308, 363, 402, 564
Develop and evaluate inferences and predictions that are based on data	pp. 26, 50, 74, 108, 140, 176, 194, 232, 420, 456, 474, 510, 512, 542, 562, 578, 586
Understand and apply basic concepts of probability	pp. 34, 122, 194, 247, 268, 564
Problem Solving	
Apply and adapt a variety of appropriate strategies to solve problems	pp. 81, 124, 130, 402, 472, 510, 578
Solve problems that arise in mathematics and in other contexts	pp. 4, 20, 36, 52, 74, 92, 108, 124, 140, 162, 178, 194, 216, 232, 254, 270, 292, 310, 326, 348, 364, 388, 404, 420, 442, 458, 474, 496, 512, 528, 544, 564, 570, 586, 600, 602, 618,
Build new mathematical knowledge through problem solving	pp. 4, 20, 36, 52, 74, 92, 108, 124, 140, 162, 178, 194, 214, 232, 233, 254, 270, 292, 310, 326, 348, 364, 388, 404, 420, 442, 458, 474, 494, 512, 528, 544, 564, 586, 602, 618
Monitor and reflect on the process of problem solving	pp. 66, 168, 192, 268, 380, 434, 600

National Science Education Standards	
Content Standard A Students should develop abilities necessary to do scientific inquiry, understandings about scientific inquiry	pp. 45, 117
Content Standard B Students should develop an understanding of the structure of atoms, structure and properties of matter, chemical reactions, motions and forces, conservation of energy and increase in disorder, and interactions of energy and matter	pp. 149, 224, 428
Content Standard C Students should develop understanding of the cell; molecular basis of heredity; biological evolution; interdependence of organisms; matter, energy, and organization in living systems; and behavior of organisms	pp. 12, 240, 335
Content Standard D Students should develop an understanding of energy in the earth system, geochemical cycles, origin and evolution of the earth system, origin and evolution of the universe	pp. 28, 398
Content Standard E Students should develop abilities of technological design, understandings about science and technology	pp. 39, 143, 203, 264, 318, 334, 369, 391, 408, 450, 500, 572, 610
Content Standard F Students should develop understanding of personal and community health; population growth; natural resources; environmental quality; natural and human-induced hazards; science and technology in local, national, and global challenges	pp. 12, 24, 60, 61, 133, 171, 202, 278, 300, 319, 358, 408, 414, 451, 467, 484, 505, 520, 538, 572, 573, 627
Content Standard G Students should develop understanding of science as a human endeavor, nature of scientific knowledge, historical perspectives	pp. 12, 24, 85, 102, 187, 369, 372, 557, 595

National Council of Teachers of English Standards for the English Language Arts

NCTE 1 Students read a wide range of print and non-print texts to build an understanding of texts, of themselves, and of the cultures of the United States and the world; to acquire new information; to respond to the needs and demands of society and the workplace; and for personal fulfillment. Among these texts are fiction and nonfiction, classic and contemporary works.	pp. 4-637
NCTE 2 Students read a wide range of literature from many periods in many genres to build an understanding of the many dimensions (e.g., philosophical, ethical, aesthetic) of human experience.	pp. 14, 24, 39, 50, 60, 78, 100, 118, 132, 143, 170, 181, 203, 220, 242, 262, 275, 295, 318, 334, 352, 369, 391, 408, 430, 450, 462, 382, 500, 517, 533
NCTE 3 Students apply a wide range of strategies to comprehend, interpret, evaluate, and appreciate texts. They draw on their prior experience, their interactions with other readers and writers, their knowledge of word meaning and of other texts, their word identification strategies, and their understanding of textual features (e.g., sound-letter correspondence, sentence structure, context, graphics).	pp. 18, 31, 51, 63, 66, 67, 90, 91, 106, 107, 122, 138, 176, 192, 193, 205, 230, 243, 246, 268, 324, 325, 340, 402, 418, 419, 456, 472, 510, 511, 526, 542, 575, 578, 579, 597, 616, 632
NCTE 4 Students adjust their use of spoken, written, and visual language (e.g., conventions, style, vocabulary) to communicate effectively with a variety of audiences and for different purposes.	pp. 14, 66, 118, 132, 151, 380, 453, 578
NCTE 5 Students employ a wide range of strategies as they write and use different writing process elements appropriately to communicate with different audiences for a variety of purposes.	pp. 90, 103, 154, 309, 321, 381, 399, 488, 523
NCTE 6 Students apply knowledge of language structure, language conventions (e.g., spelling and punctuation), media techniques, figurative language, and genre to create, critique, and discuss print and non-print texts.	pp. 35, 51, 123, 151, 208, 209, 268, 284, 308, 324, 469, 472, 510, 539
NCTE 7 Students conduct research on issues and interests by generating ideas and questions, and by posing problems. They gather, evaluate, and synthesize data from a variety of sources (e.g., print and non-print texts, artifacts, people) to communicate their discoveries in ways that suit their purpose and audience.	pp. 14, 15, 24, 31, 34, 60, 173, 181, 189, 203, 205, 227, 265, 275, 295, 305, 318, 337, 369, 377, 399, 418, 430, 431, 434, 453, 456, 462, 488, 507, 523
NCTE 8 Students use a variety of technological and information resources (e.g., libraries, databases, computer networks, video) to gather and synthesize information and to create and communicate knowledge.	pp. 31, 39, 50, 170, 208, 220, 227, 242, 246, 284, 305, 308, 321, 334, 352, 369, 408, 415, 482, 517, 572, 607, 616, 626
NCTE 9 Students develop an understanding of and respect for diversity in language use, patterns, and dialects across cultures, ethnic groups, geographic regions, and social roles.	pp. 23, 57, 96, 119, 127, 165, 173, 198, 237, 243, 274, 281, 314, 353, 393, 424, 461, 501, 531, 567, 605
NCTE 10 Students whose first language is not English make use of their first language to develop competency in the English language arts and to develop understanding of content across the curriculum.	pp. 242, 275, 358, 418
NCTE 11 Students participate as knowledgeable, reflective, creative, and critical members of a variety of literacy communities.	pp. 14, 15, 78, 87, 100, 138, 143, 262, 265, 337, 359, 362, 450
NCTE 12 Students use spoken, written, and visual language to accomplish their own purposes (e.g., for learning, enjoyment, persuasion, and the exchange of information).	pp. 63, 87, 119, 135, 281, 334, 359, 362, 377, 391, 431, 469, 485, 500, 507, 526, 542, 575, 597, 600, 601, 629

Make *your* TEACHING FLEXIBLE

90 Day

and **adaptable** *to* *ANY* *SCHEDULE.*

180 Day

INTEGRATE *academics*
and *workplace SKILLS*

Standards-Based Lesson Planning

Content Standards Correlations

Each chapter interleaf includes a table of content-related competencies included in the chapter and their location.

Skills and Competencies

Each chapter interleaf includes a chart of the 21st Century Skills, Foundation Skills, and Workplace Competencies that students will develop as the study the chapter.

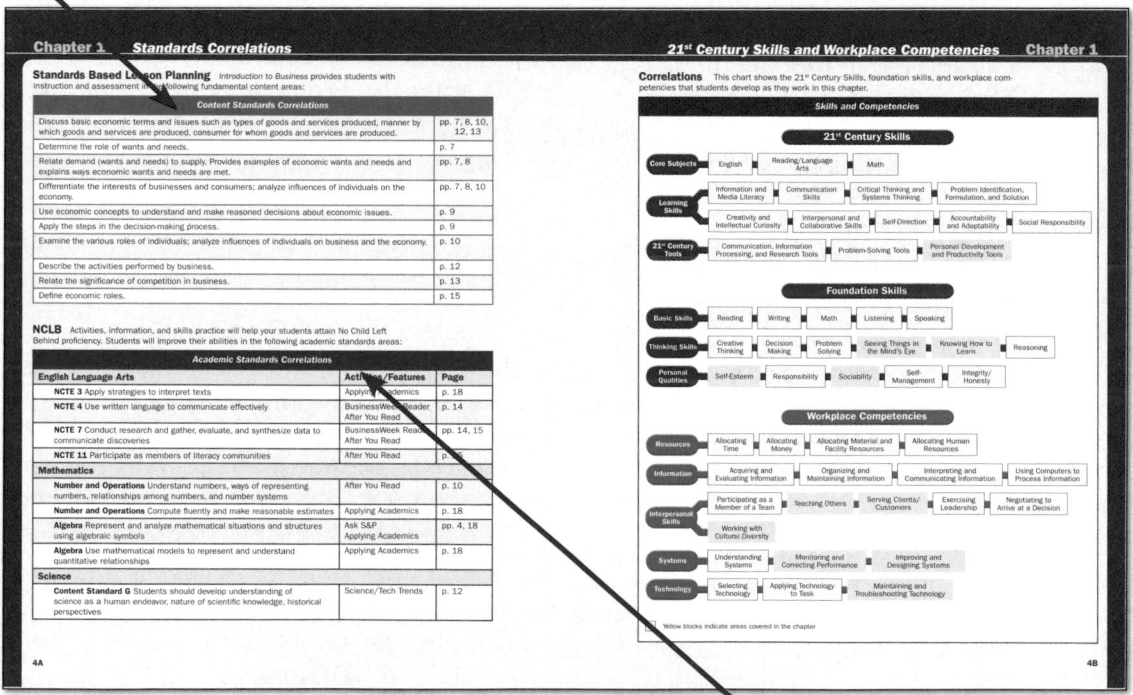

Academic Standards Correlations

Each chapter interleaf includes a table of English Language Arts, Mathematics, and Science standards correlations that show the locations of features and activities that will help your students achieve No Child Left Behind proficiency.

into the APPLIED LEARNING classroom.

NCLB

Brackets on the reduced student pages correspond to activities that help students practice and improve their abilities in Mathematics, English Language Arts, and Science.

Ask Standard & Poor's

Ask Standard & Poor's features are correlated to national Math standards

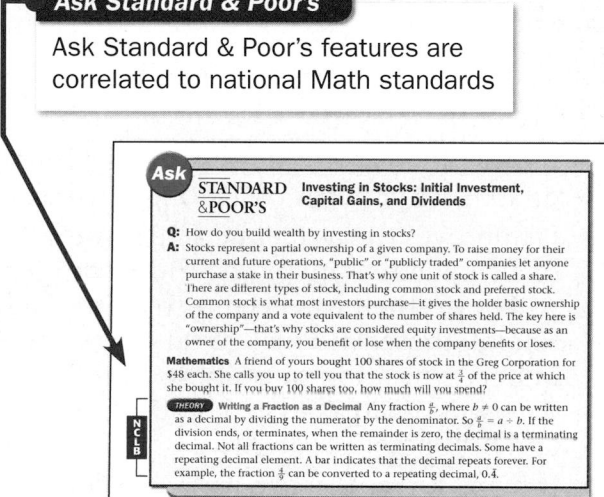

Academic Standards

Academics Standards listed in the Reading Guide at the beginning of each section correlate to features and section content..

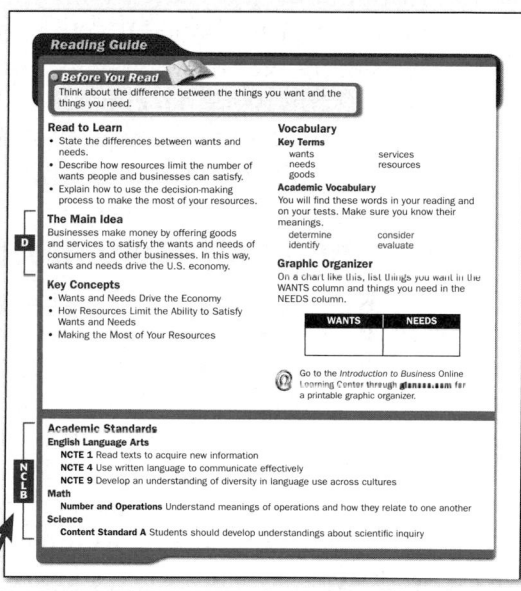

Academic Activities

Academics Activities in the After You Read section reviews are correlated to Math and English Language Arts standards

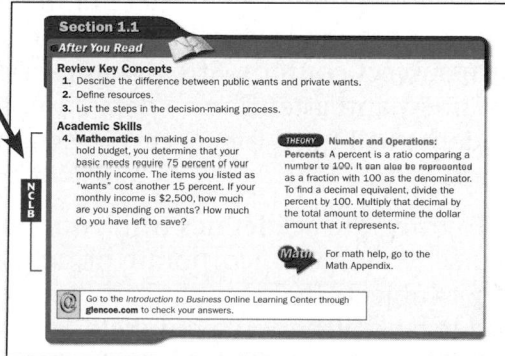

Science/Tech Trends

Science/Tech Trends features are correlated to national Science standards.

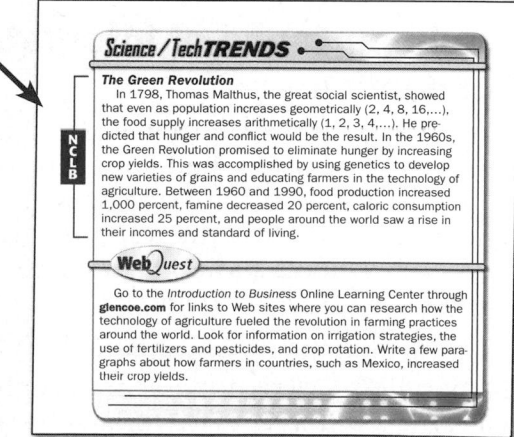

RAISE *the* BAR *and* help STUDENTS clear it.

Academic Integration

Academic skills are crucial for success both inside and outside the classroom. In addition to traditional academic skills, your students will need communication skills, interpersonal skills, and strong technology skills in order to compete in the workplace. Basic skills will support your students in completing the tasks that their jobs and lives will demand.

The No Child Left Behind Act

The No Child Left Behind Act of 2001 emphasizes student achievement in basic academic subjects. It introduces strict accountability measures for schools in the form of standardized testing. Traditionally, core academic subjects have been defined as language arts, science, and mathematics. No Child Left Behind names the following academic subjects:

- English
- Reading/Language Arts
- Mathematics
- Science
- World Languages
- Civics and Government
- Economics
- Art
- History
- Geography

The Importance of Integrating Academics

In a recent survey of high school graduates—many of whom had gone directly to work rather than into postsecondary education—more than half the respondents said their high schools should have placed more emphasis on basic academic skills.

Unfortunately, these students—like so many others—were not able to recognize the relevance of their course work while they were in high school. By explicitly integrating academic skills into the business curriculum, you can make students more aware of the connections between schoolwork and the real world.

Integrated learning offers the following additional benefits to students:

- It provides real-world learning and thus establishes patterns of lifelong learning.
- It improves the academic achievement of all students—including those who will begin their careers directly after high school, those who will go on to postsecondary education or training, and those who will obtain four-year college degrees and beyond.
- It helps students make realistic plans for their own careers and education.

Academics in the Business Curriculum

Integrate academic skills into the classroom as a regular part of your classroom activities. For example, by having students read class assignments and texts, write letters and reports, give presentations, and perform mathematics exercises, you are helping them improve their academic skills. Make expectations clear. For example, if you ask your students to prepare a written report, explain that grammar, spelling, and presentation will be evaluated along with subject content. Stress that clear writing, accuracy, and attention to detail are skills that students will need for success in school and at work.

To integrate academics into your business course, you must incorporate principles from other subjects in a way that students can understand either on a concrete level or on metaphoric terms. This type of teaching will help those students who learn best when they are exposed to a variety of examples.

Deliver *EFFICIENT* INSTRUCTION to all students.

Accountability

A consequential result of the No Child Left Behind Act, and the reauthorization of the Perkins Act through 2012, is that more states require testing for graduation at the secondary level. Accountability measures new to the Perkins reauthorization bill include:

- Academic proficiency as measured by the state criteria developed under NCLB;
- Graduation rates, also as defined by NCLB;
- Number of students to continue to post-secondary education;
- Number of students to complete state or industry certification or licensure; and
- Student achievement on assignments aligned with industry standards.

Connection to Relevance

With the mandatory requirements for proven test scores and graduation numbers, how can we assure that our students are learning? Most educators agree it is by connecting the relevance of education to life.

ACTE president Bob Scarborough says the Perkins reauthorization "ensures we are providing all students with an education that will help them succeed in the workplace and in life." William Daggett writes in "Achieving Academic Excellence through Rigor and Relevance,"

> What is important is that students enter the global economy with the ability to apply what they learned in school to a variety of ever-changing situations that they couldn't foresee before graduating.

The Rigor/Relevance Framework, developed at the International Center for Leadership in Education, illustrates leveled learning processes that enable students to perform high-level thinking. The learning process defines student performance in four sequential categories: aquisition, application, assimilation and adaptation.

As educators, our goal is to teach students to adapt their acquired knowledge and skills in complex ways to any situations, known and unknown. As educators, we are committed to provide the connectivity between classroom learning and real-world application.

Applications

Studies show that students understand and retain knowledge when they experience or apply it to relevant situations. The authors of *Introduction to Business* are dedicated to meet the challenge. Every chapter in Introduction to Business is filled with ways to engage students in experiential learning and applying their knowledge to their lives.

Features designed to help students find the relevance in content include:

- Real-World Business and Career Profile
- Unit Thematic Project (featuring skills self-assessment, career exploration, and connection to the community)
- Ask Standard & Poor's
- Ethics in Business
- Business in the Real World
- *BusinessWeek* Reader and Case Study
- Science/Tech Trends
- International Business with Examples of Language Across Cultures
- Real-Life Skills
- Cool Business Careers
- Business in the Real World
- Role-Play (competitive event practice)

The content and teaching strategies in *Introduction to Business* are designed to help applied learning students acclimate into the real world and to prepare them for high skill, high wage, and high demand professions.

Gather the TOOLS you'll need to

Universal Access

by Douglas Fisher, Ph.D.

Today's classroom includes students from many backgrounds with a variety of learning styles, strengths, and challenges. As teachers, we face the challenge of helping all of our students reach their educational potential. With careful planning, you can address the needs of all students in your classroom. The basis for this planning is universal access. When classrooms are planned with universal access in mind, fewer students require specific accommodations.

Universal Design

Universal design was first conceived as an architectural design concept when business people, engineers, and architects began making adjustments to allow for physical access to buildings. The idea was to plan the environment in advance to ensure that everyone had access. As a result, the environment would not have to be changed later for people with physical disabilities, people pushing strollers, workers who had injuries, or others for whom the environment would be difficult to negotiate. The Center for Universal Design **www.design.ncsu.edu/cud** defines Universal Design as: The design of products and environments to be usable by all people, to the greatest extent possible, without the need for adaptation or specialized design.

Universal Design and Access in Education

Researchers, teachers, and parents have expanded the development of built-in adaptations and inclusive accommodations from architectural space to the educational experience, especially in the area of curriculum.

In 1998, the National Center to Improve the Tools of Educators, with the partnership of the Center for Applied Special Technology, proposed an expanded definition of universal design focused on education: In terms of learning, universal design means the design of instructional materials and activities that allows learning goals to be achievable by individuals with wide differences in their abilities to see, hear, speak, move, read, write, understand English, attend, organize, engage, and remember.

Universal design and access in education suggests the following:

- **Inclusive Classroom Participation**—Curricula should be designed with all students and their needs in mind. The Glencoe/McGraw-Hill texts and materials are designed to accommodate a wide range of students. For example, understanding that English learners and students who struggle with reading will be using this textbook, vocabulary is specifically taught and reinforced. Teacher-support materials provide multiple instructional methods to meet the needs of the students in the class. The text is written to identify the main idea for all learners. Activating prior knowledge an identifying connections between what students know and think about are made within the text.
- **Maximum Text Readability**—In universally designed classrooms that provide access for all students, texts use direct language, clear noun-verb agreements, and clear construct-based wording. In addition to these factors, *Introduction to Business* uses embedded definitions for key terms and academic vocabulary, provides for specific instruction in reading skills, uses a number of visual representations, and includes note-taking guides.
- **Adaptable and Accommodating**— The content in this textbook can be easily translated, read aloud, or otherwise

REACH EVERY student.

changed to meet the needs of students in the classroom. The section and end-of-chapter assessments provide students with multiple ways to demonstrate their content knowledge and activities to help them see the connection between course study and the real world.

Differentiated Instruction

To differentiate instruction, teachers must appreciate student differences in background knowledge and current reading, writing, and English language skills. They must also consider student learning styles and preferences, interests, and needs, so they can react accordingly. There are a number of general guidelines for differentiating instruction in the classroom to reach all students, including:

- **Link Assessment with Instruction**—Assessments should occur before, during, and after instruction to ensure that the curriculum is aligned with what students do and do not know. Using assessments in this way allows you to plan instruction for whole groups, small groups, and individual students. Backward planning, where you establish the assessment before you begin instruction is also important.
- **Clarify Key Concepts and Generalizations**—Students need to know what concepts are essential and how this information can be used in their future learning. In addition, students need to develop a sense of the Big Ideas—ideas that transcend time and place.
- **Emphasize Critical and Creative Thinking**—The content, process and classroom should require students to think about what they are learning. While some students may require support, additional motivation, varied tasks, materials, or equipment, the overall focus on critical and creative

thinking allows all students to participate in the lesson.

- **Include Teacher- and Student-Selected Tasks**—A differentiated classroom includes both teacher- and student-selected tasks and activities. At some points in the day or lesson, the teacher must provide instruction and assign learning activities. In other parts of the lesson, students should be provided with choices in how they engage with the content. A balance of guided and chosen activities increases motivation, engagement, and learning.

Support for Individual Students

The vast majority of students will thrive in a universal access classroom that is focused on differentiated instruction. However, wise teachers recognize that no single option will work for all students and that there may be students who require unique systems of support to be successful.

Tips for Instruction

The following tips for instruction can support your efforts to help all students reach their maximum potential:

- Survey students to discover their individual differences. Use interest inventories to learn their unique talents so you can encourage contributions in the classroom.
- Be a model for respecting others. Adolescents crave social acceptance. Students with learning differences are especially sensitive to correction and criticism, particularly when it comes from a teacher. Your behavior will set the tone for how students treat one another.
- Expand opportunities for success. Provide a variety of instructional activities that reinforce skills and concepts.

- Establish measurable objectives and decide how you can best help students who meet them.
- Celebrate successes and make note of and praise "work in progress."
- Keep it simple. Point out problem areas if doing so can help a student effect change. Avoid overwhelming students with too many goals at one time.
- Assign cooperative group projects that challenge all students to contribute in solving a problem or creating a product.

Students with Learning Disabilities

- Provide support and structure. Clearly specify rules, assignments, and responsibilities.
- Practice skills frequently. Use games and drills to help maintain student interest.
- Incorporate many modalities into the learning process. Provide opportunities to hear, speak, write, read, and act out important concepts and information.
- Link new skills and concepts to those that have already been mastered.
- If possible, allow students to record answers on audiotape.
- Allow extra time to complete assessments and assignments.
- Let students demonstrate proficiency with alternative presentations, including oral reports, role plays, art projects, and musical presentations.
- Provide outlines, notes, or tape recordings of lecture materials.
- Pair students with peer helpers, and provide class time for pair interaction.

Students with Behavioral Challenges

- Provide a structured environment with clear-cut schedules, rules, seat assignments, and safety procedures.
- Reinforce appropriate behavior and model it for students.
- Cue distracted students back to the task using verbal signals as well as teacher supervision.

- Set goals that can be achieved in the short term. Work for long-term improvement in the big areas.

Students with Physical Challenges

- Openly discuss any uncertainties you have about when to offer aid with the student.
- Ask family members or therapists and students what special devices or procedures are needed and whether any special safety precautions need to be taken.
- Welcome students with physical challenges into all activities, including field trips, special events, and projects.
- Provide information about needed support to class members and adults.

Students with Visual Impairments

- Facilitate independence. Modify assignments as needed.
- Teach classmates how and when to serve as visual guides.
- Limit unnecessary noise in the classroom if it distracts students with visual impairments.
- Provide tactile models whenever it is possible.
- Foster a spirit of inclusion. Describe people and events as they occur in the classroom. Remind classmates that students with visual impairments cannot interpret gestures and other forms of nonverbal communication.
- Provide taped lectures and reading assignments for use outside the classroom.
- Team students with a sighted peer for written work.

Students with Hearing Impairments

- Seat students where they can see your lip movements easily and where they can avoid any visual distractions.
- Avoid standing with your back to the window or to a light source.
- Use an overhead projector so you can maintain eye contact while writing notes for students.

- Write all assignments on the board, or hand out written instructions.
- If the student has a manual interpreter, allow both the student and interpreter to select the most favorable seating arrangements.
- Teach students to look directly at each other when they speak.

English Language Learners

- Remember, a student's ability to speak English does not reflect his or her academic abilities.
- Try to incorporate the student's cultural experience into your instruction. The help of a bilingual aid may be effective.
- Avoid any references in your instruction that could be construed as cultural stereotypes.
- Preteach important vocabulary and concepts.
- Encourage students to preview text before they begin reading, noting headings.
- Remind students to use graphic organizers, photographs, and maps take advantage of the information contained in these visuals.
- Use realia and photographs whenever possible to build background knowledge and understanding.

Gifted Students

- Make arrangements for students to take selected subjects early and to work on independent projects.
- Ask "what if" questions to develop high-level thinking skills. Establish an environment safe for risk-taking in your classroom.
- Emphasize concepts, theories, ideas, relationships, and generalizations about the content.
- Promote interest in the past by inviting students to make connections to the present.
- Let students express themselves in alternate ways such as through creative writing, acting, debates, simulations, drawing, or music.
- Provide students with a catalog of helpful resources, listing such things as agencies that provide free and inexpensive materials, appropriate community services and programs, and community experts who might be called upon to speak to your students.
- Assign extension projects that allow students to solve real-life problems related to their communities.

Empower *your* students
with the

How Can I Motivate Students to Read?

As a teacher, your role is to help students make personal connections in order to understand "Why do I need to learn this?" Emphasize that reading is not only a necessity for work and for life; it can also bring enjoyment and enlightenment.

Ask your students, "What role does reading play in your life?" You can open this discussion by modeling examples: I love historical biographies; I read menus and order meals in Spanish; I read magazines and the Internet to stay up-to-date on my favorite sports teams.

> **Improving or fine-tuning reading skills will help your students:**
>
> - Improve grades
> - Read faster and more efficiently
> - Improve their study skills
> - Remember more information accurately
> - Improve their writing

The Reading Process

Good reading skills build on one another, overlap, and spiral in much the same way that a winding staircase goes around and around while leading readers to a higher place. The Reading Skills Handbook is designed to help your students find and use the tools to use **before, during,** and **after** reading.

> **Reading Strategies**
>
> - Identify, understand, and learn new words
> - Understand why you read
> - Take a quick look at the whole text
> - Try to predict what you are about to read
> - Take breaks during reading and ask questions about the text
> - Take notes
> - Keep thinking about what will come next
> - Summarize

Vocabulary Development

Word identification and vocabulary skills are the building blocks of reading and writing. By learning to use a variety of strategies to build word skills and vocabulary, your students will become stronger readers.

Use Context to Determine Meaning

The best way for your students to expand and extend vocabulary is to read widely, listen carefully, and participate in a rich variety of discussions. When

READING SKILLS *they will use* *in the* REAL WORLD.

reading independently, students can often figure out the meanings of new words by looking at their **context,** the other words and sentences that surround them.

Predict a Possible Meaning

Another way to determine the meaning of a word is to take the word apart. If a reader understands the meaning of the **base,** or **root,** part of a word, and knows the meanings of key syllables added either to the beginning or end of the base word, it becomes easy to figure out what the word means.

Word Origins   Since Latin, Greek, and Anglo-Saxon roots are the basis for much of our English vocabulary, having some background in one of these languages can be a useful vocabulary tool. For example, *astronomy* comes from the Greek root *astro*, which means "relating to the stars." *Stellar* also has a meaning referring to stars, but its origin is Latin. Knowing root words in other languages can help readers determine meanings, derivations, and spellings in English.

Prefixes and Suffixes   A prefix is a word part that can be added to the beginning of a word. For example, the prefix *semi* means "half" or "partial," so *semicircle* means "half a circle." A suffix is a word part that can be added to the end of a word. Adding a suffix often changes a word from one part of speech to another.

Using Dictionaries   A dictionary provides the meaning or meanings of a word. Look at the sample dictionary entry in the student edition Reading Skills Handbook to see what other information it provides.

Thesauruses and Specialized Reference Books   A thesaurus provides synonyms and often antonyms. It is a useful tool to use to expand vocabulary. Remind students to check the exact definition of the listed words in a dictionary before using a thesaurus. Specialized dictionaries such the *Barron's Dictionary of Business Terms* or *Black's Law Dictionary* list terms and expressions not commonly included in a general dictionary. See **glencoe.com** for direct links to online dictionaries.

Glossaries   Many textbooks and technical works contain condensed dictionaries that provide an alphabetical listing of words used in the text and their specific definitions.

Recognize Word Meanings Across Subjects   Words often have different meanings when used for different purposes. The word *product* may mean one thing in math and another in science. For example:

Math After you multiply the two numbers, explain how you arrived at the ***product.***

Science *One **product** of photosynthesis is oxygen.*

Economics *The Gross National **Product** is the total dollar value of goods and services produced by a nation.*

Help Students Understand What They Read

Reading comprehension means understanding—deriving meaning from—what has been read. Using a variety of strategies can help improve comprehension and make reading more interesting and more fun.

Read for a Reason

To get the greatest benefit from reading, teach students to **establish a purpose for their reading.** In school, some of the reasons for reading include:

- To learn and understand new information
- To find specific information
- To review before a test
- To complete an assignment
- To prepare (research) before you write

As reading skills improve, you will notice that your students apply different strategies to fit the different purposes for reading. For example, a person reading for entertainment may read quickly, but reading to gather information or follow directions might require reading more slowly, taking notes, constructing a graphic organizer, or rereading sections of text.

Draw on Personal Background

Drawing on personal background, or activating prior knowledge, helps students connect their culture and experiences to their reading. Before introducing a new topic, you may want to encourage students to ask:

- What have I heard or read about this topic?
- Do I have any personal experience relating to this topic?

You can also set common background knowledge with discussion before reading. For example, to prepare students to read "A Farewell to Arms," you might lead a discussion about these common background themes:

- World War I
- Italy (You might ask a student to show Italy on a map)
- Other Ernest Hemingway titles
- The Nobel Prize in literature

Having this historical background will help to set the scene for students as they read.

Using a KWL Chart A KWL chart is a good device for organizing information gathered before, during, and after reading. In the first column, students list what they already know, then list what they **want** to know in the middle column. They use the third column to review and assess what they **learned.** You or your students can add more columns to record places where they found information and places where they can look for more information.

K (What I already know)	W (What I want to know)	L (What I have learned)

Adjust Your Reading Speed Reading speed is a key factor in how well students understand what they read. Reading speed can vary depending on the purpose for reading.

Scanning *means running one's eyes quickly over the material to look for words or phrases. Readers scan to find a specific piece of information.*

Skimming *means reading a passage quickly to find its main idea or get an overview. Skim a passage as a preview to determine what the material is about.*

Reading for detail *involves careful reading while paying attention to text structure and monitoring understanding. Readers read for detail to learn concepts, follow complicated directions, or prepare to analyze a text.*

Techniques to Help Students Understand and Remember What They Read

Preview

Previewing strategies help students begin at a visual level, then drill down to evaluate, predict, draw conclusions, and use contextual clues about what they will read.

> **Previewing Strategies**
>
> **Read** the title, headings, and subheadings of the selection.
> **Look** at the illustrations and notice how the text is organized.
> **Scan** the selection. Glance at the whole thing.
> **Skim** the passage for an overview.
> **Decide** what the main idea might be.
> **Predict** what a selection will be about.

Predict

As students read, they take educated guesses about story events and outcomes. They **make predictions** before and during reading. This helps them focus their attention on the text and that focus improves understanding.

Determine the Main Idea

When students look for the **main idea,** they are looking for the most important statement in a text. Depending on what kind of text they read, the main idea can be located at the very beginning (news stories in newspaper or a magazine) or at the end (scientific research document).

Encourage students to ask these questions to determine the main idea:

- What is each sentence about?
- Is there one sentence that is more important than all the others?
- What idea do the details support or point out?

Keep track of the text's structure (see below). Looking at headers and content structure will give students important clues about the main idea.

Taking Notes

Cornell Note-taking system: There are many methods for note taking. The **Cornell Note-taking System** is a well-known method that can help students organize what they read. To the right is a note-taking activity based on the Cornell Note-taking System.

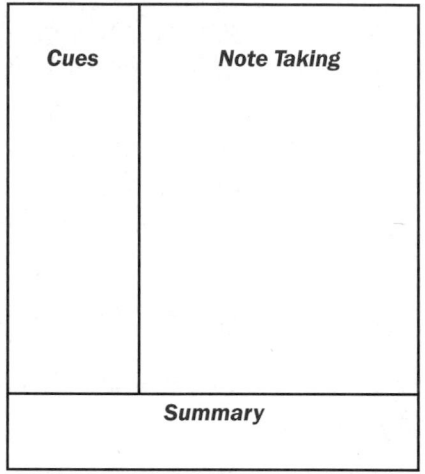

Graphic organizers: Using a graphic organizer to retell content in a visual representation will help students remember and retain content. Encourage students to make **charts** or **diagrams** to organize what they have read. Some good examples are:

Venn diagrams: A Venn diagram is a good way to organize information in a compare-and-contrast text structure. The outer portions of the circles show how two characters, ideas, or items contrast, or are different, and the overlapping part compares two things, or shows how they are similar.

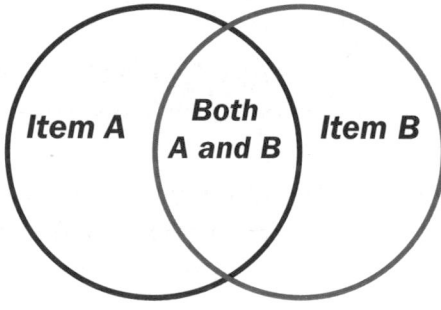

Flow charts: Students can a track sequence of events or cause and effect on a flow chart. Demonstrate how to arrange ideas or events in their logical, sequential order. Then draw arrows between ideas to indicate how one idea or event flows into another.

Go to **glencoe.com** for more information about note taking and additional study tools.

Visualize

Encourage students to try to form a mental picture of scenes, characters, and events as they read. This helps them to use the details and descriptions the author gives readers. If students can **visualize** what they read, they will become more interested and will remember the information better.

Question

Tell students to ask questions about the text while they read. Encourage them to ask about the importance of the sentences they read, how the sentences relate to one another, whether they understand what they just read, and what they think is going to come next.

Clarify

Encourage students to try these techniques when they don't understand meaning (through questioning):

What Students Should Do When They Do Not Understand

- ◆ Reread confusing parts of the text.
- ◆ Diagram (chart) relationships between chunks of text, ideas, and sentences.
- ◆ Look up unfamiliar words.
- ◆ Separate the text out of one's self. Pretend to tell it to someone else.
- ◆ Read the passage once more.

Review

Make sure students take time to stop and review what they have read. Use note-taking outlines or any other graphic organizers, charts or visual aids.

Monitor Your Comprehension

Teach students to continue to check their understanding using the following two strategies:

Summarize   Pause and state the main ideas of the text and the key supporting details. Try to answer the following questions: Who? What? When? Where? Why? and How?

Paraphrase   Pause, close the book, and try to retell what they have just read in their own words. It helps students to retell, or paraphrase reading into their own words.

Understanding Text Structure

Good writers do not just put together sentences and paragraphs, they organize their writing with a specific purpose in mind. That organization is called text structure. When students understand and follow the structure of a text, it is easier to remember the information they read. There are many ways text may be structured. Each type of structure usually makes use of some specific words. Teach students to watch for these **signal words:** They will help them follow the text's organization (remind them to use these techniques as they write).

Comparison and Contrast

This structure shows similarities and differences between people, things, and ideas. This is often used to demonstrate that things that seem alike are really different, or vice versa.

Signal words: *similarly, more, less, on the one hand / on the other hand, in contrast, but, however*

Cause and Effect

Writers use the cause and effect structure to explore the reasons for something happening and to examine the results or consequences of events.

Signal words: *so, because, as a result, therefore, for the following reasons*

Problem and Solution

When writers organize text around the question *how*, they state a problem and suggest solutions.

Signal words: *how, help, problem, obstruction, overcome, difficulty, need, attempt, have to, must*

Sequence

Sequencing tells readers in which order to consider thoughts or facts. Examples of sequencing are:

Chronological order refers to the order in which events take place.

Signal words: *first, next, then, finally*

Spatial order describes the organization of things in space (to describe a room, for example).

Signal words: *above, below, behind, next to*

Order of importance lists things or thoughts from the most important to the least important (or the other way around).

Signal words: *principal, central, main, important, fundamental*

Thinking about Reading

It is important for students to think about what they are reading to get the most information from a text, to understand the consequences of what the text says, to remember the content, and to form their own opinions about what they read.

Interpret

Interpreting involves asking, "What is the writer really saying?" and then using what students already know to answer the question.

Infer

Writers do not always state exactly everything they want readers to understand. They sometimes imply certain information by providing clues and details. An **inference** involves using reasoning and experience to develop the idea, based on what an author implies or suggests. What is most important when drawing inferences is to be sure that readers have accurately based their guesses on supporting details from the text. If students cannot point to a place in the selection to help back up an inference, encourage them to rethink that guess.

Draw Conclusions

A conclusion is a general statement a reader can make and explain using reasoning or supporting details from a text.

Analyze

To understand persuasive nonfiction (a text that lists facts and opinions to arrive at a conclusion), readers must analyze statements and examples to see if they support the main idea. To understand an informational text, students need to keep track of how the ideas are organized to find the main points.

> **Hint:** *Have students use graphic organizers and note-taking charts.*

Distinguish Facts and Opinions

This is one of the most important reading skills students can learn. A fact is a statement that can be proven. An opinion is what the writer believes. A writer may support opinions with facts, but an opinion cannot be proven. For example:

> **Fact:** *California produces fruit and other agricultural products.*

> **Opinion:** *California produces the best fruit and agricultural products.*

Evaluate

Remind students that to rely on accurate information, they will need to consider who wrote it and why. Where did the writer get information? Is the information one-sided? Can readers verify the information?

Reading for Research

To guide students in reading actively to research a topic, encourage them to follow these directions:

- generate an interesting, relevant, and researchable question
- categorize that information
- evaluate the information
- organize information in a new way for a specific audience
- draw conclusions about the original research question

Link ACADEMIC vocabulary

What Is Academic English?

by Robin Scarcella, Ph.D.

Academic English is the language commonly used in business and education. It is the language used in academics, business, and courts of law. It is the type of English used in professional books, including textbooks, and it contains specific linguistic features that are associated with all disciplines. Proficiency in reading and using academic English is strongly related to long-term success in all parts of life.

What Is Academic Vocabulary?

By the time children have completed elementary school, they must have acquired the knowledge needed to understand academic vocabulary. How many words should they acquire to be able to access their textbooks? A basic 2,000-word vocabulary of high-frequency words makes up 87% of the words. Three percent of the remaining words are technical words. The remaining 2% are low-frequency words. There may be as many as 123,000 low-frequency words in academic texts.

Why Should Students Learn Academic Vocabulary?

English language learners who have mastered a basic 2,000-word vocabulary are ready to acquire the majority of general words found in their texts and on standardized tests.

Knowledge of academic words, combined with continued acquisition of general words, can significantly boost an English learner's comprehension level of academic texts. English learners who learn and practice these words before they graduate from high school are likely to be able to master academic material with more confidence and speed. They waste less time and effort in guessing words than those students who know only the basic 2,000 words that characterize general conversation.

Academic Vocabulary and Academic English in the Business Classroom

Teachers can provide their students with rich samples of academic vocabulary and help students understand the academic English of their text. To develop academic English, students must have already acquired a large amount of basic proficiency in the grammar of everyday English.

Academic English should be taught within contexts that make sense. Academic English arises not only from a knowledge of linguistic code and cognition but also from social practices in which academic English is used to

to BUSINESS content.

accomplish communicative goals. The acquisition of academic vocabulary and grammar is necessary to advance the development of academic English.

Tips for Teaching Academic Vocabulary:

- **Expose Students to Academic Vocabulary**—Students learn academic vocabulary through use and in reading content. You do not need to call attention to all academic words students are learning because they will acquire them subconsciously.

- **Do Not Correct Students' Mistakes When Using Academic Vocabulary**—All vocabulary understanding and spelling errors are developmental and will disappear once the student reads more.

- **Help Students Decode the Words Themselves**—Once they learn the alphabet, they should be able to decode words. Decoding each word they do not recognize will help them more than trying to focus on sentence structure. Once they can recognize words, they can read "authentic" texts.

- **Do Not Ignore the English Learner in This Process**—They can learn academic vocabulary before they are completely fluent in spoken English.

- **Helping Students Build Academic Vocabulary Leads to Broader Learning**—Students who have mastered the basic academic vocabulary are ready to continue acquiring words from the rest of the vocabulary groups. Use the Internet to find lists of appropriate vocabulary word lists.

There are a number of guidelines that teachers can follow when teaching academic English and vocabulary:

Guidelines for Teaching Academic Vocabulary

1. Use direct and planned instruction.
2. Employ models that have increasingly difficult language.
3. Focus attention to form by pointing out linguistic features of words.
4. Provide practice opportunities.
5. Motivate student interest and self-confidence.
6. Provide instructional feedback.
7. Use assessment tools on a regular basis.

Generate *the* BEST

Assessment

In response to the growing demand for accountability in the classroom, educators must use multiple assessment measures to accurately gauge student performance. In addition to quizzes, tests, essay exams, and standardized tests, assessment today incorporates a variety of performance-based measurements and portfolio opportunities.

Performance assessment activities provide hands-on approaches to learning concepts. Through activities students are able to actually experience these concepts rather than just reading and listening about them. These types of activities also help students become aware of diverse audiences for their work. Performance assessment tasks are based on what is most essential in the curriculum and what is interesting to the student.

Performance-Based Assessments

One good way to present a performance assessment is in the form of an open-ended question.

- Journals—Students write from the perspective of a businessperson or a consumer of a particular historical era.
- Letters—Students write a letter from one businessperson to another or from a businessperson to another audience.
- Position Paper or Editorial—Students explain a controversial issue and present their own opinions and recommendations, supported with strong evidence and convincing reasons.
- Newspaper—Students write stories from the perspective of a business reporter. This could also involve the writing of editorials or letters to the editor.

- Biographies and Autobiographies—Students write about business leaders either from the third person point of view (biography) or from the first person (autobiography).
- Creative Stories—Students integrate business events into a piece of fiction.
- Poems and Songs—Students follow the conventions of a particular type of song or poem as they tell about a business event or person.
- Research Reports—Students synthesize information from a variety of sources into a well-developed research report.

Oral Presentations

Oral presentations allow students to demonstrate their business literacy in front of an audience. Oral presentations are often group efforts, although this need not be the case.

- Simulations—Students hold simulations of actual events, such as a role-play in a business scenario.
- Debates—Students debate two or more sides of a business policy or issue.
- Interview—Students conduct a mock interview of a business leader or worker.
- Oral Reports—Students present the results of research efforts in a lively oral report. This report may be accompanied by visuals.
- Skits and Plays—Students use business events as the basis for a play or skit.

Visual Presentations

Visual presentations allow students to demonstrate their understanding in a variety of visual formats. Visual presentations can be either group or individual projects.

- Model—Students make a model to demonstrate or represent a business process.

performance
FROM YOUR students.

- Museum Exhibit—Students create a rich display of materials around a topic. Typical displays might include models, illustrations, photographs, videos, writings, and presentation software.
- Graph or Chart—Students analyze and represent data in a line graph, bar graph, table, or other chart format.
- Drawing—Students represent a business event or period through illustration, including cartoons.
- Posters and Murals—Posters and murals may include maps, time lines, diagrams, illustrations, photographs, and written explanations that reflect students' understanding of business information.
- Quilt—Students sew or draw a design for a patchwork quilt that shows a variety of perspectives, events, or issues related to a key topic.
- Videotapes—Students film a video to show a simulation of a business event.
- Multimedia Presentation—Students create a computer-generated multimedia presentation or slide show containing business information and analysis.

How Are Performance Assessments Scored?

There are a variety of means used to evaluate performance tasks. Some or all of the following methods may be used.

- Scoring Rubrics—A scoring rubric is a set of guidelines for assessing the quality of a process and/or product. It sets out criteria used to distinguish acceptable responses from unacceptable ones, generally on a scale from excellent to poor. Rubrics may be used as guidelines as the students prepare their products. They are also commonly used for peer-to-peer assessment and self-assessment.

- Models of Excellent Work—Teacher-selected models of excellent work concretely illustrate expectations and help students set goals for their own projects.
- Student Self-Assessment—Common methods of self-assessment include ranking work in relation to the model, using a scoring rubric, and writing their own goals and then evaluating how well they have met the goals they set for themselves. Regardless of which method or methods students use, they should be encouraged to evaluate their behaviors and processes, as well as the finished product.
- Peer or Audience Assessment—Many of the performance tasks target an audience other than the classroom teacher. If possible, the audience of peers should give feedback. Have the class create rubrics for specific projects together.
- Observation—As students carry out their performance tasks, you may want to formally observe them at work. Start by developing a checklist, identifying all the specific behaviors and understandings you expect students to demonstrate. Then observe students as they carry out performance tasks and check off behaviors as you observe them.
- Interviews—As a form of ongoing assessment, you may want to conduct interviews with students, asking them to analyze, explain, and assess their participation in performance tasks. When projects take place over an extended period of time, you can hold periodic interviews as well as exit interviews. In this way the interview process allows you to gauge the status of the project and to guide the students' efforts along the way.

PREPARE *your* STUDENTS WELL,

Test-Prep Strategies

Students can follow the steps below to prepare for the standardized assessments they are required to take.

- Read About the Test—Students can familiarize themselves with the format, the types of questions, and the amount of time they will have to complete the test. Emphasize that it is very important for students to budget their time during test-taking.

- Review the Content—Consistent study will help students build knowledge and understanding. If there are specific objectives or standards that are tested on the exam, help students review facts or skills.

- Practice—Provide practice, ideally with real tests, to build students' familiarity with the content, format, and timing of the real exam. Students should practice all the types of questions they will encounter on the test.

- Pace—Students should pace themselves differently depending on how the test is administered. As students practice, they should try to increase the number of questions they can answer correctly. If students have trouble with an item, they should mark it and come back to it later.

- Analyze Practice Results—Help students improve test-taking performance by analyzing their test-taking strengths and weaknesses. Help students identify what kinds of questions they found most difficult. Look for patterns in errors and tailor instruction to review the appropriate test-taking skills or content.

Test-Taking Strategies

It's not enough for students to learn facts and concepts—they must be able to show what they know in a variety of test-taking situations.

Objective Tests

Apply the following strategies to help students do their best on objective tests.

Multiple-Choice Questions

- Students should read the directions carefully to learn what answer the test requires—the best answer or the right answer. This is especially important when answer choices include "all of the above" or "none of the above."

- Advise students to watch for negative words in the questions, such as not, except, unless, never, and so forth.

- Students should try to mentally answer the question before reading the answer choices.

- Students should read all the answer choices and eliminate those that are obviously wrong.

True/False Questions

- It is important that students read the entire question before answering. For an answer to be true, the entire statement must be true. If one part of a statement is false, the answer should be marked false.

- Remind students to watch for words such as *all, never, every,* and *always.* Statements containing these words are often false.

Matching Questions

- Students should read through both lists before they mark any answers.

- Unless an answer can be used more than once, students should cross out each choice as they use it.

- Using what they know about grammar can help students find the right answer. For instance, when matching a word with its definition, the definition is often the same part of speech (noun, verb, adjective, and so forth) as the word.

and you will **IMPROVE** *their* **PERFORMANCE.**

Essay Tests

Essay tests require students to provide thorough and well-organized written responses, in addition to telling what they know. Help students use these strategies on essay tests.

Read the Question

The key to writing successful essay responses lies in reading and interpreting questions correctly. Teach students to identify and underline key words to guide them in understanding what the question asks.

Plan and Write the Essay

Students should follow the writing process to develop their answer. Encourage students to follow these steps to plan and write their essays.

1. Map out an answer. Make lists, webs, or an outline to plan the response.
2. Decide on an order in which to present the main points.
3. Write an opening statement that directly responds to the essay question.
4. Write the essay. Expand on the opening statement. Support key points with specific facts, details, and reasons.
5. Write a closing statement that brings the main points together.
6. Proofread to check for spelling, grammar, and punctuation.

Writing Strategies	
Analyze	To analyze means to systematically and critically examine all parts of an issue or event.
Classify or Categorize	To classify or categorize means to put people, things, or ideas into groups, based on a common set of characteristics.
Compare and Contrast	To compare is to show how things are similar, or alike. To contrast is to show how things are different.
Describe	To describe means to present a sketch or impression. Rich details, especially details that appeal to the senses, flesh out a description.
Discuss	To discuss means to systematically write about all sides of an issue or event.
Evaluate	To evaluate means to make a judgment and support it with evidence.
Explain	To explain means to clarify or make plain.
Illustrate	To illustrate means to provide examples or to show with a picture or other graphic.
Infer	To infer means to read between the lines or to use knowledge and experience to draw conclusions, make a generalization, or form a prediction.
Justify	To justify means to prove or to support a position with specific facts and reasons.
Predict	To predict means to tell what will happen in the future, based on an understanding of prior events and behaviors.
State	To state means to briefly and concisely present information.
Summarize	To summarize means to give a brief overview of the main points of an issue or event.
Trace:	To trace means to present the steps or stages in a process or event in sequential or chronological order.

BASE *your* teaching ON BEST PRACTICES,

Critical Thinking

One of the factors that determines workplace success is a person's ability to deal with the varied demands of the fast-paced business world. This requires insightful decision making, creative problem solving, and interactions with diverse groups: employees, management, investors, customers, or clients. Thus, teaching critical thinking equips your students with the skills necessary to achieve success.

The Value of Critical Thinking

Critical thinking is the process of reasonably or logically deciding what to do or believe. It involves the ability to:

- Compare and contrast
- Solve problems
- Make decisions
- Analyze and evaluate
- Synthesize and transfer knowledge
- Engage in metacognition

Critical thinking skills are important for these reasons:

- They help students investigate their own problem-solving mechanisms.
- They help students find creative resolutions.
- They lead students to compare and contrast what they know with unknowns.
- They allow students to make decisions about their own learning while making them aware of their learning processes.

Cognitive Development

All learning requires thinking. Benjamin Bloom's Taxonomy of the Cognitive Domain is probably the most widely recognized schema of levels of thinking. Each of Bloom's six cognitive categories lists various thinking skills and indicates the types of behavior students are expected to perform to fulfill specific learning goals. See chart below.

CATEGORY	GOAL	EXPECTED STUDENT RESPONSE	APPROPRIATE QUESTIONS/PROMPTS
Knowledge	Identify and recall of information	Define, recognize, recall, identify, label, show, collect, understand, examine	Who…? What…? When…? Where…? How…? Describe….
Comprehension	Organize and select facts and ideas	Translate, interpret, explain, describe, summarize, extrapolate	Retell in your own words…. What is the main idea of…?
Application	Use facts, rules, and principles	Apply, solve, show, experiment, predict	How is…an example of…? How is…related to…?
Analysis	Separate a whole into component parts	Connect, relate, differentiate, classify, arrange, check, group, distinguish, organize, categorize, detect, compare, infer	Classify…according to…. How does… compare/contrast with…?
Synthesis	Combine ideas to form a new whole	Produce, propose, design, construct, combine, formulate, compose, plan, hypothesize	What would you predict/infer from…? What might happen if you combined…with…?
Evaluation	Develop opinions, judgments, or decisions	Appraise, judge, criticize, decide	What do you think about…? Prioritize….

and your STUDENTS *WILL* BENEFIT.

Cooperative Learning

Studies show that students learn faster and retain more information when they are actively involved in the learning process. Cooperative learning is one method that gets students actively involved in learning and at the same time allows for peer teaching.

Using Cooperative Learning

Your business course provides many opportunities for students to learn and apply the skills necessary for positive interpersonal relationships. Through the use of cooperative learning, you can offer a structured method of teaching team-building, collaborative social skills, and team decision making while teaching basic concepts— essential skills for the workplace.

Cooperative Learning in this Text

In *Introduction to Business*, students and teachers have a variety of materials to assist with cooperative learning activities. Many of the features and section and chapter assessment activities can be completed in a cooperative learning environment.

The Benefits of Cooperative Learning

- Cooperative learning emphasizes working toward group goals rather than the traditional emphasis on individual competition and achievement.
- Students discover that not only must they learn the material themselves, but they are also responsible for helping everyone in the group learn the material.
- Cooperative learning increases academic achievement and develops essential social skills.
- Students learn valuable problem-solving, team-building, and creativity skills that transfer to real-world occupations and work environments.
- People who help each other and work together toward a common goal generally begin to feel more positive about themselves and each other.
- Students have the opportunity to perceive other students as colleagues rather than competitors. As a result, they recognize the value of helping others rather than working competitively.

School-to-Career

A major goal set by the No Child Left Behind Act and the Perkins Act, reauthorized through 2012, is to prepare students to succeed in the constantly changing work world. *Introduction to Business* successfully integrates work skills preparation with course content and academics. Each chapter in this Teacher Wraparound Edition is preceded by a 21st Century Skills and Workplace Competencies correlations chart that previews the essential skills to be developed in chapter content and activities. Using the charts as guidelines, you can target the needs of your class and the needs of students as individuals to prepare them all for high skill, high wage, and high demand professions.

School-to-career programs are important developments in providing students a sense of relevance in their learning. These programs assume different forms in order to meet the needs of different communities, schools, and students.

Benefits of School-to-Career Programs

All school-to-career programs provide these benefits to students:

- An improved understanding of self,
- An appreciation of the relevance of school learning to "real life," and
- A clearer vision of a productive future and how to make that vision a reality,
- Familiarity with a wide range of career options,
- Increased motivation to stay in and to succeed in school.

An effective school-to-career program involves a close relationship between schools and local businesses. This relationship can result in benefits to schools and to businesses alike, as well as to parents and the community.

PURPOSES OF SCHOOL-TO-CAREER PROGRAMS
• To facilitate the creation of a universal, high-quality school-to-career transition system to enable students to identify and pursue paths to progressively more rewarding roles in the workplace;
• To utilize workplaces as learning environments in the educational process by making employers and educators joint partners in providing opportunities for students to participate in high-quality, work-based learning;
• To promote the formation of partnerships dedicated to linking the worlds of school and work among secondary schools and private and public employers, labor organizations, government, community-based organizations, parents, students, state and local educational agencies, and training and human services agencies;
• To increase knowledge and improve student skills by integrating academic and occupational learning and building links between secondary and postsecondary educational institutions;
• To motivate all students to stay in or return to school and strive to continue their education in postsecondary institutions;
• To expose students to a broad array of career opportunities and facilitate the selection of major areas of study, based on individual interests, goals, and abilities.

Technology

Technology affects how all people work, interact, and live. Technology will affect your students in the work world. For example, they may keep records using a computer, advertise on the Internet, or telecommute. It will also affect your students as consumers. An increasing number of people buy products on the Web. It is critical that your students become familiar and comfortable with technology now in order to prepare for successful careers.

Activities

Introduction to Business helps you integrate technology into your teaching with technology-based activities:

- Features and assessments provide a link the *Introduction to Business* **Online Learning Center** (OLC) through **glencoe.com** to assist students in finding answers and to further research the topic or find a project.
- The section opening **Reading Guide** provides a link to the OLC for students to download the printable graphic organizer for each section.
- Each section **After You Read** review sends students to the OLC to check their answers.
- The Science/Tech Trends feature provides a **WebQuest** research activity through the OLC at **glencoe.com**.
- Each *BusinessWeek* Reader and Case Study sends students to the OLC for a printable Case Study activity.
- The OLC provides outside reading suggestions for each chapter.
- Students can use assessment rubrics on the OLC to self-evaluate their thematic projects.

Using the Internet Effectively

There are steps you can take to use the Internet effectively in the classroom:

- Look for sites that are created by the government or universities (their URLs typically end in .gov or .edu). These are reliable sites with factual integrity and stability.
- Find out who created the site. If the purpose and creator of the Web site are unclear, its content may be unreliable.
- Use multiple search engines when you are looking for information on a topic. This will help you find as many of the pertinent sites as possible.
- Combine your Internet research with traditional research methods. Ask librarians and experts for information and sources. Use books and magazines.

Ethics

Helping students learn about ethical behavior and how to consider the effects of a decision before it is made are important life skills for your students preparing for the business world.

The Benefits of Integrating Ethics

The goal of teaching ethical decision-making skills is not to teach values. It is to help students clarify their ethical beliefs and learn how to evaluate ethical situations. Make your classroom a risk-free environment in which students can discuss issues and make ethical decisions. Students need to learn how to evaluate their actions and to ask questions such as, "Will I be proud of myself if I take this action?" and "Would I want others to know about my actions?"

The Ethical Decision Model

Your students will learn to analyze ethical situations better if they have a model to use in deliberating the issues that helps them to understand how a decision can effect others. Several decision models exist, but the basic steps for an ethical decision model are as follows:

1. Determine the ethical issue.
2. Identify the actions for handling the situation.
3. Identify the people affected by the situation.
4. Analyze how the situation affects the people involved.
5. Decide which of the actions to take.

Classroom Strategies

Ethics in Business features and a Business Ethics review activities provide real-world situations posing ethical conundrums. Both features can be catalysts for lively classroom discussion. In addition, you might lead discussion about topical ethics issues or have students bring in newspaper or magazine articles which suggest ethical dilemmas. Have students analyze the situations in class and, perhaps, write short reports on their analyses and conclusions. Some formats, such as learning groups, role-plays, and debates, are particularly well suited to teaching students about ethics.

Cooperative Learning Groups

Small groups of students are especially well suited to discuss cases and share their ideas about ethical issues. Divide students into groups of four or five. Observe groups and encourage all students to participate. Allow each group to reach its own conclusions, and then ask a member of each group to share their ideas with the class.

Role-Plays and Debates

Have your students role-play ethical situations, using their own ideas about how to respond to a given situation. Discuss class responses to the role-play, guiding students in using the ethical decision model. Set up debate teams to present different sides of an ethical issue.

?ETHICS in Business

A Conflict of Interest

■ **Critical Reading** Life is full of important decisions. Think about the kinds of decisions that you make as you read the question below.

You work as an event planner for a local company. You are in charge of hiring a caterer for the company's 10th anniversary celebration. You have bids from four caterers in town. One of the bids is from a caterer who is an old friend. His bid is higher than the three others.

■ **Decision Making** Would your relationship with the caterer affect which company you would hire? Explain your answer.

Diversity

Introduction to Business is designed to help students recognize and discuss issues of cultural diversity. During class activities, you may also find it appropriate to integrate questions related to cultural diversity. For example, you might expand a class discussion by asking:

- Would your response change if the customer or vendor did not speak the same language as you speak? If so, how?
- Would you direct your employee differently if his or her ethnic background were different from yours?
- Would your decision change if your co-worker were a male or female? From your own ethnic background? From a different background? Why?

Integrating Cultural Diversity

As future business professionals, your students will be faced with a diverse world in which people of many different cultures are both workers and consumers. Cultural knowledge may be the difference between success and failure in conducting business in the global economy. For students to become productive workers and responsible citizens, they must be open to cultural differences.

As students learn about skills needed to be successful, they should keep in mind the wide diversity of the people they are likely to encounter in every aspect of their working and personal lives. In the classroom and in one-on-one conferences, you can help your students consider the diversity of the U.S. population, not only in terms of ethnicity, but also in terms of customs, attitudes, religious beliefs, language backgrounds, and physical capabilities. High school students need to understand that ability and success are not related to skin color or gender.

Multicultural Education

Multicultural education incorporates the idea that all students—regardless of their gender and social class, and their ethnic, racial, or cultural characteristics—should have an equal opportunity to learn in school. Learning about other cultures concurrently with their own culture helps students recognize similarities and appreciate differences, without perceiving inferiority or superiority of one or the other. To foster cultural awareness:

- Recognize that all students are unique, having special talents and abilities.
- Promote uniqueness and diversity as positive traits.
- Know, appreciate, and respect the cultural backgrounds of your students.
- Use authentic situations to provide cultural learning and understanding.
- Make sure people of all cultures are represented fairly and accurately.
- Make sure that historical information is accurate and nondiscriminatory.
- Make sure that materials do not include stereotypical roles.
- Make sure there is gender equity.
- Welcome family and community involvement.
- Use current news stories or advertisements to call students' attention to cultural differences that influence the marketing of products.

Treasure Hunt

Introduction to Business contains a wealth of information. The trick is to know where to look to access all the information in the book. Guide students through the Treasure Hunt to preview the text and help them understand its organization.

1 How many chapters are in the book? How many units?
35 chapters, 11 units

2 What part of the textbook will show you where the Better Business Bureau is taught?
index

3 Where do you find the Ask Standard & Poor's features?
on the chapter opener page

4 What business is featured in the Unit 4 Real-World Business and Career Profile? Where do you first find the business name?
Expeditiontrips.com, the Table of Contents

5 If you need help with one of the math applications, where would you look?
Math Appendix

6 Where can you learn the definitions of **oligopoly**, **recruitment**, and **consumer**?
Glossary

7 What skill do you practice in Chapter 13, Section 13.1, After You Read?
Mathematics

8 Where do you find a Unit Thematic Project?
at the end of a unit

9 What is the URL that takes you to the *Introduction to Business* Online Learning Center?
glencoe.com

Table of Contents

Table of Contents

Table of Contents

Table of Contents

Unit 6 | *Financial and Technological Resources* | **290**

Table of Contents

Table of Contents

Table of Contents

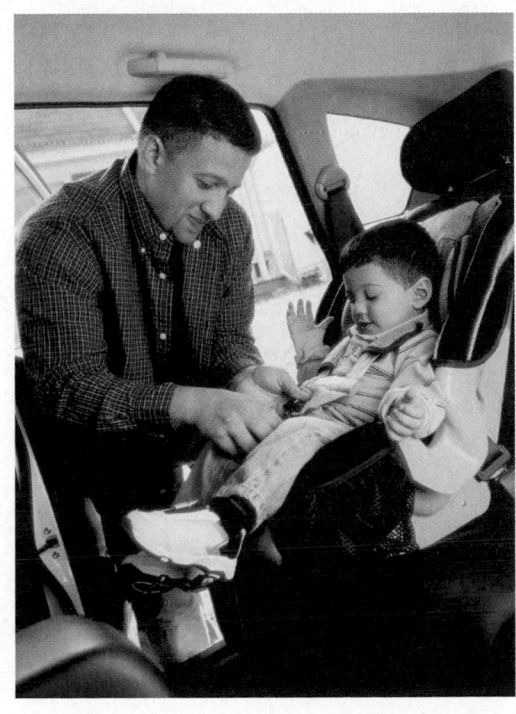

Table of Contents

Treasure Hunt

Introduction to Business contains a wealth of information. The trick is to know where to look to access all the information in the book. If you go on the Treasure Hunt with your teacher, you will discover how the textbook is organized, and how to get the most out of your reading and study time. Let's go!

1 How many chapters are in the book? How many units?

2 What part of the textbook will show you where the Better Business Bureau is taught?

3 Where do you find the Ask Standard & Poor's features?

4 What business is featured in the Unit 4 Real-World Business and Career Profile? Where do you first find the business name?

5 If you need help with one of the math applications, where would you look?

6 Where can you learn the definitions of **oligopoly, recruitment,** and **consumer**?

7 What skill do you practice in Chapter 13, Section 13.1, After You Read?

8 Where do you find a Unit Thematic Project?

9 What is the URL that takes you to the *Introduction to Business* Online Learning Center?

How is Introduction to Business Organized?

Introduction to Business contains 11 units that are logically organized into 35 chapters. The chapters include two sections. This structure presents your business lessons clearly and simply. Your book also includes a wide variety of features to reinforce the lessons and tie them to real-life situations.

Units

Units serve as an introduction to major themes of business. They show you "the big picture." Activities and interviews bring the real world of business to life.

Real-World Business and Career Profile Preview

This feature introduces you to a real-world business. You will learn more about the business and its owners when you finish studying the unit.

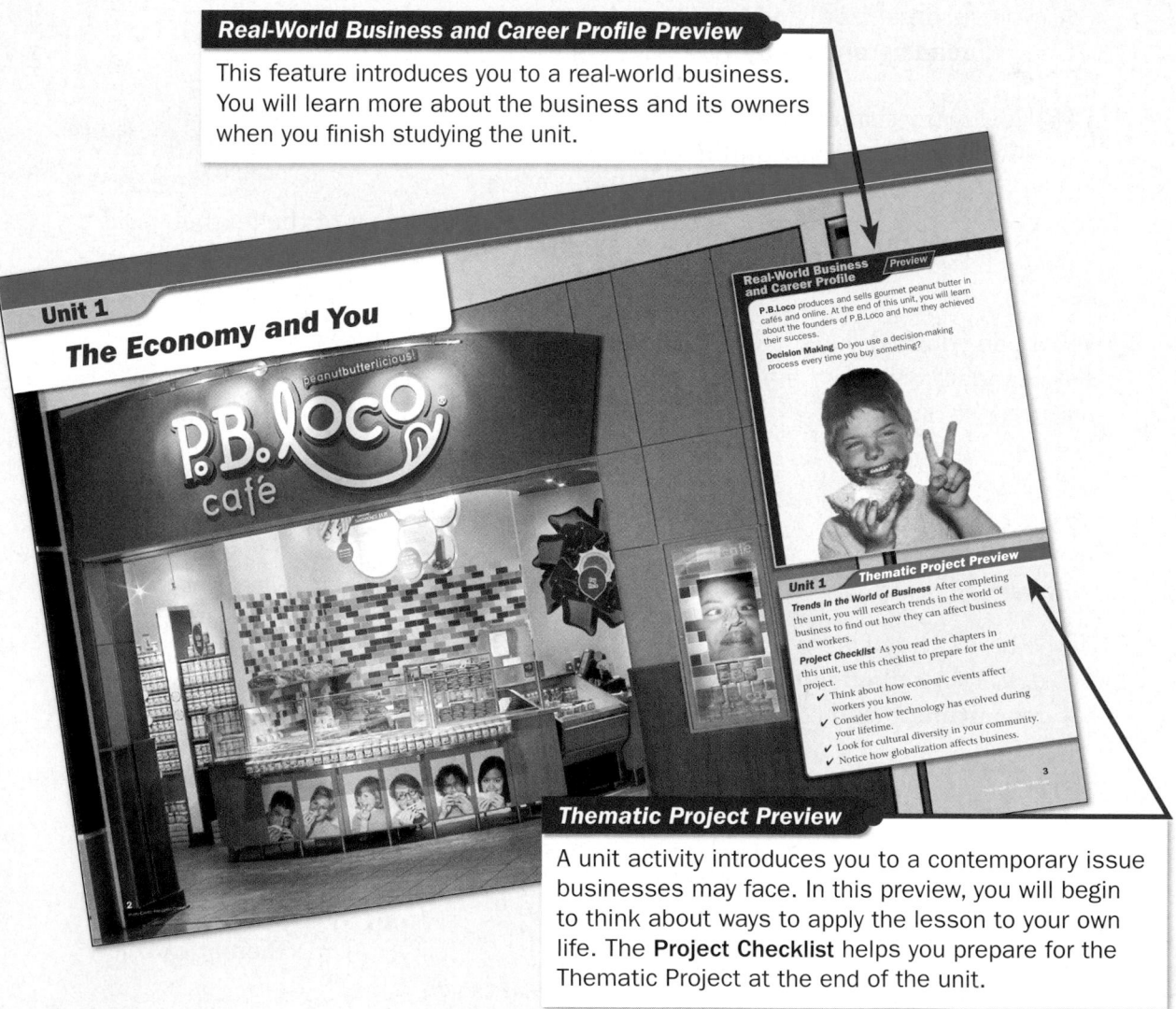

Thematic Project Preview

A unit activity introduces you to a contemporary issue businesses may face. In this preview, you will begin to think about ways to apply the lesson to your own life. The **Project Checklist** helps you prepare for the Thematic Project at the end of the unit.

Real-World Business and Career Profile

This end-of-unit feature provides an interview with the owners of a successful and eclectic business. These entrepreneurs provide practical answers to important questions about how they achieved their success. A critical thinking question prompts you to think more deeply about how you would address real decisions business owners make every day.

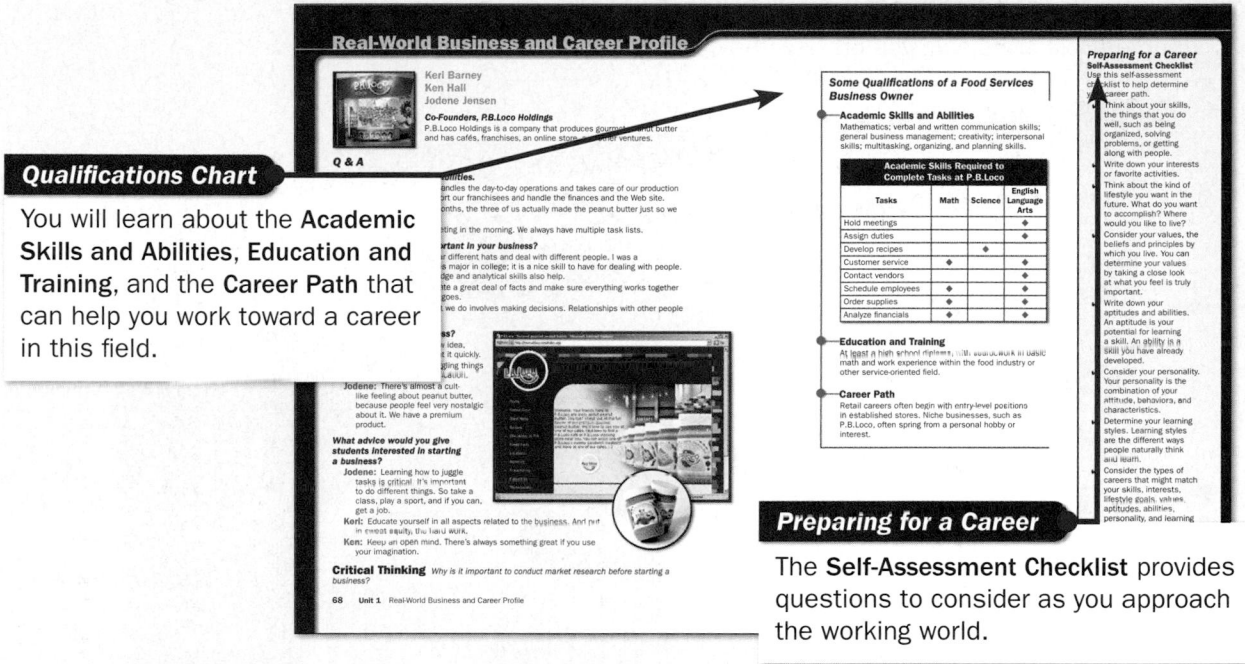

Qualifications Chart

You will learn about the **Academic Skills and Abilities**, **Education and Training**, and the **Career Path** that can help you work toward a career in this field.

Preparing for a Career

The **Self-Assessment Checklist** provides questions to consider as you approach the working world.

Thematic Project

Every Unit concludes with a Thematic Project that explores an important issue in the dynamic world of business. To complete each project, you will make decisions, conduct research, connect to your community, and develop a report.

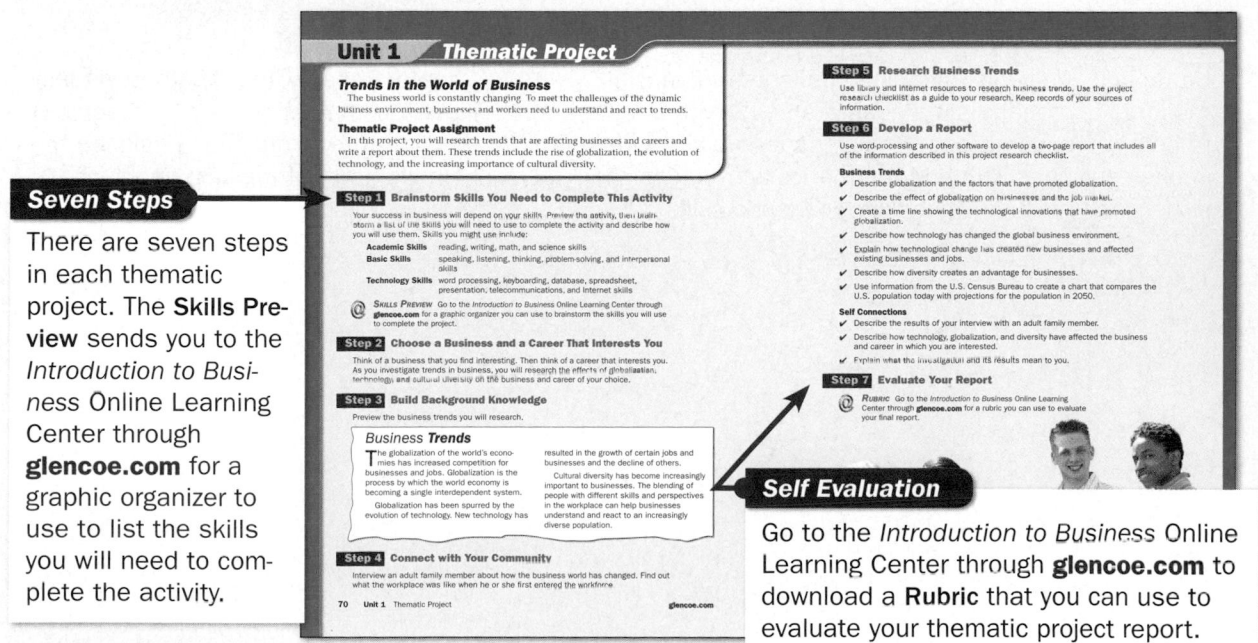

Seven Steps

There are seven steps in each thematic project. The **Skills Preview** sends you to the *Introduction to Business* Online Learning Center through **glencoe.com** for a graphic organizer to use to list the skills you will need to complete the activity.

Self Evaluation

Go to the *Introduction to Business* Online Learning Center through **glencoe.com** to download a **Rubric** that you can use to evaluate your thematic project report.

To the Student

Chapters

The chapters of *Introduction to Business* are organized around major businesses issues. They are divided logically into two sections and offer numerous learning strategies that will help you get the most from your studies.

Chapter Objectives

Chapter Objectives help you preview the content you will learn.

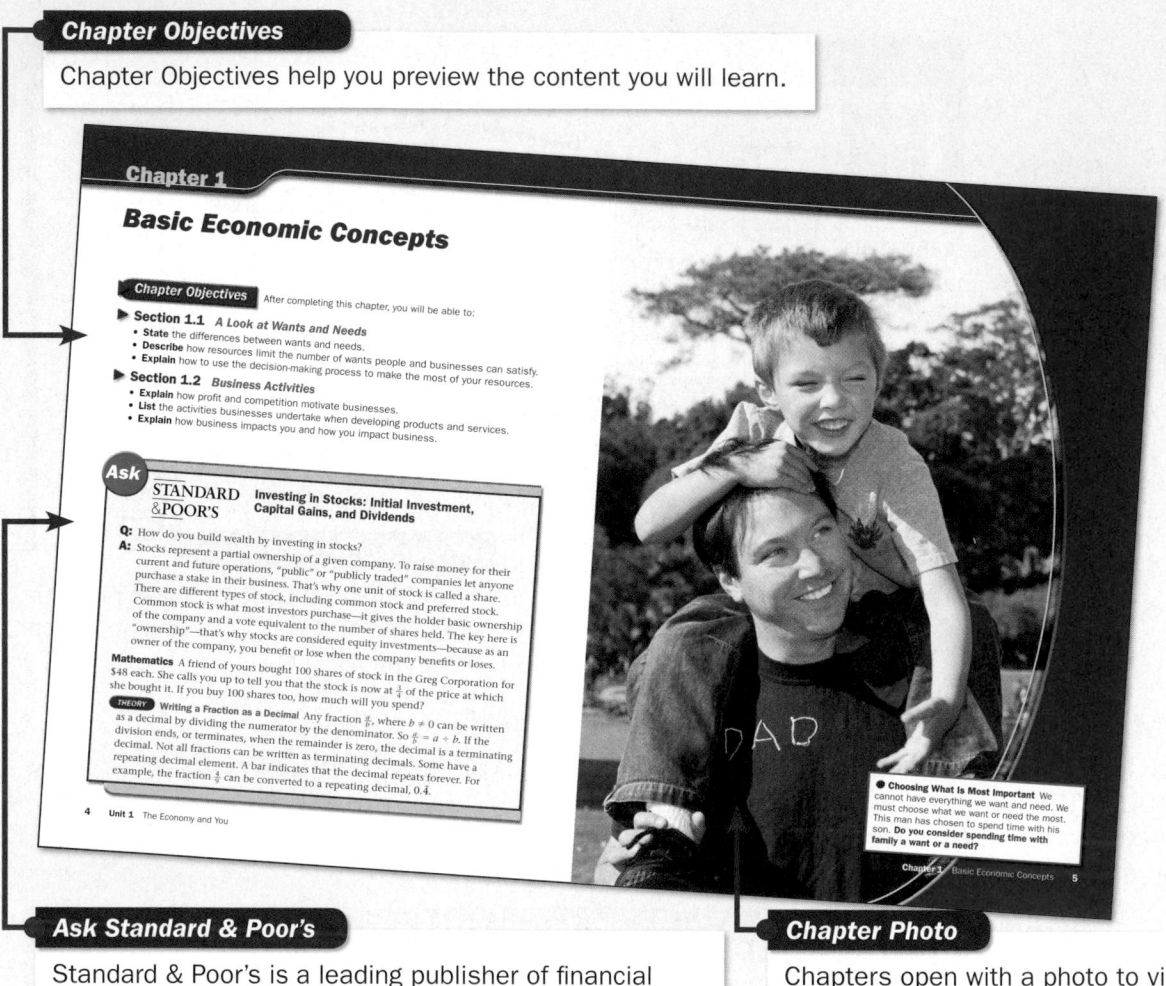

Ask Standard & Poor's

Standard & Poor's is a leading publisher of financial research and analysis. All chapters begin with a feature to help you understand financial issues. Ask Standard & Poor's concludes with a **Mathematics** activity designed to help you practice using your academic skills.

Chapter Photo

Chapters open with a photo to visually illustrate chapter content. The caption is followed by a question designed to help you to start thinking about what you will read.

Chapter Review and Activities

The Chapter Review and Activities allow you to practice your skills and reinforce your understanding of key concepts in the chapter. It organizes the chapter's key concepts to help you review the main ideas.

Review

Section Summaries, Vocabulary Review, and Key Concepts Review provide comprehension assessment.

Activities

Thinking, writing, technology, and ethics activities provide opportunities to assess your skills and apply content to varied real-world situations.

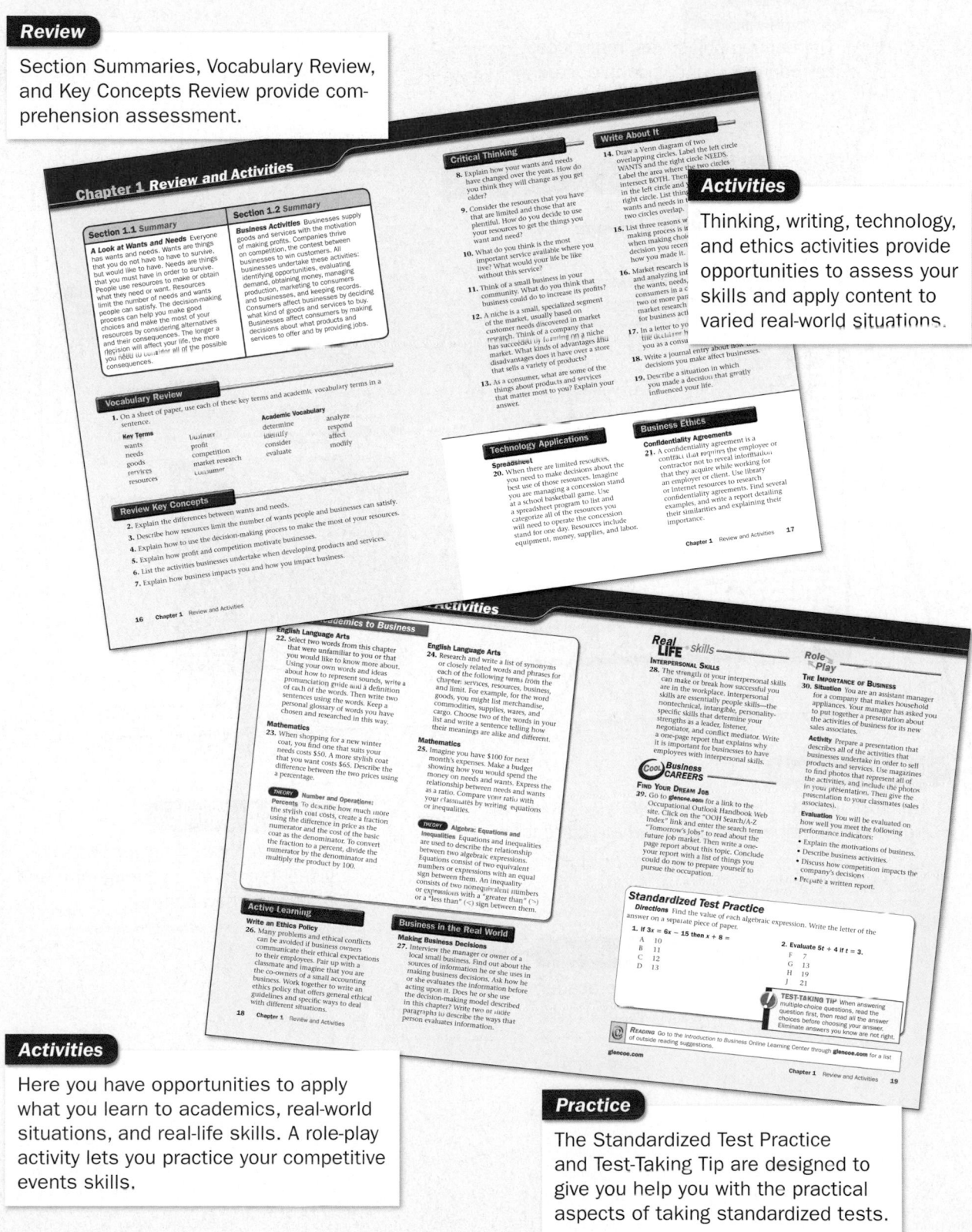

Activities

Here you have opportunities to apply what you learn to academics, real-world situations, and real-life skills. A role-play activity lets you practice your competitive events skills.

Practice

The Standardized Test Practice and Test-Taking Tip are designed to give you help you with the practical aspects of taking standardized tests.

Sections

Each chapter section begins with a Reading Guide to give you a preview of section content.

Reading Guide

The section objectives, main idea, key concepts, and vocabulary are previewed here.

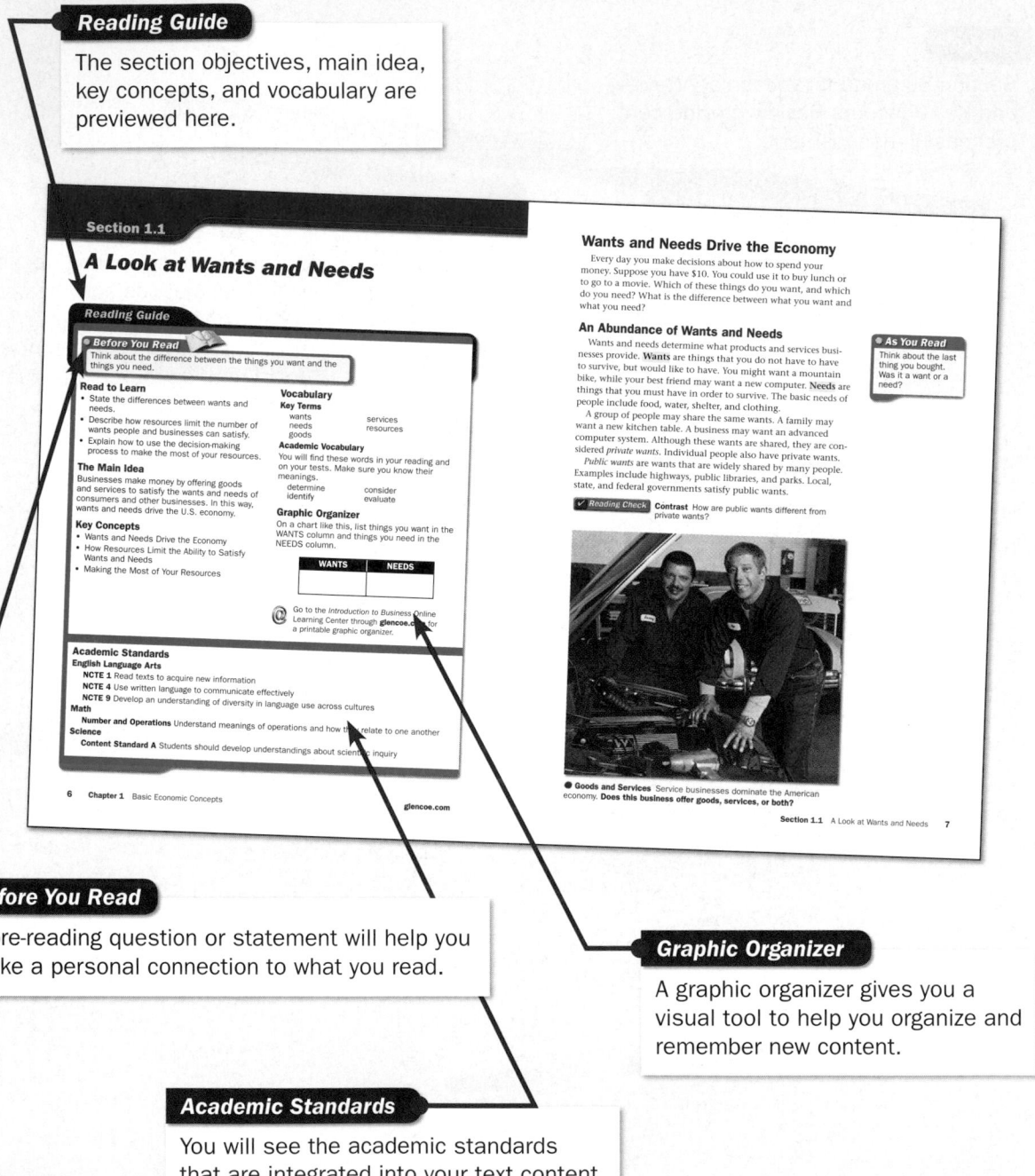

Before You Read

A pre-reading question or statement will help you make a personal connection to what you read.

Graphic Organizer

A graphic organizer gives you a visual tool to help you organize and remember new content.

Academic Standards

You will see the academic standards that are integrated into your text content.

Reading Strategies

Glencoe is committed to your reading success. Every section of *Introduction to Business* includes a number of reading strategies that will help you master this crucial skill.

As You Read

As You Read provides a cue to connect what you already know to what you are reading.

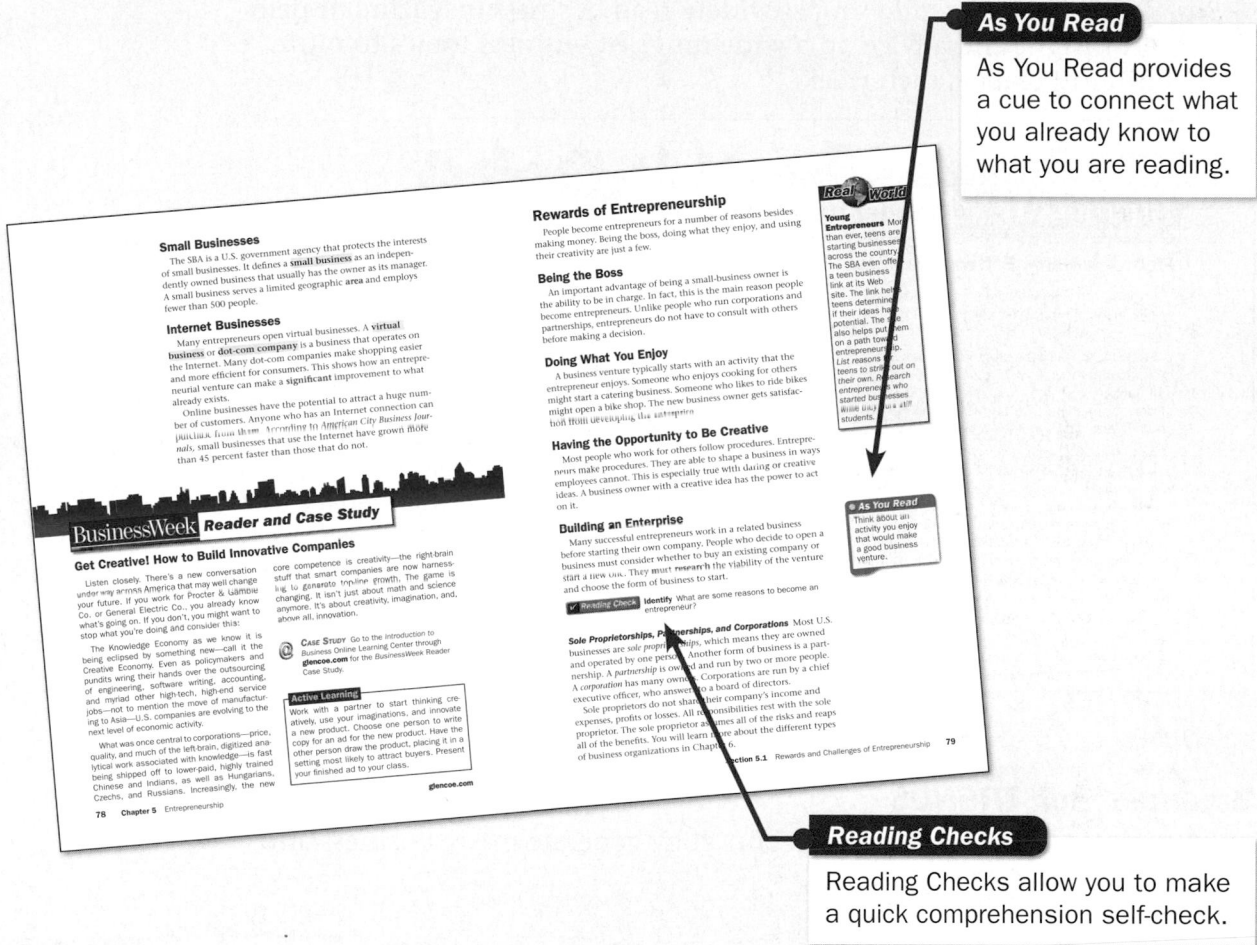

Reading Checks

Reading Checks allow you to make a quick comprehension self-check.

After You Read

Reviewing your reading is a powerful study skill. **Review Key Concepts** will help you organize and process your understanding of what you have read. **Academic Skills** will connect content to academics.

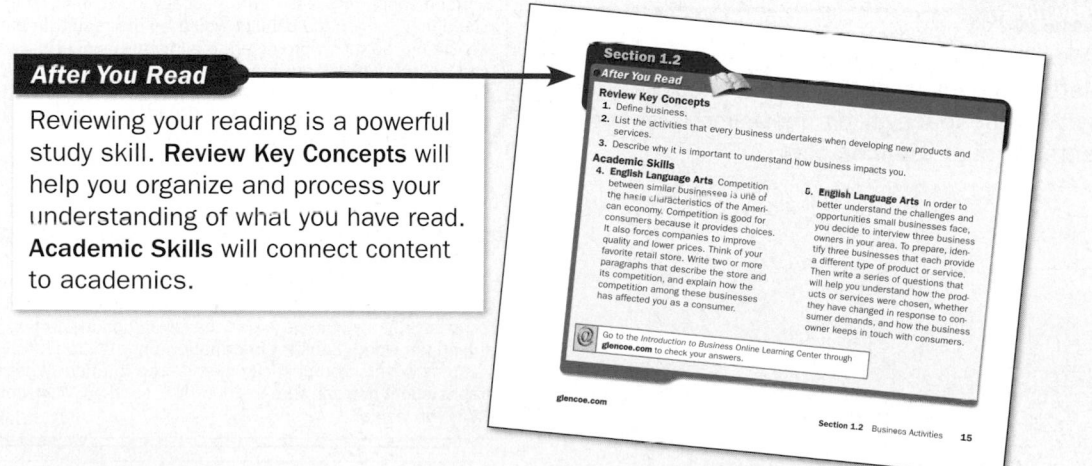

Features

The features in each chapter help you see the relevance between what you read and the real world.

BusinessWeek Reader and Case Study

BusinessWeek is the world's most widely read business magazine. It delivers expert insight and advice on a wide range of business topics to more than 8 million readers each week.

BusinessWeek *Reader and Case Study*

From Adversity, Software Success

An idea for a new business can strike anywhere: In the shower, in the car, even in a dream. Mike Jetter got his in a cancer ward.

In 1994, the German programmer was stuck in a hospital room in Munich, following his second leukemia relapse and his second bone-marrow transplant. Given a 50% chance to live another year, Jetter needed a distraction badly.

At the time, so-called mind-mapping was all the rage in Europe. Hailed as a more creative way to think, it involves organizing ideas in a visual way, with big concepts written in a circle in the middle of a page, surrounded by smaller ideas that branch off from them. But with pencil and paper, you couldn't drag and drop, edit, or collaborate. So Jetter set out to write a computer program.

After his release from the hospital, he and his wife Bettina handed marketing for the product over to a German CD-ROM distributor,

assuming not much would come of it. Today the software has spawned a $20 million-a-year business called Mindjet, headquartered in San Francisco.

Now the Jetters are turning this desktop product into something companies can use broadly to help brainstorm, plan, collaborate, and organize a host of business activities.

 CASE STUDY Go to the *Introduction to Business* Online Learning Center through **glencoe.com** for the *BusinessWeek* Reader Case Study.

Active Learning

Team up with a classmate and work together to identify and research a successful company with a unique business concept. Write a brief presentation about the business. Give the presentation to your class.

Case Study and Active Learning

The *BusinessWeek* Reader is an excerpt from BusinessWeek magazine. After reading the excerpt, you can go to the Online Learning Center through **glencoe.com** for a follow-up **Case Study** activity to print and complete. An **Active Learning** activity gives you the opportunity to work on an extended activity individually or with a team.

Science/Tech TRENDS

Current trends in science and technology generate many business and career opportunities.

Science/TechTRENDS

The Green Revolution

In 1798, Thomas Malthus, the great social scientist, showed that even as population increases geometrically (2, 4, 8, 16,…), the food supply increases arithmetically (1, 2, 3, 4,…). He predicted that hunger and conflict would be the result. In the 1960s, the Green Revolution promised to eliminate hunger by increasing crop yields. This was accomplished by using genetics to develop new varieties of grains and educating farmers in the technology of agriculture. Between 1960 and 1990, food production increased 1,000 percent, famine decreased 20 percent, caloric consumption increased 25 percent, and people around the world saw a rise in their incomes and standard of living.

WebQuest

Go to the *Introduction to Business* Online Learning Center through **glencoe.com** for links to Web sites where you can research how the technology of agriculture fueled the revolution in farming practices around the world. Look for information on irrigation strategies, the use of fertilizers and pesticides, and crop rotation. Write a few paragraphs about how farmers in countries, such as Mexico, increased their crop yields.

WebQuest

A WebQuest activity provides practice using related technology skills. You can access the WebQuest activity on the Online Learning Center through **glencoe.com**.

Ethics in Business

Ethics in Business gives you the opportunity to form opinions and make decisions about ethical questions that arise in real life and in business.

?ETHICS in Business

A Conflict of Interest

- **Critical Reading** Life is full of important decisions. Think about the kinds of decisions that you make as you read the question below.

  You work as an event planner for a local company. You are in charge of hiring a caterer for the company's 10th anniversary celebration. You have bids from four caterers in town. One of the bids is from a caterer who is an old friend. His bid is higher than the three others.

- **Decision Making** Would your relationship with the caterer affect which company you would hire? Explain your answer.

Critical Reading

The feature begins with a **Critical Reading** statement to prepare you to evaluate the ethical situation. In **Decision Making**, you have the opportunity to answer a question about how you would handle the situation.

International Business

Here you will learn about cross-cultural business practices and concepts related to global trade.

International Business

Global Marketplace

More businesses that used to operate exclusively within the United States now market their products around the world. From farmers to fast-food franchisees to theme-park operators, businesspeople in every sector of the economy are considering entering the global marketplace. Even though companies may operate successfully in the U.S. market, an increasing number of them are thinking about "going international."

Examples of Language Across Cultures

Q: In Italian, how do you say: "Hello, how are you?"
A: **Salve, come sta?** (pronounced: Sǎlvā, kōmā stǎ?)

What are some other reasons a company might choose to enter a foreign market? What are some questions companies should ask before they enter a foreign market?

Language Across Cultures

You will be introduced to words and phrases in other languages, and asked a follow-up question.

To the Student

Assessment

Assessment is an important part of the learning process. Knowing what you have learned is a good way to find out what you need to study further.

Section Assessment

Each section ends with review and academic questions.

After You Read

Assess your own comprehension with **Review Key Concepts** questions. Connect content to academics with the **Academic Skills** questions.

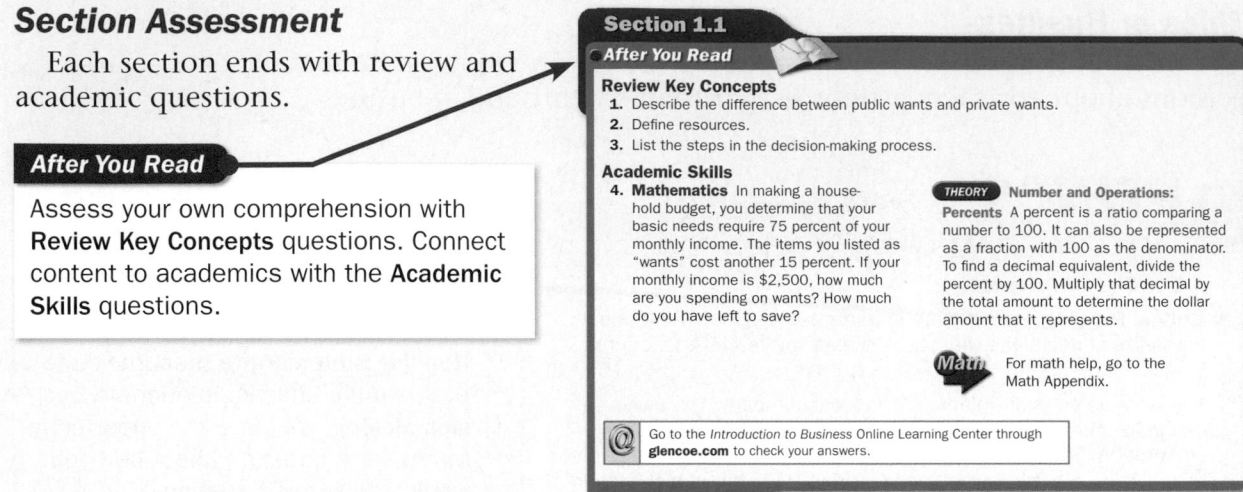

Section 1.1

After You Read

Review Key Concepts
1. Describe the difference between public wants and private wants.
2. Define resources.
3. List the steps in the decision-making process.

Academic Skills
4. **Mathematics** In making a household budget, you determine that your basic needs require 75 percent of your monthly income. The items you listed as "wants" cost another 15 percent. If your monthly income is $2,500, how much are you spending on wants? How much do you have left to save?

THEORY Number and Operations:
Percents A percent is a ratio comparing a number to 100. It can also be represented as a fraction with 100 as the denominator. To find a decimal equivalent, divide the percent by 100. Multiply that decimal by the total amount to determine the dollar amount that it represents.

Math For math help, go to the Math Appendix.

@ Go to the *Introduction to Business* Online Learning Center through **glencoe.com** to check your answers.

Chapter Review and Activities

The Chapter Review and Activities contains varied review and activities.

Critical Thinking

The Critical Thinking activities ask you to think more deeply to relate text to real situations.

Write About It

Here you will practice different types of writing.

Chapter 1 Review and Activities

Section Summaries

The Section Summaries restate the main concepts of the section.

Section 1.1 Summary

A Look at Wants and Needs Everyone has wants and needs. Wants are things that you do not have to have to survive, but would like to have. Needs are things that you must have in order to survive. People use resources to make or obtain what they need or want. Resources limit the number of needs and wants people can satisfy. The decision-making process can help you make good choices and make the most of your resources by considering alternatives and their consequences. The longer a decision will affect your life, the more you need to consider all of the possible consequences.

Section 1.2 Summary

Business Activities Businesses supply goods and services with the motivation of making profits. Companies thrive on competition, the contest between businesses to win customers. All businesses undertake these activities: identifying opportunities, evaluating demand, obtaining money, managing production, marketing to consumers and businesses, and keeping records. Consumers affect businesses by deciding what kind of goods and services to buy. Businesses affect consumers by making decisions about what products and services to offer and by providing jobs.

Vocabulary Review

The Vocabulary Review lists words you will need to know.

Vocabulary Review

1. On a sheet of paper, use each of these key terms and academic vocabulary terms in a sentence.

Key Terms
wants
needs
goods
services
resources

business
profit
competition
market research
consumer

Academic Vocabulary
determine
identify
consider
evaluate

analyze
respond
affect
modify

Review Key Concepts

Questions in the Review Key Concepts activity will review your comprehension.

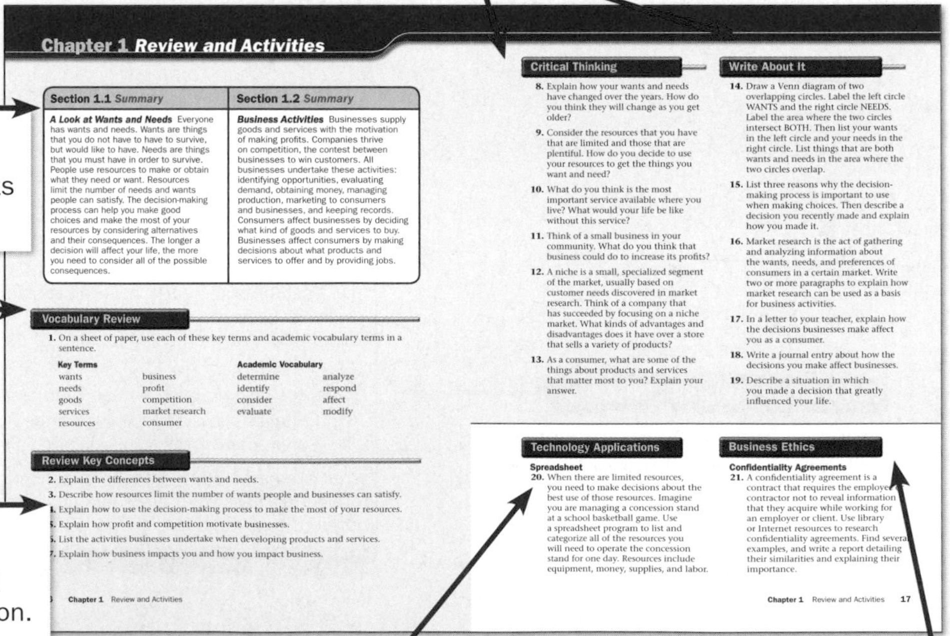

Review Key Concepts

2. Describe the differences between wants and needs.
3. Describe how resources limit the number of wants people and businesses can satisfy.
4. Explain how to use the decision-making process to make the most of your resources.
5. Explain how profit and competition motivate businesses.
6. List the activities businesses undertake when developing products and services.
7. Explain how business impacts you and how you impact business.

Chapter 1 Review and Activities

Critical Thinking

8. Explain how your wants and needs have changed over the years. How do you think they will change as you get older?
9. Consider the resources that you have that are limited and those that are plentiful. How do you decide to use your resources to get the things you want and need?
10. What do you think is the most important service available where you live? What would your life be like without this service?
11. Think of a small business in your community. What do you think that business could do to increase its profits?
12. A niche is a small, specialized segment of the market, usually based on customer needs discovered in market research. Think of a company that has succeeded by focusing on a niche market. What kinds of advantages and disadvantages does it have over a store that sells a variety of products?
13. As a consumer, what are some of the things about products and services that matter most to you? Explain your answer.

Write About It

14. Draw a Venn diagram of two overlapping circles. Label the left circle WANTS and the right circle NEEDS. Label the area where the two circles intersect BOTH. Then list your wants in the left circle and your needs in the right circle. List things that are both wants and needs in the area where the two circles overlap.
15. List three reasons why the decision-making process is important to use when making choices. Then describe a decision you recently made and explain how you made it.
16. Market research is the act of gathering and analyzing information about the wants, needs, and preferences of consumers in a certain market. Write two or more paragraphs to explain how market research can be used as a basis for business activities.
17. In a letter to your teacher, explain how the decisions businesses make affect you as a consumer.
18. Write a journal entry about how the decisions you make affect businesses.
19. Describe a situation in which you made a decision that greatly influenced your life.

Technology Applications

Spreadsheet
20. When there are limited resources, you need to make decisions about the best use of those resources. Imagine you are managing a concession stand at a school basketball game. Use a spreadsheet program to list and categorize all of the resources you will need to operate the concession stand for one day. Resources include equipment, money, supplies, and labor.

Business Ethics

Confidentiality Agreements
21. A confidentiality agreement is a contract that requires the employee contractor not to reveal information that they acquire while working for an employer or client. Use library or Internet resources to research confidentiality agreements. Find several examples, and write a report detailing their similarities and explaining their importance.

Chapter 1 Review and Activities **17**

Technology Applications

Practice your technology skills and applications.

Business Ethics

Opportunities to consider the ethical consequences of business decisions.

Applying Academics

Four activities give you practice applying your academic skills to business content.

Real-Life Skills

Activities to help you develop strong workplace and interpersonal skills.

Role Play

Role-play scenarios give you practice for competitive events. You will also learn how your performance will be evaluated.

Chapter 1 Review and Activities

Applying Academics to Business

English Language Arts

22. Select two words from this chapter that were unfamiliar to you or that you would like to know more about. Using your own words and ideas about how to represent sounds, write a pronunciation guide and a definition of each of the words. Then write two sentences using the words. Keep a personal glossary of words you have chosen and researched in this way.

Mathematics

23. When shopping for a new winter coat, you find one that suits your needs costs $50. A more stylish coat that you want costs $65. Describe the difference between the two prices using a percentage.

THEORY Number and Operations:
Percents To describe how much more the stylish coat costs, create a fraction using the difference in price as the numerator and the cost of the basic coat as the denominator. To convert the fraction to a percent, divide the numerator by the denominator and multiply the product by 100.

English Language Arts

24. Research and write a list of synonyms or closely related words and phrases for each of the following terms from the chapter: services, resources, business, and limit. For example, for the word goods, you might list merchandise, commodities, supplies, wares, and cargo. Choose two of the words in your list and write a sentence telling how their meanings are alike and different.

Mathematics

25. Imagine you have $100 for next month's expenses. Make a budget showing how you would spend the money on needs and wants. Express the relationship between needs and wants as a ratio. Compare your ratio with your classmates by writing equations or inequalities.

THEORY Algebra: Equations and Inequalities Equations and inequalities are used to describe the relationship between two algebraic expressions. Equations consist of two equivalent numbers or expressions with an equal sign between them. An inequality consists of two nonequivalent numbers or expressions with a "greater than" (>) or a "less than" (<) sign between them.

Active Learning

Write an Ethics Policy

26. Many problems and ethical conflicts can be avoided if business owners communicate their ethical expectations to their employees. Pair up with a classmate and imagine that you are the co-owners of a small accounting business. Work together to write an ethics policy that offers general ethical guidelines and specific ways to deal with different situations.

Business in the Real World

Making Business Decisions

27. Interview the manager or owner of a local small business. Find out about the sources of information he or she uses in making business decisions. Ask how he or she evaluates the information before acting upon it. Does he or she use the decision-making model described in this chapter? Write two or more paragraphs to describe the ways that person evaluates information.

18   Chapter 1   Review and Activities

Real LIFE skills

INTERPERSONAL SKILLS

28. The strength of your interpersonal skills can make or break how successful you are in the workplace. Interpersonal skills are essentially people skills—the nontechnical, intangible, personality-specific skills that determine your strengths as a leader, listener, negotiator, and conflict mediator. Write a one-page report that explains why it is important for businesses to have employees with interpersonal skills.

Cool Business CAREERS

FIND YOUR DREAM JOB

29. Go to glencoe.com for a link to the Occupational Outlook Handbook Web site. Click on the "OOH Search/A-Z Index" link and enter the search term "Tomorrow's Jobs" to read about the future job market. Then write a one-page report about this topic. Conclude your report with a list of things you could do now to prepare yourself to pursue the occupation.

Role Play

THE IMPORTANCE OF BUSINESS

30. **Situation** You are an assistant manager for a company that makes household appliances. Your manager has asked you to put together a presentation about the activities of business for its new sales associates.

Activity Prepare a presentation that describes all of the activities that businesses undertake in order to sell products and services. Use magazines to find photos that represent all of the activities, and include the photos in your presentation. Then give the presentation to your classmates (sales associates).

Evaluation You will be evaluated on how well you meet the following performance indicators:
• Explain the motivations of business.
• Describe business activities.
• Discuss how competition impacts the company's decisions.
• Prepare a written report.

Standardized Test Practice

Directions Find the value of each algebraic expression. Write the letter of the answer on a separate piece of paper.

1. If $3x = 6x - 15$ then $x + 8 =$
   A 10
   B 11
   C 12
   D 13

2. Evaluate $5t + 4$ if $t = 3$.
   F 7
   G 13
   H 19
   J 21

TEST-TAKING TIP When answering multiple-choice questions, read the question first, then read all the answer choices before choosing your answer. Eliminate answers you know are not right.

READING Go to the Introduction to Business Online Learning Center through glencoe.com for a list of outside reading suggestions.

glencoe.com   Chapter 1   Review and Activities   19

Active Learning

Here you have an opportunity to "learn by doing," either on your own or as part of a team.

Business in the Real World

Activities that will help you connect to your local business community.

Cool Business Careers

Exploring careers can help you set goals that can lead you to career success.

Standardized Test Practice

These activities give you an opportunity to sharpen your test-taking skills. The activities also includes a valuable **Test-Taking Tip**.

Online Learning Center

Follow these steps to access the textbook resources at the *Introduction to Business* Online Learning Center.

Step 1

Go to **glencoe.com**.

Step 2

Select your state from the pull-down menu.

Step 3

Select Student/Parent.

Step 4

Select Business Administration.

Step 5

Click ENTER.

Step 6

Click Introduction to Business © 2008.

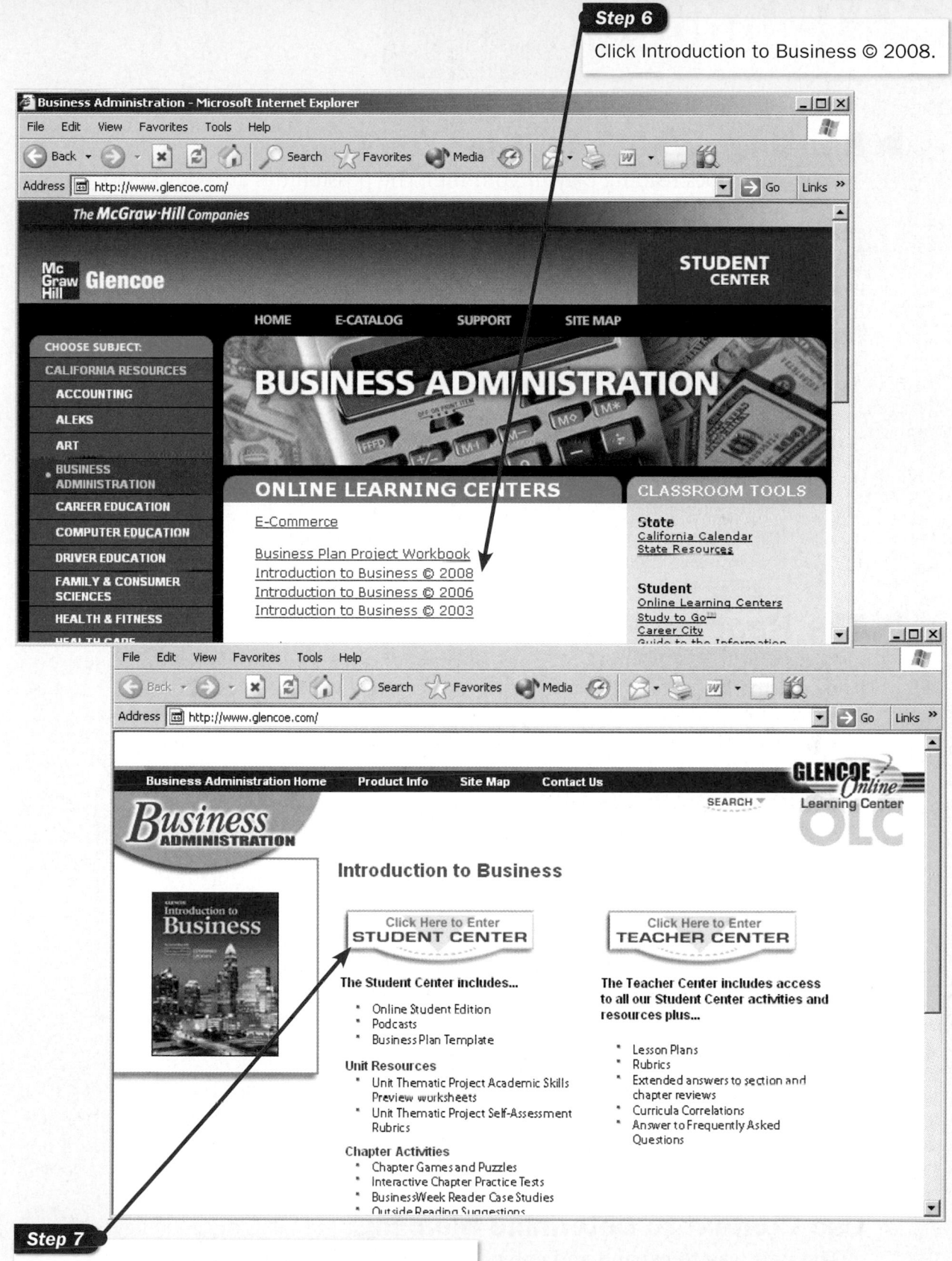

Step 7

Click Student Center to access student resources.

Reading Skills Handbook

▶ Reading: What's in It for You?

What role does reading play in your life? The possibilities are countless. Are you on a sports team? Perhaps you like to read about the latest news and statistics in your sports or find out about new training techniques. Are you looking for a part-time job? You might be looking for advice about résumé writing, interview techniques, or information about a company. Are you enrolled in an English class, an algebra class, or a business class? Then your assignments require a lot of reading.

Improving or Fine-tuning Your Reading Skills Will:

◆ Improve your grades
◆ Allow you to read faster and more efficiently
◆ Improve your study skills
◆ Help you remember more information accurately
◆ Improve your writing

▶ The Reading Process

Good reading skills build on one another, overlap, and spiral around in much the same way that a winding staircase goes around and around while leading you to a higher place. This handbook is designed to help you find and use the tools you'll need **before, during,** and **after** reading.

Strategies You Can Use

◆ Identify, understand, and learn new words
◆ Understand why you read
◆ Take a quick look at the whole text
◆ Try to predict what you are about to read
◆ Take breaks while you read and ask yourself questions about the text
◆ Take notes
◆ Keep thinking about what will come next
◆ Summarize

▶ Vocabulary Development

Word identification and vocabulary skills are the building blocks of the reading and the writing process. By learning to use a variety of strategies to build your word skills and vocabulary, you will become a stronger reader.

Use Context to Determine Meaning

The best way to expand and extend your vocabulary is to read widely, listen carefully, and participate in a rich variety of discussions. When reading on your own, though, you can often figure out the meanings of new words by looking at their **context,** the other words and sentences that surround them.

Tips for Using Context

Look for clues such as:

A synonym or an explanation of the unknown word in the sentence:
*Elise's shop specialized in **millinery**, or **hats for women.***

A reference to what the word is or is not like:
*An **archaeologist,** like a **historian,** deals with the past.*

A general topic associated with the word:
*The **cooking** teacher discussed the best way to **braise** meat.*

A description or action associated with the word:
*He used the **hoe** to **dig up** the garden.*

Predict a Possible Meaning

Another way to determine the meaning of a word is to take the word apart. If you understand the meaning of the **base,** or **root,** part of a word, and also know the meanings of key syllables added either to the beginning or end of the base word, you can usually figure out what the word means.

Word Origins Since Latin, Greek, and Anglo-Saxon roots are the basis for much of our English vocabulary, having some background in languages can be a useful vocabulary tool. For example, *astronomy* comes from the Greek root *astro,* which means "relating to the stars." *Stellar* also has a meaning referring to stars, but its origin is Latin. Knowing root words in other languages can help you determine meanings, derivations, and spellings in English.

Prefixes and Suffixes A prefix is a word part that can be added to the beginning of a word. For example, the prefix *semi* means "half" or "partial," so *semicircle* means "half a circle." A suffix is a word part that can be added to the end of a word. Adding a suffix often changes a word from one part of speech to another.

Using Dictionaries A dictionary provides the meaning or meanings of a word. Look at the sample dictionary entry on the next page to see what other information it provides.

Thesauruses and Specialized Reference Books A thesaurus provides synonyms and often antonyms. It is a useful tool to expand your vocabulary. Remember to check the exact definition of the listed words in a dictionary before you use a thesaurus. Specialized dictionaries such as *Barron's Dictionary of Business Terms* or *Black's Law Dictionary* list terms and expressions that are not commonly included in a general dictionary. You can also use online dictionaries.

See **glencoe.com** for direct links.

Glossaries Many textbooks and technical works contain condensed dictionaries that provide an alphabetical listing of words used in the text and their specific definitions.

Dictionary Entry

Forms of
the word

Numbered
definitions

Usage label

Part of
speech

Example
of use

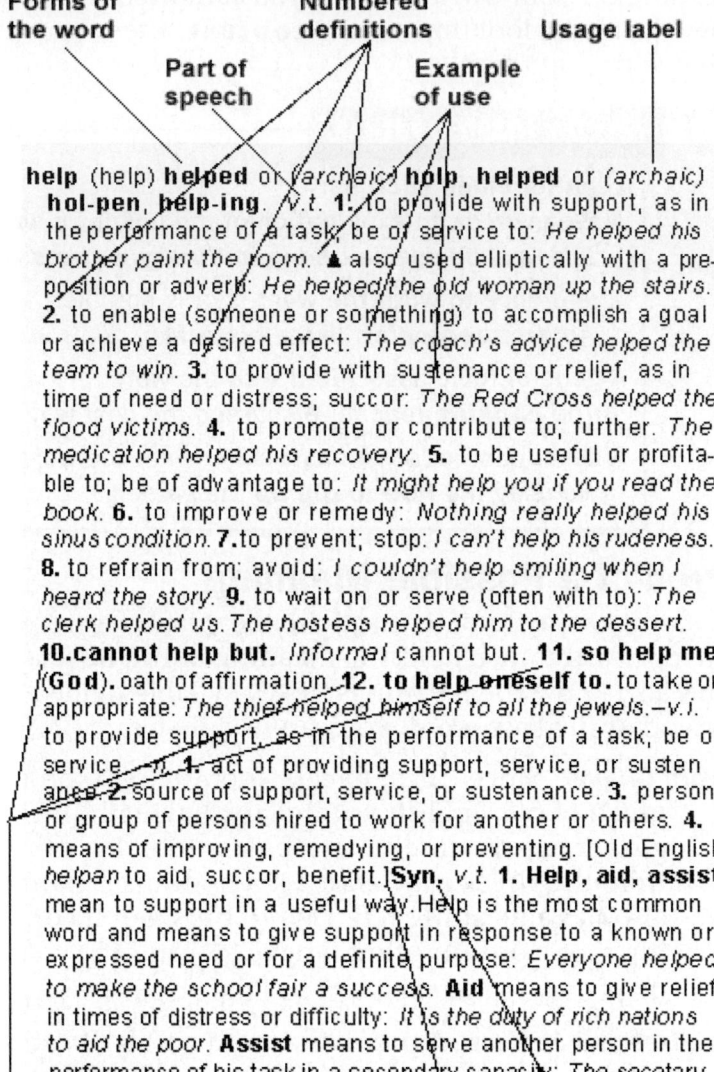

help (help) **helped** or *(archaic)* **holp, helped** or *(archaic)*
hol-pen, help-ing. *v.t.* **1.** to provide with support, as in
the performance of a task; be of service to: *He helped his
brother paint the room.* ▲ also used elliptically with a pre-
position or adverb: *He helped the old woman up the stairs.*
2. to enable (someone or something) to accomplish a goal
or achieve a desired effect: *The coach's advice helped the
team to win.* **3.** to provide with sustenance or relief, as in
time of need or distress; succor: *The Red Cross helped the
flood victims.* **4.** to promote or contribute to; further. *The
medication helped his recovery.* **5.** to be useful or profitable to; be of advantage to: *It might help you if you read the
book.* **6.** to improve or remedy: *Nothing really helped his
sinus condition.* **7.** to prevent; stop: *I can't help his rudeness.*
8. to refrain from; avoid: *I couldn't help smiling when I
heard the story.* **9.** to wait on or serve (often with to): *The
clerk helped us. The hostess helped him to the dessert.*
10. cannot help but. *Informal* cannot but. **11. so help me
(God).** oath of affirmation. **12. to help oneself to.** to take or
appropriate: *The thief helped himself to all the jewels.*—*v.i.*
to provide support, as in the performance of a task; be of
service. —*n.* **1.** act of providing support, service, or susten
ance. **2.** source of support, service, or sustenance. **3.** person
or group of persons hired to work for another or others. **4.**
means of improving, remedying, or preventing. [Old English
helpan to aid, succor, benefit.] **Syn.** *v.t.* **1. Help, aid, assist**
mean to support in a useful way. Help is the most common
word and means to give support in response to a known or
expressed need or for a definite purpose: *Everyone helped
to make the school fair a success.* **Aid** means to give relief
in times of distress or difficulty: *It is the duty of rich nations
to aid the poor.* **Assist** means to serve another person in the
performance of his task in a secondary capacity: *The secetary
assists the officer by taking care of his corresponding.*

Idioms

Origin
(etymology)

Synonyms

Recognize Word Meanings across Subjects Have you learned a new word in
one class and then noticed it in your reading for other subjects? The
word might not mean exactly the same thing in each class, but you
can use the meaning you already know to help you understand what
it means in another subject area. For example:

Math *After you multiply the two numbers, explain how you arrived at the*
product*.*

Science *One **product** of photosynthesis is oxygen.*

Economics *The Gross National **Product** is the total dollar value of goods
and services produced by a nation.*

▶ Understanding What You Read

Reading comprehension means understanding—deriving meaning from—what you have read. Using a variety of strategies can help you improve your comprehension and make reading more interesting and more fun.

Read for a Reason

To get the greatest benefit from what you read, you should **establish a purpose for reading.** In school, you have many reasons for reading. Some of them are:

- To learn and understand new information
- To find specific information
- To review before a test
- To complete an assignment
- To prepare (research) before you write

As your reading skills improve, you will notice that you apply different strategies to fit the different purposes for reading. For example, if you are reading for entertainment, you might read quickly, but if you read to gather information or follow directions, you might read more slowly, take notes, construct a graphic organizer, or reread sections of text.

Draw on Personal Background

Drawing on personal background may also be called activating prior knowledge. Before you start reading a text, ask yourself questions like these:

- What have I heard or read about this topic?
- Do I have any personal experience relating to this topic?

Using a KWL Chart A KWL chart is a good device for organizing information you gather before, during, and after reading. In the first column, list what you already **know,** then list what you **want** to know in the middle column. Use the third column when you review and you assess what you **learned.** You can also add more columns to record places where you found information and places where you can look for more information.

K (What I already know)	W (What I want to know)	L (What I have learned)

Adjust Your Reading Speed Your reading speed is a key factor in how well your understand what you are reading. You will need to adjust your speed depending on your reading purpose.

Scanning *means running your eyes quickly over the material to look for words or phrases. Scan when you need a specific piece of information.*

Skimming *means reading a passage quickly to find its main idea or to get an overview. Skim a text when you preview to determine what the material is about.*

Reading for detail *involves careful reading while paying attention to text structure and monitoring your understanding. Read for detail when you are learning concepts, following complicated directions, or preparing to analyze a text.*

▶ Techniques to Understand and Remember What You Read

Preview

Before beginning a selection, it's helpful to **preview** what you are about to read.

> **Previewing Strategies**
>
> **Read** the title, headings, and subheadings of the selection.
> **Look** at the illustrations and notice how the text is organized.
> **Skim** the selection: Take a glance at the whole thing
> **Decide** what the main idea might be.
> **Predict** what a selection will be about.

Predict

Have you ever read a mystery, decided who committed the crime, and then changed your mind as more clues were revealed? You were adjusting your predictions. Did you smile when you found out you guessed the murderer? You were verifying your predictions.

As you read, take educated guesses about story events and outcomes; that is, **make predictions** before and during reading. This will help you focus your attention on the text and it will improve your understanding.

Determine the Main Idea

When you look for the **main idea**, you are looking for the most important statement in a text. Depending on what kind of text you are reading, the main idea can be located at the very beginning (news stories in newspaper or a magazine) or at the end (scientific research document). Ask yourself:

- What is each sentence about?
- Is there one sentence that is more important than all the others?
- What idea do details support or point out?

Taking Notes

Cornell Note-Taking System: There are many methods for note taking. The **Cornell Note-taking System** is a well-known method that can help you organize what you read. To the right is a note-taking activity based on the Cornell Note-taking System.

Graphic organizers: Using a graphic organizer to retell content in a visual representation will help you remember and retain content. You might make a **chart** or **diagram,** organizing what you have read. Here are some examples of graphic organizers:

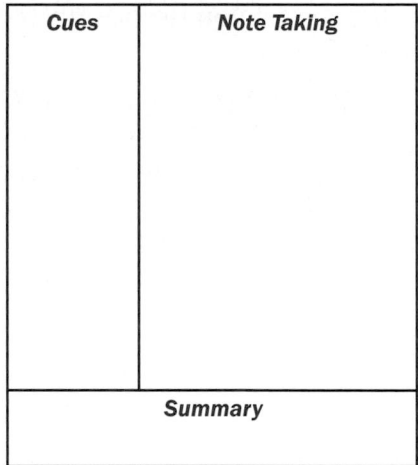

Venn diagrams: When mapping out a comparison-and-contrast text structure, you can use a Venn diagram. The outer portions of the circles will show how two characters, ideas, or items contrast, or are different, and the overlapping part will compare two things, or show how they are similar.

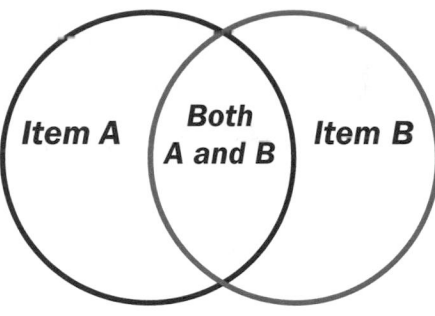

Flow charts: To help you track the sequence of events, or cause and effect, use a flow chart. Arrange ideas or events in their logical, sequential order. Then draw arrows between your ideas to indicate how one idea or event flows into another.

Go to **glencoe.com** for more information about note taking and more study tools.

Visualize

Try to form a mental picture of scenes, characters, and events as you read. Use the details and descriptions the author gives you. If you can **visualize** what you read, it will be more interesting and you will remember it better.

Question

Ask yourself questions about the text while you read. Ask yourself about the importance of the sentences, how they relate to one another, if you understand what you just read, and what you think is going to come next.

Clarify

If you feel you do not understand meaning (through questioning), try these techniques:

> **What to Do When You Do not Understand**
>
> ◆ Reread confusing parts of the text.
> ◆ Diagram (chart) relationships between chunks of text, ideas, and sentences.
> ◆ Look up unfamiliar words.
> ◆ Talk out the text to yourself.
> ◆ Read the passage once more.

Review

Take time to stop and review what you have read. Use your note-taking tools (graphic organizers or Cornell notes charts). Also, review and consider your KWL chart.

Monitor Your Comprehension

Continue to check your understanding by using the following two strategies:

Summarize   Pause and tell yourself the main ideas of the text and the key supporting details. Try to answer the following questions: Who? What? When? Where? Why? How?

Paraphrase   Pause, close the book, and try to retell what you have just read in your own words. It might help to pretend you are explaining the text to someone who has not read it and does not know the material.

▶ Understanding Text Structure

Good writers do not just put together sentences and paragraphs, they organize their writing with a specific purpose in mind. That organization is called text structure. When you understand and follow the structure of a text, it is easier to remember the information you are reading. There are many ways text may be structured. Watch for these **signal words**: They will help you follow the text's organization (also, remember to use these techniques when you write).

Compare and Contrast

This structure shows similarities and differences between people, things, and ideas. This is often used to demonstrate that things that seem alike are really different, or vice versa.

> **Signal words:** *similarly, more, less, on the one hand / on the other hand, in contrast, but, however*

Cause and Effect

Writers used the cause and effect structure to explore the reasons for something happening and to examine the results or consequences of events.

> **Signal words:** *so, because, as a result, therefore, for the following reasons*

Problem and Solution

When they organize text around the question "how?" writers state a problem and suggest solutions.

> **Signal words:** *how, help, problem, obstruction, overcome, difficulty, need, attempt, have to, must*

Sequence

Sequencing tells you in which order to consider thoughts or facts. Examples of sequencing are:

Chronological order refers to the order in which events take place.

> **Signal words:** *first, next, then, finally*

Spatial order describes the organization of things in space (to describe a room, for example).

> **Signal words:** *above, below, behind, next to*

Order of importance lists things or thoughts from the most important to the least important (or the other way around).

> **Signal words:** *principal, central, main, important, fundamental*

▶ Reading for Meaning

It is important to think about what you are reading to get the most information out of a text, to understand the consequences of what the text says, to remember the content, and to form your own opinion about what the content means.

Interpret

Interpreting is asking yourself, "What is the writer really saying?" and then using what you already know to answer that question.

Infer

Writers do not always state exactly everything they want you to understand. By providing clues and details, they sometimes imply certain information. An **inference** involves using your reason and experience to develop the idea on your own, based on what an author implies or suggests. What is most important when drawing inferences is to be sure that you have accurately based your guesses on supporting details from the text. If you cannot point to a place in the selection to help back up your inference, you may need to rethink your guess.

Draw Conclusions

A conclusion is a general statement you can make and explain with reasoning, or with supporting details from a text. If you read a story describing a sport where five players bounce a ball and throw it through a high hoop, you may conclude that the sport is basketball.

Analyze

To understand persuasive nonfiction (a text that discusses facts and opinions to arrive at a conclusion), you need to analyze statements and examples to see if they support the main idea. To understand an informational text (a text, such as a textbook, that gives you information, not opinions), you need to keep track of how the ideas are organized to find the main points.

> **Hint:** *Use your graphic organizers and notes charts.*

Distinguish Facts and Opinions

This is one of the most important reading skills you can learn. A fact is a statement that can be proven. An opinion is what the writer believes. A writer may support opinions with facts, but an opinion cannot be proven. For example:

> **Fact:** *California produces fruit and other agricultural products.*

> **Opinion:** *California produces the best fruit and other agricultural products.*

Evaluate

Would you take seriously an article on nuclear fission if you knew it was written by a comedic actor? If you need to rely on accurate information, you need to find out who wrote what you are reading and why. Where did the writer get information? Is the information one-sided? Can you verify the information?

▶ Reading for Research

You will need to **read actively** in order to research a topic. You might also need to generate an interesting, relevant, and researchable **question** on your own and locate appropriate print and nonprint information from a wide variety of sources. Then you will need to **categorize** that information, evaluate it, and **organize** it in a new way in order to produce a research project for a specific audience. Finally, **draw conclusions** about your original research question. These conclusions may lead you to other areas for further inquiry.

Locate Appropriate Print and Nonprint Information

In your research, try to use a variety of sources. Because different sources present information in different ways, your research project will be more interesting and balanced when you read in a variety of sources.

Textbooks Texts include any book used as a basis for instruction or a source of information.

Book Indices A book index, or a bibliography, is an alphabetical listing of books. Some book indices list books on specific subjects; others are more general. Other indices list a variety of topics or resources.

Periodicals Magazines and journals are issued at regular intervals, such as weekly or monthly. One way to locate information in magazines is to use the *Readers' Guide to Periodical Literature.* This guide is available in print form in most libraries.

Technical Manuals A manual is a guide or handbook intended to give instruction on how to perform a task or operate something. A vehicle owner's manual might give information on how to operate and service a car.

Reference Books Reference books include encyclopedias and almanacs, and are used to locate specific pieces of information.

Electronic Encyclopedias, Databases, and the Internet There are many ways to locate extensive information using your computer. Infotrac, for instance, acts as an online readers guide. CD encyclopedias can provide easy access to all subjects.

Organize and Convert Information

As you gather information from different sources, taking careful notes, you will need to think about how to **synthesize** the information, that is, convert it into a unified whole, as well as how to change it into a form your audience will easily understand and that will meet your assignment guidelines.

1. First, ask yourself what you want your audience to know.
2. Then, think about a pattern of organization, a structure that will best show your main ideas. You might ask yourself the following questions:
   - When comparing items or ideas, what graphic aids can I use?
   - When showing the reasons something happened and the effects of certain actions, what text structure would be best?
   - How can I briefly and clearly show important information to my audience?
   - Would an illustration or even a cartoon help to make a certain point?

Chapter	Section	Unit Objectives
Chapter 1 *Basic Economic Concepts*	1.1	**State** the differences between wants and needs.
		Describe how resources limit the number of wants people and businesses can satisfy.
		Explain how to use the decision-making process to make the most of your resources.
	1.2	**Explain** how profit and competition motivate businesses.
		List the activities businesses undertake when developing products and services.
		Explain how business impacts you and you impact business.
Chapter 2 *Economic Resources and Systems*	2.1	**Explain** how scarcity requires individuals and nations to make decisions about resources.
		Describe the four factors of production.
	2.2	**Describe** the three basic economic questions each country must answer in order to make decisions about using their resources.
		Contrast the way a market economy and a command economy answer the three economic questions.
Chapter 3 *Economic Activity in a Changing World*	3.1	**Describe** the four types of economy the United States has experienced.
		Describe what is shown by GDP, unemployment rate, rate of inflation, and national debt.
	3.2	**Explain** how individuals and the government influence the economy.
		Describe the four stages of the business cycle.
Chapter 4 *Business Ethics and Social Responsibility*	4.1	**Define** ethics and business ethics.
		Describe why ethical behavior is good for business.
		List the steps for dealing with an ethical dilemma.
	4.2	**Define** what is meant by the social responsibility of business.

Understanding the Coding

Brackets Brackets on the reduced student edition page correspond to teaching strategies and activities in the Teacher Wraparound Edition. As you teach the lesson, the brackets show you exactly where to use the teaching strategies and activities.

Letters The letters on the reduced student edition page identify the type of strategy or activity. See the key below to learn about the different types of strategies and activities.

Ability Levels Leveled teaching strategies are identified by one of three codes to give you an idea of their suitability for students of varying learning styles and abilities.

Resources Key program resources are listed in each chapter. Icons indicate the format of resources.

KEY to Letters

D **Develop Concepts** activities help teachers gauge and plan for students' concept development.

R **Reading Strategy** activities help you teach reading skills and vocabulary.

C **Critical Thinking** strategies help students apply and extend what they have learned.

U **Universal Access** activities provide differentiated instruction for English language learners and suggestions for teaching various types of learners.

S **Skill Practice** provides leveled instruction for meeting individual needs and learning styles.

W **Writing Support** activities provide writing opportunities to help students comprehend the text.

NCLB **No Child Left Behind** activities help students practice and improve their abilities in academic subjects.

KEY to Ability Levels

L1 Strategies should be within the ability range of all students. Often full class participation is required.

L2 Strategies are for average to above-average students or for small groups. Some teacher direction is necessary.

L3 Strategies are designed for students able and willing to work independently. Minimal teacher direction is necessary.

KEY to Resource Icons

📁 Print Material

💿 CD-ROM

📡 Online Learning Center with Podcasts

BusinessWeek *Reader and Case Study*

In Unit 1, your students can learn more about business in the real world through the following *BusinessWeek* Readers and Case Studies:

From Adversity, Software Success

An idea for a new business can strike anywhere—in the shower, in the car, even in a dream. Mike Jetter got his in a cancer ward. (page 14)

Graphing the Development Gap

Hans Rosling's brainchild, a nonprofit called Gapminder, uses interactive design to render global statistics comprehensible. (page 24)

Net or Newspapers?

Newspapers have always been a part of our lives. But the Internet has Wall Street analysts concerned about the future of the daily paper. (page 39)

It's Getting Easier Being Green

Interest in integrating business with the needs of the environment is prompting a harder look at achieving a sustainable economy. (page 60)

Chapter Features and Activities

 STANDARD &POOR'S

BusinessWeek *Reader and Case Study*

Science/Tech TRENDS

ETHICS in Business

International Business

Section	Feature Title	Page
1.1	Service Business	8
1.1	Local Brands	10
1.2	Target Market	13
2.1	Being *Resourceful*	24
2.2	Supply and Demand	29
3.1	Unsung Heroes	40

Section	Feature Title	Page
3.1	Worker Shortage	41
3.2	Depressionproof	46
4.1	Cultural Etiquette	55
4.2	Earth-Friendly Products	61
4.2	Independent Films	62

Reading Strategies

Before You Read

Section	Page
1.1	6
1.2	11
2.1	22
2.2	27
3.1	38
3.2	43
4.1	54
4.2	59

Graphic Organizer

Chapter	Section	Title	Page
1	1.1	Wants and Needs	6
	1.2	Business Activities	11
2	2.1	Factors of Production	22
	2.2	Market and Command Economies	27
3	3.1	Economic Timeline	38
	3.2	The Business Cycle	43
4	4.1	Ethical Decision Making	54
	4.2	Business Responsibilities	59

As You Read

Section	Page
1.1	7, 8
1.2	12
2.1	23
2.2	28, 31
3.1	39, 40
3.2	44, 45
4.1	55, 57, 58
4.2	60, 63

✔ Reading Check

Section	Page
1.1	7, 9
1.2	12
2.1	23, 24, 25
2.2	29
3.1	41
3.2	44, 46
4.1	55
4.2	60, 63

After You Read

Section	Page
1.1	10
1.2	15
2.1	26
2.2	31
3.1	42
3.2	47
4.1	58
4.2	63

Unit Overview

Introduce the Unit

Introduce the unit by describing the main concepts of each chapter in the unit.

Unit 1 is about economic activity and how it affects everyday life.

Chapter 1 explains the difference between wants and needs and examines how businesses satisfy consumer wants and needs.

Chapter 2 introduces scarcity and the four factors of production and describes economic systems.

Chapter 3 describes types of economic measurements and explains the four phases of the business cycle.

Chapter 4 explains the importance of ethics in business and describes the social responsibility of business.

00:00 OUT OF TIME?

If class time is too short to cover all of the chapters in this unit, have students:

- Write down the vocabulary terms and their definitions.
- Read the chapter summaries at the beginning of each chapter review.
- Go to the *Introduction to Business* Online Learning Center through **glencoe.com** to download free Study-to-Go content to their PDAs or cell phones.

The Economy and You

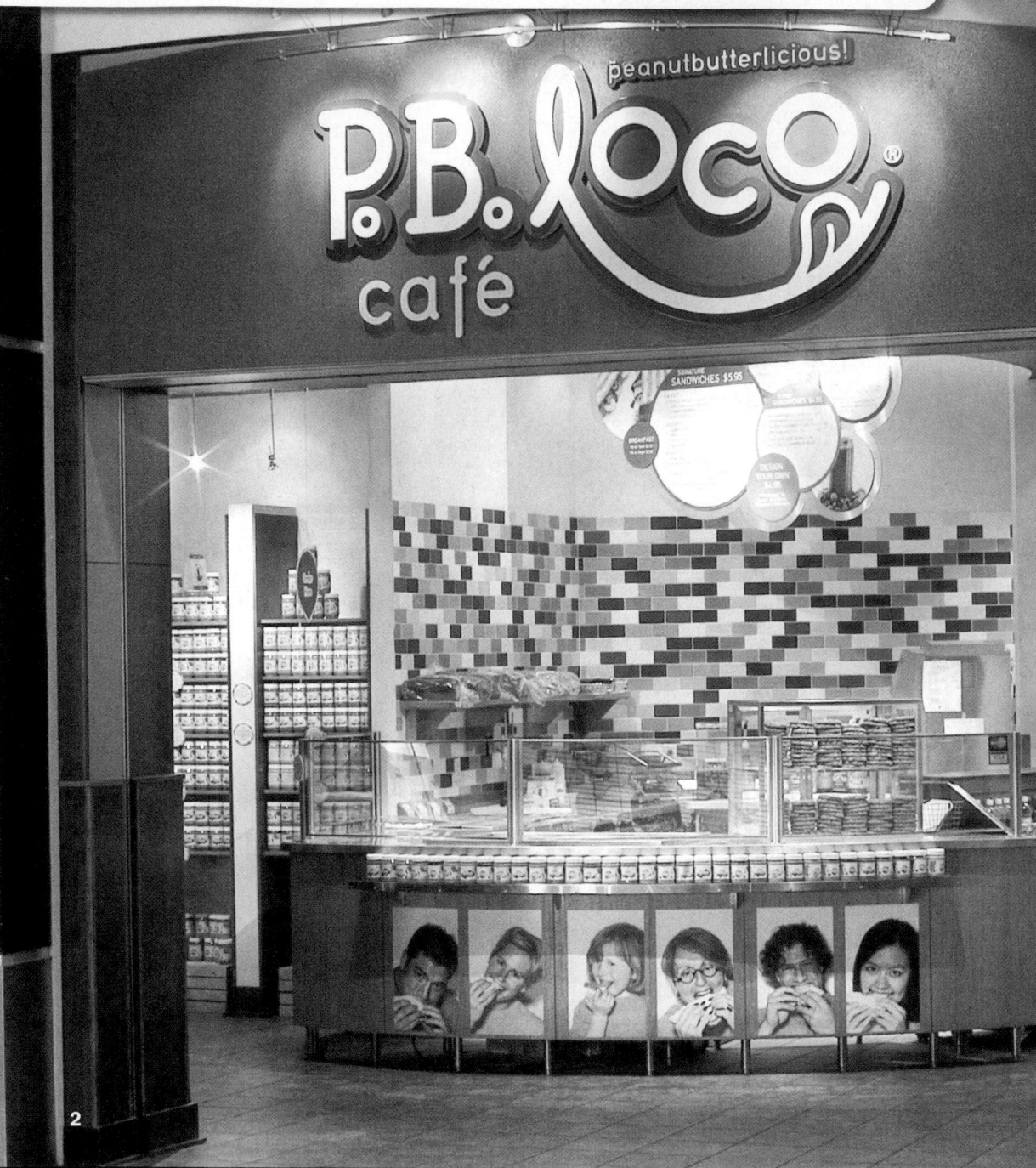

Real-World Business and Career Profile — Preview

P.B.Loco Tell students that at the end of this unit, they will learn about the founders of P.B.Loco and how they achieved their success. P.B.Loco produces and sells gourmet peanut butter in cafés, franchises, and online. Friends Jodene Jensen, Ken Hall, and Keri Barney chose to work together and sell a product that they all loved. Ask students to give reasons why P.B.Loco's business concept has been successful. (Answers will vary. Students might suggest that their idea was simple and unique and that it offers online and retail sales.)

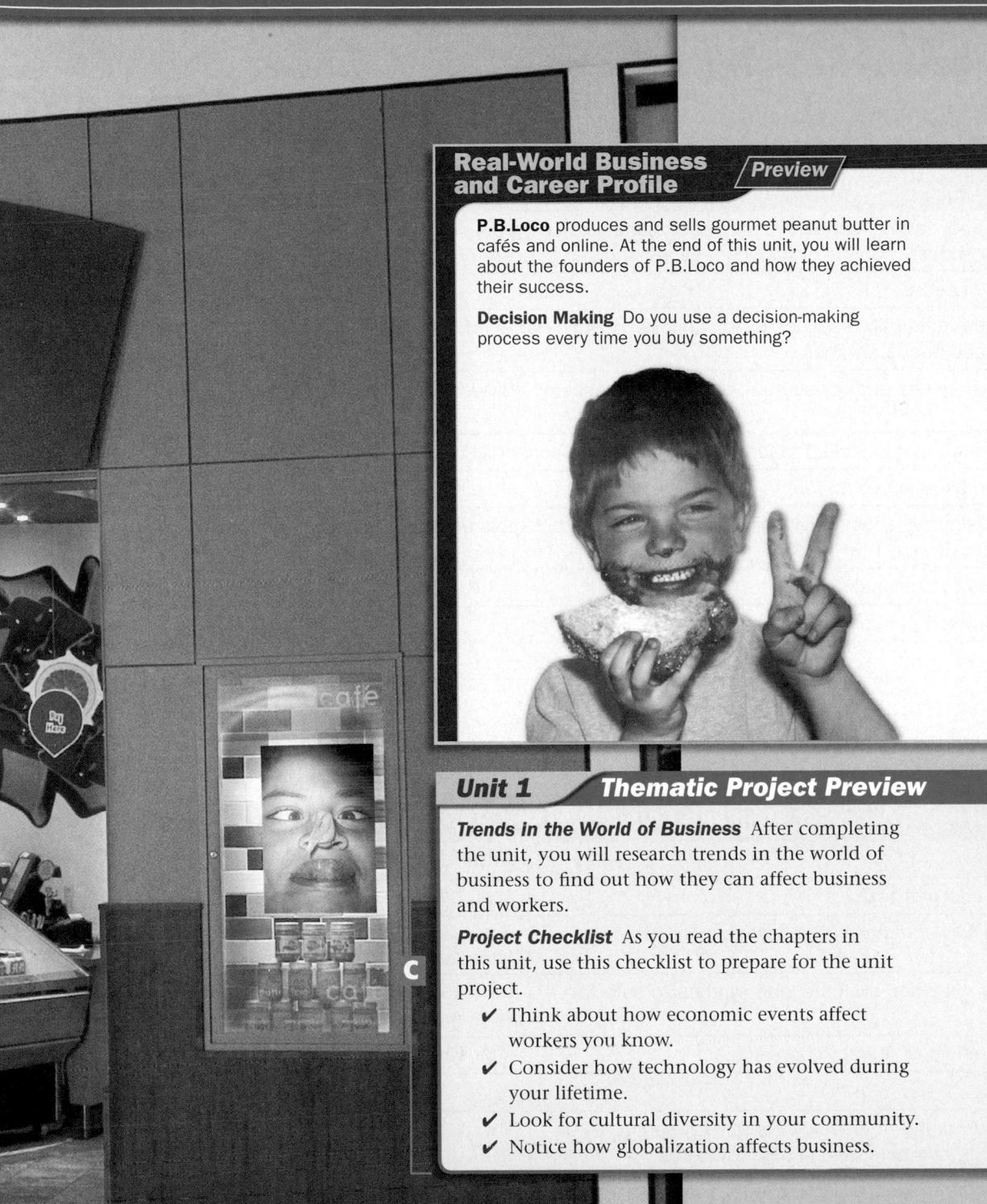

Real-World Business and Career Profile *Preview*

P.B.Loco produces and sells gourmet peanut butter in cafés and online. At the end of this unit, you will learn about the founders of P.B.Loco and how they achieved their success.

Decision Making Do you use a decision-making process every time you buy something?

Unit 1 Thematic Project Preview

Trends in the World of Business After completing the unit, you will research trends in the world of business to find out how they can affect business and workers.

Project Checklist As you read the chapters in this unit, use this checklist to prepare for the unit project.

- ✔ Think about how economic events affect workers you know.
- ✔ Consider how technology has evolved during your lifetime.
- ✔ Look for cultural diversity in your community.
- ✔ Notice how globalization affects business.

3

3

Standards Based Lesson Planning

Introduction to Business provides students with instruction and assessment in the following fundamental content areas:

Content Standards Correlations	
Discuss basic economic terms and issues such as types of goods and services produced, manner by which goods and services are produced, consumer for whom goods and services are produced.	pp. 7, 8, 10, 12, 13
Determine the role of wants and needs.	p. 7
Relate demand (wants and needs) to supply. Provides examples of economic wants and needs and explains ways economic wants and needs are met.	pp. 7, 8
Differentiate the interests of businesses and consumers; analyze influences of individuals on the economy.	pp. 7, 8, 10
Use economic concepts to understand and make reasoned decisions about economic issues.	p. 9
Apply the steps in the decision-making process.	p. 9
Examine the various roles of individuals; analyze influences of individuals on business and the economy.	p. 10
Describe the activities performed by business.	p. 12
Relate the significance of competition in business.	p. 13
Define economic roles.	p. 15

NCLB

Activities, information, and skills practice will help your students attain No Child Left Behind proficiency. Students will improve their abilities in the following academic standards areas:

Academic Standards Correlations		
English Language Arts	**Activities/Features**	**Page**
NCTE 3 Apply strategies to interpret texts	Applying Academics	p. 18
NCTE 4 Use written language to communicate effectively	BusinessWeek Reader After You Read	p. 14
NCTE 7 Conduct research and gather, evaluate, and synthesize data to communicate discoveries	BusinessWeek Reader After You Read	pp. 14, 15
NCTE 11 Participate as members of literacy communities	After You Read	p. 15
Mathematics		
Number and Operations Understand numbers, ways of representing numbers, relationships among numbers, and number systems	After You Read	p. 10
Number and Operations Compute fluently and make reasonable estimates	Applying Academics	p. 18
Algebra Represent and analyze mathematical situations and structures using algebraic symbols	Ask S&P Applying Academics	pp. 4, 18
Algebra Use mathematical models to represent and understand quantitative relationships	Applying Academics	p. 18
Science		
Content Standard G Students should develop understanding of science as a human endeavor, nature of scientific knowledge, historical perspectives	Science/Tech Trends	p. 12

Correlations   This chart shows the 21st Century Skills, foundation skills, and workplace competencies that students develop as they work in this chapter.

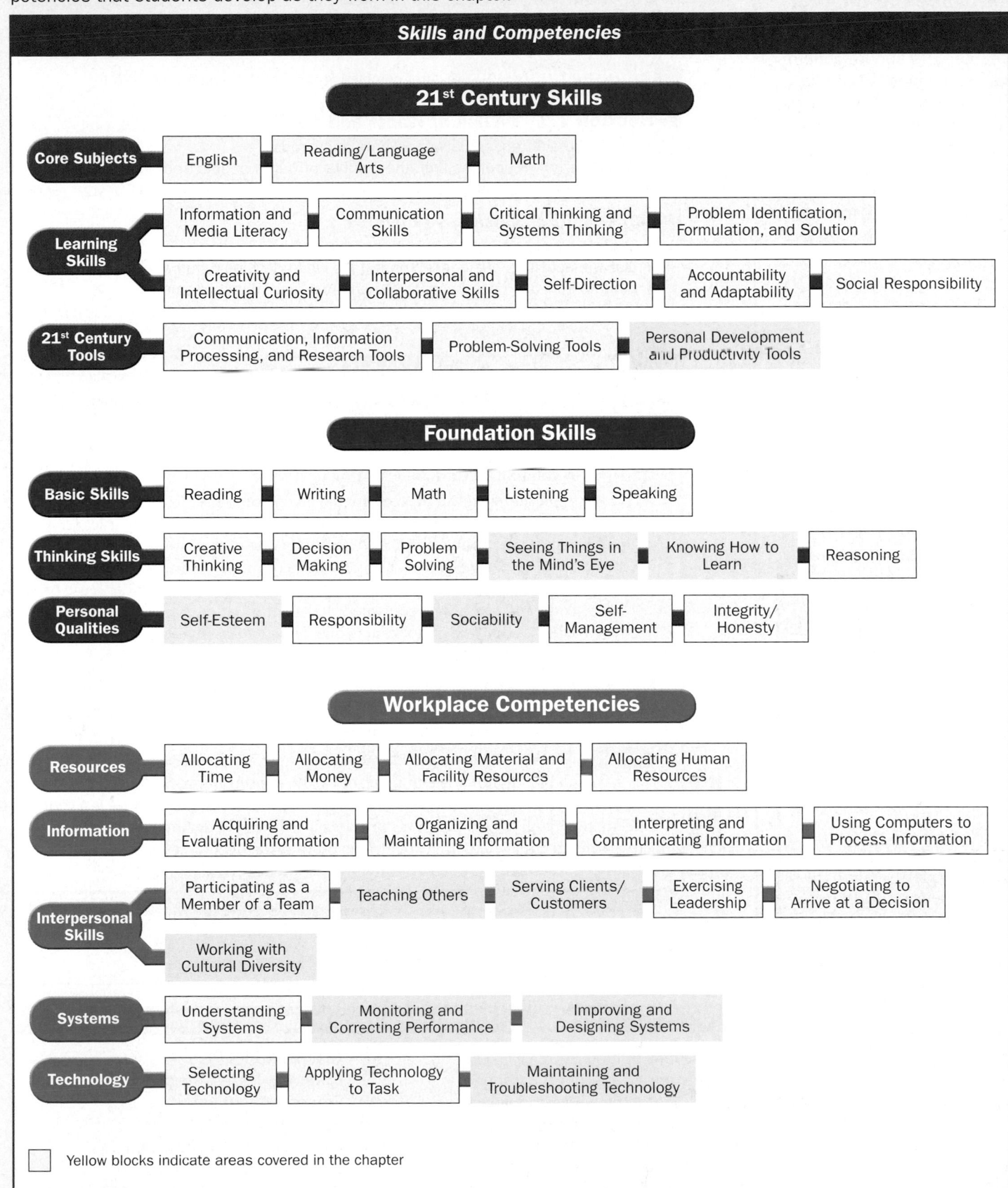

Skills and Competencies

21st Century Skills

Core Subjects
- English
- Reading/Language Arts
- Math

Learning Skills
- Information and Media Literacy
- Communication Skills
- Critical Thinking and Systems Thinking
- Problem Identification, Formulation, and Solution
- Creativity and Intellectual Curiosity
- Interpersonal and Collaborative Skills
- Self-Direction
- Accountability and Adaptability
- Social Responsibility

21st Century Tools
- Communication, Information Processing, and Research Tools
- Problem-Solving Tools
- Personal Development and Productivity Tools

Foundation Skills

Basic Skills
- Reading
- Writing
- Math
- Listening
- Speaking

Thinking Skills
- Creative Thinking
- Decision Making
- Problem Solving
- Seeing Things in the Mind's Eye
- Knowing How to Learn
- Reasoning

Personal Qualities
- Self-Esteem
- Responsibility
- Sociability
- Self-Management
- Integrity/Honesty

Workplace Competencies

Resources
- Allocating Time
- Allocating Money
- Allocating Material and Facility Resources
- Allocating Human Resources

Information
- Acquiring and Evaluating Information
- Organizing and Maintaining Information
- Interpreting and Communicating Information
- Using Computers to Process Information

Interpersonal Skills
- Participating as a Member of a Team
- Teaching Others
- Serving Clients/Customers
- Exercising Leadership
- Negotiating to Arrive at a Decision
- Working with Cultural Diversity

Systems
- Understanding Systems
- Monitoring and Correcting Performance
- Improving and Designing Systems

Technology
- Selecting Technology
- Applying Technology to Task
- Maintaining and Troubleshooting Technology

☐ Yellow blocks indicate areas covered in the chapter

Introduce the Chapter

Basic Economic Concepts
Chapter 1 is about economics. Economics is the study of how people satisfy unlimited and competing wants and needs through the careful use of limited resources.

Building Background
The term "economy," from which we get "economics," comes most directly from the Old French word "economie," meaning "management of a household." The French adopted the term from the Latin word "oeconomia," which was in turn derived from the Greek word "oikonomia." Oikonomia came from the word "oikonomos," which separates into "oikos," meaning house, and "-nomos" meaning managing.

STANDARD &POOR'S

>> Math Answer
Convert $\frac{3}{4}$ to a decimal by dividing: $3 \div 4 = 0.75$. Now multiply: $\$48 \times 0.75 = \$36$. Mulitply again to get the answer: $\$36 \times 100 = \$3,600$.

>> Extension Activity
Have students calculate the price for 100 shares of each of these stocks: Apple, $54.10 per share; Bank of America, $48.44 per share; Yahoo, $26.97 per share. Have students name the company that would raise the most (Apple) and the least (Yahoo) by selling stock.

N C L B Activity correlates to Math standards.

Basic Economic Concepts

Chapter Objectives After completing this chapter, you will be able to:

▶ **Section 1.1** *A Look at Wants and Needs*
- **State** the differences between wants and needs.
- **Describe** how resources limit the number of wants people and businesses can satisfy.
- **Explain** how to use the decision-making process to make the most of your resources.

▶ **Section 1.2** *Business Activities*
- **Explain** how profit and competition motivate businesses.
- **List** the activities businesses undertake when developing products and services.
- **Explain** how business impacts you and how you impact business.

Ask STANDARD &POOR'S

Investing in Stocks: Initial Investment, Capital Gains, and Dividends

Q: How do you build wealth by investing in stocks?

A: Stocks represent a partial ownership of a given company. To raise money for their current and future operations, "public" or "publicly traded" companies let anyone purchase a stake in their business. That's why one unit of stock is called a share. There are different types of stock, including common stock and preferred stock. Common stock is what most investors purchase—it gives the holder basic ownership of the company and a vote equivalent to the number of shares held. The key here is "ownership"—that's why stocks are considered equity investments—because as an owner of the company, you benefit or lose when the company benefits or loses.

Mathematics A friend of yours bought 100 shares of stock in the Greg Corporation for $48 each. She calls you up to tell you that the stock is now at $\frac{3}{4}$ of the price at which she bought it. If you buy 100 shares too, how much will you spend?

THEORY **Writing a Fraction as a Decimal** Any fraction $\frac{a}{b}$, where $b \neq 0$ can be written as a decimal by dividing the numerator by the denominator. So $\frac{a}{b} = a \div b$. If the division ends, or terminates, when the remainder is zero, the decimal is a terminating decimal. Not all fractions can be written as terminating decimals. Some have a repeating decimal element. A bar indicates that the decimal repeats forever. For example, the fraction $\frac{4}{9}$ can be converted to a repeating decimal, $0.\overline{4}$.

N C L B

Classroom Resources

- Student Edition
- Teacher Wraparound Edition
- Student Activity Workbook with Academic Integration
- Student Activity Workbook with Academic Integration TAE
- *Fast File*, Unit 1 Resources
- Inclusion in the Business Education Classroom

- TeacherWorks Plus
- *ExamView Assessment Suite*
- Presentation Plus!
- Vocabulary PuzzleMaker
- Interactive Student Edition
- Online Student Edition
- Online Learning Center with Podcasts

● **Choosing What Is Most Important** We cannot have everything we want and need. We must choose what we want or need the most. This man has chosen to spend time with his son. **Do you consider spending time with family a want or a need?**

Review the Objectives
Introduce the chapter by reviewing the chapter objectives:

Section 1.1 *Objectives*
State the differences between wants and needs. (A need is required for survival; a want is something that you do not have to have to survive.)

Describe how resources limit the number of wants and needs people and businesses can satisfy. (Few people have enough resources to satisfy all of their wants.)

Explain how the decision-making process can help you to make the most of your resources. (It can help you to make the right choices about what to buy.)

Section 1.2 *Objectives*
Explain how profit and competition motivate businesses. (Businesses compete against each other to win customers and make a profit.)

List the activities businesses undertake when developing products and services. (Businesses identify opportunities, evaluate demand, obtain funding, manage production, market goods and/or services, and keep records.)

Explain how business impacts you and how you impact business. (Consumers affect businesses by deciding what kind of goods and services to buy. Businesses affect consumers by making decisions about what goods and services to produce.)

Discuss the Photo
● **Choosing What Is Most Important** Read the photo caption to students: We cannot have everything we want and need. We must choose what we want or need the most. This man has chosen to spend time with his son.

Ask students to give examples of how this concept applies to their lives. (Answers should involve making decisions from among many choices about how to use resources, such as money and time.)

5

FOCUS

 Bell Ringer Activity

A Look at Wants and Needs

Write these statements on the board and have students complete them: Things I need to survive include _____. Things I want include _____.
Ask students: How do you distinguish between your needs and wants?
(Needs are necessary for survival, while wants are not.)

Preteaching

Presentation Plus!
The Presentation Plus! CD provides visual teaching aids for this section.

PuzzleMaker
Use the Vocabulary PuzzleMaker to create a puzzle of this section's key terms. Students can complete the puzzle on paper or on a computer.

Graphic Organizer
Tell students to go to the Online Learning Center through **glencoe.com** for a printable graphic organizer. (Graphic organizers will vary but should properly classify wants and needs.)

N C L B Academic correlations to book content.

A Look at Wants and Needs

 **Reading Guide**

Before You Read
Think about the difference between the things you want and the things you need.

Read to Learn
- State the differences between wants and needs.
- Describe how resources limit the number of wants people and businesses can satisfy.
- Explain how to use the decision-making process to make the most of your resources.

D

The Main Idea
Businesses make money by offering goods and services to satisfy the wants and needs of consumers and other businesses. In this way, wants and needs drive the U.S. economy.

Key Concepts
- Wants and Needs Drive the Economy
- How Resources Limit the Ability to Satisfy Wants and Needs
- Making the Most of Your Resources

Vocabulary
Key Terms
wants   services
needs   resources
goods

Academic Vocabulary
You will find these words in your reading and on your tests. Make sure you know their meanings.
determine   consider
identify   evaluate

Graphic Organizer
On a chart like this, list things you want in the WANTS column and things you need in the NEEDS column.

WANTS	NEEDS

 Go to the *Introduction to Business* Online Learning Center through **glencoe.com** for a printable graphic organizer.

Academic Standards
English Language Arts
N C L B
    NCTE 1 Read texts to acquire new information
    NCTE 4 Use written language to communicate effectively
    NCTE 9 Develop an understanding of diversity in language use across cultures
Math
    Number and Operations Understand meanings of operations and how they relate to one another
Science
    Content Standard A Students should develop understandings about scientific inquiry

Reading Guide

Before You Read
Point out to the class that there is a category of things called needs that people can not live without. Needs are required for survival.

D Develop Concepts
The Main Idea Ask students: How do wants and needs drive the economy? (Wants and needs drive the economy because they determine what goods and services businesses produce and sell.)

Wants and Needs Drive the Economy

Every day you make decisions about how to spend your money. Suppose you have $10. You could use it to buy lunch or to go to a movie. Which of these things do you want, and which do you need? What is the difference between what you want and what you need?

An Abundance of Wants and Needs

Wants and needs determine what products and services businesses provide. **Wants** are things that you do not have to have to survive, but would like to have. You might want a mountain bike, while your best friend may want a new computer. **Needs** are things that you must have in order to survive. The basic needs of people include food, water, shelter, and clothing.

A group of people may share the same wants. A family may want a new kitchen table. A business may want an advanced computer system. Although these wants are shared, they are considered *private wants*. Individual people also have private wants.

Public wants are wants that are widely shared by many people. Examples include highways, public libraries, and parks. Local, state, and federal governments satisfy public wants.

✔ Reading Check **Contrast** How are public wants different from private wants?

● **Goods and Services** Service businesses dominate the American economy. **Does this business offer goods, services, or both?**

● **As You Read**

Think about the last thing you bought. Was it a want or a need?

TEACH

Discussion Starter
Personal Wants and Needs
Ask students to list the things they need between the time they leave their house in the morning and lunchtime. (transportation, food, clothing, shelter, and/or assistive technologies)

● **As You Read**

Ask a volunteer to answer the question: Was the last thing you bought a want or a need? Then discuss how to discern between wants and needs.

R Reading Strategy

Create a Table Ask students to create a table that lists the wants and needs of consumers and the wants and needs of businesses. (Consumer needs include food, water, shelter, clothing, medicine, and/or assistive technologies. Business needs may include money, office space, essential equipment, and employees. Business wants will vary but may include technology and non-essential equipment.)

✔ Reading Check

Contrast Public wants are wants that are widely shared by many people, while private wants are wants of smaller groups of people, such as families and businesses.

Discuss the Photo

● **Goods and Services** A mechanic offers services, such as car repair and servicing. If the mechanic also sells car parts, such as wiper blades and tires, then it sells goods, too.

S Skill Practice

Guided Practice

List Ask students to make a list of classroom resources. (audiovisual equipment, books, desks, computers, and white boards) **L1**

Explain Have students write a paragraph about how each resource meets a classroom need or want. (Books satisfy the need for information; audiovisual equipment satisfies the want for a way to display information.) **L2**

Classify Ask students to write a paragraph that explains why they would classify some classroom resources as wants rather than needs. (Many classroom resources such as computers are not absolutely necessary for learning.) **L3**

● As You Read

Ask a volunteer to describe a recent decision about how to use resources. Have a discussion about how everyone makes decisions about using resources.

ASSESS

Review Key Terms

Have students write sentences using each key term.

 **Study-to-Go** Have students go to the Online Learning Center through **glencoe.com** to download **Study-to-Go** content to their PDAs or cell phones.

Service Businesses H & R Block and Jackson Hewitt are businesses that offer tax preparation services. Even the Internal Revenue Service will help you with your taxes. Look in your local business directory and list three businesses in your community that offer tax preparation services.

● As You Read

Think of a decision you have made about how to use your resources.

Satisfying Wants and Needs

Businesses provide goods and services to satisfy wants and needs. **Goods** are physical products. Skates, groceries, and telephones are examples of goods.

Services are tasks that businesses perform for consumers. These include tasks that people or machines do. Like goods, services are provided for a fee. For example, when you pay H & R Block to prepare your taxes, you are buying a service. Insurance, sports and entertainment, tourism, banking, and education involve offering services. Most companies that sell goods also provide services to their customers.

How Resources Limit the Ability to Satisfy Wants and Needs

Most people have unlimited wants for goods and services. In the United States, most consumers are able to satisfy their basic needs. Marketers promote goods and services that will appeal to people's wants.

S The more money you make, the more goods or services you can buy. However, few people have enough resources to satisfy all of their wants. **Resources** are items that people can use to make or obtain what they need or want. Examples of resources include money, fuel, and labor.

Resources limit the number of needs and wants people can satisfy. For example, you may want a new pair of jeans and a new camera. You may have only enough money to buy one of these things. Businesses and governments are influenced by the same problem. They lack the resources to do all the things that they want to do. To make the best use of limited resources, **determine** what your needs are and satisfy them first, then wants.

? ETHICS in Business

A Conflict of Interest

■ **Critical Reading** Life is full of important decisions. Think about the kinds of decisions that you make as you read the question below.

You work as an event planner for a local company. You are in charge of hiring a caterer for the company's 10th anniversary celebration. You have bids from four caterers in town. One of the bids is from a caterer who is an old friend. His bid is higher than the three others.

■ **Decision Making** Would your relationship with the caterer affect which company you would hire? Explain your answer.

Real World

Service Businesses Lists will vary but should include accountants, tax attorneys, and franchise tax preparation businesses. Ask students if these types of businesses sell goods as well as services. (Tax preparation businesses usually provide only services, not goods.)

? ETHICS in Business

Decision Making The event planner should recuse himself or herself from the decision-making process due to the conflict of interest. The employee has an ethical obligation to act in the best interest of the company.

Making the Most of Your Resources

Every day you make choices about how you will spend your resources to satisfy your needs and wants. You should make these important decisions carefully. You can make the most of your resources by making the best choices about what to buy.

✔ **Reading Check** **Explain** How can you make the most of your resources?

The Decision-Making Process

The decision-making process can help you make good choices. It helps you to **identify** and **consider** your various alternatives and their consequences before you make a final decision. The essential steps of the process are outlined in **Figure 1.1**.

Figure 1.1 — *The Decision-Making Process*

> **Step 1: Identify the situation.**
> Whether the problem is one that occurs daily or comes up only a few times in a lifetime, identifying the problem is the first step.

> **Step 2: Identify possible courses of action.**
> Take time to think through the situation so you can identify and consider all the important alternatives.

> **Step 3: Determine the pros and cons.**
> Consider your values and goals when determining the advantages and disadvantages of each alternative. You can use this information to compare and evaluate your choices.

> **Step 4: Make a decision.**
> Use the information you gathered to rank the alternatives and make a decision. Once you have made your decision, you can plan how to reach your goal.

> **Step 5: Evaluate your decision.**
> Once your decision is put into effect, ask yourself whether you achieved the results you expected. Would you make the same choice again?

● **Making Better Choices** The decision-making process can be used to make all kinds of decisions. **What major decisions have you made recently?**

✔ **Reading Check**

Explain Nobody has enough resources to satisfy all of their needs and wants. Individuals, companies, and nations must use the decision-making process to make the best use of limited resources and satisfy needs first, then wants.

Figure 1.1

● **Making Better Choices** Answers will vary but may involve setting goals or deciding how to spend money or time. Remind students that one of the biggest decisions they will make in their lives is choosing a career, and that will require serious planning.

RETEACH

W Writing Support
Independent Practice
Resources Tell students that they are planning to spend a day with a friend. They have $20 to spend. They need to buy lunch and they want entertainment. Have students write down how much they will spend, what they will buy, and why. (Remind students to use the five-step decision-making process. Answers and situations will vary. Encourage students to recognize that their money will go farther if they buy lunch at the grocery store and avoid dining in restaurants. Also remind students that there are many low-cost ways to entertain themselves, such as visiting a book store or watching movies at home.)

R Reading Strategy
Draw a Diagram Ask students to draw a diagram that shows the steps of the decision-making process. (Diagrams will vary but should include all of the steps in **Figure 1.1**.)

U Universal Access
Visual Impairments Plan for the challenges of students with visual impairments by giving a verbal description of **Figure 1.1**.

Student Activity Workbook ☞ Assign the Section 1.1 Activities.

RETEACH (cont.)

C Critical Thinking

Connect to the Community

Ask students: Should citizens consider the effect of their decisions on the local and global community? Why? (If citizens consider the effects of their decisions on the world around them, they can help to change the world in a positive way.)

Local Brands Remind students that supporting local businesses is good for their communities.

ASSESS

After You Read

Have students complete the Section 1.1 After You Read section review.

Online Study Tools

Have students go to the Online Learning Center through **glencoe.com** to:

- Take the Section 1.1 **Practice Test**.
- Download free **Study-to-Go**  content to their PDAs or cell phones.

CLOSE

Culminating Activity
Needs and Environment

Have students create a presentation showing the needs for survival in another climate. (Someone living in a big city has different needs than someone living on a small island.)

Local Brands
Besides national orange juice brands such as Tropicana and Minute Maid, there are local brands, too. Go to your local grocery store. List the brands it sells.

N C L B Activity correlates to Math standards

Personal Decision Making You may not use all of the steps of the decision-making process every time you buy something. When you decide to buy orange juice, you may always buy the same brand, such as Tropicana. However, many decisions need more careful thought. A bike can be an important purchase because you are likely to keep it for some time. When you consider what kind of bike to buy at what price, you will probably use all five steps of the decision-making process. The longer a decision will affect your life, the more you need to **evaluate** your options and consider the possible consequences.

Business Decision Making Competition among businesses is intense. For this reason, businesses must decide how to best use and conserve their resources. Businesses must make thoughtful decisions that are consistent with their goals. Business managers constantly make decisions. Most companies allow managers to make routine decisions independently. Higher-level business managers usually make more important decisions that affect the future of their companies.

Section 1.1

After You Read

Review Key Concepts
1. Describe the difference between public wants and private wants.
2. Define resources.
3. List the steps in the decision-making process.

Academic Skills
N C L B
4. **Mathematics** In making a household budget, you determine that your basic needs require 75 percent of your monthly income. The items you listed as "wants" cost another 15 percent. If your monthly income is $2,500, how much are you spending on wants? How much do you have left to save?

THEORY **Number and Operations:**
Percents A percent is a ratio comparing a number to 100. It can also be represented as a fraction with 100 as the denominator. To find a decimal equivalent, divide the percent by 100. Multiply that decimal by the total amount to determine the dollar amount that it represents.

 For math help, go to the Math Appendix.

 Go to the *Introduction to Business* Online Learning Center through **glencoe.com** to check your answers.

Section 1.1

Review Key Concepts
1. Public wants are shared by many people; individuals or small groups of people have private wants.
2. things people use to make or obtain what they need or want
3. identify the situation, list alternatives, determine pros and cons, make a decision, evaluate the decision

Academic Skills
4. **Mathematics** $2,500 × .15 = $375
You are spending $375 per month on "wants." 75% + 15% = 90%
100% − 90% = 10%
$2,500 × .10 = $250
You have $250 left to save each month.

Business Activities

Reading Guide

Before You Read

Think about all the things a business must do in order to sell products and services.

Read to Learn

- Explain how profit and competition motivate businesses.
- List the activities businesses undertake when developing products and services.
- Explain how business impacts you and how you impact business.

The Main Idea

Businesses seek profit by providing goods and services in exchange for money. Companies thrive on competition, the contest between businesses to win customers. Competition and profit motivate businesses to continually strive to find new ways to satisfy customers.

Key Concepts

- How to Define Business
- Business Activities
- Business and You

Vocabulary

Key Terms

business
profit
competition
market research
consumer

Academic Vocabulary

You will find these words in your reading and on your tests. Make sure you know their meanings.

analyze
respond
affect
modify

Graphic Organizer

On a chart like the one below, list the six activities businesses undertake when developing products or services.

Business Activities
1 _____
2 _____
3 _____
4 _____
5 _____
6 _____

 Go to the *Introduction to Business* Online Learning Center through **glencoe.com** for a printable graphic organizer.

Academic Standards

English Language Arts

NCTE 5 Use different writing process elements to communicate effectively

NCTE 8 Use information resources to gather information and create and communicate knowledge

---

🔔 Bell Ringer Activity

Business Activities
Ask students to name a favorite product and brainstorm all of the things that have to happen before they see the product in the store. (Answers will vary but may include identifying conducting market research to determine opportunities, obtaining funding, managing the production, marketing, and distributing the product or service.)

Preteaching

Presentation Plus! 💿

The Presentation Plus! CD provides visual teaching aids for this section.

PuzzleMaker 💿

Use the Vocabulary PuzzleMaker to create a puzzle of the section's key terms. Students can complete the puzzle on paper or on a computer.

Graphic Organizer

Tell students to go to the Online Learning Center through **glencoe.com** for a printable graphic organizer. (Graphic organizer answers should include the six activities outlined on page 14.)

NCLB Academic correlations to book content.

Reading Guide

Before You Read

Lead students to understand that there are several categories of activities all businesses undertake in order to market their goods and services.

D Develop Concepts

The Main Idea Ask students: Why do businesses provide goods and services and compete with each other? (Businesses provide goods and services and compete with each other to make profits.)

Discussion Starter
The Motives of Business
Ask students: Why do businesses supply goods and services? (The opportunity to make profits provides the motivation.) Call on a volunteer to use the term *profit* in a sentence. (Profit is the reward for satisfying the needs and wants of consumers and businesses.)

● **As You Read**
Ask a volunteer to name a local business and describe the activities of the business. Categorize them as the six business activities described in the text.

R **Reading Strategy**
Make a List Ask students to make a list of reasons people start their own business. Why? (Most students will say that their motive is to make money.) Remind students that starting a business can result in profits but it also involves risk, or the chance of losing money.

NCLB Activity correlates to Science standards.

● **As You Read**
Think about the types of businesses in your community and the activities they do to sell their products and services.

How to Define Business

Whether you need to buy food for dinner or want a new bike, your wants and needs are usually satisfied by business. **Business** is any commercial activity that seeks profit by providing goods and services to others in exchange for money. **Profit** is the money left over after a business has paid the cost of providing its goods and services.

Businesses provide consumers and other businesses with necessities, such as food, clothing, housing, medical care, and transportation. Businesses also provide goods and services that make life easier and better. For entrepreneurs, owning a business also offers an opportunity to earn a good living.

✔ **Reading Check** **Apply** Think of your favorite retail store. What companies are its competition?

The Motive of Business: To Make a Profit

R Businesses supply goods and services with the motivation of making profits. Without profit, a company cannot survive. Profit is the reward for satisfying the needs and wants of consumers and businesses. The wealth created by businesses benefits the entire community because businesses pay taxes and provide jobs.

Science/Tech TRENDS

NCLB

The Green Revolution
In 1798, Thomas Malthus, the great social scientist, showed that even as population increases geometrically (2, 4, 8, 16,…), the food supply increases arithmetically (1, 2, 3, 4,…). He predicted that hunger and conflict would be the result. In the 1960s, the Green Revolution promised to eliminate hunger by increasing crop yields. This was accomplished by using genetics to develop new varieties of grains and educating farmers in the technology of agriculture. Between 1960 and 1990, food production increased 1,000 percent, famine decreased 20 percent, caloric consumption increased 25 percent, and people around the world saw a rise in their incomes and standard of living.

WebQuest

Go to the *Introduction to Business* Online Learning Center through **glencoe.com** for links to Web sites where you can research how the technology of agriculture fueled the revolution in farming practices around the world. Look for information on irrigation strategies, the use of fertilizers and pesticides, and crop rotation. Write a few paragraphs about how farmers in countries, such as Mexico, increased their crop yields.

✔ **Reading Check**

Apply Answers will vary depending on students' interests. Encourage students to recognize that nearly all traditional retailers compete with other bricks-and-mortar retailers as well as online stores and mail-order businesses.

Science/Tech TRENDS

WebQuest

The Green Revolution Answers will vary, but paragraphs might describe new crop cultivars; irrigation techniques, such as tubewells and electric pumps, which provide more water than traditional methods; new fertilizers; and pesticides.

The Significance of Competition

Companies thrive on **competition**, the contest between businesses to win customers. For example, Skechers competes with other shoe retailers, such as Foot Locker, for business. Competition is a direct response to those wants and needs.

Competition is possible because companies have the freedom to produce the products they think will be the most profitable. Because the American economy is based on freedom and voluntary exchange, buyers can compete to find the best products at the lowest prices. The result is that goods and services are produced and sold at the lowest possible cost.

Competition among businesses has never been greater than it is today. Some companies find a competitive edge by focusing on making high-quality products. Others compete by focusing on making products with no defects. However, simply making a high-quality, defect-free product is not enough to allow a company to stay competitive in the global marketplace. For companies to successfully compete in the global economy, they must offer quality products with outstanding service at competitive prices.

Target Market A target market is a group of people identified as those most likely to become customers. The target market of Foot Locker is 12- to 20-year-olds, and the target market of Skechers is 12 to 25-year-olds. Develop a list of shoe stores in your area and the likely target market for each.

● **The Functions of Business** The success of a business depends on how well key activities are coordinated, managed, and performed. **Why should businesses use market research when making important decisions?**

Section 1.2   Business Activities   **13**

TEACH (cont.)

S Skill Practice
Guided Practice

List Have students make a list of different ways businesses can compete. (Answers will vary. Business can compete by offering superior customer service, the fastest service, or by demonstrating concern for the community, employees, and the environment.) **L1**

Apply Ask students to describe two ways that companies can compete on the basis of concern for the environment. (Companies can work to cause minimal damage to the environment. They can make efforts to conserve and recycle and promote the ethical treatment of animals.) **L2**

Report Write a report on the global competitive environment. How are leading companies competing in the 21st century? (Global competition has dramatically changed the business environment. Many leading companies are competing by becoming more customer-driven.) **L3**

ASSESS

Review Key Terms
Have students write sentences using each key term.

 **Study-to-Go**
Have students go to the Online Learning Center through **glencoe.com** to download **Study-to-Go** content to their PDAs or cell phones.

Discuss the Photo
● **The Functions of Business** Market research provides information that can help a business identify opportunities and evaluate demand. Businesses use this information to make informed decisions about market goods and services.

Target Market Lists and target markets will vary depending on the types of stores in your area. Different types of shoe stores have different target markets. Some shoe stores have more than one target market.

RETEACH

 **Writing Support**

Independent Practice

Market Research Ask students to interview a local business owner and ask about the types of market research he or she uses when making business decisions. Have students write a summary of the interview. (Summaries will vary but may suggest that market research provides insight into the attitudes and behaviors of consumers.)

Virtual Business

Introduce market research to students using the Virtual Business Retailing Market Research activity. In this simulation, students learn why market research is important to the success of a business.

Cooperative Learning
Business Activities

Write the six catergories of business activities on the board. Organize students into small groups. Ask groups to brainstorm a list of 20 things that businesses do in order to sell their products and services. Ask volunteers to read their lists, and as they do, ask them to assign each item to one of the categories written on the board. (Paying taxes, for example, should be categorized as Keeping Records. Advertising should be classified as Marketing. Creating products should be classified as Managing Production.)

Student Activity
Workbook ☞ Assign the Section 1.2 Activities.

Business Activities

You might be surprised to know all the activities a business undertakes when developing products or services. They must:

- identify opportunities for products or services;
- evaluate the demand for products or services;
- obtain start-up money and operating capital;
- manage the production of goods and/or services;
- market the goods and/or services;
- keep records to satisfy government requirements and improve processes.

W Some business activities should be supported by market research. **Market research** is the act of gathering and analyzing information about the wants, needs, and preferences of consumers in a certain market. Market research provides information that can help a business identify opportunities, **analyze** demand, and **respond** to consumer demand for goods and services.

BusinessWeek *Reader and Case Study*

From Adversity, Software Success

An idea for a new business can strike anywhere: In the shower, in the car, even in a dream. Mike Jetter got his in a cancer ward.

In 1994, the German programmer was stuck in a hospital room in Munich, following his second leukemia relapse and his second bone-marrow transplant. Given a 50% chance to live another year, Jetter needed a distraction badly.

At the time, so-called mind-mapping was all the rage in Europe. Hailed as a more creative way to think, it involves organizing ideas in a visual way, with big concepts written in a circle in the middle of a page, surrounded by smaller ideas that branch off from them. But with pencil and paper, you couldn't drag and drop, edit, or collaborate. So Jetter set out to write a computer program.

After his release from the hospital, he and his wife Bettina handed marketing for the product over to a German CD-ROM distributor,

assuming not much would come of it. Today the software has spawned a $20 million-a-year business called Mindjet, headquartered in San Francisco.

Now the Jetters are turning this desktop product into something companies can use broadly to help brainstorm, plan, collaborate, and organize a host of business activities.

 CASE STUDY Go to the *Introduction to Business* Online Learning Center through **glencoe.com** for the *BusinessWeek* Reader Case Study.

Active Learning

Team up with a classmate and work together to identify and research a successful company with a unique business concept. Write a brief presentation about the business. Give the presentation to your class.

BusinessWeek *Reader and Case Study*

From Adversity, Software Success

CASE STUDY Have students go to the *Introduction to Business* Online Learning Center through **glencoe.com** to download a Case Study activity that corresponds to the article. The activity and answer key are also available on the TeacherWorks Plus CD.

Active Learning

Encourage students to use good presentation skills. Remind them to maintain eye contact with the audience, stand up straight with both feet on the ground, use natural hand gestures, speak clearly and at a reasonable volume, and show an interest in the topic.

Business and You

Businesses make many decisions that impact you, the consumer. A **consumer** is a person who uses goods or services. Businesses decide what goods and services to produce to meet the needs and wants of consumers. Businesses also **affect** consumers when they **modify** or discontinue products. The decision to stop manufacturing products is often because there is a decreasing demand for them. Businesses affect you as a wage earner. In order to make goods and provide services, businesses hire people to work.

Consumers also affect businesses. Consumers decide what kinds of goods and services they want and where they will buy them. You reward companies by making the decision to purchase their products. When consumers choose not to purchase a business's products or services, the business usually fails. To avoid failure, a business can modify its products, services, and business practices to satisfy consumers.

 Activity correlates to English Language Arts standards

Section 1.2

After You Read

Review Key Concepts
1. Define business.
2. List the activities that every business undertakes when developing new products and services.
3. Describe why it is important to understand how business impacts you.

Academic Skills
4. **English Language Arts** Competition between similar businesses is one of the basic characteristics of the American economy. Competition is good for consumers because it provides choices. It also forces companies to improve quality and lower prices. Think of your favorite retail store. Write two or more paragraphs that describe the store and its competition, and explain how the competition among these businesses has affected you as a consumer.

5. **English Language Arts** In order to better understand the challenges and opportunities small businesses face, you decide to interview three business owners in your area. To prepare, identify three businesses that each provide a different type of product or service. Then write a series of questions that will help you understand how the products or services were chosen, whether they have changed in response to consumer demands, and how the business owner keeps in touch with consumers.

> @ Go to the *Introduction to Business* Online Learning Center through **glencoe.com** to check your answers.

Section 1.2

Review Key Concepts
1. any activity involving the exchange of money for goods or services
2. identify opportunities, evaluate demand, obtain money, manage production, market products, keep records
3. because the actions of businesses will affect you

Academic Skills
4. **English Language Arts** Paragraphs should state that competition affects consumers by offering more choices and lowering prices.
5. **English Language Arts** Questions will vary but should elicit information about how the businesses maintain relationships with their customers.

RETEACH (cont.)

C Critical Thinking

Diagram to Compare Ask students to create a diagram that shows how businesses affect consumers and how consumers affect businesses. (Diagrams will vary. Businesses affect consumers by providing jobs and goods and services. Consumers affect businesses by choosing which businesses to support and which goods and services to buy.)

ASSESS

After You Read

Have students complete the Section 1.2 After You Read section review.

Online Study Tools
Have students go to the Online Learning Center through **glencoe.com** to:
- Take the Section 1.2 **Practice Test**.
- Download free **Study-to-Go** content to their PDAs or cell phones.

CLOSE

Culminating Activity
Types of Businesses
Have students make a table of 10 companies that operate in your community. In the table, have students identify whether the business provides goods, services or both; the size of the business (large or small); and the market (business or consumer).

15

Vocabulary Review

1. Students should write complete sentences using each term correctly.

Review Key Concepts

2. Wants are things that you do not need to survive, but would like to have. Needs are things that you must have to survive.

3. Few people have enough resources to satisfy all of their needs and wants. To make the best use of limited resources, satisfy needs first, then wants.

4. The decision-making process helps you to consider your alternatives and their consequences. It can help you make the careful decisions about the use of your resources.

5. Businesses are motivated by profit, the reward for satisfying the needs and wants of consumers and businesses. Competition is the contest among businesses to win customers.

6. identifying opportunities, evaluating demand, obtaining money, managing production, marketing, and keeping records

7. Consumers affect businesses by deciding what kind of goods and services to buy. Businesses affect consumers by hiring people to work and by releasing and discontinuing products.

Section 1.1 *Summary*

A Look at Wants and Needs Everyone has wants and needs. Wants are things that you do not have to have to survive, but would like to have. Needs are things that you must have in order to survive. People use resources to make or obtain what they need or want. Resources limit the number of needs and wants people can satisfy. The decision-making process can help you make good choices and make the most of your resources by considering alternatives and their consequences. The longer a decision will affect your life, the more you need to consider all of the possible consequences.

Section 1.2 *Summary*

Business Activities Businesses supply goods and services with the motivation of making profits. Companies thrive on competition, the contest between businesses to win customers. All businesses undertake these activities: identifying opportunities, evaluating demand, obtaining money, managing production, marketing to consumers and businesses, and keeping records. Consumers affect businesses by deciding what kind of goods and services to buy. Businesses affect consumers by making decisions about what products and services to offer and by providing jobs.

Vocabulary Review

1. On a sheet of paper, use each of these key terms and academic vocabulary terms in a sentence.

Key Terms		Academic Vocabulary	
wants	business	determine	analyze
needs	profit	identify	respond
goods	competition	consider	affect
services	market research	evaluate	modify
resources	consumer		

Review Key Concepts

2. Explain the differences between wants and needs.

3. Describe how resources limit the number of wants people and businesses can satisfy.

4. Explain how to use the decision-making process to make the most of your resources.

5. Explain how profit and competition motivate businesses.

6. List the activities businesses undertake when developing products and services.

7. Explain how business impacts you and how you impact business.

16   **Chapter 1**   Review and Activities

Critical Thinking

8. Students might refer to how their needs and wants as children (food, toys) are different from their needs and wants as adults (money, a car).

9. Students might say they prioritize their wants and needs and take care of their needs first.

10. One response could be the service that hospitals provide to patients.

11. Students may offer a wide range of answers, including offering a good or service that is unavailable, update inventory, redecorate, hire more employees, and lower prices.

12. The niche store would sell a wider selection of its main product or service, and its employees would be more familiar with the products. Disadvantages include having a limited focus and higher prices.

Critical Thinking

8. Explain how your wants and needs have changed over the years. How do you think they will change as you get older?

9. Consider the resources that you have that are limited and those that are plentiful. How do you decide to use your resources to get the things you want and need?

10. What do you think is the most important service available where you live? What would your life be like without this service?

11. Think of a small business in your community. What do you think that business could do to increase its profits?

12. A niche is a small, specialized segment of the market, usually based on customer needs discovered in market research. Think of a company that has succeeded by focusing on a niche market. What kinds of advantages and disadvantages does it have over a store that sells a variety of products?

13. As a consumer, what are some of the things about products and services that matter most to you? Explain your answer.

Write About It

14. Draw a Venn diagram of two overlapping circles. Label the left circle WANTS and the right circle NEEDS. Label the area where the two circles intersect BOTH. Then list your wants in the left circle and your needs in the right circle. List things that are both wants and needs in the area where the two circles overlap.

15. List three reasons why the decision-making process is important to use when making choices. Then describe a decision you recently made and explain how you made it.

16. Market research is the act of gathering and analyzing information about the wants, needs, and preferences of consumers in a certain market. Write two or more paragraphs to explain how market research can be used as a basis for business activities.

17. In a letter to your teacher, explain how the decisions businesses make affect you as a consumer.

18. Write a journal entry about how the decisions you make affect businesses.

19. Describe a situation in which you made a decision that greatly influenced your life.

Technology Applications

Spreadsheet
20. When there are limited resources, you need to make decisions about the best use of those resources. Imagine you are managing a concession stand at a school basketball game. Use a spreadsheet program to list and categorize all of the resources you will need to operate the concession stand for one day. Resources include equipment, money, supplies, and labor.

Business Ethics

Confidentiality Agreements
21. A confidentiality agreement is a contract that requires the employee or contractor not to reveal information that they acquire while working for an employer or client. Use library or Internet resources to research confidentiality agreements. Find several examples, and write a report detailing their similarities and explaining their importance.

Chapter 1 Review and Activities **17**

Critical Thinking

13. Explanations could be based on factors such as low prices, quality of materials used, speed of service, ease of use, durability, customer service, and technological innovation.

Write About It

14. Needs should include food, water, and shelter. Wants will vary according to students' desires. Similarities may include things that make life comfortable.

15. It is important to use the decision-making process because it makes you consider all of your alternatives and the consequences of each alternative.

16. Market research provides information that can help a business identify opportunities and evaluate demand. When a business does market research to support a business decision, its risk is reduced.

17. Letters will vary but should express that businesses affect consumers by providing jobs and selling or choosing not to sell goods and services.

18. Journal entries should express that consumers affect business by choosing from which businesses to buy products and services.

19. Situations will vary but may include decisions about education and career planning.

Technology Applications

20. Lists will vary but should include equipment for the storage and preparation of the food and beverages that will be served.

Business Ethics

21. Reports should state that confidentiality agreements and understandings can take many forms, but are all to be taken very seriously. Any information covered by such an understanding must be treated in confidence and not disclosed to anyone else, except as set out in the agreement or understanding.

Applying Academics to Business

22. Answers will vary, but you might ask students to discuss the words they have chosen and tell what they learned from researching them.

23. $\frac{15}{50} = 30\%$
The more stylish coat costs 30 percent more.

24. Sentences should elaborate on the shades of meaning for each of the chosen words.

25. Answers will vary, but make sure students understand the difference between a ratio that stands for "needs versus wants" and a ratio that stands for "wants versus needs."

Active Learning

26. Policies will vary but should include general ethical guidelines as well as specific ways to deal with different situations. Policies should explain that unethical practices can damage a company's reputation.

Business in the Real World

27. Answers should identify the source of information and compare that person's decision-making process with the one outlined in the text.

Applying Academics to Business

English Language Arts
22. Select two words from this chapter that were unfamiliar to you or that you would like to know more about. Using your own words and ideas about how to represent sounds, write a pronunciation guide and a definition of each of the words. Then write two sentences using the words. Keep a personal glossary of words you have chosen and researched in this way.

Mathematics
23. When shopping for a new winter coat, you find one that suits your needs costs $50. A more stylish coat that you want costs $65. Describe the difference between the two prices using a percentage.

> **THEORY** **Number and Operations:**
> **Percents** To describe how much more the stylish coat costs, create a fraction using the difference in price as the numerator and the cost of the basic coat as the denominator. To convert the fraction to a percent, divide the numerator by the denominator and multiply the product by 100.

English Language Arts
24. Research and write a list of synonyms or closely related words and phrases for each of the following terms from the chapter: services, resources, business, and limit. For example, for the word goods, you might list merchandise, commodities, supplies, wares, and cargo. Choose two of the words in your list and write a sentence telling how their meanings are alike and different.

Mathematics
25. Imagine you have $100 for next month's expenses. Make a budget showing how you would spend the money on needs and wants. Express the relationship between needs and wants as a ratio. Compare your ratio with your classmates by writing equations or inequalities.

> **THEORY** **Algebra: Equations and**
> **Inequalities** Equations and inequalities are used to describe the relationship between two algebraic expressions. Equations consist of two equivalent numbers or expressions with an equal sign between them. An inequality consists of two nonequivalent numbers or expressions with a "greater than" ($>$) or a "less than" ($<$) sign between them.

Active Learning

Write an Ethics Policy
26. Many problems and ethical conflicts can be avoided if business owners communicate their ethical expectations to their employees. Pair up with a classmate and imagine that you are the co-owners of a small accounting business. Work together to write an ethics policy that offers general ethical guidelines and specific ways to deal with different situations.

Business in the Real World

Making Business Decisions
27. Interview the manager or owner of a local small business. Find out about the sources of information he or she uses in making business decisions. Ask how he or she evaluates the information before acting upon it. Does he or she use the decision-making model described in this chapter? Write two or more paragraphs to describe the ways that person evaluates information.

ExamView Assessment Suite **CD** allows you to print out ready-made unit and chapter tests, complete with answer keys. You can also create customized tests.

TeacherWorks Plus provides complete teacher resources in one convenient package. It includes customizable lesson plans in calendar format, and instant access to many print program resources.

 **Real LIFE** • skills

INTERPERSONAL SKILLS

28. The strength of your interpersonal skills can make or break how successful you are in the workplace. Interpersonal skills are essentially people skills—the nontechnical, intangible, personality-specific skills that determine your strengths as a leader, listener, negotiator, and conflict mediator. Write a one-page report that explains why it is important for businesses to have employees with interpersonal skills.

 **Business CAREERS**

FIND YOUR DREAM JOB

29. Go to **glencoe.com** for a link to the Occupational Outlook Handbook Web site. Click on the "OOH Search/A Z Index" link and enter the search term "Tomorrow's Jobs" to read about the future job market. Then write a one-page report about this topic. Conclude your report with a list of things you could do now to prepare yourself to pursue the occupation.

Role Play

THE IMPORTANCE OF BUSINESS

30. Situation You are an assistant manager for a company that makes household appliances. Your manager has asked you to put together a presentation about the activities of business for its new sales associates.

Activity Prepare a presentation that describes all of the activities that businesses undertake in order to sell products and services. Use magazines to find photos that represent all of the activities, and include the photos in your presentation. Then give the presentation to your classmates (sales associates).

Evaluation You will be evaluated on how well you meet the following performance indicators:

- Explain the motivations of business.
- Describe business activities.
- Discuss how competition impacts the company's decisions.
- Prepare a written report.

Standardized Test Practice

Directions Find the value of each algebraic expression. Write the letter of the answer on a separate piece of paper.

1. If $3x = 6x - 15$ then $x + 8 =$

A   10
B   11
C   12
D   13

2. Evaluate $5t + 4$ if $t = 3$.

F   7
G   13
H   19
J   21

 **TEST-TAKING TIP** When answering multiple-choice questions, read the question first, then read all the answer choices before choosing your answer. Eliminate answers you know are not right.

 READING Go to the *Introduction to Business* Online Learning Center through **glencoe.com** for a list of outside reading suggestions.

 **STRATEGIES FOR STANDARDIZED TEST PREP SUCCESS**

Test Savvy Explain to students that muliple-choice items on stardardized tests consist of a stem, or question, and distractors, or answer choices. Often, test-takers will read the stem, glance at the distractors, and quickly choose the one they think is right. Help students develop the habit of reading the stem and all the distractors before deciding. If they are unsure, have them eliminate distractors they know aren't correct before deciding among the remaining choices.

Real LIFE • skills

28. Reports will vary, but should explain that employers value interpersonal skills, because they are important indicators of job performance.

Business CAREERS

29. A wide range of educational backgrounds is suitable for this occupation, but many employers prefer those with experience in related occupations. Employers prefer a bachelor's degree in marketing. Courses in business law, economics, accounting, finance, mathematics, and statistics are advantageous.

Role Play

30. Presentations should address the competencies noted in the role play. Businesses are motivated by profit and competition. In order to operate, businesses identify opportunities, evaluate demand, obtain funding, manage production, market products, and keep records. Competition influences businesses to develop better and cheaper goods and services, which benefits consumers.

Standardized Test Practice
1. D
2. H

Standards-Based Lesson Planning
Introduction to Business provides students with instruction and assessment in the following fundamental content areas:

Content Standards Correlations	
Analyze the impact scarcity has on various economic systems.	p. 23
Identify factors of production.	pp. 23–26
Differentiate among the types of economic resources.	pp. 23–26
Summarize how economic decisions are made.	p. 28
Differentiate between the types of economic systems.	pp. 29–31
Describe characteristics of the free enterprise system.	pp. 29–30
Explain the economic role played by business in satisfying customer needs and wants in a free enterprise system.	p. 29
Evaluate the role of an individual within the free enterprise system as a producer, a consumer, and a citizen.	p. 29
Relate the significance of competition in business.	p. 29
Relate demand (wants and needs) to supply.	pp. 29–30

NCLB
Activities, information, and skills practice will help your students attain No Child Left Behind proficiency. Students will improve their abilities in the following academic standards areas:

Academic Standards Correlations		
English Language Arts	Activities/Features	Page
NCTE 1 Read texts to acquire new information	After You Read	p. 31
NCTE 3 Apply strategies to interpret texts	Applying Academics to Business	p. 34
NCTE 6 Apply knowledge of language structure and conventions to discuss texts	Standardized Test Practice	p. 35
NCTE 7 Conduct research and gather, evaluate, and synthesize data to communicate discoveries	After You Read / Applying Academics to Business	pp. 31, 34
NCTE 8 Use information resources to gather information and create and communicate knowlege	After You Read	p. 31
Mathematics		
Data Analysis and Probability Formulate questions that can be addressed with data and collect, organize, and display relevant data to answer them	After You Read	p. 26
Data Analysis and Probability Select and use appropriate statistical methods to analyze data	Applying Academics to Business	p. 34
Algebra Use mathematical models to represent and understand quantitative relationships	Applying Academics to Business	p. 34
Algebra Represent and analyze mathematical situations and structures using algebraic symbols	Standardized Test Practice	p. 35
Science		
Content Standard D Students should develop an understanding of energy in the earth system, geochemical cycles, origin and evolution of the earth system, origin and evolution of the universe	Science/Tech Trends After You Read	pp. 28, 31

Correlations   This chart shows the 21ˢᵗ Century Skills, foundation skills, and workplace competencies that students develop as they work in this chapter.

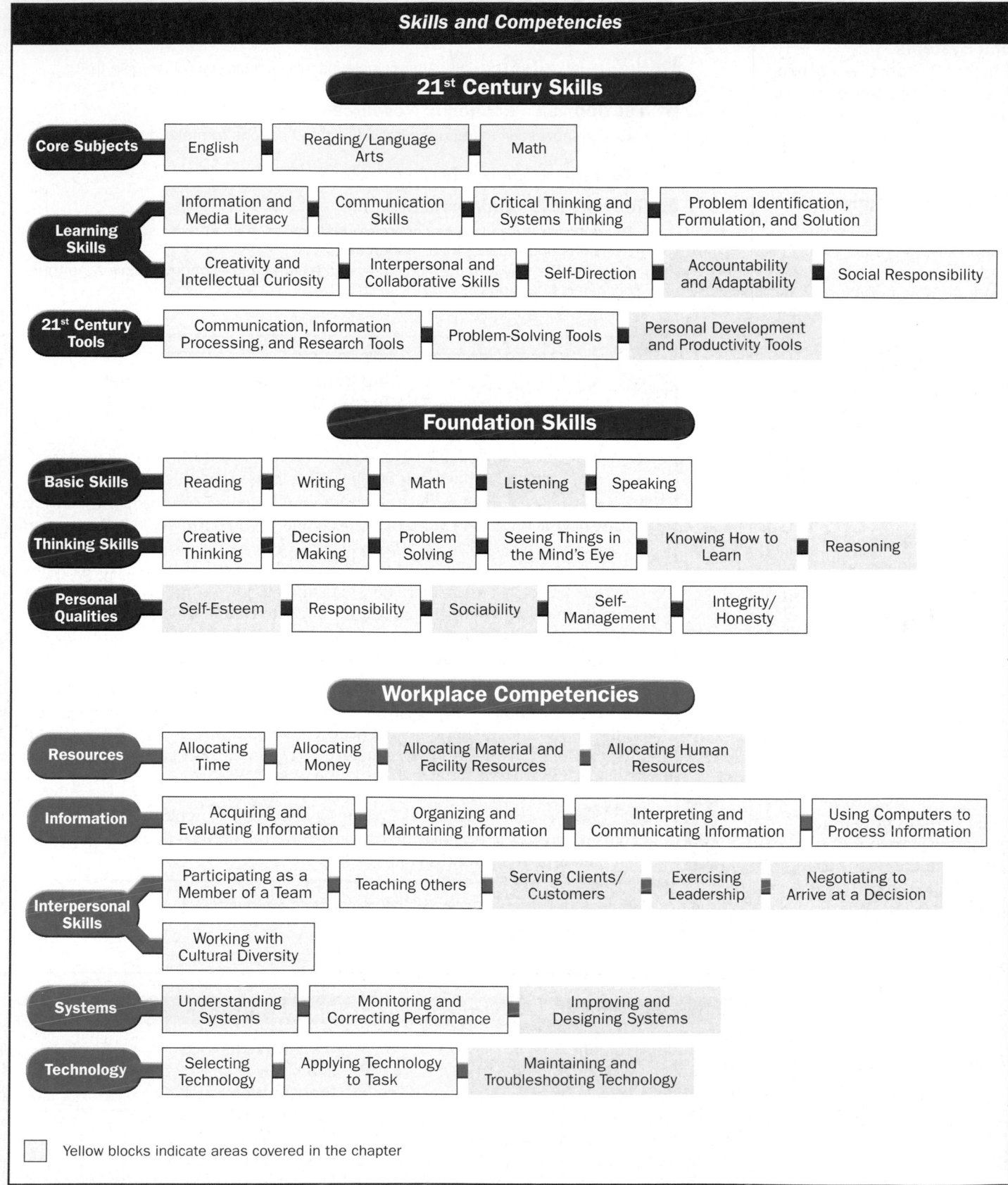

Skills and Competencies

21ˢᵗ Century Skills

Core Subjects
- English
- Reading/Language Arts
- Math

Learning Skills
- Information and Media Literacy
- Communication Skills
- Critical Thinking and Systems Thinking
- Problem Identification, Formulation, and Solution
- Creativity and Intellectual Curiosity
- Interpersonal and Collaborative Skills
- Self-Direction
- Accountability and Adaptability
- Social Responsibility

21ˢᵗ Century Tools
- Communication, Information Processing, and Research Tools
- Problem-Solving Tools
- Personal Development and Productivity Tools

Foundation Skills

Basic Skills
- Reading
- Writing
- Math
- Listening
- Speaking

Thinking Skills
- Creative Thinking
- Decision Making
- Problem Solving
- Seeing Things in the Mind's Eye
- Knowing How to Learn
- Reasoning

Personal Qualities
- Self-Esteem
- Responsibility
- Sociability
- Self-Management
- Integrity/Honesty

Workplace Competencies

Resources
- Allocating Time
- Allocating Money
- Allocating Material and Facility Resources
- Allocating Human Resources

Information
- Acquiring and Evaluating Information
- Organizing and Maintaining Information
- Interpreting and Communicating Information
- Using Computers to Process Information

Interpersonal Skills
- Participating as a Member of a Team
- Teaching Others
- Serving Clients/Customers
- Exercising Leadership
- Negotiating to Arrive at a Decision
- Working with Cultural Diversity

Systems
- Understanding Systems
- Monitoring and Correcting Performance
- Improving and Designing Systems

Technology
- Selecting Technology
- Applying Technology to Task
- Maintaining and Troubleshooting Technology

☐ Yellow blocks indicate areas covered in the chapter

Chapter Overview

Introduce the Chapter

Economic Resources and Systems
Chapter 2 is about economic resources, scarcity, economic systems, the factors of production, and the three basic economic questions.

Building Background
In a market economy, business owners create goods and/or services to make a profit. In a planned economy, the government decides how resources should be used to benefit all citizens. Discuss the pros and cons of the different types of economies.

>> Math Answer
The interest rate is about:

$0.05 \div 12 \approx 0.0041666$;
$\$40,000 \times 0.0041666 \approx$
$\$166.66$; the first payment includes $\$166.66$ in interest.

>> Extension Activity
Have students determine the monthly payment for Franco's loan. ($921.17) Ask students to calculate how much interest Franco will pay over the life of the loan. ($4,216.24); the total principal and interest paid over the life of the loan ($921.17 × 48 = $44,216.24); and the total interest paid on the loan ($44,216.24 − $40,000.00 = $4,216.24).

N C L B Activity correlates to Math standards.

Economic Resources and Systems

Chapter Objectives After completing this chapter, you will be able to:

▶ **Section 2.1** *Economic Resources*
- **Explain** how scarcity requires individuals and nations to make decisions about resources.
- **Describe** the four factors of production.

▶ **Section 2.2** *Economic Systems*
- **Describe** the three basic economic questions each country must answer to make decisions about using their resources.
- **Contrast** the way a market economy and a command economy answer the three economic questions.

Ask STANDARD &POOR'S **Getting Your Financial Life in Order: The Proper Use of Credit Cards**

Q: I know that many people have too much credit card debt. Why is credit card debt such a problem, and when is it appropriate to use a credit card?

A: The effect of compounding interest is to seriously increase the rate you are actually paying on credit card debt. For example, if you borrow $40,000 at an annual percentage rate of 5%, you'll pay almost $6,400, or 16% of the total if you make the minimum payment of $644 each month. Debt is generally a barrier to financial success. Use debt as an alternative to taking money out of savings or money tied up in another investment that earns more interest than the rate at which you are borrowing. When buying a home, keep in mind that interest on a mortgage loan is often tax deductible, allowing you to better manage a large loan.

Mathematics Franco borrowed $40,000 for four years at an annual percentage rate of 5%. He is scheduled to make a payment each month. His first payment includes interest due on the unpaid portion of the debt. The interest due is found by multiplying the unpaid amount by the annual rate divided by the number of payments made in a year.

How much of Franco's first payment is interest?

THEORY **Percents and Decimals** When solving real-life problems, it is often easier to convert percents to decimals. To convert, move the decimal point two places to the left, and drop the percent sign.

N C L B

Classroom Resources

- ✐ Student Edition
- ✐ Teacher Wraparound Edition
- 📂 Student Activity Workbook with Academic Integration
- 📂 Student Activity Workbook with Academic Integration TAE
- 📂 *Fast File*, Unit 1 Resources
- 📂 Inclusion in the Business Education Classroom

- ◉ TeacherWorks Plus
- ◉ *ExamView Assessment Suite*
- ◉ Presentation Plus!
- ◉ Vocabulary PuzzleMaker
- ◉ Interactive Student Edition
- ◌ Online Student Edition
- ◌ Online Learning Center with Podcasts

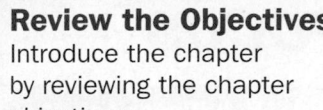

Scarcity Many people have to deal with scarcity issues, such as having few funds to make purchases. Countries also deal with scarcity of resources. **How do nations deal with the problem of scarcity and determine how resources are to be used?**

Photo Credit: David Young Wolff/PhotoEdit

Discuss the Photo

● **Scarcity** Read the caption on the photo to students: Many people have to deal with scarcity issues, such as having few funds to make purchases. Countries also deal with scarcity of resources.

Ask students to talk about how nations should decide how to spend limited resources. (Encourage students to recognize that it is wise to use the decision-making process when deciding how to use limited resources. People should also satisfy their needs first, then their wants.)

Review the Objectives

Introduce the chapter by reviewing the chapter objectives:

Section 2.1 *Objectives*
Explain how scarcity requires individuals and nations to make decisions about resources. (Limited resources prevent individuals and societies from being able to have all they want, so they must decide what to do with their limited resources.)

Describe the four factors of production. (Natural resources: raw materials from nature. Labor resources: individuals who make the goods and services. Capital resources: used to produce goods and services. Entrepreneurial resources: people who recognize opportunities and start businesses.)

Section 2.2 *Objectives*
Describe the three basic economic questions each country must answer to make decisions about using their resources. (What should be produced? [What items will be produced with limited economic resources] How should it be produced? [The procedures and ingredients that will be used] Who should share in what is produced? [Who will be able to own the items]).

Contrast the way a market economy and a command economy answer the three economic questions. (A market economy focuses on individuals through the interaction of supply and demand. A command system focuses on a central authority, such as the government making those decisions.)

21

Economic Resources

Economic Resources
Hold up a product and ask students to identify the resources that are used to produce it. Record students' answers on the board. (One example is a prewashed salad. Vegetables are natural resources. Labor resources include growers, packagers, and truckers. Capital resources include the food preparation and distribution centers. The people who thought of the "salad in a bag" are the entrepreneurial resources.)

Preteaching

Presentation Plus!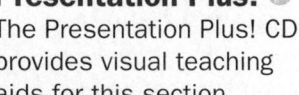
The Presentation Plus! CD provides visual teaching aids for this section.

PuzzleMaker
Use the Vocabulary PuzzleMaker to create a puzzle of the section's key terms. Students can complete the puzzle on paper or on a computer.

Graphic Organizer
Tell students to go to the Online Learning Center through **glencoe.com** for a printable graphic organizer. (Answers are: natural resources, labor resources, capital resources, and entrepreneurial resources.)

 Connects academics to content.

Reading Guide

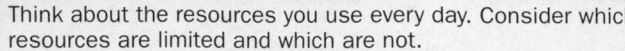

● Before You Read
Think about the resources you use every day. Consider which resources are limited and which are not.

Read to Learn
- Explain how scarcity requires individuals and nations to make decisions about resources.
- Describe the four factors of production.

The Main Idea
Both people and countries must deal with the problem of scarcity. Nations do not have enough factors of production to produce everything that their population wants. Factors of production are all the economic resources necessary to produce a society's goods and services.

Key Concepts
- Making Economic Decisions
- Factors of Production

Vocabulary
Key Terms
> scarcity
> factors of production
> natural resources
> labor resources
> capital resources
> entrepreneurial resources
> entrepreneurship
> entrepreneur

Academic Vocabulary
You will find these words in your reading and on your tests. Make sure you know their meanings.
> factor
> process
> labor
> individual

Graphic Organizer
Write the four factors of production in a figure like the one below.

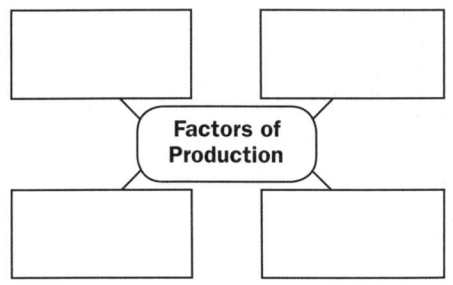

Factors of Production

 Go to the *Introduction to Business* Online Learning Center through **glencoe.com** for a printable graphic organizer.

Academic Standards
English Language Arts
> **NCTE 1** Read texts to acquire new information
> **NCTE 9** Develop an understanding of diversity in language use across cultures

Mathematics
> **Data Analysis and Probability** Formulate questions that can be addressed with data and collect, organize, and display relevant data to answer them

Reading Guide

● Before You Read
Have students brainstorm the resources used to create a backpack. Point out that resources are used to make every product.

D Develop Concepts
The Main Idea Ask students: How do individuals and groups deal with the problem of scarcity? (Individuals and groups adopt systems to determine how to use their resources.)

Making Economic Decisions

Just as individuals have to deal with a shortage of resources, so do societies. In this case resources are the items that go into the making of goods and services. This lack of resources is called **scarcity**. The principle of scarcity states that there are limited resources for satisfying unlimited wants and needs.

Because resources are in limited supply, to have one thing may mean giving up something else. For example, a restaurant owner may forgo plans for a costly new décor to have more money to put into kitchen equipment. A city government might decide to cut expenses for most services to be able to hire more police officers. When dealing with scarcity, it is important to think of the best way to use the item that is in short supply.

> ✔ **Reading Check** **Identify** What is scarcity?

Factors of Production

R **Factors of production** are all the economic resources necessary to produce a society's goods and services, such as the wheat that grows in the ground, the tractor that harvests it, the labor that turns it into flour, and the distribution system that delivers it to the marketplace. There are four **factors** of production: natural resources, labor resources, capital resources, and entrepreneurial resources.

> ● **As You Read**
> Think of a product you own. What factors of production were involved in creating it?

International Business

Global Marketplace
More businesses that used to operate exclusively within the United States now market their products around the world. From farmers to fast-food franchisees to theme-park operators, businesspeople in every sector of the economy are considering entering the global marketplace. Even though companies may operate successfully in the U.S. market, an increasing number of them are thinking about "going international."

Examples of Language Across Cultures
Q: In Italian, how do you say: "Hello, how are you?"
A: **Salve, come sta?** (pronounced: Săl̄vā, kō̄mā stă?)

What are some other reasons a company might choose to enter a foreign market? What are some questions companies should ask before they enter a foreign market?

International Business

Global Marketplace Answers will vary, but students should identify that companies enter foreign markets in order to utilize excess capacity or expertise, to take advantage of relationships that exist in other countries, to achieve growth that is not available with a single market strategy, and to take advantage of an opportunity in a nearby area. Questions companies should ask include: What are the costs? Can we compete? How will expanding affect our existing operations?

TEACH

Discussion Starter
Scarcity
Scarcity is shortage of resources. Ask students if they have ever had to decide how to spend their money when they wanted to buy more than one thing. (Students should respond that everyone has to make decisions about using resources because everyone has limited resources.) Jump-start the discussion by explaining that even the wealthiest people in the world can't have everything they want.

R **Reading Strategy**

Create a Table Instruct students to create a table illustrating the four factors of production using two examples—one for a service and the other for a product. Students may work in pairs. (Tables will vary depending on the goods and services selected, but they should include the four factors of production as headings for the appropriate rows or columns.)

> ● **As You Read**
> Encourage students to consider all four factors of production. Write the volunteers' answers on the board and challenge the class to think of other factors to add to the list.

> ✔ **Reading Check**

Identify Scarcity is an economic principle that states that there are limited resources for satisfying unlimited wants and needs.

TEACH (cont.)

S Skill Practice

Guided Practice

Classify Ask students to write a paragraph explaining the difference between renewable and nonrenewable natural resources. (Paragraphs should state that renewable resources can be reproduced, while nonrenewable resources are limited.) **L1**

Research Ask students to write a one-page paper about the resources used to produce both paper and plastic grocery bags. (Students should identify trees as a resource for paper and petroleum as a resource for plastic.) **L2**

Investigate Have students make a tourism brochure about the natural resources found near their homes, explaining how each relates to the local economy. (Brochures will vary. For example, a nearby lake might have an economic impact because of tourism.) **L3**

✔ Reading Check

Contrast Renewable resources can be reproduced; nonrenewable resources are limited. Ask for examples of both. Tell students that the time required for the renewal of resources varies.

Being *Resourceful*
Answers may include tighter conservation measures and developing more energy-saving technology.

Being *Resourceful*
Like the United States, Japan is dependent on outside sources for oil. During the world oil crisis in 1973, Japan was able to reduce its dependence on oil and enhance productivity through conservation and alternative sources of industrial energy. *Describe some ways that the U.S. government could ease American dependence on foreign oil.*

Natural Resources

Natural Resources are raw materials from nature that are used to produce goods. Trees, water, and grains are natural resources. Natural resources can often be **processed** in various ways to create goods. Even synthetic or artificially produced materials are made by combining or changing natural resources. For example, nylon is a synthetic material derived from coal, water, and air.

The economy of many countries is primarily based on its natural resources. For example, some Latin American countries rely on their coffee and banana crops. Other countries, such as Japan, have little land and scarce natural resources and must get them from somewhere else.

Some natural resources, such as wheat and cattle, are *renewable*. They can be reproduced. You can breed cattle to make more cattle. Other resources are limited, or *nonrenewable*. Coal, iron, and oil are nonrenewable. The amount of natural resources available to a society has a direct effect on its economy.

✔ Reading Check **Contrast** How are renewable resources different from nonrenewable resources?

BusinessWeek *Reader and Case Study*

Graphing the Development Gap

Hans Rosling's brainchild, a nonprofit called Gapminder, uses interactive design to render global statistics comprehensible.

In the late 1990s, Dr. Hans Rosling became frustrated by the x-axis, which—as all middle-schoolers know—is the part of a graph used to measure time. But for Rosling's global-development students at the Karolinska Institutet in Stockholm, it was also the obstacle to their understanding of the health and economic trends that were shaping the globe.

"The students didn't have a fact-based worldview," says Rosling, who helps kick off this year's TED conference—that's technology, education, and design—on Feb. 22. "They talked about 'we' and 'them' the whole time—and even the official terminology of 'industrialized' and 'developing' countries failed to communicate that there is a continuity from the world's poorest nations to the richest."

So Rosling did what any medical doctor and public-health researcher who had spent countless hours playing video games with his children would do: He enlisted his son's help in creating a short animated movie, with floating bubbles representing nations' progress along both health and economic indicators.

 CASE STUDY Go to the *Introduction to Business* Online Learning Center through **glencoe.com** for the *BusinessWeek* Reader Case Study.

Active Learning

Gapminder is a nonprofit organization dedicated to better communicating and disseminating global-development statistics—as a means to "mind the gap" between the world's rich and poor, sick and healthy. Make a set of charts to compare the key development statistics of two nations.

BusinessWeek *Reader and Case Study*

Graphing the Development Gap

CASE STUDY Have students go to the *Introduction to Business* Online Learning Center through **glencoe.com** to download a Case Study activity that corresponds to the article. The activity and answer key are also available on the TeacherWorks Plus CD.

Active Learning

Charts will vary but should include key development figures of two nations, including population, health and wealth, gross domestic product per capita, and average life span.

ASSESS

Review Key Terms
Have students write sentences using each key term.

 **Study-to-Go**
Have students go to the Online Learning Center through **glencoe.com** to download free **Study-to-Go** content to their PDAs or cell phones.

RETEACH

W Writing Support
Enrichment
Labor Resources Have students write a three-paragraph essay about an economy's need for different kinds of labor resources such as skilled, unskilled, physical, and intellectual labor. (Essays will vary, but the works should show evidence of understanding that a variety of labor resources are needed.)

R Reading Strategy
Illustrate Have students draw or find a picture that can be used to illustrate the concept of capital resources. Instruct students to include a caption. The caption should include a question and answer that relates to the illustration. (Answers will vary. Instruct students to use the photo caption as a guide.)

Labor Resources

Every type of business needs labor resources to produce goods and provide services. **Labor resources** are people who make the goods and services for which they are paid. Labor can be skilled or unskilled, physical or intellectual. Teachers, coal miners, bank managers, and farm workers are all human resources. Whether you are a cashier or a news anchor, you are a labor resource.

W

Capital Resources

Capital resources make up another factor of production. Capital resources are not the same as capital, or money. **Capital resources** are the things used to produce goods and services, such as buildings, materials, and equipment. They are also called capital goods. They include delivery trucks, supermarkets, cash registers, and medical supplies. A tractor that a farmer uses to harvest wheat is a capital resource. The headquarters of a major firm is a capital resource. If you are a writer or an accountant, the computer you use is a capital resource.

R

● **An American Pastime**
Capital goods are things used to create goods and services. The capital goods needed to create and sell the entertainment service of baseball include bats, balls, uniforms, and a ballpark.
Name two other capital goods in this picture.

✔ **Reading Check** **Contrast** How are capital resources different from capital?

✔ **Reading Check**

Identify Capital is money, while capital resources are things that are used to produce goods and services. Money is used to buy capital resources, but it is not a capital resource. Capital resources are not the same as capital or money.

Discuss the Photo
● **An American Pastime** In addition to bats, balls, uniforms, and the ballpark, students may suggest ticket machines, mitts, bases, and concessions stands.

C Critical Thinking

Entrepreneurial Thinking
Have students read and discuss an article about a local entrepreneur. Ask: What characteristics do entrepreneurs need to be successful? Do you have what it takes to be an entrepreneur? (Students should recognize traits such as leadership, and the risks and rewards of entrepreneurship.)

Student Activity Workbook 📁 Assign the Section 2.1 Activities.

ASSESS

● After You Read

Have students complete the Section 2.1 After You Read section review.

Online Study Tools
Have students go to the Online Learning Center through **glencoe.com** to:

- Take the Section 2.1 **Practice Test**.
- Download free **Study-to-Go** content to their PDAs or cell phones.

CLOSE

Culminating Activity
Entrepreneurship
Have students write a one-page profile about an entrepreneur. Instruct students to use all the key terms in this section. (Profiles will vary but the key terms should be used correctly.)

26

Entrepreneurial Resources

Entrepreneurial resources meet society's changing wants and needs. **Entrepreneurial resources** are used by the people who recognize opportunities and start businesses.

Entrepreneurship is the process of recognizing a business opportunity, testing it in the market, and gathering the resources necessary to start and run a business. An **entrepreneur** is an individual who undertakes the creation, organization, and ownership of a business. He or she accepts the risks and responsibilities of business ownership to gain profits and satisfaction. Being *entrepreneurial* means acting and thinking like an entrepreneur.

Entrepreneurial resources are different from **labor** resources, even though people provide both. Entrepreneurial resources are **individuals** who start and direct businesses to produce goods and services to satisfy needs or wants. Labor resources are people who produce the goods or services.

NCLB Activity correlates to Math standards.

Section 2.1

● After You Read

Review Key Concepts
1. Why do all nations face the problem of scarcity?
2. Identify one similarity and one difference between labor and entrepreneurial resources.
3. List five different natural resources.

Academic Skills
4. **Mathematics** Jeanne makes costume jewelry and sells it at art fairs. She has tried different pricing strategies and gets different results. Here is a chart of results over the last seven months:

NCLB

Month	Price	Number of items sold
April	$10	300
May	$12	290
June	$14	280
July	$20	250
August	$15	280
September	$13	320
October	$12	340

Describe a graph that you might make from this data. Write a sentence or two about what it would show.

 THEORY **Data Analysis and Probability: Line Graphs** A line graph is useful in displaying information about quantities that change over time. In this case, there are three variables to analyze: time, price, and quantity sold.

 Math For math help, go to the Math Appendix.

@ Go to the *Introduction to Business* Online Learning Center through **glencoe.com** to check your answers.

Section 2.1

Review Key Concepts
1. No nation has enough resources to satisfy all of its wants and needs.
2. Entrepreneurial resources initiate businesses to make new goods and services; labor resources produce goods and services.
3. Answers will vary. Examples include water, oil, iron ore.

Academic Skills
4. **Mathematics** A three-dimensional graph would show that lower priced items sell in greater quantities. A graph of sales dollars generated each month would show that higher priced items sell in smaller quantities and the sales dollars generated are greater than sales of items sold at a lower price.

Economic Systems

FOCUS

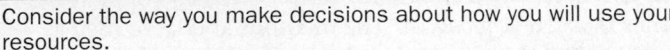

Reading Guide

D

Before You Read

Consider the way you make decisions about how you will use your resources.

Read to Learn

- Describe the three basic economic questions each country must answer to make decisions about using their resources.
- Contrast the way a market economy and a command economy answer the three economic questions.

The Main Idea

Scarcity of economic resources forces every country to develop an economic system that determines how resources will be used. Each economic system has its advantages and disadvantages.

Key Concepts

- Basic Economic Questions
- Different Types of Economies

Vocabulary

Key Terms

economics	demand
economic systems	equilibrium price
market economy	price
price	command economy
supply	mixed economy

Academic Vocabulary

You will find these words in your reading and on your tests. Make sure you know their meanings.

relationship	observed
interact	control

Graphic Organizer

In the left oval, write notes about market economies. In the right oval, write notes about command economies. In the overlapping section, write notes that apply to both.

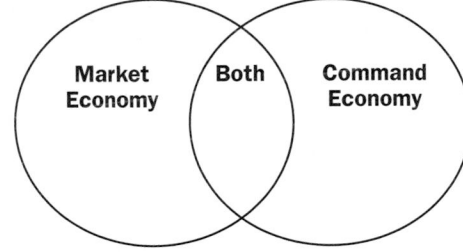

Market Economy — Both — Command Economy

 Go to the *Introduction to Business* Online Learning Center through **glencoe.com** for a printable graphic organizer.

Academic Standards

English Language Arts Correlation

NCLB

NCTE 4 Use written language to communicate effectively

NCTE 7 Conduct research and gather, evaluate, and synthesize data to communicate discoveries

NCTE 8 Use information resources to gather information and create and communicate knowledge

Science

Content Standard D Students should develop an understanding of energy in the earth system, geochemical cycles, origin and evolution of the earth system, origin and evolution of the universe

Bell Ringer Activity

Economic Systems

Ask: Which economic system does the United States have? (market economy) Then ask students to describe a market economy. (Students should describe an economic system in which economic decisions are made in the marketplace where buyers and sellers meet to exchange goods and services.)

Preteaching

Presentation Plus!

The Presentation Plus! CD provides visual teaching aids for this section.

PuzzleMaker

Use the Vocabulary PuzzleMaker to create a puzzle of this section's key terms. Students can complete the puzzle on paper or on a computer.

Graphic Organizer

Tell students to go to the Online Learning Center through **glencoe.com** for a printable graphic organizer. (Answers are: Top oval: Economic decisions are made in the marketplace where buyers and sellers meet to exchange goods and services, usually for money. Bottom oval: A central authority makes the key economic decisions. Overlapping: Methods that societies choose to use and distribute resources.)

NCLB Academic correlations to book content.

Reading Guide

Before You Read

Have students think about the decisions they make about using their resources. Then explain that nations establish economic systems to make these types of decisions.

D Develop Concepts

The Main Idea Ask students: Why does a country have to develop an economic system? (Because of the scarcity of economic resources, every country has to develop an economic system that answers how resources will be used and who will receive them.)

27

TEACH

Discussion Starter
Basic Economic Questions
Write these three words on the board: What, How, Who. Invite three students to complete the three basic economic questions. (What should be produced? How should it be produced? Who should share in what is produced?)

R Reading Strategy

Make a Table Have students make a two-column table with four rows. Instruct students to write "Basic Economic Questions" in the first cell in the first column and write "Notes" in the first cell in the second column. Ask students to complete the table as they read the page. (What should be produced? Using a resource for one purpose means not using it for others. [opportunity cost] How should it be produced? [Factors include methods, labor, quality, etc.] Who should share in what is produced? [Income determines who will share in what is produced.])

Virtual Business
Introduce supply and demand to students using Virtual Business Retailing Supply and Demand activity. In this simulation, students learn why supply and demand are important to a business.

N C L B Activity correlates to Science standards.

Basic Economic Questions

Economics is the study of how individuals and groups of individuals strive to satisfy their needs and wants by making choices. All societies have to make choices to deal with some form of scarcity. No society has enough productive resources available to produce everything people want and need. Societies make economic decisions about how to meet the needs of people by answering three basic economic questions.

What should be produced? Deciding to use a resource for one purpose means giving up the opportunity to use it for something else. This is called an *opportunity cost.*

How should it be produced? The methods and labor used as well as the quality of items produced are important factors. In a country with many workers but few capital resources, it is likely that little equipment and larger amounts of labor are used in producing goods.

Who should share in what is produced? In most societies, people can have as many goods and services as they can afford to buy. The amount of income people receive determines how many goods and services they can have.

● **As You Read**
People make choices every day. What economic decisions have you made recently?

Science/Tech TRENDS

Finding Natural Resources
Earth's crust contains more than 100 naturally occurring elements. For example, gold can be concentrated with other minerals in veins that form in igneous rocks deep underground. Forces related to plate tectonics uplift these rocks and form mountain ranges. Weathering and erosion expose the veins at Earth's surface, and some of the gold is eventually deposited as nuggets, flakes, or flour-size material in stream and river sediment. The gold is sometimes extracted directly from sedimentary rocks in the streambed. The use of satellite imagery has become a valuable tool for geologists. Geologists are now able to perform large-scale surveys of remote, unexplored regions for the presence of geologic structures and key minerals that may indicate areas favorable for mineral deposits.

Web Quest
Go to the *Introduction to Business* Online Learning Center through **glencoe.com** for links to Web sites where you can find satellite images of Earth's geologic structures. Look for companies whose business involves extracting natural resources from Earth's crust. List at least three companies. Write a paragraph or two about one of them, discussing how they might use satellite imagery to support research and exploration. Include a discussion about types of geologic structures.

Science/Tech TRENDS

Web Quest

Finding Natural Resources Answers will vary, but mining companies, oil and gas companies, and computer chip manufacturers are all involved in extracting mineral deposits from Earth's crust.

● **As You Read**
Students may answer that they have made economic decisions about how to spend their money. Encourage students to recognize that all people make economic decisions every day.

Different Types of Economies

Economic systems are the methods societies use to distribute resources. Different economic systems answer the three basic economic questions in different ways. Two basic types of economic systems are a market economy and a command economy.

Market Economies

A **market economy** is an economic system in which economic decisions are made in the marketplace. The marketplace is where buyers and sellers meet to exchange goods and services, usually for money. A market economy can also be called a private enterprise system, the free enterprise system, or capitalism.

In a market economy, resources are privately owned. Citizens can own their own homes, land, and businesses. Business owners decide how their businesses will be run, what to produce and sell, and how much to charge. The government works to promote free trade and prevent unfair trade practices. Consumers choose their occupations and decide where to live, where to shop, and what to buy. People who have labor skills that are in demand earn higher incomes than those who do not. There is an uneven distribution of income. In a market economy, individuals are responsible for being informed and making careful decisions.

✔ Reading Check **Explain** What is the role of the individual within the free enterprise system?

Price, Supply, and Demand There is a **relationship** between price, supply, and demand. The price for an item is determined through the interactions of supply and demand. **Price** is the amount of money given or asked for when goods and services are bought or sold. **Supply** is the amount of goods and services that producers will provide at various prices. Producers want a price for their goods and services that will cover their costs and result in a profit. **Demand** is the amount or quantity of goods and services that consumers are willing to buy at various prices. The higher the price, the less consumers will buy. The lower the price, the more consumers will buy.

Supply and demand **interact** with each other, as shown in **Figure 2.1** on page 30. The **equilibrium price** is the point at which the quantity demanded and the quantity supplied meet.

Competition and Profit In a market economy, competition is **observed**. Competition between similar businesses is one of the basic characteristics of a free enterprise system. It encourages businesses to produce better products at lower prices to attract more customers. Entrepreneurs take risks to make profits. *Profit motive* is the desire to make a profit, and profit is the reward for taking a risk and starting a business.

Supply and Demand
The price of a TV set with a 3-inch screen was $125 in 1938, which would equal approximately $1,721 today. The cheapest model with a 12-inch screen was $445 ($6,256 today). Only 0.5% of U.S. households had a TV set in 1946, 55.7% had one in 1954, and 90% by 1962. *What factors do you think contributed to the large increase in TV ownership?*

✔ Reading Check

Explain In a market economy, individuals are responsible for being informed and making careful decisions. In a command economy, individuals have fewer responsibilities because the government handles much of the decision making.

Supply and Demand Answers will vary but should include a discussion of supply and demand, as well as expansion of programming offered by television networks, a drop in set prices because of mass production, and additional individual income.

Section 2.2

TEACH (cont.)

S Skills Practice

Guided Practice

Illustrate Have students draw a graph to show the relationship of price, supply, and demand in a market economy. Have students label their graph and write a caption to explain it. (Illustrations should be similar to **Figure 2.1**. Supply, demand, and equilibrium price should be labeled.) **L1**

Compare Have students use a table to compare the two basic types of economic systems. (Market economy: economic decisions are made in the marketplace; prices are determined through supply and demand. Command economy: a central authority makes the key economic decisions and sets prices.) **L2**

Specify Have students find an encyclopedia entry about a foreign economy and develop a list of words used to describe it. (Words and phrases may include: market economy, mixed economy, command economy, standard of living, privatization, growth, recession, inflation.) **L3**

ASSESS

Review Key Terms

Have students write sentences using each key term.

STUDY TO GO **Study-to-Go** Have students go to the Online Learning Center through **glencoe.com** to download free **Study-to-Go** content to their PDAs or cell phones.

29

RETEACH

C Critical Thinking

Read the Graph Have students refer to **Figure 2.1**. Tell them to work in pairs to take the roles of consumer and producer. Have the student acting as a consumer be willing to buy the number of DVDs that will be supplied if the price is $5. Ask the supplier to only be willing to sell the number of DVDs that will be supplied if the price is $5. Have students analyze the conflict that would result. Ask if they would feel differently if, instead of DVDs, the item was gasoline, or any other necessity. (At a price of $5, there would be a shortage. A supplier would only be willing to supply 1 DVD, but the consumer would want to buy 6 DVDs. Encourage students to recognize that the conflicts over the equilibrium price are more urgent when an item is a need rather than a want.)

Independent Practice
Individual Responsibility

Ask students to write a paragraph about the role of individual responsibility in a market economy and in a command economy. (In a market economy, individuals are responsible for being informed and making careful decisions. In a command economy, individuals have fewer responsibilities because the government handles most decisions. Students should recognize the importance individual responsibility plays in a market economy as opposed to a command economy.)

● **The Effect of Price** There is a direct relationship between price and the number of items produced and purchased. **What is the equilibrium price for DVDs? At that price, approximately how many DVDs will consumers demand?**

Figure 2.1 — *Supply, Demand, and Equilibrium*

Demand Curve for DVDs
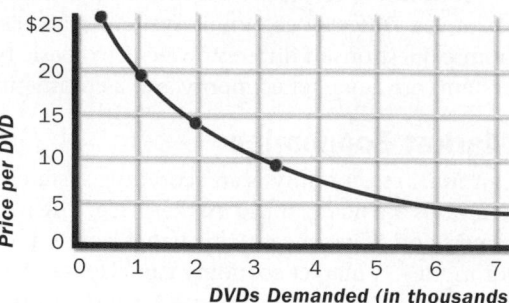

Supply Curve for DVDs
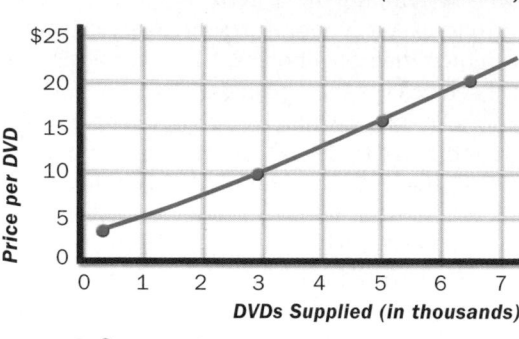

Demand and Supply Curve for DVDs
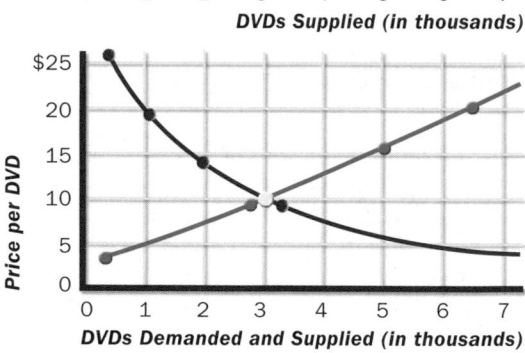

Command Economies

R A **command economy** is an economic system in which a central authority makes the key economic decisions. The government dictates what will be produced, how it will be produced, and who will get the goods. The government owns and controls all the resources and businesses. There is little choice of what to buy. Goods that are not considered necessities are often unavailable. Prices are controlled by the state. There is no incentive to produce a better product since there is no competition. Highly skilled workers may earn the same wages as low-skilled workers.

In a moderate command economy, also called *socialism,* there is some form of private enterprise. The state owns major resources, such as airlines and steel companies and makes the key economic decisions. Individuals own some businesses.

R Reading Strategy

Create a List Ask students to create a bulleted list to summarize the concept of a command economy. After the lists are completed, ask students to work in pairs to refine and improve their lists. Point out that this strategy can be used for other concepts.

Figure 2.1

● **The Effect of Price** The equilibrium price is the point at which the quantity demanded and the quantity supplied meet. The equilibrium price for DVDs is $10. At that price, consumers will demand approximately 3 DVDs.

Mixed Economies

In reality, few nations have a pure market economy or a pure command economy. Most nations have a mixed economy in which private ownership of property and individual decision making are combined with government intervention and regulations. A **mixed economy** is an economy that contains both private and public enterprises. A mixed economy combines elements of capitalism and socialism. In the United States, for example, the government provides things such as defense, education, and aid to those with lower incomes. These are characteristics of a command economy. Yet the United States is primarily a market economy. That means the market makes more of the decisions regarding the allocation of resources than the government. This is also true of Japan. France, Germany, and Sweden are also classified as market economies. However, many of their major industries, such as steel and health care, are owned by the government. In other words, their governments have more **control** of the resources than U.S. and Japanese governments. These economies are considered more socialistic because of greater governmental control of resources.

N C L B Activity correlates to English Language Arts standards.

Section 2.2

● After You Read

Review Key Concepts

1. How does a market system decide what will be produced?
2. In a market system, what determines how many goods and services an individual can buy?
3. Some nations can produce more goods with fewer workers than other countries that have more workers. How can that be true?

Academic Skills

4. **English Language Arts** An economy is not only affected by the decisions that are made in the marketplace. Factors such as natural disasters, war, or political changes can also impact an economic system. Observe a news program, or read a newspaper, magazine, or Internet article on a current event. Write a one- or two-page paper on how the event has impacted a national economic system.

5. **English Language Arts** Choose a country with a different economic system than the U.S. system. Use reference materials such as encyclopedias, Internet sources, history books, and magazines to gather research on the economic systems of both countries. Then prepare a three-minute presentation comparing and contrasting the systems. Illustrate at least one or more of the points you make using a visual aid.

@ Go to the *Introduction to Business* Online Learning Center through **glencoe.com** to check your answers.

Section 2.2

Review Key Concepts

1. A market system decides what is to be produced through supply and demand in the marketplace.
2. It is through one's income—mostly generated by working.
3. More technology is used in the country with fewer workers, increasing worker productivity.

Academic Skills

4. **English Language Arts** Papers should describe the event as well as the effects it causes.
5. **English Language Arts** You might suggest that students investigate countries that were part of the former Soviet Union.

RETEACH (cont.)

C Critical Thinking

Mixed Economy Ask students why it is unlikely that the public role in many mixed economies will completely be eliminated. (Some services are too important or not profitable enough to be left to the market.)

● As You Read

In a market economy, citizens can start their own businesses and make decisions about where they live and work.

Student Activity Workbook 📂 Assign the Section 2.2 Activities.

ASSESS

● After You Read

Have students complete the Section 2.2 After You Read section review.

Online Study Tools

Have students go to the Online Learning Center through **glencoe.com** to:

- Take the Section 2.2 **Practice Test**.
- Download free **Study-to-Go** content to their PDAs or cell phones.

CLOSE

Culminating Activity
Developing Economies
Have students work in pairs to create a presentation about the economy of a developing country.

31

● As You Read

Think about the freedoms you enjoy by living as a citizen in a market economy.

Vocabulary Review

1. Students should write complete sentences using each term correctly.

Review Key Concepts

2. Individuals and societies must decide what to do with their limited resources.

3. Natural resources: raw materials from nature. Labor resources: the people who make the goods and services. Capital resources: items used to produce goods and services. Entrepreneurial resources: the people who create new goods and services through a new business.

4. What should be produced? How should it be produced? Who should share in what is produced?

5. A market economy answers the three questions through individual decision making in the marketplace. A central authority makes the decisions in a command economy.

Critical Thinking

6. Because of scarcity, each country must decide how to use the limited resources and who will get those resources.

7. A market economy encourages business development because of the profit motive, individual decision making, and private enterprise.

Section 2.1 *Summary*

Economic Resources Just as individuals have to deal with a lack of resources, so do societies. Resources are necessary to make what people want and need. A shortage of resources is called scarcity. Individuals and groups of individuals have to deal with the problem of scarcity. Nations do not have enough economic resources or factors of production to satisfy all of the wants and needs of their people. Factors of production that go into making goods and services include natural, labor, capital, and entrepreneurial resources.

Section 2.2 *Summary*

Economic Systems Because all nations must deal with the scarcity of economic resources, each must set up an economic system that determines what and how much will be produced, how items will be produced, and who will receive what is produced. There are two primary types of economic systems. A market economy focuses on individuals answering the three economic questions through the interaction of supply and demand. In a planned economy, the government makes those decisions. Each country has attributes of both.

Vocabulary Review

1. On a sheet of paper, use each of these key terms and academic vocabulary terms in a sentence.

Key Terms		Academic Vocabulary
scarcity	economic systems	factors
factors of production	market economy	processed
natural resources	price	labor
labor resources	supply	individuals
capital resources	demand	relationship
entrepreneurial resources	equilibrium price	interact
entrepreneurship	command economy	observed
entrepreneur	mixed economy	control
economics		

Review Key Concepts

2. Explain how scarcity requires individuals and nations to make decisions about resources.

3. Describe the four factors of production.

4. Describe the three basic economic questions that each country must answer to make decisions about using their resources.

5. Contrast how a market economy and a command economy answer the three economic questions.

32   **Chapter 2**   Review and Activities

8. Capital goods are items that make other items. Money is used to buy capital goods but does not go into making other goods.

9. There is a risk in starting a business. One major incentive is the possibility of making a profit.

10. Yes, it all depends on the supply and demand for the item.

11. The greater supply relative to the demand will receive a lower price.

12. Such price increases are allowed. Because toys are not meeting a basic need, the government should not control the price. The higher price tells other toy producers to start producing similar toys. With more supply, the price will decline or not continue to increase.

Critical Thinking

6. Why does a country need an economic system?

7. In the last 10 to 20 years, several nations have moved toward having a market economy with less emphasis on planned economies. Why do you think some nations choose to adopt a more market-based economy?

8. Explain the reason for the difference between capital and capital goods.

9. Why is the profit motive considered an incentive in a market system?

10. Are some natural resources more valuable than others? Explain.

11. Countries have different levels of scarcity of their economic resources or factors of production. Think of two countries with different levels of scarcity for the same item. How does that affect the economic choices the nations make?

12. A company produces a new toy that is in great demand. It raises its price because there is no competition. Supplies cannot keep up with demand, so the company raises its price again. Are such price increases allowed in a market system? Should the government control the price? What are other toy producers likely to do?

Write About It

13. Write a diary entry about a career you might be interested in pursuing. What capital resources would you need?

14. In a one-page essay, describe at least two situations in which competition has been beneficial to you.

15. Which factor of production do you believe is the most important in the production of goods and services? Write an e-mail to your teacher. Give reasons for your opinion.

16. Write a paper either supporting or rejecting the following statement: "The market system in America focuses too much on individual achievement and not enough on the needs of society."

17. How does recycling help bridge the gap between renewable and nonrenewable resources? Write two or more paragraphs explaining your answer.

18. Create a table that compares and contrasts the quality differences between machine-made products and handmade products.

19. Write two or more paragraphs discussing reasons that trade-offs between labor and capital resources might impact the supply and demand for a product.

Technology Applications

Web Page Design

20. Research a country that has recently moved from a command economy to a mixed or market economy. Prepare a Web page that includes a report on the transitional process. Describe the conditions that led to it. Discuss the rights and responsibilities of businesses, consumers, and the government before and afterward.

Business Ethics

Ethics and Economies

21. Economists study how society distributes scarce resources to produce goods and services. They conduct research, collect and analyze data, monitor economic trends, and develop forecasts. Do you think ethics should be considered when making economic decisions? Explain your answer.

Chapter 2   Review and Activities   **33**

22. The word *capital* comes from the Latin word *capitalis* meaning "of the head." Sentences should include *capital* in the sense of serious (a *capital* crime, a *capital* virtue), important (a *capital* city), wealth (*capital* available for investment), and top part (*capital* of a column). Related words include: chief, cap, capital letter, and capitalist.

23. If the prices don't vary much, the range will be small and ratio will be small. But if the prices are widely different, the range will be greater and ratio will be greater.

24. Answers should include discussion about the financial impact of the event on individuals and on the economy as a whole.

25. The graph for a situation where demand is in decline will typically plot time along the *x*-axis and level of demand along the *y*-axis. The graph will show a line falling from left to right.

Active Learning

26. Answers will vary depending on the businesses chosen and the goods and services as well.

Business in the Real World

27. Answers will vary depending on the businesses chosen.

Applying Academics to Business

English Language Arts

22. The main part of the word *capitalism* is *capital,* which has several meanings and can be used in different contexts. Research the original word in Latin and tell what it means. Then read its various definitions and write a few sentences to demonstrate the meanings of the English word. Finally, list synonyms and a few related words.

Mathematics

23. List five things you buy often, several places where you can buy them, and the price charged at each place. Find the range and median of the prices for each item, and write a ratio comparing the range to the median. How would a ratio for a product with a small range of prices differ from the ratio for a product with a large range of prices?

THEORY **Data Analysis and Probability** The range of a set of data is the difference between the greatest and smallest elements in the set. The mean is the average of the elements in the set, the median is the middle number—or the average of the middle two numbers—when the elements are listed from least to greatest, and the mode is the most frequently occurring number.

English Language Arts

24. Select a current economic event that you are familiar with from reading the newspaper or watching the news. Think about how the economic event impacts the lives of those directly involved and those who are related to the event in some way. Try to find information about the positive and negative economic impacts of the event. Write two or three paragraphs summarizing the economic event and its impacts.

Mathematics

25. Because of warmer-than-expected weather in the winter months, the demand for heating oil has decreased. Sketch a graph showing what a demand curve for heating oil might look like.

THEORY **Algebra/Graphing/Quantitative Relationships** Two-dimensional line graphs can be used to show how two changing values act relative to one another. In this case, as time progresses, demand for heating oil declines.

Active Learning

Community Survey

26. Develop a list of five goods or services. Use a local business directory to determine how many firms in the community offer those goods or services. Rank the goods or services from those with the most competition to those with the least competition.

Business in the Real World

Competition and Product Differentiation

27. Select an article from a recent business publication on how one business is trying to differentiate its products or services in order to attract more customers. Write a letter to your teacher about how each competitor differentiates its products from others in the market.

ExamView Assessment Suite CD allows you to print out ready-made unit and chapter tests, complete with answer keys. You can also create customized tests.

TeacherWorks Plus provides complete teacher resource in one convenient package. It includes customizable lesson plans in a calendar format and instant access to many print program resources.

Real LIFE skills

ASSESSING YOUR WORKPLACE BASIC SKILLS

28. The skills and qualities essential for success in the workforce include basic skills (reading, writing, mathematics, listening, and speaking), thinking skills, and personal qualities. Create a table of these skills and qualities. Then use a 1–5 ranking scale to evaluate your proficiency at these skills. Write an essay that describes how you plan to improve your greatest weakness.

Business CAREERS

FIND YOUR DREAM JOB

29. Go to the *Introduction to Business* Online Learning Center through **glencoe.com** for a link to the Occupational Outlook Handbook Web site. Click on the "OOH Search/A-Z Index" link and enter the job title "customer service representative." Then write a one-page report about this type of occupation. Conclude your report with a list of things you could do now to prepare yourself to pursue the occupation.

Role Play

THE ADVANTAGES OF MARKET ECONOMIES

30. **Situation** You are an economist who consults politicians and other economists in a country that wants to move from a command economy to a market economy.

Activity Prepare and give a presentation on the differences between a command economy and a market economy.

Evaluation You will be evaluated on how well you meet the following performance indicators:

- Explain the characteristics of a market economy, including: profit; competition; private ownership; the ability of individuals to start businesses; freedom of the individual to make career, consumer, and business decisions.
- Explain the characteristics of a command economy.
- Prepare a logical outline of the talk with correct grammar and punctuation.

Real LIFE skills

28. Answers will depend on the student's assessment of ways to improve the weakest skill.

Business CAREERS

29. Nature of the work: Provide direct contacts with customers. Working conditions: Indoors at work stations or in cubicles. Helping people and solving problems is rewarding; dealing with irate customers can be stressful. Training and qualifications: A high-school diploma is required. Some positions require college degrees, licenses, and often ongoing training. Communication and listening skills are important. A second language can be helpful. Opportunities for advancement: Experienced CSRs have opportunities for supervisory and management positions. Job outlook: Excellent. In preparation, improve communication and computer skills.

Role Play

30. Presentations should explain the main concepts of the chapter clearly, succinctly, and logically.

Standardized Test Practice

Directions Choose the letter of the best answer. Write the letter for the answer on a separate piece of paper.

1. In the sentence below, which underlined word or phrase contains a spelling error?

   <u>Cheryl's</u> paper comparing <u>capitalism and socialism</u> was written <u>hurriedly,</u> but she <u>recieved</u> a high mark from the teacher.

   A Cheryl's
   B capitalism and socialism
   C hurriedly,
   D recieved

TEST-TAKING TIP Study for tests over a few days or weeks, and continually review class material. Do not wait until the night before and try to learn everything at once.

READING Go to the *Introduction to Business* Online Learning Center through **glencoe.com** for a list of outside reading suggestions.

Standardized Test Practice
1. D

STRATEGIES FOR STANDARDIZED TEST PREP SUCCESS

Frequent Reviews Help students prepare for standardized tests by planning review sessions two or three times a week so they continually review class material. Vary the approach so that students sometimes work with a study partner, or are responsible for a two-or-three minute presentation on a review topic. Remind them that cramming the night before won't help them do well on standardized tests, and they will be better served by getting a good night's sleep.

Standards-Based Lesson Planning   *Introduction to Business* provides students with instruction and assessment in the following fundamental content areas:

Content Standards Correlations	
Relate the historical basis for the four types of economy the United States has experienced.	p. 39
Discuss basic economic terms: gross domestic product, standard of living, inflation, deflation, deficit, surplus, business cycle, prosperity, recession, depression, recovery.	pp. 38–47
Analyze economic indicators and how they affect the business cycle.	p. 42
Analyze the relationship between inflation and purchasing power.	p. 41
Describe the phases of the business cycle.	pp. 44–47
Interpret data needed to analyze the business cycle.	pp. 44–47
Examine factors influencing the condition of the U.S. economic system.	pp. 40–47
Explore career opportunities in economics.	p. 51

NCLB   Activities, information, and skills practice will help your students attain No Child Left Behind proficiency. Students will improve their abilities in the following academic standards areas:

Academic Standards Correlations		
English Language Arts	Activities/Features	Page
NCTE 2 Read literature to build an understanding of the human experience	Applying Academics to Business	p. 50
NCTE 3 Apply strategies to interpret texts	After You Read Standardized test Practice	pp. 47, 51
NCTE 6 Apply knowledge of language structure and conventions to discuss texts	Standardized test Practice	p. 51
NCTE 8 Use information resources to gather information and create and communicate knowledge	Applying Academics to Business	p. 50
Mathematics		
Data Analysis and Probability Formulate questions that can be addressed with data and collect, organize, and display relevant data to answer them	Ask S&P Applying Academics to Business	pp. 36, 50
Number and Operations Understand numbers, ways of representing numbers, relationships among numbers, and number systems	Applying Academics to Business	p. 50
Number and Operations Understand the meanings of operations and how they relate to one another	After You Read	p. 42
Science		
Content Standard A Students should develop abilities necessary to do scientific inquiry, understandings about scientific inquiry	Science/Tech Trends	p. 45
Content Standard F Students should develop understanding of population growth, science, and technology in local, national, and global challenges	Science/Tech Trends	p. 45

Correlations This chart shows the 21st Century Skills, foundation skills, and workplace competencies that students develop as they work in this chapter.

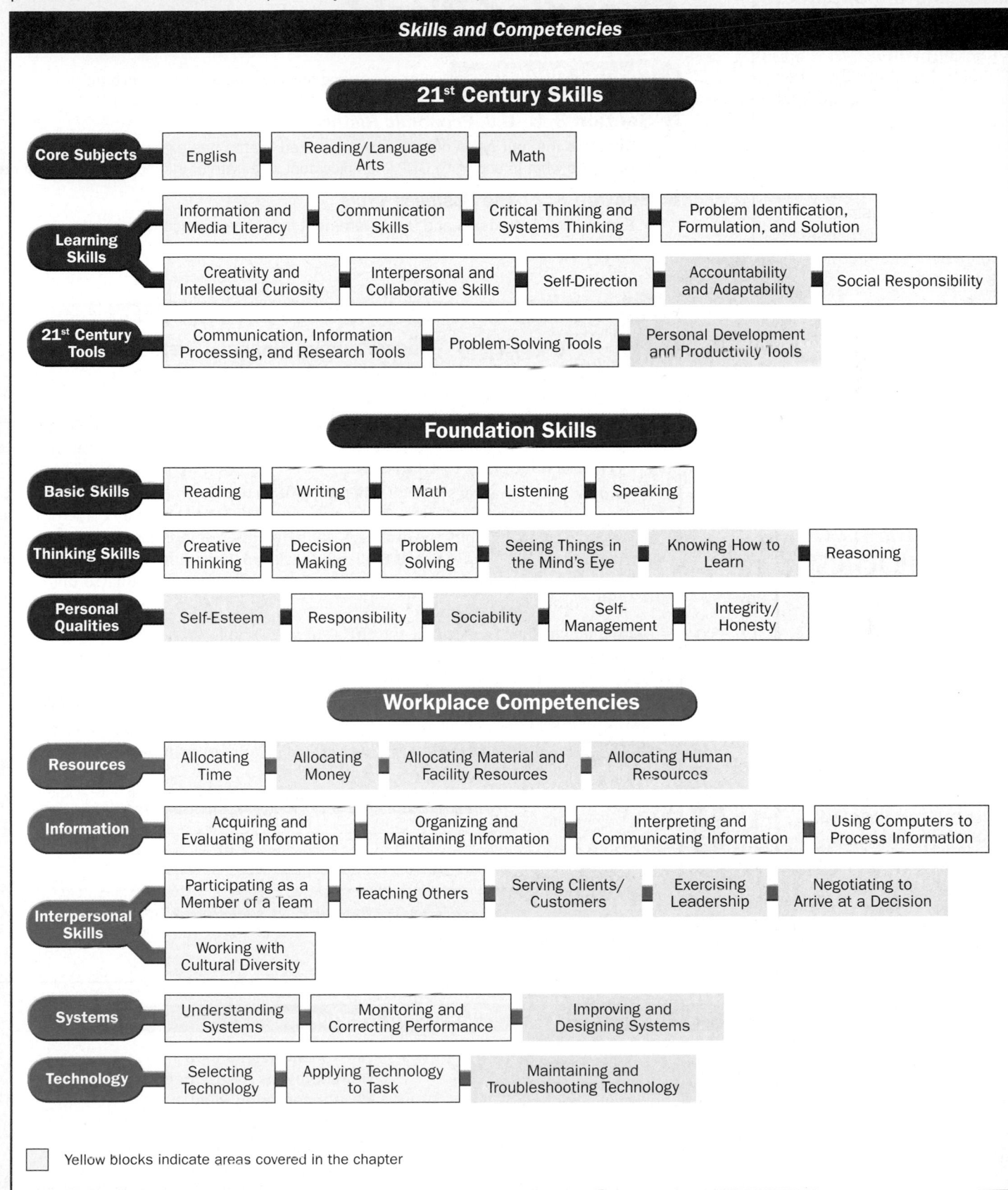

Skills and Competencies

21st Century Skills

Core Subjects: English | Reading/Language Arts | Math

Learning Skills: Information and Media Literacy | Communication Skills | Critical Thinking and Systems Thinking | Problem Identification, Formulation, and Solution | Creativity and Intellectual Curiosity | Interpersonal and Collaborative Skills | Self-Direction | Accountability and Adaptability | Social Responsibility

21st Century Tools: Communication, Information Processing, and Research Tools | Problem-Solving Tools | Personal Development and Productivity Tools

Foundation Skills

Basic Skills: Reading | Writing | Math | Listening | Speaking

Thinking Skills: Creative Thinking | Decision Making | Problem Solving | Seeing Things in the Mind's Eye | Knowing How to Learn | Reasoning

Personal Qualities: Self-Esteem | Responsibility | Sociability | Self-Management | Integrity/Honesty

Workplace Competencies

Resources: Allocating Time | Allocating Money | Allocating Material and Facility Resources | Allocating Human Resources

Information: Acquiring and Evaluating Information | Organizing and Maintaining Information | Interpreting and Communicating Information | Using Computers to Process Information

Interpersonal Skills: Participating as a Member of a Team | Teaching Others | Serving Clients/Customers | Exercising Leadership | Negotiating to Arrive at a Decision | Working with Cultural Diversity

Systems: Understanding Systems | Monitoring and Correcting Performance | Improving and Designing Systems

Technology: Selecting Technology | Applying Technology to Task | Maintaining and Troubleshooting Technology

☐ Yellow blocks indicate areas covered in the chapter

Chapter Overview

Introduce the Chapter

Economic Activity in a Changing World

Chapter 3 is about the types of economic measurements such as gross domestic product (GDP), unemployment rate, rate of inflation, and national debt. The four phases of the business cycle—prosperity, recession, depression, and recovery—are introduced.

Building Background

This chapter will help students to better understand the economic news they read, hear, and see in newspapers, on the radio, or television.

Ask STANDARD &POOR'S

>> Math Answer
The least expensive option is the first, $7,500 at 7% interest.

>> Extension Activity
Have students compare the interest rates on basic savings accounts and on Certificate of Deposit (CD) accounts over the past year. Ask: Would the drummer have earned more interest if he put $7,500 in a regular savings account or in a CD? Answers will vary. In most cases, a CD will pay a higher interest rate. However, there is usually a penalty if the saver wishes to withdraw money before the term ends.

NCLB Activity correlates to Math standards.

Economic Activity in a Changing World

Chapter Objectives After completing this chapter, you will be able to:

▶ **Section 3.1** *U.S. Economic History*
- **Describe** the four types of economy the United States has experienced.
- **Describe** what is shown by GDP, unemployment rate, rate of inflation, and national debt.

▶ **Section 3.2** *The Business Cycle*
- **Explain** how individuals and the government influence the economy.
- **Describe** the four stages of the business cycle.

Ask STANDARD &POOR'S **Understanding Financial Risk**

Q: I am a drummer in a band. I can't decide if I should buy a new drum set now, or wait until next year when we go on the road. Should I buy now, or wait until next year and hope prices don't go up?

A: Financial risk is always a factor when making major purchasing decisions. You have identified one risk—inflation. Prices may go up, but they also may come down. If you need a loan to buy the drum set, changing interest rates represent another risk. You also have liquidity risk. If the band breaks up, how long will it take you to sell your drums so you can pay off your loan? Some risks can be evaluated mathematically, others cannot.

Mathematics You can calculate the effects of price and interest rate fluctuation on purchases. For example, if a drum set costs $7,500, and the interest rate for one year is 7 percent, the total cost will be (0.07 × $7,500) + $7,500 = $8,025. Calculate the total cost with interest for each of the scenarios in the comparison chart and determine the least expensive option.

THEORY **Comparison Charts** A chart can help in comparing different scenarios of price and interest rates.

Price	Interest Rate
$7,500	7%
$7,450	8%
$8,200	5%

NCLB

Classroom Resources

- Student Edition
- Teacher Wraparound Edition
- Student Activity Workbook with Academic Integration
- Student Activity Workbook with Academic Integration TAE
- *Fast File*, Unit 1 Resources
- Inclusion in the Business Education Classroom

- TeacherWorks Plus
- *ExamView Assessment Suite*
- Presentation Plus!
- Vocabulary PuzzleMaker
- Interactive Student Edition
- Online Student Edition
- Online Learning Center with Podcasts

● **Ups and Downs** A market economy has its ups and downs. **How is the business cycle similar to a roller-coaster ride?**

Review the Objectives
Introduce the chapter by reviewing the chapter objectives:

Section 3.1 *Objectives*
Describe the four types of economy the United States has experienced. (agricultural, industrial, service, and information technology)

Describe what is shown by GDP, unemployment rate, rate of inflation, and national debt. (GDP: total amount of goods and services produced in a country in one year. Unemployment rate: measures the number of people who are able to work and are looking for a job during a particular period. Rate of inflation: a general increase in the costs of goods and services comparing one period to another. National debt: the total amount of debt of the national government.)

Section 3.2 *Objectives*
Explain how individuals and government influence the economy. (Individuals are participants in the market; government has an additional role to play by passing laws that encourage commerce and labor and through its ability to influence the market with its fiscal and monetary policy.)

Describe the four stages of the business cycle. (Prosperity: the peak of economic activity. Recession: economic activity slows down. Depression: a deep recession that lasts for several years. Recovery: the economy begins to rebound from a recession or depression.)

Discuss the Photo
● **Ups and Downs** Read the photo caption to students: A market economy has its ups and downs. How is the business cycle similar to a roller-coaster ride?

Ask students to give examples they have heard of good and bad times in the country's economic history. (Point out that all economies experience rises and falls. In a market economy, there is an economic cycle, which includes four stages: prosperity, recession, depression, and recovery. These booms and slumps in economic activity are associated with increased/decreased unemployment and increased/decreased productivity and GDP. The resulting graph looks much like a roller-coaster track.)

37

FOCUS

Bell Ringer Activity

U.S. Economic History
Make copies of a recent news article about the local economy and distribute them to students. Ask: How would you describe the local economy? (Answers will vary depending on the current state of the local economy.)

Preteaching

Presentation Plus!
The Presentation Plus! CD provides visual teaching aids for this section.

PuzzleMaker
Use the Vocabulary PuzzleMaker to create a puzzle of the section's key terms. Students can complete the puzzle on paper or on a computer.

Graphic Organizer
Tell students to go to the Online Learning Center through **glencoe.com** for a printable graphic organizer. (When complete, the graphic organizer should indicate the following time spans: 1700s: Agricultural; 1800s: Industrial; Services: 1700s to 2000s; Information Technology: 1900s to 2000s.)

NCLB Connects academics to content.

U.S. Economic History

Reading Guide

Before You Read

Think of some factors that affect the health of the U.S. economy.

D

Read to Learn
- Describe the four types of economy that the United States has experienced.
- Describe what is shown by GDP, the unemployment rate, rate of inflation, and national debt.

The Main Idea
Throughout the years, the U.S. economic system has changed. Each change affected what was produced and how people were employed. To gauge the health of our economic system, we use a variety of economic indicators.

Key Concepts
- The Changing U.S. Economy
- Measuring Economic Activity

Vocabulary
Key Terms
> gross domestic product (GDP)
> standard of living
> inflation
> deflation
> budget deficit
> national debt
> budget surplus

Academic Vocabulary
You will find these words in your reading and on your tests. Make sure you know their meanings.
> shifts
> emphasis
> sum
> period

Graphic Organizer
Use a timeline like this one to indicate the changes in the U.S. economy from the 1700s to the 2000s. Mark the timeline to designate the following eras: Agricultural, Industrial, Production of Services, and Information Technology.

1700	1800	1900	2000

 Go to the *Introduction to Business* Online Learning Center through **glencoe.com** for a printable graphic organizer.

NCLB

Academic Standards
Text
> **NCTE 1** Read texts to acquire new information

Mathematics
> **Number and Operations** Understand meanings of operations and how they relate to one another

---

Reading Guide

Before You Read

Students might mention unemployment, interest rates, or things that affect them directly such as the cost of gasoline and the cost of their favorite foods.

D Develop Concepts

The Main Idea Ask students: Based on history, what has happened each time our economic system faced changes? (Each change affected what was produced and how people were employed.)

The Changing U.S. Economy

Sometimes major **shifts** in certain growth areas can change the **emphasis** of the U.S. economy. The United States has experienced four major economic shifts.

During the early 1600s, the colonists bartered, or traded, goods and services. This created our service-based economy. In the 1700s, farming was a common way of life. This formed the agriculture-based economy. In the mid-1850s, the Industrial Revolution enabled the advent of big machines for producing goods. This started the industry-based economy. The 1900s saw the rapid movement of information, with the invention of the computer. This created the information-based economy. Computers have transformed the ways that goods and services are produced, delivered, and sold.

While we live in the information age, we also still rely upon aspects of the other types of economies. Agriculture, industry, services, and information all contribute to the health of the U.S. economy.

BusinessWeek *Reader and Case Study*

Net or Newspapers?

No matter what is introduced into the media ecosystem, the oldest of the Big Media survives. Despite decades of doomsayers, newspapers prospered through radio, through TV and cable, through video games, through the Internet...

Not so fast. Suddenly, even sober Wall Street analysts think something new is afoot.

What looms now "is different from all other threats," says Lauren Rich Fine, a Merrill Lynch & Co. analyst who has covered the industry since the 1980s. Consumers are shifting decisively to online information, says Fine, especially the young, and are no longer yoked to the local newspaper. "Ads are following the eyeballs to where they make transactional decisions." Fine recently forecast that newspapers' profit margins are set to enter a long period of decline.

The new and troubling reality for newspapers is that, even if they excel as purveyors of information to appreciative audiences, they still face tough business terrain. "They can try to be the

destination where you go online and [can] be really successful with citizen journalism and blogs," says Fine. But such innovations are "not going to pay a lot of bills."

 CASE STUDY Go to the *Introduction to Business* Online Learning Center through **glencoe.com** for the *BusinessWeek* Reader Case Study.

Active Learning

Newspapers have had to compete as sources of information for a long time. Radio, TV, cable, and the Internet all provide news coverage. Each provides it differently, however, to take the most advantage possible of the distinct features of its medium. Research the same story on TV news, in a newspaper, and on the Internet. How are the presentations similar? How are they different?

glencoe.com

Section 3.1

TEACH

Discussion Starter
The Changing U.S. Economy
Changes in the U.S. economy affect production and employment. Ask students to provide some examples of products, services, and occupations that emerged as the emphasis of the U.S. economy shifted. Then ask students to identify products, services, and occupations that have disappeared. (Answers will vary. For example, the automobile has largely replaced horses as transportation and is responsible for tires, gasoline pumps, car washes, auto mechanics, and used car dealers.)

● **As You Read**

Results will vary. Students are likely to mention technological changes in their answers.

R Reading Strategy

Apply Knowledge Invite volunteers to share knowledge about the economy that they may have gained from history and social studies classes. (Students probably studied the building of railroads and factories in the industrialized North before the Civil War. Point out that the proliferation of cars and planes in the twentieth century created changes in the economy that were just as dramatic as the information technology revolution being experienced today).

BusinessWeek *Reader and Case Study*

Net or Newspapers?

 CASE STUDY Have students go to the *Introduction to Business* Online Learning Center through **glencoe.com** to download a Case Study activity that corresponds to the article. The activity and answer key are also available on the TeacherWorks Plus CD.

Active Learning

Answers will vary, depending on the story chosen for research, but should include some discussion of differences in story length, reliance on visual vs. verbal information presentation, proximity of/interruptions by advertisements, depth of coverage, etc.

TEACH (cont.)

S Skill Practice

Guided Practice

List Ask: List the four main components of the gross domestic product (GDP). (goods and services sold to consumers, to businesses, to the government, and to other countries) **L1**

Compare Have students make a poster comparing the United States and another country's GDP per capita for the previous year. (Posters should compare U.S. GDP to another country's GDP.) **L2**

Chart Have students create a pie chart from this GDP data: United States, $12.370 trillion; European Union, $12.180 trillion; China, $8.158 trillion; Japan, $3.867 trillion; India, $3.678 trillion; Other countries, $19.127 trillion. (United States, 21%; European Union, 21%; China, 14%; Japan, 7%; India, 6%; Other countries, 31%) **L3**

ASSESS

Review Key Terms

Have students write sentences using each key term.

Study-to-Go Have students go to the Online Learning Center through **glencoe.com** to download free **Study-to-Go** content to their PDAs or cell phones.

● As You Read

Students may refer to sports statistics or grade-point averages.

Unsung Heroes
Each nation's economy has had its unsung heroes and heroines. One hero of the Industrial Revolution might have been French-born Joseph Jacquard, who conceived the Jacquard loom, a system for the mass production of woven fabrics. *Who are the unsung heroes or heroines of our information age?*

● As You Read

Economic indicators are figures that measure economic performance. What figures do you use to measure events or performances in your everyday life?

Measuring Economic Activity

Baseball fans know that batting averages, strikeouts, RBIs, and ERAs are figures used to measure a player's performance. Figures are also used to measure economic performance. These figures are called *economic indicators*. They measure things such as how much a country is producing, whether its economy is growing, and how it compares to other countries.

Gross Domestic Product

One way of telling how well an economy is performing is to measure how many goods and services it produces. The total value of the goods and services produced in a country in a given year is called its **gross domestic product (GDP)**. GDP is one of the most important indicators of the status of an economy. To calculate the GDP, economists compute the **sum** of goods and services sold to businesses, consumers, the government, and other countries. The United States has a very high GDP compared to other countries.

Standard of Living

Another important measure of a country's economic health is its standard of living. The **standard of living** is the level of material comfort as measured by the goods and services that are available. The more goods and services produced per person, the higher the standard of living.

The United States has a high standard of living largely because of its productive workforce. The standard of living refers to the amount of goods and services people can buy with the money they have. In the free-enterprise system, the wealth created by businesses benefits the entire community because businesses pay taxes and provide jobs.

❓ETHICS in Business

Environmental Awareness

■ **Critical Reading** Life is full of important decisions. Think about the kinds of decisions that you make as you read the question below.

You are a purchasing agent for a large furniture manufacturer. You have received several bids from lumber companies for a supply of teak, a very dense and decay-resistant type of wood. The lowest bid comes from a lumber company that has been known for not placing a strong emphasis on local environmental concerns, especially resource depletion, when it cuts down trees.

■ **Decision Making** How does the lumber company's reputation affect your decision? Explain your answer.

Real World

Unsung Heroes Students may research recent technology to find out who started these new technologies, such as Jean Armour Polly and Tim Berners-Lee. Polly, a librarian also known as "NetMom," coined the phrase "surfing the Internet" in 1992.

❓ETHICS in Business

Decision Making Students might suggest that all aspects of the company's reputation should be considered before making a decision to buy from the company.

● **A Changing Economy**
Our economy has been affected by many developments. The development of information technology has transformed the ways goods and services are produced. **What other changes have affected the U.S. economy?**

Unemployment Rate

The *unemployment rate* measures the number of people who are able and willing to work but cannot find work during a given **period**. Changes in the unemployment rate show whether an economy is picking up or slowing down.

✔ Reading Check **Identify** What does the unemployment rate measure?

Rate of Inflation

Another important measure of economic strength is the rate of inflation. **Inflation** is a general increase in the price of goods and services. With inflation, one's buying power decreases because it costs more to buy goods and services.

Inflation has many causes. It can occur after a war because scarce resources were transferred to the war effort. Inflation can be caused by increases in the costs of raw materials, expenses, and salaries. Inflation can also occur when the government allows too much money to circulate in the economy.

When the supply of goods is greater than demand, deflation can result. **Deflation** is a general decrease in the price of goods and services. When an economy produces more goods than people want, sellers have to lower prices and cut production. As a result, people have less money to buy goods, so the demand continues to go down.

Worker Shortage
In recent years, Japan has found that it does not have enough workers. Corporations have had to react by retaining their skilled laborers. Toyota Motor Corporation is preparing for a shrinking workforce by offering one-year contracts to top employees who turn 60. Japan's largest untapped source is its women. *What steps do you think Japan might take to ease its current labor shortage?*

Section 3.1 U.S. Economic History **41**

RETEACH

W Writing Support
Enrichment
Types of Unemployment
Have students write a short report on unemployment including explanations of frictional, seasonal, structural, and cyclical unemployment. (Frictional: caused by changing jobs, is temporary with little effect on the economy. Seasonal: workers are only needed part of the year. Structural: new technology replaces workers, requiring new skills, or companies merge and eliminate jobs. Cyclical: the entire economy slows down.)

R Reading Strategy
Investigate and Report
Have students investigate and write a short report on the national and local unemployment rates for the last ten years and to compare them to employment in Japan. (Answers will vary depending on where students live and the date of the assignment.)

U Universal Access
Auditory Learners Invite a student to read aloud from the textbook while classmates listen. Ask another volunteer to summarize what was read. All students can benefit from this activity.

✔ Reading Check

Identify The unemployment rate measures the percentage of people in the economy who are looking for a job but are not able to find one.

Discuss the Photo
● **A Changing Economy** Information technology is the most recent development. Other changes are the product of shifts in the demographics of the workforce, such as increases in the number of women working. Also, the increasingly global economy has shifted many jobs overseas.

Worker Shortage Answers will vary. Japan might try to ease its current labor shortage by enticing women to join the workforce with services such as daycare facilities, flexible hours, and other benefits.

RETEACH (cont.)

C Critical Thinking

National Debt Have students work in groups to locate information about the national debt. Instruct students to prepare a summary of their findings with reference citations for class discussion. (Students can find basic information from government sources, encyclopedias, business publications, and academic journals.)

Student Activity Workbook ☞ Assign the Section 3.1 Activities.

ASSESS

● After You Read

Have students complete the Section 3.1 After You Read section review.

Online Study Tools

Have students go to the Online Learning Center through **glencoe.com** to:

- Take the Section 3.1 **Practice Test**.
- Download free **Study-to-Go** content to their PDAs or cell phones.

CLOSE

Culminating Activity

Economic Activity in the Changing World

Organize the class into six groups and have each group prepare a short presentation about a topic from the chapter. (Presentations will vary. Make sure that all key terms and concepts are covered.)

National Debt

Countries can run up large debts. The main source of income for a government is taxes. Governments use tax money to pay for programs such as defense, education, and Social Security. When the government spends more on programs than it collects in taxes, the difference in the amount is called a **budget deficit**. To pay for the difference, governments borrow money from the public, banks, and even other countries. The total amount of money a government owes is its **national debt**. If the debt gets too large, a nation can become dependent on other nations or unable to borrow more money. This is the case in many developing nations.

Sometimes, a government's revenue can exceed its expenditures. When a government's revenue exceeds its expenditures during a one-year period, it has a **budget surplus**. The United States experienced several years of budget surpluses in the late 1990s. The government often uses a surplus to cut taxes, reduce the national debt, or increase spending for certain programs.

N C L B Activity correlates to Math standards.

Section 3.1

● After You Read

Review Key Concepts

1. When did the service-based economy begin?
2. What do economic indicators measure?
3. What is the difference between a budget surplus and a budget deficit?

Academic Skills

4. **Mathematics** Suppose a recent study shows the U.S. Gross Domestic Product (GDP) is $11.5 trillion. The study also shows that personal spending accounts for 70.4 percent of the total GDP. How much is personal spending in dollars?

THEORY **Number and Operations: Percents**
A percent is a ratio comparing a number to 100. It can also be represented as a fraction, with 100 as the denominator. To find a decimal equivalent, divide the percent by 100. Multiply that decimal by the total amount to determine the dollar amount that it represents.

 For math help, go to the Math Appendix.

@ Go to the *Introduction to Business* Online Learning Center through **glencoe.com** to check your answers.

Review Key Concepts

1. The service economy started in colonial times, when colonists traded among themselves for services.
2. Economic indicators measure the economic health of the nation.
3. A budget surplus occurs when revenue is more than expenses whereas a budget deficit occurs when expenses are more than revenue.

Academic Skills

4. **Mathematics** $11,500,000,000,000 × .704 = $8,096,000,000,000

The Business Cycle

FOCUS

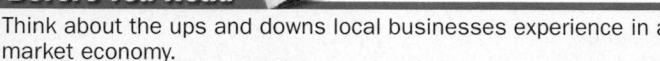

Reading Guide

● Before You Read

Think about the ups and downs local businesses experience in a market economy.

Read to Learn

- Describe the four stages of the business cycle.
- Explain how individuals and government influence the economy.

The Main Idea

In a market economy, there is an economic cycle, which includes four stages: prosperity, recession, depression, and recovery. These are also the four stages of the business cycle. In the last few decades, we have experienced the economic cycle a number of times.

Key Concept

- Guiding the Economy
- Four Stages of the Business Cycle

Vocabulary

Key Terms

business cycle	depression
prosperity	recovery
recession	

Academic Vocabulary

You will find these words in your reading and on your tests. Make sure you know their meanings.

enormous	purchase
policy	decline

Graphic Organizer

On a figure like the one below, label each of the four boxes with the appropriate stage of the business cycle.

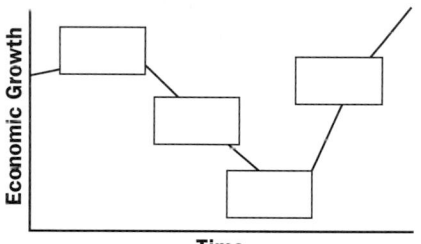

 Go to the *Introduction to Business* Online Learning Center through **glencoe.com** for a printable graphic organizer.

Academic Standards

English Language Arts

NCTE 1 Read texts to acquire new information

NCTE 4 Use written language to communicate effectively

NCTE 3 Apply strategies to interpret texts

Science

Content Standard A Students should develop abilities necessary to do scientific inquiry, understandings about scientific inquiry

Content Standard F Students should develop understanding of population growth, science and technology in local, national, and global challenges

---

Bell Ringer Activity

The Business Cycle
Ask students to think about a local sports team. Discuss winning and losing streaks, and compare them to the economy. (Students should realize that all teams have ups and downs over time.) **Ask:** What stage of the business cycle do they see and hear about In the media? (Answers will vary depending on the current health of the economy.)

Preteaching

Presentation Plus!
The Presentation Plus! CD provides visual teaching aids for this section.

PuzzleMaker
Use the Vocabulary PuzzleMaker to create a puzzle of the section's key terms. Students can complete the puzzle on paper or on a computer.

Graphic Organizer
Tell students to go to the Online Learning Center through **glencoe.com** for a printable graphic organizer. ([1] prosperity, [2] recession, [3] depression, and [4] recovery.)

N C L B Connects academics to content.

Reading Guide

● Before You Read

Answers will vary. Students might describe successful, struggling, and failed businesses.

D Develop Concepts

The Main Idea Ask students: What are the four stages of the economic cycle in a market economy? (The four stages are prosperity, recession, depression, and recovery.)

43

TEACH

Discussion Starter
Four Stages of the Business Cycle
Ask students how prosperity in another country might affect the economy in the United States. (Students should recognize that prosperity in other countries generally provides a market for U.S. goods and services.)

R **Reading Strategy**

Summarize Have students work in pairs to summarize and discuss with the class the events that occur during the business cycle. (Answers will vary. Some students might describe the expansion and contraction of the economy. Others might focus more on the cyclical nature of the economy.)

● **As You Read**

Answers will vary. Students may explain that a new company in town creates jobs, provides incomes, and allows residents to buy more goods and services. Layoffs in a community will have an adverse effect, affecting many businesses in the community.

✔ **Reading Check**

Identify The four stages of the business cycle are prosperity, recession, depression, and recovery. Follow up by asking volunteers to look up the definitions of these words in the glossary and read the definitions aloud.

Guiding the Economy

The U.S. economy is shaped by a mix of public and private forces. Individuals have an **enormous** role on the market for goods and services. Congress and the President enact laws that impact fiscal **policy**. Whenever tax money is spent, it has an effect on the economy. These expenditures are often planned to guide the economy. The Federal Reserve, informally called "the Fed," is a government agency that guides the economy by regulating the amount of money in circulation, controlling interest rates, and controlling the amount of money loaned. State and local governments may also take steps to influence their local economies.

● **As You Read**

One country's economy can affect other countries. How does the economy of your community affect you and your family?

Four Stages of the Business Cycle

Economies go through ups and downs. This can happen for many reasons, including wars, foreign competition, changes in technology, and changes in consumers wants. Over long periods of time, these changes form patterns. For example, the U.S. economy went through slumps in the 1930s, the 1950s, the 1970s, and the early part of 2000. These slumps in economic activity with increased unemployment were followed by new waves of increased productivity and rises in GDP. The rise and fall of economic activity over time is called the **business cycle**. There are four stages of the business cycle—prosperity, recession, depression, and recovery. **Figure 3.1** illustrates the business cycle.

In a global economy, one country's economy can affect other trading partners. If a nation is in a period of economic expansion, it may **purchase** goods and services from other countries, promoting expansion in those countries.

✔ **Reading Check** | **Identify** What are the four stages of the business cycle?

Figure 3.1 – **Business Cycle Model**

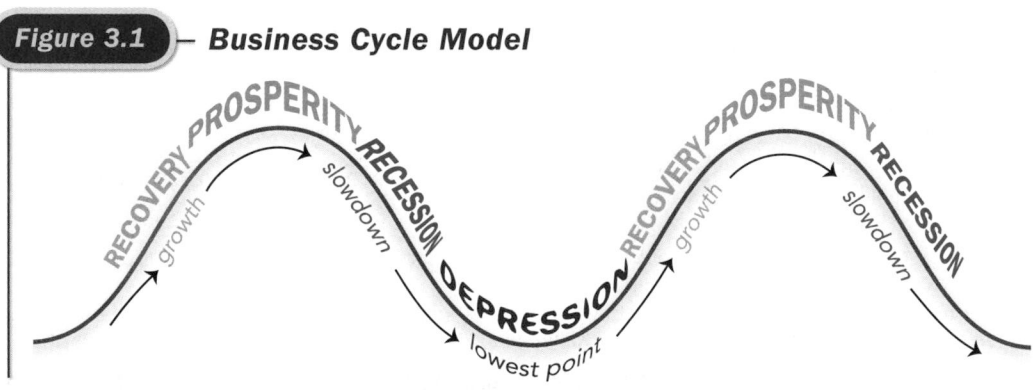

● **The Business Cycle** The repeated rise and fall of economic activity over time is called a business cycle. **Does every business cycle have all four of these stages?**

Figure 3.1

● **The Business Cycle** Not every business cycle has all four stages. Many business cycles proceed from recovery to prosperity to recession and back to recovery.

Prosperity

When unemployment is low, production of goods and services is high, new businesses open, and there is prosperity. **Prosperity** is a peak of economic activity. This condition spreads throughout the economy. Wages are usually higher, so workers have more income. There is a greater demand for goods to be produced. More people can buy houses, which creates more work for builders. People also want to buy more goods from other countries, which benefits those countries as well.

Recession

During a **recession**, economic activity slows down. Businesses produce less, so they need fewer workers. As the unemployment rate increases, people have less money to spend. Without a steady source of income, unemployed workers consume fewer goods and services. The general drop in the total production of goods and services makes GDP decline.

In a recession there are downturns in many industries. A downturn in one industry can affect others. For example, a recession in the auto-making industry can lead to a recession in businesses that make parts for cars. When this happens, it is called the ripple effect. Because of the ripple effect, downturns in major industries can bring on a recession.

• As You Read

When an economy enjoys prosperity, there is a greater demand for goods. What new technologies were developed in the last few decades as a result of good economic conditions?

Science/Tech TRENDS

Jobs in Your Future

Job opportunities result from the relationships between the population, the labor force, and the demand for goods and services. Population changes influence the demand for goods and services. When the population changes, the size and makeup of the labor force change as well.

The Bureau of Labor Statistics recently released a report stating that nearly all of the 20 fastest growing occupations between now and 2014 are related to health care or computers. These occupations include home health aides, network systems specialists, and data communications analysts. During the same period, retail salespeople and registered nurses are expected to gain the most new jobs—more than 700,000 each.

Web Quest

Go to the *Introduction to Business* Online Learning Center through **glencoe.com** for links to Web sites where you can research population trends between now and 10 years from now. Make some predictions about how the demand for goods and services will change over the next 10 years.

TEACH (cont.)

S Skill Practice
Guided Practice

Clarify Ask students to compare the definitions of prosperity and recession. (Prosperity is a peak in economic activity whereas a recession is a slowdown in the economy.) **L1**

Outline Have students create an outline for the prosperity and recession stages of the business cycle. (Each stage should have a main topic and a few bullet points.) **L2**

Outline Have students create an outline for all four stages of the business cycle. (Each stage should be a main topic and a few bullet points.) **L3**

ASSESS

Review Key Terms
Have students write sentences using each key term.

 Study-to-Go Have students go to the Online Learning Center through **glencoe.com** to download free **Study-to-Go** content to their PDAs or cell phones.

• As You Read

Some examples are the Internet and e-commerce Web sites.

 Activity correlates to Science standards.

Science/Tech TRENDS

Web Quest

Jobs in Your Future Numbers will grow, the number of women will grow at a faster rate, and percent of men in the labor force is expected to decrease. The group aged 16 to 24 is expected to slightly decrease. The primary working age group, 25 to 54 years old, is projected to decline. Workers 55 and older are projected to increase due to the aging of the baby-boomer generation. Childcare needs will increase, as will more demand for housing, and an aging population will increase the demand for health services.

RETEACH

● **Different Scenes for Different Stages of the Business Cycle** When workers go on strike, they usually want more wages or benefits. **At what stage of the business cycle would this type of event most likely occur?**

Real World

R **"Depressionproof"** During the Great Depression, millions of people lost their homes and livelihoods. However, a large percentage of middle-class Americans were able to keep their jobs. These people were in professions considered "depressionproof." *What professions do you think are more secure during a depression, and why?*

Depression

During a depression there is high unemployment and low production of goods and services. A **depression** is a deep recession that affects the entire economy and lasts for several years. It can be limited to one country but usually spreads to related countries. During a depression, many people are out of work, and fewer goods and services are produced. There is also a lot of unused manufacturing facilities. Fortunately, depressions are rare.

W The stock market crash on October 29, 1929, or "Black Tuesday," marked the beginning of the Great Depression. Between 1929 and 1933, GDP fell from approximately $103 billion to $55 billion—a **decline** of nearly 50 percent. At the same time, the number of people out of work rose nearly 800 percent—from 1.6 million to 12.8 million. During the worst years of the Depression, one out of every four workers was jobless. Even workers who had jobs suffered. The average manufacturing wage, which had reached 55 cents an hour by 1929, plunged to five cents an hour by 1933.

U Many banks across the country failed. The FDIC did not exist at the time, so depositors were not protected. To prevent panic withdrawals, the federal government declared a "bank holiday" in March 1933. Every bank in the country closed for several days, and many never reopened. The money supply fell by one-third. Currency was in such short supply that towns, counties, chambers of commerce, and other civic bodies resorted to printing their own money.

✔ **Reading Check** **Describe** What happens to the economy during a depression?

46 **Chapter 3** Economic Activity in a Changing World

Recovery

During a recovery, production starts to increase. A **recovery** is a rise in business activity after a recession or depression. People start going back to work and have money to purchase goods and services. The new demand for goods and services stimulates more production, and the GDP grows. Recovery leads back to prosperity as new businesses open and existing businesses increase productivity.

A recovery can take a long time or it can happen quickly. In 1939, the United States was only beginning to recover from the depression when World War II began. During the war, the United States recovered much faster because of the demand for war production.

During a recovery, some businesses innovate—meaning that they bring out new goods and services. These innovations can be different from what they previously produced. They could also be different from what their competitors make. If the innovation is popular with consumers, sales increase dramatically, their per unit costs decrease, and profitability increases. Businesses thus grow and economic activity soars.

 Activity correlates to English Language Arts standards.

Section 3.2

After You Read

Review Key Concepts

1. What is the stage that follows a recession or depression?
2. What is the difference between a recession and a depression?
3. Why may innovation play an important role in the recovery stage of the business cycle?

Academic Skills

4. **English Language Arts** The business cycle is often described using terms that describe how large bodies of water behave. Two of those terms are *ebb and flow* and *ripple effect*. Write a few sentences about each of these terms. Explain what they mean and why they are good metaphors for different aspects of the business cycle.

5. **English Language Arts** The words listed below are all synonyms, or closely related in meaning. They all can be used to describe negative movement in the business cycle. Notice that some of the words imply a more serious fall in the economy than others. Rewrite the list so that the words are, in your best judgment, ordered from least serious to most serious. Then write a few sentences explaining why you ordered the words as you did.

recession   slump   depression
decline   downturn

@ Go to the *Introduction to Business* Online Learning Center through **glencoe.com** to check your answers.

Section 3.2

Review Key Concepts

1. The recovery stage can happen after either a recession or a depression.
2. A recession is a slight downturn; a depression is a major downturn.
3. Innovation creates demand that leads to more employment and production, which leads to more demand.

Academic Skills

4. **English Language Arts** *Ebb and flow:* rising and falling tides. *Ripple effect:* what happens to the surface of water when touched. Both are good metaphors because the economy rises and falls in a pattern.
5. **English Language Arts** downturn, decline, slump, recession, depression

RETEACH (cont.)

C Critical Thinking

Innovation During Recovery
During the Depression, the U.S. government established the Tennessee Valley Authority. Have students visit the TVA Web site and write a short report on how it spurred recovery. (Students might focus on the electricity generated by their dams that brought increased production.)

Student Activity Workbook Assign the Section 3.2 Activities.

ASSESS

After You Read

Have students complete the Section 3.2 After You Read section review.

Online Study Tools
Have students go to the Online Learning Center through **glencoe.com** to:

- Take the Section 3.2 **Practice Test**.
- Download free **Study-to-Go** content to their PDAs or cell phones.

CLOSE

Culminating Activity
Stage of the Economy
Have students form groups to discuss which stage the economy is in. (Students are likely to be influenced by local conditions.)

47

1. Students should write complete sentences using each term correctly.

2. See page 37.
3. See page 37.
4. See page 37.
5. See page 37.

6. Cars made in this country by a foreign-owned company are included in GDP. However, items made in a foreign country by an American company would not be included.

7. Babysitting is probably not included in the GDP. Day-care centers would probably be reported and included.

8. Unemployment figures only include people who are willing and able to work and looking for work. Full-time students and retired people are not looking for work.

9. Retired people's income stays the same and the cost of goods and services increases under inflation.

10. Deflation is a general decrease in the price of goods and services. When sellers lower prices or cut production, people have less money to buy goods, so demand goes down.

11. No. Inflation is a general price increase over an array of items.

Section 3.1 Summary

U.S. Economic History Throughout the years, our economic system has evolved and changed. In colonial times, the United States had begun its service-based economy. The 1700s saw the rise of the agriculture-based economy. The Industrial Revolution in the 1850s brought about the industrial economy, characterized by the large-scale manufacturing of goods. During the latter part of the 20th century, the information technology economy revolutionized the business world. To measure the health of our economic system, we use a variety of economic indicators, including GDP, unemployment rate, rate of inflation, and national debt.

Section 3.2 Summary

The Business Cycle In a global economy, one country's economy can affect the economy of its other trading partners. The Fed adjusts monetary policies to try to level out the ups and downs of the economy. An economic cycle includes four stages: prosperity, recession, depression, and recovery. Prosperity is the peak of economic activity. Recession is a slowdown in economic activity. Depression is a deep recession that affects the entire economy and lasts for several years. A recovery is a rise in business activity after a recession or depression. Fortunately, the United States has not had a depression since the 1930s.

Vocabulary Review

1. On a sheet of paper, use each of these key terms and academic vocabulary terms in a sentence.

Key Terms

gross domestic product (GDP)
standard of living
inflation
deflation
budget deficit
national debt

budget surplus
business cycle
prosperity
recession
depression
recovery

Academic Vocabulary

shifts
emphasis
sum
period

enormous
policy
purchase
decline

Review Key Concepts

2. Describe the four types of economy the United States has experienced.

3. Describe what is shown by GDP, unemployment rate, rate of inflation, and national debt.

4. Explain how individuals and the government influences the economy.

5. Describe the four stages of the business cycle.

12. Personal bankruptcies increase during recession or depression because job loss means people cannot pay their bills. Business formations increase during recovery and prosperity because there is more demand for goods.

13. The standard of living is high because of productivity. We produce an abundance of goods and services because of technology, access to raw materials, an educated workforce, and the entrepreneurial spirit.

Critical Thinking

6. Would the cars made in this country by a foreign-owned company be included in GDP? Why or why not?

7. Which would be included in GDP: babysitting at home or working at a day-care center?

8. Why are people who are unemployed but not looking for work not included in the unemployment figures?

9. Why is inflation especially difficult for retired people?

10. Why might deflation be a bad thing?

11. Suppose you go to a store to buy a soda but notice the price is 20 cents higher than it was last week. Other item's prices are unchanged. Is this an example of inflation? Why or why not?

12. In which stage or stages of the business cycle would there be more personal bankruptcies? More business formations?

13. Explain why the standard of living is higher in the United States than in many other countries.

Write About It

14. Many economists believe that some unemployment is necessary because many of the unemployed are between jobs. Write an essay explaining why this might be true.

15. To pay for expenses, the federal government issues bonds. Many of these bonds are bought by foreign countries. Write a paragraph indicating whether you think this is good or bad for America.

16. Write a letter to your school counselor that explains how understanding the unemployment rate can be beneficial to you as you look for a job.

17. Assume the current inflation rate is 3 percent. Write an e-mail to your teacher explaining how that might help you decide where to put your savings.

18. Write a summary of the pros and cons of your starting a new business in the prosperous stage of the business cycle.

19. The unemployment rate in your community has increased considerably because of the closure of two firms. Write a letter to the editor of the newspaper explaining what steps you might take in your business as a result.

Technology Applications

Web Pages
20. You want to do business on the Internet. You know what kind of business you want to open. Use the Internet to research several businesses that might be considered your competition. Write a report that evaluates their Web sites. Print pages from each Web site and include them in your report.

Business Ethics

Dealing With Ethical Systems
21. You are the president of a biotechnology company that produces vaccines. A foreign government has asked to buy a vaccine to help stop a deadly infectious disease, but the negotiator expects a bribe. Should you look the other way so that you can get the vaccine to people who need it?

Chapter 3 Review and Activities **49**

Write About It

14. Essays will vary but should describe why there is always some unemployment because some of the unemployed are simply between jobs.

15. It is bad because it causes the United States to become too dependent on foreign nations. It is good because it encourages interdependence between nations.

16. If the unemployment rate is high, you will probably have more difficulty. If the unemployment rate is low, job markets are good.

17. To ensure that the buying power of your savings dollars will keep up with the inflation rate, select savings or investments that pay more than 3%. If return on investments is less than 3%, the purchasing power of money will decline unless the inflation rate declines too.

18. Pros: If prosperity continues, there will be high demand for products and services. Cons: Owner might not be able to sell all of his products or services, leading to bankruptcy for a business and personal financial trouble for owner.

19. Letters should describe the need to determine how closings are affecting your business, ways to cut costs without sacrificing quality, and how to diversify by attracting new businesses.

Technology Applications

20. Answers will vary depending on the Web sites visited. Students should include print-outs of some of the Web pages they evaluated.

Business Ethics

21. Some students will think that preventing the outbreak of an infectious disease is most important and there is an ethical obligation to help. Others will think that bribery is too wrong to overlook.

Applying Academics to Business

22. Students' bibliographies should include such works as Steinbeck's *The Grapes of Wrath* and Fitzgerald's *The Great Gatsby*.

23. $18\% = \frac{18}{100}$

$\frac{18}{100} = \frac{9}{50}$

$\frac{9}{50} + \frac{1}{50} = \frac{10}{50} = \frac{1}{5}$

$\frac{5}{5} - \frac{1}{5} = \frac{4}{5} = 80\%$

The service sector represents $\frac{4}{5}$ or 80% of the U.S. economy.

24. *Inter-* means between or among. Other words include *intercom* and *intermediate*. *Pro-* means moving forward or ahead. Words include *proceed* and *process*.

25. Graphs should reflect high unemployment during the Depression, low unemployment during World War II, rising unemployment during the 50s, falling in the 60s, and fluctuating unemployment in the 70s, 80s, and 90s.

Active Learning

26. Encourage students to relate their report or presentation to the materials in the chapter.

Business in the Real World

27. For the most part, businesses will have experienced financial difficulties during economic downturns and will have experienced prosperity when the economy was doing well.

Applying Academics to Business

English Language Arts

22. Major novelists of the 1920s, a time of prosperity in the United States, and the 1930s, the time of the Great Depression, include John Steinbeck, William Faulkner, F. Scott Fitzgerald, Ernest Hemingway, and John Dos Passos. Find out more about their work and the work of other writers of the period. Make a bibliography of novels that portray everyday life during the 1920s and 1930s. Choose one to read and write a review of it to share with your classmates.

Mathematics

23. The Agriculture sector of the U.S. economy produces $\frac{1}{50}$ of the GDP while the Industry sector produces 18 percent. The rest is produced by the Service sector. What percent of GDP is contributed by the service sector?

THEORY **Number and Operations: Comparing Numbers** After converting the two numbers $\frac{1}{50}$ and 18 percent so that they are either both percents or both fractions, they can be added together and then subtracted from the whole to find the part contributed by the service sector.

English Language Arts

24. The words Internet, interdependent, and international have the same prefix. Write a sentence in your own words telling what the prefix is and what it means. Give examples of other words that use the same prefix, and write sentences using them. Do the same for productivity and prosperity. Then check your work by looking in a dictionary or other resource.

Mathematics

25. Find unemployment statistics for the years 1933, 1944, 1955, 1966, 1977, 1988, 1999, and the most recent year for which statistics are available. Present the information in a bar graph. Write a few sentences discussing the reasons for the differences shown in the graph.

THEORY **Data Analysis and Probability: Bar Graphs** Bar graphs are great for making multiple comparisons, showing frequencies, and displaying trends. They are sometimes confused with histograms, which are used to graphically show the distribution of a set of data. In this case, the bar graph will show how unemployment levels rose and fell with the cycles of the economy.

Active Learning

Track News Stories

26. During a two-week period, read the newspaper or watch the national news on television. Pick out three articles or report on three sequences of television news programming that relate to one of the topics discussed in this chapter, such as unemployment, inflation, deflation, and national debt. Write a report or give an oral presentation to the class on your findings.

Business in the Real World

Interview a Businessperson

27. Identify a businessperson in your community who has been in business for several years and experienced a number of business cycles. Interview the business owner to find out how his or her company performed during periods of recession and periods of prosperity. Then write a report summarizing the business owner's responses.

50 **Chapter 3** Review and Activities

***ExamView Assessment Suite* CD** allows you to print out ready-made unit and chapter tests, complete with answer keys. You can also create customized tests.

TeacherWorks Plus provides complete teacher resources in one convenient package. It includes customizable lesson plans in calendar format, and instant access to many print program resources.

Real LIFE skills

ASSESSING YOUR SKILLS

28. These skills are needed by all employees: creative thinking, decision making, and problem solving. Give an example of how you have implemented each skill in the last month. Then indicate which skills you believe you are fairly good at doing. Recommend how you can become better at doing the skill or skills in which you need work.

 **Business CAREERS**

FIND YOUR DREAM JOB

29. Go to the *Introduction to Business* Online Learning Center through **glencoe.com** for a link to the Occupational Outlook Handbook Web site. Click on the "OOH Search/A-Z Index" link and enter the job title "economist." Then write a one-page report about this type of occupation. Conclude your report with a list of things you could do now to prepare yourself to pursue the occupation.

Role Play

ANALYZING ECONOMIC INDICATORS

30. **Situation** You are an intern for a federal bureau that collects and analyzes economic data. You have been asked to research recent economic indicators.

Activity Choose a sector of the economy to measure how well the economy is doing. Give a presentation to the bureau's economists. Sectors include housing construction, gross domestic product, and retail and food services.

Evaluation You will be evaluated on how well you meet the following performance indicators:

• Research an economic sector.
• Interpret economic data.
• Answer questions about your findings.
• Present clear and relevant information.
• Project your voice, and use correct grammar and English.

Real LIFE skills

28. Answers will vary depending on the student's skills and experiences.

Business CAREERS

29. Nature of work: How society distributes scarce resources to produce goods and services for a variety of organizations, including corporations and government agencies.

Working conditions: structured schedules; often work alone but may be part of team. Pressure of deadlines. Travel may be required.

Training and qualifications: Bachelor's degree for entry-level positions. Master's degree or Ph.D. for advancement.

Job outlook: Expected to grow more slowly than average.

Earnings: Median annual earning in 2004 was approximately $73,000. As preparation, develop quantitative, computer, and communication skills.

Role Play

30. Students should attempt to apply the concepts developed in the chapter to interpret economic data and to answer questions about their findings.

Standardized Test Practice
1. C

Standardized Test Practice

Directions Read the paragraph and answer the question that follows. Write the letter for the answer on a separate piece of paper.

Some reasons for unemployment represent more of a problem for the economy than others. For example, recently graduated students and those who are voluntarily looking for a new job are only temporarily unemployed. Some workers are seasonal workers and only unemployed during part of the year. However, those workers who have lost their jobs because the economy has slowed down may be out of work until the economy recovers.

1. Which best describes the way the paragraph is organized?

A   sequence of events
B   comparison
C   statement and example
D   cause and effect

 TEST-TAKING TIP When studying from a textbook, read the chapter summaries. They usually do a good job at summarizing important points.

 READING Go to the *Introduction to Business* Online Learning Center through **glencoe.com** for a list of outside reading suggestions.

 **STRATEGIES FOR STANDARDIZED TEST PREP SUCCESS**

Test Prep Remind students that when studying from a textbook they should begin by rereading section and chapter introductions and summaries, information graphics, and photographs with the purpose of identifying main ideas. Then they should read any end-of-chapter study questions and skim the text to find specific details to answer the questions. Make them aware of how to use the table of contents, index, feature articles, and sidebars to find information related to content.

Standards-Based Lesson Planning   *Introduction to Business* provides students with instruction and assessment in the following fundamental content areas:

Content Standards Correlations	
Define ethics in business.	pp. 55, 64
Analyze the relationship between ethics and the law.	pp. 56, 65–67
Relate the consequences of social and civic responsibility to business ownership (environmental issues, business ethics, consumerism, employee issues).	pp. 57, 60–63, 65–67
Relate the ethical decision-making process to business situations.	pp. 58, 65–67
Demonstrate work ethics that include integrity, honesty, and perseverance.	p. 60
Research benefits and consequences resulting from the practice of business ethics.	pp. 57, 60–63, 65–67
Distinguish between ethical and unethical business practices.	pp. 57, 60–63, 65–67
Analyze the benefits and consequences of ethical conduct in business.	pp. 57, 60–63, 65–67
Analyze ethical issues related to business responsibilities.	pp. 57, 60–63, 65–67

NCLB   Activities, information, and skills practice will help your students attain No Child Left Behind proficiency. Students will improve their abilities in the following academic standards areas:

Academic Standards Correlations		
English Language Arts	**Activities/Features**	**Page**
NCTE 3 Apply strategies to interpret texts	Applying Academics to Business Standardized Test Practice	pp. 66–67
NCTE 4 Use written language to communicate effectively	After You Read	p. 63
NCTE 12 Use language to accomplish individual purposes	After You Read	p. 63
Mathematics		
Algebra Represent and analyze mathematical situations and structures using algebraic symbols	Ask S&P	p. 52
Number and Operations Compute fluently and make reasonable estimates	Applying Academics to Business	p. 66
Number and Operations Understand meanings of operations and how they relate to one another	After You Read Applying Academics to Business	pp. 58, 66
Problem Solving Monitor and reflect on the process of problem solving	Applying Academics to Business	p. 66
Science		
Content Standard F Students should develop understanding of population growth, science, and technology in local, national, and global challenges	Science/Tech Trends	p. 61

Correlations   This chart shows the 21ˢᵗ Century Skills, foundation skills, and workplace competencies that students develop as they work in this chapter.

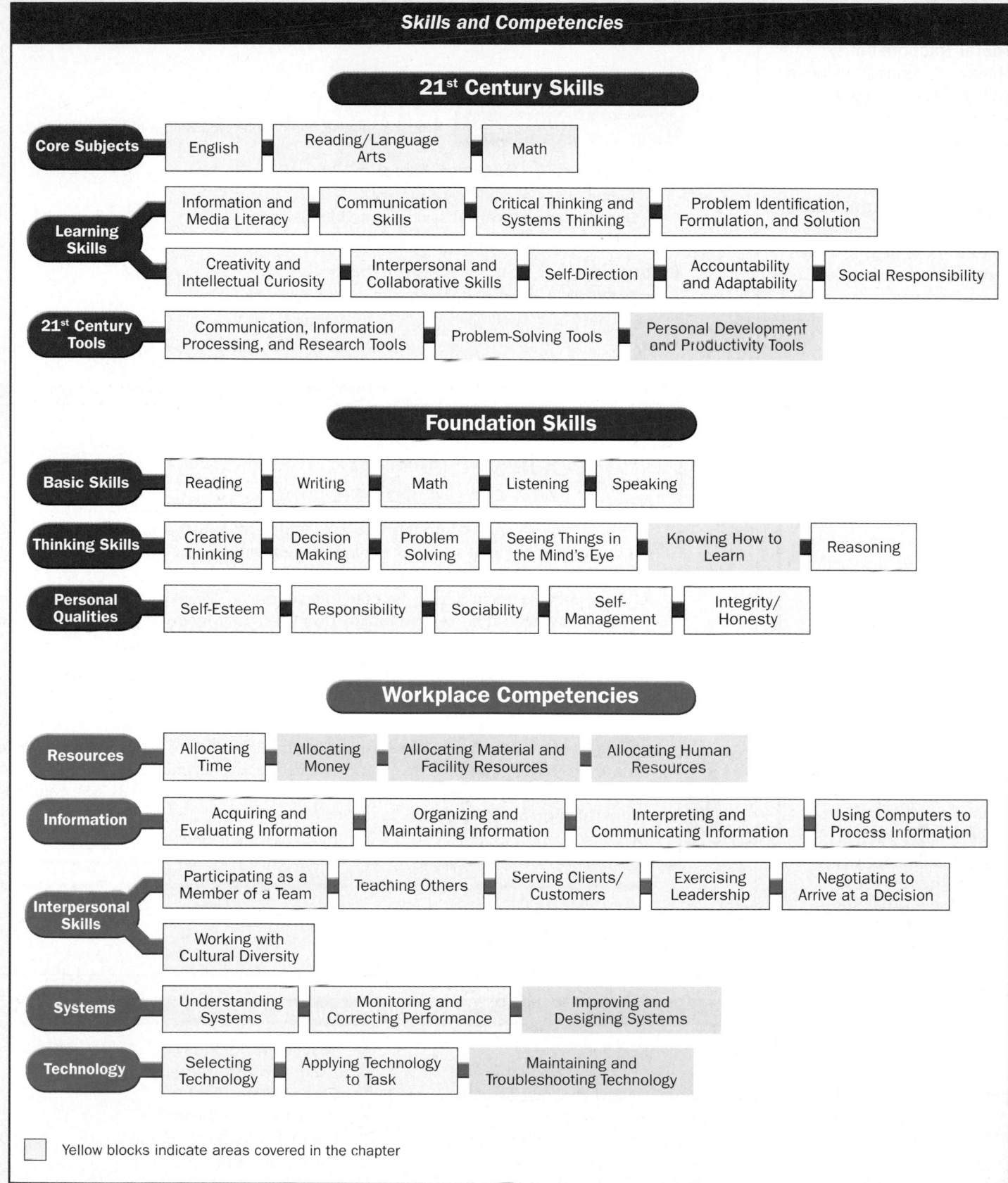

Skills and Competencies

21ˢᵗ Century Skills

Core Subjects: English | Reading/Language Arts | Math

Learning Skills: Information and Media Literacy | Communication Skills | Critical Thinking and Systems Thinking | Problem Identification, Formulation, and Solution | Creativity and Intellectual Curiosity | Interpersonal and Collaborative Skills | Self-Direction | Accountability and Adaptability | Social Responsibility

21ˢᵗ Century Tools: Communication, Information Processing, and Research Tools | Problem-Solving Tools | Personal Development and Productivity Tools

Foundation Skills

Basic Skills: Reading | Writing | Math | Listening | Speaking

Thinking Skills: Creative Thinking | Decision Making | Problem Solving | Seeing Things in the Mind's Eye | Knowing How to Learn | Reasoning

Personal Qualities: Self-Esteem | Responsibility | Sociability | Self-Management | Integrity/Honesty

Workplace Competencies

Resources: Allocating Time | Allocating Money | Allocating Material and Facility Resources | Allocating Human Resources

Information: Acquiring and Evaluating Information | Organizing and Maintaining Information | Interpreting and Communicating Information | Using Computers to Process Information

Interpersonal Skills: Participating as a Member of a Team | Teaching Others | Serving Clients/Customers | Exercising Leadership | Negotiating to Arrive at a Decision | Working with Cultural Diversity

Systems: Understanding Systems | Monitoring and Correcting Performance | Improving and Designing Systems

Technology: Selecting Technology | Applying Technology to Task | Maintaining and Troubleshooting Technology

☐ Yellow blocks indicate areas covered in the chapter

Chapter Overview

Introduce the Chapter

Business Ethics and Social Responsibility
Chapter 4 defines business ethics and tells how ethics affect business and the social responsibility of business.

Building Background

This chapter provides a framework to help students understand the concepts of ethics and social responsibility, as well as examples in the business world.

Ask STANDARD &POOR'S

›› Math Answer
If you start with $4,000 in a savings account earning 5% interest, your balance after 50 years will be $45,870. Ask how someone might achieve the goal of having a million dollars saved for retirement. (Students should understand that a larger initial investment or a higher interest rate would yield a higher return and that making yearly investments would increase the amount in the account at retirement.)

›› Extension Activity
Have students create a spreadsheet that shows how long it will take to accumulate more than a million dollars by saving $4,000 per year in an account earning 5% per year. (It will take almost 53 years to accumulate one million dollars.)

N C L B
Activity correlates to Math standards.

52

Business Ethics and Social Responsibility

Chapter Objectives After completing this chapter, you will be able to:

▶ **Section 4.1** *Business Ethics*
- **Define** ethics and business ethics.
- **Describe** why ethical behavior is good for business.
- **List** the steps for dealing with an ethical dilemma.

▶ **Section 4.2** *Social Responsibility*
- **Define** what is meant by the social responsibility of business.

Ask STANDARD &POOR'S **The Time Value of Money**

Q: This past summer I worked as a carpenter. I saved close to $4,000. I'm thinking about buying a new computer with my savings. My father said that if I didn't spend the money, but let it sit in my savings account without touching it, I would be a millionaire when I retire. Could that be true?

A: Your father is teaching you the time value of money. Because of compounding interest, savings can grow substantially over time. That is why it is important to start saving and investing money early in your life.

Mathematics The balance your account has grown to in the future is known as the *future value* of your starting principal. Calculate the future value of your $4,000 in 50 years.

THEORY **Calculating Future Value** To find a formula for future value, write P for your starting principal, r for the rate of return expressed as a decimal, and n for the number of years in the future. (Assume that the interest rate is 5%, so r equals .05). Your balance will grow according to the following formula:

$$FV = P(1 + r)^n$$

N C L B

Classroom Resources

- 📖 Student Edition
- 📖 Teacher Wraparound Edition
- 📁 Student Activity Workbook with Academic Integration
- 📁 Student Activity Workbook with Academic Integration TAE
- 📁 *Fast File*, Unit 1 Resources
- 📁 Inclusion in the Business Education Classroom

- 💿 TeacherWorks Plus
- 💿 *ExamView Assessment Suite*
- 💿 Presentation Plus!
- 💿 Vocabulary PuzzleMaker
- 💿 Interactive Student Edition
- 💿 Online Student Edition
- 💿 Online Learning Center with Podcasts

Review the Objectives
Introduce the chapter by reviewing the chapter objectives:

Section 4.1 *Objectives*
Define ethics and business ethics. (Ethics: set of moral principles by which people conduct themselves personally, socially, or professionally. Business ethics: rules, often based on moral principles, by which a business conducts itself.)

Describe why ethical behavior is good behavior for business. (Ethical behavior encourages consumers to buy the firm's products, employees to be productive, members of society to feel good about the firm, creditors to lend money to the firm, and in corporations, investors to buy stock in the firm.)

List the steps for dealing with an ethical dilemma. (Identify the dilemma, discover alternative actions, decide who might be affected, list the probable effects of the alternatives, and select the best alternative.)

Section 4.2 *Objectives*
Define what is meant by the social responsibility of business. (It is the duty to do what is best for the good of society, such as sponsor cultural events, provide materials for schools, encourage employees to participate in community projects. In some developing countries, they build schools and hospitals.)

● **Duty-Bound** Businesses and customers both have ethical responsibilities. **What are some of your ethical responsibilities?**

Discuss the Photo
● **Duty-Bound** Read the caption aloud: Businesses and customers both have ethical responsibilities.

Ask students: What are some of your ethical responsibilities? (Students are likely to be more aware of their duties to their family and friends than they are of their responsibilities as consumers. Some may recognize that they have duties to society, including the duty to be honest, or to recycle, or even a duty to work hard in school to pay back the investment society makes in them. Point out that the responsibilities people have to society are the source of the responsibility to maintain honesty and fair play in the business environment.)

FOCUS

Bell Ringer Activity

Business Ethics

Pose this scenario to students: A neighbor offered you $15 for picking up her mail. Afterward, she gives you $20 and refuses change. She actually gave you two twenties that were stuck together. What do you do? (Students should return one of the twenties.)

Preteaching

Presentation Plus!

The Presentation Plus! CD provides visual teaching aids for this section.

PuzzleMaker

Use the Vocabulary PuzzleMaker to create a puzzle of the section's key terms. Students can complete the puzzle on paper or on a computer.

Graphic Organizer

Tell students to go to the Online Learning Center through **glencoe.com** for a printable graphic organizer. (Ethical questions: Does it violate the law? How would I feel? Sacrificing long-term benefits for short-term gains? Steps to take: Identify dilemma. Discover alternatives. Decide who is affected. List effects of alternatives, select the best.)

N C L B Connects academics to content.

Business Ethics

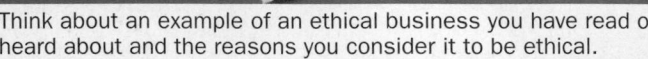

Reading Guide

● Before You Read

Think about an example of an ethical business you have read or heard about and the reasons you consider it to be ethical.

Read to Learn

- Define ethics and business ethics.
- Describe why ethical behavior is good for business.
- List the steps for dealing with an ethical dilemma.

The Main Idea

Ethics are moral principles by which people conduct themselves personally, socially, and professionally. Business ethics are rules that guide the behavior of a business and its employees. Business ethics are generally based on moral principles. In business, good ethics is beneficial for long-term profitability and success.

Key Concepts

- The Nature of Ethics
- Ethics as Good Business
- Ethical Questions

Vocabulary

Key Terms

ethics	sweatshop
business ethics	conflict of interest
code of ethics	

Academic Vocabulary

You will find these words in your reading and on your tests. Make sure you know their meanings.

principles	encounter
conduct	alternative

Graphic Organizer

Print or draw a graphic like the one below. In the left column, list three questions you need to ask when facing an ethical dilemma. In the right column, list the five steps to take to decide which choice to make.

Ethical Questions	Steps to Take
1.	1.
	2.
2.	3.
	4.
3.	5.

 Go to the *Introduction to Business* Online Learning Center through **glencoe.com** for a printable graphic organizer.

Academic Standards

English Language Arts

NCTE 1 Read texts to acquire new information

NCTE 9 Develop an understanding of diversity in language use across cultures

Mathematics

Number and Operations Understand the meanings of operations and how they relate to one another

Reading Guide

● Before You Read

Answers will vary. Students may cite businesses that refused to charge for services or suggested ways to save them money.

D Develop Concepts

The Main Idea Ask students: Why do you think ethical behavior is beneficial for long-term profitability and successes? (Some students might indicate businesses engaging in ethical behavior earn a good reputation, which translates into sales.)

The Nature of Ethics

Ethics are moral **principles** by which people **conduct** themselves personally, socially, or professionally. For example, you do not cheat on a test or lie to friends or your family because of your personal honor and integrity. For the good of society, you may recycle to take care of the environment. **Business ethics** are rules based on moral principles about how businesses and employees ought to conduct themselves. Most businesses are committed to providing safe products, creating jobs, treating their employees fairly, protecting the environment, and being truthful about their financial situation.

The effects of unethical behavior by customers are not always obvious. However, to make up for problems caused by unethical behavior, businesses have to charge more for their products. As a result, customers have to pay more.

Different cultures, businesses, and industries have different ethical standards. For example, in some cultures, including the United States, excessive gift giving is considered bribery, which is unethical. Bribery occurs when gifts, money, or favors are offered to encourage a business deal. In other cultures, excessive gift giving is overlooked or considered ethical.

> **✔ Reading Check** **Identify** What are three kinds of ethics?

● **As You Read**

Think about some businesses that you consider to be run ethically. In what ways are they ethical?

● **Business Ethics** Businesses have a set of moral principles that they follow. **In what ways can a business behave ethically toward its employees?**

Section 4.1 Business Ethics **55**

Section 4.1

TEACH

Discussion Starter
The Nature of Ethics
Ask students what they would do if they found a copy of a midterm exam or what they would do if they found a diamond ring in the restroom at a restaurant. Encourage multiple answers for these questions and for a consensus. (Students might suggest taking the exam to the office without reading it. The ring should be given to the restaurant manager or the police.)

R Reading Strategy

Make a Bulleted List Have students create a bulleted list illustrating ways people conduct themselves ethically in their personal, social, and professional lives. (Answers will vary but should demonstrate an understanding of ethical behavior.)

✔ Reading Check

Identify The three kinds of ethics are personal, social, and professional. Answers will vary. Keeping accurate score while playing golf is an example of personal ethics. Choosing to drive a hybrid car is an example of social ethics. Treating employees fairly is an example of professional ethics.

● **As You Read**

Students should distinguish between companies that only promise ethical commitments and those that actually do what they promise.

Discuss the Photo
● **Business Ethics** A business can behave ethically toward employees by creating safe working conditions and providing fair wages and procedures for fair resolution of disputes.

TEACH (cont.)

S Skill Practice

Guided Practice

Search and List Have students find the link for teen workers at www.osha.gov and make a list of the responsibilities shown. (Follow rules and safe work practices. Tell an adult if you feel threatened or endangered. Be aware of your environment. Trust your instincts. Stay sober.) **L1**

Read and Summarize Ask students to choose an apparel maker, browse the apparel maker's Web site for initiatives that protect workers' rights, and write a summary. (Summaries will vary depending on the site visited and the current content of the site.) **L2**

Find and Report Have students use the Internet to identify a U.S. government agency that was set up to protect society. Have students print a copy of the agency's home page and write a brief description of the agency's mission. (Agencies include the Federal Trade Commission (FTC) and Federal Communications Commission (FCC.) **L3**

ASSESS

Review Key Terms
Have students write sentences using each key term.

 **Study-to-Go** Have students go to the Online Learning Center through **glencoe.com** to download free **Study-to-Go** content to their PDAs or cell phones.

Cultural Etiquette
In Thailand, it is customary to exchange gifts during a second business meeting. In China, however, gift giving is considered a form of bribery and is illegal. *Do you think it is unethical for businesspeople not to observe another country's rules of etiquette in the global marketplace?*

Law and Ethics

Ethics involve a system of moral principles that govern the appropriate conduct for a person or group. Laws involve rules for conduct that may be used to punish violators. In business, people follow rules as well as a code of ethics. A **code of ethics** is a set of guidelines for maintaining ethics in the workplace. Most businesses follow their own code of ethics. **Figure 4.1** includes some findings about how employees feel about ethical behavior in their workplace.

Many unethical behaviors lead to the passage of legislation that makes those behaviors illegal. In the United States, bad working conditions are not only unethical, they are also illegal. On March 25, 1911, a fire at the Triangle Shirtwaist Factory Company in New York City killed 146 workers—mostly young female immigrants. The business's inadequate exit doors and fire escapes along with overcrowded conditions led to the deaths of the workers. This industrial tragedy brought about changes in laws governing conditions in sweatshops. A **sweatshop** is a shop or factory in which workers are employed for long hours at low wages and under unhealthy conditions.

The Occupational Safety and Health Administration (OSHA) is a division of the U.S. Department of Labor. OSHA sets and enforces work-related health and safety rules. Other agencies protect consumers, address discrimination in the workplace, and promote truthfulness in financial reporting.

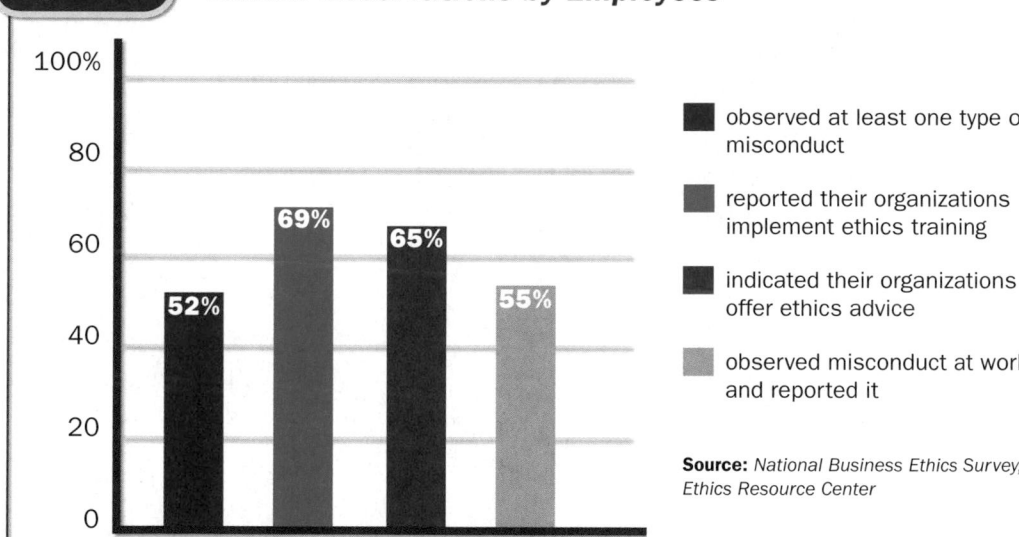

Figure 4.1 — *Ethical Observations by Employees*

- observed at least one type of misconduct
- reported their organizations implement ethics training
- indicated their organizations offer ethics advice
- observed misconduct at work and reported it

Source: *National Business Ethics Survey, Ethics Resource Center*

● **A National Survey of Employees** These are some of the key findings of a recent National Business Ethics Survey. **Does American business seem to be becoming more or less concerned about ethical behavior?**

56   Chapter 4 Business Ethics and Social Responsibility

Cultural Etiquette Answers will vary. Students should discuss that closing a deal may depend on an awareness of the other country's culture, customs, and etiquette. Not observing the rules may actually be considered unethical in some countries.

Figure 4.1

● **A National Survey of Employees**
American businesses are becoming more concerned about ethics. Explain to students that corporate scandals have caused some businesses to focus their attention on ethics and have empowered consumers and stockholders to demand ethical behavior.

Ethics as Good Business

Most businesses police themselves with codes of ethics. Professionals such as doctors, lawyers, journalists, and teachers have their own codes of ethics. A code of ethics can cover issues such as employee behavior and environmental safety.

Unethical business practices include lying, offering merchandise known to be substandard, or treating customers or employees unfairly. If a business violates government regulations, the owner can be fined or go to jail. If an employee violates a company or professional code of ethics, the employee might be fired or lose his or her license. Not all unethical practices are covered by the law. Unethical business practices affect businesses indirectly.

Suppose you own an auto-body paint shop. To increase your profits, you charge top price and use the cheapest paint. One of your customers complains about the quality of the paint, but you do not care because she has already paid. What is one customer, right? The fact is that most businesses (especially small businesses) rely on repeat customers and word of mouth to get new customers. The amount you make in profits from one unhappy customer may not be worth the lost business.

Treating employees unethically can also backfire. Suppose you manage a small film distribution company. You hire Jaime fresh out of business school to run the office. You teach him how to use the computer system, how to deal with customers, and how the business works. You also pay him very little, make him do all your work, and treat him poorly. The first chance Jaime gets, he quits and ends up being hired by one of your competitors. You now have to retrain a new employee to take his place. Meanwhile, your competition now has a well-trained employee, who is much more efficient.

Conflicts of Interest

Another major ethical question that is generally not illegal relates to conflict of interest. A **conflict of interest** is a conflict between self-interest and professional obligation. Suppose that a manager of a small business hires his sister to do some work in the firm, but she is clearly unqualified to do the work. Giving the position to the sister will help out the family but will create morale problems with the other employees. It may also damage the business if her work does not get done. When making business decisions, employees have an ethical obligation to act in the best interest of the company.

International Business

Trade Barriers

Before a business can enter a foreign market, its managers must first recognize the barriers to trade that it faces. For example, a fast-food hamburger restaurant chain will face considerable barriers if it tries to expand into India, a place where beef is seldom eaten. A U.S. company wanting to market its products in Cuba will face prohibitions and regulations from the U.S. government. From cultural barriers to legal and political barriers, there are a lot of things a company needs to consider when looking at expanding into international markets.

Examples of Languages Across Cultures

Q: In Bahasa-Indonesian, how do you say: "Hello"?

A: Halo (pronounced: Hă-lōw)

What are some cultural differences that might create barriers to trade? How can they be overcome?

● **As You Read**

Think about how your school operates and the practices that could be included in a school code of ethics.

● **As You Read**

Students might focus on areas such as cheating and safety.

International Business

Trade Barriers Citizens of countries that have fought recent wars often continue to have lingering hostility that creates cultural trade barriers. Government policies can help reduce tensions, however.

RETEACH

W **Writing Support**
Writing Practice

A Code of Ethics Provide students with a copy of a code of ethics for a local business or a professional organization such as the Society of Professional Journalists. Have students read the document and use it as a guide for writing a personal code of ethics. (Answers will vary depending on the code of ethics provided and each student's personal values.)

R **Reading Strategy**

Apply Knowledge Ask students to look at the examples of unethical behavior that appear on this page. Ask students for another example of an unethical situation. (Answers will vary based on students' personal experiences.)

U **Universal Access**

Auditory Learners Have students work in pairs. Instruct the pairs to have one student read the paragraph on conflicts of interest aloud while the other student takes notes. Instruct students to switch roles. This time one student reads aloud as the other reviews and improves the notes. Although reading aloud is especially important to some learners, all students can benefit from this activity.

RETEACH (cont.)

C Critical Thinking

Ethical Decision Making
Ask: Should employees report behavior that violates ethics policies? (Employees should report any behavior that violates company policy.)

Student Activity Workbook 📂 Assign the Section 4.1 Activities.

ASSESS

After You Read

Have students complete the Section 4.1 After You Read section review.

Online Study Tools

Have students go to the Online Learning Center through **glencoe.com** to:

• Take the Section 4.1 **Practice Test**.

• Download free **Study-to-Go** content to their PDAs or cell phones.

As You Read

Students may list conflicts between work schedules, study, and recreational time.

CLOSE

Culminating Activity
Ethical Questions
Have students use the ethical questions and steps for ethical decision-making shown on this page to consider an example presented in this section. (Answers will vary depending on the situation.)

As You Read

Consider conflict of interest you have encountered in your life. How did you resolve it?

C

N C L B Activity correlates to Math standards.

Ethical Questions

When you **encounter** an ethical decision and must choose a course of action, ask yourself these important questions:

• Is it against the law? Does it violate company or professional policies?
• Even if everyone is doing it, how would I feel if someone did this to me?
• Am I sacrificing long-term benefits for short-term gains?

The Ethical Decision-Making Process

Here are some steps to take if you find yourself in an ethical dilemma:

1. Identify the ethical dilemma.
2. Discover **alternative** actions.
3. Decide who might be affected.
4. List the probable effects of the alternatives.
5. Select the best alternative.

Using this process will enable you to make a more informed ethical choice. Making an ethical decision involves more people than just you.

Section 4.1

After You Read

Review Key Concepts
1. What is the difference between personal and business ethics?
2. Describe some of the ways that unethical business practices can affect a business.
3. What is the relationship between illegal behaviors of business and unethical behaviors of business?

N C L B

Academic Skills
4. **Mathematics** A large company decided it would give $\frac{1}{8}$ of its profits to charity. If the amount given was spread equally among five different charities, what fraction of the company's profits was given to each? What percent of the company's profits is this?

 THEORY **Number and Operations: Dividing Fractions** To divide a fraction, invert the divisor and multiply.

 For math help, go to the Math Appendix.

@ Go to the *Introduction to Business* Online Learning Center through **glencoe.com** to check your answers.

Section 4.1

Review Key Concepts
1. Personal ethics: moral principles that guide an individual; business ethics: rules, based on moral principles, used by a business.
2. Customers will not patronize the business. It is hard to retain employees. If the behavior is illegal, the business might be fined.

3. Generally, illegal behaviors of business are also considered unethical but there are some unethical behaviors that are not illegal.

Academic Skills
4. **Mathematics** Each charity would receive $\frac{1}{40}$, or 2.5% of the company's profits.

Social Responsibility

FOCUS

Reading Guide

● Before You Read

Think about some things a business can do to be socially responsible.

Read to Learn
- Define what is meant by the social responsibility of business.

The Main Idea

Social responsibility is the duty to do what is best for the good of society. Producing goods and services that are beneficial to society and providing jobs for people are not sufficient for a business to be considered socially responsible. They are expected to do more. Many businesses provide money for projects that benefit society.

Key Concept
- Business and Social Responsibility

Vocabulary

Key Term
social responsibility

Academic Vocabulary

You will find these words in your reading and on your tests. Make sure you know their meanings.

integrity   benefit
integral   sufficient

Graphic Organizer

In a figure like the one below, list four responsibilities of each business.

Business Responsibilities

 Go to the *Introduction to Business* Online Learning Center through **glencoe.com** for a printable graphic organizer.

Academic Standards

English Language Arts

NCTE 1 Read texts to acquire new information

NCTE 4 Use written language to communicate effectively

NCTE 12 Use language to accomplish individual purposes

Science

Content Standard F Students should develop an understanding of science and technology in local, national, and global challenges

---

Bell Ringer Activity

Social Responsibility

Locate and read a news article about a local firm's commitment to social responsibility to the students and ask them why the company is involved in this kind of activity. (Students should understand that many organizations participate in such activities to better their communities.) Follow up by asking for other businesses that have made similar commitments. (Answers will vary depending on students' experiences.)

Preteaching

Presentation Plus!

The Presentation Plus! CD provides visual teaching aids for this section.

PuzzleMaker

Use the Vocabulary PuzzleMaker to create a puzzle of the section's key terms. Students can complete the puzzle on paper or on a computer.

Graphic Organizer

Tell students to go to the Online Learning Center through **glencoe.com** for a printable graphic organizer. (The four responsibilities are to customers, to employees, to society, and to creditors and owners.)

Academic correlations to book content.

Reading Guide

● Before You Read

Students might mention protecting the environment, contributing to charities, and encouraging employees to give to charity and to volunteer.

D Develop Concepts

The Main Idea Ask students: What motivates businesses to be socially responsible? (In some cases stockholders and customers demand it. In other cases businesses participate to attract media attention. There also are cases where owners, directors, or employees have a personal connection to a project.)

TEACH

Discussion Starter
Business and Social Responsibility

Ask students for examples of how companies can integrate social responsibility into all aspects of the business. (Answers will vary. Computer manufacturers might protect the environment during manufacturing, sponsor recycling, donate computer equipment to schools, and encourage employees to volunteer at computer literacy workshops.)

R Reading Strategy

Visualize an Idea Have students choose one of the examples in this section and create a visual aid to illustrate the idea. Consider allowing students to work in pairs. (Visual aids will vary but should clearly refer to one of the examples.)

● **As You Read**

Individuals could participate in curbside recycling. Schools could encourage recycling beverage containers in the school cafeteria. Businesses could provide recycling bins for office workers.

✔ **Reading Check**

Explain Companies can protect the environment, care for their customers, care for their employees.

● **As You Read**

Think about the damage that is done to the environment when people do not recycle.

Business and Social Responsibility

Business ethics focus on decisions considered good or bad, correct or incorrect. The social responsibility of business takes into consideration all that business does or does not do to solve the problems of society. **Social responsibility** is the duty to do what is best for the good of society. Businesses that follow ethical standards value **integrity** and honesty in employees. Ethics are an **integral** part of their business practices.

R Some people believe that if a company produces goods that **benefit** society, it is fulfilling its social responsibility. However, many people and businesses do not think that is **sufficient**. They consider social responsibility to be more than that.

Some firms are very concerned about limiting the damage that they do to the environment. The *Los Angeles Times,* a daily newspaper with more than 1 million readers, uses recyclable paper and environmentally friendly soy-based ink. Automakers such as Honda and Toyota offer eco-cars, which reduce air pollution.

✔ **Reading Check** **Explain** What ways can a business fulfill its social responsibilities?

BusinessWeek *Reader and Case Study*

It's Getting Easier Being Green

Interest in integrating business with the needs of the environment is prompting a harder look at achieving a sustainable economy.

Justin DeKoszmovszky, a rising second-year student at the S.C. Johnson School of Management at Cornell University in Ithaca, N.Y., is spending his summer living and working with small-scale farmers in Kenya. As part of a six-person team, he's exploring new opportunities for communities, entrepreneurs, government organizations, local universities, and S.C. Johnson, the school's benefactor. The team has many goals, including finding ways to diversify crops.

Many MBA students are following DeKoszmovszky's path and pursuing careers involving sustainable development, which is defined as a job or project that meets the needs of the present generation without compromising the ability of future generations to succeed.

Usually, sustainability is focused on the environment, but it can also include finding ways for factories to reduce carbon emissions to fundraising for patients who need medicine in Africa. It's the latest "it" field for MBAs.

 CASE STUDY Go to the *Introduction to Business* Online Learning Center through **glencoe.com** for the *BusinessWeek* Reader Case Study.

Active Learning

Form a group to explore new opportunities to achieve a sustainable economy in your community. Write a brief presentation to present to an entrepreneur, government official, or local university professor to propose ways to implement your group's ideas.

60 **Chapter 4** Business Ethics and Social Responsibility **glencoe.com**

BusinessWeek *Reader and Case Study*

It's Getting Easier Being Green

 CASE STUDY Have students go to the *Introduction to Business* Online Learning Center through **glencoe.com** to download a Case Study activity that corresponds to the article. The activity and answer key are also available in the TeacherWorks Plus CD.

Active Learning

Presentations will vary depending on the entrepreneur, government official, or local university professor interviewed.

Science/Tech**TRENDS**

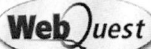

Biotechnology

Biotechnology is any technique that uses living organisms to make or modify products, improve plants, or develop microorganisms to serve a specific purpose. The work scientists have done in the biotechnology field has impacted the agricultural industry, the health-care and medical industries, and environmental protection.

Web**Quest**

Go to the *Introduction to Business* Online Learning Center through **glencoe.com** for links to Web sites where you can research different examples of how biotechnology has been used by businesses. Write a few paragraphs describing the impact biotechnology has had and the ethical issues, if any, that might arise.

Responsibility to Customers

Customers are a business's first responsibility. Businesses should offer a good, safe product or service at a reasonable price. The Federal Trade Commission (FTC) is a federal government agency that protects consumers from dangerous or falsely advertised products. Most companies obey the government's rules.

Some companies do not act responsibly in the marketplace, especially when it comes to fair competition. Fair competition between businesses is necessary for the marketplace to operate effectively. It is a major component of a market economy. The market economy relies chiefly on market forces to allocate goods, services, and other resources, and to determine prices. Some companies use unethical tactics to eliminate competition. One of the most common means is to conspire with other companies to control the market for a product. Together, the companies can control the supply of a product and the prices they charge.

When companies restrict competition, consumers are affected. Consumers have fewer choices in what they can buy and how much they have to pay. When a company does not have to compete, its productivity decreases. This can backfire on a business. When the market changes or new markets open up, a company can find itself unprepared to compete. For example, in the 1940s, a handful of entertainment studios controlled the film industry. They kept control by owning most of the theaters. Smaller studios could make movies, but they could not get them shown anywhere. The government sued the big studios and forced them to sell their theaters. As a result, small studios were able to compete in the marketplace.

Earth-Friendly Products Many beauty-product companies include mission statements regarding the environment in their advertising and on their labels. Origins™, for one, promises to preserve the earth, animals, and the environment. *What products do you have at home that promise to be environmentally friendly?*

Real World

Earth-Friendly Products Students may name products packaged in recyclable plastic, energy-saving appliances, hybrid vehicles, or energy-efficient windows.

Science/Tech**TRENDS**

Web**Quest**

Biotechnology Students should discuss profitability for biotech businesses that are discovering new ways to cure disease and save lives.

TEACH (cont.)

S Skill Practice

Guided Practice

Apply Ask students to name some warnings they have seen on labels that demonstrate firms' responsibility to consumers. (Examples of common warnings include to use chemicals in a well ventilated area or to keep cleaning products out of reach of children.) **L1**

Categorize Have groups of students select a food product package, list all the information, and then put the information into two categories: information intended to help consumers and information intended to sell the product. (The nutritional label is intended to help; other information is intended to sell.) **L2**

Search and Report Ask students to visit the FDA Web site and create a table with product categories it regulates in one column and examples in the next. (The first column should include the products. Examples in the second column will vary.) **L3**

ASSESS

Review Key Terms
Have students write sentences using each key term.

Study-to-Go
Have students go to the Online Learning Center through **glencoe.com** to download free **Study-to-Go** content to their PDAs or cell phones.

Activity correlates to Science standards.

RETEACH

W Writing Practice

Independent Practice

Explaining Instruct students to research and write a short paper explaining the relationships between independent and large studios. Remind students to include proper reference citations. (Papers will vary depending on the current issues studios are facing.)

R Reading Strategy

Discuss Organize students into small groups and ask them to read and discuss the four paragraphs about responsibility to employees. Ask students to write a quiz question, including the answer, for each paragraph. (Quiz questions will vary but should relate to the content.)

U Universal Access

Artistic/Visual Learners

Ask students to pick a concept from this page and draw a cartoon to illustrate the concept. Consider allowing students to work in pairs. (Cartoons will vary, but should clearly illustrate a concept on this page. For example, a cartoon might show volunteers participating in a community project.)

Student Activity Workbook ☞ Assign the Section 4.2 Activities.

● **A Community Concert** People enjoy going to community concerts. **How could a business demonstrate social responsibility by participating in an event like this?**

Real World

W **Independent Films** Independent studios, including Lions Gate, Fox Searchlight, Focus Features, and Fine Line Features, have flourished since the 1940s. Some of these studios are subsidiaries of larger studios. They focus on developing less commercial, more character-driven films. *What advantages or disadvantages do you think an independent studio has compared to a large studio?* **R**

U

Responsibility to Employees

Some businesses provide work experience for people with limited job skills. Many of these people are public assistance recipients. The purpose of such programs is to develop the skills and confidence levels necessary for success.

Volunteerism is another way businesses tackle societal problems. Some companies allow employees to take one or more paid days off during the year to work on community projects.

Businesses have a social responsibility to provide employees with safe working conditions, equal treatment, and fair pay. Less than 100 years ago, however, workers had few rights. Over the years the government has passed laws to protect workers from a range of issues, from child labor abuses to the rights of workers to organize. As the workplace has changed, the government has passed new laws. The Equal Pay Act (passed in 1964) requires that men and women be paid the same wages for doing equal work. More than 40 years later, however, the gap still exists. Another law, the Americans with Disabilities Act, bans discrimination against people with physical or mental disability. More than 50 million workers are likely to be covered by this law.

It is in a company's best interest to treat its workers fairly. Otherwise, it may suffer from low morale, poor production, and a high turnover rate.

62 **Chapter 4** Business Ethics and Social Responsibility

Discuss the Photo

● **A Community Concert** Answers will vary but students are likely to mention principles of community involvement, prompting unity, and improving living conditions for residents.

Independent Films Answers will vary. Students may discover that independents have more control, but less money and fewer distribution channels.

Responsibility to Society

Businesses have responsibilities not only to customers and employees but also to society. One of the biggest social issues facing businesses today is environmental responsibility.

In 1970, the U.S. government created the Environmental Protection Agency (EPA), which enforces rules that protect the environment and control pollution.

✔ Reading Check **Identify** What is one of the biggest social issues facing businesses today?

Responsibility to Creditors and Owners

In the late 1990s and the early part of the 21st century, a number of major corporations reportedly kept inaccurate accounting records. Records showed that the firms had higher profits than they reported. Their behaviors were unethical and unlawful. Such behaviors are harmful to creditors (those who loan money) and outside shareholders (those who are owners but do not work in the business). Because of these behaviors, the federal government passed additional legislation. The Sarbanes-Oxley Act mandates truthful reporting and makes the CEO more accountable for the actions of the financial managers of a firm.

C

● As You Read

Think about owning a business. What type of project would you like your employees to do to benefit your community?

Section 4.2

● After You Read

Review Key Concepts
1. How is producing a good or service a way of being socially responsible?
2. What is the mission of the Food and Drug Administration?
3. What is one of the biggest social issues that businesses face today?

Academic Skills
4. **English Language Arts** Situations involving ethics and social responsibility are not found only in the business world. They come up in everyone's day-to-day life. Write a paragraph explaining an ethical decision made by you or someone you know. Explain what made it an ethical decision and the steps that were taken to make the final decision.

5. **English Language Arts** The terms below all relate to business ethics. Imagine that you are asked to explain these terms to a group of sixth-grade students who are just beginning to study how businesses work. Plan a talk designed to define each term. Give examples that might help a sixth grader understand the ideas.

| code of ethics | conflict of interest |
| social responsibility | volunteerism |

 Go to the *Introduction to Business* Online Learning Center through **glencoe.com** to check your answers.

NCLB

Vocabulary Review

1. Students should write complete sentences using each term correctly.

Review Key Concepts

2. Ethics: the set of moral principles by which people conduct themselves personally, socially, or professionally. Business ethics: rules, often based on moral principles, by which a business conducts itself with groups with whom it deals.

3. Ethical behavior encourages consumers to buy the firm's products, employees to be productive, members of society to feel good about the firm, creditors to lend money to the firm, and for corporations, investors to buy stock in the firm.

4. Identify the ethical dilemma, discover alternative actions, decide who might be affected, list the probable effects of alternatives, and select best alternative.

5. It is the duty to do what is best for the good of society. Businesses sponsor sporting and cultural events. They provide materials for schools. In some developing countries, they build schools and hospitals. They encourage their employees to become involved in community projects.

Section 4.1 *Summary*

Business Ethics Ethics are the set of moral principles by which people conduct themselves personally, socially, and professionally. Business ethics are guidelines for how businesses should conduct themselves. Many unethical business practices are against the law. The guidelines that can be used when facing ethical dilemmas are a lot like the steps of the problem-solving process. Good ethics can be beneficial for the long-run profitability and success of a business.

Section 4.2 *Summary*

Social Responsibility Social responsibility is the duty to do what is best for the good of society. In today's society, producing goods and services that are beneficial to society is not enough for a business to be considered socially responsible. Businesses must also be ethical and fair to consumers, workers, creditors, and society in general. Businesses also have a responsibility to the environment. In a corporation, management must be truthful about the financial health of the firm.

Vocabulary Review

1. On a sheet of paper, use each of these key terms and academic vocabulary terms in a sentence.

Key Terms	Academic Vocabulary
ethics	principles
business ethics	conduct
sweatshop	encounter
code of ethics	alternative
conflict of interest	integrity
social responsibility	integral
	benefit
	sufficient

Review Key Concepts

2. Define ethics and business ethics.

3. Describe why ethical behavior is good behavior for business.

4. Using the ethical decision-making process, list the steps for dealing with an ethical dilemma.

5. Define what is meant by the social responsibility of business.

Critical Thinking

6. Students should discuss the difference between legal and ethical behavior in their answers.

7. Some students will say that we should not trade with these countries. Other will say that trading with these countries provides jobs and income for poor workers.

8. Some students will say that when people understand the ethical behavior expected of them, they are more likely to exhibit those behaviors. Other students might say that fear of discipline might motivate workers.

9. Younger managers may be less secure and feel the need to participate in unethical behavior in order to achieve goals. Mature managers may have a better understanding of what is ethical.

Critical Thinking

6. Give an example of an unethical decision that is not illegal. Can a legal decision also be an unethical one?

7. Do you think the United States should trade with countries that have a poor human rights record? Why or why not?

8. Why do you think businesses with written codes of ethics and ethics programs for their employees have fewer ethical problems than other companies?

9. One study showed that young, inexperienced managers are twice as likely to feel pressured to compromise ethical standards as their older counterparts. Why do you think that is true?

10. Why do you think that some employees tell their managers about unethical behaviors of other workers? Do you think this is a good development?

11. Imagine that your manager says she cannot give you a raise but will allow some personal items in your travel expense report. What impression does that give you of her professional ethics?

12. Is ethical behavior always easy? Why or why not? What can a person do to make the best decision regarding an ethical dilemna?

Write About It

13. Some people believe that to solve social problems, money should come from government, not businesses. Write a letter to the editor of your local newspaper about your opinion of this stance.

14. Imagine that you discover your company is cheating the government out of thousands of dollars each year. Write a short essay about your options in this case.

15. In a paragraph or two, describe a situation in which you showed ethical behavior that resulted in some positive reactions from others.

16. Think of a business that you believe shows ethical behavior. Write a letter to the business owner about your observations.

17. Write an e-mail to your teacher discussing whether the drive to maximize profits is the reason some businesses are ethical and others are unethical.

18. Businesses have an ethical responsibility to their employees. Describe the type of ethics you would look for in an employer.

19. Write at least two paragraphs detailing ways that the government has helped working people.

Technology Applications

Internet
20. Using the Internet, select three codes of ethics from various professions (such as the medical, legal, educational, and accounting fields) or businesses. Compare and contrast the codes of ethics. Report your findings to the class.

Business Ethics

Making Ethical Decisions
21. What would you do if a friend at work was making about $100 worth of personal phone calls each month? Would your answer be different if the cost were $10 a month? Use the ethical decision-making process to determine what you should do.

Technology Applications
20. Answers will vary depending on the codes of ethics the students use when completing this assignment.

Business Ethics
21. Answer will vary. Some students will say that they would talk to the friend and point out the consequences of this unethical behavior. Others will say that they would talk to a supervisor about the situation. Most students will recognize that the behavior is unethical regardless of the dollar amount.

Critical Thinking

10. Misconduct can affect everyone. Some may do it because of increased legal protection for whistle blowers. Some may think it makes people more accountable, while others may feel that it could cause distrust.

11. The manager is sending a signal that unethical behavior will be tolerated.

12. It is not easy to behave ethically when others set a bad example.

Write About It

13. Business should also be expected to provide resources for solving social problems.

14. When managers and executives set a bad example, employees may fear the consequences. However, students should recognize they have an individual ethical responsibility.

15. Examples will vary depending on students' experiences.

16. Letters will vary but should describe ethical behaviors.

17. Students should understand that the statement is true.

18. Payment of wages on time, good working conditions, and respect and fair treatment of employees are all important.

19. OSHA ensures better working conditions. The Equal Pay Act and the Americans With Disabilities Act protect workers in various ways.

Applying Academics to Business

22. A. The auxiliary verb *be* is needed to complete the verb phrase: "Businesses *must be concerned* with environmental issues."

B. *Social* and *responsible* are both adjectives. To make the sentence correct, add "-ly" to *social*: "Most nonprofit organizations are *socially* responsible."

23. $58,000 $\times \frac{1}{36}$ = $1,611

$1,611 $\times \frac{1}{8}$ = $201

Jimmy could not accept the TV because its value, $250, is greater than $201.

24. The underlined words modify the noun and are therefore adjectives.

25. The additional dividend paid to shareholders is: 8,000,000 $\times$ $2 = $16,000,000 $\times$ $40% = 6.4 million.

The reserve is $15 million.

$6.4 million + $15 million = 21.4 million

Since $20 million is less than $21.4 million, there is not enough money to do both.

Active Learning

26. Answers should describe an ethical situation and the outcome. Some students will report that the situation was not resolved.

Business in the Real World

27. Answers will vary depending on whether or not the business has a code of ethics.

Applying Academics to Business

English Language Arts

22. Each of the following sentences contains a grammatical mistake. Identify the errors, and rewrite the sentences to make them correct.

    A. Businesses must concerned with environmental issues.

    B. Most nonprofit organizations are social responsible.

Mathematics

23. Jimmy's company had a code of ethics that only allowed its sales representatives to accept gifts from clients if they cost less than $\frac{1}{8}$ of the employee's yearly bonus. The bonuses were equal to $\frac{1}{36}$ of the employee's total sales for the year. If Jimmy's total sales equaled $58,000, could he ethically accept a $250 TV from a client?

> **THEORY**   **Number and Operations: Multiplying Fractions** Multiply fractions by multiplying the numerators and then multiply the denominators. To find how much Jimmy's bonus will be, multiply $58,000 by $\frac{1}{36}$. Then multiply that product by $\frac{1}{8}$.

English Language Arts

24. Read the following phrases and note the underlined words. Write a sentence describing what they have in common and naming their part of speech.

<u>decision-making</u> process

<u>short-term</u> goals

Mathematics

25. A manufacturing company with 8 million shareholders normally pays a $2 dividend per share at year-end. Because of an unexpected $20 million windfall in profits, one member of the board of directors proposes raising the dividend by 40 percent and reserving $15 million for future environmental cleanup operations. Is there enough extra money to do both?

> **THEORY**   **Problem Solving** Solving word problems sometimes requires several mathematical steps. Read the situation described carefully in order to figure out what the steps should be. To better understand the problem, you might try restating the question: *Is $20 million greater than the additional dividend paid to shareholders plus the $15 million reserve?*

Active Learning

Dealing With a Dilemma

26. Ask a family member if he or she have ever been faced with an ethical issue at work. If so, find out what happened and how it was resolved. Ask that person to explain the steps in making an ethical decision. Write two paragraphs listing what you learned from your conversation.

Business in the Real World

Interview a Businessperson

27. Interview a manager of a business in the local community. Ask the manager if the business has a code of ethics and how it is enforced. What are some common violations of the code? Ask for at least three experiences in which ethical behavior was beneficial to the firm. Then prepare a report based on your findings.

ExamView Assessment Suite CD allows you to print out ready-made unit and chapter tests, complete with answer keys. You can also create customized tests.

TeacherWorks Plus provides complete teacher resources in one convenient package. It includes customizable lesson plans in calendar format, and instant access to many print program resources.

Real LIFE · skills

DEVELOP ETHICAL SKILLS

28. As a class, create a formal code of ethics for the classroom. Be sure to include the purpose of the code, the rules for classroom behavior, the steps for making ethical decisions, and the consequences of breaking the code. Use the code of ethics in the class for the remainder of the year. Revise as needed.

Business CAREERS

FIND YOUR DREAM JOB

29. Go to the *Introduction to Business* Online Learning Center through **glencoe.com** for a link to the Occupational Outlook Handbook Web site. Click on the "OOH Search/A-Z Index" link and enter the job title "paralegals and legal assistants" Then write a one-page report about this type of occupation. Conclude your report with a list of things you could do now to prepare yourself to pursue the occupation.

Role Play

BUILDING ON A HISTORIC SITE

30. Situation Your firm wants to put up an apartment building on a site where the oldest building in town currently rests. The people in the area are very interested in historical preservation.

Activity When the initial planning for the apartment building was made, there was no idea that this property was historically significant. Prepare a report to the president of your firm with recommendations for the project.

Evaluation Your report will be evaluated on how well you meet the following performance indicators:

- Explain alternate courses of action.
- Explain the ethical implications of proceeding with the project.
- Describe the community's reaction to the project.
- Demonstrate an understanding of the ethical decision-making process.

Standardized Test Practice

Directions Choose the answer that is the most effective substitute for each underlined part of the sentence. If no substitution is necessary, choose "Leave as is."

1. **Consider your values and goals when determining the advantages and disadvantages of <u>alternatives: you can</u> use this information to compare and evaluate your choices.**

   A   alternatives, you can
   B   alternatives; you can
   C   alternatives. You can
   D   Leave as is

 **TEST-TAKING TIP** Budget your time. Make sure you have sufficient time to study so that you are well prepared for the test.

 READING Go to the *Introduction to Business* Online Learning Center through **glencoe.com** for a list of outside reading suggestions.

Real LIFE · skills

28. The code should reflect the four points in the assignment and focus on classroom behavior.

Business CAREERS

29. Nature of work: Helping lawyers prepare for trials, drafting documents, performing research. Working conditions: Office or law library. Mostly 40-hour workweek, working for law firms, government agencies, and corporations. Training and qualifications: Associate's degree in paralegal studies or bachelor's degree plus a certificate in paralegal studies. Opportunities for advancement: More with experience. In large organizations, opportunities for supervisory positions. Job outlook: Projected to grow faster than average. Earnings: Median annual earning in 2004 was approximately $39,000. In preparation: improving communication, organizational skills; develop computer and research skills.

Role Play

30. Presentations should address the competencies noted in the Role Play.

Standardized Test Practice
   1. C

 **STRATEGIES FOR STANDARDIZED TEST PREP SUCCESS**

Test Prep Help students develop a structured plan for studying in preparation for taking a standardized test. Explain that standardized tests are usually designed to examine what a student has learned over time, and so cramming is not helpful. Instead, have them start a month or so in advance, and spend 15 or 20 minutes every other day engaged in such activities as reviewing textbooks for content, answering practice-test questions, and familiarizing themselves with how to use machine scorable answer sheets.

FOCUS

Bell Ringer Activity

Favorite Foods

Ask volunteers to name their favorite foods. (Answers will depend on students' tastes and cultural backgrounds.) Write a list of the foods on the board. Ask students if they think a business that specializes in selling one type of food could be successful in their town. Ask students to brainstorm a list of local restaurants that specialize in one type of food. (Students may mention pizza parlors and restaurants that specialize in regional food such as Mexican and Italian fare.)

TEACH

Teaching Points
Factors of Production

Ask students to define and list the four factors of production. (The factors of production are all the economic resources necessary to produce a society's goods and services. They are natural resources, labor resources, capital resources, and entrepreneurial resources.) Ask students to categorize the factors of production involved with running P.B.Loco. (Natural resources include peanuts and other ingredients used to make the peanut butter. Labor resources include the company's staff. Capital resources include the company's factory, stores, and equipment. Its entrepreneurial resources are its owners.)

Keri Barney
Ken Hall
Jodene Jensen

Co-Founders, P.B.Loco Holdings
P.B.Loco Holdings is a company that produces gourmet peanut butter and has cafés, franchises, an online store, and other ventures.

Q & A

Describe your job responsibilities.

Jodene: Right now Keri handles the day-to-day operations and takes care of our production facility. Ken and I support our franchisees and handle the finances and the Web site.

Ken: For the first three months, the three of us actually made the peanut butter just so we would know how.

Keri: We have a daily meeting in the morning. We always have multiple task lists.

What skills are most important in your business?

Keri: Knowing how to wear different hats and deal with different people. I was a communications studies major in college; it is a nice skill to have for dealing with people. Basic business knowledge and analytical skills also help.

Ken: You have to assimilate a great deal of facts and make sure everything works together as far as your strategy goes.

Jodene: So much of what we do involves making decisions. Relationships with other people are also important.

What is your key to success?

Ken: When we have a new idea, we're able to implement it quickly.

Keri: We're constantly juggling things and staying in communication.

Jodene: There's almost a cult-like feeling about peanut butter, because people feel very nostalgic about it. We have a premium product.

What advice would you give students interested in starting a business?

Jodene: Learning how to juggle tasks is critical. It's important to do different things. So take a class, play a sport, and if you can, get a job.

Keri: Educate yourself in all aspects related to the business. And put in sweat equity, the hard work.

Ken: Keep an open mind. There's always something great if you use your imagination.

Critical Thinking Why is it important to conduct market research before starting a business?

Critical Thinking

Businesses need information to make the right decisions and compete effectively, and market research supplies that information. Market research can help a business identify opportunities and challenges and find information. It can help a business determine what customers have purchased in the past and what they are likely to want to purchase in the future. Businesses can reduce the risk of failure by using market research to learn about the people and the products in a specific market.

Some Qualifications of a Food Services Business Owner

Academic Skills and Abilities

Mathematics; verbal and written communication skills; general business management; creativity; interpersonal skills; multitasking, organizing, and planning skills.

Academic Skills Required to Complete Tasks at P.B.Loco			
Tasks	Math	Science	English Language Arts
Hold meetings			◆
Assign duties			◆
Develop recipes		◆	
Customer service	◆		◆
Contact vendors			◆
Schedule employees	◆		◆
Order supplies	◆		◆
Analyze financials	◆		◆

Education and Training

At least a high school diploma, with coursework in basic math and work experience within the food industry or other service-oriented field.

Career Path

Retail careers often begin with entry-level positions in established stores. Niche businesses, such as P.B.Loco, often spring from a personal hobby or interest.

Preparing for a Career
Self-Assessment Checklist

Use this self-assessment checklist to help determine your career path.

✔ Think about your skills, the things that you do well, such as being organized, solving problems, or getting along with people.

✔ Write down your interests or favorite activities.

✔ Think about the kind of lifestyle you want in the future. What do you want to accomplish? Where would you like to live?

✔ Consider your values, the beliefs and principles by which you live. You can determine your values by taking a close look at what you feel is truly important.

✔ Write down your aptitudes and abilities. An aptitude is your potential for learning a skill. An ability is a skill you have already developed.

✔ Consider your personality. Your personality is the combination of your attitude, behaviors, and characteristics.

✔ Determine your learning styles. Learning styles are the different ways people naturally think and learn.

✔ Consider the types of careers that might match your skills, interests, lifestyle goals, values, aptitudes, abilities, personality, and learning styles.

69

ASSESS

Write About It
P.B.Loco

Ask students to write a summary of what they like about P.B.Loco's business concept. (Students may say that they like the fun product idea and the freedom that the owners have to create their own income.)

Academic Vocabulary
Career Planning

Ask students to read the Self-Assessment Checklist, then write one or more paragraphs about preparing for a career. Have students use some words from the Academic Vocabulary Glossary. (Example: When preparing for a career, students should consider careers that might match their skills, interests, lifestyle, and goals. They should also determine the standard of living they want in the future. Doing research allows students to identify potential careers that will help them eventually find the right career.)

CLOSE

Cooperative Learning
Technology Applications

Ask students to work in pairs and develop an idea for a specialty food service business. Have them work together to develop an advertisement for the business. Encourage students to use technology applications to design the brochure and integrate images and text in the form of marketing copy and nutritional information. (Brochures should include marketing copy, visuals, and nutritional information.)

Preparing for a Career
Career Decision Making The decision-making process can be used to make all kinds of decisions. Remind students that one of the biggest decisions they will make in their lives is choosing a career, and that will require serious planning. Ask students: What major decisions have you made recently? (Answers will vary but may involve setting goals or deciding how to spend money or time.) Tell students that they will have an opportunity to think about careers and the career-planning process as they read the Self-Assessment Checklists in this book.

FOCUS

Discussion Starter

Lead a discussion about technology in society at the present time. Ask students to project how the evolution of technology will change society.

Step 1

Brainstorm Skills

Have students go to the *Introduction to Business* Online Learning Center through **glencoe.com** for a graphic organizer they can use to brainstorm the skills needed to complete the project.

Step 2

Choose a Business and a Career

Students can use the Occupational Outlook Handbook Web site to explore occupations.

TEACH

Step 3

Build Background

Technology Have students brainstorm ways workers will use technology in the future. (Technology will be used to perform a wide range of tasks, including sending, receiving, sharing, and analyzing information.)

Diversity Ask students why the workforce is becoming more diverse. (The workforce is becoming more diverse because the population is growing more diverse.) Ask students how diversity benefits businesses. (A diverse workforce can help businesses understand a diverse population.)

Trends in the World of Business

The business world is constantly changing. To meet the challenges of the dynamic business environment, businesses and workers need to understand and react to trends.

Thematic Project Assignment

In this project, you will research trends that are affecting businesses and careers and write a report about them. These trends include the rise of globalization, the evolution of technology, and the increasing importance of cultural diversity.

Step 1 Brainstorm Skills You Need to Complete This Activity

Your success in business will depend on your skills. Preview the activity, then brainstorm a list of the skills you will need to use to complete the activity and describe how you will use them. Skills you might use include:

Academic Skills	reading, writing, math, and science skills
Basic Skills	speaking, listening, thinking, problem-solving, and interpersonal skills
Technology Skills	word processing, keyboarding, database, spreadsheet, presentation, telecommunications, and Internet skills

 SKILLS PREVIEW Go to the *Introduction to Business* Online Learning Center through **glencoe.com** for a graphic organizer you can use to brainstorm the skills you will use to complete the project.

Step 2 Choose a Business and a Career That Interest You

Think of a business that you find interesting. Then think of a career that interests you. As you investigate trends in business, you will research the effects of globalization, technology, and cultural diversity on the business and career of your choice.

Step 3 Build Background Knowledge

Preview the business trends you will research.

Business *Trends*

The globalization of the world's economies has increased competition for businesses and jobs. Globalization is the process by which the world economy is becoming a single interdependent system.

Globalization has been spurred by the evolution of technology. New technology has resulted in the growth of certain jobs and businesses and the decline of others.

Cultural diversity has become increasingly important to businesses. The blending of people with different skills and perspectives in the workplace can help businesses understand and react to an increasingly diverse population.

Step 4 Connect with Your Community

Interview an adult family member about how the business world has changed. Find out what the workplace was like when he or she first entered the workforce.

Globalization Ask students to write an essay stating the arguments for and against globalization. (Arguments for globalization may say that the expansion of free trade has created enormous wealth in both rich and previously poor nations. Arguments against globalization may express concerns about environmental protection and allowing international organizations to make decisions that affect all of society.)

Step 4

Connect with Your Community

Ask students to describe what the word *community* means to them. Write their ideas on the board. (A community is a group of people who have something in common.) Ask students to think of ways they could get involved in their communities. (Students may suggest community service or volunteer work.)

Step 5 | Research Business Trends

Use library and Internet resources to research business trends. Use the project research checklist as a guide to your research. Keep records of your sources of information.

Step 6 | Develop a Report

Use word processing and other software to develop a two-page report that includes all of the information described in this project research checklist.

Business Trends

✔ Describe globalization and the factors that have promoted globalization.

✔ Describe the effect of globalization on businesses and the job market.

✔ Create a time line showing the technological innovations that have promoted globalization.

✔ Describe how technology has changed the global business environment.

✔ Explain how technological change has created new businesses and affected existing businesses and jobs.

✔ Describe how diversity creates an advantage for businesses.

✔ Use information from the U.S. Census Bureau to create a chart that compares the U.S. population today with projections for the population in 2050.

Self Connections

✔ Describe the results of your interview with an adult family member.

✔ Describe how technology, globalization, and diversity have affected the business and career in which you are interested.

✔ Explain what the investigation and its results mean to you.

Step 7 | Evaluate Your Report

@ **RUBRIC** Go to the *Introduction to Business* Online Learning Center through **glencoe.com** for a rubric you can use to evaluate your final report.

TEACH (cont.)

Step 6
Develop a Report
Give students these tips on report writing:

- Know your audience.
- Organize your report by developing an outline and using titles and subtitles.
- Write concisely (briefly but completely).
- Write in easy-to-read, simple language.

ASSESS

Step 7
Evaluate Your Report
Rubric Encourage students to use the rubric to evaluate their final reports.

CLOSE

Culminating Activity
Career Interviews
Have students form pairs and interview each other about the businesses and careers they researched. Make sure they discuss how their opinions and perceptions of the businesses and careers evolved during the course of the project. (Interviews will vary depending on students' business and career choices and reactions to their research.)

Step 5
Research Business Trends
Students can go to the *Introduction to Business* Online Learning Center through **glencoe.com** for a rubric they can use as a content checklist when researching their reports.

71

Chapter	Section	Unit Objectives
Chapter 5 *Entrepreneurship*	5.1	**Define** entrepreneur and entrepreneurship.
		List at least five rewards of being an entrepreneur.
		Identify at least four challenges of being an entrepreneur.
		Discuss why entrepreneurs are important to the American economy.
	5.2	**Discuss** the initial steps in setting up a business.
		Identify the parts of a business plan.
Chapter 6 *Business Ownership and Operations*	6.1	**Describe** the advantages and disadvantages of the three major forms of business organizations.
		Describe how cooperatives and nonprofits are like and unlike corporations and franchises.
	6.2	**Differentiate** the six types of businesses.
		Describe the five functions of business.
		Discuss how the five functions of business relate to each other.
Chapter 7 *Business Management*	7.1	**Describe** the overall purpose of management.
		Discuss the four functions of management.
	7.2	**Identify** the differences between management structures.
		Name six skills necessary for effective management.
Chapter 8 *Leadership in Management*	8.1	**Define** leadership.
		Describe the qualities of a leader.
		Name at least three ways in which an individual can develop leadership skills.
	8.2	**Identify** and describe the autocratic, democratic, and free rein leadership styles.
		Describe the self-managed team approach and the two ways in which such an approach is organized.
Chapter 9 *Technology and Business*	9.1	**Describe** how technological inventions have an effect on business.
		Give examples of how technology has changed jobs in business.
	9.2	**Explain** why doing business on the Internet has become a major factor in many industries.

Understanding the Coding

Brackets　Brackets on the reduced student edition page correspond to teaching strategies and activities in the Teacher Wraparound Edition. As you teach the lesson, the brackets show you exactly where to use the teaching strategies and activities.

Letters　The letters on the reduced student edition page identify the type of strategy or activity. See the key below to learn about the different types of strategies and activities.

Ability Levels　Leveled teaching strategies are identified by one of three codes to give you an idea of their suitability for students of varying learning styles and abilities.

Resources　Key program resources are listed in each chapter. Icons indicate the format of resources.

KEY　to Letters

D **Develop Concepts** activities help teachers gauge and plan for students' concept development.

R **Reading Strategy** activities help you teach reading skills and vocabulary.

C **Critical Thinking** strategies help students apply and extend what they have learned.

U **Universal Access** activities provide differentiated instruction for English language learners and suggestions for teaching various types of learners.

S **Skill Practice** provides leveled instruction for meeting individual needs and learning styles.

W **Writing Support** activities provide writing opportunities to help students comprehend the text.

NCLB **No Child Left Behind** activities help students practice and improve their abilities in academic subjects.

KEY　to Ability Levels

L1 Strategies should be within the ability range of all students. Often full class participation is required.

L2 Strategies are for average to above-average students or for small groups. Some teacher direction is necessary.

L3 Strategies are designed for students able and willing to work independently. Minimal teacher direction is necessary.

KEY　to Resource Icons

🗀　Print Material

💿　CD-ROM

🎧　Online Learning Center with Podcasts

BusinessWeek *Reader and Case Study*

In Unit 2, your students can learn more about business in the real world through the following *BusinessWeek* Readers and Case Studies:

How to Build Innovative Companies
There's a new conversation under way across America that may well change your future. (page 78)

For the Poor, Help from MBAs
They're bringing business development to many impoverished developing nations. (page 100)

A Board of Your Own
Small companies turn to each other for objective advice in peer groups. (page 118)

Memo to Students: Writing Skills Matter
B-schools face a challenge in teaching writing and communications skills to undergrads. (page 132)

Wherever You Go, You're on the Job
A dramatic mobility shift is changing work. (page 143)

Chapter Features and Activities

BusinessWeek *Reader and Case Study*

Science/Tech TRENDS

?ETHICS in Business

International Business

Real World

Reading Strategies

Before You Read

Graphic Organizer

As You Read

✔ Reading Check

After You Read

Unit Overview

Introduce the Unit

Introduce the unit by describing the main concepts of each chapter in the unit.

Unit 2 is about the skills that are necessary parts of owning and operating a business.

Chapter 5 is about entrepreneurship and small businesses—what they are and their advantages and disadvantages.

Chapter 6 introduces the different forms of business ownership and the five main types of businesses.

Chapter 7 is about different managerial structures and the different levels and functions of management.

Chapter 8 is about leadership qualities and styles of leadership.

Chapter 9 is about how technology has influenced business. It describes the e-workforce and virtual business.

00:00 OUT OF TIME?

If class time is too short to cover all of the chapters in this unit, have students:

- Write down the vocabulary terms and their definitions.
- Read the chapter summaries at the beginning of each chapter review.
- Go to the *Introduction to Business* Online Learning Center through **glencoe.com** to download free Study-to-Go content to their PDAs or cell phones.

Owning and Operating a Business

72

Real-World Business and Career Profile   Preview

Seventh Generation Tell students that at the end of this unit, they will learn about the founder of Seventh Generation and how he achieved his success. Seventh Generation is the leading brand of environmentally safe household products in the country. Jeffery Hollender is president of the company. He has written a book entitled, *How to Make the World a Better Place: A Beginner's Guide to Doing Good.* Ask students to give reasons why a business that specializes in making products that are good for the environment might be successful. (There is increasing demand for products that do not harm the environment. Also, Seventh Generation is a socially responsible business, which appeals to consumers.)

Real-World Business and Career Profile

Preview

Seventh Generation makes environmentally safe household products such as dish soap and laundry detergent. At the end of this unit, you will learn about Seventh Generation® founder Jeffrey Hollender and how he achieved his success.

Decision Making What type of ownership would you use if you decided to open a company?

Unit 2   Thematic Project Preview

Entrepreneurship in a Global World After completing this unit, you will research to find out how entrepreneurs conduct business in a global economy.

Project Checklist As you read the chapters in this unit, use this checklist to prepare for the unit project.

✔ Think about how globalization affects entrepreneurs.

✔ Analyze how technology helps entrepreneurs build global businesses.

✔ Look for entrepreneurial businesses in your community that are working in the global marketplace.

✔ Discover how different entreprencurial businesses can increase their market share through globalization.

73

Build Background

Ask students these questions to activate prior knowledge:

Chapter 5
Are all potential entrepreneurs alike? (Some would-be entrepreneurs never get past the dreaming phase while others are driven to make their dreams a reality.)

Chapter 6
Do you think you need to know about how businesses are run even if you do not want to own a business or a piece of a business? (There are some basics of business ownership that everyone should know about. Knowing how businesses operate makes it easier to function as workers, consumers, and citizens.)

Chapter 7
What do you know about the concept of management? (The word *manage* is part of our everyday vocabulary. In their personal lives, people manage stress, time, money, and relationships.)

Chapter 8
What do you know about leadership? (Some students have already served as leaders in school, athletics, and community activities. All students have seen people demonstrate leadership.)

Chapter 9
What changes in technology do you think your family members have seen in their lifetimes? (Today they use cell phones, but they may remember party lines and dialing the phone.)

Unit   Thematic Project Preview

Entrepreneurship in a Global World
Tell students that when they complete this unit, they will learn about how technology and globalization have changed the world for entrepreneurs. They will consider how different the world will be in the future for entrepreneurs. Encourage students to think about how these changes could affect the types of jobs and careers they might consider choosing.

C Critical Thinking

Ask students: What effect will globalization have on future entrepreneurs? (Encourage students to recognize that in the future there will be competition as well as opening the marketplace. Prices could become highly competitive as suppliers compete on a worldwide basis.)

73

Standards-Based Lesson Planning
Introduction to Business provides students with instruction and assessment in the following fundamental content areas:

Content Standards Correlations	
Discuss opportunities for business ownership.	pp. 77–79
Explore the role of an entrepreneur and apply the concepts of entrepreneurship.	pp. 76–81, 88–91
Prepare to become entrepreneurs by drawing from their general understanding of all aspects of business.	pp. 76–81, 88–91
Evaluate entrepreneurship concepts.	pp. 76–81, 88–91
Compare and contrast other forms of business with a sole proprietorship.	p. 79
Analyze the pros and cons of small business ownership.	pp. 79–81, 88–91
Evaluate the impact of small businesses in the U. S. and global economies.	p. 81
Examine the traits and skills required for a successful career as an entrepreneur.	pp. 77, 81, 88–91
Analyze a business plan for organizing a small business.	pp. 83–87
Explore career opportunities in business ownership.	pp. 76–81

NCLB
Activities, information, and skills practice will help your students attain No Child Left Behind proficiency. Students will improve their abilities in the following academic standards areas:

Academic Standards Correlations		
English Language Arts	Activities/Features	Page
NCTE 3 Apply strategies to interpret texts	Applying Academics to Business Standardized Test Practice	pp. 90, 91
NCTE 5 Use different writing process elements to communicate effectively	Applying Academics to Business	p. 90
NCTE 7 Conduct research and gather, evaluate, and synthesize data to communicate discoveries	After You Read	p. 87
NCTE 11 Participate as members of literacy communities	After You Read	p. 87
NCTE 12 Use language to accomplish individual purposes	After You Read	p. 87
Mathematics		
Algebra Represent and analyze mathematical situations and structures using algebraic symbols	Ask S&P	p. 74
Problem Solving Apply and adapt a variety of appropriate strategies to solve problems	After You Read	p. 81
Number and Operations Compute fluently and make reasonable estimates	Applying Academics to Business	p. 90
Number and Operations Understand numbers, ways of representing numbers, relationships among numbers, and number systems	Applying Academics to Business	p. 90
Science		
Content Standard G Students should develop understanding of science as a human endeavor, nature of scientific knowledge, historical perspectives	Science/Tech Trends	p. 85

Correlations   This chart shows the 21st Century Skills, foundation skills, and workplace competencies that students develop as they work in this chapter.

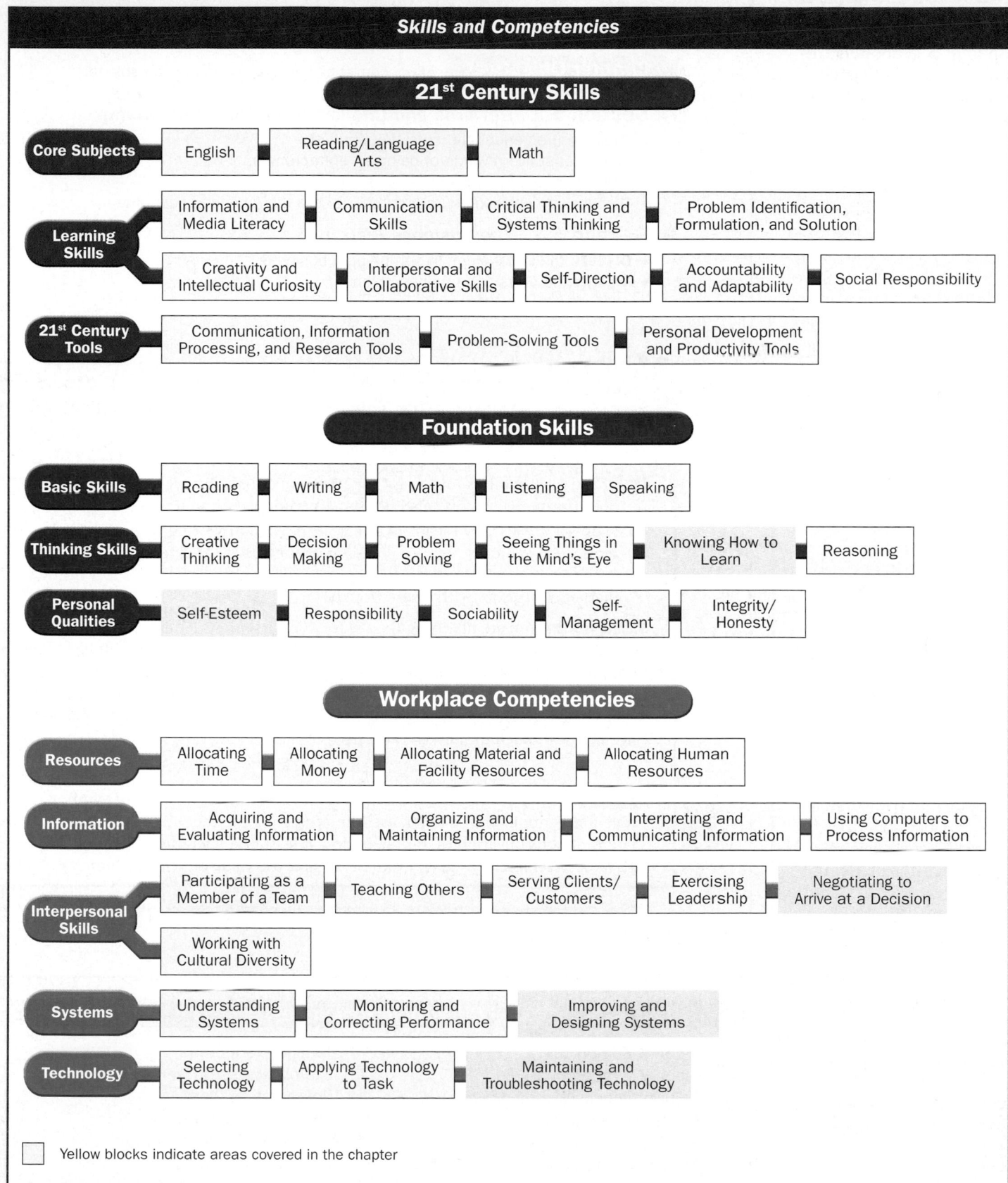

Skills and Competencies

21st Century Skills

Core Subjects
- English
- Reading/Language Arts
- Math

Learning Skills
- Information and Media Literacy
- Communication Skills
- Critical Thinking and Systems Thinking
- Problem Identification, Formulation, and Solution
- Creativity and Intellectual Curiosity
- Interpersonal and Collaborative Skills
- Self-Direction
- Accountability and Adaptability
- Social Responsibility

21st Century Tools
- Communication, Information Processing, and Research Tools
- Problem-Solving Tools
- Personal Development and Productivity Tools

Foundation Skills

Basic Skills
- Reading
- Writing
- Math
- Listening
- Speaking

Thinking Skills
- Creative Thinking
- Decision Making
- Problem Solving
- Seeing Things in the Mind's Eye
- Knowing How to Learn
- Reasoning

Personal Qualities
- Self-Esteem
- Responsibility
- Sociability
- Self-Management
- Integrity/Honesty

Workplace Competencies

Resources
- Allocating Time
- Allocating Money
- Allocating Material and Facility Resources
- Allocating Human Resources

Information
- Acquiring and Evaluating Information
- Organizing and Maintaining Information
- Interpreting and Communicating Information
- Using Computers to Process Information

Interpersonal Skills
- Participating as a Member of a Team
- Teaching Others
- Serving Clients/Customers
- Exercising Leadership
- Negotiating to Arrive at a Decision
- Working with Cultural Diversity

Systems
- Understanding Systems
- Monitoring and Correcting Performance
- Improving and Designing Systems

Technology
- Selecting Technology
- Applying Technology to Task
- Maintaining and Troubleshooting Technology

Yellow blocks indicate areas covered in the chapter

Chapter Overview

Introduce the Chapter

Entrepreneurship
Chapter 5 is about entrepreneurship and small business—what they are and their advantages and disadvantages.

Building Background
Some entrepreneurs are motivated by the idea of being in charge and doing things their own way. Others want to turn a hobby into a livelihood. Some never get past the dreaming phase, while others are driven to make their dreams a reality.

 **STANDARD &POOR'S**

>> Math Answer
The amount needed for 20 years is $700,000 ($20 \times \$35,000 = \$700,000$).

>> Extension Activity
Explain to students that the reason this problem was calculated "in today's dollars" is that the Time Value of Money concept means that $35,000 is worth more today than it will be when they retire. Have students calculate what $35,000 will be worth in one year, assuming 5% interest, using the equation $PV = amt / (1 + r)^n$. ($PV = \$35,000 / (1 + .05)^1 = \$35,000 / 1.05 = \$33,333.33$). For an extension exercise that calculates the present value of a payment stream, go to page 77.

 Activity correlates to Math standards.

74

Entrepreneurship

Chapter Objectives After completing this chapter, you will be able to:

▶ **Section 5.1** *Rewards and Challenges of Entrepreneurship*
- **Define** entrepreneur and entrepreneurship.
- **List** at least five rewards of being an entrepreneur.
- **Identify** at least four challenges of being an entrepreneur.
- **Discuss** why entrepreneurs are important to the American economy.

▶ **Section 5.2** *The Business Plan*
- **Discuss** the initial steps in setting up a business.
- **Identify** the parts of a business plan.

Ask **STANDARD &POOR'S** **The Value of a Long-Term Investment Strategy**

Q: I have read that it is important for a new investor to invest for the long-term. What does this mean, why is this important, and how do I do it?

A: "Long-term" usually means five years or beyond. Investments meant for the long term, such as stocks, tend to fluctuate. Money designated for short-term events is best kept in safer havens, such as savings accounts. The risk of loss in the stock market diminishes with time, though.

Mathematics You are planning to save for 20 years of retirement. Just before you retire, your annual salary will be the equivalent of about $50,000 in today's dollars. You will need 70% to 80% of your pre-retirement income to maintain your lifestyle. Based on this rule, you would need a minimum of $35,000 for your first year of retirement. Replace the variables in the algebraic expression below and evaluate the expression to calculate how much money you will need to retire.

$$\text{Evaluate } x \bullet y \text{ if } x = 20 \text{ and } y = \$35,000$$

THEORY **Algebra: Variables and Expressions** Algebra is a language of symbols. A variable is a symbol, often a letter, used to represent a number. Algebraic expressions are combinations of variables, numbers, and at least one operation. Once the variables have been replaced, you can evaluate, or find the value of, the algebraic expression.

74 Unit 2 Owning and Operating a Business

Classroom Resources

- Student Edition
- Teacher Wraparound Edition
- Student Activity Workbook with Academic Integration
- Student Activity Workbook with Academic Integration TAE
- *Fast File*, Unit 2 Resources
- Inclusion in the Business Education Classroom

- TeacherWorks Plus
- *ExamView Assessment Suite*
- Presentation Plus!
- Vocabulary PuzzleMaker
- Interactive Student Edition
- Online Student Edition
- Online Learning Center with Podcasts

● **Realizing a Dream** The opening of a new
business is a proud moment for entrepreneurs.
**What dreams might entrepreneurship turn into
reality in your life?**

Chapter 5 Entrepreneurship **75**

Review the Objectives
Introduce the chapter
by reviewing the chapter
objectives:

Section 5.1 *Objectives*
Define entrepreneur and
entrepreneurship. (Entrepreneur: Recognizes a business
opportunity. Entrepreneurship: Recognizing and testing an opportunity in the
market.)

List at least five rewards
of being an entrepreneur.
(Being the boss, doing what
you enjoy, being creative,
setting own schedule, possible substantial rewards.)

Identify at least four challenges of being an entrepreneur. (Getting funds, being
fully responsible, uncertain
income, risking time and
money.)

Discuss why entrepreneurs
are important to the
American economy.
(Entrepreneurs bring out
new goods and services and
improve on existing goods
and services. Small busi-
nesses also generate jobs.)

Section 5.2 *Objectives*
Discuss the initial steps
in setting up a business.
(Decide what to produce.
Then research competitors,
consumer wants and needs,
and costs.)

Identify the parts of a business plan. (Executive summary, management team
plan, company description,
products and service plan;
vision and mission state-
ments; industry overview;
market and competitive
analyses; marketing, operational, organizational, financial, growth, and contingency
plans; cover and title page
and table of contents.)

Discuss the Photo
● **Realizing a Dream** Read the photo caption to students: The opening of a new business is a proud moment for entrepreneurs.

Ask students to discuss their entrepreneurial dreams. (Answers will vary. Encourage
students to think seriously about the success they might find in a range of business
activities. These might include owning retail establishments that sell goods and/or
services such as restaurants, cleaners, ice cream shops, or record stores, law firms,
doctor's offices, or hair salons, or manufacturing businesses such as clothing manufacturers. Encourage students to understand that, with careful planning, they can be
successful entrepreneurs.)

FOCUS

Rewards and Challenges of Entrepreneurship

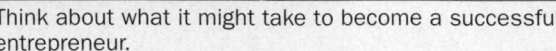
Reading Guide

● Before You Read

Think about what it might take to become a successful entrepreneur.

🔔 Bell Ringer Activity

Rewards and Challenges of Entrepreneurship
Ask students to identify a student-run business. (Answers might include a lawn service or a dog-walking service.) Follow up with some advantages of running your own business. (Being the boss, doing what you enjoy, opportunity to be creative, and flexible work schedule.)

Preteaching

Presentation Plus!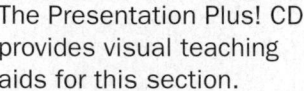
The Presentation Plus! CD provides visual teaching aids for this section.

PuzzleMaker
Use the Vocabulary PuzzleMaker to create a puzzle of the section's key terms. Students can complete the puzzle on paper or on a computer.

Graphic Organizer
Tell students to go to the Online Learning Center through **glencoe.com** for a printable graphic organizer. (Rewards: being the boss, doing what you enjoy, being creative, flexibility. Challenges: getting money to start, uncertain income, risking time and money, and working long hours.)

N C L B Connects academics to content.

Read to Learn
- Define entrepreneur and entrepreneurship.
- List at least five rewards of being an entrepreneur.
- Identify at least four challenges of being an entrepreneur.
- Discuss why entrepreneurs are important to the American economy.

The Main Idea
An entrepreneur is someone who recognizes a business opportunity and organizes, manages, and assumes the risks of starting a business. Entrepreneurs face many challenges. However, those who succeed see many rewards.

Key Concepts
- Entrepreneurship
- Rewards of Entrepreneurship
- Challenges of Entrepreneurship
- The Impact of Small Businesses

Vocabulary
Key Terms
small business
virtual business or dot-com company

D

Academic Vocabulary
You will find these words in your reading and on your tests. Make sure you know their meanings.
area
significant
research
estimate

Graphic Organizer
In a chart like the one below, list four rewards and four challenges of being an entrepreneur as you read.

Rewards	Challenges
1. _____	1. _____
2. _____	2. _____
3. _____	3. _____
4. _____	4. _____

 Go to the *Introduction to Business* Online Learning Center through **glencoe.com** for a printable graphic organizer.

Academic Standards
English Language Arts
  NCTE 1 Read texts to acquire new information
  NCTE 4 Use written language to communicate effectively
Mathematics
  Problem Solving Apply and adapt a variety of appropriate strategies to solve problems

N C L B

Reading Guide

● Before You Read

Students should recognize that a good idea, money, time, and energy are necessary.

D Develop Concepts

The Main Idea Students might assume small businesses do not play a significant role in the local economy. Ask students to name the employers of several people they know and if they think small businesses are important to the local community. (Students should recognize that many people own or work for small businesses.)

Entrepreneurship

If you have ever thought about going into business for yourself, then you have thought about becoming an entrepreneur. An entrepreneur is a person who recognizes a business opportunity and organizes, manages, and assumes the risks of starting and operating a business. Entrepreneurship is the process of recognizing an opportunity, testing it in the market, and gathering the resources necessary to go into business.

Creating and running a business venture requires a variety of skills. A *venture* is a new business undertaking that involves risk. Even if you do not become an entrepreneur, the lessons you learn about entrepreneurship will help you in any job. Knowing more about business will also benefit you as a consumer.

Personal Characteristics of Entrepreneurs

Most entrepreneurs have similar characteristics. The Small Business Administration (SBA) created a checklist to help people see if they have the recommended traits for a career in entrepreneurship. These traits include leadership, decision-making, self-discipline, planning, and people skills.

As You Read

Think about a business opportunity offering a service that could be improved. What type of service would you choose?

Figure 5.1 — *Twelve Characteristics of Successful Entrepreneurs*

Persistent Entrepreneurs are willing to work until a job is done, no matter how long it takes.

Risk-taking Entrepreneurs take risks, but they are not reckless.

Self-confident Entrepreneurs believe in themselves.

Restless Once entrepreneurs achieve their goals, they start looking for new challenges.

Goal-oriented Entrepreneurs set and achieve goals.

Action-oriented Entrepreneurs are doers instead of spectators. They take action.

Responsible Entrepreneurs take responsibility for their decisions and actions.

Self-demanding Entrepreneurs have high expectations.

Creative Entrepreneurs look for new ways to solve old problems.

Independent Entrepreneurs want to make their own decisions.

Inquisitive Entrepreneurs conduct research and ask questions to solve problems.

Enthusiastic Entrepreneurs are energetic and passionate about their pursuits.

● **Ranking the 12 Traits** Entrepreneurs plan for success by setting goals. **In what order would you rank the importance of these entrepreneurial characteristics?**

As You Read

Answers will vary. For example an appliance repair service might narrow the time window for a service call to two hours instead of four.

Figure 5.1

● **Ranking the 12 Traits** Answers will depend on students' opinions on the importance of each characteristic. Encourage students to understand that although they are likely to be naturally inclined in several of these areas, they should strive to practice each of the traits throughout their studies.

TEACH

Discussion Starter
Entrepreneurship
Ask students if they have ever seen a new product or service and wondered, "Why didn't I think of that?" Point out that an entrepreneur recognizes a business opportunity and then takes action.

R Reading Strategy

Provide Examples Refer students to **Figure 5.1** (showing traits of successful entrepreneurs). Point out that most people have many of these traits. Have students look at the list of traits and write an example related to their own life for a few of the traits listed. Ask volunteers to share their examples. (Answers will vary. Examples will likely relate to academics, sports, extracurricular activities, hobbies, and family responsibilities.)

Extension Activity Point out that the Ask S&P calculation on page 74 assumes that on the first day of retirement the retiree has $700,000 in an account that pays no interest. It is more likely that the money would be invested in an interest-bearing account. Have students use a spreadsheet to calculate the minimum amount needed at retirement. Instruct students to use the present value function: PV(rate, nper, pmt, [fv], [type]). Assume 20 annual payments of $35,000 at an annual interest rate of 5%. Set FV = 0 and type as 1. (Based on the above data, the amount needed at retirement is $457,986.23.)

TEACH (cont.)

S Skill Practice

Guided Practice

Express an Opinion Ask students whether it is a good idea to start a business on the Internet. (Answers will vary. Students are likely to base their opinions on their own experiences with Internet-based businesses. Encourage students to think more deeply and consider reasons Internet businesses might be easier to start than traditional stores or services businesses because they do not need to find and rent physical premises.) **L1**

Illustrate the Idea Have students create an illustration for information presented in the "Internet Businesses" section. (Illustrations should reflect the content.) **L2**

Summarize Ask students to find an article that contains information about starting an Internet-based business and to write a brief summary of the article with a properly formatted reference citation. (Provide students with an example of the format you want them to use for the citation.) **L3**

ASSESS

Review Key Terms

Have students write sentences using each key term.

 **Study-to-Go** Have students go to the Online Learning Center through **glencoe.com** to download free **Study-to-Go** content to their PDAs or cell phones.

Small Businesses

The SBA is a U.S. government agency that protects the interests of small businesses. It defines a **small business** as an independently owned business that usually has the owner as its manager. A small business serves a limited geographic **area** and employs fewer than 500 people.

Internet Businesses

Many entrepreneurs open virtual businesses. A **virtual business** or **dot-com company** is a business that operates on the Internet. Many dot-com companies make shopping easier and more efficient for consumers. This shows how an entrepreneurial venture can make a **significant** improvement to what already exists.

Online businesses have the potential to attract a huge number of customers. Anyone who has an Internet connection can purchase from them. According to *American City Business Journals*, small businesses that use the Internet have grown more than 45 percent faster than those that do not.

BusinessWeek *Reader and Case Study*

Get Creative! How to Build Innovative Companies

Listen closely. There's a new conversation under way across America that may well change your future. If you work for Procter & Gamble Co. or General Electric Co., you already know what's going on. If you don't, you might want to stop what you're doing and consider this:

The Knowledge Economy as we know it is being eclipsed by something new—call it the Creative Economy. Even as policymakers and pundits wring their hands over the outsourcing of engineering, software writing, accounting, and myriad other high-tech, high-end service jobs—not to mention the move of manufacturing to Asia—U.S. companies are evolving to the next level of economic activity.

What was once central to corporations—price, quality, and much of the left-brain, digitized analytical work associated with knowledge—is fast being shipped off to lower-paid, highly trained Chinese and Indians, as well as Hungarians, Czechs, and Russians. Increasingly, the new

core competence is creativity—the right-brain stuff that smart companies are now harnessing to generate top-line growth. The game is changing. It isn't just about math and science anymore. It's about creativity, imagination, and, above all, innovation.

 CASE STUDY Go to the *Introduction to Business* Online Learning Center through **glencoe.com** for the *BusinessWeek* Reader Case Study.

Active Learning

Work with a partner to start thinking creatively, use your imaginations, and innovate a new product. Choose one person to write copy for an ad for the new product. Have the other person draw the product, placing it in a setting most likely to attract buyers. Present your finished ad to your class.

BusinessWeek *Reader and Case Study*

Get Creative! How to Build Innovative Companies

 CASE STUDY Have students go to the *Introduction to Business* Online Learning Center through **glencoe.com** to download a Case Study activity that corresponds to the article. The activity and answer key are also available on the TeacherWorks Plus CD.

Active Learning

Products and ads will vary. Encourage students to explain how they came up with the product and ad. Encourage the class to provide feedback that will help students refine their innovation process.

Rewards of Entrepreneurship

People become entrepreneurs for a number of reasons besides making money. Being the boss, doing what they enjoy, and using their creativity are just a few.

Being the Boss

An important advantage of being a small-business owner is the ability to be in charge. In fact, this is the main reason people become entrepreneurs. Unlike people who run corporations and partnerships, entrepreneurs do not have to consult with others before making a decision.

Doing What You Enjoy

A business venture typically starts with an activity that the entrepreneur enjoys. Someone who enjoys cooking for others might start a catering business. Someone who likes to ride bikes might open a bike shop. The new business owner gets satisfaction from developing the enterprise.

R ### Having the Opportunity to Be Creative

Most people who work for others follow procedures. Entrepreneurs make procedures. They are able to shape a business in ways employees cannot. This is especially true with daring or creative ideas. A business owner with a creative idea has the power to act on it.

Building an Enterprise

Many successful entrepreneurs work in a related business before starting their own company. People who decide to open a business must consider whether to buy an existing company or start a new one. They must **research** the viability of the venture and choose the form of business to start.

✔ Reading Check   **Identify** What are some reasons to become an entrepreneur?

U ***Sole Proprietorships, Partnerships, and Corporations*** Most U.S. businesses are *sole proprietorships,* which means they are owned and operated by one person. Another form of business is a partnership. A *partnership* is owned and run by two or more people. A *corporation* has many owners. Corporations are run by a chief executive officer, who answers to a board of directors.

Sole proprietors do not share their company's income and expenses, profits or losses. All responsibilities rest with the sole proprietor. The sole proprietor assumes all of the risks and reaps all of the benefits. You will learn more about the different types of business organizations in Chapter 6.

Young Entrepreneurs More than ever, teens are starting businesses across the country. The SBA even offers a teen business link at its Web site. The link helps teens determine if their ideas have potential. The site also helps put them on a path toward entrepreneurship. *List reasons for teens to strike out on their own. Research entrepreneurs who started businesses while they were still students.*

W

● **As You Read**

Think about an activity you enjoy that would make a good business venture.

RETEACH

W Writing Support

Enrichment
Profile an Entrepreneur
Instruct students to write a short profile of a young entrepreneur who has been featured in the media. In addition to the profile, have them write a probing question they would like to ask the entrepreneur about the challenges of entrepreneurship. (Profiles should include basic information about the person and his or her business.)

R Reading Strategy

Compare and Contrast
Have students create a chart to compare and contrast the importance of the rewards from doing what they enjoy with the importance of being able to be creative. (Answers will vary depending on the student's values, interests and goals.)

U Universal Access

Reading Comprehension
Ask students to use a dictionary to look up the meaning of the word *proprietor*. Point out that this paragraph introduces forms of business ownership that will be presented in more detail in Chapter 6.

✔ Reading Check

Identify Students may choose being their own boss, being creative, or making their own hours.

Young Entrepreneurs Students may identify factors such as making money, creating their own hours, having an interest in a particular activity, seeing an opportunity to meet a need. They may talk about Michael Dell, Steve Jobs, Tony Hawk, or others who started businesses as students.

● **As You Read**

Students who like watching movies could start a new movie rental store or buy an existing one; those who enjoy reading could buy or open a bookstore; and those who like karate could buy or open a karate studio.

RETEACH (cont.)

R Reading Strategy

Paraphrase Ask students to paraphrase the section entitled "Other Reasons for Entrepreneurship." (Discussions will vary but should include both the benefits of entrepreneurship and types of businesses that can be started.)

W Writing Support

Develop an Argument
Pitch Your Idea Ask students to brainstorm a list of five or more reasons that other people should invest in a business they might like to start. Have students assemble the parts of the list into a short argument that they could use to pitch the idea to someone who might lend them the money. (Lists and arguments should vary depending on the type of business selected, the student's perception of the growth potential for the business, and to whom they will make the pitch.)

✔ Reading Check

Identify Answers may include: consulting services, editing services, housekeeping, bookkeeping, and technology services such as graphic design and Web-site design.

Virtual Business

Introduce market segmentation to students using Virtual Business Retailing Marketing Segmentation activity. In this simulation, students learn why market segmentation is important to the success of a business.

80

? ETHICS in Business

Facing Money Problems

■ **Critical Reading** Life is full of important decisions that must be made. Think about the kinds of decisions that you make as you read the question below.

You are an entrepreneur trying to build a new business. One of your most important clients is late paying your recent invoice because its computerized accounting system is down. You face a cash-flow problem. Since your client has not paid you, you cannot pay all of your bills. However, you could get by if you did not pay your rent for the month.

■ **Decision Making** What are some ways of handling this situation so that you maintain relationships with your clients, landlord, and other vendors while acting ethically? Explain your answer.

Real World

Home-Based Businesses Some home-business experts say the best opportunities to start a home-based business stem from tasks employees do for their employer. *What tasks might an employee of an Internet bookstore perform as part of a home-based business?*

Other Reasons for Entrepreneurship

 Entrepreneurs enjoy developing their own schedule. Many run home-based businesses, such as consultancies, or editing, housekeeping, and bookkeeping services. They make an economic contribution to their community through investment and the creation of jobs. Entrepreneurs are rewarded for assuming risk.

✔ Reading Check
Identify Name some types of home-based businesses.

Challenges of Entrepreneurship

There are rewards to becoming an entrepreneur. There are also some challenges that business owners deal with in order to be successful.

Getting Funds to Start the Business

One of the biggest obstacles in starting a business is obtaining financing. Most people must borrow money to start their business. It is often difficult to get loans from financial institutions. They are concerned about whether the business would succeed and they would be repaid.

Being Fully Responsible for the Business

Business owners are responsible for more than just decision making. They must see that everything gets done—from sweeping the floors and paying the bills, to hiring employees and making repairs. Duties include handling financial records as well as training employees.

Real World

Home-Based Businesses Answers may vary, but tasks could include reviewing and processing orders, notifying customers of deliveries and delays, or managing the company's Web site.

? ETHICS in Business

Decision Making Answers might suggest that being honest with everyone up front will help you maintain good relationships. It would also be appropriate to let your client know that their late payment is affecting you.

Other Challenges for Entrepreneurs

Entrepreneurs also face the challenge of feeling alone and insecure about making the right decisions. They work long hours, especially during start-up. They also face uncertain income levels and the risk of losing their investment if the business fails. About four out of five small businesses fail in their first five years. Most failures are due to inadequate financial planning and management, and a poor response to change.

The Impact of Small Businesses

More than 99 percent of U.S. firms are small businesses. Small businesses employ more than 50 percent of the U.S. workforce. A majority of them are one-person operations that generate more than half the nation's income. Small businesses are also the principal source of new jobs. Some **estimate** that two-thirds of all new jobs are generated by small businesses. The number of virtual businesses continues to increase. This allows more small businesses to enter the global marketplace and other economies.

 Activity correlates to Math standards.

● **As You Read**

Think about ways you could lose an investment in a new business. What can be done to help prevent this from happening?

Section 5.1

● **After You Read**

Review Key Concepts
1. What are some characteristics of successful entrepreneurs?
2. What reward is the main reason most people become an entrepreneur?
3. Identify some of the challenges of entrepreneurship.

Academic Skills
4. **Mathematics** Rick is thinking about starting his own business. The start-up costs he has identified include $12,000 to lease an office, $25,000 for inventory, and $30,000 for the first year's payroll. For the first year, he projects that he would make a slight profit of $3,250. Would it be better to use the money to open the business or to invest the money in a savings bond with a first-year return of 5.99 percent?

THEORY Problem Solving: Adapt Strategies Read word problems carefully to make sure you know what you are being asked. It sometimes helps to restate the question in your own words. In this problem, you are asked to make a judgment about which is more valuable, $3,250 in profit from a new business or 5.99 percent of the sum of $12,000 + $25,000 + $30,000.

 For math help, go to the Math Appendix.

@ Go to the *Introduction to Business* Online Learning Center through **glencoe.com** to check your answers.

Section 5.1

Review Key Concepts
1. risk-taking, self-confident, restless, goal-oriented, independent, inquisitive, and enthusiastic
2. being your own boss
3. getting funds to start the business and being fully responsible for it

Academic Skills
4. **Mathematics** The savings bond would yield more that $3,250 in the first year. 5.99% ($12,000 + $25,000 + $30,000) = $4,013.30. Investing in a new business that is profitable in the first year could be much more valuable in the long run.

Section 5.1

RETEACH (cont.)

C Critical Thinking

Connect to the Global Marketplace Ask students why an increase in the number of virtual businesses allows small businesses to enter the global marketplace. (Virtual businesses are not limited by geography. Virtual entrepreneurs can develop customers all over the globe.)

● **As You Read**

Knowing your market, pricing your product or service appropriately, having some prior experience.

Student Activity Workbook Assign the Section 5.1 Activities.

ASSESS

● **After You Read**

Have students complete the Section 5.1 After You Read section review.

Online Study Tools
Have students go to the Online Learning Center through **glencoe.com** to:
- Take the Section 5.1 **Practice Test**.
- Download free **Study-to-Go** content to their PDAs or cell phones.

CLOSE

Culminating Activity Think Like an Entrepreneur Ask students to develop an idea for goods or services. (Answers should include a description of the product or service.)

81

FOCUS

Bell Ringer Activity

The Business Plan
Point out that planning is the key to success in many areas. Teachers have lesson plans, healthcare providers have treatment plans, and coaches have game plans. Ask students to provide some examples of plans from their own lives. (Some students might mention career plans or more immediate plans for a vacation.)

Preteaching

Presentation Plus!
The Presentation Plus! CD provides visual teaching aids for this section.

PuzzleMaker
Use the Vocabulary PuzzleMaker to create a puzzle of the section's key terms. Students can complete the puzzle on paper or on a computer.

Graphic Organizer
Tell students to go to the Online Learning Center through **glencoe.com** for a printable graphic organizer. (The graphic organizer should include all parts of the business plan as shown on **Figure 5.2**.)

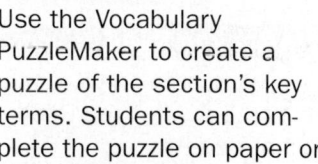 Connects academics to content.

82

The Business Plan

Reading Guide

● Before You Read

Think of some reasons for having a business plan before starting a business.

Read to Learn
- Describe how to prepare for your own business.
- Discuss the parts of a business plan.

The Main Idea
Once an entrepreneur discovers a good business opportunity, the next step is to do market research. Market research helps to determine whether there will be a demand for a new product or service. It can also uncover issues to address in a business plan.

Key Concepts
- Initial Steps in Setting up a Business
- Parts of a Business Plan

Vocabulary
Key Terms
business plan
executive summary
vision statement
mission statement

Academic Vocabulary
You will find these words in your reading and on your tests. Make sure you know their meanings.

section   established
concept   data

Graphic Organizer
Using a figure like the one below, fill in the parts of a business plan as you read.

 Go to the *Introduction to Business* Online Learning Center through **glencoe.com** for a printable graphic organizer.

Academic Standards
English Language Arts
> **NCTE 1** Read texts to acquire new information
> **NCTE 4** Use written language to communicate effectively
> **NCTE 7** Conduct research and gather, evaluate, and synthesize data to communicate discoveries
> **NCTE 11** Participate as members of literacy communities
> **NCTE 12** Use language to accomplish individual purposes

Science
> **Content Standard G** Students should develop understanding of science as a human endeavor, nature of scientific knowledge, and historical perspectives

---

Reading Guide

● Before You Read

Students may identify planning as a way of getting organized, identifying goals, or figuring out how much their idea would cost.

D Develop Concepts

The Main Idea Ask students: Why is market research an important part of developing a new product? (Students should understand that just because they think something is a good idea does not guarantee that others will want their product or service.)

Initial Steps in Setting up a Business

Before you decide to start a particular business, you need to see if there is a demand for your product or service. This requires doing market research. If your market research shows that your business has the potential to succeed, then develop a business plan. A **business plan** is a written description of a new business venture that describes all aspects of the business. It helps entrepreneurs focus on what they want to do, how they will do it, and what they expect to accomplish. The business plan is used by potential investors and financing agencies that new entrepreneurs go to for start-up funds.

Checklist for Starting a Venture

A checklist is a good way to organize your thinking when you begin planning your own business. Entrepreneurs should keep these questions and their answers in mind as they develop and write their business plan.

Here are some questions to consider:

- What will I produce?
- Who are my main competitors?
- Why is my product or service needed?
- How much will my product or service cost to produce?
- How many people will I need to run the business?
- What physical facilities will I need?
- What licenses, permits, or other legal documents do I need?
- How much money will I need to get started?

✔ Reading Check | **Identify** List some questions to consider before starting a business.

Parts of a Business Plan

A business plan must be well organized and easy to read. It must also follow a logical format. There are 15 essential parts of a business plan.

Executive Summary

The **executive summary** is a brief account of the key points contained in a business plan. It should be no more than two pages and should include the most important information from each section of the plan. It should open with a compelling story to persuade the reader that the business is going to succeed. Then it should support that statement with evidence gathered through market research.

Section 5.2 The Business Plan **83**

● **As You Read**

Examples of acceptable answers include: The business plan provides a snapshot of the business to help investors see the entrepreneur's vision. It helps the entrepreneur organize the business before starting it. It helps the entrepreneur set goals.

● **Selling the Business Plan** Most lenders prefer to meet with entrepreneurs before giving them a loan based on a business plan. **Why do they want to meet with the entrepreneur?**

Management Team Plan

This section presents your qualifications and those of any partners you might have. You must describe your team's capabilities to execute your business **concept**. You should discuss how you will fill gaps in expertise. You may need to hire consultants, or form partnerships or advisory boards.

Company Description

The description of the firm provides an outline of the business. It helps investors understand the size, scope, and type of business you plan to start. It describes the business opportunity and explains why the venture will succeed.

Product and Service Plan

Describe the product or service you want to offer. The nature of your business should be clear. You should note the unique features of the product or service and possible spin-offs. Spin-offs are additional products and services that you might offer when the business is more **established**. They show that the venture has growth potential.

● As You Read

Prospective entrepreneurs must convince potential investors, such as banks, that they are capable of making their business a success. What qualifications do you have that could be presented in your business plan? How would you handle the gaps in experience you might have?

S

Vision and Mission Statements

The vision and mission statements section states the guiding principles by which a business functions. A **vision statement** establishes the scope and purpose of a company and reflects its values and beliefs. A **mission statement** expresses the specific aspirations of a company, the major goals it will try to reach.

84 **Chapter 5** Entrepreneurship

● As You Read

Students might include informal work experience and skills they have gained through extracurricular activities. Students might suggest their willingness to work hard and learn new things. They also might suggest using a partner to help bridge the gap.

Discuss the Photo
● **Selling the Business Plan** Lenders prefer to meet with entrepreneurs in order to get answers to questions about the plan and the proposed business. They also want the face-to-face meeting to help determine if the individual has the skills necessary to be successful.

Industry Overview

This section presents your research of the industry. Every business operates within an industry. Think of your industry as companies that provide similar, complementary, or different products and services. Discuss trends and growth within the industry.

Market Analysis

This section presents research about your customer profile. The results help you determine your overall marketing and sales strategies. In addition, this section analyzes your customers and the competition. Include geographic, economic, and demographic **data** about the target market and business location.

Competitive Analysis

Indicate how the proposed business has an advantage over its competitors. You can gather information on competitors by viewing their Web sites; talking to their customers, vendors, suppliers, and employees; and attending trade shows. See if any articles have been written about them.

Marketing Plan

A marketing plan discusses how a company makes its customers aware of its products or services. It includes features such as the market niche, pricing, company image, marketing tactics, a media plan, and a marketing budget.

Real World

Mission Statements
A mission statement should clearly express a company's main goals. Find an example of a good mission statement on the Internet. *What makes your example a good model?*

W

Science/Tech TRENDS

The Technology Sector
Digital technology has the ability to improve our personal and business lives in many ways. Technology is one of the fastest growing sectors of our economy. The increasing demand for consumer electronics, such as iPods and digital cameras, the popularity of cell phones, and the opening up of new markets around the world have fueled the impressive growth of this sector. For the individual investor, buying shares in a technology sector mutual fund is a way to capitalize on this growth. However, investing in a single sector of the economy carries with it greater risk than does a more diversified approach to investing.

Web Quest

Go to the *Introduction to Business* Online Learning Center through **glencoe.com** for links to Web sites where you can find more information about technology sector mutual funds. List one or two mutual funds as examples. Then write a sentence or two describing their investment strategies, goals, and objectives.

glencoe.com

RETEACH

W Writing Support

Enrichment Many organizations—including schools, government agencies, and nonprofit organizations—have developed vision statements and mission statements. Ask students to write a vision statement and mission statement for this class. If your school has a vision statement and mission statement, share them with students before they begin writing. (Statements will vary. The vision statement should establish the scope and purpose of the course and reflect the values and beliefs shared by the students and teacher. The mission statement should express the specific aspiration of the class.)

R Reading Strategy

Make a List Have students draw a diagram or picture to illustrate the ideas presented under the heading "Competitive Analysis." (Illustrations will vary. The advantages the proposed business has over competitors should be clear.)

U Universal Access

Visual Learners Ask students to use presentation software to illustrate the contents presented under the heading "Marketing Plan." Invite a volunteer to present the information to the class.

NCLB Activity correlates to Science standards.

Real World

Mission Statements Students should point out examples that display clear core beliefs and values, what the company is about, or the company's purpose. Suggest that students look at a government agency or a university's Web site for examples.

Science/Tech TRENDS

Web Quest

The Technology Sector Students might note that technology sector funds typically invests a minimum of 65% of assets in the technology sector. Funds focusing on this sector are growth-oriented and likely to invest in equities, the stocks of fast-growing companies.

RETEACH (cont.)

 Critical Thinking

Planning Ahead

Organizational Plan Ask students these questions: Why is an organizational plan an important part of a business plan? Ask students if the organizational plan should include room to make changes. (Answers will vary. Students should realize that the organizational plan sets the hierarchy of who will make the important decisions. However, as the company grows and changes, it will be necessary to change the organization to accommodate growth.)

 Writing Support

Supporting the Main Idea

Growth Plan Ask students to research the history of a large company like Microsoft or Apple that has undergone explosive growth over a period of only a few decades. Have the students write several paragraphs of details that support the idea that investors and lenders need to know that a company has plans to deal with growth. (Answers will vary depending on the company chosen but are likely to include milestones such as the hiring of staff and business incorporation as well as business challenges caused by the need to grow the company.)

Operational Plan

The operational plan includes the business processes that result in production and delivery of the product or service.

Organizational Plan

C This part looks at the people who will run the firm as well as management's philosophy. The form of business organization that is chosen, such as a sole proprietorship, is also discussed.

Financial Plan

This section presents forecasts for the business. Data are usually shown in financial statements. The plan provides proof that the new business will be financially healthy.

Growth Plan

W The growth plan looks at how the business will expand in the future. Investors and lenders like to know that a business has plans to grow and deal with growth.

Figure 5.2 — *Parts of a Business Plan*

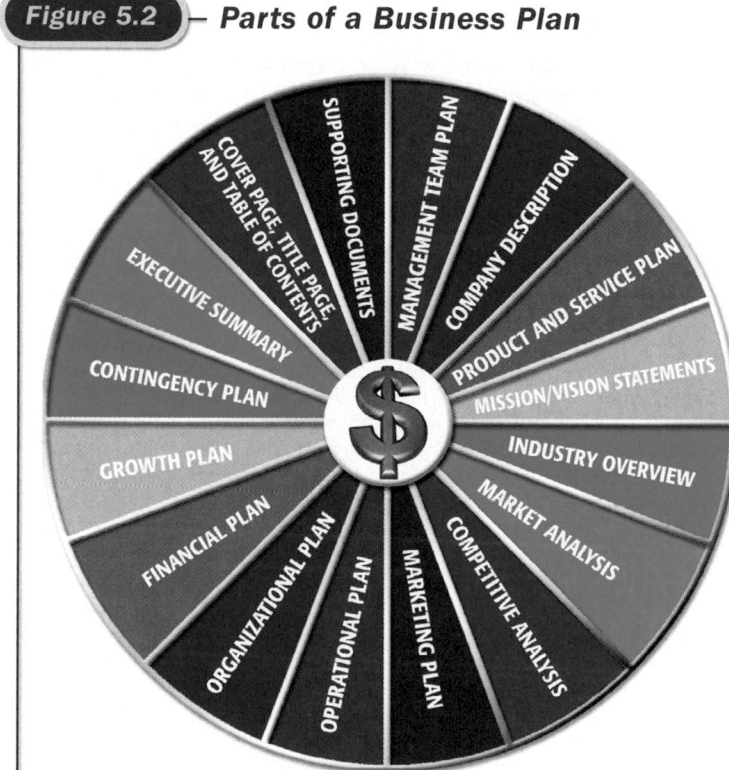

● **Creating a Business Plan** There are several steps involved in creating a business plan. **Do you think one part of the business plan is more important than the others?**

Figure 5.2

● **Creating a Business Plan** Students should explain their choices. For example, a student may think the market analysis is most important. Encourage students to understand that each part of the business plan will be important to potential lenders and investors so that they understand the need to give careful thought to polishing each aspect of their plan. Have students refer to the Business Plan Appendix for a detailed, step-by-step approach to creating a business plan.

Contingency Plan

 The contingency plan looks at likely risks to the business, such as lower-than-expected sales and emergencies that might affect it. It then suggests a way to minimize risk.

Cover Page, Title Page, Table of Contents, and Supporting Documents

The cover page should include the company's name, address, phone number, Web site and e-mail addresses, and logo. The title page follows the cover page. It includes the company name; the names, titles, and addresses of the owners; the date the plan was submitted; and the name of its preparer. The table of contents details the components of the business plan. Supporting documents include exhibits and other information relevant to the business.

N C L B Activity correlates to English Language Arts standards.

Section 5.2

After You Read

Review Key Concepts

1. Why is a business plan important?
2. Why should entrepreneurs carefully study their competitors before starting a business?
3. Why is a growth plan important to include in a business plan?

Academic Skills

4. **English Language Arts** With a partner or small group, brainstorm and write questions you can use to interview two or three entrepreneurs or small-business owners. Think of questions that will get the interviewees to tell how their lives changed as a result of starting or running a small business. Present the interview results to the class as part of a panel discussion. Compare and contrast the stories with information presented in the text.

5. **English Language Arts** You want to strengthen your entrepreneurial skills. Complete these steps to learn more about other entrepreneurs and yourself:

   - Reading: Go online or to the library and read articles and books about entrepreneurial activities.
   - Writing: Write about individuals you know who are entrepreneurs and the obstacles they had to overcome.
   - Watching: Find films about athletes, businesspeople, or others who achieved success.
   - Practice: Find case studies that involve goals, creativity, and risk taking.

@ Go to the *Introduction to Business* Online Learning Center through **glencoe.com** to check your answers.

glencoe.com

87

Chapter 5 Review and Activities

Vocabulary Review

1. Students should write complete sentences using each term correctly.

Review Key Concepts

2. An entrepreneur recognizes a business opportunity and organizes, manages, and assumes the risk of starting and operating it. Entrepreneurship is the process of recognizing an opportunity, testing it in the market, and gathering the necessary resources to start.

3. being the boss, being creative, building an enterprise, setting own schedule, contributing to the community

4. getting start-up funds, being fully responsible, feeling alone, working long hours, possibility of losing investment

5. Entrepreneurs improve existing goods and bring out new goods.

6. Entrepreneurs should ask themselves: What will I produce? Who are my competitors? Why will consumers want or need my product or service? How much will it cost to produce?

7. executive summary, management team plan, company description, product and service plan, vision and mission statements, industry overview, market and competitive analysis; marketing, operational, organizational, financial, growth, and contingency plans; cover page, title page, and table of contents

---

Section 5.1 Summary

Rewards and Challenges of Entrepreneurship An entrepreneur is a person who recognizes a business opportunity, tests it in the market, and gathers the resources necessary to start and operate a business. Entrepreneurs make or sell products or services to meet consumers' wants and needs. Some advantages of being an entrepreneur include being the boss, doing what you enjoy, having the opportunity to be creative, building an enterprise, and possibly making a substantial income. Challenges include getting start-up funds, risk of failure, and having an uncertain income. Small businesses are important to the U.S. economy because they provide goods and services, and jobs.

Section 5.2 Summary

The Business Plan Before you decide to start a particular business, you need to see if there is demand for your product or service. This requires doing market research. If research shows that you have a viable business, then develop a business plan. A business plan is a written description of a new business venture. It describes all aspects of the business. It also helps entrepreneurs to focus on exactly what they want to do, how they will do it, and what they expect to accomplish. The business plan is an essential tool to attract potential investors and financing agencies for start-up funds. It includes a description of the firm, market analysis, competitive analysis, and financial information.

Vocabulary Review

1. On a sheet of paper, use each of these key terms and academic vocabulary terms in a sentence.

Key Terms	Academic Vocabulary	
small business	area	section
virtual business or dot-com company	significant	concept
business plan	research	established
executive summary	estimate	data
vision statement		
mission statement		

Review Key Concepts

2. Define entrepreneur and entrepreneurship.

3. Describe five rewards of being an entrepreneur.

4. Describe four challenges of being an entrepreneur.

5. Describe the reasons entrepreneurs are important to the American economy.

6. Describe how to prepare for your own business.

7. Discuss the parts of a business plan.

Critical Thinking

8. Many Internet businesses fail for the same reasons as traditional businesses: owners have inadequate management skills, inadequate experience, or little start-up capital; they extend credit too freely, or kept poor records.

9. Entrepreneurs must do everything that needs to be done without someone else's direction.

10. The owner looks after all aspects of the business, including finishing tasks that employees leave undone.

Critical Thinking

8. Many Internet businesses have started and failed. Why do you think some virtual businesses fail?

9. It is important that entrepreneurs be take-charge, self-directed people. Why do you think this is true?

10. What are some reasons the owner of a business usually puts in more hours at work than an employee?

11. Why is it important for small-business owners to keep good financial records?

12. The industry overview section of the business plans calls for the entrepreneur to analyze the trends of the industry in which the entrepreneurial venture falls. Why is this information an important part of the business plan?

13. Give reasons why some small businesses fail if they do not respond quickly to change. Why do you think it is difficult for small businesses to respond quickly to change?

14. Is there a difference between being self-disciplined and self-motivated? Explain.

15. Review the 12 characteristics of successful entrepreneurs. Think about the traits that you have. Why do you think you have these traits? How could they benefit you as an entrepreneur?

Write About It

16. Look for an opportunity that you think could be turned into a small business. Write a one-page essay outlining the nature of the opportunity and why you think it has potential.

17. Select three business opportunities to pursue in your community. Talk to someone who knows the business community in your area, such as the head of the chamber of commerce. Determine whether these are good ideas. Then write an e-mail to the business leader reviewing your discussion.

18. Visit a nearby library and select a book or articles on the life of an entrepreneur. The entrepreneur could be living or deceased. Read the account, and write a report on his or her life, noting your subject's influences, obstacles, education, and experience with starting a business.

19. Go to the U.S. Census Bureau's Web site and research the latest survey of small business. Determine how many jobs are created and how much income is generated by small business. Write a 500-word report based on your findings. Discuss the importance of small businesses to economies.

Technology Applications

Internet

20. Use word-processing software to create a survey that can be sent to local small-business owners and entrepreneurs. Find out what technical skills they possess and will need in the future. As a class, compile the results using spreadsheet or database software.

Business Ethics

Making Ethical Decisions

21. For the grand opening of your hardware store, you issue flyers advertising lawn mowers for $1. However, you have only five mowers. Should you encourage customers to buy more expensive ones or issue rain checks for the advertised price?

Critical Thinking

11. to spot potential problems and determine if the business is making a profit

12. It lets readers know the entrepreneur has an understanding of trends and the nature of the business's industry.

13. If a small business does not make timely changes, competition could lure its customers away.

14. Yes. Self-disciplined people control their actions without outside direction. Self-motivated people do not need orders to set goals to get work done.

15. Answers will depend upon the students' traits. Being responsible is important in running a business because the entrepreneur must handle all aspects of the company.

Write About It

16. Answers could relate to students' surroundings while in class or on campus. Students could see opportunities for new products such as clothes, electronics, or learning materials.

17. Answers will depend upon the business opportunities students identify.

18. Choices include cosmetics maker Mary Kay Ash or Famous Amos cookie maker Walter Amos.

19. Answers should discuss the importance of small businesses to job growth and to the national economy.

Technology Applications

20. Answers will depend on replies to the surveys and databases compiled from the results.

Business Ethics

21. Definitely not. In most states, this is called bait and switch advertising and is illegal. You will create ill will. If you run out of stock, give customers a rain check.

Applying Academics to Business

22. Synonyms and related words for innovative include *groundbreaking*, *pioneering*, *inventive*, *original*, *new*, *novel*, and *modern*. Antonyms include *stale*, *unoriginal*, *worn-out*, *old-fashioned*, and *traditional*.

23. $(1.3 \times 10^{12}) \div 0.20 = 6.5 \times 10^{12} = 6.5 \times 10^{12}$

$(4.3 \times 10^{12}) \div 0.32 = 13.4 \times 10^{12} = 13.4 \times 10^{12}$

$(13.4 - 6.5) \times 10^{12} = 6.9 \times 10^{12} = \$6,900,000,000,000$

The total purchasing power of the country will grow $6.9 trillion.

24. Paragraphs might begin with a topic sentence followed by supporting details. A cause and effect paragraph might use words and phrases such as *because* or *as a result*.

25. ($3.4 million − $2.8 million) $\times 0.155 = \$93,000$

$93 thousand would be invested in research and development.

Active Learning

26. Answers will depend on family members' responses, which could include the location of the business or relationship with the owner.

Business in the Real World

27. Answers will depend on students' findings, including requirements for licensing, zoning, and permits.

Applying Academics to Business

English Language Arts

22. The ability to innovate is a key skill for a successful entrepreneur. What does it mean to be innovative? Write a sentence or two explaining what it means to be innovative. List synonyms, antonyms, and related words.

Mathematics

23. In one year, the combined purchasing power of minority groups in the United States was $1.3 trillion, or 20 percent of the country's purchasing power. It is estimated that, in 40 years, minority-group purchasing power will equal $4.3 trillion, or 32 percent of the total. By how much will the country's total purchasing power grow over 40 years?

THEORY **Numbers and Operations: Working With Large Numbers** Problems like this can be solved more easily by expressing large numbers using scientific notation. A number expressed in scientific notation is the product of a decimal between 1 and 10 and a power of 10. For example, $1,100 = 1.1 \times 10^3$.

English Language Arts

24. In one type of paragraph, a statement is followed by examples that support it. In another type, a cause is presented followed by a description of its effect. Write two paragraphs about the special skills an entrepreneur needs. Use a statement-and-example organization for one and cause-and-effect for the other.

Mathematics

25. The business plan for a large corporation called for 15.5 percent of annual profits to be reinvested in research and development (R & D) of new products. If this company shows $3.4 million in revenue and $2.8 million in expenses, how much would be invested in R & D?

THEORY **Number and Operations: Decimals and Percents** A percent can be converted to a decimal by moving the decimal point two places to the left and dropping the percent sign. To solve this problem, multiply profits (revenue less expenses) by 0.155.

Active Learning

Investigate Product Loyalties

26. Create an inventory of the products and services you and your family use that are produced or offered by small businesses. Categorize them by family member. Then interview each family member. Discover why he or she purchases the products or services from a small business. Make a report of your results. Share it with the class.

Business in the Real World

Research a Small-Business Idea

27. With a classmate, research the requirements for setting up a small business venture in your community. Investigate areas such as government regulations, financing, and the cost of leasing space and buying equipment. The local chamber of commerce might direct you in your research. Write a report on your findings.

ExamView Assessment Suite CD allows you to print out ready-made unit and chapter tests, complete with answer keys. You can also create customized tests.

TeacherWorks Plus provides complete teacher resources in one convenient package. It includes customizable lesson plans in calendar format, and instant access to many print program resources.

 **Real LIFE** • skills

INCREASING YOUR ENTREPRENEURIAL SKILLS

28. Turn back to Figure 5.1 and assess how many entrepreneurial skills you have. Identify three characteristics that you think could be improved. Write a 250-word essay on how you could improve in those areas.

 **Business CAREERS**

FIND YOUR DREAM JOB

29. Go to the *Introduction to Business* Online Learning Center through **glencoe.com** for a link to the Occupational Outlook Handbook Web site. Click on the "OOH Search/A-Z Index" link and enter the job title "operations research analyst." Then write a one-page report about this type of occupation. Conclude your report with a list of things you could do now to prepare yourself to pursue the occupation.

 **Role Play**

SUBMITTING A BUSINESS PLAN

30. Situation You are seeking funds to start a new business venture. Along with a business plan, you must give an oral presentation to a banker to consider before loaning you the money.

Activity Create a presentation that focuses on various aspects of the business plan.

Evaluation You will be evaluated on how well you meet the following performance indicators:

- Describe the new business venture.
- Cover at least seven of the parts of a business plan.
- Use visuals when necessary.
- Make persuasive arguments.
- Use clear diction and correct grammar

Standardized Test Practice

Directions Choose the letter of the best answer. Write the letter for the answer on a separate piece of paper.

1. Which word or phrase should be left out of the following sentence in order to change it from passive voice to active voice?

A <u>successful</u> owner <u>of a small business</u> <u>is one who</u> possesses <u>multiple</u> skills.

  A   successful
  B   of a small business
  C   is one who
  D   multiple

 **TEST-TAKING TIP** When answering multiple-choice questions, ask yourself if each option is true or false. This may help you find the best answer if you are unsure.

 READING Go to the *Introduction to Business* Online Learning Center through **glencoe.com** for a list of outside reading suggestions.

 **Real LIFE** • skills

28. Answers will vary depending on skills chosen.

 **Business CAREERS**

29. Nature of the work: Determine better ways to coordinate materials, equipment, and people by applying analytical methods. Requires a master's degree in operations research or in computer science, engineering, mathematics. Dual degrees in operations research and computer science are attractive. Positions as technical specialists or supervisors. Some operations research analysts become consultants. Employment is expected to grow more slowly than average. As preparation, develop math and logic skills along with computer and communication skills.

Role Play

30. Presentations should address the competencies noted but should cover at least seven areas of the business plan.

Standardized Test Practice
  1. C

 **STRATEGIES FOR STANDARDIZED TEST PREP SUCCESS**

Test Savvy Help students develop a variety of strategies for choosing the best answer choice when they're not sure of the answer to a multiple-choice question. In addition to reading each choice carefully and eliminating options they know are incorrect, they can apply the true/false test to each answer choice. Give students practice in analyzing answer choice options to determine the best one. Remind them to be careful, however, because an answer choice may be a true statement, but not the best answer to the question.

Standards-Based Lesson Planning *Introduction to Business* provides students with instruction and assessment in the following fundamental content areas:

Content Standards Correlations	
Identify the types of business.	pp. 94–98, 100–101, 104–107
Compare the forms of business ownership.	pp. 94–98, 104–107
Evaluate the role of different types of businesses and the various forms of business ownership in the United States.	pp. 94–98, 99–103, 104–107
Identify the five functions of business (accounting, finance, production, marketing, and management).	pp. 101–103, 104–107
Analyze the various functions of business operations.	pp. 101–103
Understand the interrelationships of different functional areas of business and the impact of one component on another.	pp. 101–103, 104–107
Explain the interrelationships between accounting, finance, production, marketing, and management.	pp. 101–103, 104–107
Examine the various roles of individuals; analyze influences of individuals on business and the economy.	pp. 101–103, 104–107

NCLB Activities, information, and skills practice will help your students attain No Child Left Behind proficiency. Students will improve their abilities in the following academic standards areas:

Academic Standards Correlations		
English Language Arts	Activities/Features	Page
NCTE 3 Apply strategies to interpret texts	Applying Academics to Business Standardized Test Practice	pp. 106, 107
NCTE 5 Use different writing process elements to communicate effectively	After You Read	p. 103
Mathematics		
Algebra Represent and analyze mathematical situations and structures using algebraic symbols	Applying Academics to Business	p. 106
Data Analysis and Probability Formulate questions that can be addressed with data and collect, organize, and display relevant data to answer them	After You Read	p. 98
Number and Operations Understand meanings of operations and how they relate to one another	Ask S&P	p. 92
Number and Operations Compute fluently and make reasonable estimates	Applying Academics to Business Standardized Test Practice	pp. 106, 107
Geometry Analyze characteristics of 2- and 3-dimensional geometric shapes and develop mathematical arguments about geometric relationships	Applying Academics to Business	p. 106
Science		
Content Standard G Students should develop understanding of science as a human endeavor, nature of scientific knowledge, historical perspectives	Science/Tech Trends	p. 102

Correlations This chart shows the 21st Century Skills, foundation skills, and workplace competencies that students develop as they work in this chapter.

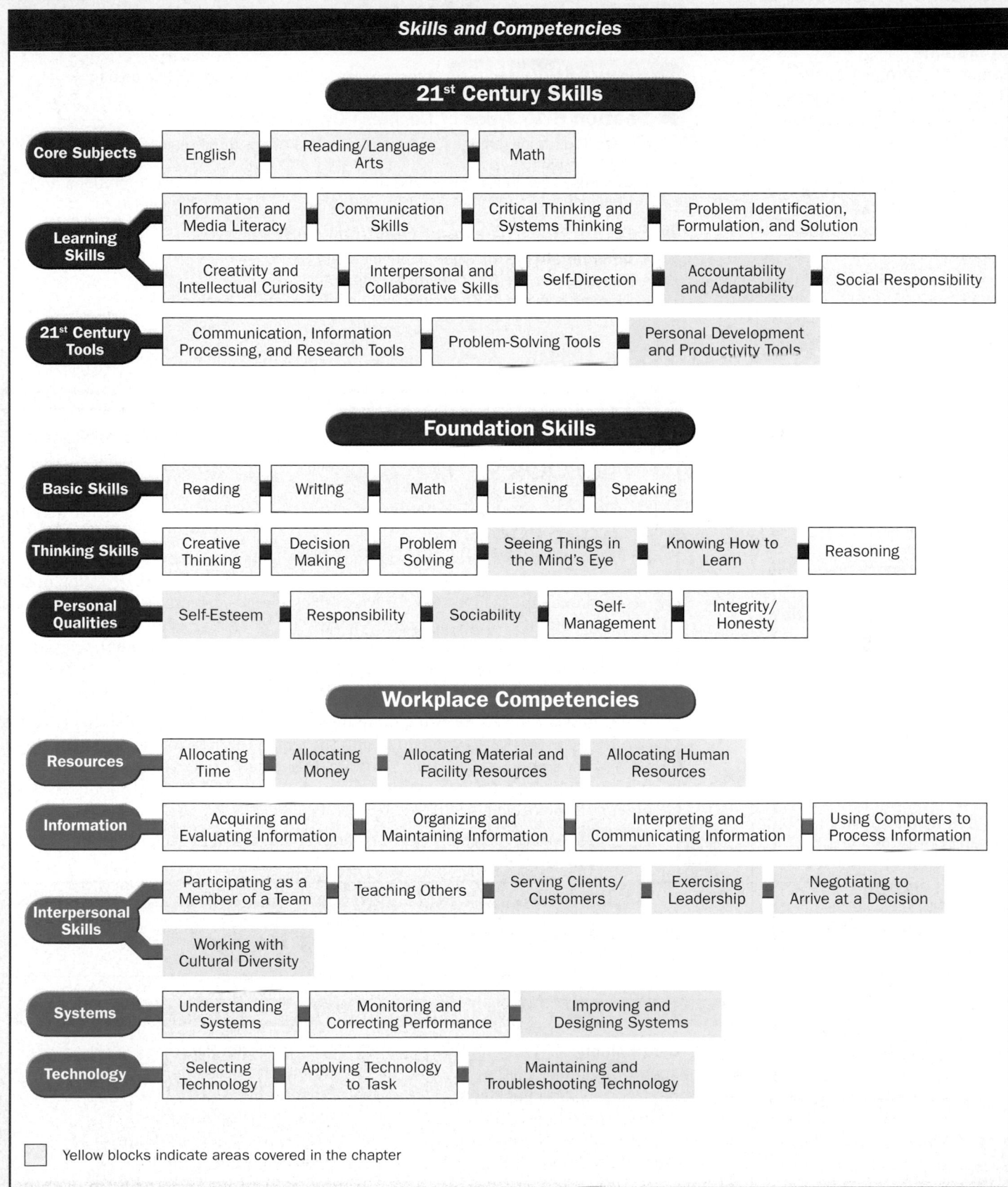

Skills and Competencies

21st Century Skills

Core Subjects: English | Reading/Language Arts | Math

Learning Skills: Information and Media Literacy | Communication Skills | Critical Thinking and Systems Thinking | Problem Identification, Formulation, and Solution | Creativity and Intellectual Curiosity | Interpersonal and Collaborative Skills | Self-Direction | Accountability and Adaptability | Social Responsibility

21st Century Tools: Communication, Information Processing, and Research Tools | Problem-Solving Tools | Personal Development and Productivity Tools

Foundation Skills

Basic Skills: Reading | Writing | Math | Listening | Speaking

Thinking Skills: Creative Thinking | Decision Making | Problem Solving | Seeing Things in the Mind's Eye | Knowing How to Learn | Reasoning

Personal Qualities: Self-Esteem | Responsibility | Sociability | Self-Management | Integrity/Honesty

Workplace Competencies

Resources: Allocating Time | Allocating Money | Allocating Material and Facility Resources | Allocating Human Resources

Information: Acquiring and Evaluating Information | Organizing and Maintaining Information | Interpreting and Communicating Information | Using Computers to Process Information

Interpersonal Skills: Participating as a Member of a Team | Teaching Others | Serving Clients/Customers | Exercising Leadership | Negotiating to Arrive at a Decision | Working with Cultural Diversity

Systems: Understanding Systems | Monitoring and Correcting Performance | Improving and Designing Systems

Technology: Selecting Technology | Applying Technology to Task | Maintaining and Troubleshooting Technology

Yellow blocks indicate areas covered in the chapter

Chapter Overview

Introduce the Chapter

Business Ownership and Operations
Chapter 6 introduces the different forms of business ownership and the five main types of businesses.

Building Background
Most people think they know someone who owns a business or a piece of a business. But they might not have the whole story. There are some basics of business ownership that everyone should know.

STANDARD &POOR'S

>> Math Answer
Linda needs to sell 12.5% of her stock. Her current stock holdings are 80% of the $100,000 portfolio, worth $80,000. She needs to sell $10,000 of stock and redistribute the proceeds in order for her stocks to be 70% of her portfolio. The $10,000 represents 12.5% of her current stock holdings.

>> Extension Activity
Liam is only five years away from retirement and has diversified his $187,000: 45% stock, 30% bonds, and 15% money market fund. Have students calculate the value of the three segments of Liam's portfolio. (Stock: $84,150; bonds: $74,800; and money market fund: $28,050.)

N C L B Activity correlates to Math standards.

Business Ownership and Operations

Chapter Objectives After completing this chapter, you will be able to:

▶ **Section 6.1** *Types of Business Ownership*
- **Describe** the advantages and disadvantages of the three major forms of business organizations.
- **Describe** how cooperatives and nonprofits are like and unlike corporations and franchises.

▶ **Section 6.2** *Types and Functions of Businesses*
- **Differentiate** the six types of businesses.
- **Describe** the five functions of business.
- **Discuss** how the five functions of business relate to each other.

Ask

STANDARD &POOR'S **The First Steps in Investing: Diversification**

Q: What is "portfolio diversification," and how can it help me achieve my investment goals?

A: Diversification is spreading your money throughout a number of investments in order to reduce risk. You can diversify through asset allocation, investing in more than one type of investment, such as stocks, bonds, or cash. You can also diversify your holdings within an asset category. With stocks, for example, you might own 20 stocks scattered across different industries. In addition, you might consider owning stocks from countries outside the United States. Economies and markets are cyclical, and diversification helps you avoid the pitfalls of those cycles.

Mathematics Linda is investing for retirement 30 years from now. She wants 70% of her money in stocks, 20% in bonds, and the remaining 10% in a money market fund. Stocks now comprise 80% of her portfolio, so she needs to rebalance her portfolio. If her portfolio is worth $100,000, what percent of her stock holdings should she sell in order to rebalance?

THEORY **Finding Percents** Percent means "per hundred." To figure out what percent of a number, a, another number, b, is, divide b by a.

N C L B

92 **Unit 2** Owning and Operating a Business

Classroom Resources

- Student Edition
- Teacher Wraparound Edition
- Student Activity Workbook with Academic Integration
- Student Activity Workbook with Academic Integration TAE
- *Fast File*, Unit 2 Resources
- Inclusion in the Business Education Classroom

- TeacherWorks Plus
- *ExamView Assessment Suite*
- Presentation Plus!
- Vocabulary PuzzleMaker
- Interactive Student Edition
- Online Student Edition
- Online Learning Center with Podcasts

● **Meeting Diverse Needs** Businesses are of different types and sizes. **Why do you think there is so much variation in the sizes and forms of businesses?**

Chapter 6 Business Ownership and Operations **93**

Review the Objectives
Introduce the chapter by reviewing the chapter objectives:

Section 6.1 *Objectives*
Describe the advantages and disadvantages of the three major forms of business organizations. (See pages 95–97 of the textbook for discussion.)

Describe how cooperatives and nonprofits are like and unlike corporations and franchises. (Cooperatives are also profit-seeking but their members are the owners and have lower tax rates. Nonprofits are similar to corporations in that they need a charter and board of directors, but are not profit-making.)

Section 6.2 *Objectives*
Differentiate the six types of businesses. (Producer: develops or gathers raw products; processor changes the raw materials into more finished goods. Manufacturer: makes finished products. Intermediary: moves goods from one business to another or to the consumer. Wholesaler: buys goods from manufacturers and resells the goods to customers. Retailer: purchases goods from wholesaler and sells them to consumer.)

Describe the five functions of business. (The functions are production, procurement, marketing, management, and finance and accounting.)

Discuss how the five functions of business relate to each other. (Nearly all business activities involve ideas from all functions of business.)

Discuss the Photo
● **Meeting Diverse Needs** Read the photo caption to students. Businesses are of many types and sizes.

Ask students: Why do you think there is so much variation in the sizes and forms of businesses. (Answers will vary but students should recognize that the size and form of a business will depend on the goods or services that it produces.)

93

Section 6.1

FOCUS

Bell Ringer Activity

Types of Business Ownership

Identify three local businesses that will be familiar to students. Try to include one business of each type—sole proprietorship, partnership, and corporation. Ask students if they know how each of the businesses is organized. (Answers will vary depending on the local businesses you identify.)

Preteaching

Presentation Plus!

The Presentation Plus! CD provides visual teaching aids for this section.

PuzzleMaker

Use the Vocabulary PuzzleMaker to create a puzzle of the section's key terms. Students can complete the puzzle on paper or on a computer.

Graphic Organizer

Tell students to go to the Online Learning Center through **glencoe.com** for a printable graphic organizer. (When completed the graphic organizer will include the three major types of business organizations: sole proprietorships, partnerships, and corporations.)

N C L B Connects academics to content.

Types of Business Ownership

Reading Guide

● Before You Read

Think about a business you would like to start, the form of organization you would use, and the type of business it would be.

Read to Learn

- Describe the advantages and disadvantages of the three major forms of business organizations.
- Describe how cooperatives and nonprofits are like and unlike corporations and franchises.

The Main Idea

Sole proprietorships, partnerships, and corporations are the most common forms of business organization. Cooperatives and nonprofits are other forms.

Key Concepts

- Organizing a Business
- Other Ways to Organize a Business

Vocabulary

Key Terms

sole proprietorship	limited liability
unlimited liability	cooperative
partnership	nonprofit organization
corporation	franchise

Academic Vocabulary

You will find these words in your reading and on your tests. Make sure you know their meanings.

sole	partners
income	regulates

Graphic Organizer

In boxes like the ones below, list the types of business organizations.

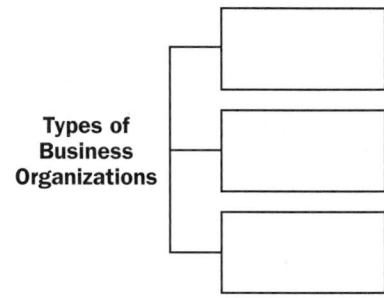

Types of Business Organizations

 Go to the *Introduction to Business* Online Learning Center through **glencoe.com** for a printable graphic organizer.

Academic Standards

English Language Arts

NCTE 1 Read texts to acquire new information

NCTE 9 Develop an understanding of diversity in language use across cultures

Mathematics

Data Analysis and Probability Formulate questions that can be addressed with data and collect, organize, and display relevant data to answer them

Reading Guide

● Before You Read

Ask students: What type of business? What form of organization you would use?

D Develop Concepts

The Main Idea Discuss the main idea with students. Ask students: Why does an entrepreneur need to know about the different types of business ownership? (Students should understand that there are advantages and disadvantages to each type of ownership.)

Organizing a Business

There are three main types of business organizations: sole proprietorships, partnerships, and corporations. As part of a business plan, entrepreneurs must decide which type best fits their situation and describe their choice and the reasons for it. During the life of a business, its form can change. These changes often occur when a business is growing.

Sole Proprietorships

About three-quarters of all businesses in the United States are sole proprietorships. A **sole proprietorship** is a business owned by one person. **Figure 6.1** includes the percentage of U.S. sole proprietorships, partnerships, and corporations.

Advantages of Owning a Sole Proprietorship Starting a sole proprietorship is easy to do. Depending on local laws, the sole proprietor might need only a license or a permit to start. Sole proprietors are in charge of their businesses. They can make all the decisions and run the companies as they see fit. As the **sole** owner, they can also keep all the profits. Finally, their income taxes are usually lower than a corporation's. Income from a sole proprietorship is taxed once. However, income from corporations can be taxed twice. A corporation pays taxes on the income it receives. Then a corporation's stockholders pay taxes on the income they receive as dividends on stock. A sole proprietor's personal tax rate is often lower than the corporate tax rate.

● **As You Read**

Suppose you decide to make and sell jewelry as a business. Why might you want to be the sole owner of the business?

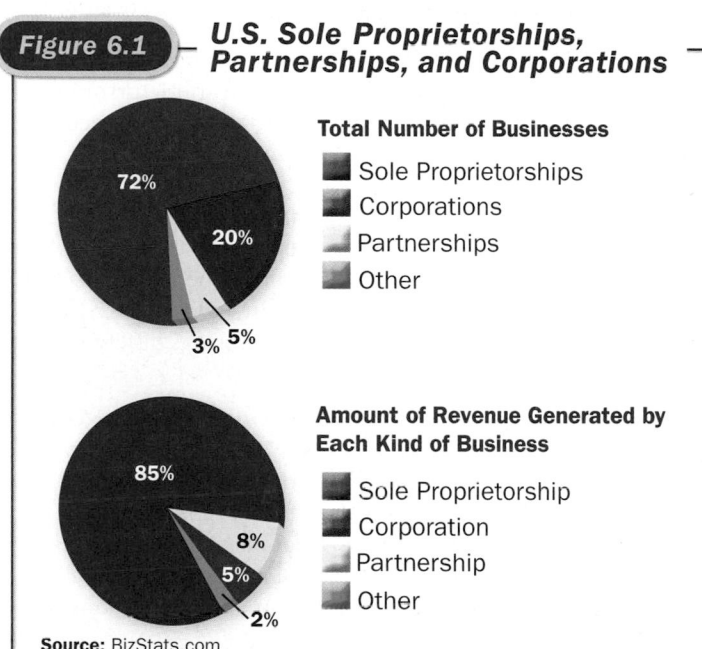

Figure 6.1

U.S. Sole Proprietorships, Partnerships, and Corporations

Total Number of Businesses

- Sole Proprietorships — 72%
- Corporations — 20%
- Partnerships — 3%
- Other — 5%

Amount of Revenue Generated by Each Kind of Business

- Sole Proprietorship — 85%
- Corporation — 8%
- Partnership — 5%
- Other — 2%

Source: BizStats.com

● **Businesses and the Revenues They Create** Various types of businesses have effects on the economy. **Which kind is most prevalent? Which kind generates the most revenue?**

TEACH

Discussion Starter
Sole Proprietorship
Ask students this question: Why do some people want to own their own business? (Answers will vary. Students might suggest some of the following: being your own boss, doing what you like to do, setting your own hours, and the potential for making lots of money.)

R Reading Strategy

Create a List Have students create a list of the advantages of the sole proprietorship form of business ownership. (Students' lists will vary slightly. Advantages include: A sole proprietorship is easy to start. The owner is in charge of the business. The owner keeps all the profit. Income taxes generally are lower than if the business was organized as a corporation.)

● **As You Read**

Answers will vary. Students should mention that it is easy to start, taxes are lower, and the owner makes all of the decisions.

Figure 6.1

● **Businesses and the Revenues They Create** Sole proprietorships are the most prevalent. Corporations generate the most revenues. Asking students to explain how the largest number of businesses can be responsible for such a small percentage of revenue. Students should understand that most sole proprietorships are small businesses. The revenue of a single large corporation can be much greater than the combined revenue of many small businesses.

TEACH (cont.)

S Skill Practice

Guided Practice

Create Bulleted Lists Have students list the advantages and disadvantages of the partnership using two bulleted lists. (Advantages: Easy to start, easier to obtain capital, partners bring different skills, and income taxed only once. Disadvantages: Partners share profits and risks, unlimited liability, and limited life.) **L1**

Illustrate an Idea Have students create a poster illustrating the advantages and disadvantages of a partnership. (All advantages and disadvantages should be included.) **L2**

Write a Vignette Have students develop a short sketch to illustrate the advantages and disadvantages of the partnership. (All advantages and disadvantages should be included.) **L3**

ASSESS

Review Key Terms

Have students write sentences using each key term.

Study-to-Go

Have students go to the Online Learning Center through **glencoe.com** to download free **Study-to-Go** content to their PDAs or cell phones.

✔ Reading Check

Identify Unlimited liability, limited access to credit, not all skills necessary to run the business, the business ends when the owner dies.

International Business

Understanding Cultural Differences

The first time you travel for business internationally, you'll probably need help with things such as booking hotels, renting a car, managing the effects of jet lag, and understanding the cultural differences of the people at your destination. A whole information industry has developed around helping the international business traveler. Now, books, magazines, and Web sites are devoted to helping unravel the mysteries of other countries and cultures so that commerce can flourish.

Examples of Languages Across Cultures

Q: In Russian, how do you say: "Do you understand?"

A: Вам понятно? (pronounced: Văm pă-nyắt-nă?)

What kinds of information do you think a first-time international business traveler needs?

● As You Read

Say you had a partner who made a bad business decision that caused your business to lose money. What steps could you take to correct the situation?

S

Disadvantages of Owning a Sole Proprietorship A major disadvantage of owning a sole proprietorship is that the owner has unlimited liability. **Unlimited liability** means the owner is responsible for the company's debts. If the owner has more debt than she or he receives in **income**, then the owner has to make up the difference.

Limited access to credit is another disadvantage. If the potential owner does not have much experience or money saved, lenders will be reluctant to offer credit. Many proprietorships fail because they run out of money. A third disadvantage is that the person in charge may not have all of the skills needed to run the business. For instance, the owner of a bakery might know everything about making cakes, but nothing about record keeping. A fourth disadvantage is that the sole proprietorship ends when the owner dies.

✔ Reading Check

Identify What are four disadvantages of owning a sole proprietorship?

Partnerships

A **partnership** is a business owned by two or more people who share its risks and rewards. To start a partnership, you need a partnership agreement. This agreement is a contract that outlines the rights and responsibilities of each partner.

Advantages of Owning a Partnership There are several advantages of owning a partnership. As with a sole proprietorship, partnerships are easy to start. Potential **partners** might need only to obtain a license. Unlike a sole proprietorship, it is easier for partnerships to obtain capital. Also, each partner usually contributes money to start the business. Another advantage is that banks are often more willing to lend money to partnerships than to sole proprietorships. Partnerships are not dependent on a sole person. As with a sole proprietorship, the income of a partnership is taxed only once. Lastly, each partner brings different skills and talents to the business.

Disadvantages of Owning a Partnership One disadvantage is that all the partners share the business risks. Problems occur when partners do not get along or one of them decides to leave. In that case, the other owners must end the partnership and reorganize the business since the original partnership no longer exists. Partners also share unlimited legal and financial liability. If one partner makes a bad decision, all partners are responsible.

● As You Read

Because partners are responsible for debts in a partnership, you must pay your share of the debt. If the partner makes other bad decisions you might decide to end the partnership to limit further losses.

International Business

Understanding Cultural Differences

Students might suggest that international business travelers will need help understanding how to handle language barriers, meeting people and introducing themselves, business negotiations, after-hours entertainment, gift-giving, business dress, and conversation.

Corporations

A **corporation** is a company that is registered by a state and operates apart from its owners. To form a corporation, the owners must get a corporate charter from the state where their main office will be located. A corporate charter is a license to run a corporation. To raise money, the owners can sell stock, or shares in the company. The company also must have a board of directors, who will govern the corporation.

Advantages of Forming a Corporation A major advantage of a corporation is limited liability. **Limited liability** holds a firm's owners responsible for no more than the capital that they have invested in it. Another advantage is its ability to raise money when people buy stock. A third advantage is that the corporation does not end if an owner dies. If that happens, the deceased owner's shares are sold, and the business continues.

Disadvantages of Forming a Corporation Corporations face several disadvantages. They pay taxes on their income, and stockholders pay taxes on profits issued to them. That is called double taxation. There are some special types of corporations, such as S corporations and limited liability companies, which do not have double taxation. However, they have other restrictions. The government **regulates** corporations more than other types of businesses. Corporations are also difficult and costly to start.

● **Corporations and Big Business** Many corporations are big businesses, with more than 500 employees. **Which advantage allows corporations to raise funds for expansion?**

Discuss the Photo
● **Corporations and Big Business**
Limited liability of owners makes it easier for money to be raised to build large structures and offer many products and services.

RETEACH

W **Writing Support**
Enrichment
Write a Letter Have students assume the role of a business owner who has decided to form a corporation to write a letter to the company's employees explaining the process of starting the corporation. (Letters should mention the intention to form a corporation, the need to get a charter from the state, and plans to appoint a board of directors.)

R **Reading Strategy**
Make Lists Have students make lists of the advantages and disadvantages of the corporate form of business ownership. (Lists should include the following information. Advantages of forming a corporation: limited liability, ability to raise funds, and unlimited life of the corporation. Disadvantages of forming a corporation: time and expense involved in formation, double taxation, and more government regulation.)

U **Universal Access**
Learners with Limited Reading Comprehension Skills Students who have difficulty answering questions should be encouraged to read all the text, then the question, and then reread the same information. Many students can benefit from this technique.

Student Activity Workbook Assign the Section 6.1 Activities.

RETEACH (cont.)

C Critical Thinking

Apply Skills

Cooperatives Ask: Why does a cooperative make sense? (Members have much in common and benefit from working together.)

ASSESS

● **After You Read**

Have students complete the Section 6.1 After You Read section review.

Online Study Tools

Have students go to the Online Learning Center through **glencoe.com** to:

• Take the Section 6.1 **Practice Test**.

• Download free **Study-to-Go** content to their PDAs or cell phones.

Car Sharing Some students might car share to save money on insurance and parking. Others would rather enjoy the freedom of their own car.

CLOSE

Culminating Activity

Have five groups each prepare a short presentation on one of these topics: sole proprietorships, partnerships, corporations, cooperatives, and nonprofit organizations. Ask each group to select a representative to a panel to combine the content into one. Select a panelist to show the final presentation.

98

Car Sharing Car sharing is a popular European process in which many households share vehicles. Mobility Car-Sharing cooperative in Switzerland has over 50,000 clients. *Do you think car sharing could become popular in the United States?*

NCLB Activity correlates to Math standards.

Other Ways to Organize a Business

There are other ways to organize a business venture.

A **cooperative** is an organization that is owned and operated by its members. When groups of businesses, such as small farms, pool their resources, they form a cooperative. The purpose is to save money on the purchase of certain goods and services. A cooperative can make marketing of goods and services more efficient and profitable. Juice maker Ocean Spray is a cooperative of cranberry growers.

A **nonprofit organization**, or nonprofit, is a type of organization that focuses on providing a service, but not to make a profit. Nonprofits must also register with the government. Because they do not make a profit, they do not pay taxes.

A **franchise** is a contractual agreement to use the name and sell the products or services of a company in a designated geographic area. Fast-food restaurant Taco Bell and cleaning service Merry Maids are two common franchises. To run a franchise, you have to invest money and pay franchise fees or a share of the profits. In return, the franchiser offers a well-known name and a business plan.

Section 6.1

● **After You Read**

Review Key Concepts
1. What is the difference between a sole proprietorship and a partnership?
2. If a partner makes a bad decision, what responsibility do the other partners have?
3. Why are cooperatives formed?

Academic Skills
4. **Mathematics** Approximately 22% of businesses are corporations, 7% are partnerships, and the rest are sole proprietorships. In a sentence or two, describe how to construct a circle graph about the various forms of business ownership using this information.

THEORY **Data Analysis and Probability: Circle Graphs** A circle graph, also called a pie chart, uses wedge-shaped pieces to represent all the parts of the whole. If a part is 20% of the whole, then the wedge takes up 20% of the circle. In other words, the angle of the wedge is 20% of 360°.

 Math For math help, go to the Math Appendix.

 Go to the *Introduction to Business* Online Learning Center through **glencoe.com** to check your answers.

Section 6.1

Review Key Concepts
1. A sole proprietorship is owned by one person. A partnership is owned by two or more people.
2. All partners share responsibility for a bad decision.
3. so that the members have advantages in buying and selling products and services

Academic Skills
4. **Mathematics** There should be one wedge for corporations, 22% of 360°, or 79°; one for partnerships, 7% of 360°, or 25°; and one for sole proprietorships (100% − 22% − 7%) = 71% of 360°, or 256°.

Types and Functions of Businesses

Reading Guide

● Before You Read

Think about the tasks that are performed by businesses to get goods and services to consumers.

Read to Learn

- Differentiate the six types of businesses.
- Describe the five functions of business.
- Discuss how the five functions of business relate to each other.

The Main Idea

There are many different types of businesses. The five functions of business are involved in every one.

Key Concepts

- Types of Businesses
- Functions of Business
- How the Functions of Business Are Interdependent

Vocabulary

Key Terms

producer	production
processor	procurement
manufacturer	marketing
intermediary	management
wholesaler	finance
retailer	accounting

Academic Vocabulary

You will find these words in your reading and on your tests. Make sure you know their meanings.

distributes	functions
tasks	involves

Graphic Organizer

In a box like the one below, arrange the six types of businesses in the order in which their tasks would be performed.

1.	
2.	
3.	
4.	
5.	
6.	

wholesaler

processor

manufacturer

retailer

producer

intermediary

 Go to the *Introduction to Business* Online Learning Center through **glencoe.com** for a printable graphic organizer.

Academic Standards

English Language Arts

NCTE 4 Use written language to communicate effectively

NCTE 5 Use different writing process elements to communicate effectively

Science

Content Standard G Students should develop understanding of science as a human endeavor, nature of scientific knowledge, historical perspectives

---

FOCUS

🔔 Bell Ringer Activity

Types and Functions of Businesses
Write the types of businesses on the board as column headings—*producers, processors, manufacturers, wholesalers and intermediaries, retailers, and services.* Ask students to identify local businesses and categorize them according to type. Make sure they list at least one business for each category.

Preteaching

Presentation Plus!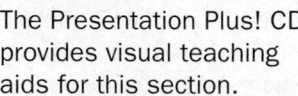

The Presentation Plus! CD provides visual teaching aids for this section.

PuzzleMaker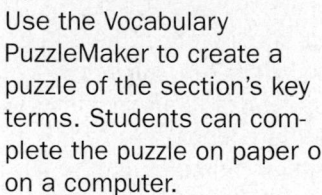

Use the Vocabulary PuzzleMaker to create a puzzle of the section's key terms. Students can complete the puzzle on paper or on a computer.

Graphic Organizer

Tell students to go to the Online Learning Center through **glencoe.com** for a printable graphic organizer. (When complete, the graphic organizer should show the businesses in this order: 1. producer, 2. processor, 3. manufacturer, 4. intermediary, 5. wholesaler or distributor, and 6. retailer.)

N C L B Connects academics to content.

Reading Guide

● Before You Read

Point out to students that even a product as simple as milk must travel through several types of businesses before it makes it to the consumer.

D Develop Concepts

The Main Idea Ask students: Why do you think the different types of businesses each use the same basic functions? (Different types of businesses may *produce* different goods and services, but they must still manage their resources, market their products, and make a profit.)

100

TEACH

Discussion Starter
Types of Businesses
Point out that it is easy to limit your ideas about business to the businesses in your own community or the retail businesses that you frequent. Remind students that there are many types of businesses involved in the global economy.

R Reading Strategy

Create a Memory Device
Point out that in addition to remembering the types of businesses involved in producing goods that people consume, it is important to remember the order in which the businesses are involved. Ask students to work in pairs to create a memory device to help remember the correct order. (Memory devices will vary, but should reflect the correct order—producer, processor, manufacturer, intermediary, wholesaler, and retailer. Some students may form acronyms or acrostics or develop a visual that will help them remember the correct order.)

● As You Read

Answers will vary. Students should categorize the business correctly.

Types of Businesses

R As previously discussed, the business environment consists of many forms of organizations. There are many different types of businesses and various ways to classify them. One way is to group them by the kinds of activities they perform.

● As You Read

Think of a product you own. What kind of business made the product?

Producers

A **producer** is a business that gathers raw goods. Raw goods are materials gathered in their original state from natural resources such as land or water. Agriculture, mining, fishing, and forestry are some of the industries that produce raw goods.

Processors

A **processor** changes raw materials into more finished products. Processed goods are made from raw goods that require further processing. For example, sugar cane is turned into sugar, crude oil into gasoline, and iron ore into steel.

Manufacturers

A **manufacturer** is a business that makes finished products out of processed goods. Manufacturers turn raw or processed goods into finished goods. Goods are material products such as cars, CDs, and computers.

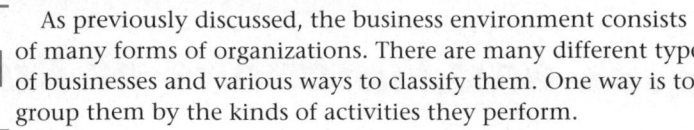

BusinessWeek *Reader and Case Study*

For the Poor, Help from MBAs

They're bringing microfinancing, business development—and eventually a consumer economy—to many impoverished developing nations.

Sue Igoe, a second-year MBA student at Columbia Business School in New York, is returning from her summer internship invigorated and ready to learn how to make a profit—and a difference.

Igoe, who originally sought to intern at a media outlet in New York, instead spent 11 weeks in Nicaragua assisting in the launch of Agora Partnerships, an enterprise that helps young entrepreneurs in Central America develop socially responsible businesses. "I was attracted to this job in part because it had such heart," says Igoe.

@ **CASE STUDY** Go to the *Introduction to Business* Online Learning Center through **glencoe.com** for the *BusinessWeek* Reader Case Study.

Active Learning

With a partner, think about other opportunities that can help give purchasing power to people in developing nations. Write a two-page report about a country you would like to help. Describe socially responsible businesses that already exist in that country. Finally, prepare an oral presentation based on your report.

BusinessWeek *Reader and Case Study*

For the Poor, Help from MBAs

@ **CASE STUDY** Have students go to the *Introduction to Business* Online Learning Center through **glencoe.com** to download a Case Study activity that corresponds to the article. The activity and answer key are also available on the TeacherWorks Plus CD.

Active Learning

Reports and presentations should include descriptions of socially responsible businesses and how they help people in a developing nation.

● **The Interdependence of Businesses** Many businesses rely on other businesses. **Which types of businesses might be involved in the manufacture of an automobile?**

Intermediaries and Wholesalers

An **intermediary** is a business that moves goods from one business to another. It buys goods, stores them, and then resells them. A **wholesaler distributes** goods. Wholesalers are also known as distributors. A clothing wholesaler, for example, may buy thousands of jackets from several manufacturers. The wholesaler then divides the large quantities into smaller ones and sells them to retailers.

Retailers and Service Businesses

A **retailer** purchases goods from a wholesaler and sells them to consumers, the final buyers of the goods. Service stations, record stores, and auto dealers are examples of retailers.

Service businesses perform **tasks** rather than provide goods. Some service businesses meet needs, such as medical clinics and law firms. Others provide conveniences, such as taxi companies and copy shops. Service businesses employ about three-quarters of the workforce and are rapidly increasing in numbers.

Functions of Business

There are five main **functions** involved in the operation of all types of businesses. They are production and procurement; marketing; management; finance; and accounting.

✔ **Reading Check** **Identify** What are the five main functions of business?

Discuss the Photo
● **The Interdependence of Businesses**
First the iron ore is mined (producer). Second, the ore is processed by a steel company (processor). Third, steel is used at an automobile plant (manufacturer).

✔ **Reading Check**

Identify Production, marketing, management, finance, and accounting.

TEACH (cont.)

S Skill Practice
Guided Practice
List Examples Have students make a list of two additional examples of retailers that would buy merchandise from wholesalers. (Examples may include grocery stores, restaurants, and furniture stores) **L1**

Draw a Picture Have students draw a series of pictures illustrating how a raw material gets from wholesalers to retailers to consumers. (Some students will draw goods being shipped by boat, rail, truck, or by mail or other shipping service. Some students may draw customers at a retail store.) **L2**

Investigate Have students research a company that handles its own wholesaling and retailing. Ask students to prepare a short presentation about the way manufacturing their own product allows them to "skip the middleman." (Presentations should focus on the impact shortening the distribution chain has on the business.) **L3**

ASSESS

Review Key Terms
Have students write sentences using each key term.

 **Study-to-Go** Have students go to the Online Learning Center through **glencoe.com** to download free **Study-to-Go** content to their PDAs or cell phones.

101

RETEACH

W Writing Support

Restating

Production Have students find an article in a business magazine about the production of a product and write a summary of the article. (Abstracts will vary depending on the article chosen.)

R Reading Strategy

Marketing Have students use a dictionary to look up the words *marketing* and *market*. Ask them what the difference is between the words. (Students should note that although "market" is the root of the word "marketing," they have different meanings. "Market" has several meanings, including the customers for a particular product or service or a gathering place for buying and selling. "Marketing" is the processes involved in selling and distributing products or services.)

U Universal Access

Visual Learners Use a projector to show students an accounting program and several reports it will generate for use by management, such as an index of cost of goods sold.

Student Activity Workbook 📂 Assign the Section 6.2 Activities.

 Activity correlates to Science standards.

● As You Read

Think about starting a surfboard business that sells boards you design and make. Would your business be involved in production or procurement?

Production and Procurement

W **Production** is the process of creating, expanding, manufacturing, or improving goods and services. Most retailers procure goods from producers for resale. **Procurement** is the buying and reselling of goods that have already been produced. Wholesalers buy goods from producers to resell to retailers and other wholesalers.

Marketing

R **Marketing** is the process of planning, pricing, promoting, selling, and distributing ideas, goods, and services. Marketing **involves** getting consumers to buy a product or service. Marketers make decisions based on market research of trends and consumer habits.

Management

Management is the process of achieving company goals by planning, organizing, directing, controlling, and evaluating the effective use of resources.

Finance and Accounting

U **Finance** is the business or art of money management. It requires analyzing financial statements to make future decisions. **Accounting** involves maintaining and checking records, handling bills, and preparing financial reports for a business.

---

*Science/Tech*TRENDS

NCLB

The History of Information Technology

The information technology (IT) practices of today have evolved and developed through several stages, each with the goal of solving the input, processing, output, and communication problems of the time. During the Premechanical Age, from 3000 BC to AD 1450, writing and alphabets developed, books and libraries were invented, and the first calculator, the abacus, came into popular use. The Mechanical Age, from 1450 to 1840, brought with it the first real computers. During the Electromechanical Age, from 1840 to 1940, the discovery of ways to harness electricity meant knowledge and information could be converted into electrical impulses. From 1940 to the present, the Electronic Age has brought the ongoing communications revolution we see in our homes and places of business.

Go to the *Introduction to Business* Online Learning Center through **glencoe.com** for links to Web sites where you can find out more about the history of information technology. Write a few paragraphs about a person, invention, or time period that interests you.

● As You Read

Answers will vary. Students should recognize that the business is primarily involved with production—making the boards. They may also be involved in procurement if they decide to carry related items or boards manufactured by others.

---

*Science/Tech*TRENDS

WebQuest

The History of Information Technology Answers will vary, but students should identify a particular person, invention, or time period.

How the Functions of Business Are Interdependent

The functional areas of business depend on each other. For example, say a furniture maker's sales have been decreasing. The accounting and finance departments have noted the drop in sales. If the products are too high-priced, then more efficient procedures will have to be implemented. This will involve management and production. A new marketing plan may be required. Accounting and finance will have to closely monitor the effects that new efforts have on profits.

Sometimes the functional areas conflict with each other. Suppose management wants to increase sales by 20 percent within three years. The production department suggests improving quality to attract more customers. However, changing the quality would add to costs. Meanwhile, the marketing department says the problem is that there is not enough marketing being done. It requests more funds for projects. Accounting then says neither plan is good since both would lower profits by raising costs. It suggests improving production efficiency. The final plan involves ideas from all functions of business. Companies benefit when all functional areas work together.

Real World

To Advertise or Not
Advertising is used to influence consumers to buy one product or service over another. *Do you think you could run a successful business without doing major advertising? Why or why not?*

Activity correlates to English Language Arts standards.

Section 6.2

After You Read

Review Key Concepts
1. What is the difference between a producer and a processor?
2. Identify the five functions of business.
3. Give an example of how the accounting and finance functions can affect a business's marketing and production processes.

Academic Skills
4. **English Language Arts** Brainstorming is a technique you can try to come up with ideas to use in your writing. Imagine that you have written a book encouraging high school students to start their own part-time business. Work with a group to brainstorm titles for your book. Ask the group to think of titles that would be intriguing to high school students.

5. **English Language Arts** Write a three-sentence summary of the material in this section. Share it with four classmates, and ask them to either add a sentence containing something you missed, correct any errors they find, comment about how you could write a better summary, or compare their summary to yours. Then rewrite your summary, incorporating any ideas or corrections you feel are appropriate.

Go to the *Introduction to Business* Online Learning Center through **glencoe.com** to check your answers.

Section 6.2

Review Key Concepts
1. A producer gathers or creates raw products. A processor changes raw products into more finished products.
2. production and procurement, marketing, management, finance, and accounting
3. If the financials show little profits, new marketing plans may be developed and new production procedures may be implemented.

Academic Skills
4. **English Language Arts** Lists will vary but should include some usable titles.
5. **English Language Arts** The paragraphs should be error free and describe the various types of businesses covered in the section.

RETEACH (cont.)

C Critical Thinking
Extrapolate
Functional Interdependence
Have students write another example than that in the text to illustrate the interdependence of the functions of business. (Students might describe an established company that is facing a new aggressive competitor.)

Real World

To Advertise or Not
It is important to get the word out about a product, but advertising is only one part of marketing.

ASSESS

After You Read
Have students complete the Section 6.2 After You Read section review.

Online Study Tools
Have students go to the Online Learning Center through **glencoe.com** to:

- Take the Section 6.2 **Practice Test**.
- Download free **Study-to-Go** content to their PDAs or cell phones.

STUDY TO GO

CLOSE

Culminating Activity
Visualize a Concept
Ask students to pick a topic from this section and develop a visual representation that they can use as a study tool. (Students might create tables, drawings, or outlines.)

Vocabulary Review

1. Students should write complete sentences using each term correctly.

Review Key Concepts

2. Sole proprietorship: easy setup, owner makes decisions, single taxation; difficulty raising funds, unlimited liability, reliance on one person, limited life of business. Partnerships: easy fundraising, more skills, single taxation; sharing profits and risks, unlimited liability, and limited life. Corporations: limited liability, easy fundraising, and unlimited life; expensive and hard to form, double taxation, government regulation.

3. Cooperatives: for profit; need charter and board of directors; issue dividends; members are owners; have lower tax rates. Nonprofits: need charter and board of directors; are not-for-profit; do not sell stock; raise funds from donations.

4. producer, processor, manufacturer, intermediary, wholesaler, retailer

5. production and procurement, marketing, management, finance, accounting

6. Answers will vary, but should describe the interdependence of the functions.

Section 6.1 *Summary*

Types of Business Ownership Three primary forms of business ownership are sole proprietorships, partnerships, and corporations. A major advantage of sole proprietorships and partnerships is their ease of formation. One advantage corporations have over sole proprietorships and partnerships is limited liability. Limited liability means an owner cannot suffer a loss that is more than he or she invested. An advantage partnerships and corporations have over sole proprietorships is better access to capital. Nonprofits, cooperatives, and franchises are other forms of organizations.

Section 6.2 *Summary*

Types and Functions of Businesses There are different types of businesses. Most can be categorized as producers, processors, manufacturers, intermediaries, or retail or service businesses. There are five functions of business: production and procurement; marketing; management; finance; and accounting. These functions take place in every company. The functional areas are interdependent and must work together for the business to succeed. Sometimes the functional areas are in conflict with one another. Conflicts can be resolved by considering ideas from all functional areas.

Vocabulary Review

1. On a sheet of paper, use each of these key terms and academic vocabulary terms in a sentence.

Key Terms

sole proprietorship
unlimited liability
partnership
corporation
limited liability
cooperative
nonprofit organization

franchise
producer
processor
manufacturer
intermediary
wholesaler
retailer

production
procurement
marketing
management
finance
accounting

Academic Vocabulary

sole	distributes
income	tasks
partners	functions
regulates	involves

Review Key Concepts

2. Describe the advantages and disadvantages of three major forms of business organizations.

3. Describe how cooperatives and nonprofits are like and unlike corporations and franchises.

4. Differentiate the six types of businesses.

5. Describe the five functions of business.

6. Discuss how the five functions of business relate to each other.

Critical Thinking

7. Partnership allows risks and rewards to be shared, and partners bring different strengths to benefit the business.

8. Answers will vary. One advantage is that teams benefit from having the talents and skills of more than one person. Team members also can encourage one another. A disadvantage is that some team members may not do a good job or could have low expectations. Also, their poor decisions or performance might reflect negatively on the entire team.

9. Sole proprietorships are easy to form and have low startup costs. The owner is the boss and gets to keep all the profits. Income is taxed only once.

Critical Thinking

7. Why might two or more people decide to form a partnership instead of each forming a sole proprietorship?

8. Working as a team member is similar to being in a partnership. What are some advantages and disadvantages of working with others?

9. There are more sole proprietorships than partnerships or corporations in the United States. Why do you think so many businesses are organized as sole proprietorships?

10. Identify what happens during the production, processing, and delivery stages within each type of business responsible for the manufacturing and sale of a loaf of bread.

11. Explain how a producer, a processor, and a manufacturer are not involved in producing a service.

12. How can accountants in a firm provide an idea of the general financial health of the company?

13. Imagine that you and a friend have developed a new engine and would like to manufacture the engine and sell it to major automakers. What form of business organization would you select for your company? Why?

Write About It

14. Write an e-mail to a friend, explaining the reasons for the differences between the cost of manufacturing a product and its final sales price.

15. Interview a business partner. Ask why he or she entered into a partnership. What are the challenges of being in a partnership? Write a report based on the person's responses.

16. Form groups. Have each member interview someone who works in finance, marketing, production, human resources, management, or sales. Ask them about the responsibilities of their positions. How do their departments fuction within their companies? Write a report on your findings.

17. Look in reference books for information about what is included in the articles of incorporation. Write a one-page report about your findings.

18. Research the characteristics of an S corporation or a limited liability company. In two or more paragraphs, discuss how they are like and unlike a conventional corporation.

19. Interview the director of a nonprofit. Find out how its functions are similar to or different from a for-profit business. Prepare a one-page report on your findings.

Technology Applications

Creating a Database

20. Compile a database of at least 10 businesses from a phone book. Include fields for the name, address, telephone number, and the category of business. Find at least one business that is a producer, a processor, a manufacturer, an intermediary, and a retail or service business.

Business Ethics

Go Solo or Form a Partnership?

21. Imagine that you and a friend invent a new material for fixing leaky faucets. You would like to sell this new product. Your friend wants to be your partner. Since he worked with you on the new invention, should you form a partnership with him? Write a letter to your friend discussing your decision.

Technology Applications

20. Databases will vary depending on the businesses that students list. Make sure that they include at least one producer, processor, manufacturer, intermediary, and retail or service business.

Business Ethics

21. Answers will vary. If you and your friend both contributed to the invention, you should both share in the potential rewards. Cutting your friend out of the business would be unethical. A partnership would allow the two of you to share any profits derived from as well as the risks associated with starting and operating a business.

Critical Thinking

10. A farmer produces wheat; a processor makes flour; the manufacturer makes bread; an intermediary sells it to a retailer who sells to customers.

11. A service does not require gathering raw materials, or processing and making them into more finished products.

12. Accountants track the firm's profitability, debt, and sales increases or decreases.

13. A partnership is easy to form, and owners can keep all of the profits and make the decisions. However, there is a possibility of losing your investment if the business fails.

Write About It

14. There are costs involved in producing, distributing, and selling goods.

15. Answers will depend on the responses of the person interviewed.

16. Answers will vary depending on the people interviewed.

17. Articles of incorporation include: name, address, and purpose of the business, the number of shares to be issued, and when the shares will be issued.

18. S corporations have more restrictions and do not face double taxation. An LLC ends when an owner withdraws from the company.

19. Answers will depend on the nonprofit that is chosen.

22. The base words are *produce, manufacture, wholesale,* and *retail.* The suffix for each word is *–er.* The suffix *-er* in each case means "one who." The suffix is often used with the names of occupations or professions. There are many examples of this suffix in English words, including *skater, maker, packer, geographer,* and *lawyer.* The suffix *-or* in *editor* and *monitor* has a similar meaning, as does the suffix *-ist* in *botanist* and *druggist.*

23. $0.75x = \$.87$

$x = \$.87 \div 0.75 = \$1.16$, the regular price of the bread.

24. The Latin word *corpus,* which means body, is the common ancestor of all these words. A corporation is like a body in that it is comprised of various parts that all work together to make a whole.

25. The slope is in the shape of a rectangle, and the formula for the area of a rectangle is $A = l \times w$. Converting the length to yards, we have $822 \div 3 = 274$. Therefore, $A = 274 \times 65 = 17,810$ square yards. Converting the width to feet, we have $65 \times 3 = 195$ feet. $822 \times 195 = 160,920$ square feet. Since there are 9 square feet in a square yard, we can check our work: $17,810 \times 9 = 160,290$ square feet.

Applying Academics to Business

English Language Arts
22. List the words *producer, manufacturer, wholesaler,* and *retailer.* Underline the base word within each and circle the suffix. Write a definition for the suffix and list a few other words that use it in the same way. What other suffixes have a similar meaning? Give some examples.

Mathematics
23. The neighborhood bakery makes bread, cakes, cookies, and pies. At the end of the day, the prices of all the leftover products are reduced by 75%. If bread sells for 87¢ at the end of the day, what is its regular price?

> **THEORY** **Algebra: Equations** Using the information given in the problem, you can write an algebraic equation and find the solution. Let *x* stand for the regular price of the bread.

English Language Arts
24. The word *corporation* is related to other words in the English language that might not seem connected such as *corps,* as in *Marine Corps, corpulent* (meaning obese), and *corpus delicti* (meaning the facts that prove a crime was committed). Research the origins of these words, and explain why they are related.

Mathematics
25. Zack wanted to open a business having to do with his favorite sport, skiing. Since he lives in a warm climate, he decided to open an indoor ski park. The beginner's slope is 822 feet long and 65 yards wide. What is its area?

> **THEORY** **Geometry: Finding Areas** The areas of two-dimensional geometric figures can be found using various formulas. Area is measured in square units. In solving this problem, decide which units to use.

Active Learning

Learning from Working
26. Most nonprofit organizations provide charitable services to people and communities. They rely upon volunteers to conduct much of their business. Volunteer to work in a nonprofit organization. Find out what workers do, how they do it, how the nonprofit is set up, what people like about working there, how it is funded, and what challenges it faces. Write a one-page report about your findings. Present your report to the class.

Business in the Real World

Comparing Business Organizations
27. Invite local businesspeople from sole proprietorships, partnerships, and corporations to serve on a panel discussion in your class. If there is a cooperative in your community, have a representative from the organization attend. Ask the panel members about the advantages and disadvantages of their type of business ownership, how they got their start, and the qualities they feel are important for success. Be sure to thank them for their time.

ExamView Assessment Suite CD allows you to print out ready-made unit and chapter tests, complete with answer keys. You can also create customized tests.

TeacherWorks Plus provides complete teacher resources in one convenient package. It includes customizable lesson plans in calendar format, and instant access to many print program resources.

Real LIFE skills

ASSESSING YOUR SKILLS

28. Successful business ownership requires several personal qualities. They include: responsibility, self-esteem, sociability, self-management, integrity, and honesty. In your own words, write definitions of these qualities and rate your possession of them from 1 to 5, with 5 being your strongest quality and 1 being your weakest. What can you do to develop the two qualities that you have ranked as the lowest?

(COOL) Business CAREERS

FIND YOUR DREAM JOB

29. Go to the *Introduction to Business* Online Learning Center through **glencoe.com** for a link to the Occupational Outlook Handbook Web site. Click on the "OOH Search/A-Z Index" link and enter the job title "top executive." Then write a one-page report about this type of occupation. Conclude your report with a list of things you could do now to prepare yourself to pursue the occupation.

Role Play

FUNCTIONAL AREAS OF BUSINESS

30. **Situation** You are the sales manager of a company that makes bicycles. Your salespeople report that several bicycles have been returned because of a faulty brake.

   Activity The president wants to know what you think should be done to correct the problem. You need to prepare a report for him that demonstrates what you think should be done. Your report should include the actions to take in the functional areas of the business.

   Evaluation You will be evaluated on how well you meet the following performance indicators:

   - Make valid recommendations for each department.
   - Describe each department function.
   - Understand how the five functions of business depend on each other.
   - Prepare a written report.
   - Speak clearly and use correct grammar.

Standardized Test Practice

Directions Choose the letter of the best answer. Write the letter for the answer on a separate piece of paper.

1. **Which word or phrase best completes the sentence?**

   Many people _____ hard over the years to make the business a success.

   A   work
   B   will work
   C   works
   D   have worked

   TEST-TAKING TIP When taking a test, work on a problem only until you get stuck. Think about it for a minute or two, and if nothing comes to mind, then move on to another problem.

 READING Go to the *Introduction to Business* Online Learning Center through **glencoe.com** for a list of outside reading suggestions.

STRATEGIES FOR STANDARDIZED TEST PREP SUCCESS

Test Timing Tell students that timed multiple-choice tests usually provide a little more than a minute to answer each question. Therefore, they should answer 10 questions in about 10 minutes and 20 questions in about 20 minutes. Encourage them to pace themselves in this way through a test neither going too slowly nor rushing too quickly. Remind them that if they use the one-minute-per-question rule, they should have enough time at the end to look over their answers.

Active Learning

26. Answers will vary based on the nonprofit that is chosen.

Business in the Real World

27. Panels will vary, but students should try to get at least one business-person for each type of business.

Real LIFE skills

28. Answers will vary. Students should identify ways to work on the skill they perceive as lacking.

(COOL) Business CAREERS

29. Top executives must devise strategies to ensure that an organization's goals and objectives are met while working under intense pressure. CEOs often become members of boards of directors. Preparation includes developing analytical, leadership, and communications skills along with self-confidence.

Role Play

30. Presentations should address the competencies noted in the Role Play. Answers will depend on how each student approaches the situation but should make valid recommendations that reflect the interdependence of business functions.

Standardized Test Practice
   1. D

Standards-Based Lesson Planning
Introduction to Business provides students with instruction and assessment in the following fundamental content areas:

Content Standards Correlations	
Discuss the importance of record keeping.	p. 114
Explain the importance of common managerial responsibilities.	pp. 111–114, 120–123
Assess processes that incorporate effective business practices.	pp. 111–114, 120–123
Describe managerial skills necessary for maintaining a high quality work environment, goals, and strategic planning in business settings.	pp. 111–114, 120–123
Evaluate management functions.	pp. 111–114, 120–123
Analyze advantages and disadvantages of organizational business structures.	pp. 116–119, 120–123
Evaluate organizational structures and cultures for managing project teams.	pp. 116–119, 120–123
Manage data from all of the functional areas of business needed to make wise management decisions.	pp. 111–114, 120–123
Demonstrate human relations, self-management, organizational, and professional leadership skills.	pp. 120–123
Explore career opportunities in business management.	p. 123

NCLB
Activities, information, and skills practice will help your students attain No Child Left Behind proficiency. Students will improve their abilities in the following academic standards areas:

Academic Standards Correlations		
English Language Arts	**Activities/Features**	**Page**
NCTE 3 Apply strategies to interpret texts	Applying Academics to Business	p. 122
NCTE 6 Apply knowledge of language structure and conventions to discuss texts	Standardized Test Practice	p. 123
NCTE 9 Develop an understanding of diversity in language use across cultures	After You Read	p. 119
NCTE 12 Use language to accomplish individual purposes	After You Read	p. 119
Mathematics		
Algebra Represent and analyze mathematical situations and structures using algebraic symbols	Applying Academics to Business	p. 122
Data Analysis and Probability Select and use appropriate statistical methods to analyze data	Applying Academics to Business	p. 122
Number and Operations Understand numbers, ways of representing numbers, relationships among numbers, and number systems	Standardized Test Practice	p. 123
Problem Solving Apply and adapt a variety of appropriate strategies to solve problems; Monitor and reflect on the process of mathematical problem solving	After You Read	p. 114
Science		
Content Standard A Students should develop abilities necessary to do scientific inquiry and understandings about scientific inquiry	Science/Tech Trends	p. 117

Correlations   This chart shows the 21st Century Skills, foundation skills, and workplace competencies that students develop as they work in this chapter.

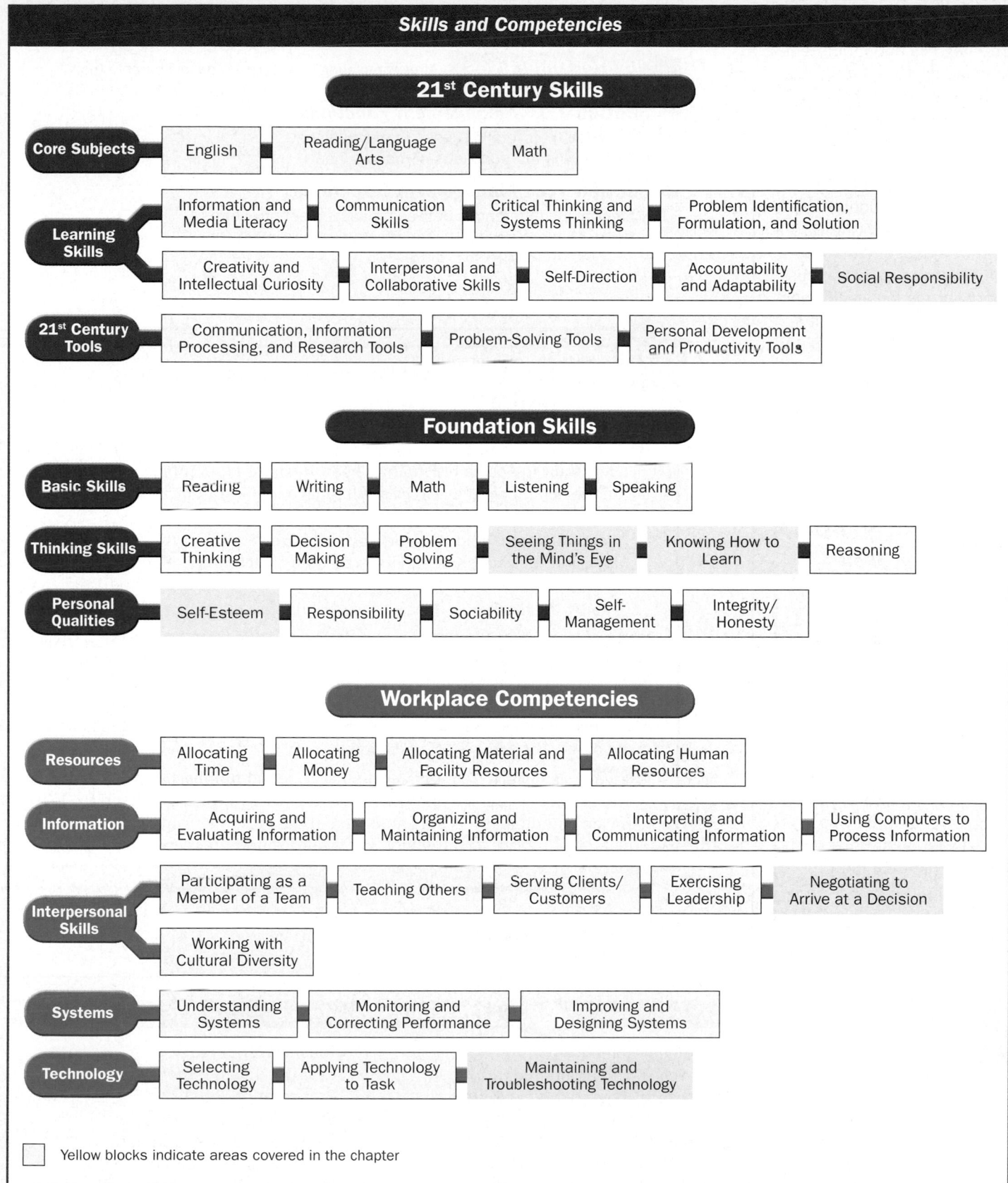

Skills and Competencies

21st Century Skills

Core Subjects
- English
- Reading/Language Arts
- Math

Learning Skills
- Information and Media Literacy
- Communication Skills
- Critical Thinking and Systems Thinking
- Problem Identification, Formulation, and Solution
- Creativity and Intellectual Curiosity
- Interpersonal and Collaborative Skills
- Self-Direction
- Accountability and Adaptability
- Social Responsibility

21st Century Tools
- Communication, Information Processing, and Research Tools
- Problem-Solving Tools
- Personal Development and Productivity Tools

Foundation Skills

Basic Skills
- Reading
- Writing
- Math
- Listening
- Speaking

Thinking Skills
- Creative Thinking
- Decision Making
- Problem Solving
- Seeing Things in the Mind's Eye
- Knowing How to Learn
- Reasoning

Personal Qualities
- Self-Esteem
- Responsibility
- Sociability
- Self-Management
- Integrity/Honesty

Workplace Competencies

Resources
- Allocating Time
- Allocating Money
- Allocating Material and Facility Resources
- Allocating Human Resources

Information
- Acquiring and Evaluating Information
- Organizing and Maintaining Information
- Interpreting and Communicating Information
- Using Computers to Process Information

Interpersonal Skills
- Participating as a Member of a Team
- Teaching Others
- Serving Clients/Customers
- Exercising Leadership
- Negotiating to Arrive at a Decision
- Working with Cultural Diversity

Systems
- Understanding Systems
- Monitoring and Correcting Performance
- Improving and Designing Systems

Technology
- Selecting Technology
- Applying Technology to Task
- Maintaining and Troubleshooting Technology

☐ Yellow blocks indicate areas covered in the chapter

Chapter Overview

Introduce the Chapter

Business Management
Chapter 7 is about different managerial structures used by businesses, as well as the different levels and functions of management.

Building Background
Point out that students are already familiar with the concept of management. The word *manage* is part of our everyday vocabulary. In their personal lives people manage stress, time, money, and relationships. Students can use their current knowledge as a building block for learning more about business management.

Ask STANDARD &POOR'S

» Math Answer
Answers will vary but should include an estimate of the capital required with a list of initial expenses and of recurring expenses.

» Extension Activity
Ask students to think about common examples of rounding and estimating. (Answers will vary. Students might point out the people frequently round up to the nearest dollar when leaving a tip for a restaurant server.)

N C L B
Activity correlates to Math standards.

108

Business Management

Chapter Objectives After completing this chapter, you will be able to:

▶ **Section 7.1** *Management Functions*
- **Describe** the overall purpose of management.
- **Discuss** the four functions of management.

▶ **Section 7.2** *Management Structures*
- **Identify** the differences between management structures.
- **Name** six skills necessary for effective management.

Ask STANDARD &POOR'S **Establishing Investment Goals**

Q: Next year I plan to attend college and major in food management. When I graduate, I want to open a restaurant. I know it takes a lot of money to get started, so my first restaurant will have to be small—maybe a take-out pizza shop. How can I start investing money now to meet my goal?

A: Identifying your goals is a good first step. However, an investment plan requires a specific, measurable goal. First, you need to determine how much money you will need to open your restaurant. Then you can develop a plan for how you will acquire the funds.

Mathematics To start, estimate the capital required to open the business. Create a list of all your initial expenses. Include items that you will need to purchase once, such as pizza ovens, pans, plates, and other service items. Then make another list of recurring costs, such as rent, ingredients, and paper products. Next to each expense, estimate how much that item will cost. If it is a recurring cost, estimate how much you will spend during the first year of operation.

THEORY **Estimation** To estimate your needs, round numbers to the nearest hundred or thousand. To round a number, look at the place to the left of the place to which you are rounding. If you are rounding to thousands, for example, look at the digit in the hundreds place. If the digit is 5 or greater, round up; if it is 4 or less, round down.

N C L B

Classroom Resources

- ✐ Student Edition
- ✐ Teacher Wraparound Edition
- 📁 Student Activity Workbook with Academic Integration
- 📁 Student Activity Workbook with Academic Integration TAE
- 📁 *Fast File*, Unit 2 Resources
- 📁 Inclusion in the Business Education Classroom

- ⊙ TeacherWorks Plus
- ⊙ *ExamView Assessment Suite*
- ⊙ Presentation Plus!
- ⊙ Vocabulary PuzzleMaker
- ⊙ Interactive Student Edition
- ⟆ Online Student Edition
- ⟆ Online Learning Center with Podcasts

● **Communication Is Key** Effective managers have good communication and people skills. **Why do you think effective managers need to be good communicators?**

Review the Objectives
Introduce the chapter by reviewing the chapter objectives:

Section 7.1 *Objectives*
Describe the overall purpose of management. (To set and meet goals efficiently and effectively to make a profit.)

Discuss the four functions of management. (Planning: creating goals and strategies to meet them; organizing: arranging resources in an orderly and functional way to accomplish goals; leading: providing direction and vision; controlling: keeping company on track and making sure goals are met.)

Section 7.2 *Objectives*
Identify the difference between different management structures. (Line authority: managers at the top are in charge of those beneath them. Line and staff authority: shows the authority lines as well as the advisory staff. Centralized authority: most major decision-making ability goes to top-level managers. Decentralized authority: more major decisions made at lower level. Formal structure creates a clear-cut organization, generally within departments. Informal structure allows most employees to offer input and work together.)

Name six different traits necessary for effective management. (Ability to perform varied tasks, work under pressure, effective communication skills, interpersonal skills, technical skills, and conceptual skills.)

Discuss the Photo
● **Communication is Key** Read the caption on the photo to students: Effective managers have good communication and people skills.

Ask students: Why do you think effective managers need to be good communicators? (Answers will vary but should include a recognition that one of the basic functions of a manager is to communicate job roles and responsibilities to his or her employees.)

FOCUS

Bell Ringer Activity

Management Functions
Write the four management functions—planning, organizing, leading, and controlling—on the board and ask students to relate them to their own lives. (Planning: career planning, college search, and class scheduling. Organizing: keeping track of assignments and commitments. Leading: participating in school and community activities and taking on responsibilities at home. Controlling: finding time to exercise, eating nutritious meals.)

Preteaching

Presentation Plus!
The Presentation Plus! CD provides visual teaching aids for this section.

PuzzleMaker
Use the Vocabulary PuzzleMaker to create a puzzle of the section's key terms. Students can complete the puzzle on paper or on a computer.

Graphic Organizer
Tell students to go to the Online Learning Center through **glencoe.com** for a printable graphic organizer. (Answer: Top-level managers sets goals and plans for future; middle managers carry out top managers' decisions; operational manager is responsible for daily business operations.)

Connects academics to content.

110

Management Functions

Reading Guide

● Before You Read
Think about the processes involved in managing a baseball team and how they might apply in business.

Read to Learn
- Describe the overall purpose of management.
- Discuss the four functions of management.

The Main Idea
The purpose of management is to set goals for the company and to help meet those goals as efficiently and effectively as possible. There are four functions of management: planning, organizing, leading, and controlling.

Key Concepts
- Introduction to Management
- The Four Functions of Management

Vocabulary
Key Terms
management
planning
organizing
organizational chart
top-level manager
middle manager
operational manager
leading
controlling

Academic Vocabulary
You will find these words in your reading and on your tests. Make sure you know their meanings.

focus   teams
goals   enforce

Graphic Organizer
In a figure like the one below, write examples of the types of positions that might be held by top-level managers, middle managers, and operational managers.

Top-Level Manager	Middle Manager	Operational Manager

 Go to the *Introduction to Business* Online Learning Center through **glencoe.com** for a printable graphic organizer.

Academic Standards
English Language Arts
  NCTE 1 Read texts to acquire new information
Mathematics
  Problem Solving Apply and adapt a variety of appropriate strategies to solve problems; monitor and reflect on the process of mathematical problem solving

glencoe.com

Reading Guide

● Before You Read
Point out that there are aspects of managing a baseball team that have nothing to do with playing baseball—someone needs to order the hot dogs and peanuts.

D Develop Concepts
The Main Idea Ask students: What is the ultimate purpose of management for all business organizations? (The purpose of business management is to make a profit.)

Introduction to Management

Entrepreneurs who start and run businesses by themselves do not have to manage other people. They have to manage themselves. However, if the firm has employees, then some type of management plan is necessary. **Management** includes the processes or functions of planning, organizing, leading, and controlling.

For example, suppose you have created your own comic book and want to start a comic book company. Do you want to produce comic books and market them as well? Do you also want to produce cartoons, video games, and action figures based on your comic books? Because of the complexity of your business, you will need employees to help. Managers can help by supervising and directing employees.

Management helps businesses **focus** on setting and meeting **goals** efficiently and effectively so that a profit can be made. The word *management* also refers to the people who are in charge of running a business. Managers need a thorough understanding of business operations, which involve all the activities of a company. They develop the objectives for a firm or a department and then figure out how to meet those objectives through people, work processes, and equipment.

The Four Functions of Management

Most managers carry out four different functions of management: planning, organizing, leading, and controlling. Some managers may primarily focus on one or two of them. These functions are indicated in the order in which they occur. Planning must be completed first, then organization can take place. Organization allows managers to lead and control employees and activities to get work done. Leading involves providing guidance to employees so they can fulfill their responsibilities effectively. Controlling involves measuring how the business performs to ensure that financial and operational goals are met.

A challenge for many managers, especially in small businesses, is dealing with multiple objectives, each at a different functional level. For example, suppose your company's manager discusses plans to produce a new comic book with the marketing and production **teams**. The manager directs the marketing team to research the national and global markets for comic books. The manager also tells the production team to prepare to produce the new product.

● As You Read

Think about all the things that are involved in managing your local grocery store.

❓ETHICS in Business

A Conflict of Interest

- **Critical Reading** Life is full of important decisions. Think about the kinds of decisions that you make as you read the question below.

  You and your best friend, Jeremiah, were helping your little brother figure out how to make molded cars from melted crayons using a kit you gave him. You decide to sell the cars at a local toy shop. Jeremiah hears you talking with your business teacher about your new business idea, and he wants to be a partner.

- **Decision Making** Since Jeremiah was involved in the initial experiment, do you have an obligation to make him a partner in your business venture? What about your little brother? Should he also own a piece of the new business? What are the advantages and disadvantages of a partnership? Explain your answer.

Section 7.1 Management Functions **111**

TEACH (cont.)

S Skill Practice

Guided Practice

Define Have students write definitions for *goal* and *objective*. Ask if they can be used interchangeably. (Both can be defined as something toward which effort is directed, or, a goal is a broad statement you hope to accomplish, an objective is specific, measurable behavior.) L1

Describe Ask students to describe reasons the company's goals and objectives should be important when managers make decisions about organizing and staffing. (A company can't be well organized or adequately staffed if its goals and objectives are not met.) L2

Develop a Handout Have students create a handout including a description of planning, organizing and staffing functions of management with examples. (Handouts will vary but should include descriptions and examples.) L3

ASSESS

Review Key Terms

Have students write sentences using each key term.

Study-to-Go Have students go to the Online Learning Center through **glencoe.com** to download free **Study-to-Go** content to their PDAs or cell phones.

It is up to the manager to organize, analyze, and monitor the project to assure that the production process works efficiently and effectively. Communicating with employees at all times helps assure that objectives are met. **Figure 7.1** describes the four functions of management.

✓ Reading Check **Describe** What are the four functions of management?

Planning

Planning is the act or process of creating goals and objectives as well as the strategies to meet them. Planning also involves figuring out the resources that are needed and the standards that must be met.

Organizing and Staffing

S **Organizing** is getting the resources arranged in an orderly and functional way to accomplish goals and objectives. A manager must organize people, work processes, and equipment so that the work is well coordinated. Managers also hire and train employees—and fire them when necessary. They are responsible for making sure employees have all the tools they need to do their jobs well.

Figure 7.1 — ***Management Functions***

PLANNING
Setting objectives and making long- and short-term plans for meeting the objectives

ORGANIZING
Obtaining and coordinating resources so that a business's objectives can be met

CONTROLLING
Setting standards for work, evaluating performance, and solving problems that prevent certain tasks' completion

LEADING
Influencing, guiding, and directing people under one's management to carry out their assigned tasks

● **Management Functions** Managers carry out four different functions. **Which function involves coordinating resources?**

Figure 7.1

● **Management Functions** The organizing function involves coordinating resources so that a business's objectives can be met.

✓ **Reading Check**

Identify planning, organizing, leading, and controlling

Levels of Management   Another important part of organizing is determining how different individuals in the firm relate to one another. An **organizational chart** shows how the firm is structured and who is in charge of whom.

A **top-level manager** is responsible for setting goals and planning for the future as well as leading and controlling the work of others. There is only one top-level manager at the Small Wonders Comic Book Company because it is a small business. In larger firms, top-level management can be composed of a chief executive officer (or CEO), a president, and at least one vice president.

A **middle manager** carries out the decisions of top management. Middle managers are often responsible for various departments in a business, such as the production, marketing, and accounting departments. Middle management is responsible for the organizing function as well as leading and controlling the work of others. Although middle managers do some planning, they are usually responsible for carrying out plans made by top management.

An **operational manager** is responsible for the daily operations of a business. Supervisors, office managers, and crew leaders are types of operational managers. Operational managers also do some planning and organizing. However, their main duties include overseeing workers and meeting deadlines (leading and controlling).

Leading

Good management also requires good leadership. There is more to leading than just giving orders. **Leading** means providing direction and vision. You have to create a vision of the company to inspire your employees. You need to set standards, such as deadlines and sales quotas, so your managers and workers know their goals. Leaders also have to delegate work, **enforce** policies, oversee time management, and provide feedback on employees' work. Resolving conflicts between workers is also a leadership task.

● **As You Read**

Many companies have eliminated middle managers to save money. Do you think this is a good business practice?

● **Responsibilities of a Manager**
A manager has many different responsibilities. **What responsibility is this manager fulfilling?**

Section 7.1   Management Functions   **113**

● **As You Read**

Answers will vary. Some students might say that saving money by eliminating middle managers will allow firms to be more profitable. Others might say middle managers are necessary to carry out plans of top management.

Discuss the Photo
● **Responsibilities of a Manager** The responsibility to train employees and to oversee their work is illustrated in this photograph.

RETEACH

W Writing Support
Enrichment
Levels of Management
Have students locate and print two examples of organizational charts and to write a paragraph describing their observations about their examples. (Students might note the similarities and differences in the appearance or content of the charts.)

R Reading Strategy
Draw a Diagram Ask students to draw an organizational chart depicting this structure: Dawna Kemper is the president of Keepsake Gifts. It has three managers: Cindy Halowski manages the warehouse, Lara Sighn manages the retail store, and Bob Kemper manages the online store. There are three retail sales associates, a Webmaster, an online sales associate, and two warehouse workers. (Organizational charts should show Kemper as the only top-level manager. Halowski, Sighn, and Kemper should all be on the same level. The employees should appear below their managers.)

U Universal Access
English Language Learners
Identify and explain words that are used in an unexpected context. For example, the word *vision* is used here to mean an image or concept in the imagination. The traditional definition is merely the ability to see.

Student Activity Workbook ☛ Assign the Section 7.1 Activities.

RETEACH (cont.)

Real World
Incentive Plans
Satisfied employees are more productive and contribute to success.

✔ **Reading Check**

Analyze Leaders provide direction and vision, set standards, delegate work, enforce policies, provide feedback, and motivate others.

ASSESS

● **After You Read**

Have students complete the Section 7.1 After You Read section review.

Online Study Tools
Have students go to the Online Learning Center through **glencoe.com** to:

• Take the Section 7.1 **Practice Test**.
• Download free **Study-to-Go** content to their PDAs or cell phones.

CLOSE

Culminating Activity
Management Functions
Assign the functions of management to each of four groups to develop presentations about how their function relates to others.

Incentive Plans
Some companies try to motivate employees with incentives such as on-site child care and bonuses. *How do you think offering such benefits can add to a company's costs?*

N C L B Activity correlates to Math standards.

Good managers lead by example. This is especially important when leading a team. Showing respect to others, honesty, loyalty, courtesy, and a strong work ethic can have a positive effect on employees. Managers who show motivation, initiative, cooperation, and punctuality demonstrate to employees the importance of each person's contribution.

✔ **Reading Check** **Analyze** Why is there more to leading than giving orders?

Controlling

Controlling the operation means keeping the company on track and making sure goals are met. Managers keep track of the budget, the schedule, and the quality of the products or services they provide. They also monitor their employees and review their performance according to standards. Taking corrective action when goals are not met is another management task.

Controlling also involves monitoring customer satisfaction. Your marketing manager can measure the success of your comic book by studying sales figures and reviews. You might find out your comic book sold well in certain parts of the country but sold poorly in others. If your comic book is more popular with adults than children, you might want to develop a new marketing plan.

Section 7.1

After You Read

Review Key Concepts
1. What is management?
2. What are three levels of management?
3. Which of the three levels is most involved in the day-to-day supervision of employees?

Academic Skills
N C L B
4. **Mathematics** You are a delivery manager at Blue Bag, a wholesale bakery. The bakery employs two drivers and owns two trucks. Each truck can deliver up to 175 crates of bread per day. The bakery has standing orders for 340 crates a day, but a new supermarket is opening up, and you expect orders to increase 225%. If you hire two more drivers, you can run two shifts. Will it be enough? Write a paragraph explaining how you found your answer.

THEORY **Problem Solving: Reflect on the Problem-Solving Process** Solving complex word problems such as this requires thinking through different scenarios, writing equations to match those scenarios, solving those equations, and comparing the results.

Math For math help, go to the Math Appendix.

@ Go to the *Introduction to Business* Online Learning Center through **glencoe.com** to check your answers.

glencoe.com

Section 7.1

Review Key Concepts
1. The aspect of business that involves planning, organizing, leading, and controlling.
2. top, middle, and operational
3. operational management

Academic Skills
4. **Mathematics** You are capable of delivering 175 × 2 = 350 crates of bread daily. If you double your driving staff, you will be able to deliver 350 × 2 = 700 crates. If standing orders increase by 225%: 340 × 225% = 765 crates, hiring two more drivers won't be enough.

Management Structures

FOCUS

Reading Guide

● Before You Read

Think about the characteristics you would need to be an effective manager.

D

Read to Learn
- Identify the differences between management structures.
- Name six skills necessary for effective management.

The Main Idea
Businesses have many different management structures that they can adopt. People who are interested in management should pay attention to the skills and knowledge needed to be an effective manager.

Key Concepts
- Managerial Structures
- Is Being a Manager for You?

Vocabulary
Key Terms
> line authority
> line and staff authority
> centralized organization
> decentralized organization
> departmentalization
> entry-level job

Academic Vocabulary
You will find these words in your reading and on your tests. Make sure you know their meanings.

> structure   evident
> authority   sector

Graphic Organizer
In a figure like the one below, list the qualities you need to be a good manager as you read.

Skills Needed by Managers

 Go to the *Introduction to Business* Online Learning Center through **glencoe.com** for a printable graphic organizer.

N C L B

Academic Standards
English Language Arts
> **NCTE 1** Read texts to acquire new information
> **NCTE 4** Use written language to communicate effectively
> **NCTE 9** Develop an understanding of diversity in language use across cultures
> **NCTE 12** Use language to accomplish individual purposes

Science
> **Content Standard A** Students should develop abilities necessary to do scientific inquiry and understandings about scientific inquiry

Section 7.2   Management Structures   **115**

Bell Ringer Activity

Management Structures
Point out that many people would like to be the boss. Ask students: What do you think it takes to be an effective manager? (Answers will vary. Students might suggest some of the traits outlined in this section along with some others such as dedication, stamina, competitiveness, etc.)

Preteaching

Presentation Plus!
The Presentation Plus! CD provides visual teaching aids for this section.

PuzzleMaker
Use the Vocabulary PuzzleMaker to create a puzzle of the section's key terms. Students can complete the puzzle on paper or on a computer.

Graphic Organizer
Tell students to go to the Online Learning Center through **glencoe.com** for a printable graphic organizer. (Answers include: The skills you need to be a good manager include: the ability to perform many tasks, the ability to work under pressure solving problems, communication skills, interpersonal skills, technical skills, and conceptual skills.)

N C L B   Connects academics to content.

Reading Guide

● Before You Read

In order to be effective, managers need certain abilities and sets of skills.

D Develop Concepts

The Main Idea Ask students: Why do businesses have different management structures? (Management structures have advantages and disadvantages. Depending on the firm, one structure might work better than the others.)

Discussion Starter
Managerial Structures
Ask students: Why are clear lines of authority important? (Answers will vary. Students should recognize that having clear lines of authority helps to clarify responsibilities.)

R **Reading Strategy**

Compare Ask students to compare the concepts of line authority and line and staff authority by thinking of some examples where one of the management structures seems to have a clear advantage. (Answers will vary. Students might suggest that a company that has to move quickly and make rapid decisions might benefit from a line authority structure because it gives clear lines of authority. Students also might suggest that small firms would not have enough staff to have a line and staff authority structure.)

Managerial Structures

There are several ways to organize a management **structure**. **Line authority** is an organizational structure in which managers on one level are in charge of those beneath them. An advantage of the line authority structure is that **authority** is clearly defined. Each employee knows to whom she or he reports. A disadvantage to line authority is that the managers have few specialists who **R** help with their responsibilities.

A **line and staff authority** organizational chart shows the direct line of authority (indicated by solid lines) as well as staff who advise the line personnel (indicated by dotted lines). **Figure 7.2** shows a line and staff organizational chart. The line and staff authority structure enables managers to get advice. However, a disadvantage is that it can lead to overstaffing, which can be costly.

Some firms have a **centralized organization** that puts authority in one place—with top management. This helps managers throughout the firm to be consistent in decision making.

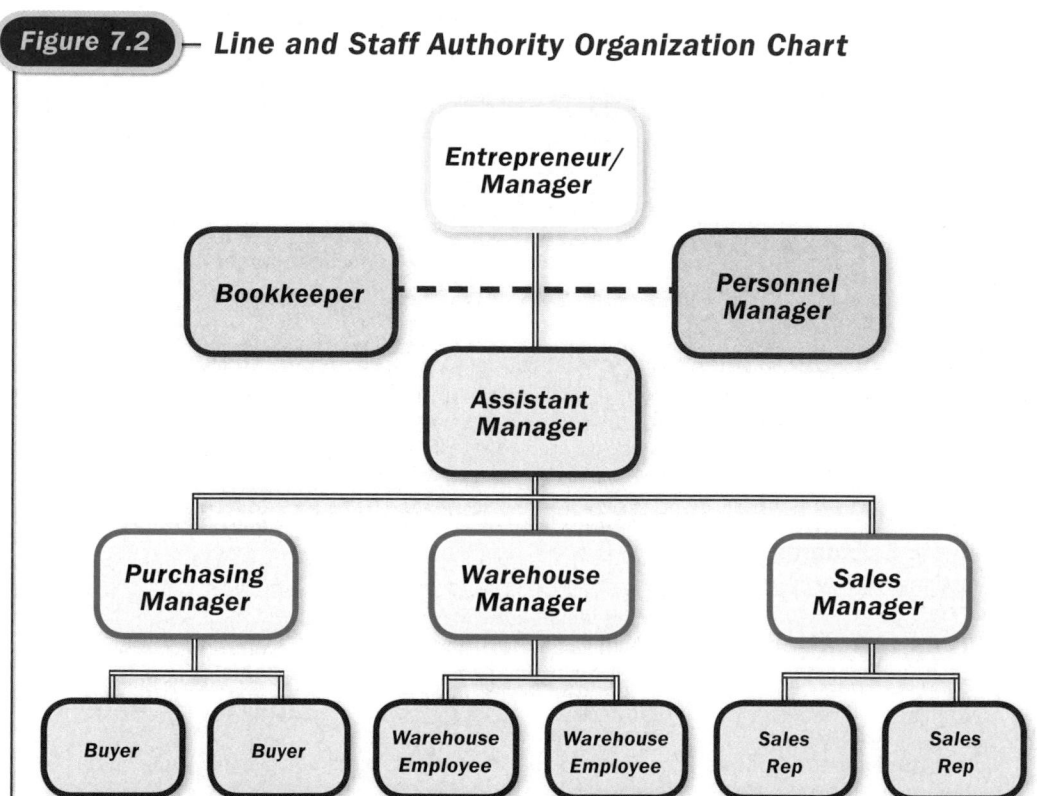

Figure 7.2 — *Line and Staff Authority Organization Chart*

● **Solid and Dotted Lines** A line and staff organizational chart shows different roles of staff with different types of lines. **What is the difference between the personnel linked by solid lines and staff positions linked by dotted lines?**

Figure 7.2

● **Solid and Dotted Lines** The personnel linked by solid lines are in direct lines of authority. Personnel who are shown linked by dotted lines are outside those direct lines of authority, but they work together and are able to give advice to each other.

Decentralized organization gives authority to a number of different managers. Decentralized organizations are often evident in international businesses. Some U.S. managers working in foreign countries have more decision-making power because they know their markets well.

✔ **Reading Check** **Contrast** What is the advantage and the disadvantage of line authority?

Formal Structure

Formal structures are usually departmentalized. **Departmentalization** divides responsibility among specific units, or departments. Departments can be organized many different ways, such as by geographical location, function, customer groups, and product.

Informal Structure

Smaller businesses can be run informally. If a business does not need a big marketing or distribution network, it does not need a lot of managers. Employees can be more flexible and share duties. For example, partners can work on projects alone or together. The informal structure often works well for them.

Employee Input
Forward-looking companies are on a new track to encourage worker participation, new ways of thinking, and a move away from a formal structure. *How is this good for business?*

● **As You Read**
Think about an informal business you have seen or read about. Do you think this type of business can be successful?

NCLB

Decision Science

Solving highly complex business problems requires a manager to be an effective decision maker. Effective decision makers seek input from many sources and gather varied data to inform their thinking about business problems. Since the 1940s, the field of decision science, also known as management science or success science, has developed new ways to use mathematics and the scientific method to make decisions. Business managers faced with the need to analyze mounds of data and choose among risky alternatives can hire decision scientists to help them. These consultants offer data analysis services, education in mathematical concepts, and data analysis tools and techniques.

WebQuest

Decision science evolved from game theory, which deals largely with how individuals interact with one another in an effort to win. Go to the *Introduction to Business* Online Learning Center through **glencoe.com** for links to Web sites where you can research more about how game theory and decision science have developed since the 1940s. Write a paragraph or two describing how an understanding of game theory and decision science could help a person make complex business decisions.

TEACH (cont.)

S Skill Practice
Guided Practice
Make a List Ask students to make a list of the ways departmentalized companies are organized. (geographical location, function, or customer groups) **L1**

Draw a Chart Have students draw an organizational chart for a departmentalized structured company. (Departmentalization should be illustrated clearly.) **L2**

Compare and Contrast Ask students to name a circumstance where an informal management structure would be a better choice. (Answers include: businesses that foster teamwork and creativity.) **L3**

✔ **Reading Check**

Contrast When lines of authority are clearly defined, each employee knows who is boss, but few specialists are available to help managers.

ASSESS

Review Key Terms
Have students write sentences using each key term.

 Study-to-Go Have students go to the Online Learning Center through **glencoe.com** to download free **Study-to-Go** content to their PDAs or cell phones.

● **As You Read**
Informality can allow for creativity, which can lead to success.

Decision Science
People who understand game theory are likely to win games. Managers who use decision science can use similar strategies to gather and analyze complex information.

Employee Input Encouraging workers to participate allows them to use their skills and talents. Some workers feel more comfortable in a less structured setting.

117

RETEACH

W Writing Support

Enrichment

Interpersonal Skills Have students write a short essay about a skill like interpersonal skills or one of the other traits of effective managers that they might exhibit. Ask students to consider how the trait affects the manager, employees, and the firm. (Essays will vary, but should indicate an understanding of the meaning, importance, and dynamic nature of the chosen trait.)

R Reading Strategy

Make a Bulleted List Have students create a bulleted list of key information about effective communication as a trait of effective managers. Encourage students to flesh out the list with additional information. (Students might add information about body language, presentation skills, and eye contact.)

U Universal Access

Auditory Learners Organize students into pairs and ask them to focus on the information about managers' needs for listening skills. Instruct students to read the text aloud and discuss what they have read. Suggest that students work together to decide what should be included in their class notes. This activity is helpful for students who learn well by listening and talking.

Student Activity Workbook ✎ Assign the Section 7.2 Activities.

Is a Manager's Job for You?

W Most managers begin their career in an entry-level job. An **entry-level job** is a beginner-level position. New employees who gain experience and show certain qualities can be promoted to higher positions, including management.

Skills Needed by Managers

R Managers are usually task-oriented. This means that they can handle many tasks at the same time. They have to plan their time and decide which tasks are most important. They also must keep accurate business records. A manager often has to work under pressure and solve many small problems. Good problem-solving and time-management skills are a must. Every manager must communicate well. Most of a manager's day is spent interacting with other people. This involves listening, an important part of communication. Managers need human relations skills, **U** or skills in dealing with people. All managers must have some knowledge about the technical aspects of their business.

BusinessWeek *Reader and Case Study*

A Board of Your Own

Where can small companies turn for objective advice? To each other, thanks to peer groups such as The Alternative Board.

When Daryl Rossman, president of Merco Manufacturing, wanted feedback about expanding his family-owned aerospace parts manufacturer or needed advice on strategy and marketing, his options were limited. He could go to the expense of hiring an outside accountant, lawyer, or business consultant. Or he could discuss his views internally with one of his 16 employees.

"Being a small business, I didn't really have anybody to sound off my ideas with other than my own employees," he says. "But I always felt they were biased. They would say what I wanted to hear and give me the response I was looking for."

However, since last March, Rossman has sought the objective advice of The Alternative Board (TAB), a peer advisory group that brings together small- and midsize-business owners from noncompeting companies to share their collective wisdom and act as a professional sounding board. A kind of small-business think tank that meets on a monthly basis, TAB offers a forum for entrepreneurs to discuss everything from personnel to management and finance issues, and come up with goals and plans to address them.

 CASE STUDY Go to the *Introduction to Business* Online Learning Center through **glencoe.com** for the *BusinessWeek* Reader Case Study.

Active Learning

Entrepreneurs often have to fill several different roles—at the same time. Write an e-mail to your teacher comparing and contrasting reasons a manager might or might not want to go to employees for advice. How can adding employees who specialize in a single function help a business grow?

118 **Chapter 7** Business Management

glencoe.com

BusinessWeek *Reader and Case Study*

A Board of Your Own

 CASE STUDY Have students go to the *Introduction to Business* Online Learning Center through **glencoe.com** to download a Case Study activity that corresponds to the article. The activity and answer key are also available on the TeacherWorks Plus CD.

Active Learning

Entrepreneurs who start businesses may have to assume any or all the roles performed by employees in a large business. Like entrepreneurs, top managers also have responsibility for guiding the company's direction, but they can direct middle and operational managers to take responsibility for parts of the enterprise.

Managers, especially top-level managers, must be able to understand how various parts of the company relate to the whole business. This includes knowing how economic conditions and competition can affect the business. Higher-level managers have to know what is happening in the world and in their **sector** of the business world. Otherwise, they will have trouble conceptualizing and solving problems that the company faces.

Advantages of Being a Manager

Managers usually earn more money than employees in non-management jobs. People become managers because they have the ability to lead. Managers who are good leaders are respected. Being a respected manager builds prestige. Managers have more influence and authority than other employees because they plan, organize, direct, and control company resources. They also have greater control over their time.

Disadvantages of Being a Manager

There are several disadvantages to being a manager. Managers are often blamed when things go wrong, even if they did not cause the problem. Their mistakes can be very costly to a company so they are under a lot of pressure to make the right decisions.

> ● **As You Read**
>
> Think about an opportunity to manage a local restaurant. Would you want to take on the responsibility? Why or why not?

NCLB Activity correlates to English Language Arts standards.

Section 7.2

● **After You Read**

Review Key Concepts
1. What is an advantage of a line and staff authority organization structure over a line authority organization?
2. Why do some businesses use a decentralized organization?
3. What are some characteristics of an effective manager?

Academic Skills

4. **English Language Arts** Work with a partner to role play two business situations involving a manager and an employee. If possible, choose a partner who has a different cultural background from your own. Each of you should take the role of manager in one of the situations you choose. List the management responsibilities and skills that you and your partner think are important for handling the situations you examined.

5. **English Language Arts** In which kind of organization would you like to work? Should it have a formal or informal structure? Write a short description of the ideal business environment for you. Then imagine starting a garden design and maintenance business. Decide what jobs you will need to hire people to fill. Create an organizational chart for your company.

 Go to the *Introduction to Business* Online Learning Center through **glencoe.com** to check your answers.

Section 7.2

Review Key Concepts
1. Line and staff authority structure enables management to get advice from staff personnel.
2. They allow decisions to be made at the local level where managers are more familiar with the problems and have the resources to solve them.
3. task-oriented, able to work under pressure, effective communicator, work well with others, and technical knowledge

Academic Skills
4. **English Language Arts** effective communication and interpersonal skills
5. **English Language Arts** The chart should show a formal or informal structure.

Vocabulary Review

1. Students should write complete sentences using each term correctly.

Review Key Concepts

2. to set and meet goals as effectively as possible so that a profit can be made

3. Planning: the act or process of creating goals and objectives and the strategies to meet them. Organizing: getting the resources arranged in an orderly and functional way to accomplish goals and objectives. Leading: providing direction and vision for people. Controlling: keeping employees on track to make sure goals are met.

4. Line authority: managers at the top of the line are in charge of those beneath them. Line and staff authority: shows the authority lines and the staff who advise the manager. Centralized authority: major decision-making ability goes to top-level managers. Decentralized authority: more major decisions are made at lower level. Formal structure creates a clear-cut organization, generally with departments. Informal structure allows most employees to offer input and to work together.

5. the ability to perform varied tasks, work under pressure, communication skills, interpersonal skills, technical skills, conceptual skills

Section 7.1 *Summary*

Management Functions Management includes the processes or functions of planning, organizing, leading, and controlling. Most managers carry out all four of the functions. However, some spend more time on some of the functions than others. There are generally three levels of management: top-level, middle, and operational. Top-level managers usually spend more time on planning than operational managers. Middle managers spend more time organizing. They also lead and control the work of others. Operational managers generally spend more time on leading and controlling than do top-level managers.

Section 7.2 *Summary*

Management Structures There are several different management structures, including line authority; line and staff authority; centralized or decentralized authority; and formal or informal authority. Each has its own advantages and disadvantages. A business should adopt the structure that makes it operate at its best to maximize profits. Successful managers are task-oriented and able to work under pressure. Many people aspire to become managers because of advantages such as increased income, prestige, and the ability to make things happen. Disadvantages of being a manager include stress and accepting responsibility for other people's mistakes.

Vocabulary Review

1. On a sheet of paper, use each of these key terms and academic vocabulary terms in a sentence.

Key Terms

management
planning
organizing
organizational chart
top-level manager
middle manager
operational manager
leading

controlling
line authority
line and staff authority
centralized organization
decentralized organization
departmentalization
entry-level job

Academic Vocabulary

focus
goals
teams
enforce
structure
authority
evident
sector

Review Key Concepts

2. Describe the overall purpose of management.

3. Discuss the four functions of management.

4. Identify the differences between management structures.

5. Name six skills necessary for effective management.

Critical Thinking

6. If you do not have a good plan, the results will not be successful.

7. Many top-level managers welcome input and will consider changing plans if warranted.

8. Top-level and operational managers have had to assume more of the responsibilities that were previously handled by middle managers.

9. It helps to build morale while promoting efficiency. It also helps to prepare employees for promotion.

10. Some people enjoy the stability of a formally structured organization. Others feel more comfortable with the relaxation of an informal structure.

11. Answers should include characteristics of a good manager presented in this chapter.

Critical Thinking

6. Some people believe that the planning function is the most important one for a manager. Why might that be true?

7. Suppose top-level management decides how to produce and market a new product. Do you think the plans might change during the organizing, leading, and controlling stages?

8. Since companies are using fewer middle managers, how have the jobs of top-level management and operational managers changed?

9. Why do you think it is a good idea for workers to have more decision-making duties and provide input to managers?

10. Give reasons for working within either a formal or an informal business structure.

11. Describe the qualities of a manager for whom you would like to work someday.

12. One problem with line and staff authority as compared to line authority is that some line and staff managers tend to overanalyze a problem. Why might that happen?

13. Why might a manager decide to change an informally structured organization into a formally structured one?

Write About It

14. In what ways are an entrepreneur and a manager alike? In what ways are they different? Write an e-mail to your teacher on your thoughts.

15. Imagine you are in charge of the next school dance. In one page, indicate some tasks that you would complete in each function of management.

16. What are reasons some managers are hired from within a company? Why are some hired from outside a company? Write two or more paragraphs explaining your answers.

17. Research the requirements for a management major at a local two- or four-year college. Determine the types of courses that students must take. In a one-page article, describe the required courses in the program.

18. One requirement of a good manager is effective communication skills. Write a short essay about the importance of communication to managers. Be sure to include listening skills.

19. Managers generally receive more pay than the workers they manage. Write two or more paragraphs indicating why you believe this is fair or unfair.

Technology Applications

Organization Chart

20. Work in small groups. Imagine you are starting a greeting card company. Decide what functions your team members will perform. Consider each person's talents and interests. Will your company be structured formally or informally? Make a chart using presentation software to show how you organized your company. Present your chart to the class.

Business Ethics

Managerial Decision Making

21. You are an operations manager for a ceramics manufacturer. The president's son is assigned to work for you, but after two weeks, you notice that he spends a lot of time on the Internet, does little work, and does not get along with other workers. If you do nothing, then production will be affected. What should you do?

Critical Thinking

12. Line and staff advisors may provide too much analysis.

13. When growth demands increased accountability in the company.

Write About It

14. Entrepreneurs must take on many of the roles of a manager because they do not have as large a staff, but have more freedom.

15. Planning: deciding on a theme and location. Organizing: assigning volunteers. Leading: working with volunteers. Controlling: making sure that volunteers are following through.

16. Managers from within a company are likely to have experience facing the challenges of that company. Managers from outside are likely to be able to bring a diverse perspective.

17. Managers should take courses in science, mathematics, communication, computers, history, social science, arts, and business.

18. Communication skills allow managers to direct staff, but listening skills allow managers to take advantage of employee skills.

19. Some will indicate that higher pay is fair because managers have more responsibility. Others may think wages should be equal because both groups contribute to the success of the enterprise.

Technology Applications

20. Students should indicate the different functions of the company that will be covered by team members and why they have chosen to follow a formal or informal management structure. The organization chart should include the different levels of management.

Business Ethics

21. Students should recognize that as a manager, your first step is to discuss the problem with the production assistant and offer suggestions for improvement. If there is no improvement, the next step is to discuss the matter with your immediate superior and follow his or her direction.

22. Answers will vary, but students' examples of proper nouns might include the names of companies or brands that use hyphens, such as Wal-Mart® and Coca-Cola®.

23. [$500 + (3 × $350)] 108.15% = x

24. Successful managers are able to carry out varied tasks, perform under pressure, communicate effectively, relate to people, and grasp and use information. Managers have prestige, influence, and power; however, they usually experience a lot of pressure, too.

25. Range: 12; Mean: 7.7; Median: 7; Mode: 5

Active Learning

26. Answers will vary depending on where the interviewee works.

Business in the Real World

27. Answers will depend on the type of business chosen, the type of manager interviewed, and his or her responses.

Applying Academics to Business

English Language Arts
22. Hyphens and dashes are used in several situations. Look through this textbook and note two examples of each of the following: a dash separating parts of a sentence; a hyphen separating syllables in a word that turns a line; hyphenated adjectives; and hyphenated proper nouns.

Mathematics
23. Fran, a merchandising manager for Blue Bag, is planning her department's yearly budget. She earns $500 a week and is in charge of three employees, each earning $350 a week. The business pays FICA (Federal Insurance Contributions Act) taxes of 8.15% on employee earnings to cover the cost of Social Security. Write an equation Fran could use to figure how much her department needs to budget to pay salaries and FICA taxes for the year.

> **THEORY** **Algebra: Writing Equations**
> Simplify your equation by multiplying the total of the departmental salaries by a percent, greater than 100, that represents total salaries increased by the percent for FICA taxes.

English Language Arts
24. Copy the following paragraph onto a piece of paper and add the correct punctuation. Successful managers are able to carry out varied tasks perform under pressure communicate effectively relate to people and grasp and use information. Managers have prestige influence and power however they usually experience a lot of pressure too.

Mathematics
25. Fred tracked the number of days members of his department were absent. For the second quarter, the results were: 5, 3, 5, 6, 9, 13, 15, 12, 8, 7, 5, 7, and 5. What are the range, mean, median, and mode of the data?

> **THEORY** **Data Analysis and Probability: Measures of Central Tendency** For any given set of data, the range is the difference between the greatest and least value; the mean is the average; the median is the middle value when all values are ordered from least to greatest; and the mode is the most frequently occurring value.

Active Learning

Workplace Organization
26. Ask a family member how his or her workplace is organized. How is the management structured? Is the company divided into different divisions? How many employees are there in each division, if any? Does the company operate in more than one location? Create a poster summarizing your findings.

Business in the Real World

Managers as Leaders
27. Interview a business manager to find out how he or she uses leadership skills and resources on the job. Ask about job duties, delegating, what the manager most likes about his or her job, and what his or her greatest challenges are. Then ask how much time is spent on each of the four functional areas of management. Use this information to write a report of 250 words of more.

ExamView Assessment Suite CD allows you to print out ready-made unit and chapter tests, complete with answer keys. You can also create customized tests.

TeacherWorks Plus provides complete teacher resources in one convenient package. It includes customizable lesson plans in calendar format, and instant access to many print program resources.

Real LIFE *skills*

EVALUATING MANAGEMENT SKILLS

28. Review the six different traits necessary for effective management. These traits include technical and conceptual skills. Choose a successful entrepreneur, and research how she or he became successful. Identify the traits that helped this businessperson reach his or her goals. Write at least a one-page report on your findings.

Cool Business CAREERS

FIND YOUR DREAM JOB

29. Go to the *Introduction to Business* Online Learning Center through **glencoe.com** for a link to the Occupational Outlook Handbook Web site. Click on the "OOH Search/A-Z Index" link and enter the job title "medical and health services manager." Then write a one-page report about this type of occupation. Conclude your report with a list of things you could do now to prepare yourself to pursue this occupation.

Role Play

INTERVIEWING FOR A MANAGEMENT JOB

30. Situation Last summer you planned and implemented an educational trip for 30 young people for three weeks. Now you are interviewing for a summer job managing a recreational program for 8- to 10-year-olds in your community. You would be developing this program on your own.

Activity Discuss the experiences you have that show the skills and background needed for the job.

Evaluation You will be evaluated on how well you meet the following performance indicators:

- Mention how you used the four functional areas of management.
- Demonstrate how you have at least five of the management skills mentioned in the chapter.
- Make concise and clear statements while showing self-confidence.
- Use correct grammar.

Standardized Test Practice

Directions Choose the letter of the best answer. Write the letter for the answer on a separate piece of paper.

1. Which could be added to 4 to get an integer x that is less than -2?

A   any integer greater than -3
B   any integer less than 0
C   any integer less than -6
D   any integer greater than -6

> **TEST-TAKING TIP** You can improve your score on multiple-choice items by covering the options while you read the question and try to answer it. Then select the option that most closely matches your answer.

@   **READING** Go to the *Introduction to Business* Online Learning Center through **glencoe.com** for a list of outside reading suggestions.

Real LIFE *skills*

28. Answers will depend on the entrepreneur chosen, but should discuss each of the traits, whether or not that businessperson has them.

Cool Business CAREERS

29. Nature of the work: Plan, direct, and coordinate health care in a variety of settings. A specialist manages a specific department; a generalist manages a system. Managers need a master's degree in health services administration, health sciences. Some require certification. Preparation includes science and business classes and volunteering at a health care facility.

Role Play

30. Presentations should mention how the four functional areas of management were used and demonstrate that students have at least five management skills mentioned in the chapter.

> *Standardized Test Practice*
> **1.** C

STRATEGIES FOR STANDARDIZED TEST PREP SUCCESS

Test Savvy Answer choices on multiple-choice test items are called distractors because they do just that. Incorrect answer choices, especially those that look similar, can distract the test-taker's attention from that answer which is the best. A strategy that many students find effective is to cover the answer choices before reading the stem of the question, answering the question, and then reading the answer choices. In this way, the student has an answer in mind when he or she chooses, and will be less likely to be distracted. Tell students to look for the answer choice that most closely matches the answer they came up with on their own.

Standards-Based Lesson Planning

Introduction to Business provides students with instruction and assessment in the following fundamental content areas:

Content Standards Correlations	
Students will understand the personal qualities that are the basis for developing leadership skills.	pp. 127–130, 136–139
Identify and use leadership skills in a variety of individual and group work situations.	pp. 127–130, 136–139
Demonstrate interpersonal, teamwork, and leadership skills necessary to function in multicultural business settings.	pp. 127–130, 136–139
Examine the characteristics of a good leader.	pp. 127–130, 132–135, 136–139
Demonstrate human relations, self-management, organizational, and professional leadership skills.	pp. 127–130, 136–139
Examine the role of leadership skills in business success.	pp. 127–130, 132–135, 136–139
Discuss the role of the worker as a team member.	pp. 134–135, 136–139
Plan, organize, and assume responsibility for effective meetings.	pp. 134–135, 137–138
Students will understand the personal qualities that are the basis for developing leadership skills.	pp. 127–130, 136–139
Identify and use leadership skills in a variety of individual and group work situations.	pp. 127–130, 136–139

NCLB Activities, information, and skills practice will help your students attain No Child Left Behind proficiency. Students will improve their abilities in the following academic standards areas:

Academic Standards Correlations		
English Language Arts	Activities/Features	Page
NCTE 3 Apply strategies to interpret texts	Applying Academics to Business	p. 138
NCTE 11 Participate as members of literacy communities	Applying Academics to Business	p. 138
NCTE 12 Use language to accomplish individual purposes	After You Read	p. 135
Mathematics		
Geometry Use visualization, spatial reasoning, and geometric modeling to solve problems	Applying Academics to Business	p. 138
Measurement Apply appropriate techniques, tools, and formulas to determine measurements	Applying Academics to Business	p. 138
Number and Operations Compute fluently and make reasonable estimates	Standardized Test Practice	p. 139
Problem Solving Apply and adapt a variety of appropriate strategies to solve problems	Ask S&P After You Read	pp. 124, 130
Science		
Content Standard F Students should develop understanding of personal and community health, science, and technology in local, national, and global challenges	Science/Tech Trends	p. 133

Correlations   This chart shows the 21st Century Skills, foundation skills, and workplace competencies that students develop as they work in this chapter.

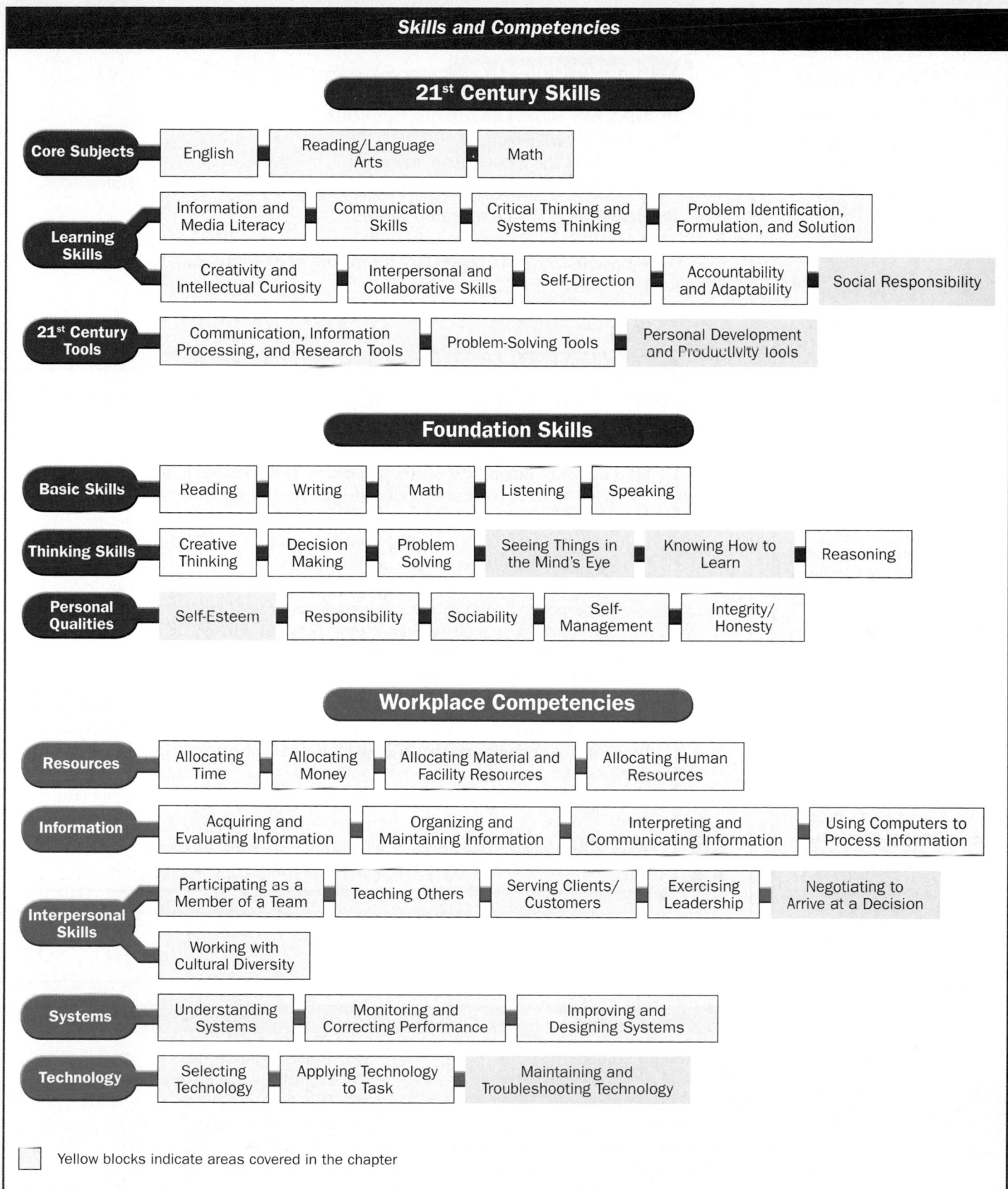

Skills and Competencies

21st Century Skills

Core Subjects
- English
- Reading/Language Arts
- Math

Learning Skills
- Information and Media Literacy
- Communication Skills
- Critical Thinking and Systems Thinking
- Problem Identification, Formulation, and Solution
- Creativity and Intellectual Curiosity
- Interpersonal and Collaborative Skills
- Self-Direction
- Accountability and Adaptability
- Social Responsibility

21st Century Tools
- Communication, Information Processing, and Research Tools
- Problem-Solving Tools
- Personal Development and Productivity Tools

Foundation Skills

Basic Skills
- Reading
- Writing
- Math
- Listening
- Speaking

Thinking Skills
- Creative Thinking
- Decision Making
- Problem Solving
- Seeing Things in the Mind's Eye
- Knowing How to Learn
- Reasoning

Personal Qualities
- Self-Esteem
- Responsibility
- Sociability
- Self-Management
- Integrity/Honesty

Workplace Competencies

Resources
- Allocating Time
- Allocating Money
- Allocating Material and Facility Resources
- Allocating Human Resources

Information
- Acquiring and Evaluating Information
- Organizing and Maintaining Information
- Interpreting and Communicating Information
- Using Computers to Process Information

Interpersonal Skills
- Participating as a Member of a Team
- Teaching Others
- Serving Clients/Customers
- Exercising Leadership
- Negotiating to Arrive at a Decision
- Working with Cultural Diversity

Systems
- Understanding Systems
- Monitoring and Correcting Performance
- Improving and Designing Systems

Technology
- Selecting Technology
- Applying Technology to Task
- Maintaining and Troubleshooting Technology

Yellow blocks indicate areas covered in the chapter

Chapter Overview

Introduce the Chapter

Leadership in Management
Chapter 8 is about leadership qualities and styles of leadership.

Building Background

Students already know something about leadership, having served as leaders in school, athletics, and community activities, and observing classmates and teammates demonstrate leadership.

Ask STANDARD &POOR'S

>> Math Answer
The equation for calculating the fee is shown below. Students may or may not use parentheses. The letter *p* represents the unknown.

$p = (\$100,000 \times 0.02) + (\$60,000 \times 0.005)$

$p = \$2,000 + \$300$

$p = \$2,300$

>> Extension Activity
Point out that fees for financial planning are calculated in different ways. Mary Ann's brother uses a financial planner who does not charge a separate fee for stock purchases. She charges 2.2% for the amount under management. How much would Mary Ann pay if she used her brother's financial planner? ($2,200)

N C L B
Activity correlates to Math standards.

Leadership in Management

Chapter Objectives After completing this chapter, you will be able to:

▶ **Section 8.1** *Leadership Qualities*
- **Define** leadership.
- **Describe** the qualities of a leader.
- **Name** at least three ways in which an individual can develop leadership skills.

▶ **Section 8.2** *Leadership Styles*
- **Identify** and describe the autocratic, democratic, and free-rein leadership styles.
- **Describe** the self-managed team approach and the two ways in which such an approach is organized.

Ask STANDARD &POOR'S **Getting Professional Help with Investing**

Q: I have just inherited some money and need help making investment decisions. What kinds of professional services are available to new investors?

A: The service that is best for you depends partly on how much time and effort you want to spend tending to your investments. Certified financial planners can help you look at the larger picture, identify goals, and structure a portfolio. Stockbrokers can help you buy and sell individual stocks. You'll want to investigate credentials and experience, and get recommendations from other clients before choosing. Investment help is also available from publications such as Standard & Poor's *The Outlook*. Finally, investment clubs are a great way for like-minded people to share their investing experiences. You might consider joining one.

Mathematics Mary Ann hired a certified financial planner to help her invest $100,000 she inherited. When she asked the CFP how he would be paid, he said his fee would be 2% of the amount under management plus a half-percent commission on any stock purchase. Mary Ann chose to invest $60,000 in stocks and the rest in other types of investments. Write an equation that shows what she paid her financial planner (*p*) for his services.

N C L B

THEORY **Choosing Operations** Solving most real-world problems requires several steps. Read carefully to make sure you understand which operations to use.

124 **Unit 2** Owning and Operating a Business

📖 **Classroom Resources**

- 📑 Student Edition
- 📑 Teacher Wraparound Edition
- 📁 Student Activity Workbook with Academic Integration
- 📁 Student Activity Workbook with Academic Integration TAE
- 📁 *Fast File*, Unit 2 Resources
- 📁 Inclusion in the Business Education Classroom

- 💿 TeacherWorks Plus
- 💿 *ExamView Assessment Suite*
- 💿 Presentation Plus!
- 💿 Vocabulary PuzzleMaker
- 💿 Interactive Student Edition
- 💻 Online Student Edition
- 💻 Online Learning Center with Podcasts

● **Captain of the Team** All kinds of groups need leaders. **Why do you think it is good to have a leader?**

Chapter 8 Leadership in Management **125**

Introduce the chapter by reviewing the chapter objectives:

Section 8.1 *Objectives*
Define leadership. (taking a company and its employees in a direction based on a vision)

Describe the qualities of a leader. (motivation, confidence, communication skills, and integrity)

Name at least three ways in which an individual can develop leadership skills. (reading books, working with someone who has leadership skills, and volunteering for projects that provide leadership opportunities)

Section 8.2 *Objectives*
Identify and describe the autocratic, democratic, and free-rein leadership styles. (Autocratic leaders run everything and make all decisions without consulting others. Democratic leaders work with employees to make decisions, still make the final decisions, but explain their reasons for their decisions. Free-rein leaders set goals for managers and employees, then leave the employees alone so they can get the job done.)

Describe the self-managed team approach and the two ways in which such an approach is organized. (Team members with a varied skills and talents work together to complete assigned tasks using the means they deem best. They are organized in two ways: (1) each team member has a special skill with no team leader or (2) the team selects one team leader.)

Discuss the Photo
● **Captain of the Team** Read the caption on the photo to students: All kinds of groups need leaders.

Ask students: Why is it good to have a leader? (For instance, a winning quarterback has all four leadership qualities—motivation, communication, integrity, and confidence. In any setting where decisions need to be made, it is good to have one person who can be counted on to make decisions. Leaders set goals so that a team of people who work can achieve more than any individual could accomplish alone.)

125

FOCUS

🔔 Bell Ringer Activity

Leadership Qualities

Ask students if they think some people are "born leaders." (Some students will indicate that leaders are born and others will say that leadership can be learned. Other students might suggest that leadership is based on a combination of innate talent and learned skills.) Follow up by pointing out that leadership can be developed through a number of different avenues.

Preteaching

Presentation Plus! 💿

The Presentation Plus! CD provides visual teaching aids for this section.

PuzzleMaker 💿

Use the Vocabulary PuzzleMaker to create a puzzle of the section's key terms. Students can complete the puzzle on paper or on a computer.

Graphic Organizer

Tell students to go to the Online Learning Center through **glencoe.com** for a printable graphic organizer. (Answers include: The essential qualities of leaders include motivation, confidence, communication skills, and integrity.)

NCLB Connects academics to content.

Leadership Qualities

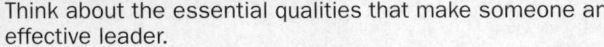

Reading Guide

📖 Before You Read

Think about the essential qualities that make someone an effective leader.

Read to Learn
- Define leadership.
- Describe the qualities of a leader.
- Name at least three ways in which an individual can develop leadership skills.

D

The Main Idea

Leaders develop a vision for the organization that they are leading. They move employees and their organization toward that vision. The qualities of leaders include motivation, confidence, communication skills, and integrity.

Key Concepts
- Managing and Leading Others
- Developing Leadership Skills

Vocabulary
Key Terms
leadership
initiative
human relations
integrity

Academic Vocabulary

You will find these words in your reading and on your tests. Make sure you know their meanings.

vision	conflict
trends	techniques

Graphic Organizer

List and define the qualities of a good leader in a figure like the one below.

Leadership

 Go to the *Introduction to Business* Online Learning Center through **glencoe.com** for a printable graphic organizer.

Academic Standards

English Language Arts
    NCTE 1 Read texts to acquire new information
    NCTE 9 Develop an understanding of diversity in language use across cultures
Mathematics
    Problem Solving Apply and adapt a variety of appropriate strategies to solve problems

N C L B

Reading Guide

📖 Before You Read

Leaders are highly motivated, self-confident, demonstrate integrity, and have good communication skills.

D Develop Concepts

The Main Idea Ask students: Is it possible for someone to be a leader and not a manager? (Not all leaders are managers.)

Managing and Leading Others

Leadership means taking a company and its employees in a direction based upon a **vision**. Leaders see the big picture and never lose sight of their goal. Good leaders manage others by inspiring them.

There is more to leadership than just being in charge. In today's world, true leaders know their business and the capabilities of their employees, analyze current **trends**, and steer their business on the right course. Some people who are managers are not leaders. They may focus on specific tasks to make sure work gets done, but they may not be visionaries or inspire others.

Good leadership is needed not only in the business world but also in areas such as nonprofits, education, and sports. For example, a football team depends on its quarterback to call the signals and direct the offensive play. The quarterback has to think quickly and counts on his teammates to follow through after a decision is made. Ideally, the person in charge of a business or business team is also a leader.

Leaders also make sure that the basic operations of an organization are running smoothly. That could involve making sure office duties get done; handling records management; and planning, organizing, and running meetings. Being a good leader takes several qualities. Motivation, confidence, communication skills, and integrity are among them.

> ● **As You Read**
>
> Think about some people you know who are managers.

✔ Reading Check **Identify** What does leadership involve in today's world?

International Business

Total Quality Management

After World War II, Japan had a reputation for producing poorly made products. In order to bring about change, Japanese business leaders hired Dr. W. Edwards Deming, an American management consultant. Deming promised that if they followed his directions, they could achieve the desired outcome in five years. The system he implemented came to be known as TQM—total quality management. Deming is now known as the father of the Japanese postwar industrial revival. For his efforts, he was awarded the Second Order of the Sacred Treasure by Emperor Hirohito in 1960.

Examples of Languages Across Cultures

Q: In Japanese, how do you say: "Happy birthday?"

A: めでとう! 誕生日お (pronounced: Ōtǎn-jō-bā ōmādātō!)

Deming believed in the right to have pride in your workmanship. Why do you think pride in workmanship is important in improving quality?

TEACH

Discussion Starter
Leadership Qualities
Ask students to explain this statement: Good leaders manage others by inspiring them. (Answers will vary. Students should understand that employees are inspired to do their best when they have a leader who is committed to and excited about goals; who has the confidence and the ability to communicate the vision to employees, investors, and customers; and who demonstrates integrity through fairness and honesty.)

R Reading Strategy

Develop Examples Ask students to visualize examples of good leadership and relate them to the text. (Answers will vary. Many students will think of characters from movies who have demonstrated leadership qualities under adversity. Others may cite historical figures or leaders in their communities. Encourage students to recognize that leadership qualities are an everyday necessity. Organizations need good leaders in both good times and bad, and sometimes good leadership involves simple hard work.)

✔ Reading Check

Identify In today's world leadership involves knowing the business you are leading and the capabilities of your employees, analyzing current trends that affect your business, having a vision, and steering the business on the right course.

● **As You Read**

Managers tell others what to do, but leaders look at the "big picture" and motivate others. Great managers are also leaders.

International Business

Total Quality Management Students should mention the connection between the desire to do a good job and the likelihood that a quality product will be the result.

S Skill Practice

Guided Practice

Make a List Have students define the three components of motivation. (inspiring others, having initiative, and having a goal) **L1**

Explain Your Motivation Instruct students to write a paragraph relating the three components of motivation to their situation. (Students might write about the motivation needed to do their homework or to improve their game.) **L2**

Provide an Example Instruct students to read the passage about Dr. Martin Luther King and write a similar passage based on another example of motivation. (Encourage students to find examples from their own community.) **L3**

ASSESS

Review Key Terms

Have students write sentences using each key term.

Study-to-Go Have students go to the Online Learning Center through **glencoe.com** to download free **Study-to-Go** content to their PDAs or cell phones.

✔ Reading Check

Explain Inspiring others, having initiative, and having a goal.

128

Quiet Leadership
On December 1, 1955, Rosa Parks, an African-American seamstress, was ordered to give her bus seat to a white male passenger in Montgomery, Alabama. Her refusal and subsequent arrest sparked the Montgomery bus boycott, which was a significant event in the civil rights movement. *Have you ever taken a stand that motivated others to action? Why?*

● **As You Read**

Think about a mistake you have made. What did you learn from it?

Motivation

Motivation has three different components. One involves inspiring others. Good leaders have the ability to motivate others to meet goals. Some do this by inspiring them with their energy, enthusiasm, and charisma as well as their personal efforts.

Another component is initiative. **Initiative** is the ability to act and make decisions without the help or advice of others. People with initiative do not wait to be told what to do. Initiative is an important quality of entrepreneurs and good leaders. Generally, it involves taking risks.

Most important, motivation means having a goal, whether it is to create the best video game or to make the best skateboard. A true leader is motivated by a vision and uses it to inspire others. Activist and theologian Dr. Martin Luther King, Jr. delivered many powerful speeches during the civil rights movement. In his famous "I Have a Dream" speech, he painted a vivid picture of a future in which all people were treated equally. One year later Congress passed the Civil Rights Act of 1964.

✔ Reading Check **Explain** What are the three components of motivation?

Confidence

Leaders also need self-confidence. Being self-confident means knowing what to do and taking action. Self-assurance makes others feel confident in their leader's abilities. The more others are convinced that their leader knows what to do, the more confidence they will have in him or her.

A confident leader is also decisive. Suppose you run a student magazine. The latest issue has come back from the printer with a big mistake on the cover. You could sell it as it is, remove the covers, or send it back to the printer. You could get advice from your workers, but you need to make the final decision. If your decision turns out to be wrong, you must take responsibility for it. People have confidence in a leader who is willing to make decisions and learn from them.

Communication Skills

Being able to communicate and discuss employee issues helps leaders deal effectively with different situations. A leader must be good at human relations. **Human relations** is the study of how people interact in the workplace and how communication can be improved. Most large companies have a human relations department, which handles employee hiring, records, and problems. To deal with some human relations problems, leaders have to apply **conflict** resolution **techniques**.

● **As You Read**

Answers will vary and students may feel reluctant to discuss the mistake itself. Students should recognize, however, that it is frequently possible to learn things from mistakes that they cannot learn from success and that humility, compassion, and the ability to overcome one's mistakes are some of the most important qualities of leaders.

Quiet Leadership Answers will depend on students' individual circumstances.

Good communication also involves mentoring. A *mentor* is a trusted counselor or guide. Mentors usually have more experience than the people they counsel. They should also be good listeners. Leaders need to listen to people to be informed about what they are doing, and what their strengths and weaknesses are. As mentors, leaders can better understand employees and their needs. This is especially important when working with teams and trying to increase productivity. Leaders must also communicate the types of behavior that are considered acceptable at the organization. **Figure 8.1** asks you to evaluate your communication skills.

Integrity

Integrity is an adherence to a code of ethical values such as honesty, loyalty, and fairness. Integrity is the most highly valued quality in a leader. Leaders need to set a good example and follow standards. If they are willing to sacrifice the quality of their product to make a bigger profit, people are not going to have much faith in their vision.

✔ **Reading Check** **Explain** What is the difference between initiative and integrity?

Figure 8.1 — *How Good Are Your Communication Skills?*

Communication Skills
1. People usually understand what I am saying.
2. I find it easy to see things from someone else's point of view.
3. I listen actively to keep my mind from drifting.
4. When I am wrong, I am not afraid to admit it.
5. I rarely jump to conclusions.
6. I try to put myself in the other person's shoes when we are talking.
7. It helps me understand if people tell me that they disagree with me.
8. When I work with others, I try to do my fair share of the work.

● **The Importance of Good Communication Skills** Evaluate your communication skills. **Do these traits apply to you?**

Figure 8.1

● **The Importance of Good Communication Skills** The more traits you can say "yes" to, the better your skills are as a communicator. All skills can be learned. Knowing the traits you need to strengthen is the first step in becoming a better communicator.

✔ **Reading Check**

Explain Initiative is the desire to take action and get things done. Integrity is holding on to principles such as honesty and loyalty.

RETEACH

W Writing Support
Enrichment
Mentoring Have students write a summary of an article in a business magazine about mentoring in the workplace as opposed to a school-based program. (Summaries will vary depending on the article selected.)

R Reading Strategy
Make an Outline Have students create an outline for the description of integrity. (Outlines should include ethical values, the need to set a good example, and willingness to stand up for a vision.)

U Universal Access
Learners with Cognitive Limitations Instruct students to use the list in **Figure 8.1** to generate examples of behaviors that exhibit each quality and to use them to explain the reason the skill is important. (Some examples: I know that people usually understand what I am saying because they answer back. When we are engaged in a conversation, I am able to learn from them and I feel that they can learn from me. That makes me feel valuable and appreciated.)

Student Activity Workbook ☞ Assign the Section 8.1 Activities.

RETEACH (cont.)

C Critical Thinking

Developing Leadership Skills Have students write a short paper about their leadership skills with examples of how they use them and how to improve them. (Students might suggest that they use leadership skills at home, at school, and in the community. Ideas for improving leadership skills might include reading or joining an organization that focuses on developing leadership skills.)

ASSESS

● After You Read

Have students complete the Section 8.1 After You Read section review.

Online Study Tools

Have students go to the Online Learning Center through **glencoe.com** to:

- Take the Section 8.1 **Practice Test**.
- Download free **Study-to-Go** content to their PDAs or cell phones.

CLOSE

Culminating Activity
Make a Poster
Have students make a poster or collage related to leadership. (Posters will vary but the theme of leadership should be evident in the work.)

Developing Leadership Skills

C Some people say leaders are born and not made. However, while some people have natural leadership abilities, others can develop them over time. A person with charisma, such as a star athlete or a popular person in class, is often mistaken for a natural born leader. Charisma alone, however, does not make somebody a good leader.

To manage activities successfully, you must draw on a specific set of skills. These include human relations, communication, networking, problem solving, and decision-making skills.

Leadership qualities are learned through knowledge and experience. Skills can be developed in a number of ways, such as

- through reading books, watching videos, and taking courses on leadership.
- by working with someone who has leadership ability and studying what he or she does.
- by joining a club, a team, a drama group, or a community organization.
- by taking initiative at school, at work, or in club activities.

NCLB Activity correlates to Math standards.

Section 8.1

● After You Read

Review Key Concepts
1. Why are some managers not leaders?
2. What are the three motivational qualities that leaders have?
3. How can leadership skills be developed?

Academic Skills
4. **Mathematics** Your manager at the Burger Barn wants each employee to sell $350 worth of hamburgers and fries during his or her shift. Yesterday, your sales totaled $330. Today, your sales total $440. Determine the percentage you achieved above or below the goal for yesterday and today.

THEORY **Problem Solving: Make a Plan** Many problems require more than one step to solve. Think through your approach, and make a plan before you choose the operations to use.

 For math help, go to the Math Appendix.

@ Go to the *Introduction to Business* Online Learning Center through **glencoe.com** to check your answers.

Section 8.1

Review Key Concepts
1. Some managers are not leaders because they do not have a vision for the organization and do not inspire others to work toward a vision.
2. The three motivational qualities that leaders have are initiative, ability to motivate others, and ability to set goals.
3. by taking courses on leadership, studying a leader, joining a club, or taking initiative

Academic Skills
4. **Mathematics** ($330 + $440) ÷ ($350 + $350) = $770 ÷ $700 = 110%. For the two days, you exceeded your quota by 10%.

Leadership Styles

Reading Guide

Before You Read

Think about the difference in leadership styles between a football coach and a doctor.

Read to Learn

- Identify and describe the autocratic, democratic, and free-rein leadership styles.
- Describe the self-managed team approach and the two ways in which such an approach is organized.

The Main Idea

Leaders differ in the leadership styles that they use. Autocratic, democratic, and free-rein leadership are common styles. The leadership style that should be used depends on the work to be done and the type of worker being managed.

Key Concepts

- Types of Leadership
- Leadership in Teams

Vocabulary

Key Terms

autocratic leadership
democratic leadership
free-rein leadership
delegating
self-managed teams

Academic Vocabulary

You will find these words in your reading and on your tests. Make sure you know their meanings.

inclined   approach
role   theory

Graphic Organizer

As you read, write notes about the three types of leadership styles in a figure like the one below.

AUTOCRATIC	DEMOCRATIC	FREE-REIN

 Go to the *Introduction to Business* Online Learning Center through **glencoe.com** for a printable graphic organizer.

Academic Standards

English Language Arts

NCTE 1 Read texts to acquire new information

NCTE 4 Use written language to communicate effectively

NCTE 12 Use language to accomplish individual purposes

Science

Content Standard F Students should develop understanding of personal and community health, science, and technology in local, national, and global challenges

---

Bell Ringer Activity

Leadership Styles
Ask students: Why do you think leadership styles vary? (Leadership styles might be influenced by a leader's personality, the firm's culture, the work being done, or the situation.)

Preteaching

Presentation Plus!
The Presentation Plus! CD provides visual teaching aids for this section.

PuzzleMaker
Use the Vocabulary PuzzleMaker to create a puzzle of the section's key terms. Students can complete the puzzle on paper or on a computer.

Graphic Organizer
Tell students to go to the Online Learning Center through **glencoe.com** for a printable graphic organizer. (Answers include: With autocratic leadership, one person runs everything and makes all decisions without consulting others. With democratic leadership, managers work with employees to make decisions. Free-rein leadership requires the leader to set goals for managers and employees and then leave them alone to get the job done. This style shows the most trust in workers.)

N C L B Connects academics to content.

Reading Guide

Before You Read

Ask students to think about the difference in leadership styles of a football coach and a doctor.

D Develop Concepts

The Main Idea Ask students: Is there one leadership style that is better than the others? (The leadership style that should be used depends on the work to be done and the type of worker who is being managed.)

TEACH

Discussion Starter
Types of Leadership
Point out that every leadership style has drawbacks. Ask students: What are some of the drawbacks of autocratic leadership? (Answers will vary. Students might suggest that some people do not like to work for autocratic leaders.)

R Reading Strategy

Create Bulleted Lists Have students create two bulleted lists, one for the attributes of an autocratic leader and another for the circumstances where autocratic leadership works well. (Lists will vary. The attributes of an autocratic leader include making all the decisions and not consulting others. Circumstances where autocratic leadership works well include when it is important to obey orders, when there is no time for consultation, and when workers are new or unskilled.)

● As You Read
Answers will vary. Students might point this type of leadership is well-suited in situations where employees are not allowed to make their own decisions.

● As You Read
There are some situations in which autocratic leadership is necessary. What situations can you think of in which it would be necessary to rule in an autocratic manner?

Types of Leadership

Different leaders have different styles. Some rule with strict discipline while others leave employees alone to do their work. Many leaders use more than one style. There are three basic styles of leadership: autocratic, democratic, and free-rein.

Autocratic Leadership

An **autocratic leadership** style is one in which one person runs everything and makes all decisions without consulting others. When autocratic leaders give orders, they expect them to be obeyed without question. Autocratic leaders assume others must have decisions made for them and that workers have to be watched all the time. A major problem that autocratic leaders face is that many people do not like to work for them.

Autocratic leadership is useful in situations in which it is important to obey orders without question. Firefighters, combat troops, and police officers have autocratic leadership.

BusinessWeek *Reader and Case Study*

Memo to Students: Writing Skills Matter

B-schools face a challenge in teaching writing and communications skills to undergrads more comfortable with cell phones and IMs.

The thought of tackling a 15-page English paper scared David Rodriguez to pieces as an undergraduate finance major at the University of Miami. Proposals and memos for his business-focused communication sections were more applicable to his life, easier to get through, and more enjoyable. Luckily for him, at his current job in the Mortgage Capital Group at Lehman Brothers, Rodriguez has left long reports and literary analyses behind him.

While his writing skills may not have been up to par when he entered Miami, Rodriguez acknowledges that they improved by taking required courses common to many B-school curriculums. Business undergraduates are faced with a dual challenge once they enter college—writing mature research papers for general courses

and expressing themselves clearly, confidently, and concisely for a professional audience. In B-school courses, undergrads learn to write presentations, memos, notes, proposals, and reports for different business audiences.

 CASE STUDY Go to the *Introduction to Business* Online Learning Center through **glencoe.com** for the *BusinessWeek* Reader Case Study.

Active Learning
Many business leaders write several memos a day. Research the form of a business memo. Compare it to the structure of a business letter. Write an e-mail to your teacher explaining the ways that memos, letters, and e-mail are similar to each other and the ways they are different.

132   **Chapter 8**   Leadership in Management

glencoe.com

BusinessWeek *Reader and Case Study*

Memo to Students: Writing Skills Matter

 CASE STUDY Have students go to the *Introduction to Business* Online Learning Center through **glencoe.com** to download a Case Study activity that corresponds to the article. The activity and answer key are also available on the TeacherWorks Plus CD.

Active Learning
Answers should include differences in format, style of language used, and intended audience. Students should appropriately target these differences and explain why they are important.

Democratic Leadership

Democratic leadership is a style in which managers work with employees to make decisions. Everyone meets, discusses a situation, and listens to each other's opinions. New ideas are encouraged in such workplace environments. Democratic leaders still make the final decisions, but they might explain their reasons for making them. A democratic leader assumes that people have ideas and are **inclined** to contribute.

✔ **Reading Check** **Contrast** How do the leadership styles of an autocratic leader and a democratic leader differ?

Free-Rein Leadership

Free-rein leadership requires the leader to set goals for managers and employees and then leave them alone to get the job done. This style places the most trust and confidence in workers. Another name for this type of leadership style is *hands-off leadership*. Free-rein leaders deal with broader decision making. They have to be available to answer questions and resolve problems.

Giving managers and employees the power to run things and make decisions is called **delegating**. There are several reasons for a leader to delegate:

- The managers do not have time to do everything.
- The managers can focus on more important work.
- Employees have more ownership of the production process.
- Employees have a chance to develop their own potential.

Science/Tech**TRENDS**

Contamination Crisis

In 1996, Odwalla Inc., a producer of fresh-fruit beverages, faced a crisis. Its apple juice had caused an outbreak of *E. coli*. One child died. Odwalla executives ordered an immediate recall of all products containing apple or carrot juice, costing the company about $6.5 million. The next step was to tackle the problem of contamination. Odwalla used unpasteurized juice because it tasted best. They moved quickly to introduce a process called "flash pasteurization" to destroy bacteria, while leaving the best flavored juice possible.

WebQuest

Go to the *Introduction to Business* Online Learning Center through **glencoe.com** for links to Web sites where you can find out more about flash pasteurization. Write a few paragraphs explaining how decisive leadership and good science helped a company survive a crisis.

Science/Tech**TRENDS**

WebQuest

Contamination Crisis Students might explain that within months of the outbreak, the company had in place a comprehensive quality control and safety system. Decisive leadership saved the company's reputation.

N C L B Activity correlates to Science standards.

TEACH (cont.)

S Skill Practice

Guided Practice

List Have students make a list of reasons a leader delegates. (A manager cannot do everything. He or she needs time to focus on more important work. Employees can develop potential.) **L1**

Make a Table Have students make a table to illustrate why managers delegate, using *Managers* and *Employees* as the column heads. (The title might be Reasons Managers Delegate. The Manager column should indicate the manager cannot do everything. The Employee column should include entries about ownership and potential.) **L2**

Research Have students create a role-play scenario that illustrates the reasons to delegate and the reasons not to delegate. (Scenarios will vary but should reflect appropriate content.) **L3**

ASSESS

Review Key Terms

Have students write sentences using each key term.

STUDY TO GO **Study-to-Go** Have students go to the Online Learning Center through **glencoe.com** to download free **Study-to-Go** content to their PDAs or cell phones.

✔ **Reading Check**

Contrast Autocratic leaders assume that employees need to have decisions made for them. Democratic leaders expect employees to make decisions.

133

RETEACH

R Reading Strategy

Illustrate an Idea Have students work in teams to create a drawing or sketch that illustrates the idea of leadership in teams. Have the teams share their work with the class. (Illustrations and leadership within the teams will vary.)

W Writing Support

Enrichment

Self-Managed Teams Have students locate a magazine article from the 1970s or early 1980s that describes the introduction of self-managed teams to American businesses. Instruct students to write a summary of the article and include a correctly formatted reference citation. (Summaries will vary depending on the article chosen.)

U Universal Access

Kinesthetic Learners Invite students with athletic ability to give a short presentation about leadership in teams. Ask the student to explain the leadership role of the coach or manager and the leadership role of team captain.

Student Activity Workbook 📂 Assign the Section 8.2 Activities.

✔ Reading Check

Explain In a self-managed team, the team leader makes decisions with the team rather than alone. The leader also learns a range of jobs rather than just one.

134

● As You Read

Think of a task that you have had to delegate. Why did you make that choice?

There are also reasons not to delegate. Shifting responsibility because of laziness or a lack of interest or self-confidence is not good leadership. Choosing the right people to delegate power to is a test of your leadership skills. Hiring workers who are experienced, reliable, and knowledgeable leads to success.

Leadership in Teams

R Thirty to forty years ago, autocratic leadership was the main style used in most U.S. businesses. As companies learned the value of giving workers more power, they started using a more democratic or free-rein style. Today, the trend is to go even further. Many companies have been putting workers in self-managed teams. **Self-managed teams** are work groups that supervise themselves. With these teams, the manager's **role** is replaced by the team leader's role.

Self-Managed Teams

W The use of the self-managed team **approach** started in Japan and came to the United States in the 1980s. U.S. companies had emphasized people working as individuals on separate jobs. Japanese companies had stressed people working in teams and making decisions as a group. The Japanese method was such a success that American companies also started using it.

U In a self-managed team, the leader is a team player rather than a boss. A team leader makes decisions with the team rather than alone. This person learns a range of jobs instead of just one. The team usually works on a single project, such as designing a video game. This way the project is more goal-oriented rather than task-oriented.

✔ Reading Check **Explain** What is the position of the leader in a self-managed team?

● Problem Solving When groups brainstorm, more ideas can develop. **What is the leadership style that is apparent here?**

134 **Chapter 8** Leadership in Management

● As You Read

Reasons may include the need for another person's perspective, recognition of another person's superior skill, or a distaste for the task itself. Encourage students to recognize that delegation can lead to a more efficient use of resources.

Discuss the Photo

● Problem Solving Because the workers are interacting with each other, the leadership style might be democratic or free-rein.

The Organization of Self-Managed Teams

Self-managed teams are organized in two ways: (1) the team selects one team leader, or (2) each team member employs specialized skills, but there is no team leader.

The first type of self-managed team appoints a team leader. A team leader is not so much a manager as a team captain. If you are a team leader, your job is not to give orders but to motivate your team and get the members to work toward a shared goal. Team members usually evaluate each other's performance.

 The **theory** behind self-managed teams is that the whole is greater than the sum of its parts. Self-managed teams have many advantages:

- They are more goal-oriented than task-oriented.
- Team members have a chance to learn each other's job and obtain new skills.
- Team members learn to participate and cooperate.
- Self-managed teams learn to solve their own problems.

The disadvantage of self-managed teams is that some people do not have the skills and initiative to work together productively.

NCLB Activity correlates to English Language Arts standards.

Section 8.2

● After You Read

Review Key Concepts
1. In which situations is an autocratic style of leadership useful?
2. Why should a manager delegate authority?
3. Name a similarity and a difference between free-rein management and self-managed teams.

Academic Skills

4. **English Language Arts** Locate and read articles about effective leadership styles. Become familiar with the characteristics of different leadership styles. Then write an essay. In the first paragraph, explain the range of possible styles a leader might exhibit. In the second paragraph, compare and contrast two or three of the styles identifying both positive and negative aspects. In the final paragraph, discuss which style fits your personality best.

5. **English Language Arts** Your company has developed a new video game for girls aged 11 to 14. You are the team leader assigned to develop a marketing campaign. The team includes an art director, a market researcher, and a copywriter. Write a memo to your team explaining the goals of the project. Think about the leadership qualities and approaches you wish to exhibit and incorporate them into your memo. Read your memo to the class.

 Go to the *Introduction to Business* Online Learning Center through **glencoe.com** to check your answers.

Section 8.2

Review Key Concepts
1. when dealing with unmotivated or unskilled employees or in emergency situations
2. when a job is time consuming, requires special skills, or to give workers more responsibility
3. Both give freedom to the employee. Free-rein management involves individuals working alone. Several people are involved in a self-managed team.

Academic Skills
4. **English Language Arts** Students should describe and compare and contrast leadership styles.
5. **English Language Arts** The memo should describe leadership styles.

Chapter 8 *Review and Activities*

Vocabulary Review

1. Students should write complete sentences using each term correctly.

Review Key Concepts

2. taking a company in a direction based upon a vision

3. motivation, confidence, communication skills, and integrity

4. reading books, taking courses, working with a leader, joining a group to develop better skills, and volunteering for projects with leadership opportunities

5. Autocratic leadership: one person runs everything and makes all decisions. Democratic leadership: leaders work with employees to make decisions, still make the final decisions, but explain their reasons. Free-rein leadership: the leader sets goals for managers and employees. Then the free-rein leader leaves the employees alone.

6. Team members with varied skills work together to complete assigned tasks using the means they deem best and are organized in two ways: (1) each team member has a special skill with no team leader or (2) the team selects one team leader.

Section 8.1 *Summary*

Leadership Qualities A leader has a vision for the firm and inspires others to work toward that vision. Being a manager is not necessarily the same as being a leader. Many managers tell people what to do and make sure they do it. However, managers who lack a vision and do not inspire others are not leaders. In today's world, true leaders know their business and the capabilities of their employees. They analyze trends to steer their business on the right course. They also make sure that the basic operations run smoothly. Good leadership traits include motivation, confidence, integrity, and communication skills.

Section 8.2 *Summary*

Leadership Styles The three basic styles of leadership are autocratic, democratic, and free-rein. An autocratic leader is one who runs everything and makes all of the decisions. A democratic leader is one who seeks input from his or her employees before making decisions. A free-rein leader sets goals and permits employees to work alone to get their jobs done. Today's leadership trend is toward self-managed teams. Self-managed teams govern themselves. They determine how to produce their business's goods and services using the expertise of individual team members. Many of today's leaders use a combination of leadership styles.

Vocabulary Review

1. On a sheet of paper, use each of these key terms and academic vocabulary terms in a sentence.

Key Terms		**Academic Vocabulary**	
leadership	democratic leadership	vision	inclined
initiative	free-rein leadership	trends	role
human relations	delegating	conflict	approach
integrity	self-managed teams	technique	theory
autocratic leadership			

Review Key Concepts

2. Define leadership.

3. Describe the qualities of a leader.

4. Name at least three ways in which an individual can develop leadership skills.

5. Identify and describe the autocratic, democratic, and free-rein leadership styles.

6. Describe the self-managed team approach and the two ways in which such an approach is organized.

Critical Thinking

7. Leaders are needed to provide vision and goals that can serve to keep our institutions up to date and current in fulfilling the needs of our society.

8. It is essential that a successful leader have integrity because people will not follow individuals they do not trust.

9. Many professionals have motivation and initiative and like to "think outside the box." This means they like to come up with different ideas and methods of handling situations. Thus, they perform better with a free-rein leadership style than an autocratic leadership style.

Critical Thinking

7. Good leadership is needed in the business world as well as in areas such as government, nonprofits, education, and sports. Why do all institutions need leaders?

8. Why is it essential that a leader have integrity?

9. Why are professionals such as engineers and doctors usually managed with a free-rein style rather than an autocratic management style?

10. Imagine that you have five employees—a bookkeeper with years of experience, two college students who have worked with you for six months, and two high school students who started last week. What leadership style(s) will you use with each of your employees?

11. What are some instances in which self-managed teams will not work?

12. Why do managers who use leadership styles that empower employees have to think differently than those who use the autocratic style?

13. What traits must workers have if self-managed teams are to operate efficiently and effectively?

14. Explain how a leader can use different leadership styles.

Write About It

15. Working on a team project requires you to exercise different skills than you would use if you did the assignment alone. Write an essay about the pros and cons you have experienced working on a team for a project.

16. Find an article in a current issue of a business magazine that focuses on the experiences of a CEO. In a one-page report, describe the characteristics you believe he or she possesses that make this person a leader.

17. Michael Eisner, former CEO of Disney, said business leaders must be willing to take intelligent risks. He also said they must encourage failure, because "you will not get success without it." Write a one-page essay either agreeing or disagreeing with his statement.

18. Leaders often have different ways of inspiring the people who work for them. Write a brief essay discussing reasons why leaders delegate.

19. In a one-page report, indicate three important communication skills that you believe a good leader should have. Share them with a group of other people. List the communication skills that your group believes are most important.

Technology Applications

Technological Leadership

20. Technology offers many tools that help leaders be more effective, from telephones to computers to software that helps track employee performance. Research five ways leaders can use technology tools to help them be more effective. Write a one-page article about the benefits and costs associated with using these tools.

Business Ethics

When a Leader Wants Your Help

21. Imagine your manager has been asked to speak at a national trade show and tells you to write the speech. Later, she is asked to write a book on the topic. Her name will be on the cover. Would it be appropriate for her manager to ask you to write the book? In two or more paragraphs, discuss some of the ethical issues involved.

Chapter 8 Review and Activities **137**

137

Applying Academics to Business

22. Free-rein, carte blanche, and laissez-faire can mean hands-off. High-handed can mean bossy, so it should be crossed out. Other phrases include hands-off, full authority, and complete discretion.

23. Since Maya works from 8 A.M. to 1 P.M., she works 5 hours a day, three days a week. She couldn't finish the job in two days. Similarly, Susan only works 4 hours and 45 minutes each day. Kyle, who works $5\frac{1}{2}$ hours each day, or $27\frac{1}{2}$ hours during a week, is the best choice. He will have 17 hours left for other duties.

24. Pamphlets should address interpersonal business issues.

25. Since V = lwh, h = V ÷ lw. Therefore, 2,690 ÷ (23 × 13) = 2,690 ÷ 299 = 8.99 feet. The storage facility ceiling would have to be at least 9 feet high.

Active Learning

26. Students should exhibit some of the same leadership qualities indicated.

Business in the Real World

27. If students are employed but have little experience, then they might observe that their manager leads in an autocratic style. The manager might use a different style with other employees.

Applying Academics to Business

English Language Arts
22. Read the following list of two-word phrases. Think about their meanings. Use a dictionary to learn more about them. Then cross out the phrase that does not belong with the others, and add another phrase that does belong.

free-rein   high-handed
carte blanche   laissez-faire

Mathematics
23. Imagine that you need to train an employee to manage purchasing. It takes $10\frac{1}{2}$ hours a week, and the employee needs to work on it two days a week. Your staff has the following work hours:

- Maya: 8:00 A.M. to 1:00 P.M., Monday, Wednesday, and Friday
- Susan: 9:15 A.M. to 3:00 P.M., Monday through Friday, with an hour lunch
- Kyle: 11:30 A.M. to 5:30 P.M., Monday through Friday, with a half-hour lunch

Who would be the best choice? How many hours a week will this person have available to work on other tasks?

THEORY **Measurement: Time** Think about elapsed time when calculating duration.

English Language Arts
24. Your work team at Tropic Aquaria has been assigned to plan and write a pamphlet describing how to run successful teams. In a small group, create a pamphlet with helpful tips and guidelines.

Mathematics
25. You are in charge of finding storage facilities for your company's surplus inventory. The inventory is stored on pallets and has a total volume of 2,690 cubic feet. You find a storage site with an area that fits your needs. If the floor measures 23 feet by 13 feet, how high would the ceiling have to be to accommodate your inventory?

THEORY **Geometry: Volume** The volume of a three-dimensional geometric figure is measured in cubic units. You can memorize the formulas for finding the volumes of various figures, or you can look them up in a math glossary. To find the volume of a rectangular solid, multiply length by width by height.

Active Learning

Attend a Student Council Meeting
26. At a student council meeting, notice how each council member communicates. In a one-page article for your school newspaper, identify the person who demonstrated leadership qualities and how he or she did so at the meeting. Indicate other people's reactions to the council member's leadership styles.

Business in the Real World

Observe a Manager
27. Observe the activities of a manager for a one-week period. What leadership styles does the manager use? Are employees organized into teams? If so, how effective do you think they are? Present your findings in a two-page report. (Note: If you are not employed, observe the activities of a teacher for one week.)

ExamView Assessment Suite CD allows you to print out ready-made unit and chapter tests, complete with answer keys. You can also create customized tests.

TeacherWorks Plus provides complete teacher resources in one convenient package. It includes customizable lesson plans in calendar format, and instant access to many print program resources.

Real LIFE skills

DEVELOPING LEADERSHIP SKILLS

28. Interview a leader in a business or your community. Ask how he or she developed leadership skills. Indicate what the biggest challenge in developing the skills was and how she or he met that challenge. In a thank-you letter to the leader, indicate what you learned from him or her.

Cool Business CAREERS

FIND YOUR DREAM JOB

29. Go to the *Introduction to Business* Online Learning Center through **glencoe.com** for a link to the Occupational Outlook Handbook Web site. Click on the "OOH Search/A-Z Index" link and enter the job title "education administrator." Then write a one-page report about this type of occupation. Conclude your report with a list of things you can do now to prepare yourself to pursue the occupation.

Role Play

CHOOSING A MANAGEMENT STYLE

30. **Situation** You are the CEO of a new automaker. The board of directors wants you to indicate the best management style to use.

Activity You are to give a presentation describing the management style that you believe should be used in your company. You expect questions from the board.

Evaluation You will be evaluated on how well you meet the following performance indicators:

- Understand the characteristics of the management style that you are promoting.
- Discuss the advantages and disadvantages of the style. Indicate how the business can deal with the disadvantages.
- Answer the board's questions effectively.
- Project your voice and provide concise explanations.

Standardized Test Practice

Directions Choose the letter of the best answer. Write the letter for the answer on a separate piece of paper.

1. $3\frac{1}{2} \div 1\frac{1}{3} =$

A $\frac{8}{12}$ B $\frac{1}{4}$ C $2\frac{5}{8}$ D $3\frac{3}{8}$

TEST-TAKING TIP Find a regular place to study where you can focus without much outside interference. Make sure that you have all the necessary materials before you begin studying.

 READING Go to the *Introduction to Business* Online Learning Center through **glencoe.com** for a list of outside reading suggestions.

Real LIFE skills

28. Answers will depend on what the leaders say but should indicate some of the leadership skills and challenges that have been discussed.

Cool Business CAREERS

29. Work involves providing instructional leadership and managing and directing daily activities of educational institutions. Work is indoors, more than 40 hours per week, 11 or 12 months a year. Training begins in the classroom and advancement requires a graduate degree. Job outlook is excellent.

Role Play

30. Presentations should address the competencies noted in the Role Play. Answers will vary, depending on the choice of leadership style chosen. However, in this instance, most leaders might want to use a different leadership style for different workers or departments.

Standardized Test Practice
1. C

STRATEGIES FOR STANDARDIZED TEST PREP SUCCESS

Test Prep Enlist the support and help of parents in preparing their students for taking standardized tests. Encourage parents to find a regular place for students to study. Suggest they organize the study area so that their student is as free of noise and interruption as possible. Depending on the student and home environment, some parents might want to reserve the kitchen before or after dinner as a study area. In this way, they can be close at hand to monitor the student's study habits and help by answering questions even as they cook or clean up.

Standards-Based Lesson Planning
Introduction to Business provides students with instruction and assessment in the following fundamental content areas:

Content Standards Correlations	
Select and apply the tools of technology as they relate to personal and business decision making.	pp. 143–146, 148–151, 152–155
Describe different types of technology and explain the role of technology in business settings.	pp. 143–146, 148–151, 152–155
Describe types of technology and their importance to businesses.	pp. 143–146, 148–151, 152–155
Give examples of how technology has changed jobs in business.	pp. 143–146, 152
Research future trends in the workplace relating to technology.	p. 153

NCLB
Activities, information, and skills practice will help your students attain No Child Left Behind proficiency. Students will improve their abilities in the following academic standards areas:

Academic Standards Correlations		
English Language Arts	Activities/ Features	Page
NCTE 4 Use written language to communicate effectively	After You Read	p. 151
NCTE 5 Use different writing process elements to communicate effectively	Applying Academics to Business	p. 154
NCTE 6 Apply knowledge of language structure and conventions to discuss texts	After You Read Standardized Test Practice	pp. 151, 155
Algebra Represent and analyze mathematical situations and structures using algebraic symbols	After You Read Applying Academics to Business Standardized Test Practice	pp. 146, 154, 155
Mathematics		
Data Analysis and Probability Formulate questions that can be addressed with data and collect, organize, and display relevant data to answer them	Ask S&P	p. 140
Number and Operations Compute fluently and make reasonable estimates	Applying Academics to Business	p. 154
Science		
Content Standard B Students should develop an understanding of structure and properties of matter, chemical reactions	Science/Tech Trends	p. 149

Correlations This chart shows the 21st Century Skills, foundation skills, and workplace competencies that students develop as they work in this chapter.

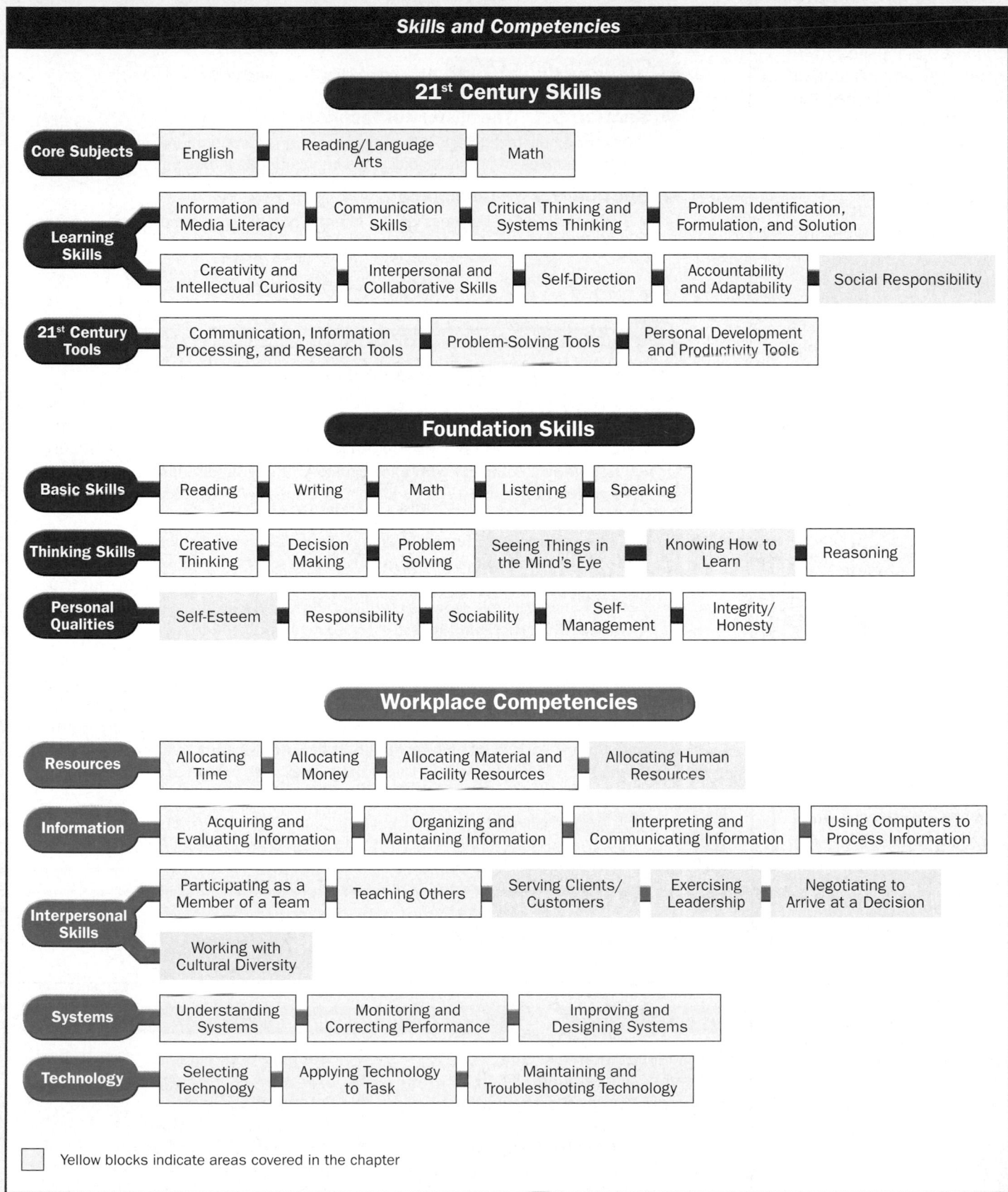

Skills and Competencies

21st Century Skills

Core Subjects
- English
- Reading/Language Arts
- Math

Learning Skills
- Information and Media Literacy
- Communication Skills
- Critical Thinking and Systems Thinking
- Problem Identification, Formulation, and Solution
- Creativity and Intellectual Curiosity
- Interpersonal and Collaborative Skills
- Self-Direction
- Accountability and Adaptability
- Social Responsibility

21st Century Tools
- Communication, Information Processing, and Research Tools
- Problem-Solving Tools
- Personal Development and Productivity Tools

Foundation Skills

Basic Skills
- Reading
- Writing
- Math
- Listening
- Speaking

Thinking Skills
- Creative Thinking
- Decision Making
- Problem Solving
- Seeing Things in the Mind's Eye
- Knowing How to Learn
- Reasoning

Personal Qualities
- Self-Esteem
- Responsibility
- Sociability
- Self-Management
- Integrity/Honesty

Workplace Competencies

Resources
- Allocating Time
- Allocating Money
- Allocating Material and Facility Resources
- Allocating Human Resources

Information
- Acquiring and Evaluating Information
- Organizing and Maintaining Information
- Interpreting and Communicating Information
- Using Computers to Process Information

Interpersonal Skills
- Participating as a Member of a Team
- Teaching Others
- Serving Clients/Customers
- Exercising Leadership
- Negotiating to Arrive at a Decision
- Working with Cultural Diversity

Systems
- Understanding Systems
- Monitoring and Correcting Performance
- Improving and Designing Systems

Technology
- Selecting Technology
- Applying Technology to Task
- Maintaining and Troubleshooting Technology

☐ Yellow blocks indicate areas covered in the chapter

Chapter Overview

Introduce the Chapter

Technology and Business
Chapter 9 discusses how technology has influenced business. It describes the e-workforce and virtual business.

Building Background

Everyone has seen dramatic changes in technology in their lifetime. Today people use cell phones and view video over the Internet. Long before iPods, teens walked down the street, earpiece in place, enjoying a CD player or even a transistor radio.

Ask **STANDARD &POOR'S**

>> Math Answer
Student's graphs should include appropriate scales with time plotted along the x-axis. The points hit should be: 1170, 1053, 1170, 800, 950, 770, and 900.

>> Extension Activity
Have students use spreadsheet software to create a graph using the following data for average interest rates for 30-year mortgage rates in 2005:

Jan 5.71%; Feb 5.63%;
Mar 5.93%; Apr 5.86%;
May 5.72%; Jun 5.58%;
Jul 5.70%; Aug 5.82%;
Sep 5.77%; Oct 6.07%;
Nov 6.33%; Dec 6.27%

Student's graphs should include appropriate scales with time plotted along the x-axis—along the bottom of the graph.

NCLB Activity correlates to Math standards.

140

Technology and Business

Chapter Objectives After completing this chapter, you will be able to:

▶ **Section 9.1** *The History of Technology*
- **Describe** how technological inventions have an effect on business.
- **Give** examples of how technology has changed jobs in business.

▶ **Section 9.2** *E-Commerce*
- **Explain** why doing business on the Internet has become a major factor in many industries.

Ask **STANDARD &POOR'S** **Researching Stocks**

Q: I'm thinking about buying stock in a company my father used to work for. It's a well-known company with a long history of paying dividends. Is there any kind of research I can do to help me figure out if this stock will continue to do well in the future?

A: There are many different ways to evaluate a stock. *Fundamental analysis* involves looking at the company behind a stock to see if it's in good financial shape. *Technical analysis* involves looking at charts and graphs to figure out where a stock may go next. However, you shouldn't rely on just one measure to assess a stock. Most successful investors evaluate a potential investment in a number of different ways.

Mathematics As part of his research into a stock he was considering, George found a graph showing the S&P 500 Price Index for 12 months beginning December 2001. The index reached a high of 1170 in mid-December, fell almost 10% by February, and climbed back to its high by March. It declined steadily to about 800 in early July, jumped 150 points by August 1, and hit its low, 770, toward the end of October. The index then rose steadily to over 900 by the end of November. Sketch George's graph.

NCLB **THEORY** **Graphing** Line graphs have an x-axis and a y-axis. The x-axis is most often used to represent time.

Classroom Resources

- Student Edition
- Teacher Wraparound Edition
- Student Activity Workbook with Academic Integration
- Student Activity Workbook with Academic Integration TAE
- *Fast File*, Unit 2 Resources
- Inclusion in the Business Education Classroom

- TeacherWorks Plus
- *ExamView Assessment Suite*
- Presentation Plus!
- Vocabulary PuzzleMaker
- Interactive Student Edition
- Online Student Edition
- Online Learning Center with Podcasts

● **On the Go** Technological devices make it possible for people to take their work, entertainment, and communication with them wherever they go. **What technological device do you rely on most? Why?**

Review the Objectives

Introduce the chapter by reviewing the chapter objectives:

Section 9.1 *Objectives*

Describe how technological inventions have an effect on business. (The Internet makes it possible for businesses to communicate instantly with clients and customers around the world. Businesses can use the Internet to show and sell their products and services. Phones and fax machines enable businesses to communicate by voice and by images immediately. Mobile phones make it possible for people to communicate, wherever they are.)

Give examples of how technology has changed jobs in business. (Technology has created a boom in online businesses. More workers work through the Internet, using Web sites and e-mail. Technology products such as computers, printers, and fax machines allow people to work easier and faster. Computer technology also has transformed the paper workflow into a digital workflow.)

Section 9.2 *Objective*

Explain why doing business on the Internet has become a major factor in many industries. (Any company can go online to sell its products or services. Businesses can sell products in stores, by mail, and online.)

Discuss the Photo

● **On the Go** Read the caption on the photo to students: Technological devices make it possible for people to take their work, entertainment, and communication with them wherever they go.

Ask students: What technological device you rely on the most and why? (Answers will vary depending on the student's access to technology and personal needs. Encourage students to understand that their technology use will change over time as their needs change.)

FOCUS

Bell Ringer Activity

The History of Technology

Technology is the practical application of knowledge. Although people tend to think technology is new, people have been applying practical knowledge throughout history by inventing things. Ask volunteers to name some significant inventions that affect business today. (Some include the sewing machine, the telephone, and the airplane.)

Preteaching

Presentation Plus!

The Presentation Plus! CD provides visual teaching aids for this section.

PuzzleMaker

Use the Vocabulary PuzzleMaker to create a puzzle of the section's key terms. Students can complete the puzzle on paper or on a computer.

Graphic Organizer

Tell students to go to the Online Learning Center through **glencoe.com** for a printable graphic organizer. (Answers include: the telegraph, telephone, trains, cars, airplanes, computers, cordless phones, cell phones, radio telephones, e-mail, video, fax machines, PDAs, the Internet, digital workflow, and more.)

N C L B Connects academics to content.

The History of Technology

Reading Guide

● Before You Read

Think about how technology has changed the way you do your work and communicate with others.

Read to Learn

- Describe how technological inventions have an effect on business.
- Give examples of how technology has changed jobs in business.

The Main Idea

Technology has changed the way people do business. Technological inventions have created new products, new markets, and new jobs.

Key Concepts

- Technology Influences Business
- Technology and the E-Workforce

Vocabulary

Key Terms
- e-workforce
- e-commerce
- digital workflow

Academic Vocabulary

You will find these words in your reading and on your tests. Make sure you know their meanings.
- technology
- edit
- images
- authors

Graphic Organizer

As you read the section, list 10 important technological advances on a figure like the one below.

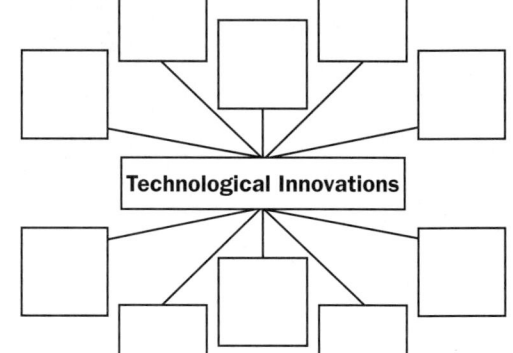

Technological Innovations

 Go to the *Introduction to Business* Online Learning Center through **glencoe.com** for a printable graphic organizer.

D

Academic Standards

English Language Arts
　NCTE 1 Read texts to acquire new information

Mathematics
　Algebra Represent and analyze mathematical situations and structures using algebraic symbols

Reading Guide

● Before You Read

Students should recognize that home computers and the Internet have caused widespread changes in the way people communicate.

D Develop Concepts

The Main Idea Ask students: Can you think of an example of how technology has changed the way people do business? (Answers will vary. Students might point out that technology has changed banking by allowing people to withdraw money from ATMs, pay for purchases with debit cards, and view their statements online.)

Technology Influences Business

Technology refers to the tools and machines that people have invented to make life easier. Inventions such as the radio and television entertain and inform us. The telegraph and then the telephone made it easier to communicate with one another. Trains, cars, and airplanes made it easier to travel. When computers were invented, they changed the way business was conducted.

Perhaps the most common technology staple in businesses today is the computer. Computers electronically store thousands of files, which saves time, labor, and space. Scanners read the prices of products and record sales instantly, making business move much faster. Accounting and bookkeeping software programs help organize, plan, and control business operations. The film industry uses digital technology to **edit** film as well as enhance colorful **images** and create animated scenes.

As You Read

Think about how a large business, such as Home Depot, would have operated before computers. What problems might they have encountered?

BusinessWeek *Reader and Case Study*

Wherever You Go, You're on the Job

A dramatic shift toward mobility is changing the way we work—and shaking up the status quo among tech titans.

Don't call Texan Sheryl Padamonsky a road warrior. Sure, she spends an average of three days a week away from her company's Austin office. But she's not on the road. She spends the time working at home and at the house of her elderly parents in Cleveland. She stays connected with a Dell laptop, equipped with built-in wireless technology to tap into the Net and a webcam for videoconferencing. And she uses a Palm Treo 650 smartphone, which makes calls, keeps her calendar, and pulls down her corporate e-mail—all while she's on the treadmill at the gym. The 40-year-old administrative assistant to John T. "Jack" McDonald, chief executive of tech consulting firm Perficient, seems shocked anyone would compare her to her always-traveling boss. "It's really about the ability to balance work life and private life in a way that's good for me, good for my company," Padamonsky says.

Once confined to jet-setting CEOs and salespeople who demand day and night access to the office, mobile corporate computing is coming to the masses. Superfast wireless networks, innovative communications software, and a slew of relatively cheap devices from notebook PCs to palm-size handhelds let practically any worker bee stay connected to the corporate hive, from wherever he or she may be.

 CASE STUDY Go to the *Introduction to Business* Online Learning Center through **glencoe.com** for the *BusinessWeek* Reader Case Study.

Active Learning

Wireless technology allows users to tap into the Net, and smartphones can let you make calls, keep your calendar, and check your e-mail. Team up with a classmate to research wireless options you could use to make your homework time more productive. Present your findings to your class.

glencoe.com

Discussion Starter
Technology Influences Business
Hold up a light bulb and ask students how its invention has influenced business. (Answers will vary. Students might suggest that the invention of the light bulb allows businesses to operate indoors and after the sun goes down.) Follow up by pointing out that technological advances continue to affect businesses.

R Reading Strategy

Apply Knowledge Ask students to think about books and movies they may have enjoyed that depict a world before computers. Ask them how they think that world was different? (Answers will vary. Students may think the pace of life seemed slower or less efficient.)

As You Read

Answers will vary. Students might identify areas of the business such as inventory control, processing customer payments, logistics, and payroll would be handled differently and would take more time and labor.

BusinessWeek *Reader and Case Study*

Wherever You Go, You're on the Job

 CASE STUDY Have students go to the *Introduction to Business* Online Learning Center through **glencoe.com** to download a Case Study activity that corresponds to the article. The activity and answer key are also available on the TeacherWorks Plus CD.

Active Learning

Students should present wireless technology options and give realistic reasons that they will make homework time more productive. Encourage students to understand that the options they identify come at a cost that must be justified by the productivity increase.

TEACH

S Skill Practice

Guided Practice

Observe Have students locate an advertisement showing an invention that has changed the way we live or do business and to write a caption identifying the invention. (Advertisement and captions will vary depending on the invention.) **L1**

Interview Have students ask a family member or acquaintance who is at least 40 years old: What technology advancement during your life has had the greatest impact on the way you live? Instruct students to write a summary of what they learned. (Examples include the personal computer and the cell phone.) **L2**

Investigate and Report

Have students write a short report on a simple invention that had a huge impact on business. (Examples include computers, software, the Internet, Post It® notes.) **L3**

ASSESS

Review Key Terms

Have students write sentences using each key term.

STUDY TO GO **Study-to-Go** Have students go to the Online Learning Center through **glencoe.com** to download free **Study-to-Go** content to their PDAs or cell phones.

The Impact of Telephones

Even the simplest invention can have a huge impact on business. Before the telephone was invented, people had to communicate face-to-face or in writing. A letter could take several days to travel from the writer to the reader. The telephone made it possible for people to communicate instantly even if they were hundreds of miles away. Telephone companies sprang up, and people were hired as phone operators. Manufacturers began producing telephones and all the related equipment and supplies needed for telephone services.

Telephones were so useful that making them became a big business. Companies specialized in making them. Machinists were needed to make parts. There was a constant demand to produce new and more efficient tools. In time, cordless phones, cell phones, and radio telephones became useful tools for business and consumers.

Since the invention of the telephone, countless new inventions have changed the way we live, work, and do business. Some of the technologies we use today were made possible by the invention of the telephone. Cell phones are not just phones—they are small computers. Aside from talking on a cell phone, you can send and receive e-mail and text messages, take photographs, and view video. Fax machines use telephone lines to send images. Mobile phones of all types help businesses to communicate at all times. Without mobile phones and fax machines, doing business would be more difficult.

✔ Reading Check **Contrast** How did life before the telephone compare to life after its invention?

? ETHICS in Business

Employment Contracts

■ **Critical Reading** Life is full of important decisions. Think about the kinds of decisions that you make as you read the question below.

After graduating from college and getting an advanced degree, you accepted a great job. The only problem is that you had to sign an employee agreement with serious restrictions on what work you could do if you left the company. You have now been at your job for three years and have been promoted several times. However, a new opportunity has come up with another company that competes with yours in a small area of the market. You want to do what is right by your current employer, but you really want this new job.

■ **Decision Making** How does the agreement you signed with your current employer affect your decision? What options could you explore?

Modern Technology

In the past 60 years, electronic devices have revolutionized business and society. Today, the economies of many countries, such as Japan and Taiwan, are based on manufacturing electronics. Business and consumers constantly demand smaller, faster, cheaper, and more powerful electronic devices.

Computers were first used only by the military. Now the computer is an important business tool, electronically storing thousands of files, saving time and space. The computer has created a boom in nearly all industries. Personal digital assistants, or PDAs, are handheld devices. They let users send e-mail, list contacts, and access the Internet. **S**

✔ Reading Check

Contrast Before the telephone, people had to communicate face to face or in writing. After its invention, people could have instant communication.

? ETHICS in Business

Decision Making You voluntarily signed the agreement. The current employer has offered several promotions. Keeping your word may not be in your immediate best interest but may be in your long-term best interest. However, the employer might be willing to compromise.

● **Technology Careers**
Computers and the Internet have created new careers and a demand for workers, such as software writers, online writers, and Web page designers. **What type of person do you think would be a good software writer?**

Technology and the E-Workforce

W
Visualize an office worker typing a report on a computer. Another is sitting at his desk and talking to a customer while placing an order on his computer. A few rows down, another is printing photos to use in a sales presentation. This is a portrait of today's electronic workforce, or e-workforce.

R
The **e-workforce** consists of people who work with computers while doing business. According to the Bureau of Labor Statistics, more than 77 million workers use computers daily. Electronic commerce, or **e-commerce**, which uses the Internet to do business, means businesses can reach customers directly anywhere in the world.

✔ **Reading Check** **Explain** What is the difference between e-commerce and the e-workforce?

Employment

U
Technology has created a boom in many industries. New markets have opened for products such as printers, fax machines, video games, and cell phones. New products are constantly being invented, developed, and manufactured. Innovation means more jobs and more people learning new skills. Technology allows people to work easier and faster.

Mapping Locations
Some companies use Web-based mapping software to find the right location for their business. Starbucks uses software to determine factors such as how many offices are located near a site and the amount of foot traffic around a block. *What other types of businesses can you list that might benefit from mapping tools?*

Section 9.1 The History of Technology **145**

Discuss the Photo
● **Technology Careers** Answers will vary. Examples might include people who have an eye for detail, people who are creative, people who are good with computers, etc.

Mapping Locations Students may indicate an interest in using the tools for their own businesses, such as baby-sitting or tutoring. Others include bookstores, health clubs, and laundries.

RETEACH

W **Writing Support**
Enrichment
Technology Awareness
Have students locate, read, and summarize a magazine or journal article about the impact of modern technology on business. Instruct students to include a properly formatted reference citation. (Summaries will vary depending on the article chosen.)

R **Reading Strategy**
Expand the Example Ask students to review the portrait of the electronic workforce described on this page. Instruct them to expand the example by identifying some of the positive aspects of being part of the e-workforce. (Examples might include the opportunity to work from home and the ability to share documents electronically.)

U **Universal Access**
Visual Learners Have students create an illustration that shows the way technology allows people to work easier and faster.

Student Activity Workbook ☞ Assign the Section 9.1 Activities.

✔ **Reading Check**

Explain E-commerce is electronic commerce, or using the Internet to do business. The e-workforce consists of people who work with computers while doing business.

C Critical Thinking

Consider the Process
Digital Workflow Ask students to describe the workflow involved in processing digital photographs. (Taking pictures with a digital camera, transferring the images to a computer, and printing the photos.)

● As You Read
Authors write articles, send them electronically to publishers, they are edited and designed, and sent to printers.

ASSESS

● After You Read
Have students complete the Section 9.1 After You Read section review.

Online Study Tools
Have students go to the Online Learning Center through **glencoe.com** to:

- Take the Section 9.1 **Practice Test**.
- Download free **Study-to-Go** content to their PDAs or cell phones.

CLOSE

Culminating Activity
New Jobs Have students write a short paragraph describing what they would need to do to qualify for an Internet-related position. (Students should identify the need for additional education and work experience.)

Digital Workflow A **digital workflow** links all the steps in a process digitally. For example, digital workflow has greatly influenced the publishing and printing industries. **Authors**, editors, marketing, manufacturing, and archiving departments can work together at a seamless electronic pace. People now have easier access to a broad range of information. Library catalogs and encyclopedias are available in digital format. Information is at your fingertips in an instant.

Paper workflow, sending information in paper form, requires workers to exchange many pages of paper. By switching to a digital format, less paper is involved.

Technology Centers The high-tech industry can be found in practically any city, but especially in technology centers such as California's Silicon Valley; New York's Silicon Alley; Oregon's Silicon Forest; and Austin, Texas's Silicon Hill.

New Jobs One important tool of the high-tech industry is the Internet. The Internet has created a demand for software writers, online writers, and Web page designers. Companies are now able to post job opportunities on their home page, in a newspaper's online classified section, and to partner with Internet job services, such as Monster.com.

● As You Read
Think about the digital workflow processes involved in creating your favorite magazine.

N C L B Activity correlates to Math standards.

Section 9.1

● After You Read

Review Key Concepts
1. What are some examples of inventions that have had a major impact on business?
2. How is digital workflow different from paper workflow?
3. What are three examples of new jobs that have been created by the Internet?

Academic Skills
4. **Mathematics** Suppose you run a business that develops Web sites for e–commerce. You charge a flat fee of $2,700 to create the Web site. One of your clients also pays you a $15 bonus for every seven people who visit the site. How many people need to visit the Web site in order for you to match your fee for creating the Web site? Write an equation and solve it.

THEORY **Algebra: Equations** As you read a word problem, think through what you know and do not know. Assign an unknown to stand for a value you want to find. In this problem, let x equal the number of people who need to visit the site.

 For math help, go to the Math Appendix.

@ Go to the *Introduction to Business* Online Learning Center through **glencoe.com** to check your answers.

Section 9.1

Review Key Concepts
1. Some examples are computers, fax machines, copy machines, and telephones.
2. All steps in a process are linked electronically in a digital workflow. There is less paper involved than in paper workflow.
3. Three examples are software writers, online writers, and Web page designers.

Academic Skills
4. **Mathematics**
$(x \div 7)15 = 2,700$
$x \div 7 = 180$
$x = 1,260$
1,260 people need to visit the site.

E-Commerce

Reading Guide

● Before You Read

Think about the products and services that you have shopped for and purchased online.

Read to Learn
- Explain why doing business on the Internet has become a major factor in many industries.

The Main Idea
Businesses offer all types of goods and services online. Consumers can research almost any product or service from their home. They can buy just about anything online.

Key Concept
- The Importance of Virtual Business

Vocabulary
Key Terms
start-up
e-tail
multi-channel retailer
brick-and-mortar
clicks-and-mortar
e-ticket

Academic Vocabulary
You will find these words in your reading and on your tests. Make sure you know their meanings.

transports   rely
methods   fee

Graphic Organizer
In a graphic like the one shown, describe each type of business indicated as you read.

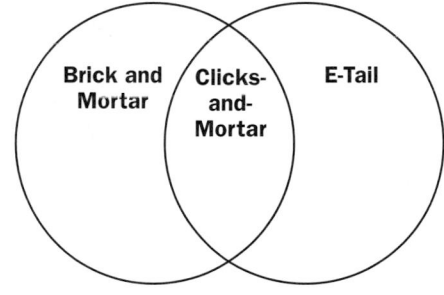

 Go to the *Introduction to Business* Online Learning Center through **glencoe.com** for a printable graphic organizer.

Academic Standards
English Language Arts
NCTE 1 Read texts to acquire new information
NCTE 4 Use written language to communicate effectively
NCTE 6 Apply knowledge of language structure and conventions to discuss texts

Science
Content Standard B Students should develop an understanding of structure and properties of matter, chemical reactions

---

🔔 Bell Ringer Activity

E-Commerce
Ask students to define e-commerce. (E-commerce is electronic commerce or business conducted on the Internet.) Tell students that e-commerce is not limited to consumers buying things online; it also facilitates business-to-business transactions.

Preteaching

Presentation Plus!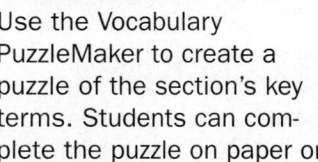
The Presentation Plus! CD provides visual teaching aids for this section.

PuzzleMaker
Use the Vocabulary PuzzleMaker to create a puzzle of the section's key terms. Students can complete the puzzle on paper or on a computer.

Graphic Organizer
Tell students to go to the Online Learning Center through **glencoe.com** for a printable graphic organizer. (Bricks-and-mortar: a business with a physical building that requires customers to visit the location. E-tail: a purely electronic business hub that sells goods or services over the Internet. Clicks-and-mortar: any of the common business types that shares both a physical and an online presence.)

N C L B Connects academics to content.

Reading Guide

● Before You Read

Answers will vary. Examples include books, songs, software, and backpacks.

D Develop Concepts

The Main Idea Ask students: What are some products and services that cannot be purchased online? (Haircuts and oil changes are not available online.) Follow up by asking: Are there products or services that you would not want to purchase online? (Students might suggest that they would use the Internet to research products such as clothing and cars, but that they would not make a purchase online.)

U **Universal Access**

Virtual Businesses Point out that virtual businesses generally do not need a store or office to conduct business. Interaction with customers, vendors, and employees is over the Internet and through e-mail.

R **Reading Strategy**

Draw a Conclusion Ask students to write a paragraph explaining the importance of virtual business. (Paragraphs will vary. Students should understand that virtual business allows for innovation, expands markets, and fuels the global economy.)

✔ Reading Check

Identify Two examples of e-commerce are e-tail and e-ticket. Follow up by encouraging students to expand their idea of e-commerce to include business-to-business activities. Ask students to describe a situation that involves e-commerce that does not involve a consumer. (Answers will vary. Students should understand that a business involved in e-tail is likely to be involved in e-commerce with vendors and suppliers.)

● **As You Read**

One of the chief benefits of virtual businesses is that they can be opened without the need to buy or lease real estate for a physical location in which to do business.

The Importance of Virtual Business

The ease of doing business via the Internet has created a boom in new online businesses. This type of business is called a virtual business. Many entrepreneurs have developed businesses that they can operate from their homes. The Internet makes it possible to communicate online with customers and clients around the world. Some Internet businesses are start-ups. A **start-up** is a newly formed business that is usually small.

Technology **transports** your mind to new places in the world. It would be nice to order a blueberry muffin and hot chocolate over the Internet and receive them in five minutes, but that is not yet possible. However, if you do not have a muffin shop in your town but still want to purchase muffin mix and hot chocolate, you can order these products from companies doing business online. **Figure 9.1** shows you what consumers buy most online.

● **As You Read** **R**

Think about a virtual business you would like to start. What advantage would your business offer over a traditional type of store?

The Basics of E-Commerce

Everyone hooked up to the Internet is a potential customer. This has not only changed the way products are sold. It has also changed the way business activities are conducted. E-tail and e-tickets are two examples of e-commerce.

✔ Reading Check **Identify** What are two examples of e-commerce?

● **Top Consumer Purchases** People shop on the Internet for these types of purchases. **What do you think are reasons for buying these products online?**

Figure 9.1 — *What Consumers Buy Online: Top Purchases*

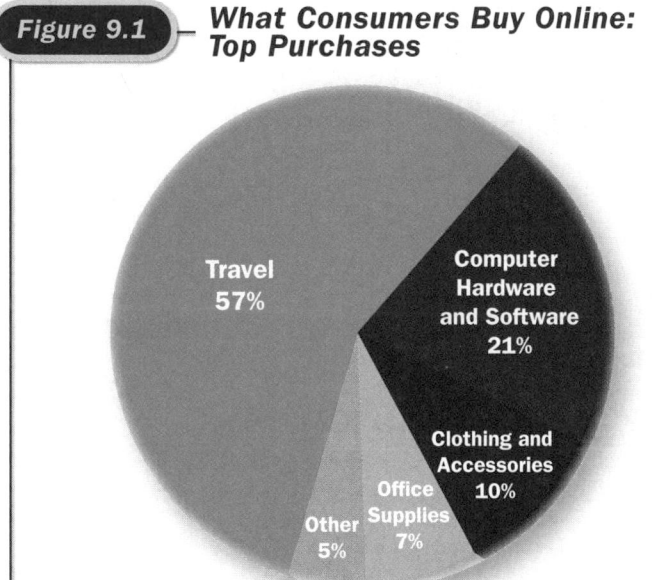

Travel 57%

Computer Hardware and Software 21%

Clothing and Accessories 10%

Office Supplies 7%

Other 5%

Source: *comScore Media Metrix.*

Figure 9.1

●**Top Consumer Purchases Online** Travel products are the most popular online purchases, probably because it is possible to purchase and print e-tickets that are essentially identical to the ones a travel agent would sell, but without a substantial commission. Purchases of all items online are probably driven by the ease of comparison shopping and the wide selection available.

Science/TechTRENDS

High-Tech Clothing

Wouldn't it be great if you could put on a lightweight, flexible ski outfit that would instantly harden into protective armor if you took a nasty spill? Does this sound impossible? It's not. At the winter 2006 Olympic Games, a special material called d3o (dee-three-oh) protected U.S. and Canadian skiers from injury on the slalom runs. Skiwear company Spyder developed racing suits using d3o along the shins and forearms. Competitive skiers love it. The inspiration for d3o came when materials scientist Dr. Phil Green was nursing a bruised elbow after a snowboarding accident. "It occurred to me that all the available impact protection systems... are restrictive, uncomfortable and actually pretty ineffective. I knew if I could get a system to work at a molecular level, we could have an amazing product," Green says.

WebQuest

Go to the *Introduction to Business* Online Learning Center through **glencoe.com** for links to Web sites where you can find out more about d3o and how it works. Write a paragraph or two describing the molecular structure of the material, and suggest other uses for this futuristic material.

E-Tail **E-tail** is electronic retail. E-tailers sell products over the Internet through e-commerce. For instance, J. Crew sells clothing and accessories in stores, by mail, and online. This type of company is called a **multi-channel retailer**. It uses several **methods** to sell products. Businesses often call their stores and warehouses **brick-and-mortar**, referring to the actual buildings. Grocery stores such as Kroger are brick-and-mortar companies. Businesses that also use the Internet are called **clicks-and-mortar** operations. Bookstore chain Barnes & Noble is a clicks-and-mortar company.

E-commerce makes it easier to send catalogs of e-tailers' products to consumers. This is especially useful for companies that do a lot of mail-order business, such as Land's End. Putting catalogs on the Internet rather than shipping them by mail saves a lot of money in printing and mailing costs.

How does e-tail benefit you as a consumer? Here are the advantages:

- **Convenience** You can shop at home without going to a store. You can shop 24 hours a day, seven days a week. Your purchase can be delivered to your door.

> **As You Read**
>
> Think of some brick-and-mortar businesses that also do business online.

TEACH (cont.)

S Skill Practice

Guided Practice

Illustrate an Idea Have students illustrate one of the following: multi-channel retailer, brick-and-mortar, or clicks-and-mortar. (Illustrations will vary depending on type of business.) **L1**

Categorize Ask students in small groups to make a table to categorize retailers as multi-channel retailer, brick-and-mortar, or clicks-and-mortar, using provided retailer catalogs. (Tables will vary depending on the types of businesses.) **L2**

Create a Graph Ask students to create a line graph with the following sales data for a small retailer.

Sales	Total	E-commerce
Year 1	$10,000	$1,000
Year 3	28,000	11,000
Year 5	58,000	23,000

(Graphs should show a line for total sales and a line for e-commerce sales.) **L3**

ASSESS

Review Key Terms

Have students write sentences using each key term.

 **Study-to-Go** Have students go to the Online Learning Center through **glencoe.com** to download free **Study-to-Go** content to their PDAs or cell phones.

 Activity correlates to Science standards.

Science/TechTRENDS

WebQuest

High-Tech Clothing The material is normally flexible because the molecules can move past each with ease. But the shock of sudden impact causes the chemical bonds to strengthen and the moving molecules to lock, turning the material into a more protective shield.

> **As You Read**
>
> Remind students that this type of business is called clicks-and-mortar.

RETEACH

 **W** Writing

Enrichment Have students write an article for a magazine about price comparison Web sites. (Students might include information about the concept, the history, advantages and disadvantages, success, and the future of price comparison Web sites.)

R Reading Strategy

Paraphrase Have students paraphrase the text about the additional charges that may be associated with online purchases. (Additional charges may be for shipping, taxes, and exchanges and returns.)

U Universal Access

Visual Learners Have students compare several books from the library to their descriptions on a Web site that sells books. Ask students what information they can obtain by leafing through the book that they cannot get from the Web site or on the Web site that they cannot get from the book? Which source of information is more likely to make them want to buy and read the book? (Answers will vary.)

Student Activity Workbook ☞ Assign the Section 9.2 Activities.

✔ **Reading Check**

Identify Shipping and handling charges add to the cost, you have to wait for delivery, and you cannot rely on observation.

150

Real World

Privacy Issues
Some companies use software to track consumers. Customer-tracking software follows what customers are doing on the Web as they shop and offers to help if it seems a customer cannot find a product. *Do you think this violates your privacy? List some rules e-tailers might post to ensure customer privacy while still using tracking software.*

● **Self-Service with E-Tickets** With an electronic ticket, a traveler can use self-service check-in at many airports. **What services could this kiosk offer to travelers?**

• **Choices** The number of companies selling products online gives you more choices and makes comparing items easier. Web sites such as Shopping.com and ZDNet.com allow consumers to compare products and prices. Some online companies allow you to download music and computer games or preview movie trailers. This helps consumers make decisions about purchases.

There are some disadvantages to e-tail. They include:

• **Buying Power** It is easy to overspend online. If you are not careful, you can also order things by mistake.

• **Additional Charges** Since most products bought online are delivered by mail or express delivery services, you have to pay shipping charges and sometimes taxes. The exchange and return policies may be more strict than those of a bricks-and-mortar store.

• **Immediacy** While shopping online is convenient, you still have to wait for most products to be delivered. Most online companies promise speedy delivery, but delivery times vary.

• **Relying on Observation** It is hard to know for sure whether you like a sofa unless you see it and try it. The same can be said for clothes, CDs, or books. Online buying requires you to **rely** on pictures and descriptions instead of actually touching things yourself. In some ways, your decisions about what to buy can be easier. In others, they can be harder because you cannot examine the product before buying it.

✔ **Reading Check** **Identify** What are some disadvantages to e-tail?

Real World

Privacy Issues Some students may feel it is a violation. Others may rate convenience over privacy. Rules may include: clear notice if customer names will be sold to other businesses and offering a way to opt out; clearly telling customers that tracking is taking place.

Discuss the Photo
● **Self-Service with E-Tickets** A traveler can use a self-service terminal like this to check in, select a seat, check bags, get a boarding pass, and obtain an electronic receipt.

E-Tickets Businesses find that customers want to buy more goods and services online. Using their computers, people can now purchase an **e-ticket**, or electronic ticket. Approximately 70 percent of travelers in the United States now shop for airline tickets online. E-tickets are also available for concerts, museums, movies, and amusement parks.

Some people find purchasing an e-ticket is easier and cheaper than visiting an actual store. For example, a travel agency may charge you a $25 **fee** for handling your airline ticket. If you buy a ticket from an online travel agency, you may be charged only $1. Many customers search online for the least expensive e-tickets. Browsing the Internet gives them time to compare offers and prices.

E-ticket holders can print their boarding passes online, use self-service check-in, and avoid some of the lines in crowded terminals. However, if an airline loses your e-ticket in its computer system, you might be required to buy another ticket.

> ● **As You Read**
>
> Think about the kinds of problems that could arise from buying a ticket online.

 Activity correlates to English Language Arts standards.

Section 9.2

● **After You Read**

Review Key Concepts
1. How have virtual businesses changed the business world?
2. How is an e-tailer different from other businesses?
3. What are two advantages and two disadvantages to buying products and services via e-tail for you as a consumer?

Academic Skills
4. **English Language Arts** If you spend any time surfing the Internet, you are familiar with banner ads. These small rectangular advertisements appear on all sorts of Web pages. If you click on them, your Internet browser will take you to the advertiser's Web site. Imagine that you have just set up a Web site for your sportswear catalog company. Your target market includes four distinct groups: boys and girls ages 11 to 18, and men and women in the 18-to-35 age range. Write four banner ads designed to appeal to each group.

5. **English Language Arts** A topic sentence is the most important sentence in a paragraph. It tells what the paragraph is mostly about. Topic sentences often appear at the beginning of a paragraph, but sometimes they are found in the middle or at the end of a paragraph. Skim through the paragraphs in this section, and find an example of a paragraph with a topic sentence at the beginning and an example of one occurring at the middle or end. Then write a sentence that indicates what the paragraphs are about, based on each topic sentence you selected.

@ Go to the *Introduction to Business* Online Learning Center through **glencoe.com** to check your answers.

Section 9.2

Review Key Concepts
1. Entrepreneurs can conduct businesses from their homes, communicate with customers worldwide, and operate via the Internet.
2. An e-tailer sells products over the Internet.
3. Advantages: convenience and choice. Disadvantages: shipping charges; time for delivery; and you cannot always judge the product's quality.

Academic Skills
4. **English Language Arts** Banner ads should appeal to the four groups.
5. **English Language Arts** Students should identify the topic sentence and explain why they chose it.

RETEACH (cont.)

C **Critical Thinking**

Compare and Contrast
E-Tickets Have students compare and contrast the policies of two travel Web site airline e-tickets refund policies. (Answers will depend on Web sites chosen.)

> ● **As You Read**
>
> Problems may occur with the Web site, getting a refund, or using the ticket.

ASSESS

● **After You Read**

Have students complete the Section 9.2 After You Read section review.

Online Study Tools
Have students go to the Online Learning Center through **glencoe.com** to:

- Take the Section 9.2 **Practice Test**.
- Download free **Study-to-Go** content to their PDAs or cell phones.

CLOSE

Culminating Activity
Organize students in small groups to discuss trends in e-commerce that they have observed. Ask a spokesperson from each group to offer a summary to the class. (Summaries will vary depending on e-commerce trends.)

Vocabulary Review

1. Students should write complete sentences using each term correctly.

Review Key Concepts

2. Technological inventions make it possible for businesses to conduct their business in a different way. The Internet allows businesses to communicate instantly with clients and customers around the world. They can use the Internet to show and sell their products and services. Phones and fax machines enable them to communicate by voice and by images immediately. Mobile phones make it possible for people to communicate with co-workers from wherever they are.

3. Technology has created a boom in online businesses. More workers work through the Internet, using Web sites and e-mail. Many brick-and-mortar stores have become clicks-and-mortar businesses, using Web sites. Shoppers use Web sites to shop at any time—day or night.

4. Any company can go online to sell its products or services. Businesses can sell products in stores, by mail, and online. Catalogs can be put on the Internet for customers.

Section 9.1 *Summary*

The History of Technology Technology has changed the business world through tools and machines that make life easier. Inventions such as the radio and television entertain and inform us. Trains, cars, and airplanes make it easier to travel. The telephone makes it possible for people around the world to have instant communication. With computers and the Internet, workers are able to do business around the world and reach customers directly. Technology has created new markets for many products. Files flow digitally, placing information at your fingertips instantly. Part of the effect of technology has been to build new technology centers for high-tech companies. Those companies have created new types of jobs for people working with high-tech products.

Section 9.2 *Summary*

E-Commerce E-commerce has changed the way we do business. Virtual businesses operate through the Internet. Technology has created a boom in online businesses, providing new employment opportunities and ways for people to make purchases. Many brick-and-mortar stores have become clicks-and-mortar businesses, adding Web sites so customers can shop online. Online shopping is a way of life for many consumers. They go to an e-tailer's Web site and shop any time of the day or night. E-tickets can be used for traveling, concerts, museums, and amusement parks. Advantages of e-commerce are convenience and the availability of choices. Disadvantages are that you can easily overspend, and you must rely on pictures and descriptions.

Vocabulary Review

1. On a sheet of paper, use each of these key terms and academic vocabulary terms in a sentence.

Key Terms		Academic Vocabulary	
e-workforce	multi-channel	technology	transports
e-commerce	retailer	edit	methods
digital workflow	brick-and-mortar	images	rely
start-up	clicks-and-mortar	authors	fee
e-tail	e-ticket		

Review Key Concepts

2. Describe how technological inventions have an effect on business.

3. Give examples of how technology has changed jobs in business.

4. Explain why doing business on the Internet has become a major factor in many industries.

Critical Thinking

5. The delays in communicating would probably be the greatest difference.

6. More "wearable" computers will be available. One device may combine your computer and telephone in one device.

7. They become more interested in technology and sources of information.

Teens who do not spend time online may be interested in other pastimes, such as physical activities.

8. You may be able to use an Internet service to find companies, send electronic résumés, and find a job.

9. The kitchen can become a command center, using a computer to store information and to program the appliances.

Critical Thinking

5. Imagine your life without technology. What difference do you think you would notice in your communications?

6. Devices for downloading and storing information and music have grown in popularity. What other devices do you think may be developed in the future?

7. Online children and teens watch more TV, see more movies, and read more magazines and books than offline children and teens. What do you conclude from these facts?

8. Internet job services make it possible for people to find jobs and companies to find employees. How could you benefit by using an Internet job service?

9. In a "smart" kitchen, a refrigerator can keep track of food stored in it and remind you when you need to shop. What other technology might be possible for a smart kitchen?

10. How might a brick-and-mortar company be encouraged to or discouraged from engaging in e-commerce?

11. Smartphones combine a phone with a PDA, calendar, address book, note pad, Internet access, built-in camera, and display screen for reading documents. What other capabilities might they have someday?

Write About It

12. A number of companies have become very successful as Internet service providers (ISPs). Write an e-mail to your teacher that explores reasons ISPs are an important part of business.

13. Write a one-page story describing life in the business world without computers.

14. Why do you think the telephone had such an influence on business? Write two or more paragraphs on the subject.

15. Describe how you think the average workplace has been changed by technology.

16. Write an article on online shopping for your school newspaper. Describe the differences between shopping with a paper catalog and shopping online.

17. Using the decision-making process, write a one-page essay describing the process you would go through in choosing a product online.

18. Your friend has never bought anything on the Internet, but would like to buy the same DVD player you just bought online. In an e-mail to him, list the reasons why you would or would not advise him to use e-tail.

19. In two or more paragraphs, write about a disadvantage to e-tail that you think is most important to you.

Technology Applications

Spreadsheet
20. Choose a product such as a book, an electronic device, or a game. Check the prices of the product online, researching several companies to find what they would charge for that product. Then create a spreadsheet to compare the companies and their prices. Finally, prepare a graph that shows the companies and their prices.

Business Ethics

Online Shopping Safety
21. Identity theft is a big concern in online shopping. If a hacker gains access to your credit card information, you may find yourself a victim of it. However, you might want to buy online and pay for your purchases with your credit card. What guidelines would you advise online shoppers to follow to prevent problems?

Chapter 9 Review and Activities **153**

Critical Thinking

10. Some stores may change to clicks-and-mortar if they can identify an advantage to switching. If their competitors are online, companies also may want an online presence.

11. They may be able to hold software, function as a navigation tool, and recognize speech.

Write About It

12. They facilitate e-commerce.

13. Stories will vary.

14. It possible for businesspeople to reach one another from a distance. It also precipitated related technologies.

15. Workers can transfer information with e-mail, voice mail, and fax machines.

16. Shoppers may feel they can spend more time browsing through a paper catalog while others like the convenience of online shopping.

17. Identify the product you need, the businesses that offer the product, compare the products and identify the pros and cons, make your choice and evaluate it when you receive it.

18. You can shop at any time. However, the product might not have looked or worked as described. It might have taken longer to arrive than you anticipated.

19. Answers will vary but students should give consideration to issues in the chapter.

Technology Applications

20. Spreadsheets and graphs will vary, depending on the type of product students choose to research.

Business Ethics

21. Buy only from online sites of companies you recognize as well-known, trusted companies. Always check the security measures of the site on which you are shopping. Does it offer you the option of phoning the company to provide your credit card information? If so, you may want to choose that option.

Applying Academics to Business

22. Each of the terms originated in a different decade starting in the 1940s. 40s: TV; 50s: beatnik; 60s: instant replay; 70s: Silicon Valley; 80s: in-line skate; 90s: nanotube

23. Adding the products $4 \times 4 = 16$ and $4 \times 6 = 24$, equals 40. Multiplying by 10 days $= 400$, and multiplying by approximately $10 $ = \$4,000$.

24. Sentences will vary, but should exhibit the characteristics of simple, compound, and complex sentences.

25. $40x + 16(2x) = \$1,152$

$40x + 32x = \$1,152$

$72x = \$1,152$

$x = \$16$ per hour

Active Learning

26. Reports will vary depending on the stores in your community. Companies that do not sell to consumers include tool-and-die companies and manufacturing plants.

Business in the Real World

27. Questions may include: What are the benefits of selling online? Will selling online increase business? Will it increase profits on sales? What potential problems might arise from selling online? Would it be better to add online sales in the future?

Applying Academics to Business

English Language Arts

22. The following terms have become a common part of the English language. Find out more about these terms using a dictionary or other resource. List them in the order in which you think they first appeared in the English language. Ask family members to do the same, and compare the results.

instant replay	nanotube
TV	beatnik
Silicon Valley	in-line skate

Mathematics

23. Jason's Web business jumps in sales, and he needs to hire more people to keep up. He hires 8 people to fill the extra orders and pays them $11 per hour. Four of them work 4 hours over 10 days, and the other four work 6 hours over 10 days. Jason does some quick mental arithmetic and concludes that he owes these workers about $4,000. Describe how he might have used mental math to estimate his cost.

> **THEORY** **Numbers and Operations:**
> **Mental Math** Using basic multiplication facts and rounding can help you make mental computations.

English Language Arts

24. A simple sentence contains a subject and a verb to express a complete thought. A compound sentence contains two independent clauses joined by *for, and, nor, but, or, yet,* or *so*. A complex sentence has an independent clause joined by one or more dependent clauses. Write examples of each type of sentence on the topic of technology's impact on business.

Mathematics

25. Shannon charges clients a regular rate for the first 40 hours she spends working during a week and twice that rate for overtime. Last week, she spent 56 hours working for one client and was paid $1,152. Write an equation using x to represent her regular rate. Solve for x.

> **THEORY** **Algebra: Writing Equations**
> Read word problems carefully to understand how mathematical ideas connect and build on one another. Use symbols in equations to stand for the numbers you are trying to find.

Active Learning

Clicks-and-Mortar Businesses
26. Team up with a classmate, and list 10 businesses in your community. Select businesses that sell to consumers or businesses that sell to other businesses. Then research which of those businesses have online sites to offer their products and services. Prepare a report of at least two pages indicating which local businesses are also e-tail businesses.

Business in the Real World

Investigate E-Tailing
27. Interview a businessperson in your community about e-tailing. Does the businessperson sell products or services online? Why or why not? Ask him or her to list questions to ask when considering becoming an e-tailer. Write a report of at least one page on your findings. Be prepared to share your information with your class.

ExamView Assessment Suite CD allows you to print out ready-made unit and chapter tests, complete with answer keys. You can also create customized tests.

TeacherWorks Plus provides complete teacher resources in one convenient package. It includes customizable lesson plans in calendar format, and instant access to many print program resources.

Real LIFE • skills

INTERNET SKILLS

28. Efficient use of technology is important in our fast-paced business world. Many people waste a great deal of time browsing the Internet because they get sidetracked and spend time looking for information that does not meet their needs. Write a one-page report about how to seek information on the Internet quickly and effectively. Include tips on how to avoid getting distracted and wasting time.

FIND YOUR DREAM JOB

29. Go to the *Introduction to Business* Online Learning Center through **glencoe. com** for a link to the Occupational Outlook Handbook Web site. Click on the "OOH Search/A-Z Index" link and enter the job title "computer scientists and database administrators." Write a one-page report about this occupation. Conclude your report with a list of things you could do now to prepare yourself to pursue the occupation.

Role Play

CLICKS-AND-MORTAR COMPANIES

30. Situation You are an employee of a clicks-and-mortar company. Your manager has asked you to prepare a presentation about your company for a group of high school students who are coming for a field trip.

Activity Prepare an outline of the major points of your presentation to the high school students. Then make the presentation to your class.

Evaluation You will be evaluated on how well you meet the following performance indicators:

- Explain what a clicks-and-mortar company is.
- Describe how this company is different from a brick-and-mortar company.
- Describe how customers can buy from your company.
- Prepare a written outline.
- Speak clearly and use correct grammar.

Standardized Test Practice

Directions Choose the letter of the best answer. Write the letter for the answer on a separate piece of paper.

1. If the formula for converting from Celsius to Fahrenheit is $F = \frac{9}{5}C + 32$, what is the formula for converting from Fahrenheit to Celsius?

  A $C = \frac{5}{9}(F - 32)$ B $C = \frac{5}{9}(F + 32)$ C $C = 32 - \frac{9}{5}F$ D $C = \frac{9}{5}(F - 32)$

TEST-TAKING TIP Study for tests over a few days or weeks, and continually review class material. Do not wait until the night before to try to learn everything.

READING Go to the *Introduction to Business* Online Learning Center through **glencoe.com** for a list of outside reading suggestions.

Chapter 9 Review and Activities   **155**

Real LIFE • skills

28. Use the decision-making process. What is the problem to be solved? Identify key words, then choose a search engine. Evaluate the sites the search engine lists. Browse several sites to determine which one will help.

Business CAREERS

29. Nature of the work: Computer scientists work as theorists, researchers, or inventors. Database administrators work with database management systems software and determine ways to organize and store data. Training and qualifications require an increasing level of broad-range skills. Job outlook is favorable. As preparation, take computer science courses, and art and design courses.

Role Play

30. Presentations should address the competencies noted in the Role Play. Outlines should cover how a clicks-and-mortar company operates and how customers can make purchases.

Standardized Test Practice
  1. A

STRATEGIES FOR STANDARDIZED TEST PREP SUCCESS

Test Stress Explain to students that procrastination about studying only adds to the stress they experience when taking tests. Creating and following a study plan can relieve much of this stress. Part of planning a structured approach to studying over a period of time is setting weekly or periodic goals. You might have students create a written schedule for a week and identify what and how they intend to study at each session. During the week have them monitor their own efforts and, at week's end, evaluate their success at accomplishing their plan.

FOCUS

Bell Ringer Activity

Keeping America Clean

Ask students to name cleaning products they have used. (Students will be familiar with a wide variety of cleaning products.) Write a list of products on the board. Ask students to brainstorm groupings of cleaning products and assess whether or not they are all likely to be sold at the same store. (Examples of product groupings are: WD40, window cleaner, and car wax are likely to be sold in a hardware or auto accessory store. Laundry detergent might be sold in a wide variety of stores.)

TEACH

Teaching Points

Entrepreneurship

Ask students to define entrepreneur and entrepreneurship (An entrepreneur is someone who recognizes a business opportunity and organizes, manages, and assumes the risks of starting a business. Entrepreneurship is the process of recognizing an opportunity, testing it in the market, and gathering the resources necessary to go into business.)

Jeffrey Hollender

President/Chief Inspired Protagonist, Seventh Generation

Seventh Generation is the leading brand of environmentally safe household products in the United States. Since 1988, consumer purchases of his products have saved more than 240,000 trees, more than 1 million gallons of petroleum, 92 million gallons of water, and almost 230,000 pounds of greenhouse gases—the kind that contribute to global warming.

Q & A

Describe your job responsibilities.

Jeffrey: I manage a small team of senior managers and see my role as providing overall vision and leadership. Outside the company, I have three roles: building relationships with shareholders, public speaking, and participating in interviews.

What skills are most important in your business?

Jeffrey: You need to be clear about what you know and what you don't know so that you can find talented people who complement you. I look for an alignment of values instead of just skills when hiring new employees, especially management.

What is your key to success?

Jeffrey: Being clear about my purpose. I know who I am and what I want to do. Developing ecologically-safe products through Seventh Generation is related to my personal purpose in life: being authentic, having a positive impact on the world, and being socially just. Other keys are having a good business plan, identifying the need or product I'll fulfill or create, and knowing how much capital is needed to help grow the company until it becomes self-sustaining.

What advice would you give students interested in starting a business?

Jeffrey: Know what you're getting into. Students also need to ask themselves if they are willing to do all that is required. This includes working long hours, and managing other people, as well as doing very basic tasks.

Critical Thinking *What role does a person's belief system play in the type of company he or she develops and its products and services?*

Critical Thinking

In Jeffrey's case, his personal beliefs about the importance of solving Earth's problems influenced his decision to join an ecologically sound company. He believes that developing, selling, and promoting ecologically sound products relates to his purpose in life, which is to have a positive impact on the world.

Some Qualifications of a Manufacturing Company Owner

Academic Skills and Abilities

Biology, chemistry; marketing; interpersonal skills; general business management skills; verbal and written communication skills; multitasking, organizing, and planning skills

Academic Skills Required to Complete Tasks at Seventh Generation			
Tasks	Math	Science	English Language Arts
Hold meetings			◆
Assign duties			◆
Develop new products		◆	◆
Assess products' market performance	◆		◆
Customer service			◆
Schedule employees	◆		◆
Order supplies and equipment	◆		◆
Analyze financials	◆		◆

Education and Training

Most owners and managers need a four-year college degree in addition to experience in the industry. As in other highly technical industries, top managerial positions often are held by those with substantial technical experience.

Career Path

Owners and managers can advance without additional formal training outside the workplace, although competition is keen. In general, advancement into the highest management ranks depends on one's experience and proven ability to handle responsibility in several functional areas. Among larger, multinational firms, international experience is important for career advancement.

Preparing for a Career
Self-Assessment Checklist

Use this self-assessment checklist to help determine ways you can succeed in the global marketplace.

- ✔ Think about the goods and services people need.
- ✔ Study the marketplace for products and services you could provide.
- ✔ Talk to entrepreneurs and managers, especially if they work in your area of interest.
- ✔ Take a good look at yourself. Do you possess the personal qualities that your career path demands? If not, brainstorm ways you can start developing the qualities you will need for success.
- ✔ Be creative—sometimes the most unique idea can become a booming success in the business world.
- ✔ Remember that many successful individuals make changes in their career paths.
- ✔ View change as a positive way to learn more about yourself and your interests.
- ✔ Apply the skills and knowledge you have already acquired when you start a job.

157

Preparing for a Career

Career Preparation Preparing for success in a career is much easier when you have a concrete idea of where you are headed and what will be expected of you when you get there. Ask students to visualize their dream job and make a list of some of the things they will like about the job. (Dream jobs will vary, but students should be concrete about details they like. For instance, someone might want to be the head of a Fortune 500 company because they like the powerful lifestyle. Another student might prefer a job as a construction worker as a way to build for the future.) Remind students to keep their options open and learn more about career options as they read the Self-Assessment Checklists in this book.

ASSESS

Write About It
Seventh Generation

Ask students to write a summary of what they like about Seventh Generation's business concept. (Students may say they like the company's commitment to the environment. They may also appreciate the idea that the people in the company do work that is fulfilling.)

Academic Vocabulary
Career Planning

Ask students to read the Self-Assessment Checklist, then write one or more paragraphs about preparing for a career. Have students use some words from the Academic Vocabulary Glossary. (Example: When preparing for a career, students should *consider* careers that will provide them with opportunities for positive income growth. They should look for positions that will *involve* tasks they enjoy. If they *focus* their goals around their abilities, they are likely to succeed.)

CLOSE

Cooperative Learning
Technology Applications

Ask students to work in pairs and develop an idea for a business that will allow them to benefit the environment. (Students may describe a business concept that would reduce the need for printing and wasting paper. They may also describe other business ideas that involve communications technology that lessens the need for travel to far-flung locations.)

FOCUS

Discussion Starter

Lead a discussion about entrepreneurship in a global world. Ask students to project how entrepreneurship and globalization will change society.

Step 1

Brainstorm Skills

Have students go to the *Introduction to Business* Online Learning Center through **glencoe.com** for a graphic organizer they can use to brainstorm the skills needed to complete the project.

Step 2

Choose a Business and a Career

Students can use the Occupational Outlook Handbook Web site to explore options.

TEACH

Step 3

Build Background

Entrepreneurship Have students brainstorm ways young entrepreneurs can prepare to enter a global marketplace. (Global business means change is always happening. Global markets are fiercely competitive and foreign business-people are likely to follow different rules. In addition, the influx of immigration to this country will provide new workers but may cause other issues.)

Globalization Ask students about how they plan to prepare to face a globalized business market. (Answers will vary but may include

158

Entrepreneurship in a Global World

Globalization and technology are creating a worldwide marketplace. Smart entrepreneurs recognize the opportunities in a worldwide marketplace and adjust to doing business at a global level.

Thematic Project Assignment

In this project you will conduct an interview and create a presentation about entrepreneurship in a global world. Your interview may be in person, on the phone, or through e-mail.

Step 1 Brainstorm Skills You Need to Complete this Activity

Your success in interviewing an entrepreneur will depend on your skills. Preview the activity. Then brainstorm a list of the skills you will need to use to complete the activity and describe how you will use them. Skills you might use include:

Academic Skills	reading, writing, social studies
Basic Skills	speaking, listening, thinking, and interpersonal skills
Technology Skills	word processing, keyboarding, presentation, telecommunications, and Internet skills

 SKILLS PREVIEW Go to the *Introduction to Business* Online Learning Center through **glencoe.com** for a graphic organizer you can use to brainstorm the skills you will use to complete the project.

Step 2 Choose a Business and a Career That Interest You

Think of an entrepreneurial business that you find interesting. Then think of a career in this entrepreneurial business that interests you. As you investigate how entrepreneurs work in the global marketplace, you will research the effects of globalization and technology on the business and career of your choice.

Step 3 Build Background Knowledge

Preview entrepreneurship in a global economy.

Young **Entrepreneurs** Enter a **Global** Marketplace

The whole world is now the marketplace for young entrepreneurs. Anyone with a computer and Internet connection can enter the international marketplace almost overnight. Entrepreneurs are no longer confined to their local communities, or even to the United States. Now they can open their virtual doors to the world.

Globalization, the development of an increasingly integrated global economy, was brought on in large part by the growth of technology. The Internet allows entrepreneurs to build their businesses on an international stage, confined only by the capabilities of their technology.

---

learning more about other cultures, learning a foreign language, developing technology skills that will allow them to connect with people around the globe, etc.)

Step 4

Connect with Your Community

Ask students to describe what the word *community* means to them in a world that is increasingly without boundaries.

(Answers will vary but some students may note that their definition of friends has been changed by the Internet. They are able to find online "communities" that provide many of the traditional bounded communities. These communities are likely to be more diverse.

Step 4 Connect with Your Community

Interview two adults in your community about inconveniences they experience during the course of a day. Then think about what goods or services an entrepreneur could create or import to lessen or eliminate these inconveniences. Could these goods or services be exported to other countries?

Step 5 Research Entrepreneurship in a Global Economy

Interview a local entrepreneur to find out about entrepreneurship in a global economy. Then prepare your presentation. Use the project research checklist as a guide to help you develop your interview questions and prepare your presentation.

Step 6 Develop Your Presentation

Use presentation software to develop a 5-minute presentation that includes all of the information described in the project checklist.

Entrepreneurship in a Global Economy

✔ Create a chart that illustrates the countries in which the entrepreneur you interviewed conducts business. Use the chart in your presentation.

✔ Explain how technology helped this company become global.

✔ Explain how the economy in the United States and in other countries helps or hinders the company's success.

✔ Explain the rewards and risks this company has experienced in the global marketplace.

✔ Give examples of how this company is socially responsible.

Self Connections

✔ Describe the results of your research with a family member or other adult.

✔ Describe how the entrepreneur you interviewed influenced the business and career that interests you.

✔ Explain what the investigation and its results mean to you.

Step 7 Evaluate Your Presentation

 RUBRIC Go to the *Introduction to Business* Online Learning Center through **glencoe.com** for a rubric you can use to evaluate your final report.

159

TEACH (cont.)

Step 6

Develop a Report
Give students these tips on report writing:

- Know your audience.
- Organize your report by developing an outline and using titles and subtitles.
- Write concisely (briefly but completely).
- Write in easy-to-read, simple language.

ASSESS

Step 7

Evaluate Your Report
Rubric Encourage students to use the rubric to evaluate their final reports.

CLOSE

Culminating Activity
Career Interviews
Have students form pairs and interview each other about the businesses and careers they researched and how their opinions and perceptions of the businesses and careers evolved during the course of the project. (Interviews will vary depending on students' business and career choices and reactions to their research.)

Step 5

Research Global Trends in Entrepreneurship
Students can go to the *Introduction to Business* Online Learning Center through **glencoe.com** for a rubric they can use as a content checklist while they are researching their reports.

Chapter	Section	Unit Objectives
Chapter 10 *Business in a Global Economy*	**10.1**	**Explain** why the world has become a global economy.
		Explain why people and countries specialize in producing goods and services.
	10.2	**Describe** free trade.
		Indicate who benefits and who does not benefit from free trade.
Chapter 11 *The Role of Government in Our Economy*	**11.1**	**Name** four ways in which government regulates business.
	11.2	**Name** five aspects of the government's role in society.
		Name three items that the national government provides and three items that local governments provide.
		Explain how government can stimulate or restrict economic activities.
Chapter 12 *Money and Financial Institutions*	**12.1**	**Describe** the functions and characteristics of money.
		Discuss three main functions of a bank.
	12.2	**Compare and contrast** three types of banks that are found in our economy.
		Explain the major functions of the Federal Reserve System in the U.S. economy.

Understanding the Coding

Brackets Brackets on the reduced student edition page correspond to teaching strategies and activities in the Teacher Wraparound Edition. As you teach the lesson, the brackets show you exactly where to use the teaching strategies and activities.

Letters The letters on the reduced student edition page identify the type of strategy or activity. See the key below to learn about the different types of strategies and activities.

Ability Levels Leveled teaching strategies are identified by one of three codes to give you an idea of their suitability for students of varying learning styles and abilities.

Resources Key program resources are listed in each chapter. Icons indicate the format of resources.

KEY to Letters

D **Develop Concepts** activities help teachers gauge and plan for students' concept development.

R **Reading Strategy** activities help you teach reading skills and vocabulary.

C **Critical Thinking** strategies help students apply and extend what they have learned.

U **Universal Access** activities provide differentiated instruction for English language learners and suggestions for teaching various types of learners.

S **Skill Practice** provides leveled instruction for meeting individual needs and learning styles.

W **Writing Support** activities provide writing opportunities to help students comprehend the text.

NCLB **No Child Left Behind** activities help students practice and improve their abilities in academic subjects.

KEY to Ability Levels

L1 Strategies should be within the ability range of all students. Often full class participation is required.

L2 Strategies are for average to above-average students or for small groups. Some teacher direction is necessary.

L3 Strategies are designed for students able and willing to work independently. Minimal teacher direction is necessary.

KEY to Resource Icons

📂 Print Material

💿 CD-ROM

🖥 Online Learning Center with Podcasts

BusinessWeek *Reader and Case Study*

In Unit 3, your students can learn more about business in the real world through the following *BusinessWeek* Readers and Case Studies:

Going Global for an MBA
More B-school students are studying abroad, creating an international class of grads. (page 170)

How China Controls the Internet
Nicholas Bequelin of Human Rights Watch in Hong Kong explains, and he says U.S. companies need to take a stand against Beijing. (page 181)

Peter Kight's Excellent Adventure
How an ex-jock changed the way the world pays its bills, while he toiled in a basement in Columbus, Ohio. (page 203)

Chapter Features and Activities

BusinessWeek *Reader and Case Study*

Science/Tech TRENDS

? ETHICS in Business

International Business

Reading Strategies

● Before You Read

Graphic Organizer

● As You Read

✔ Reading Check

● After You Read

Unit Overview

Introduce the Unit
Introduce the unit by describing the main concepts of each chapter in the unit.

Unit 3 is about economic activity and how it affects everyday life.

Chapter 10 describes the global marketplace and global competition. It explains how currency exchange works. It names the types of trade barriers and major trade alliances in the world today.

Chapter 11 explains the role of government in our economy. It focuses on how government regulates business, government's role in society, how government is funded, and how governments allocate resources.

Chapter 12 describes the functions and characteristics of money. It explains the bank services and types of banks.

`00:00` OUT OF TIME?

If class time is too short to cover all of the chapters in this unit, have students:

- Write down the vocabulary terms and their definitions.
- Read the chapter summaries at the beginning of each chapter review.
- Go to the *Introduction to Business* Online Learning Center through **glencoe.com** to download free Study-to-Go content to their PDAs or cell phones.

160

Influences on Business

160

Real-World Business and Career Profile | Preview |

Jenzabar Tell students that at the end of this unit, they will learn about the founder of Jenzabar and how she achieved her success. Twice nominated for the Nobel Peace Prize, Ling Chai found herself on the Chinese government's most wanted list after her leadership role in the Tiananmen Square uprising. Now living in the United States, Ling Chai's company, Jenzabar, offers Web-based software and e-learning products and services. Ask students: What qualities make a person a strong business leader? (Answers will vary. Students will probably think the necessary qualities are having drive, good ideas, and charisma.)

Real-World Business and Career Profile

Preview

Jenzabar provides e-learning products, services, and Web-based software to colleges and universities. At the end of this unit, you will learn about Jenzabar® founder Ling Chai and how she achieved her success.

Decision Making What decisions do you think will be most important for you to make as you enter the business world?

| Unit 3 | Thematic Project Preview |

Community Outreach and Service Learning
After completing this unit, you will research how businesses come together for the good of the community, and how students and volunteers can help.

Project Checklist As you read the chapters in this unit, use this checklist to prepare for the unit project.

- ✔ Think about how a business can help a community.
- ✔ Look for ways you and your friends might volunteer to help with a community project that a local business is sponsoring.
- ✔ Reflect on how a business benefits by helping the community.
- ✔ Consider how you benefit by volunteering to help a business with a community project.

161

Standards-Based Lesson Planning
Introduction to Business provides students with instruction and assessment in the following fundamental content areas:

Content Standards Correlations	
Understand the impact of global and domestic businesses, financial concepts, and integrated business models.	pp. 165–168, 170–173, 174–177
Relate the impact of international business on the United States economy.	pp. 165–166, 170–173, 175
Compare domestic and world trade.	pp. 165–166, 175
Explain the impact of imports and exports on the United States economy.	pp. 165–166, 175–176
Explain trade and exchange rates.	pp. 165–168, 175–176
Evaluate the economic basis of domestic and global trade.	pp. 165–168, 170–173, 175–176
Relate the impact of world trade on the standard of living.	pp. 167, 175
Analyzes the significance of interdependence in world trade.	pp. 165–168, 170–173, 175
Assess ways government trade policies impact personal, business, and world economics climates.	pp. 170–173, 175

NCLB
Activities, information, and skills practice will help your students attain No Child Left Behind proficiency. Students will improve their abilities in the following academic standards areas:

Academic Standards Correlations		
English Language Arts	Activities/Features	Page
NCTE 3 Apply strategies to interpret texts	Applying Academics to Business	p. 176
NCTE 7 Conduct research and gather, evaluate, and synthesize data to communicate discoveries	After You Read	p. 173
NCTE 9 Develop an understanding of diversity in language use across cultures	After You Read	p. 173
Mathematics		
Algebra Use mathematical models to represent and understand quantitative relationships	Ask S&P	p. 162
Data Analysis and Probability Formulate questions that can be addressed with data and collect, organize, and display relevant data to answer them	Applying Academics to Business	p. 176
Measurement Apply appropriate techniques, tools, and formulas to determine measurements	Standardized Test Practice	p. 177
Problem Solving Monitor and reflect on the process of problem solving	After You Read	p. 168
Science		
Content Standard F Students should develop an understanding of environmental quality and science and technology in local, national, and global challenges	Science/Tech Trends	p. 171

Correlations   This chart shows the 21st Century Skills, foundation skills, and workplace competencies that students develop as they work in this chapter.

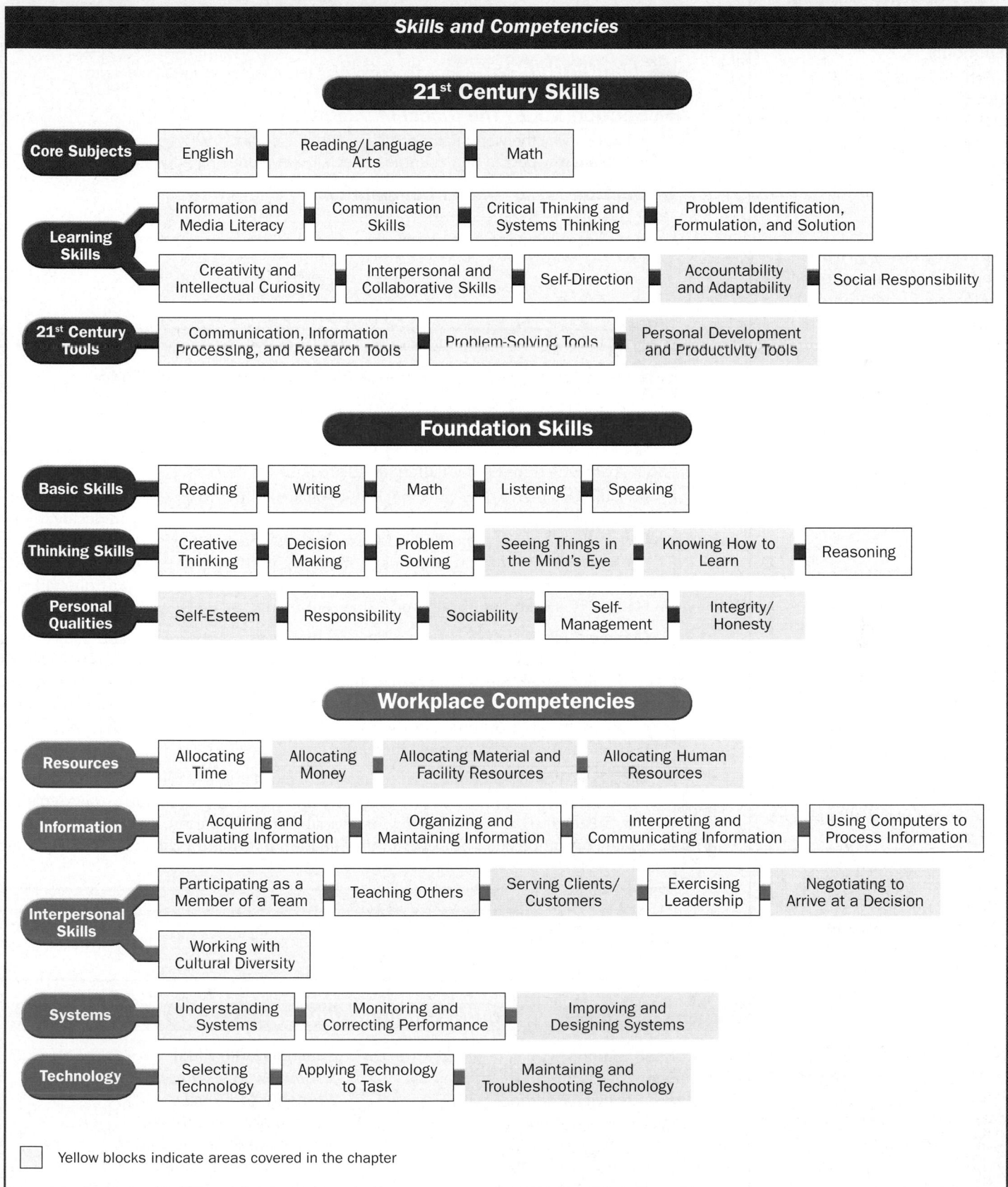

Skills and Competencies

21st Century Skills

Core Subjects
- English
- Reading/Language Arts
- Math

Learning Skills
- Information and Media Literacy
- Communication Skills
- Critical Thinking and Systems Thinking
- Problem Identification, Formulation, and Solution
- Creativity and Intellectual Curiosity
- Interpersonal and Collaborative Skills
- Self-Direction
- Accountability and Adaptability
- Social Responsibility

21st Century Tools
- Communication, Information Processing, and Research Tools
- Problem-Solving Tools
- Personal Development and Productivity Tools

Foundation Skills

Basic Skills
- Reading
- Writing
- Math
- Listening
- Speaking

Thinking Skills
- Creative Thinking
- Decision Making
- Problem Solving
- Seeing Things in the Mind's Eye
- Knowing How to Learn
- Reasoning

Personal Qualities
- Self-Esteem
- Responsibility
- Sociability
- Self-Management
- Integrity/Honesty

Workplace Competencies

Resources
- Allocating Time
- Allocating Money
- Allocating Material and Facility Resources
- Allocating Human Resources

Information
- Acquiring and Evaluating Information
- Organizing and Maintaining Information
- Interpreting and Communicating Information
- Using Computers to Process Information

Interpersonal Skills
- Participating as a Member of a Team
- Teaching Others
- Serving Clients/Customers
- Exercising Leadership
- Negotiating to Arrive at a Decision
- Working with Cultural Diversity

Systems
- Understanding Systems
- Monitoring and Correcting Performance
- Improving and Designing Systems

Technology
- Selecting Technology
- Applying Technology to Task
- Maintaining and Troubleshooting Technology

Yellow blocks indicate areas covered in the chapter

Chapter Overview

Introduce the Chapter

Business in a Global Economy

Chapter 10 is about the global marketplace and global competition, how currency exchange works, and the types of trade barriers and major trade alliances in the world today.

Building Background

Archaeologists have found evidence of trade routes in Asia and Africa that date back more than four thousand years.

Ask STANDARD &POOR'S

>> *Math Answer*

For a conservative portfolio you need to reallocate $1,150 to stocks and bonds.

$4,600 − ($23,000 × 15%) = x

$4,600 − $3,450 = x

$1,150 = x

>> *Extension Activity*

Ask students to write two additional equations to find out how much of the $4,600 to reallocate to pursue a moderate portfolio.

For the moderate portfolio you need to reallocate $2,300 to stocks and bonds.

$4,600 − ($23,000 × 10%) = x

$4,600 − $2,300 = x

$2,300 = x

N C L B Activity correlates to Math standards.

162

Business in a Global Economy

► Chapter Objectives   After completing this chapter, you will be able to:

► **Section 10.1** *The Global Marketplace*
- **Explain** why the world has become a global economy.
- **Explain** why people and countries specialize in producing goods and services.

► **Section 10.2** *Global Competition*
- **Describe** free trade.
- **Indicate** who benefits and who does not benefit from free trade.

Ask STANDARD &POOR'S   Evaluating Investment Alternatives

Q: I know that diversifying my portfolio is a key to building wealth, but how do I evaluate which investment alternatives are right for me?

A: Start by determining how much risk you are willing to accept. Take a risk tolerance test available online or from an investment advisor. Then you can decide if you need an aggressive portfolio (for example, 75 percent stocks, 20 percent bonds, and 5 percent money market funds), a moderate portfolio (60 percent stocks, 30 percent bonds, and 10 percent money markets), or a conservative portfolio (40 percent stocks, 45 percent bonds, and 15 percent money markets).

Mathematics You have chosen a conservative investment strategy, and your portfolio has grown to $23,000. According to your recent account statement, you have $4,600 in money market funds. You realize that you need to reallocate some of these funds to stocks and bonds in order to maintain a conservative approach. Write an equation you can solve to find how much of the $4,600 you need to reallocate so that only 15% of your money will be in money markets.

THEORY **Writing Equations** An equation is a mathematical sentence that states that two expressions are equal. The two expressions in an equation are always separated by an equal sign. When solving for a variable in an equation, you must perform the same operations on both sides of the equation in order for the mathematical sentence to remain true.

N C L B

Classroom Resources

- 📝 Student Edition
- 📝 Teacher Wraparound Edition
- 📂 Student Activity Workbook with Academic Integration
- 📂 Student Activity Workbook with Academic Integration TAE
- 📂 *Fast File*, Unit 3 Resources
- 📂 Inclusion in the Business Education Classroom

- 💿 TeacherWorks Plus!
- 💿 *ExamView Assessment Suite*
- 💿 Presentation Plus!
- 💿 Vocabulary PuzzleMaker
- 💿 Interactive Student Edition
- 💿 Online Student Edition
- 💿 Online Learning Center with Podcasts

● **International Markets** Trade between nations is an important part of today's world. **Why do you think international trade has grown in recent years?**

Review the Objectives
Introduce the chapter by reviewing the chapter objectives:

Section 10.1 *Objectives*
Explain why the world has become a global economy. (There is an increased amount of trading between nations.)

Explain why people and countries specialize in producing goods and services. (People and countries specialize in order to have a better standard of living. It is generally better to produce what one is good at producing and trade with others to get what they are good at producing.)

Section 10.2 *Objectives*
Describe free trade. (Free trade means that there are no protective restrictions, such as tariffs, quotas, and embargoes, against foreign-produced items being offered in a country.)

Indicate who benefits and who does not benefit from free trade. (With free trade, consumers benefit because there is more competition, lower prices, better-quality goods, and a better standard of living. Free trade also encourages cultural understanding and cooperation between countries. Those who suffer because of free trade are industries that cannot compete without restrictions. Those businesses often lay off workers and eventually shut down.)

Discuss the Photo
● **International Markets** Read the caption on the photo to students: Trade between nations is an important part of today's world.

Ask students: Why do you think international trade has grown in recent years? (Trade between different parts of the globe has always been important, but foreign goods were once costly because they were so difficult to transport. As shipping has become easier and cheaper, and as communications across the globe have become almost instantaneous, goods have become cheaper and easier to obtain.)

FOCUS

Bell Ringer Activity

The Global Marketplace
Collect 10 or 12 common products that were produced in other countries. Make sure the country of origin appears on the product or the packaging. Divide students into two teams. Hold up the first item and ask Team A to guess the country of origin. After they guess, have Team B read the country of origin. Continue switching between teams to discuss all of the products.

Preteaching

Presentation Plus! ⊙
The Presentation Plus! CD provides visual teaching aids for this section.

PuzzleMaker ⊙
Use the Vocabulary PuzzleMaker to create a puzzle of the section's key terms. Students can complete the puzzle on paper or on a computer.

Graphic Organizer
Tell students to go to the Online Learning Center through **glencoe.com** for a printable graphic organizer. (Imports: toys, games, sporting goods, electronics, fuels, clothing, bananas, automobiles, etc. Exports: airplanes, agricultural products, wheat, etc.)

N C L B
Connects academics to content.

164

The Global Marketplace

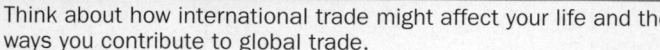

Reading Guide

● Before You Read
Think about how international trade might affect your life and the ways you contribute to global trade.

Read to Learn
- Explain why the world has become a global economy.
- Explain why people and countries specialize in producing goods and services.

D

The Main Idea
International trade has increased because more countries specialize and offer their goods and services to other countries. Also, the value of one nation's currency in relation to other currencies affects what it buys and sells to other nations.

Key Concepts
- The Global Economy
- International Trade

Vocabulary
Key Terms

global economy	imports
international trade	exports
multinational corporation	balance of trade
trade	comparative advantage
	exchange rate

@ Go to the *Introduction to Business* Online Learning Center through **glencoe.com** for a printable graphic organizer.

Academic Vocabulary
You will find these words in your reading and on your tests. Make sure you know their meanings.

specific	sustains
professionals	vehicles

Graphic Organizer
In a graphic like the one below, list items mentioned in the section that are either imported into the United States or exported from the United States.

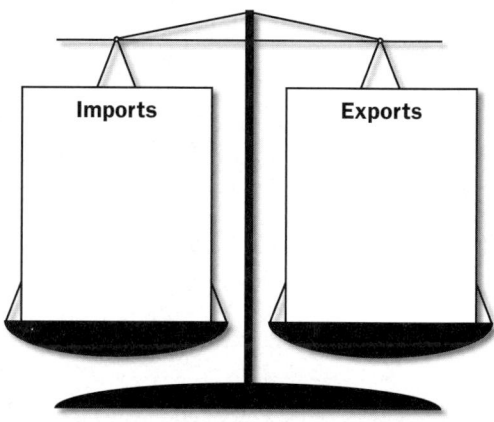

Imports | Exports

Academic Standards
English Language Arts
> **NCTE 1** Read texts to acquire new information
> **NCTE 9** Develop an understanding of diversity in language use across cultures

Mathematics
> **Problem Solving** Monitor and reflect on the process of problem solving

N C L B

Reading Guide

● Before You Read
Students might mention that they use products from other countries or know someone who works for a company that does business in other countries.

D Develop Concepts
The Main Idea Ask students: How does specialization work in the local economy? (Students should recognize that the bakery specializes in baking and selling baked goods and the auto mechanic specializes in vehicle maintenance.)

164

The Global Economy

The **global economy** is the interconnected economies of the nations of the world. We live in a global economy fueled by international trade. **International trade** involves the exchange of goods and services between nations. The development of the global economy is often referred to as globalization.

A **multinational corporation** is a company that does business in many countries and has facilities and offices around the world. Sony is a multinational corporation.

International Trade

R **Trade** has several meanings. It can be a **specific** area of business or industry, such as the book trade. It can refer to a skilled occupation, such as auto mechanics. It can also refer to the people who work in a specific area of business or industry, such as construction workers. This chapter looks at trade as the activity of buying and selling goods and services in domestic or international markets. Trading goods and services allows countries to meet their individual wants and needs as well as to help their own economy.

✔ Reading Check **Explain** What are some meanings of the word *trade*?

Types of Trade

Domestic trade is the production, purchase, and sale of goods and services within a country. *World trade* is the exchange of goods and services across international boundaries. In many cases, a country cannot produce a desired good because it does not have a suitable climate or the necessary raw materials. In other cases, businesses in one country may produce better products or services at cheaper prices than businesses in other countries. As a result, world trade takes place.

Since the 1970s, world trade has increased considerably. Better transportation and telecommunications, along with a decrease in trade barriers, enables more world trade. These changes also help many countries' economies to grow.

Imports and Exports The United States buys pepper from India, bananas from Honduras, coffee from Colombia, and automobiles from Japan. These products are called imports. **Imports** are goods and services that one country buys from another country. The United States also sells wheat and airplanes to

Section 10.1 The Global Marketplace **165**

Real World

Multinationals The top multinational companies include Sony, Coca-Cola, Toyota, and Nike. *What characteristics do multinational companies share?*

International Business

Devaluing Currency
In a global economy, countries need to closely monitor the exchange rates of their currencies. For example, when the value of the U.S. dollar goes up compared to the European euro, it is said to have a favorable exchange rate. With a favorable rate, Americans can buy more European products with their currency. However, it also means that American products become more expensive for Europeans to buy.

Examples of Languages Across Cultures

Q: In Dutch, how do you say: "What time is it?"

A: **Hoe laat is het?**
(pronounced: Who lăwt ĭss hĕt?)

Why might countries with a favorable exchange rate choose to devalue their currency?

TEACH

Discussion Starter
The Global Economy
Point out that as large and diverse as the United States is, there are some things that Americans want that cannot be produced here or cannot be produced in sufficient quantity to meet consumer demand. Even though Americans drink lots of coffee, almost all the coffee beans must be imported from countries with much warmer climates. Guatemalan Antigua is not just a fun name for a one of the coffees at Starbucks; it identifies the origin of the beans—Antigua in south central Guatemala.

R Reading Strategy
Recognize the Main Idea
Have students read the paragraph about international trade and ask them to identify the main idea. (Trading goods and services allows countries to meet their individual wants and needs as well as to help their own economy.)

✔ Reading Check

Explain The word *trade* has several meanings: a specific area of industry or business; a skilled occupation; people who work in a specific area of business; or the activity of buying and selling goods or services in domestic or international markets.

Real World

Multinationals Answers will vary. Students should recognize that the products these companies produce cross-cultures and social boundaries. These companies' goods appeal to consumers wherever they are sold.

International Business

Devaluing Currency Countries with a favorable exchange rate might choose to devalue their currency as a way to boost sales of their goods in the international marketplace.

 **Skill Practice**

Guided Practice
Extrapolate Ask students to identify a product and write a pair of sentences that describes which country imports the product and which country exports the product. (Answers will vary depending on the product selected.) **L1**

Create a Pie Chart Ask students to create a pie chart to illustrate the following data about U.S. export partners. Main Export Partners: Canada, 23%; Mexico, 13.6%; Japan, 6.7%; United Kingdom, 4.4%; China, 4.3%, Other, 48%. (The charts should reflect the given percentages.) **L2**

Research and Chart Have students use *The World Factbook* to find the most recent data about the United States' main import and export partners and to create two pie charts to illustrate the data. (There should be one chart each for import and export partners.) **L3**

ASSESS

Review Key Terms
Have students write sentences using each key term.

Study-to-Go Have students go to the Online Learning Center through **glencoe.com** to download free **Study-to-Go** content to their PDAs or cell phones.

---

countries such as Australia and Russia. These products are called exports. **Exports** are goods and services that one country sells to another country.

Countries can also invest in other nations by opening businesses there. They import and export the services of **professionals**, such as doctors and engineers. One country's exports are another country's imports. **Figure 10.1** shows the major imports and exports of the United States.

✔ **Reading Check** **Contrast** What is the difference between an import and an export?

Balance of Trade
When a country exports more than it imports, it has a trade surplus. When a country imports more than it exports, it has a trade deficit. A **balance of trade** is the difference in value between a country's imports and exports over a period of time.

A country can have a trade deficit with one country and a trade surplus with another. For instance, the United States has a favorable balance with Australia. That means it takes in more money from sales to Australia than Australia takes in from sales to the United States. The United States has an unfavorable balance with France, which means the United States takes in less money from sales to France than Frances takes in from sales to the United States.

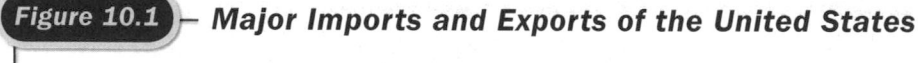
Figure 10.1 — *Major Imports and Exports of the United States*

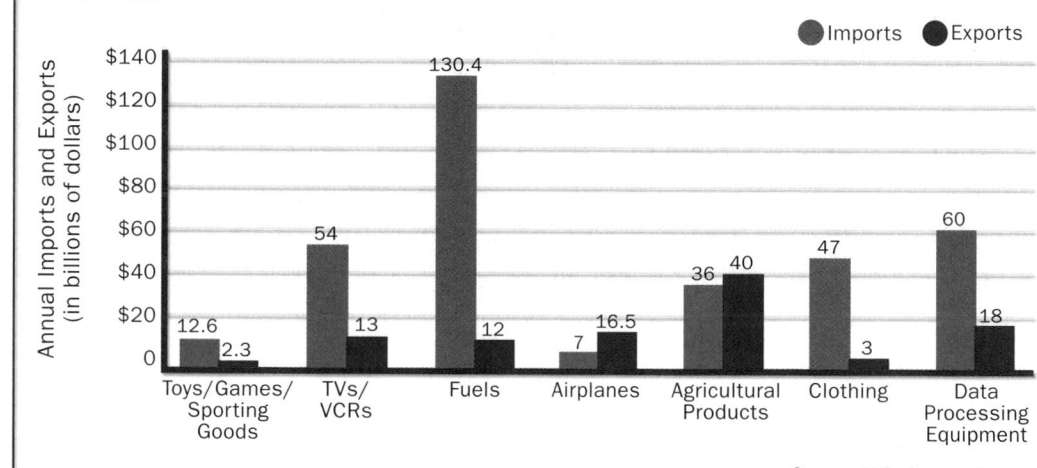

Source: U.S. Census Bureau

● **Major Imports and Exports of the United States** Look at the graph to see a comparison of products the United States imports and exports. **Name the products that the United States exports more than it imports.**

✔ **Reading Check**

Contrast Imports are goods and services that one company *buys* from another country. Exports are goods and services that one country *sells* to another country.

Figure 10.1

● **Major Imports and Exports of the United States** The United States exports more agricultural products and airplanes than it imports.

● **Currency exchange**
Financial institutions fulfill many different functions. **What does an exchange rate specify?**

Specialization

To *specialize* means to focus on a particular activity, area, or product. Specialization builds and **sustains** a market economy. Countries specialize in producing certain goods and services. Many take advantage of their specialties by trading them with other countries in the global marketplace. Similarly, individuals specialize by concentrating their activities in a particular area or field, such as carpentry, medicine, or office administration. Each worker's income buys goods and services that others have specialized in producing.

Using Resources to Specialize

Countries also specialize and trade some of the items that they produce in order to obtain other countries' goods and services. For example, the United States, Japan, and Germany are the world's top automobile producers. They have the technology, factories, and labor forces needed to produce lots of **vehicles**. Therefore, these countries have a comparative advantage in producing vehicles. A **comparative advantage** is the ability of a country or company to produce a particular good more efficiently than another country or company. Money gained from auto sales to other countries is then used to buy items that other countries produce. This helps to improve the standard of living for each country.

Currency

Countries have to pay for products and services with currency. Currency is another name for money. Just as different countries use different languages, they also use different currencies. Mexico uses pesos, Japan uses yen, and India uses rupees. Some countries use the same name for their currency. The United States, Canada, and Australia all call their currency dollars.

● **As You Read**
Think about how a comparative advantage might help a country to compete in a global marketplace.

● **As You Read**
A comparative advantage is the ability of a country or company to produce a particular good or service more efficiently than another country or company. It helps a country compete in the global marketplace, especially if it has a rare resource or skill.

Discuss the Photo
● **Currency Exchange** An exchange rate specifies the relative values of two currencies. If you are trading dollars to euros, the exchange rate will tell you how many euros a dollar will buy. There will be a separate rate to signify how many dollars you could buy with a single euro.

RETEACH

W Writing Support
Make a Poster
Specialization Have students make a poster that illustrates at least three levels of specialization for a particular occupational area. For example, a pediatrician is a physician who specializes in the health of children and teens. (Posters will vary but should illustrate the idea of specialization.)

R Reading Strategy
Figures of Speech
Comparative Advantage
Ask students to research the phrase "comparative advantage" by looking at the individual words separately and comparing the definitions to the way the phrase is defined in the text. (The word "comparative" is used to consider a relationship to something known, mentioned, or expected. An "advantage" is a superior or favorable position in relation to somebody or something. Thus, the text's definition makes sense.)

U Universal Access
Tactile Learners Bring some foreign currency to class and allow students to look at and touch it. If possible, demonstrate currency exchange using the current exchange rate.

Student Activity Workbook ☞ Assign the Section 10.1 Activities.

Section 10.1

RETEACH (cont.)

C Critical Thinking

Create a Table
Exchange Rates Have students use an online currency exchange calculator to create a table showing the value of one American dollar in six other currencies and the value of one unit of each of the other currencies in American dollars. (Tables will vary depending on currencies selected and current exchange rates.)

World Currencies It can cause confusion during the exchange of money.

ASSESS

After You Read
Have students complete the Section 10.1 After You Read section review.

Online Study Tools
Have students go to the Online Learning Center through **glencoe.com** to:

- Take the Section 10.1 **Practice Test**.
- Download free **Study-to-Go** content to their PDAs or cell phones.

CLOSE

Culminating Activity
Create a Brochure
Have students prepare a brochure about how a country they choose uses resources to specialize. (Brochures will vary but should illustrate specialization of resources.)

World Currencies
Several countries have the same currencies or use the same name for their currencies. *How might this cause confusion in the international marketplace?*

NCLB Activity correlates to Math standards.

To trade with another country, businesses and countries must convert their money into that nation's currency. To do that, their currency is exchanged on the *foreign exchange market*. The foreign exchange market is mostly made up of banks where different currencies are exchanged.

Exchange Rates Each country's currency has a value that is different from those of other countries. The price at which one currency can buy another currency is called the **exchange rate**. For example, one American dollar is worth a certain number of Mexican pesos or Japanese yen. Exchange rates change from day to day and from country to country. The amount a country's currency is worth depends on the number of other countries that want to buy its products.

Prices Companies follow the change in exchange rates to find the best prices for products. When the value of a country's currency goes up compared to another country's, it appreciates, or goes up in value. A country with an appreciated exchange rate can buy more of the other country's products. When it goes down, the currency depreciates, or goes down in value. For example, if the U.S. dollar goes up compared to the euro, it will take fewer dollars to buy French cheese or Italian furniture. It also means U.S. goods will cost more because it will take more euros to buy them.

Section 10.1

After You Read

Review Key Concepts
1. What is the global economy?
2. What is the difference between domestic trade and international trade?
3. Why would a country want its currency to appreciate?

Academic Skills
4. **Mathematics** Next week you will take an exciting biking trip in Thailand. You have saved $850 for the trip. When your plane lands in Bangkok, you will convert your U.S. dollars to Thai baht. The service charge for exchanging currency is a flat rate of 185 baht. Using the exchange rate below, how many baht will the clerk give you?

    1 U.S. dollar = 39.22 Thai baht

THEORY **Problem Solving** Solving some word problems requires more than one step. Read carefully so you can represent the problem in mathematical terms.

 For math help, go to the Math Appendix.

@ Go to the *Introduction to Business* Online Learning Center through **glencoe.com** to check your answers.

Section 10.1

Review Key Concepts
1. The global economy is the interconnected economies of the nations of the world.
2. Domestic trade is between parties within a country. International trade is between parties in different countries.
3. A country might want its currency to appreciate so that citizens can buy more goods and services in other countries.

Academic Skills
4. **Mathematics** (850 × 39.22) − 185 = 33,152 Thai baht

Global Competition

Reading Guide

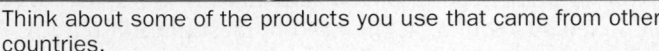

● Before You Read

Think about some of the products you use that came from other countries.

Read to Learn
- Describe free trade.
- Indicate who benefits and who does not benefit from free trade.

The Main Idea

Protectionism is the practice of putting limits on foreign trade to protect businesses at home. However, protectionism decreases competition and generally increases the prices that consumers pay for goods and services. More nations are moving toward free trade.

Key Concept
- Protectionism and Free Trade

Vocabulary

Key Terms
protectionism
tariff
quota
embargo
free trade

Go to the *Introduction to Business* Online Learning Center through **glencoe.com** for a printable graphic organizer.

Academic Vocabulary

You will find these words in your reading and on your tests. Make sure you know their meanings.

disputes   cooperate
restrict   controversy

Graphic Organizer

In boxes like the ones below, write notes about trade barriers. In the left box, write notes about tariffs. In the middle box, write notes about quotas. In the right box, write notes about embargoes.

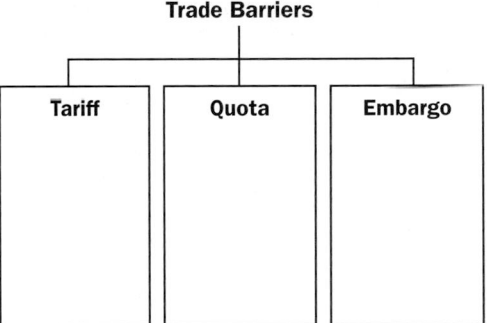

Trade Barriers

Tariff	Quota	Embargo

Academic Standards

English Language Arts
- **NCTE 1** Read texts to acquire new information
- **NCTE 4** Use written language to communicate effectively
- **NCTE 7** Conduct research and gather, evaluate, and synthesize data to communicate discoveries
- **NCTE 9** Develop an understanding of diversity in language use across cultures

---

FOCUS

🔔 Bell Ringer Activity

Global Competition
Global competition is inevitable in a global marketplace. How has global competition had a negative affect on the U.S. textile industry? (Low labor costs in other countries make foreign textiles less expensive than fabric produced in the United States.)

Preteaching

Presentation Plus! 💿
The Presentation Plus! CD provides visual teaching aids for this section.

PuzzleMaker 💿
Use the Vocabulary PuzzleMaker to create a puzzle of the section's key terms. Students can complete the puzzle on paper or on a computer.

Graphic Organizer
Tell students to go to the Online Learning Center through **glencoe.com** for a printable graphic organizer. (Answers include: Tariff: tax on imports to increase price in domestic market. Quota: limit on quantities that can be imported. Embargo: ban on import or export of a product.)

N C L B Connects academics to content.

Reading Guide

● Before You Read

The United States imports clothing from around the world. Ask students to look at the labels on their clothing to see where the garments were manufactured.

D Develop Concepts

The Main Idea Discuss the main idea with students: Ask: Why do you think countries are moving toward free trade? (Free trade generally increases competition and lowers prices. It generally stimulates the economy in both the buying and selling country.)

Discussion Starter
Protectionism and Free Trade
Write the words *protectionism* and *free trade* on the board. Explain that protectionism and free trade are two opposing points of view. Point out that most countries are involved in a variety of trade practices. Some of these practices support free trade while others support protectionism. Draw an arrow from protectionism to free trade and tell students that most countries currently are moving away from protectionism and toward free trade.

R Reading Strategy

Summarize Ask students to summarize the paragraphs about protectionism and free trade. (Paraphrases will vary but should note that there are both benefits to free trade and disputes that arise as a result.)

✔ Reading Check

Analyze The issue at the heart of most trade disputes is whether there should be limits on trade or if trade should be unrestricted.

Protectionism and Free Trade

In the global marketplace, countries benefit from buying one another's products. Countries compete by making the same products. The United States, Japan, and Germany all specialize in making cars and are major competitors in that market. China, the Ukraine, and the United States are major producers of steel.

Global competition often leads to trade **disputes**, which occur when nations put barriers on trading particular items with another country. For example, suppose the United States decides that no Chinese-made steel can be imported into the country. The Chinese may respond by not allowing any more U.S. cars to be imported into China. At the heart of most trade disputes is whether there should be limits on trade or whether trade should be unrestricted. Protectionism and free trade are two opposing points of view involved in trade disputes.

✔ Reading Check **Analyze** What is at the heart of most trade disputes?

BusinessWeek *Reader and Case Study*

Going Global for an MBA

More business school students are studying abroad, creating an international class of grads.

Soon the new MBA students at RSM Erasmus University in Rotterdam would be hunched over textbooks for their finance and marketing courses, but first it was time to pound on a goatskin stretched across a hollow piece of wood. That's part of the orientation for RSM's 96 incoming international MBA students, most from outside the Netherlands, to help them get used to crossing cultural barriers and working together as teams. Their goal: learn the art of Sewa-style African drumming—in a day. Under the tutelage of instructors from Sewa Beats, a Swiss company that specializes in corporate drumming sessions, the students became passable tribal drummers by nightfall, performing complicated Mandinka rhythms in groups and, in the judgment of one observer, rocking the house.

Across Europe these days, B-schools are using team-building exercises like this to deal with student bodies that have undergone radical changes. Once populated almost entirely by locals, many B-schools now draw from dozens of countries, and no one nationality dominates. Properly mastered, this diversity gives students an edge in the job market.

 CASE STUDY Go to the *Introduction to Business* Online Learning Center through **glencoe.com** for the *BusinessWeek* Reader Case Study.

Active Learning

MBA students at RSM play drums as a way of learning to work in harmony with people from different cultures. Another way to share cultures is to share traditional foods. Research recipes from around the world and create a cookbook using desktop publishing software.

BusinessWeek *Reader and Case Study*

Going Global for an MBA

 CASE STUDY Have students go to the *Introduction to Business* Online Learning Center through **glencoe.com** to download a Case Study activity that corresponds to the article. The activity and answer key are also available on the TeacherWorks Plus CD.

Active Learning

Answers will vary, but encourage students to incorporate recipes from the cultures of other members of the class.

Protectionism

Protectionism is the practice of the government putting limits on foreign trade to protect businesses at home. Many companies want to sell what they produce at home. They often want to keep out foreign competitors. For example, rice farming and auto production are two major contributors to the Japanese economy. To limit competition from other countries, Japan practices protectionism in these segments. Some countries also do not want to share what they produce with other countries. Reasons to **restrict** trade include the following:

- Foreign competition can lower the demand for products made at home.
- Companies at home need to be protected from unfair foreign competition.
- Industries that make products related to national defense (such as satellites, aircraft, and weapons) need to be protected.
- The use of cheap labor in other countries can lower wages or threaten jobs at home.
- A country can become too dependent on another country for important products such as oil, steel, or grain.
- Other countries might not have the same environmental or human rights standards.

Science/Tech**TRENDS**

Motoring Technology

Automobiles have been an important part of our lives for more than 100 years. Today's cars are actually designed to have human characteristics. For example, an Australian invention helps drivers read road signs. Cameras mounted in various parts of the car send pictures of what is ahead to a computer. Software is then used to detect road signs by recognizing their shapes: rectangles, diamonds, octagons, or circles. Once a sign is detected, the image is compared to a list of signs stored in the computer's memory. If it recognizes a stop sign, the computer checks to determine if the car is slowing down.

WebQuest

Go to the *Introduction to Business* Online Learning Center through **glencoe.com** for links to Web sites where you can find examples of other futuristic technology applications you may soon find on your car. Search to learn more about alternative fuel sources for cars and how they might help us reduce the dependency on oil. Write a paragraph or two describing the car of the future.

Science/Tech**TRENDS**

WebQuest

Motoring Technology Answers will vary, but students might include information about alternatives to fossil-fuel-based gasoline, such as plant oils, hydrogen fuel cells, or hybrid engines.

TEACH (cont.)

S Skill Practice
Guided Practice
Make a List Ask students to make list of six reasons for protectionism and a trigger word or phrase for each. (lowers demand, companies need to be protected, necessary for national defense, lowers wages, country becomes dependent, lower human rights standards) **L1**

Make a Table Ask students to make a three-column table to illustrate the six reasons for protectionism, with a trigger word or phrase for each in the first column, the complete corresponding sentences in the second column and an example of the problem in the third column. (Tables will vary but should include six rows and three columns.) **L2**

Research and Write Ask students to write a two-page essay about the history and consequences of real-world protectionism. (Essays should include the history, along with an analysis of the consequences to both sides.) **L3**

ASSESS

Review Key Terms
Have students write sentences using each key term.

 Study-to-Go
Have students go to the Online Learning Center through **glencoe.com** to download free **Study-to-Go** content to their PDAs or cell phones.

 Activity correlates to Science standards.

171

RETEACH

W Writing Support

Write a Thesis

Trade Embargos Have students write a thesis statement and give supporting details about the validity of the embargo that prohibits trading with Cuba. (Statements will vary. Students might include information about the original purpose of the embargo and the effect it has had since its inception in 1963.)

R Reading Strategy

Make a Table Ask students to make a two-column table to illustrate the benefits of free trade. Have students identify a trigger word or phrase for each of the six benefits and write them in the first column. Instruct students to write the complete corresponding sentences in the second column. Point out that knowing the trigger word can help you remember the more complete idea. (Tables will vary. For example, a student might choose these six trigger words: new markets, jobs, competition, choice, cooperation, and standard of living.)

U Universal Access

Peer Teaching Organize students into groups of three. Have students work together to make sure they all understand and can explain the benefits of trade alliances.

Student Activity Workbook 📂 Assign the Section 10.2 Activities.

Real World

Trade Sanctions
A government can impose a trade sanction, or penalty, on other countries, usually by adding tariffs. *Do you think there are good reasons to do this?*

Trade Barriers To limit competition from other countries, governments develop *trade barriers*. For example, the United States and Brazil both produce sugar, but Brazil can sell it for less than the United States can. The U.S. government can protect U.S. sugar producers in three different ways: with a tariff, a quota, or an embargo.

A **tariff** is a tax placed on imports to increase their price in the domestic market. By placing a tax on sugar from Brazil, the United States can make it more expensive than American sugar. A **quota** is a limit placed on the quantities of a product that can be imported. If the United States allows only a small amount of Brazilian sugar into the country, most Americans have to buy American sugar. An **embargo** is a ban on the import or export of a product. Embargoes are rare and usually are used against another country for political or military reasons.

Free Trade

Economic or foreign policy often determines which countries trade with each other. **Free trade** occurs when there are few or no limits on trade between countries. Supporters of free trade think all countries should be free to compete anywhere in the world without restrictions. Free trade offers several benefits:

- It opens up new markets in other countries. There are more than 298 million people in the United States, but more than 6 billion worldwide.
- It creates new jobs, especially in areas related to global trade, such as shipping, banking, and communications.
- Competition forces businesses to be more efficient and productive.
- Consumers have more choices in the variety, prices, and quality of products.
- It promotes cultural understanding and encourages countries to **cooperate** with each other.
- It helps countries raise their standard of living.

As You Read

Think about the controversy over NAFTA before the free trade agreement was formed.

Trade Alliances As the world economy becomes more global, many countries are moving toward a free trade system. To reduce limits on trade, nations form *trade alliances*. In a trade alliance, several countries merge their economies into one huge market. For example, NAFTA (North American Free Trade Agreement) combined the economies of the United States, Canada, and Mexico. As a result, it is easier for the United States to buy oil from Mexico and to sell its cars there.

Free trade is good in general, but it is not without problems. Some people opposed NAFTA because they feared some workers would be displaced when trade barriers were lowered. Opponents predicted that some high-paid U.S. jobs would be lost to Mexico.

Real World

Trade Sanctions Some students may feel it is unfair for more prosperous countries to claim this advantage to promote their products. Others may feel there are times when tariffs or sanctions can be a political advantage, to retaliate, or to encourage a country's industry.

As You Read

The countries involved have seen a rise in economic growth and an increase in the availability of lower-cost goods. Some workers were displaced when trade barriers were lowered. Some high-paid American jobs were lost.

That did happen in areas where Americans and Mexicans were competing. Those in favor of NAFTA predicted that trade among all three nations would increase dramatically, stimulating growth and bringing a wider variety of lower-cost goods to consumers. Indeed, that has occurred since the passage of NAFTA.

Despite the early **controversy** over NAFTA, the alliance has resulted in various business projects between the three countries. Some of the major trade alliances in the world today are:

- **North American Free Trade Agreement (NAFTA):** United States, Canada, and Mexico
- **European Union (EU):** Austria, Belgium, Cyprus, Czech Republic, Denmark, Estonia, Finland, France, Germany, Greece, Hungary, Ireland, Italy, Latvia, Lithuania, Luxembourg, Malta, the Netherlands, Poland, Portugal, Slovakia, Slovenia, Spain, Sweden, and the United Kingdom
- **Association of Southeast Asian Nations (ASEAN):** Brunei, Cambodia, Indonesia, Laos, Malaysia, Myanmar, Philippines, Singapore, Thailand, and Vietnam

DR-CAFTA
The Dominican Republic-Central America Free Trade Agreement (DR-CAFTA) encompasses Costa Rica, El Salvador, Guatemala, Honduras, Nicaragua, the Dominican Republic, and the United States. The goal of the agreement is the creation of a free trade zone, similar to NAFTA. *What advantages and disadvantages do you think DR-CAFTA has?*

 Activity correlates to English Language Arts standards.

Section 10.2

After You Read

Review Key Concepts
1. Give three reasons for protectionism.
2. Give three reasons for free trade.
3. What are some of the major trade alliances in the world today?

Academic Skills

4. **English Language Arts** In order to better understand the challenges and opportunities of selling products in global markets, interview three local business owners who export goods overseas. Write a series of questions that will help you understand these businesses and how the products or services were chosen, whether they have changed in response to consumer demands or currency values, and how the business owner keeps in touch with international customers. Present your findings to the class.

5. **English Language Arts** Today's global marketplace means that business people need to have a working knowledge in more than one language. Identify two languages other than English that would be of special benefit to a global businessperson. Write two or more paragraphs that identify the languages, and explain why you chose them. Join in a discussion with your class to compare your answers.

@ Go to the *Introduction to Business* Online Learning Center through **glencoe.com** to check your answers.

Section 10.2

Review Key Concepts
1. protects businesses from unfair competition and countries that violate U.S. human rights or environmental standards
2. encourages competition, gives consumers more choices for products, promotes cultural understanding
3. NAFTA, the EU, and ASEAN

Academic Skills
4. **English Language Arts** Students should ask questions that get at the differences between marketing and selling products locally versus internationally.
5. **English Language Arts** Answers will vary, but should address the benefits.

RETEACH (cont.)

C Critical Thinking

Analyze
NAFTA Ask students: Do you think NAFTA has had a positive effect on Americans? Why or why not? (Different people and different parts of the country have been affected differently.)

DR-CAFTA It opens new markets, helps nations modernize, creates worker protections, and improves environmental standards, but depletes agricultural lands, promotes big business, and eliminates jobs.

ASSESS

After You Read

Have students complete the Section 10.2 After You Read section review.

Online Study Tools
Have students go to the Online Learning Center through **glencoe.com** to:

- Take the Section 10.2 **Practice Test**.
- Download free **Study-to-Go** content to their PDAs or cell phones.

CLOSE

Culminating Activity
Draw a Map Have students work in pairs to draw a map of the ASEAN countries and label and indicate some of the exports for each. (Maps will vary.)

Chapter 10 *Review and Activities*

Section 10.1 *Summary*

The Global Marketplace Domestic trade is the production, purchase, and sale of goods and services within a country. Countries do not produce everything their citizens want or need and must trade with other countries. World trade is the exchange of goods and services across international boundaries. Most nations produce items in which they specialize, thus gaining a comparative advantage. A comparative advantage allows countries to trade their specialty with other countries for other things that they want or need. Items purchased across borders are bought in the currency used by the country that produced them. Foreign exchange markets allow one country's currency to be converted into another country's currency.

Section 10.2 *Summary*

Global Competition Global competition often leads to trade disputes, which occur when nations enact barriers to trade. Three common trade barriers are tariffs, quotas, and embargoes. Countries use trade barriers, or protectionism, to protect business from world competition. One reason for protectionism is that outside competition can lower the demand for domestically made products. Free trade opens up new markets, creates jobs, increases consumer choices, and promotes international cooperation. Major trade alliances that have promoted free trade include NAFTA, the EU, and ASEAN. Free trade is good in general, but it is not without problems. Some workers get displaced after an alliance is formed. However, alliances often lead to lower-cost goods.

Vocabulary Review

1. On a sheet of paper, use each of these key terms and academic vocabulary terms in a sentence.

Key Terms

global economy
international trade
multinational corporation
trade
imports
exports
comparative advantage

exchange rate
balance of trade
protectionism
tariff
quota
embargo
free trade

Academic Vocabulary

specific
professionals
sustains
vehicles

disputes
restrict
cooperate
controversy

Review Key Concepts

2. Explain why the world has become a global economy.

3. Explain why people and countries specialize in producing goods and services.

4. Describe free trade.

5. Indicate who benefits and who does not benefit from free trade.

Critical Thinking

6. Free trade encourages competition that leads to lower prices and higher-quality goods. People have more money to buy other items.

7. It is better for the nation to produce what it can do best and get the other items through trade.

8. U.S. exports will increase because the American-made goods will be cheaper.

9. Imports from Britain will increase because they will require fewer U.S. dollars to buy them.

10. An embargo means that no product from a particular nation can be imported. With tariffs, products from the foreign exporter still can be offered.

11. Protectionism limits foreign competition so consumers have fewer choices. Products are higher priced.

Critical Thinking

6. Why does free trade generally increase people's standards of living?

7. Why would a nation choose not to produce everything its citizens want?

8. If the dollar decreases in value in relation to the euro, what is the probable effect that this will have on exports to Europe?

9. If the dollar increases in value in relation to the British pound, what is the probable effect on imports from Britain?

10. Why is an embargo a stronger measure against free trade than tariffs?

11. Protectionism may help certain segments of the economy but may hurt consumers. Why might this be so?

12. If the exchange rate is fixed between the U.S. dollar and the Chinese yuan, America imports more from China than vice versa. If the exchange rate can be determined by the market, what should happen to the relative value of the dollar?

13. Should companies making items for national defense be protected by trade barriers?

Write About It

14. List the countries where 10 items of clothing from your closet were made. Write a one-page essay on why you think they were not all made in the United States.

15. Write an editorial explaining and defending your opinion on the following statement: "It is unpatriotic to buy foreign-made goods."

16. Research the three major exports for another country. Write an argument for why it may have a comparative advantage in those areas.

17. Find an article about the increasing foreign competition that American businesses are facing. Summarize the article.

18. Compare the value of two currencies over five days. Write a one-page report about what happened and why the change occurred.

19. Research the U.S. balance of trade. Is there a trade deficit or a surplus? Write an e-mail to your teacher explaining imbalances between imports and exports and giving reasons for the imbalances.

Technology Applications

Presentation Software

20. As the world economy becomes more global, many countries decide to form trade alliances or to join an existing alliance. Research a trade alliance discussed in this chapter. Make a presentation about the countries involved, the alliance's history, and the impact the alliance has on the world.

Business Ethics

Cultural Differences

21. Imagine you work as a sales manager for a U.S. firm. You have been assigned a new account in Spain. Your Spanish host, the new client, expects you to attend soccer matches with him. Should your company pay for this expense? Write a one-page essay on the matter.

Critical Thinking

12. The value of the dollar should drop and the value of the yuan should rise.

13. If nations import items for national defense, they might have to rely upon other countries to supply the defense equipment in a time of war, which could jeopardize national security.

Write About It

14. Answers will vary depending on the clothing chosen. The United States does not have a comparative advantage in the mass production of clothing. Also, foreign-made clothing is acceptable in the American marketplace.

15. Agree: Increased competition can lead to fewer domestic jobs, which can have a negative effect on the economy. Disagree: Buying some foreign-made goods helps us get better-quality and lower-priced items. Competition gives consumers more choices.

16. Answers will vary depending on the country chosen.

17. Answers will depend on article chosen.

18. Answers will depend on how the currencies perform compared to each other.

19. Answers will depend on the balance and flow of trade.

Technology Applications

20. Answers will depend on the trade alliance chosen but should reflect an understanding of the material in the text.

Business Ethics

21. Each country has its own cultural traditions, even in regard to doing business. In this case, the U.S. firm may have to adapt its policy, within the limits of U.S. law. Doing so can show the client that the U.S. firm values the client's traditions and could help assure that the deal gets made.

Applying Academics to Business

22. Sentences should elaborate on the shades of meaning for the chosen words.

23. A circle graph could be used effectively to show how parts make up a whole.

24. protectionism

embargo

levy

limit

quota

25. A scatter plot could be used. Scatter plots are similar to line graphs in that they use horizontal and vertical axes to plot data points. However, the advantage of a scatter plot is that it does not require a user to know the relationship between variables before the graph can be constructed. Instead, the position of dots can be used to infer the relationship.

Active Learning

26. Examples include ceramics from China or a coat from Russia. If these items are also made in the United States, some of the materials used might be from other countries.

Business in the Real World

27. Charts will vary, depending on the exchange rates at the time students begin their project. The list of questions should incorporate the ideas developed in the text.

Applying Academics to Business

English Language Arts
22. Research and write a list of synonyms for each of the following terms from the chapter. Write a sentence about two of the words, telling how their meanings are alike and different.

tariff   protectionism
embargo   quota

Mathematics
23. NAFTA created a total market of more than 410 million people: 30 million live in Canada, more than 280 million live in the United States, and 100 million live in Mexico. What type of graph could best be used to represent this data? Why?

THEORY   Types of Graphs A graph or chart is used to present facts in visual form. It is a drawing that displays the relative sizes of numerical quantities. A graph is one of the easiest ways to compare numbers.

English Language Arts
24. Read the following terms from the chapter. Organize the terms using one of them as the heading under which the others are listed as examples.

embargo   protectionism
limit   quota

Mathematics
25. The value of the dollar affects the values of other currencies. Morgan tracked the values of the U.S. dollar and the Mexican peso over one year to see if she could find a relationship. What kind of graph could best be used to represent her data? Why?

THEORY   Types of Graphs Graphs can be used to illustrate many types of data and are not limited to the simpler types, such as line, bar, and circle. They should be used to make facts clearer and more understandable.

Active Learning

International Products
26. Think of three different items that you and your family use that were made in another country. List the items and where each one was made. Research the type of trade relationship each country has with the United States. Find out if similar items are made in the United States. If not, explain why not. If there are, why do you buy the international product? Write a one-page report on your findings.

Business in the Real World

Chart Exchange Rates
27. Choose a country and research its currency and the current rate of exchange. As a class, create a chart that combines the countries, their currencies, and the exchange rates each student has chosen. Make a list of questions about how the bank processes currency exchanges. Then invite someone who deals with currency exchanges at a financial institution to speak to the class.

ExamView Assessment Suite **CD** allows you to print out ready-made unit and chapter tests, complete with answer keys. You can also create customized tests.

TeacherWorks Plus! provides complete teacher resources in one convenient package. It includes customizable lesson plans in calendar format, and instant access to many print program resources.

 • skills ─────────

PREPARING TO WORK ABROAD

28. With two classmates, find an individual to interview who has worked in another country. Ask about the cultural differences between working in another country and in the United States. Ask for suggestions on dealing with that culture. As a class, make a chart with the subjects' names. Compare their overseas job titles, types of work performed, the countries where they worked, and tips for preparing for work abroad.

 **Business CAREERS** ─────────

FIND YOUR DREAM JOB

29. Go to the *Introduction to Business* Online Learning Center through **glencoe.com** for a link to the Occupational Outlook Handbook Web site. Click on the "OOH Search/A-Z Index" link and enter the job title "cost estimator." Then write a one-page report about this type of occupation. Conclude your report with a list of things you could do now to prepare yourself to pursue the occupation.

Role Play ─────────

EXAMINING FREE TRADE

30. Situation Imagine that you are an economics expert for another country that is highly protectionist, with a lot of tariffs and quotas on global products. This protectionism keeps many of its major industries secure from global competition. However, the country lacks products and services that its citizens want and need.

Activity Take one of two sides—either continue the protectionist strategies or move toward free trade. Make a persuasive argument for your position.

Evaluation You will be evaluated on how well you meet the following performance indicators:

• Define protectionism and free trade.
• State all of the possible reasons for either position in a clear way.
• Use proper English grammar.
• Speak clearly.

Standardized Test Practice

Directions Choose the letter of the best answer. Write the letter for the answer on a separate piece of paper.

1. How many kilometers is 2,300,000 meters?

   A   less than 300 kilometers
   B   between 300 and 2,000 kilometers
   C   between 2,000 and 3,000 kilometers
   D   more than 3,000 kilometers

TEST-TAKING TIP When taking a test, if you have time at the end, check your answers and solutions. Did you answer each part of every question? Did you answer the questions asked? Do your answers look reasonable? Do your calculations check out?

 READING Go to the *Introduction to Business* Online Learning Center through **glencoe.com** for a list of outside reading suggestions.

Real LIFE • skills

28. Answers will vary, based on visitors' responses.

Cool Business CAREERS

29. Reports on a career as a cost estimator will vary. Information on some or all of the following topics might be included. Nature of the work: Develop cost information that business owners need to make bids for contracts or to decide whether new products will be profitable; compile and analyze data on all factors that can influence costs.

Opportunities for advancement: Management positions or consultants. Job outlook is better than average. As preparation, take a summer job in construction and develop mathematical and computer skills.

Role Play

30. Presentations should address the competencies noted in the Role Play. Answers will vary. Some students could suggest moving to free trade. Others students might argue in favor of keeping protectionism. Their arguments should reflect the materials discussed in the text.

Standardized Test Practice
1. C

STRATEGIES FOR STANDARDIZED TEST PREP SUCCESS

Test Savvy Help students develop techniques for evaluating the quality of their own work on standardized tests. Explain that all of us make careless mistakes when we are performing complicated tasks and working against a deadline. For example, we may skip a question, or add when we should have subtracted. If we are aware that mistakes will inevitably be made, and have a plan for finding those mistakes, we can better control the quality of our work. Explain that, when finishing a standardized test, asking yourself questions such as the ones suggested, and consciously answering them, can help you find errors, maintain the highest quality, and get the highest score.

Standards-Based Lesson Planning   *Introduction to Business* provides students with instruction and assessment in the following fundamental content areas:

Content Standards Correlations	
Differentiate among the roles of government in business.	pp. 181–184, 186–189, 190-191
Describe types of activities performed by governments in business.	pp. 181–184, 186–189, 190–191
Comprehend laws related to ownership (copyrights, patents, and trademarks) and their applications to business.	pp. 181–184, 191
Explain a contract.	p. 182
Distinguish ways taxes impact decisions made by individuals, businesses, and government.	pp. 186–189, 191
Debate components of government tax policies, including use and sources of tax revenue.	pp. 186–189, 191
Explain the effect and importance of taxes.	pp. 188–189, 191
Identify the key characteristics and key areas of government spending.	pp. 188–189, 191
Explain the importance of money management.	pp. 188–189, 191

NCLB   Activities, information, and skills practice will help your students attain No Child Left Behind proficiency. Students will improve their abilities in the following academic standards areas:

Academic Standards Correlations		
English Language Arts	Activities/Features	Page
NCTE 3 Apply strategies to interpret texts	Applying Academics to Business Standardized Test Practice	pp. 192, 193
NCTE 7 Conduct research and gather, evaluate, and synthesize data to communicate discoveries	After You Read	p. 189
Mathematics		
Geometry Analyze characteristics and properties of two- and three-dimensional geometric shapes and develop mathematical arguments about geometric relationships	Applying Academics to Business	p. 192
Number and Operations Understand meanings of operations and how they relate to one another	Ask S&P	p. 178
Number and Operations Understand numbers, ways of representing numbers, relationships among numbers, and number systems	After You Read	p. 184
Problem Solving Monitor and reflect on the process of problem solving	Applying Academics to Business	p. 192
Science		
Content Standard G Students should develop understanding of science as a human endeavor, nature of scientific knowledge, historical perspectives	Science/Tech Trends	p. 187

Correlations   This chart shows the 21st Century Skills, foundation skills, and workplace competencies that students develop as they work in this chapter.

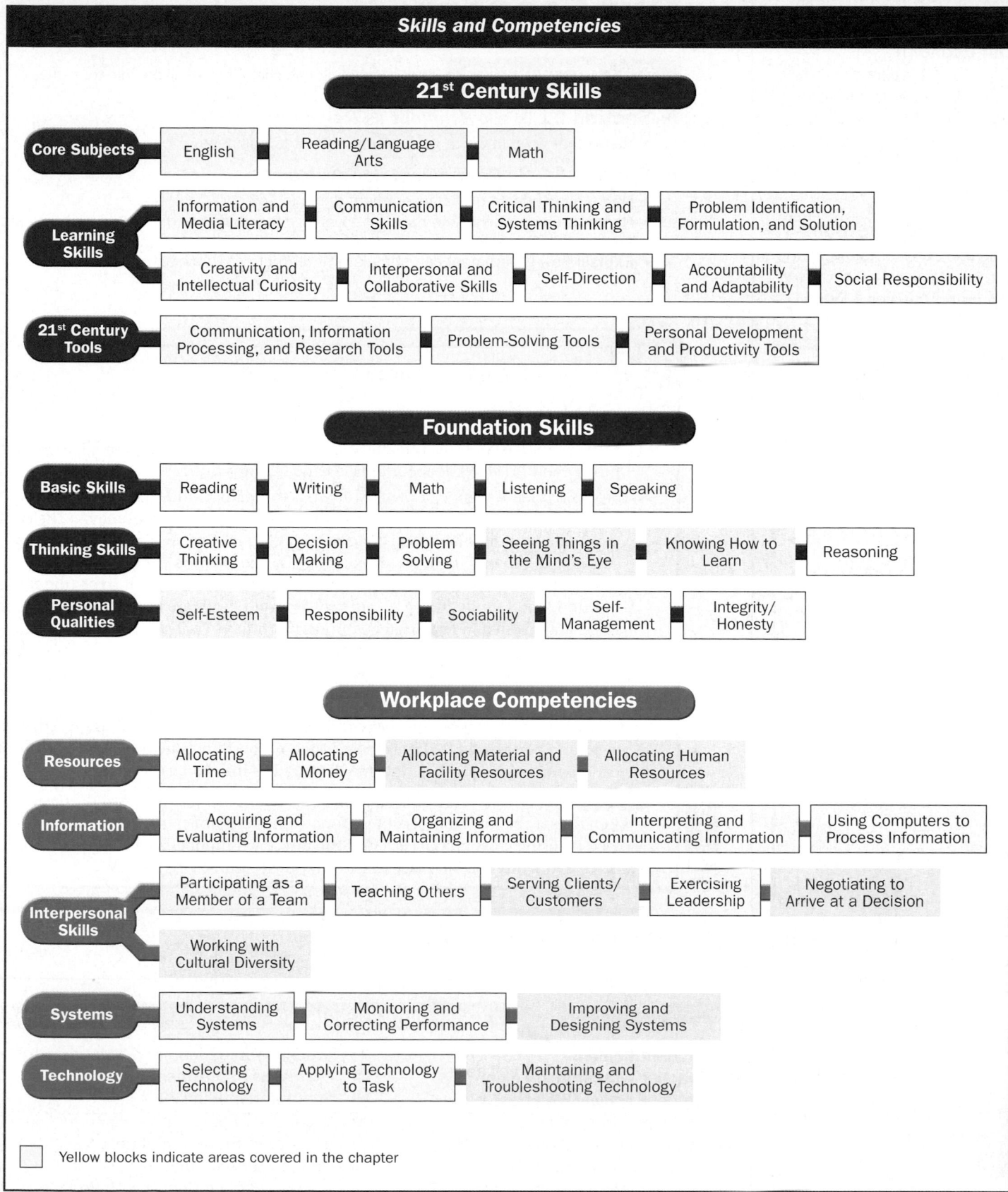

Skills and Competencies

21st Century Skills

Core Subjects
- English
- Reading/Language Arts
- Math

Learning Skills
- Information and Media Literacy
- Communication Skills
- Critical Thinking and Systems Thinking
- Problem Identification, Formulation, and Solution
- Creativity and Intellectual Curiosity
- Interpersonal and Collaborative Skills
- Self-Direction
- Accountability and Adaptability
- Social Responsibility

21st Century Tools
- Communication, Information Processing, and Research Tools
- Problem-Solving Tools
- Personal Development and Productivity Tools

Foundation Skills

Basic Skills
- Reading
- Writing
- Math
- Listening
- Speaking

Thinking Skills
- Creative Thinking
- Decision Making
- Problem Solving
- Seeing Things in the Mind's Eye
- Knowing How to Learn
- Reasoning

Personal Qualities
- Self-Esteem
- Responsibility
- Sociability
- Self-Management
- Integrity/Honesty

Workplace Competencies

Resources
- Allocating Time
- Allocating Money
- Allocating Material and Facility Resources
- Allocating Human Resources

Information
- Acquiring and Evaluating Information
- Organizing and Maintaining Information
- Interpreting and Communicating Information
- Using Computers to Process Information

Interpersonal Skills
- Participating as a Member of a Team
- Teaching Others
- Serving Clients/Customers
- Exercising Leadership
- Negotiating to Arrive at a Decision
- Working with Cultural Diversity

Systems
- Understanding Systems
- Monitoring and Correcting Performance
- Improving and Designing Systems

Technology
- Selecting Technology
- Applying Technology to Task
- Maintaining and Troubleshooting Technology

☐ Yellow blocks indicate areas covered in the chapter

Chapter Overview

Introduce the Chapter

The Role of Government in Our Economy

Chapter 11 describes how the government regulates business, the government's role in society, and how the government is funded and allocates resources.

Building Background

For many students, this chapter will inspire a new way to think about government.

Ask STANDARD &POOR'S

>> Math Answer

Mara has $1,000 invested in bonds.

To find the unknown value that represents the value of Mara's bond investment, you need to know the proportion of Frank's bond investment. Set up this equation:

Frank's Total ÷ Frank's Bonds = Mara's Total ÷ Mara's Bonds

$10,240 ÷ $2,560 = $4,000 ÷ ?

4 = $4,000 ÷ ?

$1,000 = ?

>> Extension Activity

Ask students to read an article that provides information about mutual funds and to work in groups to create a flyer explaining the advantages. (Simplicity, expert management, diversification, and limited risk.)

NCLB Activity correlates to Math standards.

The Role of Government in Our Economy

Chapter Objectives After completing this chapter, you will be able to:

▶ **Section 11.1** *Government as Regulator*
- **Name** four ways in which government regulates business.

▶ **Section 11.2** *Government as Provider*
- **Name** five aspects of the government's role in society.
- **Name** three items that the national government provides and three items that local governments provide.
- **Explain** how government can stimulate or restrict economic activities.

Ask STANDARD &POOR'S Types of Investments

Q: I think I understand the differences between stocks and bonds, but what are mutual funds and REITS? What about options and futures contracts?

A: Stocks represent equity, or ownership, in a company. Bonds represent debt. When you buy bonds, it's as if you are the bank, and you're lending money to the company. Shares of mutual funds, bond funds, and REITS are securities that sell like stocks; you can buy them on an exchange. A mutual fund is a pool of money invested by an expert manager in a variety of stocks with a specific investment goal in mind. Bond funds and REITs are similar. Bond funds are invested in bonds, and REITs are invested in real estate. Options and futures contracts offer sophisticated investors ways to gamble on future changes in the prices of securities or offset risks in their existing portfolios.

Mathematics Frank and his wife Mara have separate investment accounts. Frank's account has $7,680 invested in stocks and $2,560 in bonds. Mara's total investment in stocks and bonds is $4,000 split in the same proportion as her husband's. Write and solve a proportion to calculate how much Mara has invested in bonds.

NCLB

THEORY Proportions A proportion is an equation with equivalent ratios on each side. When one of the four numbers in a proportion is unknown, the proportion may be solved by using cross products to find the unknown number. Question marks or letters are frequently used in place of the unknown number.

Classroom Resources

- 📓 Student Edition
- 📓 Teacher Wraparound Edition
- 📂 Student Activity Workbook with Academic Integration
- 📂 Student Activity Workbook with Academic Integration TAE
- 📂 *Fast File*, Unit 11 Resources
- 📂 Inclusion in the Business Education Classroom

- 💿 TeacherWorks Plus
- 💿 *ExamView Assessment Suite*
- 💿 Presentation Plus!
- 💿 Vocabulary PuzzleMaker
- 💿 Interactive Student Edition
- 💻 Online Student Edition
- 💻 Online Learning Center with Podcasts

● **Government Roles** Governments play important roles in our economy. **How is the federal government's role different from that of a state government?**

Chapter 11 The Role of Government in Our Economy **179**

Review the Objectives
Introduce the chapter by reviewing the chapter objectives:

Section 11.1 *Objective*
Name four ways in which government regulates business. (It protects competition, creative properties, and business agreements. It also regulates the production process.)

Section 11.2 *Objectives*
Name five aspects of the government's role in society. (It provides goods, services, and incentives for the common good. Its spending decisions can affect how individual incomes are distributed. It also provides jobs, supports business, and uses many goods and services.)

Name three items that the national government provides and three items that local governments provide. (The federal government provides national defense, national highways, Social Security, and education. Local governments provide streets, libraries, parks, and education.)

Explain how government can stimulate or restrict economic activities. (Sometimes government decides to put money into certain projects. This decision can mean that other projects will not get much funding, if any. Government funding can boost an area's economy. More jobs are created when projects are funded. People with jobs tend to spend more than people without jobs. This affects the economic health of an area.)

Discuss the Photo
● **Government Roles** Read the caption on the photo to students: Governments play important roles in our economy.

Ask students: How is the federal government's role different from that of a state government? (Answers will vary but should include some discussion of their different status under the Constitution and of the scope of their powers.)

FOCUS

Government as Regulator

 Bell Ringer Activity

Government as Regulator

Locate an article in the local newspaper that includes a reference to a government regulation which affects business. Read the headline, provide a brief summary of the article, and read the passage that mentions the government regulation.

Preteaching

Presentation Plus! ⊙

The Presentation Plus! CD provides visual teaching aids for this section.

PuzzleMaker ⊙

Use the Vocabulary PuzzleMaker to create a puzzle of the section's key terms. Students can complete the puzzle on paper or on a computer.

Graphic Organizer

Tell students to go to the Online Learning Center through **glencoe.com** for a printable graphic organizer. (Answers include: Antitrust legislation protects competition. Contract laws protect business agreements. Intellectual property laws protect creative properties. Agencies like the FDA regulate the production process.)

N C L B Connects academics to content.

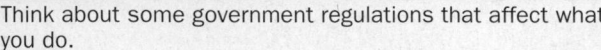 **Reading Guide**

 Before You Read

Think about some government regulations that affect what you do.

Read to Learn
- Name four ways in which government regulates business.

D

The Main Idea

Our government's role is to foster success in the economy. One way it does this is by creating rules and regulations that organizations and consumers must follow. Laws cover three aspects of the economy. They protect competition. They protect business agreements and creative properties. They are also used to regulate the production process.

Key Concept
- How the Government Regulates Business

Vocabulary

Key Terms

interstate commerce	contract
intrastate commerce	breach of contract
monopoly	copyright
oligopoly	patent
trust	trademark
antitrust laws	

Academic Vocabulary

You will find these words in your reading and on your tests. Make sure you know their meanings.

federal	symbol
enables	registered

Graphic Organizer

In a figure like the one below, write notes about government's role in the economy.

Protecting Competition	Protecting Business Agreements
Protecting Creative Properties	Regulating the Production Process

@ Go to the *Introduction to Business* Online Learning Center through **glencoe.com** for a printable graphic organizer.

Academic Standards

English Language Arts

NCTE 1 Read texts to acquire new information

NCTE 4 Use written language to communicate effectively

Mathematics

Number and Operations Understand numbers, ways of representing numbers, relationships between numbers, and number systems

N C L B

Reading Guide

Before You Read

Students might mention truancy laws, speed limits, sales tax, and copyright laws.

D Develop Concepts

The Main Idea Ask students if they can think of examples of how the government regulates business. (Answers will vary. Students might mention antitrust laws, contracts, and intellectual property laws.)

How Government Regulates Business

One of government's roles is to foster economic success. It also tries to aid in the quality of life of its citizens. In a market economy, a country's economic health depends on businesses doing well. In some cases, government helps people so that they are not abused by businesses. To fulfill these duties, local, state, and national governments pass laws to promote and regulate business.

 There are three levels of government: **federal**, state, and local. The federal government runs the country. State governments run their state. Local governments run counties, townships, cities, and towns. The federal government oversees interstate commerce. **Interstate commerce** is business that takes place between states. State governments oversee intrastate commerce. **Intrastate commerce** is business that takes place within states.

Laws govern the workings of the economy. These laws regulate the production process and protect competition, business agreements, and creative properties.

Companies that break the law can be fined, sued, or forced to close. People who do not follow the rules also face penalties.

BusinessWeek *Reader and Case Study*

How China Controls the Internet

Nicholas Bequelin of Human Rights Watch in Hong Kong explains, and he says U.S. companies need to take a stand against Beijing.

The news that Microsoft shut down a Chinese blogger's site at the request of Beijing officials is bringing a renewed focus on the role U.S. companies play in helping China control the Internet. It's no secret that Western businesses that want to enter the Internet market in China have to do some unsavory things. The Chinese government, determined to prevent dissidents from using the Net to promote taboo subjects such as the Falun Gong religious movement, formal independence for Taiwan, or an end to Communist Party rule, pressures providers to play by Chinese rules and control the content that's available for local Net surfers.

When companies do restrict what their Chinese users send or read on the Net, however, they face howls of criticism from activists, bloggers, and ordinary folks abroad who think that multinationals should not be helping Beijing police the Net.

CASE STUDY Go to the *Introduction to Business* Online Learning Center through **glencoe.com** for the *BusinessWeek* Reader Case Study.

Active Learning

The Internet is a powerful source of information—but it offers a tremendous amount of misinformation as well. Research what information is appropriate to include in a bibliography. Present a PowerPoint presentation to your class about the proper way to reference online content in a bibliography. Include reasons a Web site might not be reliable enough to reference in a research paper.

glencoe.com

BusinessWeek *Reader and Case Study*

How China Controls the Internet

CASE STUDY Have students go to the *Introduction to Business* Online Learning Center through **glencoe.com** to download a Case Study activity that corresponds to the article. The activity and answer key are also available on the TeacherWorks Plus CD.

Active Learning

Presentations should discuss a systematic referencing system such as APA. Web sites may be missing authorship information or could include out-of-date information, etc.

TEACH

Discussion Starter
How Government Regulates Business
Ask students: Why does government need to regulate business? Stimulate discussion by pointing out that many laws and regulations foster economic success and protect the public from harmful business practices. For example, copyright laws protect copyright holders and foster creative businesses.

R Reading Strategy

Identify Have students create a table that illustrates the three levels of government and names the specific governments for the location where they live. (The top level of government is the federal government of the United States of America. The second level is state government. The specific state government will vary depending on the state where you live. The third level is local government. The specific local government will vary depending on where you live. Local governments include cities, towns, villages, and townships.)

Virtual Business

Introduce pricing to students using the Virtual Business Retailing Pricing activity. In this simulation, students learn why pricing is important to the success of a business.

181

TEACH (cont.)

S Skill Practice

Guided Practice

Illustrate Have students create a set of posters to illustrate monopoly, oligopoly, and trust. (Posters will vary. Encourage students to give their posters a common design.) **L1**

Summarize Ask students to summarize an article about antitrust laws and sports. (Summaries will vary. For example, college athletes have filed lawsuits over the eligibility requirements for the NFL draft and NCAA rules governing transfers.) **L2**

Research and Present Ask students to research the Sherman Antitrust and the Clayton Acts and prepare a slide presentation. (Presentations will vary. The Sherman Antitrust Act [1890] allows the federal government to break up trusts. The Clayton Antitrust Act [1914] clarifies and strengthens the Sherman Act.) **L3**

ASSESS

Review Key Terms

Have students write sentences using each key term.

Study-to-Go
Have students go to the Online Learning Center through **glencoe.com** to download free **Study-to-Go** content to their PDAs or cell phones.

182

Monopoly, the Board Game Lizzie Magie, a young Quaker woman from Virginia, created a game that became Monopoly® in 1903. It was developed as a way to teach people about the monopoly of land ownership. *How do you think a popular game can affect or teach people about an issue?*

S

Protecting Competition

A **monopoly** occurs when a company controls an industry or is the only one to offer a product or service. An **oligopoly** occurs when a small number of companies control an industry. Monopolies are problematic for several reasons. One is that monopolies do not compete with other firms. This **enables** them to charge any price they want for products or services. Also, quality may not be their biggest concern. Both monopolies and oligopolies limit choice.

Companies can also form a monopoly by establishing a trust. A **trust** is a group of companies that band together to form a monopoly and cut out competition. The U.S. government passed antitrust laws to promote competition. **Antitrust laws** allow the federal government to break up monopolies, regulate them, or take control of them. These laws have not always stopped firms from competing unfairly. The government formed the Federal Trade Commission (FTC) to enforce antitrust laws. For example, in the 1940s, the government sued a group of studios for trying to take over the film industry. The FTC also regulates interstate trade. It keeps competition between U.S. businesses free and fair. Its job includes setting standards for honest advertising.

Protecting Business Agreements

One of the most basic ways government protects business is by enforcing contracts. A **contract** is a legally enforceable agreement between two or more parties. It can be written, verbal, or even formed over a handshake. A rental agreement, a car-repair order, and the warranty on a CD player are all types of contracts.

? ETHICS in Business

Out of State Advertising

■ **Critical Reading** Life is full of important decisions. Think about the kinds of decisions that you make as you read the question.

You own a clothing shop in a state that has a low sales tax on consumer goods; neighboring states have higher sales taxes. When an in-state customer buys clothing, you add the state tax. When an out-of-state customer buys clothing at your shop, you don't add any tax. The customer is supposed to report the purchase and pay the appropriate tax to his or her state government. Many out-of-staters from nearby towns shop at your store, and you don't know if they pay the tax they're supposed to pay.

■ **Decision Making** Knowing that some people don't pay their state sales taxes, is it appropriate for you to advertise your shop in nearby out-of-state towns? Explain your answer.

Monopoly, the Board Game Students may cite games such as Risk that teach real-world concepts. Students might say that a game is an easy way to get a concept across. Others may say a game cannot cover complex ideas.

? ETHICS in Business

Decision Making Students might suggest that it isn't appropriate to appear to be promoting tax avoidance. However, advertising your shop's goods and services is appropriate, even if the area encompasses more than one state.

Breach of contract occurs when one party fails to live up to the terms of a contract. It is easier to prove a breach of contract occurred if there is a written contract. For example, suppose you are in a band that plays at a coffeehouse, and the manager refuses to pay you. It can be very difficult to prove that the manager agreed to pay if the agreement is not written in a contract.

Protecting Creative Properties

Laws also protect the right to own creative properties. Creative properties, items such as inventions and art, can be protected with a copyright, a patent, or a trademark.

Copyrights A **copyright** gives artists the legal right to own their creations. Copyrights protect photographs, music, paintings, books, plays, and other written material. Today, a person creating an original work automatically holds the copyright to it. An artist who also registers it with the U.S. Copyright Office in Washington, D.C., gains additional legal protection. If you own the copyright to a story you wrote, others who want to use it must get your permission beforehand. A copyright usually lasts until 70 years after the owner's death.

Patents A **patent** is a legal grant for the sole right to own an invention. The federal government grants patents. No one can copy a patented product or process without permission for 20 years after the inventor filed his or her application with the U.S. Patent and Trademark Office.

> ● **As You Read**
> Think about works of art you have seen or heard that are protected by copyright laws.

● **Government as Watchdog** Federal laws limit the amount of waste factories can discharge into the environment. **Why does the government work to curb pollution?**

● **As You Read**
Students should understand that photos and music are generally protected by copyright. Using a copyrighted item without permission is illegal.

Discuss the Photo
● **Government as Watchdog** Government works to curb pollution because limiting the amount of waste factories can discharge is a way of regulating the production process that benefits all citizens.

Section 11.1

RETEACH

W Writing Support
Enrichment
Breach of Contract Have students write a fable that addresses the concept of breach of contract. Point out that a fable is a short tale with a hidden meaning or moral. Characters in most fables are animals to which human traits and behaviors have been attributed. (Students might focus on the consequences of breaking a promise or the importance of having a contract.)

R Reading Strategy
Give an Example Ask students to come up with another example of a situation where not having a copyright filed with the copyright office might be problematic. (Students might suggest situations in which the date that the work was created is in doubt or where the author shares creative credit because both these situations would allow a dispute to exist that would be settled by a registered copyright.)

U Universal Access
Visual Learners Display an assortment of items that are protected by patent. Have students find the appropriate notice on the items.

Student Activity Workbook 📂 Assign the Section 11.1 Activities.

183

RETEACH (cont.)

C Critical Thinking

Compare and Contrast
Trademarks Have students compare and contrast common trademarked names and the generic names for the same items. (Often the trademarked names are more memorable.)

✔ Reading Check

Contrast Copyright gives artists the legal right to own their creations. Patent is a legal grant for sole right to an invention.

ASSESS

● After You Read

Have students complete the Section 11.1 After You Read section review.

Online Study Tools

Have students go to the Online Learning Center through **glencoe.com** to:

- Take the Section 11.1 **Practice Test**.
- Download free **Study-to-Go** content to their PDAs or cell phones.

CLOSE

Culminating Activity
Copyrights, Patents, and Trademarks

Have students visit the United States Patent and Trademark Office Web site's FAQ. Ask: Is a trademark search necessary? (It is strongly advisable.)

Trademarks A **trademark** is a name, a **symbol**, or a characteristic that identifies a product. It is also **registered** with the government. Only the owner of the trademark can legally use it. Well-known trademarks include Frito-Lay's *Doritos*®, Kellogg's *Rice Krispies Treats*®, and *Visa*®. Trademarks are protected from being copied if they are registered appropriately.

✔ Reading Check   **Contrast** What is the difference between a copyright and a patent?

Regulating the Production Process

The government also steers economic activity by regulating the production process. It tries to stop companies from polluting by enacting laws. Some laws limit the amount of waste that factories can discharge into the environment. Worker protection laws impose safety requirements and work procedures and regulate the minimum wage. Organized labor, or labor unions, often help to report violations of worker protection regulations.

The Food and Drug Administration (FDA) regulates the manufacture and sale of drugs in the United States. Local and state governments regulate production processes, too.

 **NCLB** Activity correlates to Math standards.

Section 11.1

● After You Read

Review Key Concepts
1. What is the difference between interstate and intrastate commerce?
2. What are the ways that the government can deal with a monopoly?
3. What kinds of property are protected by copyrights?

Academic Skills
NCLB
4. **Mathematics** You are an event coordinator. You work from 8:30 A.M. to 5:00 P.M. from your office in Philadelphia. Tomorrow you need to place phone calls to an acrobatic team in New York, a specialty caterer in California, a display designer in Hawaii, and a magician in Colorado. The companies are open from 9:00 A.M. to 5:00 P.M., and the employees take lunch from noon to 1:00 P.M. Taking into account time zone differences, make a list of the times you might call each vendor.

 THEORY **Working with Time** The United States is spread across six time zones. From east to west they are: eastern, central, mountain, Pacific, Alaska, and Hawaii-Aleutian. Philadelphia is in the eastern time zone. The time is an hour earlier in each time zone as you go from east to west.

 For math help, go to the Math Appendix.

@ Go to the *Introduction to Business* Online Learning Center through **glencoe.com** to check your answers.

184   **Chapter 11**   The Role of Government in Our Economy   glencoe.com

Section 11.1

Review Key Concepts
1. Interstate commerce is business between states, overseen by the federal government. Intrastate commerce is business within a state, overseen by state or local governments.
2. It can break it up, regulate it, or take it over.
3. musical compositions, song lyrics, books, movies, plays, and photographs

Academic Skills
4. **Mathematics** One possible schedule is to call New York at 9 A.M., Colorado at 11 A.M., California at 1 P.M., and Hawaii at 3 P.M.

Government as Provider

Reading Guide

Before You Read
Think about some of the items that the government provides you or your community.

Read to Learn
- Name five aspects of the government's role in society.
- Name three items that the national government provides and three items that local governments provide.
- Explain how government can stimulate or restrict economic activities.

The Main Idea
D The different levels of government do more than regulate business activities. One of their main roles is to provide goods and services. These are provided using tax money collected from people and organizations.

Key Concepts
- Government's Role in Society
- How Government Is Funded
- How Government Allocates Resources

Vocabulary
Key Terms

revenue tax
privatization tax incentive
subsidies

Academic Vocabulary
You will find these words in your reading and on your tests. Make sure you know their meanings.

incentives ensure
welfare allocate

Graphic Organizer
In a box like the one below, list and describe five aspects of the government's role in society.

1.
2.
3.
4.
5.

 Go to the *Introduction to Business* Online Learning Center through **glencoe.com** for a printable graphic organizer.

Academic Standards
English Language Arts
　NCTE 1 Read texts to acquire new information
　NCTE 7 Conduct research and gather, evaluate, and synthesize data to communicate discoveries
Science
　Content Standard E Students should develop abilities of technological design
　Content Standard G Students should develop understanding of science as a human endeavor, nature of scientific knowledge, historical perspectives

N C L B

Reading Guide

Before You Read
Answers might include fixed potholes, collected trash, inspected meat, licensed me as a driver, protected me from criminals, etc.

D Develop Concepts
The Main Idea Ask students: How could government officials justify the use of tax revenue to build something such as a skate park? (Students should understand that it is likely that a relatively small number of residents might enjoy the direct benefits of the park; most residents would enjoy indirect benefits.)

Section 11.2

Bell Ringer Activity

Government as Provider
Ask students if they think it makes sense for the government to be in charge of some services. Point out that different communities handle some services differently. (Students might suggest that some services related to health and safety need to be provided by the government to protect all members of the community.)

Preteaching

Presentation Plus!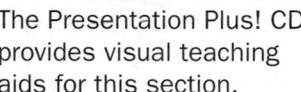
The Presentation Plus! CD provides visual teaching aids for this section.

PuzzleMaker
Use the Vocabulary PuzzleMaker to create a puzzle of the section's key terms. Students can complete the puzzle on paper or on a computer.

Graphic Organizer
Tell students to go to the Online Learning Center through **glencoe.com** for a printable graphic organizer. (Answers include: Government provides goods and services, aids citizens through transfer payments, provides employment, consumes goods and services, supports business, and provides incentives.)

N C L B Connects academics to content.

Discussion Starter

Government's Role in Society

Point out that government generally takes on things that are necessary but unprofitable for businesses to provide. Ask students to discuss how life would be different without goods and services provided by the government. (Students might mention lack of services or the expense of trying to purchase the service as an individual.)

R Reading Strategy

Outline Starting on this page, have students create an outline using the sub-heads that fall under heading "The Government's Role in Society" as their main entries. Suggest that they include several points under each main entry. (The main points of the outline should be: providing goods and services, transfer payments, providing employment, consuming goods and services, and supporting business.)

● As You Read

Government-provided goods include highways, bridges, water treatment plants, and national defense. Private goods and services include CDs, clothing, food, and housekeeping services.

Government's Role in Society

 The role of government in business is not limited to law making. Government also plays a big role in society. It provides key services to the public. It also gives **incentives** to businesses and people. Other services include providing jobs and distributing income. These activities occur at every level of government.

● As You Read

Think about the goods and services government provides and those that you buy directly from businesses.

Providing Goods and Services

Government is the largest provider of services in the country. Businesses offer goods and services to people to make a profit. However, government provides services to the public as a whole for the good of society.

Highways, bridges, water treatment plants, and national defense are examples of public goods and services. *Public goods and services* are items provided by government and paid for using tax money. They are different from private goods and services. *Private goods and services* are items that consumers purchase directly from businesses. They include CDs, clothing, food, and housekeeping services.

Other services promote social **welfare**. Government provides parks, libraries, museums, and swimming pools. These facilities improve people's quality of life. The cost of providing all these services is high. Governments pay for them with revenues they receive. **Revenue** is the income that governments get from all sources. That includes taxes and fees that consumers sometimes must pay to use certain public goods and services. Revenue is also money that comes into a business from the sale of goods and services.

In some cases, a business may provide a public good or service. **Privatization** occurs when a business offers a public good or service. The government body that pays for it oversees the business. For example, most cafés in government buildings are run by private businesses, not the government.

Aiding Citizens Through Transfer Payments

People's well-being is another concern of government. To improve their quality of life, the federal government provides transfer payments. A *transfer payment* is a government expense that is provided to help people. These payments **ensure** that people have money when they need it. Unemployment, Social Security, and veterans' benefits are forms of transfer payments.

Providing Employment

The government is the largest employer in the United States. More than 3 million people work for the federal government. State and local governments also employ millions of people. Mayors, firefighters, and the U.S. president are all public workers.

Real World

Government Jobs When more people have jobs, the unemployment rate goes down, and businesses benefit from a larger workforce. More consumers are able to buy products and services. Instruct students to visit www.usajobs.gov and use the job search tool to see what kinds of positions are currently available, find a position of interest, and provide the following: position title, agency name, salary range, duty location, and minimum education requirement.

Consuming Goods and Services

Government is also the largest consumer of goods and services. It has to buy computers, furniture, and supplies for schools and government offices. To maintain the military, it has to buy uniforms, food, ships, aircraft, and weapons. Government buys most of its equipment directly from businesses or has equipment specially made. It also hires businesses to build aircraft, courthouses, schools, and roads.

Supporting Business

The government is involved in many activities that support business. The Small Business Administration (SBA) is a U.S. agency that encourages the development of small businesses. The SBA offers loans and advice to people who want to open small businesses.

The U.S. government helps some businesses compete internationally by providing subsidies. **Subsidies** are monetary grants given to producers or consumers to encourage certain behaviors. They are usually given to firms that are considered to benefit the public. Agriculture and steel are two industries that have historically received subsidies.

Government Jobs
The U.S. federal government's official job Web site lists federal jobs and provides general employee information. The Web site also helps applicants create résumés. *How do you think the government can aid firms with its job Web site?*

Science/Tech TRENDS

Commercial Space Travel

The space shuttle looks like an airplane because it has to travel through Earth's atmosphere just like an airplane. However, the space industry has not developed in the same way that the aviation industry developed over the course of the 20th century. Aviation was largely developed by inventors and entrepreneurs, although government and the military played important roles. In the case of the space industry, however, governments in the United States, Europe, and Japan established monopolies to open the space frontier on behalf of the public. Today, with growing interest in commercial space travel, the role of government in the space industry is changing. The innovations that come from public sector space travel research help scientists and create new opportunities for business.

Go to the *Introduction to Business* Online Learning Center through **glencoe.com** for links to Web sites where you can find information on commercial space travel. What will it take to fly adventurers and commuters to the edge of space? Give a talk to your class about the future of commercial space travel. Use presentation software and include pictures taken from a spacecraft or space telescope.

---

glencoe.com

Science/Tech TRENDS

WebQuest

Commercial Space Travel Answers will vary, but students might discuss such topics as a new spaceport envisioned for New Mexico's desert, and such entrepreneurs as Burt Rutan and Richard Branson.

Activity correlates to Science standards.

TEACH (cont.)

S Skill Practice

Guided Practice

Share Examples Ask students to name examples of public goods and services they rely on that require government to act as a consumer. (Students might identify school as a service they rely on, which requires the government to consume buildings, desks, teacher services, etc.) **L1**

Create a Table Ask students to create a two-column, three-row table giving examples of public goods and services for each of the three levels of government and listing at least five examples of goods and services that are consumed at each level. (Table will vary. Some positions such as education could appear in all three rows.) **L2**

Research Have students use Internet resources to find and print an announcement of a major government contract to purchase goods and services. (Examples may include contracts to build roads or buy military airplanes.) **L3**

ASSESS

Review Key Terms
Have students write sentences using each key term.

Study-to-Go Have students go to the Online Learning Center through **glencoe.com** to download free **Study-to-Go** content to their PDAs or cell phones.

187

RETEACH

Enrichment

Government Subsidies Ask students to locate, read, and summarize a magazine, journal, or newspaper article about the costs of government subsidies. (Summaries will vary depending on the article. Encourage students to think about the subsidy from both the perspective of being taxpayers and being citizens who enjoy the benefits of the subsidy.)

R Reading Strategy

Illustrate an Idea Have students use the examples in the textbook to create an illustration showing some of the service that each level of government funds through the collection of taxes. (Illustrations will vary.)

U Universal Access

Visual Learners Direct students to visit the Small Business Administration Web site to learn more about SBA and the services it provides. Viewing another source of information is often helpful for students who learn best through a visual experience.

● **As You Read**

Students should consider that they receive indirect benefits because others they depend on use the highways. Buses use highways, too.

Student Activity Workbook 📂 Assign the Section 11.2 Activities.

● **As You Read**

Think of a government good or service that does not directly benefit you. Do you think it is fair for you to share the tax burden for something you do not use?

How Government Is Funded

A **tax** is an amount of money people and businesses pay governments to help run the nation, state, county, city, or town. For some goods, such as gasoline, taxes are included in the purchase price. If you have a job, income taxes are deducted from your wages. Your income tax revenue helps pay for public goods and services and provide money for transfer payments.

The purpose of taxes is to pay for public goods and services by spreading the cost among many people. **Figure 11.1** provides a glimpse of the amount of time it takes for taxpayers in some states to work to pay their taxes. However, some people may not receive direct benefits from all the taxes they pay. For instance, some people may never need to call a fire department. However, the fire department is important to everyone in a community.

Each level of government collects taxes for different kinds of services. For example, federal income tax pays for national highways and defense. State taxes pay for state police and motor vehicle departments. Local taxes pay for streets and parks. All three levels of government pay for public education.

✔ **Reading Check** **Analyze** Why are taxes necessary?

Figure 11.1 — **Working to Pay Taxes**

| ☆ Alaska April 2 | ★ New Jersey April 25 | ★ Alabama April 4 | ★ New York April 29 | ★ Tennessee April 6 | ★ Connecticut May 3 |

APRIL						
Sun	Mon	Tues	Weds	Thurs	Fri	Sat
			1	2	3	4
5	6	7	8	9	10	11
12	13	14	15	16	17	18
19	20	21	22	23	24	25
26	27	28	29	30		

MAY						
Sun	Mon	Tues	Weds	Thurs	Fri	Sat
					1	2
3	4	5	6	7	8	9
10	11	12	13	14	15	16
17	18	19	20	21	22	23
24	25	26	27	28	29	30
31						

Source: Tax Foundation

● **Tax Freedom Day** Tax Freedom Day is the first day of the year when the average person has earned enough to pay all of his or her annual federal, state, and local taxes. **Why does it take residents of Connecticut longer to pay all of their taxes?**

✔ **Reading Check**

Analyze Taxes are necessary so that government can pay for public goods and services and to spread the cost among many people.

Figure 11.1

● **Tax Freedom Day** It probably takes Connecticut residents longer to pay all of their taxes because they have a higher tax rate per capita than the other states shown.

Providing Incentives

C

The government provides many incentives to businesses and consumers. A **tax incentive** is a temporary reduction or elimination of a tax that is meant to encourage or discourage an activity. A *tax break* is a special tax benefit given to promote specific economic or social objectives. Tax deductions for mortgage interest and property tax expenses encourage home ownership.

Government also tries to discourage certain behaviors. For example, taxes on cigarettes have increased dramatically. The reasoning is that some people may stop smoking if they decide it is too expensive to smoke.

● **As You Read**

Think about the tax incentives your town or city might give to local businesses. Do you think it is fair for some businesses to receive tax incentives?

How Government Allocates Resources

Governments **allocate** resources by deciding the best ways to spend tax revenues. They determine which projects are priorities for funding. For example, the government may decide to pay more for projects in rural areas than projects in urban ones. Such a decision can help the economies in rural areas.

Government spending also affects the distribution of income. For example, people who receive transfer payments such as unemployment pay can see their income rise or fall if the government raises or lowers the amount of their payments.

N C L B Activity correlates to Engllsh Language Arts standards.

Section 11.2

● **After You Read**

Review Key Concepts

1. What are some services that the government provides for the public?
2. How is government funded?
3. How does the government allocate resources?

Academic Skills

N C L B

4. **English Language Arts** In a group of three or four, brainstorm a list of ways to make a business more competitive. Consider topics such as innovation, pricing, marketing, and customer service. Also brainstorm a list of reasons businesses lose their competitive edge. Use your list for a presentation about the advantages and disadvantages of government regulation of business.

5. **English Language Arts** The U.S. Department of Labor publishes various major economic indicators including the unemployment rate, the consumer price index, the producer price index, and the employment cost index. Choose one of these and find out more about it. Write a paragraph explaining what it is and why it is valuable to people in business and government.

 Go to the *Introduction to Business* Online Learning Center through **glencoe.com** to check your answers.

Section 11.2

Review Key Concepts

1. defense, education, parks, museums, libraries, roads, police, fire department, and courts
2. through taxes
3. The government decides how to spend tax revenues by determining which projects are priorities.

Academic Skills

4. **English Language Arts** Impediments include excessive government regulation and high interest rates.
5. **English Language Arts** Students may note that the consumer price index represents changes in the prices of all goods and services purchased by urban households.

Section 11.2

RETEACH (cont.)

C **Critical Thinking**

Consider the Consequences

Tax Incentives Have students write an essay about the consequences of one of the incentives or disincentives mentioned under the heading "Providing Incentives." (Answers will depend on the incentive or disincentive chosen.)

● **As You Read**

Answers will vary depending on student experiences and on the type of tax incentive.

ASSESS

● **After You Read**

Have students complete the Section 11.2 After You Read section review.

Online Study Tools

Have students go to the Online Learning Center through **glencoe.com** to:

- Take the Section 11.2 **Practice Test**.
- Download free **Study-to-Go** content to their PDAs or cell phones.

CLOSE

Culminating Activity

Tax Freedom Day

Ask students to visit www.taxfoundation.org to find Tax Freedom Day information for all the states for the current year and create an illustration showing the tax freedom day for each state. (Students might use a timeline or map.)

Vocabulary Review

1. Students should write complete sentences using each term correctly.

Review Key Concepts

2. Government protects competition, creative properties, and business agreements. It also regulates the production process.

3. Government provides goods, services, and incentives for the common good. Its spending decisions can affect how individual incomes are distributed. It also provides jobs, supports business, and uses many goods and services itself.

4. Answers will vary. For example, the federal government provides national defense, national highways, Social Security, and education. Local governments provide streets, libraries, parks, and education.

5. Sometimes government decides to put money in to certain projects in ways that influence economic activities. These decisions can mean that other projects will not get much funding, if any. Government funding can boost an area's economy. More jobs are created when projects are funded. People with jobs tend to spend more than people without jobs. This affects the economic health of an area.

Section 11.1 *Summary*

Government as Regulator There are three levels of government: federal, state, and local. The federal government runs the country. A state government runs each state. Local governments run counties, cities, towns, and townships. Each level of government oversees a different level of business. One of government's roles is to foster success in our market economy. It does this by enacting laws for organizations and people to follow. Laws protect competition, business agreements, and creative rights. They also help the government to regulate the production process. In some cases, government must approve an item before it can be produced.

Section 11.2 *Summary*

Government as Provider Government is the largest provider of services in the country. It provides goods and services that are not easy for consumers to buy on their own and for the good of society. Individuals cannot buy highways, bridges, or national defense. These public goods and services are provided by the government and paid for with tax revenues. Government provides incentives to businesses to encourage or discourage certain activities. Since governments do not have unlimited resources, they must choose how their limited resources should be used. Their decisions can affect the economic health of an area.

Vocabulary Review

1. On a sheet of paper, use each of these key terms and academic vocabulary terms in a sentence.

Key Terms

interstate commerce	copyright
intrastate commerce	patent
monopoly	trademark
oligopoly	revenue
trust	privatization
antitrust laws	subsidies
contract	tax
breach of contract	tax incentive

Academic Vocabulary

federal	incentives
enables	welfare
symbol	ensure
registered	allocate

Review Key Concepts

2. Name four ways in which government regulates business.

3. Name five aspects of the government's role in society.

4. Name three items that the national government provides and three items that local governments provide.

5. Explain how governments can stimulate or restrict economic activities.

Critical Thinking

6. Businesses provide goods and services, jobs, and tax revenues. Tax revenues pay for public goods and services. A strong economy depends on the success of businesses.

7. Competition offers consumers more choices. More choices mean businesses have to improve their products or lower prices to stay competitive.

8. Consumers ultimately pay for the cost of the pollution-control equipment when they buy goods or services produced by the company.

9. Answers will be based on students' opinions and experiences.

10. In a democracy, people vote for public servants to represent them. They make their wants known through their elected officials.

Critical Thinking

6. Why does our government want businesses to succeed?

7. How is competition a form of consumer protection?

8. Suppose a business is required by U.S. law to install pollution-control equipment. Who ultimately pays for the cost of the equipment and in what way?

9. Do you think patent protection can lead to monopolies over a patented good? Is that a good or a bad thing?

10. How do people in a democracy acknowledge their social wants so that the government can help satisfy them?

11. Why are many public goods and services being offered through privatization?

12. Are transfer payments good for society? Why or why not?

13. Imagine that you run a coffee shop in an area where there is a military base. The government decides to close the military operation. Will that have an effect on your coffee shop? Explain.

Write About It

14. Attend a city council or county board meeting in your area. Write a one-page article describing what took place. What decisions were made that might affect you and your community? Be sure to include residents' comments.

15. Write a one-page essay discussing whether you believe the federal government looks out for the well-being of all people in the country.

16. Make a list of people in your community who help pay for the cost of public goods and services but do not directly use them. In two or more paragraphs, state why you think it is right for them to contribute to the cost of these services.

17. In two or more paragraphs, discuss your opinion of high taxes on cigarettes.

18. Write a one-page letter to the mayor of your city or town expressing a problem that you would like solved. Indicate why the problem should be addressed.

19. In at least one page, argue for or against the value of government giving tax incentives to business.

Technology Applications

Internet Research

20. Research three laws that the government has created to protect individuals. Include one law in each of the following categories: environmental protection, consumer protection, and employee protection. Investigate the costs and benefits of the laws to citizens as well as their effects on business. Prepare a presentation about the role of the legal system in business and how these laws impact society.

Business Ethics

Should You "Bid" This Project Farewell?

21. Suppose you own a small business that makes nuts and bolts for machines. You would like to compete for a bid to make nuts and bolts for the U.S. military. You could submit a low bid to beat your competitors' proposals. However, you know that your costs will be higher than what is shown on your bid. Is this ethical? Explain your answer.

Critical Thinking

11. Items can be provided at lower costs and some projects are too large for governments to handle.

12. They provide income for people when they need it.

13. It will probably have a negative affect on the business.

Write About It

14. Students should discuss the role local government plays in society.

15. Some people, especially the poor, are not well represented in government.

16. People who do not have children often pay taxes for public schools.

17. Pro: High taxes discourage people from smoking. Con: Other unhealthful habits are not taxed in the same manner.

18. Students should indicate how government can address the issue through its goods and services.

19. Students may agree that tax incentives help businesses to succeed, which can mean more jobs and revenues for their community. Other students may say that businesses can compete without them.

Technology Applications

20. Answers will vary. For example, the Clean Air Act reduces smog and pollution, which helps the environment. The Humphrey-Hawkins Full Employment Act protects employees by prohibiting discrimination of employees on the basis of gender, religion, race, age, and national origin.

Business Ethics

21. No. It is unfair to the parties involved—the U.S. military, your competitors, and your company, whose employees would be affected by the large work order.

Applying Academics to Business

22. *Mono-* means one or single, and *oligo-* means small or a few. Other words are monochromatic and oligarchy.

Inter- means between or among, and *intra-* means within. Other words are intercom and intramural.

23. One way is to calculate the total cost at each location and then subtract to find the difference. Or you could just multiply $12 by .25%, or 0.0025. The CD will cost 3 cents less in the new city.

24. *Trade dress* refers to the appearance of a product or its packaging. A *trade secret* is a formula, practice, process, design, instrument, pattern, or compilation of information used by a business to obtain an advantage over competitors.

25. Converting 60 cm × 90 cm to feet, you find that the pieces need to be just under 2 ft × 3 ft. You can get 5 pieces per sheet, or 5 sheets to fill the customer's order.

Active Learning

26. Answers will depend on the school's student government.

Business in the Real World

27. Answers will vary depending on the business owner or manager who is interviewed.

Applying Academics to Business

English Language Arts
22. Use a dictionary or other resource to find out more about the prefixes in the following word pairs. Write a phrase or sentence giving the meanings of the prefixes and list other words that use them.

*mono*poly   *oligo*poly
*inter*state   *intra*state

Mathematics
23. You recently moved to a city with a lower sales tax. The sales tax where you used to live was 5.75%, and the new tax rate is a quarter percent less. Explain two different ways you could calculate how much less you would pay for a $12 CD in your new city than your old, and then solve the problem.

THEORY **Percents** A percent is a ratio that compares a number to 100. A percent can be converted to a decimal by dividing the percent number by 100.

English Language Arts
24. Copyrights, patents, and trademarks protect creative properties. This legal protection extends to *trade dress* and *trade secrets*. Research the meanings of these terms, and write a sentence or two explaining each.

Mathematics
25. You work for a lumber yard and a customer orders 25 pieces of plywood cut to 60 cm × 90 cm. You must cut them from larger sheets that measure 4 ft. by 8 ft. What is the fewest number of sheets of plywood you need to fill the customer's order?

THEORY **Geometry and Measurement** You can convert metric and U.S. customary measurements using tables found in math books, reference books, and other online resources. For example, use the formulas 1 in. = 2.54 cm, and 12 in. = 1 ft. Then use the problem-solving strategy "draw a diagram" to solve the problem.

Active Learning

Analyze Student Government
26. Write a report about your school's student government. What is its role in the school? How are officials chosen? How does your school's government look out for students' common welfare? What kind of rules and regulations does it enact, and how are they enforced? How is the government funded? How are spending decisions made?

Business in the Real World

Workplace Safety
27. Form a group and choose a local business owner or manager to interview. Ask how he or she works to avoid work-related accidents. Which rules regarding job safety apply most in this type of business? Compare your findings with those of other groups. Then as a class, list the safety rules that were discussed.

ExamView Assessment Suite CD allows you to print out ready-made unit and chapter tests, complete with answer keys. You can also create customized tests.

TeacherWorks Plus provides complete teacher resources in one convenient package. It includes customizable lesson plans in calendar format, and instant access to many print program resources.

Real LIFE skills

DEVELOPING SKILLS IN BUSINESS LAW

28. Interview someone involved in the legal field. Possible contacts include lawyers, judges, legal assistants, teachers, or job counselors. Ask the professional about career opportunities in business law. What kinds of skills are important in this field? How can you develop them? Write a report of at least one page. Share your findings with the class.

Business CAREERS

FIND YOUR DREAM JOB

29. Go to the *Introduction to Business* Online Learning Center through **glencoe.com** for a link to the Occupational Outlook Handbook Web site. Click on the "OOH Search/A-Z Index" link and enter the job category of "state and local government, excluding education and hospitals." Then write a one-page report about this area of occupation. Conclude your report with a list of things you could do now to prepare yourself to pursue this occupation.

Role Play

A CASE FOR OR AGAINST PUBLIC GOODS OR SERVICES

30. **Situation** Imagine that you are a lawyer who is asked to justify a position on a public good or service to the mayor.

    Activity Choose an existing public good or service in your community. Prepare an argument explaining why it should either continue to be provided as a public good or service or should instead be provided by the private sector.

    Evaluation You will be evaluated on how well you meet the following performance indicators:

    - Demonstrate an understanding of the difference between private and public goods and services.
    - Give reasons why the good or service should be provided in the public or private sector.
    - Deliver your presentation in a logical sequence.
    - Use correct grammar and project your voice.

Real LIFE skills

28. Answers will depend on the contact's role in the legal field, the type of law practiced, and what the interviewee says.

Business CAREERS

29. State and local government employees provide constituents with vital services. Working conditions, training, and qualifications vary depending on the occupation. Opportunities for advancement vary by occupation and jurisdiction, some based on seniority, job performance, and examination results. The job outlook is expected to be slow. As preparation, take social studies classes in history, government, and economics and prepare for the civil service examination.

Role Play

30. Presentations should address the competencies noted in the Role Play. Answers will vary, depending on the stance that students take. For instance, students could argue that a public good such as police service is vital for the safety of society. It should remain a public service because the expense is too great for the private sector.

Standardized Test Practice
1. D

Standardized Test Practice

Directions Choose the letter of the best answer. Write the letter for the answer on a separate piece of paper.

1. **Which word is spelled correctly and completes the sentence?**

   A Supreme Court decision about antitrust laws set an important _____.

   A president
   B presedent
   C precedant
   D precedent

 TEST-TAKING TIP Taking tests can be stressful. Stay relaxed. If you begin to get nervous, take a few deep breaths slowly to relax yourself. Then get back to work.

 READING Go to the *Introduction to Business* Online Learning Center through **glencoe.com** for a list of outside reading suggestions.

 **STRATEGIES FOR STANDARDIZED TEST PREP SUCCESS**

Test Stress Remind students that the kind of stress they will experience when taking standardized tests can have real physical manifestations. Depending on the severity of their reaction, they may sweat, breathe harder, experience confusion or lack of ability to concentrate. Explain that stress is normal, and properly managed, stress can actually help them do better. One of the keys is to focus and answer one question at a time. If they find their minds wandering, they should break the cycle by looking up, breathing deeply, and then refocusing on the task at hand.

Standards-Based Lesson Planning
Introduction to Business provides students with instruction and assessment in the following fundamental content areas:

Content Standards Correlations	
Explain the importance of banking among government, business, and the consumer.	pp. 197–200, 202–205, 206–207
Research and present major financial issues for the individual, for example, money management, banking system and services, saving and investing.	pp. 197–200, 202–205, 206–207
Examine banking services.	pp. 197–200, 202–205, 206–207
Compare and contrast types of banking services.	pp. 197–200, 202–205, 207
Evaluate ways that commercial banks can assist consumers with money management.	p. 200
Explain how agencies that regulate financial markets protect investors.	pp. 204–205, 206–207
Discuss technological advances and their impact on the banking industry.	p. 205
Evaluates the characteristics and costs of checking accounts and other payment methods offered by banks and credit unions.	pp. 197–200, 202–205, 207
Evaluates bank investment opportunities, such as savings accounts, money market accounts, and trusts.	pp. 202–205, 207

NCLB
Activities, information, and skills practice will help your students attain No Child Left Behind proficiency. Students will improve their abilities in the following academic standards areas:

Academic Standards Correlations		
English Language Arts	**Activities/Features**	**Page**
NCTE 3 Apply strategies to interpret texts	After You Read	p. 205
NCTE 6 Apply knowledge of language structure and conventions to discuss texts	Applying Academics to Business Standardized Test Practice	pp. 208, 209
NCTE 7 Conduct research and gather, evaluate, and synthesize data to communicate discoveries.	After You Read	p. 205
NCTE 8 Use information resources to gather information and create and communicate knowledge	Applying Academics to Business	p. 208
Mathematics		
Data Analysis and Probability Select and use appropriate methods to analyze data	Ask S&P	p. 194
Measurement Understand measurable attributes of objects and the units, systems, and processes of measurement	After You Read	p. 200
Number and Operations Understand the meanings of operations and how they relate to one another	Applying Academics to Business	p. 208
Number and Operations Compute fluently and make reasonable estimates	Applying Academics to Business	p. 208
Science		
Content Standard F Students should develop an understanding of science and technology in local, national, and global challenges	Science/Tech Trends	p. 202

Correlations   This chart shows the 21st Century Skills, foundation skills, and workplace competencies that students develop as they work in this chapter.

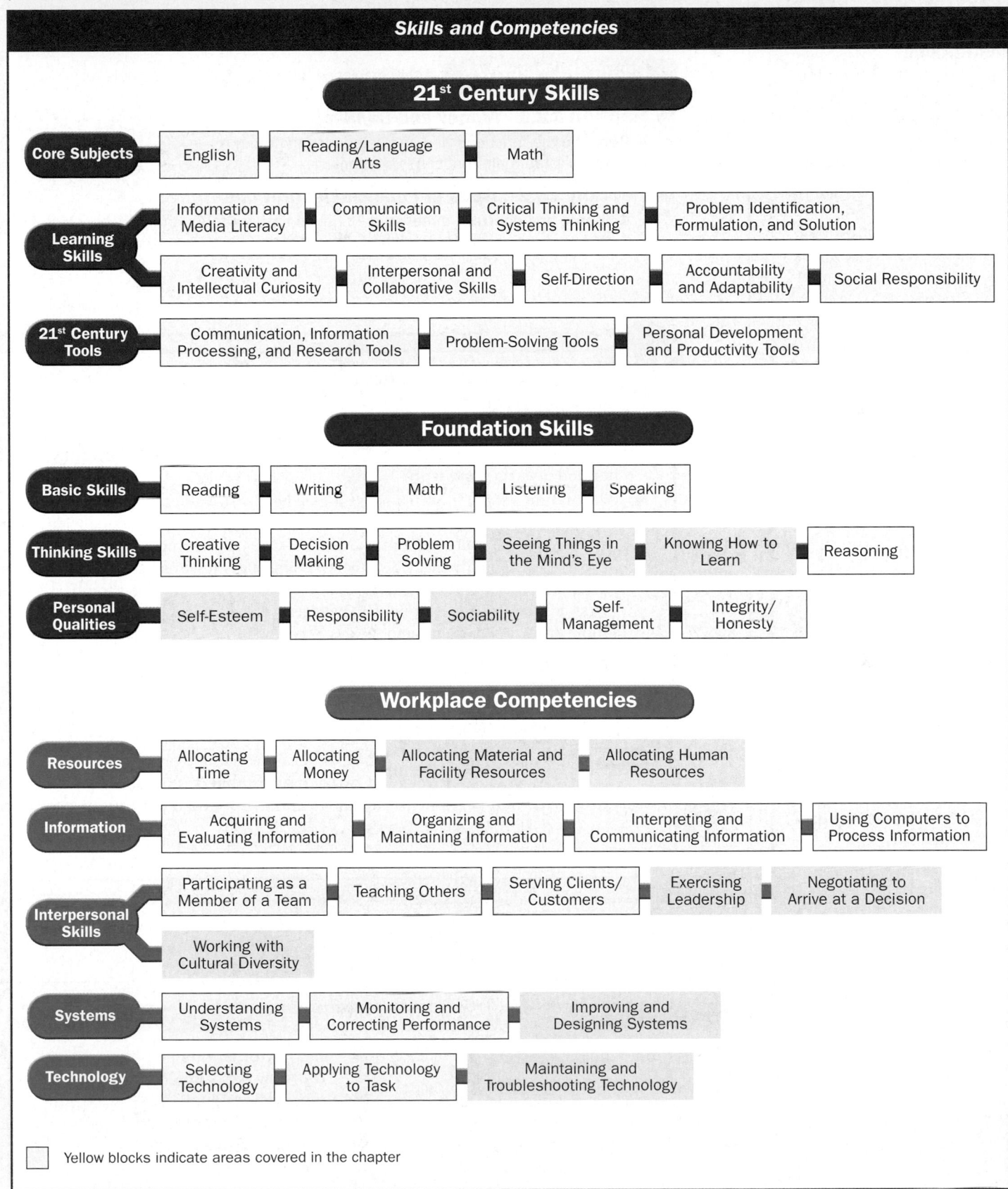

Skills and Competencies

21st Century Skills

Core Subjects
- English
- Reading/Language Arts
- Math

Learning Skills
- Information and Media Literacy
- Communication Skills
- Critical Thinking and Systems Thinking
- Problem Identification, Formulation, and Solution
- Creativity and Intellectual Curiosity
- Interpersonal and Collaborative Skills
- Self-Direction
- Accountability and Adaptability
- Social Responsibility

21st Century Tools
- Communication, Information Processing, and Research Tools
- Problem-Solving Tools
- Personal Development and Productivity Tools

Foundation Skills

Basic Skills
- Reading
- Writing
- Math
- Listening
- Speaking

Thinking Skills
- Creative Thinking
- Decision Making
- Problem Solving
- Seeing Things in the Mind's Eye
- Knowing How to Learn
- Reasoning

Personal Qualities
- Self-Esteem
- Responsibility
- Sociability
- Self-Management
- Integrity/Honesly

Workplace Competencies

Resources
- Allocating Time
- Allocating Money
- Allocating Material and Facility Resources
- Allocating Human Resources

Information
- Acquiring and Evaluating Information
- Organizing and Maintaining Information
- Interpreting and Communicating Information
- Using Computers to Process Information

Interpersonal Skills
- Participating as a Member of a Team
- Teaching Others
- Serving Clients/Customers
- Exercising Leadership
- Negotiating to Arrive at a Decision
- Working with Cultural Diversity

Systems
- Understanding Systems
- Monitoring and Correcting Performance
- Improving and Designing Systems

Technology
- Selecting Technology
- Applying Technology to Task
- Maintaining and Troubleshooting Technology

☐ Yellow blocks indicate areas covered in the chapter

Chapter 12

Chapter Overview

Introduce the Chapter

Money and Financial Institutions
Chapter 12 describes the functions and characteristics of money and banks.

Building Background
Understanding how money and financial institutions fit into the economy and individual lives will help students become more financially responsible.

Ask STANDARD &POOR'S

›› Math Answer
Average price of Cynthia's stocks on the first day: $13.59; the second day: $13.04

13.58 − 13.042 = .547

Average decrease: .547

Emphasize that comparing a few stocks does not really give analysts enough statistical information.

›› Extension Activity
Have students calculate the following average:

Derek's work schedule varied on his last six weekly paychecks: July 2, 25 hours; July 9, 17 hours; July 16, 29 hours; July 23, 19 hours; July 30, 22 hours; August 6, 14 hours. On average, how many hours per week did Derek work? (21 hours per week. Add all the hours together and divide by the number of weeks: 126 ÷ 6 = 21.)

N C L B Activity correlates to Math standards.

Money and Financial Institutions

Chapter Objectives After completing this chapter, you will be able to:

▶ **Section 12.1** *Money and Banking*
- **Describe** the functions and characteristics of money.
- **Discuss** three main functions of a bank.

▶ **Section 12.2** *Types of Financial Institutions*
- **Compare and contrast** three types of banks that are found in our economy.
- **Explain** the major functions of the Federal Reserve System in the U.S. economy.

Ask STANDARD &POOR'S **Statistical Analysis**

Q: What are statistics, and how do they help analysts predict which investments will be good over the long term?

A: One minute a stock is up. The next it may be down. Values can fluctuate from day to day and minute to minute. Financial analysts must consider a wide variety of data every day to forecast market trends. One of their most powerful tools is a branch of mathematics called statistics. Using statistics, analysts use powerful computers to "crunch" numbers. The results allow analysts to predict trends. One way stocks are evaluated uses weighted averages to compare companies. You can use a simple averaging technique to see one way statistics help analysts.

Mathematics Cynthia picked five stocks yesterday. Their closing prices were $17.09, $13.80, $2.81, $26.16, and $8.08. Today their closing prices, respectively, are $17.22, $13.93, $2.84, $23.43, and $7.79. Average the values for each day, and compare them for a broader view of what is happening in the overall market.

THEORY **Average (Mean):** The average, or mean, is a single number used to represent a group of numbers. The average of two or more numbers is the sum of the numbers divided by the number of items added. The formula for each day's mean stock price is:

$$\frac{\text{Stock}_1 + \text{Stock}_2 + \text{Stock}_3 + \text{Stock}_4 + \text{Stock}_5}{5}$$

N C L B

Classroom Resources

- Student Edition
- Teacher Wraparound Edition
- Student Activity Workbook with Academic Integration
- Student Activity Workbook with Academic Integration TAE
- *Fast File*, Unit 3 Resources
- Inclusion in the Business Education Classroom

- TeacherWorks Plus
- *ExamView Assessment Suite*
- Presentation Plus!
- Vocabulary PuzzleMaker
- Interactive Student Edition
- Online Student Edition
- Online Learning Center with Podcasts

● **Financial Institutions** Banks are intermediaries that help with the flow of money between borrowers and lenders. **What other financial institutions serve as intermediaries between lenders and borrowers?**

Chapter 12 Money and Financial Institutions **195**

Review the Objectives
Introduce the chapter by reviewing the chapter objectives:

Section 12.1 *Objectives*
Describe the functions and characteristics of money. (Money functions as a medium of exchange and is accepted by people in exchange for goods and services. It also functions as a standard of value and is used to place a value on goods and services. It functions as a store of value. That means it holds its value after time and can be stored or saved.)

Discuss three main functions of a bank. (Banks provide a safe place to put money. They transfer money from one bank to another and lend money to businesses and people.)

Section 12.2 *Objectives*
Compare and contrast three types of banks that are found in our economy. (Commercial banks, savings and loans, and credit unions are all full-service. They all offer most of the same products and services. Commercial banks and savings and loans make a profit. Credit unions are non-profits for members only.)

Explain the major functions of the Federal Reserve System in the U.S. economy. (The Federal Reserve System clears checks, acts as the federal government's fiscal agent, supervises member banks, regulates the money supply, sets the reserve requirements for banks, and supplies paper currency.)

Discuss the Photo
● **Financial Institutions** Read the caption on the photo to students: Banks are intermediaries that help with the flow of money between borrowers and lenders.

Ask students: What other financial institutions serve as intermediaries between lenders and borrowers? (Savings and loans, credit unions, mortgage and finance companies, insurance companies, and brokerage firms.)

195

FOCUS

Bell Ringer Activity

Money and Banking
Ask students to make a list of things they paid for the past week. Ask students: If money did not exist, how would you pay for these? How would you compare the costs of different products?
(Answers will vary.)

Preteaching

Presentation Plus!
The Presentation Plus! CD provides visual teaching aids for this section.

PuzzleMaker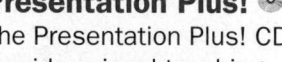
Use the Vocabulary PuzzleMaker to create a puzzle of the section's key terms. Students can complete the puzzle on paper or on a computer.

Graphic Organizer
Tell students to go to the Online Learning Center through **glencoe.com** for a printable graphic organizer. (Medium of exchange: anything accepted as a measure of value in a particular country or region. Standard of value: fixed means for measuring weight, amount, size, or value of something. Store of value: holds its value over time and can be stored.)

 Connects academics to content.

Money and Banking

Reading Guide

● Before You Read
Think about how bartering, or trading goods or services, might work in your life.

Read to Learn
• Describe the functions and characteristics of money.
• Discuss three main functions of a bank.

The Main Idea
Money functions as a standard of value, a medium of exchange or payment, and a store of value. Most countries create and circulate their own money. Banks are in the business of handling money.

Key Concepts
• The Purpose of Money
• The Functions of Banks

Vocabulary
Key Terms
money
monetary system
financial institution
bank account
deposit
withdrawal
interest

electronic funds transfer (EFT)
direct deposit
collateral
mortgage
safe-deposit box

Academic Vocabulary
You will find these words in your reading and on your tests. Make sure you know their meanings.
acquire   primary
stable   secure

Graphic Organizer
As you read, write notes about the functions of money in a box like the one below.

The Functions of Money	
Medium of Exchange	
Standard of Value	
Store of Value	

 Go to the *Introduction to Business* Online Learning Center through **glencoe.com** for a printable graphic organizer.

Academic Standards
English Language Arts
NCTE 1 Read texts to acquire new information
NCTE 9 Develop an understanding of diversity in language use across cultures
Mathematics
Measurement Understand measurable attributes of objects and the units, systems, and processes of measurement

Reading Guide

● Before You Read
Bartering could work well between two people who have things to swap, but it is difficult to barter for all wants and needs.

D Develop Concepts
The Main Idea Ask students: How might your dealings with a bank expand or change in the future? (Some students might have checking accounts or debit cards. They may plan to get a car loan or borrow money for college.)

The Purpose of Money

Money enables people and businesses to buy and sell goods and services more easily around the world. **Money** is a standard of value and a means of exchange or payment. It can be anything that people accept as a standard for payment. In the past, people used shells, stones, corn, parrot feathers, and even gopher tails for money. Modern society uses coins, currency, checks, and debit cards as part of the **monetary system**. Goods and services are directly exchanged using money. The seller of the goods or services can then take the money and exchange it for other goods and services.

✔ **Reading Check** **Identify** What kinds of money does modern society use?

The Functions of Money

Whether you buy a soda or sell a corporation, money changes hands. Without money, people would be forced to *barter*, or trade goods or services directly for other goods or services. Bartering can be a difficult method of exchange. Suppose you have grown a bushel of tomatoes. You would like to trade the tomatoes for new sneakers. In the barter system, you would have to find someone willing to accept tomatoes for sneakers. You would also have a hard time figuring out the value of the sneakers in relation to the tomatoes. You might have to make several trades to **acquire** something the sneaker owner would accept.

Money has three basic functions:

• It is a *medium of exchange*. A medium of exchange is anything that is generally accepted as a measure of value and of wealth. In a system that uses money, buyers and sellers agree to exchange money.

Real World

The Barter System
The barter system is still used in some business situations. More than 100,000 businesses have been involved in bartering, according to the Illinois Trade Association, a national trade group. Major corporations that barter include Xerox®, Mattel®, IBM®, Chrysler, and General Electric. *Do you know of any businesses or people who barter their goods or services?*

● **What Is Money?**
Money is most commonly considered to be coins, currency, and checking accounts. **What are some other ways that people and businesses can pay for goods and services?**

Section 12.1 Money and Banking 197

Discuss the Photo
● **What Is Money?** In addition to using cash, people and businesses can pay for goods and services by using checks, credit cards, and debit cards. Students can also barter for goods and services, or they can pay with credit or an IOU. Of course, these latter methods of payment are really only ways to postpone payment with money.

Section 12.1

TEACH

Discussion Starter
The Purpose of Money
Hold up a five-dollar bill and ask students this question: What can you do with this? (Answers will vary. Students might suggest specific items such as a dozen doughnuts at a local bakery, gasoline, a greeting card, or lunch.)

R **Reading Strategy**

Make an Outline Ask students to make an outline of the paragraph under the title, "The Purpose of Money." (Outlines will vary but should focus on the following points: used to buy goods and services; is a standard of value and means of exchange or payment; it can be anything people accept as a standard of payment; modern society uses set items—coins, currency, checks, debit cards—as part of the monetary system; seller can take the money and exchange it for other goods and services.)

✔ **Reading Check**

Identify Modern society uses coins, currency, checks, and debit cards.

The Barter System
Students may tell about exchange programs, through which people trade homes for vacations, for example. They may talk about personal bartering they have done, such as trading babysitting services for tutoring.

TEACH

S Skill Practice

Guided Practice

List Have students make a list of the characteristics of money. (It must be stable, scarce, accepted, divisible, portable, and durable.) **L1**

Make a Table Have students make a two-column table of the characteristics of money, using the first column for the characteristics and the second column for an explanation. (Students should include the six characteristics and a brief explanation of each.) **L2**

Produce a Skit Have students work in groups of six to write, rehearse, and perform a skit about the characteristics of money. (Skits should demonstrate an understanding of the concept.) **L3**

ASSESS

Review Key Terms

Have students write sentences using each key term.

 **Study-to-Go** Have students go to the Online Learning Center through **glencoe.com** to download free **Study-to-Go** content to their PDAs or cell phones.

✔ Reading Check

Explain It must be stable in value, accepted, divisible, portable, and durable.

International Business

Investment Banking
Investment banks are not like other types of banks. The investment banker's job is to help businesses and governments issue securities, and find the capital they need to grow. They also help investors purchase and trade securities, manage financial assets, and provide financial advice. Some investment banks operate regionally or specialize in a particular industry. Big investment banks have offices all over the world. Investment banking is an exciting, fast-paced environment, and thousands of college students look to enter this field each year.

Examples of Languages Across Cultures

Q: In Greek, how do you say: "How much does that cost?"

A: Πόσο κάνει;
(pronounced: Pō-sō kă-nēē?)

What are some skills and talents an investment bank would look for when hiring a recent graduate?

● As You Read

Think about what would happen if your money had little or no value in your country. What would you use as a medium of exchange?

- Money functions as a *standard of value*. A standard is a way to measure the weight, amount, size, or value of something. Money provides a means of measuring the value of goods and services.
- Money functions as a *store of value*. That means it holds its value over time and can be stored or saved. Money that is saved can build wealth.

Characteristics of Money

Paper money and coins are common forms of money. For money to carry out its functions, it must have these characteristics. Money must be *stable* in value. Money that is **stable** has little if any change in value. To be used as money, an item must be *scarce*. If the supply of an item is overly plentiful, it loses its value and cannot serve as money or a store of value since it would have little worth. People would lose faith in its value as a medium of exchange.

Money must be *accepted*. People have to be willing to take money in exchange for goods and services. It should be *divisible* into parts. Money also has to be *portable* and *durable*. Finally, it must be hard to counterfeit. To *counterfeit* means to make a copy of something in order to defraud or deceive people.

S

✔ Reading Check

Explain What are the characteristics of money?

The Functions of Banks

A **financial institution** is a firm that manages money. Banks are the main types of financial institutions. Banks offer a variety of financial services. They help other businesses and consumers manage their money. **Figure 12.1** shows how banks and customers interact.

Storing Money

One of the main services banks provide is storing money in bank accounts. To *store* money means to place or leave it for preservation or later use. A **bank account** is a record of the amount of money a customer has deposited into or withdrawn from a bank. The money put in a bank account is called a **deposit**. The money taken out is called a **withdrawal**. Keeping your money in a bank prevents you from losing it, spending it, or having it stolen easily.

198 **Chapter 12** Money and Financial Institutions

International Business

Investment Banking Students should identify that investment banks are looking for top-notch students with excellent grades, superior communications skills including foreign languages, and an understanding of finance.

● As You Read

Answers will vary. Students may explain that they would be unable to buy even basic food or shelter. They may try bartering. Some might try to introduce their own currency.

The two main types of bank accounts are checking accounts and savings accounts. Checking accounts are used for storing money in the short term. Banks usually charge a fee for checking accounts. Savings accounts are used for storing money over a longer period of time. An advantage of a savings account is that it earns more interest than most checking accounts. **Interest** is a rate that the bank pays customers for keeping their money.

● **As You Read**

Think about some ways you protect your money. Do you believe that having your money in a bank is the best way to keep from spending it?

Transferring Money

Banks use checks and electronic funds transfers to move money. Checks are primarily used to transfer money from one party to another. **Electronic funds transfer (EFT)** allows money to be transferred from one bank account to another through a network of computers. **Direct deposit** is the electronic transfer of a payment directly from the payer's bank account to that of the party being paid. Many employers issue payroll checks this way.

Lending Money

Lending money is the **primary** way banks generate profits. The money you deposit in a bank makes it possible for the bank to lend money to other customers. Just as banks pay customers interest on their savings, customers pay interest on the money they borrow from banks. Banks then use the interest they earned to pay interest on customers' savings accounts. Most bank loans require some form of collateral. **Collateral** is property or goods pledged by a borrower to use as security against a loan if it is not repaid.

Figure 12.1 — **The Business of Banks**

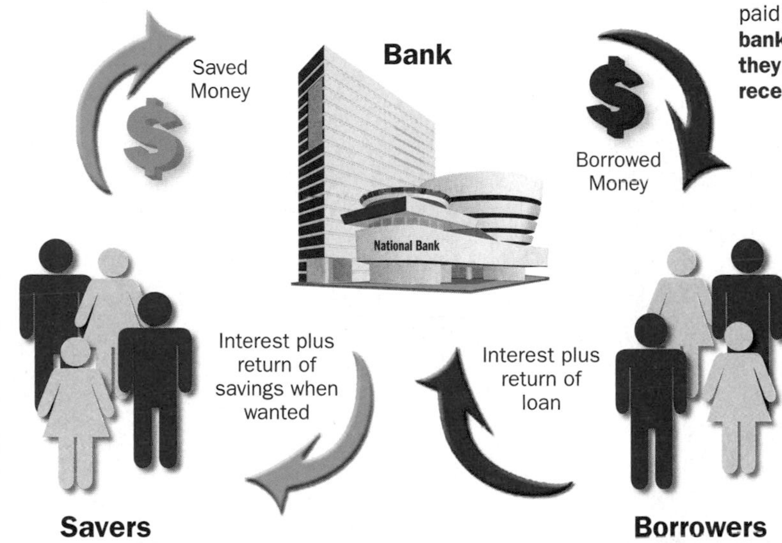

● **How Banks Profit**
Banks pay interest and are paid interest. **Explain how banks can make money if they both pay interest and receive interest.**

Bank

Saved Money

Borrowed Money

Interest plus return of savings when wanted

Interest plus return of loan

Savers

Borrowers

National Bank

● **As You Read**

Answers will vary. Students may feel that they can easily write checks or use credit cards, or that they can save their money in other ways.

Figure 12.1

● **How Banks Profit** Banks make a profit because the interest received is greater than the interest they pay.

RETEACH

W Writing Support
Quoting
Types of Bank Accounts
Have students interview a local bank officer about the types of bank accounts that are available and write a magazine article based on their interview. (Articles should mention both savings and checking accounts and should address the differences between the accounts.)

R Reading Strategy
Outline Have students create an outline for the content under the heading "Transferring Money." (Outlines will vary, but should reflect the content of this page.)

U Universal Access
Tactile Learners Pass out brochures from a local bank that explain the basics of loans. Ask students to read the information and ask questions about what they have read. Allow students to keep the brochures.

Student Activity Workbook 📂 Assign the Section 12.1 Activities.

Virtual Business
Introduce promotion to students using the Virtual Business Retailing Promotion activity. In this simulation, students learn why promotion is important to the success of a business.

C Critical Thinking

Write an Abstract

Types of Loans Have students read a recent article related to types of loans and write an abstract of the article. Point out that an abstract usually includes a complete reference citation and a brief description of the article. (Abstracts should provide enough information about types of loans.)

As You Read

Some students may not want to risk losing their collateral. Others may feel that, if the loan is for something worthwhile, it is worth the risk.

ASSESS

After You Read

Have students complete the Section 12.1 After You Read section review.

Online Study Tools

Have students go to the Online Learning Center through **glencoe.com** to:

- Take the Section 12.1 **Practice Test**.
- Download free **Study-to-Go** content to their PDAs or cell phones.

CLOSE

Culminating Activity

Take a Virtual Tour

Have students visit the Web site of a local bank, print a copy of the bank's home page, and add annotations about the main links. (Annotations should be logical.)

200

As You Read

Think about whether you would be willing to use your collateral to borrow money.

There are four main types of loans that banks offer to businesses and individuals:

- A *mortgage loan* is a loan used to buy real estate, such as a house or an office building. A **mortgage** is an agreement in which a borrower gives a lender the right to take the property if the loan is not repaid.
- A *commercial loan* is a loan made to businesses to buy supplies and equipment.
- An *individual loan* is a loan made to an individual to pay for personal items, such as a car, home repairs, or a vacation.
- A *line of credit* is a credit arrangement in which a financial institution agrees to lend a specific amount of money to be used at any time for any purpose.

Other Financial Services

Banks also offer other services. Many provide financial advice on managing and investing money. Banks not only store money, they can also store valuable items, such as jewelry and birth certificates, in a safe-deposit box. A **safe-deposit box** is a **secure** box in a bank's vault used for the safe storage of a customer's valuables. As another service, many banks offer debit cards and credit cards, such as MasterCard® or Visa®. Banks also have trust departments that manage money for individuals and organizations.

NCLB Activity correlates to Math standards.

Section 12.1

After You Read

Review Key Concepts
1. What is a major advantage of using money over bartering in buying goods and services?
2. What are at least five characteristics that money must have?
3. What are four types of loans that a bank makes?

Academic Skills

NCLB

4. **Mathematics** Imagine that the U.S. Mint has issued a new coin that is worth $1 and weighs 0.5 ounce. Find the total weight of the new coins you would need to purchase the following items with cash. Express the weights using the most appropriate unit: a pizza for $16, a new sports car for $32,000, and a new condo for $96,000.

THEORY Weights and Measures
Choosing the best unit of measure to express a quantity can help you avoid excessively large numbers.

 For math help, go to the Math Appendix.

Go to the *Introduction to Business* Online Learning Center through **glencoe.com** to check your answers.

Section 12.1

Review Key Concepts
1. Money makes buying and selling goods and services easier.
2. All money shares these characteristics: stable, scarce, acceptable, divisible, portable, and hard to counterfeit.
3. Four types of bank loans are mortgage loans, commercial loans, individual loans, and lines of credit.

Academic Skills
4. **Mathematics** You would need 16 coins weighing 8 ounces for a supreme pizza. You would need 32,000 coins weighing 1,000 pounds for the car, and 96,000 coins weighing 1.5 tons for the condo.

Types of Financial Institutions

Reading Guide

● Before You Read

Think about the different banking services you and your family use every day.

Read to Learn
- Compare and contrast three types of banks that are found in our economy.
- Explain the major functions of the Federal Reserve System in the U.S. economy.

The Main Idea
There are three types of institutions that operate as banks. They are commercial banks, savings and loan associations, and credit unions. A Federal Reserve Bank is a banker's bank. The Federal Reserve System manages the banking system and controls the money supply.

Key Concepts
- Financial Institutions
- Functions of the Federal Reserve System

Vocabulary
Key Terms

commercial banks
savings and loan
 associations
credit unions
mortgage companies

finance companies
insurance companies
brokerage firms
Federal Reserve System
reserves

Academic Vocabulary
You will find these words in your reading and on your tests. Make sure you know their meanings.

granted
bonds

monitors
flexible

Graphic Organizer
As you read, write notes about the types of financial organizations on a figure like the one below.

Types of Financial Institutions	
Commercial Bank	
Savings and Loan	
Credit Union	
Mortgage Company	
Finance Company	
Insurance Company	
Brokerage	

 Go to the *Introduction to Business* Online Learning Center through **glencoe.com** for a printable graphic organizer.

Academic Standards
English Language Arts
  NCTE 1 Read texts to acquire new information
  NCTE 3 Apply strategies to interpret texts
  NCTE 4 Use written language to communicate effectively
  NCTE 5 Use different writing process elements to communicate effectively
Science
  Content Standard F Students should develop an understanding of science and technology in local, national, and global challenges

---

Reading Guide

● Before You Read

Students might mention making deposits, paying bills online, writing checks, paying for purchases with a debit card, and withdrawing cash at an ATM.

D Develop Concepts

The Main Idea Ask students: Which financial institutions are likely to be more local in scope? (Credit unions are frequently limited to a single geographic area or local community.)

FOCUS

🔔 Bell Ringer Activity

Types of Financial Institutions
Have students find banks, savings and loans, and credit unions in a local business telephone directory, and make a list of five financial institutions for each. (In some communities listings are limited.)

Preteaching

Presentation Plus!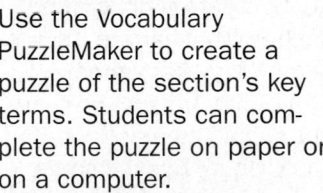
The Presentation Plus! CD provides visual teaching aids for this section.

PuzzleMaker ⊙
Use the Vocabulary PuzzleMaker to create a puzzle of the section's key terms. Students can complete the puzzle on paper or on a computer.

Graphic Organizer
Tell students to go to the Online Learning Center through **glencoe.com** for a printable graphic organizer. (Commercial banks offer entire range of banking services; savings and loan associations offer interest-bearing accounts; credit unions are members only not-for-profit organizations; mortgage companies provide home or business loans; finance companies offer higher-rate short-term loans; insurance companies offer business and consumer loans; brokerage firms offer a variety of services.)

N C L B Connects academics to content.

201

TEACH

Discussion Starter
Financial Institutions
Ask students what types of financial services they think a business owner might need. (Answers will vary. Students might suggest some of the following: a loan to start a business, a checking account to deposit revenue and to pay for goods and services needed to operate the business including paying employees, banking services needed to process credit cards, and insurance.)

 Reading Strategy

Illustrate an Idea Have students create a drawing or diagram to illustrate the way commercial banks make a profit. (Illustrations will vary but should clearly show that commercial banks charge more interest on the money they lend than the interest they pay.)

✔ Reading Check

Explain Banks have to meet special requirements, apply for a charter from the federal or state government, and have enough capital.

Real World

Universal Banks
Answers will vary. Students may point out that customer demand has required banks to furnish many services, but also may be risky because banks have more defaults and losses from bad loans.

Real World

Universal Banks
Universal banks, also known as financial services companies, are diversified businesses involved in both retail banking and investment banking. For example, Citigroup®, a major U.S. bank, is involved in commercial and retail lending, business banking, investment banking, and private banking. *Do you think universal banking is a good business practice for large banks?*

Financial Institutions

Banks operate on state, national, and international levels. There are strict rules for starting one because banks handle large amounts of money. To open a federal or a state bank in the United States, the owners have to meet special requirements. They must also apply for a charter from the federal or state government. The owners need to prove they have enough capital to start a bank. In the United States, there are three main types of banks. They are commercial banks, savings and loan associations, and credit unions.

✔ Reading Check **Explain** What are some of the rules for starting a bank?

Commercial Banks

Most of the banks in the United States are commercial banks. **Commercial banks** offer the entire range of banking services, such as checking and savings accounts, loans, and financial advice. They are often called *full-service banks*. Commercial banks serve individuals and businesses. They are authorized to conduct business through a charter, or license, that is **granted** by either the federal government or a state government. To make a profit, commercial banks charge more interest on the money that they lend than the interest they pay on savings accounts.

Science/Tech TRENDS

Digital Cash

Star Trek fans may recall that members of the Federation abolished money a long time ago. Perhaps they were able to create a moneyless society because they had invented a replicator machine that allowed them to make copies of everything from food to cars to clothing and homes. That is not possible in our world, but some communities are experimenting with digital cash to replace bills and coins. For example, New Haven, Connecticut, became one of the first cities to use the new "smart card" payment system for parking and retail. The card can be bought and loaded with $100, used to pay for parking meter fees, lattes at a coffee shop, and books at bookstores. When the value on the card runs low, it can be refilled.

Web Quest

Go to the *Introduction to Business* Online Learning Center through **glencoe.com** for links to Web sites where you can find out more about smart card technology. How do smart cards work? Where are they being used? What are the advantages and disadvantages of using them?

NCLB Activity correlates to Science standards.

Science/Tech TRENDS

Web Quest

Digital Cash Smart cards contain a microprocessor, which enhances security. Smart cards are popular in Europe but are just starting to take off in the United States. Concerns about the security of information on a smart card are the most frequently cited cons.

Savings and Loan Associations

Savings and loan associations are financial institutions that hold customers' funds in interest-bearing accounts and invest mainly in mortgage loans. Savings and loans were originally set up to offer savings accounts and home mortgage loans. Their purpose was to encourage people to save money and make it easier to buy a home or start a business. To do this, they charged lower interest rates on loans and paid higher interest on savings accounts than banks.

In 1982, the government passed new regulations allowing them to charge higher interest rates and offer more services. In the late 1980s, about 20 percent of savings and loan associations failed. In response, new regulations were passed. The services offered by savings and loan associations today are very similar to the services offered by commercial banks and credit unions.

> ✓ **Reading Check** **Define** What is a savings and loan association?

BusinessWeek *Reader and Case Study*

Peter Kight's Excellent Adventure

How an ex-jock changed the way the world pays its bills, while he toiled in a basement in Columbus, Ohio

If anyone can claim to be the pioneer of electronic bill payment, it's Peter Kight. The former college decathlete was managing a handful of health clubs in Texas in the late 1970s when he saw firsthand how hard it was for gyms like his to collect monthly dues from members. So Kight convinced the gym's owner to buy a small IBM computer, then he devised a way for a local bank to deduct the monthly dues from each member's account—and history was made.

In the early 1980s, Kight moved back to his hometown Columbus, Ohio, set up shop in his grandmother's basement, and began building a business devoted to handling payments from consumers electronically.

Fast forward to the present: Kight's Atlanta-based company, CheckFree®, now handles more than half of all electronic payments, generating more than $700 million in revenues.

glencoe.com

 CASE STUDY Go to the *Introduction to Business* Online Learning Center through **glencoe.com** for the *BusinessWeek* Reader Case Study.

Active Learning

CheckFree allows clients to access the money in their bank accounts to pay bills online. One of the advantages of electronic bill-paying is that funds can be transferred instantly. No checks have to clear. Research other bill-paying options. Prepare a spreadsheet listing at least five payment strategies. Make a column for the time required for a single payment to become effective, the cost associated with each transaction, and any associated inconveniences or security concerns. Write an e-mail to your teacher recommending the best options. Attach the spreadsheet to your message.

Section 12.2 Types of Financial Institutions **203**

TEACH (cont.)

S Skill Practice
Guided Practice

Explain Ask students to explain how savings and loan associations are similar to commercial banks. (Commercial banks and savings and loan associations offer similar services.) **L1**

Research Have students identify a savings and loan and find out what lending requirements are. (Loans might be limited to purchases that can be used as collateral. Loans to people with low incomes or poor credit might be limited.) **L2**

Compare Have students research and compare three savings and loans and present their findings in a short oral report. (One might have locations in many states. Another might promote its commitment to the community. A third emphasizes its commitment to its members.) **L3**

ASSESS

Review Key Terms
Have students write sentences using each key term.

STUDY TO GO **Study-to-Go** Have students go to the Online Learning Center through **glencoe.com** to download free **Study-to-Go** content to their PDAs or cell phones.

> ✓ **Reading Check**

Define They are financial institutions that hold customers' funds in interest-bearing accounts and invest mainly in mortgage loans.

RETEACH

W Writing Support

Develop an Argument Have students make a table to show how credit unions are similar to and different from banks. List similarities in the first column and differences in the second column. (Tables will vary but should include the information presented in the textbook.)

R Reading Strategy

Draw Conclusions Have students visit the Federal Reserve System Web site to learn more about the Fed and to draw conclusions about the most important function of the Fed's role as "the banker's bank." (Encourage students to support their conclusions.)

U Universal Access

Visual Learners Have students use the map of the Federal Reserve districts in **Figure 12.2** to locate the district that includes their state. Ask students to discuss some of the things they find on the Web site. (Students will find a variety of information that is similar from one district to another.)

As You Read

Students may discuss the advantage of higher rates that credit unions pay on savings and checking accounts, or as a disadvantage the fact that credit unions do not have many branches.

Student Activity Workbook ✍ Assign the Section 12.2 Activities.

As You Read

Credit unions offer a variety of services to their members. Do you think it would be better for you to open an account at a credit union or a bank?

Credit Unions

Credit unions are not-for-profit banks set up by organizations for their customers to use. Credit union customers are also called members. Credit unions offer members credit cards, checking accounts, low-interest loans, and high interest savings accounts. Many of them also pay interest on checking accounts.

Other Financial Institutions

There are other financial institutions that offer some of the same services as banks. **Mortgage companies** provide loans specifically for buying a home or business. **Finance companies** offer short-term loans to businesses and consumers, but at much higher interest rates than banks charge. **Insurance companies** not only provide protection against problems such as fire and theft, but they also offer loans to businesses and consumers. **Brokerage firms** that sell stocks and **bonds** may also offer a wide range of financial services to their customers.

The Federal Reserve System

The **Federal Reserve System** (or Federal Reserve) is the central bank of the United States. Also known as "The Fed," the Federal Reserve is the banker's bank. It **monitors** the money supply. **Figure 12.2** shows a map of the 12 Federal Reserve Districts.

Figure 12.2 — *The Federal Reserve System*

● **The Federal Reserve System** The Federal Reserve System is based in Washington, D.C., and has 12 districts. **In which Federal Reserve District is your community?**

204 **Chapter 12** Money and Financial Institutions

Figure 12.2

● **The Federal Reserve System** Answers will vary depending on locale. In areas where Federal Reserve System district boundaries are not contiguous with state borders, encourage students to go online to verify their understanding of the district boundaries.

Congress set up the Federal Reserve System in 1913. Its mission is to provide the United States with a safe, flexible, and stable monetary and financial system. The Federal Reserve System consists of 12 regional Federal Reserve Banks and 25 branch banks. It also has about 5,000 member banks. The Federal Reserve is run by the Board of Governors. It supervises the 12 district banks and regulates activity of the member banks. The Federal Reserve has six functions:

1. **Clearing Checks** Funds are transferred from one bank to another when someone writes or deposits a check.
2. **Acting as the Federal Government's Fiscal Agent** The Federal Reserve distributes money to Federal Reserve member banks and commercial banks. It also tracks the deposits and holds a checking account for the U.S. Treasury.
3. **Supervising Member Banks** The Fed regulates banks that are members of the Federal Reserve System.
4. **Regulating the Money Supply** The primary responsibility of the Federal Reserve is to determine the amount of money in circulation and either increase or decrease it.
5. **Setting Reserve Requirements** Member banks must keep a certain percentage of deposits as reserves. **Reserves** are funds set aside for emergencies, such as a rush of withdrawals.
6. **Supplying Paper Currency** The Federal Reserve is responsible for printing and maintaining U.S. paper currency.

The Federal Reserve One of the Federal Reserve's main duties is to monitor the inflation rate. Inflation is a general increase in the cost of goods and services. *When the inflation rate is high, why is it important for the Federal Reserve to take action?*

N C L B Activity correlates to English Language Arts standards.

Section 12.2

After You Read

Review Key Concepts
1. How is a credit union different from a commercial bank?
2. List the seven types of financial institutions discussed in the section.
3. What is the mission of the Federal Reserve?

Academic Skills
4. **English Language Arts** Banks operate on several levels from local to international. We use the word *federal* to describe some banks. Write a definition for the word *federal* and use it in a sentence. List some synonyms and antonyms for *federal*.

5. **English Language Arts** Interview a family member about their experience with banks. Ask them to describe how their experience of banking has changed over the years. Is banking more customer-friendly today? How has technology changed banking? Write a paragraph summarizing your findings.

@ Go to the *Introduction to Business* Online Learning Center through **glencoe.com** to check your answers.

RETEACH (cont.)

C Critical Thinking

Develop a Presentation
Functions of the Federal Reserve Have students create a presentation about the functions of the Federal Reserve, including how the functions affect daily life. (Presentation should include all six functions.)

The Federal Reserve The Federal Reserve usually takes action to help lower the inflation rate to keep costs from rising, allowing businesses and consumers to buy more.

ASSESS

After You Read

Have students complete the Section 12.2 After You Read section review.

Online Study Tools

Have students go to the Online Learning Center through **glencoe.com** to:

- Take the Section 12.2 **Practice Test**.
- Download free **Study-to-Go** content to their PDAs or cell phones.

CLOSE

Culminating Activity
Create a Collage

Have students create a collage for this section, with an image that relates to each heading. (The images should relate to the headings.)

Section 12.2

Review Key Concepts
1. Credit unions are nonprofits. Banks seek profits.
2. commercial banks, savings and loan associations, credit unions, mortgage companies, insurance companies, and brokerage firms
3. It provides a safe, flexible, and stable monetary and financial system.

Academic Skills
4. **English Language Arts** *Federal:* Union of states with a central authority and some powers and responsibilities at the state level. Synonyms: *national, central,* and *nationwide.* Antonyms *state, local,* and *regional.*
5. **English Language Arts** Summaries should describe the changes to banking.

205

Chapter 12 Review and Activities

1. Students should write complete sentences using each term correctly.

Review Key Concepts

2. Money functions as a medium of exchange. It also functions as a standard of value and as a store of value.

3. Banks provide a safe place for people to put their money. They transfer money from one bank to another and lend money to businesses and people.

4. Commercial banks, savings and loans, and credit unions are all full-service banks. They all offer most of the same products and services. However, there are more commercial banks than savings and loans and credit unions. Commercial banks and savings and loans are profit-making businesses. Credit unions are members-only nonprofits.

5. The Fed clears checks, acts as the federal government's fiscal agent, supervises member banks, regulates the money supply, sets the reserve requirements for banks, and supplies paper currency.

Critical Thinking

6. To use depositors' money to make loans at higher rates.

Section 12.1 *Summary*

Money and Banking Money functions as a medium of exchange, a standard of value, and a store of value. It enables people and businesses to buy and sell goods and services more easily. For money to carry out its functions, it must have several characteristics. It must be scarce, acceptable, portable, divisible, durable, and hard to counterfeit. Financial institutions such as banks manage money. They store, transfer, and lend it. The products and services banks offer help other businesses and consumers manage their money.

Section 12.2 *Summary*

Types of Financial Institutions The three main types of banks are commercial banks, savings and loan associations, and credit unions. Mortgage, finance, and insurance companies offer some of the same services as banks. The Federal Reserve is the central bank of the United States. It provides the country with a safe, flexible, and stable monetary and financial system. It consists of 12 regional Federal Reserve Banks, 25 branch banks, and about 5,000 member banks. The Federal Reserve's most important function is regulating the money supply.

Vocabulary Review

1. On a sheet of paper, use each of these key terms and academic vocabulary terms in a sentence.

Key Terms		Academic Vocabulary
money	mortgage	acquire
monetary system	safe-deposit box	stable
financial institution	commercial banks	primary
bank account	savings and loan associations	secure
deposit	credit unions	granted
withdrawal	mortgage companies	bonds
interest	finance companies	monitors
electronic funds transfer (EFT)	insurance companies	flexible
	brokerage firms	
direct deposit	Federal Reserve System	
collateral	reserves	

Review Key Concepts

2. Describe the functions and characteristics of money.

3. Discuss three main functions of a bank.

4. Compare and contrast three types of banks that are found in our economy.

5. Explain the major functions of the Federal Reserve System in the U.S. economy.

206 **Chapter 12** Review and Activities

---

7. Using a credit card involves borrowing money from the credit card company, which must be repaid using money.

8. Coins are more durable and most hold their value longer than paper.

9. There is less money circulating in the economy and fewer goods and services will be purchased.

10. If all depositors requested their deposits at the same time, banks would not have enough currency to cover all the withdrawals. The Fed monitors the money supply and banks by requiring banks to reserve a percentage of their deposits for emergencies.

Critical Thinking

6. Why do you think banks pay interest on deposits left in savings accounts?

7. Credit cards can be used to make purchases. However, credit cards are not considered money. Why do you think this is so?

8. Why do you think coins have been a more desirable form of money than paper currency throughout history?

9. How can the reserve requirement for banks be used to slow the economy's growth?

10. What do you think would happen if all the depositors of a bank requested their deposits at the same time? What is done to keep this from happening?

11. The British pound cannot be used in most U.S. stores to buy goods and services. Why do you think this is so?

12. Loans with collateral generally have a lower interest rate than loans without collateral. Why?

13. Is it unfair to require banks and savings and loans to pay federal income taxes on their income but not credit unions, which do not have to pay taxes because they are nonprofit organizations? Explain your answer.

Write About It

14. Research a bank to see which kinds of trust services are available. Find out how their trust accounts differ from their other accounts. Write a 250-word article about trust services offered by that bank.

15. Visit or contact a bank. Find out about its interest rates and the terms on its checking and savings accounts. Write a report comparing the accounts.

16. How has the Internet affected competition in the area of financial services? Write at least two paragraphs explaining your response.

17. Research the history of U.S. currency. Create a timeline with explanations for the development of money from colonial times to the present.

18. Go online to research the history of counterfeiting. Then write a two-page report on your findings. Include strategies that are being used to combat it.

19. Observe the recent activities or decisions of the Federal Reserve Board. Then write a two-page essay on your findings. Be sure to discuss the effects their decisions have on the economy.

Technology Applications

Access Cards and Digital Cash

20. Although cash and checks are still commonly used, various access cards are becoming more popular. Gift cards are examples of access cards. Digital cash refers to buying goods and services with funds that are transferred from one account to another through computers. Research access cards and digital cash. Write an essay on your findings. Include whether you think cash and checks will soon be outdated.

Business Ethics

Banks as Citizens of the Community

21. When Hurricane Katrina hit Louisiana, it caused a break in the levee system. Most of New Orleans was flooded. The coasts of Mississippi and Alabama also suffered heavy damage that caused a humanitarian crisis on a vast scale. Hurricane Katrina was one of the most costly natural disasters in U.S. history. In situations such as this, what is the responsibility of banks? What ethical issues do they face?

Chapter 12 Review and Activities **207**

Critical Thinking

11. It is not divisible by other U.S. currency or coins.

12. Less risk is involved.

13. Credit unions are nonprofit and technically have no income, but it may be considered unfair competition because many credit unions offer full-service banking.

Write About It

14. One bank may offer a family trust, which allows a person's assets to be passed down to his or her children or other heirs.

15. Checking accounts generally carry a lower interest rate, because there are more costs to the bank than with a savings account.

16. The Internet has increased competition because bank customers now have more choices.

17. Some of the events that might appear on a timeline include: Massachusetts issues the first paper money in the colonies (1690). Congress charters the first Bank of the United States and authorizes it to issue paper bank notes to eliminate confusion and simplify trade (1791).

18. Counterfeiting is one of the world's oldest crimes. Color printers and copiers have made it easier to create fake currency.

19. Answers will vary, depending on recent board activities.

Technology Applications

20. Gift cards are access cards that contain stored prepaid monetary values. Digital cash is a system that lets consumers pay for goods and services by sending information from one computer to another. Digital cash numbers are unique, represent a specific amount of money, and are reusable.

Business Ethics

21. Because banks are part of the community, they have a responsibility to help in such situations. One way they can help is by extending the time customers affected by disasters have to make loan payments. Banks also can waive fees and lower loan requirements, allowing more people and businesses to buy goods.

Applying Academics to Business

22. Students should identify how the institutions are alike and different.

23. $5000 × 6% × 3 = $900

Pauline will pay $900 in interest.

24. Sentences will vary. Here are some examples:

I have a financial interest in my parent's business.

We are interested in what you have to say.

We got a low interest rate on our loan.

Can I interest you in a game of tennis?

25. $\frac{1}{5} × 52 = 10.4$

Another way to think about this is that Heather spends 4 weeks in town and the 5th week out of town. Therefore, she will be out of town during the 5th, 10th, 15th, 20th, . . . 50th week each year. Heather spends 10 weeks out of town during a year.

$3 × 10 × $1.50 = 45.00

She will spend $45 on ATM services during a year.

Active Learning

26. Answers will vary, depending on the Federal Reserve Bank branch that is contacted.

Business in the Real World

27. Answers will depend on the interviewee's responses.

Applying Academics to Business

English Language Arts

22. Collect various types of advertisements for financial institutions. Include a commercial bank, a savings and loan, and a mortgage company or credit union. Based on the ads you collect, chart the different services offered. Write a paragraph or two comparing and contrasting the institutions.

Mathematics

23. Pauline needs to get a $5,000 loan to buy a car. Her bank offers a loan at 6% simple interest, which she will pay back in three years. If she takes this loan, how much interest will she pay?

> **THEORY** **Simple Interest** The formula for finding simple interest is $I = prt$, where I is the amount of the interest, p is the principal, r is the interest rate, and t is time.

English Language Arts

24. As a noun, the word *interest* has several meanings. It can also be used as a verb. Look at the definition of *interest* in at least two different dictionaries. Then write four sentences using the word or one of its forms to illustrate four of its meanings. One of your sentences should use it as a verb.

Mathematics

25. Heather uses an ATM three times a week. She spends a week out of town for work every fifth week, and has to use an ATM that charges her $1.50 in service fees each time she uses it. How many weeks does she spend out of town each year? How much will she spend on service fees in a year?

> **THEORY** **Multiplying Fractions** To multiply a fraction by a whole number, multiply the whole number by the numerator of the fraction and then divide by the denominator.

Active Learning

Research the Federal Reserve

26. Write a letter to the Federal Reserve Bank in your area. Ask for information about the Federal Reserve System. Find out how the branch fulfills the Federal Reserve mission. Request information about the member banks in your area. Share the information you receive with your classmates.

Business in the Real World

Interview a Loan Officer

27. Interview a business loan officer at a local bank about business loans. Ask about the size of a typical loan and the percentage of loans backed by collateral. Find out why some business loans have no collateral. Also, ask about the length of a typical loan. Why are some loans not repaid? Share what you find with the rest of the class.

ExamView Assessment Suite CD allows you to print out ready-made unit and chapter tests, complete with answer keys. You can also create customized tests.

TeacherWorks Plus provides complete teacher resources in one convenient package. It includes customizable lesson plans in calendar format, and instant access to many print program resources.

Real LIFE skills

SKILLS NEEDED IN BANKING

28. Research the training and qualifications that are required to be a bank teller. Get this information from banks' Web sites, bank employees, the Occupational Outlook Handbook, or other sources. Write a one-page report that includes this information. Indicate if you think you would be interested in preparing for this position.

Business CAREERS

FIND YOUR DREAM JOB

29. Go to the *Introduction to Business* Online Learning Center through **glencoe.com** for a link to the Occupational Outlook Handbook Web site. Click on the "OOH Search/A-Z Index" link and enter the job category "loan counselors and officers." Then write a one-page report about this area of occupation. Conclude your report with a list of things you could do now to prepare yourself to pursue the occupation.

Role Play

CURRENCY FOR AN ISLAND ECONOMY

30. Situation Imagine that you live on an island that has few modern conveniences. You and your neighbors want to figure out something you can use for currency.

Activity Make a presentation about items you would consider using as currency and why.

Evaluation You will be evaluated on how well you meet the following performance indicators:

- Know the characteristics of money.
- Accurately relate the characteristics of money to the characteristics of the items that are suggested as currency.
- Use correct grammar.
- Organize your presentation in a logical way.

Standardized Test Practice

Directions Choose the letter of the best answer. Write the letter for the answer on a separate piece of paper.

1. Which sentence contains an error in the use of commas?

- A   All over the world, paper money and coins are common forms of money.
- B   Without money, buying and selling is difficult.
- C   With money, however transactions become easy.
- D   As a standard of value, money makes it possible to set a fixed value on a product.

TEST-TAKING TIP Even though the first answer choice you make is often correct, do not be afraid to change an answer if you change your mind after thinking about it.

@ **READING** Go to the *Introduction to Business* Online Learning Center through **glencoe.com** for a list of outside reading suggestions.

glencoe.com

STRATEGIES FOR STANDARDIZED TEST PREP SUCCESS

Test Savvy Help students develop their critical thinking ability by first modeling the thinking that takes place when figuring out the best answer to a multiple-choice test item, and then providing them with practice. Analyze individual items as a class and have students explain their thinking as they made their choices.

Real LIFE skills

28. high school diploma, know how to work in an office or in customer service, experience with handling cash, good communication skills, computer savvy

Business CAREERS

29. Nature of the work: Facilitate lending money, determine client creditworthiness.

Working conditions: 40-hour week, but may work longer; office setting.

Training and qualifications: Bachelor's degree. Experience in banking, lending, or sales. Opportunities for advancement: Advance to larger branches or managerial positions. A Certified Mortgage Banker (CMB) designation enhances opportunities. Job outlook: Projected to increase more slowly than average. As preparation: business and college-prep classes.

Role Play

30. For example, on an island, coconuts, bananas, tree leaves, rocks, sand, and water are not scarce so they are not money. Whale's teeth will be scarce because it will be hard to capture a whale to get them. They are also divisible and portable. Therefore, they could be used as currency.

Standardized Test Practice
1. C

Ling Chai
Founder, President, and COO, Jenzabar
Jenzabar offers Web-based software and e-learning products and services to colleges and universities. Its founder, Ling Chai, is also known for her leadership role in the Tiananmen Square democracy movement, which landed her on the Chinese government's most wanted list. She has been nominated for the Nobel Peace Prize twice.

Q & A

Describe your job responsibilities.
Ling: I am involved in almost every aspect of the business, with a particular focus on the company's product development and product marketing.

What skills are most important in your business?
Ling: A solid academic, technology, and business background, which is particularly key to my type of business and marketplace. In becoming a manager, it is essential to develop and maintain people skills, knowing what it takes to create and motivate a team. Defining culture is the key to managing a company—in our case a service-oriented, customer-centric culture.

What is your key to success?
Ling: Success comes through hard work and dedication to an idea. Persistence has been a key attribute for me, and certainly a little luck helps, too.

What advice would you give students interested in starting a business?
Ling: Most important is a solid educational background. Go for it, and follow your heart. Do something that makes you want to wake up and go do it every day, because you'll need that attitude to support the hard work and persistence necessary to be successful.

How has your experience in China, especially Tiananmen Square protests, shaped who you are today?
Ling: My leadership in Tiananmen Square protests helped shape the democracy movement in terms of organizing people in a disorderly situation, and developing an action plan. There are similarities between leading a political movement and running a business. Both deal with managing people, developing a mission, handling situations and issues as they emerge, and maintaining a direction.

Critical Thinking *Why is it important to maintain a balance of education, experience, and networking while developing and running a business?*

Critical Thinking
Education and lifelong learning are critical to long-term success in business and in life. Experience, or the accumulation of knowledge or skill, gives a business vital insight. Businesses that employ networking techniques build relationships with people who might bring business opportunities.

Some Qualifications of the Owner of a Software Development Company

Academic Skills and Abilities

Computer science; mathematics; information systems; computer programming; interpersonal skills; general business management; verbal and written communication skills; multitasking, organizing, and planning skills

Academic Skills Required to Complete Tasks at Jenzabar			
Tasks	Math	Science	English Language Arts
Hold meetings			◆
Assign duties			◆
Develop new products	◆	◆	◆
Assess marketplace opportunities	◆	◆	◆
Customer service			◆
Schedule employees	◆		◆
Order supplies and equipment	◆		◆
Analyze financials	◆		◆

Education and Training

Occupations in the software publishing industry require varying levels of education. The level of education and type of training required depend on the employer's needs, which often change due to changes in technology and business conditions. Another factor driving employers' needs is the time frame within which a project must be completed.

Career Path

Computer software engineers need a broad knowledge of and experience with computer systems and technologies. Usual degree concentrations for applications software engineers are computer science or software engineering; for systems software engineers, usual concentrations are computer science or computer information systems. Graduate degrees are preferred for some of the more complex software engineering jobs.

Preparing for a Career
Self-Assessment Checklist

Use this self-assessment checklist to help determine ways you can succeed in the marketplace of ideas.

✔ Evaluate price fluctuations for products and services you might be able to provide.

✔ Ask for advice or assistance when you need it—and be prepared to provide help in return.

✔ Always look for new opportunities to update your technological skills.

✔ Investigate the unfulfilled business needs of your own community.

✔ Brainstorm with friends and find a partner with whom you work well.

✔ Be realistic about job requirements and necessary skills.

✔ Be persistent. It may take some time for your plan to become a success.

✔ Perform further research about business plans and create one for your own business idea.

211

ASSESS

Write About It
Jenzabar

Ask students to write a summary of what they like about Jenzabar's business concept. (Students may say that they like the opportunity to share educational materials in ways that are exciting, engaging, visually stimulating, and portable.)

Academic Vocabulary
Career Planning

Ask students to read the Self-Assessment Checklist and write one or more paragraphs about preparing for a career. Have students use words from the Academic Vocabulary Glossary. (Example: Education *enables* people to have successful careers. Professionals usually have a high *degree* of training in their specialty. A broad education, with additional *specialized* training, gives people the most choices down the road.)

CLOSE

Cooperative Learning
Technology Applications

Ask students to work in pairs and develop an idea for an e-learning product. Have them use presentation software to develop an oral report about their product. (Presentations will vary but should include mock-ups of the product as well as descriptions and visuals of the product.)

Preparing for a Career

Developing Academic Skills and Abilities for Career Growth The education students receive in your classroom calls on students to exercise knowledge from many different disciplines. Remind students that business people in the real world will use math, science, and English Language Arts skills in ways that may seem surprising. Ask students to research the academic skills and abilities required for their dream job and have them draw a diagram of how those skills will interrelate to make them successful in their chosen career. (Diagrams will vary but should be a realistic picture of the academic abilities and skills necessary for the career chosen.)

FOCUS

Discussion Starter

Lead a discussion about the role of community outreach and service learning in business. Ask students to project how being involved in their communities will help them be better businesspeople.

Step 1

Brainstorm Skills

Have students go to the *Introduction to Business* Online Learning Center through **glencoe.com** for a graphic organizer they can use to brainstorm the skills needed to complete the project.

Step 2

Choose a Business and a Career

Students can use the library and Internet resources to explore options.

TEACH

Step 3

Build Background

Community Organizations
Have students brainstorm ways they could use technology skills to help a community organization. (Students may be able to create flyers or presentations that will recruit others in their community service project. They may also be used to encourage donations.)

Diversity Ask students: why do community organizations serve so many diverse interests? (Communities have many diverse needs. Just as no two people are alike, no two problems are alike either. Community organiza-

tions may be organized to serve specific groups of people, to preserve the environment, or even to rescue sick or injured animals. Having a diversity of community organizations allows communities to build a better future.)

Community Outreach and Service Learning

Community outreach and service learning are smart business practices. Community outreach is good public relations. It helps keep the community strong and healthy, brings in new customers to a business, and helps mentor young people through service learning.

Thematic Project Assignment

In this project you will research and then write a news story, with pictures, about a business that is working on a community project. Include information about student volunteers for the project and how they acquire knowledge while working in service to the community.

Step 1 Brainstorm Skills You Need to Complete This Activity

Your success in researching and writing a news feature story will depend on your skills. Preview the activity. Then brainstorm a list of the skills you will need to use to complete the activity and describe how you will use them. Skills you might use include:

Academic Skills	reading, writing, art/photography
Basic Skills	speaking, listening, thinking, and interpersonal skills
Technology Skills	word processing, keyboarding, presentation, and Internet skills

 SKILLS PREVIEW Go to the *Introduction to Business* Online Learning Center through **glencoe.com** for a graphic organizer you can use to brainstorm the skills you will use to complete the project.

Step 2 Choose a Business and a Career That Interest You

Use your local newspaper, business magazines, and the Internet to find news stories about businesses that interest you that are helping communities. Make sure they offer a career in which you are interested and are using student volunteers with the project.

Step 3 Build Background Knowledge

Preview the stories and look for the who, what, when, where, and why in each story.

Local **Business** Helps Clean Up **Community** Park

Young volunteers from local schools helped Montgomery Hardware clean up downtown Community Park and build new playground equipment. Organized by Montgomery Hardware, the Saturday event brought out 44 students. Montgomery Hardware donated tools and supplies. The students, who were supervised by members of the carpenter's union, did the work.

"It was a whole team effort," states Edwin Hubble, president of Montgomery Hardware. "Students were mentored by carpenters, so they have a step-up when wanting to get jobs in the industry."

Step 4 Connect with Your Community

Interview a local business owner about the company's involvement in community projects. Find out how the owner benefited. Ask if he or she had student volunteers and how the volunteers benefited.

Step 4

Connect with Your Community

Ask students to describe what steps they can take to form a better connection to their community. (Most students will agree that volunteering is a good first step.) Encourage students to understand that there is no "best" way to be involved in their community. Desire and commitment are what is important.

Step 5 — Research Community Outreach

Use library and Internet resources to research community outreach. Use the project checklist as a guide to your research. Keep records of your sources of information.

Step 6 — Develop a News Feature Story

Use word processing or page design software to write a 350- to 400-word newspaper feature story, with photos. Use your imagination to create the "facts" for your story. Stage your friends for the photos. Include all the information described in this checklist.

News Feature

✔ Use the stories you have already read as models for your story.

✔ Write a draft of your story. Include the who, what, when, where, why, and how.

> **Who:** Who is the story about? What is the name of the business? Who are the student volunteers? Who had the idea?
>
> **What:** What is the community project? What is the company philosophy about community outreach?
>
> **When:** When did the business and students get together to tackle the project? When did they first meet? How did the business find student volunteers?
>
> **Where:** Where did the project take place?
>
> **Why:** Why did the business decide to take on this community project?
>
> **How:** How did the company benefit? How did the student volunteers benefit?

✔ Stage your friends for the photos. Have a few friends dress in clothing appropriate for your story and do things that illustrate the story. For example, if your story is about cleaning up a park, have your friends wear outdoor clothing and plant flowers or rake leaves.

Self Connections

✔ Describe the results of your research to a family member or other adult.

✔ Describe how businesses you are interested in benefit by helping the community, and how volunteers acquire knowledge while servicing the community.

✔ Explain what the investigation and its results mean to you.

Step 7 — Evaluate Your News Story

@ *RUBRIC* Go to the *Introduction to Business* Online Learning Center through **glencoe.com** for a rubric you can use to evaluate your final report.

213

Unit 3

TEACH (cont.)

Step 6

Develop a Report
Give students these tips on report writing:

- Know your audience.
- Organize your report by developing an outline and using titles and subtitles.
- Write concisely (briefly but completely).
- Write in easy-to-read, simple language.

ASSESS

Step 7

Evaluate Your Report
Rubric Encourage students to go use the rubric to evaluate their final reports.

CLOSE

Culminating Activity
Community Outreach Interviews
Have students form pairs and interview each other about the community organizations they researched and how their opinions and perceptions of community outreach evolved during the course of the project. (Interviews will vary depending on students' community outreach research and reactions to what they learned.)

Step 5

Research Business Trends
Students can go to the *Introduction to Business* Online Learning Center through **glencoe.com** for a rubric they can use as a content checklist when researching their reports.

Chapter	Section	Unit Objectives
Chapter 13 *Marketing in Today's World*	**13.1**	**Define** marketing.
		Identify the functions of marketing.
		List the elements of the marketing mix.
	13.2	**Describe** the kinds of market research a company may use.
		Identify the steps in developing a new product.
Chapter 14 *Advertising*	**14.1**	**Define** advertising.
		List types of media that businesses use to reach potential customers.
	14.2	**List** the components of media measurement.
		Identify how advertising costs are measured.
		Describe how media rates are determined.

Understanding the Coding

Brackets Brackets on the reduced student edition page correspond to teaching strategies and activities in the Teacher Wraparound Edition. As you teach the lesson, the brackets show you exactly where to use the teaching strategies and activities.

Letters The letters on the reduced student edition page identify the type of strategy or activity. See the key below to learn about the different types of strategies and activities.

Ability Levels Leveled teaching strategies are identified by one of three codes to give you an idea of their suitability for students of varying learning styles and abilities.

Resources Key program resources are listed in each chapter. Icons indicate the format of resources.

KEY to Letters

D **Develop Concepts** activities help teachers gauge and plan for students' concept development.

R **Reading Strategy** activities help you teach reading skills and vocabulary.

C **Critical Thinking** strategies help students apply and extend what they have learned.

U **Universal Access** activities provide differentiated instruction for English language learners and suggestions for teaching various types of learners.

S **Skill Practice** provides leveled instruction for meeting individual needs and learning styles.

W **Writing Support** activities provide writing opportunities to help students comprehend the text.

NCLB **No Child Left Behind** activities help students practice and improve their abilities in academic subjects.

KEY to Ability Levels

L1 Strategies should be within the ability range of all students. Often full class participation is required.

L2 Strategies are for average to above-average students or for small groups. Some teacher direction is necessary.

L3 Strategies are designed for students able and willing to work independently. Minimal teacher direction is necessary.

KEY to Resource Icons

📁 Print Material

💿 CD-ROM

🖥 Online Learning Center with Podcasts

BusinessWeek *Reader and Case Study*

In Unit 4, your students can learn more about business in the real world through the following *BusinessWeek* Readers and Case Studies:

The Art of Chinese Relationships
Westerners entering the market had best learn the basics of *guanxi* if they want their ventures to thrive. (page 220)

TV Eyeballs Close-Up
A handful of companies are figuring out how to give advertisers better feedback on who's watching. (page 242)

Chapter Features and Activities

BusinessWeek *Reader and Case Study*

Science/Tech TRENDS

? ETHICS in Business

International Business

Reading Strategies

Before You Read

Graphic Organizer

As You Read

✔ Reading Check

After You Read

Marketing

214

214

Unit Overview

Introduce the Unit

Introduce the unit by describing the main concepts of each chapter in the unit.

Unit 4 is about marketing, the process of developing, promoting, and distributing products to satisfy customers' needs and wants.

Chapter 13 discusses the functions of marketing. It also discusses details of market research, product development, and channels of distribution.

Chapter 14 describes advertising media—the different media and their advantages and disadvantages. It also discusses advertising rates.

00:00 OUT OF TIME?

If class time is too short to cover all of the chapters in this unit, have students:

- Write down the vocabulary terms and their definitions.
- Read the chapter summaries at the beginning of each chapter review.
- Go to the *Introduction to Business* Online Learning Center through **glencoe.com** to download free Study-to-Go content to their PDAs or cell phones.

Real-World Business and Career Profile | Preview

Expeditiontrips.com Tell students that at the end of this unit, they will learn about the cofounder of Expeditiontrips.com and how she achieved her success. Expeditiontrips.com is an Internet-based adventure travel company specializing in trips on small cruise ships to remote locations like Antarctica, the Arctic, and the Amazon. They are a small company that seeks to be the best at a very specialized niche, expedition cruising and nature-based travel. Ask students why a travel business that specializes in going to hard-to-reach parts of the world might be a success. (Students should recognize that there are only a few companies that specialize in travel to exotic locales such as Antarctica and the Arctic.)

Real-World Business and Career Profile
Preview

Expeditiontrips.com is an Internet-based company that specializes in trips on small cruise ships to remote locations such as Alaska and Antarctica. At the end of this unit, you will learn about Expeditiontrips.com co-founder Kristy Royce and how she achieved her success.

Decision Making If you were about to start an online travel business, how would you market it?

Unit 4 | *Thematic Project Preview*

Marketing in a Global Economy After completing this unit, you will develop marketing strategies for a marketing product and/or service in a foreign market.

Project Checklist As you read the chapters in this unit, use this checklist to prepare for the unit project.

✔ Think about how a country's geography and culture affect the marketplace.

✔ Think about how a country's economy and government affect the marketplace.

✔ Consider the types of goods and services that are needed and wanted in a country.

✔ Think about how our wants and needs are affected by the region and culture of a community.

215

Build Background
Ask students these questions to activate prior knowledge:

Chapter 13
What is the difference between marketing and advertising? (Most students will be familiar with the word "marketing," and some of the functions of marketing. Marketing includes seven functions: distribution, financing, marketing information management, pricing, product service management, promotion, and selling. Advertising is part of marketing. The term *advertising* is familiar and some people incorrectly use the terms *marketing* and *advertising* interchangeably.) Ask: Do you know any other functions of marketing? (Responses will vary but may include selecting target markets and product development.)

Chapter 14
Record a current television advertisement and play it for your students. Ask: What do you remember about the ad? (Some students will only remember phrases or images. Other students will remember details about the product that was being advertised.) Ask: Do you think the ad will motivate people to buy the product? (Answers will depend on the advertisement and students' opinions of it.)

Unit | Thematic Project Preview

Marketing in a Global Economy
Tell students that when they complete this unit, they will know about marketing in a global economy. Encourage students to think about how the geography and culture of a country affect the needs of consumers.

C Critical Thinking
Ask students to analyze how the geography where they live and the culture in which they live affect their choice of goods and services. (Students should recognize that weather, religion, cultural traditions, age, economics, and peer pressure affect their choice of goods and services.)

Standards-Based Lesson Planning   *Introduction to Business* provides students with instruction and assessment in the following fundamental content areas:

Content Standards Correlations	
Examine the functions of marketing.	pp. 219–222, 228–229
Explain components of the marketing mix.	pp. 221–222, 228–231
Explain the principles of the production and marketing of goods and services.	pp. 219–222, 224–227
Develop the ability to market the assets each individual has whether they be in the labor market or in the consumer goods market.	p. 229
Describe concepts of the market and market identification.	pp. 224–225

NCLB   Activities, information, and skills practice will help your students attain No Child Left Behind proficiency. Students will improve their abilities in the following academic standards areas:

Academic Standards Correlations		
English Language Arts	**Activities/Features**	**Page**
NCTE 3 Apply strategies to interpret texts	Applying Academics to Business	p. 230
NCTE 7 Conduct research and gather, evaluate, and synthesize data to communicate discoveries	After You Read	p. 227
NCTE 8 Use information resources to gather information and create and communicate knowledge	After You Read	p. 227
Mathematics		
Algebra Represent and analyze mathematical situations and structures using algebraic symbols	After You Read	p. 222
Data Analysis and Probability Formulate questions that can be addressed with data and collect, organize, and display relevant data to answer them	Ask S&P	p. 216
Geometry Analyze characteristics of 2- and 3- dimensional geometric shapes and develop mathematical arguments about geometric relationships	Applying Academics to Business	p. 230
Number and Operations Understand the meanings of operations and how they relate to one another	Applying Academics to Business	p. 230
Number and Operations Compute fluently and make reasonable estimates	Standardized Test Practice	p. 231
Science		
Content Standard B Students should develop an understanding of structure and properties of matter, chemical reactions, interactions of energy and matter	Science/Tech Trends	p. 224

Correlations   This chart shows the 21st Century Skills, foundation skills, and workplace competencies that students develop as they work in this chapter.

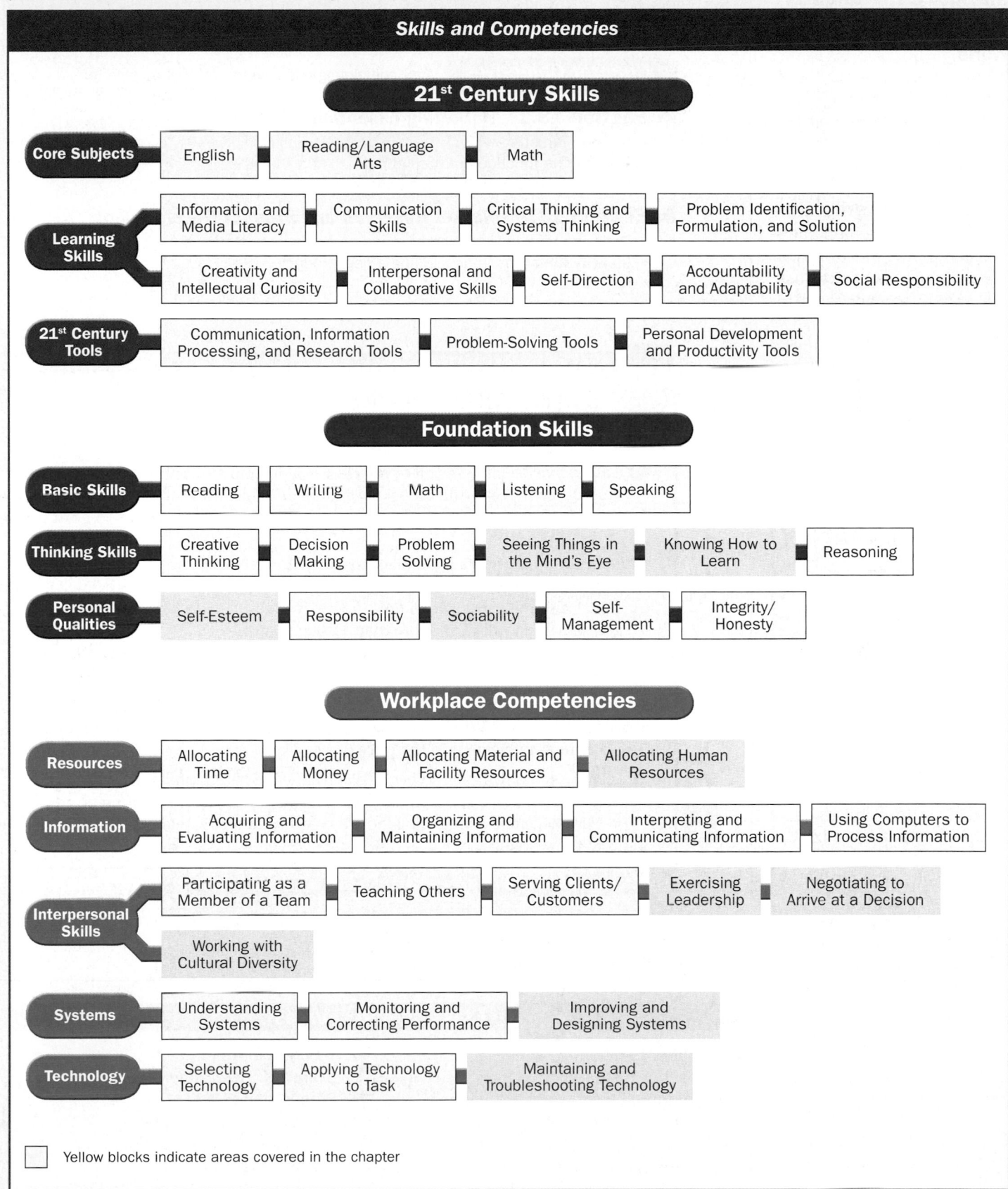

Skills and Competencies

21st Century Skills

Core Subjects
- English
- Reading/Language Arts
- Math

Learning Skills
- Information and Media Literacy
- Communication Skills
- Critical Thinking and Systems Thinking
- Problem Identification, Formulation, and Solution
- Creativity and Intellectual Curiosity
- Interpersonal and Collaborative Skills
- Self-Direction
- Accountability and Adaptability
- Social Responsibility

21st Century Tools
- Communication, Information Processing, and Research Tools
- Problem-Solving Tools
- Personal Development and Productivity Tools

Foundation Skills

Basic Skills
- Reading
- Writing
- Math
- Listening
- Speaking

Thinking Skills
- Creative Thinking
- Decision Making
- Problem Solving
- Seeing Things in the Mind's Eye
- Knowing How to Learn
- Reasoning

Personal Qualities
- Self-Esteem
- Responsibility
- Sociability
- Self-Management
- Integrity/Honesty

Workplace Competencies

Resources
- Allocating Time
- Allocating Money
- Allocating Material and Facility Resources
- Allocating Human Resources

Information
- Acquiring and Evaluating Information
- Organizing and Maintaining Information
- Interpreting and Communicating Information
- Using Computers to Process Information

Interpersonal Skills
- Participating as a Member of a Team
- Teaching Others
- Serving Clients/Customers
- Exercising Leadership
- Negotiating to Arrive at a Decision
- Working with Cultural Diversity

Systems
- Understanding Systems
- Monitoring and Correcting Performance
- Improving and Designing Systems

Technology
- Selecting Technology
- Applying Technology to Task
- Maintaining and Troubleshooting Technology

Yellow blocks indicate areas covered in the chapter

216

Chapter Overview

Introduce the Chapter

Marketing in Today's World

Chapter 13 discusses the functions of marketing, including market research, product development, and channels of distribution.

Building Background

Advertising is the marketing function that is most familiar. Some people incorrectly use the word interchangeably with "marketing." Most students will be familiar with the importance of product, place, price, and promotion but not associate them with marketing.

Ask STANDARD &POOR'S

›› Math Answer

A line graph would be best. To predict change in the future, you could use a scatter plot and draw a line of best fit.

›› Extension Activity

Suggest that students visit a Web portal that has a financial section and look up the company symbol and key it into the quote box. Ask students to find the stock chart, explore the options, and print a one-year line chart showing the stock's performance in comparison to the S&P 500. (Follow up by asking students to visit the company's Web site and click on "investor relations" to see what kind of information is posted.)

N C L B Activity correlates to Math standards.

Marketing in Today's World

Chapter Objectives After completing this chapter, you will be able to:

▶ **Section 13.1** *Marketing Essentials*
- **Define** marketing.
- **Identify** the functions of marketing.
- **List** the elements of the marketing mix.

▶ **Section 13.2** *Market Research and Product Development*
- **Describe** the kinds of market research a company may use.
- **Identify** the steps in developing a new product.

Ask STANDARD &POOR'S **Industry Surveys**

Q: Lately, I've been buying all of my clothes at a couple of online outlet Web sites. I think they're great, and I'll bet that companies like these are poised for big growth. Is there a way for me to find out more about this type of business so I can consider investing?

A: Your local library is a good place to start. Most libraries carry *The Value Line Investment Survey,* a weekly publication providing data on 1,700 stocks. Standard & Poor's also publishes *The Outlook,* a weekly investment advisory newsletter; *Stock Guide,* with key data on more than 11,000 securities; *Industry Surveys,* which provides in-depth analyses of 53 different industries; and *Stock Reports,* which covers about 2,000 companies.

Mathematics Which type of graph would be best to show the fluctuation in the price of a stock over time? Why? Describe a graphing technique that you could use to predict the short-term movement in the price of a stock.

THEORY **Graphs** Different types of graphs include bar graphs, line graphs, circle graphs, scatter plots, and stem-and-leaf plots. They are used for different purposes. For example, circle graphs show how the parts of a whole relate in size to each other and to the whole.

N C L B

Classroom Resources

- Student Edition
- Teacher Wraparound Edition
- Student Activity Workbook with Academic Integration
- Student Activity Workbook with Academic Integration TAE
- *Fast File,* Unit 4 Resources
- Inclusion in the Business Education Classroom

- TeacherWorks Plus
- *ExamView Assessment Suite*
- Presentation Plus!
- Vocabulary PuzzleMaker
- Interactive Student Edition
- Online Student Edition
- Online Learning Center with Podcasts

Marketing Business Businesses provide a wide array of products and services in stores, online, and through catalogs. **How do businesses attract buyers?**

Review the Objectives

Introduce the chapter by reviewing the chapter objectives:

Section 13.1 *Objectives*

Define marketing. (Marketing is the process of creating, promoting, and presenting a product to meet the wants and needs of consumers in the target market(s).)

Identify the functions of marketing. (The seven functions of marketing are distribution, financing, marketing information management, pricing, product/service management, promotion, and selling.)

List the elements of the marketing mix. (The four Ps are product, place, price, and promotion. Some people include a fifth P for people,)

Section 13.2 *Objectives*

Describe the kinds of market research a company may use. (A company may use phone calls, e-mails, surveys, or focus groups to gather information from potential customers.)

Identify the steps in developing a new product. (The steps in developing a new product are: generate ideas, screen ideas, develop a business plan, create the product, test-market the product, introduce the product, and evaluate customer acceptance.)

Discuss the Photo

● **Marketing Business** Read the caption on the photo to students: Businesses provide a wide array of products and services in stores, online, and through catalogs.

Ask students: How do businesses attract buyers? (Businesses attract buyers for their products through marketing. They promote and present a product to meet the wants and needs of consumers, wherever they are.)

FOCUS

Bell Ringer Activity

Marketing Essentials

For this activity you will need several sets of grocery store sales receipts and the companion strips of coupons generated by the cash register. Ask the students why the specific coupons were generated during that visit to the store. (Students should be able to locate the item on the receipt that triggered the coupon. For example, the purchase of shampoo might generate a coupon for conditioner made by the same company.)

Preteaching

Presentation Plus!

The Presentation Plus! CD provides visual teaching aids for this section.

PuzzleMaker

Use the Vocabulary PuzzleMaker to create a puzzle of the section's key terms. Students can complete the puzzle on paper or on a computer.

Graphic Organizer

Tell students to go to the Online Learning Center through **glencoe.com** for a printable graphic organizer. (When completed the graphic organizer will include the following labels: product, place, price, and promotion.)

 Connects academics to content.

218

Marketing Essentials

Reading Guide

● Before You Read

Think about the role marketing plays in your life and how it affects your buying decisions.

D

Read to Learn

- Define marketing.
- Identify the functions of marketing.
- List the elements of the marketing mix.

The Main Idea

To sell their products or services, businesses engage in marketing activities. They find and analyze potential customers and then try to meet their wants and needs.

Key Concepts

- The Basics of Marketing
- The Functions of Marketing
- The Marketing Mix

Vocabulary

Key Terms

market
marketing
relationship marketing
marketing mix
channel of distribution
direct distribution
indirect distribution
break-even point

Academic Vocabulary

You will find these words in your reading and on your tests. Make sure you know their meanings.

genders
physical
located
aware

Graphic Organizer

As you read, write the four parts of the marketing mix in a graphic like the one below.

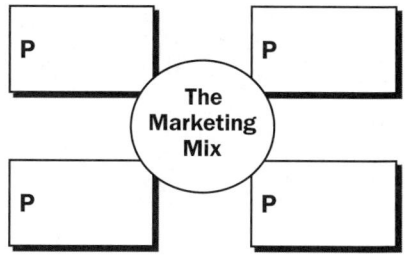

 Go to the *Introduction to Business* Online Learning Center through **glencoe.com** for a printable graphic organizer.

Academic Standards

N C L B

English Language Arts

NCTE 1 Read texts to acquire new information

NCTE 9 Develop an understanding of diversity in language use across cultures

Mathematics

Algebra Represent and analyze mathematical situations and structures using algebraic symbols

---

Reading Guide

● Before You Read

Students should recognize that marketing pervades life in the United States. For example, if the clerk asks for your ZIP code when you make a purchase, the store is gathering information about its customers.

D Develop Concepts

The Main Idea Ask students: Are marketing and selling a product the same thing? (Marketing and selling are not the same thing. Students should understand that selling is one of seven marketing functions.)

The Basics of Marketing

Marketing a CD requires a different strategy than marketing diamond earrings. Each item appeals to people of different ages, **genders**, and income ranges. Every holiday season more gadgets, toys, and clothes hit stores. The companies that make these and other items do research before developing and selling them. To market a product successfully, a company has to understand what people want to buy and why they want to buy it.

It all comes down to knowing your market. From a marketing viewpoint, a **market** is a group of customers who share common wants and needs. These people have the ability to purchase the product or service. In the global marketplace, many countries can make up a market for a product. **Marketing** is the process of creating, promoting, and presenting a product or service to meet the wants and needs of consumers, wherever they are.

Marketing involves a number of stages, from studying what people want to buy to designing a product's packaging. For example, you might be part of the $11 billion market for recorded music and music video purchases. Businesses want you to buy their products, so they perform detailed research to find and analyze potential customers in their market. Knowing what groups of people want and need helps companies decide how and what to sell.

The Functions of Marketing

There are seven functions of marketing. These functions define all the aspects that are part of marketing.

1. *Distribution* is the process of getting goods and services to customers. The process includes purchasing, stock handling, inventory control, and **physical** distribution. Goods are usually transported by trucks, trains, airplanes, and ships. Distribution also involves the systems that track products so they can be **located** at any time.

2. *Financing* is getting the money that is necessary for setting up and running a business. Finance also includes protecting investments through risk management.

3. *Marketing information management* is gathering and analyzing information about consumers, trends, and competitors' products. Making informed decisions requires good research and development.

● As You Read

Think about the "hot" new product that appealed to you this year. Was there a marketing strategy that influenced your decision to want the product?

?ETHICS in Business

Marketing Questions

■ **Critical Reading** Life is full of important decisions. Think about the kinds of decisions that you make as you read the question below.

Imagine that you have just gotten a job working for a toy company as a marketing director specializing in action figures for boys ages 7 to 12. In planning a special promotion, a team member under your direction suggests a contest. Children would fill out a questionnaire about their preferences and have a chance to win a chest full of toys and games. You can then use the information compiled from the questionnaires to design an action figure children will want.

■ **Decision Making** To prepare for your new assignment, you do some research into ethical marketing to children and understand that you have a special responsibility in communicating with children. What are some guidelines you would use in designing a promotional contest for children? Explain your answer.

TEACH

Discussion Starter
The Basics of Marketing
Ask a volunteer to define "market." (A market is a group of customers who share common wants and needs.) Ask students to identify some specific markets. As they offer suggestions, ask them if they can identify a narrower market. (Answers will vary. Students might mention baby boomers. This could be narrowed down to retired baby boomers or to retired baby boomers who like to travel.)

R Reading Strategy

Create a Caption Ask students to describe the market for a product that is advertised in a current magazine. Provide a stack of magazines and allow students to tear out the advertisements they choose. Have students create a caption for the ad that describes the market for the product. (Captions will vary depending on the selected advertisements. Students should recognize that the market is a group of customers who share common wants and needs. They should realize that all segments of the market might not be represented in a single advertisement.)

Virtual Business

Introduce merchandising to students using the Virtual Business Retailing Merchandising activity. In this simulation, students learn why merchandising is important to the success of businesses.

● As You Read

Students may talk about videogame players or sneakers and the ways these products were presented, noting celebrity involvement, a manufactured "scarcity," or other techniques used to get their attention.

?ETHICS in Business

Decision Making Privacy is an important issue when marketing to children. Marketing interactions directed to children, including requests for personal information, should require the express consent of the child's parent or guardian.

TEACH (cont.)

S Skill Practice

Guided Practice

List Have students list the functions of marketing. (distribution, financing, marketing information management, pricing, product/service management, promotion, and selling) **L1**

Create a Table Have students create a two-column table listing the functions of marketing in the first column and an explanation in the second column. (Tables should include all seven marketing functions.) **L2**

Illustrate an Idea Have students create an icon for each of the functions of marketing. Suggest that students look at magazines and Web sites to see how groups of icons generally share some characteristics. (Icons should have some logical connection to the functions of marketing.) **L3**

✔ Reading Check

Identify distribution, financing, marketing information management, pricing, product/service management, promotion, and selling

ASSESS

Review Key Terms
Have students write sentences using each key term.

 **Study-to-Go** Have students go to the Online Learning Center through **glencoe.com** to download free **Study-to-Go** content to their PDAs or cell phones.

---

4. *Pricing* is deciding how much to charge for a product or service so the business can make a profit.

5. *Product/service management* is obtaining, developing, maintaining, and improving a product or product mix in response to market opportunities.

6. *Promotion* is any effort to inform, persuade, or remind potential customers about a business's products or services.

7. *Selling* is providing customers with the goods and services they choose to buy. A popular trend today is using relationship marketing. Companies use **relationship marketing** to build and maintain relationships with their customers.

✔ Reading Check **Identify** What are the seven functions of marketing?

BusinessWeek *Reader and Case Study*

The Art of Chinese Relationships

Westerners entering the market had best learn the basics of *guanxi* if they want their ventures to thrive

As a Scottish citizen, Rod MacGregor, who founded the U.S.-based NanoMuscle® in 1998 with venture capital from Germany, Switzerland, Italy, and France, knows a thing or two about international business. But when he started moving production and R&D of the company's miniature motors to China, MacGregor quickly realized that while it's nearly impossible to make a fatal mistake in other Western countries, doing business in China is an entirely different story.

Here's an example: Once when MacGregor went to visit a powerful factory owner in the south of China, an American business associate he was traveling with handed over his business card with a nonchalant, one-handed grasp rather than the more respectful and deliberate two-handed technique typically used in China. The factory owner accepted the card but didn't offer one of his own. Later, his people called MacGregor and told him to never bring that man back again.

The key to avoiding such deal-killers is understanding the etiquette of business in China.

How to present your card is important. But even more crucial is understanding the web of relationships that defines business in China. That's why, after recently launching China Corp., a company that specializes in helping Western companies enter the Chinese market, one of MacGregor's first moves was to compile a guidebook to doing business in China that devotes plenty of attention to *guanxi* (pronounced GUAN-SHEE), or the art of relationship development.

 CASE STUDY Go to the *Introduction to Business* Online Learning Center through **glencoe.com** for the *BusinessWeek* Reader Case Study.

Active Learning

Greeting customs vary from one culture to the next. The two-handed handshake is typically used in China. Research greetings customs from three different countries and practice them with a friend. Demonstrate one in class.

BusinessWeek *Reader and Case Study*

The Art of Chinese Relationships

CASE STUDY Have students go to the *Introduction to Business* Online Learning Center through **glencoe.com** to download a Case Study activity that corresponds to the article. The activity and answer key are also available on the TeacherWorks Plus CD.

Active Learning

Presentations will vary but may include such rituals as bowing, cheek-kissing, shaking hands, kissing the hand, raising a hat, tipping a hat, kowtowing, and waving.

The Marketing Mix

The **marketing mix** consists of four basic marketing strategies: product, place, price, and promotion, collectively known as the *four Ps*. In recent years, many people have begun to include a fifth P for people because the success of a marketing mix depends on people: good employees and customers.

Product

First, marketing is used to find out if there is a demand for a product. Then it is concerned with how to make the product appeal to consumers. Packaging is a major part of marketing. It includes the design, color, size, and brand name of a product.

Place

Marketers have to decide how and where customers will buy their goods and services. For example, a company is more likely to sell snowshoes in Maine than in Texas because of the snowy weather in Maine. Then marketers have to consider in *what kind of location* to sell their product. Does the product need to be in a large department store or a boutique?

To make place decisions, marketers select the right channel of distribution. A **channel of distribution** is a pathway to direct products to consumers. **Direct distribution** occurs when goods or services are sold from the producer directly to the customer. **Indirect distribution** involves one or more intermediaries. Distribution decisions affect the price of products. The cost of distributing a product has to be added to its price.

As You Read

Imagine that you have designed a new line of sunglasses for teens. Think about a particular location you would choose to sell your sunglasses.

● **Product Strategies**
Businesses make product strategy decisions when developing new products for their markets. **Do you think this product will appeal to consumers? Why?**

As You Read

Sunny locations where lots of people go, such as the beach or parks, or sporting-goods establishments or swimsuit shops.

Discuss the Photo

● **Product Strategies** Some students are likely to think that the robot is "cool" and will catch consumer attention. Others are likely to note that it will probably be very expensive because of the technology involved in making a robot that can walk, and will thus think that the "coolness" of the product is unlikely to overcome the high price.

RETEACH

W **Writing Support**
Enrichment
Marketing Research Have students describe a real product in terms of the four Ps. Suggest that they answer the four questions posed in the textbook: Who will want the product? How much should it cost? Where should it be sold? What is the best way to tell people about it? (Answers will vary depending on the product selected.)

R **Reading Strategy**
Create a Poster Have students create a poster for a product. Suggest that they use words and graphics to identify and explain how the product fits into the four Ps. (Posters will vary. The four Ps should be clearly identified and explained.)

U **Universal Access**
Spacial Learners Have students create a graphic of the channels of distribution. Encourage students to use maps and icons to show the physical relationships between different locations in the channel of distribution. Students who are spacial learners might benefit most from help with mapping out concepts, but all students can benefit from this activity.

Student Activity Workbook 📂 Assign the Section 13.1 Activities.

RETEACH (cont.)

C Critical Thinking

Pros and Cons

Distribution Channels What are some advantages and disadvantages of distributing a product without intermediaries? (Online selling can increase profits; cutting out intermediaries might limit the market.)

Celebrity Endorsements
Students may list soft drinks, clothing, and insurance. Some celebrities have image problems that can hurt promotions. Consumers may buy products promoted by a celebrity.

ASSESS

After You Read

Have students complete the Section 13.1 After You Read section review.

Online Study Tools

Have students go to the Online Learning Center through **glencoe.com** to:

- Take the Section 13.1 **Practice Test**.
- Download free **Study-to-Go** content to their PDAs or cell phones.

CLOSE

Culminating Activity

Display Have students create a display highlighting forms of promotion.
(Displays should have relevance to promotion.)

Activity correlates to Math standards.

Real World

Celebrity Endorsements Many big companies hire celebrities to endorse what they sell. A *celebrity endorsement* is public support from a well-known person for a product or service. Companies put celebrities in their TV commercials and print ads. *List some of the products and services that you have seen celebrities endorse. Then write reasons why you think the ads helped or hurt sales.*

C | **Channel Members** It takes an intermediary to move a product from the manufacturer to the final user. As discussed in Chapter 6, intermediaries can include distributors, wholesalers, or retailers. Even the Internet can be considered an intermediary. It allows people and businesses to interact with each other.

Price

To determine the price of a product, a marketer considers three questions: (1) How much are customers willing to pay? (2) Is the price competitive with other products? and (3) Can the company make a profit? Marketers must find the break-even point. The **break-even point** is the point at which total revenues, or sales, equal total costs and expenses of developing and offering a product or service.

Promotion

Promotion involves making customers **aware** of a product. The most familiar form of promotion is advertising, which will be covered in Chapter 14. Automakers spend billions of dollars each year on ads. There are, however, many other ways companies can promote a product. One way is to offer discounts in the form of coupons, rebates, and sales. They can also give away items.

Section 13.1

After You Read

Review Key Concepts
1. Define marketing.
2. What are the seven functions of marketing?
3. What four elements are in the marketing mix? What is sometimes considered a fifth element?

Academic Skills
4. **Mathematics** You are manager of the sweatshirt department at Trends, a clothing manufacturer. Trends plans to produce 25,000 sweatshirts. The sweatshirts will be sold to stores for $16 each. The cost of manufacturing and marketing each sweatshirt is $10. How many sweatshirts need to be sold for the company to break even? Write an equation using x for the unknown that could be used to solve this problem.

THEORY **Writing Equations** The unknown quantity in this problem is the number of sweatshirts that, when sold at $16 apiece, equals the manufacturing cost of all the sweatshirts.

 For math help, go to the Math Appendix.

> Go to the *Introduction to Business* Online Learning Center through **glencoe.com** to check your answers.

Section 13.1

Review Key Concepts
1. the process of creating, promoting, and presenting a product or service to meet the wants and needs of consumers
2. distribution, financing, marketing information management, pricing, product/service management, promotion, and selling
3. Product, place, price, and promotion. Some people include a fifth P for people.

Academic Skills
4. **Mathematics** $\$16x = 25{,}000 \times \$10$
$x = \$250{,}000 \div \$16 = 15{,}625$
15,625 sweatshirts need to be sold for the company to break even.

Market Research and Product Development

Reading Guide

● Before You Read

Think about how businesses decide when to market new products and when to discontinue old products.

D

Read to Learn
- Describe the kinds of market research a company may use.
- Identify the steps in developing a new product.

The Main Idea
Businesses must know their markets to provide products that will sell. They do market research to collect information and then develop products that will meet their customers' wants and needs.

Key Concepts
- Market Research
- The Seven Steps of Product Development

Vocabulary
Key Terms
- market research
- marketing concept
- demographics
- target marketing
- market segmentation
- test-market

Academic Vocabulary
You will find these words in your reading and on your tests. Make sure you know their meanings.

surveys   strategy
potential   crucial

Graphic Organizer
In a graphic organizer like the one below, list the seven steps of product development as you read.

1.
2.
3.
4.
5.
6.
7.

 Go to the *Introduction to Business* Online Learning Center through **glencoe.com** for a printable graphic organizer.

Academic Standards

N C L B

English Language Arts
- **NCTE 1** Read texts to acquire new information
- **NCTE 4** Use written language to communicate effectively
- **NCTE 6** Apply knowledge of language structure and conventions to discuss texts
- **NCTE 7** Conduct research and gather, evaluate, and synthesize data to communicate discoveries

Science
- **Content Standard B** Students should develop an understanding of structure and properties of matter, chemical reactions, interactions of energy and matter

---

FOCUS

🔔 Bell Ringer Activity

Market Research and Product Development
Bring several different brands of shampoo to class. Ask students to identify the target market of each. Ask students how the marketers of these products determined a marketplace need. (They used marketing research.)

Preteaching

Presentation Plus! 💿
The Presentation Plus! CD provides visual teaching aids for this section.

PuzzleMaker 💿
Use the Vocabulary PuzzleMaker to create a puzzle of the section's key terms. Students can complete the puzzle on paper or on a computer.

Graphic Organizer
Tell students to go to the Online Learning Center through **glencoe.com** for a printable graphic organizer. (Answers include: generate ideas, screen ideas, develop a business plan, develop the product, test-market the product, introduce the product, and evaluate acceptance.)

N C L B Connects academics to content.

Reading Guide

● Before You Read

Companies market new products when a need or want is identified. Pants with cell phone pockets appeared soon after cell phones became popular. Products are discontinued when sales decline or when they become obsolete.

D Develop Concepts

The Main Idea Ask students: Why do you think businesses need to know their markets? (to understand and respond to the wants and needs of their potential customers)

TEACH

Discussion Starter
Market Research versus Marketing Research
Ask students this question: What is the difference between market research and marketing research? (Market research is the gathering and analysis of information on the size, location, and makeup of a product market. Marketing research is research on how to promote, sell, and distribute a product or service.)

R **Reading Strategy**

Identifying Sources Explain that American FactFinder is a resource developed by the U.S. Census Bureau. It contains demographic data about the American population and it is available online at www.census.gov. Ask students why they think the U.S. Census Bureau serves as such a key source of demographic data? (The U.S. Census Bureau has a vast array of data compiled directly from the U.S. population. Because census data covers all segments of the population from every region of the country, it is uniquely able to provide vital statistics that can be used to show trends in a variety of subgroups.)

✔ Reading Check

Identify Market research is the gathering and analysis of information on the size, location, and makeup of a market.

 Activity correlates to Science standards.

224

Market Research

Market research helps businesses make decisions. **Market research** is the gathering and analysis of information on the size, location, and makeup of a market.

Market researchers ask shoppers to answer questions or give an opinion about new foods, or watch a new commercial. This helps businesses discover consumers' wants and needs. Market research helps companies to produce and market products and services that attract customers. This is known as the marketing concept. The **marketing concept** involves determining the wants and needs of customers and providing them more efficiently and effectively than competitors.

✔ Reading Check **Identify** What is market research?

Information About Consumers

Before a product is put on the market, marketers gather information about the people who make up the market. They analyze and label their markets by demographics. **Demographics** are facts about the population. These facts include age, gender, location, and income. This information comes from **surveys**, sales figures for current products, databases, and the census.

Science/Tech **TRENDS**

Flat-Screen TVs

Liquid crystal displays (LCDs) are used in all kinds of devices used every day—from laptop computers to cell phones to microwave ovens. LCDs have helped manufacturers transform the bulky, boxy TV into a slim screen that can hang on a wall. LCDs offer an environmental advantage over the cathode ray TV tube they replace because they draw much less power and are therefore more energy-efficient. LCDs also have some advantages over Plasma technology when it comes to TV screens. Just what are liquid crystals? The term "liquid crystal" sounds like a contradiction. We think of a crystal as a solid material such as quartz, usually as hard as rock, and a liquid is obviously different. How could any material combine qualities of the two?

Web **Quest**

Go to the *Introduction to Business* Online Learning Center through **glencoe.com** for links to Web sites where you can find out more about LCDs and how they work. List the products in which they are used. Make a chart to compare the advantages and disadvantages of LCDs versus plasma displays in flat-screen TVs. Write a report about how flat-screen TVs with LCDs are being marketed. What do advertisers say about these new products?

Science/Tech **TRENDS**

Web **Quest**

Flat Screen TVs Liquid crystals are more like a liquid than a solid because of the way their molecules move. In TVs, LCD screens offer a slightly wider viewing angle and don't have the burn-in problem. Some adjectives used in advertising for LCD TVs are *slim, beautiful, elegant,* and *high performance.*

After studying a market, firms can aim their product or service at a group of **potential** customers. **Target marketing** helps companies focus on the people most likely to buy their goods or services. Once marketers know the demographics of a market, companies can make products to fit that group. **Market segmentation** is the division of a market for a product into groups of customers who have the same needs and traits. **Figure 13.1** shows different ways businesses can reach customers.

● **As You Read**

Think about the target markets to which a marketer might seek to sell a new computer football game.

The Seven Steps of Product Development

New products energize the marketplace. Companies take seven steps in developing a new product. You could use these to develop a car, dish soap, a book, or even clothing.

Step 1: Generate Ideas

It usually takes more than one person to come up with new ideas. Workers often get together to think of new products. This is called *brainstorming*. People from a company's development department, the market research staff, and even outside market researchers may be involved. Collaboration is key in this step.

S

Step 2: Screen Ideas

Once the team puts together a list of ideas for a product, the team must evaluate each idea. How do these ideas fit the company's mission and **strategy**? Does the new product compete with one of the company's existing products? Consumers can identify what they liked or disliked about the concept. Their responses are **crucial** as to whether the company continues with a proposed product.

Figure 13.1 — **Conducting Market Research** —

Call people on the phone

Talk to a group of people (focus group)

Talk to people face to face

Send letters through the mail

Send e-mails

Arrange an online focus group

● **Market Research** There are many ways to reach present and potential customers. **Why do businesses contact customers directly?**

Section 13.2 Market Research and Product Development **225**

● **As You Read**

A new computer football game is likely to appeal to people who like computer games and those who like football. This is most likely a market of young men.

Figure 13.1

● **Market Research** The business can find out what customers are thinking and feeling. Customers can answer questions and share new ideas that may help in marketing.

Section 13.2

TEACH (cont.)

S Skill Practice
Guided Practice
Identify and Display Have students identify and create a display for a product that did not require much work to generate because it is only a slight variation of another product. (A good example is a box of graham crackers and a box of cinnamon graham crackers.) **L1**

Illustrate the Relationship Ask students to use a diagram to illustrate the product development steps of generating and screening ideas. (Brainstorming generates ideas and screening eliminates ideas, but the brainstorming process often generates ideas that are eliminated immediately through the collaborative process.) **L2**

Brainstorm a Product Have students work in pairs to come up with a new product idea. Instruct one of the students to brainstorm ideas and the other to screen them. Then have the pairs switch tasks. (Product ideas will vary.) **L3**

ASSESS

Review Key Terms
Have students write sentences using each key term.

 Study-to-Go Have students go to the Online Learning Center through **glencoe.com** to download free **Study-to-Go** content to their PDAs or cell phones.

225

226

● **Concept Cars** Car makers develop concept cars, or prototypes, to introduce new cars to the buying public. **In the seven steps of product development, which step does this photograph illustrate?**

● **As You Read**

Think about why it is important to develop a business plan before you develop a product.

Step 3: Develop a Business Plan

W Once the creative ideas pass the screening process, one or two of the ideas are developed into a business plan. The written proposal provides a look at the market. This includes estimated sales, costs, profit potential, market trends, and competing products.

Step 4: Develop the Product

R If the company's decision makers are in favor of the product, a *prototype* will be made. A prototype is a model of the actual product. It is used to see what the new product will look like. It also tests how it can be made. If any aspects of the prototype need to be changed, now is the time to make changes. A company might experience delays in finalizing the product as it is tested.

Step 5: Test-Market the Product

U Once the product is fully developed, it should be test-marketed. To **test-market** a product means to offer it in a limited market for a limited time. The goal is to collect customers' responses to see if the product is likely to be a success. Testing may give a competitor time to produce a similar product. Then both products may enter the market at the same time, and the first firm loses its competitive advantage.

226 **Chapter 13** Marketing in Today's World

● **As You Read**

A business plan gives information on the market before a product or service becomes available. This includes estimated sales, costs, profits, trends, competition, and the risks involved. If the plan shows weaknesses, the business can fix the problem or decide not to go ahead with it.

Discuss the Photo

● **Concept Cars** The concept car in the photograph is being test-marketed, which is Step 5 in the seven steps of product development.

Step 6: Introduce the Product

When the product has passed the market test, it is ready for the marketplace. A publicity campaign introduces the product. The costs of launching a new product are often high. The company has a short time in the market before competitors start to develop similar products. This is especially true after a new product becomes successful.

C

Step 7: Evaluate Customer Acceptance

Once the product is introduced, marketers track customers and their responses to it. Their reports answer key questions that can be used in the company's research and development plans. Who are their best customers? What new products are they buying? How often do customers buy the new product? If customers like the new product, the company will continue to produce it. If not enough customers like it, it may not be on the market long.

Real World

Product Failures
Not all products that are test-marketed succeed. After Ford® introduced the Edsel in 1958, the car failed to meet sales expectations. Marketing experts say Ford did not understand U.S. consumers. *Compile a list of other commercial flops. Explain why they were not accepted.*

Section 13.2

● **After You Read**

Review Key Concepts
1. What are some tools used by market researchers?
2. What are the seven steps of product development?
3. How can a company know if its new product is succeeding?

Academic Skills

4. **English Language Arts** Find advertisements in magazines and newspapers that appeal to different demographic categories. For example, look for ads for products that teens, parents with young children, and retirees would be especially interested in buying. Mount the ads on poster board and write captions for them. Prepare a five-minute talk about the demographic groups represented, telling why the ads are well-designed for their target demographic. Discuss the ads' headlines, visual imagery, and the words used in the ad copy.

5. **English Language Arts** During the next week, save all of the advertising and promotional material that comes in the mail for you and your family. Create categories based on the types of products and services offered. Organize the material accordingly, and prepare a brief questionnaire to give to your family members. Try to find out whether they would buy any of the goods or services based on the advertising material. Which advertisements do the best job of marketing their product or service? Write a summary of your findings.

@ Go to the *Introduction to Business* Online Learning Center through **glencoe.com** to check your answers.

Section 13.2

Review Key Concepts
1. surveys, sales figures for existing products, databases, and the census
2. generate ideas, screen ideas, develop a business plan, develop the product, test-market the product, introduce the product, and evaluate acceptance
3. Companies can evaluate success by tracking customer responses.

Academic Skills
4. **English Language Arts** Students might choose ads for clothing, cars, or travel.
5. **English Language Arts** Students should form conclusions.

RETEACH (cont.)

C **Critical Thinking**

Consider Options
Test Marketing Have students discuss how a company might introduce a product. (Students might suggest coupons, free trial subscriptions, or an advertising campaign.)

Real World

Product Failures Use the Internet to find failed products, such as Coca-Cola's New Coke® and the Tucker automobile.

ASSESS

● **After You Read**

Have students complete the Section 13.2 After You Read section review.

Online Study Tools
Have students go to the Online Learning Center through **glencoe.com** to:

- Take the Section 13.2 **Practice Test**.
- Download free **Study-to-Go** content to their PDAs or cell phones.

STUDY TO GO

CLOSE

Culminating Activity
Develop a Product
Have students work in groups to develop an idea for a new product and to map out the steps they would follow to develop their new product. (Presentations should include all seven steps of product development.)

Activity correlates to English Language Arts standards.

227

Chapter 13 *Review and Activities*

Vocabulary Review

1. Students should write complete sentences using each term correctly.

Review Key Concepts

2. Marketing is the process of creating, promoting, and presenting a product to meet the wants and needs of consumers, wherever they are.

3. The seven functions of marketing are distribution, financing, marketing information management, pricing, product/service management, promotion, and selling.

4. The elements of the marketing mix are also called the four Ps: product, place, price, and promotion.

5. A company may use phone calls, e-mails, surveys, or focus groups to gather information from customers.

6. Generate ideas, screen ideas, develop a business plan, create the product, test-market the product, introduce the product, and evaluate customer acceptance.

Section 13.1 *Summary*

Marketing Essentials To market a product successfully, a company has to understand what people want to buy and why they want to buy it. Marketing is the process of creating, promoting, and presenting a product to meet the wants and needs of consumers. Marketing research studies how to promote, sell, and distribute a product or service. It helps companies determine who will buy the product or service and how much it should cost. Marketing research includes studying the marketing mix. The marketing mix consists of four marketing strategies: product, place, price, and promotion, or the *four Ps.* Some people also include a fifth P—for people.

Section 13.2 *Summary*

Market Research and Product Development Market research is the gathering and analysis of information on the size, location, and makeup of a product market. It helps companies make decisions based on demographics, which include age, gender, location, and income. Marketers use surveys, sales figures for current products, databases, and the census to gather this information. Companies generate ideas, screen the ideas, and develop a business plan. They also create the product, do test-marketing, introduce the new product, and evaluate customer acceptance. Their goal is to come up with a product that people would like to buy.

Vocabulary Review

1. On a sheet of paper, use each of these key terms and academic vocabulary terms in a sentence.

Key Terms

market
marketing
relationship marketing
marketing mix
channel of distribution
direct distribution
indirect distribution

break-even point
market research
marketing concept
demographics
target marketing
market segmentation
test-market

Academic Vocabulary

genders	survey
physical	potential
located	strategy
aware	crucial

Review Key Concepts

2. Define marketing.

3. Identify the functions of marketing.

4. List the elements of the marketing mix.

5. Describe the kinds of market research a company may use.

6. Identify the steps in developing a new product.

Critical Thinking

7. Is there a demand for my services? What skills and attributes do I have to offer the employer? What can I do to promote myself as the best person for the job?

8. The target market for a music CD will depend on the type of music offered. The target market for diamond earrings is probably adults with high incomes.

9. The target market includes families, couples, and travelers.

10. If a product is priced too high, fewer people will buy it; if too low, the business may not be able to make a profit. It might discontinue the product.

11. The security and dependability of online retailers make it more comfortable to shop online. Consumers buy travel services and easily shipped items.

Critical Thinking

7. The basics of marketing apply to more than just products and services. If you want a job, you must market yourself to your potential employer. What questions would you research before applying for the job?

8. Compare and contrast the target markets for a music CD and diamond earrings.

9. If you planned to develop and market a sit-down restaurant that offered inexpensive meals, who would be your target market? Explain your answer.

10. Why is pricing such an important part of the marketing mix?

11. Why do you think many consumers now shop on the Internet? What types of products do you think they probably buy online?

12. Companies use many kinds of promotions to attract customers besides advertising. Which types of promotions work best at persuading you to buy?

13. What types of organizations can you list that have a limited role in marketing their products or services? Why do you think those businesses do not engage in more marketing?

Write About It

14. Write a one-page story about what you think the business world would be like without marketing.

15. Imagine that you are part of a team that is developing a new cereal. List the features you would promote for it and its packaging. Write an e-mail to your teacher on how each feature would help the promotion succeed.

16. Write at least one page about the target market for a new cereal. What group or groups would you recommend your company target in marketing the product?

17. Research different trucking companies. List their names, and then write at least two paragraphs about their role in marketing products.

18. Note three products that are marketed to a highly segmented market. Write two paragraphs about each of your choices. Include reasons why these items would be for a segmented market.

19. List at least five items you have purchased recently. Write a page about where each product was produced, where you bought it, and how you think it was brought to the market.

Technology Applications

Spreadsheets and Bar Graphs
20. Survey as many people as you can in your class. Ask them to name their favorite flavor of ice cream. Summarize your data in a spreadsheet. Make a bar graph of their favorites. If you were an ice cream vendor, how would this information be useful to your marketing plan?

Business Ethics

Marketing to Children
21. You have been working on developing a new snack food. Your team has identified small children as the target market. You know this snack food is not very healthful. However, market research shows that the new snack food would very likely sell well. What should you do?

Technology Applications

20. If a large number of students chose one flavor, you might want to plan to sell more of that flavor locally. If you want to expand your market, you might begin a promotional campaign for some of the less-popular flavors.

Business Ethics

21. Students might suggest asking about healthier ingredients, or consulting a nutrition expert. Some students might point out that they would not want to work for a company that promotes unhealthy food. Others might suggest that by continuing to work for the company they might be able to promote changes.

Critical Thinking

12. Answers include: sales; two-for-one sales; offers that include a gift; products that have been endorsed by a celebrity; or coupons for immediate savings.

13. Professionals, government agencies, and universities. Some are not in a competitive market.

Write About It

14. Without marketing, people would hear about products mainly through word of mouth or personal experience or would have little incentive to change their buying habits.

15. E-mails might include price, taste, size, and packaging.

16. The company could target children by promoting taste and prizes in the package. If the company preferred to attract adults, it might point out nutrition and taste.

17. Examples are American Freight, ABF Freight, McLean Trucking. They are the primary ways of moving most products to the market. Various types of trucks are used for specialized purposes.

18. Products will vary but may include expensive items or specific music CDs.

19. Items will vary, but answers should address the country of origin and means of introduction to the market.

Applying Academics to Business

22. Advertising: paid-for communications using various media, a form of promotion. Publicity: a kind of free advertising. Promotion: making customers aware of a product. Marketing: process of matching products to customers who have particular needs.

23. 8 inches × 11 inches = 88 square inches

528 cubic inches ÷ 88 square inches = 6 inches

The box would have to be 6″ tall to have a volume of 528 cubic inches.

24. medium, bacterium, stratum, and phenomenon

25. $2.3 \times 10^3 = 2,300$

Since the company is raising the price 2 × 3 cents, they will lose 1% of their customer base, or 23 customers.

1% = 0.01
0.01 × 2,300 = 23

Active Learning

26. Some students will focus on nutrition. The slogan should be short and grab the consumer's attention. The logo might evoke the idea of health and fun.

Business in the Real World

27. Students should summarize their findings so that they can report the information. They should include answers to all of the questions included in their interview.

Applying Academics to Business

English Language Arts
22. *Advertising, publicity, promotion,* and *marketing* are listed in a thesaurus as synonyms. However, the words have slightly different meanings. Write a few sentences clarifying the meanings of these words and explaining the relationships among them.

Mathematics
23. Market research shows that people prefer rectangular boxes over cylinders. If a company switches from cylinders with a volume of 528 cubic inches to rectangular boxes with a base measuring 8″ × 11″, how tall would the boxes need to be to have the same volume?

> **THEORY** **Finding Volume** The volumes of a three-dimensional solid can be found using a formula. For a rectangle, use $V = lwh$ where V is volume, l is length, w is width, and h is height.

English Language Arts
24. The words *media, bacteria, strata,* and *phenomena* have something in common. They are all plurals. List the singular forms of these words and research their histories using a dictionary, an online source, or other reference material.

Mathematics
25. In a market research study, Acme Corporation showed that every 3¢ increase in the price charged for its widgets lost the company $\frac{1}{2}$ of 1% of its customer base to its competition. If its customer base is 2.3×10^5 people, how many customers would the company lose if it raised the price 6¢?

> **THEORY** **Scientific Notation** To express a number in scientific notation in standard form, look at the exponent. Move the decimal point in the base number that many places to the right.

Active Learning

Design a New Product
26. Packaging must be as appealing as possible to catch the attention of customers. Pair up with a classmate and design a box for a new snack food called Twirls. This new item is nutritious, tastes like your favorite candy, is low-fat, and would be a good after-school snack. Develop a theme for your box and choose colors that will catch the attention of buyers. Design a logo and write a slogan. Share your ideas with the class.

Business in the Real World

Decision Making for Marketing
27. Interview at least two people about what they consider when shopping. Ask questions about the marketing mix: product, place, price, and promotion. Which part of the marketing mix do they consider to be the main factor when making buying decisions? Prepare a written report of your findings. Give an oral presentation to the class about the considerations your subjects considered most important.

***ExamView Assessment Suite* CD** allows you to print out ready-made unit and chapter tests, complete with answer keys. You can also create customized tests.

TeacherWorks Plus provides complete teacher resources in one convenient package. It includes customizable lesson plans in calendar format, and instant access to many print program resources.

Real LIFE • skills

WISE BUYING

28. Critics of marketing sometimes say that products would cost less if consumers did not have to pay for marketing. Others say that, without marketing, we would not know about all of the products available, and there would be less competition. Write guidelines for shoppers to follow so that they can take advantage of the benefits that marketing provides.

Cool Business CAREERS

FIND YOUR DREAM JOB

29. Go to the *Introduction to Business* Online Learning Center through **glencoe.com** for a link to the Occupational Outlook Handbook Web site. Click on the "OOH Search/A-Z Index" link and enter the job category "market and survey researchers." Then write a one-page report about this type of occupation. Conclude your report with a list of things you could do now to prepare yourself to pursue the occupation.

Role Play

MARKETING A PRODUCT

30. Situation You have been asked to give a short speech to your class about the steps a company must follow to market a new running shoe.

Activity Prepare an outline of the points you will include in your presentation on the importance of marketing.

Evaluation You will be evaluated on how well you meet the following performance indicators:

- Define and discuss marketing research.
- Describe the different ways to gather market research.
- Discuss the marketing mix involved in marketing a new running shoe.
- Give reasons why marketing is so important to the success of a product.
- Prepare a written outline of the points in your speech.
- Speak clearly and use correct grammar.

Standardized Test Practice

Directions Choose the letter of the best answer. Write the letter for the answer on a separate piece of paper.

1. By 2000, Skillful Marketing Inc. had collected 1,245,850 names of people who vacation in Mexico for its marketing database. By 2006, the database had grown to 1,594,688. What was the percentage increase in names from 2000 to 2006?

A   1.28%

B   21.87%

C   28%

D   78%

 **TEST-TAKING TIP** Concentration can reduce anxiety when you are taking a test. Do not worry about whether you should have studied more. Pay close attention to one question at a time.

 READING Go to the *Introduction to Business* Online Learning Center through **glencoe.com** for a list of outside reading suggestions.

Real LIFE • skills

28. Answers might include: Compare prices before purchasing. Clip coupons for items you know you will buy. Go online to see if local stores provide coupons on their Web sites. Use loyalty cards to get lower prices. Apply for rebates.

Cool Business CAREERS

29. Market research analysts gather and analyze data and make recommendations to their employers. Survey researchers design and conduct surveys for a variety of clients. Working conditions: Generally in offices, often alone, but may be part of a team; tight deadlines and overtime. Training and qualifications: Bachelor's degree, sometimes a master's degree, plus continuing education. Employment of market and survey researchers is expected to grow faster than average for all occupation. As preparation: Develop excellent analytical and communication skills.

Role Play

30. Presentations should address the competencies noted in the Role Play. Outlines and presentations will vary.

Standardized Test Practice

1. A

 **STRATEGIES FOR STANDARDIZED TEST PREP SUCCESS**

Test Stress Explain to students that negative thinking can undermine their performance on tests because it damages their self confidence. Thinking about how you should have studied more, or how unhappy you are with your academic efforts also crowds your mind and diverts your attention away from the task at hand. We perform our best on tests when we can achieve a state of deep concentration. Help students banish negative thoughts by stopping briefly when such thoughts occur to imagine they are in a warm, comfortable place such as a park or beach. In this way, they won't dwell on the negative and can more easily refocus their attention on the test.

Standards-Based Lesson Planning
Introduction to Business provides students with instruction and assessment in the following fundamental content areas:

Content Standards Correlations	
Describe the types of advertising media used in marketing a product or service.	pp. 235–238, 244–247
Differentiate between different types of advertising media.	pp. 235–238, 244–247
Discuss importance of advertising media.	pp. 235–238, 244–245
Evaluate effectiveness of advertising.	pp. 236, 241, 242, 245
Identify the types of advertising media and media costs.	pp. 235–238, 240–243
Select the most effective direct advertising methods.	pp. 236, 237, 245
Design an appropriate media ad.	p. 243
Calculate media costs.	pp. 240–243, 246

NCLB
Activities, information, and skills practice will help your students attain No Child Left Behind proficiency. Students will improve their abilities in the following academic standards areas:

Academic Standards Correlations		
English Language Arts	Activities/Features	Page
NCTE 3 Apply strategies to interpret texts	After You Read Applying Academics to Business	pp. 243, 246
NCTE 8 Use information resources to gather information and create and communicate knowledge	Applying Academics to Business	p. 246
NCTE 9 Develop an understanding of diversity in language use across cultures	After You Read	p. 243
Mathematics		
Data Analysis and Probability Understand and apply basic concepts of probability	Standardized Test Practice	p. 247
Number and Operations Compute fluently and make reasonable estimates	After You Read	p. 238
Number and Operations Understand numbers, ways of representing numbers, relationships among numbers, and number systems	Applying Academics to Business	p. 246
Problem Solving Build new mathematical knowledge through problem solving	Ask S&P	p. 232
Science		
Content Standard C Students should develop an understanding of the behavior of organisms	Science/Tech Trends	p. 240

Correlations

This chart shows the 21st Century Skills, foundation skills, and workplace competencies that students develop as they work in this chapter.

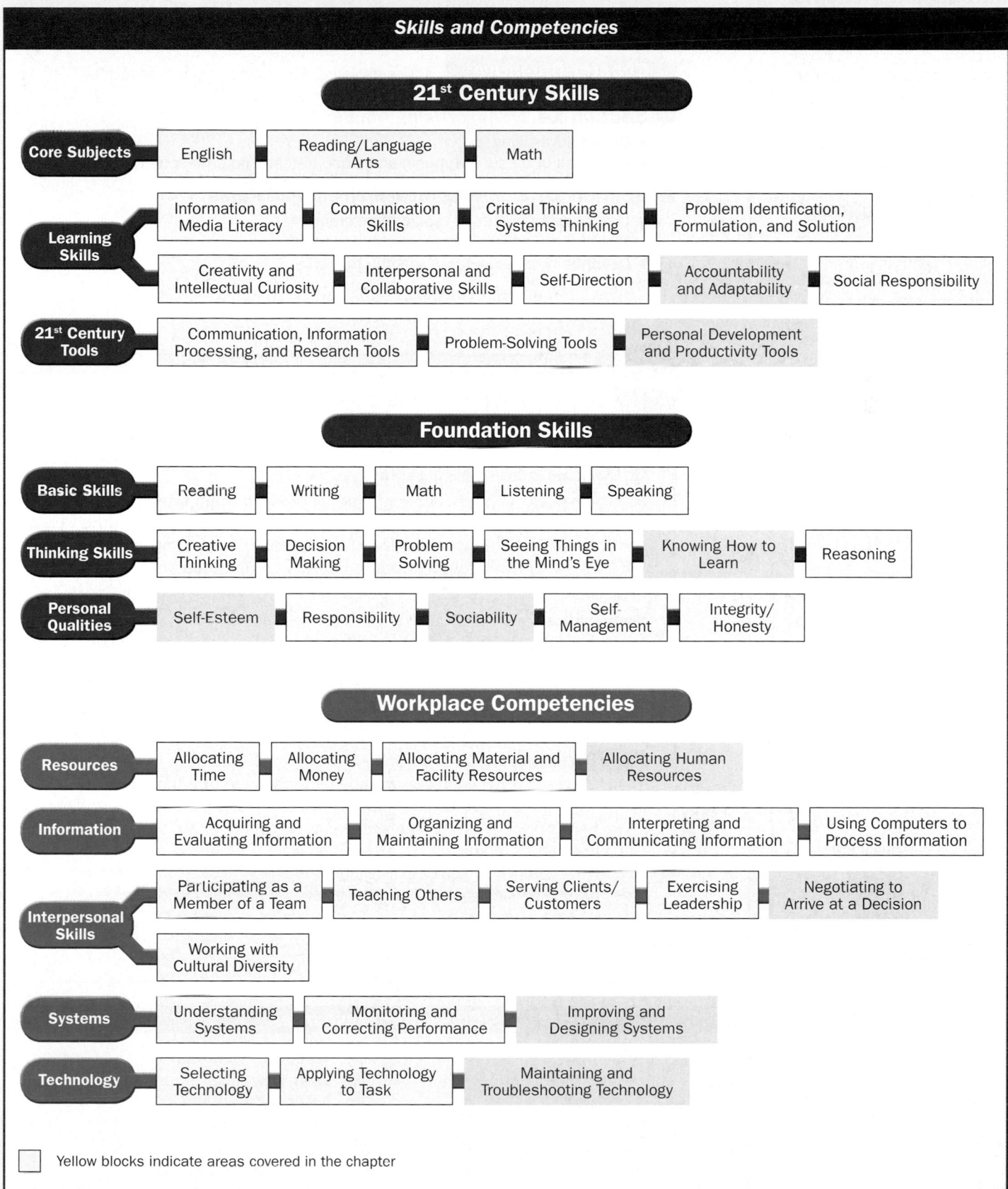

Skills and Competencies

21st Century Skills

Core Subjects
English | Reading/Language Arts | Math

Learning Skills
Information and Media Literacy | Communication Skills | Critical Thinking and Systems Thinking | Problem Identification, Formulation, and Solution
Creativity and Intellectual Curiosity | Interpersonal and Collaborative Skills | Self-Direction | Accountability and Adaptability | Social Responsibility

21st Century Tools
Communication, Information Processing, and Research Tools | Problem-Solving Tools | Personal Development and Productivity Tools

Foundation Skills

Basic Skills
Reading | Writing | Math | Listening | Speaking

Thinking Skills
Creative Thinking | Decision Making | Problem Solving | Seeing Things in the Mind's Eye | Knowing How to Learn | Reasoning

Personal Qualities
Self-Esteem | Responsibility | Sociability | Self-Management | Integrity/Honesty

Workplace Competencies

Resources
Allocating Time | Allocating Money | Allocating Material and Facility Resources | Allocating Human Resources

Information
Acquiring and Evaluating Information | Organizing and Maintaining Information | Interpreting and Communicating Information | Using Computers to Process Information

Interpersonal Skills
Participating as a Member of a Team | Teaching Others | Serving Clients/Customers | Exercising Leadership | Negotiating to Arrive at a Decision
Working with Cultural Diversity

Systems
Understanding Systems | Monitoring and Correcting Performance | Improving and Designing Systems

Technology
Selecting Technology | Applying Technology to Task | Maintaining and Troubleshooting Technology

Yellow blocks indicate areas covered in the chapter

Chapter 14

Chapter Overview

Introduce the Chapter

Advertising
Chapter 14 is about advertising media—the different types of media and their advantages and disadvantages. It also discusses advertising rates.

Building Background
Record a current TV advertisement and play it for your students. Ask the students what they remember about the spot. Discuss the spot and ask the students if they think it motivates people to buy the product or service. (Answers will depend on students' opinions.)

Ask **STANDARD & POOR'S**

>> Math Answer
Fisher Press is probably a better managed company, given its lower, more consistent gross profit.

>> Extension Activity
One way to compare companies in different industries is to use a ratio called the Price-to-Earnings Ratio (P/E ratio). The formula is:

$$P/E\ ratio = \frac{Stock\ Price}{Earnings\ per\ Share}$$

Imagine that a company's stock is trading at $40. If it announces $10 in earnings per share, what is the company's P/E ratio?

$$P/E\ ratio = \frac{\$40}{\$10}$$
$$P/E\ ratio = 4$$

N C L B
Activity correlates to Math standards.

Advertising

Chapter Objectives After completing this chapter, you will be able to:

▶ **Section 14.1** *Advertising Media*
- **Define** advertising.
- **List** types of media that businesses use to reach potential customers.

▶ **Section 14.2** *Media Measurement and Rates*
- **List** the components of media measurement.
- **Identify** how advertising costs are measured.
- **Describe** how media rates are determined.

Ask **STANDARD & POOR'S** **Industry Classifications**

Q: What are industry classifications?

A: Companies that make different types of products often face different challenges in the global economy. To make comparisons easier, analysts use industry classifications to divide the economy into a number of different economic sectors. These sectors are further subdivided into industry groups, industries, and sub-industries. Subdivisions make it easier to compare companies within and across industries.

Mathematics You are interested in two competitors in the information sector of the economy and research their financial histories to find out if one company is better than another. McLain Publishing has a gross profit of 20%, and Fisher Press has a gross profit of 17%. Graphs showing financial histories of the companies suggest that Fisher's gross profit has been steady over the years and that McClain's has fluctuated between 16% and 24%. What conclusions can you draw from this information?

THEORY **Interpreting Data** Since the two companies are in the same business, you can assume that the company with better fundamentals is a better company. When looking at gross profit (revenues minus cost of goods sold) keep in mind that the lower gross profit is as a percentage of sales, the more profitably the company can manufacture its products.

N C L B

Classroom Resources

- Student Edition
- Teacher Wraparound Edition
- Student Activity Workbook with Academic Integration
- Student Activity Workbook with Academic Integration TAE
- *Fast File*, Unit 4 Resources
- Inclusion in the Business Education Classroom

- TeacherWorks Plus
- *ExamView Assessment Suite*
- Presentation Plus!
- Vocabulary PuzzleMaker
- Interactive Student Edition
- Online Student Edition
- Online Learning Center with Podcasts

● **Target Marketing** Businesses advertise in media that will reach their intended market. **How is this an example of target marketing?**

Review the Objectives
Introduce the chapter by reviewing the chapter objectives:

Section 14.1 *Objectives*
Define advertising. (Advertising is the paid, non-personal form of communication that businesses use to promote their products or services.)

List types of media that businesses use to reach potential customers. (Mass media used to reach potential customers includes print media, such as newspapers, magazines, direct-mail advertising, and directory advertising; outdoor advertising; transit advertising; broadcast media, such as television, radio, and webcasting; and online media.)

Section 14.2 *Objectives*
List the components of media measurement. (There are four components of media measurement: audience, impression, frequency, and cost per thousand [CPM].)

Identify how advertising costs are measured. (Costs of advertising are measured by the cost of reaching 1,000 readers or viewers of an advertisement [cost per thousand, or CPM].)

Describe how media rates are determined. (Media rates are determined by the size of an ad, the number of people it reaches, how often it appears, and where it is placed.)

Discuss the Photo
● **Target Marketing** Read the caption on the photo to students: Businesses advertise in media that will reach their intended market.

Ask students: How is this an example of target marketing? (Answers will vary, but students should note that the placement of an ad in a magazine that appeals to young people is a way of targeting the youth market.)

FOCUS

Bell Ringer Activity

Advertising Media
Ask students: Where do companies advertise? (Answers include television, radio, magazines, the Internet, and billboards.)

Preteaching

Presentation Plus!
The Presentation Plus! CD provides visual teaching aids for this section.

PuzzleMaker
Use the Vocabulary PuzzleMaker to create a puzzle of the section's key terms. Students can complete the puzzle on paper or on a computer.

Graphic Organizer
Tell students to go to the Online Learning Center through **glencoe.com** for a printable graphic organizer. (Answers include: Newspapers: Main advertising medium in the United States. Magazines: Published weekly or monthly. Ads can be national or regional. Television: Ads reach a mass audience. Direct-mail: Ads are sent by mail to homes. Directories: Telephone books are the most common type; most useful for local businesses. Radio: Caters to travelers. Online media: Ads include pop-up, banner, and paid search ads.)

N C L B Connects academics to content.

Advertising Media

Reading Guide

● Before You Read

Think about the types of media businesses can choose from to advertise their products and services.

D

Read to Learn
- Define advertising.
- List types of media that businesses use to reach potential customers.

The Main Idea
Businesses must find ways to reach potential customers. Advertising is one type of promotion that can be used to reach local, regional, national, or even worldwide markets.

Key Concepts
- Why Companies Advertise
- Types of Media

Vocabulary
Key Terms
advertising
mass media
infomercial
direct-mail advertising
pop-up ads
banner ads
webcast

 Go to the *Introduction to Business* Online Learning Center through **glencoe.com** for a printable graphic organizer.

Academic Vocabulary
You will find these words in your reading and on your tests. Make sure you know their meanings.

media   unique
communicate   transit

Graphic Organizer
As you read, list the types of advertising media, and add notes about each in a chart like the one below.

Types of Media	Notes
Newspapers	
Magazines	
Television	
Direct-Mail	
Directories	
Radio	
Online	

Academic Standards
English Language Arts
    NCTE 1 Read texts to acquire new information
    NCTE 9 Develop an understanding of diversity in language use across cultures
Mathematics
    Number and Operations Compute fluently and make reasonable estimates

N C L B

Reading Guide

● Before You Read

Students will likely mention television, radio, magazines, billboards, and the Internet.

D Develop Concepts

The Main Idea Ask students: Why do businesses need to advertise? (Businesses must find ways to reach potential customers so that they can communicate the benefits of their products and services and increase profits.)

Why Companies Advertise

Advertising is the public promotion of something such as a product, service, business, or event, to attract or increase interest in it. Advertisements, or ads, are everywhere. The average person sees hundreds of ads every day. They are in magazines and movie theaters, and on TV and the street.

Advertisers use humor, creativity, style, and originality to create an image for their products and services. They try to get consumers' attention. Using catchy advertising slogans is one way companies get customers to remember them (see **Figure 14.1**).

Types of Media

A *medium* is a channel or system of communication. For example, television is a medium. **Media** are the members of the mass media. **Mass media** are channels of communication, such as television, radio, and newspapers. Advertisements are delivered to consumers through mass media. The type of medium an advertiser uses depends on the market it wants to reach. *Print media* use words and pictures to **communicate**. Print media include newspapers, magazines, signs, and billboards.

Newspapers

Newspapers are the main advertising medium in the United States. Newspapers allow advertisers to target people within a certain area. However, newspaper ads have a short life. Most people throw newspapers away after they read them.

● As You Read

Think about an item you recently purchased. What image do you feel was attached to the product? Did it influence your purchase?

Figure 14.1 — *Catchy Slogans*

Just do it®
When It Rains, It Pours®
The Breakfast of Champions®
The Pause that Refreshes®
Where's the Beef?®
Good to the Last Drop®
The milk chocolate melts in your mouth — not in your hands®
We bring good things to life®

Source: *Advertising Age Magazine*

● **How Many Do You Know?** Some advertising slogans have become so well known that people all over the country recognize them. *Advertising Age* magazine judged these slogans to be some of the best. How many of the products or services can you name?

● As You Read

Answers will vary. Students should be aware of images that influence them to make purchases. For example, some ads feature people having fun and give the impression that the product is the reason they are having fun.

Figure 14.1

● **How Many Do You Know?** Students are most likely to know the Nike slogan, "Just do it," and the Wheaties slogan, "The Breakfast of Champions." Point out that many popular slogans remain familiar to people long after the companies have stopped using them.

TEACH

Discussion Starter
Why Companies Advertise
Ask students: Why do companies advertise? Why do they use some media and not others? (Answers will vary. Students should understand that companies advertise to promote their products and services. They should recognize that companies choose media that are likely to be seen or heard by potential customers. For example, a local bakery with only a single store is not likely to advertise on television or even in a daily newspaper. The bakery might advertise in a weekly neighborhood newspaper.)

R **Reading Strategy**

Find Examples Provide students with newspapers from the past few weeks. Include local daily and weekly papers as well as papers that have a national audience. If possible, include several newspapers from large cities and small towns. Ask students to choose three ads from three different papers. For each ad, ask students to write a short paragraph explaining why the advertiser might have chosen to place an ad in that particular newspaper. Consider allowing students to work in pairs. (Answers should explain why the medium is well-suited to the advertised product or service. For example, an ad for a surfboard shop would be well-suited to a local beach community newspaper but not a national financial newspaper.)

235

TEACH (cont.)

S Skill Practice

Guided Practice

Find Examples Provide students with issues of three similar magazines to find ads that appear in all three. Ask why a company might run the same ad in multiple magazines. (to reach as many people as possible in the target market) **L1**

Explain Examples Have students find examples and explain the benefits of regional advertising. (Regional advertising reaches a large audience without the cost of national advertising.) **L2**

Compare Examples Have students present the similarities and differences in ads for a similar product from a newspaper and a magazine. (The printing quality in the magazine may be better. The text might be similar for both. The ads may differ, depending on the geographic reach of the different types of media.) **L3**

ASSESS

Review Key Terms

Have students write sentences using each key term.

Study-to-Go

Have students go to the Online Learning Center through **glencoe.com** to download free **Study-to-Go** content to their PDAs or cell phones.

Humor in Advertising

TV commercials try to grab viewers' attention and leave an impression about the advertised item. This must be done within a few seconds. Companies use humor in ads to help consumers remember their products or services. Think of some funny ads that you have seen. *Did they help you remember the item advertised? Explain your answer.*

S

Magazines

Most magazines are national and appear every week (such as *Time*) or every month (such as *Seventeen*). People from all over the country see national magazine ads. Many magazines offer regional editions for different parts of the country. Special-interest magazines such as *Sports Illustrated* make it possible to reach target markets on a large scale.

Magazine ads have a longer life than newspaper ads. People take their time when reading magazines. Some even save them.

Television

Television advertising combines sounds, images, and motion. TV ads can be informative, entertaining, or creative. Most TV ads are 30 seconds long. A **unique** type of TV ad is the infomercial. An **infomercial** is a 30-minute commercial.

TV ads can be shown on national, local, or cable stations. TV advertisers can reach a wide audience. They can also reach target markets by showing ads during certain types of shows.

Ads for TV can be expensive to produce and run. The more popular a show is, the more it costs to air an ad during that show. **Figure 14.2** illustrates the amount of money some corporations spend to advertise their product.

Figure 14.2 — Big Spenders

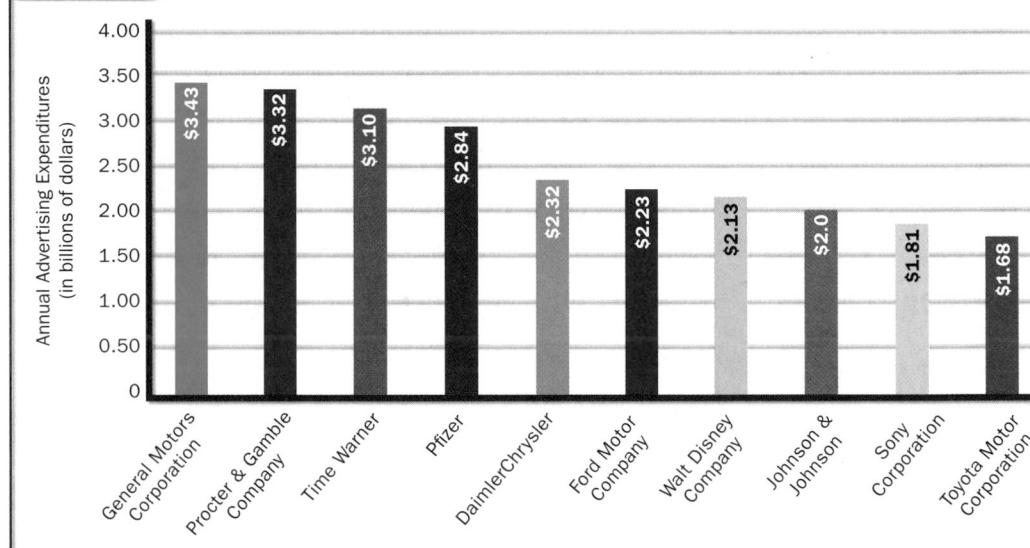

Source: *The World Almanac and Book of Facts*

● **Big Spenders** This chart shows five companies who spent the most on advertising in a recent year. General Motors Corporation, for example, spent about $3.4 billion on advertising. **Think about advertisements for these five companies. In what media have you seen their ads?**

236 **Chapter 14** Advertising

Real World

Humor in Advertising Some companies that are known for their funny ads are American Express®, Sprint®, and Pepsi®. However, some firms' ads place more emphasis on humor instead of the product, which does not help some consumers to remember what was advertised.

Figure 14.2

● **Big Spenders** Most students will have seen advertisements for products from these companies on television and in national magazines. Ask students if they can name some of the products that these companies advertise. (GM advertises cars and trucks; Procter & Gamble® advertises coffee, toothpaste, and soap.)

International Business

Cross-Cultural Advertising

One of the most difficult challenges for international marketers is communicating to people of diverse cultures. Advertising is about communicating a message to raise awareness or promote a product. When a product is marketed to an international audience, using the same advertising campaign as is used at home will in most cases result in failure. Sayings, symbols, and images speak to different people differently; cultures have different values and perceptions about what enhances status or gives convenience. Therefore, many advertising executives are turning to special consultants for help with cross-cultural advertising.

Examples of Languages Across Cultures

Q: In Spanish, how do you say: "Thank you for your time"?

A: **Gracias por su tiempo.** (pronounced: Grăh-sēē-ŭs pŏhr soo tēē-ĭm-pō)

If you were planning an international advertising campaign, what are some things you would need to know about a culture in order to be successful?

Direct-Mail Advertising

Direct-mail advertising is the biggest advertising medium after television and newspapers. **Direct-mail advertising** consists of ads sent by mail to people's homes and businesses. Direct mail allows advertisers to reach a specific target market.

Direct-mail advertisers contact consumers in a variety of ways. They use letters, flyers, postcards, and catalogs. They often include coupons or free samples. The cost of sending ads through the mail can be high. Direct mail is often referred to as "junk mail." People who receive direct-mail advertising often throw it out without ever looking at it.

Directory Advertising

Directory advertising appears mostly in phone books. It is especially useful for local advertisers. They can display an ad under a heading for the type of product or service they offer and list their phone number and address. The cost of a directory ad is usually low. A disadvantage of directory ads is that they have to compete with other similar ads.

Radio Advertising

Radio ads can reach a wide audience. However, they may not be as effective as TV or magazine ads because they cannot use images. They use music, dialogue, and sound effects to get a listener's attention.

● As You Read

Think about the junk mail your household gets. If few people actually respond to this mail, why do you think advertisers keep sending it?

Section 14.1   Advertising Media   **237**

International Business

Cross-Cultural Advertising Students might mention language, what colors and numbers mean in the culture, what motivates people, and what is considered tasteful and appropriate.

● As You Read

Answers will vary. Students may feel the approach of sending thousands, even millions, of pieces of mail will result in a certain percentage of sales, justifying the cost. Others may feel it is not a good advertising tool.

C Critical Thinking

Consider the Source
Outdoor Advertising Have students make up a checklist of at least five things to consider when creating an outdoor ad. (length, type size, graphic size, location, and community standards)

ASSESS

● **After You Read**

Have students complete the Section 14.1 After You Read section review.

Online Study Tools
Have students go to the Online Learning Center through **glencoe.com** to:

- Take the Section 14.1 **Practice Test**.
- Download free **Study-to-Go** content to their PDAs or cell phones.

CLOSE

Culminating Activity
Cyber Ads
Have students visit at least three news Web sites and to make a list of the ads on the home pages. The list should include the product advertised, a description of the ad and the type of ad. (Most will be banner ads and screen ads.)

✔ **Reading Check**

Identify pop-up ads and banner ads

Online Media

The two main types of online ads are pop-up and banner ads. **Pop-up ads** appear in a new browser window when you first log on to a Web site. **Banner ads** are displayed across the top or bottom of the Web page.

Webcasting Another way to advertise online is through webcasting. A **webcast** is a broadcast made on the Internet. It often consists of a live broadcast made using a Web camera, or cam.

✔ **Reading Check** **Identify** Name two kinds of online ads.

Other Types of Media

Billboards provide the most common form of *outdoor advertising*. Most billboards are large and placed near highways where they are very visible. The main disadvantage of them, though, is that people often drive by too quickly to notice them.

C **Transit** advertising usually consists of posters placed on the sides of buses, in subway stations, inside trains, and at airports. These ads are most common in urban areas where public transportation is often used. Just about any space that can be seen by people can be used for advertising.

NCLB Activity correlates to Math standards.

Section 14.1
● **After You Read**

Review Key Concepts
1. Why do companies advertise?
2. What are some types of media used by businesses to advertise?
3. What advantages do print and cyber ads share?

NCLB

Academic Skills
4. **Mathematics** The top rate paid one year for a 30-second TV ad during the Super Bowl was 6% greater than the previous year's top rate. If the new top rate paid was $2.4 million, what was the top rate paid the previous year?

THEORY **Working with Percents** In this problem, $2.4 million represents 106% of the previous year's rate. Percents can be converted easily to decimals by moving the decimal point two places to the left.

 For math help, go to the Math Appendix.

@ Go to the *Introduction to Business* Online Learning Center through **glencoe.com** to check your answers.

Section 14.1

Review Key Concepts
1. Companies advertise to promote a product, service, business, or event.
2. Advertising media used by businesses include print, broadcast, and online media.
3. Print and cyber ads are high quality, full color, and sent directly to consumers.

Academic Skills
4. **Mathematics** $2.4 million ÷ 1.06 = $2.26 million
The top rate paid last year was $2.26 million.

Media Measurement and Rates

Reading Guide

Before You Read

Think about how companies make plans to advertise and determine the cost of an advertisement.

Read to Learn
- List the components of media measurement.
- Identify how advertising costs are measured.
- Describe how media rates are determined.

The Main Idea
Businesses need to reach as many targeted customers as possible. Many companies do this by advertising. It is important to calculate ad costs and measure media effectiveness to best reach a potential audience.

Key Concepts
- Media Planning
- Media Measurement
- Media Rates

Vocabulary
Key Terms

media planning
advertising agency
ad campaign
audience

impression
frequency
cost per thousand (CPM)
prime time

Academic Vocabulary
You will find these words in your reading and on your tests. Make sure you know their meanings.

medium
display

prime
network

Graphic Organizer
As you read, write notes about media planning questions in a figure like the one below.

Media Planning Questions

1.	?
2.	?
3.	?

 Go to the *Introduction to Business* Online Learning Center through **glencoe.com** for a printable graphic organizer.

Academic Standards
English Language Arts
- **NCTE 1** Read texts to acquire new information
- **NCTE 3** Apply strategies to interpret texts
- **NCTE 4** Use written language to communicate effectively
- **NCTE 5** Use different writing process elements to communicate effectively
- **NCTE 9** Develop an understanding of diversity in language use across cultures

Science
- **Content Standard C** Students should develop an understanding of the behavior of organisms

---

Reading Guide

Before You Read

Costs include the development and production of the ad and the cost of running the ad.

D Develop Concepts

The Main Idea Remind students of the Taco Bell chihuahua ad campaign. Then ask: Why might an advertisement be discontinued? (Students should understand that it is important to measure the effectiveness of advertising. Even though people enjoy the ad, they might not be buying the product.)

FOCUS

Bell Ringer Activity

Media Measurement and Rates
Tell students: Advertising is a paid, nonpersonal form of communication that businesses use to promote their products and services. Ask students: To what does the word "paid" refer in the definition of advertising? (Paying a company to deliver your advertising message.) There are also costs involved in developing and producing the ad.

Preteaching

Presentation Plus!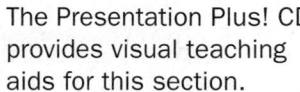
The Presentation Plus! CD provides visual teaching aids for this section.

PuzzleMaker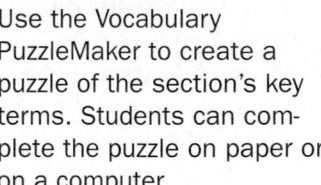
Use the Vocabulary PuzzleMaker to create a puzzle of the section's key terms. Students can complete the puzzle on paper or on a computer.

Graphic Organizer
Tell students to go to the Online Learning Center through **glencoe.com** for a printable graphic organizer. (Answers include: Can the medium present the product or service and the appropriate business image? Can the desired customers be targeted? Will the medium get the desired response rate?)

NCLB Connects academics to content.

239

TEACH

Discussion Starter
Media Planning
Ask students this question: What kinds of issues do you think need to be considered in media planning? (Answers will vary. Students might mention the marketing objective, the target market, and the cost.)

R Reading Strategy

Recognize the Main Idea
Ask students to summarize the main idea of the section under the head, "Media Planning." (Media planning is the process of selecting advertising media and deciding the time and space in which the ads should appear.)

● As You Read

Companies try to project an image that will attract the type of consumers they are targeting. Also, ads are a quick and easy way to reach the most people at one time. The images they see in ads leave an impression on them for when they buy goods and services later.

Virtual Business

Introduce advanced promotion using the Virtual Business Retailing Advanced Promotion activity. In this simulation, students learn why advanced promotion is important to the success of a business.

240

● As You Read
Think about the different images that some companies convey in their ads.

Media Planning

R

Media planning is the process of selecting advertising media and deciding the time and space in which the ads should appear. To create a media plan and select the right **medium** to use, advertisers address three basic questions:

1. Can the medium present the product or service and the appropriate business image?
2. Can the desired customers be targeted with the medium?
3. Will the medium get the desired response rate?

Effective media planning can help a business project the desired image to the target market.

Advertising Agencies

Many businesses develop advertising by hiring advertising agencies. An **advertising agency** is a business that specializes in developing ads and ad campaigns for its clients. An **ad campaign** is a series of ad messages that share a single idea and theme. Ad agencies vary in size—from small agencies that serve regional markets to large international firms.

Science/Tech **TRENDS**

NCLB

Sensory Branding

Some of the world's most recognizable brands from the 20th century are Ivory® soap, Gerber® baby food, Kodak® cameras, Coca-Cola®, and McDonald's®. These brands mean something to most people and have managed to become part of our everyday lives. How are companies creating the brands of the future? Marketing and branding guru Martin Lindstom is encouraging today's marketing professionals to appeal to all the senses, not just sight and sound. He says that touch and smell are the future when it comes to creating a brand identity. For example, chemists develop special scents, and aestheticians design sound and tactile elements. These create a deeper emotional connection to the brand. Singapore Airlines used a patented smell called Stefan Floridian Waters throughout its airplanes to differentiate its brand from others. They even put it on flight attendants' uniforms and on the hot towels they gave passengers.

Web Quest

Go to the *Introduction to Business* Online Learning Center through **glencoe.com** for links to Web sites where you can find out more about how marketers are appealing to all the senses when establishing brand identity. Give some specific examples, and explain how appealing to all the senses can help influence people's attitudes, preferences, and purchasing behavior.

Science/Tech **TRENDS**

Web Quest

Sensory Branding Answers will vary, but students might discuss the relationship between human behavior and the senses. Our senses detect stimuli in the environment around us and send signals to our brains through the nervous system.

NCLB
Activity correlates to Science standards.

Media Measurement

Media planners are concerned with the correct medium to use and its costs. They are also concerned with how to measure an ad's overall effectiveness. An effective ad will help raise a firm's sales.

To understand media measurement, you need to become familiar with several key terms. First, the number of homes or people exposed to an ad is called the **audience**. A single exposure to an advertising message is called an **impression**. **Frequency** is the number of times an audience sees or hears an ad. **Cost per thousand (CPM)** is the media cost of exposing 1,000 readers or viewers to an advertising impression. (The "M" in CPM comes from the word *mille,* which is Latin for "thousand.")

Media Audiences

TV audience measurement is based on diaries and viewer data collected by Nielsen Media Research®. The Nielsen organization takes a sample of TV viewers in more than 200 markets. Arbitron Inc.® uses listener diaries to measure radio audiences in more than 260 markets. Online audiences are measured through surveys and computer software tracking systems.

Knowing the potential audience, how frequently your ad will be seen, and its CPM can tell you if the rates charged by various media are right for your ad budget.

● **Successful Ads** The purpose of advertising is to attract attention and transmit a message. **What catches your attention in this ad?**

✔ Reading Check **Analyze** Why do advertisers rely on media measurement?

Media Rates

To reach customers, advertising uses a set format that is defined in terms of time (a 60-second TV or radio ad) or space (a half-page newspaper ad). Media costs vary greatly, not just with type of media but also with geographic location and audience.

A *media rate* or *advertising rate* is the amount of money it costs to **display** or broadcast an ad. It is separate from the amount it costs to make an ad. Ad rates are determined by several factors: the size of the ad, the number of people it reaches, how often it appears, when it appears, and where it is placed.

✔ Reading Check **Analyze** Advertisers rely on media measurement to select the correct medium to use and to evaluate its costs.

Discuss the Photo
● **Successful Ads** Answers will vary. Students are likely to be attracted to the size of the ad, the sense of motion, and the visual excitement of the image.

RETEACH

R Reading Strategy

Use Examples Have students measure four display ads in a local newspaper and calculate the cost of the ads using an ad rate of $25 per inch. Point out that ad rates vary from paper to paper and within a newspaper. (Answer for the cost of the ads will vary depending on the ad sizes. The calculation is as follows: $25 × depth in inches × number of columns.)

U Universal Access

Second Language Learners Watching TV can be an excellent way for second language learners to practice their listening comprehension skills. Have second language students practice their speaking skills by verbally answering the *BusinessWeek* Reader Active Learning activity. Be aware that a student's ability to speak the language may not be the same as his or her ability to comprehend when reading or listening.

Ad Campaigns That

Fail Answers include the cost of making and airing TV ads. The company decided the ads were not worth their cost because sales did not rise. Other ads might lead to more sales.

Student Activity Workbook ☞ Assign the Section 14.2 Activities.

Ad Campaigns That Fail Taco Bell® used to run ads featuring a Chihuahua that said, *"Yo quiero Taco Bell"* ("I want Taco Bell"). The commercials were so popular that the dog's image was put on T-shirts, window decals, and toys. After a while, the company determined that the ads did not lead to more sales, so they stopped running them. *If the ads were popular, why do you think they did not increase sales?*

Print Media Ad Rates

Ad rates for newspapers and magazines are based on circulation, or the number of people who buy them, and audience, the number of readers per issue. An advertiser usually pays a rate for every 1,000 people (CPM) a newspaper or magazine reaches.

The size of the ad also affects the cost. Newspaper and magazine ads are sold by the inch on a page. A column inch is an area that is one column wide by one inch deep. If a newspaper quotes a column inch rate, multiply the number of inches by the number of columns. This gives you the total number of column inches. Then multiply the total column inches by the rate. For example, if the rate for a column inch is $17, then an ad that measures four inches long by three columns wide will cost $204 ($17 × 4 inches × 3 columns = $204).

Magazine rates are based on circulation, the type of readership, and production techniques. *Premium position* refers to ad placement. Ads placed in **prime** positions, such as on the back cover or the inside of the first page, are more expensive to buy.

BusinessWeek *Reader and Case Study*

TV Eyeballs Close-Up

A handful of companies are figuring out how to give advertisers better feedback on who's watching television.

Ever since the advent of commercial television, advertisers have wondered exactly what they get for the megabucks they spend on 30-second spots. After all, the networks and cable companies offer only a crude approximation of who is watching what. With such thin information, advertisers can't target specific neighborhoods or consumer tastes. Yet the Web, with its sophisticated per-click metrics, does all of that billions of times a day. "The problem," says Yankee Group analyst Aditya Kishore, "is that there's not enough math in [the TV] business."

But aQuantive Inc. aims to change that. A marketing firm that also owns the Avenue A | Razorfish™ Web ad agency, aQuantive helps clients measure online audiences and tailor ads to specific surfers. Having locked up a sizable chunk of that business, the Seattle outfit is eager to bring its smarts to television, promising advertisers their first real fix on the viewing and spending habits of Americans. Despite the hoopla about advertisers moving online, the $70 billion television ad market still dwarfs the Web business 5 to 1. Says aQuantive CEO Brian P. McAndrews, once an ABC executive: "TV is the largest medium out there."

 CASE STUDY Go to the *Introduction to Business* Online Learning Center through **glencoe.com** for the *BusinessWeek* Reader Case Study.

Active Learning

Watch a TV show and write down all of the products that are advertised during the program. Use a spreadsheet to keep track of the age and gender of any people appearing in the ads. Use your results to predict the show's target demographics.

U

glencoe.com

BusinessWeek *Reader and Case Study*

TV Eyeballs Close-Up

CASE STUDY Have students go to the *Introduction to Business* Online Learning Center through **glencoe.com** to download a Case Study activity that corresponds to the article. The activity and answer key are also available on the TeacherWorks Plus CD.

Active Learning

Students should note a connection between the ages and genders of the characters in the ads and the target demographics for the show. They should also note that the products are intended to appeal to the target audience.

Broadcast Media Ad Rates

The cost of TV and radio ads depends on the size of the audience, the reach of the station, and the time of day an ad is broadcast. **Prime time** is the time period when the **network** TV or radio audience is the largest. TV audiences are usually largest between 7 P.M. and 11 P.M., when most viewers are at home. For radio, prime time on weekdays is during the morning or afternoon hours, also called drive times.

Internet Ad Rates

The cost of Internet advertising is based on the type, size, and format of ads. Types include banner ads, rich-media enhanced banner ads, and pop-up ads. The length of time an ad runs also affects the price. Like newspaper and magazine ads, Internet advertisers pay a certain amount for every 1,000 people who get the ad. Rates vary based on the volume of monthly page views.

Paid search ads are Internet ads that online advertisers bid on for search engine queries. The advertiser pays a fee to the search engine whenever someone clicks on the ad. The advertiser that bids the highest for a particular keyword has its ad show up first on the list of ads next to the search results.

● **As You Read**

Think about the different costs for magazine ads. Why would it cost more to place an ad on the back of a magazine than on the inside?

N C L B Activity correlates to English Language Arts standards.

Section 14.2
● **After You Read**

Review Key Concepts

1. What are the three basic questions advertisers must address in media planning?
2. Name the four components of media measurement.
3. Define media rate or advertising rate.

Academic Skills

4. **English Language Arts** Work with a partner to create a radio ad for a product you both like and think would interest other people your age. Write a 30-second script and use music or other sound effects to enhance the ad. Use words and music that will have special appeal to your audience. If possible, record the ad and play it for your class. Join in a discussion with your classmates about the ad's effectiveness.

5. **English Language Arts** Which type of text structure best describes these sentences: compare and contrast, cause and effect, or statement and example? Write a few sentences of your own that use the same type of structure.

Transit advertising is most common in urban areas where public transportation is widely used. For this reason, it is useful for advertising things such as concerts, public events, and local TV.

 Go to the *Introduction to Business* Online Learning Center through **glencoe.com** to check your answers.

RETEACH (cont.)

C Critical Thinking

Draw Conclusions
Setting Advertising Rates
Rates charged for broadcast time are negotiated between sponsors and stations. What affect does this policy have on advertising in broadcast media? (It creates a free market.)

● **As You Read**

Many more people see an ad on the back cover.

ASSESS

● **After You Read**

Have students complete the Section 14.2 After You Read section review.

Online Study Tools

Have students go to the Online Learning Center through **glencoe.com** to:

- Take the Section 14.2 **Practice Test**.
- Download free **Study-to-Go** content to their PDAs or cell phones.

CLOSE

Culminating Activity
Advertising Timeline
Have students work in groups to create advertising timelines. (Timelines will vary but should include significant events in advertising history.)

Section 14.2

Review Key Concepts

1. Can the medium present the product or service and the appropriate business image? Can the desired customers be targeted? Will the medium get the desired response rate?
2. audience, impression, frequency, and cost per thousand (CPM)

3. The amount of money it costs to display or broadcast an ad.

Academic Skills

4. **English Language Arts** Radio ads should communicate a clear message and appeal to the intended audience.
5. **English Language Arts** A cause-and-effect structure.

Chapter 14 *Review and Activities*

Vocabulary Review

1. Students should write complete sentences using each term correctly.

Review Key Concepts

2. Advertising is the paid, non-personal form of communication that businesses use to promote their products or services.

3. Mass media used to reach potential customers include print media, such as newspapers, magazines, direct-mail advertising, and directory advertising; outdoor advertising; transit advertising; broadcast media, such as television, radio, and webcasting; and online media.

4. There are four components of media measurement: audience, impression, frequency, and cost per thousand (CPM).

5. Costs of advertising are measured by the cost of reaching 1,000 readers or viewers of an advertisement (cost per thousand, or CPM).

6. Media rates are determined by the size of the ad, the number of people it reaches, how often it appears, and where it is placed.

Critical Thinking

7. Answers will vary depending on the student's habits and interests.

Section 14.1 *Summary*

Advertising Media Businesses use advertisements, or ads, to promote their products and services. Ads are everywhere—in movie theaters, on the street, and on the Internet. They are placed in print media, which includes newspapers, magazines, and direct mail. Commercials run on TV and radio. Businesses try to build an image for their products and services through their ads. Companies often use humor in ads to leave a lasting impression with consumers. They carefully select the types of advertising and media they will use to reach their target market.

Section 14.2 *Summary*

Media Measurement and Rates Media planning is the process of selecting advertising media and deciding when and where ads should appear to meet the marketing objective. A media plan helps advertisers present an interesting message and project the desired business image to the target market. It is important to calculate costs and measure media effectiveness to best reach an audience. Ad rates vary according to the medium in which the ad appears and how long it runs. Other factors include size, length of time, and the type of ad used.

Vocabulary Review

1. On a sheet of paper, use each of these key terms and academic vocabulary terms in a sentence.

Key Terms		Academic Vocabulary	
advertising	advertising agency	media	medium
mass media	ad campaign	communicate	display
infomercial	audience	unique	prime
direct-mail advertising	impression	transit	network
pop-up ads	frequency		
banner ads	cost per thousand (CPM)		
webcast	prime time		
media planning			

Review Key Concepts

2. Define advertising.

3. List the types of media that businesses use to reach potential customers.

4. List the components of media measurement.

5. Identify how advertising costs are measured.

6. Describe how media rates are determined.

8. Students may list auto or fashion magazines and ads for clothing, beauty products, or motorcycle accessories. They might consider buying the products because the ads make the goods appear attractive.

9. Popularity of cable, DVDs, the Internet, and other forms of media are likely to make TV less desirable than it has been in the past.

10. Advertisers may consider ways of making their TV ads more effective or interesting to prospective customers. They may also shift to other types of media.

11. Online ads can be targeted toward specific groups of people and that form of ad is relatively low-cost.

Critical Thinking

7. Think about your favorite magazine. When you read it, do you glance at the ads, or do you read them carefully? Explain your answer.

8. What products or services are advertised in your favorite magazine? Why would you purchase any of those products or services?

9. Do you think advertising on network TV will be done less or more often in the future? Why?

10. When people record a TV show, they are likely to skip the ads when they watch the show later. What do you think this means to TV advertisers?

11 Many companies advertise their goods and services on the Internet. They also sell space on their Web sites to advertisers. However, the response rates to online ads are low. Why do you think more advertisers are using online ads even if the response rates are low?

12. Why do you think a TV producer would sign a contract with an ad agency?

13. What impact do you think the increasing popularity of cable TV will have on advertising?

Write About It

14. What are some ways to promote a business besides advertising? Write a brief essay offering some examples.

15. Write one page describing an ad from a magazine. Name the product advertised, and list some product descriptions from the ad. Decide if the ad is well designed.

16. In two or more paragraphs, describe the purposes of the following characters used in ads: the Energizer Bunny® (Energizer® batteries); and Tony the Tiger (Kellogg's Frosted Flakes®).

17. Look at a newspaper, and review its ads. Write a one-page description of three ads that appear. Compare and contrast their effectiveness.

18. What will be the effect on online advertising if people use software to block pop-up ads? Write at least two paragraphs on your response.

19. Companies pay more to advertise their products and services during special events, such as the *Academy Awards* or the Olympics. Why do you think advertisers are willing to pay up to $400,000 for a 30-second ad? Write a brief summary of your thoughts.

Technology Applications

Word-Processing Software
20. Select one of the following advertising agencies to research: Ogilvy & Mather; McCann Worldgroup; TBWA Worldwide; Leo Burnett Worldwide; BBDO Worldwide; Agency.com; J. Walter Thompson Company; or Saatchi & Saatchi. Write a two-page report about the ad agency's services. Include some of its clients and the types of ads it helped create.

Business Ethics

Ethical Advertising
21. Companies must disclose all information necessary for a customer to make a safe and informed decision. If a company promotes a food product as a "diet product," what types of information do you think it should provide in order to be ethical in its advertising? What would you consider to be unethical? Write at least two paragraphs on your responses.

Critical Thinking

12. If their specialties match, the agency should be able to provide the kind of ad campaign that will reach a potential audience for a TV program.

13. As more people watch cable TV, the number of advertisers will probably grow.

Write About It

14. Essays may mention offering coupons, sponsoring special events, and donating goods and services.

15. Answers will vary depending on the ad selected.

16. McDonald's Restaurants sponsors Ronald McDonald Houses—facilities that provide housing for families of children who are hospitalized. Tony the Tiger is well known for his They're Gr-r-reat!® slogan for Frosted Flakes.

17. Answers will vary depending on the ads selected and their effectiveness.

18. The effect probably will not be less online advertising, but just a shift in the types of ads used.

19. Popular shows reach millions of viewers. Those advertisers may believe that the expense is worth the market share they may gain for their products.

Technology Applications

20. Answers will depend on the agency chosen. For example, Ogilvy & Mather indicates that it primarily helps its clients to build brands. It gathers information about products, consumers, the competition, and the environment as a way of developing a brand image for its ads.

Business Ethics

21. Answers will vary. For instance, if the product is supposed to be a diet product, the company should provide the number of calories per serving and the amount of fat contained in the product. If their product does not have fewer calories and fat than other non-diet, the company should not call it a diet product.

Applying Academics to Business

22. Smaller, more local companies tend to use radio advertising more often than others. Some companies may use all three.

23. 56% = 0.56; $\frac{1}{4}$ = 0.25; 10% = 0.10; 0.56 + 0.25 + 0.10 = 0.91; 1.00 − 0.91 = 0.9; 0.9 = 9%; Of the total revenue, 9% was generated by direct mail.

24. The word that does not belong is *infomercial* because it is a portmanteau word, not a compound word like the others. A portmanteau word combines both sounds and meanings from two or more other words, in this case, *information* and *commercial*. Some other compound words are *outdoor* and *newspaper*.

25. Let *x* equal the total cost. Then, *x* = $420,000 + $\frac{1}{3}$ ($420,000 × 12) *x* = $2,100,000

Active Learning

26. Answers will vary. For instance, ads with real people show how they use the product.

Business in the Real World

27. Answers will vary. For example, a lawn-care business may do snow removal in the winter.

Applying Academics to Business

English Language Arts
22. List businesses that advertise on TV, radio, and billboards. Are there any types of businesses that advertise using all three media? Do large, multinational corporations seem to use one type more than others? Which is used by smaller, more local businesses? Write a one-page paper explaining what you have learned.

Mathematics
23. Of a company's $140 million in sales, 56% was credited to TV ads, $\frac{1}{4}$ to magazine ads, and 10% to radio. The rest of the business came from direct mail. What percent of the total revenue was generated by direct mail?

> **THEORY** **Fractions, Decimals, and Percents** Fractions, decimals, and percents are similar in that they are all used to represent part of a whole. To solve this problem, start by converting the fractions and percents to decimals.

English Language Arts
24. List the words below on a sheet of paper. Four of them have something in common. Cross out the word that does not belong. Add a fifth word from the chapter that does belong. Write a sentence or two explaining your choices.

update   lifespan   infomercial
billboard   webcast

Mathematics
25. Production costs for a 30-second TV commercial are $420,000. Airtime costs $\frac{1}{3}$ of that each time the ad runs. Write an equation to find the total cost of creating the commercial and then running it 12 times. Write a sentence or two explaining the steps to take to find the solution.

> **THEORY** **Order of Operations** Equations are solved by first performing any operations within parentheses, then exponents, multiplication and division from left to right, and finally addition and subtraction from left to right.

Active Learning

Describe TV Ads
26. Ads sometimes convey their message by showing people using a product in their everyday life. Others present a fantasy. Some ads use a song or jingle to help people remember the product or service. Others give information. Watch three popular TV shows. List the products that are advertised during those shows. For each product, describe the approach of the ad.

Business in the Real World

Small Business Advertising
27. Interview a person who has a service business that is seasonal, such as a lawn mowing or snow removal company. Ask the business owner if he or she advertises. If so, how? Are there highs and lows in the owner's business? If so, does the owner offer other services in the off-season in order to have a steady income? How does advertising affect the business's budget?

246 Chapter 14 Review and Activities

ExamView Assessment Suite CD allows you to print out ready-made unit and chapter tests, complete with answer keys. You can also create customized tests.

TeacherWorks Plus provides complete teacher resources in one convenient package. It includes customizable lesson plans in calendar format, and instant access to many print program resources.

Real LIFE · skills

SUITABLE ADVERTISING

28. Advertisers use different types of appeals to reach their potential customers. Write a short report describing the types of appeals that are successful in persuading teens to buy products. If you could advise advertisers on marketing to teens, what advice would you give them? What can advertisers do that will convince teens to buy their products?

Business CAREERS

FIND YOUR DREAM JOB

29. Go to the *Introduction to Business* Online Learning Center through **glencoe.com** for a link to the Occupational Outlook Handbook Web site. Click on the "OOH Search/A–Z Index" link and enter "advertising, marketing, promotions, public relations, and sales managers." Then write a one-page report about this field. Conclude your report with a list of things you could do now to prepare yourself to pursue the occupation.

Role Play

A COMMUNITY PROJECT

30. Situation A *sponsor* is a person or organization that provides money to help fund an event as a form of advertising. Plan a presentation to convince a local firm to sponsor a community activity in your neighborhood.

Activity Outline the points you would make to the company about the advertising value of its sponsorship.

Evaluation You will be evaluated on how well you meet the following performance indicators:

- Explain the purpose of the community activity, its audience, and potential attendance figures.
- Outline several points about how the sponsorship is valuable to the community and how it can build a good image of the company.
- Identify what the company would do as the sponsor.
- Prepare a written outline of the points you will make in your presentation.

Standardized Test Practice

Directions Choose the letter of the best answer. Write the letter for the answer on a separate piece of paper.

1 Which are dependent events?

  A   flipping a coin, and then flipping it again

  B   taking a marble out of a bag, then taking another marble out of the bag

  C   spinning a spinner, then moving your piece that many spaces

  D   tossing a number cube, then tossing another number cube

TEST-TAKING TIP Just before taking a test, try to avoid talking about it with other students. Test anxiety can be contagious.

 READING Go to the *Introduction to Business* Online Learning Center through **glencoe.com** for a list of outside reading suggestions.

 **STRATEGIES FOR STANDARDIZED TEST PREP SUCCESS**

Test Stress Explain that everyone has experienced stress before an important test or performance. It's a good idea not to discuss your anxiety with others before a test. Help students monitor their own stress-related responses by having them look for daydreaming, confusion, tense muscles, and mental blocking and manage these effects using relaxation techniques.

Real LIFE · skills

28. Answers will vary. For example, students might suggest that advertisers include clothing and products that are popular with teens in the ads. Price is also a factor.

Business CAREERS

29. Advertising managers oversee advertising and promotion staffs. Promotions managers supervise staffs of promotion specialists. Marketing managers develop the firm's marketing strategy in detail. Public relations managers supervise public relations specialists. Most work in offices close to those of top managers. Long hours are common. A wide range of educational backgrounds is suitable for entry, but requirements vary. These positions are highly coveted, resulting in keen competition. College graduates with related experience, a high level of creativity, and strong communication skills have the best opportunities.

Role Play

30. Presentations should address the competencies noted in the Role Play. Answers will vary depending on the community activity chosen.

Standardized Test Practice
1. C

FOCUS

Kristy Royce

Vice President/Founder, Expeditiontrips.com

This Internet-based adventure travel company focuses on expeditions. They specialize in trips on small cruise ships to remote locations. The company was founded by Ashton Palmer and Kristy Royce. This interview is with Kristy Royce.

Bell Ringer Activity

Marketing

Ask volunteers to name places they would like to visit. (Answers will depend on student experiences, values, and preferences.) Write a list of exotic locations on the board. Ask students if they think a Web-based business that specializes in organizing trips to a single location could be successful.

TEACH

Teaching Points
Marketing versus Advertising

Ask students to compare and contrast the meanings of the words "marketing" and "advertising." (Marketing is the process of creating, promoting, and presenting a product to meet the wants and needs of consumers, wherever they are. Advertising, which is just one aspect of marketing, is the public promotion of something such as a product, service, business, or event, in order to attract or increase interest in it.) Ask students to categorize the marketing niche that Expeditiontrips.com fills. (Expeditiontrips.com is a specialty travel agency that appeals to people who are interested in trips on small cruise ships to remote destinations.)

Q & A

Describe your job responsibilities.

Kristy: My main job responsibilities are marketing, managing our Web site, public relations, and coordinating all in-house documents. On a typical work day, I work with our site manager to update site text, coordinate an e-mail blast, update our search engine marketing, speak with an intern about site submissions, and then edit text for trip documents.

What skills are most important in your business?

Kristy: Our business is the travel business, so the most important quality is to truly love travel. From there, great communication skills: you must be able to express yourself to others and describe a travel experience both verbally and in writing. You also need to be organized, pay attention to details, and prioritize tasks.

What is your key to success?

Kristy: Our key to success was finding a unique niche that we could fill better than anybody else. I would also say treating our clients extremely well is key to our success. If there is a problem, we fix it, no questions asked.

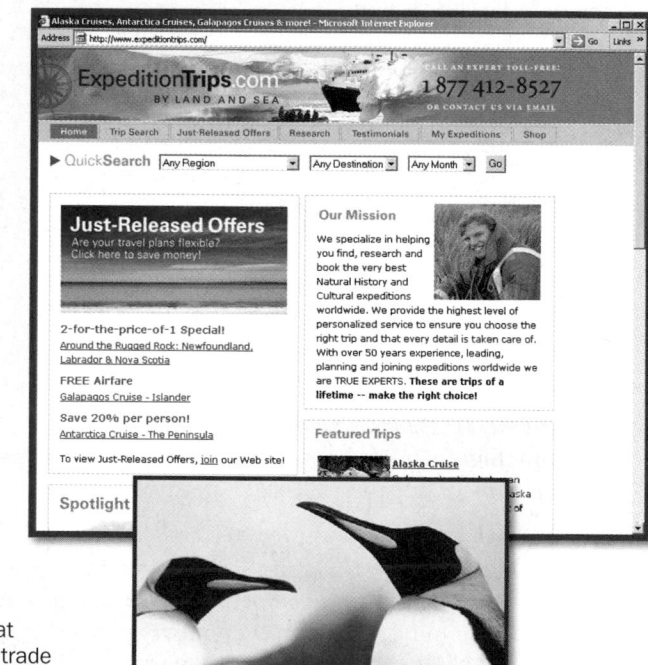

What advice would you give students interested in starting a business?

Kristy: Get an education in the field that interests you. This can be university, trade school, or work, but it is important to have an understanding of the field before you start. Everything you do prior to starting your business will help you once you start. If you fail, get up and try again.

Another very important thing is to do something that you truly love. Starting a business is very hard work, so it helps to believe in what you are doing and believe that it is an important service. In addition, you must fill a need for a service. Other people need to want whatever it is that you offer or your business will never get off the ground.

Critical Thinking *What are the pros and cons of running a Web-based business?*

Critical Thinking

Web-based businesses rely on customers being Web-savvy. Given that most vacation planning is done online, a Web-based travel company is well positioned, as long as customers can find it.

Some Qualifications of an e-Travel Business

Academic Skills and Abilities

Geography; geology; meteorology; computer skills; foreign languages; world history; interpersonal skills; general business management skills; verbal and written communication skills; multitasking, organizing, and planning skills

Academic Skills Required to Complete Tasks at Expeditiontrips.com			
Tasks	Math	Science	English Language Arts
Hold meetings			◆
Assign duties			◆
Develop itineraries	◆	◆	◆
Plan routes to minimize distance traveled and optimize weather conditions	◆	◆	
Customer service			◆
Schedule employees	◆		◆
Order supplies and equipment	◆		◆
Analyze financials	◆		◆

Education and Training

A few colleges offer bachelor's or master's degrees in travel and tourism. A college education is sometimes desired to establish a background in fields such as computer science, geography, communication, foreign languages, and world history. Courses in accounting and business management are also important for those who expect to manage or start a travel agency.

Career Path

Personal travel experience or experience as an airline reservation agent is an asset. As the Internet has become an important tool for making travel arrangements, more travel agencies are using Web sites to provide services to clients. This trend has increased the importance of computer skills in the occupation.

Preparing for a Career
Self-Assessment Checklist

Use this self-assessment checklist to help determine ways you can make your career path more satisfying.

✔ Have confidence in your own abilities and talents.

✔ Keep an open mind about careers that seem difficult or require a lot of education or training.

✔ Base career decisions on your interests, not on a high salary or others' expectations.

✔ Consider ways you can make your values a part of your career.

✔ Define clear goals.

✔ Stay informed of changes in the global business environment.

✔ Expect the best of yourself and others.

✔ Keep an open mind so that you may learn from others.

✔ Maintain a positive outlook so that you are able to see alternatives instead of obstacles.

249

Preparing for a Career

Marketing Yourself Being enthusiastic about a product is important in marketing, and being enthusiastic about your future is equally important in career planning. Remind students that even though choosing a career requires serious consideration, they should also think about ways to have some fun in the process. Ask students why it is important for them to choose a career they will enjoy. (The courses and training people choose should employ skills and abilities they enjoy using because enjoyment of their career will help them achieve long-term success.) Tell students they will have an opportunity to think about careers and the career-planning process as they read the Self-Assessment Checklists in this book.

ASSESS

Write About It
Expeditiontrips.com

Ask students to write a summary of what they like about the business concept for Expeditiontrips.com. (Students may say that they like the way it offers consumers opportunities to travel to places they have only seen in nature documentaries or other movies.)

Academic Vocabulary
Career Planning

Ask students to read the Self-Assessment Checklist then write one or more paragraphs about preparing for a career. Have students use some words from the Academic Vocabulary Glossary. (Example: In planning a career, it is important to be *aware* of the *potential* opportunities available so that you can form a successful *strategy* for the future. One skill that will be *crucial* for most careers is the ability to *communicate* your own *unique* abilities and *display* your talents. If you learn how to *network* with peers, they may be able to help you find ways to make your abilities shine.)

CLOSE

Cooperative Learning
Technology Applications

Ask students to work in pairs and develop an idea for an Internet business. Have them work together to develop an advertisement for the business. (Ads will vary but should include marketing copy, visuals, and information about the business.)

249

FOCUS

Discussion Starter

Lead a discussion about marketing in a global economy. Ask students to project how the evolution of the global economy will change marketing and society.

Step 1

Brainstorm Skills

Have students go to the *Introduction to Business* Online Learning Center through **glencoe.com** for a graphic organizer they can use to brainstorm the skills needed to complete the project.

Step 2

Choose a Business and a Career

Students can use the Occupational Outlook Handbook Web site to explore occupations.

TEACH

Step 3

Build Background

Globalization Ask students to write an essay stating the arguments for and against the globalization of marketing. (Arguments for the globalization of marketing may say that the ability to reach customers in far-flung parts of the world will help businesses compete successfully. Arguments against it may express concerns about protecting domestic markets from businesses that operate outside our country and our laws.)

Marketing in a Global Economy

Today's marketing executives base marketing strategies on global needs. Marketing researchers gather information on consumers in foreign countries, study that information, and report their findings. The research findings become the basis for marketing strategies.

Thematic Project Assignment

In this project you will prepare a market research report that recommends marketing strategies that could be implemented by an American company marketing its goods or services in another country. You will need to research factors that should be considered in the country, study that information, and then write a two-page report.

Step 1 Brainstorm Skills You Need to Complete This Activity

Your success in writing a marketing report will depend on your skills. Preview the activity. Then brainstorm a list of the skills you will need to use to complete the activity and describe how you will use them. Skills you might use include:

Academic Skills reading, writing, social studies, geography, and researching

Basic Skills speaking, listening, thinking, and interpersonal skills

Technology Skills word processing, keyboarding, telecommunications, and Internet skills

 **SKILLS PREVIEW** Go to the *Introduction to Business* Online Learning Center through **glencoe.com** for a graphic organizer you can use to brainstorm the skills you will use to complete the project.

Step 2 Choose a Business and Career That Interest You

Think of a business that you find interesting. Then think of a career related to that business. As you conduct research on marketing in a global economy, consider how it affects the business and career in which you are interested.

Step 3 Build Background Knowledge

Preview information on marketing in a global economy.

Marketing **Internationally**

Conducting business internationally can be very different from doing business in the United States. There are language barriers, international trade laws, and political, economical, cultural, and technological factors that affect international business. Marketers working on the global stage must be willing to put the time and effort into being savvy about the country in which they want to conduct business.

Businesses must study the characteristics of a country and find ways to target consumers with similar needs and wants. Then businesses must adapt their products to each country where they do business.

Step 4

Connect with Your Community

Ask students to describe ways businesses in their community interact with markets in this country and in other parts of the world. (Answers will vary, depending on the community and students' opinions.)

Ask students to think about how it might benefit businesses to communicate that they are part of a community in their marketing efforts. (People are more likely to identify with people they define as part of their community and may be more willing to make a purchase from a business if they identify with the business.)

Step 4 Connect with Your Community

Conduct a local market survey by interviewing three business owners in your community to ask in which countries they market their goods or services. Ask how they market differently in this country and in other markets.

Step 5 Research Marketing in a Global Economy

Use library and Internet resources to research factors that should be considered when marketing another country. Use the project checklist as a guide to your research. Keep records of your sources of information.

Step 6 Prepare a Report

Use word processing and other software to develop a two-page market research report that includes all of the information described in this project research checklist.

Marketing in a Global Economy

✔ Describe how a U.S. company can learn about the needs of the consumers in another country.

✔ Describe how the language barrier affects trade with this country.

✔ Describe how the political, economical, cultural, and technological factors affect doing business with this country.

✔ Explain how the climate affects the types of goods and services that could be marketed in this country.

Self Connections

✔ Describe the results of your research to a family member or other adult.

✔ Describe how marketing in a global economy affects the business and career in which you are interested.

✔ Explain what the investigation and its results mean to you.

Step 7 Evaluate Your Report

 RUBRIC Go to the *Introduction to Business* Online Learning Center through **glencoe.com** for a rubric you can use to evaluate your final report.

251

TEACH (cont.)

Step 6

Prepare a Report
Give students these tips on report writing:

- Know your audience.
- Organize your report by developing an outline and using titles and subtitles.
- Write concisely (briefly but completely).
- Write in easy-to-read, simple language.

ASSESS

Step 7

Evaluate Your Report
Rubric Encourage students to use the rubric to evaluate their final reports.

CLOSE

Culminating Activity
Career Interviews
Have students form pairs and interview each other about the businesses and careers they researched and how their opinions and perceptions of the businesses and careers evolved during the course of the project. (Interviews will vary depending on students' business and career choices and reactions to their research.)

Step 5

Research Marketing in a Global Economy
Students can go to the *Introduction to Business* Online Learning Center through **glencoe.com** for a rubric they can use as a content checklist when researching their reports.

Chapter	Section	Unit Objectives
Chapter 15 *Human Resources Management*	15.1	**Define** human resources management.
		Describe how a company attracts and rewards good employees.
		Discuss what a human resources manager should consider about job applicants.
	15.2	**Identify** responsibilities of human resources managers after they have hired a new employee.
		Describe how the status of employees changes.
Chapter 16 *Culture and Diversity in Business*	16.1	**Describe** the effect of culture on doing business globally.
		Describe how corporate cultures differ among businesses.
	16.2	**Identify** ways in which cultural diversity has an impact on business.

Understanding the Coding

Brackets Brackets on the reduced student edition page correspond to teaching strategies and activities in the Teacher Wraparound Edition. As you teach the lesson, the brackets show you exactly where to use the teaching strategies and activities.

Letters The letters on the reduced student edition page identify the type of strategy or activity. See the key below to learn about the different types of strategies and activities.

Ability Levels Leveled teaching strategies are identified by one of three codes to give you an idea of their suitability for students of varying learning styles and abilities.

Resources Key program resources are listed in each chapter. Icons indicate the format of resources.

KEY to Letters

D **Develop Concepts** activities help teachers gauge and plan for students' concept development.

R **Reading Strategy** activities help you teach reading skills and vocabulary.

C **Critical Thinking** strategies help students apply and extend what they have learned.

U **Universal Access** activities provide differentiated instruction for English language learners and suggestions for teaching various types of learners.

S **Skill Practice** provides leveled instruction for meeting individual needs and learning styles.

W **Writing Support** activities provide writing opportunities to help students comprehend the text.

NCLB **No Child Left Behind** activities help students practice and improve their abilities in academic subjects.

KEY to Ability Levels

L1 Strategies should be within the ability range of all students. Often full class participation is required.

L2 Strategies are for average to above-average students or for small groups. Some teacher direction is necessary.

L3 Strategies are designed for students able and willing to work independently. Minimal teacher direction is necessary.

KEY to Resource Icons

📂 Print Material

💿 CD-ROM

🖱 Online Learning Center with Podcasts

BusinessWeek *Reader and Case Study*

In Unit 5, your students can learn more about business in the real world through the following *BusinessWeek* Readers and Case Studies:

What Works: Eyes on the Prize
The right bonus program can unlock your company's growth. It doesn't always take expensive consultants or wholesale firings to get the company on the right track. A company that instituted a well-designed bonus program successfully tied employees' pay directly to their performance and to the company's profitability. (page 262)

Fashion, with a Conscience
CEO George Zimmer's central tenet at Men's Wearhouse? "You've got to have a company that starts with trust and fairness." Behind the scenes, Zimmer has long worked to build a corporate culture that centers first and foremost on keeping his employees happy and loyal. That culture appears to benefit Men's Wearhouse. (page 275)

Chapter Features and Activities

Ask STANDARD &POOR'S

BusinessWeek *Reader and Case Study*

Science/Tech**TRENDS**

?**ETHICS** in Business

International Business

Section	Feature Title	Page
15.1	Hiring Older Workers	259
15.2	Training Methods	262
16.2	Seeking All Qualified Workers	280

Reading Strategies

Before You Read

Section	Page
15.1	256
15.2	261
16.1	272
16.2	277

Graphic Organizer

Chapter	Section	Title	Page
15	15.1	Steps to Select the Right Candidate for a Job	256
	15.2	Employee Experiences	261
16	16.1	Corporate Culture	272
	16.2	Benefits of Diversity	277

As You Read

Section	Page
15.1	257, 258
15.2	263, 264
16.1	273, 274, 276
16.2	278, 279

Reading Check

Section	Page
15.1	257
15.2	264
16.1	275
16.2	278

After You Read

Section	Page
15.1	260
15.2	265
16.1	276
16.2	281

Unit 5

Human Resources

Unit Overview

Introduce the Unit

Introduce the unit by describing the main concepts of each chapter in the unit.

Unit 5 is about how businesses manage human resources and how culture and diversity affect business.

Chapter 15 introduces human resources management—the process of finding, selecting, training, and evaluating employees.

Chapter 16 discusses the importance of business culture both globally and within a company. It also discusses diversity in the workplace.

00:00 OUT OF TIME?

If class time is too short to cover all of the chapters in this unit, have students:

- Write down the vocabulary terms and their definitions.
- Read the chapter summaries at the beginning of each chapter review.
- Go to the *Introduction to Business* Online Learning Center through **glencoe.com** to download free Study-to-Go content to their PDAs or cell phones.

252

Real-World Business and Career Profile   Preview

Alienware Tell students that at the end of this unit, they will learn about one of the founders of Alienware and how he achieved his success. Alienware makes specialized, high-performance computers for gamers. Nelson Gonzalez was always fascinated by computers and technology. He managed a small IT shop in a post-production house and that gave him the necessary technical foundation to start Alienware. Ask students to give reasons a business that specializes in making computers that fit the needs of gamers could be a good business to be in. (Students should recognize that gamers represent a lucrative market and have specialized needs.)

Real-World Business and Career Profile | Preview

Alienware makes customized computers that are assembled specifically for high performance for gamers. At the end of this unit, you will learn about the Alienware co-founders Nelson Gonzalez and Alex Aguila and how they achieved their success.

Decision Making Why do you think it is so important for companies to make good decisions about selecting employees?

Unit 5 — Thematic Project Preview

Cultural Diversity in the Business World After completing this unit, you will understand how cultural diversity affects today's businesses.

Project Checklist As you read the chapters in this unit, use this checklist to prepare for the unit project.

✔ Think about the rich cultural heritage of different students in your school, including exchange students.

✔ Consider how the Internet, television, and movies expose you to people of different cultures.

✔ Think about how globalization is creating a more culturally diverse workforce.

✔ Consider how businesses benefit from a multinational workforce.

253

Build Background

Ask students these questions to activate prior knowledge:

Chapter 15
What do you already know about human resource management? (Answers will vary, but even students who have jobs may not know much. For example, some students' only experience with how a firm recruits employees might be seeing "help wanted" signs in the windows of local businesses.) Tell students that this chapter provides an opportunity to see the bigger picture.

Chapter 16
How are people different? (People are different because of age, gender, ethnicity, and nationality. Individual schools and neighborhoods may not reflect the diversity of the local community or of the country. For many students, their first experience with people from other cultures or ethnic backgrounds comes when they attend school or enter the workforce.) Ask: What are some of the benefits of diversity? (A diverse workforce offers a broad range of ideas and ways of looking at things. Greater diversity in the workplace helps a company better understand and serve the needs of a diverse marketplace.)

Unit — Thematic Project Preview

Cultural Diversity in the Business World
Tell students that when they complete this unit, they will understand what cultural diversity is and why cultural diversity is important in the modern business world. Encourage students to think about how a business benefits from a culturally diverse workforce.

C Critical Thinking
Ask students how exposure to students of different cultures affects their lives. (Encourage students to recognize that knowing people of other cultures enriches our lives.)

253

Standards-Based Lesson Planning   *Introduction to Business* provides students with instruction and assessment in the following fundamental content areas:

Content Standards Correlations	
Identify procedures for meeting staffing needs.	pp. 257–260, 266–267
Explain the components of compensation.	pp. 258, 262
Describe how to conduct effective searches and find the best candidates.	pp. 259, 266–267
Describe personal and interpersonal skills and attributes appropriate for the workplace.	pp. 259, 263, 267
Explain methods for developing and retaining employees.	pp. 262–265
Apply appropriate strategies to manage and resolve conflict in work situations.	pp. 268, 269
Describe the importance of retaining valued employees.	pp. 265, 269
Explain how performance management and appraisal systems can drive productivity and growth in an organization.	pp. 264, 267
Demonstrate techniques for communicating with employees to resolve issues and improve performance.	pp. 268, 269

NCLB   Activities, information, and skills practice will help your students attain No Child Left Behind proficiency. Students will improve their abilities in the following academic standards areas:

Academic Standards Correlations		
English Language Arts	**Activities/Features**	**Page**
NCTE 3 Apply strategies to interpret texts	Applying Academics to Business	p. 268
NCTE 6 Apply knowledge of language structure and conventions to discuss texts	Applying Academics to Business	p. 268
NCTE 7 Conduct research, and gather, evaluate, and synthesize data to communicate discoveries	After You Read	p. 265
NCTE 11 Participate as members of literacy communities	After You Read	p. 265
Mathematics		
Data Analysis and Probability Select and use appropriate statistical methods to analyze data	Applying Academics to Business	p. 268
Number and Operations Understand numbers, ways of representing numbers, relationships among numbers, and number systems	Ask S&P	p. 254
Number and Operations Compute fluently and make reasonable estimates	After You Read Standardized Test Practice	pp. 260, 269
Communication Analyze and evaluate the mathematical thinking and strategies of others	Applying Academics to Business	p. 268
Science		
Content Standard E Students should develop understandings about science and technology	Science/Tech Trends	p. 264

Correlations   This chart shows the 21ˢᵗ Century Skills, foundation skills, and workplace competencies that students develop as they work in this chapter.

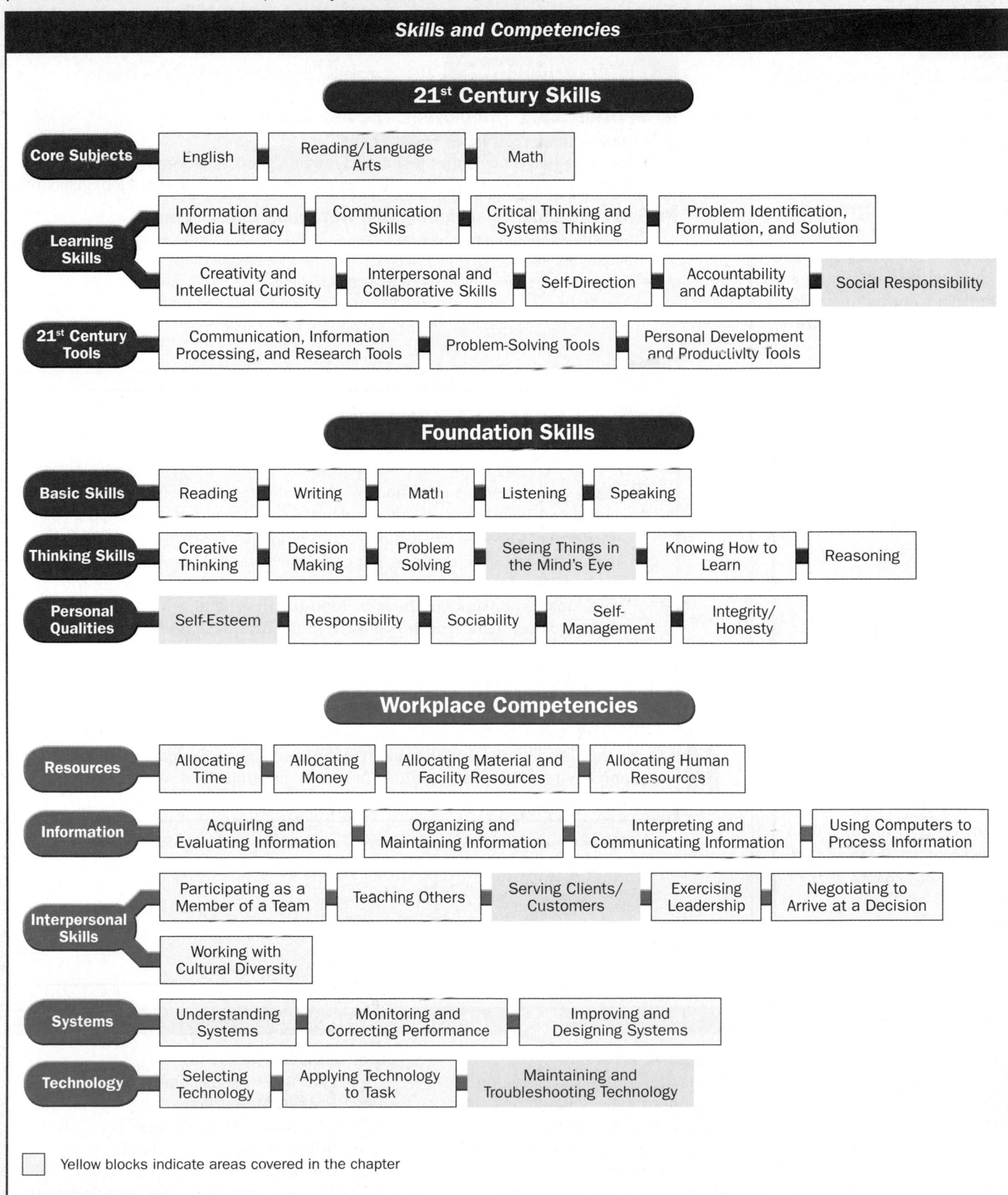

Skills and Competencies

21ˢᵗ Century Skills

Core Subjects
English | Reading/Language Arts | Math

Learning Skills
Information and Media Literacy | Communication Skills | Critical Thinking and Systems Thinking | Problem Identification, Formulation, and Solution

Creativity and Intellectual Curiosity | Interpersonal and Collaborative Skills | Self-Direction | Accountability and Adaptability | Social Responsibility

21ˢᵗ Century Tools
Communication, Information Processing, and Research Tools | Problem-Solving Tools | Personal Development and Productivity Tools

Foundation Skills

Basic Skills
Reading | Writing | Math | Listening | Speaking

Thinking Skills
Creative Thinking | Decision Making | Problem Solving | Seeing Things in the Mind's Eye | Knowing How to Learn | Reasoning

Personal Qualities
Self-Esteem | Responsibility | Sociability | Self-Management | Integrity/Honesty

Workplace Competencies

Resources
Allocating Time | Allocating Money | Allocating Material and Facility Resources | Allocating Human Resources

Information
Acquiring and Evaluating Information | Organizing and Maintaining Information | Interpreting and Communicating Information | Using Computers to Process Information

Interpersonal Skills
Participating as a Member of a Team | Teaching Others | Serving Clients/Customers | Exercising Leadership | Negotiating to Arrive at a Decision

Working with Cultural Diversity

Systems
Understanding Systems | Monitoring and Correcting Performance | Improving and Designing Systems

Technology
Selecting Technology | Applying Technology to Task | Maintaining and Troubleshooting Technology

Yellow blocks indicate areas covered in the chapter

Introduce the Chapter

Human Resources Management

Chapter 15 discusses human resources management—the process of finding, selecting, training, and evaluating employees.

Building Background

Even students who have jobs may not be familiar with human resources management. This chapter provides an opportunity to see the bigger picture.

Ask STANDARD &POOR'S

›› Math Answer

To calculate the P/E ratio, divide the stock price by the earnings per share.

In this case,

P/E ratio = $\dfrac{\$40}{\$2}$

P/E ratio = 20

›› Extension Activity

Ask students to calculate the PE ratio for each of the five companies.

Company	Stock Price	EPS
Allied	$14.38	$0.29
Kenwood	33.93	0.53
Mackee	6.35	0.16
Summit	21.12	0.79
Turpin	16.16	0.20

(Allied, 49.59; Kenwood, 64.02; Mackee, 39.69; Summit, 26.73; Turpin, 80.80.)

N C L B Activity correlates to Math standards.

Human Resources Management

Chapter Objectives After completing this chapter, you will be able to:

▶ **Section 15.1** *Employees: The Key to Success*
- **Define** human resources management.
- **Describe** how a company attracts and rewards good employees.
- **Discuss** what a human resources manager should consider about job applicants.

▶ **Section 15.2** *Developing and Retaining Employees*
- **Identify** responsibilities of human resources managers after they have hired a new employee.
- **Describe** how the status of employees changes.

Ask STANDARD &POOR'S Earnings and the P/E Ratio

Q: I've heard a lot about P/E ratio. For what purposes do investors use P/E ratio?

A: The Price/Earnings ratio is a popular indicator used to judge whether a stock is a good value. The P/E ratio compares the company's share price to its per-share earnings. A P/E of 15, for example, indicates that investors are willing to pay $15 for every dollar of yearly earnings the company generates. Investors use the P/E ratio to compare companies in the same industry. In general, a high P/E suggests that investors expect higher earnings growth in the future compared to companies with a lower P/E.

Mathematics Imagine that a company's stock is trading at $40. If it announces $2 in earnings per share, what is the company's P/E ratio?

N C L B

THEORY Using Ratios The P/E ratio is a useful way to look at the relationship between a stock's price and its underlying value. You can compare the P/E ratio of one company to another, across different sectors and industries. You can also compare similar companies to get a better idea of challenges in an industry.

Classroom Resources

- Student Edition
- Teacher Wraparound Edition
- Student Activity Workbook with Academic Integration
- Student Activity Workbook with Academic Integration TAE
- *Fast File*, Unit 5 Resources
- Inclusion in the Business Education Classroom

- TeacherWorks Plus
- *ExamView Assessment Suite*
- Presentation Plus!
- Vocabulary PuzzleMaker
- Interactive Student Edition
- Online Student Edition
- Online Learning Center with Podcasts

● **Managing Human Resources** Businesses must be careful to select the best workers for job openings. **Why do you think it is important to choose good employees?**

Discuss the Photo

● **Managing Human Resources** Read the caption on the photo to students: Businesses must be careful to select the best workers for job openings.

Ask students: Why do you think it is important to choose good employees? (Answers will vary but may include the importance of characteristics such as honesty, integrity, intelligence, necessary skills, motivation, etc.)

Review the Objectives

Introduce the chapter by reviewing the chapter objectives:

Section 15.1 *Objectives*

Define human resources management. (It is the process of finding, selecting, training, and evaluating employees.)

Describe how a company attracts and rewards good employees. (Businesses offer competitive pay—wages and salary—and benefits such as health insurance, life insurance, sick leave, retirement plans, and paid holidays.)

Discuss what a human resources manager should consider about job applicants. (Review each candidate's application and/or résumé, interview qualified candidates, conduct testing to make sure job candidates have the right skills and character for a job, conduct a background check, and check references.)

Section 15.2 *Objectives*

Identify responsibilities of human resources managers after they have hired a new employee. (Human resources managers conduct orientation sessions for new employees, assist with training and evaluation of employees, and keep track of changes in the status of employees.)

Describe how the status of employees changes. (An employee may be promoted to a higher-level job, transferred to another job within the company, or be separated from the company. Being laid off or fired, resigning, or retiring are all forms of separation.)

FOCUS

Bell Ringer Activity

Employees: The Key to Success

Ask students to explain the title *Employees: the Key to Success*. (The skills, knowledge, and attitudes that employees bring to the workplace have a direct impact on the goods and services the firm produces.)

Preteaching

Presentation Plus!

The Presentation Plus! CD provides visual teaching aids for this section.

PuzzleMaker

Use the Vocabulary PuzzleMaker to create a puzzle of the section's key terms. Students can complete the puzzle on paper or on a computer.

Graphic Organizer

Tell students to go to the Online Learning Center through **glencoe.com** for a printable graphic organizer. (Answers include: Application: An *application* lists candidates' experience, education, skills, and references; Interview: *Interviews* reveal more detailed information about candidates; Testing: *Testing* the candidates ensures they have the right skills; References: *References* are checked to make sure candidates' information is correct.)

N
C Connects academics
L to content.
B

256

Employees: The Key to Success

Reading Guide

● Before You Read

Think about the steps a business must take to find the right person for a job.

Read to Learn
- Define human resources management.
- Describe how a company attracts and rewards good employees.
- Discuss what a human resources manager should consider about job applicants.

The Main Idea
A human resources manager finds new employees for a company. Human resources staff members assist new workers through training and evaluations.

D

Key Concepts
- Human Resources
- Meeting Staffing Needs
- Considering Job Applicants

Vocabulary
Key Terms

human resources	salary
human resources management	benefits
job description	recruitment
compensation	background check
wage	reference

Academic Vocabulary
You will find these words in your reading and on your tests. Make sure you know their meanings.

temporary	summary
fund	comments

Graphic Organizer
List and write notes about the steps needed to select the right candidate for a job in a figure like the one below.

	STEP	NOTES
1.		
2.		
3.		
4.		

 Go to the *Introduction to Business* Online Learning Center through **glencoe.com** for a printable graphic organizer.

Academic Standards
English Language Arts
  NCTE 1 Read texts to acquire new information
Mathematics
  Number and Operations Compute fluently and make reasonable estimates

N
C
L
B

Reading Guide

● Before You Read

They review résumés, interview and test applicants, and check references.

D Develop Concepts

The Main Idea Ask students: What are some reasons it might be hard to find people to hire? What are some reasons it might be hard to keep employees? (Sometimes there is a shortage of people who are qualified for the positions. Keeping employees is difficult if there are other employment opportunities that are more desirable.)

Human Resources

Pioneer automaker Henry Ford once said, "You can take my factories, burn up my buildings, but give me my people and I'll build the business right back again." **Human resources** are the people employed in a business, commonly referred to as personnel. Employees provide the skills, knowledge, labor, and experience needed to make a business productive.

Managing human resources is not the same as supervising workers. **Human resources management** is the process of finding, selecting, training, and evaluating employees. The first step in this process is finding the right person for a job.

Meeting Staffing Needs

Most businesses have specific staffing needs. These needs are usually handled by a human resources manager. When filling a job, human resources managers begin by writing a job description.

Writing a Job Description

A **job description** is a detailed outline of the duties, qualifications, and conditions required to do a specific job (see **Figure 15.1**). For example, the job description for a graphic artist position could say the job involves being creative, meeting deadlines, and using a computer. The job might also require a certain level of experience and education. It could be part-time, full-time, permanent, or **temporary**.

✔ **Reading Check** **Analyze** Why is a job description essential when trying to fill a job?

● **As You Read**

Do you think automaker Henry Ford was right in believing that his employees were more important than his factories or equipment?

❓ETHICS in Business

Psychological Testing

■ **Critical Reading** Life is full of important decisions. Think about the kinds of decisions that you make as you read the question below.

Imagine you own a retail store. You are looking for a cashier and want to make sure you hire someone who won't be likely to steal from you. You know that the federal government has banned the use of lie detectors for most employment situations, but that you can ask a prospective employee to take a psychological test. These exams can predict an individual's tendency to steal by matching his or her answers to those of known thieves. Questions may be obvious ("How often do you tell the truth?") or obscure ("How often do you make your bed?").

■ **Decision Making** Do you think it is appropriate to decide whether a person will steal based on the results of a psychological test? Explain the possible consequences of your decision.

Section 15.1

TEACH

Discussion Starter
Job Description
Use the Internet to locate some examples of current job descriptions to give students an idea of the format and content. Job descriptions are available at Web sites such as Monster® and CareerBuilder® as well as company Web sites. Share the examples with students and ask them to identify the similarities and differences.

R Reading Strategy
Drawing Conclusions
Human Resources Management Ask students why they think Henry Ford put so much emphasis on the abilities of his employees? (Employees provide the skills, knowledge, labor, and experience needed to make a business productive.)

✔ **Reading Check**

Analyze A job description is necessary to describe the job in detail in order to find the most qualified person to fill the position.

Virtual Business
Introduce staffing to students using the Virtual Business Retailing Staffing activity. In this simulation, students learn why staffing is important to the success of a business.

● **As You Read**

Most students will probably feel that he was right, that the resources and expertise employees bring to a company are its most important assets.

❓ETHICS in Business

Decision Making Answers will vary but students should suggest that it might not be fair to judge a person's future behavior based on the results of a psychological test. However, it is smart for a business owner to be very cautious when hiring.

257

S Skill Practice

Guided Practice

List Ask students to make a list of benefits that employers offer to employees. (Lists might include paid time off, retirement plans, insurance, membership for organizations and fitness centers, subsidies for on-site cafeterias, day care, and education opportunities.) **L1**

Interview Have students interview two adults with full-time jobs about the kinds of benefits offered where they work and to make a list of the benefits. Create a master list. (Some companies offer adoption assistance, employee purchase programs, credit unions, and free parking.) **L2**

Research Have students visit Web sites for three companies and make a chart comparing the benefits offered by the three companies. (Tables will vary, but headings might include: Insurance, Paid Time Off, and Education.) **L3**

ASSESS

Review Key Terms
Have students write sentences using each key term.

Study-to-Go Have students go to the Online Learning Center through **glencoe.com** to download free **Study-to-Go** content to their PDAs or cell phones.

● Executive Assistant
This job description lists the duties and responsibilities of an executive assistant to the chief financial officer of a company. **What qualifications must a person have for this Executive Assistant position?**

● **As You Read**
Think about other offerings besides money that would attract you to a job.

S

Figure 15.1 — Job Description

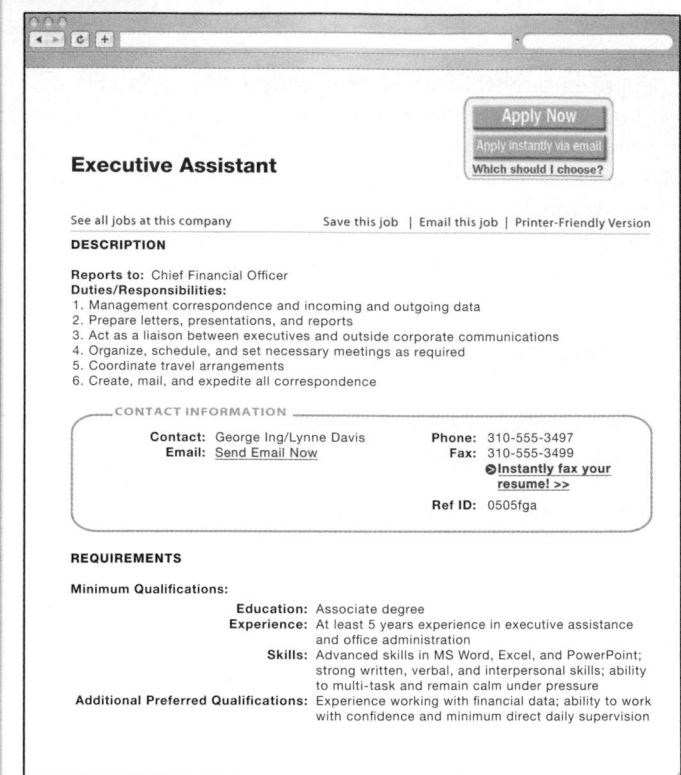

Pay and Benefits

To attract and keep good employees, businesses must offer competitive compensation. **Compensation** is pay and benefits. Pay can be in the form of a wage or a salary. A **wage** is an amount of money paid to an employee on an hourly basis. A **salary** is a fixed amount of pay for each week, month, or year. **Benefits** are extra compensation that workers receive such as health and life insurance, sick leave, holiday pay, and retirement plans. Retirement plans provide employees with money after working at a company for a certain number of years.

Some companies offer pension plans. A *pension plan* is a retirement plan that is funded at least in part by an employer. Some also offer profit-sharing plans. A *profit-sharing plan* makes an annual contribution to an employee's retirement **fund** when the company makes a profit. Another type of retirement plan is a 401(k). With a *401(k),* employees set aside a percentage of funds from each paycheck to go into their 401(k) investment account. Many employers match a percentage of an employee's contribution to a 401(k).

Figure 15.1
● Executive Assistant Associate degree; 5 years of experience in executive assistance and office administration; advanced skills in MS Word®, Excel®, and PowerPoint®; strong written, verbal and interpersonal skills; ability to multi-task and remain calm under pressure

● **As You Read**
Besides money, many companies also offer benefits such as medical and life insurance, sick and vacation leave, and retirement plans. Students might also mention flexible work hours and varied tasks to be performed.

Job Recruitment

Human resources managers often work as recruiters. **Recruitment** means actively looking for qualified people to fill a job. **Figure 15.2** illustrates qualities needed to succeed in all types of jobs. Most recruiters first consider filling a new job with someone who already works for the company. If no one is qualified, interested, or available, then the manager recruits outside the company. One way to recruit people is by placing ads in newspapers and magazines, at schools, or on the Internet. Employment agencies, referrals from employees, and job fairs are also ways to find qualified workers.

Considering Job Applicants

After recruiting job applicants, a human resources manager has to decide which one to hire. There are four steps to selecting the right person or *candidate* for the job. First, the recruiter must review each candidate's application and/or résumé. An *application* is a form companies give to potential employees to complete. It lists their work experience, education, skills, and references. Many applicants also submit a résumé. A *résumé* is a worker's **summary** of academic and work history. Reviewing the application and résumé leads to the screening step. *Screening* is a system of selecting suitable people for a job. Recruiters review applications to see which people meet their minimum qualifications. Only those who do will be considered further.

The next step is for the human resources manager to interview qualified candidates. An *interview* is a meeting in which a recruiter asks an applicant questions to see if the applicant is right for a job. It allows a company to get more details about a

Hiring Older Workers More businesses are hiring people of retirement age. Companies such as Home Depot® and Borders® have joined with the American Association of Retired Persons, or the AARP, in a commitment to hire older workers. *What advantages can older workers bring to a company?*

Figure 15.2 — *Workplace Skills*

RESPONSIBILITY

initiative

dependability

punctuality

professional dress

POSITIVE ATTITUDE

SELF-RESPECT

Integrity

RESPECT FOR OTHERS

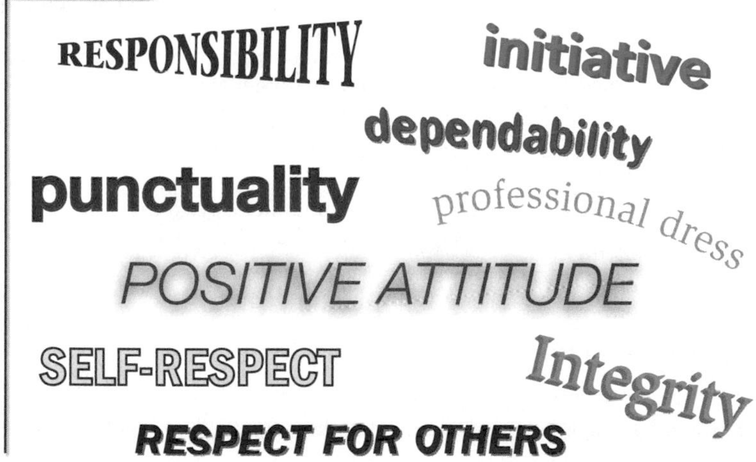

● **What Qualities Are Needed?** Here are a number of personal and interpersonal skills that are important to demonstrate in the workplace. **How can you demonstrate these skills?**

Section 15.1   Employees: The Key to Success   **259**

Hiring Older Workers Students may mention experience, a wider perspective, and years of working knowledge.

Figure 15.2

● **Workplace Skills** Answers will vary. For instance, a student might say that an employee can demonstrate dependability, responsibility, and punctuality by showing up for work on time every day. Other workplace skills exist and many workplace skills are particularly important in certain contexts.

RETEACH (cont.)

C Critical Thinking

Predict

Background Checks and References Sometimes individuals blame former employers for providing negative references. To avoid this, some employers will only confirm the dates of employment. Ask students: Why might this situation be a problem for employees and employers? (Potential employers do not learn anything about the candidate's previous performance. Employees do not have the benefit of getting an endorsement from former co-workers or supervisors.)

ASSESS

After You Read

Have students complete the Section 15.1 After You Read section review.

Online Study Tools

Have students go to the Online Learning Center through **glencoe.com** to:

- Take the Section 15.1 **Practice Test**.
- Download free **Study-to-Go** content to their PDAs or cell phones.

CLOSE

Culminating Activity
HR Professional

Invite a human resources professional from a local business to speak to the class about human resources management and to offer suggestions about the job application process.

260

---

potential employee. It shows the interviewer how the applicant communicates. Interviews also allow applicants to find out more about a company. They help applicants to see if the company is a good place to work. Many companies test job candidates as part of the interview process. *Testing* helps companies make sure that job candidates have the right skills and character for a job.

Background Checks and References

The human resources manager's final step before hiring a new employee is to check the applicant's background and references. A **background check** is the process of verifying certain information provided by a job applicant. This includes information about past and present jobs and education. Some background checks also include a review of a job applicant's financial history.

A **reference** is someone who **comments** on a job applicant's character and qualifications for a job. The statement itself is also known as a reference. References give recruiters a better idea of the kind of person the job applicant is.

It is important to be truthful on job applications and résumés, and in interviews. Failing to do so can prevent you from being hired. If it is discovered that you gave false information that led to your being offered a job, you could be fired.

N C L B Activity correlates to Math standards.

Section 15.1

After You Read

Review Key Concepts

1. What are human resources?
2. What do human resources managers do to help businesses meet staffing needs?
3. What are the four steps to selecting the right person for a job?

Academic Skills

N C L B

4. **Mathematics** Your manager at a landscaping company tells you that he wants you to stock up on gasoline for the mowing equipment for the next week. Each of the four mowers you maintain will use $1\frac{1}{2}$ gallons each day, Monday through Saturday. Gasoline costs $3.50 per gallon. Explain how you might use mental math to figure out how many gallons you need and how much the gasoline will cost.

 THEORY **Mental Math** Begin by converting the fraction to a decimal. Then use addition and multiplication to determine the total number of gallons needed. Use multiplication again to calculate the total cost of the gasoline.

 For math help, go to the Math Appendix.

@ Go to the *Introduction to Business* Online Learning Center through **glencoe.com** to check your answers.

Section 15.1

Review Key Concepts

1. the people employed in a business
2. they write a job description and advertise the position and also recruit potential employees
3. reviewing each candidate's application and/or résumé; screening people for the job; interviewing qualified candidates; and checking references

Academic Skills

4. **Mathematics** Each mower will need $1\frac{1}{2}$ (or 1.5) gallons per day for six days, so $1.5 \times 6 = 9$. For total cost of gasoline, multiply total gallons needed by cost of gasoline per gallon. So, $36 \times \$3.50 = \$126$.

Developing and Retaining Employees

Reading Guide

FOCUS

Before You Read

Think about some steps a company must take to develop good employees.

Read to Learn

- Identify responsibilities of human resources managers after they have hired a new employee.
- Describe how the status of employees changes.

The Main Idea

After employees are hired, a company has to develop their skills. New employees receive orientation, training, and evaluations. These processes help them become more valuable to a company.

Key Concepts

- Developing Employees
- Changes in Employee Status

Vocabulary

Key Terms

orientation	promotion
on-the-job training	transfer
group training	separation
performance appraisal	turnover

Academic Vocabulary

You will find these words in your reading and on your tests. Make sure you know their meanings.

demonstates	complement
relaxed	technical

Graphic Organizer

As you read, describe employee experiences on a figure like the one below.

Experience	Description
Orientation	
On-the-Job Training	
Performance Appraisal	

 Go to the *Introduction to Business* Online Learning Center through **glencoe.com** for a printable graphic organizer.

Academic Standards

English Language Arts

NCTE 1 Read texts to acquire new information

NCTE 4 Use written language to communicate effectively

NCTE 7 Conduct research, and gather, evaluate, and synthesize data to communicate discoveries

NCTE 11 Participate as members of literacy communities

Science

Content Standard E Students should develop understandings about science and technology

Reading Guide

Before You Read

Students might mention orientation and on-the-job training.

D Develop Concepts

The Main Idea Ask students: Why is evaluation a part of developing good employees? (Answers will vary. Students might suggest that evaluation helps identify employee weaknesses and inadequacies in the training process that can be corrected. It also identifies strengths that can be rewarded.)

Bell Ringer Activity

Developing and Retaining Employees
Ask students how developing and retaining employees might impact a firm's bottom line. (Students might suggest that developing employees through orientation, training, and evaluation makes employees more efficient and more effective. Retaining employees cuts down on the cost of recruiting new employees.)

Preteaching

Presentation Plus!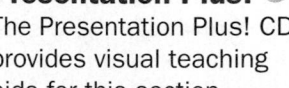
The Presentation Plus! CD provides visual teaching aids for this section.

PuzzleMaker
Use the Vocabulary PuzzleMaker to create a puzzle of the section's key terms. Students can complete the puzzle on paper or on a computer.

Graphic Organizer
Tell students to go to the Online Learning Center through **glencoe.com** for a printable graphic organizer. (Answers include: Orientation is the process of helping new employees adjust to a company; on-the-job training involves learning a new job by actually doing it; a performance appraisal is an evaluation of how well an employee is doing a job.)

NCLB Connects academics to content.

TEACH

Discussion Starter
Orientation
Orientation takes many forms. It can be informal or like a well-orchestrated production. It can vary from hours to days. Some organizations provide an orientation to the entire organization followed by departmental orientations. Ask students to discuss what new employees might expect during an orientation. (touring facilities, being introduced to other employees, watching a company video, and receiving a manual on policies and procedures)

Reading Strategy

Apply Knowledge Have students read the text under the heading "Orientation." Ask students if they have ever participated in an orientation process. If so what did they learn? (Students may have undergone orientation to a school or for a part-time job or volunteer work. Most will say they learned about the history and goals of the organization.)

Real World

Training Methods
Answers will vary. Students may favor special in-house programs because brainstorming among employees can be a more creative and productive process. Others may feel that on-the-job training and group training are more effective because there can be one-on-one instruction.

Real World

Training Methods
Dell Computer's Leadership Edge program allows its managers to go through 10 days of networking with other executives. That includes three days with Chairman Michael Dell. *Do you think special in-house training programs work better than more traditional methods, such as on-the-job training or group training?*

Developing Employees

Even people with work experience need to adjust to new jobs. They may have to learn new skills and need to keep track of how they are doing on the job. To develop as employees, they need to be oriented, trained, and evaluated. Human resources staff members assist in developing employees.

Orientation

Orientation is the process of helping new employees adjust to a company. New hires are usually taken on a tour of the building and introduced to other employees. They might also attend a group orientation session and watch a video about the company. Most new employees receive a manual that offers information on matters such as the company's organization, procedures, and safety rules. They also need to read about the company's code of ethics and policies. These documents give details about the company's goals and appropriate employee behavior.

BusinessWeek *Reader and Case Study*

What Works: Eyes on the Prize

The right bonus program can unlock your company's growth.

The 30 employees of Rockwood Retaining Walls in Rochester, Minn., are on a mission. "Everyone is talking about a common goal, which is growth," says Brian Price, who owns the company with his two brothers. Price expects this year's sales to total more than $5 million, a sizable jump from last year's $4 million.

It didn't take expensive consultants or wholesale firings to get the company on the right track. Rather, Price instituted a well-designed bonus program in 2004, tying employees' pay directly to their performance and to the company's profitability. "I think it's fantastic," says Cathy Haggerty, a nine-year front-office and call-center manager for Rockwood. "If I do my job and stay on budget and inspire people to do theirs, I have a direct effect on the money I receive."

While there's no "bonus fairy" to give entrepreneurs a bit extra this holiday season, it's worth considering a bonus program for your employees. Sure, bonuses foster goodwill, but they can also be good business, encouraging workers to think beyond their own jobs and toward a larger goal.

 CASE STUDY Go to the *Introduction to Business* Online Learning Center through **glencoe.com** for the *BusinessWeek* Reader Case Study.

Active Learning

Some companies tie bonuses to individual performance. Others tie them to the performance of the group. Calculate what your bonus would be if you were paid $300 for every 'A' you receive versus if you received $300 if your school performed in the top 20% for your state. Form groups to discuss the value of individual-versus-group performance. Use your discussion to write a persuasive article to your principal.

262 **Chapter 15** Human Resources Management

glencoe.com

BusinessWeek *Reader and Case Study*

What Works: Eyes on the Prize
CASE STUDY Have students go to the *Introduction to Business* Online Learning Center through **glencoe.com** to download a Case Study activity that corresponds to the article. The activity and answer key are also available on the TeacherWorks Plus CD.

Active Learning
Answers should include the differences between the bonus that would be received for personal achievement and the bonus received for collective achievement. Articles should weigh the pros and cons to the school of rewarding individual versus group performance.

● **Workplace Skills**
It is important to start developing workplace skills now. **How can you develop skills that will be valuable to you on the job?**

Training

New employees usually need some training for the specific job they were hired to do. **On-the-job training** involves learning a new job by actually doing it. It is usually done under the guidance of a supervisor, who **demonstrates** different tasks.

Many companies offer ways for employees to learn new skills in a more **relaxed** way and to share ideas with others. **Group training** involves teaching several employees in a class. An instructor or manager might teach a group of employees how to use a new software program at the same time.

Job rotation moves employees to different tasks or departments to help them gain experience. Sometimes if workers are absent or on leave, others have to handle their tasks. Job rotation also prevents boredom and increases morale. *Morale* is the general level of confidence or enthusiasm felt by a person or group of people.

Developing Soft Skills *Soft skills* refer to personality traits and personal abilities such as social skills, language skills, personal habits, and friendliness. Soft skills **complement** hard skills, which are the **technical** requirements of a job.

You can begin to develop soft skills now. Dress professionally and be organized. Be punctual, dependable, and take initiative and responsibility for tasks. Integrity, a positive attitude, and respect for yourself and others are important workplace characteristics. Try to improve your problem-solving, decision-making, and reasoning skills by thinking through issues. Evaluate yourself, and identify areas you can improve now.

> ● **As You Read**
>
> Think about working in a company that offers the opportunity to do a variety of different tasks.

● **As You Read**
Some students may find job rotation appealing. Others may prefer to be trained to handle only one job.

Discuss the Photo
● **Workplace Skills** Answers will vary but may include pursuing their education, taking a job that will allow them to experience on-the-job training, developing their soft skills, and doing volunteer work.

Section 15.2

TEACH (cont.)

S Skill Practice
Guided Practice
Identify Ask students to identify five soft skills. (positive attitude, punctuality, friendliness, personal responsibility, problem-solving, decision-making, anger management, and discretion) **L1**

Create a Poster Have students choose a soft skill that they would like to develop and to make a poster highlighting some of the things they could do to develop the skill. (Posters will vary but should address a skill and skill development goals.) **L2**

Act Out Organize students into small groups and ask them to create skits highlighting the importance of several soft skills. The skits should illustrate problems faced when soft skills are underdeveloped and the benefits of improving soft skills. Have each group perform in front of the class. (Skits will vary but should demonstrate the benefits of developing soft skills.) **L3**

ASSESS

Review Key Terms
Have students write sentences using each key term.

 **Study-to-Go** Have students go to the Online Learning Center through **glencoe.com** to download free **Study-to-Go** content to their PDAs or cell phones.

RETEACH

W Writing Support

Enrichment
Performance Appraisals

A business has recently experienced rapid growth and you have been hired as a human resources manager. One of the first things you want to do is formalize the process of evaluating employees. Write a letter to the CEO explaining why you want to institute a performance appraisal program. (Students should include information about the purpose, expected outcomes, and basic processes involved in employee appraisals.)

R Reading Strategy

Outline Have students create an outline for the content that falls under the heading "Changes in Employee Status." Suggest that students use the headings in the textbook as a starting point. (The headings are: promotion, transfer, and separation.)

Student Activity Workbook 📂 Assign the Section 15.2 Activities.

✔ Reading Check

Analyze An employer can review an employee's progress, strengths, and weaknesses, and communicate what changes might be necessary to help the employee become more productive. The employee gets suggestions for improvement.

 Activity correlates to Science standards.

Science/TechTRENDS

Human Resource Management Systems

Workers are not machines. They think, feel emotions, and communicate with others. Human resource management (HRM) is a business practice used to understand the human aspect of a company as well as its impact. HRM usually involves using software to help HR staff in their daily functions. Human resource management systems (HRMS) software melds these functions and information technology. It helps to reduce the manual workload by streamlining payroll; time and labor management; benefits administration; and HRM. This shift away from paper-based processes benefits employees, managers, and HR staff, resulting in reduced costs and better efficiency.

WebQuest

Go to the *Introduction to Business* Online Learning Center through **glencoe.com** for links to Web sites where you can find more information about HRMS. What are some specific ways that human resources professionals use HRMS? Write a one-page essay on your findings. Cite examples of companies that make HRMS software.

● **As You Read**

Think about the types of evaluations you have received.

Evaluating Employees

A **performance appraisal** is an evaluation of how well an employee is doing a job. Employees are evaluated periodically. The evaluation might consist of an employee and his or her manager discussing the employee's strengths and weaknesses. **W** During an evaluation, managers usually offer suggestions for improvement. Employees can also note their own progress.

 **✔ Reading Check** **Analyze** Why are performance appraisals valuable to both the employer and the employee?

Changes in Employee Status

Human resources managers keep track of changes in the status of employees. For example, an employee might be promoted to a different position, transferred to another department, or fired. As a result, the worker might need to be reoriented, retrained, or replaced. **R**

Promotion

A **promotion** gives an employee a higher-level job with more authority, responsibility, and pay. Most promotions are merit-based and encourage performance. If an employee is doing a great job, she or he might be promoted. Promotions are also given on the basis of seniority. *Seniority* is the status given to an employee based on rank or length of service.

● **As You Read**

Almost all students have received report cards, progress reports, or other school evaluations. Other evaluations include medical evaluations, volunteer-work evaluations, and internship evaluations.

Science/TechTRENDS

WebQuest

Human Resources Management Systems Students' essays will vary. For example, the HR staff can use HRMS to automate the pay process. HRMS producers include Oracle® and Microsoft®.

Transfer

A **transfer** is a move to another job within a company, usually at the same level and pay. Employees might be transferred because another department needs them or their job in their present department has been eliminated. They might also be transferred if the company moves or opens a new office.

Separation

Separation is leaving a company for any reason. A voluntary separation occurs when an employee resigns or retires. When an employee voluntarily leaves, an *exit interview* is given to pinpoint why the employee is leaving.

Involuntary separations include layoffs and terminations. A worker may be fired or *terminated* if he or she breaks rules, becomes unable to perform at the expected level, or cannot get along with others. If the company needs to *downsize,* employees might be laid off. A *layoff* occurs when there is not enough work for all employees.

Turnover It costs companies a lot of money to search for, hire, and train new employees. Therefore, businesses are concerned with keeping turnover low. **Turnover** is the number of employees who leave an organization and are replaced over time. Careful hiring decisions and sufficient training increase chances for success with new employees.

 Activity correlates to English Language Arts standards.

glencoe.com   **Section 15.2**   Developing and Retaining Employees   **265**

Section 15.2

After You Read

Review Key Concepts
1. How can a company help a new employee to develop?
2. What are three ways in which new employees can be trained?
3. What are some changes in status an employee might experience?

Academic Skills
4. **English Language Arts** Work in groups of three or four to plan, write, and illustrate a handbook for new students entering your school. Include a map of the school, behavior expectations, and information about sports and clubs.

5. **English Language Arts** Apprenticeship is one form of on-the-job training that has existed for hundreds of years. Write a 250-word paper on the history of apprenticeship. Include information about the current status of such programs.

> @ Go to the *Introduction to Business* Online Learning Center through **glencoe.com** to check your answers.

Section 15.2

Review Key Concepts
1. through orientation, training, and evaluations
2. on-the-job training, working one-on-one with a supervisor; group training; job rotation
3. The employee could be promoted, transferred, or separated from the company, either voluntarily or involuntarily.

Academic Skills
4. **English Language Arts** Handbooks will vary, depending on characteristics of the school.
5. **English Language Arts** Reports will vary but should include historical and current information.

Section 15.2

RETEACH (cont.)

C Critical Thinking

Analyze the Difference
Separation Ask students to give examples of voluntary and involuntary separation situations. (Examples of involuntary separations include losing a job because of corporate downsizing, poor performance, absenteeism, or misconduct. Examples of voluntary separation include leaving a job to return to school, to accept a position with another company, or to start your own business.)

ASSESS

After You Read

Have students complete the Section 15.2 After You Read section review.

Online Study Tools

Have students go to the Online Learning Center through **glencoe.com** to:

• Take the Section 15.2 **Practice Test**.
• Download free **Study-to-Go** content to their PDAs or cell phones.

CLOSE

Culminating Activity
HR Management
Have students research a current issue in human resources management and prepare a short oral presentation. Examples of topics might include the aging workforce, the drug-free workplace, and cultural diversity. (Presentations will vary, depending on the topic.)

265

Vocabulary Review

1. Students should write complete sentences using each term correctly.

Review Key Concepts

2. Human resources management is the process of finding, selecting, training, and evaluating employees.

3. Businesses offer competitive pay (wages and salary) and benefits such as health insurance, life insurance, sick leave, retirement plans, and paid holidays.

4. review each candidate's application and/or résumé, interview qualified candidates, conduct testing to make sure job candidates have the right skills and character for a job, conduct a background check, and review references

5. Human resources managers conduct orientation sessions for new employees, assist with training and evaluation of employees, and keep track of changes in the status of employees.

6. Employees may be promoted to a higher-level job, transferred to another job within the company, or be separated from the company. Being laid off or fired, resigning, or retiring are all forms of separation.

Section 15.1 *Summary*

Employees: The Key to Success
Human resources are the people employed in a business. Employees are also referred to as personnel. They provide the skills, knowledge, labor, and experience needed to make a business productive. Human resources managers work as recruiters. Recruiters try to find the right person for a job. They also help people develop as employees so they can do their jobs well. Human resources managers begin the recruitment process by writing a job description. The job description is included in ads for the job.

Section 15.2 *Summary*

Developing and Retaining Employees
New employees need to be oriented, trained, and evaluated. Human resources staff members assist with all the activities for developing employees. New employees usually need training to learn the specific job they were hired to do. This includes on-the-job training and job rotation. Once they have been on a job for a while, new employees must be evaluated. A performance appraisal is used to determine whether an employee should get a raise, a promotion, or more training.

Vocabulary Review

1. On a sheet of paper, use each of these key terms and academic vocabulary terms in a sentence.

Key Terms		Academic Vocabulary
human resources	reference	temporary
human resources management	orientation	fund
job description	on-the-job training	summary
compensation	group training	comments
wage	performance appraisal	demonstrates
salary	promotion	relaxed
benefits	transfer	complement
recruitment	separation	technical
background check	turnover	

Review Key Concepts

2. Define human resources management.

3. Describe how a company attracts and rewards good employees.

4. Discuss what a human resources manager should consider about job applicants.

5. Identify responsibilities of human resources managers after they have hired a new employee.

6. Describe how the status of an employee can change.

266 **Chapter 15** Review and Activities

Critical Thinking

7. developing good human relations, management, technical, organizational, communication, and leadership skills

8. Adding this line makes it possible for a supervisor to be flexible in assigning responsibilities.

9. If the employee does not work out, it will be easier to terminate the worker.

10. Students should indicate an understanding of the difference between jobs that pay a salary and those that pay a wage.

11. Answers may vary. For example, if all applicants are asked the same questions, the interviewer can compare candidates better.

Critical Thinking

7. What do you think are the most important skills that you can work on now for success in a job in the future?

8. A job description tells potential employees about the types of duties that need to be performed. Why do you think job descriptions often indicate that the employee will "perform other duties as assigned"?

9. Why would a business list a new position as temporary but intend to have an employee in the position permanently?

10. Think about some different types of jobs in your community. What types of jobs are available for workers on a salary basis?

11. Most job interviews are structured the same for all candidates. Why do you think recruiters might ask the same questions of all applicants, instead of letting applicants decide what to emphasize?

12. Who would you list as references for a job application? Why would you select those people?

13. What changes do you think will occur in the workplace because of a rise in the number of younger workers (aged 16 to 34) and older workers (aged 55 and older)?

Write About It

14. Read the job announcements in a local newspaper. In a one-page report, list the requirements or duties and responsibilities of five jobs.

15. Assume that you are a recruiter for a restaurant and need to fill a part-time job for a food server. In at least two paragraphs, write a job description for a newspaper ad.

16. In at least one page, describe the type of training that would best help you learn to do a new job entering and processing data using a computer.

17. Research a job that you would like to have someday. Use various resources for your research, including newspaper ads, the Internet, and career guides. Write two or more paragraphs about it.

18. Survey five people about their jobs. Ask them to state their job title and duties. How did they find the job they have? How long did it take to get a job with the company? How do they feel about their job? Write a two-page report summarizing their comments.

19. Write at least two paragraphs summarizing information from the yellow pages about employment agencies in your area.

Technology Applications

Presentation Software
20. As recruiters, human resources managers try to bring in qualified workers to fill openings. Their efforts help assure that companies hire the best people for their jobs. Use graphic presentation software to prepare slides outlining the steps human resources managers take to fill a position. Then give a presentation to your class.

Business Ethics

Hiring Decisions
21. You have just been put on the employment screening committee for an all-male law firm. There are two finalists being considered for a position: a man and a woman. They are equally qualified. What guidelines do you think your committee should follow in selecting the right person for the job? Should gender be a factor?

Chapter 15 Review and Activities **267**

Critical Thinking
12. Answers will vary. However, companies usually prefer references from people other than family members.

13. Younger workers will find opportunities to use the skills that they have acquired through education and technology. Older workers could need more training and education as changes arise in technology.

Write About It
14. Answers will vary depending on the announcements.

15. Answers should include qualifications and experience required, duties, hours, wages, and contact information.

16. Answers will vary but may include: people who need more extensive practice and explanation would learn best with one-on-one training; people who learn best by interacting with others may benefit most from group training. Others may prefer a combination.

17. Answers will vary but should employ appropriate resources.

18. Summaries will vary but should address the provided questions.

19. Employment agencies will provide both permanent and temporary job placement. Most will prescreen applicants and send only those with needed skills to interview with a business. Some agencies specialize in certain types of jobs.

Technology Applications
20. Slides may include: "Prepare a Job Description," "Recruit Applicants," "Review Applications and Résumés," "Screen Applicants," "Interview Qualified Applicants," "Evaluate Qualified Applicants," "Hire an Applicant."

Business Ethics
21. The law firm should encourage employment based on ability, knowledge, skills, and experience. Gender may also be a factor here because employing a woman will increase the diversity of employees in the firm.

Chapter 15 *Review and Activities*

Applying Academics to Business

Applying Academics to Business

Applying Academics to Business

22. Human resources management is the process of finding, selecting, training, and evaluating employees.

23. Mean = $56,667
Median = $60,100

24. Answers will vary. Lists could start with gerunds such as *handling, maintaining, studying.*

25. The assistant took the discount off the original price, not the new price. First apply the increase of 17% to the original price: $67 × 0.17 = $11.39. Add the increase to the original price then multiply by the discount and subtract:

$67 + $11.39 = $78.39

$78.39 × 0.08 = $6.27

$78.39 − $6.27 = $72.12

Active Learning

26. Professional and managerial workers probably acquired their skills in college. Workers with technical skills may have acquired those skills in high school or college, or by reading books and using software tutorial programs. Other workers may have completed an apprenticeship.

Business in the Real World

27. The supervisor should talk to Ashley about her situation and determine what can be done to make the situation better.

English Language Arts

22. Parallel construction is a balance of two or more similar words, phrases, or clauses. Rewrite the following sentence to solve problems with parallel construction:

Human resources management is the process of finding, selecting, to train, and to evaluate employees.

Mathematics

23. As a human resources professional for a local biomedical company, you want to offer good research workers a competitive salary. You survey similar companies in your area and find out that medical researchers are paid:

Company A: $60,100
Company B: $45,900
Company C: $64,000

What is the mean of this data? What is the median?

> **THEORY** **Data Analysis** The mean of a set of data is the average. The median is the middle number when the data is arrayed in order from least to greatest.

English Language Arts

24. Write a job description for a task you perform. Make a list of the duties and responsibilities that consists of at least four phrases or complete sentences using parallel construction.

Mathematics

25. As manager of an aircraft parts department, you need to increase prices by 17%. Customers who buy in volume will get an 8% discount. A replacement engine mount used to cost $67. To find the new price for a high-volume customer, use the following method:

17% − 8% = 9%
$67 × 9% = $6.03
$67 + $6.03 = $73.03

You calculate the price to be $72.12. What mistake was made?

> **THEORY** **Working with Percents** A discount is an amount off a selling price, often determined by multiplying the selling price by a given percent.

Active Learning

Developing Job Skills

26. Survey family, friends, or others about their work experience. Ask these questions: How did you acquire the skills and knowledge for your job? What type of training did you receive? How long was it? Is it ongoing? What type of training do you think you might need in the future? Prepare a two-page report about your findings. Present your report to your class.

Business in the Real World

Dealing with Personnel Problems

27. Ashley was hired as a Web designer. When she began work, her work was excellent, and she worked well with others. Lately, Ashley's work has slipped. She has been late to work and has been having arguments with her co-workers. What should her supervisor do to solve the problem? What would happen if her supervisor did nothing? In two or more paragraphs, discuss the supervisor's options.

ExamView Assessment Suite CD allows you to print out ready-made unit and chapter tests, complete with answer keys. You can also create customized tests.

TeacherWorks Plus provides complete teacher resources in one convenient package. It includes customizable lesson plans in calendar format, and instant access to many print program resources.

Real LIFE skills

INTERVIEW QUESTIONS

28. A job applicant cannot be asked the following questions during an interview: What nationality are you? Are you married? What are your day-care arrangements? What religious meetings or holidays do you observe? Write at least two paragraphs, explaining why these questions are considered inappropriate for a job interview.

FIND YOUR DREAM JOB

29. Go to the *Introduction to Business* Online Learning Center through **glencoe.com** for a link to the Occupational Outlook Handbook Web site. Click on the "OOH Search/A-Z Index" link and enter the job category "human resources, training, and labor relations managers and specialists." Then write a one-page report about this field. Conclude your report with a list of things you could do now to prepare yourself to pursue the occupation.

Role Play

RESOLVING CONFLICTS

30. Situation As the human resources manager of a department store, you must resolve a conflict between two members of the sales staff. Both are good at their jobs and well-liked by customers and others.

Activity Have a one-on-one talk with each of the two salespeople to determine possible solutions to resolve the conflict. Choose the best solution and present it to the employees' supervisor.

Evaluation You will be evaluated on how well you meet the following performance indicators:

- Allow both co-workers to explain their view of the situation.
- Identify the source of the conflict.
- Explain your perception of the problem and possible solution for it.
- Develop a solution to the problem.
- Speak clearly and use correct grammar.

Standardized Test Practice

Directions Choose the letter of the best answer. Write the letter for the answer on a separate piece of paper.

1. For which of these situations would you need an exact number?

A estimating the number of people who will attend a company picnic

B determining how many round trips your car can make on a full tank of gas

C ordering copies of a new employee benefits manual for present and future employees

D calculating deductions for taxes and health insurance from an employee's payroll check

 **TEST-TAKING TIP** When answering essay questions, make sure that you support generalizations with evidence. Back up your ideas with names, dates, and places. A short essay question should be answered with accurate explanations backed up by facts.

 READING Go to the *Introduction to Business* Online Learning Center through **glencoe.com** for a list of outside reading suggestions.

Real LIFE skills

28. Answers will vary. These questions are not related to the job and its requirements and could lead the interviewer to discriminate.

Cool Business CAREERS

29. Human resources staff plan, organize, and direct a wide range of training activities, conduct orientation programs and on-the-job training for new employees. A college education is required for entry-level positions. Advanced degrees are required for some jobs. Exceptional workers may be promoted to top managerial positions. The job outlook is for faster-than-average growth. As preparation, develop communication and interpersonal skills and take business and college preparation classes.

Role Play

30. Presentations should address the competencies noted in the Role Play. If they cannot work together successfully, then you might consider separating them. More training might help resolve the conflict.

Standardized Test Practice

1. D

 **STRATEGIES FOR STANDARDIZED TEST PREP SUCCESS**

Test Savvy Explain that students should carefully read essay questions to make sure they understand exactly what is expected of their answer. Then have them start by writing a topic sentence that uses wording from the question.

Standards-Based Lesson Planning   *Introduction to Business* provides students with instruction and assessment in the following fundamental content areas:

Content Standards Correlations	
Examine the significance of employment law in business.	p. 280
Analyze the characteristics of the multicultural workplace.	pp. 273–276, 278–281, 282–285
Compare patterns of behavior or interaction among various cultures.	pp. 273–276, 282–285
Identify the value of performing effectively in various environments with people of different ages, genders, cultures, socioeconomic backgrounds, attitudes, and abilities.	pp. 278–281, 282–285
Explain how diversity affects marketing.	pp. 278–281, 282–283
Explain the impact and value of diversity.	pp. 278–281, 282–285

NCLB   Activities, information, and skills practice will help your students attain No Child Left Behind proficiency. Students will improve their abilities in the following academic standards areas:

Academic Standards Correlations		
English Language Arts	Activities/Features	Page
NCTE 6 Apply knowledge of language structure and conventions to discuss texts	Applying Academics to Business	p. 284
NCTE 8 Use information resources to gather information and create and communicate knowledge	Applying Academics to Business	p. 284
NCTE 9 Develop an understanding of diversity in language use across cultures	After You Read	p. 281
NCTE 12 Use language to accomplish individual purposes	After You Read	p. 281
Mathematics		
Algebra Understand patterns, relations, and functions	Standardized Test Practice	p. 285
Number and Operations Understand numbers, ways of representing numbers, relationships among numbers, and number systems	After You Read Applying Academics to Business	pp. 276, 284
Number and Operations Understand meanings of operations and how they relate to one another	Ask S&P Applying Academics to Business	pp. 270, 284
Science		
Content Standard F Students should develop understanding of personal and community health and science and technology in local, national, and global challenges	Science/Tech Trends	p. 278

Correlations

This chart shows the 21st Century Skills, foundation skills, and workplace competencies that students develop as they work in this chapter.

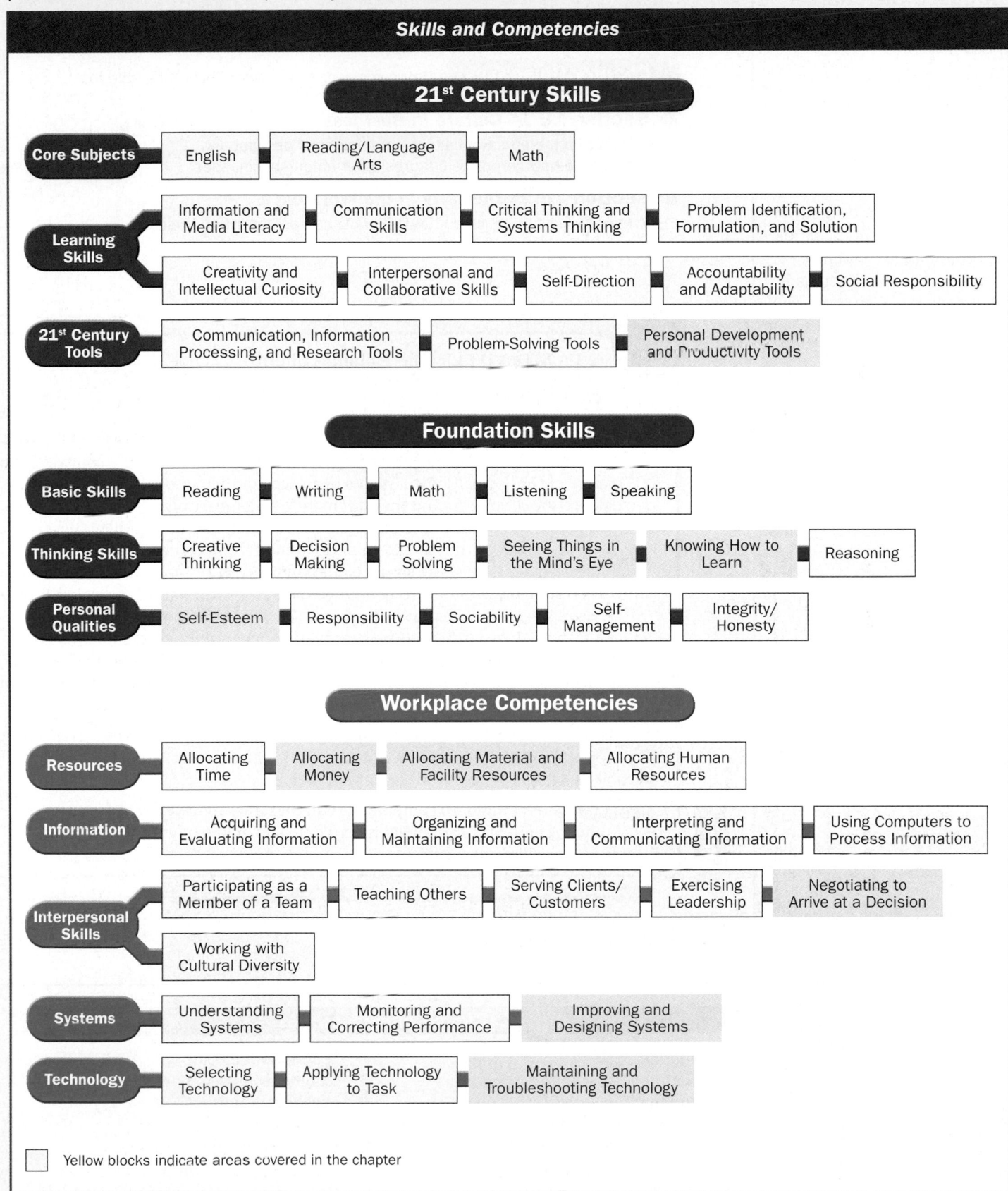

Skills and Competencies

21st Century Skills

Core Subjects
- English
- Reading/Language Arts
- Math

Learning Skills
- Information and Media Literacy
- Communication Skills
- Critical Thinking and Systems Thinking
- Problem Identification, Formulation, and Solution
- Creativity and Intellectual Curiosity
- Interpersonal and Collaborative Skills
- Self-Direction
- Accountability and Adaptability
- Social Responsibility

21st Century Tools
- Communication, Information Processing, and Research Tools
- Problem-Solving Tools
- Personal Development and Productivity Tools

Foundation Skills

Basic Skills
- Reading
- Writing
- Math
- Listening
- Speaking

Thinking Skills
- Creative Thinking
- Decision Making
- Problem Solving
- Seeing Things in the Mind's Eye
- Knowing How to Learn
- Reasoning

Personal Qualities
- Self-Esteem
- Responsibility
- Sociability
- Self-Management
- Integrity/Honesty

Workplace Competencies

Resources
- Allocating Time
- Allocating Money
- Allocating Material and Facility Resources
- Allocating Human Resources

Information
- Acquiring and Evaluating Information
- Organizing and Maintaining Information
- Interpreting and Communicating Information
- Using Computers to Process Information

Interpersonal Skills
- Participating as a Member of a Team
- Teaching Others
- Serving Clients/Customers
- Exercising Leadership
- Negotiating to Arrive at a Decision
- Working with Cultural Diversity

Systems
- Understanding Systems
- Monitoring and Correcting Performance
- Improving and Designing Systems

Technology
- Selecting Technology
- Applying Technology to Task
- Maintaining and Troubleshooting Technology

☐ Yellow blocks indicate areas covered in the chapter

Chapter 16

Chapter Overview

Introduce the Chapter

Culture and Diversity in Business

Chapter 16 is about business culture and diversity in the workplace.

Building Background

Schools and neighborhoods may not reflect the diversity of the community or country. Tell students they will probably experience people from many other cultures when they attend college or enter the workforce.

Ask STANDARD &POOR'S

>> **Math Answer**

Current Ratio = Current Assets ÷ Current Liabilities

= ($3,560 + $5,600) ÷ $4,500

= $9,160 ÷ $4,500

= 2.035

>> **Extension Activity**

Provide the following data and ask students to calculate the current ratio for each of the five companies.
(Company A, 0.75:1; Company B, 1.46:1; Company C, 1.07:1; Company D, 1.95:1; Company E, 2.23:1)

Company	Current Assets	Current Liabilities
A	3,164	4,235
B	5,583	3,820
C	13,463	12,588
D	3,558	1,821
E	27,869	12,488

NCLB Activity correlates to Math standards.

Culture and Diversity in Business

Chapter Objectives   After completing this chapter, you will be able to:

▶ **Section 16.1**   *Culture in Business*
- **Describe** the effect of culture on doing business globally.
- **Describe** how corporate cultures differ among businesses.

▶ **Section 16.2**   *Diversity in the Workplace*
- **Identify** ways in which cultural diversity has an impact on business.

Ask STANDARD &POOR'S   The Balance Sheet

Q: What is a balance sheet, and what should I look in it for when researching a stock?

A: A balance sheet is a statement of the total assets and liabilities of a company at a particular time, usually the last date of an accounting period. Using a company's balance sheet, you can find the current ratio, a comparison of current assets (assets that can be converted into cash in less than a year), and current liabilities (money owed that is due within a year) to assess liquidity. You can compare debt to shareholder's equity to see how leveraged the company is, or how much it owes. For conservative investors, a strong balance sheet is a must. If a company has little or no debt, it tends to be conservatively managed. If it has more cash and assets that can be turned into cash within a year than current liabilities and long-term debt, it is financially sound and should be able to weather financial storms. Companies publish their balance sheets in their financial reports, and you can also find them in Standard & Poor's Stock Reports, as well as in Value Line's service.

Mathematics The balance sheet for Monique's Boutique showed current assets including accounts receivable of $3,560 and cash of $5,600. Current liabilities were accounts payable of $4,500. What is the current ratio?

NCLB

THEORY   Current Ratio To compute the current ratio, divide current assets by current liabilities. A ratio of 2:1 or higher is considered favorable by creditors. It indicates that a business is able to pay its debts.

Classroom Resources

- Student Edition
- Teacher Wraparound Edition
- Student Activity Workbook with Academic Integration
- Student Activity Workbook with Academic Integration TAE
- *Fast File*, Unit 5 Resources
- Inclusion in the Business Education Classroom

- TeacherWorks Plus
- *ExamView Assessment Suite*
- Presentation Plus!
- Vocabulary PuzzleMaker
- Interactive Student Edition
- Online Student Edition
- Online Learning Center with Podcasts

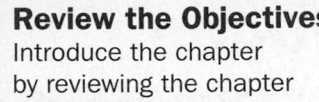

Review the Objectives
Introduce the chapter by reviewing the chapter objectives:

Section 16.1 *Objectives*
Describe the effect of culture on doing business globally. (As companies trade globally, they must be aware of different cultural and business practices. Knowing how to approach people from different cultures will give others a better impression of the company.)

Describe how corporate cultures differ among businesses. (Some companies have a formal culture, with a strict chain of command and dress codes. Other companies have an informal culture, in which employees are encouraged to make decisions, dress casually, and have flexible work hours. Most companies have a culture that is both formal and informal.)

Section 16.2 *Objectives*
Identify ways in which cultural diversity has an impact on business. (Workers have different skills, work habits, and approaches to tasks. As workers from many cultures enter the workplace, many people come into contact with people of different ages, ethnic backgrounds, and abilities for the first time. More opportunities are available for workers to advance, regardless of their cultural background. Cultural diversity among workers enables companies to anticipate the needs of culturally diverse markets.)

● **Shared Values** Many companies promote a strong corporate culture. **Why might it be important for employees in a company to share values, beliefs, and goals?**

Chapter 16 Culture and Diversity in Business **271**

Discuss the Photo
● **Shared Values** Read the caption on the photo to students: Many companies promote a strong corporate culture.

Ask students: Why might it be important for employees in a company to share values, beliefs, and goals? (Some students may think it is most important to share values so that the employees in a company will be able to work as a united team. Some may say that when employees share a similar set of beliefs, they are more likely to work in harmony. Other students may focus on the need for shared goals as a way to focus employee efforts on the same targets.)

FOCUS

Bell Ringer Activity

Culture in Business

Ask students to suggest how culture affects the way business is conducted. (Through traditions, personal space, gifts, and social status.) Follow up by asking how corporate cultures vary. (Some companies encourage competitiveness and others collaboration. Some have strict rules and others fewer rules. In some, top managers have plush offices, and in others, managers work in the open with their team.)

Preteaching

Presentation Plus!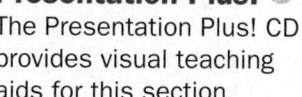

The Presentation Plus! CD provides visual teaching aids for this section.

PuzzleMaker

Use the Vocabulary PuzzleMaker to create a puzzle of the section's key terms. Students can complete the puzzle on paper or on a computer.

Graphic Organizer

Tell students to go to the Online Learning Center through **glencoe.com** for a printable graphic organizer. (Answers include: Formal: strict chain of command; several management levels; slow decision-making process; strict dress codes. Informal: encouragement of decision making; casual dress; teamwork.)

Connects academics to content.

Culture in Business

Reading Guide

● Before You Read

Think about what makes up a company's culture and how different cultures can impact a business.

Read to Learn
- Describe the effect of culture on doing business globally.
- Describe how corporate cultures differ among businesses.

D

The Main Idea
A company's culture is its shared values, beliefs, and goals that affect the way its management and employees interact. It also impacts the way it works with people in other countries with which it does business.

Key Concepts
- Culture in a Global Economy
- Corporate Culture

Vocabulary
Key Terms
    culture
    business etiquette
    corporate culture
    hierarchy
    bureaucracy

Academic Vocabulary
You will find these words in your reading and on your tests. Make sure you know their meanings.
    distinct
    ethnic
    region
    tradition

Graphic Organizer
List some attributes of a formal culture and an informal culture in a figure like the one below.

Corporate Culture

Formal	Informal

 Go to the *Introduction to Business* Online Learning Center through **glencoe.com** for a printable graphic organizer.

Academic Standards

English Language Arts

N C L B

    NCTE 1 Read texts to acquire new information
    NCTE 9 Develop an understanding of diversity in language use across cultures

Mathematics
    Number and Operations Understand numbers, ways of representing numbers, relationships among numbers, and number systems

---

Reading Guide

● Before You Read

Students might describe different corporate cultures as lacking diversity or being disconnected. Others may suggest some corporate cultures are diverse, with cohesive staffs.

D Develop Concepts

The Main Idea Ask students: Why is culture an issue in business today? (Businesses across the country interact with people and companies worldwide, more so as the U.S. population becomes more diverse.)

Culture in a Global Economy

The word "culture" can have several different meanings. In general, **culture** is the beliefs, customs, and attitudes of a **distinct** group of people. A group's culture is often considered in terms of its dress, food, language, and art. It can also be considered in terms of a group's history, geography, and religious beliefs. Culture can refer to an entire country or **ethnic** group. It can also refer to a specific social group or institution.

The global economy creates a diverse culture for business. As companies trade worldwide, they must be aware of different cultural and business practices. Each country has its own rules for etiquette, business customs, and personal interaction. Properly approaching people from various cultures can give them a better impression of you.

In business, culture has two important meanings. In the broad sense, it refers to the customs of other countries with which companies do business. A *custom* is a practice followed by people of a particular group or **region**. Business culture refers to the standards of a particular company. Companies that conduct business in other countries must be aware of differences in laws, currencies, eating habits, and even systems of measurement. Failure to understand the culture of a country with which you do business can ruin a deal or lead to a marketing disaster.

✔ Reading Check **Identify** What factors make up a group's culture?

● **Work Environment**
Different work environments reflect various types of corporate culture. **How would you describe the culture of this workplace?**

● **As You Read**

Think about the benefits of understanding other cultures.

Discussion Starter
Culture in a Global Economy
Ask students how comfortable they would be doing business in another country. Ask them to describe specific concerns. (Students might suggest that they would be comfortable doing business in some countries, but do not feel they know enough about their culture and traditions.)

R **Reading Strategy**

Give an Example Ask students to give an example of how a corporate culture might conflict with the culture where a company does business. (Casual attire that is part of a corporate culture might be seen as an insult in a country where business suits are considered more appropriate. In some countries where socializing is an important part of doing business it might be considered rude to conduct a meeting with a strict business agenda.)

✔ Reading Check

Identify dress, food, language, art, history, geography, and religion

Section 16.1 Culture in Business **273**

● **As You Read**

Answers will vary. Students may say that understanding other cultures leads to friendships, better communication, and more knowledge. Failing to understand can lead to disagreements and hostilities.

Discuss the Photo
● **Work Environment** The workplace seems to have an informal environment. The employee is wearing casual attire and is not working in an office.

TEACH (cont.)

S Skill Practice

Guided Practice

Explain Ask students why it is important to understand other cultures when doing business in a global marketplace. (so as not to offend workers, customers, and government officials) **L1**

Make a List Have students make a list of five things they might do when planning to conduct business in another country. (learning the language, visiting the country, reading about the country, hiring a consultant familiar with the country, and contacting the U.S. embassy in the country) **L2**

Summarize Ask students to read an article offering guidance about cultural issues and etiquette involved in doing business around the globe, summarize the reading, and provide a properly formatted citation. (Summaries will vary depending on the article read.) **L3**

ASSESS

Review Key Terms

Have students write sentences using each key term.

Study-to-Go

Have students go to the Online Learning Center through **glencoe.com** to download free **Study-to-Go** content to their PDAs or cell phones.

International Business

International Business

Customer Service

Today you can find a McDonald's® restaurant on every continent except Antarctica. Appealing to local tastes in some markets is an important way McDonald's has grown globally. In Uruguay you can order a "McHuevo," a hamburger with a poached egg on top. Norwegians can order a "McLaks," a grilled salmon sandwich with dill sauce; and when you're in Thailand, you can try the "Samurai Pork Burger," a sausage patty in teriyaki sauce. Because personal service is so important to customers in the Middle East and Southeast Asia, McDonald's even delivers there.

Examples of Languages Across Cultures

Q: In Bahasa-Indonesian, how do you say: "Goodbye"?
A: **Selamat tinggal** (pronounced: Slă-măt tēng-gŭll)

If you could add a local twist to a fast-food menu or restaurant in your area, what would it be?

Marketing Abroad

To market products successfully in another country, companies must research the country's languages, customs, and tastes. For example, when Pillsbury® translated "Jolly Green Giant" into Arabic, the phrase became "Intimidating Green Ogre." Soft-drink maker Coca-Cola changes the amount of carbonation and sugar in its products to suit the tastes of different countries.

Doing Business Abroad

● As You Read

Think about marketing goods in other countries. What are some obstacles you might face?

Companies doing business in other countries must be aware of cultural differences that affect the workplace. When the Walt Disney Company opened Euro Disney, French workers objected to certain practices that were typical at Disney's U.S. theme parks. As a result, 3,000 workers quit.

Business Etiquette

S **Business etiquette** is conduct that is considered socially acceptable in business. It differs from country to country. For example, in the United States, receiving a gift from a potential business partner could be seen as a bribe. In Japan, it is customary to give gifts, and there are many rituals involved. Before doing business in India, it is customary to have tea. In Mexico, throwing documents on a table during a meeting is considered an insult.

Many companies avoid cultural problems by hiring local managers in other countries. Some also prepare their own managers to live and work abroad. As more companies trade globally, there is an increased demand for people who have studied other languages and cultures.

274 **Chapter 16** Culture and Diversity in Business

● As You Read

Answers may include language barriers, differences in labor practices, and differences in customs.

International Business

Customer Service Answers will vary, but students might mention local favorites such as maple syrup in New England or Creole cooking in Louisiana.

Corporate Culture

A company's **corporate culture** is its shared values, beliefs, and goals. It can be defined formally through a company code of ethics, a written manual, and the orientation process. It can also be defined informally through dress codes, work habits, and social activities. The culture at McDonald's, for example, stresses customer service and family values. Employees are expected to be clean-cut and greet each customer with a smile. FedEx Kinko's℠, Ben & Jerry's®, and Patagonia® stress worker satisfaction and concern for the environment.

A company's founder can influence its culture. For instance, William Hewlett of computer-maker Hewlett-Packard stressed a "people first" culture. Region and **tradition** can also play big parts. A banker at a Wall Street firm in New York may be expected to wear a suit and tie. At a high-tech company in California's Silicon Valley, workers might wear T-shirts and shorts to work.

✔ Reading Check **Contrast** What other differences might you encounter if you worked at a Wall Street firm or a Silicon Valley company?

BusinessWeek *Reader and Case Study*

Fashion, with a Conscience

CEO George Zimmer's central tenet at Men's Wearhouse? "You've got to have a company that starts with trust and fairness."

As founder and CEO of Men's Wearhouse®, George Zimmer is known to the shopping public as the bearded company pitchman who declares "I guarantee it!" in his TV commercials hawking suits and sport coats.

Founded in 1973, the Men's Wearhouse chain has grown to more than 500 stores catering to the man who doesn't necessarily adore shopping. Stores are located in outdoor shopping centers, letting customers get in and out quickly. The $250 to $300 price tag for most Men's Wearhouse suits is budget-conscious. The merchandise isn't high fashion, but it is practical and functional.

Behind the scenes, Zimmer has long worked to build a corporate culture that centers first

and foremost on keeping his employees happy and loyal. That culture appears to benefit Men's Wearhouse: So far this year, its shares have risen 25%, outperforming the 1% increase in the

 CASE STUDY Go to the *Introduction to Business* Online Learning Center through **glencoe.com** for the *BusinessWeek* Reader Case Study.

Active Learning

Team up with a classmate and go shopping online or in person for business appropriate clothing. Try on at least one suit. How does it make you feel to be formally dressed? Write an advice column for your school newspaper that gives suggestions on how to best present an appropriate business image.

glencoe.com

Section 16.1 Culture in Business **275**

BusinessWeek *Reader and Case Study*

Fashion, with a Conscience

 CASE STUDY Have students go to the *Introduction to Business* Online Learning Center through **glencoe.com** to download a Case Study activity that corresponds to the article. The activity and answer key are also available on the TeacherWorks Plus CD.

Active Learning

Answers will vary but should combine expressions of the student's personal style with an appreciation of business norms.

Section 16.1

RETEACH

W Writing Support

Enrichment

Examine a Corporate Culture Have students visit the Web site of a major corporation to get some insight into its corporate culture. Ask students to write a summary of what they learn. (Summaries will vary, depending on the company's culture.)

R Reading Strategy

Explain Ask students to explain why it is important to know something about a firm's corporate culture before accepting a job. (Students might suggest that the need to be part of a team might fit in with a company that encourages teamwork.)

U Universal Access

Second Language Learners Students who speak languages other than English may be able to provide a firsthand account of another culture. Ask these students privately if they are interested in sharing their experiences and knowledge with the class. This can give them a chance to show leadership and confidence.

Student Activity Workbook ☞ Assign the Section 16.1 Activities.

✔ Reading Check

Contrast Students will point out that most Wall Street firms expect employees to dress formally. Many high-tech companies have a casual dress code.

RETEACH (cont.)

C Critical Thinking

Compare and Contrast
Formal and Informal Culture
Have students discuss the advantages and disadvantages of a formal and an informal culture. (Answers should include the pros and cons of both cultures.)

● As You Read

Top-level management has more control over the business and its employees, allowing management to control all levels of decision making.

ASSESS

● After You Read

Have students complete the Section 16.1 After You Read section review.

Online Study Tools
Have students go to the Online Learning Center through **glencoe.com** to:

- Take the Section 16.1 **Practice Test**.
- Download free **Study-to-Go** content to their PDAs or cell phones.

CLOSE

Culminating Activity
Interview
Ask students to interview an adult who is employed about the culture of his or her workplace and prepare a summary to share with the class. (Summaries will vary, depending on the adult interviewed.)

 Activity correlates to Math standards.

● As You Read

Think about working at a company with a formal culture. Why do some companies prefer this type of organization?

Formal Culture

A company's culture affects the way it is organized and does business. A formal business culture may have a strict **hierarchy**, or chain of command. A hierarchy usually has one person at the top who makes all the decisions. There might be several levels of management below. This is known as a **bureaucracy**. In formal cultures, making changes or passing down decisions can be complicated. Job titles are indicators of power and status within a company. Dress codes and work hours are strictly enforced.

C Informal Culture

At a company with an informal culture, employees are encouraged to make decisions on their own. They are allowed to dress casually and have more flexible work hours. In some cases they can even work at home. Job titles are not as important as creativity and teamwork. At computer memory maker Kingston Technology®, the founders sit in cubicles so they can interact with employees and be available to them. Few companies have a culture that is entirely formal or informal. Within one company there are often different cultures.

Section 16.1

● After You Read

Review Key Concepts
1. Why should businesses involved in global trade be aware of cultural differences?
2. How is a company's corporate culture defined?
3. What are some characteristics of a formal corporate culture?

Academic Skills
4. **Mathematics** Monica was traveling to England and France on business. She flew from London to Paris and wanted to exchange some U.S. dollars (USD) and British pounds (GBP) into euros (EUR). She went to the exchange bank and saw this sign:

Currency	Sell	Buy
GBP	1.46990 EUR	0.68032 EUR
USD	0.83399 EUR	1.19962 EUR

Compare the values of a single dollar, euro, and pound by writing an expression that orders them from least to greatest.

THEORY Inequalities Use the symbol $>$ to mean *greater than* and $<$ to mean *less than.*

 For math help, go to the Math Appendix.

 Go to the *Introduction to Business* Online Learning Center through **glencoe.com** to check your answers.

Section 16.1

Review Key Concepts
1. Properly approaching people from different cultures gives a better impression of the business.
2. Formally, through a company code of ethics, a written manual, and the orientation process. It is defined informally through dress codes, work habits, and social activities.
3. Some characteristics are a strict chain of command or hierarchy, several levels of management or a bureaucracy, importance of job titles, and strict dress codes and work hours.

Academic Skills
4. **Mathematics** 1 USD $<$ 1 EUR $<$ 1 GBP

Diversity in the Workplace

Reading Guide

Before You Read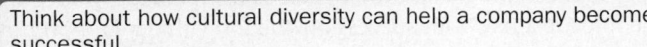

Think about how cultural diversity can help a company become successful.

Read to Learn
- Identify ways in which cultural diversity has an impact on business.

The Main Idea
Companies are more aware of the growing spending power of different consumer groups. Human resources managers find ways to draw on the strengths of culturally diverse workers.

D

Key Concept
- Cultural Diversity

Vocabulary

Key Terms

diversity	discrimination
stereotype	ageism
baby boom generation	

Academic Vocabulary

You will find these words in your reading and on your tests. Make sure you know their meanings.

diverse	prohibits
assignments	accommodation

Graphic Organizer

As you read, list the benefits of diversity in a figure like the one below.

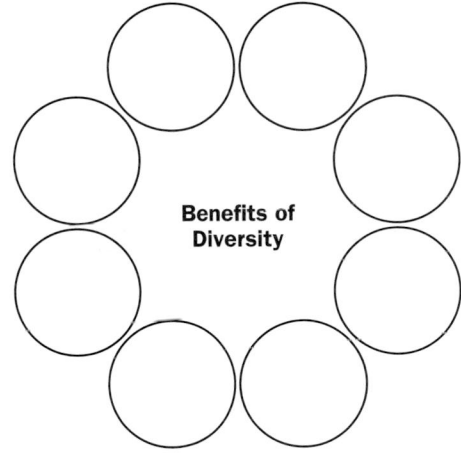

Benefits of Diversity

 Go to the *Introduction to Business* Online Learning Center through **glencoe.com** for a printable graphic organizer.

Academic Standards

English Language Arts

NCTE 1 Read texts to acquire new information

NCTE 1 Use written language to communicate effectively

NCTE 9 Develop an understanding of diversity in language use across cultures

NCTE 12 Use language to accomplish individual purposes

Science

Content Standard F Students should develop an understanding of personal and community health and science and technology in local, national, and global challenges

NCLB

Reading Guide

Before You Read

Seeking the viewpoints of their workers can help companies to serve their target markets better.

D Develop Concepts

The Main Idea Ask students: What are some of the signs the United States has become more diverse in recent years? (Students might point out that some signs are in more than one language and that it is not unusual to hear people speaking another language.)

🔔 Bell Ringer Activity

Diversity in the Workplace

Ask students how diversity enriches a community. (Communities are enriched through the heritage, arts, customs, and traditions of its members. A diverse community allows local firms to attract employees who want to live and work in a diverse environment.)

Preteaching

Presentation Plus! 💿

The Presentation Plus! CD provides visual teaching aids for this section.

PuzzleMaker 💿

Use the Vocabulary PuzzleMaker to create a puzzle of the section's key terms. Students can complete the puzzle on paper or on a computer.

Graphic Organizer

Tell students to go to the Online Learning Center through **glencoe.com** for a printable graphic organizer. (Answers include: a broader range of ideas, better understanding and service to a company's diverse market, strengthening of employees' commitment to company's goals, increased productivity and efficiency, lower turnover rates, less absenteeism, fewer legal costs from employee complaints, reduced conflicts among employees.)

NCLB Connects academics to content.

TEACH

Discussion Starter
Cultural Diversity
Point out that cultural diversity often focuses on nationality, ethnicity, and religion. Point out that the word *diverse* simply means differing from one another. Ask students to discuss how they differ from each other.

R Reading Strategy

Compare Have students work in pairs and ask them to make a list of five ways they are different. (Answers will vary but might include gender, ethnicity, talents, religion, height, and study habits.)

● As You Read

Answers will vary. Students may discuss a greater workforce from which businesses can draw and a greater emphasis on reaching diverse markets.

✔ Reading Check

Identify Ways in which people can be diverse include age, gender, ethnicity, and individual needs.

NCLB Activity correlates to Science standards.

Cultural Diversity

Companies tend to thrive when they have **diversity**, a variety of employees with different backgrounds and identities. People are **diverse** in terms of age, gender, ethnicity, and individual needs. They also differ in terms of education, marital status, income, and religious beliefs. Diversity in the workplace means differences in skills, work habits, and approaches to tasks. People with the same **assignments** will carry them out in different ways.

Some people stereotype others who are different from them. To **stereotype** people is to identify them by a single trait or as a member of a certain group rather than as individuals. In fact, no two people are alike. Your success on the job will depend on how well you work with and for people who are different from you.

● As You Read

Think about the growth of the U.S. population. What effects do you think that the increasingly diverse population will have on business in the future?

✔ Reading Check   **Identify** What are some ways in which people are diverse?

The Impact of Diversity on Business

The U.S. population is becoming more ethnically diverse. Each year, more than 1 million people come to the United States from all over the world. As total population grows, the percentages of people with African, Asian, and Hispanic or Latino

Science/Tech **TRENDS** ●

NCLB

Adaptive Technologies
Hiring people with physical disabilities and accommodating their special workplace needs is easier than ever, thanks to the development of adaptive technologies. For example, voice recognition software transforms the human voice using a computer input device that can replace the mouse and keyboard, and improves the productivity of people with movement problems. Unique authoring tools now enable Web designers to incorporate sign language into their Web sites to assist those with hearing impairment. Improvements in videoconferencing technologies are making telecommuting a reality for many who couldn't enter the workplace any other way. Fully incorporating employees with these kinds of special needs increases workplace diversity and impacts corporate culture.

Web*Quest*

Go to the *Introduction to Business* Online Learning Center through **glencoe.com** for links to Web sites where you can find out more about adaptive technologies and how they help people and companies reach their potential. Research the stories of individuals who use adaptive technologies in their daily work lives. Write a few paragraphs about how adaptive technologies are changing the diversity of the workplace.

Science/Tech **TRENDS** ●

Web*Quest*

Adaptive Technologies Paragraphs will vary but students should discuss the growing field of adaptive technology as it is related to the workplace.

heritage also grow. The fastest growing groups in the country are people of Hispanic and Asian origins. These changes are expected to continue. The growth of different cultures greatly impacts business.

The population is also living longer. More workers aged 65 and over are working past retirement age. They will account for a larger share of the U.S. labor force over the next several years. The growth rate for women in the labor force is expected to rise at a slightly faster rate than for men. Workers aged 25 to 54 are the largest share of the workforce. (See **Figure 16.1**.)

Changes in the Workplace As the population becomes more diverse, so does the workplace. There are greater numbers of women, Asians, Hispanics, and African Americans in management positions. Many workers from various cultures meet people of different ages, ethnic backgrounds, and abilities for the first time when they enter the workplace.

Changes in the Marketplace A more diverse population also means a more diverse marketplace. With more jobs, women and ethnic groups have more spending power and a larger share of the market. Companies now target several market segments. For example, many companies run ads in both English and Spanish and tailor them to different ethnic groups. The 76 million babies born in the United States between 1946 and 1964 are called the **baby boom generation**. Many members of this generation are reaching retirement age and developing specific needs.

As You Read

Think about some of your favorite TV commercials. What groups were targeted in these ads?

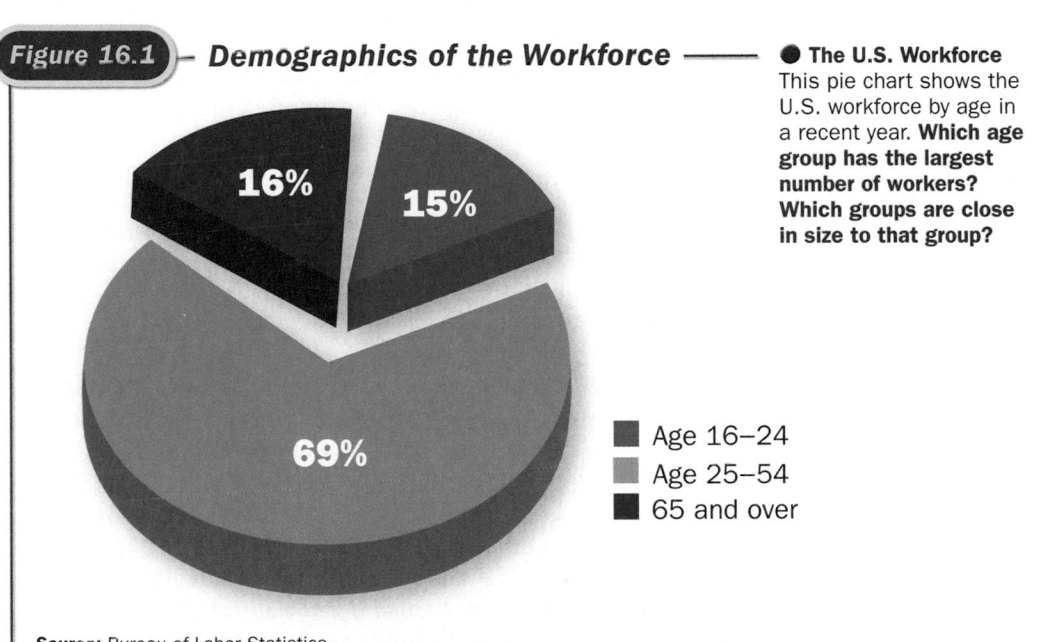

Figure 16.1 — **Demographics of the Workforce**

■ Age 16–24
■ Age 25–54
■ 65 and over

● **The U.S. Workforce** This pie chart shows the U.S. workforce by age in a recent year. **Which age group has the largest number of workers? Which groups are close in size to that group?**

Source: Bureau of Labor Statistics

Section 16.2 Diversity in the Workplace   **279**

TEACH (cont.)

S Skill Practice

Guided Practice

Calculate Have students calculate the age of the oldest and youngest baby boomers. (Answers depend on when the assignment is completed.) **L1**

Chart Data Provide the birth rate data shown below and ask students to create a line graph for 1940 to 1960. Instruct students to include a marker for each data value on the line graph.

U.S. Birth Rate—Births per Thousand

1940–45	126.2
1946–50	149.1
1951–55	125.4
1956–60	122.9

(Charts will vary but should include all data points.) **L2**

Interview and Document Invite some baby boomers to visit your class. Have students work in small groups to interview each adult and to document their interviews with summaries. (Summaries will vary, depending on the adult interviewed.) **L3**

ASSESS

Review Key Terms Have students write sentences using each key term.

 **Study-to-Go** Have students go to the Online Learning Center through **glencoe.com** to download free **Study-to-Go** content to their PDAs or cell phones.

As You Read

Students may list ads that feature African Americans, women, the elderly, Asian Americans.

Figure 16.1

● **The U.S. Workforce** The largest number of workers is in the 45–54 age group, 23 percent of the workforce. The age groups 25–34 and 35–44 are close in size to the largest group, with 22 percent and 23 percent, respectively.

U Universal Access

Students with Behavior Disorders Students with behavior disorders can at times struggle to maintain the level of attention needed to deal with challenging material. To assist these students, you may wish to outline chapter objectives on a one-on-one basis to help them feel successful.

R Reading Strategy

Make a Table Have students make a two-column table for the laws enacted to control how companies manage diversity. Instruct them to list the laws in the left column and notes in the second column. (The list of laws should include: Age Discrimination in Employment Act, Equal Employment Opportunity Act, and Americans with Disabilities Act.)

W Writing Support

Enrichment

Laws Against Discrimination Have students use Internet and library resources to learn more about one of the laws mentioned on this page. Ask students to write one or two paragraphs expanding on what is presented on this page. Instruct students to include a properly formatted reference citation. (Students might note the date of the law and present information on the law's impact.)

Student Activity Workbook Assign the Section 16.2 Activities.

● **A Diverse Workplace** The blending of people with different skills and perspectives into the workplace can help businesses understand and react to an increasingly diverse population. **How does a diverse workforce aid a business in serving a diverse market?**

Managing Diversity

Human resources managers oversee diversity. They seek ways to make the company inclusive by hiring people of different characteristics, backgrounds, and ethnicities. This diversity leads to a more realistic world view, which can lead to a competitive advantage. Employee diversity is an asset in dealing with clients and customers of various cultures. Diversity management programs try to draw on the strength of a company's melting pot.

Laws Against Discrimination **Discrimination** is unfair treatment of a person or group, usually because of prejudiced attitudes about race, ethnicity, age, religion, or gender. Many laws have been passed to prevent discrimination. For example, in the past, workers over the age of 40 were often fired or denied jobs in favor of younger workers. This form of discrimination is called **ageism**. To protect older workers, the U.S. government passed the Age Discrimination in Employment Act. It **prohibits** discrimination against workers because of their age.

The Equal Employment Opportunity Act was passed to strengthen laws that protect workers from discrimination based on race, ethnicity, religion, or gender. Workers with specific needs often could not work because buildings lacked proper access or equipment. In 1990, the Americans with Disabilities Act (ADA) was passed. ADA prohibits discrimination against qualified people who have disabilities. Employers must make a reasonable **accommodation** for a qualified person with a disability. Examples of *reasonable accommodation* include adjusting buildings so that people in wheelchairs can move around them.

Seeking All Qualified Workers Many companies state that they are equal opportunity employers in their employment ads. Some also stress that women and people with disabilities are encouraged to apply for jobs. *Why do you think companies do this?*

Seeking All Qualified Workers Answers will vary. For example, it is illegal to discriminate against people based on gender or disability. Companies that indicate that they are equal opportunity employers want to show that they follow employment laws.

Discuss the Photo

● **A Diverse Workplace** Workers with different skills, work habits, and approaches to tasks can help a company anticipate and respond to the challenges of a diverse global market.

Diversity Programs Most codes of ethics have rules against discrimination. These codes, however, are not always enough to prevent personnel problems. Some employees still have trouble working with people who are different from them. Companies offer diversity training programs to promote tolerance among workers. Diversity training breaks down stereotypes. Managers must avoid stereotyping. They must create a work environment in which prejudice is not tolerated and diversity is welcomed and respected. They must promote a corporate culture that values diversity.

Benefits of Diversity Businesses that promote diversity in the workplace have discovered many benefits:

- A diverse workforce offers a broader range of ideas and points of view.
- Greater diversity in the workplace helps a company better understand and serve diverse markets.
- Diversity improves morale among employees and strengthens their commitment to company goals.
- Companies that value diversity have increased productivity and efficiency, lower turnover rates, less absenteeism, and fewer legal costs from employee complaints. Diversity training also helps reduce conflicts among workers.

Section 16.2

After You Read

Review Key Concepts
1. In what ways are people diverse?
2. What are two laws about discrimination?
3. What are some benefits of diversity in the workforce?

Academic Skills
4. **English Language Arts** Think ahead to the time when you will be 60 years old. Create a poster that visually describes what you will be doing. Will you be working? Will you be retired? What activities will you do? What products and services will you buy? How will you provide for yourself financially? Display your poster in the classroom.

5. **English Language Arts** Spend some time observing others at a distance. Note any repeated rituals you see, such as saying hello or goodbye. What gestures or other body language tells you how people are feeling? Write a short essay about your observations, and discuss them with others.

 Go to the *Introduction to Business* Online Learning Center through **glencoe.com** to check your answers.

Section 16.2

Review Key Concepts
1. age, gender, ethnicity, individual needs, education, marital status, income, and religious beliefs
2. the Equal Employment Opportunity Act, and the Americans with Disabilities Act
3. broader range of ideas and perspectives and improved morale

Academic Skills
4. **English Language Arts** Responses will vary, but encourage students to be creative in this project.
5. **English Language Arts** Responses will vary, but students should compare and contrast their findings and note any cultural differences they observe.

RETEACH (cont.)

C Critical Thinking

Assess the Possibilities

Diversity Programs In many companies, diversity training is in place to break down stereotypes. Ask students: What do you think the impact of diversity training in companies will have in the broader culture? (Answers will vary but students should recognize the benefits of diversity training.)

ASSESS

After You Read

Have students complete the Section 16.2 After You Read section review.

Online Study Tools
Have students go to the Online Learning Center through **glencoe.com** to:

- Take the Section 16.2 **Practice Test**.
- Download free **Study-to-Go** content to their PDAs or cell phones.

CLOSE

Culminating Activity
Benefits of Diversity
Have students work in pairs to locate information about a firm's diversity programs, possibly on their Web sites, and create a presentation based on their findings. Encourage them to use presentation software. (Presentations will vary, but should include clear examples of the firm's commitment to diversity.)

 Activity correlates to English Language Arts standards.

281

Vocabulary Review

1. Students should write complete sentences using each term correctly.

Review Key Concepts

2. As companies trade globally, they must be aware of different cultural and business practices. Knowing how to approach people from differnet cultures will give others a good impression of the company.

3. Some companies have a formal culture. Other companies have an informal culture. Most companies have a culture that is both formal and informal.

4. Workers have different skills, work habits, and approaches to tasks. As workers from many cultures enter the workplace, many people come into contact with people of different ages, ethnic backgrounds, and abilities for the first time. More opportunities are available for workers to advance, regardless of their cultural background. Cultural diversity among workers enables companies to anticipate the needs of culturally diverse markets.

Critical Thinking

5. Answers will vary but should include specific examples.

6. You could talk to others who have worked there, take classes in preparation, and read about the country.

Section 16.1 *Summary*	**Section 16.2** *Summary*
Culture in Business Culture is the beliefs, customs, and attitudes of a distinct group of people. It can refer to an entire country or ethnic group as well as to a specific social group or institution. As companies trade globally, they must be aware of different cultural and business practices and etiquette. Each country has its own rules for etiquette, business customs, and personal interaction. Companies that are culturally aware are better able to market products globally. Cultural differences are also present in the workplace. Just as each country has its own culture, each corporation has its own culture. A company's corporate culture is its shared values, beliefs, and goals.	***Diversity in the Workplace*** Companies tend to thrive when they have diversity. Diversity is a variety of employees with different backgrounds and identities. People can be diverse in many ways, including age, gender, ethnicity, skills, work habits, and approaches to tasks. The U.S. population has become more ethnically diverse and is getting older and living longer. These changes affect business. Diversity in the workplace helps a company better understand and serve diverse markets. Human resources managers oversee diversity. They seek ways to make companies more inclusive by hiring different types of people. They also make sure their companies follow employment laws.

Vocabulary Review

1. On a sheet of paper, use each of these key terms and academic vocabulary terms in a sentence.

Key Terms

culture	diversity
business etiquette	stereotype
corporate culture	baby boom generation
hierarchy	discrimination
bureaucracy	ageism

Academic Vocabulary

distinct	diverse
ethnic	assignments
region	prohibits
tradition	accommodation

Review Key Concepts

2. Describe the effect of culture on doing business globally.

3. Describe how corporate cultures differ among businesses.

4. Identify ways in which cultural diversity has an impact on business.

---

7. Answers will vary depending on students' ethical beliefs and experiences.

8. Some classroom cultures may be formal. In informal classroom cultures, work is less structured.

9. Human resources managers can stress the importance of working well with others and accepting differences among workers. Employee handbooks, newsletters, and e-mails can stress the value of diversity.

10. Some examples include: many communities have local stations, newspapers, and magazines in the language spoken by a majority of their residents. More U.S. businesses make products that satisfy the tastes of global markets.

Critical Thinking

5. What cultural differences would you experience working in another country?

6. How could you prepare to fit into the culture of another country?

7. What would you do if you moved to another country and were expected to follow business practices that you considered unethical?

8. What aspects of your classroom's culture shape how you work, act, and deal with problems?

9. List some ways the management of a company can foster acceptance of diversity among workers.

10. What changes in the business world do you think are the result of our population being more diverse?

11. What changes do you think will help to eliminate discrimination?

12. If you had an opportunity to become an exchange student in another country, what would you do to learn about the culture there?

13. What types of businesses are likely to have an informal corporate culture?

Write About It

14. Research several definitions and statements on diversity. Summarize what you learned in a brief report.

15. Corporate culture has been described as "the personality of a company." Imagine that you own your own business. Write two or more paragraphs describing the business and its corporate culture.

16. A glass ceiling is an unofficial but real barrier to advancement and is usually due to discrimination. Is this fair? Write an e-mail to your teacher explaining your answer.

17. List five words or phrases that you would use to describe the culture of a company in which you would enjoy working. Is it "formal" or "informal"?

18. Describe the qualities that would make you a good employee for a company that takes pride in its diverse staff. Write a one-page essay describing your attributes as they relate to diversity.

19. Research the Americans with Disabilities Act. Write a two-page article for your school newspaper on ways businesses can accommodate people with disabilities.

Technology Applications

Spreadsheet Software
20. Use these figures about the education of U.S. residents to prepare a spreadsheet comparing the groups. Completed Grades K–9: 3.41%; Completed Grades 9–11, No Diploma: 7.48%; High School Graduate: 31.42%; Some College, No Degree: 27.37%; College: Associate's Degree: 8.10%; College: Bachelor's Degree: 15.12%; College: Graduate Degree: 7.10%

Business Ethics

Foreign Customs
21. Imagine you and a co-worker are experts in your field. One of you is female and the other is male. Your company wants to send you both to negotiate a business deal in a country whose society discriminates against women. Women who do business there must arrange for men to handle direct negotiations with its businessmen. How would you handle this situation?

Chapter 16 Review and Activities **283**

Critical Thinking

11. Answers will vary but may include education, understanding, and a willingness to learn from others.

12. Read about or interview people from the country.

13. Answers may include software development firms and advertising agencies.

Write About It

14. Diversity in the workplace means including people of different genders, races, religions, nationalities, ethnicities, ages, and physical abilities.

15. Students should recognize that the company's policies are likely to express their values and beliefs, which set the practices to be followed.

16. Answers will vary. Historically, there are some jobs that only men have held. As women excel in the workplace, many are likely to do jobs once only held by men.

17. Formal culture: traditional, well organized, direct supervision, dress code, a clear line of authority. Informal culture: no dress code, flexible work hours, few levels of management.

18. Students should express what they have learned about diversity in their answers.

19. For example, companies can adjust workspaces to allow employees with physical disabilities to do their work.

Technology Applications

20. There are more high school graduates than any other group. However, 57.69 percent of people have had at least some college. As the population grows and jobs that require new skills and education are created, those who have not achieved the levels of education required should add to their skills with further education.

Business Ethics

21. Answers will vary. Although discrimination based on gender, age, and other forms of identity is prohibited in the United States, it is allowed in other countries. It is up to the company to decide whether to do business with a country that allows discrimination.

Applying Academics to Business

22. Answers will vary but students should discuss the words they choose in the context of culture and diversity in business.

23. Standard Form: 175,000,000,000
Scientific Notation: 1.75×10^{11}

24. Answers will vary but students should be able to justify their findings with specific examples.

25. $\frac{1}{2}$ disabled peoples' spending = teen market spending; $\frac{1}{4}$ disabled peoples' spending = 8- to 12-year-olds' spending $\frac{1}{2}$ disabled people's spending + $\frac{1}{4}$ disabled people's spending = teen market spending + 8- to 12-year-olds' spending $\frac{1}{2} + \frac{1}{4} = \frac{3}{4}$ The combined spending power of 8- to 12-year-olds and teens is $\frac{3}{4}$ that of Americans with disabilities.

Active Learning

26. Answers will vary, depending on the company.

Business in the Real World

27. Reports should include the gender, age, ethnic background, and work experience of the people surveyed.

Applying Academics to Business

English Language Arts

22. Research two of the following words. How are they broken into syllables? How are they pronounced? What is their origin? What is their meaning in the context of culture and diversity in business? Do they have other meanings in different contexts? What are some synonyms and antonyms? Write a few sentences about each of the two words you choose.

hierarchy   stereotype   ageism
culture   discrimination

Mathematics

23. The Americans with Disabilities Act has opened the way for people with disabilities to join the mainstream of American life. Today, the Department of Justice estimates that people with disabilities as a group have discretionary spending power of about $175 billion a year. Write $175 billion in standard form and scientific notation.

> **THEORY** **Scientific Notation** A number written in scientific notation is written as the product of a number between 1 and 10 and a power of 10.

English Language Arts

24. Write a paragraph about a local company, predicting the type of corporate culture it has. Then contact the business and find out about its corporate culture. Ask for examples of how the company's corporate culture is formal or informal. Then write another paragraph that describes the company's corporate culture and explains how your prediction of it differed from or was similar to the company's description of it.

Mathematics

25. The Department of Justice estimates that Americans with disabilities have discretionary spending power that is twice that of the teenage market and four times that of 8- to 12-year-olds. If so, what fraction of the spending power of people with disabilities is the combined spending power of 8- to 12-year-olds and teenagers?

> **THEORY** **Inverse Operations** Multiplication and division are inverse operations. In other words, if you know that x is 2 times y, you can find y by dividing x by 2. Dividing a number by 2 is the same as multiplying it by $\frac{1}{2}$.

Active Learning

Balancing Work and Family

26. Some companies promote a corporate culture that encourages a balance between work and personal life. Work in groups and choose one of the following companies: Intel®, General Motors®, ExxonMobil®, and Amazon.com®. Visit the career pages of the company's Web site. Create a brief presentation about the services the company provides its workers.

Business in the Real World

Employee Survey

27. Survey a group of workers about the culture of their companies. Consider asking these and other questions: Does your company have a formal or an informal culture? Do members of your work group have different ethnic backgrounds, age groups, and genders? Write a two-page report of your findings.

284   **Chapter 16**   Review and Activities

ExamView Assessment Suite CD allows you to print out ready-made unit and chapter tests, complete with answer keys. You can also create customized tests.

TeacherWorks Plus provides complete teacher resources in one convenient package. It includes customizable lesson plans in calendar format, and instant access to many print program resources.

Real LIFE skills

INTERPERSONAL SKILLS

28. Interpersonal skills include the qualities that make diversity work. They include the ability to accept other people, to appreciate their differences, and to work well with them. Prepare an outline listing the qualities and skills that workers should develop that will enable them to work well with people of all types of backgrounds.

Business CAREERS

FIND YOUR DREAM JOB

29. Go to the *Introduction to Business* Online Learning Center through **glencoe.com** for a link to the Occupational Outlook Handbook Web site. Click on the "OOH Search/A-Z Index" link and enter the job category "Interpreters and translators." Then write a one-page report about this area of occupation. Conclude your report with a list of things you could do now to prepare yourself to pursue the occupation.

Role Play

HOW CUSTOMS ARE DIFFERENT

30. **Situation** You have been asked to present a skit that illustrates acceptable and unacceptable business behavior in another country. You will present your skit to your class with the help of one or more of your classmates.

Activity Choose a country to research and illustrate its business customs.

Evaluation You will be evaluated on how well you meet the following performance indicators:

- Describe the business situation you will illustrate.
- Demonstrate an awareness of the customs of the country you chose.
- Give examples of behaviors that are acceptable and unacceptable in that country.
- Describe why each behavior that you presented is acceptable or unacceptable.
- Present your skit to your classmates.

Standardized Test Practice

Directions Choose the letter of the best answer. Write the letter for the answer on a separate piece of paper.

1. **Which rule can be used to determine the *nth* term in the pattern below?**

   2, 5, 10, 17, 26...

   A $2n + 1$
   B $n^2 + 1$
   C $n^2 - 1$
   D $n^3 + 1$

 TEST-TAKING TIP When taking a test, do not use a mechanical pencil, ink pen, or correction fluid. Use a soft lead No. 2 pencil to mark your answers, and make changes with a good eraser.

 READING Go to the *Introduction to Business* Online Learning Center through **glencoe.com** for a list of outside reading suggestions.

Real LIFE skills

28. Some qualities and skills that are needed are an attitude of acceptance of others; a willingness to work with others and to assist them; an interest in others as people, and an attitude of caring about them.

Business CAREERS

29. Interpreters and translators enable cross-cultural communication, convert one spoken language into another or between spoken communication and sign language. Many freelance or work at home. Educational backgrounds vary. Those with sufficient experience move on to more difficult and prestigious assignments or start their own businesses. As preparation, take a broad range of classes including English, learning a second language, and traveling abroad.

Role Play

30. Presentations should address the competencies noted in the Role Play. Answers will vary.

Standardized Test Practice
  1. B

 **STRATEGIES FOR STANDARDIZED TEST PREP SUCCESS**

Test Prep In preparation for test day, you might give students practice marking machine-scorable answer sheets, stress that using a number 2 pencil to mark answers is a must, and direct them to erase changed answers and stray marks completely.

Real-World Business and Career Profile

FOCUS

FOCUS

Bell Ringer Activity

Favorite Games
Ask volunteers to name their favorite games. (Answers will vary depending on students' tastes and experience playing games. Some students may prefer board games, puzzles, and role-playing games; others will like electronic games best.) Write a list of games on the board. Ask students to brainstorm a list of businesses that specialize in game equipment. (Students may mention stores that sell video games, Web sites that allow gamers to "compete" against other players around the world, or even sporting goods stores that sell footballs and basketballs.)

TEACH

Teaching Points
Culture in Business
Ask students to explain why an understanding of culture is such an important factor for businesses. (Companies must be aware of different cultural and business practices. Knowing how to do business with and respond to the needs of people from different cultures will give people a better impression of the company. It also allows the company to better market its products.)

Nelson Gonzalez

CEO, Chairman, and Co-Founder, Alienware
Nelson Gonzalez and Alex Aguila started Alienware, a Miami-based company that makes customized computers for gamers. The company assembles machines specifically for performance, using only parts that gamers need.

Q & A

Describe your job responsibilities.

Nelson: When I get to the office, the first thing I do is check our sales numbers. I then meet with Alex Aguila and we speak about operational issues. Our Web site is the portal to the world. I am constantly looking at it and making suggestions in terms of design, functionality, and performance. I also do news searches for Alienware and I find out what news we've generated that day. We have a very customer-centric culture here and I believe in the importance of giving our customers a great experience. We are always in a state of change. It's my job to reinforce a culture of change and have our people embrace it and thrive on it.

What is your key to success?

Nelson: My parents emigrated from Cuba, and I came from a very modest background. I had a lot of ambition to be successful, and not just in making money, I wanted to make a difference in the work I did and products I made.

What skills are most important in your business?

Nelson: The first thing that needs to take place is the identification of a niche. I identified the opportunity because I was my own customer. Having a solid understanding of finance and accounting is essential. You also need to have a certain level of technical/engineering aptitude to feel comfortable in a high-tech business environment.

What advice would you give students interested in starting a business?

Nelson:

- Believe in the product or service you are going to offer. Passion drives success.
- It's OK to fail, but it's not OK if you never gave it a shot.
- Seek advice from experienced entrepreneurs.
- Embrace change and always be willing to entertain new ways of doing things.

Critical Thinking *How does the type of product or service dictate how a business operates?*

286   **Unit 5**   Real-World Business and Career Profile

Critical Thinking
In Alienware's case, the ever-changing computer gaming industry means that the company needs to be able to quickly react to new technology, games, and consumer demands.

Some Qualifications of the Owner of a Computer Hardware Development Company

Academic Skills and Abilities

Computer science; physics; mathematics; engineering; interpersonal skills; general business management abilities; verbal and written communication skills; multitasking, organizing, and planning skills

Academic Skills Required to Complete Tasks at Alienware			
Tasks	Math	Science	English Language Arts
Hold meetings			◆
Assign duties			◆
Design new products	◆	◆	◆
Assess marketplace opportunities	◆	◆	◆
Customer service			◆
Schedule employees	◆		◆
Order supplies and equipment	◆		◆
Analyze financials	◆		◆

Education and Training

Occupations in computer hardware engineering need a bachelor's degree in engineering for almost all entry-level engineering jobs. College graduates with a degree in a physical science or mathematics occasionally may qualify for some engineering jobs, especially in specialties that are in demand. Engineers should be creative, inquisitive, analytical, and detail-oriented. They should be able to work as part of a team.

Career Path

Computer engineering graduates usually work under the supervision of experienced engineers. As new engineers gain experience, they are assigned more difficult projects with greater independence to develop designs, solve problems, and make decisions. Engineers may advance to become technical specialists or to supervise a staff or team of engineers and technicians. Some may become engineering managers or enter other managerial or sales jobs.

Preparing for a Career
Self-Assessment Checklist

Use this self-assessment checklist to help determine ways you can design a satisfying career path.

- ✔ Consider your interests. A hobby may provide the perfect road to success.
- ✔ Avoid limiting yourself to a particular field before you have explored many options.
- ✔ Apply for an internship or part-time job in a field that interests you to gain firsthand experience.
- ✔ Volunteer at an organization that interests you to develop job skills.
- ✔ Set realistic goals regarding how you will obtain a job in the career of your choice.
- ✔ Participate in classes or school activities that will help you advance in the career of your choice.
- ✔ Do not settle for a job that will not help you advance on your chosen career path.
- ✔ Be inquisitive. Asking questions and being attuned to the answers will help you gain knowledge and will make others more willing to help.

287

ASSESS

Write About It
Alienware

Ask students to write a summary of what they like about Alienware's business concept. (Students may say they like the fact that Alienware's computers are highly customizable. They may also like Alienware's advertising.)

Academic Vocabulary
Career Planning

Ask students to read the Self-Assessment Checklist then write one or more paragraphs about preparing for a career. Have students use some words from the Academic Vocabulary Glossary. (Example: Some people gain information about careers and companies by taking part-time or *temporary* positions to gain experience. Employees in temporary *assignments* who *demonstrate* excellence may turn their jobs into careers.)

CLOSE

Cooperative Learning
Technology Applications

Ask students to work in pairs and develop an idea for a business that produces computer programs for a specialty market. Have them work together to develop an advertisement for the business. (Advertisements should include marketing copy, visuals, and information about the product.)

Preparing for a Career
Develop Cultural Sensitivity Soft skills are an important part of education and training for a career. Remind students that the ability to get along with people from all kinds of experience and backgrounds will help them advance. Ask students: What can they do to enhance their cultural sensitivity? (Answers will vary but may include having an open mind, listening to people, reading, keeping informed of international news, etc.) Tell students that they will have an opportunity to think about careers and the career-planning process more as they read the Self Assessment Checklists in this book.

FOCUS

Discussion Starter
Lead a discussion about cultural diversity in the business world. Ask students to project how diversity will change business and society.

Step 1

Brainstorm Skills
Have students go to the *Introduction to Business* Online Learning Center through **glencoe.com** for a graphic organizer they can use to brainstorm the skills needed to complete the project.

Step 2

Choose a Business and a Career
Students can use the Occupational Outlook Handbook Web site to explore occupations.

TEACH

Step 3

Build Background
Technology Have students brainstorm ways technology helps people to overcome cultural differences. (Computers and the Internet have made it quick and easy to access information that can help people relate to people who are culturally different from them.)

Diversity Ask students: Why is an understanding of diversity in the workplace important in their career planning? (To be successful, workers need to be able to relate to people of different backgrounds and cultures.)

Cultural Diversity in the Business World
Globalization has increased cultural diversity in the workplace. Smart business managers utilize the talents, backgrounds, and knowledge of every member of the workforce.

Thematic Project Assignment
In this project you will prepare an international instruction booklet. Your booklet will be used to educate businesses about different cultures.

Step 1 Brainstorm Skills You Need to Complete This Activity

Your success in writing an international instruction booklet will depend on your skills. Preview the activity. Then brainstorm a list of the skills you will need to use to complete the activity and describe how you will use them. Skills you might use include:

Academic Skills reading, writing, social studies, geography, and researching

Basic Skills speaking, listening, thinking, and interpersonal skills

Technology Skills word processing, keyboarding, telecommunications, and Internet skills

 Skills Preview Go to the *Introduction to Business* Online Learning Center through **glencoe.com** for a graphic organizer you can use to brainstorm the skills you will use to complete the project.

Step 2 Choose a Business and a Career That Interest You

Think of a business that you find interesting. Then think of a career related to the business that interests you. As you investigate cultural diversity in the business world, you will research the effects of cultural diversity on the business and career of your choice.

Step 3 Build Background Knowledge

Preview cultural diversity in the business world.

> ## Diversity *in the* **Workplace**
>
> The modern-day global economy that is creating a diverse culture for business also is creating a diverse culture in the workplace. Just as businesses that trade internationally have become aware of a country's customs and business practices, businesses in the United States must be aware of the diversity within their own borders.
>
> Employees must understand their coworkers' cultures in order to create successful and harmonious working relations. Failure to understand the diverse cultural differences among coworkers can lead to dissatisfaction and disharmony in the workplace.

Step 4 Connect with Your Community

Interview an adult you know who works in a cultural diverse workplace. Find out how his or her company does or does not take advantage of the employee's diversity.

Globalization Ask students to write an essay describing the impact of cultural diversity on globalization. (Students may focus on the need for cultural sensitivity if people and businesses are to compete in a global marketplace. Some students may feel that globalization threatens cultural values, or that one culture will begin to dominate.)

Step 4

Connect with Your Community
Ask students to describe how cultural diversity relates to their sense of community. Write their ideas on the board. (Some students may say that their sense of community is defined by cultural values. Others may say that their cultural values define their sense of community.)

Step 5 Research Cultural Diversity in the Business World

Use library and Internet resources to research cultural diversity in the business world. Use the project checklist as a guide to your research. Keep records of your sources of information.

Step 6 Develop a Booklet

Use word processing and other software to develop an international instruction booklet that educates others about different cultures and includes all the following information:

Cultural Diversity in the Business World

✔ Choose a country that does business with the business of your choice.

✔ Explain the type of government this country has and the ways that the government affects the people.

✔ Explain the language spoken in the country and any language taboos.

✔ Explain any customs of the country that would be helpful for Americans to understand.

✔ Create a pictorial that illustrates foods, traditions, and holidays that are associated with this country.

✔ Use the information form the U.S. Census Bureau to create a pie chart that illustrates the number of American citizens who were born in another country and the country of their birth.

Self Connections

✔ Describe the results of your research to a family member or other adult.

✔ Describe how cultural diversity in the business world affects the business and career in which you are interested.

✔ Explain what the investigation and its results mean to you.

Step 7 Evaluate Your Report

@ *RUBRIC* Go to the *Introduction to Business* Online Learning Center through **glencoe.com** for a rubric you can use to evaluate your final report.

289

Step 5

Research Cultural Diversity in the Business World

Students can go to the *Introduction to Business* Online Learning Center through **glencoe.com** for a rubric they can use as a content checklist when researching their reports.

TEACH (cont.)

Step 6

Develop a Booklet
Give students these tips on report writing:

- Know your audience.
- Organize your report by developing an outline and using titles and subtitles.
- Write concisely (briefly but completely).
- Write in easy-to-read, simple language.

ASSESS

Step 7

Evaluate Your Report
Rubric Encourage students to use the rubric to evaluate their final reports.

CLOSE

Culminating Activity
Interviews
Have students form pairs and interview each other about the businesses and careers they researched and how their opinions and perceptions of the businesses and careers evolved during the course of the project. (Interviews will vary depending on students' business and career choices and reactions to their research.)

Chapter	Section	Unit Objectives
Chapter 17 *Managing Business Finances*	17.1	**Identify** the six reasons for creating a financial plan.
		Explain what a budget is and how it is used.
	17.2	**Explain** the purpose of accounting.
		Describe how property rights are measured.
		Define the three components of the accounting equation.
		Describe the three main financial statements used by businesses.
Chapter 18 *Technology in the Workplace*	18.1	**Describe** the role of information technology in business.
		Identify ways that technology has changed the workplace.
	18.2	**Describe** the Internet and its components.
		Identify tools for managing threats when using the Internet.
Chapter 19 *Computer Basics*	19.1	**Describe** some ways that people use computers.
		Identify the parts of a computer system.
	19.2	**List** some types of software.

Understanding the Coding

Brackets Brackets on the reduced student edition page correspond to teaching strategies and activities in the Teacher Wraparound Edition. As you teach the lesson, the brackets show you exactly where to use the teaching strategies and activities.

Letters The letters on the reduced student edition page identify the type of strategy or activity. See the key below to learn about the different types of strategies and activities.

Ability Levels Leveled teaching strategies are identified by one of three codes to give you an idea of their suitability for students of varying learning styles and abilities.

Resources Key program resources are listed in each chapter. Icons indicate the format of resources.

KEY to Letters

D **Develop Concepts** activities help teachers gauge and plan for students' concept development.

R **Reading Strategy** activities help you teach reading skills and vocabulary.

C **Critical Thinking** strategies help students apply and extend what they have learned.

U **Universal Access** activities provide differentiated instruction for English language learners and suggestions for teaching various types of learners.

S **Skill Practice** provides leveled instruction for meeting individual needs and learning styles.

W **Writing Support** activities provide writing opportunities to help students comprehend the text.

NCLB **No Child Left Behind** activities help students practice and improve their abilities in academic subjects.

KEY to Ability Levels

L1 Strategies should be within the ability range of all students. Often full class participation is required.

L2 Strategies are for average to above-average students or for small groups. Some teacher direction is necessary.

L3 Strategies are designed for students able and willing to work independently. Minimal teacher direction is necessary.

KEY to Resource Icons

Print Material

CD-ROM

Online Learning Center with Podcasts

BusinessWeek Reader and Case Study

In Unit 6, your students can learn more about business in the real world through the following *BusinessWeek* Readers and Case Studies:

I Am My Own Accountant
Doing your own taxes isn't as crazy as it sounds. Here's one way to give your business an annual checkup. (page 295)

Math Will Rock Your World
Neal Goldman is a math entrepreneur. He works on Wall Street, where numbers rule. But he's focusing his analytic tools on a different realm altogether: the world of words. (page 318)

Digital Books Start a New Chapter
Lighter devices, better displays, and the iPod craze could make them best sellers. (page 334)

Chapter Features and Activities

Reading Strategies

Before You Read

Graphic Organizer

As You Read

Reading Check

After You Read

Unit Overview

Introduce the Unit
Introduce the unit by describing the main concepts of each chapter in the unit.

Unit 6 is about managing financial and technological resources.

Chapter 17 presents aspects of managing business finances. It discusses business accounting and financial record keeping.

Chapter 18 describes the implications of technological advances in the workplace.

Chapter 19 is about the importance of computers in the workplace. This chapter also introduces the types and parts of computers.

00:00 OUT OF TIME?

If class time is too short to cover all of the chapters in this unit, have students:

- Write down the vocabulary terms and their definitions.
- Read the chapter summaries at the beginning of each chapter review.
- Go to the *Introduction to Business* Online Learning Center through **glencoe.com** to download free Study-to-Go content to their PDAs or cell phones.

Financial and Technological Resources

290

Real-World Business and Career Profile `Preview`

Enlightened, Inc. Tell students that at the end of this unit, they will learn about the founders of Enlightened, Inc., and how they achieved their success. Antwayne Ford, Andre Rodgers, and Thomas Spann founded this information technology consulting firm. Starting their own company was something they had discussed since college. Ask students to give reasons why a business that specializes in providing information technology consulting might be a success. (Students should recognize that many businesses need help managing technology and it often makes sense to outsource this service by hiring specialists.)

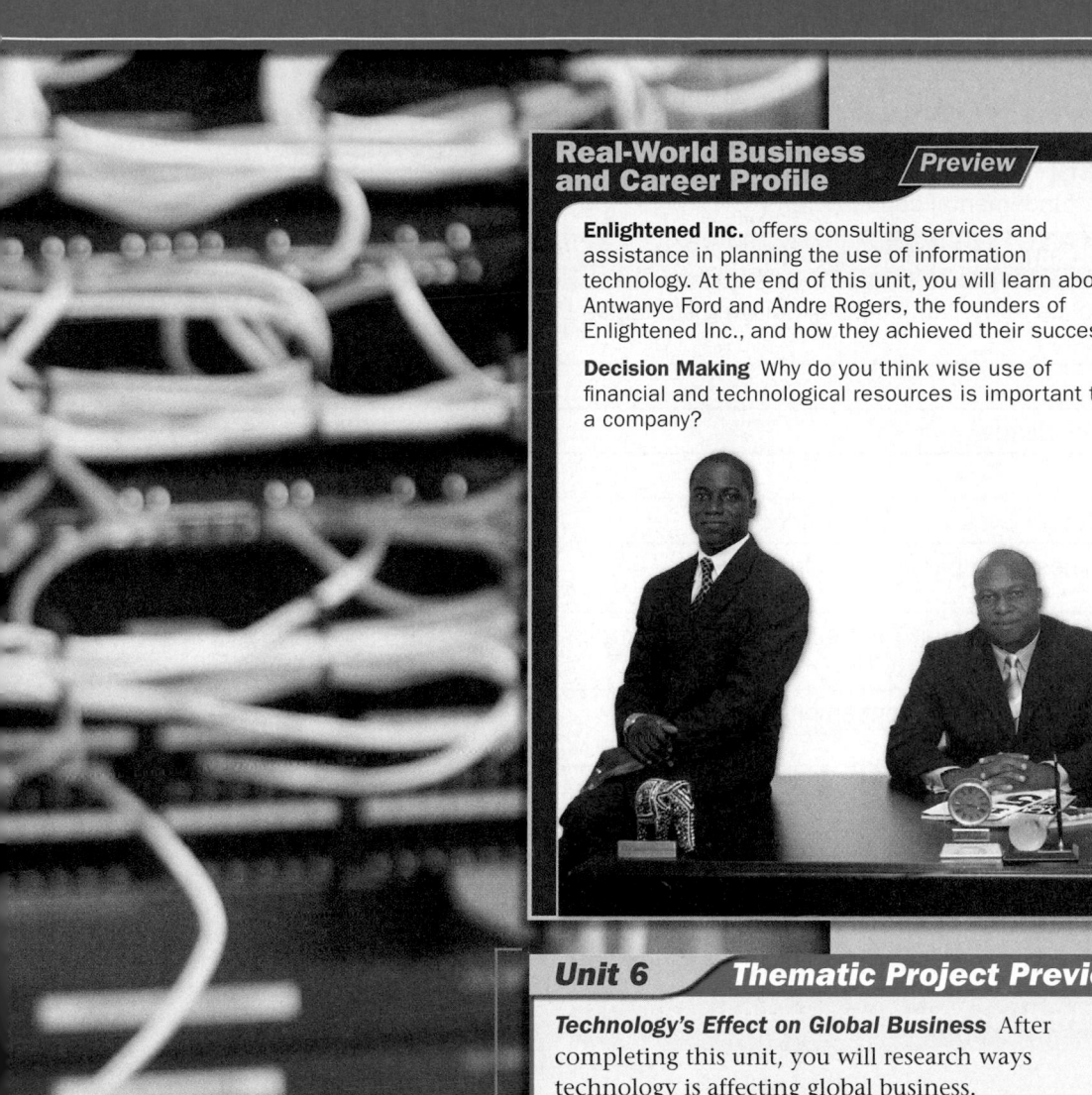

Real-World Business and Career Profile
Preview

Enlightened Inc. offers consulting services and assistance in planning the use of information technology. At the end of this unit, you will learn about Antwanye Ford and Andre Rogers, the founders of Enlightened Inc., and how they achieved their success.

Decision Making Why do you think wise use of financial and technological resources is important to a company?

Unit 6 | Thematic Project Preview

Technology's Effect on Global Business After completing this unit, you will research ways technology is affecting global business.

Project Checklist As you read the chapters in this unit, use this checklist to prepare for the unit project.

- ✔ Think about technology's effect on globalization.
- ✔ Think about how the Internet has enabled small businesses to conduct e-commerce.
- ✔ Think about how advances in telecommunications have made worldwide communication accessible to businesses.
- ✔ Think about how technology connects you to your friends in a virtual world.

291

Build Background
Ask students these questions to activate prior knowledge:

Chapter 17
What do you already know about keeping financial records? (Most students have some experience keeping financial records. At this point the records might not be too complicated and they might keep track of them in their head, but they have some experience. One situation that might apply is saving for something or figuring out what you can buy at the snack bar for five dollars or less.)

Chapter 18
How do businesses use technology? (Students often are on the forefront of technology, particularly technology used in everyday life and entertainment. It is not unusual for adults to ask young people for help when they are struggling with new technology. Point out that keeping up with technology is necessary in today's workplace and is an important way for businesses to remain competitive in the global marketplace.)

Chapter 19
What do you know about the basics of computers? (Most students know how to use a computer for certain activities—schoolwork, e-mail, and games. What they already know provides a foundation for what they will learn in this chapter.)

Unit | Thematic Project Preview

Technology's Effect on Global Business
Tell students that when they complete this unit, they will understand technology's affect on global business. Encourage students to think about how advancements in technology could affect the jobs and careers they choose.

C Critical Thinking
Ask students to predict what effect technological advances will have on business in the future. (Encourage students to brainstorm future advances that might be made in technology and how they will change the way business is conducted.)

Standards-Based Lesson Planning
Introduction to Business provides students with instruction and assessment in the following fundamental content areas:

Content Standards Correlations	
Apply mathematical operations and processes as well as financial planning strategies to commonly occurring workplace situations.	p. 292
Discuss the importance of record keeping.	p. 297
Explain basic accounting principles and procedures.	pp. 300–305
Demonstrate basic file management skills.	p. 303
Use automated accounting procedures to apply basic accounting principles.	pp. 303–305
Explain the importance of maintaining business and personal records.	pp. 295–298, 300–305, 306–309
Describe how accounting procedures can be used to make decisions about planning, organizing, and allocating resources.	pp. 300–305, 306–307
Explain the importance of budgeting and money management among government, business, and the consumer.	pp. 295–298, 306–307
Explain the importance of money handling skills.	p. 302
Explore career opportunities in finance.	p. 309

NCLB
Activities, information, and skills practice will help your students attain No Child Left Behind proficiency. Students will improve their abilities in the following academic standards areas:

Academic Standards Correlations		
English Language Arts	**Activities/Features**	**Page**
NCTE 5 Use different writing process elements to communicate effectively	Standardized Test Practice	p. 309
NCTE 6 Apply knowledge of language structure and conventions to discuss texts.	Applying Academics to Business	p. 308
NCTE 7 Conduct research and gather, evaluate, and synthesize data to communicate discoveries	After You Read	p. 305
NCTE 8 Use information resources to gather information and create and communicate knowledge	After You Read, Applying Academics to Business	pp. 305, 308
Mathematics		
Data Analysis and Probability Select and use appropriate statistical methods to analyze data	Applying Academics to Business	p. 308
Number and Operations Compute fluently and make reasonable estimates	Ask S&P, Applying Academics to Business	pp. 292, 308
Number and Operations Understand numbers, ways of representing numbers, relationships among numbers, and number systems	After You Read	p. 298
Science		
Content Standard F Students should develop understanding of science and technology in local, national, and global challenges	Science/Tech Trends	p. 300

Correlations   This chart shows the 21st Century Skills, foundation skills, and workplace competencies that students develop as they work in this chapter.

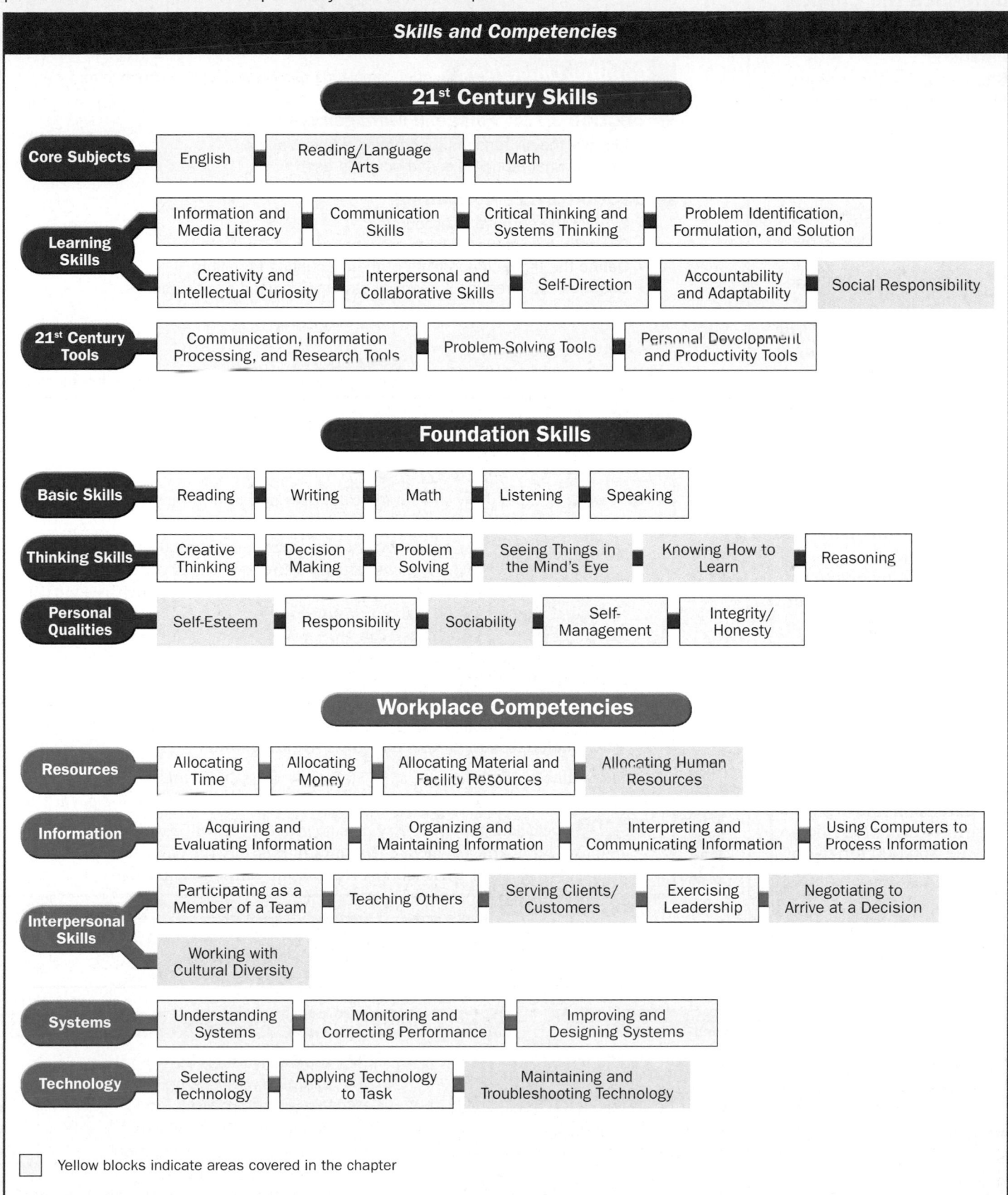

Skills and Competencies

21st Century Skills

Core Subjects
- English
- Reading/Language Arts
- Math

Learning Skills
- Information and Media Literacy
- Communication Skills
- Critical Thinking and Systems Thinking
- Problem Identification, Formulation, and Solution
- Creativity and Intellectual Curiosity
- Interpersonal and Collaborative Skills
- Self-Direction
- Accountability and Adaptability
- Social Responsibility

21st Century Tools
- Communication, Information Processing, and Research Tools
- Problem-Solving Tools
- Personal Development and Productivity Tools

Foundation Skills

Basic Skills
- Reading
- Writing
- Math
- Listening
- Speaking

Thinking Skills
- Creative Thinking
- Decision Making
- Problem Solving
- Seeing Things in the Mind's Eye
- Knowing How to Learn
- Reasoning

Personal Qualities
- Self-Esteem
- Responsibility
- Sociability
- Self-Management
- Integrity/Honesty

Workplace Competencies

Resources
- Allocating Time
- Allocating Money
- Allocating Material and Facility Resources
- Allocating Human Resources

Information
- Acquiring and Evaluating Information
- Organizing and Maintaining Information
- Interpreting and Communicating Information
- Using Computers to Process Information

Interpersonal Skills
- Participating as a Member of a Team
- Teaching Others
- Serving Clients/Customers
- Exercising Leadership
- Negotiating to Arrive at a Decision
- Working with Cultural Diversity

Systems
- Understanding Systems
- Monitoring and Correcting Performance
- Improving and Designing Systems

Technology
- Selecting Technology
- Applying Technology to Task
- Maintaining and Troubleshooting Technology

Yellow blocks indicate areas covered in the chapter

Chapter 17

Chapter Overview

Introduce the Chapter

Managing Business Finances

Chapter 17 is about aspects of managing business finances, including business accounting and record keeping.

Building Background

Most students have some experience managing finances and keeping financial records. They may be saving for something or figuring out what they can buy at the cafeteria for lunch.

Ask STANDARD &POOR'S

>> Math Answer

To calculate the total interest paid, first calculate the total amount paid. Multiply the amount of each payment by the number of loan payments ($1,000 × 60 months = $60,000). Then subtract the amount borrowed from the total amount paid ($60,000 − $51,750 = $8,250).

>> Extension Activity

Kenton and Bonnie borrowed $60,000 for 18 months at 8.7% interest. Their monthly payment is $3,567.61. What is the total amount of interest they will pay on their loan? ($4,216.98). ($3,567.61 × 18 months = $64,216.98). ($64,216.98 − $60,000 = $4,216.98)

N C L B Activity correlates to Math standards.

292

Managing Business Finances

Chapter Objectives   After completing this chapter, you will be able to:

▶ **Section 17.1** *Financial Management*
- **Identify** the six reasons for creating a financial plan.
- **Explain** what a budget is and how it is used.

▶ **Section 17.2** *Accounting*
- **Explain** the purpose of accounting.
- **Describe** how property rights are measured.
- **Define** the three components of the accounting equation.
- **Describe** the three main financial statements used by businesses.

Ask STANDARD &POOR'S   Venture Capital

Q: I want to expand my small bookstore. How do I find money to grow my business?

A: There are two ways to get the money you need: go into debt or raise equity capital. It can be difficult for a small business to raise equity capital, so ask yourself if you can get by on loans. Lenders like small businesses such as yours, especially if you have a track record of success and can offer some collateral, such as equity in your home. If you are thinking about raising equity capital, consider how much you need, how fast you think you can grow your business, and how much ownership in your business you are willing to give up. Equity investors are usually looking for high growth and high returns over a short period of time, say four to five years. Many small businesses look for angel investors, who are wealthy individuals willing to back an ongoing business in return for big payoffs down the road. Venture capitalists often look for larger companies requiring millions of dollars in investments.

Mathematics Portia borrowed $51,750 for five years at 6% interest. She is paying the loan back at the rate of $1,000 per month. How much interest will she pay in all?

N C L B

THEORY **Calculating Interest** To calculate interest you will pay on a loan when you are making the same payment every month, multiply the payment amount by the number of payments, then subtract the amount of the original loan.

Classroom Resources

- 📘 Student Edition
- 📘 Teacher Wraparound Edition
- 📂 Student Activity Workbook with Academic Integration
- 📂 Student Activity Workbook with Academic Integration TAE
- 📂 *Fast File*, Unit 6 Resources
- 📂 Inclusion in the Business Education Classroom

- 💿 TeacherWorks Plus
- 💿 *ExamView Assessment Suite*
- 💿 Presentation Plus!
- 💿 Vocabulary PuzzleMaker
- 💿 Interactive Student Edition
- 💿 Online Student Edition
- 💿 Online Learning Center with Podcasts

Managing Money All businesses use accounting and record keeping to manage finances. **Why do you think it is important for businesses to keep track of their money?**

Review the Objectives

Introduce the chapter by reviewing the chapter objectives:

Section 17.1 *Objectives*

Identify the six reasons for creating a financial plan. (Identify assets to purchase; determine needed capital; describe start-up and operating expenses; describe financial records management; forecast future finances; describe growth financing)

Explain what a budget is and how it is used. (A budget shows expected income and expenses for a future period. It is used as a guide for the business.)

Section 17.2 *Objectives*

Explain the purpose of accounting. (to collect, record, and post financial transactions that affect a business's operation)

Describe property. (anything of value that is owned or controlled)

Define the three components of the accounting equation. (Assets are property or other items of value owned by a business. Liabilities are creditors' claims to assets of a business, or a business's debts. Owner's equity is the owner's claims to the assets of the business.)

Describe the three main financial statements used by business. (The balance sheet shows the total assets, liabilities, and owner's equity during an accounting period. The income statement shows net income or loss made over a period of time. The statement of cash flow shows the cash received and spent over a period of time.)

Discuss the Photo

Managing Money Read the caption on the photo to students: All businesses use accounting and record keeping to manage finances.

Ask students: Why do you think it is important for businesses to keep track of their money? (Businesses need to keep track of their money because the decisions they make, such as developing new products, continuing to offer old ones, expanding or limiting their existing operations, hiring and firing employees, must all be made in a way that keeps the business profitable. If businesses made decisions without knowing their financial situation, they would face tremendous financial difficulties.)

FOCUS

Bell Ringer Activity

Financial Management
Ask students what kinds of information might be needed when developing a financial plan. (a list of all the business's start-up and operating expenses)

Preteaching

Presentation Plus!
The Presentation Plus! CD provides visual teaching aids for this section.

PuzzleMaker
Use the Vocabulary PuzzleMaker to create a puzzle of the section's key terms. Students can complete the puzzle on paper or on a computer.

Graphic Organizer
Tell students to go to the Online Learning Center through **glencoe.com** for a printable graphic organizer. (Answers include: identifies assets that need to be purchased and how they will be purchased; describes the capital a business will need to start and operate; describes expenses that the business will incur and how it will cover them; describes how the business will record and report financial records; forecasts future finances to project the company's profitability; explains how the business will acquire money to grow.)

N C L B
Connects academics to content.

294

Financial Management

Reading Guide

● Before You Read

Consider how a financial plan helps the entrepreneur or business manager.

D

Read to Learn
- Identify the six reasons for creating a financial plan.
- Explain what a budget is and how it is used.

The Main Idea
A financial plan outlines the essential financial facts about a new business or venture. Businesspeople use a financial plan to help them make decisions about the future. This plan shows the amount of money a business will need to start and operate. It also explains how the business will acquire money to expand.

Key Concepts
- The Purpose of the Financial Plan
- Budgets

Vocabulary
Key Terms
financial plan
capital
financial forecast
budget

Academic Vocabulary
You will find these words in your reading and on your tests. Make sure you know their meanings.
project   require
expand   predict

Graphic Organizer
In a figure like the one below, list the six items an effective financial plan identifies, describes, or explains.

An Effective Financial Plan
1.
2.
3.
4.
5.
6.

Go to the *Introduction to Business* Online Learning Center through **glencoe.com** for a printable graphic organizer.

N C L B

Academic Standards
English Language Arts
> **NCTE 7** Conduct research and gather, evaluate, and synthesize data to communicate discoveries
> **NCTE 8** Use information resources to gather information and to create and communicate knowledge

Mathematics
> **Number and Operations** Understand numbers, ways of representing numbers, relationships among numbers, and number systems

Reading Guide

● Before You Read

A financial plan helps businesspeople make decisions about how to operate and expand a business, attract investors, and identify needed assets.

D Develop Concepts

The Main Idea Ask students: How does financial planning for an existing business relate to the past, present, and future? (Data from the past helps forecast the future. The financial plan outlines how to record today's financial activities and helps businesses make decisions about the future.)

The Purpose of the Financial Plan

When starting a new business or **project** at an existing firm, managers must determine if it is likely to be financially viable. A **financial plan** is a set of documents that outline the essential financial facts about the new venture. It is a road map that can be used to guide a company into the future. A financial plan can also be used to attract investors. Lenders and investors provide money to businesses with sound financial plans. An effective financial plan

- identifies the assets that need to be purchased.
- describes the amount of money a business needs to start and operate.
- describes the expenses the business will incur and explains how a business will cover its expenses.
- describes how the business will document and report financial records.
- forecasts finances to project future profitability.
- explains how the business will acquire money to grow or **expand**.

R

✔ **Reading Check** **Explain** How is a financial plan like a road map?

BusinessWeek *Reader and Case Study*

I Am My Own Accountant

Doing your own taxes isn't as crazy as it sounds.

Here's one way to give your business an annual checkup: Do your own taxes. Sure, it's probably easier to take all the paperwork to a professional tax preparer or your certified public accountant. But think about it. Who has to collect and organize all that paperwork? Who has to come up with on-the-spot answers to all the questions about your business? What most tax guys do is fill out the forms and do the math. And to do that, they simply plug your data into their tax software. Then they plug your bill—$1,000 to $3,000 for most small corporations—into their accounting software.

Of course, there are going to be times when your taxes are too complicated to fathom yourself, or you don't have time to tackle them. Maybe you just don't have the confidence to file

your own return. After all, part of what we pay tax preparers for is their wisdom and experience. Still, consider giving tax software a try: The time you spend working through your finances will go a long way toward preparing you for that interview with your CPA.

 CASE STUDY Go to the *Introduction to Business* Online Learning Center through **glencoe.com** for the *BusinessWeek* Reader Case Study.

Active Learning

Try doing your own taxes. First, research tax forms and instructions for your state and for federal income tax. If there is an "EZ" form available, use that one. Fill out the income tax form. Write an e-mail to your teacher about what you learned about filing your taxes.

glencoe.com

TEACH

Discussion Starter
The Purpose of the Financial Plan
Ask students to explain why investors are interested in a firm's financial plan. (Students should understand that the process of creating an effective financial plan requires a business to face financial realities. Potential investors want to have a clear picture of the business before deciding whether to invest. A financial plan illustrates potential for success. It can shed light on potential problems.)

R **Reading Strategy**
Paraphrase Ask students to paraphrase the points in the bulleted list used to describe an effective financial plan. (For example, the first point could be restated as follows: It lists the building, equipment, supplies, and merchandise that we need to buy and shows how we plan to pay for these items.)

✔ **Reading Check**

Explain A financial plan can be used to guide a company into the future and tell it where it stands financially.

Virtual Business
Introduce financial statements to students using the Virtual Business Retailing Financial Statements activity. In this simulation, students learn why financial statements are important to the success of a business.

BusinessWeek *Reader and Case Study*

I Am My Own Accountant

 CASE STUDY Have students go to the *Introduction to Business* Online Learning Center through **glencoe.com** to download a Case Study activity that corresponds to the article. The activity and answer key are also available on the TeacherWorks Plus CD.

Active Learning

Answers will depend on student answers on the tax form. Even if they have filed their taxes for previous years, students are likely to report being surprised by the amount of tax people pay.

TEACH (cont.)

S Skill Practice

Guided Practice

Classify Have students make a list of start-up expenses mentioned in the textbook and a separate list for operating expenses. (Start-up expenses include business assets, remodeling, advertising, insurance, supplies, and legal permits. Operating expenses include payroll, rent, utilities, and bank fees.) **L1**

Define Have students write definitions for the terms "start-up expenses" and "operating expenses." (Start-up expenses are incurred to begin a business. Operating expenses are incurred while running the business.) **L2**

Distinguish Ask students to explain how advertising expenses might fall into both start-up and operating expense categories. (Advertising to announce the opening of a new business would be a start-up cost. Regular advertising in a community newspaper would be an operating expense.) **L3**

ASSESS

Review Key Terms

Have students write sentences using each key term.

Study-to-Go Have students go to the Online Learning Center through **glencoe.com** to download free **Study-to-Go** content to their PDAs or cell phones.

? ETHICS in Business

Recognizing Bribes

■ **Critical Reading** Life is full of important decisions. Think about the kinds of decisions you make as you read the question below.

You work as the purchasing agent for a small chain of restaurants. One of your duties is deciding where to purchase supplies, staples, and food items, such as coffee. A coffee purveyor you have bought from in the past sends you a free case of coffee beans just as you are making the purchasing decision about which coffee supplier to use for the next quarter. The coffee came with a message thanking you for purchasing from him in the past and suggesting that you try some of their new coffee blends.

■ **Decision Making** Would you consider the case of coffee a bribe? Explain how you would make the determination.

● **As You Read**

Think about the start-up expenses you would have if you wanted to start a graphic arts business from home.

Identifying Business Assets

A financial plan identifies the assets needed for the business or project. Cash, equipment, buildings, supplies, inventory, and land are examples of assets. Business owners and managers must make purchasing decisions carefully. They should research their options before buying business assets. They can analyze and compare the price of each item. The information obtained might show that buying used items instead of new ones, or renting them, would be best.

Determining Needed Capital

A financial plan estimates the amount of capital the business will need. **Capital** is money supplied by investors, banks, or owners of a business. *Start-up capital* is the money used to pay for the various assets and expenses of a new venture or business. A new business has no track record to prove that it will survive. For that reason, it may have a hard time attracting investors. Major sources of start-up capital for entrepreneurs are personal resources—friends, family, and others. These resources can include savings, loans, and investments.

Describing Start-Up and Operating Expenses

A new business or venture has start-up expenses and operating expenses. Start-up expenses often **require** a large amount of cash. Start-up expenses include the cost of business assets as well as remodeling costs, security deposits, advertising, insurance, supplies, and legal permits and licenses. Operating expenses include payroll, rent, utility bills, delivery charges, and bank fees.

296   Chapter 17   Managing Business Finances

● **As You Read**

Students may note the need for a computer and Internet connection. Other expenses are graphic design software, graphic arts courses, office supplies, and advertising.

? ETHICS in Business

Decision Making The message indicates the coffee is not a bribe. Since the supplier's business is coffee, sending a case as a sample seems appropriate. Remind students that the real determination about whether to accept the gift should come from the company's code of conduct.

Describing Financial Records Management

W A financial plan explains how a business will manage its records. It describes who will maintain the financial records and why. Some business owners maintain their own records. Others hire professionals for that purpose. A financial plan also describes any legal agreements that influence the way records are kept. For an existing business that is starting a new venture, the person who maintains the accounting records would probably keep the records regarding the new project. There are different types of accounting software available to businesses.

Forecasting Future Finances

A financial plan includes financial forecasts. A **financial forecast** is an estimate of a business's financial outlook for each of the next few years. The forecast should consider business conditions in the future, including changes in the economy. A financial forecast might show that a new business or venture will not make money in the first year. It is best to be conservative when preparing financial forecasts. Keep estimates for income low and estimates for expenses high.

Financing Expansion This business is expanding its space. **What types of financial materials does a business need to submit to creditors to get the money to finance a building expansion?**

Discuss the Photo
Financing Expansion To finance a building expansion, investors and lenders want to know that a business has thoughtfully developed strategies to finance controlled growth. The financial plan should explain the company's plans for financial growth.

RETEACH

W Writing Support
Enrichment
Financial Records Ask students to develop questions they might ask to help a business owner decide who should maintain financial records. (Do you like working with financial records? Are you good with details? Can you afford to hire a professional accountant?)

R Reading Strategy
Draw a Conclusion Have students identify changes in the economy that might be considered in a financial forecast, including things that would make the forecast brighter and others that would not bode well. (Increasing population might bode well. A lack of trained workers might predict a less-rosy future.)

U Universal Access
Gifted Learners Have students work in pairs to develop an example for the concept of being conservative when forecasting future finances. (An owner might predict income for next year to be between $50,000 and $80,000 and expenses as low as $40,000 and as high as $60,000. A conservative interpretation of this data would indicate a projected loss of $10,000 if you use a high forecast for expenses and a low forecast for income.)

Student Activity Workbook 📂 Assign the Section 17.1 Activities.

RETEACH (cont.)

C Critical Thinking

Assess the Consequences

Staying on Budget What will be necessary if a business exceeds its budget? (cut expenses, sell assets, or limit growth)

● As You Read

Responses should include a variety of businesses that have expanded.

ASSESS

● After You Read

Have students complete the Section 17.1 After You Read section review.

Online Study Tools

Have students go to the Online Learning Center through **glencoe.com** to:

- Take the Section 17.1 **Practice Test**.
- Download free **Study-to-Go** content to their PDAs or cell phones.

CLOSE

Culminating Activity
Financial Planning

Invite an accountant to speak about financial planning. Have students prepare questions to ask. Afterward, ask students to write a letter thanking the speaker and identify something the speaker said that was of particular interest. (Letters should express thanks and demonstrate knowledge of what was presented.)

298

● As You Read

Think about a business that you have seen go through an expansion.

Describing Growth Financing

Every company needs to grow in order to remain competitive. Planned growth can be very rewarding. Unplanned growth can be chaotic. Investors and lenders want to know that a business has thoughtfully developed strategies to finance controlled growth. The financial plan should explain the company's plans for financial growth.

Budgets

Financial statements indicate the financial condition of a firm in a past period. However, a budget helps guide its future. A **budget** is a plan specifying how money will be used or spent during a particular period. Budgeting helps business owners **predict** how much money the business will need. It also helps to control spending. To avoid financial problems, business owners and financial managers sometimes need to compare the business's budget to its actual income and expenses.

NCLB Activity correlates to Math standards.

There are three main types of budgets. A start-up budget is a plan for your income and expenses from the time you start a business to estimated time it will make a profit. A cash budget is a plan for the actual money the business owner spends on a daily, weekly, or monthly basis. An operating budget is a plan for the amount expected to be spent and earned over a given period of time, usually six months or a year.

Section 17.1

● After You Read

Review Key Concepts
1. What is the purpose of the financial plan?
2. What does an effective financial plan do?
3. Why do business owners use a budget?

Academic Skills
4. **Mathematics** When big companies create financial statements, they often shorten large numbers by omitting zeroes and adding a caption such as "all numbers in billions." Another way is to use scientific notation. What is 55 billion (55,000,000,000) expressed in scientific notation?

THEORY **Scientific Notation** In scientific notation, a number is expressed as the product of two factors. One is a number between one and ten, and the other is a power of 10.

 Math For math help, go to the Math Appendix.

 Go to the *Introduction to Business* Online Learning Center through **glencoe.com** to check your answers.

Section 17.1

Review Key Concepts
1. It is used as an outline of essential financial facts about a new business and to guide a business as well as to secure funding.
2. An effective plan identifies assets, determines needed capital, describes start-up and operating expenses, and describes financial records

management, forecasts future finances, and describes growth financing.
3. Budgets help business owners to predict the amount of money the business will need. They also help them to keep track of and control spending.

Academic Skills
4. **Mathematics** 55 billion = 5.5×10^{10}

Accounting

Reading Guide

Before You Read

Think about the reasons companies create and maintain financial records.

Read to Learn
- Explain the purpose of accounting.
- Describe how property rights are measured.
- Define the three components of the accounting equation.
- Describe the three main financial statements used by businesses.

The Main Idea

Accounting provides financial information about an organization. It also helps guide business decisions regarding operations and finances. Balance sheets, income statements, and statements of cash flows show the financial position of a business.

Key Concepts
- Accounting for Business
- Property Ownership and Control
- Financial Statements

 Go to the *Introduction to Business* Online Learning Center through **glencoe.com** for a printable graphic organizer.

Vocabulary

Key Terms

accounting	liabilities
generally accepted accounting principles (GAAP)	accounts payable
	owner's equity
	accounting equation
property	financial statements
assets	income statement
current assets	balance sheet
accounts receivable	cash flows
fixed assets	statement of
equity	cash flows

Academic Vocabulary

You will find these words in your reading and on your tests. Make sure you know their meanings.

converted	release
generate	formulas

Graphic Organizer

On a figure like the one below, define the components of the accounting equation.

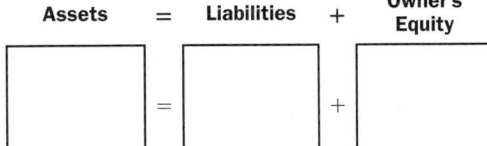

Assets	=	**Liabilities**	+	**Owner's Equity**
	=		+	

Academic Standards

English Language Arts
> **NCTE 1** Read texts to acquire new information

Science
> **Content Standard F** Students should develop understanding of science and technology in local, national, and global challenges

---

Reading Guide

Before You Read

Some are required by law. Owners and managers need financial records to make good business decisions.

D Develop Concepts

The Main Idea Ask students: Which financial document is the most important?
(Answers will vary, but students should realize that each type provides important information.)

FOCUS

🔔 Bell Ringer Activity

Accounting
Point out that every businessperson needs to understand the basics of accounting. Even if you have an accountant, you have to know the basics.

Preteaching

Presentation Plus!
The Presentation Plus! CD provides visual teaching aids for this section.

PuzzleMaker
Use the Vocabulary PuzzleMaker to create a puzzle of the section's key terms. Students can complete the puzzle on paper or on a computer.

Graphic Organizer
Tell students to go to the Online Learning Center through **glencoe.com** for a printable graphic organizer. (Answers include: Assets include cash, equipment, supplies, merchandise, and accounts receivable. Liabilities include accounts payable and money owed. Owner's equity is the owner's capital in the business.)

NCLB Connects academics to content.

299

TEACH

Discussion Starter
Accounting for Business
Ask students to explain why they think it is important for businesses to keep track of the money they spend and receive. (Answers will vary. Students might note that if a business is to be profitable, income must exceed expenditures. It is also important for a business to stick to its budget if it is to have the money needed to achieve future plans.)

 **Reading Strategy**

Recognize the Main Idea
Ask students which sentence in the second paragraph conveys the main idea. (Accounting is the systematic process of recording and reporting the financial position of a person or an organization.)

 (Real World)

Accounting Software
Answers will vary. Students may think that the software can prepare accurate records because that is what it is designed to do. Others may think you need an understanding of the transactions that the software records to be able to check the results and correctly manage the data it produces.

NCLB Activity correlates to Science standards.

Accounting for Business

Operating a business costs money. Imagine that you are planning to open a restaurant someday. You will need to buy or rent a building, equipment, and furniture. You will need to hire employees. You will also need to buy food and supplies. Before and after your business opens, you will need to keep track of the money that you spend and receive. This aspect of business is called accounting.

Accounting is the systematic process of recording and reporting the financial position of a person or an organization. The accounting system is designed to collect, record, and report financial transactions that affect the operation of a business. Small businesses usually hire an independent accountant. An *accountant* maintains and reviews business records. However, many larger companies hire accounting firms to manage or audit their financial records. An *audit* is a review of accounting records and procedures. The biggest accounting firms are known as the "Big Four." PricewaterhouseCoopers®, Deloitte Touche Tohmatsu®, Ernst & Young®, and KPMG® are accounting firms that operate worldwide.

Accounting Software There are software categories for all levels of accounting, from home use to high-end corporate use. *Do you think people who are not accountants can produce accurate financial records by using accounting software?*

Science/Tech TRENDS

EDI

Short for electronic data interchange, EDI is a convenient way for businesses and others to transfer large amounts of data using the Internet. EDI is poised to revolutionize the health-care industry because of the Health Insurance Portability and Accountability Act (HIPAA), which was passed by Congress in 1996. HIPAA requires that health-care providers, insurance companies, and others use EDI to simplify and reduce the high cost of administering health care. Those costs are huge: An average of 26¢ of each health-care dollar is spent on administrative overhead, including such tasks as enrolling individuals in health plans, paying health insurance premiums, checking eligibility, obtaining authorization to refer patients to specialists, processing claims, and notifying providers about the payment of claims. Since EDI offers a standard format for trading partners to use, it allows partners to exchange information and transact business in a fast and cost-effective way.

 Web Quest

Go to the *Introduction to Business* Online Learning Center through **glencoe.com** for links to Web sites where you can research different applications of EDI. Write a paragraph about the advantages and disadvantages of EDI in at least two different applications.

Science/Tech TRENDS

 Web Quest

EDI Answers will vary, but a good example of how EDI can be used is with the transfer of medical records between health-care providers. It is also used to facilitate e-commerce. The advantages include convenience and potential global reach. The disadvantages include privacy and security concerns.

Because it is so vital to the communication of financial information, accounting is often called the "language of business." This is because it is a way of communicating how well a business is doing. Just as a foreign language has different words and meanings, accounting has its own terminology.

Everyone involved in a business should understand some of the basics of accounting. A business manager, an employee of a firm, or an investor can use this information to gauge the health of the firm that they are working for or in which they want to invest.

Rules for Accountants

All accountants use the same set of rules, called **generally accepted accounting principles,** or **GAAP** (pronounced *gap*), to prepare reports. These rules provide a way to communicate financial information to others. *Financial reports* are summarized information about the financial status of a business. Each company sets up an accounting system according to its specific needs, but all businesses follow GAAP.

> ✔ **Reading Check** **Identify** What is an accounting system designed to do?

Property Ownership and Control

S

The right to own property is basic to a free enterprise system. **Property** is anything of value that is owned or controlled. When you own an item of property, you have a legal right or financial claim to it. Businesses also own and control property. One of the purposes of accounting is to provide financial information about property and rights to it. In accounting, property and financial claims are measured in dollar amounts. Dollar amounts measure both the cost of the property and the *property rights,* or *financial claims* to the property.

Financial Claims in Accounting

Assets are property and other items of value owned by a business. They are either current or fixed. **Current assets** are assets that are either used up or **converted** to cash during the normal cycle of the business. The normal cycle is usually one year. Cash, supplies, merchandise, and accounts receivable are all current assets. **Accounts receivable** is the total amount of money owed to a business. It represents money to be received in payments after goods or services are sold on credit. **Fixed assets** are items of value that will be held for more than one year. These include equipment and buildings. The accounting term for the financial claims to all assets is equity. **Equity** is the present value of an asset less all claims against it.

Real World

Questionable Accounting Some companies have gotten into legal trouble for committing accounting fraud. Fraud is the crime of intentionally deceiving others for financial gain or some other benefit. *Why is it important for companies to be truthful in their financial records?*

● **As You Read**

Think about the types of property you own now and might want to own in the future.

TEACH (cont.)

S Skill Practice
Guided Practice
Explain Ask students to explain why a dollar amount is attached to property. (Students should understand that the dollar amount is needed because all property is not the same and has different value.) **L1**

List Examples Ask students to list examples of something they control but do not own. (Examples will vary but may include items such as schoolbooks and the desks that they use at school, or items such as a car or their room at home.) **L2**

Report Have students research and write a one-page report on loans that are secured by property such as real estate, cars, or equipment. Ask students: How is the ownership of these items recorded? Who has the control over the items? (In many cases, the lender holds legal title to each item until the loan is paid and the person who borrowed the money for the purchase has control.) **L3**

> ✔ **Reading Check**

Identify An accounting system is designed to collect, record, and report financial transactions that affect the operation of a business.

Real World

Questionable Accounting Many people and businesses depend on accurate records to help them make important decisions. Also, all businesses must follow GAAP. Failing to do so can lead to intervention by the government.

● **As You Read**

Students might note that they own clothing, cell phones, or collectibles. They might want to own a car, a home, or a boat someday.

302

TEACH (cont.)

 R Reading Strategy

Create an Outline Have students create an outline for the content that appears under the heading "Financial Claims in Accounting." Suggest that they use the key terms as the main entries. Point out that the content began on the previous page. (Outlines should include assets, current assets, accounts receivable, fixed assets, and equity.)

W Writing Support

Restating

The Accounting Equation
Have students restate the accounting equation using the definitions of each of the three components. (Property and other items of value owned by a business = Creditors' claims to the assets of a business + Owner's claim to the assets of a business.)

ASSESS

Review Key Terms
Have students write sentences using each key term.

STUDY TO GO Study-to-Go
Have students go to the Online Learning Center through **glencoe.com** to download free **Study-to-Go** content to their PDAs or cell phones.

✔ Reading Check

Explain Assets must always equal the sum of liabilities and owner's equity. Both sides of the equation must always balance.

302

Handling Money
Financial institutions expect their tellers to keep an organized work area, verify deposits, give correct change, and keep their cash drawer balanced. Proper money handling helps banks practice theft control. *How does it affect the accounting process?*

R When a person or business buys property and agrees to pay for it later, they are buying on *credit*. The business or person selling the property is called the *creditor*. **Liabilities** are creditors' claims to the assets of a business. They are the debts of a company. Liabilities are measured by the amount of money a business owes its creditors. They include accounts payable. **Accounts payable** represents the short-term liabilities that a business owes to creditors. **Owner's equity** is an owner's claim to the assets of the business. It is also referred to as the owner's *capital* in the business. It is measured by the dollar amount of the owner's claims to the total assets of the business.

The Accounting Equation

The accounting equation ensures that all accounting records will be correct. The **accounting equation** is a rule that states that assets must always equal the sum of liabilities and owner's equity. As a result, both sides of the equation must always balance. The accounting equation is expressed as follows:

$$\text{Assets} = \text{Liabilities} + \text{Owner's Equity}$$

W The assets side of the equation shows the value of everything that the business owns or possesses. The other side shows the rights to those assets. Liabilities are the rights that creditors have to the assets. Owner's equity shows the rights that the owner has to the assets. For example, if a company's assets are worth $100,000 and liabilities against those assets are $40,000 (the amount owed creditors), then the owner has $60,000 in rights to the assets that the business possesses.

✔ **Reading Check** **Explain** What is the accounting equation?

● As You Read

Think about the types of financial decisions you have had to make.

Financial Statements

The accounting system is designed to **generate** financial statements and reports. **Financial statements** are documents that summarize the changes resulting from business transactions that occur during an accounting period. An *accounting period* is the period of time reflected by an accounting report.

Financial statements provide information that business owners use to make financial decisions. Even small sole proprietorships might prepare financial statements, but these documents are usually for the owner's use only. However, the federal government requires corporations to **release** their financial records to the public. Stockholders, employees, banks, and investment companies use financial statements to learn about the financial condition of a business. They can compare recent statements with

Real World

Handling Money Cash is a critical asset for any business, so proper money handling is important to keep the assets of the business in proper balance within the accounting equation.

● As You Read

Answers will vary but may include decisions about purchasing one item or another, or decisions to save money or to take a part-time job.

earlier ones and evaluate the business's growth or decline. The main financial statements used are income statements, balance sheets, and statements of cash flows.

Income Statement

At the end of an accounting period, you want to know how much money your business made or lost. You will want to know your total revenue in sales and where the money went. This information is reported on the income statement. The **income statement** is a report of the revenue, expenses, and *net income* or *net loss* over an accounting period. It is sometimes called a *profit and loss statement*. If a restaurant's total revenue, or earnings, is greater than its total expenses, it has a net income. If expenses are greater than revenue, then it has a net loss. Managers use income statements to see if revenues have increased or decreased from one period to another.

Income statements for different types of business operations vary in content. A service business would have sales, expenses, and net income. A merchandising business would also include the cost of merchandise purchased for resale. **Figure 17.1** shows an income statement.

Figure 17.1 – *Income Statement Using Peachtree Software*

	Current Month Actual	Current Month Budget	Year to Date Actual	Year to Date Budget
Revenues				
Sales	$ 175.00	$ 0.00	$ 175.00	$ 0.00
Sales - Aviary	5,628.01	14,583.33	50,153.16	43,749.99
Sales - Books	149.75	5,000.00	7,293.10	15,000.00
Sales - Ceramics	0.00	0.00	0.00	0.00
Sales - Equipment	15,139.29	18,000.00	57,492.78	54,000.00
Sales - Food/Fert	1,006.96	1,000.00	5,204.15	3,000.00
Sales - Furniture	15,000.00	5,000.00	15,000.00	15,000.00
Sales - Hand Tools	729.67	1,500.00	7,058.12	4,500.00
Sales - Landscape Services	7,469.43	6,000.00	16,977.53	18,000.00
Sales - Miscellaneous	0.00	0.00	45.00	0.00
Sales - Nursery	31,200.48	25,000.00	65,042.56	75,000.00
Sales - Pots	5,905.08	500.00	9,469.51	1,500.00
Sales - Seeds	1,457.43	100.00	8,661.39	300.00
Sales - Soil	655.02	2,500.00	9,082.55	7,500.00
Sales - Statuary	0.00	0.00	0.00	0.00
Sales - Topiary	0.00	0.00	0.00	0.00
Interest Income	0.00	0.00	0.00	0.00
Other Income	0.00	0.00	25,500.00	10,000.00
Finance Charge Income	0.00	0.00	0.00	0.00
Sales Returns and Allowances	0.00	0.00	0.00	0.00
Sales Discounts	(122.22)	0.00	(132.12)	0.00
Total Revenues	84,393.90	79,183.33	277,022.73	247,549.99

Bellwether Garden Supply
Income Statement
For the Three Months Ending March 31, 20--

● **Financial Information** Up-to-date financial information can provide a snapshot of how well a company is doing. **What do the total revenue figures tell you about this company?**

Section 17.2 Accounting **303**

Figure 17.1

● **Financial Information** Actual total revenues for the month and for the year to date are higher than the budgeted amounts for those periods.

Section 17.2

RETEACH

W Writing Support
Enrichment
Financial Statements Have students visit the U.S. Securities and Exchange Commission (SEC) Web site and locate the "Beginners' Guide to Financial Statements." Have students write a 100-word review of the guide. (Reviews should summarize the guide and include an opinion.)

W Writing Support
Make a Poster
Financial Statements Have students research and prepare a poster about two publicly traded companies' annual reports to find copies of their income statements. Ask students to write a brief introduction comparing and contrasting the documents. (Posters will vary, depending on the companies chosen.)

U Universal Access
Students Who Need Math Help
Ask students to copy this income statement line by line and do the math as they go. Working through the math will help students understand the income statement and realize that the math is relatively simple. This is particularly important for students who have math anxiety, but all students can benefit from this activity.

RETEACH (cont.)

R Reading Strategy

Recognize Supporting Details Have students write the definition of balance sheet and make a list of details in the paragraph that support this statement. (Details include that it is used by managers and investors. It is like a photo. It exposes problems.)

W Writing Support

Restating

Statement of Cash Flows Have students restate the paragraph to answer the following question: How is the statement of cash flows different from the income statement and the balance sheet? (The statement of cash flows shows the cash position of a business during an accounting period, which the income statement and balance sheet do not.)

C Critical Thinking

Compare and Contrast

Balance Sheet Have students compare the paragraph describing a balance sheet to the balance sheet shown in **Figure 17.1**. Ask students to locate line items on the actual balance sheet that are not mentioned in the paragraph. (Answers may include: Tools & Equipment, Employee Loans, Inventory Asset, Retainage, Undeposited Funds.)

Student Activity Workbook ☞ Assign the Section 17.2 Activities.

304

Real World

Personal Finance
You use accounting every day. At home, your family manages income, expenses, and cash flows. *What types of income and expenses would your personal financial statement show? How do you handle your cash flow?*

Balance Sheet

A **balance sheet** is a report of the balances in all assets, liability, and owner's equity accounts at the end of an accounting period. It is like a photograph of a business's finances at a specific moment. The balance sheet applies the accounting equation. When added up, the two sides of the equation are equal, or in balance. Managers and investors look at the balance sheet to determine if liabilities (claims against the assets) are increasing too much. The balance sheet can also indicate if there is too much cash available. Too much cash can mean that money is not being used efficiently. **Figure 17.2** shows a balance sheet.

Statement of Cash Flows

The income statement and balance sheet show important financial information. However, neither shows the cash position of a business during an accounting period. **Cash flows** are the money that is available to a business at any given time. The **statement of cash flows** is a financial report that shows incoming and outgoing money during an accounting period (often a month, quarter, or year).

Figure 17.2 — *Balance Sheet Using QuickBooks® Software*

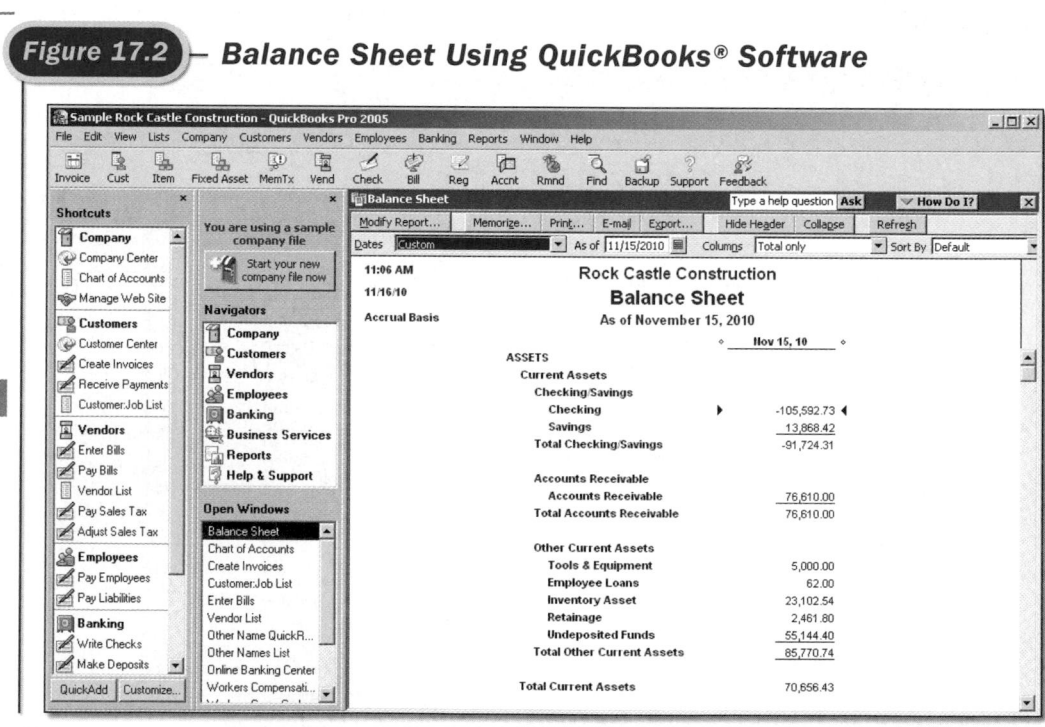

● **Computerized Accounting** Accounting programs such as QuickBooks can generate financial statements. **Which financial statement is shown here?**

Real World

Personal Finance Answers will vary. Income could come from an allowance or a part-time job. Expenses include food, clothing, and transportation. Cash flow might be handled by forecasting future expenses and income and making necessary adjustments, such as cutting back on unnecessary purchases.

Figure 17.2

● **Computerized Accounting** The financial statement is a balance sheet.

One reason that a cash flow statement is very important is that firms can run out of cash even when they make a profit. In today's world, most things are sold on credit. Credit sales are considered revenue to the firm. Businesses that do not receive credit payments from customers right away may not have cash available to pay bills. Cash flow is very important, especially for a business that wants to borrow money. Lenders and investors expect business loan applicants to be able to show a consistently positive cash flow. This gives lenders more assurance that the loan will be repaid.

● As You Read

Think about how it is possible for a business to run out of cash even though it is making a profit.

Computerized Accounting

Today, most companies use computer programs to simplify their accounting procedures. Computer spreadsheets are important tools for organizing and analyzing such data. A spreadsheet is made up of rows and columns. The columns are identified by letters, and the rows are identified by numbers. As you create a spreadsheet, you enter numbers, labels, and **formulas** into cells. Cells are the small boxes within a spreadsheet. Microsoft Excel is a spreadsheet application that is commonly used in business. Accounting software such as Peachtree Accounting and Quick-Books are programs that help people and businesses manage their finances.

NCLB Activity correlates to English Language Arts standards.

Section 17.2

● After You Read

Review Key Concepts
1. How does accounting help a business?
2. Discuss property ownership and control. How are they related to the accounting equation?
3. What are the three main financial statements used in business?

Academic Skills

4. **English Language Arts** Research the three different financial software programs mentioned in the text. Find what is available. Then write a recommendation in the form of a business memo about which would best suit a small business. Compare and contrast the software products.

5. **English Language Arts** *Liability, asset, gross profit, net profit, depreciation,* and *fiscal year* are all terms used by accountants. Find out what these words mean, and create an accounting glossary with definitions and examples of the terms used in sentences. You might want to expand the list of terms and work with others in a team to create a larger glossary.

 Go to the *Introduction to Business* Online Learning Center through **glencoe.com** to check your answers.

Section 17.2

Review Key Concepts
1. Accounting keeps track of money and shows how a business is doing.
2. The person who owns property has a financial claim to it. The accounting equation indicates the amounts of financial claims to property.
3. balance sheet, income statement, and statement of cash flows

Academic Skills
4. **English Language Arts** Students should use proper form and back up statements and recommendations with examples and facts.
5. **English Language Arts** Students' glossaries should include definitions and sample sentences.

RETEACH (cont.)

C Critical Thinking

Ask students: What do computerized accounting programs have in common with the old paper system? (They are used to create a permanent record of the business's finances.)

● As You Read

Businesses that make sales on credit do not receive their money right away, so cash may not be available when needed.

ASSESS

● After You Read

Have students complete the Section 17.2 After You Read section review.

Online Study Tools

Have students go to the Online Learning Center through **glencoe.com** to:

- Take the Section 17.2 **Practice Test**.
- Download free **Study-to-Go** content to their PDAs or cell phones.

CLOSE

Culminating Activity
Real Financial Statements
Have students work in pairs to locate three main financial statements for two large corporations for a recent year from their annual reports. Ask students to look at each of the two balance sheets, note the similarities, and to do the same for the income statement and the statement of cash flows.

Vocabulary Review

1. Students should write complete sentences using each term correctly.

Review Key Concepts

2. identify assets to purchase, determine needed capital, describe start-up and operating expenses, describe financial records management, forecast future finances, and describe growth financing

3. A budget shows the expected income and expenses for a future period and is adjusted according to new developments.

4. Accounting is used to collect, record, and post financial transactions that affect the operation of a business.

5. Property rights are measured by their monetary value.

6. Assets are items of value owned by a business. Liabilities are creditors' claims to the assets or the debts of a company. Owner's equity is an owner's claims to the assets of the business.

7. The balance sheet shows the total amount of assets, liabilities, and owner's equity during an accounting period. The income statement shows net income or net loss over a period. The statement of cash flows shows how much cash has been received and spent over a period.

Section 17.1 *Summary*

Financial Management A financial plan outlines the financial projections about a new firm or venture. Businesses use financial plans to make decisions about the future. Financial plans include the amount of money a business will need to start and operate. They also include financial forecasts. A forecast estimates the financial outlook for a business over the next few years. Financial planning also involves budgeting. A budget is a plan that specifies how money will be used or spent during a particular period.

Section 17.2 *Summary*

Accounting An accounting system collects, records, and reports financial transactions that affect the operation of a business. Accountants follow a uniform set of rules. These rules provide a consistent way to share financial information. The accounting equation is the basis of accounting. It equates assets to liabilities plus owner's equity. Key documents include the balance sheet, the income statement, and the statement of cash flows.

Vocabulary Review

1. On a sheet of paper, use each of these key terms and academic vocabulary terms in a sentence.

Key Terms
financial plan
capital
financial forecast
budget
accounting
generally accepted accounting
  principles (GAAP)
property
assets
current assets
accounts receivable

fixed assets
equity
liabilities
accounts payable
owner's equity
accounting equation
financial statements
income statement
balance sheet
cash flows
statement of cash flows

Academic Vocabulary
project
expand
require
predict
converted
generate
release
formulas

Review Key Concepts

2. Identify the six reasons for creating a financial plan.

3. Explain what a budget is and how it is used.

4. Explain the purpose of accounting.

5. Describe how property rights are measured.

6. Define the three components of the accounting equation.

7. Describe the three main financial statements used by businesses.

Critical Thinking

8. It might show that the business does not have a realistic possibility of success when income is compared to expected expenses.

9. Failure is a possibility. The business might have to lower its expenses and make other changes to increase income.

10. Credit allows people and companies to make purchases for major items. Sometimes credit allows people and companies to spend more than they can afford to repay in a timely manner.

11. The government ensures businesses are operating honestly. Stockholders and lenders rely on a company's management to make good decisions and present accurate information.

Critical Thinking

8. Why do you think an entrepreneur might realize that he or she could not secure any investors after developing a financial plan?

9. A budget helps businesses determine how money will be spent in a given period. Will a business fail if it does not meet its budget?

10. How can having and extending credit on purchases be both good and bad for business?

11. Why do you think the federal government gets involved in the way businesses create and manage their finances?

12. If a business buys $4,000 worth of new equipment on credit, which inputs to the accounting equation are affected? Is the accounting equation still in balance?

13. It is important to use financial statements on a regular basis. What might happen to a business that analyzes its finances just twice a year?

14. Why does the income statement provide an incomplete picture of a business?

15. What are some reasons a company might not have enough cash reserves?

Write About It

16. Choose a well-known corporation and research its most current income statement. Write a one-page report describing the income statement. Indicate the accounting period(s) covered.

17. Amy Sullivan has hired you to handle the accounting for her pet-grooming business. Based on the following totals, calculate the assets, liabilities, and owner's equity for the shop: cash: $200; grooming equipment: $300; accounts receivable: $500; accounts payable: $900; owner's equity: $100. Prepare a report, giving your opinion of the financial condition of the shop.

18. Accounting standards differ from country to country. Several groups are developing international accounting standards. Write a 200-word essay on the effect these standards might have on business.

19. As an investor in a certain company, would you like to see the accounts receivable on the balance sheet increase, decrease, or stay the same from one year to another? What should the company do to reach that point? Write a letter of two or more paragraphs to a financial manager supporting your answer.

Technology Applications

Automated Accounting Programs
20. Investigate different accounting software programs and the types of financial documents that can be created using them. Can these programs be used by individuals, businesses, or both? Are they for small or large businesses, or can any business or organization use them? Write a report on your findings.

Business Ethics

Confidentiality
21. Imagine that you were recently hired as the accountant for a well-known music group and have access to personal information. Your friends ask you for details about the band, such as the amount of money they make and where they live. Your friends tell you they will not give anyone else this information. What should you do?

Chapter 17 Review and Activities **307**

Critical Thinking

12. Assets are increased by $4,000 and liabilities by $4,000. The equation is still in balance.

13. The owner might discover that the business will not have enough funds to cover upcoming expenses.

14. It shows only the net income or net loss over an accounting period, not the debt or amount of available cash.

15. A business may have sold products on credit or might have had emergencies that required cash outlays.

Write About It

16. Answers will vary, depending on the company selected.

17. Assets = Liabilities + Owner's Equity. Assets are $200 + $300 + $500 = $1,000. The only liability is accounts payable ($900). The owner has $100 equity in the assets possessed.

18. Investors would be more willing to invest in a business in another country if there were standardized reports they could understand.

19. An increase can be good if there also is an increase in sales and cash. However, if the increase is because accounts receivable is not paid off, and cash is not also increasing, then the firm has extended credit to too many customers.

Technology Applications
20. Reports will vary but should describe the functionality of various accounting software programs.

Business Ethics
21. Most students will agree that it is inappropriate to give confidential information to friends.

Applying Academics to Business

22. Students' sentences should include contextual clues to help others infer the meanings of the key words.

23. The median is $76,948. The mean is $77,686.

$76,948 < $77,686.

24. Notes will vary, depending on the section chosen.

25. $42,000 ÷ 0.15 = ~~$280,000~~

Tran's company needs to generate $280,000 in revenue.

Active Learning

26. Budgets and reports will vary, based on students' assets, liabilities, and goals.

Business in the Real World

27. Answers will depend on the interviewees' responses.

Applying Academics to Business

English Language Arts
22. *Funds, capital, wealth, currency,* and *cash* are all words having to do with money. Research the meanings of the words and use each in a sentence so that someone unfamiliar with the words could infer their meanings from the context.

Mathematics
23. Three accounting supervisors in a large corporation earn different salaries based on their experience and time on the job. The median base salary is $76,948, with a range of $64,494 to $91,617. Write an inequality comparing the mean and the median.

> **THEORY** **Data Analysis: Mean, Median, and Range** The range of a set of data is the difference between the greatest and least number, the median is the number in the middle when all are listed in order from least to greatest, and the mean is the average.

English Language Arts
24. The topic sentence of a paragraph sometimes appears at the beginning. Sometimes it appears in the middle or at the end, and sometimes it is not directly stated in the paragraph, but must be inferred. Take notes from one of the sections by identifying and jotting down the key words and phrases from the topic sentences of each paragraph.

Mathematics
25. Tran, an entrepreneur, wants his computer business to earn $42,000 in profits. His research shows that the average net profit for his type of business is 15%. If Tran's business earns the average net profit percentage, how much revenue must be generated to deliver that net profit?

> **THEORY** **Working with Percents** If you know that a number, *x*, is a certain percent of an unknown, *y*, divide *x* by the percent to find *y*.

Active Learning

Financial Statements
26. Prepare a personal balance sheet. Price your assets at the cost that you paid for them. Next, use spreadsheet software, such as Excel, to prepare a personal budget for the next six months. Then write a one-page report on your financial goals for the future. Lastly, create separate folders for your balance sheet, personal budget, and goals.

Business in the Real World

Interview a Financial Manager
27. In groups of three or four, interview a financial manager or an accountant for a business. Ask about the business's long-term plans; the way financial forecasting is done and used; the software used for financial management of the firm; and the most common financial mistakes businesses make. As a group, prepare a written report on the interview.

308   **Chapter 17**   Review and Activities

***ExamView Assessment Suite* CD** allows you to print out ready-made unit and chapter tests, complete with answer keys. You can also create customized tests.

TeacherWorks Plus provides complete teacher resources in one convenient package. It includes customizable lesson plans in calendar format, and instant access to many print program resources.

Real LIFE skills

PERSONAL QUALITIES OF ACCOUNTANTS

28. General skills and abilities needed by accountants include the following: aptitude in math; ability to analyze, compare, and interpret data; communication skills; people skills; and a high level of integrity. Write at least two paragraphs indicating whether you have the interests and abilities necessary to pursue this type of career. Discuss ways you think you might overcome any weaknesses.

Cool Business CAREERS

FIND YOUR DREAM JOB

29. Go to the *Introduction to Business* Online Learning Center through **glencoe.com** for a link to the Occupational Outlook Handbook Web site. Click on the "OOH Search/A-Z Index" link and enter the job category "accountants and auditors." Then write a one-page report about this area of occupation. Conclude your report with a list of things you could do now to prepare yourself to pursue the occupation.

Role Play

THE ACCOUNTING DEPARTMENT'S FUNCTION

30. **Situation** You are an accountant at a movie studio. Your manager asks you for reasons why the company needs such a large accounting department. She wonders if it would cost less to pay an outside accounting firm to perform the same services.

Activity You are called upon to justify the importance of the accounting department's function to the business.

Evaluation You will be evaluated on how well you meet the following performance indicators:

- Demonstrate a knowledge of business operations.
- Demonstrate knowledge of the important contributions that accounting makes to the health of the business.
- Organize comments in a logical way.
- Project your voice well and make good eye contact.

Real LIFE skills

28. Answers will depend on students' assessment of their personal qualities and interest in accounting.

Cool Business CAREERS

29. Nature of the work: Accounting professionals help ensure that firms run efficiently, that their public records are kept accurately, and taxes are paid properly. Some work long hours during tax season. Training and qualifications include a bachelor's degree in accounting or a related field. Most states require CPA candidates to complete 150 semester hours of college coursework. The job outlook is for faster-than-average growth. As preparation, develop computer and business skills.

Role Play

30. Presentations should address the competencies noted in the Role Play. For example, the presentation could start with a statement about the purpose of accounting. Accountants who work within a business will know the company better than an outside accounting firm. The studio will know its employees better, too.

Standardized Test Practice

Directions Choose the letter of the best answer. Write the letter for the answer on a separate piece of paper.

1. **Which sentence best develops the topic sentence below?**

   Effective financial managers deserve to earn a high salary.

   A They spend all their time thinking about numbers.
   B Some live lavishly and have lots of expenses.
   C They make even more for their clients.
   D Every financial manager deserves to do well financially.

 TEST-TAKING TIP When taking a test, always read the directions before you work on a section. Failing to read directions can cause you to completely misinterpret what the test is asking you to do.

 **READING** Go to the *Introduction to Business* Online Learning Center through **glencoe.com** for a list of outside reading suggestions.

STRATEGIES FOR STANDARDIZED TEST PREP SUCCESS

Test Savvy To help students make a habit of carefully reading directions for a test, organize the class into groups. Give each group a game to play that they find unfamiliar. Have them read the directions before they begin, and refer back to the directions as they play. After students are proficient, have individuals write the directions from memory and compare their directions with others. Ask the group to compile a list of complete directions for the game.

Standardized Test Practice
1. C

Standards-Based Lesson Planning   *Introduction to Business* provides students with instruction and assessment in the following fundamental content areas:

Content Standards Correlations	
Describe types of technology and their importance to businesses.	pp. 313–316, 318–321, 322–325
Discuss electronic communications in productive business situations.	pp. 313–316, 318–321, 322–325
Develop skills necessary to function effectively in a variety of electronic offices.	pp. 313–316, 318–321, 322–325
Identify and describe communications and networking systems used in workplace environments.	pp. 313–316, 318–321, 322–325
Use technology to apply and enhance communication skills.	pp. 319, 321, 325
Describe the threat of viruses to a computer network, methods of avoiding attacks, and options in dealing with a virus attack.	pp. 320–321, 322–323
Identify potential abuse and unethical uses of computers and networks.	pp. 320–321, 323–324
Explore career opportunities in computer technology.	pp. 323, 325
Select and use appropriate modes of communication for specific job and work situations.	p. 325

NCLB   Activities, information, and skills practice will help your students attain No Child Left Behind proficiency. Students will improve their abilities in the following academic standards areas:

Academic Standards Correlations		
English Language Arts	Activities/Features	Page
NCTE 3 Apply strategies to interpret texts	Applying Academics to Business Standardized Test Practice	pp. 324, 325
NCTE 5 Use different writing process elements to communicate effectively	After You Read	p. 321
NCTE 6 Apply knowledge of language structure and conventions to discuss texts	Applying Academics to Business	p. 324
NCTE 8 Use information resources to gather information and communicate knowledge	After You Read	p. 321
Mathematics		
Algebra Represent and analyze mathematical situations and structures using algebraic symbols	After You Read	p. 316
Measurement Apply appropriate techniques, tools, and formulas to determine measurements	Applying Academics to Business	p. 324
Number and Operation Understand numbers, ways of representing numbers, relationships among numbers, and number systems	Applying Academics to Business	p. 324
Problem Solving Build new mathematical knowledge through problem solving	Ask S&P	p. 310
Science		
Content Standard F Students should develop understanding of personal and community health	Science/Tech Trends	p. 319

Correlations   This chart shows the 21st Century Skills, foundation skills, and workplace competencies that students develop as they work in this chapter.

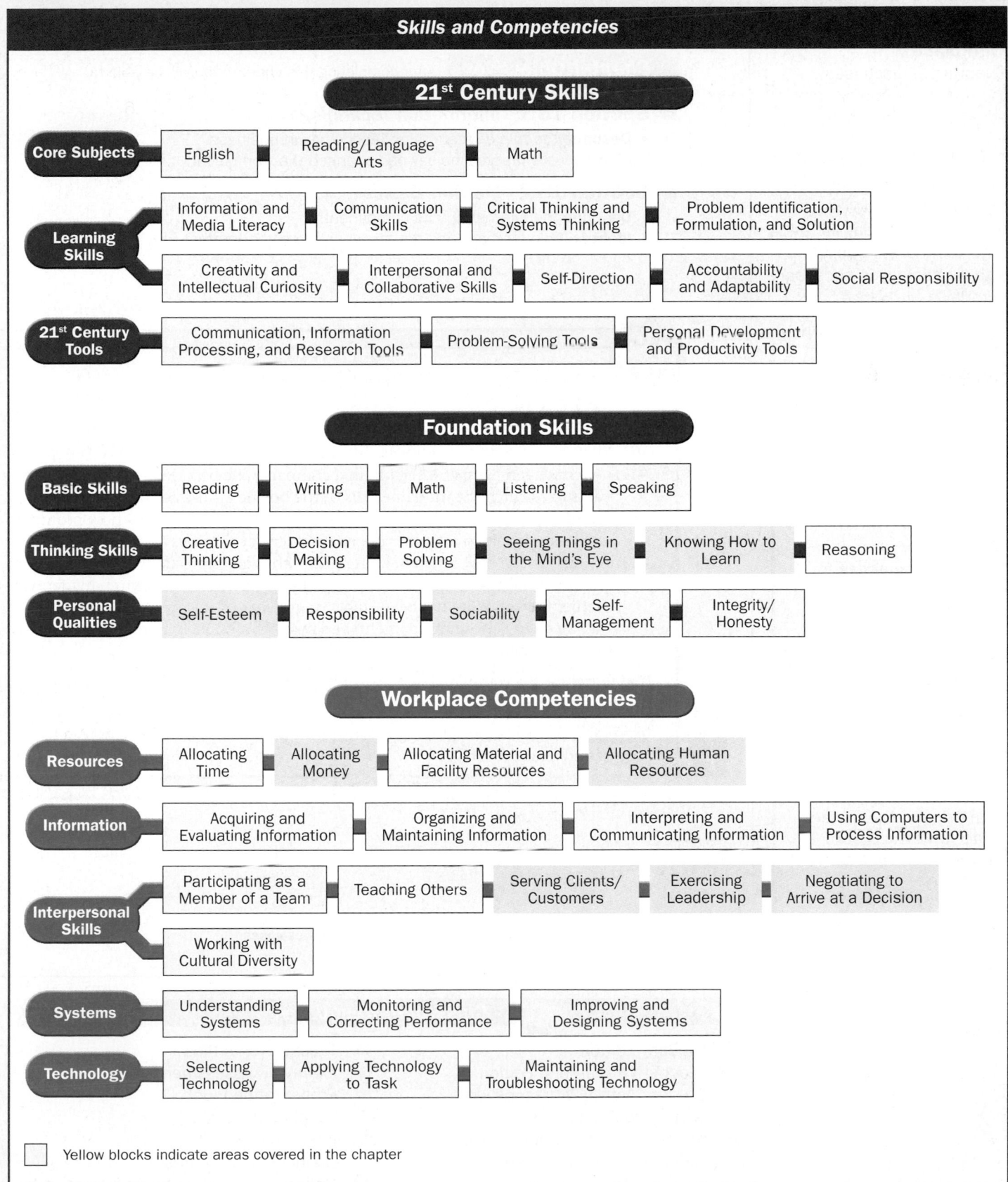

Skills and Competencies

21st Century Skills

Core Subjects
- English
- Reading/Language Arts
- Math

Learning Skills
- Information and Media Literacy
- Communication Skills
- Critical Thinking and Systems Thinking
- Problem Identification, Formulation, and Solution
- Creativity and Intellectual Curiosity
- Interpersonal and Collaborative Skills
- Self-Direction
- Accountability and Adaptability
- Social Responsibility

21st Century Tools
- Communication, Information Processing, and Research Tools
- Problem-Solving Tools
- Personal Development and Productivity Tools

Foundation Skills

Basic Skills
- Reading
- Writing
- Math
- Listening
- Speaking

Thinking Skills
- Creative Thinking
- Decision Making
- Problem Solving
- Seeing Things in the Mind's Eye
- Knowing How to Learn
- Reasoning

Personal Qualities
- Self-Esteem
- Responsibility
- Sociability
- Self-Management
- Integrity/Honesty

Workplace Competencies

Resources
- Allocating Time
- Allocating Money
- Allocating Material and Facility Resources
- Allocating Human Resources

Information
- Acquiring and Evaluating Information
- Organizing and Maintaining Information
- Interpreting and Communicating Information
- Using Computers to Process Information

Interpersonal Skills
- Participating as a Member of a Team
- Teaching Others
- Serving Clients/Customers
- Exercising Leadership
- Negotiating to Arrive at a Decision
- Working with Cultural Diversity

Systems
- Understanding Systems
- Monitoring and Correcting Performance
- Improving and Designing Systems

Technology
- Selecting Technology
- Applying Technology to Task
- Maintaining and Troubleshooting Technology

Yellow blocks indicate areas covered in the chapter

310B

Chapter Overview

Introduce the Chapter

Technology in the Workplace
Chapter 18 discusses the use of technological advances in the workplace.

Building Background
Students often are on the forefront of technology, particularly in everyday life and entertainment. Keeping up with technology is necessary in today's workplace.

Ask STANDARD & POOR'S

>> Math Answer
The cost of manufacturing the products is 80% of the price charged in the marketplace. The relationship between the price a company charges for its products and the cost of manufacturing is the inverse of the gross margin. If the gross margin is 20%, the cost of manufacturing the goods is 80% (100% − 20%).

>> Extension Activity
Ask students to describe the relationship between the price in the marketplace and the cost of manufacturing a product if the gross margin is: Company A, 15%; Company B, 27%; and Company C, 34%. (Company A's cost is 85%. Company B's cost is 73%. Company C's cost is 66%.)

Activity correlates to Math standards.

Technology in the Workplace

Chapter Objectives After completing this chapter, you will be able to:

▶ **Section 18.1** *Information Technology*
- **Describe** the role of information technology in business.
- **Identify** ways that technology has changed the workplace.

▶ **Section 18.2** *Internet Basics*
- **Describe** the Internet and its components.
- **Identify** tools for managing threats when using the Internet.

Ask STANDARD & POOR'S **Fundamental Research**

Q: What do I look for when researching a company whose stock interests me?

A: Since stock represents ownership in a company, the best way to gauge a stock's appeal is to research the fundamentals of the business—the company's basic financial condition. You might look at aspects such as gross margin to see how profitably a company is able to manufacture its products; at earnings and the price to earnings ratio to see how much of a premium other investors are willing to pay for a company's future earnings; and at the company's history of paying dividends to tell whether the company has been stable or growing over time. All the information you'll need to perform fundamental analysis on a publicly traded company is available to the public.

Mathematics If a company has a gross margin of 20%, what is the cost of manufacturing its products?

THEORY **Gross Margin** Gross margin is profit divided by net sales. It is usually expressed as a percentage.

Classroom Resources

- ✎ Student Edition
- ✎ Teacher Wraparound Edition
- 📁 Student Activity Workbook with Academic Integration
- 📁 Student Activity Workbook with Academic Integration TAE
- 📁 *Fast File*, Unit 6 Resources
- 📁 Inclusion in the Business Education Classroom

- ◉ TeacherWorks Plus
- ◉ *ExamView Assessment Suite*
- ◉ Presentation Plus!
- ◉ Vocabulary PuzzleMaker
- ◉ Interactive Student Edition
- 🖉 Online Student Edition
- 🖉 Online Learning Center with Podcasts

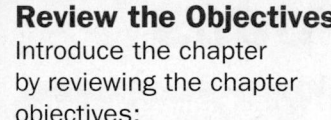

Review the Objectives
Introduce the chapter by reviewing the chapter objectives:

Section 18.1 *Objectives*
Describe the role of information technology in business. (Information technology enables workers to create, process, store, and communicate information. Workers can use computers, telephones, fax machines, and handheld devices to access and send information.)

Identify ways that technology has changed the workplace. (Mobile technology allows people to telecommute by working from home or anyplace outside the office. Wearable computers also make the office more mobile. Robots and machine tools help to improve the manufacturing process. Workers can learn new tasks through simulation training.)

Section 18.2 *Objectives*
Describe the Internet and its components. (The Internet is a global computer network that connects many computer networks. Its components include the World Wide Web, Web browsers, and search engines.)

Identify tools for managing threats when using the Internet. (Many kinds of software can be used to protect computer systems and information. Firewalls act as a security wall between a computer and the Internet. Anti-virus software protects against viruses and worms. Spyware-protection software protects against tracking while browsing the Web.)

● **Telecommuting to Work** Technology makes it possible to move the worker from the workplace to the home. **What technologies could allow you to do work at home?**

Chapter 18   Technology in the Workplace   **311**

Discuss the Photo
● **Telecommuting to Work** Read the caption on the photo to students: Technology makes it possible to move the worker from the workplace to the home.

Ask students: What technologies could allow you to do work at home? (Telephones, fax machines, computers, e-mail, and the Internet are technologies that telecommuters frequently rely on to allow them to work from home.)

FOCUS

 Bell Ringer Activity

Information Technology

Using your own recent experiences, provide students with a few examples of how technology is used when businesses interact with customers and clients. Ask students to share some examples. (Students might mention sending digital pictures to a photo finisher for pickup at the local drugstore, or tracking a package at a delivery service Web site.)

Preteaching

Presentation Plus!

The Presentation Plus! CD provides visual teaching aids for this section.

PuzzleMaker

Use the Vocabulary PuzzleMaker to create a puzzle of the section's key terms. Students can complete the puzzle on paper or on a computer.

Graphic Organizer

Tell students to go to the Online Learning Center through **glencoe.com** for a printable graphic organizer. (Answers include: Advantages: comfort of working from home, flexible work hours, less traveling, fewer absences. Some advantages of working in an office are: more distractions at home, better supervision, face-to-face contact with other workers, no cost of home office equipment.)

 Connects academics to content.

Information Technology

Reading Guide

● Before You Read

Think about ways information technology is used for business and personal reasons.

Read to Learn

- Describe the role of information technology in business.
- Identify ways that technology has changed the workplace.

The Main Idea

People want instant access to information. At home and at work, they use hardware and software to create, store, and communicate information. Information technology allows people to access information from anywhere.

Key Concepts

- The Role of Information Technology
- How Technology Has Changed the Workplace

Vocabulary

Key Terms

information technology (IT)
telecommunications
telecommuting
wearable computer
computer-aided design (CAD)
virtual reality

Academic Vocabulary

You will find these words in your reading and on your tests. Make sure you know their meanings.

transmit   simulate
automatic   visual

Graphic Organizer

In a figure like the one below, list the advantages of telecommuting in the left column and the advantages of working in an office in the right column.

Advantages of Telecommuting	Advantages of Working in an Office

 Go to the *Introduction to Business* Online Learning Center through **glencoe.com** for a printable graphic organizer.

D **Academic Standards**

English Language Arts

   NCTE 1 Read texts to acquire new information

Mathematics

   Algebra Represent and analyze mathematical situations and structures using algebraic symbols

Reading Guide

● Before You Read

Students might mention laptop computers, cell phones, personal music devices, and digital assistants.

D Develop Concepts

The Main Idea Ask students: How important is it to you to have instant access to information? Is it a need or a want? (Students should distinguish between the need for critical information and wanting less-important information.)

The Role of Information Technology

People depend on getting information quickly and easily. **Information technology (IT)** uses computing, electronics, and telecommunications to process and distribute information in digital and other forms. **Telecommunications** is the transmission of information over communication lines. This covers many technologies, including telephones and computer networks.

Computers are an important part of information technology. So are telephones, fax machines, personal digital assistants (PDAs), and other handheld devices. MP3 players digitally store music for listening anywhere. Wireless technology (wireless fidelity, or WiFi) lets people with a wireless-enabled computer or PDA connect to the Internet. Buildings wired for WiFi can transfer information from one part of a computer system to another. Computers used to design and make new products have improved the manufacturing process. Millions of employees work from home. IT makes these innovations possible.

● **As You Read**
Think about changes in technology that have taken place at your school in the last decade.

✔ **Reading Check** **Identify** What are some forms of information technology?

How Technology Has Changed the Workplace

New technology makes it possible to do tasks in different ways. When computers were first used in business, they were too big and heavy to take from the office. Today, mobile computers are light enough to take anywhere. *Electronic mail,* or e-mail, allows workers to communicate with others electronically. Wearable computers, manufacturing technology, and specialized software allow more work flexibility. Wireless phones, broadband access, and voice technology also let the workspace become mobile. For example, Capital One Financial Corp. replaces traditional offices and cubicles with mobile work areas and a casual environment. At hospitals, nurses can use a wireless computer to enter information about patients from anywhere in the facility. Through *WiFi,* the information is sent to a database available to the doctors, technicians, and others who need it.

● **Internet Tools** Technological innovation has changed the way people and businesses interact. **How can a business use technology to improve sales?**

Section 18.1 Information Technology 313

Discuss the Photo
● **Internet Tools** Many businesses have started Web sites that sell their products and services online. Other businesses have established "presence" Web sites that allow them to market directly to consumers, even though the actual point of sale is another catalog, store, or Internet business. Still others have started advertising campaigns centered around banner ads and e-mail solicitation to improve their sales.

Section 18.1

TEACH

Discussion Starter
The Role of Information Technology
Ask students how information technology makes it possible for employees to work from their homes. (Students should understand that information technology systems allow users to transfer data and voice signals between locations. This includes communication between people working at home with their co-workers, clients, and vendors regardless of their location.)

Ⓡ **Reading Strategy**
Illustrate an Idea Have students create a drawing to illustrate one of the ideas presented under the heading "The Role of Information Technology." (Illustrations will vary. A student might draw a picture of someone sitting in a café using a laptop computer.)

● **As You Read**
Answers will vary. Computers, e-mail, use of the Internet, and software programs have enabled students and teachers to learn and communicate faster and more efficiently.

✔ **Reading Check**

Identify Forms of information technology include computers, telephones, fax machines, cell phones, MP3 players, and wireless systems.

314

TEACH (cont.)

S Skill Practice

Guided Practice

Describe Ask students to identify a job where telecommuting would be impossible and to explain why. (Answers should indicate that telecommuting is not possible with certain jobs that require employees to have direct physical contact with other people or things. Some examples include dentist, sanitation worker, carpet installer, and dry cleaner.) **L1**

Categorize Have students categorize the advantages and disadvantages of telecommuting listed in the textbook as benefiting or hurting the worker or employer. (For example, students should indicate that spending less time traveling to and from work benefits the employee.) **L2**

Express an Opinion Ask students to write an essay about why they would or would not enjoy telecommuting. (Essays will vary.) **L3**

ASSESS

Review Key Terms

Have students write sentences using each key term.

 **Study-to-Go** Have students go to the Online Learning Center through **glencoe.com** to download free **Study-to-Go** content to their PDAs or cell phones.

314

Telecommuting

Telecommuting is an arrangement that allows employees to work at home while communicating with the workplace by phone, fax, or modem. Telecommuting has advantages. It decreases traffic in busy areas since workers spend less time traveling. It allows for flexible work hours. Companies also find that the quality of work often improves for telecommuters. Many employees are absent less often than when they worked full-time at the office.

Telecommuting also has disadvantages. Some employees dislike the lack of contact with other workers. Many miss the social part of the office. Some also find that they get distracted at home and cannot get their work done. For employers, a major problem is supervising an employee at a remote site. Telecommuters must have computers and other equipment to do their work. In many cases, this adds to company expenses. **Figure 18.1** shows that younger people use computers more frequently than older people.

Wearable Computers

Ever more portable computers are being developed by the IT industry. One goal is to make more wearable computers. A **wearable computer** is a small portable computer designed to be used while it is worn on the body. Some can be worn as wristbands; others work as headsets or clip onto a belt or backpack. For example, portable music players may be able to understand and record speech by workers who need to take dictation.

Real World

Open-Source Systems An *operating system* is the basic set of programs and utilities that make your computer run. Users can modify and redistribute open-source operating systems such as Linux®. *What are some issues that computer users should consider before using open-source systems?*

International Business

Telecommuting Telecommuting is an invaluable employment tool for many people. Some of the opportunities telecommuting offers international business include offshore outsourcing and allowing companies to be open almost all the time.

Open-Source Systems Computer users should consider security risks using systems that are used and changed by other users. Risks include hacking and viruses. Parents might want to supervise their children's computer use of open source systems.

Technology in Manufacturing

Computers have also made a difference in the way products are designed and made. **Computer-aided design (CAD)** is software for designing products with a computer. With CAD, engineers can design without paper. They can change designs quickly and easily. By using CAD and computer-aided manufacturing (CAM) programs together, companies can custom-design and make products.

Most manufacturing plants are partly automated. Robots and computer-controlled machine tools do much of the work. They can do many of the hard or monotonous jobs that were done by people in the past, freeing workers to direct the robots and machine tools. Workers usually receive technical training to do these jobs.

Electronic Information Transfer

Electronic information transfer allows tasks to be done quicker. For example, many companies electronically transfer paychecks to employees' bank accounts. A national sales manager uses electronic mail to **transmit** sales figures to regional managers. Consumers use electronic information transfer, too. They can use an **automatic** teller machine (ATM) or their own computer to transfer funds from one bank account to another.

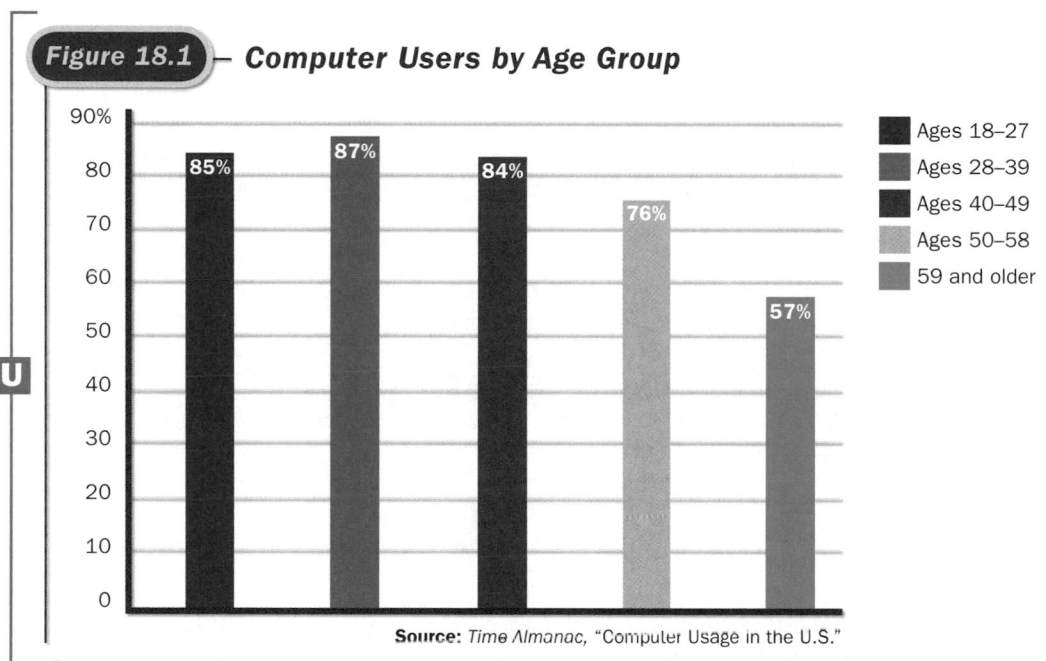

Figure 18.1 — *Computer Users by Age Group*

Legend:
- Ages 18–27
- Ages 28–39
- Ages 40–49
- Ages 50–58
- 59 and older

85%, 87%, 84%, 76%, 57%

Source: *Time Almanac*, "Computer Usage in the U.S."

● **Tools for Everyone** This chart shows the percentages of people in the United States who used computers in a recent year. **What changes do you predict will happen over the next several years in these figures?**

Section 18.1 Information Technology **315**

Virtual Business

Introduce purchasing to students using the Virtual Business Retailing Purchasing activity. In this simulation, students learn why purchasing is important to the success of a business.

Figure 18.1

● **Tools for Everyone** Computer use will probably increase in all groups. People will increasingly use computers at home and at work.

W **Writing Support**

Enrichment

Technology in Manufacturing Have students use library or Internet resources to identify a situation where technology is used in manufacturing. Ask students to write a paragraph describing their findings. Instruct students to include a properly formatted reference citation. (Paragraphs will vary.)

R **Reading Strategy**

Apply Knowledge Ask students to use their own experience to construct another example that could be used under the heading "Electronic Information Transfer." (Examples will vary. Students might suggest that the use of key cards to allow drivers access to parking garages or point of sale scanners that approve and record credit card purchases.)

U **Universal Access**

Computer Users Have students investigate trends in the age groups involved in the use of computers and share their findings with the class. Allow students to choose the medium for sharing their new knowledge. For example, students might create posters, produce short videos, or write reports. Making choices is especially important to some learners and all students can benefit from this activity.

Student Activity Workbook ☞ Assign the Section 18.1 Activities.

RETEACH (cont.)

C Critical Thinking

Think of Examples
Virtual Training Have students identify a situation where they think virtual training could be useful and to describe one advantage over other types of training. (Answers include driver's education, pilots, etc.)

As You Read

Playing a simulation game is good training in handling future business situations and recognizing situations you may see at work.

ASSESS

After You Read

Have students complete the Section 18.1 After You Read section review.

Online Study Tools

Have students go to the Online Learning Center through **glencoe.com** to:
- Take the Section 18.1 **Practice Test**.
- Download free **Study-to-Go** content to their PDAs or cell phones.

CLOSE

Culminating Activity
Technology Usage
Have students work in groups to research and graph some aspects of technology usage. Ask students to provide source information for their data. (Graphs will vary depending on the type of technology chosen.)

As You Read

Think about computer games that use virtual reality and how they might help you in the business world.

N C L B Activity correlates to Math standards.

Virtual Training

Virtual training allows people to **simulate** a real situation using a computer. For instance, a computer-run flight simulation program allows pilots to learn how to fly aircraft. Pilots enter a room equipped with cockpit controls and a video screen, and practice flying the "aircraft." The screen shows them the results of their actions. The entire room is movable, with its motion controlled by a computer. In this case, virtual training offers pilots a safe way to learn to fly. Schools use computer-based science labs. Students try different science experiments using a computer. Menus allow them to choose chemicals to combine and tell them the amounts to use. Experiments done on computers are safe, with no danger involved if students make mistakes.

Virtual reality is also used in training. **Virtual reality** is an artificial, three-dimensional **visual** world created by a computer. In a *virtual world,* the computer recreates places and actions that seem real. Users wear special goggles and fiber-optic gloves called data gloves. They enter and move about, and interact with objects as if inside the virtual world. The data gloves are the input devices, relaying movements of the user's hand to the computer. The senses of sight, sound, motion, and touch give the illusion of real objects or places. For example, in medical training, computers allow surgeons to practice procedures without real patients.

Section 18.1

After You Read

Review Key Concepts
1. What are some forms of information technology?
2. How has technology, especially mobile technology, changed the workplace?
3. What are some of the pros and cons of telecommuting?

Academic Skills
4. **Mathematics** At a Silicon Valley computer networking company, 17,000 people, or 47% of its workforce, telecommute for part or all of the workday. Write a sentence or two describing how you could determine the number of employees who do not telecommute.

THEORY **Proportions** A proportion is an equation stating that two ratios are equivalent.

 For math help, go to the Math Appendix.

 Go to the *Introduction to Business* Online Learning Center through **glencoe.com** to check your answers.

Section 18.1

Review Key Concepts
1. computers, telephones, PDAs
2. making it possible to work outside the office, especially from home
3. pros: work at home, work without physical supervision, less travel time, flexible work hours; cons: lack of contact with co-workers, distractions, problems in supervision, cost of equipment

Academic Skills
4. **Mathematics** Write and solve a proportion to find the total number of employees; subtract the number of telecommuters:

$17,000 : 0.47 = x : 1; 0.47x = 17,000$

$x = 36,170.2$ employees

$36,170 - 17,000 = 19,170$ employees don't telecommute.

Internet Basics

Reading Guide

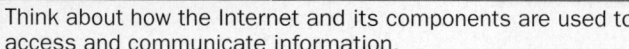

● Before You Read

Think about how the Internet and its components are used to access and communicate information.

Read to Learn

- Describe the Internet and its components.
- Identify tools for managing threats when using the Internet.

The Main Idea

The Internet has changed the way business is done. However, it poses risks to the information that is stored on computers. Companies and people must protect their computers from threats.

Key Concepts

- The Internet
- Managing Technology Threats

Vocabulary

Key Terms

Internet
World Wide Web
Web browser
search engine
intranet
extranet
hacker
cookies
virus

Academic Vocabulary

You will find these words in your reading and on your tests. Make sure you know their meanings.

guidelines   reject
authorized   insert

Graphic Organizer

In a figure like the one below, define intranet in the left circle and extranet in the right circle. Write notes about similarities among intranets and extranets in the area where the two circles overlap.

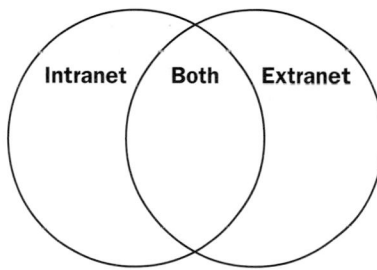

Intranet   Both   Extranet

 Go to the *Introduction to Business* Online Learning Center through **glencoe.com** for a printable graphic organizer.

Academic Standards

English Language Arts

NCTE 1 Read texts to acquire new information

NCTE 5 Use different writing process elements to communicate effectively

NCTE 8 Use information resources to gather information and communicate knowledge

Science

Content Standard F Students should develop understanding of personal and community health

Bell Ringer Activity

Internet Basics
Ask: What is the difference between the Internet and the World Wide Web? (Internet: a large library of huge databases. World Wide Web: a means of accessing, organizing, and moving through the information on the Internet; part of the Internet.)

Preteaching

Presentation Plus!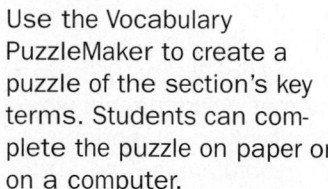

The Presentation Plus! CD provides visual teaching aids for this section.

PuzzleMaker

Use the Vocabulary PuzzleMaker to create a puzzle of the section's key terms. Students can complete the puzzle on paper or on a computer.

Graphic Organizer

Tell students to go to the Online Learning Center through **glencoe.com** for a printable graphic organizer. (Answers include: left: employee handbook and directory, code of ethics; right: sharing information with other companies, and managing and communicating with customers, vendors, and suppliers with secure Web sites; middle: software and hardware that allow businesses and Internet users to access these networks.)

Connects academics to content.

Reading Guide

● Before You Read

Businesses use the Internet to facilitate e-mail with customers, suppliers, and employees, advertise products and services.

D Develop Concepts

The Main Idea Ask students: Why are Internet users concerned about viruses, hackers, and spyware? (Viruses, hackers, and spyware cost computer users time, money, and energy.)

317

TEACH

Discussion Starter
The Internet

Explain that no one actually owns the Internet. Ask students how they think the Internet works if no one really owns it. (Answers will vary. Students should understand that the W3C is able to control the Internet because so many organizations cooperate in an effort to make the Internet widely available.)

R Reading Strategy

Draw a Conclusion Point out that standards on the World Wide Web are merely a system for accessing, changing, and downloading a large set of hypertext-linked documents and other files located on computers connected through the Internet. Ask students why they think it is important for people around the world to agree on a single set of standards for a language to link most data transmission on the Internet. (Students should be able to recognize that, without cooperation, their computers would be unlikely to speak the same "language" as computers around the globe.)

✔ Reading Check

Explain The Internet is a global computer network. It connects many computer networks, allowing information to flow freely around the world.

318

The Internet

The **Internet** is a global computer network. It connects many computer networks, allowing information to flow freely around the world. People access the Internet through their telephone lines or digital subscriber line (DSL) service, which provides a high-speed connection. Other high-speed connections can be established over cable or Ethernet connections. These connections are possible through modems, devices used to send data from one computer to another.

✔ Reading Check   **Explain** What is the Internet?

The World Wide Web

R The World Wide Web is part of the Internet. The **World Wide Web** (or simply the Web) is a system for accessing, changing, and downloading a large set of hypertext-linked documents and other files located on computers connected through the Internet. *Hypertext* is a computer language that allows Internet users to access stored images, text, and other files. It enables direct links to related text, images, sound, and other data.

BusinessWeek *Reader and Case Study*

Math Will Rock Your World

Neal Goldman is a math entrepreneur. He works on Wall Street, where numbers rule. But he's focusing his analytic tools on a different realm altogether: the world of words.

Goldman's start-up, Inform Technologies LLC, is a robotic librarian. Every day it combs through thousands of press articles and blog posts in English. It reads them and groups them with related pieces. Inform doesn't do this work alphabetically or by keywords. It uses algorithms to analyze each article by its language and context. It then sends customized news feeds to its users, who also exist in Inform's system as—you guessed it—math.

How do you convert written words into math? Goldman says it takes a combination of algebra and geometry. Imagine an object floating in space that has an edge for every known scrap of information. It's called a polytope and it has near-infinite dimensions, almost impossible to conjure up in our earthbound minds. It contains every topic written about in the press. And every article that Inform processes becomes a single line within it. Each line has a series of relationships.

 CASE STUDY Go to the *Introduction to Business* Online Learning Center through **glencoe.com** for the *BusinessWeek* Reader Case Study.

Active Learning

Ciphers are another method of turning words into math. One of the simplest types of ciphers turns each letter into a corresponding number. ASCII (pronounced askey) code is just such a cipher type—and is the way computers and communications devices process words. Research the ASCII code symbols and write your name in ASCII code.

318   **Chapter 18**   Technology in the Workplace   glencoe.com

BusinessWeek *Reader and Case Study*

Math Will Rock Your World

 CASE STUDY Have students go to the *Introduction to Business* Online Learning Center through **glencoe.com** to download a Case Study activity that corresponds to the article. The activity and answer key are also available on the TeacherWorks Plus CD.

Active Learning

Answers should be composed of a string of ones and zeroes. Each letter in ASCII code is eight characters long, so the answer should contain a multiple of eight digits.

Science/Tech TRENDS

Ergonomics

Ergonomics is the understanding of how the interaction of humans and other elements in a system or setting affects people's health. The study of ergonomics goes back to the 1700s, when Italian physician Bernardino Ramazzinni published "De Morbis Artificum (Diseases of Workers)." During World War II, ergonomics was first used in the design of products to reduce workplace medical issues. At that time, ergonomically designed cockpit controls were invented and greatly reduced the sort of pilot error that led to plane crashes. In the time since WWII, the study of ergonomics has grown a great deal. With so many people using computers today, new health challenges have surfaced. It is the task of the designers to create technological tools that not only accomplish their purpose but also keep us healthy.

Web Quest

Go to the *Introduction to Business* Online Learning Center through **glencoe.com** for links to Web sites where you can research the different ways that ergonomics can be applied in the design of products. Look at examples of things in various fields. Write a few paragraphs about how items are designed ergonomically and the health concerns they are intended to affect.

Who Sets Standards for the Internet? The Internet is not owned or controlled by any one person or country. The World Wide Web Consortium (W3C) is an international association in which member organizations, a full-time staff, and the public work together to develop Web standards. The group oversees research and sets standards and **guidelines** for many areas of the Internet. More than 500 organizations from around the world are members of W3C.

The Web connects sources of information. However, there are too many Web sites for people to visit. To access the information they need, computer users use Web browsers and search engines.

A **Web browser** is a program used for displaying and viewing pages on the Web. The inclusion of design, graphics, and sound on the Web makes it more enjoyable to *surf*, or search for information. Browsers include Mozilla Firefox®, Netscape®, and Microsoft Internet Explorer®. A **search engine** is a computer program that can produce a list of documents related to a given topic. Users find information that they need by giving the search engine a key word. The search engine then sifts through countless Web pages and creates a list of documents related to the key word. Some search engines are Yahoo!®, MSN®, and Lycos®.

glencoe.com
Section 18.2 Internet Basics 319

Science/Tech TRENDS

Web Quest

 Activity correlates to Science standards.

Ergonomics Answers will vary. For example, some office chairs are designed to prevent back strain. Computer keyboards and mouse pads are made to prevent carpal tunnel syndrome.

RETEACH

W **Writing Support**

Enrichment

Managing Technology Threats Some hackers are only interested in demonstrating their abilities and vulnerabilities of systems. Ask students to write a short essay about if and how hackers should be punished. (Some may suggest that they provide a service by identifying security problems. Others might feel that hackers should be punished but that their crimes are not as bad as hackers who steal or destroy data.)

R **Reading Strategy**

Explain Ask students to explain, in their own words, how cookies work. (The information resides on the user's hard drive.)

U **Universal Access**

Creative Learners Have students work in groups to create a skit based on the information in the photo and caption about "Computer Protection."

✔ **Reading Check**

Contrast An intranet is closed to public access. An extranet is a semi-private network.

● **As You Read**

Cookies are a form of tracking users. They give personalized aspects to Web sites.

Student Activity Workbook ☞ Assign the Section 18.2 Activities.

320

Real World

Collaboration Software Many businesspeople find they can communicate better with their customers and employees using collaboration software. WebEx™, Microsoft's Live Meeting®, and IBM Lotus Sametime® are some types of this software. *What do you think are some advantages of collaboration software?*

● **As You Read**

Think about how cookies affect you when you surf the Internet.

Intranets and Extranets

Unlike the Internet, an intranet is closed to access by the public. An **intranet** is a computer network used by an organization. It works like the Internet, but its access is restricted to **authorized** users. A company might keep its employee directory and code of ethics on an intranet. An **extranet** is an extension of the intranet of a company or organization. It gives authorized users controlled access to the intranet. This semi-private network allows more than one company to access the same information. With an extranet, companies can share information and collaborate.

✔ **Reading Check** **Contrast** What is the difference between an intranet and an extranet?

Managing Technology Threats

Privacy and security risks are threats to users of computer technology. A **hacker** is a person who illegally gains access to and sometimes tampers with information in a computer system. Internet users are especially open to security risks. To avoid privacy and security threats, do not click on pop-up ads unless you know and trust the company. These ads may not be secure.

W

Privacy Issues

Companies use software tools to track computer users online. Many Web sites that users visit send cookies to their computer. **Cookies** are bits of information about a computer user that are stored on that computer's hard drive. The information is accessed by a server when the user revisits a Web site. Users who visit online stores can have their personal information stored even if they do not buy anything. Some computer users see cookies as a convenience. Others see them as an invasion of privacy. Those who do not want companies to store and use their personal information must **reject** or delete cookies.

R

● **Computer Protection** As more companies' computer networks are connected to the Internet, the need for computer security has become increasingly important. **What types of protection does this software offer?**

U

Real World

Collaboration Software Ability to manage projects, gain access to databases, reach distant clients or workers, hold videoconferences, and have group interaction.

Discuss the Photo

● **Computer Protection** Specialized computer software is designed to protect computers against hackers. Programs like this work to isolate viruses, worms, and Trojan Horses before they can damage a computer or the files on it.

Protection for Data A computer **virus** is a program that can **insert** copies of itself into a computer without the user's knowledge, often damaging stored data. Viruses are a problem for computer users. They may do little harm, or they may destroy computer files. A worm is a special virus that invades a computer network and multiplies itself as it spreads throughout the network. Security programs such as anti-virus software protect against different types of viruses. New viruses are created every day, so updates of anti-virus software must be installed regularly.

Spyware is software that tracks what a user does on the Internet. Users can download free software or buy special software to prevent spyware. Some software packages offer several kinds of protection.

Software packages can protect users from other types of security threats. A *firewall* is computer software that prevents unauthorized access to system software or data on a user's computer. It acts as a security wall between your computer and the Internet. Firewalls can also reduce spam. *Spam* is unwanted e-mail.

A security breach occurs when someone manages to obtain unauthorized access to your system. Finding and fixing the security breach can be time-consuming and costly.

N C L B Activity correlates to English Language Arts standards.

Section 18.2
After You Read

Review Key Concepts
1. How would you describe the Internet and the World Wide Web?
2. How does a search engine work?
3. How can a computer user protect against spam, viruses, worms, and spyware?

Academic Skills
4. **English Language Arts** Choose a type of technology that is important to business such as cell phones, telecommuting, WiFi, wearable computers, or expert systems. Research the technology so that you can describe how it is used in a business setting, the solutions it offers, and how you think it will develop in the future. Present a brief oral presentation or write a three- or four-paragraph paper about your topic.

5. **English Language Arts** Imagine that the company you work for has grown, and your manager has decided to switch from an older system of independent computers to one in which each worker's computer is linked to a network with Internet access. Write a list of the advantages a network offers and the precautions to take to keep company information secure.

 Go to the *Introduction to Business* Online Learning Center through **glencoe.com** to check your answers.

Section 18.2

Review Key Concepts
1. The Internet is a global computer network of interconneted documents and files.
2. It looks through countless Web pages and creates a content index for each.
3. install firewall software, anti-virus, and spyware-protection software

Academic Skills
4. **English Language Arts** Responses will vary, but encourage students to be creative in this project.
5. **English Language Arts** Benefits: file sharing, ready access to shared information. Precautions: controlling access to sensitive information.

RETEACH (cont.)

C Critical Thinking
Explain
Protection for Data Ask students to explain why an individual or group would want to install spyware on personal and business computers. Are there legitimate uses for spyware? (A business might install spyware to track employees' Internet activities to make sure they are not wasting company time with personal shopping, playing games, or looking at inappropriate content.)

ASSESS

After You Read
Have students complete the Section 18.2 After You Read section review.

Online Study Tools
Have students go to the Online Learning Center through **glencoe.com** to:
- Take the Section 18.2 **Practice Test**.
- Download free **Study-to-Go** content to their PDAs or cell phones.

STUDY TO GO

CLOSE

Culminating Activity
Create a Brochure
Have students work in pairs to create a brochure for new computer users based on the information in this section. Encourage students to be creative while providing basic information. (Some students might focus on defining terms and others might use a FAQ format.)

Vocabulary Review

1. Students should write complete sentences using each term correctly.

Review Key Concepts

2. Information technology enables workers to create, process, store, and communicate information.

3. See answer on p. 311.

4. The Internet is a global computer network that connects many computer networks.

5. Many kinds of software can be used to protect computer systems and information.

Critical Thinking

6. Answers may vary. One of the risks is that strangers will intercept their communications and use the information they gather in ways that harm users.

7. Companies often are able to reduce office space. It allows people without transportation, and people with physical disabilities or illnesses, or who live in remote areas, to work.

8. With more robots and tools to do work that was once done by people, many manufacturing plants need fewer workers. Jobs require highly skilled people. Many jobs are not available to people without technical skills.

Section 18.1 *Summary*

Information Technology Information technology (IT) has changed the way business is done. Computers are an important part of IT. So are telephones, fax machines, PDAs, and other handheld devices. Wireless technology lets people with a wireless-enabled computer or PDA connect to the Internet. E-mail lets them communicate with others electronically. Wearable computers help workers to become more mobile. All of these technologies enable business to be done more quickly and easily. Telecommuting can help employees decrease their travel time. Virtual training lets people simulate real situations using a computer to help them learn new tasks.

Section 18.2 *Summary*

Internet Basics The Internet connects many computer networks. It allows information to flow freely around the world. The World Wide Web is part of the Internet. The Web consists of stored files and images. A Web browser is a program that displays Web pages. Users find information they need by giving key words to a search engine, which produces a list of Web pages related to the key words. Some companies use intranets and extranets as ways of communicating with their employees. Computers can be threatened by privacy and security risks. Security programs such as anti-virus software protect against threats.

Vocabulary Review

1. On a sheet of paper, use each of these key terms and academic vocabulary terms in a sentence.

Key Terms		Academic Vocabulary
information technology (IT)	Web browser	transmit
telecommunications	search engine	automatic
telecommuting	intranet	simulate
wearable computer	extranet	visual
computer-aided design (CAD)	hacker	guidelines
virtual reality	cookies	authorized
Internet	virus	reject
World Wide Web		insert

Review Key Concepts

2. Describe the role of information technology in business.

3. Identify ways that technology has changed the workplace.

4. Describe the Internet and its components.

5. Identify tools for managing threats when using the Internet.

---

9. Orders that are placed and received electronically do not require a paper trail. Electronic transfer lets companies save on postage and delivery costs. Communication is fast, bills can be paid, and money can be transferred quickly. It also helps the environment.

10. Virtual reality is used in architecture and construction. Changes in design can be explored before they become final. Virtual reality is also used in video games.

11. To track an online order, a number of technologies are necessary. The buyer uses the Internet to go to the company's Web site, accessing it with a tracking number they received by e-mail. Computers and scanners keep track of the parcel.

Critical Thinking

6. Wireless technology, which makes it possible to transfer information without cables, is less secure than wired technology. What risks do people take when they use wireless technology?

7. What are some reasons why a company might encourage an employee to telecommute?

8. How is the workforce affected by technical advances developed for manufacturing processes?

9. The electronic transfer of information has replaced much of the paper used in offices. What are some benefits of using less paper in the office?

10. Virtual reality is used by business for training. What is another way that virtual reality is used?

11. What kinds of technology are involved in tracking an online order?

12. Computer users can delete cookies from their machines. When do you think you would delete cookies?

13. Suppose you are hired to work in an office that uses the latest technology related to its business. How would you prepare to use new technology?

Write About It

14. With mobile technology, workers can be in touch with their workplace all the time. Write an e-mail to your teacher about the pros and cons of mobile technology.

15. Research the work of a computer software engineer. Write a one-page report that describes this career.

16. Look up future trends in technology that will affect the workplace. Write a 500-word article for your school newspaper on the impact some of these trends may have on the business world.

17. People who work with computers in business are often referred to as knowledge workers. Write at least two paragraphs describing the relationship between computers and knowledge in business.

18. Telephones are often used in customer service. Write a skit that involves using the telephone to resolve a customer complaint. Present your skit in class.

19. Research the different types of electronic communications that businesses use, including videoconferencing and telephone conferencing. Write a one-page report on your findings.

Technology Applications

Research Security Software

20. Using the Internet, research companies that provide security software packages. These companies include Symantec®, McAfee®, Trend Micro™, and Kaspersky Lab®. Use the information you collect to develop a database of software information. Include prices and facts about the types of security risks each company's products address.

Business Ethics

Ethical Computer Use

21. Explain why the following statements about the ethical use of computers are true. (1) Computer users should respect the privacy of other users' computer files. (2) You do not have a right to share software with your friends. (3) It is your responsibility to secure your computer. (4) Information on a Web site does not always belongs to the Web site owner.

Critical Thinking

12. To stop pop-up ads, or if personal information changes. Cookies contain data that will appear the next time you visit the Web site.

13. Ask co-workers. Read manuals. Check for online tutorials on software and work-related tasks. Investigate training options.

Write About It

14. Pros: Workers are constantly connected to their workplace. Cons: Being in constant contact with the office can be stressful.

15. It is one of the fastest-growing occupations. Engineers design, develop, test, and evaluate software and computer systems. It requires using math and logic extensively.

16. Answers should address growth, power, software advances, and portability in new technology.

17. A knowledge worker creates information that can be used to make business decisions.

18. Skits will vary but should communicate the issues discussed in the text.

19. Reports should discuss various types of mass communication and their uses, including videoconferencing and telecommunication.

Technology Applications

20. Answers will vary but should include prices and facts regarding a company's security package.

Business Ethics

21. (1) Hackers do damage to other users' data. (2) Software makers can restrict the ability to share software. (3) You must choose the type of protection that meets your needs. (4) Web sites often contain material that is copyrighted, patented, or trademarked.

Applying Academics to Business

22. Definitions should be complete and include facts about origins.

23. 9×10^8 or 900,000,000

24. Microsoft Internet Explorer, a Web browser, is a program that makes it easier to search for information on the Internet.

Expert systems, applications that store the kind of knowledge that humans use, are used in many businesses.

25. Minimum Area = $3.14 \times 0.5^2 =$ 0.785 square miles

Maximum Area = $3.14 \times 5^2 =$ 78.5 square miles

Active Learning

26. Answers could include a statement about the importance of computers and networks in business. Employees could be restricted from opening spam. Other restrictions: no personal Web browsing while working, or viewing of explicit material.

Business in the Real World

27. Summaries might discuss changes caused by information technology; an estimate of expenses for new computers and software; or ways the Internet is used to research prices, order supplies, and accept orders. The owner may use e-mail to contact suppliers and customers.

Applying Academics to Business

English Language Arts

22. As new technologies come into use, new words are added to the English language to describe them. Below are several terms that have come into common usage in recent years. Write a definition for each, and tell something about its origin.

blog   dodgy   domain   hot spot

Mathematics

23. An executive at a large telecommunications company claimed that $1.9 billion in operating expenses could be saved if the company merged with a competitor. What is the place value of the 9 in 1.9 billion? Write your answer in two ways.

THEORY **Place Value** In the base 10 number system we use most often, each place in a number has a value that is a power of 10. The value of a number in the ones place is 10^0; the value of a number in the tens place is 10^1; the value of a number in the hundreds place is 10^2, and so on.

English Language Arts

24. An appositive describes words or phrases that refer to the same person or thing and have the same relationship to other parts of the sentence. Combine each pair of sentences below by using an appositive. Use commas correctly.

Microsoft Internet Explorer is a program that makes it easier to search for information on the Internet. Microsoft Internet Explorer is a Web browser.

Expert systems are applications that store the kind of knowledge that humans use. Expert systems are used in many businesses.

Mathematics

25. A cell tower has an effective range of between 0.5 mile and 5 miles. What is the minimum and maximum coverage area for the cell tower?

THEORY **Area** The range represents the radius and is the distance from the center of a circle to any point on the circle. To find the minimum and maximum areas, find the area of the circles. The area of a circle can be found using the formula $A = \pi r^2$.

Active Learning

Create a Computer-Use Policy

26. Many companies develop a policy on the personal use of computers at work. Rules that restrict workers from visiting certain Web sites or downloading software help to protect computer networks from security risks. Pair up with a classmate. Imagine that you are the co-owners of a small delivery service. Write a policy on employees' use of computers at work. Be sure to consider telecommuters.

Business in the Real World

Technology's Effect on Business

27. Interview a small-business owner in your community to learn how technology affects his or her business. What changes have been made because of information technology? What additional expenses were incurred? Is the Internet used for business? If so, how? After the interview, prepare a summary of your results, and share it with your class.

ExamView Assessment Suite **CD** allows you to print out ready-made unit and chapter tests, complete with answer keys. You can also create customized tests.

TeacherWorks Plus provides complete teacher resources in one convenient package. It includes customizable lesson plans in calendar format, and instant access to many print program resources.

 *skills*

TELECOMMUTING HABITS AND SKILLS

28. Some employees choose to telecommute. Telecommuters usually work at home at least one day a week. Create a list of habits and skills that you think are important to a technical writer who telecommutes. Include the personal characteristics and technical skills that would be important for someone who works at home. Be prepared to share your list in class.

FIND YOUR DREAM JOB

29. Go to the *Introduction to Business* Online Learning Center through **glencoe.com** for a link to the Occupational Outlook Handbook Web site. Click on the "OOH Search/A-Z Index" link and enter the job title "computer systems analysts." Then write a one-page report about this type of occupation. Conclude your report with a list of things you could do now to prepare yourself to pursue the occupation.

 *Role Play*

USING THE INTERNET SAFELY

30. Situation You have been asked to give a short presentation to a group of consumers about proper procedures for shopping online. Most of your audience members have not used the Internet for online shopping.

Activity Prepare an outline of your presentation, stressing ways to use the Internet. Give your audience some "do's and don'ts" about Internet use.

Evaluation You will be evaluated on how well you meet the following performance indicators:

- Explain the advantages and disadvantages of shopping online.
- Explain concepts such as security software, a secure Web site, a Web site shopping cart, cookies, and online payment.
- List at least three guidelines to follow when shopping online.
- Prepare a written outline of your presentation.

Standardized Test Practice

Directions Choose the letter of the best answer. Write the letter for the answer on a separate piece of paper.

1. Which is a synonym for *virtual*?

A   secondary

B   actual

C   precise

D   near

 TEST-TAKING TIP Real learning occurs through studying that takes place over a period of time. Relate the information you are learning to what you already know, and you will be better able to understand and retain it. Plan more than one review session.

 **READING** Go to the *Introduction to Business* Online Learning Center through **glencoe.com** for a list of outside reading suggestions.

 ## STRATEGIES FOR STANDARDIZED TEST PREP SUCCESS

Test Prep Help students tap into their knowledge base by using K-W-L charts when introducing a content area topic: *What I Know, What I Want to Learn,* and *What I Learned.* When reading literature, have students write about how characters or events in a story remind them of things in their own lives.

 *skills*

28. Personal characteristics: honesty, dependability. Skills: time management and organization; computer knowledge; good grammar, spelling, and writing.

Business CAREERS

29. Analysts solve computer problems and apply computer technology to meet the individual needs of an organization. Employees work in comfortable offices or labs. Telecommuting is common. Training required: Bachelor's degree in computer science, information science, or management information systems. Job outlook: stronger than average. As preparation, develop basic computer skills, take computer programming and business classes.

Role Play

30. Presentations should address the competencies noted in the Role Play. Advantages of shopping online include shopping at any time, and being able to compare products and services. Disadvantages include the possibility of overspending and relying on pictures and descriptions. Make the audience aware of security risks when shopping online.

Standardized Test Practice
1. D

Standards-Based Lesson Planning
Introduction to Business provides students with instruction and assessment in the following fundamental content areas:

Content Standards Correlations	
Relate the uses of computer applications to business and marketing.	pp. 334–337, 338–341
Demonstrate knowledge, skill, and application of information systems to accomplish job objectives and enhance personal performance in relation to the workplace.	pp. 329–332, 334–337, 338–341
Develop keyboarding skills to enter and manipulate text and data.	p. 341
Describe and use current and emerging computer technology and software to perform personal and business-related tasks.	pp. 332, 334–335, 337–341
Use reference materials such as online help, vendor bulletin boards, tutorials, and manuals available for application software.	pp. 339, 341
Research ways to troubleshoot problems with computer software, hardware, peripherals, and other office equipment.	p. 339
Discuss ergonomic principles applicable to the configuration of computer workstations.	pp. 330, 339
Select and use word-processing software to enhance written business communications.	p. 341
Use database, spreadsheet, presentation, scheduling, and integrated software packages to enhance communications.	pp. 334–337, 338–341
Create business and personal presentations using multimedia technology.	pp. 340–341
Outline the role of computers in business.	pp. 329–332
Describe ethical issues and problems associated with computers and information systems.	pp. 330, 339

NCLB
Activities, information, and skills practice will help your students attain No Child Left Behind proficiency. Students will improve their abilities in the following academic standards areas:

Academic Standards Correlations		
English Language Arts	Activities/Features	Page
NCTE 3 Apply strategies to interpret texts	Applying Academics to Business	p. 340
NCTE 7 Conduct research and gather, evaluate, and synthesize data to communicate discoveries	After You Read	p. 337
NCTE 11 Participate as members of literacy communities	After You Read	p. 337
Mathematics		
Geometry Analyze characteristics and properties of two- and three-dimensional geometric shapes and develop mathematical arguments about geometric relationships	Applying Academics to Business Standardized Test Practice	pp. 340, 341
Number and Operations Compute fluently and make reasonable estimates	Ask S&P	p. 326
Number and Operations Understand numbers, ways of representing numbers, relationships among numbers, and number systems	After You Read Applying Academics to Business	pp. 332, 340
Science		
Content Standard C Students should develop an understanding of the behavior of organisms	Science/Tech Trends	p. 335

Correlations This chart shows the 21ˢᵗ Century Skills, foundation skills, and workplace competencies that students develop as they work in this chapter.

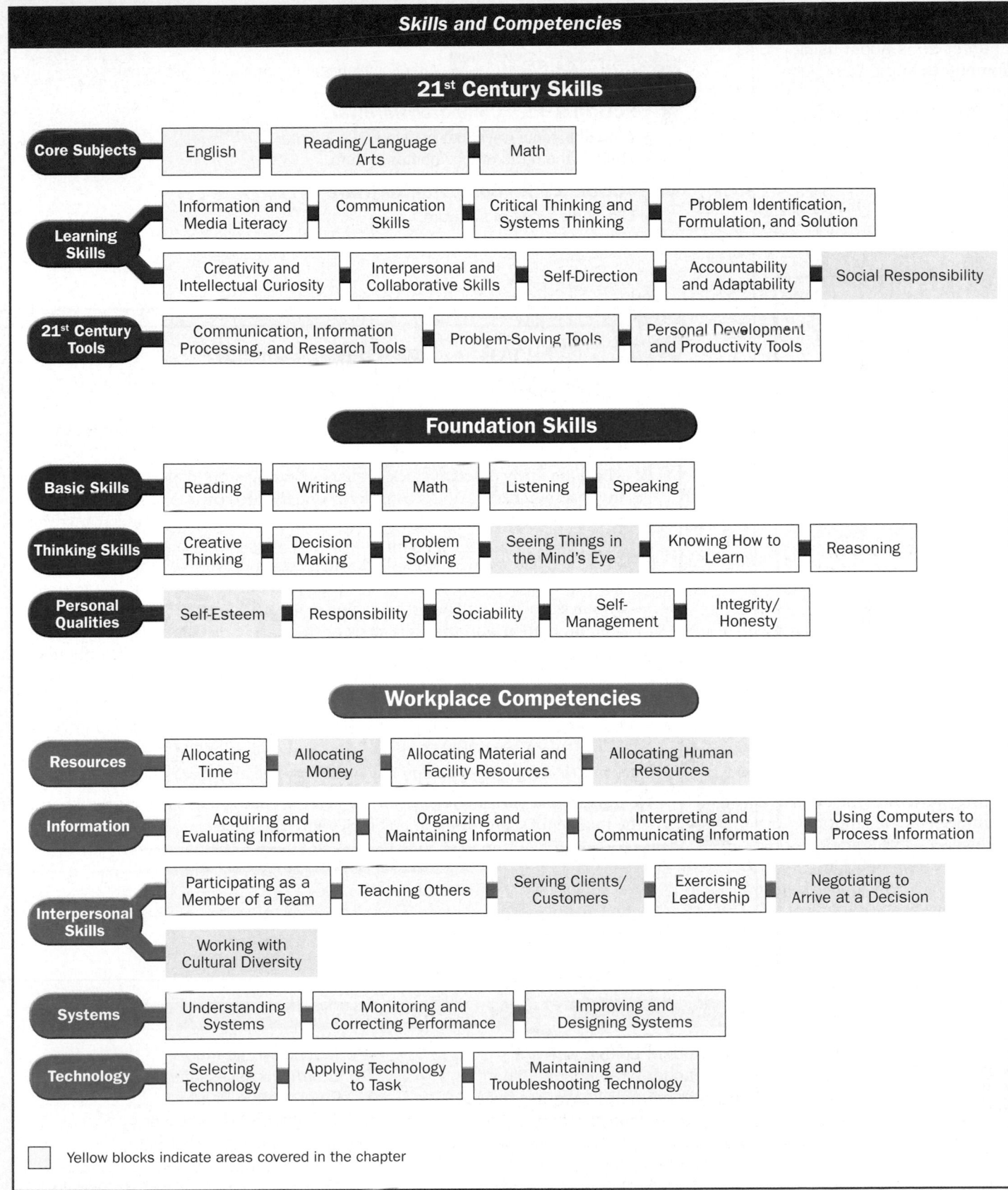

Skills and Competencies

21ˢᵗ Century Skills

Core Subjects — English | Reading/Language Arts | Math

Learning Skills — Information and Media Literacy | Communication Skills | Critical Thinking and Systems Thinking | Problem Identification, Formulation, and Solution

Creativity and Intellectual Curiosity | Interpersonal and Collaborative Skills | Self-Direction | Accountability and Adaptability | Social Responsibility

21ˢᵗ Century Tools — Communication, Information Processing, and Research Tools | Problem-Solving Tools | Personal Development and Productivity Tools

Foundation Skills

Basic Skills — Reading | Writing | Math | Listening | Speaking

Thinking Skills — Creative Thinking | Decision Making | Problem Solving | Seeing Things in the Mind's Eye | Knowing How to Learn | Reasoning

Personal Qualities — Self-Esteem | Responsibility | Sociability | Self-Management | Integrity/Honesty

Workplace Competencies

Resources — Allocating Time | Allocating Money | Allocating Material and Facility Resources | Allocating Human Resources

Information — Acquiring and Evaluating Information | Organizing and Maintaining Information | Interpreting and Communicating Information | Using Computers to Process Information

Interpersonal Skills — Participating as a Member of a Team | Teaching Others | Serving Clients/Customers | Exercising Leadership | Negotiating to Arrive at a Decision

Working with Cultural Diversity

Systems — Understanding Systems | Monitoring and Correcting Performance | Improving and Designing Systems

Technology — Selecting Technology | Applying Technology to Task | Maintaining and Troubleshooting Technology

Yellow blocks indicate areas covered in the chapter

Chapter 19

Computer Basics

Chapter Overview

Introduce the Chapter

Computer Basics
Chapter 19 is about using computers in the workplace.

Building Background

Most students know how to use a computer for certain activities, which provides a foundation for what they will learn in this chapter.

Ask STANDARD &POOR'S

>> *Math Answer*
You will buy 111 shares. You buy 30 shares in January ($180 ÷ $6 = 30), 36 shares in February ($180 ÷ $5 = 36), and 45 shares in March ($180 ÷ $4 = 45).

>> *Extension Activity*
You decide to increase your monthly investment to $200 on April 1.
You buy stock at the following prices: April, $5.00; May, $6.00; June, $6.50; July, $6.00; August, $6.50; September, $7.00; October, $7.00; November, $7.50; December, $8.00. How many shares of stock will you own at the end of the year? (388 shares. Divide your monthly investment by the stock price. The total number of shares is the sum of the quantities you purchased each month.)

Activity correlates to Math standards.

> **Chapter Objectives**   After completing this chapter, you will be able to:

▶ **Section 19.1** *Computer Hardware*
  • **Describe** some ways that people use computers.
  • **Identify** the parts of a computer system.

▶ **Section 19.2** *Computer Software*
  • **List** some types of software.

Ask STANDARD &POOR'S   **Stock Buying Strategies**

Q: What are some strategies I can use to acquire stocks if I'm investing for the long term?

A: There are many different stock strategies floating around out there. Value investing involves purchasing stocks considered undervalued by one or more fundamental measures. Growth investing focuses on companies that have quickly increased their earnings or revenues. Market-timing investors aggressively buy and sell based on their prediction of whether a stock will go up or down. For example, daytraders buy and sell with all activity occurring within a single day. But for a long-term investor, a strategy such as dollar cost averaging makes the most sense. You invest a fixed amount of money in the same stock or stocks on a regular basis. In this way you establish a position in a stock over a long, steady period of time. During that time, the stock price is likely to fluctuate, and you can take advantage of periods of weakness by buying more shares for the same amount of money.

Mathematics You are investing $180 each month in stock in the McKay Brick Company. The stock sells for $6 in January, and drops to $5 in February and $4 in March. How many shares do you buy over the three months?

> **THEORY** **Dollar Cost Averaging** Since you are spending a fixed amount each month, the number of shares you can buy varies with the price.

> **Classroom Resources**

- Student Edition
- Teacher Wraparound Edition
- Student Activity Workbook with Academic Integration
- Student Activity Workbook with Academic Integration TAE
- *Fast File*, Unit 6 Resources
- Inclusion in the Business Education Classroom

- TeacherWorks Plus
- *ExamView Assessment Suite*
- Presentation Plus!
- Vocabulary PuzzleMaker
- Interactive Student Edition
- Online Student Edition
- Online Learning Center with Podcasts

● **Computer Applications** Businesses use many different types of software applications. **What software applications do you use on your computer that a business might also use?**

Chapter 19 Computer Basics **327**

Introduce the chapter by reviewing the chapter objectives:

Section 19.1 *Objectives*
Describe some ways that people use computers. (Companies use computers to record information and keep track of records. Computers are used to research products and services, design products, prepare reports, and analyze sales figures. PDAs and other handheld devices are used to list appointments, phone numbers, and other data.)

Identify the parts of a computer system. (A computer system includes hardware, software, and data. Hardware includes processors, memory, input and output devices, and storage devices.)

Section 19.2 *Objectives*
List some types of software. (Major types of software include office suites with word-processing, spreadsheet, database management, and presentation programs. Other types are: desktop publishing programs; accounting programs; communication software; groupware; and Web site development programs.)

Discuss the Photo
● **Computer Applications** Read the caption on the photo to students: Businesses use many different types of software applications.

Ask students: What software applications do you use on your computer that a business might also use? (Answers will vary but are likely to include word-processing programs, e-mail, Internet browsers, spreadsheets, presentation software, and photo-editing software.)

FOCUS

Bell Ringer Activity

Computer Hardware
Show students a 3.5" disk that stores 1.44 megabytes of information or an older 5.25" floppy with 360-kilobyte capacity. Then show the most recent storage device you have, such as a 750-megabyte zip drive. Ask why it is easier to store and transport computer data today. (Although computer programs and files are much larger today, new devices have been created that allow vast amounts of data to be stored and transported with ease.)

Preteaching

Presentation Plus!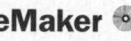
The Presentation Plus! CD provides visual teaching aids for this section.

PuzzleMaker
Use the Vocabulary PuzzleMaker to create a puzzle of the section's key terms. Students can complete the puzzle on paper or on a computer.

Graphic Organizer
Tell students to go to the Online Learning Center through **glencoe.com** for a printable graphic organizer. (Answers include: a computer's hardware system includes a processor, memory, input and output devices, and storage.)

Connects academics to content.

Computer Hardware

Reading Guide

Before You Read
Think about the ways you use computer systems for your personal use.

D

Read to Learn
- Describe some ways that people use computers.
- Identify the parts of a computer system.

The Main Idea
Each day, businesses and individuals use computers to perform different tasks. Desktop computers, laptops, tablet PCs, and handheld devices allow many tasks to be done easily and quickly. Hardware enables a computer system to function properly.

Key Concepts
- The Importance of Computers
- Parts of a Computer System

Vocabulary
Key Terms
computer
ergonomics
e-learning
hardware
random access memory (RAM)

Academic Vocabulary
You will find these words in your reading and on your tests. Make sure you know their meanings.

linked   element
quotes   random

Graphic Organizer
In a figure like the one below, list four components of a computer's hardware system.

Hardware

1. _____
2. _____
3. _____
4. _____

 Go to the *Introduction to Business* Online Learning Center through **glencoe.com** for a printable graphic organizer.

NCLB

Academic Standards
English Language Arts
  NCTE 1 Read texts to acquire new information
Mathematics
  Number and Operations Understand numbers, ways of representing numbers, relationships among numbers, and number systems

glencoe.com

Reading Guide

Before You Read
Students may use computers for homework, e-mail, and games.

D Develop Concepts
The Main Idea Ask students: How do you think businesses use computers? (Answers will vary. Students might suggest that businesses use computers for e-mail, word processing, financial records, customer databases, inventory records, etc. They also might know that computers are used in manufacturing and distribution.)

The Importance of Computers

People depend on computers to handle all kinds of tasks. When a person pays a bill online, buys gasoline, or withdraws money from a bank, computers handle the transactions. Computers also handle different tasks in the workplace. Businesses of all sizes use computers to collect data and keep track of records. Laptops and tablet PCs allow people to work outside the office. Handheld devices track appointments, telephone numbers, and other data. Most businesses consider computers to be essential.

Computers for Business

A **computer** is an electronic device that accepts, processes, stores, and outputs data at high speeds, based on programmed instructions. A *personal computer,* or PC, is a small computer that is intended to be used by one person. A *desktop computer* is a personal computer that is small enough to fit in an individual workspace. PCs and desktop computers are generally the same. Dell and Hewlett-Packard are two of the world's top PC makers. Apple is also a leading computer maker. Its Macintosh systems are personal computers, too. However, they are usually called "Macs" rather than PCs.

In most companies, computers are **linked** through either a central mainframe computer or a network. A *mainframe* is a fast, powerful computer with a large storage capacity. It can accommodate several users at the same time. Linking workstations allows users to share files, data, and printers, send e-mails, and access the Internet.

Computers in Marketing Nielsen Media Research® is the top media researcher in the United States. It is best known for its TV ratings. Nielsen uses small computers to gather data from 10,000 TV meters placed in U.S. homes. They record the viewing activities of participants and transmit these records nightly to Nielsen. *Why are computers important in this type of research?*

Digital Security Biometric devices such as this fingerprint reader can be used to limit access to computers and data. **How can these devices save time, too?**

Section 19.1 Computer Hardware **329**

TEACH (cont.)

S Skill Practice

Guided Practice

Paraphrase Ask students to paraphrase the content related to ergonomics. (Answers will vary according to each student's choice of words.) **L1**

Illustrate an Idea Ask students to create a drawing and use the labels "minimize" and "maximize" to illustrate ergonomics. (Illustrations should indicate the use of ergonomics to maximize productivity and minimize worker discomfort.) **L2**

Demonstrate Have students locate some suggestions for setting up an ergonomically correct computer workstation. (Demonstrations should include adjusting the chair, the computer screen, and the keyboard.) **L3**

ASSESS

Review Key Terms

Have students write sentences using each key term.

 **Study-to-Go** Have students go to the Online Learning Center through **glencoe.com** to download free **Study-to-Go** content to their PDAs or cell phones.

● As You Read

Answers will vary. Students should recognize that Macs are often used in creative jobs. Macs can handle large files. They use software such as Adobe Photoshop and Illustrator for creating designs.

❓ ETHICS in Business

Intellectual Property

■ **Critical Reading** Life is full of important decisions. Think about the kinds of decisions that you make as you read the question below.

You work in the human resources department of a large computer company. The company is developing a new software platform, but the developers are having problems working out the bugs, and the project is behind schedule. Your manager asked you to contact a friend who works in the information technology department of a competitor to see if she would be interested in joining your company. You find out that she is working on a secret project that's very similar and would surely be able to help you solve your problems.

■ **Decision Making** Is it appropriate to hire a competitor's employee who can help you solve a problem even if it means she will use your competitor's company secrets to do it? Explain your answer.

● As You Read

Think about special computers and how they might affect your work. If you worked in a graphic arts studio, what type of computer do you think you would need?

The Computer Workstation A well-organized computer workstation is important for both business and home use. **Ergonomics** are design factors for the workplace that are intended to maximize productivity by minimizing a worker's discomfort. Well-designed workstations can help workers reduce stress and avoid straining their eyes, neck, shoulders, and wrists. They also help to increase efficiency.

To create a safe and comfortable computer workstation:

S

- Place the tools you need most close to you.
- Place your monitor at or just below eye level and at arm's length.
- Keep your wrists straight when you type.
- Use a chair that is adjustable, and keep it at a height that suits you.
- Position your chair so that it supports your lower back.
- Keep your feet flat on the floor or on a footrest.

Computers as Learning Tools Businesses also use computers to provide workers with the information, tools, and training they need to do their job. **E-learning**, or electronic learning, is the process of learning online. For instance, a large insurance company uses a Web-based system to train new employees to handle **quotes** and claims. Some training companies specialize in online education and tutorials for workers. Training with simulation software lets employees practice new tasks at their own pace. With e-learning, workers can be trained in an efficient and cost-effective way.

❓ ETHICS in Business

Decision Making Answers should focus on the definition of intellectual property and the ethical issues involved. Have students think about what can be done to ensure intellectual property is secure.

Parts of a Computer System

A computer system includes three main parts: hardware, software, and data. The physical components of a computer system are the **hardware**. Computer systems include at least four hardware **elements**: a microprocessor; memory; input and output devices; and data storage devices. Computers control data made up of characters, sound, graphics, and numbers. Here is a closer look at the parts of the system.

> ✔ **Reading Check** **Identify** What are the three main parts of a computer system?

Microprocessors

A *microprocessor* is a small computer chip. It is the brain of a computer. It is also called the central processing unit (CPU), or microchip. A microprocessor receives instructions and carries them out at extremely high speeds. Each chip contains millions of circuits for data storage. A circuit is an electrical device that provides a path for the flow of electricity. Devices such as calculators, PDAs, electronic toys, and mobile phones also use computer chips.

Memory

Memory is hardware that stores information for instant retrieval and processing. It can be thought of as a kind of scratch pad. The computer uses its **random access memory (RAM)** to hold all the data and instructions required during operations. When a computer is using information, it stores it in **random** access memory. As long as your computer is on, the information remains in this temporary memory so that the computer can use it quickly. As soon as you turn off the computer, RAM loses information. For that reason, data storage devices are a very important part of a computer.

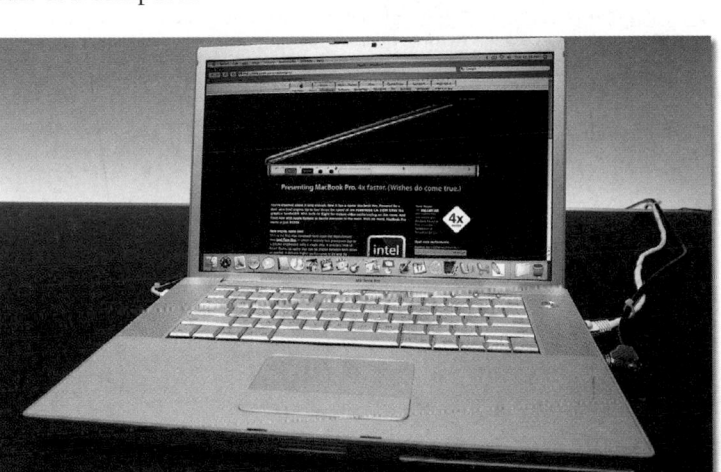

● **Portable Hardware** Laptop computers contain several hardware devices in a single product. **Where are the input devices on this computer? Where are the output devices?**

Section 19.1 Computer Hardware **331**

Discuss the Photo
● **Portable Hardware** The keyboard and touchpad are input devices. The screen and speakers are output devices.

RETEACH

W Writing Support
Enrichment
Input and Output Devices
Ask students to write an essay that compares the human brain to a microprocessor and to input and output devices. (Students may suggest that the abilities to process facts and reason are the microprocessor; the abilities to read, hear, or see data are input devices; and the abilities to write or speak are output devices.)

R Reading Strategy
Provide Examples Have students list devices that contain a microprocessor but are not personal computers. (Students may list devices such as calculators, MP3 players, automobiles, DVD players, TV sets, cell phones, and microwave ovens.)

U Universal Access
Hands-On Learners Have students identify all the visible parts of a computer system. Hands-on activities are especially important to some learners, but all students can benefit from this activity.

Student Activity Workbook 📂 Assign the Section 19.1 Activities.

> ✔ **Reading Check**

Identify The parts are hardware, software, and data.

RETEACH (cont.)

C Critical Thinking

Analogize
Memory Aids Ask students: What hardware and software would make it easy to quickly access information about everyone in the class? (Students may suggest a computer's RAM, a database program, and a data storage device.)

● As You Read
Students may use a computer mouse, an MP3 player, computer keyboard, or some other device.

ASSESS

● After You Read
Have students complete the Section 19.1 After You Read section review.

Online Study Tools
Have students go to the Online Learning Center through **glencoe.com** to:

- Take the Section 19.1 **Practice Test**.
- Download free **Study-to-Go** content to their PDAs or cell phones.

CLOSE

Culminating Activity
The Importance of Computers
Have students list the age and species of their pets. Write the results on the board. Discuss how a computer could sort the data.

● As You Read
Think about some input and output devices in your home or school and ways that you use them.

Input and Output Devices
An *input device* is hardware that is used for entering data into a machine, such as a computer. Input devices include keyboards, computer mice, touchpads, joysticks, and scanners. An *output device* is hardware that is used for producing results from a machine. Output devices include computer monitors, printers, fax machines, and speakers.

Data Storage Devices
C There are a variety of devices for storing large amounts of data. *Data storage devices*—which include hard drives, CD-ROM drives, and DVD drives—save information for later use. Portable storage devices are also popular because they can easily be moved from one machine to another. Disks, flash drives, and DVDs are widely used for portable storage. Data storage helps to protect important information. Data storage is measured in

- kilobytes (1,024 bytes),
- megabytes (1,024 kilobytes),
- gigabytes (1,024 megabytes), and
- terabytes (1,024 gigabytes).

N C L B Activity correlates to Math standards.

Section 19.1

● After You Read

Review Key Concepts
1. What are some ways that people use computers at work?
2. What are the parts of a computer system?
3. Name five data storage devices.

Academic Skills
4. **Mathematics** *Kilo-, mega-, giga-, tera-,* and *peta-* are prefixes used to note the quantity of something, such as a bit in computing. Sometimes called *prefix multipliers*, these prefixes can denote powers of 10. For example, bits per second is a measurement used to express the transmission rate of data. 1 kbps (1 kilobit per second) is 1×10^3 bits per second. Express 10^3, 10^4, and 10^5 as numbers in standard form.

THEORY **Exponents** An exponent tells how many times the base number is multiplied by itself.

 Math For math help, go to the Math Appendix.

@ Go to the *Introduction to Business* Online Learning Center through **glencoe.com** to check your answers.

Section 19.1

Review Key Concepts
1. Businesses of all sizes use computers to record data and keep track of records.
2. hardware, software, and data
3. hard drives, CD-ROM drives, DVD drives, disks, flash or thumb drives, and DVDs

Academic Skills
4. **Mathematics**
$10^3 = 1,000$
$10^4 = 10,000$
$10^5 = 100,000$

Computer Software

Reading Guide

● Before You Read
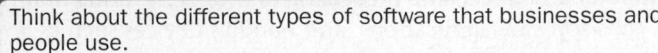
Think about the different types of software that businesses and people use.

Read to Learn
- List some types of software.

The Main Idea
Without software, a computer is just a collection of parts. Software tells a computer what to do. Programs such as word-processing and spreadsheet applications allow the creation of documents for business and personal use.

Key Concept
- Software Programs

Vocabulary

Key Terms

software	database management
operating system	presentation program
word processing	desktop publishing
spreadsheet	

@ Go to the *Introduction to Business* Online Learning Center through **glencoe.com** for a printable graphic organizer.

Academic Vocabulary
You will find these words in your reading and on your tests. Make sure you know their meanings.

creating	schedules
incorporate	facilitate

Graphic Organizer
In a figure like the one below, list and describe 10 different types of software.

Software	Purpose
1.	
2.	
3.	
4.	
5.	
6.	
7.	
8.	
9.	
10.	

D

NCLB

Academic Standards

English Language Arts

NCTE 1 Read texts to acquire new information

NCTE 4 Use written language to communicate effectively

NCTE 7 Conduct research and gather, evaluate, and synthesize data to communicate discoveries

NCTE 9 Develop an understanding of diversity in language use across cultures

NCTE 11 Participate as members of literacy communities

Science

Content Standard C Students should develop an understanding of the behavior of organisms

Reading Guide

● Before You Read
Students may mention word processing, presentation, or database software or other computer programs.

D Develop Concepts
The Main Idea Ask students: Where is software stored, and how does it get there? (It is stored on the computer's hard drive or on a network server. It may be installed by copying files from a CD or downloaded from the company's Web site.)

FOCUS

🔔 Bell Ringer Activity

Computer Software
Write 22, 267, 38, 90, 127, 302, 159, and 211 on the board. Tell students that the numbers were the sizes of one year's high school graduating class in a county in Michigan. Their task is to calculate the average size of a graduating class. (152 (1,216 ÷ 8). To get the answer, add the numbers to get a sum of 1,216 and divide the sum by 8.)

Preteaching

Presentation Plus!
The Presentation Plus! CD provides visual teaching aids for this section.

PuzzleMaker
Use the Vocabulary PuzzleMaker to create a puzzle of the section's key terms. Students can complete the puzzle on paper or on a computer.

Graphic Organizer
Tell students to go to the Online Learning Center through **glencoe.com** for a printable graphic organizer. (Answers will vary. Purposes will depend on the programs named.)

NCLB Activity connects academics to content.

Discussion Starter
Software Programs

Ask students: How many ways are there to bake a chocolate cake? Students are likely to know about recipes that use different types of chocolate or different amounts of flour, oil, or eggs. They may discuss baking from scratch or with a mix. Ask students to explain how these options are similar to and different from the options available from various software programs they can use to write a letter on a computer.

R Reading Strategy

Paraphrase Ask students to paraphrase the functions software programs perform that allow a computer to complete tasks. (Students should explain that software contains directions that tell a computer's microprocessor how to use data to complete a desired task, including composing written documents, completing mathematical calculations, or creating an image.)

As You Read

Students may cite Word® for word processing and report writing, PowerPoint® for presentations, iTunes® for music, or Mail® for e-mail.

As You Read

Think about some software programs that you use.

Software Programs

R Computers are just machines. They cannot do anything without instruction from people. **Software** is a computer program that contains a set of instructions that tells a computer what to do. Software is also referred to as a program or an application. Some software programs tell a computer how to calculate numbers or arrange words.

Operating Systems

An **operating system** is software that controls the operation of a computer and directs the processing of programs. It maintains files, runs software applications, and handles devices such as a computer mouse and printer. The most widely used operating system is Microsoft Windows®. Windows-based PCs are used in most businesses and perform many tasks, such as **creating** word processing documents, presentations, and spreadsheets. Apple uses its own operating system, called OS X. Newer Macs can also run using the Windows operating system. Macs are often used to create graphic designs and illustrations.

BusinessWeek *Reader and Case Study*

Digital Books Start a New Chapter

Lighter devices, better displays, and the iPod craze could make them best-sellers

Richard D. Warren, a 58-year-old lawyer in California, is halfway through Ken Follett's novel *Jackdaws*. But he doesn't bother carrying around the book itself. Instead, he has a digital version of Follett he reads on his Palm® Treo™ each morning as he commutes by train to San Francisco from his home in Berkeley. He's a big fan of such digital books. Usually, there are around seven titles on his Treo, and he buys at least two new ones each month. "It's just so versatile," he says. "I've tried to convert some friends to this, but they think it's kind of geeky."

Geeky? For now, maybe, but not for much longer. Many experts are convinced that digital books, after plenty of false starts, are finally ready for takeoff. "Every other form of media has gone digital—music, newspapers, movies," says Joni Evans, a top literary agent who just left the William Morris Agency® to start her own company that will focus on books and technology. "We're the only industry that hasn't lived up to the pace of technology. A revolution is around the corner."

 CASE STUDY Go to the *Introduction to Business* Online Learning Center through **glencoe.com** for the *BusinessWeek* Reader Case Study.

Active Learning

For thousands of years, people have been making books based on stories about their lives. Write a story of at least 500 words. Print it on both sides of several sheets of paper and staple them together so that it can be read as a book. Present the book to a family member.

BusinessWeek *Reader and Case Study*

Digital Books Start A New Chapter

 CASE STUDY Have students go to the *Introduction to Business* Online Learning Center through **glencoe.com** to download a Case Study activity that corresponds to the article. The activity and answer key are also available on the TeacherWorks Plus CD.

Active Learning

Student stories will vary, and students' skill at printing and binding their books will also vary. This activity is intended to encourage student creativity.

Office Suites

A *suite* is a collection of integrated application programs or software applications that works as a single program. In a suite, each program can **incorporate** data from the others, eliminating the need to re-enter or transfer data. An office suite usually includes word-processing, spreadsheet, database management, presentation, and communications software. Microsoft Office, Lotus® SmartSuite®, Corel® WordPerfect Office®, and Sun Microsystems™ StarOffice are office suites.

✓ Reading Check **Define** What is a suite?

S

Application Programs Application programs handle different tasks. Each type of application program performs a specific function for the user. **Word processing** is the writing, editing, and production of documents, such as letters and reports, through the use of a computer program. Word-processing software, such as Microsoft Word, is used to create, edit, and print documents. A **spreadsheet** program is a computerized worksheet for entering and charting data. Sales figures, quantities, prices, and production costs can be listed and compared with a spreadsheet.

Science/Tech TRENDS

Heads-Up Display

A Heads-Up display, or HUD as it is commonly known, is any display that doesn't alter the user's view when it displays data. HUD was first used in military aircraft but can now be seen in a wide variety of applications. Many games include HUDs. One example is the speedometers and instrument panels on the screen in racing games. The two types of HUD are fixed and helmet-mounted. The fixed type would typically be mounted to a surface such as an aircraft's airframe. The helmet-mounted display moves with the user's head. The user must wear a helmet or other headgear that is secured to the head. Two characteristics of any HUD are that the image is transparent, and the information is projected with its focus at infinity, which allows users to change their focus of attention between the data and the outside world without having to refocus their eyes.

Web Quest

Go to the *Introduction to Business* Online Learning Center through **glencoe.com** for links to Web sites where you can research different applications of Heads-Up displays. Look for ways HUD has helped the industries in which they are used. Write a few paragraphs describing what you find.

glencoe.com

TEACH (cont.)

S Skill Practice
Guided Practice
Define Ask students to write a definition of word-processing, spreadsheet, and database management programs. (Word-processing software: create, edit, and print documents. Spreadsheet program: computerized worksheet for entering and charting data. Database management program: stores data for rapid search and retrieval.) **L1**

Provide Examples Ask students to describe a situation in which the use of a presentation program would be appropriate. (Students will discuss various situations in which the use of presentation software would be appropriate.) **L2**

Illustrate Have students illustrate functions of a software suite and indicate how the functions work together. (Student illustrations should show the different types of software programs and how they relate to each other.) **L3**

ASSESS

Review Key Terms
Have students write sentences using each key term.

 Study-to-Go Have students go to the Online Learning Center through **glencoe.com** to download free **Study-to-Go** content to their PDAs or cell phones.

 Activity correlates to Science standards.

✓ Reading Check
Define A suite is a collection of integrated application programs or software that works as a single program.

Science/Tech TRENDS
Web Quest
Heads-Up Display Answers might describe how HUD has affected the aviation industry and medicine.

335

RETEACH

As You Read

Think about how you could create a presentation without presentation software.

A **database management** program is used to store data organized especially for rapid search and retrieval. With database software, lists can be updated, changed, or rearranged.

A **presentation program** includes software for creating slide shows for presentations. Data from word-processing documents and spreadsheets can be put into graphs, charts, or figures as part of a presentation.

Desktop publishing software is used to produce publications such as reports, newsletters, and magazines. A user can write, design, and lay out documents on a computer like a professional publisher. Users can create high-quality publications with art and illustrations. Desktop publishing software can be a part of an office suite. Adobe® InDesign® and QuarkXPress® are desktop publishing software packages. The illustration below shows some of the options available in Microsoft Office Publisher, which is also used for desktop publishing.

There are many other types of software that businesses depend on in their day-to-day operations. *Accounting software* helps people keep accurate records and prepare reports. Intuit® QuickBooks® is a well-known accounting program. *Communications software* allows access to databases, accounts, **schedules**, and other shared files. It makes it possible for computers to communicate or transfer files. With communications software, users can receive faxes and voice mail directly on their computer. Microsoft Outlook® is a communications program. *Speech recognition software* allows a user to enter text and give commands to the computer by speaking into a microphone. Philips® SpeechExec Pro® is a speech recognition program.

● **Software Options**
Many software programs come with preformatted templates for you to customize. **What software templates have you used?**

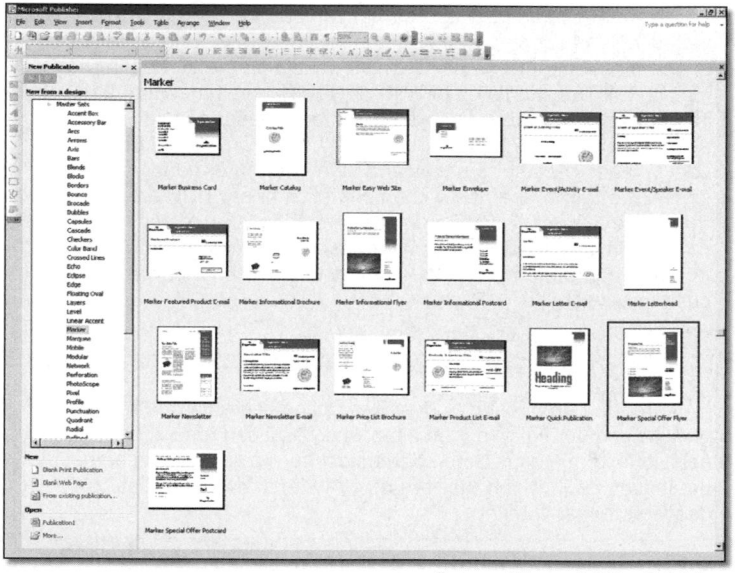

Source: Microsoft Office Publisher

● **As You Read**

Point out that desktop publishing software enables users to create professional-looking publications.

Discuss the Photo

● **Software Options** Answers will vary but may include various kinds of presentation software, including software used to build Web pages.

Groupware

Groupware is project management software. It provides tools for groups of users on a computer network to plan, develop, and complete a project. Team members on the same network can use groupware to track costs, schedules, and tasks for a project.

There are three categories of groupware: communication tools, conferencing tools, and collaborative management (or coordination) tools. Communication tools send messages, files, data, or documents between people. Examples include e-mail, faxing, voice mail, and Web publishing. Conferencing tools also **facilitate** the sharing of information, but in a more interactive way. Internet forums, chat rooms, and videoconferencing are conferencing tools. Collaborative management tools facilitate and manage group activities. They include electronic calendars (or time management software) and project management software.

Web Site Development Programs

The Internet plays an important part in many businesses' ability to reach consumers around the world. Web pages make it possible for companies to market their goods and services globally. Web site development programs allow users to choose from several templates or designs, or to customize their site according to their needs. Macromedia Dreamweaver® and Microsoft Front-Page® are Web site development programs.

Collaborative Software Lotus Notes® is a popular groupware program. It integrates work on a single project by several computer users at separate workstations. By planning an entire project for workers, the software makes it possible to complete the project more efficiently. *How does communications software differ from collaborative software?*

Activity correlates to English Language Arts standards.

Predict
Groupware Ask students to describe a situation in which using groupware would be helpful. (Answers will vary. Students might mention a situation in which many people had to perform multiple steps and meet deadlines.)

Collaborative Software Communications software can be used to meet individual needs. Collaborative software provides tools for groups of users to work together.

ASSESS

● After You Read

Have students complete the Section 19.2 After You Read section review.

Online Study Tools
Have students go to the Online Learning Center through **glencoe.com** to:

• Take the Section 19.2 **Practice Test**.
• Download free **Study-to-Go** content to their PDAs or cell phones.

CLOSE

Culminating Activity
Write a Proposal
Have students write a proposal to buy a computer system with cost estimates. (Proposals should include the basic components of a computer system.)

Section 19.2

● *After You Read*

Review Key Concepts
1. What is software?
2. Name three types of software programs and their purposes.
3. What kind of software is useful for managing team projects?

Academic Skills
4. **English Language Arts** Locate and read a review of a software program commonly used in or designed for use in business. Write a one-paragraph summary of the review. Explain what the software is designed to do, describe its positive and negative characteristics, and tell whether the reviewer recommends the software.

5. **English Language Arts** Work in groups of four. Choose a category of software. List four to six popular software programs that fit within the category you have chosen. Use software to create a chart showing cost, features, benefits, and the availability of each program.

 Go to the *Introduction to Business* Online Learning Center through **glencoe.com** to check your answers.

Section 19.2

Review Key Concepts
1. a computer program that tells a computer what to do
2. Answers will vary, depending on the software programs selected.
3. Groupware is useful for managing team projects.

Academic Skills
4. **English Language Arts** Students' writing should focus on the main ideas presented in the article.
5. **English Language Arts** Students' charts will vary but should include the information described in the activity.

Section 19.1 *Summary*

Computer Hardware People and businesses depend on computers to handle all kinds of tasks. Computers record data and keep track of records. Businesses also use them to provide workers with the information, tools, and training they need to do their jobs. Many people use a personal computer at home and at work, where they may be part of a network. A computer system includes three main parts: hardware, software, and data. Its physical components make up the hardware. The four hardware elements found in each computer system—a processor; memory; input and output devices; and storage devices—enable a computer to function as needed.

Section 19.2 *Summary*

Computer Software A computer needs instructions to perform tasks. Software tells it what to do. There are many different types of software. An operating system is software that controls the operation of a computer. It maintains files, runs software applications, and handles devices such as computer mice and printers. Application programs handle specific task-oriented functions. Word-processing software is used to create, edit, and print documents. Spreadsheet software is an electronic worksheet for entering and charting data. These and other forms of software allow users to do certain tasks easily and quickly.

Vocabulary Review

1. On a sheet of paper, use each of these key terms and academic vocabulary terms in a sentence.

Key Terms

computer
ergonomics
e-learning
hardware
random access memory (RAM)
software

operating system
word processing
spreadsheet
database management
presentation program
desktop publishing

Academic Vocabulary

linked
quotes
elements
random

creating
incorporate
schedules
facilitate

Review Key Concepts

2. Describe some ways that people use computers.

3. Identify the parts of a computer system.

4. List some types of software.

Critical Thinking

5. You will probably have difficulty finding a job that is right for you.

6. Users should back up important files and store the backup safely.

7. They allow computer users to communicate and share information, but participants have to schedule a time to meet. Some participants make inappropriate or discourteous comments.

8. Help workers reduce stress and increase efficiency and productivity.

9. Just as the brain controls the body, a microprocessor receives information and processes it, sending messages throughout the computer.

10. E-learning lets businesses train people in an efficient and cost-effective way, so it is likely to be used more in the future.

Critical Thinking

5. If you leave high school with very few computer skills, what problems might you face in the future?

6. What advice would you give users about protecting information on their computer?

7. A *chat room* is a form of groupware that lets computer users communicate instantly. What are some advantages and disadvantages of using chat rooms?

8. What can companies that make computer hardware and other items do to improve ergonomics?

9. Why is a microprocessor called the "brain of a computer"?

10. Describe the ways e-learning helps business. Do you think e-learning will become more or less popular in the future? Explain your answer.

11. Some people list four components of computer systems: hardware, software, data, and *people*. Why do you think it is important to include people as part of the system?

12. What types of businesses can you think of that do not use computers or that use them infrequently?

13. Discuss some ways to make sure both the classroom and computer equipment are safe.

Write About It

14. With two classmates, research ways to avoid computer problems. Use software to prepare a demonstration presentation on tips for keeping your computer running smoothly.

15. Ask family members and friends about the ways they use computers and the types of software they use. Write a report of at least one page about your findings.

16. Interview someone who works with your school's computer system. Ask him or her about the types of problems that occur and how they are addressed. Write a one-page article based on your interview.

17. Technology usually improves an old invention. In two or more paragraphs, describe how the PC improved on the typewriter.

18. List ways in which business software may be used. Include the types of documents that can be created using software.

19. Research speech recognition software. How does it work? Why do businesses use it? What type of equipment is needed to use speech recognition? Write a one-page report on your findings.

Technology Applications

Software Programs
20. Go to a computer lab or use your own computer to research database, spreadsheet, presentation, scheduling, and integrated software packages. Use tutorials, online help, or information from the software maker to find out how each can be used to enhance communications. Then write a report of at least one page on your findings.

Business Ethics

Using Computers Ethically
21. Ethics are the principles and standards we use to decide how to act. Your behavior while using a computer is also guided by ethics. Team up with a classmate. Develop a list of at least three ethical situations and problems associated with computers. Then list possible reactions to these issues and problems.

Chapter 19 Review and Activities **339**

Chapter 19

Critical Thinking

11. Computers are just machines. People make the decisions necessary to produce useful information.

12. Small businesses that mainly depend on manual labor may not use computers often.

13. Computer equipment can be kept safe by placing it on sturdy tables or shelves. Computer cables should be out of the walkway or seating area. No food or drinks should be near the equipment.

Write About It

14. Users should delete unneeded files from their hard drive regularly, back up files, empty the recycle bin, install security software, and update it regularly.

15. Answers will be based on respondents' replies.

16. Answers will depend on the school's systems.

17. PCs allow users to make changes easily and neatly. Spell-check and grammar-check features help users to find and correct mistakes.

18. to create letters, invoices, and bills, create financial reports, to store personnel records, inventory, and customer files

19. Reports should detail the process and how it works. This software is helpful to physically disabled workers and in customer service phone calls.

Technology Applications

20. Most people use Microsoft Office, an integrated software package. Excel is a spreadsheet program. PowerPoint is presentation software. Access is database software. The Outlook program can be used to send and receive e-mail.

Business Ethics

21. Answers will vary. For instance, in one situation, you notice that a co-worker has left his e-mail open. Possible reactions: Read the e-mail or tell the co-worker. Telling the co-worker is the ethical reaction.

339

Applying Academics to Business

22. The prefix *bio-* means life, or from living things. It appears in *biology, biography,* and *biochemical.* The word *metric* is the system of measurement based on the meter and gram. It appears in *parametric* and *metrical. Biometrics* is the branch of biology that deals with mathematical analysis of data.

23. $(3x)^2 + (4x)^2 = (4x)^2$

$x = 15$

$20^2 + 15^2 = c^2$

$400 + 225 = c^2$

$625 = c^2$

$25 = c$

The diagonal of the screen is 25 inches.

24. Examples include database, desktop, everywhere, groupware, hardware, and keystroke.

25. The factors of 128 are: 2, 4, 8, 16, 32, and 64. The factors of 256 are: 2, 4, 8, 16, 32, 64, and 128. The number 256 has one more factor because it includes all of the factors of 128, but also includes 128.

Active Learning

26. Answers will depend on the items that are demonstrated and students' observations of them.

Business in the Real World

27. Answers will vary, depending on the companies researched.

Applying Academics to Business

English Language Arts

22. Biometric devices identify people by physical traits such as fingerprints, voices, and faces. Separate the word *biometric* into its prefix and base word. Write a definition of each part and list other words in which they appear. Then write a definition for the word *biometrics.*

Mathematics

23. The relationship between the width and height of a computer screen is 4:3. How could you use the Pythagorean theorem to figure out the length of the diagonal of a screen that is 15 inches in height?

> **THEORY** **Geometry** The Pythagorean Theorem states that the square of the hypotenuse of a right triangle equals the sum of the squares of the lengths of the other two sides: $a^2 + b^2 = c^2$.

English Language Arts

24. Compound words are words made up of two or more parts, each of which can stand alone as a word. Compound words can often mean something very different from the meaning the two words would have if they were used separately. Skim the chapter, and list as many compound words as you can. Alphabetize your list.

Mathematics

25. Clarice bought a 128 MB memory chip and a 256 MB memory chip to upgrade the memory in her computer. List the factors of 128 and 256, and explain why 128 has an even number of factors and 256 has an odd number of factors.

> **THEORY** **Factoring** Factors are the numbers you multiply to get another number.

Active Learning

Hold a Tech Fair

26. Work in small groups. Set up booths in your classroom for a tech fair. Each group should bring in a technology item or a picture of one. Categorize the hardware as an input, output, or storage device, or as other computer hardware. Decide ahead of time which device each group should bring. Be prepared to demonstrate or explain the item and answer questions about it. Afterward, write a short essay on what you learned about the different items.

Business in the Real World

Technology Product Development

27. Form groups. Go online to research a company that makes hardware or software. Contact the company for more information. Ask how it learns about ways that consumers use its products. How does it decide if something should be changed or discontinued? What does the company do when another company offers a new technology that is successful? Write a report on your findings. Present your report to the class.

340 **Chapter 19** Review and Activities

ExamView Assessment Suite CD allows you to print out ready-made unit and chapter tests, complete with answer keys. You can also create customized tests.

TeacherWorks Plus provides complete teacher resources in one convenient package. It includes customizable lesson plans in calendar format and instant access to many print program resources.

Real LIFE skills

DEVELOPING KEYBOARDING SKILLS

28. Open a Microsoft Word file that contains a previous assignment. Click "Help" on the menu bar. Go to "Keyboard shortcuts for Word" and find the quick reference link. Practice using the shortcuts listed by retyping the first paragraph from your assignment. Include the following in a printout: Make the letters of the first word bold and italic; decrease the font size of the second word to 9 points; and increase the font size of the third word to 16 points.

Business CAREERS

FIND YOUR DREAM JOB

29. Go to the *Introduction to Business* Online Learning Center through **glencoe.com** for a link to the Occupational Outlook Handbook Web site. Click on the "OOH Search/A-Z Index" link and enter the job title "computer programmer." Then write a one-page report about this type of occupation. Conclude your report with a list of things you could do now to prepare yourself to pursue the occupation.

Role Play

USING SOFTWARE FEATURES

30. **Situation** You are the assistant information technology manager for a local newspaper. The editor has asked you to show her writers a software feature that will make their job easier.

Activity Plan and demonstrate how to use the feature. If necessary, use online help, tutorials, or manuals for the software.

Evaluation You will be evaluated on how well you meet the following performance indicators:

- Explain ways in which the feature can be used.
- Present the feature in steps that your audience can follow easily.
- Answer questions from your audience about the feature and how to use it.
- Prepare a written outline of the points of your presentation.
- Speak clearly and use correct grammar.

Standardized Test Practice

Directions Choose the letter of the best answer. Write the letter for the answer on a separate piece of paper.

1. **The hypotenuse of a triangle measures 20 mm. Which could be the lengths of the legs?**

   A   6 mm and 8 mm
   B   9 mm and 16 mm
   C   12 mm and 16 mm
   D   13 mm and 14 mm

TEST-TAKING TIP Make sure you do not read too much into test questions. Avoid imagining detailed scenarios in which the answer could be true. In most cases, "trick questions" are not as difficult as you think.

 READING Go to the *Introduction to Business* Online Learning Center through **glencoe.com** for a list of outside reading suggestions.

Real LIFE skills

28. Bold: CTRL+B; italic: CTRL+I; decrease font size (to 9 points): CTRL+SHIFT+<; and increase font size (to 16 points): CTRL+SHIFT+>.

Business CAREERS

29. Computer programmers conceive, design, and test logical structure for solving problems. They work long hours. Telecommuting is common. Training and qualifications: bachelor's degree and continuing education are important. Certification and experience can lead to promotion to lead programmer and supervisory responsibility. Job outlook: Expected to grow more slowly than the average. As preparation: develop basic computer skills, and take computer programming and business classes.

Role Play

30. Presentations should address the competencies noted in the Role Play. Answers will vary, depending on the software and features chosen.

Standardized Test Practice
1. C

STRATEGIES FOR STANDARDIZED TEST PREP SUCCESS

Test Savvy Explain to students that while some items on standardized tests can be "tricky," they are generally not designed to be so complicated or deceptive that they will trick all but the most wary of students. Suggest that they can come back to the question later with a fresh approach.

FOCUS

 Bell Ringer Activity

Technology Consulting
Write a list of computer peripherals on the board. Ask students if they think a business that specializes in helping businesses use technology could be successful in your town. Ask students to brainstorm a list of services such a business could offer. (Students might suggest setting up computer systems for businesses or consumers or providing phone or Internet-based support systems for businesses.)

TEACH

Teaching Points
Information Technology
Ask students to describe the role of information technology in business. (People depend on getting information quickly and easily. Businesses use information technology such as computing, electronics, and telecommunications to process and distribute information in digital and other forms.) Ask students to categorize the businesses' uses of information technology. (All types of businesses use information technology for processes from manufacturing to sales to financial management and more. In the future, many new applications are likely to become vital to business.)

Antwanye Ford
President/CEO/Co-Founder, Enlightened Inc.

Andre Rogers
CFO/Co-Founder, Enlightened Inc.

Enlightened Inc. is an information technology consulting firm based in Washington, D.C. Friends and founders Antwanye Ford, Andre Rogers, and Thomas Spann met at George Washington University.

Q & A

Describe your job responsibilities.

Antwanye: As the President of the company, I am responsible for the general direction and vision of the company. This is done by establishing the corporate goals and objectives, and ensuring we have the necessary people in place to achieve those goals.

Andre: I am in charge of two main areas, all financial and administrative duties, and all technical projects. My daily duties include ensuring that projects are done on time and on budget, while making certain that the customer receives more than they expect.

What skills are most important in your business?

Antwanye: Passion, vision, belief in yourself, a thick skin, an ability to deal with failure, self-motivation, and persistence. Interpersonal and academic skills are also essential.

Andre: The most important aspect of being an entrepreneur is passion. There will be some things that a person would be natural at doing, while others would be a stretch. But drive and passion will allow a person to do both.

What is your key to success?

Antwanye: I believe that you must see what others cannot see, and see it as if it already exists.

Andre: Relationships have been key to obtaining customers. Delivering high-quality services and exceeding customers' expectations have allowed us to retain several of our customers for years.

What advice would you give students interested in starting a business?

Antwanye: You need to find something you have passion for beyond what money you might make.

Andre: If it is your passion, then do it! Don't let anything stop you. Learn as much as you can about your passion. Value your relationships. Find a mentor—no one knows everything.

Critical Thinking *Why is being known for a product or service—developing a brand identity—important to a company?*

Critical Thinking

If a company has brand recognition, it is often seen as a market leader. This recognition can prompt new customers to buy the product or service, and encourage customer loyalty, too.

Some Qualifications to be the Owner of an Information Technology Consulting Company

Academic Skills and Abilities

Computer science; mathematics; information systems; computer programming; interpersonal skills; general business management skills; verbal and written communication skills; multitasking, organizing, and planning skills

Academic Skills Required to Complete Tasks at Enlightened Inc.			
Tasks	**Math**	**Science**	**English Language Arts**
Hold meetings			◆
Assign duties			◆
Monitor developments in technology	◆	◆	◆
Assess marketplace opportunities	◆	◆	◆
Customer service	◆	◆	◆
Schedule employees	◆		◆
Order supplies and equipment	◆		◆
Analyze financials	◆		◆

Education and Training

Despite employers' preference for those with technical degrees, people with degrees in a variety of majors find employment in information technology. The level of education and the type of training that employers require depend on their needs. One factor affecting these needs is changes in technology.

Career Path

Computer scientists employed in private industry may advance into managerial or project leadership positions. Database administrators may advance into managerial positions on the basis of their experience managing data and enforcing security. Computer specialists with work experience and considerable expertise in a particular subject or a certain application may find lucrative opportunities as independent consultants or may choose to start their own computer consulting firms.

Preparing for a Career
Self-Assessment Checklist

Use this self-assessment checklist to help determine ways you can build your professionalism.

✔ Be informed about careers. Search the newspaper and the Internet for available jobs in your field of interest.

✔ Take advantage of resources available through teachers or your school's guidance counselor.

✔ Create a résumé that highlights your professional and personal strengths.

✔ Write a cover letter that advertises your best qualities.

✔ Utilize all your contacts for networking, including friends and family members.

✔ Prepare for interviews by researching the company and by dressing professionally.

✔ Have confidence in yourself and in your abilities.

✔ Be personable, professional, organized, and ready to take advantage of good opportunities.

343

ASSESS

Write About It
Enlightened, Inc.

Ask students to write a summary of what they like about Enlightened, Inc.'s business concept. (Students may say that they like the idea of providing technology services that can help businesses to grow and be successful.)

Academic Vocabulary
Career Planning

Ask students to read the Self-Assessment Checklist then write one or more paragraphs about preparing for a career. Have students use some words from the Academic Vocabulary Glossary. (Example: One of the hardest skills to learn is the ability to *predict* what will happen in the future so that you can *develop* the skills events will *require*. However, career planning can give you information that will *facilitate* success.)

CLOSE

Cooperative Learning
Technology Applications

Ask students to work in pairs and develop an idea for an information technology service. Have them work together to develop an advertisement for the business. Encourage students to use technology applications to develop a slide show or Web page using images and marketing copy that offer information about the business and service. (Slide shows or Web pages should include marketing copy, visuals, and information about the business and service.)

343

Preparing for a Career

Using Information Technology Information technology is so important to many businesses that it is likely to be a vital part of most students' careers. Remind students that the experiences they have in writing e-mails, developing slide-shows, and building Web pages are likely to be skills they can use to achieve success in the business world. Ask students: What technology skills do you think will be most important to your future careers? (Answers will vary but are likely to include communication tools.) Tell students that they will have an opportunity to think about ways to build their futures by thinking about careers and the career planning process as they read the Self-Assessment Checklists in this book.

Unit 6 / Thematic Project

FOCUS

Discussion Starter

Lead a discussion about technology's effect on global business. Ask students to project how the evolution of technology will change the business world.

Step 1

Brainstorm Skills

Have students go to the *Introduction to Business* Online Learning Center through **glencoe.com** for a graphic organizer they can use to brainstorm the skills needed to complete the project.

Step 2

Choose a Business and a Career

Students can use the Occupational Outlook Handbook Web site to explore options.

TEACH

Step 3

Build Background

Technology Have students brainstorm ways they will use information technology in the future. (Ideas will vary. For example, future technology will likely include using small, portable communications devices that will allow people to be instantaneously connected to coworkers around the globe.)

Technology's Effect on Global Business

Improvements in technology have had an enormous impact on international trade. Information exchange that once took days or weeks now takes place in seconds with development of the Internet, fax machines, e-mail, and telecommunication advances.

Thematic Project Assignment

In this project you will conduct research and design a Web page that illustrates technology's effect on global business. Technology includes the Internet, fax machines, teleconferencing, digital TV, Web conferencing, and other technology used in international business.

Step 1 · Brainstorm Skills You Need to Complete This Activity

Your success in designing your Web site depends on your skills. Preview the activity. Then brainstorm a list of the skills you will need to use to complete the activity and describe how you will use them. Skills you might use include:

Academic Skills	reading, writing, social studies
Basic Skills	speaking, listening, thinking, and interpersonal skills
Technology Skills	word processing, keyboarding, presentation, telecommunications, and Internet skills

 SKILLS PREVIEW Go to the *Introduction to Business* Online Learning Center through **glencoe.com** for a graphic organizer you can use to brainstorm the skills you will use to complete the project.

Step 2 · Choose a Business and a Career That Interest You

Think of a business that you find interesting. Then think of a career related to the business that interests you. As you investigate technology's effects on global business, you will research the effects of technology on the business and career of your choice.

Step 3 · Build Background Knowledge

Preview technology's effects on the global business that you will research.

Technology's Influence on Global Business

The 21st century has seen technology revolutionize global business. Today, the economies of many countries are based on international trade. E-commerce, or electronic commerce, has made it possible for businesses to directly reach customers anywhere in the world.

For example, the Internet allows a business in India to sell goods to a student in New Mexico. Telecommunications allows for corporate meetings to take place via TV screens with managers being in different parts of the world. Fax machines allow for contracts to be delivered, signed, and returned in a matter of minutes instead of days or weeks.

Globalization Ask students to write a paragraph stating the effects of globalization on technology. (Students should recognize that technology builds on ideas. Now that people all around the world can share ideas quickly and easily, it is likely that the speed of technological advancement will only increase.)

Step 4

Connect with Your Community

Ask students to describe the effect technology has had on their community. (Effects will vary, depending on the community. Students should recognize that people once defined their communities very narrowly, both culturally and geographically.)

Step 4 Connect with Your Community

Interview an older family member about the advances in technology in his or her lifetime. Find out what computers were like when he or she first entered the workplace. Ask how he or she communicated with other workers or companies.

Step 5 Research Technology's Effects on Global Business

Use library and Internet resources to research technology's effects on global business. Use the project research checklist as a guide to your research. Keep records of your sources of information.

Step 6 Develop a Web Site

Use word processing and other software to develop a Web site that includes all of the information described in the project checklist.

Technology's Effects on Global Business

✔ Write a summary that explains the effects of technology on global business. Include information that explains how technology helps companies become global.

✔ Make a list of the newest trends and products in technology that are used in business. Identify how the new products and developments impact the way global business is conducted.

✔ Explain how businesspeople can keep up with new developments in technology.

✔ Create a time line that illustrates technological advances in the last 50 years.

✔ Prepare a map of the world and illustrate it with graphics to show how the world is connected through technology.

✔ Use the Internet to find an article on a new technology that is being used in international business. Write a summary of the article. Include your source.

Self Connections

✔ Discuss the results of your research with a family member or other adult.

✔ Describe how technology effects the business and career in which you are interested.

✔ Explain what the investigation and its results mean to you.

Step 7 Evaluate Your Presentation

 RUBRIC Go to the *Introduction to Business* Online Learning Center through **glencoe.com** for a rubric you can use to evaluate your final report.

345

Step 5

Research Technology's Effects on Global Business

Students can go to the *Introduction to Business* Online Learning Center through **glencoe.com** for a rubric they can use as a content checklist when researching their reports.

Chapter	Section	Unit Objectives
Chapter 20 *Career Planning*	**20.1**	**Discuss** the importance of career planning.
		Define at least five attributes you should know about yourself when analyzing careers.
		Describe how work is changing.
	20.2	**Name** four sources where you can learn about careers.
		Describe some aspects of the working world that may affect a worker.
		Define short-, medium-, and long-term goals.
		Identify the three lists needed to make a career plan.
Chapter 21 *Getting a Job*	**21.1**	**Discuss** the importance of understanding employers' wants and needs.
		Describe some of the qualifications employers seek in employees.
	21.2	**Discuss** the parts of a résumé.
		Describe the elements involved in the application process.
		Discuss how employers and job candidates both benefit from a job interview.

Understanding the Coding

Brackets Brackets on the reduced student edition page correspond to teaching strategies and activities in the Teacher Wraparound Edition. As you teach the lesson, the brackets show you exactly where to use the teaching strategies and activities.

Letters The letters on the reduced student edition page identify the type of strategy or activity. See the key below to learn about the different types of strategies and activities.

Ability Levels Leveled teaching strategies are identified by one of three codes to give you an idea of their suitability for students of varying learning styles and abilities.

Resources Key program resources are listed in each chapter. Icons indicate the format of resources.

KEY to Letters

D **Develop Concepts** activities help teachers gauge and plan for students' concept development.

R **Reading Strategy** activities help you teach reading skills and vocabulary.

C **Critical Thinking** strategies help students apply and extend what they have learned.

U **Universal Access** activities provide differentiated instruction for English language learners and suggestions for teaching various types of learners.

S **Skill Practice** provides leveled instruction for meeting individual needs and learning styles.

W **Writing Support** activities provide writing opportunities to help students comprehend the text.

NCLB **No Child Left Behind** activities help students practice and improve their abilities in academic subjects.

KEY to Ability Levels

L1 Strategies should be within the ability range of all students. Often full class participation is required.

L2 Strategies are for average to above-average students or for small groups. Some teacher direction is necessary.

L3 Strategies are designed for students able and willing to work independently. Minimal teacher direction is necessary.

KEY to Resource Icons

📁 Print Material

💿 CD-ROM

🖱 Online Learning Center with Podcasts

BusinessWeek *Reader and Case Study*

In Unit 7, your students can learn more about business in the real world through the following *BusinessWeek* Readers and Case Studies:

Picture Your Business with a Logo
More than just printing up business cards, a logo can create the kind of brand identity that becomes instantly recognizable to customers and also communicates that this is a serious business. (page 352)

These Technicians Are Better Than Robots
Japan is turning to hyper-skilled *supaa ginosha,* or super technicians, to preserve its manufacturing edge. (page 369)

Chapter Features and Activities

Section	Feature Title	Page
20.1	Online Self-Assessment	353
20.1	Shifting Careers	354
20.2	Career Clusters	356
20.2	Regrouping After Job Loss	357

Section	Feature Title	Page
20.2	Employment Agencies	359
21.1	Work Permits	367
21.2	Looking for Openings	374
21.2	Accepting a Job Offer	377

Reading Strategies

● Before You Read

Section	Page
20.1	350
20.2	355
21.1	366
21.2	371

Graphic Organizer

Chapter	Section	Title	Page
20	20.1	Things I Need to Know About Myself	350
	20.2	Planning for a Career	355
21	21.1	Qualifications Employers Want	366
	21.2	Five Places to Start a Job Search	371

● As You Read

Section	Page
20.1	351, 352
20.2	358
21.1	368
21.2	372

✔ Reading Check

Section	Page
20.1	351, 353
20.2	356
21.1	367
21.2	374

● After You Read

Section	Page
20.1	354
20.2	359
21.1	370
21.2	377

Unit Overview

Introduce the Unit
Introduce the unit by describing the main concepts of each chapter in the unit.

Unit 7 is about career planning in a global economy.

Chapter 20 discusses the three steps in career planning. It focuses on self-awareness, learning about careers, setting goals, and making a plan.

Chapter 21 describes the skills needed to get a job. Employability skills and the job search process are discussed. Preparing a resume, contacting potential employers, and interviewing for jobs are also covered.

00:00 OUT OF TIME?

If class time is too short to cover all of the chapters in this unit, have students:

• Write down the vocabulary terms and their definitions.

• Read the chapter summaries at the beginning of each chapter review.

• Go to the *Introduction to Business* Online Learning Center through **glencoe.com** to download free Study-to-Go content to their PDAs or cell phones.

Career Planning in a Global Economy

346

Real-World Business and Career Profile — Preview

Girlstart Tell students that at the end of this unit, they will learn about Girlstart founder Rachel Muir and how she achieved her success. This organization runs after-school programs for underserved low-income schools, free Saturday camps and summer camps at the Girlstart Tech Center, and free online courses in HTML and graphic design. Girlstart is based in Austin, Texas. Ask students to name ways that teaching math and science can lead to success. (Math teaches problem solving. Science teaches how to investigate our world. Workers with strong math and science skills have more job opportunities.)

Real-World Business and Career Profile
Preview

Girlstart runs after-school programs, Saturday camps, and summer camps to empower girls in mathematics, science, and technology. At the end of this unit, you will learn about Girlstart® founder Rachel Muir and how she achieved her success.

Decision Making Have you started making decisions about the career you will pursue?

Unit 7 | Thematic Project Preview

Lifelong Learning After completing this unit, you will research to find out how lifelong learning will help you in your career throughout your life.

Project Checklist As you read the chapters in this unit, use this checklist to prepare for the unit project.

✔ Think about how changes in the world are affecting the job opportunities in the career of your choice.

✔ Think about how lifelong learning will increase job opportunities in adult education.

✔ Look for opportunities for adult learning experiences in your community and in different career choices.

✔ Consider how lifelong learning will affect your future.

347

Build Background
Ask students these questions to activate prior knowledge:

Chapter 20
Why should you consider different careers? (There are thousands of different careers from which to choose. The path to a choosing career starts with considering your hopes and dreams for the future. Selecting a career that matches your interests, abilities, and skills will make your working life more enjoyable.)

Chapter 21
Why do you need to understand how to get a job? (Employers screen job applicants through job applications, resumes, cover letters, and interviews. It is important to project a positive image of yourself in person and through these important documents. To stand our in a competitive job market, it is important to research a company before an interview and be prepared to ask intelligent questions about the company and the industry.)

Unit | Thematic Project Preview

Lifelong Learning
Tell students that when they complete this unit, they will understand that lifelong learning is essential. Students will understand that globalization increases competition among qualified people for good jobs. Encourage students to think about how these changes could affect the types of jobs and careers they might choose.

C Critical Thinking

Ask students what types of lifelong learning experiences they might need. (To compete in the job market, they may need more training as their jobs and industry change. Lifelong learning might mean returning to college or getting specialized training.)

Standards-Based Lesson Planning
Introduction to Business provides students with instruction and assessment in the following fundamental content areas:

Content Standards Correlations	
Understand the career preparation and job-acquisition skills required for employment, professional growth, and employment transitions in business.	pp. 351–354, 356–359, 360–363
Discuss the potential impact of local and global trends on career plans and life goals.	pp. 353–354, 357, 361
Research careers and apply skills needed for initial and continued employment.	pp. 356, 358, 361–363
Assess personal strengths and weaknesses.	pp. 361–362
Design, initiate, refine, and implement a plan to facilitate personal growth and skill development related to anticipated job requirements and career expectations.	p. 361
Examine a domestic and an international career of interest.	p. 361
Experience work-based learning through volunteerism, job shadowing, mentoring, and/or e-coaching.	p. 361
Create a follow-up (thank you) letter.	p. 361
Incorporate knowledge gained from individual assessment and job/career exploration to design an individual career plan that reflects the transition from school to work, lifelong learning, and personal and professional goals.	p. 363

NCLB
Activities, information, and skills practice will help your students attain No Child Left Behind proficiency. Students will improve their abilities in the following academic standards areas:

Academic Standards Correlations		
English Language Arts	Activities/Features	Page
NCTE 11 Participate as members of literacy communities	After You Read Applying Academics to Business	pp. 359, 362
NCTE 12 Use language to accomplish individual purposes	After You Read Applying Academics to Business	pp. 359, 362
Mathematics		
Data Analysis and Probability Formulate questions that can be addressed with data, and collect, organize, and display relevant data to answer them	Applying Academics to Business	p. 362
Data Analysis and Probability Select and use appropriate statistical data to analyze data	Standardized Test Practice	p. 363
Number and Operations Compute fluently and make reasonable estimates	Ask S&P After You Read	pp. 348, 354
Algebra Represent and analyze mathematical situations and structures using algebraic symbols	Applying Academics to Business	p. 362
Science		
Content Standard F Students should develop understanding of personal and community health	Science/Tech Trends	p. 358

Correlations   This chart shows the 21st Century Skills, foundation skills, and workplace competencies that students develop as they work in this chapter.

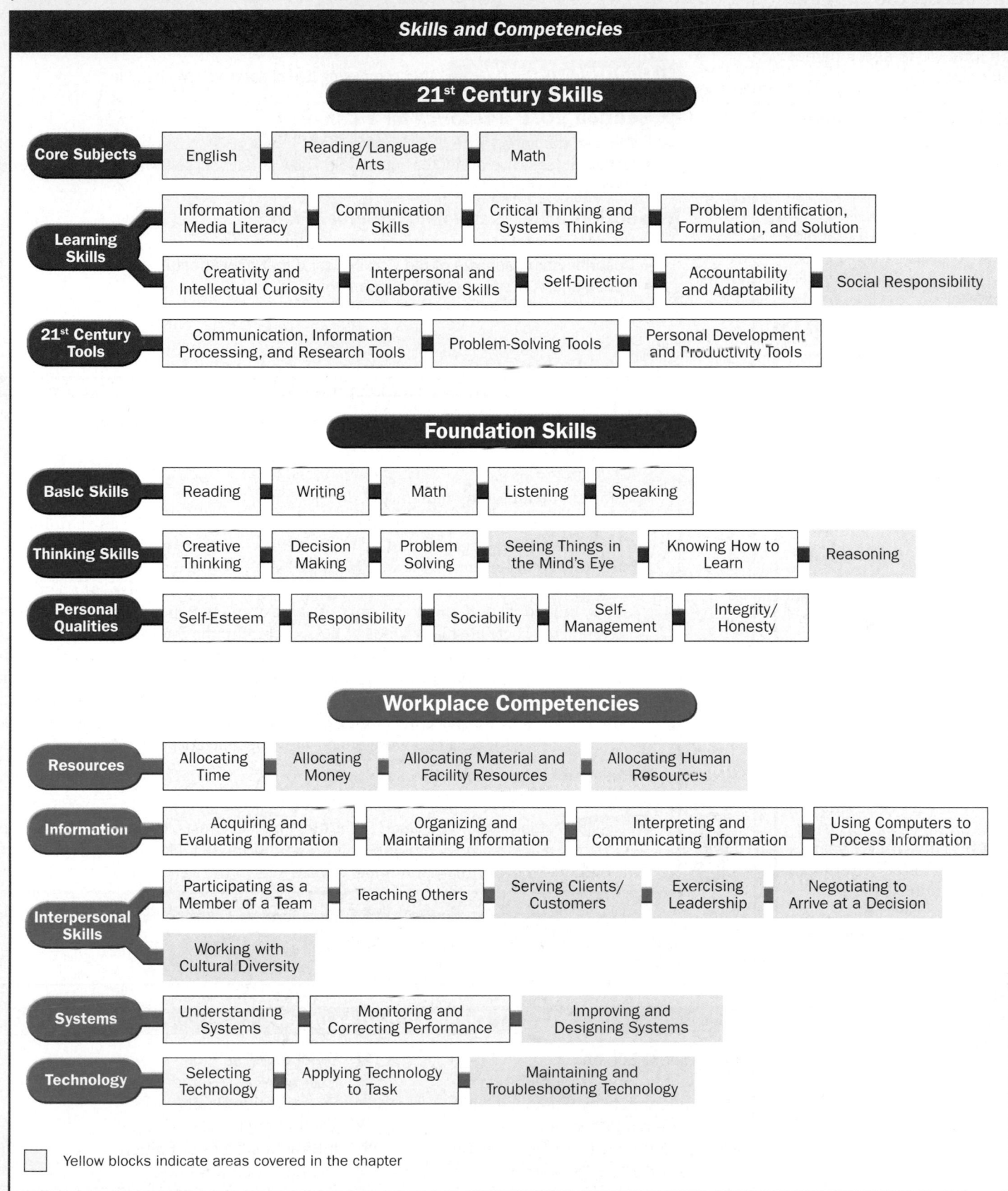

Skills and Competencies

21st Century Skills

Core Subjects
| English | Reading/Language Arts | Math |

Learning Skills
| Information and Media Literacy | Communication Skills | Critical Thinking and Systems Thinking | Problem Identification, Formulation, and Solution |
| Creativity and Intellectual Curiosity | Interpersonal and Collaborative Skills | Self-Direction | Accountability and Adaptability | Social Responsibility |

21st Century Tools
| Communication, Information Processing, and Research Tools | Problem-Solving Tools | Personal Development and Productivity Tools |

Foundation Skills

Basic Skills
| Reading | Writing | Math | Listening | Speaking |

Thinking Skills
| Creative Thinking | Decision Making | Problem Solving | Seeing Things in the Mind's Eye | Knowing How to Learn | Reasoning |

Personal Qualities
| Self-Esteem | Responsibility | Sociability | Self-Management | Integrity/Honesty |

Workplace Competencies

Resources
| Allocating Time | Allocating Money | Allocating Material and Facility Resources | Allocating Human Resources |

Information
| Acquiring and Evaluating Information | Organizing and Maintaining Information | Interpreting and Communicating Information | Using Computers to Process Information |

Interpersonal Skills
| Participating as a Member of a Team | Teaching Others | Serving Clients/Customers | Exercising Leadership | Negotiating to Arrive at a Decision |
| Working with Cultural Diversity |

Systems
| Understanding Systems | Monitoring and Correcting Performance | Improving and Designing Systems |

Technology
| Selecting Technology | Applying Technology to Task | Maintaining and Troubleshooting Technology |

☐ Yellow blocks indicate areas covered in the chapter

Chapter 20

Chapter Overview

Introduce the Chapter

Career Planning
Chapter 20 is about career planning.

Building Background
Lead a discussion about careers students know, through school, family members, and friends. Talk about your own path to a teaching career.

STANDARD &POOR'S

>> *Math Answer*
After five years Cyndie's IRA will be worth $4,831.53. Calculate the interest for each year and add it to the balance before calculating the interest for subsequent years. If Cyndie now withdraws the money, the tax is: .20($4,831.53 − $3,000) = .20($1,831.53) = $366.30. If she subtracts her expected taxes, her IRA will yield $4,831.53 − $366.30 = $4,465.23.

>> *Extension Activity*
Have students calculate the value of $2,500 in a Roth IRA after 5 years at 9% interest. After five years the IRA will be worth $3,845.56.

N C L B
Activity correlates to Math standards.

Career Planning

Chapter Objectives After completing this chapter, you will be able to:

▶ **Section 20.1** *Preparing for a Career*
- **Discuss** the importance of career planning.
- **Define** at least five attributes you should know about yourself when analyzing careers.
- **Describe** how work is changing.

▶ **Section 20.2** *Developing a Career Plan*
- **Name** four sources where you can learn about careers.
- **Describe** some aspects of the working world that may affect a worker.
- **Define** short-, medium-, and long-term goals.
- **Identify** the three lists needed to make a career plan.

Ask

STANDARD &POOR'S **Developing a Retirement Plan: IRAs**

Q: How do I plan for my retirement?

A: While planning for retirement is something everyone should do, an alarming number of people never get around to opening even one retirement account. According to the Employee Benefit Research Institute (EBRI), 49 percent of workers with an annual income between $30,000 and $60,000 don't have a retirement account. IRAs, individual retirement accounts, are an extremely popular way to save for retirement. There are many kinds of IRAs, including the traditional IRA, which is tax-deductible, and the Roth IRA, which is nondeductible. It's important to start investing early. Be sure to allocate your assets appropriately, and don't touch what you've already put in! Many people borrow against what they've saved, promising themselves they'll replace the money later, but they never get around to doing so. Finally, it's a good idea to choose one or more beneficiaries for your investments.

Mathematics How much will a Roth IRA be worth in 5 years if you invest $3,000 now? Assume a 20% future tax rate and 10 percent annual earnings.

THEORY **Multiplying by a Decimal** To multiply by a decimal, count the total number of decimal places in the two numbers you are multiplying. Place the decimal point in the product by counting that number of places from the right.

N C L B

Classroom Resources

- 📖 Student Edition
- 📖 Teacher Wraparound Edition
- 📁 Student Activity Workbook with Academic Integration
- 📁 Student Activity Workbook with Academic Integration TAE
- 📁 *Fast File,* Unit 7 Resources
- 📁 Inclusion in the Business Education Classroom

- 💿 TeacherWorks Plus
- 💿 *ExamView Assessment Suite*
- 💿 Presentation Plus!
- 💿 Vocabulary PuzzleMaker
- 💿 Interactive Student Edition
- 🖥 Online Student Edition
- 🖥 Online Learning Center with Podcasts

● **Learning from Experience** One of the best ways to learn about occupations is to experience the work firsthand and talk to people about their jobs. **What lessons do you think you could learn from a more experienced worker?**

Review the Objectives

Introduce the chapter by reviewing the chapter objectives:

Section 20.1 *Objectives*
Discuss the importance of career planning. (It allows you to assess potential, analyze work options, and prepare for the future.)

Define at least five attributes you should know about yourself when analyzing careers. (aptitudes; interests; abilities; values; personality)

Describe how work is changing. (Companies do business via e-commerce. Technology enables work to be performed quickly, easily, and in more cost-effective ways.)

Section 20.2 *Objectives*
Name four sources where you can learn about careers. (written sources, career counselors, networks, and work)

Describe some aspects of the working world that may affect a worker. (outsourcing and the supply of and demand for jobs)

Define short-, medium-, and long-term goals. (short-term goal: something that can be started and reached right away; medium-term goal: takes longer to achieve; long-term goal: may take a long time to reach)

Identify the three lists needed to make a career plan. (graduation plan, education and training plan, and experience plan)

Discuss the Photo

● **Learning from Experience** Read the caption on the photo to students: One of the best ways to learn about occupations is to experience the work firsthand and talk to people about their jobs.

Ask students: What lessons could you learn from a more experienced worker? (Answers will vary, but students should mention that people who have real world experiences are a valuable resource.)

Section 20.1

FOCUS

Bell Ringer Activity

Preparing for a Career
Ask students why they need to start planning for a career now. (Some might suggest that it is too soon to think about a career. Others will point out that they need to figure out in which types of work they would find enjoyment and success. They also need to figure out what they have to do to get ready.)

Preteaching

Presentation Plus!
The Presentation Plus! CD provides visual teaching aids for this section.

PuzzleMaker
Use the Vocabulary PuzzleMaker to create a puzzle of the section's key terms. Students can complete the puzzle on paper or on a computer.

Graphic Organizer
Tell students to go to the Online Learning Center through **glencoe.com** for a printable graphic organizer. (Answers include: your interests, values, skills, abilities, aptitudes, personality, and goals.)

Connects academics to content.

Preparing for a Career

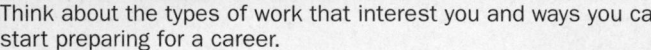

Reading Guide

● Before You Read
Think about the types of work that interest you and ways you can start preparing for a career.

Read to Learn
- Discuss the importance of career planning.
- Define at least five attributes you should know about yourself when analyzing careers.
- Describe how work is changing.

The Main Idea
Choosing a career is one of the most important decisions that you will make. Career planning can help put you on the right path. It involves considering your interests and skills.

Key Concepts
- Making Decisions About Work
- Self-Awareness
- How Work Is Changing

Vocabulary
Key Terms

full-time job	values
job	skill
occupation	ability
career	aptitude
interests	personality

Academic Vocabulary
You will find these words in your reading and on your tests. Make sure you know their meanings.

pursuing	via
overseas	adaptable

Graphic Organizer
In a graphic like the one shown, note five things you need to know about yourself before you begin career planning.

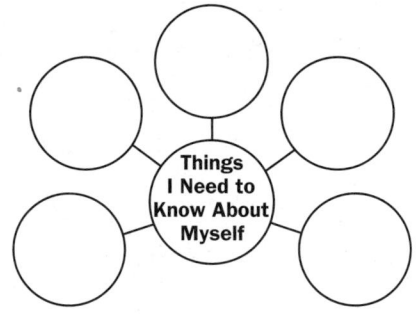

Things I Need to Know About Myself

 Go to the *Introduction to Business* Online Learning Center through **glencoe.com** for a printable graphic organizer.

Academic Standards
English Language Arts
   NCTE 1 Read texts to acquire new information
   NCTE 4 Use written language to communicate effectively
   NCTE 9 Develop an understanding of diversity in language use across cultures
Mathematics
   Number and Operations Compute fluently and make reasonable estimates

Reading Guide

● Before You Read
Students might mention classes they are taking or plans they are making for college or other training.

D Develop Concepts
The Main Idea Ask students: Why should you consider your interests and skills when planning for a career? (Students should recognize that many people choose careers based on things that interest them or their skills.)

Making Decisions About Work

Choosing a career is an important decision that everyone must make. The decision will affect the rest of your life. It will affect the amount of money you will earn. It will also affect the amount of satisfaction you will get from your work and life. A **full-time job** requires at least 40 hours of work every week. Most full-time workers spend 2,000 hours working each year. That is time you will want to spend doing something you enjoy.

Jobs and Careers

Work is essential to almost everyone's economic and social well-being. It includes jobs, occupations, and careers. A **job** or **occupation** is work that people engage in to earn pay. A **career** is a work history of one or more jobs in the same or related fields of interest. Each occupation in a career builds on interest, knowledge, training, and experience from the other jobs.

Pursuing a career requires career planning. *Career planning* consists of assessing your potential, analyzing your options, and preparing for the future. That preparation could include education or training as well as developing specialized skills or abilities.

✔ **Reading Check**   **Contrast** What is the difference between a job and a career?

> ● **As You Read**
>
> Think about some jobs you might like to do.

Self-Awareness

Before you start thinking about careers, you should note what interests you. Knowing yourself is a key part of your journey into the working world. Who are you? What do you value most? Answering these and other questions can help steer you down the right career path.

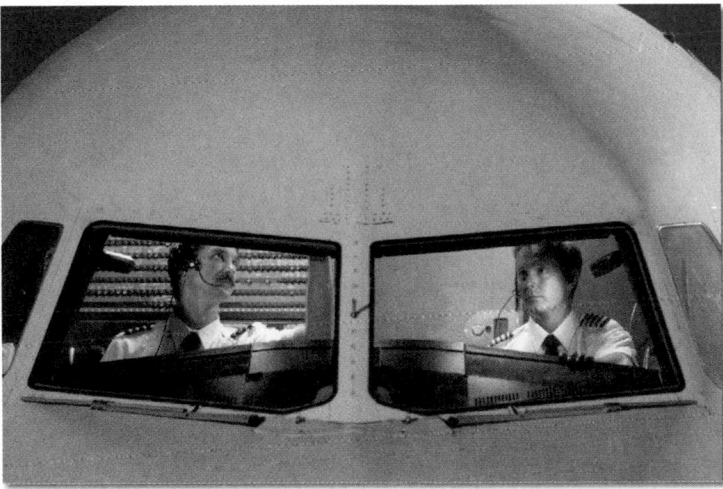

● **Careers in Aviation**
Carefully consider the unique characteristics of the careers in which you are interested. **What is the work environment for people who work in commercial aviation?**

TEACH

Discussion Starter
Making Decisions About Work
Ask students what kinds of jobs they have had. List the jobs on the board. Ask them how these jobs fit into their career plan. (Students might note that these jobs help develop interpersonal skills and work habits.)

R Reading Strategy

Illustrate an Idea Have students create an illustration to explain how a single job relates to a career. (Answers should clearly show how one job is part of a career.)

✔ **Reading Check**

Contrast A job is work that people do for pay. A career is a work history of one or more jobs in the same or related fields of interest.

● **As You Read**

Students may be interested in work that involves creativity or decision-making, such as management positions or entrepreneurship.

Discuss the Photo

● **Careers in Aviation** For pilots, the work environment is an enclosed space. A pilot's "office" is the cockpit, which includes the controls, instruments, and electronic equipment needed to fly the aircraft. Flight attendants must also work in small spaces, thousands of feet in the air.

TEACH (cont.)

S Skill Practice

Guided Practice

Identify and Explain Ask students to identify some of their interests and explain how they could lead to a career they would enjoy. (Answers will depend on students' interests.) **L1**

Create a Table Have students create a two-column table, listing in the first column three careers related to their interests. In the second column, list a current activity or interest related to each career. (Answers will vary, based on each student's career options, interests, and current activity.) **L2**

Brainstorm Have students work in groups to create a list of questions that might help individuals become more aware of their interests, values, skills, aptitudes, and personality. (Lists will vary, according to each student's characteristics.) **L3**

● As You Read

Answers will vary, depending on the jobs selected.

ASSESS

Review Key Terms

Have students write sentences using each key term.

 **Study-to-Go** Have students go to the Online Learning Center through **glencoe.com** to download free **Study-to-Go** content to their PDAs or cell phones.

● As You Read

Your talents and hobbies are also part of your interests. Think about a particular talent you have or a hobby you like to do. How could you use this in a particular job or career?

Your Interests

Your **interests** are your favorite activities. They could lead to a career that you would enjoy. Make a list of your interests. What are your favorite things to do? What school subjects do you enjoy? Which types of books do you read, and what TV shows and films do you watch? You might see patterns in your list of interests. Things that you enjoy doing may involve working with people, information, technology, or all three.

S Most people who enjoy working with others have a friendly demeanor. If you are interested in working with people, then you might enjoy being a salesperson or a nurse. However, several careers deal with information. Jobs that require handling information usually involve reading or doing research. Maybe you enjoy visiting libraries or learning about history. If so, then you might like being a detective or a lawyer. Many people interested in technology enjoy making or fixing things. If this sounds like you, then you might find reward in being a video producer or an electrician.

BusinessWeek *Reader and Case Study*

Picture Your Business with a Logo

Logoworks.com creates affordable logos and identities for small businesses. Doing most of the work online keeps it cheap.

Sarah Hawley, a 10-year public relations veteran, was moving from a job at a large agency to launch her own business, Mockingbird PR, out of her home in Gilbert, Arizona. She soon discovered that her experience bringing in clients wasn't enough. Appearances mattered, too.

It was time to get a logo. More than just printing up business cards, a logo can create the kind of brand identity that becomes instantly recognizable to customers and also communicates that this is a serious business. Hawley analyzed a few different logo vendors and decided upon Logoworks.com, a five-year-old online provider of logo services for small businesses based in Lindon, Utah.

"I liked that their designers were spread out [across the country]," she says. "So none of the designs looked the same, and they weren't influencing each other." She also liked the ease of the process and the turnaround time.

But most important, she really liked the cost. Hawley chose the firm's Platinum Package, which gave her 10 designs to choose from and unlimited revisions for $600—a fraction of the cost of getting a logo from an agency, which can start at $5,000.

 CASE STUDY Go to the *Introduction to Business* Online Learning Center through **glencoe.com** for the *BusinessWeek* Reader Case Study.

Active Learning

Develop your own status symbol—a logo for your own business. First, decide on a particular business within a particular industry. Next, research companies in that industry to see what is appropriate. Finally, use a sketchpad to try out at least three different options. Present your research and logo options to your class. Ask for feedback on which logo makes the strongest impact.

BusinessWeek *Reader and Case Study*

Picture Your Business with a Logo

@ **CASE STUDY** Have students go to the *Introduction to Business* Online Learning Center through **glencoe.com** to download a Case Study activity that corresponds to the article. The activity and answer key are also available on the TeacherWorks Plus CD.

Active Learning

Research, logos, and presentations will vary but should be appropriate to the type of business chosen.

Your Values

Values are what you believe to be important. They are the beliefs and ideas by which you live. Your values help you to make all kinds of decisions—from choosing friends to choosing a career. Your *work values* are the aspects of work that are important to you. Understanding your work values will help you select a career that suits you.

Your Skills, Abilities, Aptitudes, and Personality

Once you have some idea of your interests and values, you should consider your skills, abilities, aptitudes, and personality. A **skill** is proficiency for performing a task that is developed through training and experience. An **ability** is a natural or acquired skill or talent. Besides basic skills such as reading and writing, you may have a special ability to learn languages or to play a sport. An **aptitude** is your potential for learning a skill. Having an aptitude is like having a knack for something.

Personality is the set of characteristics that make someone special. It is the sum total of your feelings, actions, habits, and thoughts. If someone asked you to describe your personality, what would you say? You might start naming some of your characteristics. What are some of the first words that come to mind?

 **Explain** What are values?

International Business

Offshore Outsourcing

Offshore outsourcing is the term used when jobs are transferred to countries overseas. In the past, outsourcing was a way to reduce costs, primarily with blue-collar jobs. More recently, there has been a growing shift in the number of white-collar jobs being outsourced, such as software development and medical and financial services jobs. This has raised a debate over how outsourcing will affect the U.S. unemployment rate and overall economy. Some argue that this trend will lead to decreased U.S. wages. Others claim that the United States has an edge with its innovation. They argue that this innovation will continue creating high-paying positions and that the recent increase in white-collar outsourcing is insignificant.

Examples of Languages Across Cultures

Q: In German, how do you say: "It's nice to meet you"?
A: **Es hat mich sehr gefreut, Sie kennenzulernen.** (pronounced: Ĕs hŭll mekh zăĭr ghĕ-froyt, zēē kĕn-nĕn-tsŏŏ-lăĭr-nĕn.)

Do you think outsourcing is good or bad for American workers? Explain your answer.

Online Self-Assessment
Online firms such as Monster.com® and CareerBuilder.com™ help match employers with employees. They also offer job seekers self-assessment services to help them decide which careers will bring them the most satisfaction and success. *How do you think you could benefit from using online self-assessment services?*

Section 20.1 Preparing for a Career **353**

Section 20.1

RETEACH

R Reading Strategy

Apply Knowledge Have students use their own words to explain the difference between a skill, an ability, and an aptitude. (Explanations will vary. Students might explain that an aptitude is the potential a person has to learn a skill, while a skill is proficiency for performing a task that is developed through training. An ability is a natural or acquired skill.)

W Writing Support

Enrichment

Personality Testing Explain that in some countries teens are required to take a series of tests that determine their career path. Ask students to write a short essay about personality tests. (Some students might suggest that personality tests would be helpful. Others might point out that many people do not discover what truly interests them until they are older.)

Student Activity Workbook ☞ Assign the Section 20.1 Activities.

✔ Reading Check

Explain Values are the beliefs and ideas by which people live.

Real World

Online Self-Assessment These services are a convenient way for students to consider future plans and get more insight into careers. They also can help students determine their strengths and weaknesses.

International Business

Offshore Outsourcing Answers will vary, but possible solutions might include tax breaks for companies that keep jobs in the United States. Remedies might also focus on increasing education and training.

 **Critical Thinking**

Identify Skills
Adapting to Change Ask students to identify skills that are transferable.
(Answers include reading, writing, problem-solving, and decision-making skills.)

Real World

Shifting Careers Later generations tend to consider options that benefit them, such as higher-paying jobs.

ASSESS

After You Read

Have students complete the Section 20.1 After You Read section review.

Online Study Tools
Have students go to the Online Learning Center through **glencoe.com** to:

• Take the Section 20.1 **Practice Test**.

• Download free  **Study-to-Go** content to their PDAs or cell phones.

CLOSE

Culminating Activity
List Career Options
Have students interview a partner to develop a list of career values, interests, aptitudes, and skills. Working from the lists, have the pairs come up with some logical career choices to investigate. (Lists and career ideas will vary, depending on each student's characteristics.)

Real World

Shifting Careers
Many baby boomers will have begun and ended their career at one company. However, studies show that the generations that follow the baby boom generation will have between five and nine different careers during their lifetime. *Why do you think this change has occurred?*

NCLB Activity correlates to Math standards.

How Work Is Changing

The world of work is constantly changing. Some businesses fail, while new ones start. Certain workers are no longer needed. Others are in demand. The way people work is also changing. As previously discussed, technology enables work to be performed more quickly, easily, and in more cost-effective ways.

The working world is no longer limited by U.S. borders. The global economy continues to grow. People around the world want many goods and services that U.S. businesses sell. More U.S. companies are opening offices abroad, and **overseas** firms are operating within the United States. Companies do business **via** e-commerce. These changes create more job opportunities for workers.

Adapting to Change

Today's workers must be **adaptable** and willing to learn new technologies and ways of working. Every day you should work to improve your basic skills, develop thinking skills, and build personal skills. You will use these skills in all kinds of work later. They will help you adjust to new technologies and to change. They will also help you to compete with others in the working world.

Section 20.1

After You Read

Review Key Concepts
1. What is the difference between a job and a career?
2. What is the difference between an aptitude and an ability?
3. Discuss some ways that work is changing.

Academic Skills
4. **Mathematics** George got his dream job after graduating from college. He became a construction manager, helping to build commercial buildings. His starting salary was $40,000. He will receive a 3% raise in six months and, if he does well, another 5% raise at the end of the year. Will he then be earning more, less, or equal to $42,923, the average salary offered to new graduates for this job according to the *Occupational Outlook Handbook?*

THEORY Percents A percent increase in a number can be found by multiplying the number by the sum of 100% and the percent increase.

 For math help, go to the Math Appendix.

@ Go to the *Introduction to Business* Online Learning Center through **glencoe.com** to check your answers.

Section 20.1

Review Key Concepts
1. job: work that is done to make money; career: a work history of one or more jobs in a field
2. An aptitude is the potential to learn a skill. An ability is a natural or an acquired skill or talent.
3. Answers vary. For example, companies can do business online.

Academic Skills
4. **Mathematics** $40,000 \times 103\% =$ $41,200
$41,200 \times 5\% = \$43,260$
$43,260 > \$42,923$
George will be earning more than the average salary.

Developing a Career Plan

Reading Guide

Before You Read

Think about ways to get information about careers to help you make plans about your future.

Read to Learn

- Name four sources where you can learn about careers.
- Describe some aspects of the working world that may affect a worker.
- Define short-, medium-, and long-term goals.
- Identify the three lists needed to make a career plan.

The Main Idea

After you identify potential careers, you should research them. The information you gather will enable you to pinpoint the right career for you.

Key Concepts

- Finding Information on Careers
- Understanding the Working World
- Setting Goals
- Making a Career Plan

@ Go to the *Introduction to Business* Online Learning Center through **glencoe.com** for a printable graphic organizer.

Vocabulary

Key Terms

networking	volunteerism
job shadowing	entry-level job
internship	outsourcing

Academic Vocabulary

You will find these words in your reading and on your tests. Make sure you know their meanings.

series	challenging
internal	ultimate

Graphic Organizer

In each box of a graphic like the one shown, note the preparation you will need to develop a career.

Graduation Plan	Education and Training Plan	Experience Plan

Academic Standards

English Language Arts

NCTE 1 Read texts to acquire new information

NCTE 9 Develop an appreciation of diversity in language use across cultures

NCTE 10 Use first language to develop competency in English language arts and develop an understanding of content across the curriculum

NCTE 11 Participate as members of literacy communities

NCTE 12 Use language to accomplish individual purposes

Science

Content Standard F Students should develop understanding of personal and community health

Bell Ringer Activity

Developing a Career Plan

Ask the school librarian, media specialist, or guidance counselor to introduce students to career resources that are available at school. Encourage students to ask questions about the different resources.

Preteaching

Presentation Plus!

The Presentation Plus! CD provides visual teaching aids for this section.

PuzzleMaker

Use the Vocabulary PuzzleMaker to create a puzzle of the section's key terms. Students can complete the puzzle on paper or on a computer.

Graphic Organizer

Tell students to go to the Online Learning Center through **glencoe.com** for a printable graphic organizer. (Graduation Plan: courses, activities, and experiences that are related to student career goals; Education and Training Plan: education and training the student will need after high school; Experience Plan: experiences that will lead to their specific career choice.)

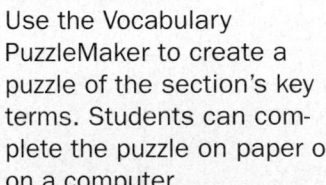

Connects academics to content.

Reading Guide

Before You Read

Students might use the library, the Internet, and career-day activities to get information about careers.

D Develop Concepts

The Main Idea Ask students: If you know the kind of work you want to do, why do you need to research the career and develop a plan? (Most careers require some sort of preparation, including training or education.)

Discussion Starter
Finding Information on Careers

Write these phrases on the board: Nature of Work; Working Conditions; Training, Other Qualifications, and Advancement; Employment; Job Outlook; Earnings; Related Occupations; and Sources of Additional Information. Point out that these are the headings used in the *Occupational Outlook Handbook* for each occupation. Ask students how the information in each section can help when making a career decision. (Answers will vary. If students have not already used the OOH Web site, this would be a good time to introduce it. See Question 29 at the end of each chapter for a suggested activity.)

R Reading Strategy

Compare and Contrast
Have students compare and contrast information from written sources, career counselors, and networks. Suggest that they use a table. (Tables will vary, based on the information that is collected.) Follow up by pointing out that networking is an excellent way to build relationships with people who will provide information about careers and to open up new career opportunities.

✔ Reading Check

Explain It is important to research careers because it enables you to pinpoint the right career and develop a career plan.

356

Career Clusters The U.S. Department of Education has organized more than 28,800 different careers into 16 career clusters. *Career clusters* are groups of similar occupations and industries. Go to the *Career Clusters Series* Online Learning Center through **glencoe.com**. Click on the "Hospitality & Tourism" link. *What are some jobs included in this career cluster?*

Finding Information on Careers

After you identify potential careers, it is time to do some research. The information you gather will enable you to pinpoint the right career and develop a career plan. There are many sources of job information. **Figure 20.1** offers a list of relevant skills and qualities to investigate when doing career research.

✔ Reading Check **Explain** Why is it important to research careers?

Written Sources

There is a lot of written information about careers at libraries and on the Internet. Also, the *Occupational Outlook Handbook* (OOH) describes hundreds of jobs. It lists the fastest-growing fields and gives addresses of places to write for more information.

Career Counselors

A *career counselor* is someone who is trained to provide information and guidance on choosing a career. A career counselor can also help you learn more about your interests and abilities. Most school counselors can provide career counseling.

Networks

Another way to get information is by networking. **Networking** is the practice of building informal relationships with people whose friendship could bring advantages such as job or business opportunities.

Figure 20.1 – *Skills for Success*

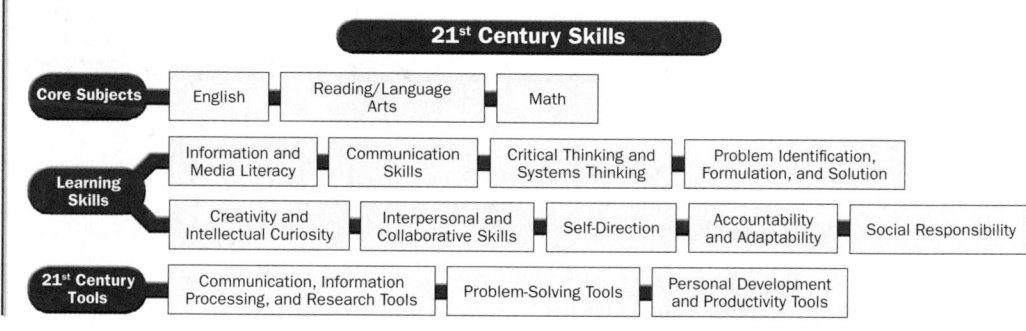

● **Workplace Skills** To succeed in the 21st century job market, all workers need information, communication and media literacy skills, thinking and problem-solving skills, and interpersonal and self-directional skills. **Why do you think creativity and intellectual curiosity are important?**

Career Clusters travel agent; hotel manager; concierge; waiter or waitress; and lifeguard

Figure 20.1

● **Workplace Skills** Answers may include: Creativity allows workers to "think outside the box" and gives workers incentives to find greater satisfaction in work. Intellectual curiosity drives workers to find solutions that are not obvious and encourages workers to make the most of a dynamic work environment.

Work

The best way to learn about a career is to work. New workers often benefit from **job shadowing**, which involves following another worker on the job for a few days. Internships are another option. An **internship** is a temporary paid or unpaid position that involves direct work experience in a career field. You might also consider **volunteerism**, or working without pay.

Understanding the Working World

There are some general aspects about the working world that you should know. They may affect you at some point during your career.

The Career Ladder

Most occupations have career ladders. A *career ladder* is a **series** of different jobs within a career. You might start with an **entry-level job**, which is suitable for a worker who is new to a job, field, or subject. From there you might be promoted to a higher level job with more responsibilities. Continually improving your skills will help you to succeed by climbing a career ladder.

Outsourcing

While U.S. companies face global competition for sales, some U.S. workers face global competition for jobs. Many U.S. firms outsource work to other countries. **Outsourcing** is using outside sources to do tasks traditionally handled by **internal** staff. It is usually done to cut costs.

The Role of Supply and Demand

Many people think that supply and demand affect only the prices they pay for goods and services. However, supply and demand also affect the job market. If there are more qualified people than there are openings for a job, then it will be difficult for a worker to get the position. People who have special skills, talents, or knowledge are also highly sought after for jobs. The more demand there is for a worker's set of skills, the easier it will be for him or her to get a job.

● **Supply and Demand** The supply of workers relative to the demand for workers affects job opportunities in an area. **Does this business have a demand for workers? How can you tell?**

Regrouping After Job Loss In recent years, some U.S. companies have moved parts of their operations to other countries in order to cut production costs. As a result, many U.S. workers have lost their jobs. *In a situation such as this, what can a worker do after losing a job?*

Discuss the Photo
● **Supply and Demand** Yes. The help-wanted sign indicates that the business has a demand for workers. The business is looking for experienced help, but it is also willing to train someone who is unexperienced.

Regrouping After Job Loss American workers can increase their chances for employment by updating their skills. They can take courses in areas relevant to the job they are seeking.

TEACH (cont.)

S Skill Practice
Guided Practice
Construct a Diagram Ask students to construct a diagram of a career ladder showing the position of an entry-level job. (The entry-level job should be on the lowest rung of the ladder.) **L1**

Explain Ask students to write a short explanation of how outsourcing affects a firm, its workers, and people in other countries. (Firms benefit by reducing costs, some of the firm's employees lose their jobs, and people in other countries get jobs.) **L2**

Draw a Conclusion Ask students to write a few paragraphs about how they can use supply and demand to their advantage when planning their career. (The number of positions is expected to grow or there will be opportunities as a result of retirements. Students could also specialize in a field such as engineering or medicine.) **L3**

ASSESS

Review Key Terms
Have students write sentences using each key term.

 Study-to-Go Have students go to the Online Learning Center through **glencoe.com** to download free **Study-to-Go** content to their PDAs or cell phones.

RETEACH

W Writing Support

Enrichment

Setting Goals Have students write their goals. Ask them to identify each goal as short-, medium-, or long-term. (Goals will vary. For example, goals might include signing up for the correct classes, going to college, and having a home and family.)

R Reading Strategy

Illustrate Have students use a timeline to illustrate the relationships between short-, medium-, and long-term goals. (Timelines will vary. Students should understand that short-term goals are accomplished in a relatively short period of time. It takes longer to achieve a medium-term goal than a short-term goal. Long-term goals take longer to achieve than short- and medium-term goals.)

U Universal Access

English Language Learners
The job-search process can be a challenge to people who are learning to speak English as a second language. Encourage students to think of ways to capitalize on an ability to speak more than one language as part of a career plan.

Student Activity Workbook ☞ Assign the Section 20.2 Activities.

Activity correlates to Science standards.

Science/TechTRENDS

Job Stress and Healthy Careers

Many otherwise exciting jobs can also be quite stressful. Police officers and air traffic controllers have some of the more stressful jobs. Studies have found that a machine-controlled pace can also lead to job stress. Working alone at a monotonous job can be stressful. Over time, job stress can lead to serious health concerns. High blood pressure and heart attacks are extreme examples of how a job with high stress levels can affect the human body. Research into what a healthy career looks like has begun, but stress researchers hope to offer solutions that will enhance both productivity and worker health.

WebQuest

Go to the *Introduction to Business* Online Learning Center through **glencoe.com** for links to Web sites where you can research what makes a healthy career. Look for ways researchers can gauge stress levels in people and the ways they determine the stress levels of different jobs. Write a paragraph about what you find.

● As You Read
Make sure your goals are realistic. Aim high, but aim at what is possible.

Setting Goals

Before you reach your career goal, you must first set and reach other goals. Goals can be short-, medium-, or long-term. A *short-term goal* is something you might start and reach quickly. A *medium-term goal* is usually more **challenging** and takes longer to achieve. A *long-term goal* may take a long time to reach. Short- and medium-term goals can help you achieve a long-term goal. When setting goals, be as specific about each one as you can. Specific goals are easier to aim for and achieve.

Making a Career Plan

As you can see, making a career plan takes effort. You can create one now for one of your career choices. It is a good way to prepare for future career decisions.

Plot Your Career Course

Now that you have seen the process of career planning, get started with your own career. First, write your **ultimate** goal at the top of a sheet of paper. Then use library and Internet resources to research and make three lists. Your teacher, school counselor, and family can also help.

Graduation Plan In the first list, identify and select current courses, activities, and experiences that are related to your career goal. This list could lead to a specific career choice.

Science/TechTRENDS

WebQuest

Job Stress and Healthy Careers
Answers will vary but might describe things such as using employee questionnaires to judge stress levels. Paragraphs could also discuss the use of data such as the amount of sick time an employee takes.

● As You Read
Discuss the importance of planning and self-assessment to reach one's goals.

Education and Training Plan In the second list, detail the education or training you will need after high school. Be specific. List and explain your education and training alternatives, including courses you might take, and certificates or degrees you must earn.

Experience Plan In the third list, note experiences that will lead to your specific career choice. Include internships and volunteer, part-time, and temporary jobs.

Set Your Goals Once your lists are complete, determine whether each of the items listed is a short-, medium-, or long-term goal. Chart your goals in the order in which they will happen. Think about when you might start and complete each one. What can you do now? What will you do one, three, or five years from now? How long will it take to reach your ultimate goal?

Achieving Your Goals

The more specific and realistic your goals are, the more likely you are to achieve them. However, your goals and the time you spend on them may change over time. If you are not reaching your goals, do not lose motivation. Find out why you are stuck. As you review and revise your goals, you must also renew your motivation. The most important thing is to have a plan that gets you moving toward your ultimate career goal.

Employment Agencies Adecco is the world's largest employment agency. Each day, the Swiss company helps more than 700,000 people find work. Its services include temporary staffing, permanent placement, project assistance, and outsourcing. The firm also trains workers to meet local needs. *How can an employment agency help you as you enter the workforce?*

 Activity correlates to English Language Arts standards.

Section 20.2
After You Read

Review Key Concepts
1. Identify some sources to use for career research.
2. What are some ways to gain work experience?
3. What are short-, medium-, and long-term goals, and how do they relate to a career plan?

Academic Skills
4. **English Language Arts** Work in a small group with other students to produce a print advertisement, radio ad, or television spot designed to recruit applicants with certain aptitudes and skills to a specific position. For example, you might recruit recent law school graduates for positions.

5. **English Language Arts** Find a partner and write a role play about a job interview. Perform your role play for the class and conduct a discussion about it.

@ Go to the *Introduction to Business* Online Learning Center through **glencoe.com** to check your answers.

glencoe.com | **Section 20.2** Developing a Career Plan | **359**

Section 20.2

Review Key Concepts
1. libraries, the Internet, networks, career counselors, and work
2. internships, volunteerism, and job-shadowing
3. Short-term goals can be reached quickly. Medium-term goals are more challenging and take longer. Long-term goals take a long time to reach.

Academic Skills
4. **English Language Arts** Students should clearly identify the skills and aptitudes required for the position they have advertised.
5. **English Language Arts** Role plays will vary, but students should express experiences that can be expected as part of a job interview.

C Critical Thinking

Predict
Achieving Your Goals Ask students to write an essay that answers the question: Can you achieve any career goal that you set? (Students might note that you can set realistic goals, revise them, and then achieve them.)

Employment Agencies Agencies offer tools and testing to help identify workers' strengths and weaknesses; training; and work opportunities that are not widely advertised.

ASSESS

After You Read

Have students complete the Section 20.2 After You Read section review.

Online Study Tools
Have students go to the Online Learning Center through **glencoe.com** to:
• Take the Section 20.2 **Practice Test**.
• Download free **Study-to-Go** content to their PDAs or cell phones.

CLOSE

Culminating Activity
Create a Career Plan
Have students create a plan for a career that interests them. (Career plans will vary depending on students' interests.)

Chapter 20 *Review and Activities*

Vocabulary Review

1. Students should write complete sentences using each term correctly.

Review Key Concepts

2. It allows people to assess their potential, analyze their work options, and prepare for the future.

3. aptitudes; interests; abilities; values; and personality

4. As the global economy grows, more opportunities become available for U.S. companies and workers. Companies do business via e-commerce. Technology enables work to be performed more efficiently and in more cost-effective ways.

5. written sources, career counselors, networks, and work

6. the career ladder, outsourcing, and the supply of and demand for jobs

7. A short-term goal is something that can be reached right away. A medium-term goal usually is more challenging and takes longer. A long-term goal may take a long time to reach.

8. Graduation plan, education and training plan, and experience plan.

Section 20.1 *Summary*

Preparing for a Career Choosing a career is one of the most important decisions that you will make. While a job is work that people do for pay, a career usually builds on interest, knowledge, training, and experience from one or more jobs. Career planning can help you determine the right path to take. It involves considering factors such as your interests and skills. Other aspects to consider are changes that have affected the working world, such as the growth of the global economy and e-commerce. These and other changes create more job opportunities for workers.

Section 20.2 *Summary*

Developing a Career Plan After you identify potential careers, you should research them. Research sources include libraries, the Internet, networks, and work. New workers can learn more about careers through job shadowing, internships, and volunteering. They should also be aware of aspects of the working world that might affect them, such as career ladders and outsourcing. Setting short-, medium-, and long-term goals can give you direction. The more specific and realistic your goals are, the more likely you will achieve them and reach your ultimate career goal.

Vocabulary Review

1. On a sheet of paper, use each of these key terms and academic vocabulary terms in a sentence.

Key Terms		Academic Vocabulary	
full-time job	aptitude	pursuing	series
job	personality	overseas	internal
occupation	networking	via	challenging
career	job shadowing	adaptable	ultimate
interests	internship		
values	volunteerism		
skill	entry-level job		
ability	outsourcing		

Review Key Concepts

2. Discuss the importance of career planning.

3. Define at least five attributes you should know about yourself when analyzing careers.

4. Describe how work is changing.

5. Name four sources where you can learn about careers.

6. Describe some aspects of the working world that may affect a worker.

7. Define short-, medium-, and long-term goals.

8. Identify the three lists needed to make a career plan.

Critical Thinking

9. Knowing your strengths can help you choose the right career and jobs that will help you meet a career goal. Choosing the right career can enrich your personal development and help you meet your life goals. While weaknesses can have a negative effect, they can be addressed through professional and personal growth.

10. It could mean that it would take longer to find a job. If you have planned for this career, and your skills are in demand, then you might decide to continue pursuing it. Another option would be to adjust your career plan.

Critical Thinking

9. How can your strengths and weaknesses affect your job objectives, career choice, personal development, and life goals?

10. Suppose you have developed a plan for a career that has a good outlook. If the outlook became negative by the time you were ready to pursue the career, what would you do?

11. A *profession* usually requires a high level of education, such as law or medicine. A *trade* requires a high level of manual or technical skills, such as mechanics. Which one would you most likely pursue? Explain your answer.

12. Besides the resources mentioned, what other resources could you use to find information about careers?

13. Why might it be helpful to research information about careers in other countries?

14. Think about your personality. Write a list of words that describe you, such as outgoing, energetic, caring, loyal, quiet, serious, confident, friendly, creative, or shy. What potential business careers might fit your personality?

Write About It

15. Research the impact new technologies and global competition have on U.S. jobs. How do changes in technology and global competition affect workers? Write a one-page report on your findings.

16. Select two careers—one in business and the other in a different field that interests you. Research the careers. Use different techniques, such as job shadowing, volunteering, watching videos, or doing interviews. Write a review of each career.

17. Talk to a guidance counselor about your interests and skills. Develop a plan for personal growth and skill development. Write a thank-you letter to your counselor reviewing your plan.

18. Research types of self-assessment tools. See if there are any specific tools offered for people seeking business careers. Then write a two-page report summarizing your findings.

19. A *mentor* acts as an advocate, offering advice as a trusted counselor or guide. In two or more paragraphs, discuss how a mentor can help you prepare for a career.

Technology Applications

Spreadsheets and Written Reports
20. Create a spreadsheet listing your interests, values, skills, aptitudes, and personality traits. Identify and research two potential business careers—one in the United States and one in another country. Compare and contrast the careers. Choose one. Write a report assessing your skills and the education or training you might need for the chosen career.

Business Ethics

Job Shadowing
21. Imagine you just started an internship at a large phone company. You spend the first day job shadowing a longtime employee. During a tour of the office, you are given access to confidential information about the company's customers. Is this right or wrong? Explain your answer.

Critical Thinking

11. Answers will depend on students' self-assessments.

12. You could use books, magazines, and newspapers.

13. Everyone is part of the global economy. Therefore, employment developments in other countries can affect the U.S. job market.

14. Answers will vary, depending on the students' personalities and self-assessments.

Write About It

15. New technologies mean people must learn the latest procedures for their work. Global competition can mean fewer jobs in the United States.

16. Reviews should indicate an understanding of available career resources and research methods.

17. Each student will develop a different plan and letter.

18. Answers will vary. For example, Monster.com offers several tools for workers, including targeted advice.

19. Students could choose a mentor in a field that interests them with whom they could discuss their goals. Students could choose an e-coach in a particular field who can help the student develop skills and capabilities.

Technology Applications

20. Answers will be based on the careers students choose.

Business Ethics

21. Answers will vary. Companies usually choose their best employees to help train new workers through job shadowing. However, even some of them can have lapses in good judgment. In such cases, it is important for the person who gains access to the information to keep it confidential.

Applying Academics to Business

Applying Academics to Business

English Language Arts

22. Write an e-mail or letter introducing yourself to someone working in a career that interests you. Describe why you are interested in the career and request an information interview. Include a list of at least six questions for the person.

22. Letters and e-mails should be concise, formal, and respectful in tone.

23. Graphs should include information about at least five different careers.

24. Answers will vary, but students should discuss ways in which others perceive their strengths.

25. $35,670 × 101.5% = $36,205

$36,205 × 101.5% = $36,748

Mathematics

23. Using the *Occupational Outlook Handbook,* research the median annual salaries for five or six different careers that interest you. Consider careers suchs as architect, fire fighter, flight attendant, teacher, lawyer, or salesperson. Make a bar graph to compare the data you have gathered.

> **THEORY** **Graphs** A bar graph is a chart that uses either horizontal or vertical bars to show comparisons among categories. One axis of the chart shows the specific categories being compared, and the other axis represents a discrete value.

English Language Arts

24. Others can often see strengths in a person that the person himself or herself does not recognize. Pair up with another student you know fairly well. Each of you should list four or five strengths of your partner, and then exchange the lists and discuss them. Write a sentence or two telling what you learned about yourself from the experience.

Mathematics

25. The average earnings of a real estate agent in a medium-sized midwestern city have been growing at a rate of 1.5% per year for several years. If the average earnings were $35,670 last year, what are they likely to be next year?

> **THEORY** **Word Problems** Read carefully to make sure you understand the question. To solve this problem, ask yourself how many time periods are in question. Round to the nearest dollar.

Active Learning

26. Answers will depend on interviewees' responses.

Active Learning

Diagram Career Paths

26. Interview a family member or a friend of the family about his or her career ladder. Create a diagram that shows the jobs the interviewee has had. Then connect the skills, experience, education, and leadership roles that led to advanced positions on the ladder. Write a brief report about the interview, and share your work with the class.

Business in the Real World

27. Answers will depend on the types of programs that are offered in the school and community.

Business in the Real World

School-to-Work Programs

27. Create a chart of the programs in your school and community that link school to work. Ask your guidance counselor and teachers to help you. Include names, addresses, and telephone numbers of people to contact. Then, as a class, compile all the charts, and prepare a document that can be shared with the rest of your school.

ExamView Assessment Suite **CD** allows you to print out ready-made unit and chapter tests, complete with answer keys. You can also create customized tests.

TeacherWorks Plus provides complete teacher resources in one convenient package. It includes customizable lesson plans in calendar format, and instant access to many print program resources.

 **Real LIFE • skills**

ANALYZE ENTRY-LEVEL JOB SKILLS

28. Interview the personnel manager of a large firm or the person who hires employees for a small firm. Determine the qualities that the manager looks for in an entry-level employee. Ask about the noted strengths and weaknesses of today's applicants. Then prepare a brief report of your findings. Share it with the class.

 **Business CAREERS**

FIND YOUR DREAM JOB

29. Go to the *Introduction to Business* Online Learning Center through **glencoe.com** for a link to the Occupational Outlook Handbook Web site. Click on the "OOH Search/A-Z Index" link and enter the job title "architects, except landscape and naval." Then write a one-page report about this type of occupation. Conclude your report with a list of things you could do now to prepare yourself to pursue the occupation.

Role Play

CREATING A CAREER PLAN

30. Situation Imagine you are a career counselor for a state employment agency. A nearby high school asks you to talk to students about developing a career plan.

Activity Develop a presentation on the steps of a career plan.

Evaluation You will be evaluated on how well you meet the following performance indicators:

- Convey the importance of career planning.
- Outline the steps to complete a career plan.
- Give a well-organized presentation.
- Answer questions about planning a career.
- Project your voice, and use correct English and grammar.

Standardized Test Practice

Directions Choose the letter of the best answer. Write the letter for the answer on a separate piece of paper.

1. Given the following set of data, which is greatest?

{1, 3, 4, 5, 5, 7, 8, 8, 8, 9, 10, 10}

A   mean
B   median
C   mode
D   the mean and median are equal

 **TEST-TAKING TIP** Look for key words in test directions and questions such as *choose, describe, explain, compare, identify, similar, except, not,* and *but.*

 READING Go to the *Introduction to Business* Online Learning Center through **glencoe.com** for a list of outside reading suggestions.

 **STRATEGIES FOR STANDARDIZED TEST PREP SUCCESS**

Test Savvy Looking for key words (*describe, explain, compare*) as students read test directions can help them quickly understand the task, improve their ability to concentrate and manage stress, and help them pace themselves efficiently through the test. *Except, but,* and *not* provide clues that will help select the best answer.

 **Real LIFE • skills**

28. Answers will depend on interviewees' responses.

 **Business CAREERS**

29. Architects are professionals focusing on appearance, function, and safety as they design structures. Working conditions: comfortable consulting with clients, developing reports and drawing, and working with other professionals. Training and qualifications: licensure required with college degree in architecture, practical training, and passing score on the Architect Registration Examination. Job outlook is for average growth. As preparation, take math, science, art, and computer courses; develop interpersonal and presentation skills.

Role Play

30. Presentations should address the competencies noted in the Role Play. Career planning helps people to choose the right career. A career plan should begin with an ultimate career goal and include a graduation plan, an education and training plan, and an experience plan. It should indicate whether goals are short-, medium-, or long-term.

Standardized Test Practice
1. C

Standards-Based Lesson Planning
Introduction to Business provides students with instruction and assessment in the following fundamental content areas:

Content Standards Correlations	
Engage in the employment process.	pp. 367–370, 372–377, 378–381
Assess the job market and identify job-seeking skills required for entry-level employment.	pp. 372–377, 379–381
Analyze skills and traits necessary to gain employment and advance within a career (ethical behavior, teamwork, and personal traits).	pp. 367–370, 372–377, 378–381
Analyze employment characteristics necessary for the workplace.	pp. 367–370, 379–381
Compare a variety of workplaces.	pp. 369, 372, 379, 381
Describe the components of an employment portfolio, which could include work samples, inquiry letters, cover letters, a résumé, employment applications, follow-up letters, acceptance letters, and/or resignation letters.	pp. 379–381
Devise a career plan to include writing a résumé, completing a job application, preparing for an interview, and dressing appropriately.	pp. 379–380
Practice social skills in personal and professional situations.	pp. 377, 379–381
Discuss the importance of etiquette in a job interview.	p. 377
Participate in mock job interviews and demonstrate effective interview techniques.	pp. 377, 379–381
Accept constructive criticism.	pp. 377, 380–381

NCLB Activities, information, and skills practice will help your students attain No Child Left Behind proficiency. Students will improve their abilities in the following academic standards areas:

Academic Standards Correlations		
English Language Arts	**Activities/Features**	**Page**
NCTE 4 Use written language to communicate effectively	Applying Academics to Business	p. 380
NCTE 5 Apply knowledge of language structure and conventions to discuss texts	Standardized Test Practice	p. 381
NCTE 7 Conduct research and gather, evaluate, and synthesize data to communicate discoveries	After You Read	p. 377
NCTE 11 Participate as members of literacy communities	After You Read	p. 377
Mathematics		
Algebra Represent and analyze mathematical situations and structures using algebraic symbols	Ask S&P Applying Academics to Business	pp. 364, 380
Number and Operations Understand numbers, ways of representing numbers, relationships among numbers, and number systems	After You Read	p. 370
Problem Solving Monitor and reflect on the process of problem solving	Applying Academics to Business	p. 380
Science		
Content Standard G Students should develop understanding of science as a human endeavor	Science/Tech Trends	p. 372

Correlations   This chart shows the 21st Century Skills, foundation skills, and workplace competencies that students develop as they work in this chapter.

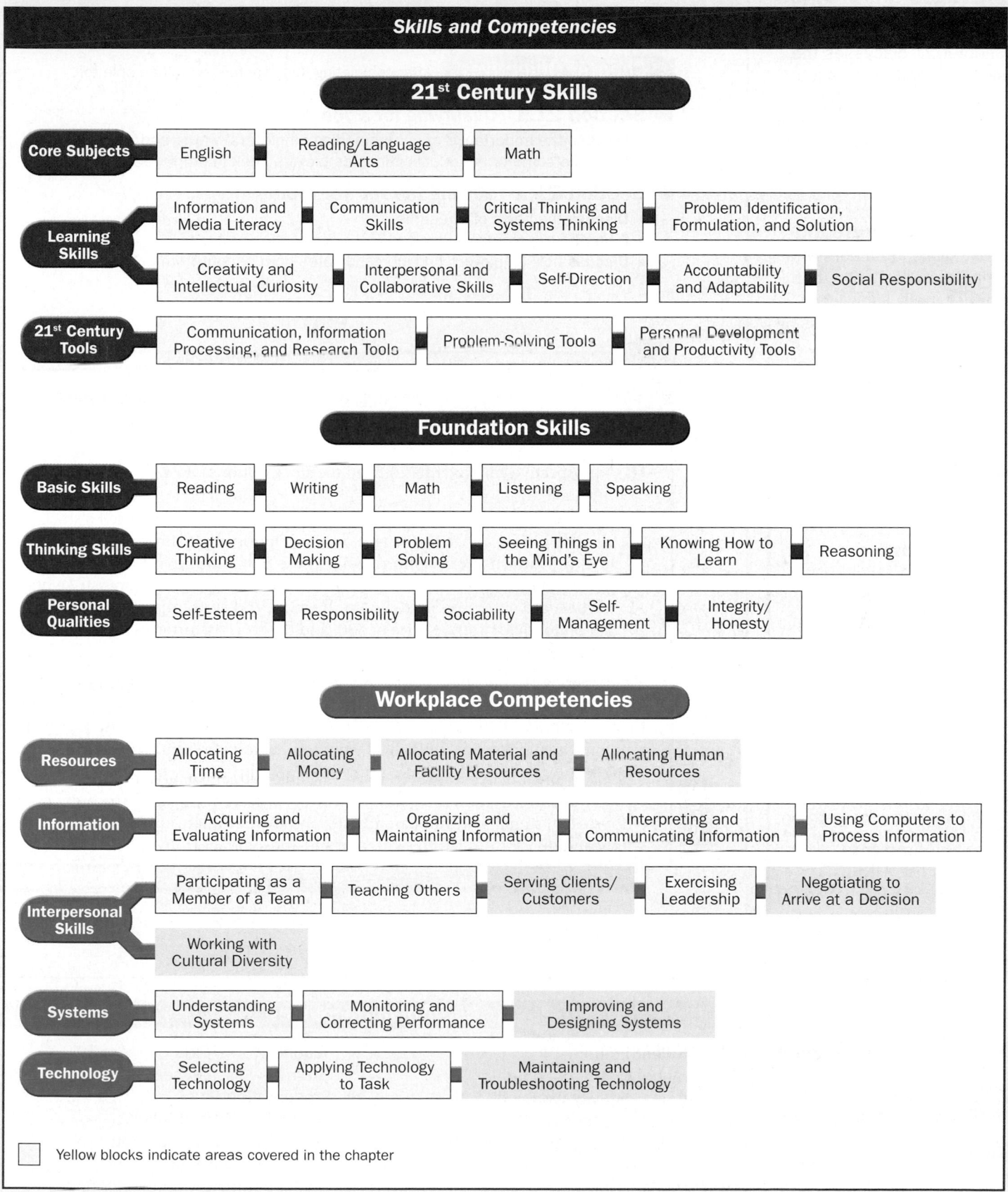

Skills and Competencies

21st Century Skills

| Core Subjects | English | Reading/Language Arts | Math |

Learning Skills
- Information and Media Literacy
- Communication Skills
- Critical Thinking and Systems Thinking
- Problem Identification, Formulation, and Solution
- Creativity and Intellectual Curiosity
- Interpersonal and Collaborative Skills
- Self-Direction
- Accountability and Adaptability
- Social Responsibility

21st Century Tools
- Communication, Information Processing, and Research Tools
- Problem-Solving Tools
- Personal Development and Productivity Tools

Foundation Skills

Basic Skills
- Reading
- Writing
- Math
- Listening
- Speaking

Thinking Skills
- Creative Thinking
- Decision Making
- Problem Solving
- Seeing Things in the Mind's Eye
- Knowing How to Learn
- Reasoning

Personal Qualities
- Self-Esteem
- Responsibility
- Sociability
- Self-Management
- Integrity/Honesty

Workplace Competencies

Resources
- Allocating Time
- Allocating Money
- Allocating Material and Facility Resources
- Allocating Human Resources

Information
- Acquiring and Evaluating Information
- Organizing and Maintaining Information
- Interpreting and Communicating Information
- Using Computers to Process Information

Interpersonal Skills
- Participating as a Member of a Team
- Teaching Others
- Serving Clients/Customers
- Exercising Leadership
- Negotiating to Arrive at a Decision
- Working with Cultural Diversity

Systems
- Understanding Systems
- Monitoring and Correcting Performance
- Improving and Designing Systems

Technology
- Selecting Technology
- Applying Technology to Task
- Maintaining and Troubleshooting Technology

☐ Yellow blocks indicate areas covered in the chapter

Chapter Overview

Introduce the Chapter

Getting a Job
Chapter 21 discusses the skills needed to get a job. Employability skills, the job search process, preparing a résumé, contacting potential employers, and interviewing for jobs are covered.

Building Background

Most students understand a "help wanted" sign, but do they really know what employers want? Assessing qualifications and skills is crucial in developing an effective résumé and mounting a successful job search.

>> Math Answer
The investor would pay $9,275. The equation is: (call amount + strike prices) × number of shares + commission = amount spent to purchase the stock or ($2 + $90) × 100 + $75 = $9,275.

>> Extension Activity
Write this option listing on the board:
TGT Mar 43 Call at $3.00

Ask a volunteer to explain the listing.
(TGT Mar 43 Call at $3.00 means that the investor could purchase for $3 a TGT call option that will expire in March for a strike price of $43 a share.)

N C L B Activity correlates to Math standards.

Getting a Job

Chapter Objectives After completing this chapter, you will be able to:

▶ **Section 21.1** *Qualifying for a Job*
- **Discuss** the importance of understanding employers' wants and needs.
- **Describe** some of the qualifications employers seek in employees.

▶ **Section 21.2** *Getting the Job You Want*
- **Discuss** the parts of a résumé.
- **Describe** the elements involved in the application process.
- **Discuss** how employers and job candidates both benefit from a job interview.

Ask **STANDARD &POOR'S** **Getting a Job: Employee Stock Options**

Q: A prospective employer has offered me stock options. How do I know if they are valuable?

A: Options are contracts that permit their holders to either buy or sell a stock at a preset price during a specified length of time. Options that allow investors to purchase stock are known as call options, while those that allow investors to sell stock are called put options. When a stock's current price makes an option's strike price attractive, the option is said to be "in the money." For example, if you're holding a call option with a strike price of $30, and the stock is currently trading at $35, your option is "in the money."

Mathematics A *Wall Street Journal* options listing reads: IBM Oct 90 Call at $2.00. This means that you could purchase an IBM call option for $2 that will expire in October for a strike price of $90 a share. If you decide to buy 100 shares because the stock is currently in the money, how much will you spend if you also must pay a $75 commission?

THEORY **Order of Operations** To solve a complex equation, it is important to write the equation correctly, and solve it in the correct order. This is called the order of operations. First, simplify within parentheses, and then evaluate any exponents. Then multiply and divide from left to right, and add and subtract from left to right.

Classroom Resources

- 📖 Student Edition
- 📖 Teacher Wraparound Edition
- 📁 Student Activity Workbook with Academic Integration
- 📁 Student Activity Workbook with Academic Integration TAE
- 📁 *Fast File*, Unit 7 Resources
- 📁 Inclusion in the Business Education Classroom

- 💿 TeacherWorks Plus
- 💿 *ExamView Assessment Suite*
- 💿 Presentation Plus!
- 💿 Vocabulary PuzzleMaker
- 💿 Interactive Student Edition
- 🖥 Online Student Edition
- 🖥 Online Learning Center with Podcasts

● **Extracurricular Activities** Employers prefer applicants who are involved in activities, such as sports and student government, as well as their school classes. **What extracurricular activities do you like the most?**

Review the Objectives
Introduce the chapter by reviewing the chapter objectives:

Section 21.1 *Objectives*
Discuss the importance of understanding employers' wants and needs. (Workers should know the requirements for a job to determine if they are qualified for it. Each job has its own responsibilities and required tasks and requires a different level and type of skills.)

Describe some of the qualifications employers seek in employees. (Employers look for education, skills, and work experience needed to do a particular job. They also look for basic skills that a worker needs to get a job, keep it, and do it well.)

Section 21.2 *Objectives*
Discuss the parts of a résumé. (A résumé is a summary of a worker's skills, education, and work experience.)

Describe the elements involved in the application process. (Preparing the cover letter and the job application; taking an employment test, and doing an interview are part of the application process.)

Discuss how employers and job candidates both benefit from a job interview. (Employers benefit because it helps them decide whom to hire. Job candidates benefit because interviews provide a chance to see if they really want the job.)

Discuss the Photo
● **Extracurricular Activities** Read the caption on the photo to students: Employers prefer applicants who are involved in activities, such as sports and student government, as well as their school classes.

Ask students: What extracurricular activities do you like the most? (Answers will vary, but students should be encouraged to think of activities that express the full range of their interests, from organized sports, to camping or knitting.) Ask students to consider ways these activities connect dynamically to their lives and have strengthened their dedication to the community. Possible answers include that these activities help students develop leadership skills and show the impact of teamwork.

FOCUS

Bell Ringer Activity

Qualifying for a Job
Organize students into small groups. Provide a page of the classified advertising section from the local newspaper to each group. Ask the groups to spend 10 minutes looking over the newspaper page and making a list of qualifications that employers list in their ads. (Lists may include years of experience, a college degree, or specific skills.)

Preteaching

Presentation Plus!
The Presentation Plus! CD provides visual teaching aids for this section.

PuzzleMaker
Use the Vocabulary PuzzleMaker to create a puzzle of the section's key terms. Students can complete the puzzle on paper or on a computer.

Graphic Organizer
Tell students to go to the Online Learning Center through **glencoe.com** for a printable graphic organizer. (The completed graphic organizer may describe five of these qualifications: level of education, required skills, work experience, character/ personality, extracurricular activities, and ability to get along with others.)

Connects academics to content.

Qualifying for a Job

Reading Guide

● Before You Read
Think about the skills you have that will help you stand out when pursuing a job.

Read to Learn
- Discuss the importance of understanding employers' wants and needs.
- Describe some of the qualifications employers seek in employees.

The Main Idea
Businesses and nonprofits provide different products and services. They need all kinds of workers to perform various tasks. You need to know what employers look for in an employee.

Key Concepts
- Finding a Job
- Your Qualifications and Skills

Vocabulary
Key Terms
qualifications
employability skills
body language
extracurricular activities

Academic Vocabulary
You will find these words in your reading and on your tests. Make sure you know their meanings.
administrator
accessing
seek
attitude

Graphic Organizer
In a table like the one below, list five qualifications employers look for in an employee, and describe what those qualifications mean to you.

Employment Qualifications	Description

Go to the *Introduction to Business* Online Learning Center through **glencoe.com** for a printable graphic organizer.

Academic Standards
English Language Arts
    NCTE 1 Read texts to acquire new information
Mathematics
    Number and Operations Understand numbers, ways of representing numbers, relationships among numbers, and number systems

366   **Chapter 21**   Getting a Job   glencoe.com

Reading Guide

● Before You Read
Students might mention their computer skills, interpersonal skills, or problem-solving skills help them to stand out when pursuing jobs.

D Develop Concepts
The Main Idea Ask students: What are some of the traits that employers look for in potential employees, regardless of the industry, company, or position? (Students might suggest honesty, dependability, a positive attitude, and a good work ethic.)

Finding a Job

Once you have an idea of what you want to do, you can take the next step and start your job search. As you search for a job, you will learn more about the various qualities employers look for in employees.

Knowing What Employers Want and Need

Businesses and nonprofits provide different products and services. They need all kinds of workers to perform different tasks. For example, a hospital needs doctors, nurses, cooks, janitors, supervisors, and an **administrator** who oversees operations. A department store needs retail buyers, sales associates, stock clerks, assistant managers, and a store manager who supervises everything. Each of these jobs carries tasks and a certain level of responsibility. Each also requires a different level and type of skills. You need to know what employers want and need in an employee.

Your Qualifications and Skills

Different jobs require different **qualifications**, or the education, skills, and work experience needed to do a particular job. What is important for one job might be less important for another. Employers look for more than job qualifications. They also look for employability skills. **Employability skills** are basic skills that you need to get a job, keep a job, and do well at a job.

✔ Reading Check **Define** What are employability skills?

Work Permits Most people under the age of 16 must obtain a work permit to have a job. In some states the age requirement is 18. A work permit is a legal document that allows a minor to hold a job. It shows the number of hours a minor can work and the kinds of jobs that can be held. *Why do you think the government requires work permits for minors?*

②ETHICS in Business

Applying for a Job

■ **Critical Reading** Life is full of important decisions. Think about the kinds of decisions that you make as you read the question below.

You are in the process of applying for a position at a large accounting firm. In a discussion with a friend who also applied for the position, you learn that applicants with more experience than you are being hired.

■ **Decision Making** Would learning about the applicants with more experience make you change your application, résumé, cover letter, or answers in an interview to make yourself look more qualified? Explain your answer.

TEACH

Discussion Starter
What Employers Need and Want
Start a discussion by asking students: Why is it important to know what employers want and need? (Students should understand that different jobs require different levels and types of skills.)

R Reading Strategy
Identify and List Ask students to identify and make a list of their current qualifications for employment. (Answers will vary. Students should include education, skills, and work experience.)

✔ Reading Check

Define Employability skills are basic skills that you need to get a job, keep a job, and do well at a job.

Work Permits The government expects minors to attend school. Many state work permits require young workers to maintain adequate high school grades. If minors' grades fall below certain levels, their work permits are revoked.

②ETHICS in Business

Decision Making Answers should emphasize the fact that a résumé is both a summary of your education and experience as well as the first impression a company has of you. Remind students that getting a job based on misleading statements on a résumé will invariably lead to problems in one's career.

TEACH (cont.)

S Skill Practice

Guided Practice

Explain Ask students to explain the relationship between a high school diploma and job opportunities. (Students should understand that without a high school diploma, job opportunities are limited. With a diploma, there are more opportunities.) **L1**

Draw a Conclusion Ask students to explain why most employers require a job applicant to have a high school diploma. (Answers will vary. Students should understand that having a high school diploma usually indicates the job candidate has the basic skills required for employment.) **L2**

Create a Poster Have students create a poster that illustrates the advantages of having a high school diploma. (Posters may include graphs, charts, or other statistical data as well as visual images to represent this data.) **L3**

ASSESS

Review Key Terms
Have students write sentences using each key term.

 Study-to-Go
Have students go to the Online Learning Center through **glencoe.com** to download free **Study-to-Go** content to their PDAs or cell phones.

Figure 21.1 — *Median Earnings of Full-Time Workers*

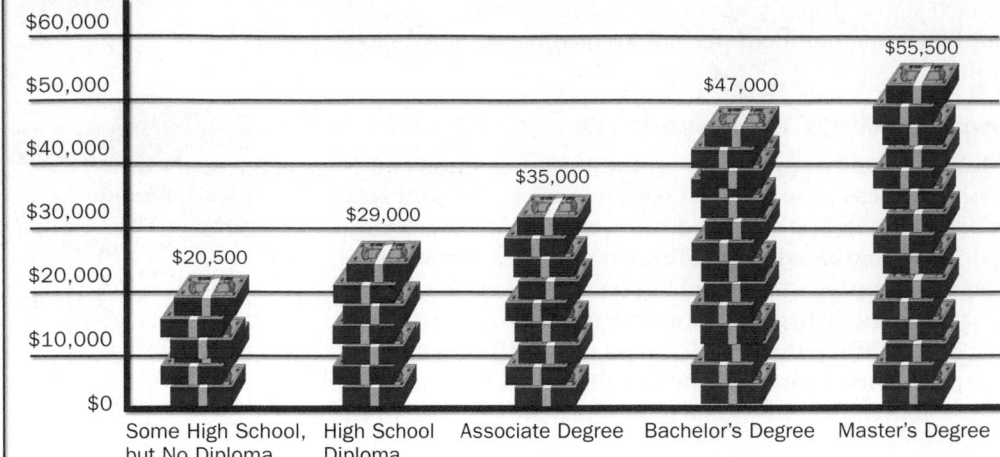

Source: Bureau of the Census, Bureau of Labor Statistics

● **Education and Earnings** One of the many advantages of education is that it increases your earnings potential. **What is the difference in the annual earnings of a high school dropout and a high school graduate?**

Level of Education

 For most jobs, employers want applicants to have at least a high school diploma. High school dropouts have fewer job opportunities, especially if they have no previous work experience. The more skills and education a worker has, the wider the job market will be for him or her. **Figure 21.1** illustrates the median income for workers based on their level of education.

Basic Skills

Almost all jobs require basic skills. Employees must be able to read well enough to function in their job. They should be able to do simple mathematical problems. They must also be able to communicate with others. Basic computer skills, such as entering or **accessing** data, are necessary. Many jobs also require basic work-related skills. For instance, a warehouse worker may need to know how to operate a forklift or specific machinery.

Work Experience

Experienced workers have proven skills and a familiarity with a job. They need less training to do a new job. That is why many employers want workers who have some work experience. It is important to get some kind of experience. Most jobs that require skills and experience pay more than those that do not.

368 **Chapter 21** Getting a Job

● **As You Read**

Students might say they would need specific skills, such as writing skills, or experience in production. Others may feel they would need a work record that shows a good work ethic.

Figure 21.1

● **Education and Earnings** The annual difference in earnings is $8,500.

Character and Personality

Skills are important, but employers also **seek** certain character traits in potential employees. Employers value hard work, honesty, dependability, and an ability to finish tasks. They also look for a good **attitude** toward work, a desire to do the job well, and the ability to work with others. Workers who can follow instructions as well as take initiative are also wanted. Sometimes, having strong character and personality traits can make up for weaknesses in other areas, such as experience. An employer can learn about these traits in several ways.

Body Language Body language often says more about you than spoken or written words. Your **body language**, or nonverbal communication, includes your posture, eye contact, facial expressions, and gestures. They can either add to or detract from the impression you make. For example, if you fidget during interviews, you may appear to lack interest in the job.

BusinessWeek *Reader and Case Study*

These Technicians Are Better Than Robots

Japan is turning to hyper-skilled *supaa ginosha*, or super technicians, to preserve its manufacturing edge.

Behind the locked doors of a Sharp® Corp. factory in the central Japanese city of Nara, Rina Masuda spends her days at a task most people would find both mind-numbing and infuriating. With the searing tip of a soldering iron, she guides droplets of molten metal on a circuit board to the edges of a microchip. In less than a minute she has the chip standing on dozens of tiny metal legs separated by a hair's breadth to keep electrons flowing smoothly. Masuda's job seems at odds with the bank of machines just a few yards away that spit out hundreds of circuit boards every hour. Yet Masuda doesn't fear losing her job to automation, at least not until the equipment is as precise as she is. When the machines botch a job, she's called in to fix up the chips. "The soldering I do by hand is far superior to anything the machines can do," says the 33-year-old.

glencoe.com

Japan has thousands of workers like Masuda, with talents so extraordinary that no machine can do their jobs. Their skills have amounted to the X factor that has given Japan a manufacturing edge for decades.

 CASE STUDY Go to the *Introduction to Business* Online Learning Center through **glencoe.com** for the *BusinessWeek* Reader Case Study.

Active Learning

Research the manufacturing processes that are used to create microchips. Use a device that does not contain a microchip (such as a pen or pencil) to write a letter to your teacher about the ways microchips have made your life easier.

Section 21.1 Qualifying for a Job **369**

Section 21.1

RETEACH

W Writing Support
Enrichment
Explain a Preference
Ask students to write an essay that explains why an employer might hire a worker who has a positive attitude instead of a disagreeable person with more experience. (Students might suggest that a disagreeable person is likely to hurt a business while a positive person can learn needed skills over time.)

U Universal Access
Students with Learning Disabilities Encourage students with learning disabilities to focus on the skills that they have developed. Point out that there are many rewarding careers available.

R Reading Strategy
Provide Examples Ask students to provide examples of body language that they should avoid when they talk to a potential employer. (Answers will vary. Students might suggest slouching, fidgeting, frowning, scratching, or always looking at their feet.)

Student Activity Workbook ☞ Assign the Section 21.1 Activities.

BusinessWeek *Reader and Case Study*

These Technicians Are Better Than Robots

CASE STUDY Have students go to the *Introduction to Business* Online Learning Center through **glencoe.com** to download a Case Study activity that corresponds to the article. The activity and answer key are also available on the TeacherWorks Plus CD.

Active Learning

Answers will vary but may include that computers have made it easier to communicate. Microchips are also in various products, such as cars and watches, are important to traffic-light timing, and form a vital part of our defense infrastructure.

369

RETEACH (cont.)

C Critical Thinking

Investigate

School Records Ask students to find out what information your school releases to prospective employers and college admission offices. Have students write a brief statement explaining the policy. (Answers will depend on school policies.)

ASSESS

• After You Read

Have students complete the Section 21.1 After You Read section review.

Online Study Tools

Have students go to the Online Learning Center through **glencoe.com** to:

- Take the Section 21.1 **Practice Test**.
- Download free **Study-to-Go** content to their PDAs or cell phones.

CLOSE

Culminating Activity
Make the Most of School

Ask students to develop a list of suggestions that can help students prepare for future work. Organize students into small groups, and ask the groups to create a poem that can be recited to the class. (Lists and poems will vary.)

School Performance Employers might check school records to see how a potential employee performs. Good grades show motivation and a willingness to apply oneself to a task. Some employers check attendance records. Even if you do not have the best grades, good attendance and punctuality indicate that you are reliable and will show up for work on time.

Extracurricular Activities **Extracurricular activities** are activities that you do besides schoolwork. They indicate extra effort and interests on your part, as well as possible leadership ability. For example, taking part in team sports shows an ability to work in a group. Volunteer work shows commitment and responsibility. Your efforts in and out of school create a record that future employers may want to see.

Your Overall Impression Think of a personnel director with three piles of job applications. One pile is labeled "Yes." One is labeled "Maybe." One is labeled "No." Your goal is to get your application into the "Yes" pile. Consider the way you present yourself. Your writing, problem solving, creative thinking, and reasoning skills will show. Employers will be influenced by the way you dress and whether you are well-groomed. They will also notice if you use slang or anything other than standard English. A good first impression increases your chances of getting hired.

NCLB Activity correlates to Math standards.

Section 21.1

• After You Read

Review Key Concepts

1. Why is it important to know what employers look for in an employee?
2. What are employability skills?
3. What are some of the qualifications that employers consider for potential new employees?

Academic Skills

4. **Mathematics** Mike got a job offer from Loom Inc. He would earn \$25,000 a year plus benefits. The value of the premiums the company pays to the insurance company is $\frac{3}{5}$ of 10% of his base salary. How much are the premiums for a year?

THEORY **Numbers and Operations: Fractions, Decimals, and Percents** Fractions, percents, and decimals are three ways to express numbers between 0 and 1. You can convert one to another. To solve this problem, convert "$\frac{3}{5}$ of 10%" to a decimal, and multiply by \$25,000.

 For math help, go to the Math Appendix.

 Go to the *Introduction to Business* Online Learning Center through **glencoe.com** to check your answers.

Section 21.1

Review Key Concepts

1. Workers need to know what employers want to determine if they have the necessary qualifications.
2. Employability skills are basic skills that you need to get, keep, and do well at a job.
3. education, basic skills, work experience, character and personality, body language, school records, and extracurricular activities

Academic Skills
4. **Mathematics** $\frac{3}{5} \times 10\% = 0.6 \times 0.1 = 0.06$
   $\$25,000 \times 0.06 = \$1,500$

Getting the Job You Want

Reading Guide

Before You Read

Think about some ways that potential employers can get more information about job applicants.

D

Read to Learn
- Discuss the parts of a résumé.
- Describe the elements involved in the application process.
- Discuss how employers and job candidates both benefit from a job interview.

The Main Idea
One of the first steps in finding a job is to prepare a resume. A resumé tells an employer what a worker has to offer. Cover letters, job applications, and interviews also provide information about potential employees.

Key Concepts
- Beginning Your Job Search
- Contacting Potential Employers
- Interviewing for Jobs

Vocabulary

Key Terms
résumé
chronological résumé
job objective
cover letter
job interview

Academic Vocabulary
You will find these words in your reading and on your tests. Make sure you know their meanings.

assess   transferable
achievements   objective

Graphic Organizer
In a figure like the one below, note five sources you can use to find a job.

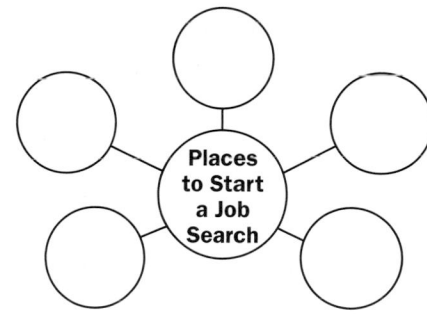

Places to Start a Job Search

 Go to the *Introduction to Business* Online Learning Center through **glencoe.com** for a printable graphic organizer.

Academic Standards
English Language Arts
NCTE 1 Read texts to acquire new information
NCTE 7 Conduct research, and gather, evaluate, and synthesize data to communicate discoveries
NCTE 11 Participate as members of literacy communities
Science
Content Standard G Students should develop understanding of science as a human endeavor

NCLB

Reading Guide

Before You Read

Résumés, job applications, and personal interviews are ways for employers to get information about applicants.

D Develop Concepts

The Main Idea Ask students: Why do employers ask applicants to fill out a job application if the potential employee has already submitted a résumé? (A résumé and a job application contain different information.)

Bell Ringer Activity

Getting the Job You Want
Finding a job requires convincing an employer to hire you. Ask students to identify some of their best "features" that they could use to sell themselves to an employer. (Students might include attributes such as being hard working, dependable, amiable, organized, and willing to learn, or mention specific skills that they have.)

Preteaching

Presentation Plus! ●
The Presentation Plus! CD provides visual teaching aids for this section.

PuzzleMaker ●
Use the Vocabulary PuzzleMaker to create a puzzle of the section's key terms. Students can complete the puzzle on paper or on a computer.

Graphic Organizer
Tell students to go to the Online Learning Center through **glencoe.com** for a printable graphic organizer. (Answers include: leads from family, friends, community leaders; school placement offices; want ads, Internet sites, and employment agencies.)

NCLB Connects academics to content.

TEACH

Discussion Starter
Beginning Your Job Search
Read each of the following achievements and ask students to decide if they should be included in a résumé. For the items that should be included, discuss where they might appear and how they might be worded. (1) I got an A in Computer Business Applications. (2) I help my father keep records for his business. (3) My mother is an insurance agent. (4) I am certified in CPR. (5) I can type 55 words per minute. (6) I played first base on my school's baseball team. (With the exception of item 3, all of these things could be worked into a résumé, but instead of listing the grade for one class, a student might describe his or her computer skills.)

R Reading Strategy

Identify Ask students to identity three bullet points that could complete this statement: To make a good first impression, my résumé should be _____. (organized, neat, error-free, and limited to one page)

● As You Read
Answers will be based on students' skills, interests, and opinions.

● As You Read
Think about jobs you might like most and might be able to do best.

Beginning Your Job Search

Before you begin looking for a job, you need to discover which jobs you would like most and would be able to do best. You should avoid limiting your search to one type of job. **Assess** the job market objectively. Some jobs require little or no experience. Other jobs require work experience. Still others might require certain skills.

Preparing Your Résumé

One of the first steps in finding a job is to prepare a résumé. A **résumé** is a summary of your skills, education, and work experience. It tells an employer what you can offer as a worker. Its purpose is to persuade potential employers to interview you. Some people also list their hobbies on their résumé to provide an indication of their personal interests and other work-related qualifications.

Your résumé gives an employer his or her first impression of you. If it is disorganized and full of mistakes, your chances of getting an interview will be slim. Check your grammar and spelling before submitting your résumé. Make sure it is neat and that the information in it is correct. Try to limit it to one page.

There are different types of résumés. The most common type is the chronological résumé. A **chronological résumé** lists your **achievements** in time order. It has five parts: the heading, the job objective, a skills summary, work experience, and education. **Figure 21.2** shows an example of a chronological résumé.

Science/Tech**TRENDS**

Becoming an Astronaut
Many young people want to be astronauts someday. What does it take to become an astronaut? While there is no real step-by-step way to ensure employment as an astronaut, there are some things you can do that will put you on the right path. A bachelor's degree in science or mathematics is the first step toward a career in space travel. Extracurricular activities such as participating in your school's science club can also help you reach your goal of becoming an astronaut. An understanding of the physical challenges of space travel is also important.

WebQuest

Go to the *Introduction to Business* Online Learning Center through **glencoe.com** for links to Web sites where you can research how someone would become an astronaut. Look for examples of how astronauts can be affected by space travel. Write a few paragraphs describing what steps you would take to become an astronaut.

Science/Tech**TRENDS**

WebQuest

Becoming an Astronaut Answers will vary but should include both the educational requirements and the physical challenges of becoming an astronaut.

NCLB Activity correlates to Science standards.

Figure 21.2 — *Résumé*

24 Mill Creek Road   Phone (850) 555-0123
Sunnyville, FL 32300   TPhilips@school.edu

Teri Philips

Job Objective	Full-time administrative position in law office.
Skills Summary	• Dependable, responsible, and hard-working.
	• Strong interpersonal and communication skills.
	• Maintain confidentiality working with legal documents.
	• Knowledge of word-processing and database software.
	• Bilingual in English and Spanish.
	• Typing speed: 70 wpm.

Work Experience   Jan. 2005–present, O'Malley Law Firm, Bremerton, FL
Administrative Assistant (part-time)
• Perform essential administrative tasks such as scheduling, filing, managing correspondence, and answering phones
• Transcribe case files and notes.

Feb. 2003–Dec. 2004, Sunnyville Museum, Sunnyville, FL
Staff Assistant (part-time)
• Performed administrative and managerial duties such as handling phone calls, assisting at museum events, filing, and answering questions from visitors.
• Coordinated projects for exhibits.

Nov. 2002–Feb. 2005, Community Law Center, Morgantown, FL
Volunteer Staff Assistant (part-time)
• Assist lawyers in providing free legal services to community residents.
• Perform administrative tasks such as typing documents and corresponding with clients.

Education   2003, Morgantown High School, Morgantown, FL
High School Diploma
• Course work in criminal justice and introduction to law.
• Participation in statewide Law Honors Project.
• Three semesters of computer applications courses.

● **Market Yourself** A résumé is a tool you can use to market yourself to prospective employers. It tells who you are, what you want to do, what you have done, and what you can do. **What are some things you should emphasize on your résumé?**

TEACH (cont.)

S Skill Practice
Guided Practice

Identify Ask students to name the parts of a résumé. (1. heading, 2. job objective, 3. skills, 4. work experience, 5. education) **L1**

Classify Ask students to classify each of these résumé facts according to where they should be placed.

(1) I have a driver's license.
(2) I will graduate In June.
(3) I live at 6432 Elm.
(4) I worked as a lifeguard.
(5) I want to operate a backhoe. ((1) skills summary, (2) education, (3) heading, (4) work experience, and (5) job objective) **L2**

Express an Opinion Tell students to explain whether a job applicant's problems should be included in a résumé. (No. They can be explained at an interview if they relate to the job.) **L3**

ASSESS

Review Key Terms
Have students write sentences using each key term.

 Study-to-Go Have students go to the Online Learning Center through **glencoe.com** to download free **Study-to-Go** content to their PDAs or cell phones.

Figure 21.2

● **Market Yourself** Answers will vary but should include consideration of the students' strengths and most marketable skills.

● **Perfect Attendance**
Employers value employees who understand the importance of attendance and punctuality. **Why is it important that all participants in a meeting are on time?**

The Parts of a Résumé The first part of the résumé is the heading. The heading contains your name and contact information. Include your street address, city, state, zip code, home phone number, and e-mail address. The second part, the **job objective**, is a statement about the type of job you want. The third part, the skills summary, includes job-specific skills such as keyboarding, computer use, and **transferable** skills. The fourth part, the work experience section, lists the jobs you have done. The fifth part, the education section, shows your secondary and postsecondary education. List the name and location of each school, and the date you finished or the date you will finish.

✔ Reading Check  **Identify** What are the essential parts of a résumé?

Real World

Looking for Openings A *job lead* is information about a job opening. Job leads can come from several sources, including a network of people who could help you. Some of them might also give you a *referral*, or a recommendation to an employer or another job lead. *What are some other ways you can find out about job openings?*

Contacting Potential Employers

Once you have prepared a résumé and found interesting job openings, you can tailor your résumé to each job. Then start to apply for the jobs. The process of applying for a job can include submitting a cover letter, filling out a job application, taking an employment test, and being interviewed.

Cover Letter

You should always include a cover letter with your résumé. A **cover letter** tells the employer about you and why you are applying for a job. It can also be used to inquire about possible job openings. As with your résumé, your cover letter also needs to make a good impression. It should be formatted and error-free. **Figure 21.3** shows an example of a cover letter.

374 **Chapter 21** Getting a Job

Figure 21.3 — Cover Letter

Teri Philips
24 Mill Creek Road • Sunnyville, FL 32300
Phone: (850) 555-0123 • **tphilips@school.edu**

October 30, 20--

Thomas L. Warren
T.L. Warren & Associates
300 Commerce Center Plaza
Miami, FL 33109

Dear Mr. Warren:

Peter Cortez suggested that I write to you about a full-time administrative position in your law firm.

I am dependable, efficient, and personable. I pay attention to detail, have excellent communication and organizational skills, and enjoy working with people.

I have three years of experience working in an office environment. That includes doing volunteer work for a nonprofit organization that provides free legal services to community residents. I have handled incoming and outgoing phone calls, and typed and distributed documents. Please see my enclosed résumé to learn more about my qualifications.

Thank you very much for considering me for a position with your firm. I look forward to speaking with you and telling you more about what makes me a good match for the job.

Sincerely,

Teri Philips

Teri Philips

Enclosure

● **Introduce Yourself** A cover letter introduces you to a prospective employer. It should be tailored to the position of interest to you. **What should accompany the cover letter?**

Figure 21.3

● **Introduce Yourself** A résumé and any supporting documents, such as references, should accompany the cover letter.

RETEACH (cont.)

W Writing Support

Enrichment

The Inside Address of a Formal Letter Have students consult an authoritative source to determine the appropriate way to format the inside address for a formal letter. Encourage students to carefully verify the correct spelling of the recipient's name, title, and street address. Ask a volunteer to explain the reason such care is crucial to a job applicant's success. (No one likes to have his or her name misspelled, and mistakes in the title and address can cause amusement or keep the proper recipient from receiving the application. By devoting the time to do it right, an applicant can display a level of care and respect that can be crucial in setting the tone for this important first meeting.)

R Reading Strategy

Formatting for Clarity Ask students why they think the writer of this letter left so much white space between paragraphs by using a block-style format instead of indenting each paragraph and following one paragraph immediately with another? (The block-style has a clean look and creates a strong visual distinction between the ideas in one paragraph and those in another.)

RETEACH (cont.)

W Writing Support

Preparation

The Job Application Have students create a spreadsheet with information that will help them fill out job applications. (Commonly requested information includes: residences for the last 10 years; school names, addresses, and phone numbers; dates and names of any special certifications; and names and addresses of references.)

R Reading Strategy

Compare and Contrast Ask students: How do you think a driving test for a job might present different stresses than one for a license? (Every testing circumstance creates stress for most people. Sometimes, however, reactions to stress depend on whether there is a "second chance.") Follow up by asking what students can do to alleviate stress. (Practicing is probably the best option.)

C Critical Thinking

Plan for Confidence

Interviewing for Jobs Ask students to explain why it is important to prepare answers to common interview questions. (Knowing the answers to common questions will allow the interviewee to be more relaxed during the interview.)

Student Activity Workbook ☞ Assign the Section 21.2 Activities.

The Job Application

W A job application form is a printed sheet with blank spaces that you fill in to apply for a job. The person who applies for a job is called a job applicant. Like your résumé, an application form presents you to a potential employer. It is easier to fill out if you have a résumé and a list of available references.

Employment Testing

R When you apply for a job, you might be asked to take a test to see if you have the required skills. For example, truck drivers must take a driving test before being hired. Jobs for government or law enforcement may require drug and lie-detector testing.

Interviewing for Jobs

C After you have found a job opening, filled out an application, and sent your cover letter and résumé, an employer may call you for a interview. A **job interview** is a formal face-to-face discussion between an employer and a potential employee. Employers use interviews to make hiring decisions. It is important to do well in an interview.

Interviews are also helpful to job candidates. They provide a chance to see if you really want the job. They also allow you to see whether you and the employer are a good match. You can do well in an interview if you prepare. Research the company. Prepare answers to common interview questions. Think of questions to ask the interviewer. Practice your interview skills.

● **The Job Interview** The job interview is an important part of the job search process. Suppose this is an interview for a management trainee position. **Is the person being interviewed dressed appropriately?**

Discuss the Photo

● **The Job Interview** The person being interviewed looks clean and neat. She is probably dressed appropriately for most positions. However, she is being greeted by a woman wearing a jacket, a signal that positions for management trainees at this company require slightly more formal dress.

Job Interview Tips

Before you go on a job interview, keep these things in mind:

- *Do some homework.* Find out about the job.
- *Be on time.* Otherwise, you may be considered disrespectful.
- *Wear appropriate clothes.* Dress neatly and in a style appropriate for the job you are seeking.
- *Put your best foot forward.* Shake the interviewer's hand. Be courteous. Be aware of your body language.
- *Ask questions about the job.* You need to find out if it is right for you.
- *Ask about the next step.* After the interview, say, "I am very interested in this job. What is the next step?"
- *Do not expect an answer right away.* The employer will need time to decide who to hire.

Follow up after the interview by calling or writing a letter thanking the interviewer. In the letter, restate your **objective** and describe how your skills and experiences are well-suited to the job. This shows your interest in the job and allows you to add anything you forgot to mention. Learn from each experience, and work on your weaknesses. Doing so will increase your chances of getting the job you want.

Accepting a Job Offer Job offers often come over the phone. However, writing a letter of acceptance is an appropriate way to begin a professional relationship. An acceptance letter states when the new employee expects to start work, what position he or she will be filling, the agreed-upon wage, and other known terms of employment. *Why would you want to accept a job offer in writing?*

 Activity correlates to English Language Arts standards.

Section 21.2

After You Read

Review Key Concepts
1. What is a résumé? What is its purpose?
2. Explain what is usually involved in the process of applying for a job.
3. How can an employer and a job applicant both benefit from a job interview?

Academic Skills
4. **English Language Arts** Read the employment want ads in your local newspaper for a week. Write three paragraphs about the kinds of jobs advertised in your area, the salary ranges for those jobs, the benefits available, and the qualifications or work experience required.

5. **English Language Arts** Working in a group of three, participate in mock job interviews for a grocery store clerk, lifeguard, and newspaper delivery person. Have group members take turns role-playing the interviewer, job applicant, and observer. The observer should provide written feedback to the interviewer and job applicant.

> Go to the *Introduction to Business* Online Learning Center through **glencoe.com** to check your answers.

RETEACH (cont.)

C Critical Thinking
Practice
Job Interview Tips Have students prepare a spreadsheet of the tips on this page. In one column, place the tips. In the next column, have them discuss a way to address each tip. (Spreadsheets will vary but should list and discuss tips.)

Accepting a Job Offer It provides a written document to assure that the employee and the employer are in agreement over the terms of employment.

ASSESS

After You Read

Have students complete the Section 21.2 After You Read section review.

Online Study Tools
Have students go to the Online Learning Center through **glencoe.com** to:

- Take the Section 21.2 **Practice Test**.
- Download free **Study-to-Go** content to their PDAs or cell phones.

CLOSE

Culminating Activity
Prepare a Résumé
Ask students to prepare a résumé to obtain a part-time job. (Résumés will vary depending on students' experiences and objectives.)

Section 21.2

Review Key Concepts
1. A summary of a worker's qualifications. Its purpose is to persuade potential employers to interview a job candidate.
2. Submitting a cover letter, filling out a job application, taking an employment test, and being interviewed.
3. Interviews provide a face-to-face opportunity that allows employers to get information about whom to hire and job applicants a chance to learn about the job.

Academic Skills
4. **English Language Arts** Answers will vary according to the types of jobs available in your area.
5. **English Language Arts** Feedback will vary.

Vocabulary Review

1. Students should write complete sentences using each term correctly.

Review Key Concepts

2. Each job has its own responsibilities and required tasks. Each also requires different levels and types of skills.

3. Employers look for qualifications needed to do a particular job. They also look for employability skills.

4. A résumé is a summary of a worker's skills, education, and work experience.

5. preparing the cover letter and the job application; taking an employment test, and doing an interview

6. Employers benefit because it helps them decide whom to hire. Job candidates benefit because interviews provide a chance to see if they really want the job.

Critical Thinking

7. to determine whether you will like the job and would be able to do it

8. people who have problems communicating could have difficulty working with others

Section 21.1 *Summary*

Qualifying for a Job Within an organization, each job carries a certain level of responsibility and tasks to be done. Jobs also require different levels and types of skills. As a worker, you need to know the qualifications employers look for in an employee. Skills are important, but employers also seek certain character traits in potential employees. Employers value hard work, honesty, dependability, and an ability to finish tasks. They also look for good personality traits in workers.

Section 21.2 *Summary*

Getting the Job You Want Before you begin looking for a job, you should discover which jobs you would like most and would be able to do best. One of the first steps in finding a job is to prepare a résumé, which tells an employer about your qualifications. Its purpose is to persuade potential employers to interview you. The process of applying for a job can include submitting a cover letter, filling out a job application, taking an employment test, and being interviewed.

Vocabulary Review

1. On a sheet of paper, use each of these key terms and academic vocabulary terms in a sentence.

Key Terms	Academic Vocabulary
qualifications	administrator
employability skills	accessing
body language	seek
extracurricular activities	attitude
résumé	assess
chronological résumé	achievements
job objective	transferable
cover letter	objective
job interview	

Review Key Concepts

2. Discuss the importance of understanding employers' wants and needs.

3. Describe some of the qualifications employers seek in employees.

4. Discuss the parts of a résumé.

5. Describe the elements involved in the application process.

6. Discuss how employers and job candidates both benefit from a job interview.

9. You should first review the résumé for errors in spelling, dates, and information. You also should run spell-check and grammar-check applications to catch mistakes.

10. A job lead is information about an available job, but a referral is a recommendation for a job. A job lead can be seen by many people. However, a referral can give a worker an advantage over other job candidates.

11. Answers should indicate an understanding of the differences between a job and a career. The accounting firm will have more career opportunities than the small grocery store.

Critical Thinking

7. Why is it important to find out as much as possible about a position before being offered the job?

8. How does your personality affect your relationships with your coworkers?

9. What are some ways to ensure that your résumé is correct before sending it to an employer?

10. Why is a referral considered to be better than a job lead?

11. Imagine you just received a college degree in accounting. You interview for two jobs: an entry-level job at a large accounting firm and a lead accountant position at a small grocery store. Which job would you prefer? Explain your answer.

12. Why might an employer want to know whether an applicant for an entry-level job has developed leadership skills while in high school or college?

13. Indicate how you affect your own employability as a student today.

14. *Productivity* is the rate at which a company or worker produces goods or services. What traits enhance a worker's productivity? What traits hinder it?

Write About It

15. Suppose you would like to get a summer job. Write a letter inquiring about possible job opportunities at a company where you would like to work.

16. A personnel assistant contacts you about your letter of inquiry. He says the company will have several summer jobs for which you might qualify. Prepare a résumé and a cover letter for a specific summer job at the company.

17. Imagine you have been interviewed for an office job at a company that makes machines. You would do a variety of tasks. You would receive a good salary. However, you would work in a very noisy area. Consider your likes and dislikes about the job. Write a thank-you letter to the interviewer.

18. Get a job application. You might get one from a teacher, a school career center, a business, a library, an employment agency, or the Internet. Complete the form. List the items that are on the application form that are not covered in your résumé.

19. Imagine that you have been offered the job you wanted. Write a letter of acceptance to the employer.

Technology Applications

Word-Processing Software

20. Analyze the job market. The Internet, newspaper want ads, and job boards are all sources of current information. Which fields seem to have the most job openings? Which ones have the fewest? What types of entrepreneurial opportunities are available? What seems to be the current outlook for the types of jobs that interest you? Write a one-page report on your conclusions. Include information on job duties and requirements, pay, and benefits.

Business Ethics

Stretching the Truth

21. Suppose you completed $3\frac{1}{2}$ years of college but did not graduate. You see an ad for a job that you really want, but the job description states that you must have a college degree. You meet all the other requirements and feel that you would be perfect for the job. If you state that you received a college degree, you will increase your chances of being interviewed and subsequently hired. What should you do?

Chapter 21 Review and Activities **379**

Critical Thinking

12. The employer most likely wants to see that the candidate has potential for advancement.

13. Students can research various companies and industries, and read about current events, especially those that affect their potential career field. They also can work in part-time, temporary, or volunteer jobs.

14. Being dedicated and willing to learn can result in high productivity. Having a poor work ethic can result in low productivity.

Write About It

15. The letter should explain the student's background and describe why he or she is interested in working for the company.

16. Students' letters and résumés will vary.

17. If you want the job, it is important not to speak negatively about it or the company. If the noise level will be a problem, you could think of a way to solve it and include your suggestion in your letter.

18. Answers will vary, but lists may include a Social Security number and a question about eligibility to work in this country.

19. Acceptance letters should include the elements discussed as well as a statement about the student's enthusiasm.

Technology Applications

20. Answers will depend on students' observations and the types of jobs chosen for research.

Business Ethics

21. Make sure students understand that they should not state anything that is not true on a résumé. Applicants can emphasize their other qualifications and their interest in the position.

379

Applying Academics to Business

22. Responses will vary, but students should avoid using forms of the verb *to be*.

23. Once the student solves for *x* in the proportion above, he or she can multiply by 20, the number of trips per month, subtract the total from $2,000, and compare the result with $1,920.

24. Here is a sample answer:
- presented a session on teamwork at new-employee training session
- graduated from management training program
- developed part-time employees' weekly schedule

25. Compute the cost of the eggs, and then subtract 10% and compare the result to $5.00 (4 × $1.60) − .1 (4 × $1.60) = $5.76. The customer still does not have enough money.

Active Learning

26. Interviewees should be courteous, ask questions, and give details about their background. Interviewers should only ask appropriate questions.

Business in the Real World

27. Most job applications require the names and addresses of current and previous employers; dates of employment; and reasons for leaving.

Applying Academics to Business

English Language Arts
22. Résumés usually include an employment objective. Write three different employment objectives for different types of jobs. Make your objectives brief and to the point, and use the active voice.

Mathematics
23. Imagine that you have two job offers. The first pays $2,000 a month and requires a 48-mile round-trip commute. The second is closer to home and you could easily walk or ride a bike to work, but it pays only $1,920 a month. You will be working five days a week. Taking into account the current price of gas and a car that gets 20 miles per gallon, how much will the commute to the first job cost? Which job will benefit you more?

THEORY **Algebra: Solving for the Unknown** One of the steps in solving this problem is to write and solve a proportion: mileage / one gallon = 48 / *x* gallons. The letter *x* represents the unknown quantity—number of gallons used per trip. Plug in the known quantities, and solve for the unknown.

English Language Arts
24. Linda read the following list of responsibilities and accomplishments at a former job on an applicant's resume. Rewrite the list using parallel construction.

- presented a session on teamwork at new-employee training session
- management training program graduate
- figuring out weekly schedules for part-time employees

Mathematics
25. Franklin works as a cashier. A customer bought four dozen eggs at $1.60 a dozen, and a carton of yogurt for 80¢ to the checkout counter. The customer also had a promotional coupon worth 10% off on any purchase. When the customer tried to pay with a $5 bill, Franklin told him it was not enough, so the customer put back the yogurt. Did he then have enough for the eggs? Explain how you would figure out if he had enough to buy the eggs.

THEORY **Problem Solving** When thinking through an approach to solving a problem, disregard extraneous information.

Active Learning

Mock Interview
26. Break into groups of three. Select an interviewer, a job candidate, and an observer. Participate in a mock interview for a job as a cook, bus driver, or cashier. After 10 minutes, the observer should provide feedback. Repeat until everyone has been in each role.

Business in the Real World

Job Applications
27. Most job applications require a lot of personal information. Look at an employment application to determine the information needed to complete it. Then create a spreadsheet or word-processing document listing the information you would need to provide.

380 **Chapter 21** Review and Activities

ExamView Assessment Suite CD allows you to print out ready-made unit and chapter tests, complete with answer keys. You can also create customized tests.

TeacherWorks Plus provides complete teacher resources in one convenient package. It includes customizable lesson plans in calendar format and instant access to many print program resources.

 **Real LIFE • skills**

PREPARING FOR AN INTERVIEW

28. Interview two relatives or family friends who work. Ask how they prepare for job interviews. What types of questions have they been asked? How did they respond? What advice would they give on preparing for an interview? Summarize your findings in a report. Note similarities and differences in their statements. Present it to the class.

 **Business CAREERS**

FIND YOUR DREAM JOB

29. Go to the *Introduction to Business* Online Learning Center through **glencoe.com** for a link to the Occupational Outlook Handbook Web site. Click on the "OOH Search/A-Z Index" link and look up the job title "teacher" (preschool, kindergarten, elementary, middle, and secondary). Then write a one-page report about this type of occupation. Conclude your report with a list of things you could do now to prepare yourself to pursue the occupation.

Role Play

KNOWING WHAT COMPANIES WANT

30. Situation Imagine that you are a recruiter for a large corporation. You have been asked to participate in a community job fair.

Activity With other students acting as job candidates, make a presentation on the types of jobs at your company and the requirements for them.

Evaluation You will be evaluated on how well you meet the following performance indicators:

- Research the types of jobs that are available at your chosen corporation.
- Indicate the qualifications your company requires.
- Discuss job openings and how résumés are handled.
- Answer questions from the job candidates.
- Organize your thoughts.
- Project your voice, make eye contact, and use correct grammar.

Standardized Test Practice

Directions Choose the letter of the best answer. Write the letter for the answer on a separate piece of paper.

1. Which underlined word in the paragraph below uses the apostrophe incorrectly?

Businesses often post job <u>notice's</u> on bulletin boards in supermarkets or in shopping malls. You can also call a <u>company's</u> personnel office to see if they have jobs open. You might find help-wanted signs in <u>businesses'</u> windows. Sometimes you can find a job by walking into a local business and asking if <u>they're</u> hiring.

A   notice's
B   company's
C   businesses'
D   they're

 **TEST-TAKING TIP** Read and consider all of the answer choices before you choose the one that best responds to the question. Examine each choice and think about how it differs from the others.

 READING Go to the *Introduction to Business* Online Learning Center through **glencoe.com** for a list of outside reading suggestions.

 **STRATEGIES FOR STANDARDIZED TEST PREP SUCCESS**

Test Savvy Sometimes students will spot answers to multiple-choice questions quickly and think that they do not have to read the stem and distractors of the question completely before moving on to the next item. This technique can lead to careless errors. Have students read directions, question stems, and all answer choices carefully before choosing the best answer.

 **Real LIFE • skills**

28. Answers will depend on comments made by family members and/or friends.

Business CAREERS

29. Teachers help students learn and apply concepts in a wide range of subjects and interact with students, parents, and school administrators. Working conditions varies widely. They include long hours for approximately 10 months with a two-month vacation during the summer. Licenses are required, except for private schools in most states. A college degree, completion of a teacher-training program, and passing a test of basic skills are required, plus continuing education for license renewal. Average job growth is expected, except in areas where the population is growing. As preparation, tutor and take classes to meet college-entrance requirements.

Role Play

30. Presentations should address the competencies noted in the Role Play. Answers will depend on the type of corporation that is chosen.

Standardized Test Practice
1. A

Favorite Subjects
Ask volunteers to name their favorite academic subjects. (Answers will vary depending on student tastes and abilities.) Write a list of the subjects on the board. Ask students if they think an organization that specializes in helping students with academics could be successful in their town. Ask students to brainstorm a list of local people and organizations that can help students improve their academic abilities. (Students may mention school programs, tutors, and after-school groups.)

TEACH

Teaching Points
Qualifying for a Job
Ask students to define qualifications and employability skills. (Qualifications are the education, skills, and work experience needed to do a particular job. Employability skills are the basic skills that you need to get a job, keep a job, and do well at a job.) Ask students to characterize the qualifications and employability skills involved with running Girlstart. (Ambition, communication, and creativity are key. An education that includes math and science training as well as knowledge of teaching techniques is important, as are organizational skills.)

Rachel Muir

Fearless Leader/Founder/Executive Director, Girlstart
Girlstart is a nonprofit organization that aims to empower girls in mathematics, science, and technology. It teaches girls the fun part of academic achievement and runs after-school programs for underserved schools, free Saturday camps, and summer camps.

Q & A

Describe your job responsibilities.
Rachel: I lead my staff, helping them achieve results, solve problems, prioritize our goals and support my board. I make sure that I am proud of everything that leaves this office, be it a brochure, a T-shirt, or an intern going to lead a program.

What skills are most important in your business?
Rachel: Bravery, generosity, compassion, thoughtfulness, creativity, passion, ambition, confidence, thirst for knowledge, respectfulness, admiration, gratitude, and inclusiveness are ones that come to mind.

What is your key to success?
Rachel: My three key skills for success are ambition, communication, and creativity. I believed in my idea to create Girlstart, and this determination to succeed helped me get through the tough times. Being an effective communicator is vital. It helps me solve problems, apply for grants, give presentations, and work with staff and volunteers. Creativity means being open to new ideas, and to also accept that I don't have to have all the answers. My job is to find the people who do.

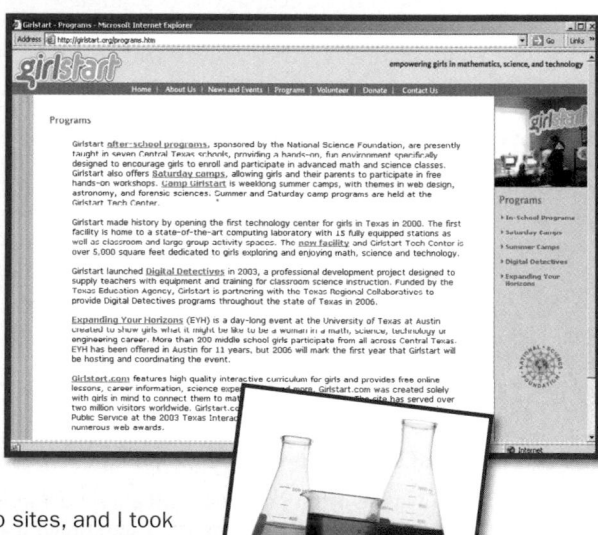

Your Web site mentions that you weren't good at math, hence your idea to create Girlstart. What steps did you take to improve your math?
Rachel: A friend taught me how to build Web sites, and I took programming and accounting classes. If you can get over your lack of confidence and believe that you can totally do this, you will succeed. Don't be limited by what you don't know. Turn your weakness into your strength by identifying it and making changes. Never give up on your idea. If you love what you do, you will work as hard as it takes to be successful.

What advice would you give students interested in starting a business?
Rachel: You will never know until you try! Be afraid, and do it anyway. Thank others every step of the way in every inventive way that you can, and be patient with yourself and those around you.

Critical Thinking *Why is identifying a target market vital to shaping an organization?*

Critical Thinking
Businesses need to consider who their target market will be before they can develop their products. Understanding their customers allows companies to better meet the needs of their market base.

Some Qualifications Needed to be a Director of an Educational Camp

Academic Skills and Abilities

Computer science; mathematics; student literacy training; teaching skills; interpersonal skills; general business management skills; verbal and written communication skills; multitasking, organizing, and planning skills

Academic Skills Required to Complete Tasks at Girlstart			
Tasks	Math	Science	English Language Arts
Hold meetings			◆
Assign duties			◆
Develop curricula	◆	◆	◆
Assess student achievement	◆	◆	◆
Customer service			◆
Schedule employees	◆		◆
Order supplies and equipment	◆		◆
Analyze financials	◆		◆

Education and Training

The minimum educational requirement is a bachelor's degree, usually in education, but a master's or higher degree is preferable. State licensing is necessary for instructional coordinators in public school systems, although specific requirements vary by state. In some states, a teaching license is needed, while in others an education administrator license is needed as well as training in curriculum development and instruction, or in the specific field for which the director is responsible, such as mathematics or science.

Career Path

To successfully empower students, directors must have a good understanding of how to teach specific groups of students, in addition to expertise in developing educational materials. As a result, many people become instructional coordinators after working for several years as teachers. Work experience in an education administrator position, such as principal or assistant principal, can also be beneficial.

Preparing for a Career
Self-Assessment Checklist
Use this self-assessment checklist to help determine ways you can develop winning career habits.

✔ Be willing to take both the credit and the blame for your actions.

✔ Think about past successes and challenges to develop an ability to predict what is likely to happen in the future on the basis of experience.

✔ Strive to succeed and to be the best.

✔ Be able and willing to face difficulties and to take risks.

✔ Exhibit trustworthiness.

✔ Display clarity of purpose and determination.

✔ Be tenacious.

✔ Develop a clear vision of your future successes.

383

FOCUS

Discussion Starter

Lead a discussion about life-long learning. Ask students how lifelong learning can enhance their careers.

Step 1

Brainstorm Skills

Have students go to the *Introduction to Business* Online Learning Center through **glencoe.com** for a graphic organizer they can use to brainstorm the skills needed to complete the project.

Step 2

Choose a Business and Career That Interest You

Students can use the Occupational Outlook Handbook Web site to explore occupations.

TEACH

Step 3

Build Background

Technology Have students brainstorm ways they will use technology as part of their plan for lifelong learning. (Technology is revolutionizing the ability to learn by allowing people to take courses that are taught in remote locations at all hours of the day and night.)

Globalization Ask students to write an essay about the impact of globalization on their plans for lifelong learning. (Trends in outsourcing of jobs to workers in other countries make it critical to remain abreast of developments in your field so that you can remain competitive.)

Lifelong Learning

Regardless of the career choice, lifelong learning will most likely play a factor in the future of today's students. Changes in technology, globalization, and greater competition among qualified job candidates are creating the need for continuing adult education. At the same time, adult education is an emerging new industry.

Thematic Project Assignment

In this project you will design and write a brochure that describes the benefits of lifelong learning for adults and the types of careers available in adult education.

Step 1 Brainstorm Skills You Need to Complete This Activity

Your success in designing and writing a brochure will depend on your skills. Preview the activity, then brainstorm a list of the skills you will need to use to complete the activity and describe how you will use them. Skills you might use include:

Academic Skills   reading, writing, designing/art/photography

Basic Skills   speaking, listening, and thinking

Technology Skills   word processing, keyboarding, design and photo programing, and Internet skills

 SKILLS PREVIEW Go to the *Introduction to Business* Online Learning Center through **glencoe.com** for a graphic organizer you can use to brainstorm the skills you will use to complete the project.

Step 2 Choose a Business and a Career That Interest You

Make a list of businesses that interest you. Add to the list any careers within this business that interest you. Think about the lifelong learning you might need in these careers. Then think of adult education courses that might help people in these businesses and careers. For example, if you are interested in overseeing an assembly line in a large factory, you might need lifelong education in robotics or other technology. Some careers in adult education might include teaching robotics, being an administrator at a school that teaches robotics, or writing manuals for the classes.

Step 3 Build Background Knowledge

Preview information on lifelong learning.

Lifelong **Learning**

Thousands of adults return to college every year or engage in training within their companies. Some take classes for self-development or personal interest. Most, however, return to the classroom to keep up with the demands of their jobs, learn a new skill, or gain a new qualification or certification.

New career opportunities in adult education are not to be overlooked by anyone interested in education. As with traditional education, many jobs require advanced degrees, but not all. On-the-job experience counts when teaching adults.

Step 4

Connect with Your Community

Ask students to describe how their community affects their options for lifelong learning. (Community colleges and peer groups can be wonderful resources for lifelong learning.)

Step 4 Connect with Your Community

Interview two adults in your community who have returned to college, taken a course at a community education center, or been involved in training at the workplace. Ask them about why they went back to school and what their experience was like. Ask them how they benefited. Then think about the people who were involved in their education, such as enrollment counselors, financial aid assistants, and instructors.

Step 5 Research Lifelong Learning

Use library and Internet resources to research lifelong learning. Keep records of your sources of information. Then prepare a brochure. Use the project research checklist as a guide to help you.

Step 6 Develop Your Brochure

Use design, photo, and other software to develop a three-fold brochure that includes all of the information described in the project checklist.

Lifelong Learning

✔ Make a list of the main points and supporting details on the benefits of lifelong learning.

✔ Use the main points to write headings and subheadings. Include information on the benefits of lifelong learning, how lifelong learning is becoming a major trend as more adults participate, and how this trend is creating more career opportunities associated with adult education.

✔ Write the supporting details under each heading and subheading.

✔ Use computer software to add graphic designs to your brochure.

✔ Edit and proofread your brochure to make sure everything is correct.

✔ Print the brochure and fold it into three panels.

Self Connections

✔ Discuss the results of your research with the adults you interviewed.

✔ Describe how the adults you interviewed benefited by lifelong learning.

✔ Explain what the investigation and its results mean to you.

Step 7 Evaluate Your Presentation

@ *RUBRIC* Go to the *Introduction to Business* Online Learning Center through **glencoe.com** for a rubric you can use to evaluate your final report.

385

TEACH (cont.)

Step 6

Develop a Brochure
Give students these tips on writing:

- Know your audience.
- Organize your plan by developing an outline and using titles and subtitles.
- Write concisely (briefly but completely).
- Write in easy-to-read, simple language.

ASSESS

Step 7

Evaluate Your Brochure
Rubric Encourage students to use the rubric to evaluate their final brochures.

CLOSE

Culminating Activity
Lifelong Learning Interviews
Have students form pairs and interview each other about what they learned about lifelong learning and how their opinions and perceptions of lifelong learning evolved during the course of the project. (Interviews will vary depending on what students learned and reactions to their research.)

Step 5

Research Lifelong Learning
Students can go to the *Introduction to Business* Online Learning Center through **glencoe.com** for a rubric they can use as a content checklist when researching their brochures.

Chapter	Section	Unit Objectives
Chapter 22 *Making Consumer Decisions*	22.1	**Identify** four decisions that consumers make when they buy goods and services.
		Compare brand-name and generic products.
		Identify choices that consumers must make about when to buy.
		List several choices that consumers have when selecting a store to make purchases.
		Describe tools that consumers can use to compare prices for goods and services.
	22.2	**Identify** types of information that can be helpful to a consumer in making wise shopping decisions.
Chapter 23 *Consumer Rights and Responsibilities*	23.1	**Describe** several protections that are included in the Consumer Bill of Rights.
	23.2	**Describe** the responsibilities of consumers.
Chapter 24 *Protecting Consumers*	24.1	**Explain** the steps consumers can take to find solutions to consumer problems.
		List nongovernmental consumer organizations that advocate for consumers.
		List some federal and state agencies that provide consumer information and protection.
	24.2	**Describe** ways that consumers are protected by laws related to the marketplace.
		List ways that the business community assists with consumer protection.

Understanding the Coding

Brackets Brackets on the reduced student edition page correspond to teaching strategies and activities in the Teacher Wraparound Edition. As you teach the lesson, the brackets show you exactly where to use the teaching strategies and activities.

Letters The letters on the reduced student edition page identify the type of strategy or activity. See the key below to learn about the different types of strategies and activities.

Ability Levels Leveled teaching strategies are identified by one of three codes to give you an idea of their suitability for students of varying learning styles and abilities.

Resources Key program resources are listed in each chapter. Icons indicate the format of resources.

KEY to Letters

D **Develop Concepts** activities help teachers gauge and plan for students' concept development.

R **Reading Strategy** activities help you teach reading skills and vocabulary.

C **Critical Thinking** strategies help students apply and extend what they have learned.

U **Universal Access** activities provide differentiated instruction for English language learners and suggestions for teaching various types of learners.

S **Skill Practice** provides leveled instruction for meeting individual needs and learning styles.

W **Writing Support** activities provide writing opportunities to help students comprehend the text.

NCLB **No Child Left Behind** activities help students practice and improve their abilities in academic subjects.

KEY to Ability Levels

L1 Strategies should be within the ability range of all students. Often full class participation is required.

L2 Strategies are for average to above-average students or for small groups. Some teacher direction is necessary.

L3 Strategies are designed for students able and willing to work independently. Minimal teacher direction is necessary.

KEY to Resource Icons

📁 Print Material

💿 CD-ROM

🌐 Online Learning Center with Podcasts

BusinessWeek *Reader and Case Study*

In Unit 8, your students can learn more about business in the real world through the following *BusinessWeek* Readers and Case Studies:

All Together Now
How collaboration software can make your company more efficient. (page 391)

HP Wants Your Old PCs Back
It's pushing states to force recycling of TVs, computers, and other e-gear. The movement to recycle electronic refuse, or "e-waste," is spreading across the nation, and so is HP's clout. (page 408)

How to Stand Up to the Nickel-and-Dimers
In a world of fees gone wild, what's a consumer to do? In some industries, such as banking, complaining customers can sometimes get fees rolled back. In others, such as telecom, it may be best to seek out competitors without fees. When a charge seems especially underhanded, an individual may want to join a consumer-action group. (page 430)

Chapter Features and Activities

BusinessWeek *Reader and Case Study*

Science/Tech*TRENDS*

?ETHICS in Business

International Business

Section	Feature Title	Page
22.1	Global Brands	391
22.1	Unit Prices	394
22.2	Consumer Advocates	397
23.1	Consumer Resources	409
23.1	Consumer Awareness	410

Section	Feature Title	Page
23.2	Who Is Responsible?	412
24.1	Testing for Safety	423
24.2	Product Recalls	428
24.2	Better Businesses, Better Charities	430

Reading Strategies

Before You Read

Section	Page
22.1	390
22.2	395
23.1	406
23.2	411
24.1	422
24.2	427

Graphic Organizer

Chapter	Section	Title	Page
22	22.1	Four Consumer Decisions	390
	22.2	Steps in Preparation for Shopping	395
23	23.1	Consumer Rights and Benefits	406
	23.2	Six Consumer Responsibilities	411
24	24.1	Consumer Protection Role of Government Agencies	422
	24.2	Types of Warranties	427

As You Read

Section	Page
22.1	392, 393
22.2	396, 398
23.1	407, 408
23.2	413, 414
24.1	423
24.2	429

Reading Check

Section	Page
22.1	391
22.2	396, 398
23.1	408
23.2	412, 414
24.1	424
24.2	428

After You Read

Section	Page
22.1	394
22.2	399
23.1	410
23.2	415
24.1	426
24.2	431

Unit Overview

Introduce the Unit

Introduce the unit by describing the main concepts of each chapter in the unit.

Unit 8 discusses buying goods and services.

Chapter 22 is about the choices consumers have to make. The four decisions consumers make when buying goods and services are introduced and suggestions for becoming a smart consumer are presented.

Chapter 23 describes consumers' rights and their impact on consumers' lives. In addition, consumer responsibilities are presented and explained.

Chapter 24 is about consumer power. It explains how government and private organizations protect and help consumers.

00:00 OUT OF TIME?

If class time is too short to cover all of the chapters in this unit, have students:

- Write down the vocabulary terms and their definitions.
- Read the chapter summaries at the beginning of each chapter review.
- Go to the *Introduction to Business* Online Learning Center through **glencoe.com** to download free Study-to-Go content to their PDAs or cell phones.

Buying Goods and Services

386

Real-World Business and Career Profile

Preview

New Leaf Paper Tell students that at the end of this unit, they will learn about New Leaf Paper founder Jeff Mendelsohn, and how he achieved his success. Based in San Francisco, New Leaf Paper produces recycled paper. A couple of years ago, the company teamed up with the Canadian publisher of the "Harry Potter" series to print an installment on 100 percent recycled and chlorine-free paper. Ask students why producing recycled paper could be good business. (Answers will vary. Students might suggest that there is a strong demand for paper goods and that using recycled paper helps the environment.)

Real-World Business and Career Profile

New Leaf Paper makes environmentally friendly recycled paper that is 100 percent post-consumer, processed, and chlorine-free paper. At the end of this unit, you will learn about New Leaf Paper co-founder Jeff Mendelsohn and how he achieved his success.

Decision Making Do you think it is important to buy goods and services that do not harm the environment?

Unit 8 | Thematic Project Preview

How the Consumer Movement Affects Business
After completing this unit, you will research to find how the consumer movement affects business and your life and career.

Project Checklist As you read the chapters in this unit, use this checklist to prepare for the unit project.

✔ Think about what the consumer movement is, and how the consumer movement affects the way business is conducted.

✔ Think about how the Internet has given voice to the consumer movement.

✔ Consider how the consumer movement affects you as a consumer.

✔ Consider how the consumer movement could affect your future job and career.

387

Build Background
Ask students these questions to activate prior knowledge:

Chapter 22
Why is it important to become smart consumers? (Students buy things all the time—food, clothing, and entertainment are regular purchases for most students. Learning to be a smart consumer can help students achieve their personal financial goals.)

Chapter 23
Do you know that you have consumer rights and responsibilities? (Young consumers may or may not be aware that they have rights and responsibilities. As they plan for their future and start to make important consumer decisions such as purchasing a car or appliance, now is a good time for students to learn about these rights and responsibilities.)

Chapter 24
Why is it important to know about government and private organizations that provide consumer protection? (Most consumer transactions go smoothly, however, the occasional problem can be frustrating, expensive, and time consuming. Learning how the government and private organizations protect and help consumers is a way for students to learn to help themselves.)

Unit | Thematic Project Preview

How the Consumer Movement Affects Business
Tell students that when they complete this unit, they will understand what the consumer movement is and how it affects the way business is conducted. Encourage students to think about how these changes could affect the types of jobs and careers they might choose.

C Critical Thinking
Ask students how they think the consumer movement affects them. (Answers will vary. Encourage students to recognize that as consumers, they have a voice. As consumers' voices grow, so does the need for business and industry to listen.)

Standards-Based Lesson Planning
Introduction to Business provides students with instruction and assessment in the following fundamental content areas:

Content Standards Correlations	
Analyze the factors that influence customer buying decisions.	pp. 391–394, 396–399, 400–403
The student researches consumer issues and determines financial implications for the individual.	pp. 401–403
Examine purchasing decisions and various products with respect to value, service, maintenance, and price.	pp. 401–403
Evaluate information available to make wise buying decisions. Compare and contrast sources of useful consumer information. Use the decision-making process to determine effective uses of money.	pp. 391–394, 396–399, 400–403
Demonstrate understanding of buying decisions.	pp. 392, 394, 401–403
Function as economically literate citizens through the development of personal consumer economic skills, a knowledge of social and government responsibility, and an understanding of business operations.	pp. 388, 392, 394, 397, 401–403

NCLB
Activities, information, and skills practice will help your students attain No Child Left Behind proficiency. Students will improve their abilities in the following academic standards areas:

Academic Standards Correlations		
English Language Arts	Activities/Features	Page
NCTE 3 Apply strategies to interpret texts	Applying Academics to Business	p. 402
NCTE 5 Use different writing process elements to communicate effectively	After You Read	p. 399
NCTE 7 Conduct research and gather, evaluate, and synthesize data to communicate discoveries	After You Read	pp. 399, 402
Mathematics		
Data Analysis and Probability Select and use appropriate statistical methods to analyze data	Applying Academics to Business	p. 402
Measurement Apply appropriate techniques, tools, and formulas to determine measurements	After You Read	p. 394
Number and Operations Compute fluently and make reasonable estimates	Standardized Test Practice	p. 403
Number and Operations Understand numbers, ways of representing numbers, relationships among numbers, and number systems	Ask S&P	p. 388
Problem Solving Apply and adapt a variety of appropriate strategies to solve problems	Applying Academics to Business	p. 402
Science		
Content Standard D Students should develop an understanding of origin and evolution of the earth system	Science/Tech Trends	p. 398

Correlations   This chart shows the 21st Century Skills, foundation skills, and workplace competencies that students develop as they work in this chapter.

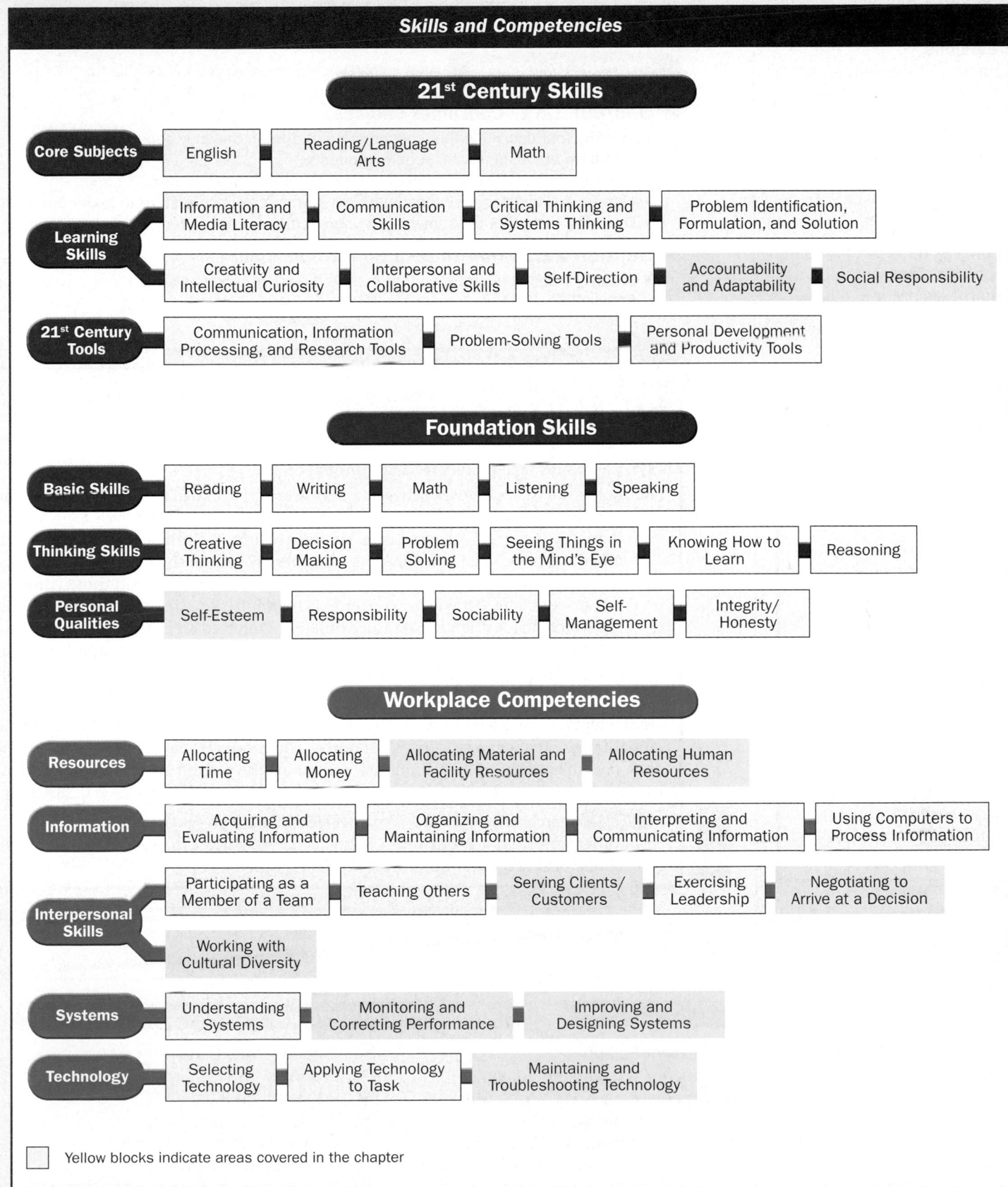

Skills and Competencies

21st Century Skills

Core Subjects
- English
- Reading/Language Arts
- Math

Learning Skills
- Information and Media Literacy
- Communication Skills
- Critical Thinking and Systems Thinking
- Problem Identification, Formulation, and Solution
- Creativity and Intellectual Curiosity
- Interpersonal and Collaborative Skills
- Self-Direction
- Accountability and Adaptability
- Social Responsibility

21st Century Tools
- Communication, Information Processing, and Research Tools
- Problem-Solving Tools
- Personal Development and Productivity Tools

Foundation Skills

Basic Skills
- Reading
- Writing
- Math
- Listening
- Speaking

Thinking Skills
- Creative Thinking
- Decision Making
- Problem Solving
- Seeing Things in the Mind's Eye
- Knowing How to Learn
- Reasoning

Personal Qualities
- Self-Esteem
- Responsibility
- Sociability
- Self-Management
- Integrity/Honesty

Workplace Competencies

Resources
- Allocating Time
- Allocating Money
- Allocating Material and Facility Resources
- Allocating Human Resources

Information
- Acquiring and Evaluating Information
- Organizing and Maintaining Information
- Interpreting and Communicating Information
- Using Computers to Process Information

Interpersonal Skills
- Participating as a Member of a Team
- Teaching Others
- Serving Clients/Customers
- Exercising Leadership
- Negotiating to Arrive at a Decision
- Working with Cultural Diversity

Systems
- Understanding Systems
- Monitoring and Correcting Performance
- Improving and Designing Systems

Technology
- Selecting Technology
- Applying Technology to Task
- Maintaining and Troubleshooting Technology

☐ Yellow blocks indicate areas covered in the chapter

Chapter 22

Chapter Overview

Introduce the Chapter

Making Consumer Decisions
Chapter 22 discusses the choices consumers have to make.

Building Background

Students buy things all the time—food, clothing, and entertainment are regular purchases for most students. Learning to be a smart consumer can help students achieve their personal financial goals.

 **STANDARD &POOR'S**

» Math Answer
The composite earning rate over the six month period is 2.28%. To determine the composite rate, locate the correct period. Add the fixed rate and the inflation rate to get the composite rate: 2.00% + 0.28% = 2.28%.

» Extension Activity
Have students determine the composite earning rate for Nov. 1, 2001, to Apr. 30, 2002 if the fixed rate was 2.00% and the inflation rate was 1.19% (3.19%).

N C L B Activity correlates to Math standards.

Making Consumer Decisions

Chapter Objectives After completing this chapter, you will be able to:

▶ **Section 22.1** *Consumer Choices*
- **Identify** four decisions that consumers make when they buy goods and services.
- **Compare** brand-name and generic products.
- **Identify** choices that consumers must make about when to buy.
- **List** several choices that consumers have when selecting a store to make purchases.
- **Describe** tools that consumers can use to compare prices for goods and services.

▶ **Section 22.2** *How to Be a Smart Consumer*
- **Identify** types of information that can be helpful to a consumer in making wise shopping decisions.

Ask **STANDARD &POOR'S** **Making Consumer Decisions: Buying Bonds**

Q: Can bonds help protect me against inflation?

A: Bonds are basically IOUs between a borrower and a lender. Governments and corporations borrow billions of dollars a year from investors, and bonds are a common way for them to do so. Like a savings account, the initial amount borrowed is called the principal, while the lender is generally paid in the form of interest. There are two main types of bonds: those issued by the government and those issued by private companies. If you are concerned about inflation, there are two kinds of U.S. government securities, the Treasury Inflation Protected Securities (TIPS) and the Series I Savings Bond (or I Bond), that are guaranteed to rise more rapidly than inflation. This is because their rates of return are directly tied to a common measure of inflation—the CPI-U, or Consumer Price Index for All Urban Consumers.

Mathematics The interest rate on an I Bond has two parts: a 30-year fixed rate and an inflation rate that changes every six months. The composite earning rate is the fixed rate plus the semiannual inflation rate. Determine the interest on a $5,000 I Bond over a six month period in which the fixed rate is 2% and the inflation rate is 0.28%.

THEORY **Percents Less Than 1** Percents less than 1 represent values less than $\frac{1}{100}$. In other words, 0.1% is one-tenth of one percent, which can also be represented in decimal form as 0.001, or in fraction form as $\frac{1}{1,000}$.

Classroom Resources

- Student Edition
- Teacher Wraparound Edition
- Student Activity Workbook with Academic Integration
- Student Activity Workbook with Academic Integration TAE
- *Fast File*, Unit 8 Resources
- Inclusion in the Business Education Classroom

- TeacherWorks Plus
- *ExamView Assessment Suite*
- Presentation Plus!
- Vocabulary PuzzleMaker
- Interactive Student Edition
- Online Student Edition
- Online Learning Center with Podcasts

Conserving and Recycling It is important for businesses and people to conserve and recycle. **What can young people do to promote a healthy environment?**

Review the Objectives

Introduce the chapter by reviewing the chapter objectives:

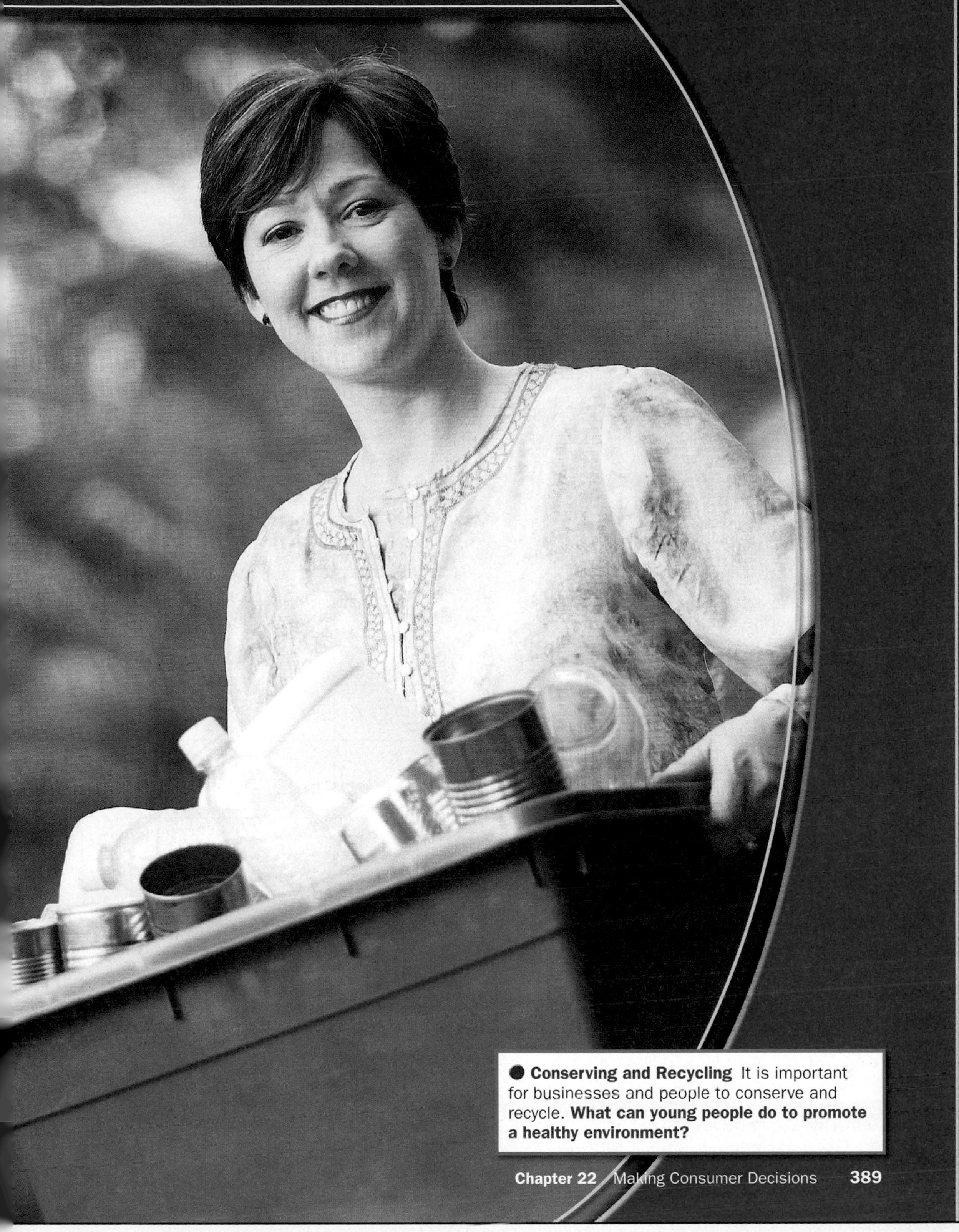

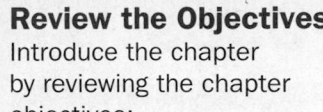

Section 22.1 ***Objectives***

Identify four decisions that consumers make when they buy goods and services. (what to buy, when to buy, where to buy, and how much to pay)

Compare brand-name and generic products. (A brand-name product helps distinguish it from other products. Generic products are plainly labeled, unadvertised, and sold at lower prices.)

Identify choices that consumers must make about when to buy. (whether to wait to buy a product when it is out of season, on sale, or when first available)

List several choices that consumers have when selecting a store to make purchases. (department stores, discount stores, off-price and outlet stores, the Internet, or catalogs)

Describe tools that consumers can use to compare prices for goods and services. (advertisements and consumer publications for tests and ratings, comparing sales and regular prices)

Section 22.2 ***Objective***

Identify types of information that can be helpful to a consumer in making wise shopping decisions. (Advertisements, consumer publications, shopping, and labels provide information about products. Warranties provide protection.)

Discuss the Photo

Conserving and Recycling Read the caption on the photo to students: It is important for businesses and people to conserve and recycle.

Ask students: What can young people do to promote a healthy environment? (Young people can promote a healthy environment by taking environmental policies into consideration when making buying decisions.)

FOCUS

Bell Ringer Activity

Making Consumer Decisions

Display three pairs of products with a generic product and a name brand product in each pair. Ask students: What are some of the advantages and disadvantages of generic or brand-name products? (Students might suggest that generic brands are generally less expensive or that brand-name products are of higher quality.)

Preteaching

Presentation Plus!

The Presentation Plus! CD provides visual teaching aids for this section.

PuzzleMaker

Use the Vocabulary PuzzleMaker to create a puzzle of the section's key terms. Students can complete the puzzle on paper or on a computer.

Graphic Organizer

Tell students to go to the Online Learning Center through **glencoe.com** for a printable graphic organizer. (Answers include: what to buy, when to buy, where to buy, how much to pay.)

N C L B Connects academics to content.

Consumer Choices

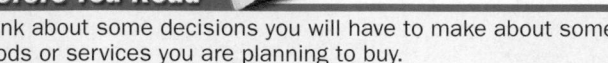

Reading Guide

● Before You Read

Think about some decisions you will have to make about some goods or services you are planning to buy.

Read to Learn

- Identify four decisions that consumers make when they buy goods and services.
- Compare brand-name and generic products.
- Identify choices that consumers must make about when to buy.
- List several choices that consumers have when selecting a store to make purchases.
- Describe tools that consumers can use to compare prices for goods and services.

D The Main Idea

Consumers must make many buying decisions. They must decide what, when, and where to buy goods and services, and how much to pay for them.

Key Concepts

- Buying Goods and Services
- Deciding What to Buy
- Deciding When to Buy
- Deciding Where to Buy
- Deciding How Much to Pay

@ Go to the *Introduction to Business* Online Learning Center through **glencoe.com** for a printable graphic organizer.

Vocabulary

Key Terms
consumer   generic products
brand name   comparison shopping

Academic Vocabulary

You will find these words in your reading and on your tests. Make sure you know their meanings.

disposes   version
priority   bulk

Graphic Organizer

In boxes like those on the figure below, list four decisions a consumer must make before buying goods or services.

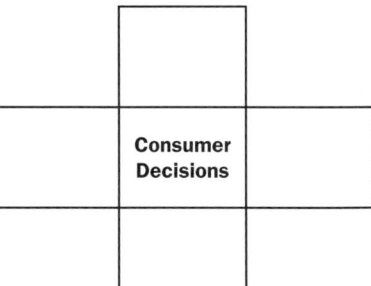
Consumer Decisions

N C L B Academic Standards

English Language Arts

NCTE 1 Read texts to acquire new information

NCTE 9 Develop an understanding of diversity in language use across cultures

Mathematics

Measurement Apply appropriate techniques, tools, and formulas to determine measurements

390 **Chapter 22** Making Consumer Decisions

glencoe.com

Reading Guide

● Before You Read

Students might mention routine purchases or they might focus on big-ticket items, such as a car.

D Develop Concepts

The Main Idea Ask students: What did you buy? When did you buy it? Where did you buy it? How much did you pay for it? (Answers will be based on students' purchases.)

Buying Goods and Services

When shopping, making choices is not always easy. A **consumer** (a person who selects, purchases, uses, and **disposes** of goods and services) is faced with many buying options. Making consumer decisions involves determining what is most important to you.

If you had unlimited money, you could buy whatever you wanted. However, no one has unlimited funds. They have to budget their money to satisfy their wants and needs. A *budget* is a plan that specifies how resources—particularly money—will be allocated or spent during a particular period.

Consumers must make many decisions about buying goods and services. They must decide what, when, and where to buy, and how much to pay.

✔ **Reading Check** **Define** What is a budget?

BusinessWeek *Reader and Case Study*

All Together Now

How collaboration software can make your company more efficient

Michael Richards is through schlepping bags of documents to clients of his $1 million auditing firm, Michael Richards & Associates in Yorba Linda, California. In April of last year, Richards signed up for WebEx™ WebOffice, a shared online workspace where he and his 10 employees can store and edit documents. Now when Richards visits clients, he simply logs on to a shared Web site to find the paperwork he needs. "This has really revolutionized our business," he says.

The revolution was painless. Within minutes after Richards signed up with WebEx, he had a special Web site that he and his employees could use to manage projects, update their calendars, and gain access to a shared database. "Without the site, we would have two or three more employees managing paper," says Richards. The site is working so well that he recently signed up for a second site he'll use

to collaborate with his 100 clients. All told, Richards will spend $9,000 a year for the two sites, plus unlimited Web conferencing for 25 people. He reckons he'll save $50,000 this year in administrative salaries. Clients are happy, too. "There's a little bit of a learning curve with clients, but once we show them how it works, they can't believe we didn't do it sooner," says Richards.

 CASE STUDY Go to the *Introduction to Business* Online Learning Center through **glencoe.com** for the *BusinessWeek* Reader Case Study.

Active Learning

One popular type of collaboration software is the shared calendar. Research electronic calendar programs and use one to set up an appointment with a classmate to study this chapter.

glencoe.com

Section 22.1 Consumer Choices **391**

TEACH

Discussion Starter
Ask students why budgets are helpful and why some people have difficulty sticking to budgets. (Students might suggest that budgets help people spend the limited resources they have to meet their needs and wants. Sticking to a budget is difficult because it is hard to delay gratification.)

R Reading Strategy
Provide Examples Ask students to provide some examples of products that are recognized by their brand name without including a description of the actual product. Ask students to include a brief description. (Students might name products such as Tylenol® as a brand of acetaminophen, Kleenex® as a brand of facial tissue, Tide® as a brand of laundry detergent, Post-it® as a brand name for "sticky notes.")

✔ **Reading Check**

Define It is a plan specifying how resources will be allocated or spent during a particular period.

Global Brands Some brand names might be offensive or difficult to understand when translated into another language. Also, some cultures may have different tastes. Their consumers might prefer ingredients or materials that are popular in their country to be used in the goods they purchase.

BusinessWeek *Reader and Case Study*

All Together Now
 CASE STUDY Have students go to the *Introduction to Business* Online Learning Center through **glencoe.com** to download a Case Study activity that corresponds to the article. The activity and answer key are also available on the TeacherWorks Plus CD.

Active Learning

Invitations to study and the programs students choose to use will vary.

TEACH (cont.)

S Skill Practice

Guided Practice

Identify Ask students to identify items that might have generic counterparts. (Answers will vary. Examples include bleach, aspirin, sugar, and flour.) **L1**

Explain Ask students to explain why some products are more likely to have generic counterparts than others. (Answers will vary. Simple products that have few ingredients or components are likely to have generic counterparts. For example, bleach contains chlorine whether it has a brand name or comes in a plain bottle.) **L2**

Explain Ask students to explain why some consumers are willing to pay more for a brand-name sugar than a generic. (Answers will vary. Some students might suggest that some consumers might think the brand-name sugar is of higher quality or that the brand-name producer has cleaner facilities. In some cases the actual products are the same but the brand-name item might have an easy-pour package.) **L3**

ASSESS

Review Key Terms
Have students write sentences using each key term.

STUDY TO GO **Study-to-Go** Have students go to the Online Learning Center through **glencoe.com** to download free **Study-to-Go** content to their PDAs or cell phones.

392

● As You Read
Think of some items on which you would not mind spending a little more money for the brand-name version and some things that are fine as generic items.

Deciding What to Buy

Consumers must first decide what product they want to buy. Usually they decide what is a top **priority** for them. Then they can choose to buy either a brand-name product or a generic product. A **brand name** is the trade name for a product or service produced by a particular company. Familiar brand names include Nike®, Kellogg's®, and Pepsi®. Buyers often associate quality with brand names.

Generic products are plainly labeled, unadvertised products that are sold at lower prices than brand-name goods. Many brand-name medicines and grocery items have a generic **version**. Despite the difference in cost, they may be equal in quality to some brand-name products. **Figure 22.1** illustrates a comparative graph for making a buying decision.

Deciding When to Buy

Prices for many items change during different times of the year. Postponing or planning a purchase can sometimes save you money. For example, you would probably save more money if you bought an air conditioner in the winter instead of in the summer. There is less demand for air conditioners during cold months, which means prices for them are lower then.

Stores often run special promotions during and after holidays, just before a school year begins, and at the end of a season. There are often more choices when products are first available. However, you may find better prices if you wait until the items go on sale.

Figure 22.1 — *Making Consumer Decisions*

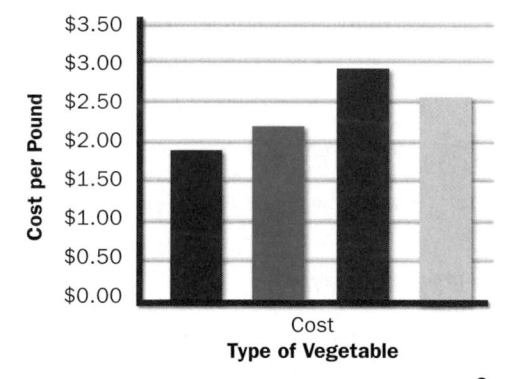

Comparison of Vegetable Prices

◆ Canned (generic brand) 1lb.

◆ Canned (brand name) 1lb.

◆ Fresh 1lb.

◇ Packaged Frozen 1lb.

Source: http://retailtrafficmag.com/mag/retail_america_shops

● **Your Choices at the Supermarket** Generic brands usually cost less than brand-name products. Food products may come fresh, frozen, or canned. **Which would you choose from these different vegetable products?**

392 **Chapter 22** Making Consumer Decisions

● As You Read
Some students may feel that brand-name products last longer. Others might think that some generic items cost less and perform as well.

Figure 22.1

● **Your Choices at the Supermarket**
If price is important, you might choose a canned generic brand. If your family likes frozen vegetables best, you might choose frozen. If fresh is best in your opinion, you may pay extra for fresh.

Deciding Where to Buy

Along with choosing what to buy, consumers have to decide where to shop. There are three factors that affect a consumer's decision on where to shop: the kinds of goods and services sold, prices, and convenience.

Department Stores

Department stores sell a wide variety of goods. Because they offer name brands and customer service, their prices may be higher than other types of stores. Most sell many lines of products, such as furniture, clothing, and shoes. They include Sears, JCPenney®, and Macy's®.

Discount Stores

Discount stores also sell a variety of goods. However, discount stores generally offer lower prices. They can sell for less because they offer fewer services and keep large quantities of goods. They include Wal-Mart® and Kmart®.

Off-Price and Outlet Stores

These types of stores carry well-known brand names at bargain prices. They offer big discounts because the items they sell may have flaws, may be out of season, or may be discontinued merchandise. Examples are T.J. Maxx®, Stein Mart®, and Loehmann's®.

Limited-Line Retailers

Limited-line retailers, or specialty stores, sell an assortment of goods in one product line or a few related lines. They often have a variety of items and high levels of service and expertise. Foot Locker®, PetSmart®, and Ace Hardware® are specialty stores.

Superstores

Superstores are like supermarkets but sell items such as books, hardware, sporting goods, and clothing as well as groceries. Like supermarkets, they are also self-serve. Kroger®, Wal-Mart, and Safeway® operate superstores.

Convenience Stores

As their name implies, convenience stores provide easy access to products that consumers often buy as necessities or impulse items. They offer limited lines of products, mostly grocery items. The world's largest chain of convenience stores is run by 7-Eleven®.

● **As You Read**

Think about an item you are planning to purchase. Do you think you could save money if you waited to buy it?

International Business

Adapting to New Cultures
Wal-Mart is one of the leading U.S. retailers. In December 2005, it acquired 545 stores in South America and Japan. Wal-Mart purchased the Sonae retail company's operations in Brazil, which will add a variety of new retail formats to Wal-Mart's already diverse catalog. Wal-Mart Canada is in the process of expanding its stores to include fresh food and a wider selection of products. All of the stores will keep the basic "feel" of the stores in America while offering products that are more fitting to the country in which they are sold.

Examples of Languages Across Cultures

Q: In Brazilian Portuguese, how do you say: "What time should I arrive?"

A: A que horas devo chegar?
(pronounced:
Ah kā ōr-dăs dāy-voo shā-găr?)

Why is it important for a company to adapt to new cultures? What types of changes does a company need to adopt when entering a foreign market?

Section 22.1

RETEACH

W **Writing Support**
Enrichment
Department Stores Ask students to identify a department store that they like and write a review that explains the three main reasons consumers choose where to shop. (Some students might prefer to drive farther to get to a particular store and pay more because the store carries their favorite brands.)

R **Reading Strategy**
Apply Knowledge Ask students for their opinions about discount stores. (Some students may feel that they offer value at a low price. Other students may express that their quality is not as good as that offered at department stores.)

U **Universal Access**
Students with Speech/ Language Impairments
Students with speech impairments may have problems with articulation or voice strength. When students with speech impairments speak in class about their shopping preferences, use normal communication patterns and refrain from completing words or phrases for the student.

Student Activity Workbook ☞ Assign the Section 22.1 Activities.

● **As You Read**
Answers will depend on the item students plan to purchase and on their saving habits.

International Business

Adapting to New Cultures Answers may vary. Students should understand that adapting to another country's culture enables the company to win customers. The changes that a company needs to adopt include the rules of etiquette, new business customs, and rules for personal interaction.

RETEACH (cont.)

C Critical Thinking

Evaluate
Superstores and Warehouse Stores Have students research superstores and warehouse stores and write an essay on their impact on communities. (Issues include jobs, traffic, and the economic impact.)

ASSESS

After You Read

Have students complete the Section 22.1 After You Read section review.

Online Study Tools
Have students go to the Online Learning Center through **glencoe.com** to:

- Take the Section 22.1 **Practice Test**.
- Download free **Study-to-Go** content to their PDAs or cell phones.

Real World

Unit Prices Brand B. Divide the price by the number of units. Brand A: $2 ÷ 10 = $0.20 or 20 cents per ounce. Brand B: $2.85 ÷ 15 = $0.19 or 19 cents per ounce.

CLOSE

Culminating Activity
Comparison Shopping
Have the class create a 10-item list of products. Organize groups to visit a particular store to get prices for the items. Have groups create a comparison chart.

Unit Prices Some products come in many different sizes, making it hard to determine the best buy. In this situation, look at the unit price. The *unit price* is the cost of an item divided by a standard unit of measurement, such as an ounce. Suppose a store offers two brands of milk. Brand A is 10 ounces and costs $2. Brand B is 15 ounces and costs $2.85. *Which brand offers the lowest unit price?*

N C L B Activity correlates to Math standards.

Warehouse Stores

Warehouse stores are typically about the size of a football field. They carry a huge selection of food and nonfood items at low prices and in **bulk** quantities. Some require customers to become members to get buying privileges and discounts. They include Costco and Sam's Club.

Shopping at Home

Consumers can shop at home through TV channels, catalogs, or the Internet. Some companies such as Service Merchandise sell items only on the Internet. Others offer catalog and online services. Some retail stores, such as Crate & Barrel and Eddie Bauer, also mail catalogs.

Deciding How Much to Pay

Comparison shopping is an important factor in buying products or services. **Comparison shopping** is comparing the prices and the characteristics of competing brands or stores. It is most important for major purchases because the difference in cost can be significant. Some people think the most expensive item is always the best product. However, sometimes the least expensive item or the one in the middle might be the best buy for the money.

Section 22.1

After You Read

Review Key Concepts
1. What are four decisions that consumers must make when they buy goods and services?
2. Compare brand-name and generic products.
3. Identify choices that consumers must make when they buy.

Academic Skills
4. **Mathematics** Paper towels come in two sizes, regular and jumbo. A regular roll costs 89¢ and contains 80 sheets, each 11 × 9 inches. A jumbo roll costs $1.37 and contains 146 sheets, each also 11 × 9 inches. What is the difference in the cost per square foot of the two sizes?

THEORY **Finding Areas** The formula for finding the area of a rectangle is $A = l \times w$. To convert square inches into square feet, divide the number of square inches in the roll by 12 × 12, the number of square inches in one square foot.

 For math help, go to the Math Appendix.

@ Go to the *Introduction to Business* Online Learning Center through **glencoe.com** to check your answers.

Section 22.1

Review Key Concepts
1. what to buy, when to buy, where to buy, and how much to pay
2. Brand-name products are identified with a brand. Generic products are plainly labeled and lower priced.
3. They must choose whether to buy now or wait until items go on sale.

Academic Skills
4. **Mathematics**
11 × 9 × 80 ÷ 144 = 55 sq. ft.
$0.89 ÷ 55 = $0.0162
11 × 9 × 146 ÷ 144 = 100 sq. ft.
$1.37 ÷ 100 = $0.0137
$0.0162 − $0.0137 = 0.0025
The difference is about a quarter of a cent.

How to Be a Smart Consumer

FOCUS

Reading Guide

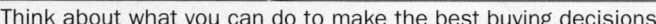

● *Before You Read*

Think about what you can do to make the best buying decisions.

Read to Learn
- Identify types of information that can be helpful to a consumer in making wise shopping decisions.

The Main Idea
To get the most value for your shopping dollar, you can collect information to make an informed decision when you shop. You should plan ahead so that you can make the best choices and get the best buys.

Key Concept
- Preparing to Shop

Vocabulary
Key Terms
promotional sale
clearance sale
loss leaders
impulse buying
warranty

Academic Vocabulary
You will find these words in your reading and on your tests. Make sure you know their meanings.

convince · · · · · · label
publications · · · document

Graphic Organizer
In a figure like the one below, list the steps you need to take when you prepare to shop.

Preparing to Shop

 Go to the *Introduction to Business* Online Learning Center through **glencoe.com** for a printable graphic organizer.

D

N C L B

Academic Standards
English Language Arts
  NCTE 1 Read texts to acquire new information
  NCTE 4 Use written language to communicate effectively
  NCTE 5 Use different writing process elements to communicate effectively
  NCTE 7 Conduct research and gather, evaluate, and synthesize data to communicate discoveries
Science
  Content Standard D Students should develop an understanding of origin and evolution of the Earth system

Bell Ringer Activity

How to Be a Smart Consumer
Ask students: What are some of the benefits of being a smart consumer? (Students might suggest that being a smart consumer means that you spend less money or get better value for the money you spend.)

Preteaching

Presentation Plus!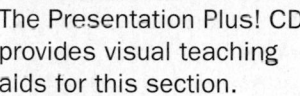
The Presentation Plus! CD provides visual teaching aids for this section.

PuzzleMaker
Use the Vocabulary PuzzleMaker to create a puzzle of the section's key terms. Students can complete the puzzle on paper or on a computer.

Graphic Organizer
Tell students to go to the Online Learning Center through **glencoe.com** for a printable graphic organizer. (Answers include the following suggestions for consumers: study advertisements, read consumer publications, shop at sales, use shopping lists, resist pressure and gimmicks, and read labels and warranties.)

N C L B Connects academics to content.

Reading Guide

● *Before You Read*

Students might suggest comparing prices at different stores, comparing unit prices, and reading reviews.

D Develop Concepts

The Main Idea Ask students: Why is it important to plan ahead when you shop?
(Planning ahead allows you to make the best choices and get the best buys.)

395

TEACH

Discussion Starter
Preparing to Shop
Project or write on the board the list of things a smart consumer should do before shopping. Ask students to elaborate on and discuss the benefits of each point on the list.

R Reading Strategy

Classify Number and display 15 print advertisements from various publications. Make sure that you include examples of rational and emotional advertising. Have each student number a piece of paper from 1 to 15. Pass the ads around the room and ask students to classify each ad as rational or emotional, recording their answers next to the appropriate number. When all students have seen all the ads, invite a volunteer to hold up the first ad and explain why it is classified as rational or emotional. Continue until all the ads have been reviewed. (Answers will depend on the advertisements chosen.)

✔ Reading Check

Identify Before purchasing a product or service, a smart consumer should study advertisements, read consumer publications, shop at sales, use shopping lists, resist pressure and gimmicks, and read labels and warranties.

396

Preparing to Shop

Consumers have to decide what a bargain is to them. You can become a smart consumer by planning in advance. Before making a purchase, a smart consumer should

R
- study advertisements.
- read consumer publications.
- shop at sales.
- use shopping lists.
- resist pressure and gimmicks.
- read labels and warranties.

✔ **Reading Check** **Identify** What should a smart consumer do before purchasing a product or service?

● **As You Read**
Think about some recent ads that have attracted your attention. Why did they appeal to you?

Study Advertisements

To be a wise consumer, you must learn how to read ads for information that will be helpful. Most ads are one of two types. *Rational advertising* attempts to **convince** consumers with facts and information. It tries to persuade buyers to choose a specific product because it is the best one for their purposes. *Emotional advertising* appeals to people's feelings. For example, it might suggest that if consumers buy a particular car, they will be popular.

When you look at advertising, decide whether it provides useful information. An ad that simply says, "The best buy in town!" will not necessarily help you become a smarter consumer. However, an ad that says, "6 oz. Sparkle-Plenty Toothpaste, $1.99," might be very helpful. If you know that this toothpaste is good and usually sells for $2.79 for 6 ounces, then you will know that the sale is a good buy.

● **Advertisers Provide Information**
Advertisers help you make shopping choices. **What types of advertising inserts are provided to consumers?**

396 **Chapter 22** Making Consumer Decisions

● **As You Read**
Students should discuss the reasons emotional and rational ads have appeal and the disadvantages of each.

Discuss the Photo
● **Advertisers Provide Information**
Individual stores print advertising inserts, especially if they have a sale. Some inserts include information and coupons for a variety of products available from a number of stores or online sources.

Figure 22.2 — *Shopping Choices*

Selection	Convenience	Price
Always in stock	Convenient location	Good value for the price
Have what I want	Good service	High quality
Unique merchandise	Products easily accessible	Low or fair prices

Source: http://retailtrafficmag.com/mag/retail_america_shops

● **What Consumers Want** There are many things that are important to consumers when they shop. **What do you consider to be the most important reason for choosing a particular store?**

Read Consumer Publications

Publications such as *Consumer Reports and Consumers' Research Magazine* give detailed information about goods that have been tested and rated. If you need to buy an expensive item, you can begin comparison shopping by studying what these magazines say about the competing brands.

Consumer magazines examine and rate products ranging from bottled iced teas to travel agencies. Many specialty magazines, such as those for photographers or hikers, rate equipment such as cameras or hiking boots. Libraries and online services are good places to find these **publications**.

Shop at Sales

Stores often use sales to attract customers. A **promotional sale** is one that offers a special buy on a new product or a product that is in season. It is usually held at a time when consumer purchases are down, such as after holidays. A **clearance sale** is a sale to clear out goods that are going out of season or are no longer profitable. These sales often make room for new merchandise. Clearance sales often mark the end of a season. Many businesses also hold other sales throughout the year.

During a sale, look for products that are advertised as selling at a loss or below cost. **Loss leaders** are advertised products that sell at a loss to bring customers into a store. Even though a store does not make money on them, their low prices are intended to attract more customers. Store managers hope consumers will buy other items along with loss leaders. **Figure 22.2** shows why consumers shop at certain stores.

Consumer Advocates Several organizations represent consumers. For instance, the Association of Community Organizations for Reform Now (ACORN) advocates for low- and moderate-income families. Other organizations include the National Consumers League and American Association of Retired Persons. *What kinds of issues would cause you to contact a consumer advocate?*

Section 22.2 How to Be a Smart Consumer   **397**

Section 22.2

TEACH (cont.)

S Skill Practice
Guided Practice
Define Ask students to use their own words to define these key terms: promotional sale, clearance sale, and loss leader. (Answers will be based on students' understanding of the key terms and their choice of words.) **L1**

Identify Examples Organize students into pairs and provide each pair with two advertising supplements from a Sunday newspaper. Instruct students to look for examples of loss leaders. Ask volunteers to explain why they think the item is a loss leader. (Answers will depend on students' examples.) **L2**

Illustrate a Concept Have students work in pairs to create a full-page newspaper advertisement for a promotional sale or a clearance sale. Instruct them to date the page and use text and illustration for their ads. (Advertisements will vary. For example, students might use a date in November and create a grocery store advertisement for a Thanksgiving dinner promotional sale.) **L3**

ASSESS

Review Key Terms
Have students write sentences using each key term.

 **Study-to-Go** Have students go to the Online Learning Center through **glencoe.com** to download free **Study-to-Go** content to their PDAs or cell phones.

Figure 22.2

● **What Consumers Want** Answers will vary but may include the selection of products, convenience, and price.

Consumer Advocates Students may note that they would contact a consumer advocate after exhausting all other resources. Reasons might include not receiving a refund after a product breaks, or not receiving an advertised service after paying for it.

RETEACH

W Writing Support

Enrichment

Shopping Lists Ask students to write a poem about the value of using shopping lists. Consider allowing them to work in pairs. (Poems will vary but should include helpful information about the benefits of using shopping lists.)

R Reading Strategy

Apply Knowledge Ask students to use their knowledge of impulse buying to explain the placement of magazines, candy, and small toys near checkout areas. (Students should recognize that retailers are hoping that people will buy these items as they wait to pay for their items.)

U Universal Access

Second Language Learners

Students whose native language is other than English may find the legal terminology used in extended warranties or credit applications overwhelming. You may need to spend extra time going over this vocabulary. Allow time for students to ask questions and receive clarification of any unfamiliar terminology.

Student Activity Workbook ☞ Assign the Section 22.2 Activities.

✔ Reading Check

Analyze Some consumers make impulse purchases because they did not make a shopping list.

Activity correlates to Science standards.

Science/TechTRENDS

Asteroids

NCLB

In 2001, a spacecraft landed on an asteroid for the first time. It took a journey of more than 2 billion miles to get there. NASA named that first spacecraft NEAR Shoemaker to honor the famous scientist, Eugene Shoemaker. The asteroid is named Eros. Scientists once thought asteroids were made of solid iron that could be mined. Eros was not. Instead, it is made of solid rock. Covered in more than 100,000 craters, about 1 million boulders the size of a house litter its surface. The spacecraft sent back images that solved some of the scientific mysteries about the solar system. However, it also created new mysteries for scientists to explore.

Web**Quest**

Go to the *Introduction to Business* Online Learning Center through **glencoe.com** for links to Web sites where you can learn more about asteroids. Look for information on what asteroids are made of and how they form. Find images that were sent back by NEAR Shoemaker. Develop a presentation using presentation software featuring some of the images you find.

● As You Read

Stores are in business to make a profit. Think about the reasons a store would sell a product at a loss.

Use Shopping Lists

Impulse buying is the act of making unplanned purchases. Impulse buying can ruin a consumer's budget and result in buying items that are not needed. To cut down on unplanned buying, use a shopping list. It might keep you from making unnecessary shopping trips because you forgot something you need. It can also save you money, because you can decide in advance what to buy and how much to spend.

Resist Pressure and Gimmicks

Some salespeople use high-pressure tactics to get consumers to buy their goods and services. They can be very persuasive. You should always ask yourself if what the salesperson is saying is true, if you need the product or service, and if you can afford it.

Sales gimmicks, such as ads for prizes or "super-low prices," are meant to grab consumers' attention and get them into a store to buy something. For example, you might get a notice in the mail that says you have won a prize. However, after reading closely, you realize you will not get the prize unless you buy something. Always examine any deal that seems too good to be true.

✔ Reading Check

Analyze Why do some consumers make impulse purchases?

Science/TechTRENDS

Web**Quest**

Asteroids Presentations will vary. Students should use photos from the spacecraft that illustrate the asteroid's composition as well as its formation.

● As You Read

Loss leaders are advertised products that sell at a loss to bring customers into a store. Store managers hope customers will buy profitable items along with loss leaders.

Read Labels and Warranties

Before buying a product, read its **label**. You might find information on it that will lead you to decide not to buy the product. For instance, before buying fruit juice, read the food label for the contents. What you thought was 100 percent fruit juice could mainly be corn syrup and water.

Many items come with a warranty. A **warranty** is a written guarantee from the manufacturer or distributor that states the conditions under which the product can be returned, replaced, or repaired. It is a legal **document** that states the rights and responsibilities of the consumer and the store or manufacturer. Federal law requires sellers of products that cost more than $15 (and that have a warranty) to make the warranty available to customers before a purchase. It is often printed on the package.

Warranties are divided into two basic types: implied and express. *Implied warranties* are unwritten guarantees that cover certain aspects of a product or its use. An implied warranty of mechantability guarantees that a product is fit for its intended use. *Express warrantees,* which are usually written, come in two forms. *Full warranties* state that the seller will repair or replace a product that does not work, usually free of charge, or give a refund. Full warranties are usually good for a stated time period, such as 90 days or one year. *Limited warranties* cover only certain parts of a product. They may require the buyer to pay a portion of the repair costs.

NCLB Activity correlates to English Language Arts standards.

Section 22.2

●After You Read

Review Key Concepts
1. What can you do before shopping that can help you make a wise choice?
2. Describe promotional sales and clearance sales.
3. What types of protection do a full warranty and a limited warranty provide to consumers?

Academic Skills
4. **English Language Arts** List products that you would buy at a store that is convenient to you. Then list products for which you shop around at several stores even if you have to travel to get to them. Write a paragraph comparing the lists.

5. **English Language Arts** With a partner, create a poster to advise students about ways to be a smart shopper and to avoid getting "taken in" by ads and promotions. Use some of this chapter's key words in your poster.

 Go to the *Introduction to Business* Online Learning Center through **glencoe.com** to check your answers.

Section 22.2

Review Key Concepts
1. study advertisements and read consumer publications
2. Promotional sale: offers a special buy on a product; clearance sale: clears out goods to make room for new merchandise
3. A full warranty promises replacement or refund for defective products.

A limited warranty covers only certain parts of the product.

Academic Skills
4. **English Language Arts** Answers may include products in different price ranges.
5. **English Language Arts** Students should incorporate chapter content into their posters.

RETEACH (cont.)

C Critical Thinking

Express an Opinion
Warranties Have students write a summary of an article about warranties and express an opinion about the value of extended warranties. (Summaries should include recognition that extended warranties offer consumers extra protections.)

ASSESS

● After You Read

Have students complete the Section 22.2 After You Read section review.

Online Study Tools
Have students go to the Online Learning Center through **glencoe.com** to:
- Take the Section 22.2 **Practice Test**.
- Download free **Study-to-Go** content to their PDAs or cell phones.

CLOSE

Culminating Activity
Shopping Challenge
Bring copies of grocery-store flyers to class. Organize students into teams and give each a flyer to use to "shop." Instruct students that they must stay within a certain budget. Have groups display their "purchases" and discuss how price played a factor.

399

Vocabulary Review

1. Students should write complete sentences using each term correctly.

Review Key Concepts

2. what to buy, when to buy, where to buy, and how much to pay

3. Brand names help consumers distinguish items from other products. Consumers often associate them with quality. Generic products are usually plainly labeled, unadvertised, and sold at lower prices.

4. wait until it is out of season or goes on sale, or buy a product when it is first available

5. department stores, off-price and outlet stores, superstores, or warehouse stores, through TV shopping channels, the Internet, or catalogs

6. study advertisements, read consumer publications, or compare sales and regular prices

7. Advertisements can provide facts and information. Consumer publications report tests and ratings. A shopping list can help a consumer to avoid impulse buying. Labels provide information. Warranties provide protection.

Section 22.1 *Summary*

Consumer Choices Making shopping decisions is not always easy, especially when there are many options available. Most people have limited funds. As consumers, they have to budget their money to satisfy their wants and needs. Consumers must decide what, when, and where to buy goods and services as well as how much to pay for them. They must also decide whether to buy generic or brand-name items. The best buy depends on what is important to the individual consumer.

Section 22.2 *Summary*

How to Be a Smart Consumer You can become a smart consumer by planning in advance. Smart consumers study advertisements, read consumer publications, and shop at sales. They also use shopping lists, resist pressure and gimmicks to buy goods and services, and read labels and warranties. Many consumers turn to consumer magazines when researching products and services. Planning helps them to avoid impulse buying and allows consumers to get the best warranty.

Vocabulary Review

1. On a sheet of paper, use each of these key terms and academic vocabulary terms in a sentence.

Key Terms	Academic Vocabulary
consumer	disposes
brand name	priority
generic products	version
comparison shopping	bulk
promotional sale	convince
clearance sale	publications
loss leaders	label
impulse buying	document
warranty	

Review Key Concepts

2. Identify four decisions that consumers make when they buy goods and services.

3. Compare brand-name and generic products.

4. Identify choices that consumers must make about when to buy.

5. List several choices that consumers have when selecting a store to make purchases.

6. Describe tools that consumers can use to compare prices for goods and services.

7. Identify types of information that can be helpful to a consumer in making wise shopping decisions.

Critical Thinking

8. Answers will vary. For example, spring months often see sales of summertime goods, such as patio furniture. "White sales" are often held in the winter.

9. These stores offer an extensive choice to shoppers, and they cater to special groups. Although higher priced, the quality of merchandise and service are factors in bringing in customers.

10. Answers will vary. For example, any item that will not spoil or decay may be a good buy in large quantities.

11. Answers will vary. For example, three common items are snack foods, soft drinks, and CDs purchased from convenience, discount, or grocery stores, or vending machines. If they did not compare prices beforehand, convenience might have been a factor.

Critical Thinking

8. What time(s) of the year would be best for department stores to offer sales because of a decrease in consumer purchases?

9. Some specialty stores set higher prices and still find a niche with shoppers. What factors do you think make them successful?

10. What types of products do you think consumers should consider buying in large quantities to save money?

11. Think about three items you have bought recently. Where did you buy each one? Did you comparison shop before you made the purchases? Why or why not?

12. In many stores, racks by the checkout counter have a wide range of "convenience goods" on display. These goods include candy, magazines, batteries, and chewing gum. Why do you think they are placed here?

13. Warehouse stores offer a wide variety of items. Why do you think consumers and small businesses choose to shop at them?

14. Do you think consumers can make informed decisions without advertising?

Write About It

15. Choose an ad from your local newspaper for a department store where you like to shop. Write two or more paragraphs describing the products that are featured in the ad. Include your ideas about why these products are being featured at this time of year.

16. Use your local phone book and prepare a list of 10 stores in your shopping community. Classify each store as one of the types of stores you have read about in this chapter.

17. Choose a store in one of the categories discussed in this chapter. Visit the store's Web site and research the types of information it offers to consumers. Write two or more paragraphs on your findings.

18. Go to a library and find an issue of a consumer magazine such as *Consumer Reports* or *Consumers Digest*. Write a short summary of the magazine features.

19. Visit a Web site for a large company that sells appliances, electronic equipment, or computers. Search for information on warranties. Summarize what you find in a brief report.

Technology Applications

Database Software

20. Research the stores that offer an item you want to buy. Use database software to create a database of the stores. Include names, addresses, telephone numbers, Web site addresses, prices, and any other information to use in comparison shopping. Use the information to determine the best place to buy the item.

Business Ethics

The Ethics of Advertising

21. A store in your neighborhood announces it will hold a sale. You know that the store raised prices before the sale was announced, but everything was later discounted for the sale. Is this ethical? What can consumers do in response?

Chapter 22 Review and Activities **401**

Critical Thinking

12. These items are often impulse buys. Most of the items are low priced, so consumers are more likely to buy them at the checkout counter.

13. Answers will vary. For example, if they can buy in large quantities at good prices, consumers can store their purchases and save money.

14. Without it, most people would not know about new goods or services. Ads also aid comparison shopping. Some students may say advertising is not influential because they do not pay attention to it.

Write About It

15. Answers will vary, depending on the items and store selected.

16. Answers will vary, depending on the stores in the community.

17. Answers will depend on the Web site, but many stores allow consumers to apply for credit cards online. Most sites provide a list of product lines they carry. Warehouse stores provide information about membership.

18. Answers will vary, depending on the magazine chosen.

19. Large stores that sell electronics usually offer manufacturers' warranties on products they carry. Most do not offer their own warranty.

Technology Applications

20. Answers will be based on the types of items desired and the stores that are researched.

Business Ethics

21. This is not ethical. Regular customers who realize that the sale is not real may lose confidence in store management. They may decide not to shop there again. They may contact upper management or consult a consumer advocate.

Applying Academics to Business

22. Students' rational ads should focus on concrete benefits and the emotional ads should communicate how the product will make you feel.

23. $45 ÷ 750 = 6%
6% of the cost went to paying for the warranty.

24. Answers may include: brand name, generic product, discount store, clearance sale, comparison shopping, unit price, impulse buying, and loss leader.

25. Answers will vary, depending on the coupons for products chosen.

Active Learning

26. Some ideas to include: If you plan to buy expensive items, do your homework. Find out about places where you can buy them and check for ads in newspapers and online. Prepare a list of questions to ask sales associates about different brands. Ask about warranties and service plans.

Business in the Real World

27. In almost all cases, students will find the generic prices of items to be lower than the brand-name items.

Applying Academics to Business

English Language Arts
22. Ads use writing that is designed to persuade. Choose a product you like and use often. Write both a rational and an emotional ad for it. Include an attention-grabbing headline and two or three sentences describing features of the product. Present your ads to the class and lead a discussion about their differences.

Mathematics
23. The computer you bought includes a one-year service warranty. The cost of servicing computers averages about $45 in parts and labor per service. If the retail price of the computer was $750, about what percentage of that price covers the cost of the warranty?

THEORY **Problem Solving** It is often helpful to restate the problem in your own words before solving. In this case you are asked to express the cost of the warranty as a percent of the cost "per computer."

English Language Arts
24. Sort the words below to make a list of eight two-word phrases about making consumer decisions.

generic	brand
clearance	discount
comparison	name
buying	unit
leader	shopping
product	price
store	impulse
sale	loss

Mathematics
25. Go through a coupon mailer or flyer for a local grocery store. List the face value for at least 20 coupons. Find the mean and median of the data.

THEORY **Data Analysis** The mean of a set of numbers is their average; the median is the middle number, or the average of the two middle numbers, when the data are listed from least to greatest.

Active Learning

Wise-Shopping Presentation
26. Prepare a short presentation for your class on wise-shopping tips for buying an electronic device of your choice. Include some ideas in your presentation for making the best choices when preparing for a shopping trip and during shopping. Include information about the best places to shop in your community for the product you chose. Present your ideas to the class.

Business in the Real World

Generic Brands
27. Visit a grocery store or supermarket. Choose five items that are available as generic products. Record their prices. Then find brand-name versions of those items and record their prices. Calculate the unit prices of the 10 items. Prepare a chart showing the unit price of each item and the amount a shopper could save by buying the generic products.

ExamView Assessment Suite CD allows you to print out ready-made unit and chapter tests, complete with answer keys. You can also create customized tests.

TeacherWorks Plus provides complete teacher resources in one convenient package. It includes customizable lesson plans in calendar format and instant access to many print program resources.

Real LIFE skills

CONSUMER ISSUES AND DECISION MAKING

28. Sometimes the government or a business that produces a good or a service makes a decision about a consumer issue that greatly affects consumers' finances. Research a consumer issue, and determine the financial implications for consumers. What might consumers do in response to this action?

Business CAREERS

FIND YOUR DREAM JOB

29. Go to the *Introduction to Business* Online Learning Center through **glencoe.com** for a link to the Occupational Outlook Handbook Web site. Click on the "OOH Search/A-Z Index" link and enter the job title "sales representative" (wholesale and manufacturing). Then write a one-page report about this type of occupation. Conclude your report with a list of things you could do now to prepare yourself to pursue the occupation.

Role Play

SHOPPING FOR A NEW COMPUTER

30. Situation With two or three of your classmates, discuss the points you need to consider in deciding to buy a new computer.

Activity Plan a short skit that your group will present to your class, demonstrating the questions you would ask before you make your decision.

Evaluation You will be evaluated on how well you meet the following performance indicators:

- Describe some different types of computers from which you could choose.
- Outline at least five questions your group will discuss.
- Identify the best choice.
- Prepare a written outline of the points in your skit.

Standardized Test Practice

Directions Choose the letter of the best answer. Write the letter for the answer on a separate piece of paper.

1. What is 559,607 rounded to the nearest hundred thousand?

  A   500,000
  B   560,000
  C   559,600
  D   600,000

 **TEST-TAKING TIP** When answering an essay question on a test, focus on one main idea per paragraph. Do not write long introductions and conclusions. Spend most of your time answering the question asked.

 READING Go to the *Introduction to Business* Online Learning Center through **glencoe.com** for a list of outside reading suggestions.

glencoe.com   **Chapter 22** Review and Activities   **403**

 **STRATEGIES FOR STANDARDIZED TEST PREP SUCCESS**

Test Prep Present students with a list of essay questions taken from released tests, or tests you have given in the past. For each question, have the students identify the key words in the directions that tell them what to do. For example, if they are asked to *explain* something, they should go beyond a basic definition or list of information to include information and examples that tell about why and how.

Real LIFE skills

28. Answers will depend on the consumer issue researched.

Business CAREERS

29. Sales representatives demonstrate products; market products to manufacturers, wholesale and retail establishments, and other institutions. Working conditions involve travel, mostly by car. Training and qualifications vary. Increasingly a bachelor's degree is required. Opportunities for advancement: Larger account or territory, training and leadership positions and positions in purchasing, advertising, or marketing research. Job outlook: Average growth. Earnings are usually a combination of salary and commission or salaries plus bonus. As preparation: developing good communication and interpersonal skills.

Role Play

30. Presentations should address the competencies noted in the Role Play. Answers will vary, but students should indicate a clear understanding of wise shopping.

Standardized Test Practice
  1. C

Standards-Based Lesson Planning

Introduction to Business provides students with instruction and assessment in the following fundamental content areas:

Content Standards Correlations	
Analyze the U.S. business system in order to function as a productive citizen, consumer, and worker.	pp. 407–410, 412–415, 416–419
Identify consumer rights.	pp. 407–410, 416–419
Analyze the role of the consumer as a responsible citizen.	pp. 412–419
Identify consumer responsibilities.	pp. 412–415, 416–419
Interpret and explain consumer rights and responsibilities.	pp. 407–410, 412–415, 416–419
Analyze information on money and responsible consumerism.	pp. 409, 412–415, 417–419
Distinguish between the rights and responsibilities needed to be an informed consumer. Compare consumer rights and responsibilities and relate them to government protection policies.	pp. 409, 412, 417–419
Research consumers' legal responsibilities associated with consumerism. Examine duties of consumers and consequences of ignoring those duties.	pp. 417, 419
Calculate taxes, discounts, and/or miscellaneous charges for purchases.	p. 418

NCLB Activities, information, and skills practice will help your students attain No Child Left Behind proficiency. Students will improve their abilities in the following academic standards areas:

Academic Standards Correlations		
English Language Arts	**Activities/Features**	**Page**
NCTE 3 Apply strategies to interpret texts	Applying Academics to Business Standardized Test Practice	pp. 418, 419
NCTE 7 Conduct research and gather, evaluate, and synthesize data to communicate discoveries	Applying Academics to Business	p. 418
NCTE 8 Use information resources to gather information and create and communicate knowledge	After You Read	p. 415
Mathematics		
Algebra Represent and analyze mathematical situations and structures using algebraic symbols	After You Read	p. 410
Algebra Use mathematical models to represent and understand quantitative relationships	Ask S&P	p. 404
Number and Operations Compute fluently and make reasonable estimates	Applying Academics to Business	p. 418
Number and Operations Understand meanings of operations and how they relate to one another	Applying Academics to Business	p. 418
Science		
Content Standard F Students should develop understanding of environmental quality and science and technology in local, national, and global challenges	Science/Tech Trends	p. 414

Correlations This chart shows the 21ˢᵗ Century Skills, foundation skills, and workplace competencies that students develop as they work in this chapter.

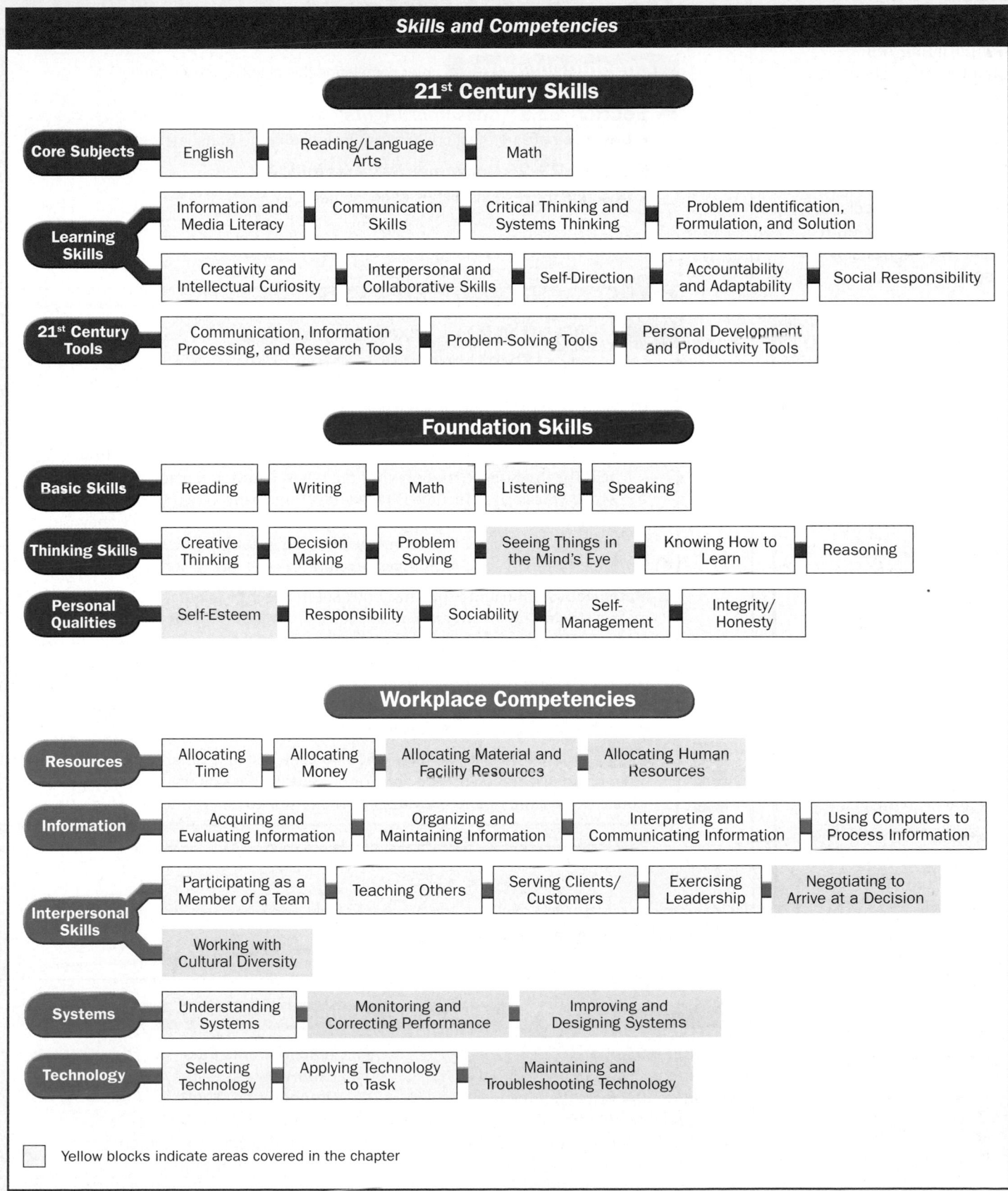

Skills and Competencies

21ˢᵗ Century Skills

Core Subjects
- English
- Reading/Language Arts
- Math

Learning Skills
- Information and Media Literacy
- Communication Skills
- Critical Thinking and Systems Thinking
- Problem Identification, Formulation, and Solution
- Creativity and Intellectual Curiosity
- Interpersonal and Collaborative Skills
- Self-Direction
- Accountability and Adaptability
- Social Responsibility

21ˢᵗ Century Tools
- Communication, Information Processing, and Research Tools
- Problem-Solving Tools
- Personal Development and Productivity Tools

Foundation Skills

Basic Skills
- Reading
- Writing
- Math
- Listening
- Speaking

Thinking Skills
- Creative Thinking
- Decision Making
- Problem Solving
- Seeing Things in the Mind's Eye
- Knowing How to Learn
- Reasoning

Personal Qualities
- Self-Esteem
- Responsibility
- Sociability
- Self-Management
- Integrity/Honesty

Workplace Competencies

Resources
- Allocating Time
- Allocating Money
- Allocating Material and Facility Resources
- Allocating Human Resources

Information
- Acquiring and Evaluating Information
- Organizing and Maintaining Information
- Interpreting and Communicating Information
- Using Computers to Process Information

Interpersonal Skills
- Participating as a Member of a Team
- Teaching Others
- Serving Clients/Customers
- Exercising Leadership
- Negotiating to Arrive at a Decision
- Working with Cultural Diversity

Systems
- Understanding Systems
- Monitoring and Correcting Performance
- Improving and Designing Systems

Technology
- Selecting Technology
- Applying Technology to Task
- Maintaining and Troubleshooting Technology

☐ Yellow blocks indicate areas covered in the chapter

Chapter 23

Chapter Overview

Introduce the Chapter

Consumer Rights and Responsibilities
Chapter 23 is about consumers' rights and responsibilities.

Building Background
As they start to make important consumer decisions, students need to learn about their rights and responsibilities.

>> Math Answer
Set up the following expression: $10,000a = $1,500. Solve for *a* by dividing both sides by $10,000 ($a = $1,500 ÷ $10,000). John's tax rate is 15% ($a = 0.15$)

>> Extension Activity
Calista and Nia each made a short-term investment of $20,000 in the same stock. They each earned $3,000 on their investment. Calista owes $840 in income taxes. Nia owes $750. At what rate was each woman taxed? (Calista was taxed at 28% and Nia at 25%.

Calista's tax rate:
$3,000$b$ = $840
b = $840 ÷ $3,000
b = .28 = 28%
Nia's tax rate: $3,000$c$ = $750
c = $750 ÷ $3,000
c = .25 = 25%)

N C L B Activity correlates to Math standards.

Consumer Rights and Responsibilities

Chapter Objectives After completing this chapter, you will be able to:

▶ **Section 23.1** *Consumer Rights*
- **Describe** seven protections that are included in the Consumer Bill of Rights.

▶ **Section 23.2** *Consumer Responsibilities*
- **Describe** the responsibilities of consumers.

Ask

STANDARD &POOR'S **Taxes and Investing**

Q: What responsibilities do I have for paying taxes on my investment earnings?

A: Everyone is required to pay taxes on investments. The amount of taxes you owe on an investment is dependent on how much your investment grew, how long you held the investment, and on your tax bracket. Your tax bracket is the amount at which your regular income is taxed. It is important to figure taxes into your calculations when comparing your investment choices. The difference they can make is startling. In fact, the tax advantage afforded to long-term capital gains is another big reason why long-term investing approaches work so well.

Mathematics John and Esperanza both fall in the 35% tax bracket. John decides to make a single $10,000 investment at the beginning of the year and hold it into the next year. Esperanza moves her $10,000 from stock to stock throughout the year. John's investment doubles to $20,000, while Esperanza's increases by 125% to $22,500. However, because John's investment qualifies as a long-term investment, he owes only $1,500 in taxes. Esperanza owes the full 35%, $5,250, because she bought and sold multiple times. At what rate was John taxed?

N C L B

THEORY **Use a Variable to Represent a Percent** Just as a variable can represent an integer, it can also represent a decimal or percent. Just as you would solve any other algebraic expression, isolate the variable on one side to determine its value.

Classroom Resources

- 📖 Student Edition
- 📖 Teacher Wraparound Edition
- 📂 Student Activity Workbook with Academic Integration
- 📂 Student Activity Workbook with Academic Integration TAE
- 📂 *Fast File*, Unit 8 Resources
- 📂 Inclusion in the Business Education Classroom

- 💿 TeacherWorks Plus
- 💿 *ExamView Assessment Suite*
- 💿 Presentation Plus!
- 💿 Vocabulary PuzzleMaker
- 💿 Interactive Student Edition
- 🖥 Online Student Edition
- 🖥 Online Learning Center with Podcasts

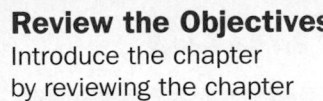

Review the Objectives
Introduce the chapter by reviewing the chapter objectives:

Section 23.1 *Objective*
Describe seven protections that are included in the Consumer Bill of Rights. (The seven protections for consumers are the right to be informed, the right to choose, the right to safety, the right to be heard, the right to have problems corrected, the right to consumer education, and the right to service.)

Section 23.2 *Objective*
Describe the responsibilities of consumers. (Consumer responsibilities: to be informed, to choose carefully, to use products safely, to speak out, to seek remedy, and to learn consumer skills)

● **Knowledge Is Power** Consumers can learn about ingredients by reading the labels on food products. **Do you compare the labels of food products before deciding which product to buy?**

Chapter 23 Consumer Rights and Responsibilities   **405**

Discuss the Photo
● **Knowledge Is Power** Read the caption on the photo to students: Consumers can learn about ingredients by reading the labels on food products.

Ask students: Do you compare the labels of food products before deciding which product to buy? (Answers will vary. Encourage students to understand that making careful buying decisions is a critical aspect of making the most of your resources.)

FOCUS

Section 23.1

Bell Ringer Activity

Consumer Rights
Ask students: During your first day of training as a sales associate, your supervisor asks, "How will you treat your prospective customers, and why?" (with respect and fairness; the way you would want to be treated)

Preteaching

Presentation Plus!
The Presentation Plus! CD provides visual teaching aids for this section.

PuzzleMaker
Use the Vocabulary PuzzleMaker to create a puzzle of the section's key terms. Students can complete the puzzle on paper or on a computer.

Graphic Organizer
Tell students to go to the Online Learning Center through **glencoe.com** for a printable graphic organizer. (Answers include: the right to be informed: lets consumers make good choices; right to choose: consumer freedom; right to safety: quality and security; right to be heard: ability to enforce consumer rights; right to have problems corrected: right to refund or exchange; right to consumer education: ability to understand consumer rights; and right to service: freedom from discrimination.)

 Connects academics to content.

Consumer Rights

Reading Guide

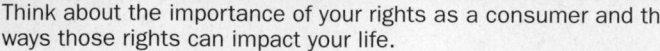
Before You Read

Think about the importance of your rights as a consumer and the ways those rights can impact your life.

Read to Learn
• Describe seven protections that are included in the Consumer Bill of Rights.

The Main Idea
Consumers are protected by the Consumer Bill of Rights. The bill states that consumers have the right to be informed, the right to choose, the right to safety, the right to be heard, the right to have problems corrected, the right to consumer education, and the right to service.

Key Concept
• The Consumer Bill of Rights

Vocabulary
Key Terms
consumer rights
consumer movement
product liability
bait and switch

Academic Vocabulary
You will find these words in your reading and on your tests. Make sure you know their meanings.
accurate
devices
resolved
scenario

Graphic Organizer
List the benefits of each of the seven basic consumer rights in a figure like the one below.

Consumer Right	Benefit of that Right
The Right to Be Informed	
The Right to Choose	
The Right to Safety	
The Right to Be Heard	
The Right to Have Problems Corrected	
The Right to Consumer Education	
The Right to Service	

@ Go to the *Introduction to Business* Online Learning Center through **glencoe.com** for a printable graphic organizer.

Academic Standards
English Language Arts
   NCTE 1 Read texts to acquire new information
Mathematics
   Algebra Represent and analyze mathematical situations and structures using algebraic symbols

Reading Guide

Before You Read

Students might suggest being treated fairly and having mechanisms to resolve complaints.

D Develop Concepts

The Main Idea Ask students: What are the seven consumer rights? (the right to be informed, to choose, to safety, to be heard, to have problems corrected, to consumer education, and to service)

The Consumer Bill of Rights

Imagine that you just bought an MP3 player. The first time you play it, you do not hear a sound. The good news is that you have rights as a consumer. These rights protect you when a product is defective.

In 1962, President John F. Kennedy outlined what he called the Consumer Bill of Rights. The bill stated that every person has four basic **consumer rights**—the right to be informed, the right to choose, the right to safety, and the right to be heard. These rights received a lot of attention from the **consumer movement**, a movement to pass laws protecting consumers from unfair and unsafe business practices. Over the years, three other rights were added: the right to have problems corrected, the right to consumer education, and the right to service.

The Right to Be Informed

As a consumer, you have a right to receive **accurate** information. Consumers can make wise decisions only if they have the information they need. Businesses are required to provide certain details about their products. For example, drug companies must list the complete contents of every medicine. Clothing manufacturers must list the fibers used in materials. Packaged foods must show all ingredients, with the main one listed first. Companies provide this information through product labeling.

The Right to Choose

Because the United States has a market economy, its consumers can choose from a wide variety of goods and services. Businesses compete with each other to sell their products to consumers. They offer new products, lower prices, higher quality, or improved services to get you to choose their products. Competition provides choices. A lack of it hurts consumers.

● As You Read

Think about your rights as a consumer. Have you ever observed your consumer protection rights when dealing with a defective product you purchased?

?ETHICS in Business

Product Safety

■ **Critical Reading** Life is full of important decisions. Think about the kinds of decisions that you make as you read the question below.

A product your company makes has a slight design flaw. You are the only one who knows about the problem, and the chances of it causing someone harm are negligible. The warning label that was printed, although thorough, does not address the design flaw. To reprint the warning labels would put this product over budget.

■ **Decision Making** Would you have the warning labels reprinted? Explain your answer.

Section 23.1   Consumer Rights   **407**

Section 23.1

TEACH

Discussion Starter
The Consumer Bill of Rights
Start a discussion by asking students to think about a recent shopping experience and new products that they have purchased or received as gifts. Ask them to describe how the Consumer Bill of Rights might have had an impact on their experience. (Students might mention getting information about the store's return policies—through signage at the store, comments by the clerk, and a written message on the receipt. They might also mention instructions for how to use a product or care for a garment.)

R Reading Strategy

Create a Memory Aid Have students work in pairs to create a device to help them remember the seven consumer rights. (Answers will vary, but should include all seven rights: the right to be informed, right to choose, right to safety, right to be heard, right to have problems corrected, right to consumer education, and right to service.)

● As You Read

Some students may say that they have not, while others may say they have if they were denied an acceptable remedy.

?ETHICS in Business

Decision Making Answers should emphasize the importance of product safety and the consumer's right to be told of any possible danger. Remind students of the ethical obligation companies have in protecting the consumer. In the case of product safety those increased costs can come in the form of legal liability.

TEACH (cont.)

S Skill Practice

Guided Practice

Evaluate Provide the packaging from several products and ask students to identify information related to the right to safety. (Students might suggest that a warning not to immerse electrical items in water is a safety warning.) **L1**

Create a Poster Have students create a poster showing safety warnings for several electronic items. (Posters will vary.) **L2**

Create a Display Have students work in pairs to create a display illustrating the right to safety, including products or pictures. Caution students against including items that are hazardous or that are not permitted on school grounds. (Displays will vary.) **L3**

● As You Read

Students may say they are affected by a lack of competition at events sponsored by only one seller.

✔ Reading Check

Explain A free-market economy

ASSESS

Review Key Terms

Have students write sentences using each key term.

 **Study-to-Go** Have students go to the Online Learning Center through **glencoe.com** to download free **Study-to-Go** content to their PDAs or cell phones.

● As You Read

Think about how businesses compete to sell their products to consumers. Have you ever been affected by a lack of competition?

The federal government has the power to keep markets competitive. It can use antitrust laws to break up monopolies or keep them from forming. Sometimes it will prevent a large company from buying a smaller one if the purchase would lead to control of a market.

✔ Reading Check **Explain** What type of economy gives its citizens the right to choose from a wide variety of goods and services?

The Right to Safety

S You have a right to products that are safe to use. **Product liability** is the legal responsibility that manufacturers have to make a safe product. For example, tools and appliances must include safety **devices** for your protection. Federal laws ensure that clothing, food, toys, and other items will not harm consumers. The U.S. Consumer Product Safety Commission enforces product-safety standards.

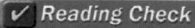

BusinessWeek *Reader and Case Study*

HP Wants Your Old PCs Back

It's pushing states to force recycling of TVs, computers, and other e-gear. Here's why.

A few years ago, when environmentalists in Washington State began agitating to rid local dumps of toxic old computers and televisions, they found an unexpected ally: Hewlett-Packard Co. Teaming up with greens and retailers, HP took on IBM, Apple Computer, and several major TV manufacturers, which were resisting recycling programs because of the costs.

Aided by HP's energetic lobbying, the greens persuaded state lawmakers to adopt a landmark program that forces electronics companies to foot the bill for recycling their old equipment. "This bill puts our market-based economy to work for the environment," said Washington Governor Christine O. Gregoire as she signed the plan into law on Mar. 24.

The movement to recycle electronic refuse, or "e-waste," is spreading across the nation,

and so is HP's clout. The company helped the greens win a big battle in Maine in 2004 when the state passed the nation's first e-waste "take-back" law.

 CASE STUDY Go to the *Introduction to Business* Online Learning Center through **glencoe.com** for the *BusinessWeek* Reader Case Study.

Active Learning

Research the components that are used to make a computer and the reasons those components should not end up in a landfill. Write a letter to your state representative. Explain the reasons it is important to your future for your state to preserve the environment.

408 **Chapter 23** Consumer Rights and Responsibilities

glencoe.com

BusinessWeek *Reader and Case Study*

HP Wants Your Old PCs Back

CASE STUDY Have students go to the *Introduction to Business* Online Learning Center through **glencoe.com** to download a Case Study activity that corresponds to the article. The activity and answer key are also available on the TeacherWorks Plus CD.

Active Learning

Answers will vary but are likely to discuss the hazards associated with toxic materials in computer components in landfills.

The Right to Be Heard

Consumers who have complaints about products or services have a right to be heard. Suppose you buy a bike helmet from a sporting goods store. After wearing the helmet a few times, you find that the chinstrap keeps coming loose. You have the right to let the store know you are not satisfied with the helmet. Businesses rely on customer satisfaction. The purpose of the customer service department is to listen to the concerns of customers.

The Right to Have Problems Corrected

Sometimes products do not work properly after they are purchased. Usually if a customer takes a defective item back to a store with a receipt, the business will replace it or issue a refund. If a business cannot or will not correct a problem, consumers can write to the manufacturer to find out how to get the matter **resolved**. If the manufacturer will not help, a government agency might be your next step. **Figure 23.1** asks you to match each **scenario** with the appropriate consumer right.

Consumer Resources Consumer.gov is an online resource for consumer information from the federal government. It is designed so that consumers can locate information by category—such as food, health, product safety, money, and transportation. *How might this consumer resource be useful to you?*

Figure 23.1 — *Know Your Consumer Rights*

Consumer Issue	Consumer Right
1. An automaker recalls its new model after some of its seat belts fail to keep children safe.	Right to be heard
2. A restaurant asks you to fill out a comment card after eating your meal.	Right to choose
3. An advertisement for a new TV informs the consumer about the total cost and interest rate.	Right to service
4. An electronics store displays three competing brands of computers from which to choose.	Right to safety
5. A shoe store replaces your new shoes after you discover a problem with the soles.	Right to be informed
6. *Consumer Reports* educates consumers who are researching different models of cameras.	Right to have problems corrected
7. You pay an auto repair service to rebuild your car's engine.	Right to consumer education

● **Consumer Rights** The Consumer Bill of Rights states that every person has the right to be informed, to choose, to be safe, to be heard, to have problems corrected, to receive consumer education, and to receive service. **Can you match the consumer issue with the appropriate consumer right?**

Section 23.1   Consumer Rights   **409**

RETEACH (cont.)

C Critical Thinking

Assess the Impact

The Right to Consumer Information Ask students to write a paragraph explaining the Internet's impact on the right to consumer education. (It is possible to find extensive information about virtually any product online.)

Consumer Awareness Fraud, false advertising, and invasion of privacy are possible themes.

ASSESS

After You Read

Have students complete the Section 23.1 After You Read section review.

Online Study Tools

Have students go to the Online Learning Center through **glencoe.com** to:

• Take the Section 23.1 **Practice Test**.

• Download free **Study-to-Go** content to their PDAs or cell phones.

CLOSE

Culminating Activity

Consumer Rights—A Business Point of View Organize students into seven groups. Ask each group to discuss one of the consumer rights from the point of view of manufacturers, retailers, and service providers and to share the group's ideas with the class. (Presentations will vary.)

410

Real World

Consumer Awareness In the United States, National Consumer Protection Week highlights consumer protection and education efforts. Whether you are investing in a business opportunity, taking part in an online auction, or looking for a scholarship, it pays to be aware as a consumer. *What issue might be a theme for the next National Consumer Protection Week?*

NCLB Activity correlates to Math standards.

The Right to Consumer Education

Consumers have the right to learn how a market system works. You should know how to get the best value and satisfaction for your money. When you decide to buy an item, you should know that different stores might charge different prices. You should know how to comparison shop to find the best buy. Check the information required by law on labels, and read fact sheets about products.

The Bait-and-Switch Tactic There are always some businesses that do not operate in the best interests of the consumer. Some might try a tactic known as bait and switch. **Bait and switch** is a sales tactic in which buyers are tempted by an advertised bargain but are then persuaded to buy a more expensive item instead.

The Right to Service

Customers have a right to be treated in a respectful and courteous manner. You have the right to expect prompt delivery of goods or services that meet the standard of quality a business claims. You also have the right to be served without discrimination on the basis of your race, gender, income, or age. These rights apply wherever you are being served.

Section 23.1

After You Read

Review Key Concepts

1. What are four basic consumer rights provided by the 1962 Consumer Bill of Rights?
2. What three consumer rights have been added to the Consumer Bill of Rights since 1962?
3. How does the bait-and-switch tactic work? Why is it unfair to consumers?

Academic Skills

4. **Mathematics** Today you found the tablecloth you wanted to buy on sale for the bargain price of $20. At other stores the same tablecloth costs $23. Write an expression that could be used to determine the percent discount of the bargain tablecloth.

THEORY **Percent Discount** Percent discount is a ratio of the difference in price divided by the original price. To convert a decimal to a percent, multiply by 100 by moving the decimal point two places to the right.

 For math help, go to the Math Appendix.

Go to the *Introduction to Business* Online Learning Center through **glencoe.com** to check your answers.

Review Key Concepts

1. right to be informed, to choose, to safety, and to be heard
2. right to have problems corrected, to consumer education, and to service
3. A business advertises an item at a lower price to bring customers into the store, but the store does not have that item. The salesperson then tries to persuade the customer to buy a more expensive item. It is unfair because the intent is to deceive customers.

Academic Skills

4. **Mathematics**
$x = [(\$23 - \$20) \div \$23]100$
$x = 13\%$

Consumer Responsibilities

Reading Guide

● Before You Read

Think about your responsibilities as a consumer and the ways those responsibilities can impact businesses.

Read to Learn
- Describe the responsibilities of consumers.

The Main Idea
Along with your consumer rights, you have responsibilities. You must use information provided to you, choose carefully, use products safely, and learn consumer skills. It is your responsibility to speak out and seek a remedy when problems occur.

Key Concept
- Your Responsibilities as a Consumer

Vocabulary

Key Terms

pollution	recycling
conservation	boycott

Academic Vocabulary

You will find these words in your reading and on your tests. Make sure you know their meanings.

adjust	contact
manuals	adequate

Graphic Organizer

In a table like the one shown, list examples of each of the six responsibilities of consumers.

Consumer Responsibility	Example
The Responsibility to Be Informed	
The Responsibility to Choose Carefully	
The Responsibility to Use Products Safely	
The Responsibility to Speak Out	
The Responsibility to Seek a Remedy	
The Responsibility to Learn Consumer Skills	

 Go to the *Introduction to Business* Online Learning Center through **glencoe.com** for a printable graphic organizer.

Academic Standards

English Language Arts

NCTE 1 Read texts to acquire new information

NCTE 8 Use information resources to gather information and create and communicate knowledge

Science

Content Standard F Students should develop understanding of environmental quality and science and technology in local, national, and global challenges

---

Reading Guide

● Before You Read

Students might mention businesses use recycled materials in response to consumer responsibility to conserve.

D Develop Concepts

The Main Idea Ask students: How are consumer rights related to responsibilities? (Answers will vary. For example, a consumer has the right to know the ingredients in a food product and the responsibility to be informed.)

FOCUS

🔔 Bell Ringer Activity

Consumer Responsibilities
Project or write the following statement on the board: If all else fails, read the instructions. Ask students if they think consumers have a responsibility to read instructions. (Answers will be based on students' opinions.)

Preteaching

Presentation Plus! ⊙
The Presentation Plus! CD provides visual teaching aids for this section.

PuzzleMaker ⊙
Use the Vocabulary PuzzleMaker to create a puzzle of the section's key terms. Students can complete the puzzle on paper or on a computer.

Graphic Organizer
Tell students to go to the Online Learning Center through **glencoe.com** for a printable graphic organizer. (Answers include the responsibility to be informed: hearing about a recall on the news; to choose carefully: reading a consumer report before making a purchase; to use products safely: following safety instructions; to speak out: complaining about defective merchandise; to seek a remedy: returning defective merchandise; to learn consumer skills: comparing prices.)

NCLB Connects academics to content.

TEACH

Discussion Starter
Your Responsibilities as a Consumer
Start a discussion by asking students: How do consumer rights and responsibilities relate? (Students should demonstrate an understanding that rights and responsibilities go hand in hand. Students might mention that people have the right to vote, but they need to take responsibility for actually going to the polls and casting their vote.)

R Reading Strategy

Make a List Ask students to make a list of resources consumers might use when they take responsibility for being informed. (Resources include labels, fact sheets, Web sites of consumer organizations and manufacturers, and publications such as *Consumer Reports* and *Consumers' Research Magazine*.)

✓ Reading Check

Contrast Product labels tell you what the product contains, such as nutritional facts in food or fibers in clothes. Fact sheets rate products on safety, performance, and value.

Who Is Responsible? Some consumers have sued a leading fast-food giant because of the contents and preparation of its food items. Some states have also sued the tobacco industry because of the contents of its products and its sales tactics. In both instances, the complaint was that the products contributed to some consumers' poor health. *Do you think a company is responsible if a consumer's health is negatively affected by its products?*

● **Stay Informed** It is your responsibility to learn about products before buying them. **How is this person taking responsibility as a consumer?**

Your Responsibilities as a Consumer

Along with rights come responsibilities. As a consumer, you have the responsibility to educate yourself. If information about a product is available, you have the responsibility to read that information and to use the product the way it is intended.

The Responsibility to Be Informed

Responsible consumers know what they are buying. When you shop for food, read the labels for nutritional facts. Product labels can tell you how much salt, sugar, fat, or protein a product contains. When you shop for clothes, read the labels to find out what materials they contain. The labels will also indicate how the clothes should be cleaned.

Before making a major purchase, you should always do some homework. Some consumers read the fact sheets from the U.S. Consumer Product Safety Commission. The fact sheets tell how a product is rated on safety, performance, and value. There is also lots of information on the Internet. Read consumer magazines such as *Consumer Reports* and *Consumers' Research Magazine,* which evaluate and rate products. Most consumer organizations and manufacturers have Web sites. **Figure 23.2** shows the Web site for J.D. Power and Associates®, a leading market research and consumer information firm.

✓ Reading Check **Contrast** How do product labels and fact sheets from the U.S. Consumer Product Safety Commission differ?

Real World
Who Is Responsible? Answers will vary. Most students will say companies have a responsibility to inform consumers about what is in their products, but consumers have the responsibility of deciding what is best for them.

Discuss the Photo
● **Stay Informed** Consumers can take responsibility by reading about products before making a buying decision.

Figure 23:2 — *Making Educated Choices*

● **Information for Consumers** The J.D. Power Web site offers valuable information for consumers. **If you were going to buy a new car, what type of information would you want to know before deciding which car to buy?**

The Responsibility to Choose Carefully

Responsible consumers make comparisons to find the best product or service at the best price. Which electronics company offers the best guarantee? Which cars have the best record for reliability? Which computer will best fit your budget and your needs? It pays to take time to make comparisons. You can examine the options and prices and then make an educated choice.

Choices That Affect the Environment Many consumer choices can affect the environment. Some vehicles emit more exhaust than others. Some materials, such as certain plastics, cannot be recycled and do not decompose easily. Illegal dumping can harm natural habitats. All of these things contribute to **pollution**, the contamination of air, water, and land. Pollution is caused by waste from products as well as the ways we use them. People and businesses must help to reduce it by making choices that are good for the environment.

Conserving Resources As the population grows, the demand for resources increases. **Conservation** is the process of preserving, protecting, and planning the management of resources. For example, as more people move into an area, the demand for water rises. Some areas may experience water shortages. Consumers should be aware of the limited supplies of certain resources and **adjust** their consumption accordingly.

● **As You Read**

Think about ways consumers can reduce pollution.

Figure 23.2

● **Information for Consumers** Answers will vary but may include reliability, gas mileage, safety features, passenger space, cost of maintenance, and resale value.

● **As You Read**

Answers will vary. For example, exhaust fumes from vehicles are another major pollutant. To reduce pollution from exhaust fumes, students could agree to walk or ride a bicycle instead of using a car or truck.

TEACH (cont.)

S Skill Practice
Guided Practice

Describe Ask students to describe some sources of pollution. (Answers will vary. Students might mention auto exhaust, air pollutants from manufacturing and energy production, or water pollution from waste disposal.) **L1**

Create a Poster Ask students to design a poster that encourages consumers to dispose of their trash in an environmentally responsible way. (Students' posters may emphasize proper disposal as a way to protect the health of their community.) **L2**

Investigate and Report
Have students investigate how consumers should properly dispose of hazardous material such as used engine oil, old household chemicals, and batteries. Ask students to report their findings to the class. (Reports will vary, but should indicate that hazardous materials should not be put in with regular household trash.) **L3**

ASSESS

Review Key Terms
Have students write sentences using each key term.

 Study-to-Go Have students go to the Online Learning Center through **glencoe.com** to download free **Study-to-Go** content to their PDAs or cell phones.

RETEACH

R Reading Strategy

Illustrate Concepts Ask students to illustrate these concepts: reducing, reusing, and recycling. (Illustrations will vary.)

U Universal Access

Students with Hearing Impairments Many students with hearing impairments use sign language. When they write, they actually use English as a second language. Their language skills can improve with increased use, correction, and exposure. Encourage students to understand that their safety depends, on their ability to communicate with others.

W Writing Support

Enrichment

The Responsibility to Speak Out Ask students to work in pairs to write a short article on ways consumers can solve concerns about products and business practices. (Students might mention calling customer service, writing a complaint letter, filling out a comment card, speaking to a manager, or posting comments on a blog.)

Student Activity Workbook ☞ Assign the Section 23.2 Activities.

✔ **Reading Check**

Define Collecting products for processing so that they can be used again.

 Activity correlates to Science standards.

414

Science/Tech**TRENDS** ●

Eco-Friendly Packaging

N C L B

If something is biodegradable, living organisms can break it down into simpler structures. This reduces the length of time it affects the environment. Packaging producers have increased research into the chemicals they use, looking for materials that can be broken down faster. A majority of packaging material is made of some form of ordinary plastic. While many plastics can be recycled, they are not biodegradable. This leaves it up to voluntary recycle programs to reduce the environmental impact.

WebQuest

Go to the *Introduction to Business* Online Learning Center through **glencoe.com** for links to Web sites where you can research how packaging manufacturers are trying to lessen the environmental impact of their products. Write a paragraph describing what companies are doing in this area.

R **Recycling** Part of conservation is learning to avoid waste. Consumers can help by reducing, reusing, and recycling materials in their daily lives. **Recycling** involves collecting products for processing so that they can be used again. Many cities have programs to collect products made of paper, plastic, metal, and glass for recycling.

✔ **Reading Check** **Define** What is recycling?

● **As You Read**

Think about a product you bought that was defective. What did you do to speak out about the defective product?

The Responsibility to Use Products Safely

U Consumers must follow the instructions provided in product **manuals** or other materials on the safe use of products. For example, a consumer must read the label of a cold remedy to find out its recommended dosage. If you know a product is unsafe, first contact the seller or producer about it. If no action is taken by the company, **contact** a consumer protection agency.

The Responsibility to Speak Out

W Responsible consumers can help improve the policies and products of the businesses where they shop. They can let a company know if they are dissatisfied with its products or policies. Consumers also have a responsibility to report unfair, unsafe, and illegal business practices. This helps to protect other consumers from problems. If you object to a company's policies or products, you could organize a **boycott**, a refusal to buy its goods or services. Boycotting is usually a last resort for consumers who have not received an **adequate** response from a company.

● **As You Read**

Answers will vary. There are many options, including informing the company, writing an editorial to a local newspaper, and contacting the community's chamber of commerce or a consumer advocacy group.

Science/Tech**TRENDS** ●

WebQuest

Eco-Friendly Packaging Answers will vary but paragraphs might describe how companies are replacing Styrofoam-based materials with those made from cornstarch or how research is being done to make more plastics that will break down in landfills.

The Responsibility to Seek a Remedy

Part of being a good consumer is getting the best value for your money. You have a responsibility to seek a remedy for a defective product. If you plan to exchange an item or get a refund, you must bring back the item, the receipt, and any warranties or guarantees that came with it. If the store cannot solve the problem to your satisfaction, you should contact the manufacturer or a consumer organization for help.

The Responsibility to Learn Consumer Skills

Find information to help you make consumer decisions. It is a bit overwhelming to think of researching every purchase before it is made. However, there are several ways to develop your consumer skills:

- Read information on labels and packages.
- Compare prices at different stores, and look for sales.
- Pay attention to the media to become aware of illegal practices.
- Read consumer information publications.
- Attend classes or workshops on consumer issues and problems.

Many purchases that you make will not require any research. Still, remember that the more informed you are about products and services, the better your consumer decisions will be.

 Activity correlates to English Language Arts standards.

Section 23.2

After You Read

Review Key Concepts

1. Where can you find information before making a major purchase?
2. Identify three steps you can take as a consumer to conserve resources.
3. If you object to a company's practices, what can you do as a consumer?

Academic Skills

4. **English Language Arts** Work together with one or two other students to create a bulletin-board display called "Consumers Speak Out!" Collect newspaper and magazine articles from consumer publications that illustrate how consumers have influenced businesses to change their policies or improve their products.

5. **English Language Arts** Write a 250-word report on how government regulations, such as those related to automobile safety, food and drug labeling, and secondhand smoke in stores and restaurants, have affected the safety of consumers.

@ Go to the *Introduction to Business* Online Learning Center through **glencoe.com** to check your answers.

Section 23.2

Review Key Concepts

1. fact sheets, the Internet, product labels, and consumer publications
2. Reduce use of disposable materials, reuse products, and recycle materials.
3. Report any unfair, unsafe, or illegal business practices; let the company know; contact a consumer organization.

Academic Skills

4. **English Language Arts** Students' bulletin boards will vary but should represent everyone's shared effort.
5. **English Language Arts** Students' reports will vary but should include evidence to support claims that government regulations have affected safety.

Section 23.2

RETEACH (cont.)

C Critical Thinking

Plan for Contingencies
The Responsibility to Seek a Remedy Ask students to explain why it is important to have a receipt when exchanging or returning a product. (Students should understand that having a receipt protects the consumer and the merchant.)

ASSESS

● **After You Read**

Have students complete the Section 23.2 After You Read section review.

Online Study Tools

Have students go to the Online Learning Center through **glencoe.com** to:

- Take the Section 23.2 **Practice Test**.
- Download free **Study-to-Go** content to their PDAs or cell phones.

CLOSE

Culminating Activity
Be a Responsible Consumer
Ask students to create a table that links each of the six consumer responsibilities to a benefit it provides that can help them be more satisfied with their consumer choices. (Students may link being informed with knowing what to buy, choosing carefully with getting the lowest price, product safety with avoiding accidents, and consumer skills with evaluating alternatives to make the most satisfying buying choice.)

415

Vocabulary Review

1. Students should write complete sentences using each term correctly.

Review Key Concepts

2. The seven protections for consumers are the right to be informed, the right to choose, the right to safety, the right to be heard, the right to have problems corrected, the right to consumer education, and the right to service.

3. Consumer responsibilities: to be informed, to choose carefully, to use products safely, to speak out, to seek remedy, and to learn consumer skills

Critical Thinking

4. People who wanted to protect the rights of consumers used that bill of rights to call attention to problems in the marketplace and passed consumer protection laws.

5. Some consumers do not complain when they have a problem with a product or service.

6. Consumer education is available from consumer education courses, publications, Web sites, instruction, and other sources.

7. If a loss leader runs out and the customer is urged to buy a higher-priced item, it can turn into a bait and switch.

Section 23.1 *Summary*

Consumer Rights The U.S. Consumer Bill of Rights states that every person has seven basic consumer rights. The first four are the right to be informed, the right to choose, the right to safety, and the right to be heard. Since the bill was developed in 1962, three other rights have been added to it: the right to have problems corrected, the right to consumer education, and the right to service. As a consumer, you are protected if you buy a defective product or receive poor service. However, it is up to you to make sure that your rights are observed.

Section 23.2 *Summary*

Consumer Responsibilities Along with rights come responsibilities. It is your responsibility to educate yourself before making consumer decisions. If you plan to make a major purchase, you can read and investigate your choices so that you can make a wise decision. Comparison shop by reading consumer magazines, checking companies' Web sites, and visiting different stores. Reducing pollution, conserving resources, and recycling are also responsibilities. If you take your consumer responsibilities seriously, you can get the best value for your money.

Vocabulary Review

1. On a sheet of paper, use each of these key terms and academic vocabulary terms in a sentence.

Key Terms	Academic Vocabulary
consumer rights	accurate
consumer movement	devices
product liability	resolved
bait and switch	scenario
pollution	adjust
conservation	manuals
recycling	contact
boycott	adequate

Review Key Concepts

2. Describe four protections for consumers that are included in the Consumer Bill of Rights.

3. Describe the responsibilities of consumers.

8. In many cases, the number of salespeople has been reduced, automated processes are used in place of people, or self-service is expected. Also, salespeople who are rushed or overworked or who are not people-oriented may not be as courteous and helpful as expected.

9. Answers may vary. Manufacturers could improve the information by reorganizing it, making it clear and concise, or enlarging the print. They also could refer consumers to their Web sites.

Critical Thinking

4. After the Consumer Bill of Rights was developed, the consumer movement was a strong force for consumer protection. Why do you think the consumer movement became so strong at that time?

5. In what ways do you think that consumers may not exercise their right to be heard?

6. Where can people go for help in making consumer decisions?

7. When might a loss leader (product sold below cost) become a bait and switch?

8. What do you think causes poor customer service?

9. Check the label on an item of clothing. How would you suggest the manufacturer improve the label?

10. How does it help consumers to have information about a single serving on food labels?

11. What do you think would justify a consumer boycott of a store or company?

12. What do you think is the most important thing that consumers can do to protect their interests when they buy goods and services?

Write About It

13. Write two or more paragraphs about why you think auto-repair complaints have led the list of consumer concerns for several years.

14. List several reasons why you think large companies often have entire departments devoted to consumer affairs.

15. List an item you recently bought that you are not satisfied with now. Write a short essay about actions you could take to resolve the matter.

16. Research the proper ways to dispose of items such as old clothes and used oil. Then write an essay on your findings.

17. Choose a company and write a short paper on the consumer information it provides. How can consumers remedy a problem with the company's product or service?

18. Find out about environmental issues in your community. List three pollution problems and discuss ways consumers can help solve them.

19. Research different consumer scams. Use the Internet, newspaper articles, and other materials. Write a news article on ways to avoid them.

Technology Applications

Spreadsheet Software

20. Study a label for canned or packaged food. Answer these questions: What is the serving size? How many servings are there per can or package? How many calories per serving? How many calories per can or package? What vitamins and minerals does the food provide? Develop a spreadsheet of your findings. Share your results with the class.

Business Ethics

Consumer Ethics Policy

21. Consumers have rights and responsibilities. Ethical behavior is one of the most important consumer responsibilities. Write a policy that offers general ethical guidelines and lists specific ways consumers should act when they shop. Discuss your policy with your classmates.

Chapter 23 Review and Activities **417**

Critical Thinking

10. The distinctions allow consumers to see how much they will consume in a single serving or in the whole amount, which is important for people watching what they consume.

11. As a last resort, if companies provide unsafe products and refuse to recall them or address the problem, a boycott is justified.

12. They can gather information so they can make informed decisions.

Write About It

13. Answers should indicate that millions of people rely on their automobiles. Sometimes repair costs and times can exceed the quotes, which can frustrate customers.

14. Large companies recognize the importance of the Consumer Bill of Rights and other consumer laws and that business can be lost if customers are unhappy.

15. Items and actions taken will vary.

16. Students should suggest ways that do not pollute the environment.

17. Answers will vary, depending on the company and its policies.

18. Answers should include definitive solutions.

19. Answers will depend on the scams researched.

Technology Applications

20. Answers should present a spreadsheet with data about serving size, servings per package, calories per serving, calories per package, and vitamins and minerals contained.

Business Ethics

21. Answers will vary. Students may report seeing signs that provide facts about different models. There may be a brochure for each item. For appliances, brochures may list various models available, make comparisons in size or capacity, and provide information about operating costs.

Applying Academics to Business

22. Students should point out that in 1880, Capt. Charles Cunningham Boycott, an English land agent in Ireland, was so ruthless in evicting tenants that his employees refused all cooperation with him. Another example is the American colonists' refusal to buy British goods after the Stamp Act of 1765.

23. $9 \times \$130 = \$1,170$

$(10 \times \$130) - .10$
$(10 \times \$130) = \$1,170$

There is no difference.

24. Students might point out similarities for recalls such as recalling toys because of small parts that can be ingested by infants.

25. $14.98 rounds to $15, and 208 rounds to 200. $15 times 200 is $3,000.

Active Learning

26. Survey responses will vary. Both businesses and consumers may have curbside recycling service. Most probably recycle used paper, plastic, and glass. Environmental problems may include pollution from factories.

Business in the Real World

27. Answers will vary. For appliances, brochures may list various models available, make comparisons in size or capacity, and provide information about operating costs.

Applying Academics to Business

English Language Arts
22. Research the etymology, or history, of the word *boycott*. How and why did it come into use? What are some important ways boycotts have been used over the years? Write two or three paragraphs about what you discover.

Mathematics
23. Francine has nine cousins. By coincidence, they are all getting married this year. Francine decides to buy each one an engraved silver pitcher as a wedding gift. She finds that the pitcher she wants to buy costs $130. However, if she buys 10, she will get a 10% discount. What is the difference in cost for 9 pitchers versus 10?

> **THEORY** **Percent Discount** Percent discount is a ratio of the difference in price divided by the original price. To find a discounted price, multiply the original price by the discount and subtract the product from the original price.

English Language Arts
24. Manufacturers sometimes recall products that have been discovered to be unsafe. Consumer magazines and Web sites post recall notices. Become familiar with at least three recalls of related products in a category such as infant products or electrical components. Describe the reasons for the recalls and the procedures for resolving the problem.

Mathematics
25. VidMania sells DVDs for $14.98 each. In January, the store sold 208 DVDs. The manager wanted to compute the total sales of DVDs for the month. If you were to estimate the answer using mental math, what would be an appropriate estimate?

> **THEORY** **Mental Math** Simplifying numbers and computation by rounding and estimating makes it possible to solve problems in your head.

Active Learning

Environmental Awareness
26. Work in a team of two or three to develop a survey about awareness of environmental issues. Survey local businesspeople and consumers. Possible questions to include: Which items do you recycle? How do you dispose of hazardous materials? Then prepare a report of your findings.

Business in the Real World

Consumer Information
27. Visit one or more stores in your community that sell large appliances or electronic equipment. Ask for brochures, pamphlets, or warranty information they may provide to customers. Based on the information you receive, from which company would you most likely make a purchase? Write a brief report on your findings and response.

***ExamView Assessment Suite* CD** allows you to print out ready-made unit and chapter tests, complete with answer keys. You can also create customized tests.

TeacherWorks Plus provides complete teacher resources in one convenient package. It includes customizable lesson plans in calendar format, and instant access to many print program resources.

Real LIFE skills

DEVELOP COMPARISON SHOPPING SKILLS

28. Think of a product that you plan to purchase soon. Then comparison shop. What are different companies' return policies? Which offers the best guarantee? Which offers the best value? Are there any customer reviews to consider? Prepare a report of your findings.

Business CAREERS

FIND YOUR DREAM JOB

29. Go to the *Introduction to Business* Online Learning Center through **glencoe.com** for a link to the Occupational Outlook Handbook Web site. Click on the "OOH Search/A-Z Index" link and enter the job category "public relations specialists." Then write a one-page report about this area of occupation. Conclude your report with a list of things you could do now to prepare yourself to pursue the occupation.

Role Play

PRACTICE CUSTOMER SERVICE SKILLS

30. Situation You are a clothing store manager. The store's return policy states that customers without a receipt may exchange a returned item. A sales associate asks you to talk to a customer, who wants to return an item without a receipt.

Activity With two partners, prepare and perform a skit on how you would handle the customer.

Evaluation You will be evaluated on how well you meet the following performance indicators:

- Listen to both the sales associate and the customer.
- Explain the store's policy on returns.
- Describe what you can do to resolve the matter.
- Speak confidently, courteously, and tactfully.

Standardized Test Practice

Directions Choose the letter of the best answer. Write the letter for the answer on a separate piece of paper.

1. Which sentence contains two independent clauses?

A   When one company controls the market, it has a monopoly.

B   In 1962, President Kennedy signed the Consumer Bill of Rights.

C   The population has stayed the same, but consumer demand has increased.

D   Part of conservation is learning to avoid waste.

 **TEST-TAKING TIP** Take tests seriously. Schools use them to measure and then improve education. Tests can tell schools that they need to strengthen courses or change teaching techniques. Other tests are used to compare students by schools, school districts, or cities. All tests determine how well you are doing.

 READING Go to the *Introduction to Business* Online Learning Center through **glencoe.com** for a list of outside reading suggestions.

Chapter 23

Real LIFE skills

28. Answers will vary. Allow students to choose the way they wish to share their findings, but encourage them to share the steps they took to develop their comparisons.

Business CAREERS

29. Public relations specialists advocate for businesses and organizations, handling media, and consumer relations. PR specialists work in offices, usually 40 hours a week. Unpaid overtime is common. Most positions require a college degree and many require prior experience. Keen competition exists for entry-level positions. The job outlook is for faster-than-average growth. As preparation, develop communication and interpersonal skills.

Role Play

30. Presentations should address the competencies noted in the Role Play. The store manager should keep in mind consumers' right to be informed, to be heard, and to have problems corrected. The responsibility to be informed, to choose carefully, and to seek a remedy may also apply. A factor may be whether the return policy was clearly given at the time of purchase.

> *Standardized Test Practice*
> **1.** C

 **STRATEGIES FOR STANDARDIZED TEST PREP SUCCESS**

Test Prep Make sure your students understand the nature of a test, its purpose, and how the information obtained from it will be used to help people make judgments. Explain how they will receive the results of the test and when they will receive them.

Standards-Based Lesson Planning
Introduction to Business provides students with instruction and assessment in the following fundamental content areas:

Content Standards Correlations	
Identify sources of consumer information.	pp. 423–426, 430–434
Identify methods that can be used to protect consumer rights.	pp. 423–426, 428–435
Analyze government's role in consumer protection and how it affects consumers' rights.	pp. 424–426, 428–430, 433–434
Examine functions of government that relate to business activities. Research and report on governmental laws related to consumer protection and ways of seeking protection under the law.	pp. 424–426, 428–430, 433–434
Evaluate information available to make wise buying decisions. Compare and contrast sources of useful consumer information. Use the decision-making process to determine effective uses of money.	pp. 429–430, 431, 433–434
Distinguish between the rights and responsibilities needed to be an informed consumer. Compare consumer rights and responsibilities and relate these to government protection policies.	pp. 433–434

NCLB
Activities, information, and skills practice will help your students attain No Child Left Behind proficiency. Students will improve their abilities in the following academic standards areas:

Academic Standards Correlations		
English Language Arts	Activities/Features	Page
NCTE 7 Conduct research and gather, evaluate, and synthesize data to communicate discoveries	After You Read Applying Academics to Business	pp. 431, 434
NCTE 12 Use language to accomplish individual purposes	After You Read	p. 431
Mathematics		
Data Analysis and Probability Formulate questions that can be addressed with data and collect, organize, and display relevant data to answer them	After You Read	p. 426
Number and Operations Compute fluently and make reasonable estimates	Standardized Test Practice	p. 435
Number and Operations Understand meanings of operations and how they relate to one another	Applying Academics to Business	p. 434
Number and Operations Understand numbers, ways of representing numbers, relationships among numbers, and number systems	Ask S&P	p. 420
Problem Solving Monitor and reflect on the process of mathematical problem solving	Applying Academics to Business	p. 434
Science		
Content Standard B Students should develop an understanding of motions and forces	Science/Tech Trends	p. 428

Correlations This chart shows the 21st Century Skills, foundation skills, and workplace competencies that students develop as they work in this chapter.

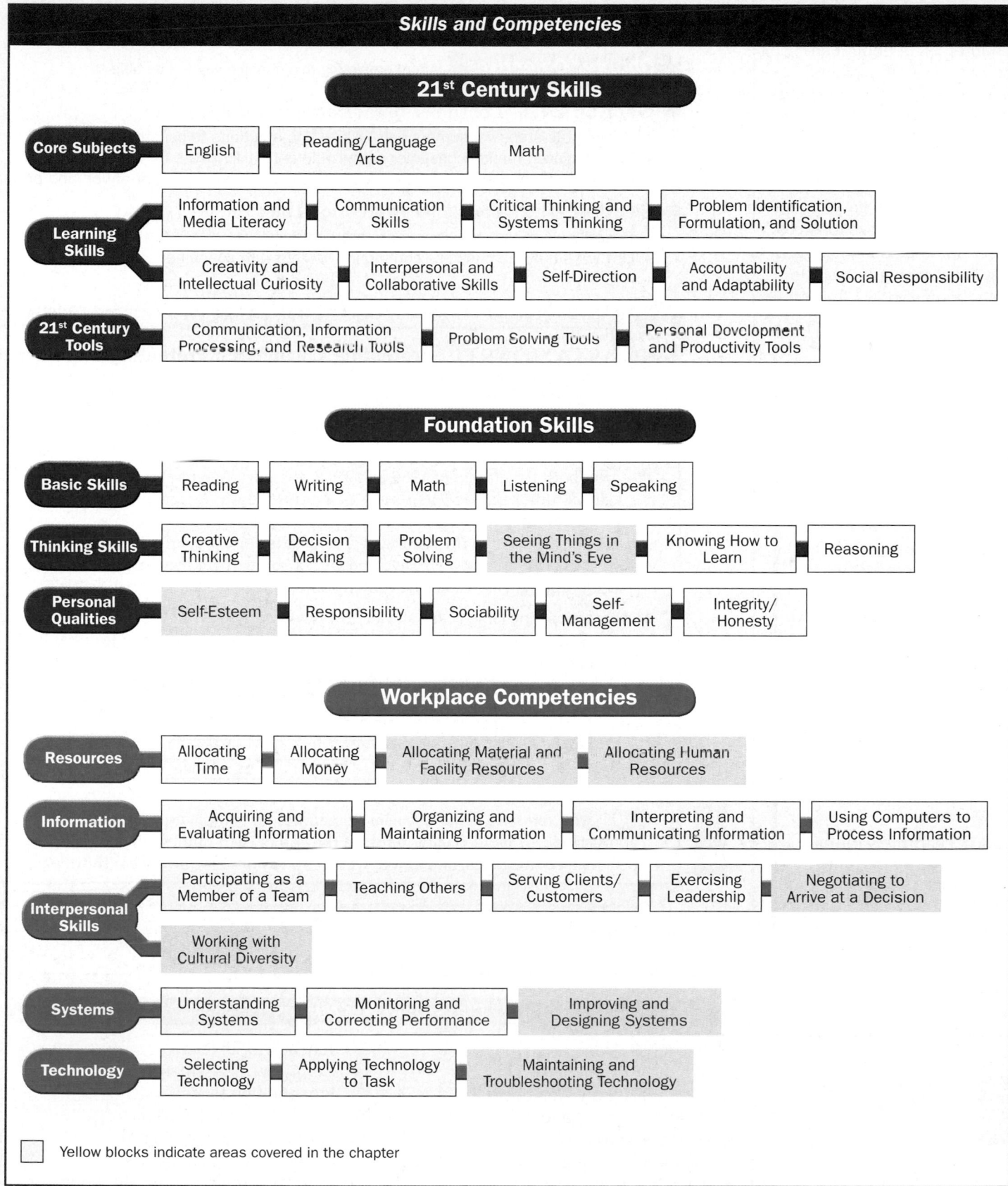

Skills and Competencies

21st Century Skills

Core Subjects
- English
- Reading/Language Arts
- Math

Learning Skills
- Information and Media Literacy
- Communication Skills
- Critical Thinking and Systems Thinking
- Problem Identification, Formulation, and Solution
- Creativity and Intellectual Curiosity
- Interpersonal and Collaborative Skills
- Self-Direction
- Accountability and Adaptability
- Social Responsibility

21st Century Tools
- Communication, Information Processing, and Research Tools
- Problem Solving Tools
- Personal Development and Productivity Tools

Foundation Skills

Basic Skills
- Reading
- Writing
- Math
- Listening
- Speaking

Thinking Skills
- Creative Thinking
- Decision Making
- Problem Solving
- Seeing Things in the Mind's Eye
- Knowing How to Learn
- Reasoning

Personal Qualities
- Self-Esteem
- Responsibility
- Sociability
- Self-Management
- Integrity/Honesty

Workplace Competencies

Resources
- Allocating Time
- Allocating Money
- Allocating Material and Facility Resources
- Allocating Human Resources

Information
- Acquiring and Evaluating Information
- Organizing and Maintaining Information
- Interpreting and Communicating Information
- Using Computers to Process Information

Interpersonal Skills
- Participating as a Member of a Team
- Teaching Others
- Serving Clients/Customers
- Exercising Leadership
- Negotiating to Arrive at a Decision
- Working with Cultural Diversity

Systems
- Understanding Systems
- Monitoring and Correcting Performance
- Improving and Designing Systems

Technology
- Selecting Technology
- Applying Technology to Task
- Maintaining and Troubleshooting Technology

Yellow blocks indicate areas covered in the chapter

Chapter Overview

Introduce the Chapter

Protecting Consumers
Chapter 24 is about consumer power. It explains how government and private organizations protect and help consumers.

Building Background
Learning how the government and private organizations protect and help consumers is a way for students to learn to help themselves.

Ask STANDARD &POOR'S

>> Math Answer
To get the correct answer, move the decimal point, add the appropriate number of zeros, and include a dollar sign. Answers: 1929: $101,400,000,000; 1931: $84,300,000,000; 1933: $68,300,000,000; 2004: $12,151,000,000,000

>> Extension Activity
Write the following information on the board. Ask students to express the numbers including all the zeros.

2004 Leading National Advertisers—in millions: General Motors, $3,997.4; Procter & Gamble, $3,919.7; and Time Warner, $3,283.1. ($3,997,400,000; $3,919,700,000; $3,283,100,000)

N C L B
Activity correlates to Math standards.

420

Protecting Consumers

Chapter Objectives   After completing this chapter, you will be able to:

▶ **Section 24.1** *Consumer Organizations and Agencies*
- **Explain** the steps consumers can take to find solutions to consumer problems.
- **List** nongovernmental consumer organizations that advocate for consumers.
- **List** some federal and state agencies that provide consumer information and protection.

▶ **Section 24.2** *Consumer Protection Laws*
- **Describe** ways that consumers are protected by laws related to the marketplace.
- **List** ways that the business community assists with consumer protection.

Ask STANDARD &POOR'S   Protecting Consumers: Protecting Investors

Q: The U.S. government regulates the credit industry. How does it regulate the securities industry?

A: After both the crashes of 1929 and 1987, the government passed laws to protect against future crashes. The Securities Act of 1933 was designed to better regulate the market. In addition, the Securities and Exchange Commission was created in 1934 to ensure that the trading of securities is done properly. To this end, the SEC requires people intimately involved with a company to regularly disclose their stock holdings, as well as their intentions to buy or sell additional shares.

Mathematics The table below shows how devastating the stock market crash was to the economy. Read the table and write out the full amount that each number in the table represents.

Year	GNP*
1929	101.4
1931	84.3
1933	68.3
2004	12,151.00

* In billions of dollars

N C L B

THEORY **Expressing Large Numbers** Sometimes, for simplicity sake, large numbers are abbreviated. To avoid placing zeros on the end of each number in a table, the numbers may be shortened, and a note will let you know how they were shortened.

Classroom Resources

- 📖 Student Edition
- 📖 Teacher Wraparound Edition
- 📁 Student Activity Workbook with Academic Integration
- 📁 Student Activity Workbook with Academic Integration TAE
- 📁 *Fast File*, Unit 8 Resources
- 📁 Inclusion in the Business Education Classroom

- TeacherWorks Plus
- *ExamView Assessment Suite*
- Presentation Plus!
- Vocabulary PuzzleMaker
- Interactive Student Edition
- Online Student Edition
- Online Learning Center with Podcasts

● **Consumer Information** Advertisements provide information to consumers. **What types of information would you want to know before buying a dishwasher?**

Discuss the Photo
● **Consumer Information** Read the caption on the photo to students: Advertisements provide information to consumers.

Ask students: What types of information would you want to know before buying a dishwasher? (Answers may vary, but students may identify the price, size, features, and warranty as important considerations in making a major purchase such as a dishwasher.)

Review the Objectives
Introduce the chapter by reviewing the chapter objectives:

Section 24.1 *Objectives*
Explain the steps consumers can take to find solutions to consumer problems. (review their receipts and warranties, contact seller, take the problem to a higher level, contact a consumer organization, consider filing a claim in small claims court)

List nongovernmental consumer organizations that advocate for consumers. (They include the Consumer Federation of America, the National Consumers League, and the Consumers Union.)

List some federal and state agencies that provide consumer information and protection. (Federal Trade Commission, U.S. Department of Agriculture, the Food and Drug Administration, the National Highway Traffic Safety Administration, and the Consumer Product Safety Commission; state agencies include public utilities and insurance commissions)

Section 24.2 *Objectives*
Describe ways that consumers are protected by laws related to the marketplace. (Price discrimination laws prohibit unfair pricing. The Fair Packaging and Labeling Act requires that labels provide truthful information about products.)

List ways that the business community assists with consumer protection. (By providing information through labels, brochures, and manuals. The Better Business Bureau also helps consumers.)

FOCUS

 Bell Ringer Activity

Consumer Organizations and Agencies
Organize students into groups and give each group a box of cereal. Ask students: Which agency would regulate the label on the box? (the Food and Drug Administration)

Preteaching

Presentation Plus!
The Presentation Plus! CD provides visual teaching aids for this section.

PuzzleMaker
Use the Vocabulary PuzzleMaker to create a puzzle of the section's key terms. Students can complete the puzzle on paper or on a computer.

Graphic Organizer
Tell students to go to the Online Learning Center through **glencoe.com** for a printable graphic organizer. (Answers include: FTC: regulates trade; USDA: indicates the level of quality of foods; FDA: duties include regulating labeling and safety of food; NHTSA: sets and enforces motor vehicle safety standards; Consumer Product Safety Commission: oversees product safety; state public utilities commissions: regulates state utility rates; state insurance commissions: regulates state insurer activities; state licensing agencies: issues business permits)

 N C L B Connects academics to content.

422

Consumer Organizations and Agencies

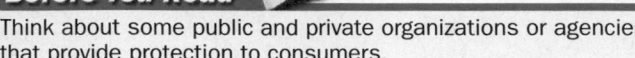 **Reading Guide**

● **Before You Read**

Think about some public and private organizations or agencies that provide protection to consumers.

Read to Learn
- Explain the steps consumers can take to find solutions to consumer problems.
- List nongovernmental consumer organizations that advocate for consumers.
- List some federal and state agencies that provide consumer information and protection.

D

The Main Idea
Many public and private organizations work on behalf of consumers. Federal, state, and local agencies provide information and enforce laws that protect consumers. Consumer advocates work to protect, inform, and defend consumers.

Key Concepts
- Nongovernmental Consumer Organizations
- Government Consumer Organizations

Vocabulary
Key Terms

consumer advocates   legal monopoly
grade labels   licenses
recall

Academic Vocabulary
You will find these words in your reading and on your tests. Make sure you know their meanings.

behalf   supplements
panels   assurance

Graphic Organizer
In a figure like the one below, describe the consumer protection roles of the governmental agencies as you read the section.

Agencies that Protect Consumers	Agency Function
Federal Trade Commission	
Department of Agriculture	
Food and Drug Administration	
National Highway Traffic Safety Administration	
Consumer Product Safety Commission	
State Public Utilities Commissions	
State Insurance Commissions	
State Licensing Agencies	

 Go to the *Introduction to Business* Online Learning Center through **glencoe.com** for a printable graphic organizer.

Academic Standards
N C L B

English Language Arts
NCTE 1 Read texts to acquire new information
NCTE 9 Develop an understanding of diversity in language use across cultures
Mathematics
Data Analysis and Probability Formulate questions that can be addressed with data and collect, organize, and display relevant data to answer them

---

Reading Guide

● **Before You Read**

Public organizations include governmental agencies such as the Federal Trade Commission. Private organizations include the National Consumers League.

D Develop Concepts

The Main Idea Ask students: What do consumer advocates do? (Consumer advocates work to protect, inform, and defend consumers.)

Finding Solutions to Consumer Problems

At some point, you may have trouble with a product or service. There are things you can do to resolve the matter yourself. When faced with a purchasing problem, review your receipts and warranties. Contact the seller and explain the problem. Bring your receipts. If the seller does not resolve the situation, take the problem to a higher level. Contact the seller's customer service department and then its headquarters. Consumer organizations may be able to help. If you do not get the results you want, you might decide to file a claim in small claims court.

Nongovernmental Consumer Organizations

R There are many organizations that work on **behalf** of consumers. Groups and individuals who work to protect, inform, and defend consumers are called **consumer advocates**. Many consumer advocates are private, nonprofit groups. Some test products and report their findings. Many work to promote consumer protection laws.

The Consumer Federation of America

The Consumer Federation of America (CFA) works to inform the public and government about consumer issues. It works with public officials to promote policies that benefit consumers and to ensure a fair and balanced debate about issues that are important to consumers. It studies federal laws that affect consumers and lets its members know so they can help to support legislation to help the public.

The National Consumers League

The National Consumers League is the nation's oldest nonprofit consumers group with membership open to anyone. It provides government agencies, businesses, and other organizations with the consumer's point of view. One of its services is a national fraud information center. It also monitors the Internet to alert consumers to fraud.

Consumers Union

Consumers Union is a nonprofit organization that publishes the magazine *Consumer Reports*. Researchers with Consumers Union test products and report their findings in the magazine. The magazine does not advertise products or allow its findings to be used in ads. Consumers Union also testifies before government agencies on consumer concerns.

Testing for Safety
Many products around your home probably are labeled "UL Listed." This is the certification by Underwriters Laboratories, a testing facility that develops standards and test procedures for materials, tools, and equipment. Underwriters Laboratories chiefly deals with product safety and utility. *What other types of products can you think of that are tested for safety?*

● **As You Read**

Consumer Reports does not accept advertising. Why do you think it has this policy?

Discussion Starter
Ask students why consumers rely on consumer organizations and government agencies to help find solutions to consumer problems. Why can't people solve their own problems? (Students should understand the power of people acting together.)

R **Reading Strategy**
Explain Ask students to explain what consumer advocates do. (Consumer advocates protect, inform, and defend consumers.)

Testing for Safety There are many products that are tested for safety, including medicine, cosmetics, automobiles, and child car seats.

● **As You Read**

Because *Consumer Reports* rates products, it needs to be unbiased. If it accepted ads, it might be accused of being partial in its ratings to businesses that advertise in the magazine.

S Skill Practice

Guided Practice

Provide an Example Ask students to provide an example of a consumer issue that might be featured on a local TV news program. (Examples could include product recalls and consumer complaints.) **L1**

Summarize Ask students to locate and summarize a recent news article that focuses on a consumer issue. (Summaries will vary. Students should describe the situation and explain how it was resolved.) **L2**

Develop an Idea Ask students to locate a recent newspaper article about a consumer issue and develop an idea for a follow-up story. Instruct students to submit a copy of the original story along with their idea for the follow-up. (Story ideas should have an obvious connection to the original story.) **L3**

ASSESS

Review Key Terms

Have students write sentences using each key term.

 **Study-to-Go** Have students go to the Online Learning Center through **glencoe.com** to download free **Study-to-Go** content to their PDAs or cell phones.

424

International Business

Import Regulations

Foreign companies wanting to sell their products in the United States are subject to a wide range of regulations. Beyond homeland security issues, there are many other things to consider. Some regulations are concerned with health and foreign foodstuffs. Others have to do with political differences between the United States and the countries from which the imports originate.

Examples of Languages Across Cultures

Q: In Arabic, how do you say: "My name is _____ "?

A: ...اسمي

(pronounced:
_____ iss-mē.)

What regulations does the United States impose on foreign companies? What is the basis for these regulations?

Major Appliance Consumer Action Program

Some industries have consumer assistance **panels**. The Major Appliance Consumer Action Program (MACAP) helps consumers solve problems with large appliances, such as washers, stoves, and freezers. Most major appliance dealers are members of MACAP.

The Media

Internet sites, radio, TV stations, and newspapers advocate for consumers. They often have a *consumer reporter* who reports on issues that are important to consumers, such as product safety, testing, and shopping. The reporter might feature one consumer's problem with a local business and visit the business to try to resolve the problem. **S**

Government Consumer Organizations

In the United States, each state has a consumer affairs division. In some states, the attorney general's office handles consumer affairs.

Many state and federal agencies have been set up to protect consumers. They publish materials to help consumers with their buying decisions and problems. They also enforce laws. The Federal Citizen Information Center is a good source for consumer information.

The Federal Trade Commission

The Federal Trade Commission (FTC) enforces federal antitrust and consumer protection laws by investigating complaints against companies. It seeks to ensure that the nation's markets function competitively by eliminating unfair or deceptive practices.

U.S. Department of Agriculture

The U.S. Department of Agriculture (USDA) inspects foods and grades them. **Grade labels** indicate the level of quality of foods. For example, meat might be graded as "prime" or "choice." Consumers can use the grades as a guide in choosing what to buy.

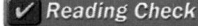 **✔ Reading Check** **Analyze** Why is it important for the government to inspect foods such as meats?

✔ Reading Check

Analyze Consumers can use the grades as a guide in choosing what to buy. Also, the inspections help to protect them from problems such as food-borne bacteria.

International Business

Import Regulations Answers will vary. For example, flora or fauna brought into the country have numerous health-related regulations attached. Students should know that the regulations imposed on foreign companies are to protect the U.S. consumer.

The Food and Drug Administration

The Food and Drug Administration (FDA) regulates the labeling and safety of food, drugs, cosmetics, dietary **supplements**, and medical devices sold in the United States. The FDA tests and approves all drugs before they can be offered to consumers. It also reviews products that are already on the market.

The National Highway Traffic Safety Administration

The National Highway Traffic Safety Administration is part of the U.S. Department of Transportation. This agency sets and enforces safety standards for motor vehicles. The administration can require an automaker to issue a recall of the automaker's vehicles. A **recall** is an order to take back and repair or replace a product that has defective parts. **Figure 24.1** shows a government Web site where consumers can find information about recalls.

The Consumer Product Safety Commission

The U.S. Consumer Product Safety Commission is a federal government agency that oversees the safety of products such as toys, cribs, power tools, electronics, and furniture. The commission has contributed significantly to a 30 percent decline in the rate of deaths and injuries associated with consumer products over the last 30 years.

Figure 24.1 — *Finding Information About Recalls*

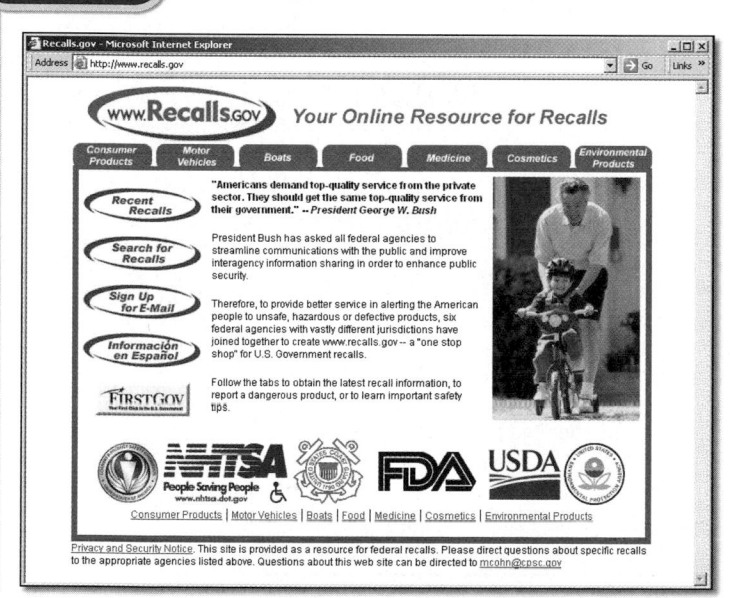

● **Consumer Product Recalls** Six federal agencies joined together to create this Web site to give consumers information about the latest recalls and to provide safety tips. It also accepts consumer reports about dangerous products. **In what other places can you find information about recalls?**

Section 24.1 Consumer Organizations and Agencies **425**

Figure 24.1

● **Consumer Product Recalls** Answers will vary but may include newspapers, television, magazines, and consumer Web sites.

425

Section 24.1

RETEACH (cont.)

C Critical Thinking

Explain
State Public Utilities Commissions Ask students to explain why it is impossible for state public utilities commissions to protect the public from increases in energy prices. (Answers will vary. Students might suggest that, even with a local monopoly, other parties around the world play a factor in prices for oil and energy produced from fossil fuels.)

ASSESS

● After You Read

Have students complete the Section 24.1 After You Read section review.

Online Study Tools

Have students go to the Online Learning Center through **glencoe.com** to:

- Take the Section 24.1 **Practice Test**.
- Download free **Study-to-Go** content to their PDAs or cell phones.

CLOSE

Culminating Activity
Consumer Advocate
Invite a consumer advocate to speak to students about consumer protection and focus on a topic that is of particular interest to students. In advance, ask students to suggest questions that they would like the speaker to answer.

State Public Utilities Commissions

C State public utilities commissions regulate the rates charged by electric, gas, and water companies. In some areas, they also regulate local telephone services. They protect consumers from unfair pricing. They do this because public utilities are legal monopolies. A **legal monopoly** is a company that is allowed to operate without competition.

State Insurance Commissions

State insurance commissions are the state government bodies responsible for regulating the activities of insurers and health plans. They control and approve insurance rates. Most have procedures for handling consumer complaints.

State Licensing Agencies

State licensing agencies issue **licenses**, or legal permits to conduct business. A license provides **assurance** to consumers that the license holder is qualified to do a service. Doctors, teachers, roofers, hair stylists, architects, and even professional wrestlers are required to have a license.

NCLB Activity correlates to Math standards.

Section 24.1

● After You Read

Review Key Concepts

1. In what ways do nongovernmental consumer organizations assist consumers?
2. What are some government agencies that help to protect consumers?
3. What is a recall?

Academic Skills

NCLB

4. **Mathematics** The Better Business Bureau is a nonprofit organization that supports consumers. The 150 BBBs in the United States handle ten million questions a year. One third of these are questions about retail businesses, one third are about home improvement companies, and one fourth are about service firms. The remaining portion of questions the BBB receives concerns other types of businesses. Draw a pie chart of this data. Record the actual number of consumer questions in each category on your chart.

 THEORY Data Analysis Pie charts are an effective way to represent the parts that make up a whole.

 Math For math help, go to the Math Appendix.

@ Go to the *Introduction to Business* Online Learning Center through **glencoe.com** to check your answers.

Section 24.1

Review Key Concepts
1. They protect, inform, and defend consumers. Some test products.
2. FTC, the USDA, the FDA, and the NHTSA
3. an order to take back and repair or replace a product that is defective

Academic Skills
4. **Mathematics** Retail businesses:
$\frac{1}{3} \times 10$ million $= 3.33$ million
Home improvement companies:
$\frac{1}{3} \times 10$ million $= 3.33$ million
Service firms: $\frac{1}{4} \times 10$ million $= 2.5$ million
Other: $\frac{1}{12}$ $(1 - \frac{2}{3} - \frac{1}{4} = \frac{1}{12})$
$\frac{1}{12}$ of 10 million is 833,333.

Consumer Protection Laws

Reading Guide

● Before You Read

Think about the ways government protects consumers and how shopping would be different without its involvement.

Read to Learn

- Describe ways that consumers are protected by laws related to the marketplace.
- List ways that the business community assists with consumer protection.

The Main Idea

A number of laws have been passed at all levels of government to protect consumers. Businesses and consumer organizations help resolve problems when consumers find a product or service to be unsatisfactory.

Key Concepts

- Laws That Protect Consumers
- How the Business Community Protects Consumers

Vocabulary

Key Terms

price discrimination
warranty
express warranty
full warranty
limited warranty
Better Business Bureau (BBB)

Academic Vocabulary

You will find these words in your reading and on your tests. Make sure you know their meanings.

justify   reveal
guarantee   community

Graphic Organizer

On a figure like the one below, write notes about consumer organizations, government organizations, and business organizations that protect consumers.

Express Warranty	Full Warranty	Limited Warranty

@ Go to the *Introduction to Business* Online Learning Center through **glencoe.com** for a printable graphic organizer.

Academic Standards

English Language Arts

    NCTE 1 Read texts to acquire new information

    NCTE 7 Conduct research and gather, evaluate, and synthesize data to communicate discoveries

    NCTE 11 Participate as members of literacy communities

Science

    Content Standard B Students should develop an understanding of motion and forces

---

FOCUS

🔔 Bell Ringer Activity

Consumer Protection Laws

Project or write the following on the board: dishonest sellers, unreasonable credit terms, unsafe products, mislabeling of products. Ask students what these things have in common. (Answers will vary, but students should realize that there are laws against all of them.)

Preteaching

Presentation Plus! 💿

The Presentation Plus! CD provides visual teaching aids for this section.

PuzzleMaker 💿

Use the Vocabulary PuzzleMaker to create a puzzle of the section's key terms. Students can complete the puzzle on paper or on a computer.

Graphic Organizer

Tell students to go to the Online Learning Center through **glencoe.com** for a printable graphic organizer. (Answers include: express warranty: explicitly stated verbally or in writing and gives conditions for return, replacement, or repair; full warranty: defective products will be repaired or returned at no cost; limited warranty: covers only certain parts or may require the customer to pay part of the cost.)

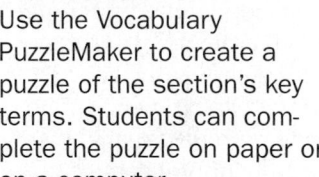 Connects academics to content.

Reading Guide

● Before You Read

The government enacts laws that regulate and restrict businesses. These laws help to preserve competition and to provide assurance to consumers regarding the products and services they purchase and use.

D Develop Concepts

The Main Idea Ask students: Where do consumers turn when they find a product or service to be unsatisfactory? (Businesses and consumer organizations help resolve problems.)

428

TEACH

Discussion Starter
Laws That Protect Consumers

Start a discussion by asking students: Why is it important for consumers and businesses to know about laws that protect consumers? (Answers will vary. Students should understand that consumers need to be aware of activities that are illegal in order to protect themselves. Businesses need to be aware so that they can follow the laws.)

R Reading Strategy

List Have students make a list of some of the reasons laws are passed to regulate businesses. (The laws regulate and restrict business practices, preserve competition, protect consumers from dishonest sellers, unreasonable credit terms, unsafe products, and mislabeling of products.)

✔ Reading Check

Explain The government enacted consumer protection laws to protect consumers, and to preserve competition and fairness in the marketplace.

 Activity correlates to Science standards.

Real World

Product Recalls
When a company has a product recall, it is usually due to safety issues. For example, Bridgestone Corporation recalled 6.5 million of its Firestone tires in response to complaints that the tires were linked to crashes involving sport utility vehicles. *How would you find out about product recalls?*

Laws that Protect Consumers

The U.S. government allows businesses to compete in the marketplace with relative freedom. However, many laws have been enacted to regulate and restrict business practices. These key trade laws were created to preserve competition. They also help to protect consumers.

R Manufacturers of products for the public must become familiar with consumer protection laws. This helps them to avoid possible recalls of their products and potential lawsuits. Most trade laws are designed to protect the consumer. These laws protect against dishonest sellers, unreasonable credit terms, unsafe products, and mislabeling of products.

✔ Reading Check **Explain** Why has government enacted consumer protection laws?

Price Discrimination Laws

Price discrimination is the act of charging more than one price for the same product or service in different markets or to different customers. The Clayton Act of 1914 and the Robinson-Patman Act of 1936 are aimed at prohibiting price discrimination. Businesses must **justify** giving one customer a lower price than another. Fair pricing means businesses must be fair to all customers when setting prices.

Science/Tech TRENDS

Safety Belts

Safety belts save approximately 13,000 lives in this country every year. According to the National Highway Traffic Safety Administration (NHTSA), an estimated 5,500 more lives could be saved each year in the United States if just 90 percent of passengers and drivers used them. Yet only 68 percent of Americans wear safety belts. When they were first invented (Edward Claghorn was the first to obtain a U.S patent for the seat belt in 1885) they were simple leather straps fastened over the operator's lap. As the technology behind cars develops, so does the technology that produces safety belts. Today, the safety belt is a system of interdependent parts and space age fabrics.

Web Quest

Go to the *Introduction to Business* Online Learning Center through **glencoe.com** for links to Web sites where you can research how safety belts do their job and the latest technologies used in safety belt systems. Write a few sentences about how new technologies have increased safety.

Real World

Product Recalls Some common sources for recall information include grocery store announcements, mailings, news reports, the Internet, and consumer magazines.

Science/Tech TRENDS

Web Quest

Safety Belts Answers will vary, but paragraphs might describe how lives have been saved with the use of seat belt reminders, pretensioners, and load limiters, as well as the emerging use of inflatable seat belts.

The Fair Packaging and Labeling Act

The Fair Packaging and Labeling Act requires that manufacturers' labels truthfully list all ingredients and raw materials used in production. Labels must include the name and place of business of the manufacturer, packer, or distributor. The act also requires the size, weight, and contents of a product to be included on the label.

The Uniform Commercial Code

The Uniform Commercial Code (UCC) is a group of laws that regulate commercial business transactions. The UCC protects the economic interests of buyers and sellers in contracts. It also regulates sales warranties. A **warranty** is a promise or **guarantee** given to a customer that a product will meet certain standards. A business may also be protected by disclaimers that describe exceptions or exclusions from a warranty. A common disclaimer limits a customer's recovery to a refund of the purchase price.

Under the UCC, a seller may make several warranties:

- An **express warranty** is a warranty that is explicitly stated, in writing or verbally. It specifies the conditions under which the product can be returned, replaced, or repaired.
- A **full warranty** is a guarantee about the quality of goods or services. With a full warranty, a purchase found to be defective within the warranty period will be repaired or replaced at no cost to the purchaser.
- A **limited warranty** covers only certain parts of the product or requires the customer to bear some of the expense in case repairs are needed.

Consumer Credit Protection Act

The Consumer Credit Protection Act requires those who give credit to reveal all the terms and conditions of their credit agreements. This law applies to anything purchased over a period of time greater than four months. Finance charges must be expressed as an annual rate so that the consumer has a clear estimate of the cost of credit. Truth-in-lending laws are enforced by the Federal Trade Commission (FTC).

● **Consumer Information** Advertisements provide information to consumers. **What types of information would you want to know before buying a laptop computer?**

● As You Read

Look at the different types of information on the labels of some products you have at home or school.

Discuss the Photo

● **Consumer Information** The size of the display, speed of the processor, types and amounts of memory, and service policies are some facts a consumer should know before buying a laptop.

● As You Read

Answers may include the ingredients, components inside a box, labels on clothing that give care instructions, and food labels with nutritional information.

TEACH (cont.)

S Skill Practice
Guided Practice

Define Ask students to define "warranty." (A warranty is a promise or guarantee given to a customer that a product will meet certain standards.) **L1**

Create a Table Have students create a two-column table. In the first column, have them list the three types of warranties. Instruct them to use the second column to explain each kind of warranty using their own words. (The three warranties are express, full, and limited. Explanations should include the information presented in the textbook.) **L2**

Research and Report Have students use library or Internet sources to learn about warranties. Ask students to share what they learned with the class. (Answers will vary. For example, some students might explain puffery or consequential damages.) **L3**

ASSESS

Review Key Terms
Have students write sentences using each key term.

 **Study-to-Go** Have students go to the Online Learning Center through **glencoe.com** to download free **Study-to-Go** content to their PDAs or cell phones.

RETEACH

U Universal Access

Gifted Learners Truth-in-Advertising Laws and the consumer protection movement are excellent topics for gifted students who are interested in working independently. Invite gifted students to choose a topic related to this chapter and prepare a short presentation for the class.

R Reading Strategy

Identify Ask students to identify some of the ways that businesses educate consumers about their products and services. (Answers should include labels, brochures, manuals, and online details.)

W Writing Support

Enrichment

Better Business Bureau Have students visit and explore the Web site for the Better Business Bureau (BBB). Instruct them to write two or three paragraphs about the site and describe a resource that consumers might find helpful. (Paragraphs should show evidence of having visited the Web site.)

Student Activity Workbook 📖 Assign the Section 24.2 Activities.

Better Businesses, Better Charities
Staying informed helps donors make good decisions about charitable giving, and it helps foster the consumer's trust.

Better Businesses, Better Charities
The Council of Better Business Bureaus Foundation merged with the National Charities Information Bureau to form the BBB Wise Giving Alliance. The alliance helps donors make informed giving decisions. *Why is it necessary to stay informed about charities?*

Truth-in-Advertising Laws

U The Federal Trade Commission Act protects consumers from false and misleading advertising with truth-in-advertising laws. Under these laws, advertising must be truthful and nondeceptive, and advertisers must have evidence to back up their claims.

How Businesses Protect Consumers

R The business **community** protects consumers by providing information. Labels, brochures, manuals, and online details are some of the ways that businesses educate consumers about their products and services.

The Better Business Bureau

W The **Better Business Bureau (BBB)** is a nonprofit organization that collects information on local businesses and handles complaints. It also shares information about problems that consumers have had and distributes consumer publications. It does not enforce laws or recommend one business over another.

BusinessWeek *Reader and Case Study*

How to Stand Up to the Nickel-and-Dimers

In a world of fees gone wild, what's a consumer to do? In some industries, such as banking, complaining customers can sometimes get fees rolled back. In others, such as telecom, it may be best to seek out competitors without fees. When a charge seems especially underhanded, an individual may want to join a consumer-action group.

In retail banking, consumers can get around certain fees if they're willing to give up some services. The first step is to get educated: Ask about the pricing and fee structure before signing up for a service. It may be possible, for example, to avoid checking-account fees, which can be as high as $20 a month, by signing up for direct deposit or forgoing the return of canceled checks.

But don't stop there. Given industry competition, banks are often willing to reduce other fees when faced with a determined customer. Call to question unreasonable or inflated charges.

"In a marketplace where prices are increasingly negotiable, complaining consumers have a fair chance of persuading sellers to reduce or eliminate individual fees," says Stephen Brobeck, executive director of the Consumer Federation of America.

 CASE STUDY Go to the *Introduction to Business* Online Learning Center through **glencoe.com** for the *BusinessWeek* Reader Case Study.

Active Learning

Research financial institutions to find out which one offers the best combination of services and fees for checking accounts. Prepare a spreadsheet that compares the services and fee structures for four different financial institutions. Write a paragraph explaining which one has the best services for the lowest fees.

BusinessWeek *Reader and Case Study*

How to Stand Up to the Nickel-and-Dimers

 CASE STUDY Have students go to the *Introduction to Business* Online Learning Center through **glencoe.com** to download a Case Study activity that corresponds to the article. The activity and answer key are also available on the TeacherWorks Plus CD.

Active Learning

Recommendations should include an evaluation of services and the fees for those services.

Customer Service Representatives

Many businesses have a customer service department. A customer service representative can answer questions or help resolve problems. Product packages often list the address, telephone number, or Web site to use to contact a customer service representative.

Advertising

Advertising can be a good source of consumer information. Although businesses use ads to promote their products, they also use them to tell consumers as much about their products as possible. Ads tell you not only a product's cost, but also the features it offers. You can use ads to compare products and services.

Magazines

Some commercial magazines are good sources of consumer information. They include articles or guides to help you make choices. *Good Housekeeping* features consumer information and endorses products with a "seal of approval." Specialty magazines on items such as cars and travel also provide information on related products.

 Activity correlates to English Language Arts standards.

Section 24.2

After You Read

Review Key Concepts

1. How do price discrimination laws protect consumers?
2. How is a full warranty different from a limited warranty?
3. What is the role of a customer service representative in consumer protection?

Academic Skills

4. **English Language Arts** Study an issue of *Consumer Reports* or *Consumers' Research Magazine*. List the types of products that are reported. Write a summary of the kinds of information provided about each product and indicate how you might find more information about the products.

5. **English Language Arts** Prepare a presentation showing how to file a complaint about a product or service. Choose a product or service that a family member has found unsatisfactory. Include a description of how to approach the business, a sample letter describing the problem and a possible solution, and the name of a private or government advocate or agency that might help you with the complaint.

@ Go to the *Introduction to Business* Online Learning Center through **glencoe.com** to check your answers.

Section 24.2

Review Key Concepts

1. They require businesses to justify giving different prices to customers.
2. full warranty: guarantees replacement or repair; limited warranty: limits protection to partial repair or replacement
3. answers questions or assists a customer in case of problems with a product or service

Academic Skills

4. **English Language Arts** Answers will vary, depending on the magazine chosen.
5. **English Language Arts** Presentations will vary but should explain the reasons the product was unsatisfactory.

RETEACH (cont.)

C Critical Thinking

Assessing Endorsements
Magazines as a Source of Consumer Information
Ask students to find out more about the Good Housekeeping Seal—How do products qualify for it? What does it mean to customers? Instruct students to summarize their findings in a brief report. (Reports will be based on students' findings and interpretations.)

ASSESS

After You Read

Have students complete the Section 24.2 After You Read section review.

Online Study Tools

Have students go to the Online Learning Center through **glencoe.com** to:

- Take the Section 24.2 **Practice Test**.
- Download free **Study-to-Go** content to their PDAs or cell phones.

CLOSE

Culminating Activity
Lemon Laws
Organize students into small groups. Ask students to learn more about their state's lemon laws and the steps that a consumer should follow to resolve the problem when a new car turns out to be a lemon. (Answers will depend on the laws of the state.)

431

Vocabulary Review

1. Students should write complete sentences using each term correctly.

Review Key Concepts

2. They can review their receipts and warranties, contact the seller, and take the problem to a higher authority if necessary. Consumer organizations may help, but further action may require filing a claim in small claims court.

3. Consumer Federation of America, the National Consumers League, the Consumers Union, and the Major Appliance Consumer Action Program (MACAP)

4. They include the Federal Trade Commission, U.S. Department of Agriculture, the Food and Drug Administration, the National Highway Traffic Safety Administration, and the Consumer Product Safety Commission. At the state level, there are public utilities and state insurance commissions, and state licensing agencies.

5. Price discrimination laws prohibit unfair pricing by businesses for consumer purchases. The Fair Packaging and Labeling Act requires that labels provide truthful information about products.

6. It assists through labels, brochures, manuals, and online details. The Better Business Bureau helps solve problems with businesses.

432

Section 24.1 Summary

Consumer Organizations and Agencies All consumers encounter purchasing problems at some point. Fortunately, there are ways that you can resolve issues yourself. Consumer advocate groups work to protect, inform, and defend consumers. Many organizations are nonprofit associations that monitor consumer information and work to prevent unfair treatment of consumers. In addition, government agencies and organizations enforce consumer protection laws and provide consumer information.

Section 24.2 Summary

Consumer Protection Laws Many laws have been passed to protect consumers, and government agencies enforce those laws. In addition, the business community provides information and services for consumer protection. Businesses may have a customer service department to assist consumers. Also, the Better Business Bureau works to resolve problems that consumers have with local businesses. These are some of the available sources that help consumers make good choices when they shop.

Vocabulary Review

1. On a sheet of paper, use each of these key terms and academic vocabulary terms in a sentence.

Key Terms

consumer advocates
grade labels
recall
legal monopoly
licenses
price discrimination

warranty
express warranty
full warranty
limited warranty
Better Business Bureau
   (BBB)

Academic Vocabulary

behalf
panels
supplements
assurance

justify
guarantee
reveal
community

Review Key Concepts

2. Explain the steps consumers can take to find solutions to consumer problems.

3. List nongovernmental consumer organizations that advocate for consumers.

4. List some federal and state agencies that provide consumer information and protection.

5. Describe ways that consumers are protected by laws related to the marketplace.

6. List ways that the business community assists with consumer protection.

Critical Thinking

7. Having fewer agencies involved in consumer protection would save money. However, without them, consumers would likely have less protection.

8. Answers may vary. For example, he should review his receipt for information about the store's return policy. He might be able to take the DVD back to the store where he bought it, explain the problem, and ask for a replacement or refund.

9. Debates will be based on students' opinions.

10. He or she should immediately notify the company that issued the card. The company must be notified quickly to stop unauthorized charges and to help identify the thief.

Critical Thinking

7. Some people argue that government should not be so involved in consumer protection. What are some arguments for and against this opinion?

8. What advice would you give a friend who purchased a movie on DVD that has a flaw that prevents him from viewing all of it?

9. Some people say consumers can make wise buying choices and do not need all of the protections that are provided. Others say consumer affairs offices and government agencies play a necessary role. Choose a partner and debate this topic.

10. What should people do if their credit card is stolen?

11. U.S. companies that furnish utilities such as water, gas, and electricity must get governmental approval before adjusting their rates. Do you think these businesses should be more or less regulated?

12. Why do you think some merchandise breaks soon after buying it?

13. Some products have grade labels, which indicate the quality of the product. Do you think most consumers pay attention to these labels?

Write About It

14. Write two or more paragraphs about ways older consumers can protect themselves from sellers who are not fair and honest.

15. Research the Federal Citizen Information Center. Write a brief summary about the types of information the center offers.

16. State governments protect consumers by requiring licenses for some professions. Write an essay of two or more paragraphs for or against the requirement of licenses.

17. Write an e-mail to your teacher about ways consumers can protect themselves when dealing with an offer that sounds too good to be true.

18. Research information from the FTC about how to solve the problem of unordered merchandise. Write a one-page summary of your findings.

19. Note the specific claims, incentives, or time limits made in an ad in the newspaper. Write a letter to the seller, supplier, or vendor to verify the information in the ad.

Technology Applications

Presentation Software

20. Using presentation software, prepare a slide show on consumer protection. Include at least six slides, with information such as resources for consumers, agencies that provide consumer protection, and advice on protection against scams, fraud, and other consumer problems.

Business Ethics

The Ethics of Advertising

21. Many packaged-food producers now provide single-serving versions of their most popular products. These items often come in smaller packages and use the same brand name as the original products. Their ads usually declare that they taste like the originals. However, some items may contain different ingredients, which can affect their look and taste. Is this ethical? Why or why not?

Chapter 24 Review and Activities **433**

Technology Applications

20. Sources of information may include FirstGov.gov, the U.S. federal government's Web site for consumers. From that site, consumers can access a number of other Web sites. Each state in the United States also has a consumer protection Web site that provides information about consumer complaints and contact information for state outreach staff.

Business Ethics

21. This practice is ethical, although somewhat misleading. Consumers who purchase the products may be disappointed if the products do not look or taste the same as the original. However, some may accept the differences as tradeoffs for the health benefits and smaller packaging.

Critical Thinking

11. Some consumers believe more regulation is better than less. Others think deregulation would lead to more choices.

12. Many consumers would say merchandise that breaks is of lesser quality. Others may say the product might not have been used correctly.

13. The labels are the basis for pricing of many products.

Write About It

14. Answers will vary. For example, they can report questionable sales tactics to a government agency.

15. The home page for FCIC has a link to the U.S. federal government Web portals, FirstGov.gov and Mymoney.gov.

16. Answers will depend on students' opinions of the regulatory power of licensing laws.

17. by being well informed, checking out products and sellers carefully, asking others about their buying experiences, and asking specific questions

18. The FTC advises consumers to be cautious. Read the fine print to find out whether you are joining a "club" with regular purchases required.

19. Students should indicate an understanding of the consumer rights, responsibilities, and protections involved.

Applying Academics to Business

Applying Academics to Business

22. Students' responses will vary, depending on the type of consumer complaint involved.

23. Multiply the number of cars by the cost of each. Multiply that product by the tariff rate:

    4,000 × $19,000 = $76 million

    $76 million × 7.5% = $5.7 million

24. Answers will depend on the product selected.

25. Answers will depend on the utility chosen and rates at the local level.

Active Learning

26. Answers will be based on students' research and ultimate purchasing decision.

Business in the Real World

27. Answers will vary. For instance, in North Carolina, the person with the complaint (the plaintiff) must file a small claim action in the county of the person or company being sued (the defendant). The plaintiff cannot sue for more than $5,000.

Applying Academics to Business

English Language Arts

22. Watch or listen to a consumer news program. Write a paragraph or two about a specific consumer complaint that is discussed, how it was resolved, and whether you would purchase the same product from the store in question.

Mathematics

23. In order to strengthen its domestic automobile industry, a country places a 7.5% tariff on all imported cars. If one foreign car company has brought 4,000 cars at $19,000 each into the country, how much will the company pay in tariffs? Write a sentence or two telling how you will solve this problem, and then solve it.

THEORY **Problem Solving** Think about which operations you will use to solve the problem.

English Language Arts

24. Sometimes new products fail in the marketplace in spite of careful market research done before the product launch. For example, New Coke with a slightly different flavor, and NutraSweet Simple Pleasure ice cream, made with a fat substitute, both seemed like sure bets. Research a product that did not sell as expected and write a paragraph summarizing your findings.

Mathematics

25. Contact one of the public utilities in your area. Find out what the rates are for the utility service. Also, find out the last time the rates were changed and calculate the percent decrease or increase.

THEORY **Percents** To calculate percent increase or decrease, find the difference between the two costs and divide by the original cost.

Active Learning

Researching Purchasing Decisions

26. Suppose you need a new digital camera. You are unaware of the latest trends in digital cameras. However, you need one that is versatile. You have about $200 to spend. Do research. Use various sources of information, such as consumer publications, company Web sites, store visits, or consumer groups. Write a report on your findings and purchasing decision.

Business in the Real World

Small Claims Court

27. Sometimes a business might refuse to satisfy a customer. In that case, the customer can take the company to small claims court. In the United States, *small claims court* settles cases involving relatively small amounts of money. Determine the small claims court limit amount in your area. Use library materials or the Internet in your research. Obtain information about filing a case. Then write a brief summary of your findings.

ExamView Assessment Suite **CD** allows you to print out ready-made unit and chapter tests, complete with answer keys. You can also create customized tests.

TeacherWorks Plus provides complete teacher resources in one convenient package. It includes customizable lesson plans in calendar format, and instant access to many print program resources.

 Real LIFE • skills

PRACTICE PROBLEM SOLVING

28. Work in teams of four or five students. Choose a product that someone has found unsatisfactory. Prepare a short presentation showing how to file a complaint about it. Be sure to include a description of how to approach the business where the product was purchased, a sample letter describing the problem and a solution, and a consumer agency that might help.

 Cool Business CAREERS

FIND YOUR DREAM JOB

29. Go to the *Introduction to Business* Online Learning Center through **glencoe.com** for a link to the Occupational Outlook Handbook Web site. Click on the "OOH Search/A-Z Index" link and enter the job title "science technician." Then write a one-page report about this type of occupation. Conclude your report with a list of things you could do now to prepare yourself to pursue the occupation.

Role Play

WHAT SHOULD YOU DO?

30. Situation You are deciding an appropriate response to resolve a consumer complaint about a product you bought. The product had a 30-day limited warranty and broke on the 31st day after you bought it.

Activity With a classmate, outline the choices you have and the action you will take to resolve your complaint.

Evaluation You will be evaluated on how well you meet the following performance indicators:

- Choose a product for this project, and describe the problem clearly.
- Outline at least two alternative actions you could take.
- Describe how you will contact the seller, consumer agencies, or other organizations about the problem.
- Prepare an outline of steps you will take to resolve your problem.

Standardized Test Practice

Directions Choose the letter of the best answer. Write the letter for the answer on a separate piece of paper.

1. What percent of 13 is 39?

A 3%
B 30%
C 33.33%
D 300%

 **TEST-TAKING TIP** When you sit down to take a math test, jot down on your scrap paper important equations or formulas that you are trying to remember. This way, you will not worry about forgetting them during the test.

 READING Go to the *Introduction to Business* Online Learning Center through **glencoe.com** for a list of outside reading suggestions.

 **STRATEGIES FOR STANDARDIZED TEST PREP SUCCESS**

Test Prep Some tests require students to be knowledgeable about technical definitions and mathematical formulas. Help students who are trying to remember these by suggesting they jot them down on scrap paper before answering the test questions. Researchers suggest that there are three keys to helping a person with memory tasks: depth, elaboration, and distinctiveness.

Real LIFE • skills

28. Answers will vary. For example, suppose a team member bought a TV that does not work. In most cases, the student can take it back to the store for a refund or replacement. A letter might be needed. It should state the problem and how to resolve it. The BBB also might be able to help.

Cool Business CAREERS

29. Science technicians develop practical applications of science to solve problems and improve production. Their working conditions vary, depending on their specialty. Training and qualifications: some jobs require a bachelor's degree; others require specialized training or an associate's degree in applied science or science-related technology. Job outlook is for average growth. To prepare, take science and math courses, and develop communication and computer skills.

Role Play

30. Presentations should address the competencies noted in the Role Play. Students should demonstrate an understanding of the basics of limited warranties.

Standardized Test Practice
1. C

FOCUS

Reasons to Use Recycled Paper

Ask volunteers to name reasons to use recycled paper. (Answers will vary but students may feel it is good for the environment.) Write a list of reasons on the board. Ask students to brainstorm a list of businesses that specialize in selling paper. (Students may mention stationers and office supply stores.)

TEACH

Teaching Points
Consumer Decisions

Ask students to identify four decisions that consumers make when they buy goods and services. (what to buy, when to buy, where to buy, and how much to pay) Ask students to characterize the consumer decisions people make when they choose to buy New Leaf Paper. (When people buy New Leaf Paper, they are making decisions about buying it versus other types of paper. They may also make decisions about different types of paper the company makes. They make decisions about when to buy on the basis of needing paper. They may buy at one store because it is convenient or has a better price. Decisions about how much to pay are likely to be based on their budgets, but people may be willing to spend more because recycled paper is better for the environment.)

Jeff Mendelsohn
Founder/President, New Leaf Paper

Jeff Mendelsohn co-founded this recycled–paper company with the belief that environmental responsibility and good business go hand in hand, and that people will prefer green paper when given the choice. A few years ago, the company teamed up with the Canadian publisher of the *Harry Potter* series to print an installment on 100 percent post-consumer, processed, and chlorine-free paper.

Q & A

Describe your job responsibilities.

Jeff: I focus on creating awareness about environmentally responsible paper in the marketplace. I also work on developing new, environmentally leading printing papers, and help with sales to large customers.

What skills are most important in your business?

Jeff: New Leaf Paper employs a very diverse group of people, but all share a commitment to our mission. Salespeople have great people skills. They are self-motivated, and have strong passion for what we do. Customer service people are level headed, have strong math and computer skills, and enjoy helping others. Managers are multitalented, they listen well, they are highly reliable, and focus on our goals. Our staff comes from a variety of educational backgrounds. Most performed very well in school because we choose people who are deeply engaged in their activities and care about the quality of their work.

What is your key to success?

Jeff: Our greatest strength is our mission statement. It very concisely sums up our main value proposition and clearly links our business success to our environmental goals.

What advice would you give students interested in starting a business?

Jeff: Be an independent thinker and be truly committed to what you do. Beyond that, it is really important, and rewarding, to truly know yourself, what you enjoy, and what your strengths and weaknesses are. With this self-awareness, you are more likely to hire people that excel at things you struggle with, and give them the authority to do their jobs.

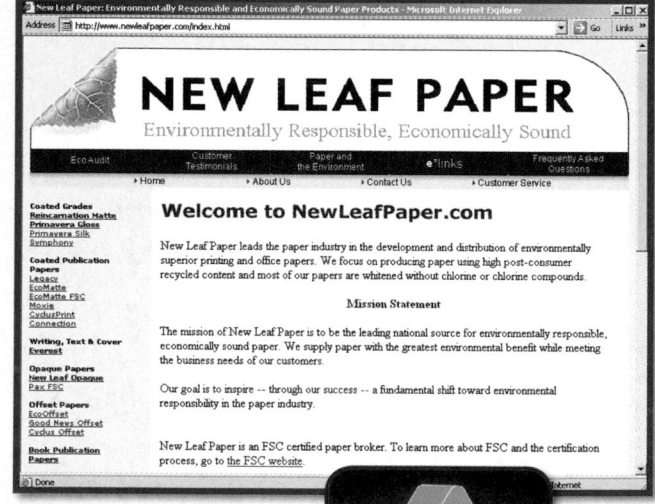

Critical Thinking *How does writing a mission statement help an entrepreneur decide which product or service his or her company will provide?*

Critical Thinking

Mission statements sum up the specific aspirations and core values of a company. Writing a mission statement is one way to solidify your company's focus.

Some Qualifications Needed to be the Owner of a Paper Manufacturing Company

Academic Skills and Abilities

Chemistry; biology; physics; mathematics; interpersonal skills; general business management skills; verbal and written communication skills; multitasking, organizing, and planning skills

Academic Skills Required to Complete Tasks at New Leaf Paper			
Tasks	Math	Science	English Language Arts
Hold meetings			◆
Assign duties			◆
Develop new products	◆	◆	◆
Assess marketplace opportunities	◆	◆	◆
Ensure quality control	◆	◆	◆
Customer service			◆
Schedule employees	◆		◆
Order supplies and equipment	◆		◆
Analyze financials	◆		◆

Education and Training

Many engineering and natural science managers begin their careers as scientists, such as chemists, biologists, geologists, or mathematicians. Some who work in applied research or other areas have a bachelor's or master's degree, or a doctorate. Science managers must be specialists in the work they supervise. Graduate programs allow scientists to augment their undergraduate training with instruction in other fields, such as management or computer technology.

Career Path

Engineering and natural sciences managers may advance to progressively higher leadership positions within their discipline. Some may become managers in nontechnical areas, such as marketing, human resources, or sales. Most begin their careers as engineers after completing a bachelor's degree in the field.

Preparing for a Career
Self-Assessment Checklist

Use this self-assessment checklist to help determine ways you can display your commitment to your work.

✔ Expand your boundaries beyond your job description.

✔ Earn the respect of your peers first; respect from higher-ups will follow.

✔ Take risks.

✔ Be ready to make mistakes.

✔ Use intuition and creativity when solving problems and developing new ideas.

✔ Set short-, medium-, and long-term goals that are aligned with your company's overall mission.

✔ In meetings, listen actively and offer suggestions.

✔ Bring a willingness to work hard to your career, even on your worst day.

437

ASSESS

Write About It
New Leaf Paper

Ask students to write a summary of what they like about New Leaf Paper's business concept. (Students may like the company's pro-environment mission and the idea of being able to build wealth by helping the environment.)

Academic Vocabulary
Career Planning

Ask students to read the Self-Assessment Checklist, then write one or more paragraphs about preparing for a career. Have students use some words from the Academic Vocabulary Glossary. (Example: If you are *committed* to your future, you will be able to see *options* over the long term that may not be obviously beneficial over the short term. To think long term, it is important to *anticipate* a *range* of *scenarios* and *evaluate* your *goals* and values so that you will not be blinded by short term difficulties.)

CLOSE

Cooperative Learning
Technology Applications

Ask students to work in pairs to develop ideas for how businesses can recycle. Have them develop a brochure promoting recycling. Encourage students to use technology applications to design the brochure and integrate images and marketing copy. (Brochures should include marketing copy, images, and information about ways businesses can recycle.)

Preparing for a Career
Education Consumption A good education is one of the most expensive investments most people will ever make. Remind students that they will have choices to make about how to get the most for their education dollar. Ask students: How can you get the best education for your money? (Answers will vary but may include getting a scholarship or going to a state university. Students should understand that shopping for the best value in the school they will attend is just as important as choosing any other service or product.) Tell students they will have an opportunity to think about careers and the career-planning process as they read the Self-Assessment Checklists in this book.

FOCUS

Discussion Starter
Lead a discussion about ways the consumer movement affects business. Ask students how they have benefited from the consumer movement.

Step 1

Brainstorm Skills
Have students go to the *Introduction to Business* Online Learning Center through **glencoe.com** for a graphic organizer they can use to brainstorm the skills needed to complete the project.

Step 2

Choose a Business and a Career
Students can use the Occupational Outlook Handbook Web site to explore options.

TEACH

Step 3

Build Background
Technology Have students brainstorm ways people can use technology to be smarter consumers. (The Internet enables people to research products quickly and efficiently. Some Web sites even specialize in providing price comparisons.)

Diversity Ask students how cultural diversity shapes the choices that are available to consumers. (Businesses are offering more choices to meet the demand of diverse markets.)

Globalization Ask students to write an essay about the impact of globalization on consumers. (International trade in consumer goods brings prices down and gives consumers more choices.)

How the Consumer Movement Affects Business
The Internet has put consumers around the world in contact with one another. People are taking an active role in speaking out for good business practices and against businesses and products that are harmful to consumers, the environment, and the world. Consumers want to buy from businesses that are socially responsible. These businesses often succeed.

Thematic Project Assignment
In this project you will work with other students to design and create a bulletin board display that describes how the consumer movement affects business.

Step 1 Brainstorm Skills You Need to Complete This Activity

Your success in designing and creating a bulletin board will depend on the skills you and your team members possess. Preview the activity, then brainstorm a list of the skills you will need to use to complete the activity and describe how you will use them. Skills you might use include:

Academic Skills	reading, writing, designing/art/photography
Basic Skills	speaking, listening, thinking, and interpersonal skills
Technology Skills	word processing, keyboarding, design and photo programs, and Internet skills

 SKILLS PREVIEW Go to the *Introduction to Business* Online Learning Center through **glencoe.com** for a graphic organizer you can use to brainstorm the skills you will use to complete the project.

Step 2 Choose a Business and a Career That Interest Your Team

Make a list of businesses that interest your team. Add to the list any careers within this business that interest your team. Then think about how the consumer movement affects these businesses. Think about how you are affected as a consumer and also how you might be affected in your future career.

Step 3 Build Background Knowledge

Preview information on how consumers affect business.

Consumers Affecting *How* **Business** *Is Conducted*

Consumers are not sitting still these days when it comes to what they like and do not like, what works and what does not work. They are coming together and speaking out in loud group voices. Businesses better listen. With the Internet connecting the world, someone in Idaho might know about a fuel-efficient vehicle being engineered in Japan almost as quickly as it could be in Detroit.

Consumers are speaking out where it hurts businesses the most—in the marketplace. This is what consumers are saying: *Build us better, more efficient products. Be more earth-friendly and socially responsible. Listen or we will take our business elsewhere. Elsewhere these days includes the whole world.*

---

438 Unit 8 Thematic Project

glencoe.com

Step 4

Connect with Your Community
Ask students to describe how their community shapes their consumer choices. (Prices in a community tend to be similar.) Ask students to think of ways their community helps them as consumers. (Students may suggest that consumer organizations and agencies protect their rights as consumers.)

Step 4 Connect with Your Community

Individually interview two adults in your community. Interview one adult who is active in a consumer movement or has taken action as a consumer. Interview another adult to learn how consumers affect the person's job or business. Bring your findings about these people's experiences to the team to use as stories for the bulletin board.

Step 5 Research How the Consumer Movement Affects Business

Use library and Internet resources to research how the consumer movement affects business. Keep records of your sources of information. Then work with your team to prepare your bulletin board. Use the project research checklist as a guide.

Step 6 Develop Your Bulletin Board

Use magazine cutouts, computer graphics, photographs, and other art supplies to create a bulletin board that includes all of the information described in the project checklist.

How the Consumer Movement Affects Business

✔ Assign tasks to team members. You will need researchers, writers, editors, and artists.

✔ Decide as a team on one type of consumer movement, such as efficient fuel for vehicles or socially responsible companies.

✔ Researchers can use library and Internet sources to find information on consumer movements and their effects on business. Look for information on how the businesses are changing because consumers are becoming active.

✔ Writers should write short paragraphs of information and picture captions.

✔ Editors should edit and proofread the information and captions.

✔ Artists should design and arrange the bulletin board.

Self Connections

✔ Individually discuss the results of your research with the adults you interviewed.

✔ Describe how the adult you interviewed spoke out as a consumer and how the other adult changed the way business was conducted.

✔ Explain what the investigation and its results mean to you.

Step 7 Evaluate Your Presentation

@ *RUBRIC* Go to the *Introduction to Business* Online Learning Center through **glencoe.com** for a rubric you can use to evaluate your final report.

439

TEACH (cont.)

Step 6

Develop a Bulletin Board
Give students these tips on writing:

- Know your audience.
- Organize your report by developing an outline and using titles and subtitles.
- Write concisely (briefly but completely).
- Write in easy-to-read, simple language.

ASSESS

Step 7

Evaluate Your Presentation
Rubric Encourage students to use the rubric to evaluate their bulletin boards.

CLOSE

Culminating Activity
Interviews
Have students form pairs and interview each other about the consumer issues they researched and how their opinions and perceptions of the consumer movement evolved during the course of the project. (Interviews will vary depending on students' opinions and reactions to their research.)

Step 5

Research How the Consumer Movement Affects Business
Students can go to the *Introduction to Business* Online Learning Center through **glencoe.com** for a rubric they can use as a content checklist when researching their bulletin boards.

Chapter	Section	Unit Objectives
Chapter 25 *The Basics of Credit*	25.1	**Define** credit and indicate three factors that affect the interest that is paid.
		Name different groups in our economy who use credit.
		Identify three advantages and disadvantages of using credit.
	25.2	**Name** the places where you can get credit, and list the three different types of credit cards.
Chapter 26 *How to Get and Keep Credit*	26.1	**Explain** how you can develop a credit history.
		Name five factors to think about when deciding which credit card to secure.
		Define the three factors that creditors consider when granting a person credit.
	26.2	**Explain** one major difference between credit cards, installment loans, and mortgages.
		Indicate at least three ways to maintain a good credit rating.
Chapter 27 *Credit and the Law*	27.1	**Discuss** state and federal regulation of credit.
		Describe federal laws that protect consumers.
	27.2	**Identify** sources of credit fraud and precautions to prevent it.
		Discuss ways to repair credit problems.

Understanding the Coding

Brackets Brackets on the reduced student edition page correspond to teaching strategies and activities in the Teacher Wraparound Edition. As you teach the lesson, the brackets show you exactly where to use the teaching strategies and activities.

Letters The letters on the reduced student edition page identify the type of strategy or activity. See the key below to learn about the different types of strategies and activities.

Ability Levels Leveled teaching strategies are identified by one of three codes to give you an idea of their suitability for students of varying learning styles and abilities.

Resources Key program resources are listed in each chapter. Icons indicate the format of resources.

KEY to Letters

D **Develop Concepts** activities help teachers gauge and plan for students' concept development.

R **Reading Strategy** activities help you teach reading skills and vocabulary.

C **Critical Thinking** strategies help students apply and extend what they have learned.

U **Universal Access** activities provide differentiated instruction for English language learners and suggestions for teaching various types of learners.

S **Skill Practice** provides leveled instruction for meeting individual needs and learning styles.

W **Writing Support** activities provide writing opportunities to help students comprehend the text.

NCLB **No Child Left Behind** activities help students practice and improve their abilities in academic subjects.

KEY to Ability Levels

L1 Strategies should be within the ability range of all students. Often full class participation is required.

L2 Strategies are for average to above-average students or for small groups. Some teacher direction is necessary.

L3 Strategies are designed for students able and willing to work independently. Minimal teacher direction is necessary.

KEY to Resource Icons

📁 Print Material

💿 CD-ROM

🖥 Online Learning Center with Podcasts

BusinessWeek *Reader and Case Study*

In Unit 9, your students can learn more about business in the real world through the following *BusinessWeek* Readers and Case Studies:

Big Plastic's Online Challenger
Gary Marino is giving e-shoppers an alternative to credit cards—and his Bill Me Later service is catching on. Is it an idea too good to survive? (page 450)

Personal Finance for Freshmen
College students need money smarts if they want to succeed after graduation. Increasingly, schools are offering assistance. (page 462)

Stopping a Scam from Spreading
Thwarted by bigger banks, ID thieves are taking aim at smaller financial institutions. One credit union provides a model for fighting back. (page 482)

Chapter Features and Activities

Section	Feature Title	Page
25.1	Credit Users	446
25.1	Credit Card Debt	447
25.2	Standard Formats	451
26.1	Credit Ratings	463

Section	Feature Title	Page
27.1	Debtors and Creditors	477
27.1	OCC	479
27.2	Bankruptcy Laws	485

Reading Strategies

Before You Read

Section	Page
25.1	444
25.2	449
26.1	460
26.2	465
27.1	476
27.2	481

Graphic Organizer

Chapter	Section	Title	Page
25	25.1	Pros and Cons of Using Credit	444
	25.2	Sources of Credit	449
26	26.1	The Three Cs of Credit	460
	26.2	Five Factors That Affect Your Credit Score	465
27	27.1	Federal Laws That Regulate Fair Credit	476
	27.2	Steps to Prevent Identity Theft	481

As You Read

Section	Page
25.1	445
25.2	450, 452, 453
26.1	461, 462, 464
26.2	466, 467
27.1	478, 480
27.2	482, 483

✔ Reading Check

Section	Page
25.1	445, 447
25.2	452
26.1	462, 463
26.2	467, 468
27.1	477, 479
27.2	483

After You Read

Section	Page
25.1	448
25.2	453
26.1	464
26.2	469
27.1	480
27.2	485

Credit

Unit Overview

Introduce the Unit

Introduce the unit by describing the main concepts of each chapter in the unit.

Unit 9 is about credit and how it affects everyday life.

Chapter 25 is about credit—it answers the question, "What is credit?" It also provides basic information about types of credit.

Chapter 26 is about applying for and maintaining credit. It describes the costs of credit and keeping good credit.

Chapter 27 describes credit laws that protect consumers and offers guidance to creditors. It also focuses on solving credit problems including identity theft.

00:00 OUT OF TIME?

If class time is too short to cover all of the chapters in this unit, have students:

- Write down the vocabulary terms and their definitions.
- Read the chapter summaries at the beginning of each chapter review.
- Go to the *Introduction to Business* Online Learning Center through **glencoe.com** to download free Study-to-Go content to their PDAs or cell phones.

440

Real-World Business and Career Profile ⟩ Preview

Geomagic Tell students that at the end of this unit, they will learn about Geomagic founder Ping Fu and how she achieved her success. Geomagic develops software that is used to model three-dimensional objects on computers Geomagic software and services are used in industries such as automotive, aerospace, medical devices, and consumer products. Ask students why producing software for businesses could be good business. (Students might suggest that businesses need computers and software to do specialized tasks.)

Real-World Business and Career Profile

Preview

Geomagic makes 3-D geometric modeling software that allows manufacturers such as Toyota® and Fisher-Price® to customize individualized products at the same cost as with mass manufacturing. At the end of this unit, you will learn more about Geomagic® founder Ping Fu and how she achieved her success.

Decision Making How do you plan to use credit in the future?

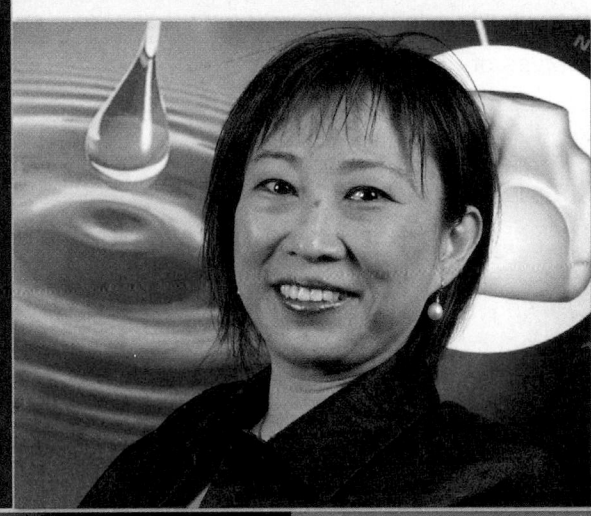

Unit 9 | *Thematic Project Preview*

Making Credit Decisions After completing this unit, you will research ways credit decisions can affect your life and career.

Project Checklist As you read the chapters in this unit, use this checklist to prepare for the unit project.

✔ Think about how to obtain credit.
✔ Analyze how to use credit wisely.
✔ Determine how unwise choices can affect your credit.
✔ Consider the types of jobs and careers in the credit industry.

441

Build Background
Ask students these questions to activate prior knowledge:

Chapter 25
Why is it important to understand credit? (Some students have credit cards in their wallets, but they might not be paying the bills. Soon they will start to receive offers to get their own cards and their own bills. Now is a good time for them to get the facts about credit.)

Chapter 26
Why is it important to understand how to get and keep credit? (It is relatively easy for young people to get their first credit card. Obtaining and using a first credit card can be a first step toward demonstrating financial responsibility.)

Chapter 27
Who do you think is likely to have credit problems? (Credit problems are not confined to individuals and families with low incomes. In fact, many people with good-paying jobs have credit problems. Some credit problems are the result of choices debtors make, but others are the result of discrimination, mistakes, and crime. All consumers can benefit from knowing the basics about credit laws and solving credit problems.)

Unit | Thematic Project Preview

Making Credit Decisions
Tell students that when they complete this unit, they will understand what credit is and how to use it wisely. Students will be able to consider how credit—both good and bad credit—affects their life.

C Critical Thinking
Ask students how they think credit affects them as a consumer. (Students should recognize that they will probably use credit to buy products, and that if they have bad credit, they cannot buy things on credit.)

Standards-Based Lesson Planning
Introduction to Business provides students with instruction and assessment in the following fundamental content areas:

Content Standards Correlations	
Analyze the concept of credit and its effect on the individual and the total economy.	pp. 445–447
Explain when and why borrowing is used for the purchase of goods and services.	pp. 445–446, 453, 455–457
Discuss major financial issues for the individual (for example, money management, the banking system and services, saving and investing, credit, taxes, and paychecks).	pp. 445–448, 450–453, 455–457
Determine the advantages and disadvantages of using credit.	pp. 446–448, 451, 454–455
Evaluate how credit can be used as a tool for financial well-being.	pp. 446–447, 455
Identify various sources of credit available to consumers, businesses, and governments.	pp. 450–453, 455–457
Evaluate the best type of payment (such as cash, mortgage, installment loans, credit cards, and debit cards) to use for different types of purchases.	pp. 455–456

NCLB
Activities, information, and skills practice will help your students attain No Child Left Behind proficiency. Students will improve their abilities in the following academic standards areas:

Academic Standards Correlations		
English Language Arts	Activities/Features	Page
NCTE 3 Apply strategies to interpret texts	Applying Academics to Business	p. 456
NCTE 4 Use written language to communicate effectively	After You Read	p. 453
NCTE 7 Conduct research and gather, evaluate, and synthesize data to communicate discoveries	After You Read / Applying Academics to Business	pp. 453, 456
Mathematics		
Data Analysis and Probability Develop and evaluate inferences and predictions that are based on data	Applying Academics to Business	p. 456
Number and Operations Compute fluently and make reasonable estimates	Ask S&P / Standardized Test Practice	pp. 442, 457
Number and Operations Understand meanings of operations and how they relate to one another	After You Read	p. 448
Number and Operations Understand numbers, ways of representing numbers, relationships among numbers, and number systems	Applying Academics to Business	p. 456
Science		
Content Standard F Students should develop understanding of science and technology in local, national, and global challenges	Science/Tech Trends	p. 451

Correlations   This chart shows the 21ˢᵗ Century Skills, foundation skills, and workplace competencies that students develop as they work in this chapter.

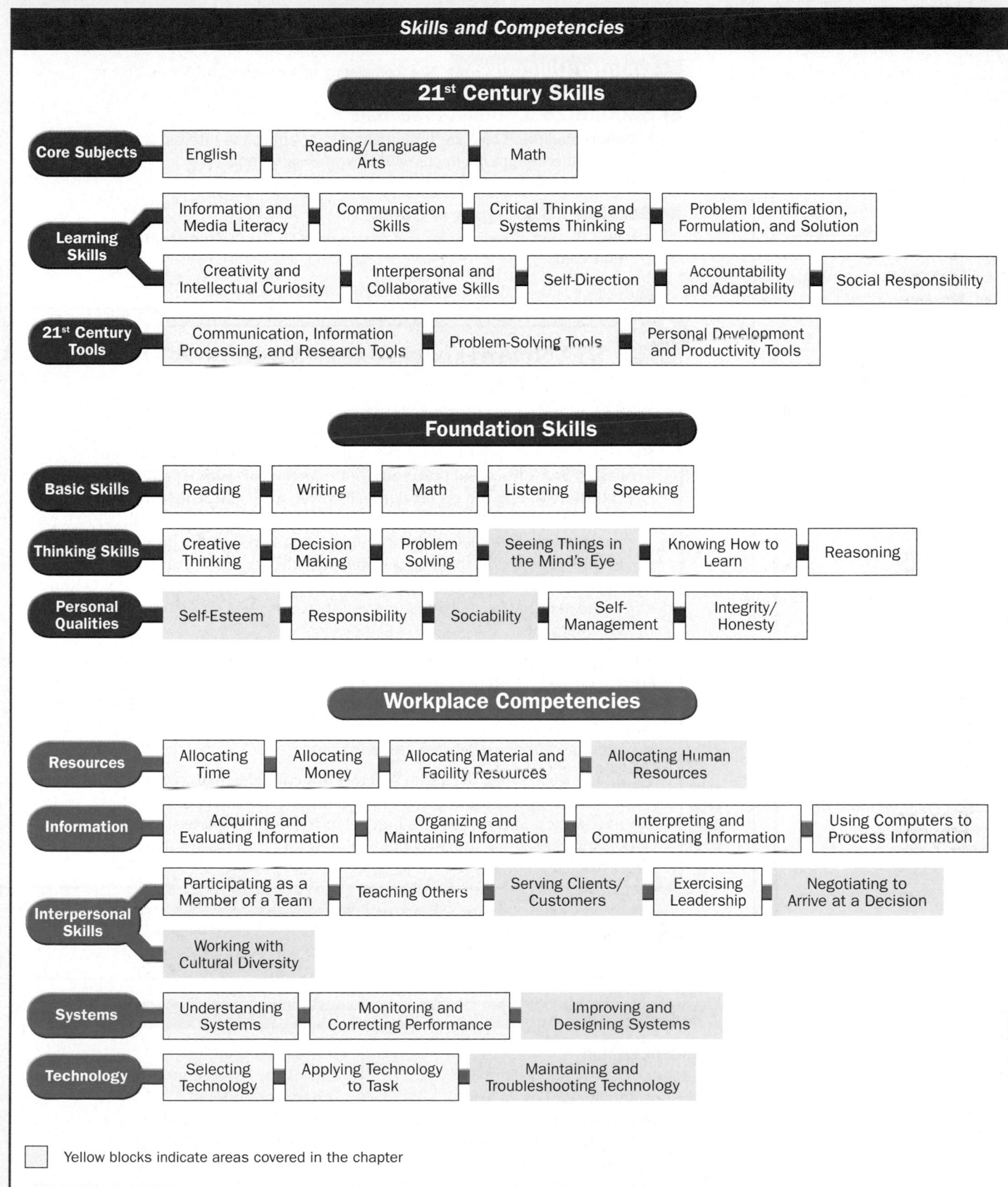

Skills and Competencies

21ˢᵗ Century Skills

Core Subjects
- English
- Reading/Language Arts
- Math

Learning Skills
- Information and Media Literacy
- Communication Skills
- Critical Thinking and Systems Thinking
- Problem Identification, Formulation, and Solution
- Creativity and Intellectual Curiosity
- Interpersonal and Collaborative Skills
- Self-Direction
- Accountability and Adaptability
- Social Responsibility

21ˢᵗ Century Tools
- Communication, Information Processing, and Research Tools
- Problem-Solving Tools
- Personal Development and Productivity Tools

Foundation Skills

Basic Skills
- Reading
- Writing
- Math
- Listening
- Speaking

Thinking Skills
- Creative Thinking
- Decision Making
- Problem Solving
- Seeing Things in the Mind's Eye
- Knowing How to Learn
- Reasoning

Personal Qualities
- Self-Esteem
- Responsibility
- Sociability
- Self-Management
- Integrity/Honesty

Workplace Competencies

Resources
- Allocating Time
- Allocating Money
- Allocating Material and Facility Resources
- Allocating Human Resources

Information
- Acquiring and Evaluating Information
- Organizing and Maintaining Information
- Interpreting and Communicating Information
- Using Computers to Process Information

Interpersonal Skills
- Participating as a Member of a Team
- Teaching Others
- Serving Clients/Customers
- Exercising Leadership
- Negotiating to Arrive at a Decision
- Working with Cultural Diversity

Systems
- Understanding Systems
- Monitoring and Correcting Performance
- Improving and Designing Systems

Technology
- Selecting Technology
- Applying Technology to Task
- Maintaining and Troubleshooting Technology

Yellow blocks indicate areas covered in the chapter

Chapter Overview

Introduce the Chapter

The Basics of Credit
Chapter 25 is about credit. It answers the question, "What is credit?" It also provides basic information about types of credit.

Building Background
Many students will start to receive offers to get their own credit cards. Now is a good time for them to learn the facts about credit.

Ask STANDARD &POOR'S

>> Math Answer
The difference between the two rates is 4.25%. (13.50% − 9.25% = 4.25%).

>> Extension Activity
Charles and Gina want to remodel their kitchen. They can take out a bank loan with an interest rate of 7.375%. They also own shares of a mutual fund with a likely return of 8.88%. Should they pay for the remodeling by borrowing from the bank or selling their mutual fund shares? (They should borrow the necessary funds from the bank because the return on their investment will be 1.535% more than the interest they would pay on the loan.)

N C L B Activity correlates to Math standards.

The Basics of Credit

Chapter Objectives After completing this chapter, you will be able to:

▶ **Section 25.1** *Credit Essentials*
- **Define** credit and indicate three factors that affect the interest that is paid.
- **Name** different groups in our economy who use credit.
- **Identify** three advantages and disadvantages of using credit.

▶ **Section 25.2** *Types of Credit*
- **Name** the places where you can get credit, and list the three different types of credit cards.

Ask STANDARD &POOR'S **The Basics of Credit: The Advantages of Debt**

Q: When is it worth going into debt for better liquidity?

A: Liquidity is simply the ease with which an asset can be bought, sold, or turned into cash. For example, suppose you need to buy a car. You have $20,000 saved that you could use to buy the car outright. However, after a little investigating, you realize that putting $10,000 toward the car, borrowing the remaining $10,000 for the car, and investing $10,000 in stocks might actually be a more profitable approach. If the interest rate on the loan is lower than the rate of increase on the stocks, going into some debt might be a good idea. Furthermore, since stocks can be more easily liquidated than a car, they allow you to access your money more quickly in case of an emergency.

Mathematics You've decided to buy that car. You're trying to choose whether to spend all of your savings on the car or to pay for part of the cost of the car now, take out a loan to pay the rest, and invest the rest of your savings. The interest rate on the loan will be 9.25% while the rate of increase on the investment is likely to be about 13.5%. What is the difference between these two rates?

THEORY **Subtracting Decimals** When subtracting decimals, write the numbers vertically, lining up the numbers by place value (the decimal points will also be lined up). If necessary, add zeros as place holders in the decimal places that do not have values, then subtract as you usually would. Do not forget to place a decimal point in the correct place in your answer.

N C L B

Classroom Resources

- Student Edition
- Teacher Wraparound Edition
- Student Activity Workbook with Academic Integration
- Student Activity Workbook with Academic Integration TAE
- *Fast File*, Unit 9 Resources
- Inclusion in the Business Education Classroom

- TeacherWorks Plus
- *ExamView Assessment Suite*
- Presentation Plus!
- Vocabulary PuzzleMaker
- Interactive Student Edition
- Online Student Edition
- Online Learning Center with Podcasts

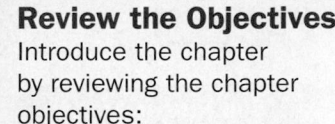

● The Importance of Good Credit Paying your bills on time and keeping your total debt low will improve your credit rating. **What does a good credit rating tell lenders?**

Review the Objectives
Introduce the chapter by reviewing the chapter objectives:

Section 25.1 *Objectives*
Define credit and indicate three factors that affect the interest that is paid. (Credit is an agreement to get money, goods, or services now in exchange for a promise to pay in the future. The amount of interest is based on the interest rate, the amount of time the borrower has the loan, and the amount of the loan.)

Name different groups in our economy who use credit. (consumers, businesses, and governments)

Identify three advantages and disadvantages of using credit. (Advantages are that it provides convenience, helps establish a credit rating, aids record keeping, and encourages economic growth. Disadvantages are that it is easy to misuse, creates the expense of interest, and requires commitment of future income.)

Section 25.2 *Objective*
Name the places where you can get credit, and list the three different types of credit cards. (Places include banks, credit unions, savings and loan associations, and other financial institutions. Sellers of goods and services, finance companies, pawn shops, and businesses that provide "borrow until payday" loans also offer credit. Three types of credit cards are single-purpose, multipurpose, and travel and entertainment cards.)

Discuss the Photo
● The Importance of Good Credit Read the caption on the photo to students: Paying your bills on time and keeping your total debt low will improve your credit rating.

Ask students: What does a good credit rating tell lenders? (A good credit rating tells lenders that you are a responsible borrower and a good credit risk.)

443

FOCUS

Bell Ringer Activity

Credit Essentials
Ask students: What promise do consumers make every time they use their credit cards? (Students should understand that when you use credit you promise to pay the funds back later.)

Preteaching

Presentation Plus!
The Presentation Plus! CD provides visual teaching aids for this section.

PuzzleMaker
Use the Vocabulary PuzzleMaker to create a puzzle of the section's key terms. Students can complete the puzzle on paper or on a computer.

Graphic Organizer
Tell students to go to the Online Learning Center through **glencoe.com** for a printable graphic organizer. (Pros: convenience, for emergencies, to take advantage of a sale, help establish credit, help keep expense records, and encourage economic growth. Cons: it can lead to overspending, interest can make an item more expensive, and it can be misused and lead to a lower credit rating.)

N C L B
Connects academics to content.

Credit Essentials

Reading Guide

● **Before You Read**
Think about the skills you need to obtain credit and to use it wisely.

Read to Learn
- Define credit and indicate three factors that affect the interest that is paid.
- Name different groups in our economy who use credit.
- Identify three advantages and disadvantages of using credit.

The Main Idea
Credit allows borrowers to purchase items that they otherwise could not afford. Consumers, businesses, and governments all borrow money. There are advantages and disadvantages to using credit.

Key Concepts
- Credit: The Promise to Pay
- Who Uses Credit?
- The Pros and Cons of Using Credit

Vocabulary
Key Terms
credit
creditor
debtor
interest
consumer credit
commercial credit
credit rating

Academic Vocabulary
You will find these words in your reading and on your tests. Make sure you know their meanings.
military
contributes
constantly
committed

Graphic Organizer
In a graphic such as the one shown, list some advantages of using credit in the PROS column and some disadvantages in the CONS column as you read.

PROS	CONS

@ Go to the *Introduction to Business* Online Learning Center through **glencoe.com** for a printable graphic organizer.

D

Academic Standards
English Language Arts
    NCTE 1 Read texts to acquire new information
Mathematics
    Number and Operations Understand meanings of operations and how they relate to one another

N C L B

Reading Guide

● **Before You Read**
Students might suggest that they need math, reading, decision-making, and organizational skills to use credit wisely.

D Develop Concepts

The Main Idea Ask students: What do you think are some good reasons to borrow money? (Answers may include buying a vehicle, starting or expanding a business, purchasing a house, and paying tuition.)

Credit: The Promise to Pay

Buying an item now and paying for it later can be an easy and convenient way to make a purchase. Consumers use credit to buy all kinds of goods and services. **Credit** is an agreement to obtain money, goods, or services now in exchange for a promise to pay in the future. When buying on credit, you are delaying the payment for an item.

A **creditor** lends money or provides credit. A **debtor** borrows money or uses credit. Credit is based on the creditor's confidence that the debtor can and will repay the debt. Creditors charge a fee for using their money, which is called **interest**. The amount of interest to be paid is based on three factors. One is the interest rate, which is a percentage of the total amount borrowed. Interest rates vary from one provider to the next. Another factor is the length of time of the loan. The longer you take to pay it off, the more interest you will have to pay. The other factor is the amount of the loan. The larger the amount, the more interest that will be charged.

> ✔ **Reading Check** **Identify** On what three factors is the amount of interest based?

Who Uses Credit?

Many people use credit. To a great extent it has replaced money as a means of making purchases. Credit is used practically everywhere. Many people use credit to pay for CDs, meals at restaurants, or even higher education.

The type of credit used by people for personal reasons is called **consumer credit**. Businesses often use credit for the same reasons that consumers do. Manufacturers borrow money to buy

> ● **As You Read**
> Think about purchases you have seen people make using credit.

? ETHICS in Business

Credit Cards

■ **Critical Reading** Life is full of important decisions. Think about the kinds of decisions that you make as you read the question below.

You work in the promotions department of a credit card company. The company instructs you to set up a booth on college campuses in an attempt to get incoming freshmen to sign up for a card. You are told to offer a pre-approved line of credit with a higher-than-average interest rate. Your manager also recommends giving a bunch of free promotional gifts to attract students to your booth.

■ **Decision Making** Would the fact that the majority of people you will be soliciting have limited, if any, disposable income affect your actions? Explain your answer.

Section 25.1 Credit Essentials **445**

TEACH

Discussion Starter
Start a discussion by asking students this question: Would you lend someone you know $5? How about $5,000? What would you expect in return for the loan? (Answers will vary. Students might suggest that they would lend someone $5 with just the promise of repayment. For a loan of $5,000, they might expect a promise of repayment and interest.)

R Reading Strategy

Define Ask students to use their own words to define *credit, creditor, debtor,* and *interest.* (Answers will vary. Credit is an agreement to get money, goods, or services now in exchange for a promise to pay in the future. A creditor is a person or an organization that lends money or provides credit. A debtor is a person or an organization that borrows money or uses credit. Interest is a fee for using their money.)

> ✔ **Reading Check**

Identify The amount of interest is based on the interest rate, the length of time for the loan, and the amount of the loan.

> ● **As You Read**
> Students may have seen people use credit at supermarkets, in restaurants, at gas stations, or at retail stores.

? ETHICS in Business

Decision Making Answers should suggest that knowingly marketing a product to people who cannot afford it is referred to as predatory marketing because it preys on people's needs regardless of their economic situation.

445

TEACH (cont.)

S Skill Practice

Guided Practice

Provide Examples Ask students to provide two examples of consumer credit and two examples of commercial credit that are used in their community. (Borrowing to buy a home or a car is consumer credit and borrowing to purchase inventory or expand a store is commercial credit.) **L1**

Classify Ask students to create a list of purchases consumers frequently make with credit and a second list of purchases they frequently make with cash. Ask them to explain differences between these types. (Students may point out that more expensive products are purchased with credit.) **L2**

Investigate Ask students to investigate how funds used to build their school were obtained. (Answers will vary, depending on the school, but bonds may have been issued.) **L3**

ASSESS

Review Key Terms
Have students write sentences using each key term.

 **Study-to-Go** Have students go to the Online Learning Center through **glencoe.com** to download free **Study-to-Go** content to their PDAs or cell phones.

Credit Users The credit card industry has terms for its customers. "Revolvers" are people who roll their balances over month to month, and never pay in full. "Rate surfers" or "gamers" are people who switch credit cards based on interest rates. *Which group do you think credit card companies prefer as customers and why?*

● **Credit Ratings** Credit scores are used for much more than financing decisions. Many employers check applicants' credit reports before making hiring decisions. **What could negatively affect your credit rating?**

---

raw materials, new machinery, factories, or trucks. Some borrow money to buy goods that they later resell. Credit used by businesses is called **commercial credit**. When businesses borrow money, however, they often pass along the cost of interest to consumers by charging higher prices.

The federal government uses credit to pay for many of the services and programs it provides to its citizens. For example, during World War II, the federal government used credit to finance **military** spending. State and local governments use credit to pay for things such as highways, public housing, stadiums, and water systems.

The Pros and Cons of Using Credit

Credit is so common in today's society that most people choose to use it. To use credit effectively, the consumer must know its advantages and disadvantages.

Advantages of Credit

An important advantage of credit is that it is convenient. You can shop and travel without carrying large amounts of cash. Instead of saving for an expensive item, such as a car, you can buy the car on credit and use it right away. Credit is especially useful in an emergency. If your car breaks down and you do not have cash to fix it, you can use credit.

Credit Users Credit card companies prefer "revolvers," because the fees and interest these customers pay generate the most income for credit card companies.

Discuss the Photo
● **Credit Ratings** Several things can lower your credit score, including using all your available credit, being close to the credit limit on several credit cards, skipping payments, and making late payments.

Figure 25.1 — *Annual Percentage Rate for Monthly Payments*

Finance Charge per $100 Borrowed at Various Interest Rates					
Number of Monthly Payments	**7.0%**	**7.5%**	**8.0%**	**8.5%**	**9.0%**
6	$2.05	$2.20	$2.35	$2.49	$2.64
12	$3.83	$4.11	$4.39	$4.66	$4.94
18	$5.63	$6.04	$6.45	$6.86	$7.28
24	$7.45	$8.00	$8.55	$9.09	$9.64
30	$9.30	$9.98	$10.66	$11.35	$12.04

● **Finding the Finance Charge** If you borrow money and do not pay it back right away, you will probably have to pay a finance charge. **What is the finance charge that you would pay if you borrowed $100 for 18 months at an APR of 9 percent?**

Buying on credit enables people to establish a credit rating. A **credit rating** is a measure of a person's ability and willingness to pay debts on time. A good credit rating tells other lenders that you are a responsible borrower and a good credit risk. Credit also helps consumers keep track of their spending. Whenever you buy something on credit, it goes on your credit card bill so you have a record of your expenses.

Finally, credit **contributes** to the growth of our economy. Credit allows consumers to buy more goods and services. Since so many consumers make credit purchases, businesses must hire more workers and produce more goods to keep up with the demand.

✔ **Reading Check** **Analyze** What factors contribute to a good credit rating?

Disadvantages of Credit

Since credit is so convenient to use, it can also be easy to misuse. With credit, it is tempting for people to buy things that they cannot afford or do not need. Advertisements and salespeople **constantly** urge consumers to buy more things. You might find it hard to resist sales or offers for more credit. Easy purchasing power should not encourage unnecessary purchases.

Items also cost more when you use credit instead of cash because of the interest. The more items you charge and the longer you take to pay off credit card debt, the more you pay in interest. Another disadvantage is that using credit means that you have **committed** some of your future income since the debt must be repaid. **Figure 25.1** shows the way total interest payments increase with higher interest rates and longer payment terms.

Credit Card Debt
The average American household carries a credit card balance of $7,500 to $8,000. *What do you think are some problems with carrying debt on your credit card?*

Section 25.1   Credit Essentials   **447**

Figure 25.1

● **Finding the Finance Charge**
You would pay $7.28.

Real World

Credit Card Debt Answers will vary. For example, carrying debt may make it difficult to pay off the balance. Also, credit card companies can raise your interest rate automatically if you make payments late.

RETEACH

W **Writing Support**
Enrichment
Credit Ratings Ask students to use Internet and library resources to create a one-page guide for building a good credit rating. (Students may suggest paying all bills on time, paying more than the minimum amount due, or limiting the number of credit applications.)

R **Reading Strategy**
List Ask students to make a list of the advantages of buying on credit. (It is convenient for everyday purchases and helps consumers keep track of spending. Credit can be used in case of an emergency. Buying on credit helps people establish a credit rating and it contributes to economic growth.)

U **Universal Access**
Students with Learning Disabilities As an alternative to using a spiral notebook to take notes, some students might find it beneficial to take notes on loose-leaf paper and copy the notes into a notebook. Rewriting the notes reinforces the concepts and helps students identify things that need to be clarified.

Student Activity Workbook ☞ Assign the Section 25.1 Activities.

✔ **Reading Check**

Analyze paying bills on time, establishing a good credit history, and paying off loans on time

C Critical Thinking

Disadvantages of Credit
Have students create an illustration that highlights one or more disadvantages of credit. (Illustrations will vary depending on the disadvantages portrayed.)

ASSESS

● **After You Read**

Have students complete the Section 25.1 After You Read section review.

Online Study Tools
Have students go to the Online Learning Center through **glencoe.com** to:

- Take the Section 25.1 **Practice Test**.
- Download free **Study-to-Go** content to their PDAs or cell phones.

CLOSE

Culminating Activity
Credit Pros and Cons
Ask students to create a chart showing a correlation between the advantages and disadvantages of credit. (Students might indicate that credit is convenient, but the convenience makes it easy to overspend.)

448

C As credit card bills pile up, you might have trouble paying them. After a while, you may reach your *credit limit,* the point where you cannot charge any more. Late or missed payments lower your credit rating, which can make it difficult to get credit in the future. Always remember when you use credit that it is not money you own, it is money you owe.

Factors to Consider Before Using Credit Imagine that you have conducted research on the Internet regarding the possibility of financing (or getting money for) a used vehicle. Before you decide to finance a major purchase by using credit, you should consider the following points:

- Do you have the cash you need for the down payment?
- Do you want to use your savings instead of credit?
- Can you afford the item?
- Could you use the credit in some better way?
- Could you put off buying the item for a while?
- What are the costs of using credit?

NCLB Activity correlates to Math standards.

As previously mentioned, one of the main factors to consider is that when you buy something on credit, you agree to pay a fee that a creditor may add to the purchase price. If you do not pay your credit card bill in full every month, you will be charged interest on the unpaid balance. Interest essentially increases the original price of the item you purchased.

Section 25.1

● **After You Read**

Review Key Concepts
1. What is credit?
2. What is the difference between commercial and consumer credit?
3. Why is it important to have a good credit rating?

Academic Skills

NCLB

4. **Mathematics** You have an unpaid balance of $100 on a credit card and plan to pay off the balance in 12 months. Your credit card company charges you 9% interest per year. You transfer the balance to a card that charges only 7% per year and plan to pay off the balance in 6 months. Use the table in **Figure 25.1** to calculate the difference in the monthly charge for interest.

THEORY **Reading Tables** To read a table, first locate the headings for the row and column requested. Reading across the row and down the column will let you compare data.

 For math help, go to the Math Appendix.

@ Go to the *Introduction to Business* Online Learning Center through **glencoe.com** to check your answers.

448   **Chapter 25**   The Basics of Credit   glencoe.com

Section 25.1

Review Key Concepts
1. an agreement to get money, goods, or services now in exchange for a promise to pay in the future
2. Commercial credit is used by business whereas consumer credit is used by the consumer.
3. It shows that a consumer is a responsible borrower and a good credit risk.

Academic Skills
4. **Mathematics** A 9% interest rate paid in 12 monthly payments costs $4.94 in interest.
A 7% interest rate paid in 6 monthly payments costs $2.05 in interest.
$4.94 − $2.05 = $2.89 in interest savings.

Types of Credit

Reading Guide

Before You Read

Think about the different types of credit that are available and the places where you can get it.

Read to Learn

- Name the places where you can get credit, and list the three different types of credit cards.

The Main Idea

There are many different types of credit plans, including charge accounts, credit cards, single payment loans, installment loans, and mortgage loans. There are also many different sources for credit.

Key Concept

- Sources of Credit

Vocabulary

Key Terms

charge account   collateral
installment loans

Academic Vocabulary

You will find these words in your reading and on your tests. Make sure you know their meanings.

available   range
annual   options

Graphic Organizer

In a table like the one below, write definitions for the different sources of credit.

Sources of Credit	Definitions
Charge account	
Credit card	
Banks/financial institutions	
Seller-provided credit	
Consumer finance company	
Payroll advance service	

 Go to the *Introduction to Business* Online Learning Center through **glencoe.com** for a printable graphic organizer.

Academic Standards

English Language Arts

NCTE 1 Read texts to acquire new information

NCTE 5 Use different writing process elements to communicate effectively

NCTE 7 Conduct research and gather, evaluate, and synthesize data to communicate discoveries

Science

Content Standard F Students should develop an understanding of science and technology in local, national, and global challenges

---

Reading Guide

Before You Read

Credit is available from bank loans, credit card companies, finance companies, and department stores.

D Develop Concepts

The Main Idea Ask students: Why are there different types of credit plans?
(Students should understand that people use different kinds of credit for different situations.)

FOCUS

Bell Ringer Activity

Types of Credit
Write the following question on the board. What do some consumers do when they need money?
(They get loans from banks and credit unions, they use credit cards or credit offered by stores, they sell or pawn their possessions, or borrow against paychecks.)

Preteaching

Presentation Plus!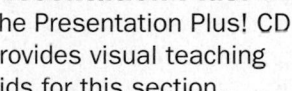
The Presentation Plus! CD provides visual teaching aids for this section.

PuzzleMaker
Use the Vocabulary PuzzleMaker to create a puzzle of the section's key terms. Students can complete the puzzle on paper or on a computer.

Graphic Organizer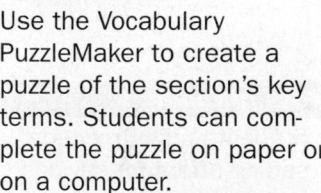
Tell students to go to the Online Learning Center through **glencoe.com** for a printable graphic organizer.
(Answers include: charge account: credit provided by a store; credit card: issued by banks for various purchases; banks/financial institutions: offer loans on specific terms; seller-provided credit: provided for specific purchases; consumer finance company: loans money to high-risk borrowers; payroll advance services: offer short-term loans)

N C L B Connects academics to content.

TEACH

Discussion Starter
Charge Accounts
Many retailers offer charge accounts that are only good in their stores. Ask students to discuss the advantages and disadvantages of such cards. (Students might suggest this type of card might be convenient, that stores sometimes offer special benefits to cardholders. Students should also understand that these cards limit consumer choices.)

R Reading Strategy

Explain Ask students to explain why stores offer charge accounts. (Stores offer charge accounts to encourage people who do not have cash to buy now and pay later.)

● As You Read
Students might mention seeing offers for savings on items purchased at a company's store; frequent flier miles; free magazine subscriptions; free travel, airline upgrades, or merchandise; and no or low interest charged for a short period.

Sources of Credit

Credit is **available** from many different sources. These sources provide different types of loans for varying lengths of time. Loans can be short-term (one year or less), medium-term (one to five years), or long-term (more than five years). The risk a creditor takes in lending money or selling on credit is the most important factor in determining the cost of credit.

Charge Accounts

R

A **charge account** is credit provided by a store or company for customers to buy its products. Customers who have charge accounts at a store can use their credit to buy now and pay later. When the bill arrives in the mail, the customer can pay part of the total amount owed or the entire amount.

● As You Read
Think about the kinds of incentives you have seen to tempt consumers to obtain a credit card.

Credit Cards

Credit cards are like charge accounts, but some can be used in many different places. Those issued by banks, for example, can be used in different stores, including companies that sell

BusinessWeek *Reader and Case Study*

Big Plastic's Online Challenger

Gary Marino is giving e-shoppers an alternative to credit cards—and his Bill Me Later® service is catching on. Is it an idea too good to survive?

Gary Marino knows more than most people about how difficult it is to create a new way for consumers to pay for goods and services.

A self-described "credit card geek" who worked for decades at Citicorp and then First USA, he watched various efforts fail over the years. "The last one that succeeded was the Discover® card in the mid-1980s, and they had to spend tens of billions to build their brand over the last 20 years." Indeed, other than PayPal®, which is used mostly for transactions between individuals on eBay®, most consumers still make their purchases the old-fashioned way: with cash, checks, or plastic when shopping online.

But Marino is making progress at creating another option. He runs a 150-person outfit

called I4 Commerce, whose Bill Me Later payment system is catching on with online merchants and shoppers.

 CASE STUDY Go to the *Introduction to Business* Online Learning Center through **glencoe.com** for the *BusinessWeek* Reader Case Study.

Active Learning
Online payments are booming, but giving money to an unknown credit company is a major issue for consumers. Research the benefits offered by Bill Me Later. With a classmate, write a 60-second commercial for the company that is designed to calm customers' fears. Film your commercial and show it to the class.

BusinessWeek *Reader and Case Study*

Big Plastic's Online Challenger
 CASE STUDY Have students go to the *Introduction to Business* Online Learning Center through **glencoe.com** to download a Case Study activity that corresponds to the article. The activity and answer key are also available on the TeacherWorks Plus CD.

Active Learning
Commercials will vary but should address issues such as identity theft and built-in consumer protections.

on the Internet. Some of the cards have **annual** fees, which can **range** from $25 to $80. Credit card companies earn money from the interest they charge as well as from annual fees and penalties.

There are three basic types of credit cards: single-purpose, multipurpose, and travel and entertainment.

Single-Purpose Cards Single-purpose cards can be used to buy goods or services only at the business that issued the card. Each month cardholders receive a statement listing all the purchases they made in the last 30 days. They can pay part of the amount owed or the entire amount. Interest is charged on the unpaid balance. Credit cards issued by oil companies and department stores, such as Shell® and Macy's®, are examples of single-purpose credit cards.

Multipurpose Cards Multipurpose cards are also called bank credit cards because banks issue them. Multipurpose cards work the way single-purpose cards do. Consumers can pay them off or pay only part of the bill, with interest due on the unpaid balance. These cards may be used at many different stores, restaurants, and other businesses all over the world. MasterCard and VISA are multipurpose cards.

Travel and Entertainment Cards These cards work a little differently than the others. Holders of travel and entertainment cards must pay the full amount due each month. Cards such as American Express® and Diners Club® are examples. They are accepted

Standard Formats
Did you ever wonder why all credit cards are the same size? The International Organization for Standardization developed a standard that defines the format for credit cards. It specifies a size of 3.370 × 2.125 inches for bank cards. *Why do you think it is necessary to formally define the size of a credit card?*

Science / Tech **TRENDS**

Smart Cards
More and more credit cards around the world have computer chips embedded in the plastic. The information in the chip can be read when waved in front of a special reader. Smart cards first became popular in Europe and Asia as stored-value cards. They could be purchased to pay for calls in phone booths or fees on toll roads. Increasingly, chips are showing up in credit cards everywhere. The chips can hold more than 100 times as much information as the magnetic strip on a standard card, which increases security for consumers using them. MasterCard, Visa, and American Express each offer a version of these smart cards.

Web Quest
Go to the *Introduction to Business* Online Learning Center through **glencoe.com** for links to Web sites where you can find out more about smart cards. What are some of the positives and negatives associated with their use?

glencoe.com

TEACH (cont.)

S Skill Practice
Guided Practice
Compare Ask students to compare single-purpose credit cards with multipurpose cards. (Single-purpose credit cards can only be used at an issuing business's stores while multipurpose cards can be used at different places.) **L1**

Explain Ask students why credit card companies offer incentives to consumers who use their cards. (They hope consumers will use their cards frequently and pay lots of interest.) **L2**

Draw a Conclusion Ask students to explain why it might be a good idea to have more than one credit card. (Answers will vary but may include that if there is a problem with one card, then another can be used.) **L3**

ASSESS

Review Key Terms
Have students write sentences using each key term.

 Study-to-Go Have students go to the Online Learning Center through **glencoe.com** to download free **Study-to-Go** content to their PDAs or cell phones.

NCLB Activity correlates to Science standards.

Standard Formats Students might suggest that the standard formats allow all cards to be used in a variety of card-reading devices.

Science / Tech **TRENDS**
Web Quest
Smart Cards Positives include faster transaction times and that these cards can be a convenient alternative to cash. A negative is that readers can capture information from your card at a distance—even if you are not buying anything.

RETEACH

W Writing Support

Enrichment

Single-Payment Loans Have students rewrite the paragraph on single-payment loans and use inference to expand the example about farmers. (Students should include the idea that the reason farmers are able to repay the loan after the harvest is because they have the proceeds from the sale of their crops.)

R Reading Strategy

Explain Ask students to explain why an installment is generally preferable to a single-payment loan. (Students should understand that most consumers would find it difficult to save enough cash to pay off a large loan all at once.)

U Universal Access

Students from Economically Diverse Backgrounds

Learning about credit can be particularly difficult for students whose families have limited experience or negative experiences with credit. Explaining the pitfalls of credit without being judgmental will help students learn the concepts and prepare them for dealing with credit in a responsible manner.

Student Activity Workbook 📂 Assign the Section 25.2 Activities.

✔ Reading Check

Analyze The bank considers the home to be collateral, which it can take if the required payments are not paid.

452

● As You Read

Think about a bank or some other financial institution where you could go to get a loan to open a computer repair business.

worldwide for expenses connected with travel, business, and entertainment, such as restaurant and hotel bills, car rentals, and airline tickets. They often have an annual fee, which is higher than the fee for a multipurpose card.

Banks and Other Financial Institutions

Financial institutions such as banks, savings and loans, and credit unions offer many types of loans. However, they tend to place many demands on the borrower, which can make it more difficult to get a loan. For example, these financial institutions only want to lend money to people with good credit ratings. Many credit unions only lend money to credit union members and employees in a certain business or field (such as a teachers credit union).

W **Single-Payment Loan** As the name suggests, the debtor pays back this type of loan in one payment, including interest (at the end of the loan period). Many farmers secure single-payment loans in the spring to pay for their seed and fertilizer. They pay back the loan in the fall, after they harvest their crops.

R **Installment Loan** Student loans, car loans, and home improvement loans are types of **installment loans**, or loans repaid in regular payments over a period of time. The debtor receives the loan money for a certain period, such as two years. Over that period, the debtor makes equal monthly payments, which cover the loan and interest.

U **Mortgage Loan** A mortgage loan is a form of an installment loan, only it is written for a long period, such as 15 to 30 years. It is used to purchase real estate, such as a home. Over the period of the loan, the debtor makes monthly payments. The home serves as **collateral**, which is something of value the bank can take if a borrower does not make the required loan payments.

✔ Reading Check   Analyze What type of collateral does the bank receive when you take out a mortgage loan?

● **Borrow Until Payday** There are businesses that specialize in providing "borrow until payday" loans, which are loans borrowed against an upcoming paycheck. **Why should you avoid using such loans?**

452   Chapter 25

● As You Read

Answers will vary. Students should mention a business plan that demonstrates their ability to repay the loan.

Discuss the Photo

● **Borrow Until Payday** The interest rate on borrow-until-payday loans is usually very high.

Seller-Provided Credit

Many stores provide credit for their customers. Clothing, furniture, and appliance stores as well as car dealerships are among those that offer credit to customers.

Consumer Finance Companies

Consumer finance companies specialize in loans to people who might not be able to get credit elsewhere. Loans from consumer finance companies cost more because there is greater risk involved.

Other Types of Loans

For people who have difficulty getting a loan, there are other **options**, although they are the most costly. *Payday advance services* offer short-term loans until payday. However, they charge high fees and interest. A *pawnshop* loan is based on the value of something you own that is left with a pawnbroker as security against money borrowed. You can later buy back your item. "Borrow until payday" loans are short-term, usually for 5 to 14 days. The cost of this kind of loan is especially high.

● As You Read

Think about high-interest loans that some companies offer. What reasons might a person have to seek a payday advance or pawnshop loan?

NCLB Activity correlates to English Language Arts standards.

Section 25.2

● After You Read

Review Key Concepts
1. Discuss the different sources of credit.
2. How is a multipurpose credit card different from a travel and entertainment card?
3. Which types of loans usually cost the most?

Academic Skills
4. **English Language Arts** Work with three or four other students to research the kinds of consumer credit used in at least two countries. Are there banks there? Are there places where you cannot use credit cards? Prepare a group presentation to present your findings.

5. **English Language Arts** Tina found a coat she liked at a department store, but it cost $20 more than she had. She did not have any credit cards and decided to leave. As she approached the exit, an employee offered her instant credit if she would apply for a store credit card. Tina signed up for the card and charged the coat. Write a sentence or two explaining various ways in which the store will benefit from extending credit to Tina.

 Go to the *Introduction to Business* Online Learning Center through **glencoe.com** to check your answers.

C Critical Thinking

Assess

Consumer Finance Companies Ask students to explain why consumer finance companies offer interest rates that are almost always higher than mortgage interest. (The mortgage rate is lower because the dwelling serves as collateral.)

● As You Read

unforeseen expenses

ASSESS

● After You Read

Have students complete the Section 25.2 After You Read section review.

Online Study Tools

Have students go to the Online Learning Center through **glencoe.com** to:

- Take the Section 25.2 **Practice Test**.
- Download free **Study-to-Go** content to their PDAs or cell phones.

CLOSE

Culminating Activity
Consumer Credit
Organize the class into three groups, and assign one of the following topics to each group (1) Credit: The Promise to Pay; (2) Pros and Cons of Using Credit; (3) Sources of Credit. Have groups develop a consumer-education segment for a television magazine show based on the content.

Section 25.2

Review Key Concepts
1. retail stores, financial institutions, and finance companies
2. Multipurpose cards are used at many stores; travel and entertainment cards can be used only for travel and entertainment expenses.
3. pawn shops, payday advance loans, and "borrow-until-payday" loans

Academic Skills
4. **English Language Arts** Answers will vary, depending on the countries studied.
5. **English Language Arts** The store will benefit by making the sale of the coat and by encouraging Tina to shop there again because she has charging privileges.

Vocabulary Review

1. Students should write complete sentences using each term correctly.

Review Key Concepts

2. an agreement to get money, goods, or services now in exchange for a promise to pay in the future; the amount of interest is based on interest rate, amount of time the borrower has the loan, and amount of the loan

3. consumers, businesses, and governments

4. Advantages: provides convenience, helps establish a credit rating, aids record keeping, and encourages economic growth; disadvantages: easy to misuse, expense of interest, and commitment of future income

5. Places include banks, credit unions, and savings and loans. Sellers of goods and services, finance companies, and pawn shops also offer credit. Three types of credit cards are single-purpose, multipurpose, and travel and entertainment cards.

Critical Thinking

6. Cash is better than credit for paying transportation costs. Credit is better when ordering items online or over the telephone and when making expensive purchases.

Section 25.1 *Summary*

Credit Essentials Credit is an agreement to get money, goods, or services now by promising to pay later. Creditors charge a fee (interest) for using their money. Consumers, businesses, and the government use credit extensively. Consumers find that credit is convenient, useful in an emergency, and helps to establish a credit rating and to keep track of one's spending. It also contributes to the growth of the economy. However, it costs more to buy items on credit, commits future income, can lead to overspending, and if handled improperly, may lower your credit rating.

Section 25.2 *Summary*

Types of Credit There are many different types of credit, including charge accounts, credit cards, single-payment loans, installment loans, mortgage loans, seller-provided credit, pawnshop loans, and "borrow until payday" loans. Loans are given by banks, credit unions, and savings and loan associations. Other financial firms specialize in specific loans (such as credit cards), and businesses that sell goods and services also offer credit. Businesses such as consumer finance companies offer loans to people who have difficulty obtaining one. However, these loans are usually costly.

Vocabulary Review

1. On a sheet of paper, use each of these key terms and academic vocabulary terms in a sentence.

Key Terms

credit
creditor
debtor
interest
consumer credit
commercial credit
credit rating
charge account
installment loans
collateral

Academic Vocabulary

military
contributes
constantly
committed
available
annual
range
options

Review Key Concepts

2. Define credit and indicate three factors which affect the interest that is paid.
3. Name different groups in our economy who use credit.
4. Identify three advantages and disadvantages of using credit.
5. Name the places where you can get credit, and list the three different types of credit cards.

7. Your credit rating plays a major role in whether lenders will issue credit or loans to you and in determining how much interest you will pay.

8. Credit card companies try to persuade you to use their cards because they earn money from every transaction and from the interest cardholders pay.

9. Using credit does not necessarily mean that someone has money problems. Many people use credit wisely and efficiently. For example, many people use credit to obtain things such as cars and homes. Without credit it would take a long time to save for these purchases.

10. Credit makes purchasing supplies, materials, and other goods and services easier. It helps companies in the process of selling their products and services to consumers.

Critical Thinking

6. Describe two situations in which cash is more convenient than credit. Then describe two situations in which credit is better to use than cash.

7. Why is it important to take care of your credit rating?

8. Why do credit card companies try so hard to persuade you to use their card?

9. If people use credit, does that mean they have money problems? Explain.

10. How do businesses use credit to help sell their products?

11. Imagine that you have a good credit rating and you want to buy a new car. Which would be the best place to get a loan for it, a bank, a consumer finance company, or a pawn shop?

12. Some people use a credit card and never pay any interest. How can that be?

13. Suppose you would like to pay for a course to improve your job skills, a new computer, and a new TV. You do not have enough cash, so you consider taking out a loan to buy at least one of them. Which one would be the best use of credit? Which would be the least wise use of it?

Write About It

14. Write at least two paragraphs either for or against this statement: "People should be charged the same interest rate, regardless of their credit rating."

15. Your friend wants to buy a ring for $400 using a credit card. He would pay 2% of the price each month, which would be $8. He would have to make payments for 95 months. Calculate the total cost of the purchase with interest. Write a letter to him about your opinion of the deal.

16. Write a short essay on whether you think it is fair or unfair for people to have to pay so much in interest on payday loans.

17. Research credit cards that offer rewards. Describe in writing the nature of the rewards you can get if you use them.

18. Write an e-mail to your teacher discussing how you will start to develop your credit rating.

19. Write a paragraph either agreeing or disagreeing with the following statement: "Businesses that charge high interest rates should be banned from the marketplace."

Technology Applications

Spreadsheet Software
20. Research interest rates and credit lines for multipurpose credit cards. Find examples of at least four and compare their rates, repayment terms, and the application process for each card. Do the companies charge an annual fee? How much are penalties for being over a credit limit or making a late payment? Develop a spreadsheet with your findings. Highlight the cells that show your choice for the best credit card to use.

Business Ethics

Borrowing from an Employer
21. You have an emergency, and you ask your employer for a loan. She gives you $100. You sign a form indicating that you received the loan and will start repaying it next month. However, you quit the job the following week. Your former manager calls and asks whether you are going to pay back the loan. You indicate that since you are a minor, the contract is voidable, meaning that you do not have to abide by it. Is it a good idea to avoid the contract?

Chapter 25 Review and Activities **455**

Critical Thinking

11. Banks charge low interest rates to consumers with good credit ratings. They offer lower rates than the other businesses mentioned.

12. Credit card users who pay off the balance every month never pay any interest.

13. The course would likely be the best use of credit because it would help the student to improve his or her job skills.

Write About It

14. Answers will depend on students' opinions.

15. Payments = $8 (95 payments) = $760; $760 − $400 = $360 in interest. The letter could indicate that the interest almost doubles the cost of the ring.

16. Some students may think it is fair for people to pay higher interest for money borrowed without security. Others may feel that it is not fair because the total cost is so high in relation to the amount people make in salaries and wages.

17. Answers will depend on the credit cards researched.

18. Students should understand a good credit rating and how to keep it.

19. Students who agree may think that a ban would protect some consumers from high rates. Those who disagree might say that these businesses allow people with a poor credit rating to get a loan.

Technology Applications

20. Spreadsheets will depend on the choices of credit cards that are researched.

Business Ethics

21. No, it is not a good idea to void the contract. The contract might be voidable, but repaying the loan is the ethical thing to do. Your actions tell the employer a lot about your character. If you void the contract, you are basically saying that you are not responsible for your commitments.

Applying Academics to Business

22. Answers should point out that *debt* and *debit* are synonyms. *Debit* is a term used in accounting to refer to the recording of a debt. Other synonyms are *charge, deduction,* and *balance due*. An antonym for both is *credit*.

23. Sam, Jill, and Tina are unlikely to receive credit. Guillermo's score is right at the cutoff, so he stands a better chance.

24. Answers will vary, depending on the situation. Students should point out that both the lender and the borrower should benefit from credit.

25. Number lines will vary, depending on the rates found for each type of institution.

Active Learning

26. Answers will depend on the ads that are chosen and on the responses of the survey takers.

Business in the Real World

27. Tables should be based on the types of applications that are reviewed.

Applying Academics to Business

English Language Arts
22. What is the difference in the meanings of the words *debt* and *debit*? List some synonyms and antonyms for each and use each in a sentence.

Mathematics
23. The Fair Isaac Corporation® (FICO) rates consumer credit worthiness according to a scale that ranges from 350 to 900 points. A good score is often considered to be 600 or greater. Banks or other companies may not give credit to those with scores below 600. List whether the following people are likely to receive credit.

Name	Credit Score
Sam	300
Jill	590
Tina	480
Guillermo	600

THEORY **Reading a Chart** Read down the column and across the row to the right to find information in a chart.

English Language Arts
24. Find newspaper and magazine articles and advertisements that demonstrate uses of credit by consumers, businesses, and governments. Write a paragraph explaining who benefits most from these examples of credit.

Mathematics
25. Research credit and the cost of credit from a variety of institutions, such as those listed below. Convert the rates to decimals, and use a number line to rank them in order from the lowest interest rate to the highest.

- consumer finance company
- revolving charge account
- travel and entertainment credit card
- credit union
- commercial bank

THEORY **Number Line** Positive decimals closer to zero on a number line are less than decimals closer to 1.

Active Learning

Analyze Advertisements
26. During the next two weeks, save all the advertisements and junk mail that try to persuade you and your family to apply for a credit card. Keep a log of the promotional offers. Conduct a mini-survey among your family and friends, and find out whether they would choose one of the cards based on the advertising material that has been sent to your home.

Business in the Real World

Comparing Credit Cards
27. Obtain a credit card application from two different retail stores or gas stations. Form groups. Compare the applications, listing similarities and differences. Be sure to examine the interest rates and repayment procedures. Then create a table using word-processing or spreadsheet software. Discuss your findings with the class.

ExamView Assessment Suite CD allows you to print out ready-made unit and chapter tests, complete with answer keys. You can also create customized tests.

TeacherWorks Plus provides complete teacher resources in one convenient package. It includes customizable lesson plans in calendar format, and instant access to many print program resources.

ADVICE ON USING CREDIT

28. Interview a consumer credit counselor or a financial adviser at a bank, asking the following questions:

a. What are the major consumer credit problems and their causes?

b. What is their advice for using credit?

c. Is a person's credit rating very important? Why or why not?

FIND YOUR DREAM JOB

29. Go to the *Introduction to Business* Online Learning Center through **glencoe.com** for a link to the Occupational Outlook Handbook Web site. Click on the "OOH Search/A-Z Index" link and enter the job category "bill and account collectors." Then write a one-page report about this area of occupation. Conclude your report with a list of things you could do now to prepare yourself to pursue the occupation.

Role Play

SHOP AROUND FOR A CAR

30. Situation You are a consumer advocate for a local news station. You are asked to prepare a news segment advising consumers on buying a car.

Activity Prepare a presentation that advocates that people shop around for credit when buying a car.

Evaluation You will be evaluated on how well you meet the following performance indicators:

- Show how consumers can save by reviewing different car loans.
- Answer questions from the newscaster(s) and/or consumers about buying a car.
- Use credit terminology correctly.
- Organize ideas in a logical sequence.
- Project your voice, and use correct English.

Standardized Test Practice

Directions Choose the letter of the best answer. Write the letter for the answer on a separate piece of paper.

1. $15\frac{1}{2}$% of [   ] = **$403**

A $6,246.5

B $60.45

C $26.00

D $2,600

 **TEST-TAKING TIP** To control the stress of test taking, approach exams with a positive attitude. View the exam as an opportunity to show how much you have studied and to receive a reward for the studying you have done.

 READING Go to the *Introduction to Business* Online Learning Center through **glencoe.com** for a list of outside reading suggestions.

glencoe.com   **Chapter 25**   Review and Activities   **457**

 **STRATEGIES FOR STANDARDIZED TEST PREP SUCCESS**

Test Stress Point out to students that controlling the anxiety associated with taking tests may not be easy, but it can be done by being well prepared, adjusting their attitude, learning some specific relaxation techniques, and monitoring their ability to concentrate during a test.

Real LIFE skills

28. Answers will depend on the interviewees' responses.

Business CAREERS

29. Bill and account collectors track overdue accounts and attempt collections. Some employers are third-party collection agencies and others work in-house for the original creditor. In-house collectors work in company offices; third-party-agency collectors work at a call center. Most work 40 hours per week. Training and qualifications include a high school diploma, but some employers prefer some college. Supervisory positions are often filled from within. The job outlook is for faster-than-average growth. As preparation, take computer and business classes, and develop your communication skills.

Role Play

30. Presentations should address the competencies noted in the Role Play. Students should indicate an understanding of the importance of comparing different loans and having good credit.

Standardized Test Practice
1. D

Standards-Based Lesson Planning
Introduction to Business provides students with instruction and assessment in the following fundamental content areas:

Content Standards Correlations	
Demonstrate an understanding of the purpose and importance of credit.	pp. 462, 467, 469, 471–473
Determine the purpose of a credit contract.	pp. 461–464
Analyze the requirements and costs of obtaining credit. Analyze characteristics of someone who would be granted credit.	p. 463
Discuss the factors on which credit is granted and the cost of credit.	pp. 463–469, 471–473
Compute cost of using credit.	pp. 464, 468–469, 471–473
Compute simple interest loans.	p. 472
Compare and contrast the use of different credit applications.	p. 473

NCLB Activities, information, and skills practice will help your students attain No Child Left Behind proficiency. Students will improve their abilities in the following academic standards areas:

Academic Standards Correlations		
English Language Arts	Activities/Features	Page
NCTE 3 Apply strategies to interpret texts	After You Read Applying Academics to Business	pp. 469, 472
NCTE 6 Apply knowledge of language structure and conventions to discuss texts	After You Read Applying Academics to Business	pp. 469, 472
NCTE 12 Use language to accomplish individual purposes	After You Read	p. 469
Mathematics		
Algebra Represent and analyze mathematical situations and structures using algebraic symbols	Ask S&P	p. 458
Number and Operations Compute fluently and make reasonable estimates	Applying Academics to Business Standardized Test Practice	pp. 472, 473
Algebra Use mathematical models to represent and understand quantitative relationships	After You Read	p. 464
Number and Operations Understand numbers, ways of representing numbers, relationships among numbers, and number systems	Standardized Test Practice	p. 473
Problem Solving Apply and adapt a variety of appropriate strategies to solve problems	Applying Academics to Business	p. 472
Science		
Content Standard F Students should develop understanding of science and technology in local, national, and global challenges	Science/Tech Trends	p. 467

Correlations   This chart shows the 21st Century Skills, foundation skills, and workplace competencies that students develop as they work in this chapter.

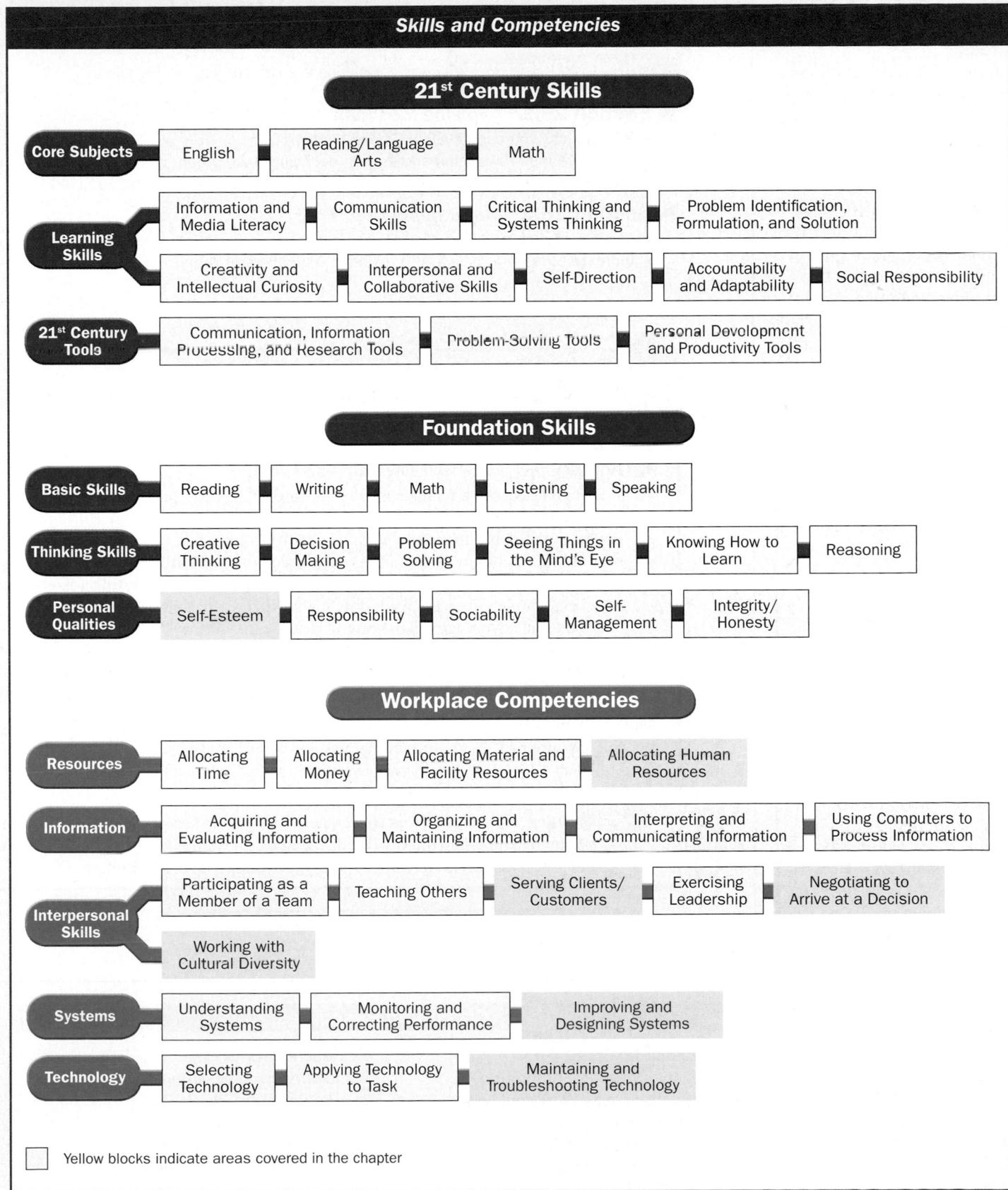

Skills and Competencies

21st Century Skills

Core Subjects
- English
- Reading/Language Arts
- Math

Learning Skills
- Information and Media Literacy
- Communication Skills
- Critical Thinking and Systems Thinking
- Problem Identification, Formulation, and Solution
- Creativity and Intellectual Curiosity
- Interpersonal and Collaborative Skills
- Self-Direction
- Accountability and Adaptability
- Social Responsibility

21st Century Tools
- Communication, Information Processing, and Research Tools
- Problem-Solving Tools
- Personal Development and Productivity Tools

Foundation Skills

Basic Skills
- Reading
- Writing
- Math
- Listening
- Speaking

Thinking Skills
- Creative Thinking
- Decision Making
- Problem Solving
- Seeing Things in the Mind's Eye
- Knowing How to Learn
- Reasoning

Personal Qualities
- Self-Esteem
- Responsibility
- Sociability
- Self-Management
- Integrity/Honesty

Workplace Competencies

Resources
- Allocating Time
- Allocating Money
- Allocating Material and Facility Resources
- Allocating Human Resources

Information
- Acquiring and Evaluating Information
- Organizing and Maintaining Information
- Interpreting and Communicating Information
- Using Computers to Process Information

Interpersonal Skills
- Participating as a Member of a Team
- Teaching Others
- Serving Clients/Customers
- Exercising Leadership
- Negotiating to Arrive at a Decision
- Working with Cultural Diversity

Systems
- Understanding Systems
- Monitoring and Correcting Performance
- Improving and Designing Systems

Technology
- Selecting Technology
- Applying Technology to Task
- Maintaining and Troubleshooting Technology

Yellow blocks indicate areas covered in the chapter

How to Get and Keep Credit

Chapter Overview

Introduce the Chapter

How to Get and Keep Credit

Chapter 26 is about choosing a credit card and using credit. It describes the costs of credit and keeping good credit.

Building Background

It is easy to get and misuse credit. Obtaining and using a first credit card can be the beginning of financial responsibility and prosperity or a gateway to financial hardship.

STANDARD &POOR'S

>> Math Answer

Determine the average monthly balance that would make the second card cost less than the first, including interest and fees. ($0.18x \geq 0.14x + 20$). Begin by subtracting $0.14x$ from each side to get $0.04x \geq 20$. Divide each side by 0.04 to get $x \geq 20 \div 0.04$ or $x \geq \$500$.

>> Extension Activity

Ask students to explain what the $500 means. (At the average monthly balance of $500, the cost of the two cards is the same. Lower average balance: the card with the higher APR costs less [no annual fee]. Higher balance: the card with the annual fee is better (interest rate is lower).

NCLB Activity correlates to Math standards.

Chapter Objectives After completing this chapter, you will be able to:

▶ **Section 26.1** *Applying for Credit*
- **Explain** how you can develop a credit history.
- **Name** five factors to think about when deciding which credit card to secure.
- **Define** the three factors that creditors consider when granting a person credit.

▶ **Section 26.2** *Maintaining Credit*
- **Explain** one major difference between credit cards, installment loans, and mortgages.
- **Indicate** at least three ways to maintain a good credit rating.

Ask STANDARD &POOR'S **How to Get and Keep Credit: Inflation Risk**

Q: How can I tell if a variable rate loan is right for me?

A: When you take out a loan or use a credit card, your interest rate will be either fixed or variable. With fixed rate plans, the interest rate does not change throughout the period of the debt. Interest rates change with variable rate plans, which may use such indices as the prime rate, the one-, three-, or six-month Treasury Bill rate, or the Federal Reserve discount rate to determine the rate to use. While a fixed rate may be a couple of percentage points higher than a variable rate at a given time, you have the advantage of knowing what the rate will be. Variable rates increase or decrease your finance charges. Fixed rates can be changed by the lender, on future purchases made on credit cards, for example, although the Truth in Lending Act requires the lender to provide 15 days' notice before changing the rate.

Mathematics You are trying to decide between a credit card that has an APR (annual percentage rate) of 18% and no annual fee, and a card that has an APR of 14% and an annual fee of $20. What would your average monthly balance need to be for the second plan to cost less in fees and interest?

NCLB **THEORY** **Using Variables to Solve an Inequality** A variable is a placeholder for an unknown value. Write an inequality inputting all of the values that you know and using a variable, such as x, to fill in for the value that you are trying to find.

Classroom Resources

- 🖋 Student Edition
- 🖋 Teacher Wraparound Edition
- 📂 Student Activity Workbook with Academic Integration
- 📂 Student Activity Workbook with Academic Integration TAE
- 📂 *Fast File*, Unit 9 Resources
- 📂 Inclusion in the Business Education Classroom

- TeacherWorks Plus
- *ExamView Assessment Suite*
- Presentation Plus!
- Vocabulary PuzzleMaker
- Interactive Student Edition
- Online Student Edition
- Online Learning Center with Podcasts

● **Responsibility** Before creditors will give you a loan, they will want to make sure that you can manage your credit responsibly. **How do creditors gauge whether a credit applicant is responsible?**

Review the Objectives
Introduce the chapter by reviewing the chapter objectives:

Section 26.1 *Objectives*
Explain how you can develop a credit history. (apply for credit, get approved, use the credit, and make payments)

Name five factors to think about when deciding which credit card to secure. (APR, fees, the grace period, whether the interest rate will change, and whether a cosigner is needed)

Define the three factors that creditors consider when granting a person credit. (the three Cs—capacity: enough cash flow to make the payments; character: trustworthiness; capital: enough assets if income flow decreases)

Section 26.2 *Objectives*
Explain one major difference between credit cards, installment loans, and mortgages. (Installment loans and mortgages both have a time limit. Credit cards do not have a time limit.)

Indicate at least three ways to maintain a good credit rating. (Do not expend more than 20 percent of your take-home pay on credit payments. Check your credit file for damaging information. Do not get another credit card If you are at the limit on one of them. Make your payments on time and try to pay more than the minimum amount due.)

Discuss the Photo
● **Responsibility** Read the caption on the photo to students: Before creditors will give you a loan, they will want to make sure that you can manage your credit responsibly.

Ask students: How do creditors gauge whether a credit applicant is responsible? (Creditors use credit reports to find out if credit applicants are a good credit risk.)

Section 26.1

FOCUS

Bell Ringer Activity

Applying for Credit

Make copies of a credit card application for students. (Consider putting an X thru the credit card company name and blacking out the "send to" information before making copies.) Ask students to work in pairs to review the application and discuss the information that an applicant must supply.

Preteaching

Presentation Plus!

The Presentation Plus! CD provides visual teaching aids for this section.

PuzzleMaker

Use the Vocabulary PuzzleMaker to create a puzzle of the section's key terms. Students can complete the puzzle on paper or on a computer.

Graphic Organizer

Tell students to go to the Online Learning Center through **glencoe.com** for a printable graphic organizer. (Answers include: the three Cs of credit—capacity: applicant's ability to repay the loan; character: whether an applicant has proven to be trustworthy in repaying debts; and capital: amount of money applicant has beyond his or her debts)

N C L B Connects academics to content.

Applying for Credit

Reading Guide

Before You Read

Consider what you know about using credit and how you might use a credit card.

Read to Learn
- Explain how you can develop a credit history.
- Name five factors to think about when deciding which credit card to secure.
- Define the three factors that creditors consider when granting a person credit.

D

The Main Idea

Developing a credit history is important. The first step will be choosing a credit card and applying for it. Before deciding to issue credit to a consumer, a creditor looks at the applicant's capacity, character, and capital.

Key Concepts
- Developing a Credit History
- Selecting a Credit Card
- Applying for a Credit Card

Vocabulary

Key Terms
- annual percentage rate (APR)
- cash advance
- cosigner
- grace period
- credit limit

Academic Vocabulary

You will find these words in your reading and on your tests. Make sure you know their meanings.
- impact
- anticipate
- submit
- minimum

Graphic Organizer

In a figure like the one below, list and describe the three Cs of credit.

The Three Cs of Credit

 Go to the *Introduction to Business* Online Learning Center through **glencoe.com** for a printable graphic organizer.

Academic Standards

English Language Arts

N C L B

    NCTE 1 Read texts to acquire new information

    NCTE 9 Develop an understanding of diversity in language use across cultures

Mathematics

    Number and Operations Understand meanings of operations and how they relate to one another

---

Reading Guide

Before You Read

Consumers can use a credit card wisely by keeping track of their spending and staying within a budget.

D Develop Concepts

The Main Idea Ask students: Why is developing a credit history important? (Lenders use a person's credit history to make decisions about granting credit and the interest rate they will charge.)

Developing a Credit History

Credit can have a major **impact** on a consumer's life. If a consumer uses credit responsibly, it can make life easier in a number of ways. If the consumer uses credit irresponsibly, his or her ability to make future purchases will be harmed. To develop a credit history, you will need to apply for credit, be approved for it, use it, and then make payments to the creditor.

How do you prove to others that you can handle credit responsibly? First, develop a credit history. Most people start by getting a credit card in their own name (if they are 18 years of age or older) or getting one with an adult family member. Before getting a credit card, though, it is important to understand how credit cards work.

● **As You Read**

Think about ways you might use credit in the future.

Selecting a Credit Card

There are several things to consider when choosing a credit card. The five main factors to consider are the interest rate, extra fees, whether the interest rate will change, whether a cosigner is needed, and whether there is a grace period. Some other questions to ask are:

- What will the cost of credit be?
- Who will accept the card?
- What is the credit limit?
- Will I be able to use the card to get cash?

The Cost of Credit

Credit cards allow people to purchase goods and services without using cash. They enable consumers to make major purchases that might otherwise take years of saving. They also provide security during emergencies. Consumers usually need a credit card to rent a car or to place a reservation for a hotel room. However, for all of their conveniences, credit cards come with a cost.

Interest Rates To gauge the cost of credit, first look at the annual percentage rate. The **annual percentage rate (APR)** determines the cost of credit on a yearly basis. For example, an APR of 18 percent means that for every $100 you owe, you pay $18 per year ($100 × .18) or $1.50 per month. It is important to note if the interest rate will change on a credit card. In many cases, a credit card might offer a low introductory rate such as 3 percent. After a few months, the rate could jump to 20 percent.

International Business

International Monetary Fund

The International Monetary Fund (IMF) is an organization of 184 nations that monitors the global financial system. In the 1930s, a majority of industrial countries began trying to defend their economies with tougher restrictions on imports. Some countries abolished foreign imports entirely, while others devalued their currency in an attempt to defend their economies. These practices eventually proved detrimental to the economies they were trying to protect, and their demise showed the need for a global financial monitoring organization.

Examples of Languages Across Cultures

Q: In Finnish, how do you say: "How do you say _____?"

A: **Kuinka sanotaan** (pronounced: Koo-ink ǎ sǎ-nō-tǎǎn)

Find out more about the IMF and how it was founded. What are the purposes of the IMF, and how have they changed since its creation?

TEACH

Discussion Starter
Developing a Credit History
Start a discussion by asking this question: How can you prove to others that you can handle credit responsibly? (Students might suggest applying for a credit card and using it responsibly. They also might suggest getting a family member to cosign for a small loan and making sure that the payments are made on time. Establishing a pattern of saving may also be suggested.)

R **Reading Strategy**
Recognize the Most Important Idea Ask which question is most important when selecting a credit card. Follow up by asking them to explain their choice. (Students should recognize the cost of credit as the most important question.)

● **As You Read**

Students should plan to show that they can pay debts on time, possibly by starting with a small loan or a credit card with an adult family member.

International Business

International Monetary Fund Answers will vary, but should indicate that some of the purposes of the IMF are to promote international monetary cooperation, facilitate balanced growth of international trade, and to promote exchange stability. The technical and financial assistance it provides as well as surveillance practices have been adapted to meet the needs of an evolving global economy.

TEACH (cont.)

S Skill Practice

Guided Practice

Explain Ask students to explain how to calculate the monthly interest rate when you know the APR. (Divide the APR by 12—the number of months in a year) **L1**

Calculate Ask students how much interest a consumer would be charged for one month on a balance of $200 with an 18% APR. (The interest is $3.00. (0.18 ÷ 12 = 0.015; $200 × 0.015 = $3.00)) **L2**

Investigate and Demonstrate Have students investigate how credit card companies calculate interest on credit card debt. Ask them to demonstrate their findings. (Demonstrations will vary but should include an explanation of the math involved.) **L3**

ASSESS

Review Key Terms

Have students write sentences using each key term.

 **Study-to-Go** Have students go to the Online Learning Center through **glencoe.com** to download free **Study-to-Go** content to their PDAs or cell phones.

● As You Read

Consumers will have to pay more if they keep using those cards.

✔ Reading Check

Explain Examine the annual percentage rate and the cost of credit on a yearly basis.

462

● As You Read

Think about how the cost of credit can increase when low introductory rates offered for credit cards rise considerably.

S **Fees** Credit card companies charge different fees for different services. Some charge an annual fee. There is usually a fee for a cash advance. A **cash advance** is a loan given in cash by a credit card company in **anticipation** of the borrower's being able to repay it. A late- or missed-payment fee is charged when a payment is missed or is not made on time. Another fee is charged if the card holder is over the credit limit.

✔ Reading Check

Explain What is the best way to gauge the cost of credit?

Other Considerations

There are other matters to consider before you will be able to get a credit card. One is that you may need a cosigner. A **cosigner** is someone who agrees to be responsible for a debt if the main applicant does not repay it. Another thing to consider is whether there is a grace period for payments. A **grace period** is an amount of time allowed to repay a debt without having to pay interest charges. There is also a grace period to make a late payment before a penalty is charged.

BusinessWeek *Reader and Case Study*

Personal Finance for Freshmen

College students need money smarts if they want to succeed after graduation. Increasingly, schools are offering assistance.

Undergrads who believe GPAs and test scores determine whether they can go to graduate school should consider another number: their credit score. Some law and medical schools encourage—and a few actually require—admitted students to submit their credit score to help the school decide if applicants have the means and commitment to complete the degree. Georgetown Law School urges students with severe credit issues to defer for a year while getting their finances in order. "The decisions they make today have a cumulative impact on practicing law," says Ruth Lammert-Reeves, Georgetown's assistant dean for financial aid. According to Lammert-Reeves, bar examiners in states such as California and New York take an applicant's observance of fiduciary responsibility into consideration. The Medical College of Wisconsin even reserves the right to deny

admittance if a student doesn't provide a clean credit report.

Such actions may seem harsh, but institutions say they want to ensure that financial ignorance doesn't jeopardize a student's graduate education or career aspirations.

 CASE STUDY Go to the *Introduction to Business* Online Learning Center through **glencoe.com** for the *BusinessWeek* Reader Case Study.

Active Learning

Consider ways the three Cs of credit apply to your life—and to your academic plans. First, develop a spreadsheet that applies each facet of creditworthiness to your personal needs and experiences. Next, create a row that applies each facet of creditworthiness to your future goals, and fill that row with the steps you will need to take to meet your goals in life.

462 **Chapter 26** How to Get and Keep Credit

glencoe.com

BusinessWeek *Reader and Case Study*

Personal Finance for Freshmen

@ CASE STUDY Have students go to the *Introduction to Business* Online Learning Center through **glencoe.com** to download a Case Study activity that corresponds to the article. The activity and answer key are also available on the TeacherWorks Plus CD.

Active Learning

Spreadsheets will vary, but students should apply the facets of creditworthiness to their lives. The goal of this exercise is to have students begin to grasp the steps they need to take to build credit so that their future financial plans can be realized.

● **A Promise Made**
Americans buy a lot of things with credit cards. **What promises are made when making a credit purchase?**

Applying for a Credit Card

W To secure a credit card, a consumer has to fill out an application form and **submit** it to the credit card company. The form asks for information about where the applicant lives and works, and what other credit the applicant has received. It also asks questions about an applicant's income and savings.

Creditworthiness: The Three Cs

R Before creditors give a consumer a charge or credit account, they want to make sure the consumer is worth the risk. They consider the applicant's capacity, character, and capital, commonly referred to as the "three Cs of credit."

✔ **Reading Check** **Identify** What are the three Cs of credit?

U *Capacity* is the applicant's ability to repay the loan. To determine an applicant's capacity to pay, creditors will verify the applicant's employment and income. If the applicant already has a lot of debt in relation to his or her level of income, lenders will be less willing to extend more credit. An applicant's *character* shows whether he or she has proven to be trustworthy in repaying debts. They will ask for credit references or check with credit bureaus, businesses that provide information about consumers' creditworthiness to companies or banks. They may ask for personal or professional references, and they may check to see if the applicant has a criminal record. An applicant's *capital* is the amount of money the applicant has beyond his or her debts. It includes savings and investments. Creditors want to know if an applicant has capital that can be used as collateral.

Credit Ratings A credit rating, or credit score, is a measure of a person's ability and willingness to pay debts on time. These ratings come from Fair Isaac Corporation (FICO). The company's FICO scores, which measure credit risk, are the most widely used credit scores in the world. *Why do you think credit issuers rely on FICO scores?*

Section 26.1 Applying for Credit **463**

Discuss the Photo
● **A Promise Made** You will pay the amount back at a later time with interest.

Credit Ratings A good credit rating tells other lenders that a consumer is a responsible borrower and a good credit risk. The ratings are based on more information than credit issuers may have. FICO ratings also allow credit issuers to compare applicants.

Section 26.1

RETEACH

W **Writing Support**
Enrichment
Applying for a Credit Card
Ask students to write a list of concerns an adult friend or relative might have about cosigning for a credit card. (Lists will vary. Students should recognize that cosigners will have the same list of concerns that lenders have.)

R **Reading Strategy**
Draw a Diagram Have students draw a diagram linking the "three Cs of credit" in a way that makes them memorable and understandable. (Diagrams may vary, but an acrostic, a triangle, or a forked branch would all be ways to distinguish the qualities.)

U **Universal Access**
Students with Difficulties in Math Calculating interest and finance charges can be confusing to students who have math difficulties. Make sure they know how to use the formulas for determining the cost of credit. Have them go through an exercise in which they make an imaginary credit purchase and must calculate and compare the costs using different interest rates. Explain that knowing how to find the best credit bargain can save them hundreds of dollars.

Student Activity Workbook ☛ Assign the Section 26.1 Activities.

✔ **Reading Check**

Identify capacity, character, and capital

463

RETEACH (cont.)

C Critical Thinking

Predict

Young Borrowers Ask students to predict the credit limits for most young people. (Credit limits are likely to be low because most young people have little property [capital] or income.)

● As You Read

Answers may include a car, a computer, or other items of value.

ASSESS

● After You Read

Have students complete the Section 26.1 After You Read section review.

Online Study Tools

Have students go to the Online Learning Center through **glencoe.com** to:

- Take the Section 26.1 **Practice Test**.
- Download free **Study-to-Go** content to their PDAs or cell phones.

CLOSE

Culminating Activity
Making Payments

Organize small groups. Have students calculate the total price of a $500 item using a credit card with an APR of 20% and a minimum payment of $20. Have students prepare a poster showing their purchase, the purchase price, the interest, and the number of payments required. (Posters should communicate the cost of credit.)

464

● As You Read

Think about the capital you have that would qualify you for a loan. What are some of your assets?

NCLB Activity correlates to Math standards.

Credit Limits

Creditors also consider capacity, character, and capital when determining the amount of a card holder's credit limit. A **credit limit** is the maximum amount a card holder can charge on a credit card. If a person pays his or her bills on time, most creditors will raise the person's credit limit.

Making the Minimum Payment

Credit card companies usually send card holders a monthly statement of their charges, the balance they owe, and the minimum amount due. If a consumer owes $2,000 on a credit card, he or she might have a minimum payment of $50 to make each month. Many people make the **minimum** payment due each month. However, consumers who pay more than the minimum amount will pay less in interest and will pay off their debt more quickly. When a consumer signs a credit card application, the application is a legal contract. The minimum payment is in the contract. If the consumer does not make at least the minimum payment, the consumer is not meeting his or her legal obligation.

Section 26.1

● After You Read

Review Key Concepts
1. How can a consumer develop a credit history?
2. What is an annual percentage rate? Why is it important?
3. What are the three Cs of credit?

Academic Skills
NCLB
4. **Mathematics** Mary Ellen bought some furniture on credit. Her total came to $1,036.29 and she qualified for interest-free financing. She made a down payment of $36.29 and agreed to pay $50 twice a month until the $1,000 balance was paid. As an alternative option, the store sent her a payment book. She could choose to use the 24 monthly payment coupons and pay the amount of $49.92. What are the differences in the two payment options?

 THEORY Interest Rate To determine the rate of interest given a sequence of payments, add up the payments, subtract the principal, and divide the difference by the principal.

 Math For math help, go to the Math Appendix.

@ Go to the *Introduction to Business* Online Learning Center through **glencoe.com** to check your answers.

Section 26.1

Review Key Concepts
1. apply for credit, be approved, use the credit, and make payments to the creditor
2. the cost of credit on a yearly basis; it determines the amount of interest that a consumer will pay on a debt
3. capacity, character, and capital

Academic Skills
4. **Mathematics** $49.92 × 24 = $1,198.08
$1,198.08 − $1,000 = $198.08
At $50 twice a month, Mary Ellen will pay no interest and will be debt free in 10 months. With the other option, she will pay an additional $198.08.

Maintaining Credit

FOCUS

Reading Guide

● Before You Read

Think about the ways that you could use credit wisely.

Read to Learn
- Explain one major difference between credit cards, installment loans, and mortgages.
- Indicate at least three ways to maintain a good credit rating.

The Main Idea
There are several similarities between credit cards, installment loans, and mortgages. There are also differences. Keeping a good credit rating is important if the consumer is interested in getting loans at a reasonable cost.

D

Key Concepts
- Understanding Loans and Mortgages
- Keeping a Healthy Credit Record

Vocabulary
Key Terms

variable rate	secured loan
fixed rate	unsecured loan
down payment	garnishment of wages
principal	repossess
finance charge	

Academic Vocabulary
You will find these words in your reading and on your tests. Make sure you know their meanings.

similar	maintain
portion	obtain

Graphic Organizer
In a table like the one below, name and give examples of the five factors that affect your credit score.

Factors Affecting Your Credit Score	Example

 Go to the *Introduction to Business* Online Learning Center through **glencoe.com** for a printable graphic organizer.

Academic Standards
English Language Arts

NCTE 1 Read texts to acquire new information

NCTE 6 Apply knowledge of language structure and conventions to discuss texts

NCTE 12 Use language to accomplish individual purposes

Science

Content Standard F Students should develop understanding of science and technology in local, national, and global challenges

NCLB

Bell Ringer Activity

Maintaining Credit
Display a car dealership advertisement with an interest rate. Ask students if everyone can get the advertised rate. (No.) Point out that people who have low credit ratings often pay interest that is three or more percentage points higher than people with better credit ratings. Ask students to calculate the total payment for an 8% loan and for an 11% loan. ($24,720 and $26,520, respectively, $1,800 difference)

Preteaching

Presentation Plus! ⊙
The Presentation Plus! CD provides visual teaching aids for this section.

PuzzleMaker ⊙
Use the Vocabulary PuzzleMaker to create a puzzle of the section's key terms. Students can complete the puzzle on paper or on a computer.

Graphic Organizer
Tell students to go to the Online Learning Center through **glencoe.com** for a printable graphic organizer. (Answers include: payment history, outstanding debt, length of credit history, recent inquiries of your report, and types of credit in use; examples will vary.)

NCLB Connects academics to content.

Reading Guide

● Before You Read

Consumers can use credit wisely by making responsible purchasing decisions and paying on time.

D Develop Concepts

The Main Idea Ask students: What is a mortgage? (Students should understand that a mortgage is a loan that is used to finance a real estate purchase.)

TEACH

Discussion Starter
How Installment Loans and Mortgages Work
Start a discussion by asking students: What makes a mortgage loan unique? (Answers will vary. When the discussion ends, students should understand that a mortgage is a loan agreement secured by property, specifically real estate.)

R Reading Strategy

Explain Ask students to explain the pros and cons of variable rate mortgages. (Students should understand that a variable rate might go up, which would mean higher payments, but it also might go down, which would mean lower payments. Follow up by pointing out that variable rate loans are attractive because the initial interest rate is usually lower than the current rate for a fixed rate mortgage.)

● **As You Read**

A house is an investment and will likely increase in value. Interest on home loans is also tax deductible.

● **As You Read**

Think about what it would be like to own a home.

Understanding Loans and Mortgages

Many of the principles of owning and using a credit card also apply to other types of credit. Loans and mortgages are **similar** to credit cards. They also allow consumers to borrow money that will be paid back with interest. Their requirements are similar to those of a credit card. However, there are some differences between credit cards and other forms of credit.

How Installment Loans and Mortgages Work

A *loan* is money lent by one party to another at interest. Most loans require collateral and are paid back in installments. Similarly, a *mortgage* is a loan agreement secured by property. This property is usually the item that the mortgage is for, such as a home. Installment loans and mortgages are written for a specific period of time. Many installment loans on appliances are written for three years. Installment loans for cars are often for five years. Mortgages are generally written for 15, 20, or 30 years.

With installment loans and mortgages, the interest rate is the same for the period of the loan except when the loan has a variable rate. A **variable rate** is an interest rate that fluctuates or changes over the life of the loan. A change in the rate causes changes in either the payments or the length of the term of the loan. With a **fixed rate**, the interest rate always remains the same.

● **Dream Home** Mr. and Mrs. Morgan are going to take out a loan to buy land and build their dream home. **What type of loan should they pursue?**

466 Chapter 26

Discuss the Photo
● **Dream Home** Read the photo caption to students: Mr. and Mrs. Morgan are going to take out a loan to buy land and build their dream home.

Ask students: What type of loan should they pursue? (a mortgage)

Science/Tech TRENDS

Online Security

Identity theft is used by criminals for stealing goods and services. In the past, identity theft wasn't a big concern, mainly because it was easy to protect against it. To guard against the theft of important "identity" factors online, be careful about the Web sites you use. Never click on links in e-mails that are sent to you by individuals who are "phishing" for secret identity information and passwords. Furthermore, it is wise to look for the SSL (secure socket layer) protection certificate symbol—signified by an "s" after the familiar "http" header on a URL—before you give out any personal data. This caution is particularly important when any aspect of your identity or financial history is at stake.

WebQuest

Go to the *Introduction to Business* Online Learning Center through **glencoe.com** for links to Web sites where you can research the technology protecting the security of people's identities. Look for information on how consumers can protect themselves as well as what businesses can do.

When purchasing an appliance, automobile, or home with an installment or mortgage loan, the applicant usually has to make a down payment. A **down payment** is a portion of the total cost that is paid when a product or service is purchased. The **principal** is the amount of borrowed money that is still owed and on which interest is based. On a *simple interest* loan, interest is based on the original principal alone.

According to the Truth in Lending Law, the lender must provide the borrower with the APR and all the finance charges of the loan. The **finance charge** is the total amount it costs the borrower to have the lender finance the loan. It includes the interest and any other charges, such as the application fee.

Secured and Unsecured Loans

When you receive an installment loan or mortgage, you must sign a written agreement to repay the loan within a certain period of time. If the loan is backed by collateral, it is called a **secured loan**. A loan that is not backed by collateral is called an **unsecured loan**. Because of the increased risk, the interest rate of an unsecured loan is often higher than that of a secured loan. A loan on a car or boat is secured. Mortgages are secured. Credit card debt is unsecured.

> **✔ Reading Check** **Contrast** What is the difference between a secured loan and an unsecured loan?

> **● As You Read**
>
> Think about the impact a down payment can have on debt. Why would you want to offer a down payment on an item such as a car or a house?

Science/Tech TRENDS

WebQuest

Online Security Answers might include firewalls for personal computers. Student should also be aware of the technology that the government is using, such as biometric fingerprinting and retina scans.

> **● As You Read**
>
> A down payment can help reduce the amount of debt that needs to be financed, which will help reduce the amount of interest the consumer pays.

TEACH (cont.)

S Skill Practice

Guided Practice

Distinguish Ask students to distinguish between a down payment and the principal of a loan. (A down payment is a portion of the total cost; principal is the amount borrowed.) **L1**

Calculate Provide students with five current real estate listings that include prices. Have students calculate the amount needed for a 20% down payment. (Answers will depend on the homes' asking prices.) **L2**

Explain a Relationship Have students explain how the amount of the loan payment stays the same, but the amount of interest and principal paid changes with each payment. (The portion applied to interest falls; the portion applied to principal rises.) **L3**

ASSESS

Review Key Terms

Have students write sentences using each key term.

 **Study-to-Go** Have students go to the Online Learning Center through **glencoe.com** to download free **Study-to-Go** content to their PDAs or cell phones.

> **✔ Reading Check**
>
> **Contrast** A secured loan is backed by collateral. An unsecured loan is not.

 Activity correlates to Science standards.

RETEACH

U Universal Access

Students with Learning Disabilities Students with learning disabilities may have trouble with symbols. Some students can more easily access the information when it is in figures or is read aloud. Students who have difficulty communicating effectively through printing or cursive writing may prefer to use a computer to perform calculations or to dictate their work to another person.

W Writing Support

Enrichment
Keeping a Healthy Credit Score Ask students to write an essay about the importance of keeping a healthy credit score. Suggest that students draw parallels between physical health and financial health. (Essays will vary. Some of the parallels include a healthy credit score and a good blood pressure reading and keeping track of expenses and counting calories.)

R Reading Strategy

Calculate Darin's take-home pay is $3,000 per month. He has school loans and owes money on his credit card. Darin wants to buy a new car with a $600-per-month payment. Based on the advice that you should not spend more than 20% of your income on credit payments, do you think he can afford it? (no, because he has other credit payments)

Student Activity Workbook ☞ Assign the Section 26.2 Activities.

468

● **Credit Score** Credit bureaus take several factors into consideration when assigning your credit score. **Which of these factors do you think is most important? Why?**

U

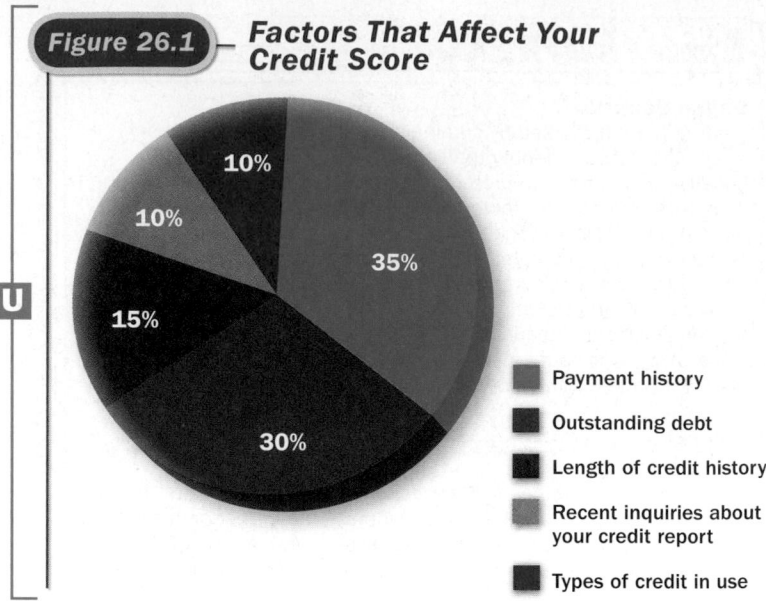

Figure 26.1 **Factors That Affect Your Credit Score**

- ■ Payment history
- ■ Outstanding debt
- ■ Length of credit history
- ■ Recent inquiries about your credit report
- ■ Types of credit in use

Keeping a Healthy Credit Record

W
Someday you might want to get a loan for a major expense, such as a house or business. You also might want to increase your credit limit or apply for a credit card. To continue using credit or to get new credit, you need to **maintain** a good credit rating or score. To get the best credit rating, you need to pay your bills on time. If not, your credit rating will decrease, which will make it more difficult to **obtain** additional credit. Consumers with low credit ratings are usually given higher interest rates and more restrictions. **Figure 26.1** shows the factors credit bureaus consider when determining credit scores.

✔ **Reading Check** **Analyze** Is it possible to get credit if you have a bad credit rating?

Staying Within Your Income Limits

R
You need to know the amount of credit you can afford to have. Experts say consumers should not use more than 20 percent of their income for credit payments. Suppose your first full-time job pays $2,000 a month. After taxes, you bring home $1,500. You have two monthly loan payments—$120 for a student loan and $160 for a car payment. You want to buy a new entertainment system that would cost you $50 a month for three years. Can you afford it? No. Twenty percent of your income is $300. Your total payments each month would be $330, which is 22 percent of your take-home pay.

✔ **Reading Check**
Analyze Yes, it is usually possible to get credit, but at a much higher interest rate and likely with more restrictions.

Figure 26.1
● **Credit Score** Answers will vary. Some students will say outstanding debt is most important, while others will say all of the factors are important.

Signs of Credit Trouble

Here are some signs of credit problems.

- You cannot make monthly loan payments and minimum monthly payments on your credit cards.
- You receive second and third payment-due notices from creditors.
- You get calls from bill collectors.
- Your wages are being garnished. Credit card companies can obtain a court order to take all or part of a debtor's paycheck if he or she stops making payments. This is called **garnishment of wages**.
- The creditor takes back the item you purchased on credit. If that item was offered as collateral and you stopped making payments for it, the creditor has the legal right to **repossess** or take back the item.

There are a number of procedures you can follow to help you get out of financial trouble. Those procedures are discussed in Chapter 27.

 Activity correlates to English Language Arts standards.

Section 26.2

After You Read

Review Key Concepts

1. Which type of loan usually carries a lower interest rate—a secured or an unsecured loan? Why?
2. What is the maximum percentage of your income that you should allocate to credit payments?
3. What is garnishment of wages?

Academic Skills

4. **English Language Arts** The word *debt* comes from the Latin word *debitum* meaning "something owed." Research and describe the origin of the word *credit* and list some related words.

5. **English Language Arts** Imagine that you have decided to attend a special summer camp related to one of your interests (for example, music, sports, government, or debating). The camp experience promises to be very valuable to you, but it will cost $1,000 for the two-week program. Write an e-mail to your teacher explaining whether this would be a good use of credit.

> @ Go to the *Introduction to Business* Online Learning Center through **glencoe.com** to check your answers.

Section 26.2

Review Key Concepts

1. a secured loan because it is backed by collateral and, therefore, involves less risk
2. 20 percent
3. a court-ordered act of taking back all or part of a debtor's paycheck if payments are stopped

Academic Skills

4. **English Language Arts** The word *credit* comes from the Latin *creditum*, meaning "a thing entrusted to another." Some related words are *trust, honor,* and *tribute*.
5. **English Language Arts** Answers should explain whether this would be a good use of credit.

RETEACH (cont.)

C Critical Thinking

Predict

Signs of Credit Trouble Ask students to review the signs of credit trouble. Have them create a list of additional early signs of trouble. (Answers will vary but may include making only the minimum payments on credit card bills or using credit to make small everyday purchases.)

ASSESS

After You Read

Have students complete the Section 26.2 After You Read section review.

Online Study Tools

Have students go to the Online Learning Center through **glencoe.com** to:

- Take the Section 26.2 **Practice Test**.
- Download free **Study-to-Go** content to their PDAs or cell phones.

CLOSE

Culminating Activity

Rules for Borrowing

Ask students to develop a list of rules that would help them use credit responsibly in the future. (Answers will vary but may include never borrowing if they can pay cash or only borrowing to purchase things that are needed.)

469

Vocabulary Review

1. Students should write complete sentences using each term correctly.

Review Key Concepts

2. apply for credit, being approved for credit, use the credit, and make payments

3. the APR, fees, the days in the grace period, whether the interest rate will change, and whether a cosigner is needed

4. the three Cs: capacity (whether there is enough cash flow to make the payments), character (whether the person is trustworthy), and capital (whether the person has enough assets in case the income flow decreases)

5. Installment loans and mortgages have a time limit—a specified number of payments are made over a specific number of months. Credit cards do not.

6. Answers may include that consumers should not expend more than 20 percent of their take-home pay on credit payments. Check your credit file for damaging incorrect information. Do not get another credit card if you are at the limit on one of them. Make your payments on time and try to pay more than the minimum amount due.

Section 26.1 *Summary*

Applying for Credit It is important to develop a credit history. Most people do this by applying for a credit card, being approved for it, using it to make purchases, and making payments on time. When looking for a credit card, there are many factors to consider, such as the APR, fees, and the grace period. When deciding whether an applicant should be granted credit, the creditor looks at the individual's capacity, character, and capital. After being approved for credit, the consumer is given a credit limit. The consumer must repay a minimum amount each month. It is wise to pay more than the minimum payment, though.

Section 26.2 *Summary*

Maintaining Credit There are several similarities and differences between credit cards, installment loans, and mortgages. Installment loans and mortgages are secured. Unlike unsecured loans, secured loans are backed by collateral and usually offer lower interest rates. Credit cards are unsecured. Installment loans and mortgages last for a fixed number of years. A fixed-rate loan requires the same payment each month. The interest rate on a variable-rate loan can be raised. To maintain a good credit rating, consumers must avoid using more credit than they can afford. They must also make payments on time.

Vocabulary Review

1. On a sheet of paper, use each of these key terms and academic vocabulary terms in a sentence.

Key Terms

annual percentage rate (APR)
cash advance
cosigner
grace period
credit limit
variable rate
fixed rate

down payment
principal
finance charge
secured loan
unsecured loan
garnishment of wages
repossess

Academic Vocabulary

impact
anticipate
submit
minimum

similar
portion
maintain
obtain

Review Key Concepts

2. Explain how you can develop a credit history.

3. Name five factors to think about when deciding which credit card to secure.

4. Define the three factors that creditors consider when granting a person credit.

5. Explain one major difference between credit cards, installment loans, and mortgages.

6. Indicate at least three ways to maintain a good credit rating.

470　**Chapter 26**　Review and Activities

Critical Thinking

7. No. The creditor makes the payment for the debtor and the use of credit delays the payment by the debtor until later.

8. Credit card companies earn money by charging consumers interest on the unpaid balance.

9. Answers will vary, according to the amount of trust students have in their friends and family members.

10. Credit limits discourage consumers from charging more than they can afford.

11. Some students may say the urgency of repayment depends on the interest rate of the debt and the prevailing interest that can be earned elsewhere.

Critical Thinking

7. When someone uses credit to buy a product or service, is he or she actually paying for the item?

8. Why would most credit card companies encourage consumers to make the minimum payment on a credit card balance instead of paying the full amount owed?

9. When you cosign on a loan, you agree to take responsibility for a debt if the primary credit applicant fails to pay it. Would you be willing to cosign a loan for a friend or family member? Why or why not?

10. A credit limit is a maximum amount of credit a lender will extend. Why do companies set credit limits on credit cards?

11. Do you think a debt should be repaid as soon as possible? Why or why not?

12. When is it possible to use a credit card and avoid paying interest?

13. Do you think most creditors want to repossess an item, such as a car, when the debtor cannot pay for it?

14. What criteria do you believe are most important in choosing a credit card? Explain your answer.

Write About It

15. Most credit card applications ask applicants to indicate the amount of time they have spent at their present residence and job. In two or more paragraphs indicate why you think companies want this information.

16. Many people who have a poor credit rating have a hard time getting a loan, an apartment, and a job. Is this fair or unfair? Write a brief essay discussing your opinions.

17. Some people use multipurpose credit cards for most of their everyday purchases. In at least two paragraphs, discuss why you think people use credit cards instead of cash or checks.

18. When people and companies do not pay their debts, businesses raise the prices of their goods and services. Write a brief e-mail to your teacher indicating whether that is fair. If you feel that is unfair, explain how would you change the practice.

19. For a fee, a credit bureau will provide potential creditors with a consumer's credit report. Use the Internet to find out more about the firms that provide credit scores. Then write a one-page report on your findings.

Technology Applications

Online Mortgage Calculators

20. Find the current annual interest rate offered on a 30-year fixed-rate mortgage for $100,000. Then use an online mortgage calculator to figure the amount of a monthly payment and the total amount of interest that will be paid over 30 years.

Business Ethics

Credit Applications

21. Suppose you have a job that pays you $15,000 a year. You receive a credit application in the mail stating that you have been pre-approved for $3,000 in credit, but that you must make at least $18,000 a year to receive the card. What should you do?

Critical Thinking

12. For most cards, it is when a consumer pays off the full balance by the due date each month.

13. No. There are a lot of costs and challenges involved with repossessing an item.

14. Answers should include the cost of the card, credit limit, and where the card is accepted.

Write About It

15. This can provide some details about an applicant's stability.

16. Some students may feel that this is fair because credit holders are responsible for creating and managing their debt. Others may feel that it is unfair because credit holders may have faced circumstances beyond their control.

17. Credit cards are convenient. They allow consumers to make more large purchases.

18. E-mail messages will vary. This practice could be deemed fair because it allows businesses to limit their losses. It could be deemed unfair because people who do pay their bills end up paying higher prices for goods and services.

19. Equifax develops credit scores that are derived from information based on a consumer's credit report.

Technology Applications

20. There are online calculators for mortgages and other loans. One bank offers a 5% annual interest rate. On a 30-year fixed loan for $100,000, the monthly payment would be $536.82. Total interest would be $93,255.20.

Business Ethics

21. You should always tell the truth on a credit application. Credit card companies usually verify the information. You could call the company and discuss the matter. You could also contact one of your present credit card companies. However, it might be better to seek an alternative to charging the repairs on a credit card.

Applying Academics to Business

22. Before you apply to First National Bank for a loan, figure out the costs to make sure you can afford it.

23. $\$3,000 \times \frac{2}{3} \times 1\% = \$20$

24. Answers will vary but should reflect a cause-and-effect relationship.

25. $\$9,000 - \$2,600 = \$6,400$

$\$6,400 \times .05 = \$320$

$\$6,400 + \$320 = \$6,720$

$\$6,720 \div 12 = \$560$

Active Learning

26. Answers will be based on students' findings.

Business in the Real World

27. Most credit counselors work for nonprofit agencies that provide money management education and budget and credit counseling. The NFCC offers a counselor certification program. All of its member counselors must complete the training program.

Applying Academics to Business

English Language Arts

22. Rewrite the following sentence using correct punctuation and capitalization.

before you apply to first national bank for a loan figure out the costs to make sure you can afford it

Mathematics

23. Your credit card has a limit of $3,000. You have charged goods totaling $\frac{2}{3}$ that amount. Your yearly APR is 12%. What is the finance charge one month?

THEORY **Finance Charges** The monthly finance charge rate is $\frac{1}{12}$ the annual rate.

English Language Arts

24. Write two or three sentences from this chapter that explain a cause-and-effect relationship. Then write two or three cause-and-effect sentences of your own about a different topic.

Mathematics

25. Total expenses for a year at college will be $9,000. You plan to pay $2,600 from your savings and finance the rest at a 5% simple interest. If you make 12 equal payments in one year, how much is each?

THEORY **Problem Solving** Computing the answer to some problems takes several steps.

Active Learning

Study Credit Habits

26. Choose a current article on the debt levels of college students, or interview someone at a local college or bank who is an expert on this topic. Find out the average debt load of college students, reasons for their debt, and how the students deal with it. Write a report of your findings. Then form groups and discuss your reports in class.

Business in the Real World

Credit Counselors

27. Research the career of a credit counselor. Find out what the job entails, the skills and formal education credit counselors should have, and the salary range for an entry-level counselor. Investigate the certification offered by the National Foundation for Credit Counseling. Write a one-page paper on your findings.

ExamView Assessment Suite CD allows you to print out ready-made unit and chapter tests, complete with answer keys. You can also create customized tests.

TeacherWorks Plus provides complete teacher resources in one convenient package. It includes customizable lesson plans in calendar format, and instant access to many print program resources.

LEARNING ABOUT LOAN APPLICANTS

28. Interview a loan officer at a bank regarding what he or she looks for in a credit applicant and why the loan officer looks for those qualities. Ask for the primary reasons people are not approved for a loan and the percent of loans that are not repaid. What action does the bank usually take when a loan is not repaid? Report your findings in writing or orally to the class.

 Business CAREERS

FIND YOUR DREAM JOB

29. Go to the *Introduction to Business* Online Learning Center through **glencoe.com** for a link to the Occupational Outlook Handbook Web site. Click on the "OOH Search/A-Z Index" link and enter the job category "credit authorizers, checkers, and clerks." Then write a one-page report about these types of occupations. Conclude your report with a list of things you could do now to prepare yourself to pursue the occupation.

Role Play

APPLYING FOR A CREDIT CARD

30. **Situation** You would like to apply for a credit card to use for most of your purchases. You must consider the different credit card options that are available.

Activity Research different types of credit cards from at least three financial institutions. Then present your creditworthiness to the institution you feel best suits your financial needs.

Evaluation You will be evaluated on how well you meet the following performance indicators:

- Demonstrate an understanding of the three Cs of credit.
- Evaluate the credit requirements of the financial institution that best suits your needs.
- Discuss the importance of maintaining a good credit score.
- Project your voice and use correct grammar.
- Answer questions about credit.

Standardized Test Practice

Directions Choose the letter of the best answer. Write the letter for the answer on a separate piece of paper.

1. **A person's "safe debt load" is often defined as $\frac{1}{3}$ of a person's after-tax income less expenses. If Devon's after-tax income is $23,930, and his expenses are $4,800 for housing, $4,900 for food, $1,280 for transportation, and $950 for clothes, what is Devon's safe debt load?**

   A $3,000
   B $4,000
   C $6,000
   D $12,000

 **TEST-TAKING TIP** If you do not know the answer to a question, make a note and move to the next question. Come back to it later, after you have answered the rest of the questions.

 READING Go to the *Introduction to Business* Online Learning Center through **glencoe.com** for a list of outside reading suggestions.

 **STRATEGIES FOR STANDARDIZED TEST PREP SUCCESS**

Test Timing Before test day, provide students with opportunities to take a multipart, timed practice test. Explain how many points each section is worth. Have them record the actual time spent on each section. Afterward, have students comment on how they planned their time and how well they followed their plan.

Standards-Based Lesson Planning
Introduction to Business provides students with instruction and assessment in the following fundamental content areas:

Content Standards Correlations	
Examine credit laws and bankruptcy.	pp. 477–480, 485, 487–488
Explain the impact of credit legislation.	pp. 477, 485, 489
Analyze laws and agencies that monitor and protect consumers' use of credit. Evaluate legal rights in regard to credit transactions.	pp. 477–480, 485, 487
Identify problems, alternative solutions, and consequences of alternative solutions. Use appropriate techniques to resolve given problems.	pp. 478, 485, 487, 489
Apply problem-solving techniques to sales-related transactions that involve monetary items such as cash, checks, debit cards, and credit cards.	pp. 478, 485, 487, 489
Use strategies appropriate to a given situation to prevent and resolve conflict.	pp. 478, 485, 487, 489
Compute cost of using credit.	p. 488

NCLB
Activities, information, and skills practice will help your students attain No Child Left Behind proficiency. Students will improve their abilities in the following academic standards areas:

Academic Standards Correlations		
English Language Arts	Activities/Features	Page
NCTE 5 Use different writing process elements to communicate effectively	Applying Academics to Business	p. 488
NCTE 7 Conduct research and gather, evaluate, and synthesize data to communicate discoveries	Applying Academics to Business	p. 488
NCTE 11 Participate as members of literacy communities	After You Read	p. 485
NCTE 12 Use language to accomplish individual purposes	After You Read	p. 485
Mathematics		
Algebra Analyze change in various contexts	Applying Academics to Business	p. 488
Measurement Understand measurable attributes of objects and the units, systems, and processes of measurement	After You Read	p. 480
Number and Operations Compute fluently and make reasonable estimates	Ask S&P Applying Academics to Business	pp. 474, 488
Number and Operations Understand meanings of operations and how they relate to one another	Standardized Test Practice	p. 489
Science		
Content Standard F Students should develop understanding of science and technology in local, national, and global challenges	Science/Tech Trends	p. 484

Correlations This chart shows the 21ˢᵗ Century Skills, foundation skills, and workplace competencies that students develop as they work in this chapter.

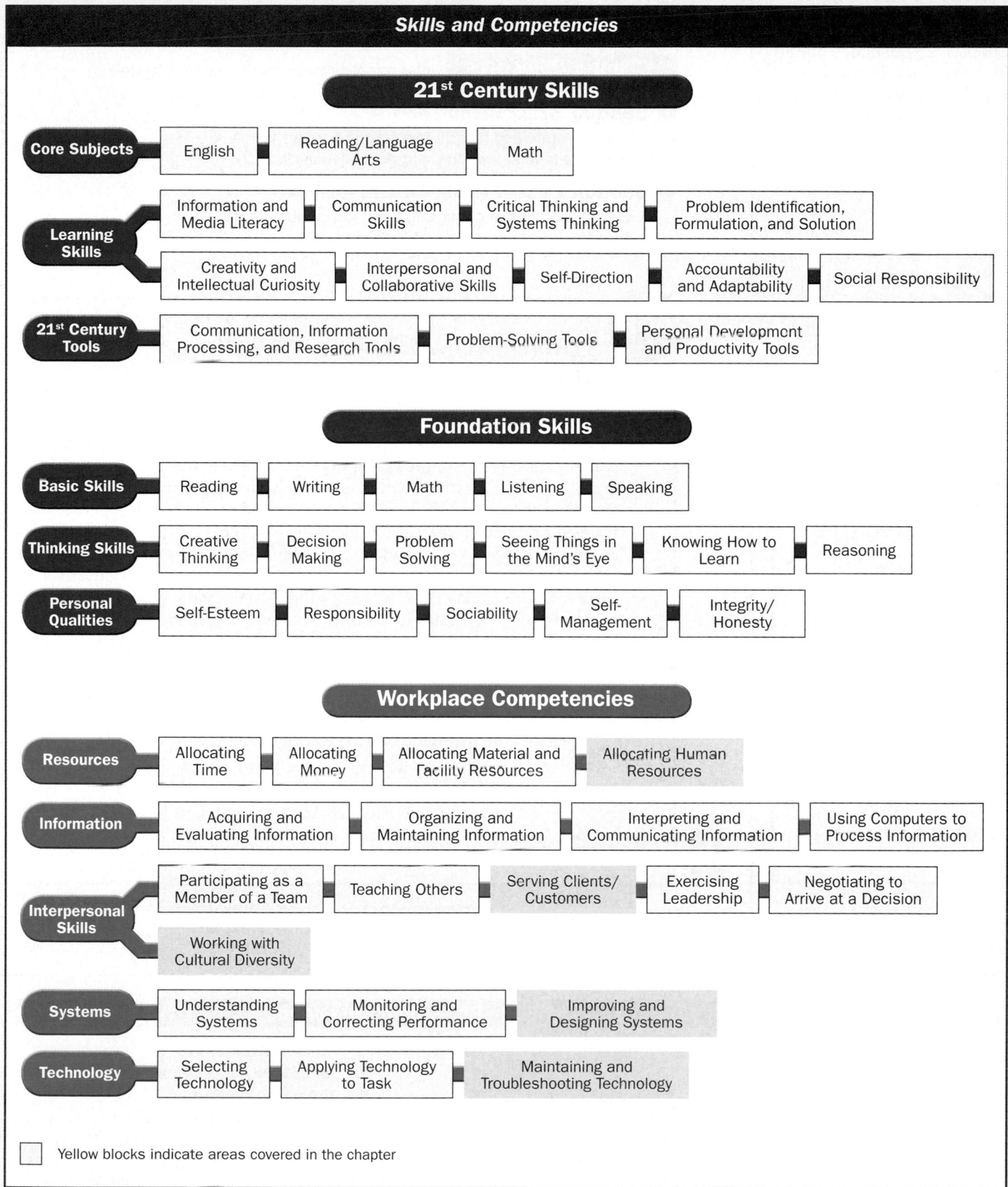

Skills and Competencies

21ˢᵗ Century Skills

Core Subjects
English | Reading/Language Arts | Math

Learning Skills
Information and Media Literacy | Communication Skills | Critical Thinking and Systems Thinking | Problem Identification, Formulation, and Solution
Creativity and Intellectual Curiosity | Interpersonal and Collaborative Skills | Self-Direction | Accountability and Adaptability | Social Responsibility

21ˢᵗ Century Tools
Communication, Information Processing, and Research Tools | Problem-Solving Tools | Personal Development and Productivity Tools

Foundation Skills

Basic Skills
Reading | Writing | Math | Listening | Speaking

Thinking Skills
Creative Thinking | Decision Making | Problem Solving | Seeing Things in the Mind's Eye | Knowing How to Learn | Reasoning

Personal Qualities
Self-Esteem | Responsibility | Sociability | Self-Management | Integrity/Honesty

Workplace Competencies

Resources
Allocating Time | Allocating Money | Allocating Material and Facility Resources | Allocating Human Resources

Information
Acquiring and Evaluating Information | Organizing and Maintaining Information | Interpreting and Communicating Information | Using Computers to Process Information

Interpersonal Skills
Participating as a Member of a Team | Teaching Others | Serving Clients/Customers | Exercising Leadership | Negotiating to Arrive at a Decision
Working with Cultural Diversity

Systems
Understanding Systems | Monitoring and Correcting Performance | Improving and Designing Systems

Technology
Selecting Technology | Applying Technology to Task | Maintaining and Troubleshooting Technology

☐ Yellow blocks indicate areas covered in the chapter

Credit and the Law

Chapter 27

Chapter Overview

Introduce the Chapter

Credit and the Law
Chapter 27 describes credit laws that protect consumers and provide guidance to creditors. It also focuses on credit problems.

Building Background
Credit problems are not confined to individuals and families with low incomes. Some credit problems are the result of choices debtors make, but others are the result of mistakes and crimes. All consumers can benefit from knowing the basics about credit laws and solving credit problems.

>> Math Answer
You can round $73.46 down to $73, and $114.81 up to $115. Now subtract: $115 − $73 = $42.

>> Extension Activity
Carter earns $137 each week as a counselor at a 9-week summer camp. Calculate his earnings rounded to the nearest $10. ($1,230: $137 × 9 = $1,233.00.)

N C L B Activity correlates to Math standards.

Chapter Objectives After completing this chapter, you will be able to:

▶ **Section 27.1** *Credit Laws*
• **Discuss** state and federal regulation of credit.
• **Describe** federal laws that protect consumers.

▶ **Section 27.2** *Solving Credit Problems*
• **Identify** sources of credit fraud and precautions to prevent it.
• **Discuss** ways to repair credit problems.

Ask
STANDARD &POOR'S **Bulls, Bears, and Crashes**

Q: How does the stock market fluctuate?

A: Various terms are used to describe fluctuations in the stock market. A bull market is a prolonged period of increasing stock prices. While there's not a true definition of a bull market, it's generally thought of as a time when major stock indices increase by 20% or more. The opposite is a bear market, and as people who have been through a number of market cycles can tell you, for every bull there will be a bear around the corner. A bear market is generally referred to as a decline of 20% from peak to trough. However, it is always a time when stock prices decline over a long period. A stock market crash is perhaps the most dramatic occurrence an investor will experience. Generally, it's a quick and severe downward movement in stock prices, often occurring in a compressed time period so as to magnify the decline's impact. Crashes generally refer to declines of at least 15–20% over a short period.

Mathematics Suppose you are analyzing a graph of stock prices during a bear market in the 1970s. You would like to estimate the difference in stock prices between the worst quarter and the highest quarter. The actual numbers are as follows:

> Worst quarter: Fourth quarter of 1974 = $73.46 a share
> Highest quarter: First quarter of 1973 = $114.81 a share
> Estimate the difference between these numbers in whole dollars.

THEORY **Estimation by Rounding** If the digit to the right of the place to which you are rounding is 5 or higher, round up. If it is lower than 5, round down.

N C L B

Classroom Resources

- Student Edition
- Teacher Wraparound Edition
- Student Activity Workbook with Academic Integration
- Student Activity Workbook with Academic Integration TAE
- *Fast File*, Unit 9 Resources
- Inclusion in the Business Education Classroom

- TeacherWorks Plus
- *ExamView Assessment Suite*
- Presentation Plus!
- Vocabulary PuzzleMaker
- Interactive Student Edition
- Online Student Edition
- Online Learning Center with Podcasts

● **Protecting Your Rights** The government regulates the credit industry to protect consumers. **What would you do if you had a complaint about credit?**

Review the Objectives
Introduce the chapter by reviewing the chapter objectives:

Section 27.1 *Objectives*
Discuss state and federal regulation of credit. (Federal and state governments control and regulate the credit industry. Most states set a maximum on interest rates for certain types of credit. The FTC is the U.S. agency that enforces credit laws and helps consumers with credit problems and complaints.)

Describe federal laws that protect consumers. (The Consumer Credit Protection Law: focuses on the right of the consumer to be informed about the cost of credit. The Equal Credit Opportunity Act: credit applications can be judged only on the basis of financial responsibility. The Fair Credit Reporting Act: the right to have an accurate credit report. The Fair Credit Billing Act: the right to receive an accurate bill from creditors. The Fair Debt Collection Practices Act: regulates collection agencies.)

Section 27.2 *Objectives*
Identify sources of credit fraud and precautions to prevent it. (credit card and identity theft, overextending credit; notify all creditors immediately so that unauthorized use can be prevented)

Discuss ways to repair credit problems. (contact creditors and negotiate a solution, talk to a credit counselor, or combine debts)

Discuss the Photo
● **Protecting Your Rights** Read the caption on the photo to students: The government regulates the credit industry to protect consumers.

Ask students: What would you do if you had a complaint about credit? (Answers will depend on student perceptions and experiences with the credit industry.)

Section 27.1

FOCUS

Bell Ringer Activity

Credit Laws
Write the names of the following laws on the board: Consumer Credit Protection Act or Truth in Lending Act, Equal Credit Opportunity Act, Fair Credit Reporting Act, Fair Credit Billing Act, and Fair Debt Collection Practices Act. Ask students to look at the names and deduce the main focus of each law. (Answers should reflect chapter content.)

Preteaching

Presentation Plus!
The Presentation Plus! CD provides visual teaching aids for this section.

PuzzleMaker
Use the Vocabulary PuzzleMaker to create a puzzle of the section's key terms. Students can complete the puzzle on paper or on a computer.

Graphic Organizer
Tell students to go to the Online Learning Center through **glencoe.com** for a printable graphic organizer. (See discussion of objectives on page 475 for answers.)

N C L B Connects academics to content.

Credit Laws

Reading Guide

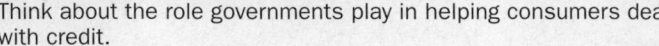

Before You Read
Think about the role governments play in helping consumers deal with credit.

D

Read to Learn
- Discuss state and federal regulation of credit.
- Describe federal laws that protect consumers.

The Main Idea
Federal and state governments both provide assistance and protection to consumers who use credit. Laws indicate the rights and responsibilities of consumers as debtors and of businesses as creditors.

Key Concepts
- State and Federal Regulation of Credit
- Federal Credit Laws

Vocabulary
Key Terms
usury law   collection agent
credit report

Academic Vocabulary
You will find these words in your reading and on your tests. Make sure you know their meanings.
comprehensive   error
plus   remove

Graphic Organizer
In a figure like the one below, write the names of the federal laws that regulate fair credit in the left column and the purpose of the laws in the right column.

Federal Law	Purpose
1.	
2.	
3.	
4.	
5.	

 Go to the *Introduction to Business* Online Learning Center through **glencoe.com** for a printable graphic organizer.

N C L B

Academic Standards
English Language Arts
    NCTE 1 Read texts to acquire new information
Mathematics
    Measurement Apply appropriate techniques, tools, and formulas to determine measurements

---

Reading Guide

Before You Read
Students might suggest that governments control and regulate the credit industry, and educate and protect consumers.

D Develop Concepts
The Main Idea Ask students: Why is it necessary for both federal and state governments to provide protection to consumers who use credit? (States regulate intrastate commerce and the federal government regulates interstate commerce.)

State and Federal Regulation of Credit

To protect consumers, both federal and state governments control and regulate the credit industry. Most states have set a maximum on the interest rates that may be charged for certain types of credit. A law restricting the amount of interest that can be charged for credit is called a **usury law**.

The Federal Trade Commission (FTC) is the U.S. agency that enforces credit laws and helps consumers with credit problems and complaints. Many city and local governments also have consumer credit protection agencies. Several states have banking or consumer protection departments that deal with credit issues. **Figure 27.1** shows a page of consumer information from the FTC's Web site.

R

> ✔ **Reading Check**   **Identify** What is the federal agency that enforces credit laws and helps consumers with credit problems?

Federal Credit Laws

A number of federal laws help inform consumers about the costs of credit and set rules concerning the credit application process, credit history information, privacy, and debt collection.

Real World

Debtors and Creditors A creditor is an entity (a bank, finance company, credit union, business, or individual) to which money is owed. A debtor is a person or business that owes money. Businesses and people can be both creditors and debtors. *In what ways have you been both a debtor and a creditor?*

Figure 27.1 — **Consumer Information**

● **Preventing Consumer Injury** The Federal Trade Commission offers many tips to help consumers. **What is the role of the Federal Trade Commission in regulating credit?**

TEACH

Discussion Starter
Usury Laws

Start a discussion by asking students why the government cares how much interest consumers have to pay for credit. (Students might suggest that without government safeguards, lenders might charge fees so high that most consumers could not afford to borrow money.)

R Reading Strategy

Identify Ask students to identify some of the government agencies that help consumers with credit problems and complaints. (Some of the groups that help consumers with credit problems and complaints are the Federal Trade Commission and state and local government agencies.)

> ✔ **Reading Check**

Identify The Federal Trade Commission (FTC) is the federal agency that enforces credit laws and helps consumers with credit problems.

Real World

Debtors and Creditors
Answers will depend on student experiences. People are creditors when they lend someone money and debtors when they borrow money.

Figure 27.1

● **Preventing Consumer Injury** The Federal Trade Commission regulates interstate credit and helps consumers with credit problems and complaints.

TEACH (cont.)

S Skill Practice

Guided Practice

Paraphrase Ask students to use their own words to describe the Equal Credit Opportunity Act. (Answers should describe it as a federal law that requires credit applications to be judged on the basis of financial responsibility.) **L1**

Create a Table Have students create a table that includes reasons a consumer can be denied credit and the bases upon which a consumer cannot be denied credit. (Only low income, large debts, and a poor payment record can be used.) **L2**

Explain Historical Context Ask students to research and describe the historical context of the Equal Credit Opportunity Act. (Enacted in 1974, it banned credit discrimination based on gender or marital status. It was later amended in 1976 to include age, national origin, race, and religion.) **L3**

ASSESS

Review Key Terms
Have students write sentences using each key term.

Study-to-Go Have students go to the Online Learning Center through **glencoe.com** to download free **Study-to-Go** content to their PDAs or cell phones.

478

? ETHICS in Business

Information Collection

■ **Critical Reading** Life is full of important decisions. Think about the kinds of decisions you make as you read the question.

You are the owner of a small business that has been open for one year. You have only been dealing in cash sales since you opened, but are now looking into credit card machines to make things more convenient for your customers. You have researched a number of providers and have narrowed it down to two. One company charges slightly more than the other for its service, but the majority of customers use credit cards issued by the second company.

■ **Decision Making** Would learning that the lower cost provider offers a discount for giving it detailed information about the purchases your customers make affect your decision? Explain your answer.

● As You Read

Think about some reasons a person might be denied a credit card.

S

? ETHICS in Business

Decision Making Tell students that the Fair Debt Collection Practices Act (FDCPA) requires lenders to notify borrowers of their privacy policy but does not forbid collecting information about consumer purchases.

Consumer Credit Protection Act

To make comparing credit costs easier, Congress passed the Consumer Credit Protection Act. The Consumer Credit Protection Act (also called the Truth in Lending Act) is a federal law that requires creditors to inform consumers about the costs and terms of credit. The law provides other protections. If your credit card is lost or stolen and someone else uses it, your payment for any unauthorized purchases will be limited to $50. Also, companies are not allowed to send a credit card to a consumer who did not request it.

The law states that advertisements for credit must communicate a fair and reasonably **comprehensive** indication of the nature and true cost of the credit. Ads must note the number of payments, the payment amount, and the period of payments if the amount of the down payment is given. The law requires that lenders inform borrowers regarding

- the cost of credit, or the total finance charge that includes the total interest **plus** required fees.
- the annual percentage rate (APR) so the borrower can compare interest rates.
- the credit terms and conditions. For instance, what happens if a payment is late?

Equal Credit Opportunity Act

The Equal Credit Opportunity Act is a federal law stating that credit applications can be judged only on the basis of financial responsibility. No person can be denied credit on the basis of marital status, gender, age, ethnicity, religion, or receipt of public assistance. The law allows only three reasons for denying credit: low income, large debts, and a poor payment record. A person who is denied credit must be given a written statement listing reasons for the denial.

Fair Credit Reporting Act

Each consumer with credit has a credit report. A **credit report**, also considered a credit history, is a record of an individual's past borrowing and repayments. It includes information about late payments and bankruptcy. You have the right to know what is in your credit report. The Fair Credit Reporting Act is a federal law that allows individuals to examine and correct information used by credit reporting agencies. Only authorized people and businesses can see your credit report. Lenders rely heavily on credit reports when they consider loan applications.

● As You Read

Low income, large debts, and a poor payment record are the only factors that can be considered.

In the United States, most credit report information is collected and kept by three credit bureaus: Experian®, Equifax®, and TransUnion®. The credit bureaus are required to provide each consumer a free copy of his or her credit report upon request each year. Consumers should order their credit report and check it annually for mistakes. If a consumer finds an **error** on a credit report, then he or she shoud take steps to **remove** it. This involves writing the credit bureaus that are reporting the incorrect information. **Figure 27.2** shows what to do if you are denied credit.

✔ **Reading Check** **Analyze** What can you do if information on your credit report is incorrect?

Figure 27.2 — *What to Do if You Are Denied Credit*

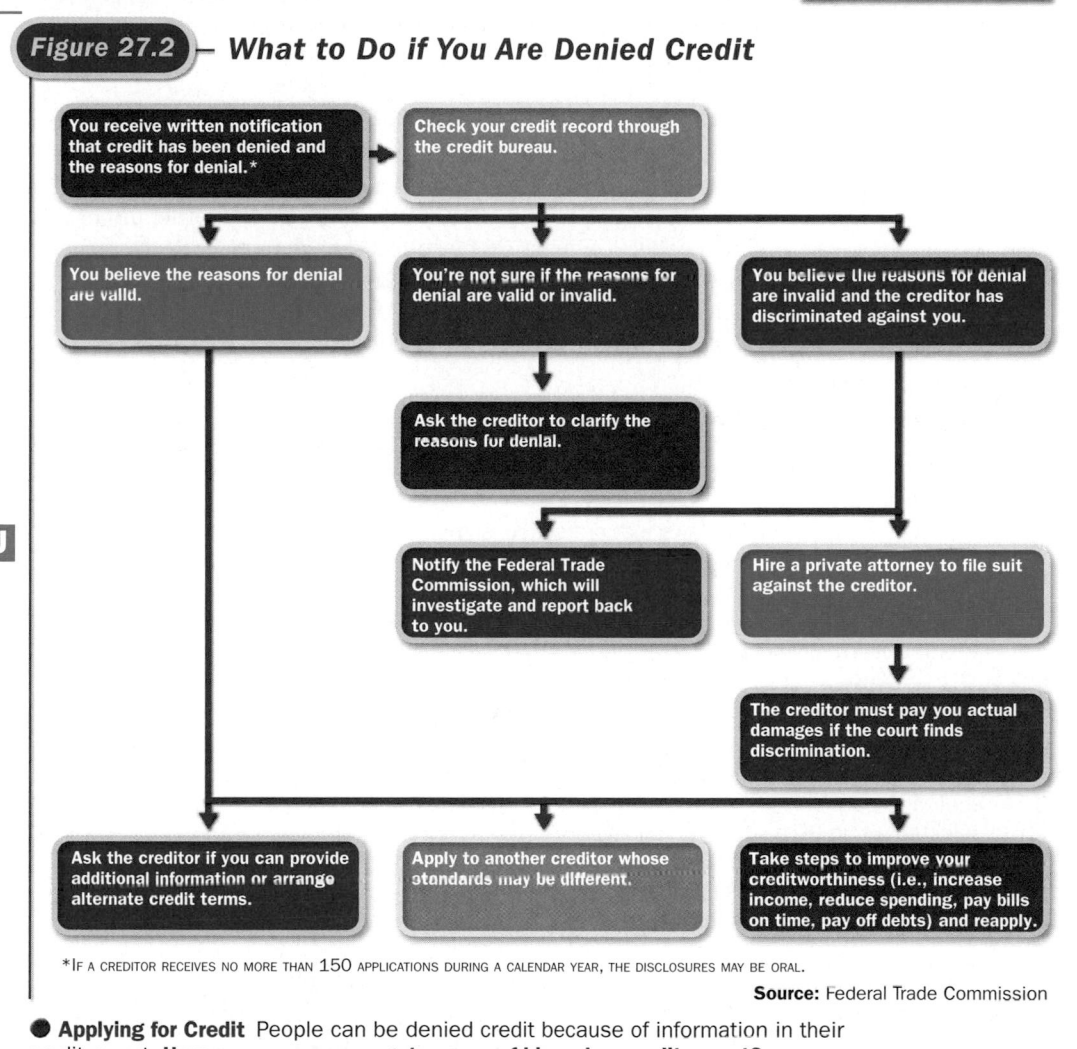

*IF A CREDITOR RECEIVES NO MORE THAN 150 APPLICATIONS DURING A CALENDAR YEAR, THE DISCLOSURES MAY BE ORAL.

Source: Federal Trade Commission

● **Applying for Credit** People can be denied credit because of information in their credit report. **How can a consumer get a copy of his or her credit report?**

RETEACH

R Reading Strategy
Recognize the Main Idea Ask students to identify the main idea in this sentence. (Most credit information is collected and kept by three credit bureaus.)

W Writing Support
Enrichment
Credit Reports Ask students to write a 200-word magazine article explaining facts that a consumer should know about his or her credit report. Suggest that students use library and Internet resources to gather information. They also might consider interviewing some adults. (Students should understand that consumers can receive a free copy of their credit report every year and that examining this information is an important way to maintain good credit.)

U Universal Access
Visual and Auditory Learners Have four volunteers team up to read the material in **Figure 27.2** to the class. Ask each student to read a different part of the flow chart while the rest of the class follows along. Visual and auditory cues are important to visual and auditory learners.

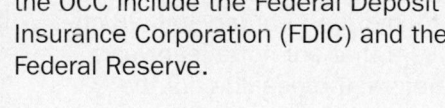

OCC Other agencies that are like the OCC include the Federal Deposit Insurance Corporation (FDIC) and the Federal Reserve.

Figure 27.2

● **Applying for Credit** Consumers can request it from one of the three credit bureaus every year. Additional copies may be purchased.

✔ **Reading Check**

Analyze You can take steps to have the error removed. This involves contacting the credit bureaus.

Student Activity Workbook ☞ Assign the Section 27.1 Activities.

RETEACH (cont.)

C Critical Thinking

Evaluate

Fair Credit Billing Act Ask students if they think it is fair to require consumers to notify creditors in writing about billing mistakes. (Students might suggest that it would be more convenient to send an e-mail or call a toll-free number.)

● As You Read

Some students may have found mistakes in grading of schoolwork and discussed the mistake with the teacher.

ASSESS

● After You Read

Have students complete the Section 27.1 After You Read section review.

Online Study Tools

Have students go to the Online Learning Center through **glencoe.com** to:

- Take the Section 27.1 **Practice Test**.
- Download free **Study-to-Go** content to their PDAs or cell phones.

CLOSE

Culminating Activity
Credit Law Posters
Have students create a poster related to one of the laws mentioned in this section. Display posters in your classroom or in a public area of the school. (Posters should reflect an accurate interpretation of the law represented.)

480

Fair Credit Billing Act

The Fair Credit Billing Act is a federal law that requires creditors to correct billing mistakes that are brought to their attention. The law also requires that consumers be informed of the steps they need to take to get an error corrected. To do this, the consumer must notify the creditor in writing. The creditor must either correct the error or explain in writing why the account is correct. If the creditor made the mistake, the consumer does not have to pay any finance charge on the incorrect amount. If there was no error, the consumer usually must pay interest plus the fee for any late payments.

The Fair Credit Billing Act also permits consumers to stop a credit payment for an item that is damaged or defective. Before stopping payment, however, consumers must attempt to resolve the problem with the company that sold it.

● As You Read

Think about what you have done in previous situations to get a mistake corrected.

Fair Debt Collection Practices Act

The Fair Debt Collection Practices Act (FDCPA) is a federal law that serves to regulate collection agencies. The purpose of the FDCPA is to prevent deception, harassment, and other unfair debt collection practices by collection agents. A **collection agent** is a person or business that collects payments for overdue bills. The FDCPA requires that collection agents respect debtors' privacy and identify themselves to debtors when they call.

NCLB Activity correlates to Math standards.

Section 27.1

● After You Read

Review Key Concepts

1. Identify some government laws that protect consumers.
2. What three things are creditors required to tell consumers under the Consumer Credit Protection Act?
3. What are the only three reasons a person can be denied credit according to the Equal Credit Opportunity Act?

Academic Skills

4. **Mathematics** The Equal Credit Opportunity Act requires that all credit applicants be informed of whether their application has been accepted or rejected within 30 days. If you submitted your application for credit on February 1 in a year that is not a leap year, what is the deadline for the response?

THEORY **Adding Calendar Dates** Since the number of days in a month varies, it is often helpful to look at a calendar when adding calendar dates.

  For math help, go to the Math Appendix.

@ Go to the *Introduction to Business* Online Learning Center through **glencoe.com** to check your answers.

Section 27.1

Review Key Concepts

1. Consumer Credit Protection Act, the Equal Credit Opportunity Act, the Fair Credit Reporting Act, the Fair Credit Billing Act, and the Fair Debt Collection Practices Act
2. to inform consumers of the cost of credit, the annual percentage rate, and the credit terms and conditions

3. low income, debts, and late payments

Academic Skills

4. **Mathematics** February has 28 days in years that are not a leap year. Therefore, the deadline for the response is March 2.

Solving Credit Problems

Reading Guide

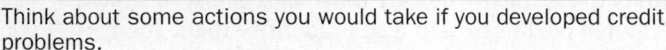

● Before You Read

Think about some actions you would take if you developed credit problems.

Read to Learn

- Identify sources of credit fraud and precautions that can prevent it.
- Discuss ways to repair credit problems.

The Main Idea

D The main credit problems that consumers face are credit card and identity theft, and overuse of credit. There are specific steps to take to resolve each issue.

Key Concept

- Preventing Credit Fraud

Vocabulary

Key Terms

identity theft   consolidation loan
credit counselor   bankruptcy

Academic Vocabulary

You will find these words in your reading and on your tests. Make sure you know their meanings.

pose   overall
restore   instances

Graphic Organizer

In a figure like the one below, write notes about the things people can do to prevent identity theft.

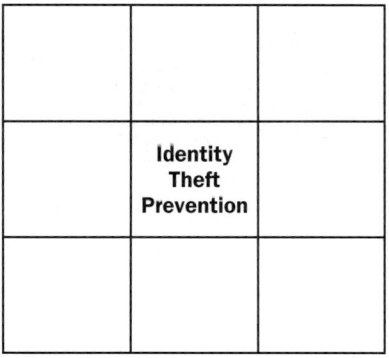

	Identity Theft Prevention	

 Go to the *Introduction to Business* Online Learning Center through **glencoe.com** for a printable graphic organizer.

Academic Standards

English Language Arts

N C L B

NCTE 1 Read texts to acquire new information

NCTE 11 Participate as members of literacy communities

NCTE 12 Use language to accomplish individual purposes

Science

Content Standard F Students should develop understanding of science and technology in local, national, and global challenges

---

Reading Guide

● Before You Read

Students might suggest that people with credit problems should contact their creditors.

D Develop Concepts

The Main Idea Ask students: What are some of the main credit problems consumers face? (Identity theft, credit card theft, and overuse of credit.)

FOCUS

🔔 **Bell Ringer Activity**

Solving Credit Problems

Write this question on the board: Is bankruptcy the only answer for credit problems? (Some students might suggest that bankruptcy is good because it wipes the slate clean. Others might suggest that bankruptcy should be a last resort.)

Preteaching

Presentation Plus!

The Presentation Plus! CD provides visual teaching aids for this section.

PuzzleMaker 💿

Use the Vocabulary PuzzleMaker to create a puzzle of the section's key terms. Students can complete the puzzle on paper or on a computer.

Graphic Organizer

Tell students to go to the Online Learning Center through **glencoe.com** for a printable graphic organizer. (Answers include: shred personal papers; make sure your card is returned to you after purchases; carry your checkbook and other cards with you only when you expect to use them; when you make purchases online, review your monthly statements for unauthorized purchases.)

N C L B Connects academics to content.

TEACH

Discussion Starter
Identity Theft

Locate a news article about identity theft that profiles a consumer's experience. Read a portion of the article aloud and ask students if they think there was anything the identity theft victim could have done to prevent the theft or to ameliorate the consequences. (Answers will be based on students' opinions and knowledge of identity theft.)

R Reading Strategy

Apply Knowledge Ask students to volunteer information that they have heard outside of class about the problem of identity theft. (Some students may have watched news stories about individuals who have had their identities stolen. Others may have read in books, magazines, or on the Internet that identity theft is a growing problem in the United States. Some students who have made purchases on the Internet will know that they should be careful to use a reputable business and to examine the Web site's security policies.)

● As You Read

Some students may say that they tried to retrace their steps to figure out how or where an item might have been lost or stolen. They might have asked others if they saw the item and/or contacted an authority, such as the police, about it.

482

● As You Read

Have you ever lost something of value or had it stolen? What steps did you take to get it back?

Preventing Credit Fraud

Credit card theft, the misuse of credit information, and identity theft are increasing problems. Fortunately, there are ways to deal with them.

Dealing with Credit Card and Identity Theft

R The first step a consumer should take when he or she gets a credit or ATM card is to write down the card issuer's phone number and other contact information. The information should be kept in a separate place from the card. This makes it easier to contact the company quickly if the card is lost or stolen.

A stolen credit card can lead to identity theft. **Identity theft** occurs when someone steals another person's financial information with the intention of committing fraud under that person's identity. People who commit identity theft often steal someone's

BusinessWeek *Reader and Case Study*

Stopping a Scam from Spreading

Thwarted by bigger banks, ID thieves are taking aim at smaller financial institutions. One credit union provides a model for fighting back

Jim Nichols, a manager at Numerica Credit Union, knew something was amiss when the customer missed his first payment. The card user, whom Nichols didn't name, looked ideal on paper, mailing in a pay stub and driver license photocopy and boasting an impeccable credit history. And then, within days of receiving a card, the person spent up to the $5,000 limit.

When the account became delinquent, Nichols sprang into action. Nichols, the accounts control manager at Spokane, Washington-based Numerica, mailed notices to the address listed on the application and left unreturned messages at home and work numbers.

Finally, after a more thorough credit check and deeper database probe, Nichols tracked down the person whose details were used and learned the "customer" had never tried to open a Numerica account. His identity had been ripped off.

482   Chapter 27   Credit and the Law

Identity theft is becoming an all-too-common problem for managers like Nichols and midsize companies like Numerica. Last year, for the first time, Numerica suffered large enough losses from ID theft that it qualified for reimbursement by its insurance policy. Nichols says a growing number of clients are getting scam e-mails from phishers or having their online résumés pillaged for names, addresses, and other personal data.

 CASE STUDY Go to the *Introduction to Business* Online Learning Center through **glencoe.com** for the *BusinessWeek* Reader Case Study.

Active Learning

Research your own identifying documents. Prepare a chart of people and institutions with whom it would and would not be appropriate to share information about each document. Write an e-mail to your teacher giving recommendations about the security attention people should pay to each document.

glencoe.com

BusinessWeek *Reader and Case Study*

Stop a Scam from Spreading

 CASE STUDY Have students go to the *Introduction to Business* Online Learning Center through **glencoe.com** to download a Case Study activity that corresponds to the article. The activity and answer key are also available on the TeacherWorks Plus CD.

Active Learning

Identifying documents will vary but are likely to include a birth certificate, driver's license, Social Security card, or passport. Other documents can also be used for identification. Encourage students to be clear about the reasons that a person is requesting personal information.

● **Credit Counseling**
Credit counselors can be very helpful for people who are over their heads in debt. **What kinds of services do credit counselors provide?**

credit cards and Social Security numbers. They can **pose** as the person to get loans or more credit cards or to make purchases. People who discover that their identity has been stolen should take the following steps:

- **Contact the Credit Bureaus** The credit bureau will flag the file with a fraud alert that will prevent new accounts from being opened without permission.
- **Contact the Creditors** Creditors should be informed about fraudulent activities immediately by phone and in writing.
- **File a Police Report** A copy of a police report is important, in case creditors need proof of the crime.

Consumers can protect their identities by being careful with the way they handle their credit and ATM cards, checks, and Social Security number. Experts advise these precautions:

- Shred personal papers that contain your account numbers and Social Security number.
- Be careful when giving out your personal information.
- Watch what salespeople do with your credit or ATM card when you give it to them.
- Make sure your card is returned to you after purchases.
- Carry your checkbook, and Social Security, ATM, and credit cards with you only when you expect to use them.
- When you make purchases online, read privacy policies and use a secure browser.
- Review your monthly bank and credit card statements for unauthorized purchases.

● As You Read

Think about some items that have your personal information on them, but that you always carry with you.

S

✔ **Reading Check** **Explain** What can you do to protect your identity from being stolen?

Section 27.2 Solving Credit Problems **483**

Discuss the Photo

● **Credit Counseling** Credit counselors can help people manage their money. They can help people set up payment plans with their creditors.

● As You Read

Answers may include a driver's license or state identification, a transit pass, an ATM card, a cell phone, or a personal digital assistant.

TEACH (cont.)

S Skill Practice
Guided Practice

List Ask students to make a list of precautions consumers can take against identity theft. (See the Graphic Organizer answer on page 481.) **L1**

Explain Ask students to choose a precaution against identity theft listed in the textbook and explain how it protects a consumer. (Students should demonstrate an understanding of chapter content.) **L2**

Find and Present Point out that banks, credit card companies, and consumer protection organizations often post lists of precautions against identity theft on their Web sites. Ask students to find such a list and share the content through a short presentation. (Presentations should reflect information gathered from a bank, credit card company, or consumer protection Web site.) **L3**

✔ Reading Check

Explain Shred all papers, be careful when giving out personal information, use a secure Web browser, and review monthly statements.

ASSESS

Review Key Terms
Have students write sentences using each key term.

Study-to-Go Have students go to the Online Learning Center through **glencoe.com** to download free **Study-to-Go** content to their PDAs or cell phones.

483

RETEACH

Science/Tech TRENDS

Becoming a Credit Scientist
Credit card companies use sophisticated mathematical models to evaluate applicants' credit risks. So do banks and multinational corporations. This branch of mathematics, called statistics, provides a means of processing raw information to simplify decision making. In mathematics, using statistics to study the economy is called econometrics. The field of econometrics has grown significantly and is likely to continue to do so in the future. Scientists who study econometrics typically need a master's degree or Ph.D. They use computer models and may work alone or as part of a team to make decisions that affect everyone's credit futures.

Web Quest

Go to the *Introduction to Business* Online Learning Center through **glencoe.com** for links to Web sites to help you find careers in math and science. Then research the cost of getting a graduate degree. Write a paragraph or two about your findings and how you might finance becoming a scientist.

Repairing Credit Problems

W Many consumers charge too many of their purchases and later realize that they cannot afford the monthly payments. To fix the problem, they have a few options to consider.

Contacting Creditors

U The first thing a consumer should do is contact the creditor. Consumers can often work out a new payment plan to lower payments. They will still owe the original balances, plus more interest since it will take longer to repay the debts.

Talking to a Credit Counselor

R Consumers who are unable to work out their credit problems should talk to a credit counselor. A **credit counselor** helps people work out a plan for getting out of debt. They also assist consumers with managing their money.

There are several different types of credit counseling services. Many credit counseling services charge a fee to "clean up" a poor credit report. However, they are seldom able to **restore** good credit to someone whose bad credit score is otherwise correct. Accurate reports of missed payments or bankruptcy cannot legally be removed from a person's credit report. If a consumer's credit rating has been unfairly damaged by inaccurate information, he or she can work with a credit bureau to correct the errors without the help of a counseling service.

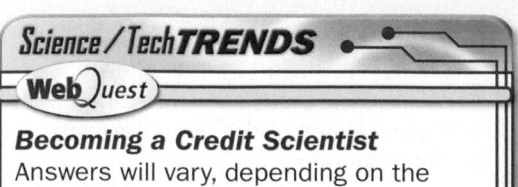

Science/Tech TRENDS

Web Quest

Becoming a Credit Scientist
Answers will vary, depending on the schools chosen.

Activity correlates to Science standards.

Combining Debts

Another possible solution is a consolidation loan. A **consolidation loan** combines a consumer's debts into one loan with lower payments. If the interest rate on a consolidation loan is better **overall**, then a consolidation loan is a good idea. However, in some **instances**, the interest rate could be higher if the debtor has a poor credit history. Another problem is that some people begin to make charges again after they pay off their cards.

Filing Bankruptcy

The last resort is to declare bankruptcy. **Bankruptcy** is a legal process in which a borrower is relieved of debts after showing an inability to pay. One kind of bankruptcy involves selling most of the debtor's assets and passing the proceeds to the creditors. The debts are forgiven even though the creditors may not be paid in full. If the reorganizational form of bankruptcy is chosen, the debtor, the creditor, and a court-appointed trustee develop a plan to repay the debt on an installment basis. The debtor gets to keep more assets with this form.

People should avoid bankruptcy because it gives a debtor a bad credit record that can last for 10 years. This can make it difficult to obtain a home or car loan, buy major appliances, or get other forms of credit. People who have declared bankruptcy are charged higher interest rates because they are considered higher risks.

Bankruptcy Laws In the United States, changes to bankruptcy laws have made it more difficult for debtors to declare bankruptcy. Before they can file, all debtors must get credit counseling. The declaration process also requires counseling on budgeting and debt management. *Do you think these laws are fair to debtors?*

 Activity correlates to English Language Arts standards.

Section 27.2

After You Read

Review Key Concepts
1. What are some credit problems that a debtor might face?
2. List some precautions to take to avoid identity theft.
3. What effect does declaring bankruptcy have?

Academic Skills
4. **English Language Arts** Write a brief summary explaining the content covered in this chapter. Then write a question about a concept that is either unclear to you or that you would like to know more about. Trade summaries and questions with a partner and write an answer to his or her question.

5. **English Language Arts** Zarina was recently denied a loan at a bank because her credit report included a statement about her non-payment of rent due to a lack of repairs that her landlord was obligated to make. On her behalf, draft a letter to the bank explaining the situation and requesting that her loan be approved.

@ Go to the *Introduction to Business* Online Learning Center through **glencoe.com** to check your answers.

Section 27.2

Review Key Concepts
1. credit card and identity theft, and over-extending their credit
2. Shred personal papers that contain identification numbers and carry financial items only when needed.
3. Creditors can take the debtor's assets. It also leaves a negative mark on a debtor's credit record for years.

Academic Skills
4. **English Language Arts** Answers will vary, but students' questions should relate to chapter content.
5. **English Language Arts** Students' letters will vary but should present the argument in a polite, concise, and logical manner.

RETEACH (cont.)

C Critical Thinking

Explain
Bankruptcy Ask students to explain the consequences of filing for bankruptcy. (Students should recognize that bankruptcy does not wipe the slate clean.)

Bankruptcy Laws Many people incur high debt because they have not been educated or informed about financial management.

ASSESS

After You Read

Have students complete the Section 27.2 After You Read section review.

Online Study Tools

Have students go to the Online Learning Center through **glencoe.com** to:

- Take the Section 27.2 **Practice Test**.
- Download free **Study-to-Go** content to their PDAs or cell phones.

CLOSE

Culminating Activity
Solving Credit Problems
Organize students into three groups and ask each group to produce a 10-minute play based on one of the topics presented in this section, helping the audience to understand how credit problems can be solved. (Plays will vary, depending on the topic.)

485

Vocabulary Review

1. Students should write complete sentences using each term correctly.

Review Key Concepts

2. Federal and state governments control and regulate the credit industry. Most states set a maximum on the interest rates that may be charged for certain types of credit. The FTC is the U.S. agency that enforces credit laws and helps consumers with credit problems and complaints.

3. Consumer Credit Protection Act, Equal Credit Opportunity Act, Fair Credit Reporting Act, Fair Credit Billing Act, Fair Debt Collection Practices Act

4. Sources include credit card and identity theft. One way to deal with identity theft is to notify all of the creditors immediately after it has occurred so that unauthorized charges can be stopped and fees can be avoided.

5. Consumers who have credit problems can contact creditors and possibly negotiate a solution, talk to a credit counselor, or combine debts. In extreme cases, consumers may need to file bankruptcy.

Section 27.1 *Summary*

Credit Laws In the United States, federal and state governments have passed several laws to help consumers avoid or handle credit problems. The Federal Trade Commission is the primary federal agency that enforces federal credit laws. Laws that protect consumers include the Consumer Credit Protection Act, the Equal Credit Opportunity Act, the Fair Credit Reporting Act, the Fair Credit Billing Act, and the Fair Debt Collection Practices Act. Several states have banking or consumer-protection departments that deal with credit issues.

Section 27.2 *Summary*

Solving Credit Problems The main credit problems consumers face are credit card and identity theft, and overuse of credit. Identity theft occurs when someone steals another person's financial information with the intention of committing fraud under that person's identity. It should be reported immediately to the proper authorities. When someone has overused credit and cannot repay it, the first step is to try to work out a new payment plan with the creditor. Credit counseling, debt consolidation, and bankruptcy are other possible solutions.

Vocabulary Review

1. On a sheet of paper, use each of these key terms and academic vocabulary terms in a sentence.

Key Terms	Academic Vocabulary	
usury law	comprehensive	pose
credit report	plus	restore
collection agent	error	overall
identity theft	remove	instances
credit counselor		
consolidation loan		
bankruptcy		

Review Key Concepts

2. Discuss state and federal regulation of credit.

3. Describe federal laws that protect consumers.

4. Identify sources of credit fraud and precautions that can prevent it.

5. Discuss ways to repair credit problems.

Critical Thinking

6. It can show how much the consumer will pay for credit and be used to comparison shop for credit.

7. Many credit holders had significant mistakes on their reports from inaccurate reporting by creditors. Legislators believed it necessary for consumers to review their credit reports for accuracy on a regular basis.

8. if she or he attempted to return the item but was denied a refund, exchange, or other remedy

9. A letter provides written documentation of your request. Moreover, it is impossible to verify supporting documents related to a claim over the phone.

10. Consumers should write a letter to the credit bureau documenting the error and provide any proof they have, such as correspondence with a creditor.

Critical Thinking

6. How can a truth-in-lending disclosure help protect consumers from credit problems?

7. People can now get free copies of their credit reports. Why do you think this change has occurred?

8. Why would a consumer need to use the Fair Credit Billing Act to stop a payment?

9. Why is it best to request changes of incorrect information in your credit report by letter rather than by phone?

10. What should a person do to correct errors on a credit report?

11. Some creditors will lower payments or interest, or even waive fees for debtors. Why do you think they are willing to make these changes?

12. Why would the Equal Credit Opportunity Act allow credit to be denied if a person has a poor credit record?

Write About It

13. Research the common ways identity theft occurs. Write a one-page paper on what you find.

14. Research credit counseling services. Write a one-page article for your school newspaper comparing and contrasting the services offered by two companies.

15. Research Chapter 7 and Chapter 13 bankruptcy. Write a report of at least 250 words discussing your findings.

16. In two or more paragraphs, describe how you could convince a credit manager that you are a good credit risk.

17. Write several reasons you might prefer using a credit card instead of cash, debit cards, or checks.

18. Write an essay about what you should do if your ATM card is stolen.

19. Research the process of filing and resolving a dispute at one of the three credit bureaus. Write a one-page report on your findings.

Technology Applications

Search the FTC's Web Site
20. The main mission of the Federal Trade Commission (FTC) is to promote consumer protection and the elimination and prevention of anticompetitive business practices. Explore the FTC's Web site. What major topics are found on consumer protection? Write a one- to two-page report summarizing your findings. Then give a brief presentation to the class.

Business Ethics

Making Credit Payments
21. Suppose you have had a difficult month financially. A couple of emergencies depleted your savings. However, you have two payments to make. One is for an installment loan on an appliance, for which you have two payments left. The other is for a credit card balance that has a minimum payment due. You can afford to make only one of the payments. What should you do?

Critical Thinking

11. From a business standpoint, it is better to make these changes so that a person can pay off the debt than to have the debtor be unable to pay anything.

12. The law protects both debtors and creditors from having a lot of unpaid debts.

Write About It

13. Topics may include "dumpster diving," skimming, and phishing.

14. Articles will vary, depending on the companies chosen.

15. With Chapter 7, the general rule is that all debts are discharged based on an order from bankruptcy court. Chapter 13 is a reorganization plan for individuals. The debtors keep their property, but must make regular payments to a trustee, who distributes the payments to the creditors.

16. You could ask what you could do to be approved in the future. You may also be able to provide payroll statements to show that you earn enough money to pay for the debt or offer collateral.

17. Credit cards enable people to purchase big-ticket items without money. Debtors pay over a period of time.

18. File a report with the police. Then notify your bank so that it can stop activity on the card.

19. Reports should reflect the credit bureau's policies.

Technology Applications

20. Presentations will vary. The FTC's Bureau of Consumer Protection is divided into divisions, such as advertising practices, privacy and identity protection, and marketing practices.

Business Ethics

21. It probably would be best to discuss your situation with both creditors. Indicate the nature of your problem, and see if you can make arrangements to pay both.

Applying Academics to Business

22. Paragraphs should represent three different structural patterns: sequence of events, statement and example, and cause and effect.

23. $750 × 0.198 = $148.50

$750 × 0.3 = $225

If she lived in Connecticut, she would pay $148.50. If she lived in New Jersey, she would pay $225.

24. Answers will vary but should include services in all three categories.

25. $\frac{1.6 \text{ mil.} - 1.4 \text{ mil.}}{1.4 \text{ mil.}} =$

$\frac{1}{7} = 14.28\%$

Active Learning

26. Answers will be based on interviewees' responses.

Business in the Real World

27. Answers will be based on interviewees' responses.

Applying Academics to Business

English Language Arts

22. Paragraphs can be structured in various ways. For example, a paragraph may present a sequence of events or be organized around a statement followed by examples. Copy an example of each of these types of paragraph from this chapter. Then write a paragraph explaining the causes and effects of bankruptcy.

Mathematics

23. States regulate the maximum annual interest rate that may be charged for credit cards. The maximum in Connecticut is 19.8%; in New Jersey, it is 30%. Marika maintained a credit card balance of $750 for a year, paying only finance charges. If she lived in Connecticut, how much would she pay in finance charges? How much would finance charges be if she lived in New Jersey?

THEORY **Percents and Decimals** To change a percent to a decimal, drop the percent sign and divide by 100 by moving the decimal point two places to the left.

English Language Arts

24. Using the local telephone book, compile a list of all the agencies that provide consumer credit counseling and protection in your community. Organize the list according to whether they operate at the local, state, or federal level.

Mathematics

25. The total number of personal bankruptcies rose overall over a five-year period. Records indicate that there were 1.4 million bankruptcies filed in U.S. courts at the beginning of the period. Five years later, there were 1.6 million filed. What is the percent increase in bankruptcies filed over the five-year period?

THEORY **Percent Increase** Percent increase is a ratio of the net change over time divided by the original value.

Active Learning

Consumer Awareness of Credit Laws

26. Interview family members about their knowledge of credit protection laws. Ask them specifically about the Truth in Lending Act, the Equal Credit Opportunity Act, and the Fair Debit Collection Practices Act. Ask them if they think the three reasons for denying credit under the Equal Credit Opportunity Act are fair. Would they add any others? Why or why not? Write a report about their responses.

Business in the Real World

Multipurpose Credit Cards

27. Interview a business owner who has a store that accepts multipurpose credit cards, such as Visa and MasterCard. Ask about dealing with the credit card companies. What are the requirements to be able to accept these cards from customers? What are the associated costs and billing procedures? Ask whether all multipurpose credit card companies work the same way. Summarize your findings and share them with the class.

ExamView Assessment Suite CD allows you to print out ready-made unit and chapter tests, complete with answer keys. You can also create customized tests.

TeacherWorks Plus provides complete teacher resources in one convenient package. It includes customizable lesson plans in calendar format, and instant access to many print program resources.

 *skills*

BEING INFORMED ABOUT CREDIT

28. Work with an adult family member to order a free copy of their credit report from one of the three U.S. credit bureaus. Then review the credit report. Is everything correct? Do any mistakes need to be corrected? Report what you did to get the credit report and the kind of information it presents.

FIND YOUR DREAM JOB

29. Go to the *Introduction to Business* Online Learning Center through **glencoe.com** for a link to the Occupational Outlook Handbook Web site. Click on the "OOH Search/A-Z Index" link and enter the job category "financial analysts and personal financial advisors." Then write a one-page report about these types of occupations. Conclude your report with a list of things you could do now to prepare yourself to pursue the occupation.

Role Play

ADVOCATE FOR OR AGAINST A USURY LAW

30. Situation The state legislature is having a session on whether it should implement a new usury law to restrict the interest rates that can be charged.

Activity Choose between being a consumer advocate who wants a usury law or a member of the banking industry who does not want a usury law. Give a presentation to the state legislature.

Evaluation You will be evaluated on how well you meet the following performance indicators:

- Explain how usury laws work.
- Consumer advocate: Give reasons why a new usury law would benefit debtors and creditors.
- Bank industry representative: Give reasons there should be less regulation of interest rates.
- Project your voice and use correct grammar.

Standardized Test Practice

Directions Choose the letter of the best answer. Write the letter for the answer on a separate piece of paper.

1. William is making interest-only payments each month on a debt he owes to a credit card company. The interest rate he pays is 18% per year, and he pays $12. Which could be used to compute the principal?

A $12 ÷ (.18 ÷ 12)

B $12 × (.18 ÷ 12)

C $12 ÷ 0.18

D $12 × 0.18

 TEST-TAKING TIP If each item on a test is worth the same number of points, do not spend too much time on questions that are confusing.

 READING Go to the *Introduction to Business* Online Learning Center through **glencoe.com** for a list of outside reading suggestions.

glencoe.com

 *skills*

28. Answers will depend on the credit users' responses.

Business CAREERS

29. Financial analysts assess economic performance of companies and industries for corporate clients. Personal financial advisors assess individuals' financial needs. Working conditions involve long hours, travel, and deadlines. A college degree is required for financial analysts and is recommended for personal financial advisors. Certifications are available for both groups. Opportunities for advancement: portfolio or financial manager. Jobs in this field are expected to increase faster than average. Developing mathematical, computer, and analytical skills is important as preparation.

Role Play

30. Presentations should address the competencies noted in the Role Play. Students should understand the differences in the roles and interests of consumer advocates and members of the banking industry.

Standardized Test Practice
1. A

 **STRATEGIES FOR STANDARDIZED TEST PREP SUCCESS**

Test Savvy Some people like to answer the multiple-choice test items they are sure of first and then go back to those questions they were unsure of, while others go in order. Either approach works, but the first response is usually correct. However, do not be afraid to change an answer you know is wrong.

FOCUS

🔔 Bell Ringer Activity

Real-World Modeling
Ask volunteers to share experiences they have had sculpting, building, or modeling three-dimensional objects. (Answers will vary but students may have made cakes, sculpted statues, or built projects in woodshop.) Write a list of objects on the board. Ask students if they think it is easier to make something when they have a plan before they start. Ask students to brainstorm reasons companies might want do their planning using modeling software on a computer. (Students may mention that computers reduce time, expense, and difficulty and improve accuracy and detail.)

TEACH

Teaching Points
The Basics of Credit
Ask students to name different groups in our economy who use credit. (Different groups in our economy who use credit include consumers, businesses, and governments.) Ask students to identify reasons it might be important for companies to have good credit. (When companies want to buy equipment and supplies, they may need to borrow money to do so. Having good credit means that companies are able to borrow money when they need it and that they will not have to pay high interest rates.)

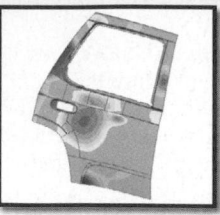

Ping Fu

Chairperson/President/CEO, Geomagic
Geomagic makes 3-D geometric modeling software for manufacturers, such as Toyota® and Fisher-Price®. The North Carolina company was co-founded by Ping Fu, who grew up in China during the Cultural Revolution. Her company allows large-scale customization of individualized products at the same cost as mass manufacturing.

Q & A

Describe your job responsibilities.
Ping: The majority of my work involves talking to and corresponding with our headquarters and offices around the world. I believe strongly in empowering people. My job is to clear obstacles and provide directions that help them meet and exceed their goals.

What skills are most important in your business?
Ping: Geomagic is a technology-driven company, so an understanding of technical matters is important. The ability to understand how technology can be applied and used to make good products and services that people want to buy is vital. A person must also have the vision and be willing to take risks to change a long-entrenched way of doing business.

What is your key to success?
Ping: Great people—I can't make the company successful by myself. I need people to help me, and it's this desire to work for the company and make a positive contribution to society at large that makes Geomagic successful. I look at business in terms of contribution, rather than success.

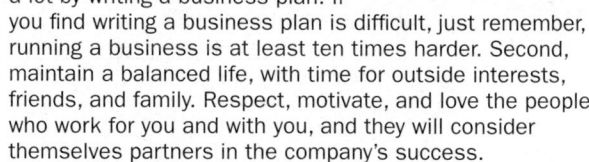

What advice would you give students interested in starting a business?
Ping: First, think about why you want to start a business and try to imagine what success looks like, not how much money you can make. Then try to write a business plan that will deliver the success that you imagined. You will learn a lot by writing a business plan. If you find writing a business plan is difficult, just remember, running a business is at least ten times harder. Second, maintain a balanced life, with time for outside interests, friends, and family. Respect, motivate, and love the people who work for you and with you, and they will consider themselves partners in the company's success.

Critical Thinking *How is launching and running a company like or unlike being a parent?*

Critical Thinking
A positive corporate environment can pave the way to a successful business. Entrepreneurs are challenged to not just persuade others to share their vision, but also to support and encourage their employees' strengths as the company grows. This guidance is much like a parent and child relationship.

Some Qualifications Needed to be the Owner of a Computer-Aided Design Company

Academic Skills and Abilities

Computer science; mathematics; information systems; computer programming; interpersonal skills; general business management skills; verbal and written communication skills; organizing and planning skills

Academic Skills Required to Complete Tasks at Geomagic			
Tasks	Math	Science	English Language Arts
Hold meetings			◆
Assign duties			◆
Determine client requirements	◆	◆	◆
Use CAD to visualize products	◆	◆	◆
Customer service			◆
Schedule employees	◆		◆
Remain technically up-to-date	◆	◆	◆
Analyze financials	◆		◆

Education and Training

Occupations in the computer-aided design (CAD) require a bachelor's degree in industrial design, architecture, or engineering. However, a master's degree or higher is preferred. Creativity and technical knowledge are crucial, as is a strong sense of the esthetic—an eye for color and detail and a sense of balance and proportion. Designers must understand the technical aspects of how products function. Despite the advancement of CAD, sketching ability remains an important advantage.

Career Path

Commercial and industrial designers usually receive on-the-job training and normally need 1 to 3 years of training before they can advance to higher-level positions. Experienced designers in large firms may advance to chief designer, design department head, or other supervisory positions. Some experienced designers open their own design firms.

Preparing for a Career
Self-Assessment Checklist

Use this self-assessment checklist to help determine ways you can improve your ability to work productively with others.

✔ Exhibit a professional attitude by listening attentively when others speak to you.

✔ Take accurate notes during meetings and conference calls.

✔ Write succinct and direct e-mails and memos, always remembering to check for errors before sending any communication.

✔ Avoid office gossip that can harm others and hurt your reputation.

✔ Show initiative by responding to concerns clearly and politely so that others know you understand problems and will do all you can to solve them.

✔ Never blame someone else for your mistakes.

✔ Treat all coworkers as skilled, competent associates.

✔ Be aware of your body language and facial expressions when responding to speakers.

491

Preparing for a Career
Paying the Bills Most people have to work to pay their bills and can get into financial trouble if their income ceases for one reason or another. Remind students that career planning should involve financial considerations that go beyond just how much money they might be able to make if they are extremely successful. Ask students: Why might teaching be a better career path than a career as an actor or professional athlete? (Answers will vary but may include having a reliable income and better prospects for a long-term career. The job outlook for teachers is excellent, too.) Tell students they will have an opportunity to think about careers and the career-planning process as they read the Self-Assessment Checklists in this book.

ASSESS

Write About It
Geomagic

Ask students to write a summary of what they like about Geomagic's business concept. (Students may say that they like the idea that computers can be used to help make models for 3-D objects. They may also like the high-tech nature of the business.)

Academic Vocabulary
Career Planning

Ask students to read the Self-Assessment Checklist, then write one or more paragraphs about preparing for a career. Have students use some words from the Academic Vocabulary Glossary. (Example: Learning to *cooperate* and work well with others is part of being able to *conduct* oneself professionally. Cooperation requires people to be *flexible* and to *function* in ways that *accommodate* other people's needs.)

CLOSE

Cooperative Learning
Technology Applications

Ask students to work in pairs and develop an idea for a software program. Have them work together to develop an advertisement for the software. Encourage students to use technology applications to design the brochure and integrate images and marketing copy that communicates information about the software. (Brochures should include marketing copy and images.)

491

FOCUS

Discussion Starter

Lead a discussion about making credit decisions. Ask students how they can make the best possible credit decisions.

Step 1

Brainstorm Skills

Have students go to the *Introduction to Business* Online Learning Center through **glencoe.com** for a graphic organizer they can use to brainstorm the skills needed to complete the project.

Step 2

Choose a Purchase You Would Like to Make

Students can use the Occupational Outlook Handbook Web site to explore options.

TEACH

Step 3

Build Background

Technology Have students brainstorm ways they can use technology to get the lowest credit costs. (People can use the Internet to shop for credit and research trends. Many people successfully lower their cost of credit by calling their credit card companies and asking for lower interest rates.)

Making Credit Decisions

Credit used wisely is a helpful way to buy large products, such as a vehicle or house. Smart consumers only use credit to buy things they need, not things they want.

Thematic Project Assignment

In this project you will write and give a speech that describes how to obtain credit and use it wisely. In your speech you also should discuss the misuse of credit and the consequences of using credit unwisely.

Step 1 | Brainstorm Skills You Need to Complete This Activity

Your success in writing and delivering a speech will depend on your skills. Preview the activity, then brainstorm a list of the skills you will need to use to complete the activity and describe how you will use them. Skills you might use include:

Academic Skills — reading, writing, and interpersonal skills
Basic Skills — speaking, listening, and thinking
Technology Skills — word processing and keyboarding

 SKILLS PREVIEW Go to the *Introduction to Business* Online Learning Center through **glencoe.com** for a graphic organizer you can use to brainstorm the skills you will use to complete the project.

Step 2 | Choose a Purchase You Would Someday Like to Make

Think about the cost of the item you want to buy. Is it a vehicle? A DVD player? A sound system? Then think of how you will pay for the item on credit, and how this can help you or hurt you.

Step 3 | Build Background Knowledge

Preview information on making credit decisions.

Buying on Credit

Most consumers buy on credit, which can work for them or against them. Credit cards come in handy when you want to buy a new CD or even a player for it. Using credit cards too much gets young people into trouble. When many young people get their first taste of credit, they feel free to buy all those things that they could not afford before. That is a mistake. Having a credit card does not mean you suddenly have more money.

Protect your credit by using credit cards and making sure you pay them each month when they become due. Pay more than the minimum payment. Someday you will want to use credit for a large purchase, such as a car. Using a credit card wisely will help you get credit for large purchases. Misusing credit will keep you from getting more credit in the future.

glencoe.com

Step 4

Connect with Your Community

Ask students to describe how credit strengthens their community. (Wise use of credit to purchase items of long-term value strengthens the community by building community wealth.)

Step 4 Connect with Your Community

Interview two adults in your community about their experiences with credit. Ask the adults what steps they take to help them obtain and then maintain credit. Think about how important it is to maintain a good credit history.

Step 5 Research How to Obtain Credit

Use library and Internet resources to research how you can obtain credit and what you need to do to maintain good credit. Also, research what happens when people misuse credit. Use the project checklist as a guide to your research. Keep records of your sources of information.

Step 6 Develop Your Oral Presentation

Use word-processing software to develop a short speech that includes all of the information described in the project checklist.

Making Credit Decisions

✔ Make a list of main ideas and supporting details that you want to cover in your speech. Then give your speech to your class.

✔ Have three main points in your speech: (1) how to obtain credit, (2) how to maintain good credit, and (3) what happens if you misuse credit.

✔ Write an introduction for your speech by opening with one of the following: (1) an interesting idea about credit, (2) a fact, such as how many people use credit cards, or (3) a story about how you have or someone you know has used credit.

✔ Include details that support your three main points.

✔ Create a chart that illustrates what a monthly payment will be on a $1,000 loan at 12.99% interest. Use this chart to show how to maintain good credit as well as what happens if you do not make the payment each month.

✔ Wrap up your speech with one of the following: (1) an interesting idea about credit, (2) a fact, such as how many people use credit cards, or (3) a story about how you have or someone you know has used credit.

✔ Practice your speech at least five or six times in front of an adult. Ask him or her to help you make your speech better.

Self Connections

✔ Discuss the results of your research with the adults you interviewed.

✔ Describe how the adults obtain and use credit.

✔ Explain what the investigation and its results mean to you.

Step 7 Evaluate Your Presentation

@ **RUBRIC** Go to the *Introduction to Business* Online Learning Center through **glencoe.com** for a rubric you can use to evaluate your final report.

493

TEACH (cont.)

Step 6
Develop an Oral Presentation
Give students these tips on speaking:

• Know your audience.
• Organize your report by developing an outline and using titles and subtitles.
• Speak concisely (briefly but completely).
• Speak in easy-to-read, simple language.

ASSESS

Step 7
Evaluate Your Presentation
Rubric Encourage students to use the rubric to evaluate their final presentations.

CLOSE

Culminating Activity
Credit Interviews
Have students form pairs and interview each other about the credit issues they researched and how their opinions and perceptions about using credit have evolved during the course of the project. (Interviews will vary depending on students' research about the use of credit and reactions to their research.)

Step 5

Research How to Obtain Credit
Students can go to the *Introduction to Business* Online Learning Center through **glencoe.com** for a rubric they can use as a content checklist when researching their presentations.

Chapter	Section	Unit Objectives
Chapter 28 *Managing Personal Finances*	28.1	**Explain** the steps involved in the financial planning process.
		Identify sources of financial information.
		Discuss sources of risk.
		Discuss the consequences of choices.
	28.2	**Discuss** importance of budgeting.
		List the steps for preparing a budget.
Chapter 29 *Checking Accounts*	29.1	**Discuss** the different types of checking accounts and how they work.
		Discuss other services and offerings that banks provide checking account holders.
	29.2	**Describe** how checking account holders manage their bank transactions.
		Describe the procedure for bringing your account into agreement with bank records.
Chapter 30 *Savings Accounts*	30.1	**Discuss** the three reasons people save money.
		Describe compound interest.
	30.2	**Differentiate** a regular savings account from a CD, a money market fund, and a money market deposit account.
		Explain two advantages and two disadvantages of savings accounts.
Chapter 31 *Investing*	31.1	**Discuss** two goals to set before you start making investments.
		Name five characteristics of bonds.
		Differentiate between types of federal, municipal government, and corporate bonds.
		Describe the advantages and disadvantages of investing in bonds.
	31.2	**Discuss** stocks and stock markets.
		Identify the advantages and disadvantages of owning stocks.
Chapter 32 *Real Estate and Other Investment Options*	32.1	**Describe** the three types of residential property.
		Discuss aspects of home buying that a potential home owner should know.
		Determine the differences between rental property and undeveloped property.
	32.2	**Describe** how precious metals, precious gems, and other commodities as well as collectibles can impact an investment plan.
		Discuss the advantages and disadvantages of buying and selling collectibles online.

Understanding the Coding

Brackets Brackets on the reduced student edition page correspond to teaching strategies and activities in the Teacher Wraparound Edition. As you teach the lesson, the brackets show you exactly where to use the teaching strategies and activities.

Letters The letters on the reduced student edition page identify the type of strategy or activity. See the key below to learn about the different types of strategies and activities.

Ability Levels Leveled teaching strategies are identified by one of three codes to give you an idea of their suitability for students of varying learning styles and abilities.

Resources Key program resources are listed in each chapter. Icons indicate the format of resources.

KEY to Letters

D **Develop Concepts** activities help teachers gauge and plan for students' concept development.

R **Reading Strategy** activities help you teach reading skills and vocabulary.

C **Critical Thinking** strategies help students apply and extend what they have learned.

U **Universal Access** activities provide differentiated instruction for English language learners and suggestions for teaching various types of learners.

S **Skill Practice** provides leveled instruction for meeting individual needs and learning styles.

W **Writing Support** activities provide writing opportunities to help students comprehend the text.

N C L B **No Child Left Behind** activities help students practice and improve their abilities in academic subjects.

KEY to Ability Levels

L1 Strategies should be within the ability range of all students. Often full class participation is required.

L2 Strategies are for average to above-average students or for small groups. Some teacher direction is necessary.

L3 Strategies are designed for students able and willing to work independently. Minimal teacher direction is necessary.

KEY to Resource Icons

Print Material

CD-ROM

Online Learning Center with Podcasts

BusinessWeek *Reader and Case Study*

In Unit 10, your students can learn more about business in the real world through the following *BusinessWeek* Readers and Case Studies:

Follow My Money
A host of young bloggers have opened their finances for all to see—and learn from. (page 500)

The Check Cashed Around the World
It's not here yet, but banks are expanding services for globe-trotting customers. (page 517)

Fiscal Fitness for Teens
Teach them that a paycheck is more than a chance to play big spender at the mall. It's an opportunity to bank on a cushier future. (page 533)

Not Your Average Science Project
As high school students select topics for the annual Intel Science Talent Search, they typically gravitate toward math, biochemistry, and medicine. Chad Sandler chose mutual-fund managers. (page 558)

Copper's Golden Hue
The not-so-precious metal's price hits an all-time record, as gold and oil also soar. Here's why this may just be the beginning. (page 572)

Chapter Features and Activities

Ask STANDARD &POOR'S

Chapter	Feature Title	Mathematics Activity	Page
28	Understanding Hedge Funds	Percent Increase on an Investment	496
29	Checking Accounts: Budgeting	Adding and Subtracting Expenditures	512
30	Savings Accounts	Comparing Investments	
31	Corporate Financial Performance and the Effect on Credit Quality	Yields on Bonds	544
32	Investing in Bonds and Real Estate: Credit Quality and Volatility	Averaging Credit Scores	564

BusinessWeek Reader and Case Study

Chapter	Feature Title	Active Learning	Page
28	Follow My Money	Develop a Budget of Your Daily Expenses	500
29	The Check Cashed Around the World	Research Traveler's Checks and Alternatives	517
30	Fiscal Fitness for Teens	Research CDs	533
31	Not Your Average Science Project	Form an Investment Group	558
32	Copper's Golden Hue	Research High-Conductive Metals	572

Science/Tech TRENDS

Chapter	Feature Title	WebQuest Activity	Page
28	Budgeting for IT Productivity	Research Ways IT Costs Influence Businesses' Investments	505
29	Biometrics	Biometric Technologies Changes to the Security Industry	520
30	Nanotechnology	Research Nanotechnology	538
31	Stock Tickers	Research Inventions	557
32	Eco-Friendly Building	Research Eco-Friendly Building Materials	573

?ETHICS in Business

Chapter	Feature Title	Page
29	Buyer's Remorse	516
31	Putting the Client First	551

International Business

Chapter	Feature Title	Page
28	The Euro	501
30	Guarding Savings Security	531
31	International Real Estate	567

Reading Strategies

Before You Read

Graphic Organizer

As You Read

✔ Reading Check

After You Read

Money Management

Unit Overview

Introduce the Unit

Introduce the unit by describing the main concepts of each chapter in the unit.

Unit 10 is about money management and how it affects everyday life.

Chapter 28 discusses personal financial planning and budgeting.

Chapter 29 explains checking account basics along with account records.

Chapter 30 is about saving and describes the various types of savings accounts.

Chapter 31 introduces investments in stocks and bonds and the markets that sell them.

Chapter 32 discusses other investment opportunities such as real estate and collectibles, as well as investment diversification.

00:00 OUT OF TIME?

If class time is too short to cover all of the chapters in this unit, have students:

- Write down the vocabulary terms and their definitions.
- Read the chapter summaries at the beginning of each chapter review.
- Go to the *Introduction to Business* Online Learning Center through **glencoe.com** to download free Study-to-Go content to their PDAs or cell phones.

494

Real-World Business and Career Profile

Preview

Integrated Management Services Engineers Tell students that at the end of this unit, they will learn about the founders of IMS Engineers, P.A., and how they achieved their success. IMS Engineers offers civil engineering services. This Jackson, Mississippi-based company is one of only a handful of minority-owned engineering firms in the country. Ask students why building roads, bridges, and water-supply systems might be a good business to pursue. (Society needs infrastructure like roads, bridges, and water-supply systems if it is to grow and progress.)

Real-World Business and Career Profile

Preview

Integrated Management Services Engineers (IMS) offers civil engineering services that range from constructing buildings to digging ditches to aviation engineering. At the end of this unit, you will learn about IMS founders John Calhoun and Rod Hill and how they achieved their success.

Decision Making What steps can you take now to begin planning your career in a global economy?

Unit 10   *Thematic Project Preview*

Building a Financial Future After completing this unit, you will research ways that building a financial future is important to your life.

Project Checklist As you read the chapters in this unit, use this checklist to prepare for the unit project.

- ✔ Think about the financial future you want to build.
- ✔ Think about ways you could build a financial future.
- ✔ Look for people and institutions in your community that will help you build a financial future.
- ✔ Think about the types of jobs and careers in the financial industry.

495

Build Background

Ask students these questions to activate prior knowledge:

Chapter 28
Why is it important to learn how to manage your finances? (If you carefully plan how to spend, save, and invest your money. you can live comfortably, have financial security, and achieve your goals.)

Chapter 29
What do you know about using a checking account? (Students' knowledge about checking accounts is likely to vary widely.)

Chapter 30
Why are savings important? (Students might be actively saving for something right now such as a car or the latest electronic gadget. They also might have heard adults talk about savings.)

Chapter 31
Why is it important to learn the basics of investing? (Learning the basics of investing can help students prepare for their financial futures and to understand everyday business activities.)

Chapter 32
Do you think buying real estate or collectibles are good ways of investing? (Students might want to own a home in the future, but they may not think of their home or hobbies as investments.)

Unit   *Thematic Project Preview*

Building a Financial Future
Tell students that when they complete this unit, they will understand what they need to do to build a good financial future for themselves. Students will be able to consider how finances affect their lives.

C Critical Thinking
Ask students how they think they will be able to build a financial future for themselves and their families. (Students should recognize that they must plan their financial futures. Help students think about financial planning and how it will affect their futures.)

Standards-Based Lesson Planning
Introduction to Business provides students with instruction and assessment in the following fundamental content areas:

Content Standards Correlations	
Explain how consumer spending affects an individual's standard of living.	pp. 499, 500, 504–507, 509–510
Discuss and develop long- and short-term financial goals.	pp. 499, 500, 504–507, 509–510
Create and analyze an individual plan for managing personal finances.	pp. 499–500, 507, 511
Develop a financial plan.	pp. 499–500, 507, 511
Design a plan for money management. Assess the need for personal, family, and business budgets.	pp. 499–500, 507, 509–511
Explain the importance of money management among consumers, businesses, and governments.	pp. 504, 509
Analyze information on budgeting and responsible consumerism.	pp. 504–507, 509–511
Explain why budgeting is essential for consumers, businesses, and governments.	pp. 504–507, 511
Research and present major financial issues for the individual, such as money management, banking systems and services, saving, and investing.	pp. 505, 509–511
Prepare and maintain a personal budget.	p. 511

NCLB
Activities, information, and skills practice will help your students attain No Child Left Behind proficiency. Students will improve their abilities in the following academic standards areas:

Academic Standards Correlations		
English Language Arts	Activities/Features	Page
NCTE 3 Apply strategies to interpret texts	Applying Academics to Business Standardized Test Practice	pp. 510, 511
NCTE 6 Apply knowledge of language structure and conventions to discuss texts	Applying Academics to Business	p. 510
NCTE 7 Conduct research and gather, evaluate, and synthesize data to communicate discoveries	After You Read	p. 507
NCTE 12 Use language to accomplish individual purposes	After You Read	p. 507
Mathematics		
Number and Operations Understand numbers, ways of representing numbers, relationships between numbers, and number systems	Ask S&P	p. 496
Data Analysis and Probability Formulate questions that can be addressed with data and collect, organize, and display relevant data to answer them	Applying Academics to Business	p. 510
Number and Operations Understand meanings of operations and how they relate to one another	After You Read	p. 502
Problem Solving Apply and adapt a variety of appropriate strategies to solve problems	Applying Academics to Business	p. 510
Science		
Content Standard F Students should develop understanding of science and technology in local, national, and global challenges	Science/Tech Trends	p. 505

Correlations   This chart shows the 21st Century Skills, foundation skills, and workplace competencies that students develop as they work in this chapter.

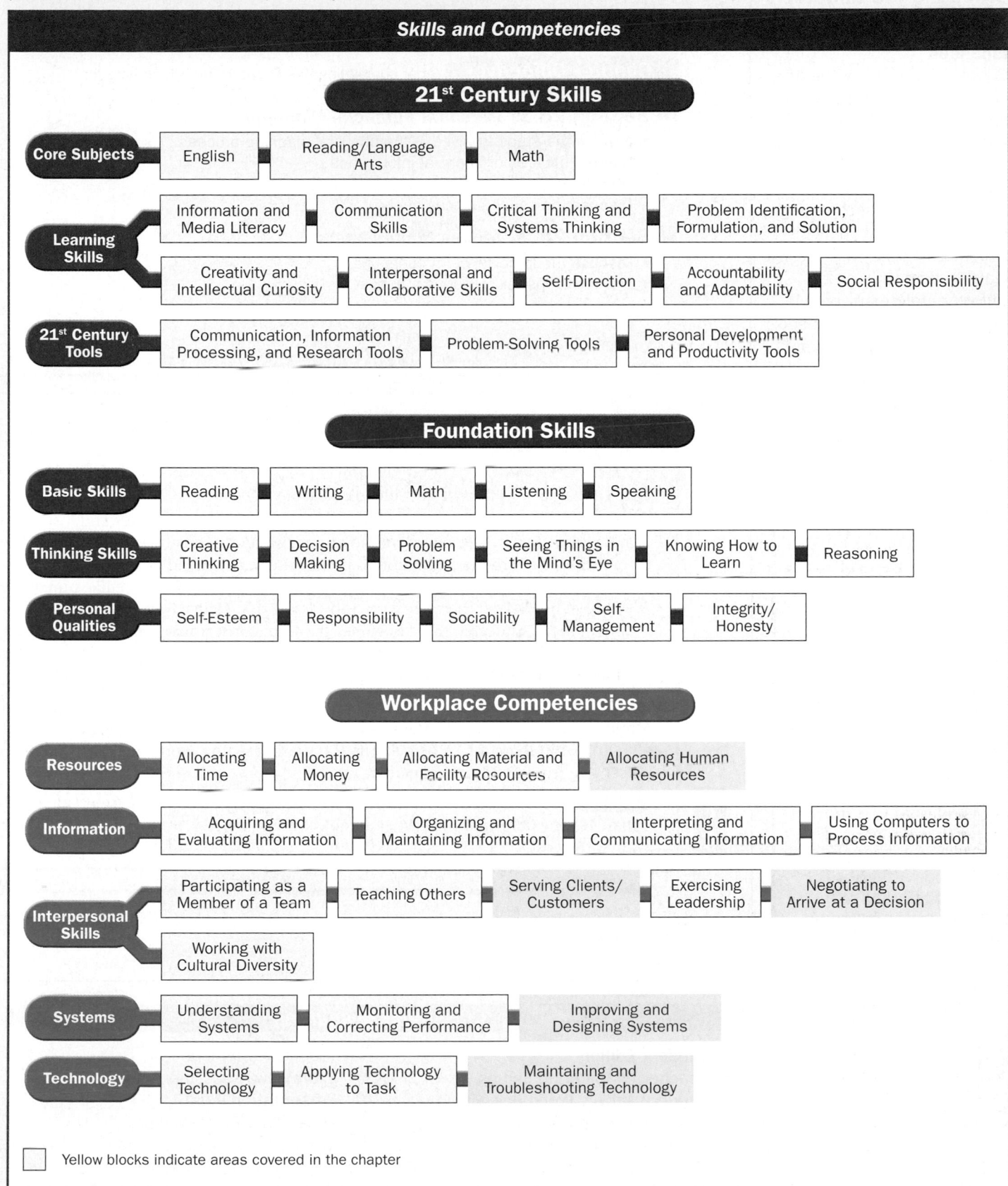

Skills and Competencies

21st Century Skills

Core Subjects
| English | Reading/Language Arts | Math |

Learning Skills
| Information and Media Literacy | Communication Skills | Critical Thinking and Systems Thinking | Problem Identification, Formulation, and Solution |

| Creativity and Intellectual Curiosity | Interpersonal and Collaborative Skills | Self-Direction | Accountability and Adaptability | Social Responsibility |

21st Century Tools
| Communication, Information Processing, and Research Tools | Problem-Solving Tools | Personal Development and Productivity Tools |

Foundation Skills

Basic Skills
| Reading | Writing | Math | Listening | Speaking |

Thinking Skills
| Creative Thinking | Decision Making | Problem Solving | Seeing Things in the Mind's Eye | Knowing How to Learn | Reasoning |

Personal Qualities
| Self-Esteem | Responsibility | Sociability | Self-Management | Integrity/Honesty |

Workplace Competencies

Resources
| Allocating Time | Allocating Money | Allocating Material and Facility Resources | Allocating Human Resources |

Information
| Acquiring and Evaluating Information | Organizing and Maintaining Information | Interpreting and Communicating Information | Using Computers to Process Information |

Interpersonal Skills
| Participating as a Member of a Team | Teaching Others | Serving Clients/Customers | Exercising Leadership | Negotiating to Arrive at a Decision |

| Working with Cultural Diversity |

Systems
| Understanding Systems | Monitoring and Correcting Performance | Improving and Designing Systems |

Technology
| Selecting Technology | Applying Technology to Task | Maintaining and Troubleshooting Technology |

☐ Yellow blocks indicate areas covered in the chapter

Managing Personal Finances

Chapter 28

Chapter Overview

Introduce the Chapter

Managing Personal Finances

Chapter 28 explains the processes involved in personal financial planning and budgeting.

Building Background

Many students think managing their personal finances is something they will learn to deal with later. Unfortunately, many people do not learn how to manage their finances until they are in financial trouble.

Ask STANDARD &POOR'S

›› Math Answer

275%. Use *x* to represent the percent increase: $2,000x = $5,500. To solve for *x*, divide both sides by $2,000 to get *x* = 2.75 or 275%.

›› Extension Activity

Carla changed jobs 10 years ago. When she left her previous employer her 401(k) was worth $45,000. She rolled the entire amount into an IRA invested in a mutual fund that has earned approximately 10% each year. Today the IRA is worth $117,000. What is the percent increase on her investment? (260%. $45,000x = $117,000 or *x* = 2.6 or 260%.)

NCLB

Activity correlates to Math standards.

496

Chapter Objectives After completing this chapter, you will be able to:

▶ **Section 28.1** *Personal Financial Planning*
- **Explain** the steps involved in the financial planning process.
- **Identify** sources of financial information.
- **Discuss** sources of risk.
- **Discuss** the consequences of choices.

▶ **Section 28.2** *Money Management*
- **Discuss** the importance of budgeting.
- **List** the steps for preparing a budget.

Ask STANDARD &POOR'S Understanding Hedge Funds

Q: What are my options if I'm able to take a big risk?

A: Hedge funds are private investment funds for wealthy individuals and institutional investors. By law you must have an annual income exceeding $250,000 and investable assets of around $1 million to participate in the world of hedge funds. This is mainly because hedge funds are limited partnerships that operate like unregulated mutual funds, and therefore carry substantial risk. Hedge funds use a variety of investment strategies, some of which are more conservative, employing little or no leverage, while others carry more risk, using leverage and derivatives. The term *leverage* means that for a given amount of money, an investor can control an asset worth a larger amount.

Mathematics Ten years ago Mateo made a valuable long-term investment. He spent $2,000 on 100 shares of XYZ stock. His 100 shares are now worth $5,500. What is the percent increase on his investment?

THEORY **Percents Greater Than 100** Percents greater than 100 represent values greater than 1. For example, if the cost of an object is 250 percent of another, it is 2.5 or $2\frac{1}{2}$ times the cost.

NCLB

Classroom Resources

- Student Edition
- Teacher Wraparound Edition
- Student Activity Workbook with Academic Integration
- Student Activity Workbook with Academic Integration TAE
- *Fast File*, Unit 10 Resources
- Inclusion in the Business Education Classroom

- TeacherWorks Plus
- *ExamView Assessment Suite*
- Presentation Plus!
- Vocabulary PuzzleMaker
- Interactive Student Edition
- Online Student Edition
- Online Learning Center with Podcasts

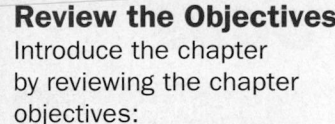

● Financial Planning Money management is the process of planning how to get the most from your income. **How can financial planning help you to have the opportunity to enjoy the luxuries of life, such as entertainment?**

Review the Objectives
Introduce the chapter by reviewing the chapter objectives:

Section 28.1 *Objectives*
Explain the steps involved in the financial planning process. (Determine your financial situation, develop your financial goals, identify alternative courses of action, evaluate your alternatives, create and use your financial plan of action, and review and revise your plan.)

Identify sources of financial information. (the Internet, magazines, and newspapers)

Discuss sources of risk. (inflation, risk that interest rates will rise or fall, risk that income will rise or fall, risks associated with personal choices, and liquidity risk)

Discuss the consequences of choices. (An opportunity cost, sometimes called a tradeoff, is what is given up when one choice is made instead of another.)

Section 28.2 *Objectives*
Discuss the importance of budgeting. (It allows individuals and businesses to manage their money and plan for using their income in a way that best meets their wants and needs.)

List the steps for preparing a budget. (Set your goals; estimate your income; budget for unexpected expenses and savings; budget for fixed expenses; budget for variable expenses; record what you spend; and review spending and saving patterns.)

Discuss the Photo
● Financial Planning Read the caption on the photo to students: Money management is the process of planning how to get the most from your income.

Ask students: How can financial planning help you to have the opportunity to enjoy the luxuries of life, such as entertainment? (Financial planning can help individuals set priorities and set aside sufficient money to meet their needs and still have the opportunity to enjoy luxuries.)

FOCUS

Bell Ringer Activity

Personal Financial Planning

Write or project these two words on the board: Wants and Needs. Ask students how these words relate to personal financial planning. (Some students might suggest that it is important to distinguish between wants and needs in order to plan personal finances.)

Preteaching

Presentation Plus!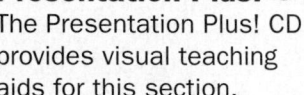

The Presentation Plus! CD provides visual teaching aids for this section.

PuzzleMaker

Use the Vocabulary PuzzleMaker to create a puzzle of the section's key terms. Students can complete the puzzle on paper or on a computer.

Graphic Organizer

Tell students to go to the Online Learning Center through **glencoe.com** for a printable graphic organizer. (When completed, the graphic organizer will include the following: determine your current financial situation, develop your financial goals, identify possible courses of action, evaluate your alternatives, implement your financial plan of action, and review and revise your plan.)

N C L B Connects academics to content.

498

Personal Financial Planning

Reading Guide

● Before You Read

Think about some ways you manage your money now and your plans to manage money in the future.

Read to Learn
- Explain the steps involved in the financial planning process.
- Identify sources of financial information.
- Discuss sources of risk.
- Discuss the consequences of choices.

D

The Main Idea
Financial planning provides a solid foundation for making financial decisions. It involves looking at your financial position and setting goals.

Key Concepts
- Making Financial Decisions
- Sources of Financial Information
- Understanding Risk
- Consequences of Choices

Vocabulary
Key Terms
personal financial planning
goals
opportunity cost

 Go to the *Introduction to Business* Online Learning Center through **glencoe.com** for a printable graphic organizer.

Academic Vocabulary
You will find these words in your reading and on your tests. Make sure you know their meanings.

sources   revise
achieve   resources

Graphic Organizer
In a figure like the one below, list the six financial planning steps.

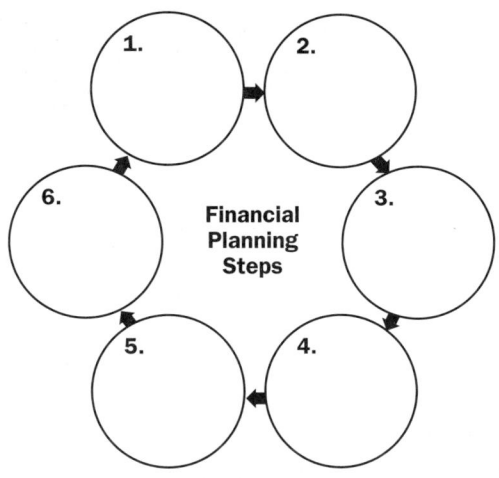

Academic Standards
English Language Arts
NCTE 1 Read texts to acquire new information
NCTE 9 Develop an understanding of diversity in language use across cultures
Mathematics
Number and Operations Understand meanings of operations and how they relate to one another

Reading Guide

● Before You Read

Students might describe how they plan the use of their allowance to cover their expenses.

D Develop Concepts

The Main Idea Ask students: What are some common financial goals? (Common financial goals include having a down payment for a house or vehicle, reducing debt, paying off student loans, or retiring.)

Making Financial Decisions

Personal finance refers to all the things in your life that involve money. **Personal financial planning** means spending, saving, and investing your money so you can enjoy the kind of life you want, along with financial security. Everyone has different financial goals. **Goals** are the things you want to accomplish. Getting a college education, buying a car, and starting a business are some examples of goals. Planning your personal finances is important because it will help you reach your goals. The financial planning process has six steps.

✔ **Reading Check** **Define** What is personal financial planning?

Step 1: Determine Your Financial Situation

Once you have determined your financial situation, you will be able to start planning. First, make a list of your savings, monthly income (money you receive, such as job earnings, an allowance, tips, gifts, and interest on bank accounts), monthly expenses (money you spend), and debts (money you owe to others). A good way to estimate your expenses is to keep a careful record of every amount you spend for one month.

Step 2: Develop Your Financial Goals

To develop clear financial goals, you will need to think about your attitude toward money. Is it more important to you to spend your money now or to save for the future? What are your wants and needs? Would you rather get a job right after high school or continue your education?

● **As You Read**

Think about how your wants and needs affect your financial goals.

● **A Beginning Step**
Planning your personal finances will help you reach your goals. **What is the first step in personal financial planning?**

TEACH

Discussion Starter
Financial Goals
Start a discussion by asking students to identify financial goals that people might have. Encourage students to think beyond their immediate circumstances. (Allow students to express their goals without judgment. Common financial goals include paying for college; buying a car; starting a business; buying a house or condo; saving for retirement; saving for a vacation; saving for a wedding; and buying a motorcycle, boat, or sports car.)

R **Reading Strategy**

Identify Ask students to identify the four components needed to determine their financial situation. (The four components are savings, monthly income, monthly expenses, and debt.)

✔ **Reading Check**

Define Personal financial planning is spending, saving, and investing your money so you can have the kind of life you want as well as financial security.

● **As You Read**

Students should prioritize their wants and needs, which will help them to prioritize their financial goals.

Discuss the Photo
● **A Beginning Step** The first step is to determine your current financial situation.

TEACH (cont.)

S Skill Practice

Guided Practice

Identify Ask students to identify the six steps in the financial planning process. (See Graphic Organizer answer on page 498.) **L1**

Illustrate an Idea Ask students to illustrate the six steps in the financial planning process. Point out that Step 6 will have a significant impact on how they interpret the steps visually. (Illustrations will vary. For instance, for Step 4, students might include a list of pros and cons regarding their alternatives.) **L2**

Explain Through Example Ask students to create a simple example appropriate to someone still in school to explain how the financial planning process works. (Answers will vary, but should include all six steps.) **L3**

ASSESS

Review Key Terms

Have students write sentences using each key term.

Study-to-Go Have students go to the Online Learning Center through **glencoe.com** to download free **Study-to-Go** content to their PDAs or cell phones.

Making Money Some students will say yes, but others may feel that they do not need to be paid for doing things they should do normally.

500

Real World

Making Money The most common way for teens to earn money is through an allowance. However, many teens do not get an allowance. Some other ways to get money may be by doing work around the house, or as a reward for receiving good grades. *Do you think you should be paid for doing chores or getting good grades?*

Step 3: Identify Possible Courses of Action

It is important to consider your options before making a decision. Generally, you will have several possible courses of action.

Step 4: Evaluate Your Alternatives

When you evaluate your alternatives, use the **sources** of financial information that are available. Look at where you are in your life, your present financial situation, and your personal values. Consider the consequences and risks of each decision you make. Your financial goals will help you determine the best option.

Step 5: Implement a Financial Plan of Action

A plan of action is a list of ways to **achieve** your financial goals. If your goal is to increase your savings, a plan of action could be to cut back on spending. If you want to increase your income, you could get a part-time job or work more hours at your present job.

Step 6: Review and Revise Your Plan

As you get older, your finances and needs will change. That means your financial plan will have to change, too. You should reevaluate and **revise** it every year.

BusinessWeek *Reader and Case Study*

Follow My Money

A host of young bloggers have opened their finances for all to see—and learn from.

Jonathan Ping is not a financial guru. He's not a certified financial planner. And he's not a millionaire (yet). He's simply a 27-year-old engineer living with his wife and dog in a rented house in Portland, Oregon. Within the next 18 months he hopes to scrape up $100,000 for a down payment on a home, and he wants to build a net worth of $1 million by age 45. So far he's at $88,953.

How do I know this? It's in bold type in the top right-hand corner of his Web log, MyMoneyBlog.com, where Ping keeps a daily tally of his progress. He's one of more than 150 bloggers, mostly 22 to 35, who have adopted an open-source approach to personal finance. Most keep their names secret, but that's about all they hide. In stark contrast to

their parents' generation, for whom comparing incomes can be awkward, if not downright taboo, bloggers list financial information down to the dollar in retirement, brokerage, and savings accounts.

 CASE STUDY Go to the *Introduction to Business* Online Learning Center through **glencoe.com** for the *BusinessWeek* Reader Case Study.

Active Learning

Use a spreadsheet to develop a budget of your daily expenses. Examine your budget carefully to determine which costs meet your values and goals and which ones you could eliminate to save money. Write a journal entry about your findings.

BusinessWeek *Reader and Case Study*

Follow My Money

 CASE STUDY Have students go to the *Introduction to Business* Online Learning Center through **glencoe.com** to download a Case Study activity that corresponds to the article. The activity and answer key are also available on the TeacherWorks Plus CD.

Active Learning

Budgets will vary, but encourage students to focus on their financial goals instead of expense reduction. Items that are considered unnecessary will depend on each student's circumstances. Students should make an attempt to distinguish between items that satisfy their needs and wants.

International Business

The Euro

In 1957, the Treaty of Rome initiated the objective of a common European market to increase economic prosperity among the people of Europe. The Single European Act of 1986 built on this objective by organizing the Economic and Monetary Union (EMU), which laid out the foundation for a single European currency. Euro banknotes and coins were put into circulation on Jan. 1, 2002. Currently the euro is the currency of several countries in the European Union.

Examples of Languages Across Cultures

Q: In Mandarin Chinese, how do you say "Please" and "Thank you"?

A: 請 (traditional) or 请 (simplified) (pronounced: Chēeng)
謝謝 (traditional) or 谢谢 (simplified) (pronounced: Shǐ-ĕ shǐ-ĕ)

What are some of the benefits of having a common currency throughout Europe? Why have only 12 countries adopted the euro?

Sources of Financial Information

When making financial decisions, the Internet is a good place to get information on social and economic conditions. Most corporations put facts about their company and financial situation on their Web site. They will also mail information that is requested. Magazines such as *BusinessWeek, Time,* and *U.S. News & World Report* and newspapers such as *The Wall Street Journal, The New York Times,* and *Financial Times* can also help.

Understanding Risk

When you make a financial decision, you also accept certain risk. Some types of financial risk include:

- **Inflation Risk** Inflation is a general increase in the cost of goods and services. If you wait to buy an item you want, you risk the possibility that the price will increase.
- **Interest Rate Risk** Interest rates rise and fall, which may affect the cost of borrowing or the profits you earn when you save or invest.
- **Income Risk** Your income may rise or fall. You could lose your job due to unexpected health problems, family ussues or other reasons. You could also find a better job or get a raise.
- **Personal Risk** Some choices increase risk. Driving for eight hours on icy mountain roads may not be worth the money you would save instead of traveling by airplane.
- **Liquidity Risk** You may have to withdraw your savings or investments. Liquidity is the ability to convert your financial resources into cash easily without a loss in value.

Section 28.1 Personal Financial Planning **501**

RETEACH

U Universal Access

Students with Learning Disabilities Many sources of financial information produce materials that might be difficult for some students to comprehend. Pair up students and instruct them to read a financial news source together, discuss it, and reread it. By rereading immediately after discussion, students can improve their comprehension skills.

W Writing Support

Enrichment

Limiting Risk Ask students to write two or three paragraphs describing how people can limit financial risk. (Paragraphs will vary. For example, students might suggest that saving for emergencies can limit income risk.)

R Reading Strategy

Explain Ask students to use their own words to explain financial risk. (Answers will vary, but students should demonstrate an understanding of the types of risk that are listed.)

Student Activity Workbook ☞ Assign the Section 28.1 Activities.

International Business

The Euro Answers may vary but might describe how a single currency allows citizens to travel more easily throughout Europe, and how the single market allows the European Union to function more efficiently and have more opportunity for growth. Only 12 countries in the EU have met the economic requirements set by the treaty to adopt the Euro.

RETEACH (cont.)

C Critical Thinking

Review and Revise

Opportunity Costs Ask students to consider the importance of opportunity costs when they are reviewing and revising a financial plan. (People must revise financial goals that might be unrealistic.)

✔ **Reading Check**

Identify inflation risk, interest rate risk, income risk, personal risk, and liquidity risk

ASSESS

● **After You Read**

Have students complete the Section 28.1 After You Read section review.

Online Study Tools

Have students go to the Online Learning Center through **glencoe.com** to:

- Take the Section 28.1 **Practice Test**.
- Download free **Study-to-Go** content to their PDAs or cell phones.

CLOSE

Culminating Activity

Who Wants to Be a Millionaire?

Divide students into groups and ask them to use a spreadsheet to calculate how long it would take to save a million dollars if you saved $2,000 each year at 7.4% interest. (almost 50 years—at the end of 49 years, $930,401, and at the end of 50 years, $1,001,399)

An important part of financial planning is understanding which risks you can afford to take and which ones you cannot. If you decide a course of action is too risky, you might decide to choose an alternative. In some cases, insurance is available to limit your exposure to risk. Diversification of your assets is another way to minimize risk.

✔ **Reading Check** **Identify** List some types of financial risks.

Consequences of Choices

C An **opportunity cost**, sometimes called a tradeoff, is what you give up when you make one choice instead of another. Suppose you want to become a full-time college student. You would like to work full time, but your work hours would conflict with your class schedule. If you choose to pursue your education, you will give up the opportunity to work full time, at least for a while. The opportunity cost of going to college is working at the full-time job. However, choosing between the alternatives involves more than just knowing what you forgo. It also involves knowing what you gain.

 Activity correlates to Math standards.

Section 28.1

● **After You Read**

Review Key Concepts

1. What are some examples of long-range financial goals that consumers may have?
2. List the steps of the financial planning process.
3. Name some types of financial risk.

Academic Skills

 NCLB

4. **Mathematics** The average U.S. family spends about 16% of its income on housing and 12% on household expenses. If a family's monthly income is $3,125, how much does it spend on housing and household expenses?

THEORY **The Distributive Property** The Distributive Property states that $a \times c + b \times c = (a + b)c$. You can multiply each percent by the monthly income then add the products, or you can add the percents and multiply their sum by the monthly income.

Math For math help, go to the Math Appendix.

@ Go to the *Introduction to Business* Online Learning Center through **glencoe.com** to check your answers.

Section 28.1

Review Key Concepts

1. getting a college education, buying a car, or starting a business
2. determine your financial situation, develop your financial goals, identify alternative courses of action, evaluate your alternatives, create and use your financial plan of action, and review and revise your plan
3. inflation risk, interest rate risk, income risk, personal risk, and liquidity risk

Academic Skills

4. **Mathematics** (16% + 12%)$3,125 = $875

The family spends $875 per month on housing and household expenses.

Money Management

Reading Guide

● Before You Read

Think about some steps you can take now in managing your money so that you can get the most from your income.

D

Read to Learn
- Discuss the importance of budgeting.
- List the steps for preparing a budget.

The Main Idea
Meeting your financial goals requires you to know your income and expenses. A budget can enable you to track your spending and make choices about your money.

Key Concepts
- The Importance of Budgeting
- Preparing a Budget

Vocabulary
Key Terms

money management	expense
budget	fixed expenses
income	variable expenses
gross pay	budget variance
deductions	surplus
net pay	deficit

@ Go to the *Introduction to Business* Online Learning Center through **glencoe.com** for a printable graphic organizer.

Academic Vocabulary
You will find these words in your reading and on your tests. Make sure you know their meanings.

utilize	intermediate
hence	major

Graphic Organizer
In a figure like the one below, list the seven steps for preparing a budget.

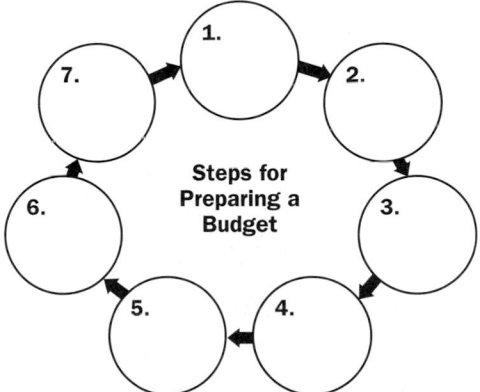

Steps for Preparing a Budget

1.
2.
3.
4.
5.
6.
7.

Academic Standards
English Language Arts

NCTE 1 Read texts to acquire new information

NCTE 7 Conduct research and gather, evaluate, and synthesize data to communicate discoveries

NCTE 12 Use language to accomplish individual purposes

Science

Content Standard F Students should develop understanding of science and technology in local, national, and global challenges

NCLB

FOCUS

🔔 Bell Ringer Activity

Money Management
Write or project the following equation on the board: Income − Expenses = Savings. Ask students to explain how this equation can be used to help people manage money. (Students should understand that the goal of money management is keeping the equation balanced.)

Preteaching

Presentation Plus! ⊙
The Presentation Plus! CD provides visual teaching aids for this section.

PuzzleMaker ⊙
Use the Vocabulary PuzzleMaker to create a puzzle of the section's key terms. Students can complete the puzzle on paper or on a computer.

Graphic Organizer
Tell students to go to the Online Learning Center through **glencoe.com** for a printable graphic organizer. (Answers include: set your goals, estimate your income, budget for unexpected expenses and savings, budget for fixed expenses, budget for variable expenses, record what you spend, and review spending/saving patterns.)

NCLB Connects academics to content.

Reading Guide

● Before You Read

Students might suggest writing down their income and expenses for a period of time.

D Develop Concepts

The Main Idea Ask students: How would tracking your spending for a week help you make better spending choices? (Students might suggest that tracking spending would help them to decide ways to reduce their expenses.)

TEACH

Discussion Starter
Preparing a Budget
Start a discussion by asking: Do you have a budget? (Some students might say they have no money, so they have no budget. Others might indicate that they get an allowance and they have to make it last all week.) Follow up by pointing out that a budget is a plan for using your income in a way that best meets your wants and needs.

R Reading Strategy

Differentiate Ask students to differentiate between money management and a budget. (Answers will vary. Students should understand that budgeting is just one part of money management. Students may suggest that money management includes making sure that you stick to your budget.)

 **Reading Check**

Analyze Income is a limited resource because most people want goods and services that they cannot afford based on their income.

Real World
Everyone Budgets If a company comes close to delivering its budgeted figures, it demonstrates that the company understands its business and has been successful in moving the company in the expected direction. If a company is not meeting its budgeted figures, its financial plan needs reevaluating.

Everyone Budgets Families, corporations, and even governments set budgets. The budget of a government is similar to your budget, setting up the intended income and expenses for the year. Nearly all large businesses reforecast their budgets on a quarterly basis. In the future, annual budgets may be replaced with monthly or rolling forecasts. *What does it mean if a company comes close to delivering its budgeted figures?*

The Importance of Budgeting

Money management is necessary for consumers, businesses, and governments. **Money management** is a method of planning to get the most from one's money. Like consumers, businesses and governments must figure out how to **utilize** their income to pay for things they want or need. Income is a limited resource for everyone. Most people want more goods and services than they **R** have money to buy. A budget helps them to set financial priorities. **Figure 28.1** shows average U.S. household expenses.

A **budget** is a plan for using your income in a way that best meets your wants and needs. It includes a record of your expected income, your planned expenses, and your planned savings over a certain period of time. **Hence**, a good budget helps people set priorities for spending and saving and tracks their money.

✔ **Reading Check** **Analyze** Why is income a limited resource for everyone?

Preparing a Budget

Planning a budget is a seven-step process: Set your goals; estimate your income; budget for unexpected expenses and savings; budget for fixed expenses; budget for variable expenses; record what you spend; and review spending and saving patterns.

Figure 28.1 — *Average Household Expenses*

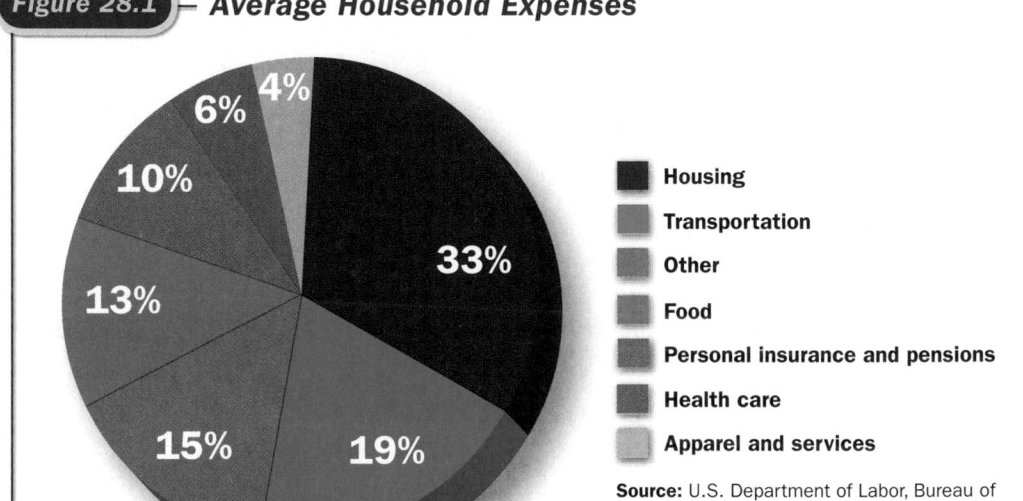

- Housing
- Transportation
- Other
- Food
- Personal insurance and pensions
- Health care
- Apparel and services

Source: U.S. Department of Labor, Bureau of Labor Statistics' Consumer Expenditure Survey

● **The Cost of Living** This graph shows how an average household in the United States spends its money. **If a family earns $3,000 a month, how much money (on average) would that family spend on housing?**

504 **Chapter 28** Managing Personal Finances

Figure 28.1

● **The Cost of Living** The family would have to spend $990, shown as follows:
0.33 × $3,000 = $990.

Science/TechTRENDS

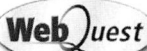

Budgeting for IT Productivity

In today's world, most business leaders believe that an organization that does not invest in information technology (IT) cannot survive. Just imagine an office without computers. IT increases productivity. However, while investments in IT are necessary, part of the role of IT professionals is to match productivity gains to technology costs. Productivity is the primary measure of technology's economic impact. It is frequently difficult to measure technology's impact, but as with every other budgetary line item, expenditures must match organizational goals to technology expenditures. When the costs for IT software and hardware are added up, decisions need to be made that narrow the difference between investments in IT and the performance it generates.

WebQuest

Go to the *Introduction to Business* Online Learning Center through **glencoe.com** for links to Web sites where you can research ways IT costs influence businesses' investments. Write a few paragraphs describing how IT affects productivity.

Step 1: Set Your Financial Goals

As you prepare to set your financial goals, you should consider several questions: What do I want to accomplish in the next month? The next year? The next five years? What is important to me? Are my goals practical? A budget should help you decide which goals you can meet with the amount of money you have. You might find it helpful to separate them into short-term, **intermediate**, and long-term goals.

Step 2: Estimate Your Income

Once you have set your goals, you can begin working on a budget. Start by recording your estimated income for the next month. Your **income** is the actual amount of money you earn or receive during a given period. Include all sources of income that you know you will receive, such as take-home pay and income on investments.

S **Pay and Deductions** Your **gross pay** is the total amount of money you earned for a specific time. Your gross pay is reduced by various **deductions**, or amounts that are taken out of your pay before you receive your paycheck. Deductions include items such as taxes, insurance premiums, retirement contributions, and union dues. Your take-home pay, or **net pay**, is your gross pay minus deductions.

Withholding Full time workers pay several kinds of taxes. *Withholding* is income tax withheld from an employee's wages and paid directly to the government by the employer. It is a form of deduction from pay. The funds are applied to the worker's federal, state, and local income taxes as well as his or her contribution to Social Security and Medicare. Self-employed people pay their taxes directly to the government. *Why do you think taxes are withheld from workers' paychecks?*

Section 28.2 Money Management **505**

TEACH (cont.)

S **Skill Practice**

Guided Practice

Define Ask students to use their own words to define *income*. (Income is the actual amount of money you earn or receive during a given period.) **L1**

Explain Ask students to explain why bonuses and gifts you expect to receive should not be included when estimating your income in the budgeting process. (It is income that you may not get.) **L2**

Illustrate an Idea Ask students to illustrate *take-home pay* using a graphic representation, including the appropriate key terms as labels. (Illustrations will vary. The following key terms should be included: gross pay, deductions, and net pay.) **L3**

ASSESS

Review Key Terms
Have students write sentences using each key term.

 **Study-to-Go** Have students go to the Online Learning Center through **glencoe.com** to download free **Study-to-Go** content to their PDAs or cell phones.

 Activity correlates to Science standards.

Real World

Withholding Withholding acts as a prepayment of tax that a worker will owe at the end of the year. It also helps to keep workers in compliance with tax-law requirements.

Science/TechTRENDS

WebQuest

Budgeting for IT Productivity If used properly as a tool, IT can improve the quality of products, reduce production time and in some cases, reduce costs.

RETEACH

Figure 28.2 — *Managing Your Money*

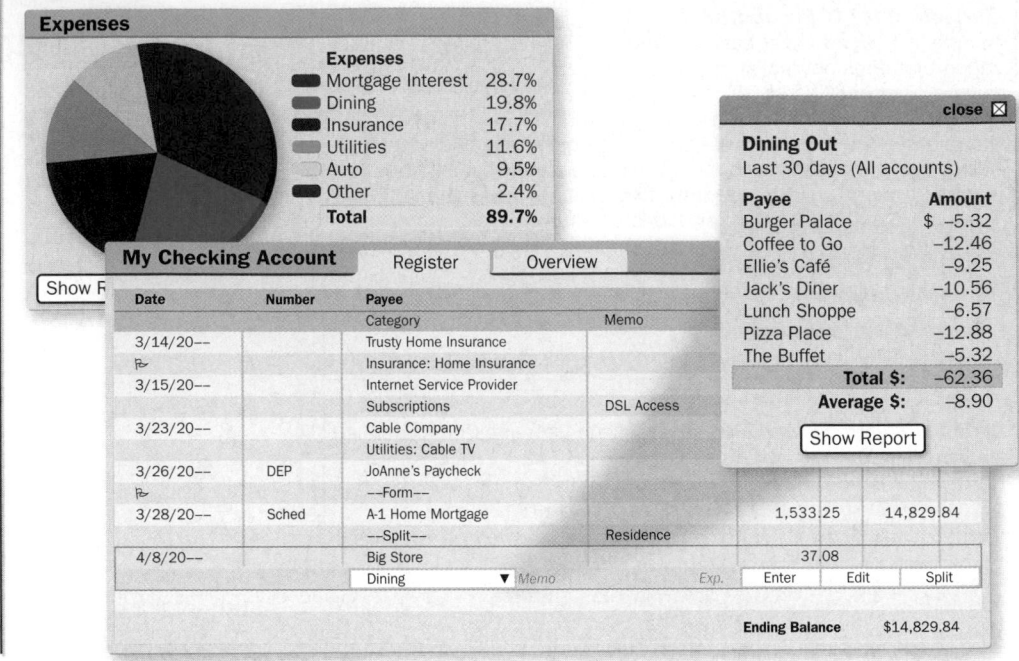

● **Budgeting Software** You can use budgeting software to create reports, charts, and graphs that quickly show you when you paid a bill, how much you paid, and to whom. **How might budgeting software make preparing your taxes easier?**

Step 3: Budget for Unexpected Expenses and Savings

W You have to plan for expenses such as food, rent, and clothing to satisfy your basic needs. An **expense** is an amount of money used to buy or do something. You must also plan for unexpected expenses, such as medical visits or accidents. Unexpected expenses could include rises in costs for items such as gasoline. **Figure 28.2** provides a glimpse of budgeting software.

R A budget must also include a plan for savings. Savings make it possible for you to meet future wants and needs. They also protect you against expenses that you did not budget for, that are higher than you expected, or that are completely unexpected. You need a savings plan if your long-term goal is to make a **major** purchase, such as a new computer or a vacation.

U When you develop your budget, make sure that the total income figure is the same as the total for planned expenses and savings. If your planned expenses and savings are more than your income, you will have to cut some expenses or find some other source of income.

● **As You Read**

Think about some unexpected expenses you have had and how they affected your budget.

506 **Chapter 28** Managing Personal Finances

Step 4: Budget for Fixed Expenses

Fixed expenses are expenses that occur regularly and are regularly paid. They include payments for rent, insurance, and a car loan. The amount of a fixed expense might sometimes change, but it is usually about the same over long periods.

Step 5: Budget for Variable Expenses

Variable expenses are expenses that change and can be controlled more easily than fixed expenses. They include expenses such as food, phone charges, entertainment, and gifts. The amounts for these expenses usually vary from month to month.

Step 6: Record What You Spend

To find out how practical your budget is, you will need to keep track of your expenses during one month and revise your budget if necessary. The difference between the budgeted amount and the actual amount that you spend is the **budget variance**. This figure can be either a surplus or a deficit. A **surplus** is extra money that can be spent or saved, depending on a person's goals and values. A **deficit** occurs when more money is spent than is earned or received.

C

Step 7: Review Spending and Saving Patterns

Budgeting is a continual process. You need to review your budget each month and consider making changes.

 **NCLB** Activity correlates to English Language Arts standards.

Section 28.2

After You Read

Review Key Concepts

1. What are the seven steps to preparing a budget?
2. What is the difference between gross pay and net pay?
3. How are fixed expenses and variable expenses different?

Academic Skills

NCLB

4. **English Language Arts** Interview someone who is responsible for a budget for a club, business, or other organization. How do goals drive the budget? How often is it revised? How is it monitored? Write a story about your interview for the organization's newsletter.

5. **English Language Arts** What are your goals for the future? Write a description of where you see yourself living and what you see yourself doing in 10 years. Then write a short plan describing the money management techniques you will use in order to meet your goals.

 Go to the *Introduction to Business* Online Learning Center through **glencoe.com** to check your answers.

Section 28.2

Review Key Concepts

1. set goals, estimate income, budget for unexpected expenses and savings, budget for fixed expenses, budget for variable expenses, record what you spend, and review spending and saving patterns
2. Gross pay: total amount earned. Net pay: gross pay minus deductions

3. Fixed expenses occur regularly. Variable expenses change and can be controlled more easily.

Academic Skills

4. **English Language Arts** Answers depend on the organization chosen and interviewees' responses.
5. **English Language Arts** Students should manage money carefully.

RETEACH (cont.)

C Critical Thinking

Assess

Review Spending and Saving Patterns Present the following: Four years into her savings plan, Claudia is disappointed that she has less than $5,000 saved. Ask students what advice they would offer. (Answers will vary. Students should understand that Claudia needs to review her spending and saving patterns and set and achieve savings goals.)

ASSESS

After You Read

Have students complete the Section 28.2 After You Read section review.

Online Study Tools

Have students go to the Online Learning Center through **glencoe.com** to:

- Take the Section 28.2 **Practice Test**.
- Download free **Study-to-Go** content to their PDAs or cell phones.

STUDY TO GO

CLOSE

Culminating Activity

What Do the Experts Say? Have students work in pairs to create a poster based on a magazine article or a book chapter that focuses on the budget process. (Examples include: paying yourself first, maximizing your employer's match to a 401(k), writing down all expenditures, and using a grocery list.)

Vocabulary Review

1. Students should write complete sentences using each term correctly.

Review Key Concepts

2. determine your financial situation, develop your financial goals, identify possible courses of action, evaluate your alternatives, implement your financial plan of action, and review and revise your plan

3. the Internet, magazines, and newspapers

4. inflation, the risk that interest rates will rise or fall, risk that income will rise or fall, risks associated with personal choices, and liquidity risk

5. An opportunity cost, sometimes called a tradeoff, is what is given up when one choice is made instead of another.

6. It allows individuals and businesses to manage their money and to plan for using their income in a way that best meets their wants and needs.

7. set your goals; estimate your income; budget for unexpected expenses and savings; budget for fixed expenses; budget for variable expenses; record what you spend; and review spending and saving patterns

Section 28.1 *Summary*

Personal Financial Planning Everyone must make financial decisions. Identifying your financial goals and planning how to get the most from your money are part of personal financial planning. If you plan well and carry out those plans, you can reach your financial goals. To create a financial plan, you need to determine your financial situation; develop your financial goals; identify possible courses of action; evaluate your alternatives; implement a financial plan of action; and review and revise your plan. Often financial planning means you must research options so that you can evaluate risk and make wise choices.

Section 28.2 *Summary*

Money Management A budget is a tool for getting the most from your income. With a budget, you can estimate your income and expenses and track your financial progress over time. Income and expenses often vary over time, so a part of budgeting is reviewing your goals, revising them, and adjusting your budget as needed. To create a budget, you need to set your financial goals; estimate your income; budget for unexpected expenses and savings; budget for fixed expenses; budget for variable expenses; record what you spend; and review your spending and saving patterns. Budgeting is an ongoing process.

Vocabulary Review

1. On a sheet of paper, use each of these key terms and academic vocabulary terms in a sentence.

Key Terms		Academic Vocabulary	
personal financial planning	deductions	sources	utilize
goals	net pay	achieve	hence
opportunity cost	expense	revise	intermediate
money management	fixed expenses	resources	major
budget	variable expenses		
income	budget variance		
gross pay	surplus		
	deficit		

Review Key Concepts

2. Explain the steps involved in the financial planning process.

3. Identify sources of financial information.

4. Discuss sources of risk.

5. Discuss the consequences of choices.

6. Discuss the importance of budgeting.

7. List the steps for preparing a budget.

508   **Chapter 28**   Review and Activities

Critical Thinking

8. Once you set goals, you can plan how to meet them.

9. In general, this statement is true. An exception may be when a person has only enough money to buy necessities and must spend that money on food and other needs.

10. If people are willing to delay spending, they will find it easier to save money to meet their long-term goals.

11. If people think of income as gross pay, they may overspend. Their gross pay is not available to them for spending. Only their net pay is. Thinking of gross pay as income is unrealistic for budgeting, unless all deductions are taken into account in the budget.

Critical Thinking

8. Why is it important to plan for spending, saving, and investing your money?

9. "People always have a choice: to use their money on a good or service, or to invest or save the money." Do you think this statement is true? Why or why not?

10. Sometimes people are willing to delay making a purchase so they can buy something better later. This concept is known as delaying gratification. What effect do you think delaying gratification can have on budgeting?

11. Some people think of their income as the total amount that they earn, not the amount that they actually receive in their paycheck. What effect will that thinking have on their ability to live within a budget?

12. What do you think is the most difficult part of budgeting? Why?

13. How do your spending habits affect your standard of living? What are some unexpected expenses that you may have that will affect your budget?

14. What suggestions would you give to someone who thinks that savings are not an important part of budgeting and money management?

Write About It

15. Estimate how much money you need for an item you would like to buy in the future. Write a brief essay about items that you could forgo buying now to have that item. When do you think you can achieve your goal?

16. Some people think money is something that they can always get. Others think that money must be conserved and used wisely or it will not be available when needed. Write two or more paragraphs about your thoughts on each statement.

17. What are your goals? In two or more pages, describe where you see yourself living and what you see yourself doing in 10 years. What personal financial planning methods will you use to meet your goals?

18. Why is opportunity cost an important concept for people to consider in their decisions about personal financial planning? Explain your answer in two or more paragraphs.

19. Check in the yellow pages of your local phone book, a local newspaper, library, or online to find information about personal financial planning assistance available in your community. Write a summary of information you find.

Technology Applications

Spreadsheet Software
20. Early planning for college or postsecondary training is important. Use a spreadsheet to prepare a summary of the costs of a college education or training program. Visit Web sites for training and education institutions to find tuition and fees, estimated room and board costs, and costs for books and supplies.

Business Ethics

Family First or Strictly Business?
21. Suppose you work as a financial planner for a well-known novelist who is also very wealthy. Your duties include advising her on personal investments. You have a brother who owns a struggling online business. He asks you to advise your client to invest in his company, pitching it as a "hot new dot-com." What should you do?

Chapter 28 Review and Activities **509**

Critical Thinking

12. For many people, it is limiting their spending to the amounts they can afford.

13. Financial goals might require more emphasis on savings. Examples of unexpected expenses include medical expenses, automobile repairs, job loss, household repairs, and exceptionally high gasoline prices.

14. Savings can form a hedge against risk and allow you to meet future financial goals.

Write About It

15. Essays will vary, depending on student preferences, income, and expenses.

16. People who see money as being like other resources probably consider money management and saving as important parts of managing that resource.

17. Each student will have different goals.

18. Answers will vary. For example, because people have limited resources, they must make choices regarding the best use of them. Decision making involves prioritizing their wants and needs—and how their finances will help consumers obtain them.

19. Summaries will depend on students' findings.

Technology Applications

20. Spreadsheets will vary, depending on students' educational goals and the school researched.

Business Ethics

21. Aside from the high-risk level involved in this type of investment, pitching it to your client would present a conflict of interest. You should not mention it to her as an investment option. Instead, perhaps you could offer some financial advice to your brother.

Applying Academics to Business

22. Students' answers will vary, but if they have difficulty finding appropriate paragraphs from this chapter, encourage them to look in earlier chapters they have already read.

23. Answers will vary, according to each student's decision about how many movies or restaurant meals he or she wants to give up. Giving up all movies and meals would enable the student to save $(3 \times \$7) + (7 \times \$9) = \$94$

24. income—expenses, outflows

gross pay—net pay

variable—fixed

unplanned—budgeted

25. Answers will vary according to the countries chosen.

Active Learning

26. Summaries will vary. For example, most people who use software for recordkeeping value the ease of finding information. Software takes much of the drudgery out of recordkeeping and makes it easier to prepare forms such as tax returns and budgets. Most people probably think they are better money managers because of it.

Business in the Real World

27. Answers will depend on the corporation that is chosen.

Applying Academics to Business

English Language Arts

22. Look for a paragraph in this chapter that describes a cause-and-effect relationship. Find another paragraph that has a topic sentence supported by details. Finally, find an example of a sequence of events.

Mathematics

23. Find a picture of a big-ticket item you would like to own. Figure out the equivalent cost in movies (at $7 per movie) and in dining out (at $9 per meal) for the item. For example, if an MP3 player costs $149, its cost-equivalent is 21 movies or 16 restaurant meals. Assuming that you see three movies per month and eat out seven times, make a plan for saving enough money to purchase your big-ticket item by eliminating one or more monthly movies and restaurant meals. Write a few sentences describing your plan.

THEORY **Problem Solving** You might start by computing how much you spend on movies and dining out each month. Then decide what you are willing to eliminate to save to buy the item you have chosen.

English Language Arts

24. Based on the concepts you have read about in this chapter, write a word that means the opposite or almost the opposite of each of the following:

income
gross pay
variable
unplanned

Mathematics

25. Americans save less than 5% of their income. Other countries have a higher percentage of savings per capita, including Belgium (22%), Denmark (16.2%), and Japan (15.7%). Research the average per capita savings of at least 10 countries and display your findings in a bar graph.

THEORY **Bar Graphs** Bar graphs can be designed so that the bars are horizontal or vertical. Each bar represents the quantity associated with a different category, in this case, the per capita savings of a country.

Active Learning

Financial Planning Software

26. Interview two or more people who use budgeting or financial planning software to organize financial information. Ask them how technology has affected their records and financial planning. Do they believe they are better money managers because they use the software? Write a summary of the information you learned.

Business in the Real World

Investing in a Corporation

27. An annual report is a corporation's yearly review of activities, especially its financial dealings. Choose a corporation, and research its annual report, either online or by contacting the company. Read the report's overview and highlights. Did the company meet its goals? Why or why not? Would you consider investing in it? In a two-page paper, explain your answers.

510 **Chapter 28** Review and Activities

***ExamView Assessment Suite* CD** allows you to print out ready-made unit and chapter tests, complete with answer keys. You can also create customized tests.

TeacherWorks Plus provides complete teacher resources in one convenient package. It includes customizable lesson plans in calendar format, and instant access to many print program resources.

Real LIFE skills

PREPARING A PERSONAL BUDGET

28. Select a college or technical school that you might like to attend after school. Obtain information on tuition and other fees. Add the cost of food, shelter, clothing, books, and any other items you think are part of the cost. Estimate the total cost of the education. Then estimate how you will pay for it. Prepare a budget for the time you will seek the education.

FIND YOUR DREAM JOB

29. Go to the *Introduction to Business* Online Learning Center through **glencoe.com** for a link to the Occupational Outlook Handbook Web site. Click on the "OOH Search/A-Z Index" link and enter "budget analysts." Write a one-page report about the job. Conclude your report with a list of things you could do now to prepare yourself to pursue the occupation.

Role Play

A BUDGET FOR YOUR MARCHING BAND

30. Situation Your school's marching band has asked for your help in preparing the band's budget for the upcoming year. You and three of your classmates are meeting to identify ways it can raise money and plan a budget.

Activity Hold a meeting to plan ways to raise money and to prepare a proposed budget. The band has $435 in the treasury.

Evaluation You will be evaluated on how well you meet the following performance indicators:

- Identify three or more ways the marching band can raise money.
- Prepare a list of expected expenses for the marching band.
- Prepare a proposed budget.
- List steps that the band members can take to meet their goals.
- Communicate with others, and use correct grammar.

Chapter 28

Real LIFE skills

28. Each student will develop a different budget.

Cool Business CAREERS

29. Budget analysts develop, analyze, and execute budgets. They work in offices for long hours and under deadline pressure. Training and qualifications include a bachelor's degree as the minimum educational requirement. Many employers prefer or require a master's degree. With a few years of experience, capable analysts can be promoted to midlevel positions. After a few more years, promotion to a senior position is possible. Senior analysts are often promoted to management positions. Average job growth is expected. As preparation, take math courses and develop good computer and communication skills.

Role Play

30. Presentations should address the competencies noted in the Role Play. Students should demonstrate an understanding of financial planning and budgeting.

Standardized Test Practice

Directions Choose the letter of the best answer. Write the letter for the answer on a separate piece of paper.

1. Which punctuation mark, if any, is needed in the sentence?

Samantha asked her accountant "Would it be better to cut my budget for housing, increase my income, or save less each month?"

A , (comma)
B . (period)
C ; (semicolon)
D The sentence is correct as it is.

 TEST-TAKING TIP Keep your family members informed about your test schedule. They can help you with your studies and provide encouragement.

 READING Go to the *Introduction to Business* Online Learning Center through **glencoe.com** for a list of outside reading suggestions.

 **STRATEGIES FOR STANDARDIZED TEST PREP SUCCESS**

Test Prep Remind your students' family members that they should not expect to know all of the answers in subjects such as math and science. If family members find the homework challenging, suggest that they ask their student to explain the homework to them. In this way, the family member can help the student identify specific questions to ask the teacher later. Also encourage family members to make sure students get plenty of rest, exercise, and eat a healthy breakfast on test day.

Standardized Test Practice
1. A

Standards-Based Lesson Planning
Introduction to Business provides students with instruction and assessment in the following fundamental content areas:

Content Standards Correlations	
Determine how to open a personal checking account.	pp. 515, 525
Learn how to make a bank deposit.	pp. 515, 516, 521–522, 525
Analyze and demonstrate how to endorse a check.	pp. 515, 522, 525
Evaluate various types of checking accounts.	p. 516
Analyze bank withdrawals.	pp. 516, 523, 527
Compare and contrast types of banking services. Evaluate the characteristics of checking accounts as well as checking account fees.	pp. 517–518, 525
Demonstrate banking skills.	pp. 521, 522, 523, 525–527
Identify proper procedures for managing a checking account.	pp. 521, 522, 523, 525–527
Utilize the correct steps to maintain an accurate checking account. Discuss the preparation of deposit slips, checks, and bank reconciliation forms.	pp. 521, 522, 523, 525, 527
Demonstrate the ability to maintain business and personal records.	pp. 521, 522, 523, 525–527
Determine how to maintain a check register.	pp. 521, 522, 523, 525–526
Analyze and demonstrate how to reconcile a bank statement.	pp. 522–523
Use appropriate computer software.	p. 525

NCLB
Activities, information, and skills practice will help your students attain No Child Left Behind proficiency. Students will improve their abilities in the following academic standards areas:

Academic Standards Correlations		
English Language Arts	Activities/Features	Page
NCTE 3 Apply strategies to interpret text	Applying Academics to Business	p. 526
NCTE 5 Use different writing process elements to communicate effectively	After You Read	p. 523
NCTE 7 Conduct research and gather, evaluate, and synthesize data to communicate discoveries	After You Read	p. 523
NCTE 12 Use language to accomplish individual purposes	Applying Academics to Business	p. 526
Mathematics		
Number and Operations Compute fluently and make reasonable estimates	Ask S&P Standardized Test Practice	pp. 512, 527
Number and Operations Understand meanings of operations and how they relate to one another	Applying Academics to Business	p. 526
Number and Operations Understand numbers, ways of representing numbers, relationships among numbers, and number systems	After You Read Applying Academics to Business	pp. 518, 526
Science		
Content Standard F Students should develop understanding of science and technology in local, national, and global challenges	Science/Tech Trends	p. 520

Correlations   This chart shows the 21st Century Skills, foundation skills, and workplace competencies that students develop as they work in this chapter.

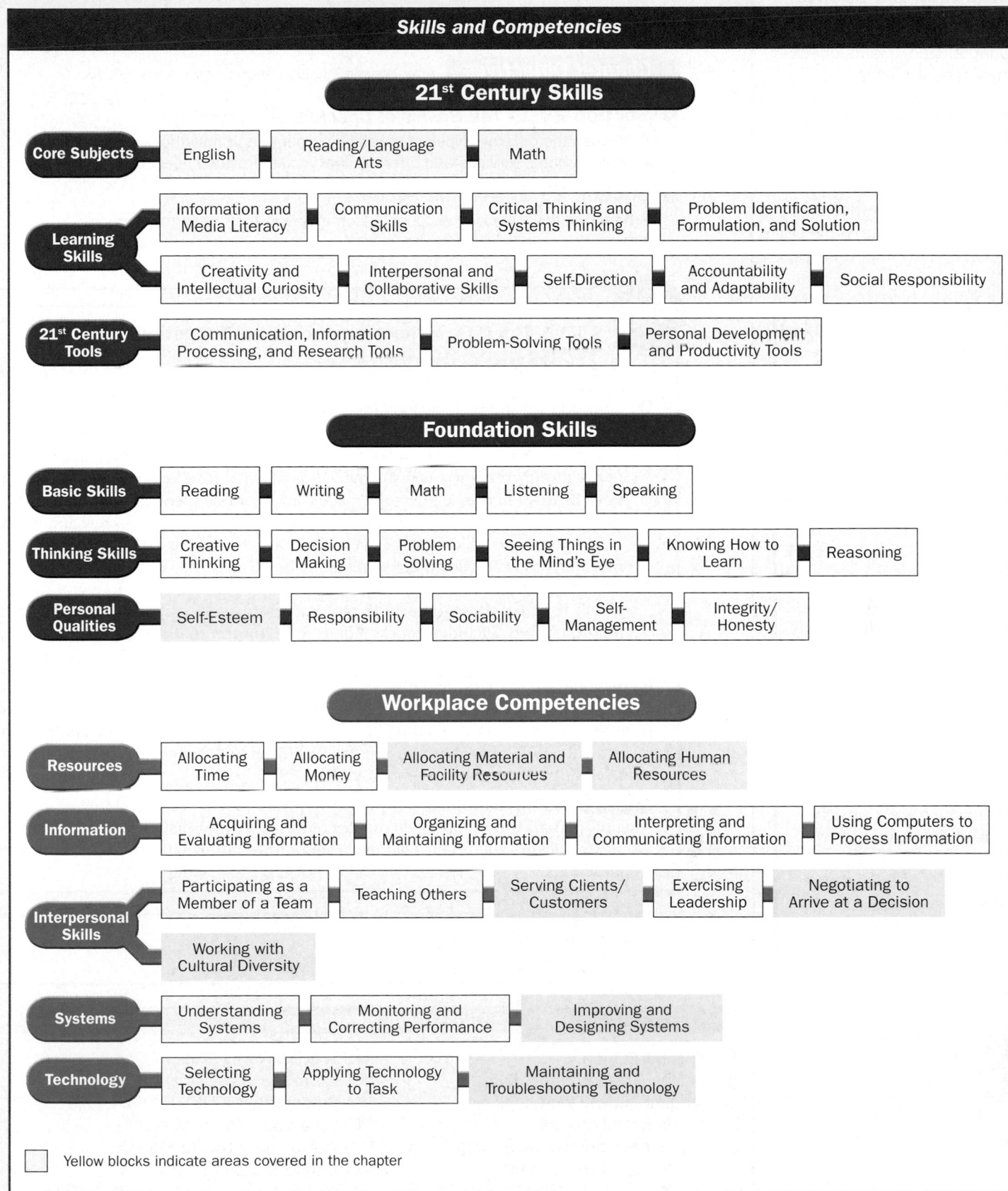

Skills and Competencies

21st Century Skills

Core Subjects
- English
- Reading/Language Arts
- Math

Learning Skills
- Information and Media Literacy
- Communication Skills
- Critical Thinking and Systems Thinking
- Problem Identification, Formulation, and Solution
- Creativity and Intellectual Curiosity
- Interpersonal and Collaborative Skills
- Self-Direction
- Accountability and Adaptability
- Social Responsibility

21st Century Tools
- Communication, Information Processing, and Research Tools
- Problem-Solving Tools
- Personal Development and Productivity Tools

Foundation Skills

Basic Skills
- Reading
- Writing
- Math
- Listening
- Speaking

Thinking Skills
- Creative Thinking
- Decision Making
- Problem Solving
- Seeing Things in the Mind's Eye
- Knowing How to Learn
- Reasoning

Personal Qualities
- Self-Esteem
- Responsibility
- Sociability
- Self-Management
- Integrity/Honesty

Workplace Competencies

Resources
- Allocating Time
- Allocating Money
- Allocating Material and Facility Resources
- Allocating Human Resources

Information
- Acquiring and Evaluating Information
- Organizing and Maintaining Information
- Interpreting and Communicating Information
- Using Computers to Process Information

Interpersonal Skills
- Participating as a Member of a Team
- Teaching Others
- Serving Clients/Customers
- Exercising Leadership
- Negotiating to Arrive at a Decision
- Working with Cultural Diversity

Systems
- Understanding Systems
- Monitoring and Correcting Performance
- Improving and Designing Systems

Technology
- Selecting Technology
- Applying Technology to Task
- Maintaining and Troubleshooting Technology

Yellow blocks indicate areas covered in the chapter

Chapter Overview

Introduce the Chapter

Checking Accounts
Chapter 29 explains checking account basics.

Building Background
This chapter presents many opportunities for students of varying academic abilities to share their knowledge of checking accounts, bank services, and account records.

Ask STANDARD &POOR'S

>> **Math Answer**
Yes, Edward needs to cut back. He spent $165 more than he received. Expenditures: $625 + $293 + $216 + $254 + $422 = $1,810. Income: $1,595 + $50 = $1,645. Income minus expenses is: $1,645 − $1,810 = −$165.

>> **Extension Activity**
Cloris needs positive cash flow to move into an apartment. Her gross pay is $2,400 per month. Her withholdings are $940. Cloris's monthly expenses total $1,420. Will she have a positive cash flow if she moves? (Yes, the difference between her net income and expenses is $40. Her gross income less withholdings and expenses is: $2,400 − $2,360 = $40)

N C L B
Activity correlates to Math standards.

512

Checking Accounts

Chapter Objectives After completing this chapter, you will be able to:

▶ **Section 29.1** *The Basics of Checking Accounts*
- **Discuss** the different types of checking accounts and how they work.
- **Discuss** other services and offerings that banks provide checking account holders.

▶ **Section 29.2** *Account Records*
- **Describe** how checking account holders manage their bank transactions.
- **Describe** the procedure for bringing your account into agreement with bank records.

Ask STANDARD &POOR'S **Checking Accounts: Budgeting**

Q: How do I get started managing my finances?

A: Basically, budgeting is about managing the money coming in (income) and the money going out (expenditures). In the business world, this coming in and going out of money is known as cash flow. The goal is to create an overall positive cash flow. Before you decide how to manage your finances, spend a month or two keeping careful track of your cash flow. Assess how you spend your money and decide where possible cutbacks can be made, for example making coffee at home in the morning or cutting down on eating out. Discipline is the key to saving money. After making cutbacks, consider your options for investing the money you've saved. You may chose to invest in physical assets, such as a car or real estate, or in financial assets, including stocks, bonds, CDs, money markets, and traditional bank accounts.

Mathematics Edward is analyzing his finances. He has determined that in the month of May he spent $625 on rent and utilities, $293 on food, $216 on gas, $254 on his car payment, and $422 on entertainment. He made only $1,595 freelancing and $50 on investments. Will Edward need to cut back on his entertainment expenditures in order to have positive cash flow?

N C L B

THEORY **Adding and Subtracting Multiple Numbers** When you are adding or subtracting more than two numbers, do one operation at a time. First, line up all of the addends vertically. Add up the columns from right to left. Finally, make the necessary subtractions.

Classroom Resources

- ✍ Student Edition
- ✍ Teacher Wraparound Edition
- 📁 Student Activity Workbook with Academic Integration
- 📁 Student Activity Workbook with Academic Integration TAE
- 📁 *Fast File*, Unit 10 Resources
- 📁 Inclusion in the Business Education Classroom

- 💿 TeacherWorks Plus
- 💿 *ExamView Assessment Suite*
- 💿 Presentation Plus!
- 💿 Vocabulary PuzzleMaker
- 💿 Interactive Student Edition
- 💻 Online Student Edition
- 💻 Online Learning Center with Podcasts

Review the Objectives

Introduce the chapter by reviewing the chapter objectives:

Section 29.1 *Objectives*
Discuss the different types of checking accounts and how they work. (Regular checking accounts allow a few checks to be written each month with no minimum amount. Interest-bearing accounts pay interest, usually have a minimum balance requirement, and allow an unlimited number of checks to be written each month with no added fee. Joint accounts are shared by two people who are equally responsible for the account.)

Discuss other services and offerings that banks provide checking account holders. (overdraft protection, stop payment orders, debit cards, and online banking)

Section 29.2 *Objectives*
Describe how checking account holders manage their bank transactions. (They use the checks' information; keep a check register; and use ATM receipts, deposit slips, and bank statements.)

Describe the procedure for bringing your account into agreement with bank records. (With the bank statement and your check register, you can identify your outstanding checks, deposits, and ATM withdrawals that have not been recorded. Use these amounts to identify differences.)

● **Bank Services** You can withdraw money from a bank account several different ways. **Why is it a good idea to keep printed copies of all banking receipts and records?**

Chapter 29 Checking Accounts **513**

Discuss the Photo
● **Bank Services** Read the caption on the photo to students: You can withdraw money from a bank account several different ways.

Ask students: Why is it a good idea to keep printed copies of all banking receipts and records? (If you keep hard copies of your banking records, you can check them against your monthly bank statement.)

FOCUS

The Basics of Checking Accounts

 Bell Ringer Activity

The Basics of Checking Accounts

Ask students: Why do most adults need a checking account? (They need a way to pay for goods and services. Cash is not always practical.) Ask for some examples of how consumers use checking accounts and how life would be different without them. (For example, many people pay their utility bills by mailing a check. Without a checking account, they would have to take cash to the company to pay.)

Preteaching

Presentation Plus!
The Presentation Plus! CD provides visual teaching aids for this section.

PuzzleMaker
Use the Vocabulary PuzzleMaker to create a puzzle of the section's key terms. Students can complete the puzzle on paper or on a computer.

Graphic Organizer
Tell students to go to the Online Learning Center through **glencoe.com** for a printable graphic organizer. (Answers include: Traditional Checking Services: checks allow depositors to draw checks payable on demand. Additional Services: interest-bearing and joint accounts.)

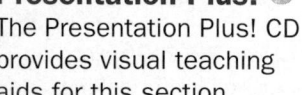 Connects academics to content.

Reading Guide

● Before You Read

Think about some types of bank services that would enable you to manage your finances.

Read to Learn
- Discuss the different types of checking accounts and how they work.
- Discuss other services and offerings that banks provide checking account holders.

The Main Idea
Checking accounts are tools that many people use to make payments. A checking account provides a way for consumers to manage their spending, make payments easily, and keep track of their funds. When they have a checking account, customers can access information online through the bank's Web site.

Key Concepts
- How Checking Accounts Work
- Account Services and Other Offerings

Vocabulary
Key Terms

check	overdrawn
direct deposit	overdraft protection
interest-bearing account	stop payment
signature card	debit card

Academic Vocabulary
You will find these words in your reading and on your tests. Make sure you know their meanings.

demand	compare
common	designed

Graphic Organizer
In a figure like the one below, describe ways you will use traditional checking services and the additional services banks now provide.

Traditional Checking Services	Additional Services

 Go to the *Introduction to Business* Online Learning Center through **glencoe.com** for a printable graphic organizer.

Academic Standards
English Language Arts
   NCTE 1 Read texts to acquire new information
   NCTE 4 Use written language to communicate effectively
Mathematics
   Number and Operations Compute fluently and make reasonable estimates

---

Reading Guide

● Before You Read

Direct deposit of paychecks, ATM withdrawals, and online bill payments allow people to better manage their money.

D Develop Concepts

The Main Idea Ask students: Why do banks offer different types of checking accounts? (People have different banking needs. Banks offer various accounts to attract customers.)

How Checking Accounts Work

It is hard to imagine how businesses and people would function without checks. A **check** is a written order directing a bank or other financial institution to pay money on **demand** to the person or company named on it. Checks are a **common** medium of exchange, or way to make payments for goods and services.

A customer opens a checking account by depositing money into a bank. The bank provides paper checks, which can then be used to pay for goods and services. The check is paid to the payee, the business or person to whom the check was written. The payee can either deposit the check or cash it. Once the money is paid, the check writer's bank voids, or cancels, the check. **Figure 29.1** shows both sides of a canceled check.

✔ Reading Check **Explain** What is a check?

Discussion Starter
Basics of Checking Accounts
Start a discussion by asking students: When do you think teens and young adults should open their first checking account? (Some students might suggest that people open checking accounts when they get their first job, when they get their first full-time job, or when they start college.)

R Reading Strategy
Paraphrase Ask students to use their own words to explain how a checking account works. (Students should understand that a customer deposits money in a checking account and writes checks to pay for goods and services. The payee cashes the check to get the amount of the check, and the amount of the check is deducted from the customer's account.)

✔ Reading Check

Explain A check is a written order to a bank directing payment on demand to the person or company named on it. Checks are common ways to make payments for goods and services.

Figure 29.1 — *Writing and Cashing a Check*

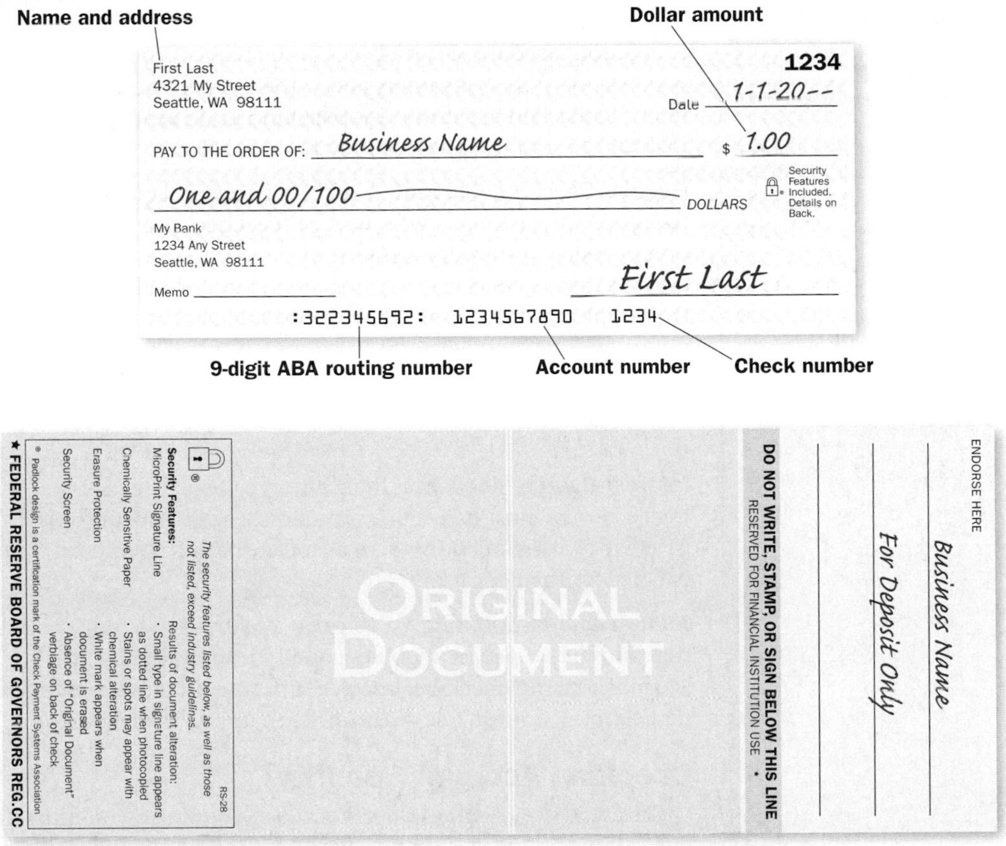

● **An Endorsed Check** Checks are a common medium of exchange. **Why is it sometimes a good idea to write a check instead of spending cash?**

Section 29.1 The Basics of Checking Accounts **515**

Figure 29.1

● **An Endorsed Check** Writing a check provides an account holder with a record of his or her payment and evidence that the payment was received.

TEACH (cont.)

S Skill Practice

Guided Practice

Identify Ask students to identify the typical customer for a regular checking account and for an interest-bearing checking account. (Regular checking account customers write few checks and do not keep a minimum balance. Interest-bearing checking account customers want to earn interest on money in the account.) **L1**

Create an Advertising Poster Ask students to create a poster for a bank advertising its checking account products. Remind students that a good advertisement includes a call to action. (Posters will vary, depending on students' assessment of desirable features.) **L2**

Compare Ask students to develop an example that showcases the difference between a regular checking account and an interest-bearing account, detailing a month's worth of activities. (Answers should be based on the differences between these accounts.) **L3**

ASSESS

Review Key Terms
Have students write sentences using each key term.

Study-to-Go Have students go to the Online Learning Center through **glencoe.com** to download free **Study-to-Go** content to their PDAs or cell phones.

516

? ETHICS in Business

Buyer's Remorse

- **Critical Reading** Life is full of important decisions. Think about the kinds of decisions that you make as you read the question below.

  You purchased a digital video camera from a local electronics store, and you paid for it with a check. Afterward, you began to regret the purchase and called the store to inquire about returns. The manager told you that there are no returns on the item you bought unless it was defective.

- **Decision Making** You wrote the check for the digital camera in good faith, but later changed your mind about buying the camera. Should you call your bank and stop payment on the check you used for the purchase? Explain your answer.

● As You Read

Think about some reasons you would want a checking account.

Types of Accounts

Most banks offer several types of checking accounts. Customer service representatives at financial institutions can answer questions about account services, fees, and charges. You might also want to ask other consumers about their experiences with different banks and accounts. Shop around and **compare** financial institutions and the services they have to offer.

Regular Checking Account A regular checking account is **designed** for customers who write a few checks each month and do not keep a minimum amount of money in the account. Withdrawals from a checking account are made through checks that the account holder has written, automatic deductions (such as bill payments), and withdrawals from automated teller machines (ATMs). **Direct deposit** allows electronic transfers of payments directly from the payer's account to the account of the person being paid.

Interest-Bearing Accounts In addition to regular checking accounts, most banks offer interest-bearing accounts. An **interest-bearing account** is an account that earns interest on the balance for the depositor.

Joint Accounts You might also open a *joint account,* an account that allows two people who are equally responsible for the account to write checks. These accounts are often used by married couples or businesses with more than one owner.

Checking Account Security

Once you decide what type of account you want, you must fill out a signature card at the financial institution. A **signature card** is a record of an account holder's signature used to verify identity.

? ETHICS in Business

Decision Making Answers may vary but should address the issue of what it means to stop payment on a check. It is not an appropriate practice to use to resolve issues of this type.

● As You Read

Some students would use a checking account as a place to store their money. It might also earn interest while providing a way for them to make purchases without cash.

If someone takes a check that the account holder has written to him or her to the branch where the account was opened, the teller can verify the account holder's signature with the card. If the signature matches, then the check will be cashed. If it does not match, the check will not be cashed.

You must also provide your address, phone number, and the answer to a security question, such as your mother's maiden name. The bank then assigns you a checking account number and issues you a book of checks.

W

U

● **As You Read**

Think about some precautions you would take when opening a checking account.

R

Account Services and Other Offerings

Banks offer various services for checking accounts. Some of these services are offered as protection to the consumer. Other services are designed to make banking more convenient.

When an account is **overdrawn**, it means that the account owner has written checks for more money than the balance in the account. An *overdraft* is the amount that is overdrawn. **Overdraft protection** is a line of credit for overdrawn checks.

BusinessWeek *Reader and Case Study*

The Check Cashed Around the World

It's not here yet, but banks are expanding services for globe-trotting customers.

Imagine being able to write a check in Madrid to send as a wedding gift to a friend in Taipei—and she can easily cash it at a local bank. Or having your checking and credit-card accounts open and waiting for you in New York City the day you arrive from your former home in Shanghai.

Banks don't typically provide such services to every retail customer, even as the industry globalizes amid a series of cross-border mergers. But some banks have been rolling out checking account services in recent years that better address the needs of globe-trotting consumers.

It's happening as multinationals and banks continue broadening their global reach. One recent example: National Bank of Greece announced plans in early April 2006 to buy a 46% stake in Turkey's Finansbank for €2.3 billion ($2.77 billion).

And speculation has been rampant this month about what—or where—global banking pioneer Citigroup will buy next, now that the Federal Reserve has lifted its prohibition against the New York financial services company's pursuit of acquisitions.

 CASE STUDY Go to the *Introduction to Business* Online Learning Center through **glencoe.com** for the *BusinessWeek* Reader Case Study.

Active Learning

Many people carry traveler's checks when they go on vacation. Research traveler's checks and alternatives to using them. Write an e-mail to your teacher about changes that make it easier to buy souvenirs while you are traveling.

glencoe.com

BusinessWeek *Reader and Case Study*

The Check Cashed Around the World

 CASE STUDY Have students go to the *Introduction to Business* Online Learning Center through **glencoe.com** to download a Case Study activity that corresponds to the article. The activity and answer key are also available on the TeacherWorks Plus CD.

Active Learning

E-mails will vary, but students should note that traveler's checks are still in use. However, credit cards and ATMs can be used in most countries, and banks may give a more favorable exchange rate. Consequently, most students will recommend against using traveler's checks.

RETEACH

W Writing Support
Enrichment
Checking Accounts Ask students to write a letter to a relative outlining the benefits of checking account security devices. (Letters should state that most checking accounts are set up to provide checks and balances that ensure security.)

R Reading Strategy
Apply Knowledge Ask students to explain how a bank with multiple branches might use a signature card to verify a customer's signature. (Large banks use digital images of signature cards so that tellers at other locations can see the signature.)

U Universal Access
Hands-On Learners Obtain a copy of a blank signature card from a local bank and make copies for students. Ask students to complete the cards and discuss why the bank might need the information requested. Afterward, have students shred their completed cards and discuss why shredding is appropriate. (Students should understand that signature cards help banks protect customer accounts from fraudulent activity and that shredding protects personal information.)

Student Activity Workbook ☞ Assign the Section 29.1 Activities.

● **As You Read**

Students may say they need to contribute to the safety of the account.

517

RETEACH (cont.)

 **C** **Critical Thinking**

Predict the Consequences

Overdraft Protection Ask students to explain the consequences of not having overdraft protection. (Banks may return checks for insufficient funds. The bank can charge a fee for the service. Businesses charge a fee for returned checks.)

E-Banking It is difficult to withdraw money or to deposit paper checks.

ASSESS

After You Read

Have students complete the Section 29.1 After You Read section review.

Online Study Tools

Have students go to the Online Learning Center through **glencoe.com** to:

- Take the Section 29.1 **Practice Test**.
- Download free **Study-to-Go** content to their PDAs or cell phones.

CLOSE

Culminating Activity
Follow the Money
Ask students to use library and Internet resources to develop a poster illustrating how an out-of-state check cashed at a local bank moves through the system. (Posters should indicate how the "money" moves.)

518

E-Banking Electronic banking over the Internet, e-banking, or online banking, is becoming more popular worldwide, but the United States still relies heavily on paper checks. A recent survey revealed that of all the households that are on the Internet, only one in five also do their banking online. *Why do you think some consumers have avoided online banking?*

N C L B Activity correlates to Math standards.

If you have overdraft protection and write a check for more than you have in the account, the bank will cover the check up to a certain amount. You may pay a service fee and interest for overdraft protection. A **stop payment** is an order for a bank not to cash a particular check. It also usually requires a fee. A **debit card** is a bank card that immediately takes money from a checking account when it is used. It is used like a credit card.

Online Banking

Technology allows consumers to handle many banking transactions over the Internet. Online banking allows consumers to check their account balances, transfer money, or pay bills at any time. With online banking, your checking account information is available to you from your home computer 24 hours a day, seven days a week. Online banking also allows you to save time and money. Banks offer the option of scheduling automatic payment of bills from the checking account, too.

You can use an Internet browser on your computer to handle online banking. With personal finance software, you can store information about your transactions for your records.

Section 29.1

After You Read

Review Key Concepts
1. How does a checking account work?
2. What are the three main types of checking accounts?
3. Discuss some additional services and offerings that banks provide checking account holders.

Academic Skills
4. **Mathematics** Vinita has a checking account at a local bank. This account pays 0.5% interest if she maintains an average balance of at least $1,500 during a month. In February, Vinita's average monthly balance was $1,120 more than the minimum. How much interest did she earn in February?

THEORY **Percents Less Than One** To convert a percent to a decimal, multiply it by 100 by moving the decimal point two places to the left. Therefore, 0.5% = 0.005.

 For math help, go to the Math Appendix.

@ Go to the *Introduction to Business* Online Learning Center through **glencoe.com** to check your answers.

Review Key Concepts
1. A customer deposits money into a checking account and receives a book of checks to use for payments and purchases. The person can cash or deposit checks.
2. regular checking accounts, interest-bearing accounts, and joint accounts

3. Overdraft protection is a line of credit for overdrawn checks. Banks also will allow a stop payment, an order for a bank not to cash a particular check. Debit cards are also offered.

Academic Skills
4. **Mathematics** ($1,500 + $1,120) × 0.005 = $13.10

Account Records

Reading Guide

● Before You Read

Think about some ways you would manage a checking account effectively.

Read to Learn

- Describe how checking account holders manage their bank transactions.
- Describe the procedure for bringing your account into agreement with bank records.

The Main Idea

You must manage your checking account so that you have an accurate picture of your finances. A bank provides you with a bank statement showing all transactions. You should check your checkbook records against that statement regularly.

Key Concepts

- Keeping Track of Financial Transactions
- Reconciling Your Account Records

 Go to the *Introduction to Business* Online Learning Center through **glencoe.com** for a printable graphic organizer.

Vocabulary

Key Terms

check register   canceled checks
endorsement   bank reconciliation
bank statement   outstanding checks

Academic Vocabulary

You will find these words in your reading and on your tests. Make sure you know their meanings.

route   valid
traces   alteration

Graphic Organizer

In a figure like the one below, write a check to Tina's Hair Salon for $25.00.

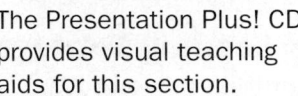

```
First Last                                              1234
4321 My Street
Seattle, WA 98111                    Date_____

PAY TO THE ORDER OF:_____ $ _____
_____ DOLLARS

My Bank
1234 Street
Seattle, WA 98111

Memo _____        _____
   :322345692:   1234567890   1234
```

Academic Standards

English Language Arts

NCTE 1 Read texts to acquire new information
NCTE 5 Use different writing process elements to communicate effectively
NCTE 7 Conduct research and gather, evaluate, and synthesize data to communicate discoveries

Science

Content Standard F Students should develop understanding of science and technology in local, national, and global challenges

---

FOCUS

🔔 Bell Ringer Activity

Account Records

Ask students if they can name some account records that are attached to a checking account. Ask a volunteer to list answers on the board. (Answers will vary. Students might mention some of the following account records: a check register, canceled check, deposit receipt, ATM receipt, and bank statement.)

Preteaching

Presentation Plus! ☉

The Presentation Plus! CD provides visual teaching aids for this section.

PuzzleMaker ☉

Use the Vocabulary PuzzleMaker to create a puzzle of the section's key terms. Students can complete the puzzle on paper or on a computer.

Graphic Organizer

Tell students to go to the Online Learning Center through **glencoe.com** for a printable graphic organizer. (Answers include: the date; payee Tina's Hair Salon; Amount: 25.00; Twenty-five and no/100; drawer: the student's signature; memo: haircut)

N C L B Connects academics to content.

Reading Guide

● Before You Read

Students might mention that they should balance the account regularly and record all ATM and debit card activity.

D Develop Concepts

The Main Idea Ask students: What does it mean to balance your checkbook and why is it a good idea? (It is done to make sure your checking account records match the bank's records, giving you a clear picture of your account.)

TEACH

Discussion Starter
Writing a Check
Draw a large rectangle on the board and ask students to help create an illustration of a check. Invite volunteers to come to the board. Instruct them to name an element, add it to the illustration, and label it. Direct students to start the illustration by creating a blank check first and then "write" the check to you for $105.39. Ask the class to discuss each element and offer suggestions for improving the illustration. (Illustrations should include all of the elements mentioned in the textbook.)

 **Reading Strategy**

Identifying the Root Word
Ask students to identify the root of the words *drawer* and *drawee*. (Both words share the same root, *draw*.) Point out that it is easier to remember the meaning of these words if people think of writing a check as a way to with*draw* money from a checking account.

Real World
The Check 21 Act
Answers will vary. Students who research the law may find that finance services are slow to adopt new technology, that it requires expensive investments in technology, and that banks do not want to receive images of checks.

The Check 21 Act
The Check Clearing for the 21st Century Act, or Check 21 Act, authorizes recipients of a check to convert it to a digital form and then transmit it to the Federal Reserve Bank for credit, as if it were an actual check. It was advocated as the start of electronic exchange and the end of paper. Yet it has progressed at a relatively slow rate of acceptance. *Why do you suppose Check 21 has been slow to gain acceptance?*

R

Keeping Track of Financial Transactions

An advantage of checking accounts is that they enable consumers to keep records of their financial transactions. The different elements of a check provide information that can be used in financial record keeping. Financial institutions also provide forms and reports (see **Figure 29.2** for an example of a checking account statement) that consumers can use to keep their checking account in order. With these records, account holders can keep track of their income and expenses.

The Parts of a Check

R There are usually three people, or parties, named on a check. The *payee* is the party to whom the check is written, or who is cashing the check. The *drawer* is the party who wrote the check and is paying the money, or drawing it from an account. The third party is the *drawee,* the financial institution where the drawer has an account.

Banks and other companies use the information printed on checks to **route** a check to your account for payment. A check must include an account number and a bank route number, which **traces** the check back to the account on which it was written. A check includes the name and location of the drawer's bank, a check number, and security features. A check presented for payment must include a **valid** date, the drawer's signature, the payee's name, and matching numerical and written amounts.

Science/Tech TRENDS

N C L B

Biometrics
With identity fraud becoming more prevalent, authorities and organizations have started looking for new ways to protect the consumer. One of the more promising technologies involves using biometrics to grant account access to consumers. Many parts of the body form patterns that are unique to each individual. The patterns formed by fingerprints, DNA, and characteristics of the eye form patterns that can last throughout a person's life. In the future, these technologies are likely to be easy to use and a highly accurate way of verifying customers' identities.

 **Web Quest**

Go to the *Introduction to Business* Online Learning Center through **glencoe.com** for links to Web sites where you can research how biometric technologies may change the security industry. Write a paragraph describing other applications of biometrics.

Science/Tech TRENDS
 Web Quest

Biometrics Answers will vary, but paragraphs might describe how iris recognition can be used by law enforcement, as a passport when traveling, and even as a key in some corporate settings.

N C L B Activity correlates to Science standards.

Figure 29.2 – *Checking Account Statements*

Louis and Ling Chung
121 Bayside Road
Fall River, OH 42119-0120

Account Number: 211-37-065

Date of Statement: 3/31/20--

PREVIOUS BALANCE	CHECKS AND CHARGES	NO. OF DEPOSITS	NO. OF CHECKS	DEPOSITS AND CREDITS	BALANCE AT THIS DATE
$535.80	$1,011.25	1	5	$814.10	$338.65

DATE	CHECKS AND OTHER CHARGES		DEPOSITS AND OTHER CREDITS	BALANCE
			Beginning Balance	$535.80
	Check No.	Amount		
3/13	106	50.00		485.80
3/19	M – Bob's Grocery	75.10		410.70
3/23	107	120.00		290.70
3/24			814.10	1,104.80
3/25	M – The Cleaner's	58.25		1,046.55
3/26	111	23.90		1,022.65
3/28	114	650.00		372.65
3/28	115	28.00		344.65
	Service Charge	6.00		338.65

Please examine your statement at once. If no error is reported in 10 days, the account will be considered correct and vouchers genuine.
All items are credited subject to final payment.

C – Certified Check   S – Service Charge   CR – Overdraft   R – Returned Check   M – Merchant Sales Draft

● **Transaction Record** Louis and Ling Chung received this bank statement. **What were their totals for checks and deposits for the month?**

Writing a Check

   When you write a check, record the check number, the amount of the check, the date, and the name of the payee in a check register. A **check register** is a checkbook log in which an account holder records checking account transactions. If you do not record the check immediately, you might forget some of the information.

✔ **Reading Check** **Identify** Who are the three parties or people named on a check?

Making Deposits

   To deposit cash or a check in your account, fill out a deposit slip. The deposit slip lists the amount of cash and checks and the total amount of the deposit. You may deposit your check at a bank or through an ATM. You will usually receive a receipt for your transaction. After you make the deposit, record it in your check register.

Section 29.2   Account Records   **521**

Figure 29.2

● **Transaction Record** Checks and charges totaled $1,011.25. Deposits and credits totaled $814.10.

✔ **Reading Check**

Identify The three parties or people named on a check are the payee, the party to whom the check is written; the drawer, the party who wrote the check; and the drawee, the financial institution where the drawer has an account.

RETEACH

R **Reading Strategy**

Describe Ask students to describe an endorsement including the proper location. (An endorsement is the signature of the payee on the back of the check.)

W **Writing Support**

Enrichment

List Ask students to write an e-mail explaining why bank statements indicate a break in check sequence. (To help customers identify outstanding checks and alert them to possible problems, such as stolen checks. For example, if the next check in your checkbook is 723 and the bank statement shows that check number 825 has been cashed, it might indicate that someone has stolen checks from you.)

U **Universal Access**

Gifted Students For students who would benefit from the additional work of an independent project, assign the task of researching the trend in the ways banks handle checks. If possible, have them arrange to visit the Web site of a bank in their community that offers online banking. Ask students to gather information on ways banks handle checks to reduce costs, increase ease of access, decrease the possibility of outside tampering, and other benefits. Have students plan a brief news report describing the trends they discover.

Student Activity Workbook ☞ Assign the Section 29.2 Activities.

R To deposit or cash a check requires an **endorsement**, or the signature of the payee on the back of the check. Endorse the check on the back (on the lines printed for the endorsement). Sign your name exactly as it is written on the front of the check. Do not sign a check until you are ready to deposit or cash it. Then you have some protection in case it is lost or stolen. When making a deposit, write "For Deposit Only" as part of the endorsement so that it cannot be cashed if lost or stolen.

Bank Statements

W Once a month, banks issue a **bank statement**, the bank's record of all the transactions in a checking account. The statement includes a record of all withdrawals, deposits, interest, and fees. It also includes a record of all **canceled checks**, or checks that have been cashed. A canceled check is proof that the money has been paid to a payee.

Handling Your Own Checks

● **As You Read**

Think about the importance of checking and keeping bank statements after receiving them.

U Checks should be handled carefully. Do not print or write your driver license, Social Security, telephone, or credit card numbers on them. Keep checks, canceled checks, deposit slips, and bank statements in a safe place. Never leave your checkbook in the open or in a car. Check your bank statements for anything unusual. Make sure your checks have security features to protect against counterfeiting and **alteration**. Unless needed for tax purposes, destroy old documents that have your account number on them. Never make a check payable to "Cash." If "Cash" is written on the payee line, anyone who has the check can cash it.

● **Balancing the Checkbook** Michael and Conchetta Hamel received this bank statement. They need to reconcile the balance in the check register shown below with a bank balance of $830.89. The statement does not include check numbers 431 and 432. Also missing is a deposit in the amount of $27.85. The bank has charged a $6 service fee. **How would you reconcile their records?**

Figure 29.3 — **A Checkbook Register**

No.	Date	Description	Payment	Deposit	Balance
					$624.83
429	10/01	Old Navy	22.95		601.88
430	10/01	Kroger	15.86		586.02
--	10/01	Paycheck		350.77	936.79
--	10/02	Cash	50.00		886.79
431	10/04	Olive Garden	46.27		840.52
432	10/04	Amazon.com	37.48		803.04
--	10/06	Sam's check		27.85	830.89

● **As You Read**

Checks and bank statements are records of all your transactions. If you have a problem, this record will show the payment. It can also be used for tax purposes.

Figure 29.3

● **Balancing the Checkbook** Subtract the amounts for checks 431 and 432 from the amount on the statement, then add the deposit and subtract the service fee. The totals for the statement and checkbook should now match.

Reconciling Your Account Records

Bank reconciliation is the process of seeing whether an account holder's records agree with the bank's records for the account. To reconcile is to bring into agreement, or balance. If the bank statement shows a different balance than your register, you should reconcile both records.

Balancing Your Checkbook

The first step to reconciling your account is to see whether the bank has processed all of your checks and deposits. With the bank statement and your check register, you can identify your **outstanding checks**, or checks that have been written but have not yet been cashed. The total dollar amount of outstanding checks should be subtracted from the balance shown on the bank statement. **Figure 29.3** shows an example of a checkbook register that must be balanced.

If you have made any deposits or ATM withdrawals that have not been recorded on the bank statement, those transactions should be factored into the bank statement balance. If the bank charged any service fees, you may not have recorded them in your check register. Subtract the service fee from the balance in your check register. If your account earns interest, add the interest shown on the bank statement to your check register.

Once the balance on the bank statement and the balance in your check register are the same, you have reconciled your check register balance with the bank statement balance.

Finding Errors If your balance differs from the bank's balance after you reconcile your account, double check the amounts in your records and all your additions and subtractions. Then check the bank's additions and subtractions. If you find a mistake, report it immediately. *Why is it important to reconcile your bank account?*

 **N C L B** Activity correlates to English Language Arts standards.

Section 29.2

After You Read

Review Key Concepts
1. What kinds of financial records help people manage their checking accounts?
2. What are some guidelines to consider when ordering and handling personal checks?
3. Describe the purpose of reconciling a bank statement and a check register.

Academic Skills
4. **English Language Arts** Work with a group of four to plan and design storyboards for a documentary called "Travels of a Check" that describes a check's life. Present your storyboards as visuals in an oral documentary.

5. **English Language Arts** Research how to balance a checking account using the monthly bank statement and check register. Write step-by-step instructions that are clear and concise describing the process.

Go to the *Introduction to Business* Online Learning Center through **glencoe.com** to check your answers.

N C L B

Section 29.2

Review Key Concepts
1. the checks themselves, a check register, ATM receipts, deposit slips, and bank statements
2. Do not print or write your personal information on your checks. Store all financial papers in a safe place.
3. to bring the two balances into agreement

Academic Skills
4. **English Language Arts** Students' presentations should reflect the combined efforts of all team members.
5. **English Language Arts** Answers will vary, but instructions should enable anyone unfamiliar with the process to successfully balance a checkbook.

Section 29.2

RETEACH (cont.)

C Critical Thinking
Explain the Significance
Outstanding Checks Ask students to explain the significance of outstanding checks. (They have been written but not cashed. They do not appear on a bank statement.)

Finding Errors to keep track of all the transactions for an account

ASSESS

After You Read

Have students complete the Section 29.2 After You Read section review.

Online Study Tools
Have students go to the Online Learning Center through **glencoe.com** to:
- Take the Section 29.2 **Practice Test**.
- Download free **Study-to-Go** content to their PDAs or cell phones.

CLOSE

Culminating Activity
Bank Reconciliation
Distribute copies of a bank reconciliation form to students. Have them reconcile the bank statement in **Figure 29.2**, using the following register entries: March 25, check 116, $36.48; March 30, ATM withdrawal, $50.00; April 1, deposit $200. (The current balance is $452.70.)

523

Vocabulary Review

1. Students should write complete sentences using each term correctly.

Review Key Concepts

2. Answers will discuss regular, interest-bearing, and joint checking accounts. See page 513.

3. overdraft protection, stop payments, debit cards, and online banking

4. They refer to the checks themselves, which include a date, their signature, the payee's name, and the numerical and written amounts. Account holders also keep a check register for their transactions, and use ATM receipts, deposit slips, and bank statements.

5. See whether the bank has processed all of your checks and deposits, identify outstanding checks, deposits, and ATM withdrawals that have not been recorded on the statement, and use these amounts to identify differences.

Critical Thinking

6. Otherwise, the account might be closed or have insufficient funds if another check is cashed before the date indicated.

7. Your name and mailing address, to send bank statements to you; your Social Security number; your initial deposit; and your signature on the signature card as identification.

Section 29.1 *Summary*

The Basics of Checking Accounts
Banks, credit unions, and other financial institutions provide checking account services for individuals and businesses. Customers can write checks to transfer money easily to others. Banks offer a selection of checking accounts to meet their customers' needs. Some accounts are designed for those who need to write only a few checks. Others are designed for those who need more extensive banking services. Many banks offer their checking account customers additional services, such as overdraft protection, stop-payment services, debit cards, and online banking.

Section 29.2 *Summary*

Account Records A checking account provides a way to keep track of financial transactions. There are usually three people, or parties, named on a check. There are specific steps that must be followed to write and deposit checks and to keep blank checks safe. A bank periodically sends each customer a record of all transactions recorded for the customer's account. With those statements, customers can reconcile the bank's records with their own records. This enables customers to find possible errors. It also helps them to manage their money and determine the correct information to start the next month.

Vocabulary Review

1. On a sheet of paper, use each of these key terms and academic vocabulary terms in a sentence.

Key Terms

check	debit card
direct deposit	check register
interest-bearing account	endorsement
signature card	bank statement
overdrawn	canceled checks
overdraft protection	bank reconciliation
stop payment	outstanding checks

Academic Vocabulary

demand	route
common	traces
compare	valid
designed	alteration

Review Key Concepts

2. Discuss the different types of checking accounts and how they work.

3. Discuss other services and offerings that banks provide checking account holders.

4. Describe how checking account holders manage their bank transactions.

5. Describe the procedure for bringing your account into agreement with bank records.

---

8. Answers will vary. Taking security measures can help ensure that the consumer's personal information is safe.

9. Answers will vary. Overdraft protection allows an account holder's checks to be paid even if there is not enough money in the account, which can often save a person money that would be charged in returned-check fees.

10. Answers will vary, but some experts recommend saving all checking account records for a year. After that, canceled checks for routine spending may be destroyed. Checks for major payments, such as investments, insurance, mortgages, taxes, or household repairs, should be kept as permanent records.

Critical Thinking

6. Banks may disregard the date written on a check that has been postdated, that is, dated for a future date. Why do you think banks have this policy?

7. What types of personal information do you think banks need and for what purposes?

8. How would you answer a person who is concerned that banking online is risky?

9. Most banks offer overdraft protection to their customers, sometimes for a fee. Would you consider taking overdraft protection? Why or why not?

10. How long do you think checking account records should be kept? Explain your answer.

11. Why is overdrawing a checking account poor financial management?

12. What effect do you think customer deposits in checking accounts have on the economic system?

13. Do you think people who have a joint checking account should each have a checkbook, or should they share one? Give reasons for your opinion.

Write About It

14. In two or more paragraphs, discuss the factors to consider when deciding whether the fees associated with overdraft protection are worthwhile.

15. How would you endorse a check if your name is misspelled as the payee? How would you endorse a check if you wanted to send someone to the bank to deposit it for you? Write an example of an endorsement in each case.

16. Write a short article for your school newspaper on the precautions people should take when handling a checking account and keeping account records.

17. What effect do you think ATMs have had on customers' use of banks? Write a brief essay on your observations.

18. Why should you shop around before opening a checking account? What are some features that would appeal to you? Write a brief explanation of your response.

19. Think about the differences and similarities between debit cards and credit cards. Discuss them in at least one page.

Technology Applications

Word-Processing Software

20. Use your local phone book, newspaper advertisements, bank Web sites, or brochures to prepare a report about banks. Include information such as the number of checking accounts offered, the minimum amount needed to open an account, interest rates offered on interest-bearing accounts, transaction fees charged, service fees, and other services offered with checking accounts.

Business Ethics

Is the Bank's Loss Your Gain?

21. Suppose you have a regular checking account. One day you make a deposit at an ATM machine for $100. While your records show that you should have $500 in the account after the deposit, your ATM receipt shows a new balance of $5,000. You figure that the ATM has made a mistake and wonder what would happen if you did not tell the bank. What should you do?

Technology Applications

20. Answers will vary. For example, information for one bank is: regular checking account—$25 to open, no interest, $1.50 for each nonbank ATM transaction; $6 per month without direct deposit; free online statements; no per-check fees.

Business Ethics

21. It would be dishonest to keep money that did not belong to you. You should report bank errors as soon as possible to avoid the problems that would occur if you started to think of the money as belonging to you and the bank corrected the error when you did not have sufficient funds in your account.

Critical Thinking

11. Overdraft fees and returned-check fees decrease an account holder's funds.

12. Banks use checking account money to issue loans to businesses and individuals. They also use it to issue cash when customers need withdrawals. The ultimate effect of deposits is to stimulate the economy.

13. If both people have a checkbook, they will likely have less risk of overdrafts. A disadvantage of two checkbooks is that they must be more careful in recordkeeping.

Write About It

14. Answers include the amount of money you expect to have in the account and the number of checks you expect to write.

15. Endorse the check as your name appears on it, and then write your name correctly. Write "For Deposit Only" on it.

16. Examples include using a pen to write a check and writing legibly.

17. Customers make fewer bank visits. Most banks have fewer jobs.

18. Banks charge different fees.

19. Debit card: looks like a credit card but works like a check. When used, a direct, immediate, electronic payment comes from the cardholder's checking account. With a credit card, the payment is delayed.

22. Students should note that consumers may have less protection when they use a debit card instead of a credit card.

23. Thirty-six and 45/100 dollars

One hundred fifty-two and 79/100 dollars

Sixteen and 14/100 dollars

One thousand three hundred eleven and 35/100 dollars

24. *Interest* is a noun that can mean money paid for the use of someone else's money, or curiosity. *Draw* is a verb that can mean to withdraw from an account, or to make a picture. *Account* is a noun meaning a list of money received, paid, or owed; it is also another word for story or report.

25. $844.71 + $131.25 = $975.96

$975.96 − ($50 × 2) − $875.96

Active Learning

26. Answers will vary. For instance, the use of checks for paying bills has decreased over the past few years.

Business in the Real World

27. Answers will vary. For instance, Wells Fargo Bank offers business customers scanning equipment for scanning checks at their desks. It calls the service "anytime, anywhere" banking.

Applying Academics to Business

English Language Arts
22. Credit cards and debit cards look alike, but they are very different when it comes to consumer protection. Find out more about the differences in how consumers are protected when they use the two types of cards. Write a few sentences informing others about these differences.

Mathematics
23. You and your friend Sal spend Saturday shopping. Sal uses checks to make purchases but needs help writing out the dollar amounts. Write the following dollar amounts as you would write them on a check: $36.45, $152.79, $16.14, and $1,311.35.

> **THEORY** **Writing Numbers** When writing the name of a number in words, avoid using the word *and* except to signal the decimal point. For example, write the name in words for 1,034.5 as "one thousand thirty-four *and* five-tenths."

English Language Arts
24. The following words have specific meanings in the context of banking and financial activity, but they have other meanings as well. Write a sentence for each word identifying its part of speech and describing at least two meanings.

interest   draw   account

Mathematics
25. Your bank statement shows an ending balance of $844.71. You have recorded in your checkbook register a deposit of $131.25 that does not appear on your statement, and two checks for $50 apiece that were not returned with the statement. What is your actual balance?

> **THEORY** **Credits and Debits** Deposits are additions to your account, and checks written against the account are reductions.

Active Learning

Online Bill Paying
26. Work in teams. Survey people in your neighborhood or school about online bill paying. Ask them: Do you pay bills online? If not, why? Do you write fewer checks than you did three years ago? Will you write fewer checks in the future? What do you like most about online bill paying? What concerns you about it? Summarize your information in a short report.

Business in the Real World

Check Scanning
27. Some banks provide scanning services for businesses to make check deposits. A business can transmit customers' check images from their business location to their bank. The process saves time and costs. Research check scanning by going online or calling some banks. You could also ask local businesspeople you know about it. Write a brief report of your findings, and share it with the class.

ExamView Assessment Suite CD allows you to print out ready-made unit and chapter tests, complete with answer keys. You can also create customized tests.

TeacherWorks Plus provides complete teacher resources in one convenient package. It includes customizable lesson plans in calendar format, and instant access to many print program resources.

USING THE RIGHT ACCOUNT

28. A routing transit number (RTN) is the nine-digit code on the bottom of checks that identifies which financial institution it is drawn upon. This code is also used to process direct deposits and other automated transfers. There are two other numbers on the bottom of every check. Research companies that print personal check blanks and fill out an order form so that the printer can print them with all of the parts of a standard check.

FIND YOUR DREAM JOB

29. Go to the *Introduction to Business* Online Learning Center through **glenooc.com** for a link to the Occupational Outlook Handbook Web site. Click on the "OOH Search/A-Z Index" link and enter the field of "banking." Then write a one-page report about this type of occupation. Conclude your report with a list of things you could do now to prepare yourself to pursue the occupation.

Role Play

USE OF ATMS

30. Situation You are a consumer who uses an automated teller machine (ATM) often. Your teacher has asked you to demonstrate ways to protect yourself and your bank information while you use an ATM.

Activity Prepare an outline of actions you can take to safeguard your personal information and account at an ATM, and then demonstrate the process.

Evaluation You will be evaluated on how well you meet the following performance indicators:

- Identify ways that theft can occur through ATM use.
- Explain steps to take when approaching and using an ATM.
- Demonstrate proper procedures to protect your personal information at an ATM.
- Prepare a written outline of points in your demonstration.
- Project your voice and use correct grammar.

Standardized Test Practice

Directions Choose the letter of the best answer. Write the letter for the answer on a separate piece of paper.

1. What is $2,952.11 rounded to the nearest hundred?

- A $2,900.00
- B $3,000.00
- C $2,952.00
- D $2,952.10

 TEST-TAKING TIP Evaluate your test-taking savvy by answering these questions:
- Do I use my time well during a test?
- Does anxiety get in the way of doing my best on a test?
- How can I prepare better for my next test?

 READING Go to the *Introduction to Business* Online Learning Center through **glencoe.com** for a list of outside reading suggestions.

 **STRATEGIES FOR STANDARDIZED TEST PREP SUCCESS**

Test Savvy Help students monitor their own preparedness for taking tests by writing a journal entry concerning their attitudes, understandings, and experiences with taking tests. Ask them to identify their strengths and weaknesses and consider how they could improve their test-taking abilities.

28. Order forms will vary, but the information should be complete.

Business CAREERS

29. Banking jobs vary. Working conditions are mostly indoors. Training and qualifications vary by occupation. Most managerial positions require a college degree. Senior management positions are filled by promoting professional personnel. Jobs are expected to decline, except for teller positions. Demand will grow for computer specialists. Earnings vary dramatically. As preparation, develop basic math and computer skills, interpersonal, and communication skills. For management positions, take college-prep classes and develop problem-solving and decision-making skills.

Role Play

30. Presentations should address the competencies noted in the Role Play. Some basic precautions include using ATMs that are inside buildings, such as grocery stores. ATMs in dark locations should be avoided. Cover the keypad when you enter your personal identification number (PIN), and take your receipt with you.

Standardized Test Practice
1. B

527

Standards-Based Lesson Planning   *Introduction to Business* provides students with instruction and assessment in the following fundamental content areas:

Content Standards Correlations	
Discuss the theory of saving and investing in our economy.	pp. 531, 537, 539, 543
Analyze how saving and investing influences economic growth.	pp. 531, 534, 537, 539, 543
Research and present major financial issues for the individual, such as money management, the banking system and services, saving, and investing.	pp. 532–533, 538–539, 541, 543
Analyze factors that affect the rate of return on a given savings or investment plan and calculate the rate of return.	pp. 534, 536, 538, 543
Discuss how to open a personal savings account.	p. 536
Identify various types of savings accounts.	pp. 536–537
Compare and contrast various investment opportunities, both insured and uninsured. Evaluate bank investment opportunities, such as savings accounts, bonds, CDs, and money market accounts. Distinguish between risk factors, rates of return, and liquidity.	pp. 536–537, 540–542
Compute simple and compound interest on investments.	pp. 536, 541, 542, 543

NCLB   Activities, information, and skills practice will help your students attain No Child Left Behind proficiency. Students will improve their abilities in the following academic standards areas:

Academic Standards Correlations		
English Language Arts	Activities/Features	Page
NCTE 3 Apply strategies to interpret texts	Applying Academics to Business	p. 542
NCTE 6 Apply knowledge of language structure and conventions to discuss texts	After You Read	p. 539
NCTE 11 Participate as members of literacy communities	After You Read	p. 539
NCTE 12 Use language to accomplish individual purposes	Applying Academics to Business	p. 542
Mathematics		
Data Analysis and Probability Formulate questions that can be addressed with data and collect, organize, and display relevant data to answer them	Applying Academics to Business	p. 542
Number and Operations Compute fluently and make reasonable estimates	After You Read Applying Academics to Business Standardized Test Practice	pp. 534, 542, 543
Number and Operations Understand numbers, ways of representing numbers, relationships among numbers, and number systems	Ask S&P	p. 528
Science		
Content Standard F Students should develop understanding of science and technology in local, national, and global challenges	Science/Tech Trends	p. 538

Correlations   This chart shows the 21ˢᵗ Century Skills, foundation skills, and workplace competencies that students develop as they work in this chapter.

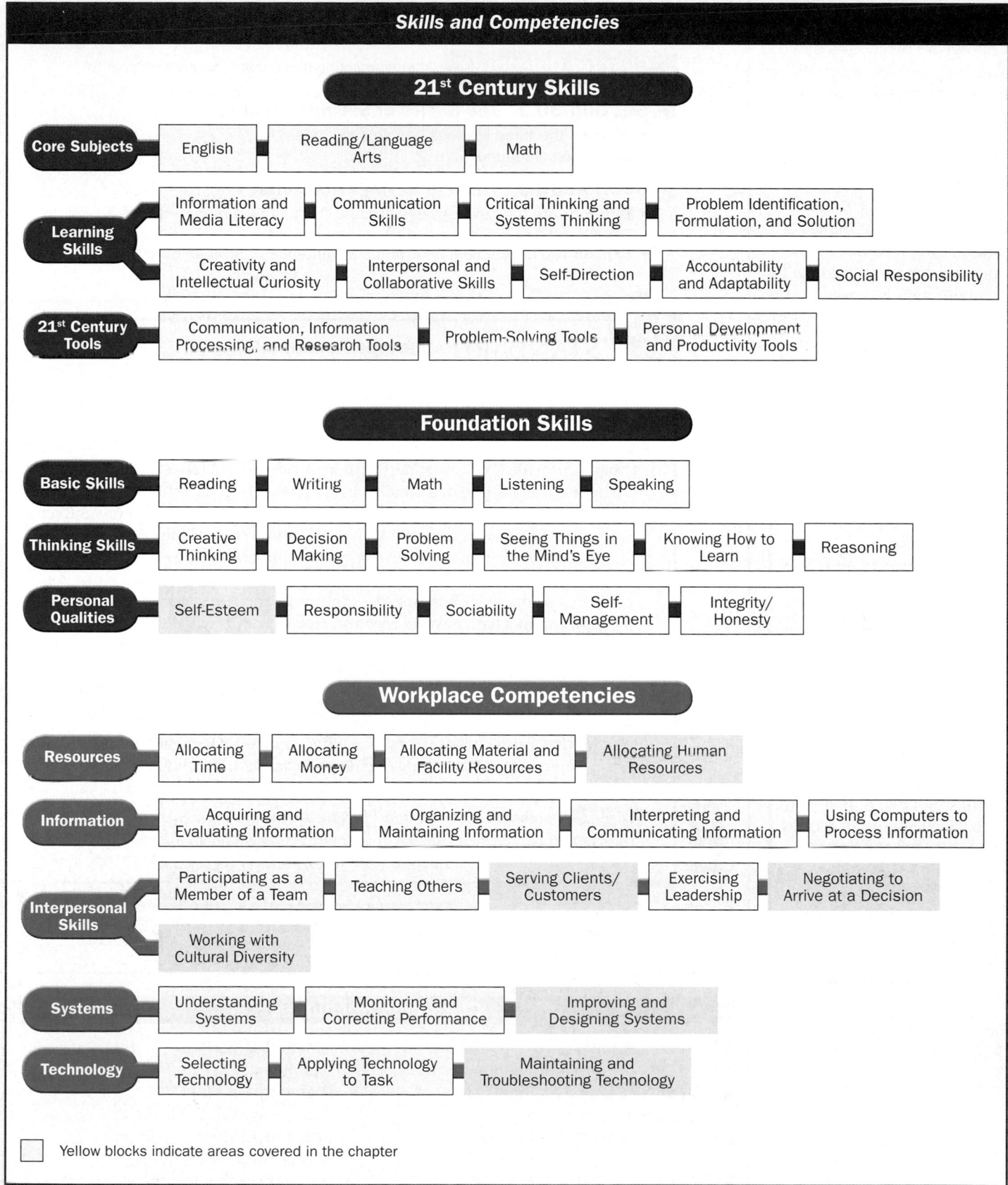

Skills and Competencies

21ˢᵗ Century Skills

Core Subjects
- English
- Reading/Language Arts
- Math

Learning Skills
- Information and Media Literacy
- Communication Skills
- Critical Thinking and Systems Thinking
- Problem Identification, Formulation, and Solution
- Creativity and Intellectual Curiosity
- Interpersonal and Collaborative Skills
- Self-Direction
- Accountability and Adaptability
- Social Responsibility

21ˢᵗ Century Tools
- Communication, Information Processing, and Research Tools
- Problem-Solving Tools
- Personal Development and Productivity Tools

Foundation Skills

Basic Skills
- Reading
- Writing
- Math
- Listening
- Speaking

Thinking Skills
- Creative Thinking
- Decision Making
- Problem Solving
- Seeing Things in the Mind's Eye
- Knowing How to Learn
- Reasoning

Personal Qualities
- Self-Esteem
- Responsibility
- Sociability
- Self-Management
- Integrity/Honesty

Workplace Competencies

Resources
- Allocating Time
- Allocating Money
- Allocating Material and Facility Resources
- Allocating Human Resources

Information
- Acquiring and Evaluating Information
- Organizing and Maintaining Information
- Interpreting and Communicating Information
- Using Computers to Process Information

Interpersonal Skills
- Participating as a Member of a Team
- Teaching Others
- Serving Clients/Customers
- Exercising Leadership
- Negotiating to Arrive at a Decision
- Working with Cultural Diversity

Systems
- Understanding Systems
- Monitoring and Correcting Performance
- Improving and Designing Systems

Technology
- Selecting Technology
- Applying Technology to Task
- Maintaining and Troubleshooting Technology

☐ Yellow blocks indicate areas covered in the chapter

Savings Accounts

Chapter Overview

Introduce the Chapter

Savings Accounts
Chapter 30 discusses savings and savings accounts. It outlines reasons for saving and describes the various types of savings accounts.

Building Background
Many students have had experience saving money and earning interest. Make sure they understand how to compute simple interest and show them how this concept is related to the way compound interest is computed.

>> Math Answer
Rewrite the percent as a decimal, 0.0178. Now multiply: $5,000 × 0.0178 = $89.

>> Extension Activity
Danica was planning to move $7,500 of her savings to a one-year CD at the same bank, where the interest rate is 5.22%. She wants to compare the interest rates offered by three other banks: 5.31%, 5.49%, and 5.63%. How much would she earn for each of the four rates? (Danica would earn $391.50 at her bank and $398.25, $411.75, and $422.25 at the other banks.)

N C L B Activity correlates to Math standards.

528

Chapter Objectives After completing this chapter, you will be able to:

▶ **Section 30.1** *The Basics of Savings Accounts*
- **Discuss** the three reasons people save money.
- **Describe** compound interest.

▶ **Section 30.2** *Types of Savings Accounts*
- **Differentiate** a regular savings account from a CD, a money market fund, and a money market deposit account.
- **Explain** two advantages and two disadvantages of savings accounts.

Ask

STANDARD &POOR'S **Savings Accounts**

Q: Which is best, passbook accounts, money markets, or CDs?

A: A basic savings account is sometimes referred to as a passbook account, since many banks provide account holders with little books used for keeping track of activity. The main advantage of a basic savings account is its accessibility—the money is pretty much there whenever you need it, and you're free to add or subtract at will. They can be opened with relatively little money, but of course, the disadvantage is that these accounts typically provide a comparably low rate of return. A money market account can be thought of as a restricted savings account since you're only allowed so many withdrawals per month. In addition, they tend to require a higher balance than a basic savings account. However, you will be rewarded with a higher interest rate. Finally, CDs, or certificates of deposit, usually provide investors with more favorable interest rates than most savings accounts and money markets. The downside is that your money would be locked away for a specific amount of time, anywhere from six months to a number of years.

Mathematics Patrick plans to open a savings account. He prefers a passbook account, but the interest rate of the money market account is 1.78% higher. How much more will he make if he puts $5,000 into a money market account?

N C L B

THEORY **Percents Less Than One** Percents less than 1 represent values less than $\frac{1}{100}$. In other words, 0.1% is one-tenth of 1 percent, which can also be represented in decimal form as 0.001 or in fraction form as $\frac{1}{1,000}$.

Classroom Resources

- Student Edition
- Teacher Wraparound Edition
- Student Activity Workbook with Academic Integration
- Student Activity Workbook with Academic Integration TAE
- *Fast File*, Unit 10 Resources
- Inclusion in the Business Education Classroom

- TeacherWorks Plus
- *ExamView Assessment Suite*
- Presentation Plus!
- Vocabulary PuzzleMaker
- Interactive Student Edition
- Online Student Edition
- Online Learning Center with Podcasts

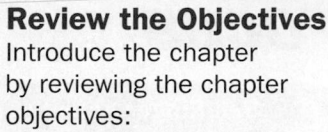

Review the Objectives
Introduce the chapter by reviewing the chapter objectives:

Section 30.1 *Objectives*
Discuss the three reasons people save money. (for major purchases, emergencies, and retirement)

Describe compound interest. (Compound interest is interest earned on both the principal and any interest earned on the principal. It is computed by dividing the annual interest rate by the number of periods, then multiplying the principal plus previously earned interest times the periodic rate.)

Section 30.2 *Objectives*
Differentiate a regular savings account from a CD, a money market fund, and a money market deposit account. (Banks offer regular savings accounts, into which a consumer can deposit even small amounts of money that earn interest. A certificate of deposit earns more interest, but requires account holders to deposit a specified amount of money in an account for a set period of time. Brokerage firms offer a money market fund. It is a kind of mutual fund, or pool of money, put into a variety of short-term debt by business and government.)

Explain two advantages and two disadvantages of savings accounts. (Advantages include insurance against loss and liquidity. Disadvantages include low rates of returns and inflation risks.)

● **Planning for the Future** Money people put aside for future use is called savings. **What are some things for which people save money?**

Chapter 30 Savings Accounts **529**

Discuss the Photo
● **Planning for the Future** Read the caption on the photo to students: Money people put aside for future use is called savings.

Ask students: What are some things for which people save money? (People save for major purchases, emergencies, and retirement.)

FOCUS

Bell Ringer Activity

Savings Account Basics
Project or write the following quote on the board: "A penny saved is a penny earned." Ask students who said it and what they think it means. (Answers will vary. The quote is attributed to Benjamin Franklin. It could mean that saving even the smallest amount can be beneficial and that saving can be a good alternative to spending.)

Preteaching

Presentation Plus!
The Presentation Plus! CD provides visual teaching aids for this section.

PuzzleMaker
Use the Vocabulary PuzzleMaker to create a puzzle of the section's key terms. Students can complete the puzzle on paper or on a computer.

Graphic Organizer
Tell students to go to the Online Learning Center through **glencoe.com** for a printable graphic organizer. (Answers include: People save for major purchases, emergencies, and retirement; reasons students should save will vary, depending on students' wants and needs.)

Connects academics to content.

Savings Account Basics

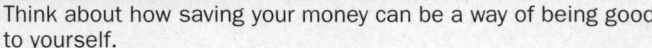
Reading Guide

● Before You Read
Think about how saving your money can be a way of being good to yourself.

Read to Learn
- Discuss the three reasons people save money.
- Describe compound interest.

The Main Idea
Savings are money people put aside for future use. Generally people use their savings for major purchases, emergencies, and retirement income. Savings accounts can earn either simple or compound interest. If one leaves money saved in an account that accumulates compound interest, interest is earned on both the amount saved and the interest earned.

Key Concepts
- A Guide to Saving
- Earning Interest on Savings

Vocabulary
Key Terms
savings
rate of return
compound interest

Academic Vocabulary
You will find these words in your reading and on your tests. Make sure you know their meanings.

experts   item
suggest   accumulate

Graphic Organizer
In a figure like the one below, list the reasons people need to save money in the left column. In the right column, give examples of reasons you will want to save in your own life.

Reasons People Save	Reasons I Should Save
1.	
2.	
3.	

Go to the *Introduction to Business* Online Learning Center through **glencoe.com** for a printable graphic organizer.

Academic Standards
English Language Arts
    NCTE 1 Read texts to acquire new information
    NCTE 9 Develop an understanding of diversity in language use across cultures
Mathematics
    Number and Operations Compute fluently and make reasonable estimates

Reading Guide

● Before You Read
Responses will vary. Students might say that saving now will help them achieve their financial goals.

D Develop Concepts
The Main Idea Ask students: What are some things for which people save?
(Students might suggest that people save for college, a car, a down payment on a home, retirement, and emergencies.)

A Guide to Saving

To achieve your financial goals, you will need a plan. Saving is putting money aside for future use. The money you save is called your **savings**. Savings plans include regular savings accounts, certificates of deposit, and money market funds.

The amount of money you save depends on how much of your income you are willing not to spend. Some personal finance **experts** say people should try to save about 10 percent of their take-home income. Many experts **suggest** that the amount to be saved should be taken from income as soon as it is received so that the saver is not tempted to spend it. However you save, it should be a part of your budget.

All savings involve some sacrifice. When you save money, you are putting off spending that money on an **item** that you might want right now. This sacrifice is called the *opportunity cost* of saving. The opportunity cost of a decision is the same as the benefit of the choice that is given up when one decision is made instead of another.

Saving is a way of being good to yourself. It helps to ensure that you will have money when you need it. People set up and maintain a savings plan for three reasons: to make major purchases, to provide for emergencies, and to have income for retirement.

✔ Reading Check **Identify** What are the three major reasons for setting up and maintaining savings plans?

International Business

Guarding Savings Security

Swiss banks have a reputation for providing customers with a secure and discreet banking environment. Accounts at banks such as Credit Suisse and UBS can be accessed worldwide. The Swiss Federal Banking Commission works to enhance this reputation by licensing banks and supervising their activities. This organization can act to protect the financial interests of account holders. The security of deposits is often a crucial feature to customers because of the important role savings accounts play in helping individuals to provide for emergencies.

Examples of Languages Across Cultures

Q: In French, how do you say: "May I have the check, please."
A: L'addition, s'il vous plait.
   (pronounced: Lă-ă-dēē-sēē-ōn sēēl vōō plā)

Why is the security of money deposited one of the most important issues for account holders?

● **As You Read**

Answers will vary. Some may feel that if what is given up is not as important as what is wanted later, it is worth it. Others may not want to wait for something in the future.

International Business

Guarding Savings Security Security is an important issue for account holders because they rely on their savings as a financial protection against emergencies, and most people save to achieve their goals. People who do not have money saved when they need it can face financial troubles.

TEACH

Discussion Starter
A Guide to Saving
Start a discussion by asking students: How hard is it to save 10 percent of your income? How would you have to change your life in order to put aside 10¢ of every dollar that you get from work, allowance, and gifts? (Answers will vary. Students should recognize that regardless of the amount of their income, saving 10 percent would require them to give up something, such as sodas, snacks, entertainment, or clothing.)

R Reading Strategy
List Ask students to list three savings plans. (Savings plans include regular savings accounts, certificates of deposit, and money market funds.)

✔ Reading Check

Identify Three major reasons for setting up and maintaining savings plans are to make major purchases, to provide for emergencies, and to have income for retirement.

Virtual Business
Introduce business turnaround to students using the Virtual Business Retailing Business Turnaround activity. In this simulation, students learn why business turnaround is important to the success of a business.

531

TEACH (cont.)

S Skill Practice

Guided Practice

Explain Ask students to explain how a regular savings plan can help when there is a financial emergency. (A savings plan can ensure that an account holder will have the funds needed to handle the emergency.) **L1**

Create Pie Charts Arlo, Bailey, and Carson all save $500 per month. Arlo earns $98,000 per year, Bailey makes $4,200 per month, and Carson earns $1,250 per week. Instruct students to calculate their savings as a percentage of their total incomes. (Arlo: 6.12%, Bailey: 11.9%, Carson: 9.23%.) **L2**

Calculate Nadia earns $48,000 per year and wants to save six months of her gross income for emergencies. How long will it take if she saves 10 percent of her income? (Five years: $48,000 ÷ 2 = $24,000 10% of income = $4,800 saved per year. Time required to achieve goal: $24,000 ÷ $4,800 = 5 years.) **L3**

ASSESS

Review Key Terms

Have students write sentences using each key term.

 **Study-to-Go** Have students go to the Online Learning Center through **glencoe.com** to download free **Study-to-Go** content to their PDAs or cell phones.

● **Saving for Retirement** Three things can have a sizable impact on your retirement fund: (1) how much you invest, (2) the rate of return you earn on your investments, and (3) the number of years those investments have to grow. **What does this chart tell you?**

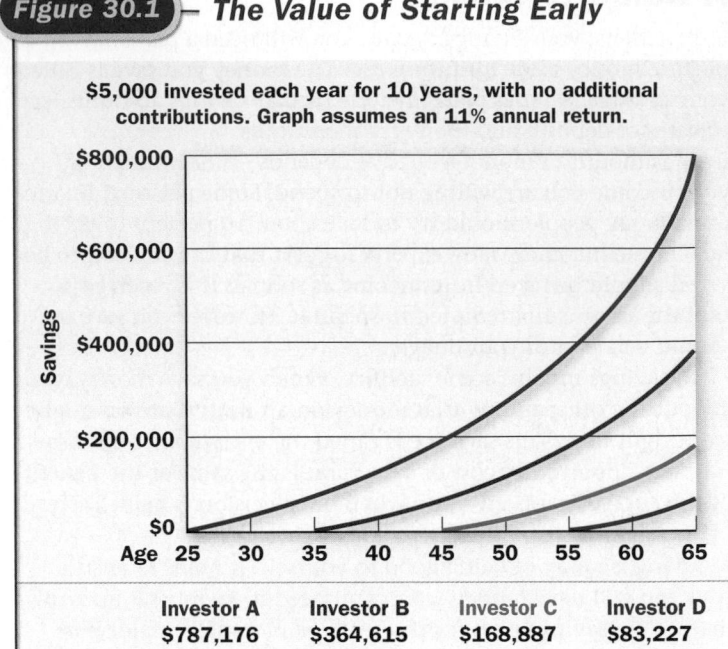

Figure 30.1 — *The Value of Starting Early*

$5,000 invested each year for 10 years, with no additional contributions. Graph assumes an 11% annual return.

	Investor A	Investor B	Investor C	Investor D
	$787,176	$364,615	$168,887	$83,227

Making Major Purchases

Most people need to save money before they can make major purchases. Common reasons people save money are to buy a home or to pay for a college education. You might also decide to save money because you want to purchase a less expensive item, such as a good sound system, a top-of-the-line guitar, or a car.

Providing for Emergencies

S You might face financial emergencies in your life. Your car could break down, you could lose your job, or you could develop a health problem. Saving your money can help you deal with the financial burden that an emergency can create. Experts recommend that people set aside at least six months of income in case of an emergency.

● **As You Read**

Think about saving for retirement. How much do you think you will need to retire someday?

Planning for Retirement

It might seem too early to think about saving for retirement, but it is best to begin early. **Figure 30.1** illustrates the average retirement account balances for people who start saving at different ages. Most U.S. workers receive Social Security income when they retire. Many people have some type of retirement plan where they work, which will provide additional income. Business owners may also set up retirement plans.

532 **Chapter 30** Savings Accounts

Figure 30.1

● **Saving for Retirement** Investors who start early will have the most money available at retirement.

● **As You Read**

Students will probably not relate to saving for retirement now but should start thinking about it.

For most people, though, Social Security and retirement plans do not provide enough money to retire comfortably. They must rely on their savings. If you start early in your life, you can **accumulate** a sizable nest egg. For example, suppose you want to retire in 35 years. If you start putting away $100 per month in an account with a return of 6 percent, by the time you retire, you will have saved about $143,000. You will have put in $42,000 and earned $101,000 in interest.

Earning Interest on Savings

Not all savings earn income. If you put your savings into a jar, a piggy bank, or under a mattress, no income is earned. To earn income on savings, you must store it in a place that will provide you with interest, such as a bank or savings and loan association. The money you put into a savings account earns interest.

If you put money into a bank's savings account, you are actually lending the bank your money. In this case, *you* are the creditor with the same conditions for lending as other creditors. The bank uses your savings to make loans to other people. Part of the interest the bank receives is used to pay interest to you.

BusinessWeek *Reader and Case Study*

Fiscal Fitness for Teens

Teach them that a paycheck is more than a chance to play big spender at the mall. It's an opportunity to bank on a cushier future.

From Standard & Poor's weekly investing newsletter, "The Outlook"

With school out, many teenagers will begin collecting their first paychecks. Now is the time for parents and grandparents to initiate a dialogue about the importance of saving as well as the value of planning and investing to meet objectives.

Start by asking your working teen plenty of goal-oriented questions, suggests David Braverman, vice president for portfolio services at Standard & Poor's and also a father of four, ages 13 to 21. Adults "may not want to see their kids spend money on short-term goals such as clothes and music, and may not realize that, to a teen, a long-range goal is a car,"

glencoe.com

Braverman says, adding that adults should use their own wisdom to help kids strike that balance between short- and long-term goals.

 CASE STUDY Go to the *Introduction to Business* Online Learning Center through **glencoe.com** for the *BusinessWeek* Reader Case Study.

Active Learning

Certificates of deposit can be a good way to achieve your long-term savings goals, but there is usually a penalty if you want to withdraw the money early. Research different CD accounts and compare penalties. Write an e-mail that gives advice to a teen about the connection between the rates on CDs and how long you must leave the money untouched.

Section 30.1 Savings Account Basics **533**

BusinessWeek *Reader and Case Study*

Fiscal Fitness for Teens

CASE STUDY Have students go to the *Introduction to Business* Online Learning Center through **glencoe.com** to download a Case Study activity that corresponds to the article. The activity and answer key are also available on the TeacherWorks Plus CD.

Active Learning

Answers will vary, depending on the prevailing interest rates and competition between banks and various investment options, but interest rates are typically higher for longer terms of investment.

RETEACH

W Writing Support
Enrichment
Relying on Social Security
Have students research a few of the changes that have been proposed for Social Security. Ask students to write a letter to the editor of their local paper about whether they think these changes will be good or bad for their generation's future security. (Answers will depend on students' perceptions of their future financial needs but should demonstrate an understanding of the current debate.)

U Universal Access
Artistic and Visual Learners
Ask students to create an artistic interpretation that helps explain how someone earns interest on savings. Encourage students to be creative when choosing media and technique. Although artistic and visual interpretation is especially important to some learners, all students can benefit from this activity.

R Reading Strategy
Recognize the Main Idea
Ask students to read the paragraphs under the heading "Earning Interest on Savings" and find the sentence in each paragraph that best states the main idea. (The last sentences in the first and second paragraphs best state the main idea.)

Student Activity Workbook Assign the Section 30.1 Activities.

RETEACH (cont.)

C Critical Thinking

Predict

The Rule of 72 Have students find the current interest rate for a savings account. Ask how long it would take them to double their money using that rate. (Answers will depend on the current rate.)

The Rule of 72 by helping savers compare returns on investments

ASSESS

● After You Read

Have students complete the Section 30.1 After You Read section review.

Online Study Tools

Have students go to the Online Learning Center through **glencoe.com** to:

- Take the Section 30.1 **Practice Test**.
- Download free **Study-to-Go** content to their PDAs or cell phones.

CLOSE

Culminating Activity

Create a Presentation Have students work in groups to produce a presentation titled "Savings: The Key to Your Future." (Presentations should reflect an understanding of chapter content.)

Activity correlates to Math standards.

The Rule of 72
Compound interest is usually earned daily, monthly, quarterly, or annually. The more often interest is compounded, the more you earn. The Rule of 72 is a rule used to calculate how long it will take to double the money in an investment. It is calculated by dividing 72 by the annual interest rate to get the number of years. For example, if you leave money in a savings account and let interest compound at 6%, you can double your savings in 12 years. *Why might knowing the Rule of 72 be useful?*

Saving is important to the economy because it generates loan money for people and businesses. Consumers use loans to buy houses and cars. Companies use loans to update their facilities and equipment. New equipment and buildings for business can enable a company to produce more goods and services. This often means that the company will need to hire more workers, which leads to economic growth.

Rate of Return

Earnings on savings can be measured by the rate of return, or yield. The **rate of return** is the percentage of increase in the value of your savings from earned interest.

Compounding

Simple interest is interest earned only on money deposited into a savings account, called the principal. When principal and interest are left in an account, it earns compound interest. **Compound interest** is interest earned on both the principal and any interest earned on the principal. Compounding may take place every year, every quarter, every month, or even every day. For example, suppose you had $50,000 in a savings account at 6 percent annual interest. After one year, you would earn $3,000 in interest. With compound interest, the $3,000 would be added to the $50,000 and you would start earning interest on $53,000. After 15 years you would earn almost $70,000, or about $20,000 more than your initial deposit.

Section 30.1

● After You Read

Review Key Concepts

1. Name three savings plans.
2. List the three main reasons people save money.
3. How is interest compounded?

Academic Skills

4. **Mathematics** Kim put the $75 she earned from babysitting on New Year's Eve into a regular savings account last year. She earned $3 in interest. What was Kim's rate of return?

THEORY **Rate of Return** To calculate the rate of return, divide the total interest by the amount of her deposit.

 For math help, go to the Math Appendix.

 Go to the *Introduction to Business* Online Learning Center through **glencoe.com** to check your answers.

Section 30.1

Review Key Concepts

1. regular savings accounts, certificates of deposit, and money market accounts
2. Most people save money for three reasons: to make major purchases, to provide for emergencies, and to have income for retirement.
3. Interest is compounded from one period to the next when interest is earned on both the principal and any interest previously earned on it.

Academic Skills

4. **Mathematics** Her rate of return was 4%. ($3 ÷ $75 = .04 or 4%)

Types of Savings Accounts

Reading Guide

● Before You Read

Think about some of the best places to save your money.

Read to Learn

- Differentiate a regular savings account from a CD, a money market fund, and a money market deposit account.
- Explain two advantages and two disadvantages of saving accounts.

The Main Idea

There are several types of savings accounts—common ones being the traditional savings account, the certificate of deposit (CD), money market fund, and money market deposit account. Each type of savings account has advantages and disadvantages.

Key Concepts

- Choosing a Savings Account
- Advantages and Disadvantages of Savings Accounts

 Go to the *Introduction to Business* Online Learning Center through **glencoe.com** for a printable graphic organizer.

Vocabulary

Key Terms
regular savings accounts
certificate of deposit (CD)
maturity date
money market fund
money market deposit accounts
liquidity
inflation risk

Academic Vocabulary
You will find these words in your reading and on your tests. Make sure you know their meanings.

institution   duration
set   mutual

Graphic Organizer

In a figure like the one below, write notes about each type of account.

Type of Savings Account	Notes
Regular Savings Account	
Certificate of Deposit	
Money Market Fund	
Money Market Deposit Account	

Academic Standards

English Language Arts

NCTE 6 Apply knowledge of language structure and conventions to discuss texts

NCTE 11 Participate as members of literacy communities

Science

Content Standard F Students should develop understanding of science and technology in local, national, and global challenges

---

Reading Guide

● Before You Read

Some students might save money in a piggy bank or jar and others might have savings accounts at banks and credit unions.

D Develop Concepts

The Main Idea Ask students: What are some of the advantages and disadvantages of savings accounts? (Advantages are that they earn interest, provide insurance against loss, and offer liquidity. Disadvantages are that they have low rates of return, inflation risks, fees, and penalties.)

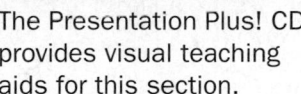

FOCUS

🔔 Bell Ringer Activity

Types of Savings Accounts
Ask: Where do people keep their savings? (Some people use jars and piggy banks for savings, but students should understand that savings accounts offer a better alternative.)

Preteaching

Presentation Plus! ◉
The Presentation Plus! CD provides visual teaching aids for this section.

PuzzleMaker ◉
Use the Vocabulary PuzzleMaker to create a puzzle of the section's key terms. Students can complete the puzzle on paper or on a computer.

Graphic Organizer
Tell students to go to the Online Learning Center through **glencoe.com** for a printable graphic organizer. (Answers include: regular savings account: passbook account at bank or savings and loan; certificate of deposit: higher interest than passbook account but money cannot be withdrawn before the end of the term without fees; money market fund: mutual fund that invests in securities; money market deposit account: money market fund at banks, savings and loans, or credit unions)

NCLB Connects academics to content.

535

Discussion Starter
Choosing a Savings Account
Start a discussion by asking students this question: Why are there choices when it comes to savings accounts? Aren't they all alike? (Answers will vary. Students should understand that savings accounts are like other goods and services in a market economy. People have different needs and wants and financial institutions offer "products" that give consumers many choices.)

R Reading Strategy

Identify Ask students to name the kinds of institutions that offer regular savings accounts. (Banks, savings and loans, savings banks, and credit unions offer regular savings accounts.)

● As You Read
Answers will vary, but students may feel it is a good choice to place the money in a bank, where it would earn interest and be safe.

✔ Reading Check

Identify The three basic types of savings accounts are regular savings accounts, certificates of deposit, and money market funds.

Choosing a Savings Account

Banks, savings and loans, savings banks, credit unions, and brokerage firms all offer several types of savings accounts. The three basic types are regular savings accounts, certificates of deposit, and money market funds. **Figure 30.2** offers a look at interest compounded in savings accounts.

✔ Reading Check   **Identify** What are the three basic types of savings accounts?

● As You Read
Think about putting your savings in a bank account or keeping it at home. Which would you prefer?

Regular Savings Accounts

Banks, savings and loans, savings banks, and credit unions all offer regular savings accounts. Traditionally called passbook accounts, **regular savings accounts** allow consumers to deposit or withdraw money at any time and to earn interest on the funds. Generally, a low minimum deposit, such as $100, is required to open a regular savings account. The interest rate varies from one financial **institution** to another. The rate can also change over time at the same institution. With a savings account, you can withdraw money without any penalty. However, the interest rate is usually low. Many banks also charge a service fee if the savings account falls below a certain minimum balance.

Figure 30.2 — *The Power of Compound Interest*

	Simple Interest			Compound Interest		
Year	Principal	6% Interest Earned	Interest Total	Principal	6% Interest Earned	Interest Total
1	$50,000	$3,000	$3,000	$50,000.00	$3,000.00	$3,000.00
2	$50,000	$3,000	$6,000	$53,000.00	$3,180.00	$6,180.00
3	$50,000	$3,000	$9,000	$56,180.00	$3,370.80	$9,550.80
4	$50,000	$3,000	$12,000	$59,550.80	$3,573.05	$13,123.85
5	$50,000	$3,000	$15,000	$63,123.85	$3,787.43	$16,911.28
6	$50,000	$3,000	$18,000	$66,911.28	$4,014.68	$20,925.96
7	$50,000	$3,000	$21,000	$70,925.96	$4,255.55	$25,181.51
8	$50,000	$3,000	$24,000	$75,181.51	$4,510.89	$29,692.40
9	$50,000	$3,000	$27,000	$79,692.40	$4,781.55	$34,473.95
10	$50,000	$3,000	$30,000	$84,473.95	$5,068.43	$39,542.38
11	$50,000	$3,000	$33,000	$89,542.38	$5,372.55	$44,914.93
12	$50,000	$3,000	$36,000	$94,914.93	$5,694.89	$50,609.82
13	$50,000	$3,000	$39,000	$100,609.82	$6,036.59	$56,646.41
14	$50,000	$3,000	$42,000	$106,646.41	$6,398.79	$63,045.20
15	$50,000	$3,000	$45,000	$113,045.20	$6,782.71	$69,827.91
	Total Interest Earned: $45,000			Total Interest Earned: $69,827.91		

● Interest on Interest Compound interest makes your money grow faster when interest is left to accrue. **Which account earned more interest? What is the difference in the account totals after 15 years?**

Figure 30.2

● Interest on Interest The account where money was left to compound earned more interest. The difference is $69,827.91 − $45,000 = $24,827.91. Expand this concept by rereading the caption. Have students calculate both simple and compound interest for Year 16 to reinforce the difference between the two methods. (Year 16 simple interest: $50,000 × .06 = $3,000. $3,000 + $45,000 = $48,000 total simple interest. Year 16 compound interest: Total principal and interest at start of Year 15: $119,827.91. $119,827.91 × .06 = $7,189.67. $69,827.91 + $7,189.67 = $77,017.58 total compound interest)

● **New Construction**
Businesses that build new buildings usually do so with borrowed money. **What is the relationship between savings and loans?**

Certificates of Deposit

Another type of savings account, called a **certificate of deposit (CD)**, requires you to deposit a specified amount of money in an account for a **set** period of time. The length of time might be three months, one year, or five years. A CD has a **maturity date**, which is when the money becomes available to you. The interest rate on a CD is higher than that on a regular savings account, but a CD's interest rate does not change over the **duration** of the CD term. If you cash in the CD before the maturity date, however, you will lose interest and might have to pay a penalty.

Money Market Funds

Brokerage firms, which buy and sell stocks and bonds, offer a special type of savings account called a money market fund. A **money market fund** is a kind of **mutual** fund, or pool of money, put into a variety of short-term debt (loans of less than one year) by business and government. In a way, you are lending your money to a business or the government to invest. The interest rate on a money market fund varies from month to month. An advantage is that you can withdraw your money at any time. You can also write checks on the account. There are, however, two disadvantages. Money market funds usually require high balances. Also, account holders can write only a limited number of checks.

Money Market Deposit Accounts Banks, savings and loans, and credit unions have their own form of money market fund called **money market deposit accounts**. They have the same basic requirements and characteristics of a money market fund. One difference is that the federal government generally insures the money in a money market deposit account.

Tracking the Money You Save No matter how or where you save your money, you must find ways to *find* the money you want to save. Write down your savings every time you decide not to buy something. Putting every penny you find or dollar you have saved into the bank will add up. *How do you think tracking every bit of your savings can help you save?*

✔ **Reading Check** **Compare** How does a money market deposit account differ from a money market fund?

537

RETEACH

U Universal Access

Students with Learning Disabilities Diagrams can help clarify information presented in a text. Ask several volunteers to draw diagrams that represent the advantages and disadvantages of savings accounts. Suggest students use word webs illustrated with simple symbols. Have students discuss the diagrams. Suggest they copy the one that seems most useful and use it as a study aid.

R Reading Strategy

List Ask students to list the advantages and disadvantages of savings accounts. (Advantages are that they earn interest, offer insurance against loss, and are liquid. Disadvantages are that they have low rates of return, inflation risks, and fees and penalties.)

W Writing Support

Enrichment

Insurance Against Loss Have students research and develop a presentation about the history of the FDIC. (It was created in 1933 because of bank failures during the Great Depression. It guarantees savings in financial institutions will be reimbursed up to $100,000. The FDIC helped to restore public faith in banks and remains an important element of the U.S. capitalist system.)

Student Activity Workbook 📂 Assign the Section 30.2 Activities.

Science/Tech **TRENDS**

N C L B

Nanotechnology

Nanotechnology is a branch of science that focuses on the behavior of matter on a very small scale. In fact, a single nanometer is only about 10 atoms wide. Scientists hope to develop nanotechnology as the next great advancement in saving data. They predict that nanotechnology will allow for storage devices with more capacity and much faster response times than are available with current digital technologies. Storage devices engineered at the scale of nanometers could, for example, allow an entire movie to be downloaded to a transportable device that is smaller than a dime.

Web**Quest**

Go to the *Introduction to Business* Online Learning Center through **glencoe.com** for links to Web sites where you can learn more about nanotechnology. Write a paragraph about applications of it.

U R Advantages and Disadvantages of Savings Accounts

Besides earning interest, savings accounts offer other advantages. However, they also have disadvantages.

Insurance Against Loss

W Banks, savings and loans, and credit unions are all insured. The Federal Deposit Insurance Corporation (FDIC), a government agency, insures bank accounts. Even if a bank fails, the FDIC will replace depositors' accounts for up to $100,000. Money market funds offered by brokerage firms are not federally insured, but most brokerage firms have insurance on their accounts.

Liquidity

Liquidity means the ability to quickly turn an investment into cash. An investment such as a car or a business is not very liquid because it has to be sold to be turned into cash. Savings accounts, however, are highly liquid because cash can easily be withdrawn.

Low Rates of Return

Since there is very little risk with a savings account, there is usually a low return. With saving and investing, there is a relationship between rate of return and risk. The lower the risk, the lower the rate of return. The higher the risk, the higher the possibility of getting a higher return.

N C L B Activity correlates to Science standards.

Nanotechnology Answers will vary but paragraphs might explain that nanotechnology is a new field of study. Some of the applications it aims for include transistors constructed of carbon molecules to reduce size and increase performance.

Inflation Risk

Inflation is a general increase in the cost of goods and services. **Inflation risk** is the risk that the rate of inflation will increase more than the rate of interest on savings. Suppose you have $1,000 in a savings account that earns 2 percent interest. During the next year, inflation is 4 percent. That means it costs $1,040 at the end of the year to buy what you could have bought at the beginning of the year for $1,000. Interest rates on most savings accounts fluctuate with inflation. However, the main risk with CDs is that their interest rates are locked in for a specific period of time.

The Costs of Savings Accounts

Savings accounts earn interest, but they can also cost money. Some accounts charge a penalty for early withdrawal or if the account balance falls below a certain minimum during a given period. Other accounts charge a fee for each deposit and withdrawal. The money you earn in interest on a savings account is also considered income. As a result, you have to pay income tax on it.

 Activity correlates to English Language Arts standards.

Section 30.2

After You Read

Review Key Concepts

1. What is the difference between a regular savings account, a certificate of deposit, and a money market fund?
2. Discuss some advantages and disadvantages of savings accounts.
3. What is the Federal Deposit Insurance Corporation, and what does it do?

Academic Skills

4. **English Language Arts** Work in a group of four to write, design, and produce a brochure titled "Saving—the Key to Your Future." Develop the content of the brochure around ways to make saving a regular habit. Include testimonials from people for whom saving has made a difference in their lives.

5. **English Language Arts** Collect brochures or other printed material from local banks containing information concerning the method each uses to compute interest. Analyze each to determine which communicate most effectively and how others might be improved. Present your findings orally and visually.

@ Go to the *Introduction to Business* Online Learning Center through **glencoe.com** to check your answers.

C Critical Thinking

Predict the Effects

Inflation Risk Ask students to explain the effect of inflation on savings account interest rates. (Students should understand that interest rates on most savings accounts increase with inflation.)

ASSESS

● **After You Read**

Have students complete the Section 30.2 After You Read section review.

Online Study Tools

Have students go to the Online Learning Center through **glencoe.com** to:

• Take the Section 30.2 **Practice Test**.

• Download free **Study-to-Go** content to their PDAs or cell phones.

CLOSE

Culminating Activity

Research Interest Rates Have students find out the current rates offered by local banks on certificates of deposit and pool their information in a chart or table. Ask volunteers to make a generalization about the relationship between the interest rate, the maturity date, and the rate of inflation. (Longer-term CDs offer higher interest rates. The interest rate may or may not be enough to cover inflation.)

Section 30.2

Review Key Concepts

1. regular savings accounts: allow consumer to deposit small amounts that earn interest; CDs: require a specified amount for a set period; money market fund: pool of money put into short-term debt instruments

2. advantages: interest, insurance against loss, and liquidity; disadvantage: low rates of return

3. a government agency that insures bank accounts for up to $100,000

Academic Skills

4. **English Language Arts** Students' brochures should include testimonials.

5. **English Language Arts** Answers will be based on students' evaluations.

539

Chapter 30 *Review and Activities*

Vocabulary Review

1. Students should write complete sentences using each term correctly.

Review Key Concepts

2. People save for major purchases, emergencies, and retirement.

3. Compound interest accrues when the interest is left with the amount saved. The next interest payment is based on the original savings plus accumulated interest.

4. Banks offer regular savings accounts, into which a consumer can deposit even small amounts of money that earn interest. A certificate of deposit earns more interest but requires account holders to deposit a specified amount of money for a set period of time. Brokerage firms offer a money market fund. It is a kind of mutual fund, or pool of money, put into a variety of short-term debt types.

5. Advantages include insurance against loss and liquidity. Disadvantages include low rates of returns and inflation risks.

Critical Thinking

6. Students should understand that having money saved affords a sense of security and provides resources when needed.

7. a CD, money market deposit account, or money market fund

Section 30.1 *Summary*

Savings Account Basics Saving is putting aside money for future use. The three main reasons for saving money are to make major purchases, for emergencies, and for retirement. Financial institutions pay interest on savings accounts in return for using savers' money. As with a credit account, the amount of interest earned depends on the interest rate, the size of the account, and the length of time you keep the account. Savings accounts earn simple interest or compound interest. Savings can grow more quickly with compound interest.

Section 30.2 *Summary*

Types of Savings Accounts Banks, savings and loans, and other financial institutions offer several types of savings accounts. Regular savings accounts, certificates of deposit, and money market funds are the major types of savings accounts. Some financial institutions have their own form of money market fund called a money market deposit account. Savings accounts earn interest, are usually secure, and have high liquidity. However, they can also cost money in fees and taxes, and generally carry a low return that may not keep up with inflation.

Vocabulary Review

1. On a sheet of paper, use each of these key terms and academic vocabulary terms in a sentence.

Key Terms
savings
rate of return
compound interest
regular savings accounts
certificate of deposit (CD)
maturity date
money market fund
money market deposit accounts
liquidity
inflation risk

Academic Vocabulary

experts	institution
suggest	set
item	duration
accumulate	mutual

Review Key Concepts

2. Discuss the three reasons people save money.

3. Describe compound interest.

4. Differentiate a regular savings account from a CD, a money market fund, and a money market deposit account.

5. Explain two advantages and two disadvantages of savings accounts.

---

8. Answers should express an understanding of the importance of savings to individuals and to the economy as a whole. FDIC insurance increases consumer confidence and probably promotes more saving.

9. Most consumers want to earn more on their savings than the rate of inflation.

10. Because it gives savers an idea of how long it will take money to double when different rates of interest are applied and compounded.

11. There is less possibility that consumers will withdraw the funds before the end of the term, enabling financial institutions to use their funds longer.

12. This allows workers to make sure they save money they might be tempted to spend from each paycheck.

Critical Thinking

6. Why is saving a way of being good to yourself?

7. If you have $1,000 to put into savings, do not need it for a year, and think that interest rates on savings will decrease, what is the best savings plan for you?

8. What do you think would happen if the FDIC did not exist?

9. How does inflation affect your savings decision?

10. Why is it a good idea to know about the Rule of 72?

11. Why are financial institutions willing to pay a higher rate of interest for a CD than for a regular savings account?

12. Many people have their employer put aside money from their paycheck for savings. Why do you think they do this?

13. Why do you think economists call banks and savings and loan associations intermediaries between savers and borrowers?

14. Why are savings important for the individual consumer and the U.S. economy?

Write About It

15. Research the savings rate of Americans compared to people in other countries. Write an e-mail to your teacher explaining the differences you note.

16. Interview a banker about the relationship between types of savings plans and the interest rates that are offered. Write at least one page about your findings.

17. Write two paragraphs about reasons people at different income levels save the same or different percentages of their income.

18. Determine the nature of the IRA, Roth IRA, and 401(k) retirement plans. Find out how each of them works. In a one-page report, discuss whether these plans encourage or discourage people from saving.

19. People rely upon different sources of income throughout their lives including their savings. Write an e-mail to your teacher listing the sources of retirement income you will rely on to live comfortably.

Technology Applications

Calculating Compound Interest

20. Compound interest is interest earned on both the principal (the money you deposit in your savings account) and any interest you earned on it. Create a spreadsheet and the formulas necessary to calculate interest compounded daily, monthly, and yearly. The spreadsheet should contain at least five different interest rates.

Business Ethics

Risking Someone Else's Future

21. You are a financial planner for Dave, who is 67 years old and retired. He wants to move his retirement account to more high-risk stocks. You would gain a great deal in fees and service charges if he turns all of his savings into stocks. However, he would face more risk if he buys the stocks. What should you do?

Critical Thinking

13. They receive money from savers and use it to make loans to borrowers. The interest borrowers pay is used in turn to pay interest to savers.

14. Savings are used to make loans used to develop new capital.

Write About It

15. The average American saves less than people in other developed countries. Many people in other developed countries have different attitudes about culture and money than Americans.

16. Answers will depend on the interviewees' responses.

17. People with different income levels are likely to have different levels of disposable income.

18. IRAs, Roth IRAs, and 401(k) retirement plans are all ways for individuals to receive tax advantages by saving for retirement. They encourage people to save.

19. Answers will vary, depending on students' perceptions of what it means to "live comfortably" and their expectations for lifetime earnings.

Technology Applications

20. Answers will depend on the interest rates calculated but should include formulas for compounding interest daily, monthly, and yearly.

Business Ethics

21. Even though you would benefit more if Dave put all of his savings into stocks, you would probably lose him as a client later if he lost his money. It probably would be best to discuss Dave's options and explain what he would gain and give up by switching to stocks. Perhaps he could invest a portion in stocks.

Applying Academics to Business

22. Answers will vary, but students should evaluate their own attitudes toward savings.

23. Scatter plots will vary, depending on the information that students gather, but they should show that, generally, interest rates increase as the time to maturity increases.

24. benefit: advantage, detriment

compound: composite, simple

inflation: price increases, deflation

deposit: place, withdraw

25. a. $1,035

b. $1,071.86

c. $1,035.56

Active Learning

26. Answers will depend on the money saved.

Business in the Real World

27. Answers will depend on the bank and brochure that are chosen.

Applying Academics to Business

English Language Arts

22. Write a paragraph or two about your savings habits. Are you currently saving money on a regular basis? For what are you saving? Do you have a plan for a regular program of saving for the future?

Mathematics

23. Research the maturity dates and related interest rates for CDs from a variety of banks or savings institutions. Make a scatter plot using your data and write a sentence or two about what it shows.

> **THEORY** **Data Analysis** Scatter plots are similar to line graphs in that they use horizontal and vertical axes. Scatter plots show how much one variable is affected by another.

English Language Arts

24. Based on the meanings of the following words as they are used in this chapter, suggest a synonym and an antonym for each:

benefit   compound
inflation   deposit

Mathematics

25. Compute the total savings on a $1,000 deposit held for one year in each of the following types of accounts:

a. a regular savings account earning 3.5% annual simple interest

b. a CD earning 7% annual interest compounded quarterly

c. a CD earning 3.5% annual interest compounded monthly

> **THEORY** **Interest Rates** When computing interest earned on an amount during a period, divide the yearly interest rate, expressed as a decimal, by the number of periods in the year.

Active Learning

Money Left Over

26. Obtain a large jar or other container and ask everyone in your family to "deposit" their change there each night when they come home. After one month, count the money. How much have you saved? As a family, decide what you would like to do with the money.

Business in the Real World

Rephrasing a Brochure

27. Businesses that offer savings accounts use brochures to convey information about their products and services. Obtain a brochure from a bank or brokerage firm that explains the different kinds of savings plans that it offers. Rewrite it so that it can be understood by a preteen.

ExamView Assessment Suite CD allows you to print out ready-made unit and chapter tests, complete with answer keys. You can also create customized tests.

TeacherWorks Plus provides complete teacher resources in one convenient package. It includes customizable lesson plans in calendar format, and instant access to many print program resources.

 **Real LIFE • skills**

FIGURING PENALTIES ON A CD

28. You called a bank to ask about its rates on a $1,000 CD. A representative told you that it earns 3% compounded quarterly. You ask what would happen if you withdrew the principal after nine months. You would lose the last six months' of interest. How much interest would you give up and how much would you get if you withdrew the money after nine months? What would be the rate of return on your savings given the return that you received?

 **Cool Business CAREERS**

FIND YOUR DREAM JOB

29. Go to the *Introduction to Business* Online Learning Center through **glencoe.com** for a link to the Occupational Outlook Handbook Web site. Click on the "OOH Search/A-Z Index" link and enter the job category "securities, commodities, and other investments." Then write a one-page report about this area of occupation. Conclude your report with a list of things you could do now to prepare yourself to pursue the occupation.

Role Play

FINANCIAL ADVISER

30. Situation You are a financial adviser who encourages people to save.

Activity Make a presentation about why people should save, including why it is important to them individually, and why it is important to the economy.

Evaluation You will be evaluated on how well you meet the following performance indicators:

- Explain the reasons saving is important for individuals.
- Describe reasons saving is important to the economy.
- Organize your presentation logically.
- Answer questions about saving.
- Project your voice and use correct grammar.

Standardized Test Practice

Directions Choose the letter of the best answer. Write the letter for the answer on a separate piece of paper.

1. How much interest was earned during the first month on a deposit of $4,000 in an account earning 6% annual interest compounded quarterly?

  A $240
  B $60
  C $40
  D $20

 **TEST-TAKING TIP** When studying in small groups, make sure your study group includes only students who are serious about studying.

 READING Go to the *Introduction to Business* Online Learning Center through **glencoe.com** for a list of outside reading suggestions.

glencoe.com

Chapter 30 Review and Activities **543**

STRATEGIES FOR STANDARDIZED TEST PREP SUCCESS

Test Prep Students working in small groups tend to be more actively involved with learning and retain more. Study teams are groups of three or four students who meet regularly over the course of a semester to review coursework, help each other with homework, and provide support. Help students divide the responsibilities fairly.

Chapter 30

Real LIFE • skills

28. Divide 3% by the number of periods in the year (4). The interest rate over a single period is .75%. Nine months is three periods of compounding ($1,000 \times 1.0075^3 =$ $1,022.67). Three months is one period of compounding ($1,000 \times 1.0075 =$ $1,007.50). The penalty is $1,022.67 $-$ $1,007.50 = $15.17. You would earn $7.50.

Cool Business CAREERS

29. The securities industry is comprised of organizations that offer financial advice, manage investments, and broker the purchase and sale of securities and commodities. More than half have a bachelor's degree. Most positions require a license and mandatory continuing education. Advancement opportunities vary widely. Employment is expected to rise. As preparation, learn about investments.

Role Play

30. Presentations should address the competencies noted in the Role Play. Answers will vary, but should indicate students' understanding of saving and savings plans.

Standardized Test Practice
  1. D

Standards-Based Lesson Planning
Introduction to Business provides students with instruction and assessment in the following fundamental content areas:

Content Standards Correlations	
Explain the theory of savings and investments in our economy.	p. 547
Summarize investing basics and various types of short-term investments.	pp. 547–552, 553–559, 560–563
Identify various ways in which money can be invested (stocks, bonds, mutual funds, etc.)	pp. 547–552, 553–559, 560–563
Analyze investment strategies.	pp. 547–552, 553–559, 560–563
Summarize various types of stock and bond investments.	pp. 547–552, 553–559, 560–563
Distinguishes between risk factors, rate of return, and liquidity for stocks and bonds.	pp. 547–552, 553–559, 560–563
Analyze factors that affect the rate of return on a given savings or investment plan.	pp. 547–552, 553–559
Calculate the rate of return.	pp. 548, 549, 552, 554, 555, 559, 563
Analyze how saving and investing influences economic growth.	pp. 547
Compare and contrast various investment opportunities, both insured and uninsured.	pp. 547–552, 553–559, 560–563
Compares and contrasts foreign investment options using exchange rate information.	p. 555

NCLB Activities, information, and skills practice will help your students attain No Child Left Behind proficiency. Students will improve their abilities in the following academic standards areas:

Academic Standards Correlations		
English Language Arts	Activities/Features	Page
NCTE 7 Conduct research and gather, evaluate, and synthesize data to communicate discoveries	After You Read Applying Academics to Business	pp. 559, 562
NCTE 11 Participate as members of literacy communities	After You Read	p. 559
Mathematics		
Algebra Represent and analyze mathematical situations and structures using algebraic symbols	After You Read Applying Academics to Business	pp. 552, 562
Data Analysis and Probability Develop and evaluate inferences and predictions that are based on data	Applying Academics to Business	p. 562
Number and Operation Represent and analyze mathematical situations and structures using algebraic symbols	Ask S&P	p. 544
Number and Operation Understand numbers, ways of representing numbers, relationships among numbers, and number systems	Ask S&P Standardized Test Practice	pp. 562
Science		
Content Standard G Students should develop understanding of historical perspectives	Science/Tech Trends	p. 557

Correlations   This chart shows the 21st Century Skills, foundation skills, and workplace competencies that students develop as they work in this chapter.

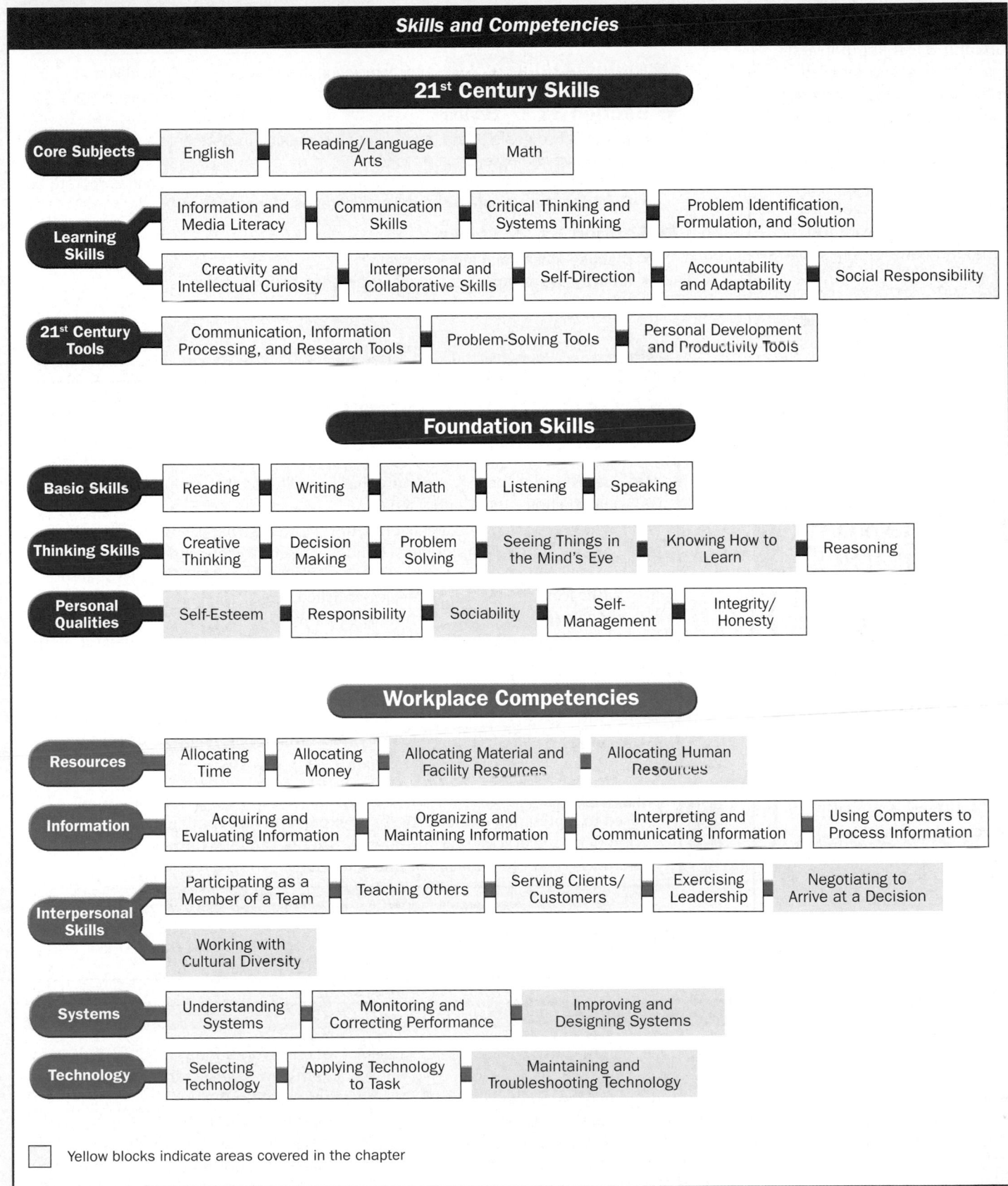

Skills and Competencies

21st Century Skills

Core Subjects
- English
- Reading/Language Arts
- Math

Learning Skills
- Information and Media Literacy
- Communication Skills
- Critical Thinking and Systems Thinking
- Problem Identification, Formulation, and Solution
- Creativity and Intellectual Curiosity
- Interpersonal and Collaborative Skills
- Self-Direction
- Accountability and Adaptability
- Social Responsibility

21st Century Tools
- Communication, Information Processing, and Research Tools
- Problem-Solving Tools
- Personal Development and Productivity Tools

Foundation Skills

Basic Skills
- Reading
- Writing
- Math
- Listening
- Speaking

Thinking Skills
- Creative Thinking
- Decision Making
- Problem Solving
- Seeing Things in the Mind's Eye
- Knowing How to Learn
- Reasoning

Personal Qualities
- Self-Esteem
- Responsibility
- Sociability
- Self-Management
- Integrity/Honesty

Workplace Competencies

Resources
- Allocating Time
- Allocating Money
- Allocating Material and Facility Resources
- Allocating Human Resources

Information
- Acquiring and Evaluating Information
- Organizing and Maintaining Information
- Interpreting and Communicating Information
- Using Computers to Process Information

Interpersonal Skills
- Participating as a Member of a Team
- Teaching Others
- Serving Clients/Customers
- Exercising Leadership
- Negotiating to Arrive at a Decision
- Working with Cultural Diversity

Systems
- Understanding Systems
- Monitoring and Correcting Performance
- Improving and Designing Systems

Technology
- Selecting Technology
- Applying Technology to Task
- Maintaining and Troubleshooting Technology

☐ Yellow blocks indicate areas covered in the chapter

Chapter Overview

Introduce the Chapter

Investing
Chapter 31 is about investing in bonds and stocks. Information about investing in bonds is presented along with descriptions of various kinds of government and corporate bonds. Stocks and stock exchanges are explained along with the pros and cons of investing in stocks.

Building Background
Owning stocks and bonds might not be a short-term goal for most students, but learning the basics of investing can help students prepare for their financial future.

Ask STANDARD &POOR'S

›› Math Answer
6 ÷ $95 = 0.0632 = 6.32%

›› Extension Activity
Write some or all of the following fractions on the board and ask students to determine which can be written as terminating decimals and which have a repeating decimal element:

$\frac{1}{2}$ Terminating 0.5

$\frac{1}{3}$ Repeating $0.333\overline{3}$

$\frac{2}{3}$ Repeating $0.6666\overline{7}$

$\frac{1}{4}$ Terminating 0.25

$\frac{1}{5}$ Terminating 0.2

$\frac{1}{6}$ Repeating $0.1666\overline{7}$

$\frac{1}{8}$ Terminating 0.125

NCLB Activity correlates to Math standards.

Investing

Chapter Objectives After completing this chapter, you will be able to:

▶ **Section 31.1** *Bonds*
- **Discuss** two goals to set before you start making investments.
- **Name** five characteristics of bonds.
- **Differentiate** between types of federal, municipal government, and corporate bonds.
- **Describe** the advantages and disadvantages of investing in bonds.

▶ **Section 31.2** *Stocks*
- **Discuss** stocks and stock markets.
- **Identify** the advantages and disadvantages of owning stocks.

Ask STANDARD &POOR'S

Corporate Financial Performance and the Effect on Credit Quality

Q: Are sectors of the U.S. economy that generate strong earnings for shareholders also a good choice for bondholders?

A: There is not always a direct correlation between what is good for shareholders and what is good for bondholders. Bonds represent the ownership of debt, and stocks represent the ownership of equity. A company may do well for its shareholders while leaving its bondholders less satisfied because acquisitions or divestures end up damaging its creditworthiness. Creditworthiness is important because bondholders assume credit risk, the chance that the bond issuer will default on its debt.

Mathematics Express the current yield of a bond as a percentage by dividing the price of the bond into the amount of the annual coupon, the interest rate stated on a bond when it is issued. What is the current yield for a $95 bond with a $6 annual coupon? Replace the variables in the algebraic expression and evaluate the expression.

Evaluate x if $x = 6 \div \$95$

THEORY **Algebra: Variables and Expressions** A variable is a symbol, usually a letter, used to represent a number. Algebraic expressions are combinations of variables, numbers, and at least one operation. Once the variables have been replaced with numbers, you can evaluate, or find the value of, the expression.

NCLB

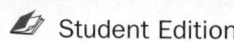

Classroom Resources

- Student Edition
- Teacher Wraparound Edition
- Student Activity Workbook with Academic Integration
- Student Activity Workbook with Academic Integration TAE
- *Fast File*, Unit 10 Resources
- Inclusion in the Business Education Classroom

- TeacherWorks Plus
- *ExamView Assessment Suite*
- Presentation Plus!
- Vocabulary PuzzleMaker
- Interactive Student Edition
- Online Student Edition
- Online Learning Center with Podcasts

● **The New York Stock Exchange®** The New York Stock Exchange provides a market for buying and selling stocks and has the highest dollar volume of any stock exchange in the world. **What are stocks?**

Chapter 31 Investing **545**

Review the Objectives
Introduce the chapter by reviewing the chapter objectives:

Section 31.1 *Objectives*
Discuss two goals to set before you start making investments. (limit credit card charges and debt; have an emergency fund)

Name five characteristics of bonds. (Bonds are debt; interest is paid; they can be sold before their maturity date; their prices rise and fall in the market; many are sold at discount, with face value paid at maturity.)

Differentiate between types of federal, municipal government, and corporate bonds. (federal: T-bills, notes, bonds, and savings bonds; municipal bonds: loans to local and state governments; corporate bonds: used to pay for new construction or equipment)

Describe the advantages and disadvantages of investing in bonds. (advantages: security, earnings, liquidity; disadvantages: minimum investment, lack of liquidity, inflation risk)

Section 31.2 *Objectives*
Discuss stocks and stock markets. (Stock is part ownership in a business; can be common or preferred; return on a stock is variable; traded on stock exchange.)

Identify the advantages and disadvantages of owning stocks. (advantage: possibility of higher rate of return than bonds and savings plans; disadvantage: more risky than savings accounts or bonds)

Discuss the Photo
● **The New York Stock Exchange** Read the caption on the photo to students: The New York Stock Exchange provides a market for selling and buying stocks and has the highest dollar volume of any stock exchange in the world.

Ask students: What are stocks? (Students should understand that stocks represent partial ownership in a corporation.) Point out to students that the man in the picture is a trader on the NYSE.

Bell Ringer Activity

Bonds

Write the words *Savings* and *Investing* on the board. Ask students to describe the difference. (Students should realize that saving is generally focused on short-term goals and preparing for emergencies. Investing has risks and is generally focused on long-term goals.)

Preteaching

Presentation Plus!

The Presentation Plus! CD provides visual teaching aids for this section.

PuzzleMaker

Use the Vocabulary PuzzleMaker to create a puzzle of the section's key terms. Students can complete the puzzle on paper or on a computer.

Graphic Organizer

Tell students to go to the Online Learning Center through **glencoe.com** for a printable graphic organizer. (Answers include: Advantages: secure investment, income from interest on bond, possible increases in value, possible tax breaks; Disadvantages: investor loses money if bond is sold or redeemed before it matures, high cost, may not keep up with inflation.)

 Connects academics to content.

Bonds

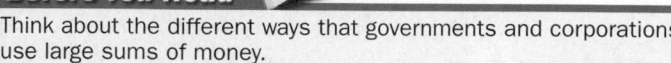

Reading Guide

 Before You Read

Think about the different ways that governments and corporations use large sums of money.

Read to Learn

- Discuss two goals to set before you start making investments.
- Name five characteristics of bonds.
- Differentiate between types of federal, municipal government, and corporate bonds.
- Describe the advantages and disadvantages of investing in bonds.

D

The Main Idea

Investing is using money to participate in a business enterprise that offers the possibility of profit. Bonds provide income opportunities for investors. They also generate money to help governments and corporations operate.

Key Concepts

- Setting Investment Goals
- Investing in Bonds
- Government and Corporate Bonds
- Advantages and Disadvantages of Investing in Bonds

 Go to the *Introduction to Business* Online Learning Center through **glencoe.com** for a printable graphic organizer.

Vocabulary

Key Terms

investing	bond discount
security	savings bonds
yield	municipal bonds
bond	corporate bonds
coupon rate	

Academic Vocabulary

You will find these words in your reading and on your tests. Make sure you know their meanings.

participate	commission
eliminate	matures

Graphic Organizer

On a figure like the one below, write notes about the advantages and disadvantages of bond ownership.

Bond Ownership

Advantages	Disadvantages

Academic Standards

English Language Arts
  NCTE 1 Read texts to acquire new information
Mathematics
  Algebra Represent and analyze mathematical situations and structures using algebraic symbols

N C L B

Reading Guide

Before You Read

Governments provide services and build infrastructure and roads. Corporations research and develop new products and build plants, warehouses, and office and retail space.

D Develop Concepts

The Main Idea Ask students: How do investors, governments, and corporations benefit from bonds? (Bonds provide income opportunities for investors. They also generate money to help governments and corporations operate.)

Setting Investment Goals

To some people, investing is an unpredictable world of formulas, symbols, and terms. Others think it is just a matter of luck and timing. Although these perceptions are generally incorrect, they are reasons some people do not invest their money. However, investing presents opportunities for people and businesses to increase their income. **Investing** is using money to **participate** in an enterprise that offers the possibility of profit. It usually involves careful planning and goal setting.

It is wise to use a practical approach when investing. You can spend money on some things that you enjoy and still save enough for an investment program. Even a small amount invested regularly can add up to a large amount over time.

As you set your investment goals, ask yourself these questions:

- How do I want to spend my money?
- How much money do I need to satisfy my goals?
- How will I get it?
- How long will it take to save it?
- How much risk am I willing to take when I invest?
- What conditions could change my investment goals?
- Are my goals reasonable, considering my circumstances?
- What will happen if I do not meet my goals?

Most people have more than one financial goal. A short-term goal might be to save enough money to pay for a vacation. A mid-term goal could be to buy a business or home. A long-term goal might be to plan for retirement. There are two goals that everyone should set before starting to invest. First, you should limit your credit card charges and reduce or **eliminate** credit card debt. In most cases, this debt generates interest charges that are higher than the investment returns you can expect to receive. Second, start an emergency fund and add to it as your income increases. It is recommended that people save enough money to cover at least six months of expenses. Once you achieve these two goals, start looking at the different investment options that are available to you.

The goals you establish when you begin to make investment plans are likely to change. It is a good idea to meet with a financial adviser annually to review your portfolio and goals.

Types of Securities

Investment options include securities. A **security** is a tradable document that shows evidence of debt or ownership. Securities include bonds, shares of stock and mutual funds, and stock options. The return on an investment is the amount of money the investment earns, or the **yield**.

As You Read

Both entrepreneurs and investors face financial risks. Both also depend on the success of the economy, which is fueled by market factors such as supply and demand.

TEACH

Discussion Starter
Setting Investment Goals
Start a discussion by asking students to use a scale of 1 to 10 to rank the importance of learning the basics of investing. Follow up by asking volunteers to explain their rankings. (Answers will vary. Some students may feel that they will never have enough money to invest, so they don't need to know the basics. Other students might suggest that they don't need to know much about investing because they plan to hire someone to take care of their finances. Students who think that learning investment basics is important might point out that you need to understand the basics in order to get started. Encourage students to recognize that it is important to understand the basics of investing even if they plan to hire a professional investment advisor.)

R Reading Strategy
Make a List Ask students to make a list of the common types of securities. (Lists should include the following common types of securities: bonds, shares of stock, shares of mutual funds, and stock options.)

Virtual Business
Introduce financing to students using the Virtual Business Retailing Financing activity. In this simulation, students learn why financing is important to the success of a business.

TEACH (cont.)

S Skill Practice

Guided Practice

Explain Ask students to explain how an investor makes money by investing in bonds. (The investor receives regular interest payments until the bond matures and then receives face value of the bond even if it was sold at a discount.) **L1**

Illustrate an Idea Ask students to create an illustration to explain a bond discount. (Illustrations will vary. Encourage students to use the following equation in their illustrations: Face value − selling price = bond discount.) **L2**

Develop the Concept Ask students to research six different bonds and to create a poster that predicts the yield from differences between the coupon rate and face value. (Posters should reflect the fact that the coupon rate is often set so that a bond will give a particular yield when compared to its face value, independent of the interest.) **L3**

ASSESS

Review Key Terms

Have students write sentences using each key term.

 **Study-to-Go** Have students go to the Online Learning Center through **glencoe.com** to download free **Study-to-Go** content to their PDAs or cell phones.

Investing in Bonds

When corporations or governments need to borrow large amounts of money, they often issue bonds. A **bond** is a certificate issued by a government or company in which it promises to pay back borrowed money at a fixed rate of interest on a specified date (the *maturity date*). It is a debt, and the buyer of a bond is the creditor (or lender) to the company or government that issued it, the debtor (or borrower).

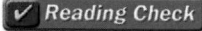 **Define** What is a bond?

Characteristics of Bonds

S

Bond Prices Bonds are rated according to their risk by several agencies, including Standard & Poor's and Moody's®. They are usually rated from *secure* (the highest rating) to *speculative* (the lowest rating). Those with more risk carry a higher interest rate than those that are more secure. Most bonds are considered safe investments. *Would you invest in a bond rated as speculative? Why?*

Investing in bonds is similar to putting money into a savings account. Both act as a source of funds to be used for business and personal loans. Both generate interest for consumers. There are several differences, though. Bonds have specific characteristics.

The rate of interest on a bond is referred to as the **coupon rate**. (This rate is also referred to as the yield.) Interest is usually paid once or twice a year. For example, a $1,000 bond with a 6 percent coupon rate will pay $60 once a year or $30 twice a year. Bonds may be sold at a discount, or below their face value. *Face value* is the value of a security that is set by the company or government that is issuing it. It is usually shown on the front of a bond. Bonds accrue interest until they reach their full value. The difference between the amount you pay for the bond and its face value is the **bond discount**. There are two types of bonds you can buy: government bonds and corporate bonds.

Government and Corporate Bonds and Securities

Federal, state, and local governments issue bonds to help raise the money to fund their regular activities. Government securities are considered almost risk-free because they are backed by our tax dollars. Because they are low risk, government bonds offer lower interest rates than other bonds. The interest paid on a bond can be higher than the interest paid on a savings account.

Federal Bonds and Securities

The U.S. Treasury Department issues four basic types of securities: Treasury bills (or T-bills), notes, bonds, and savings bonds. Investors can buy these securities through banks or brokerages, which charge a **commission**. **Figure 31.1** shows TreasuryDirect, a financial services Web site that lets investors buy and redeem securities directly from the U.S. Treasury Department without paying a commission.

✓ **Reading Check**

Define A bond is a certificate issued by a government or company promising to pay back borrowed money at a fixed rate of interest on a specified date (the *maturity date*).

Bond Prices Answers will vary. Bonds rated as speculative, sometimes called "junk bonds," offer the enticement of high returns, often for a low investment.

Figure 31.1 — Buying Treasury Bonds

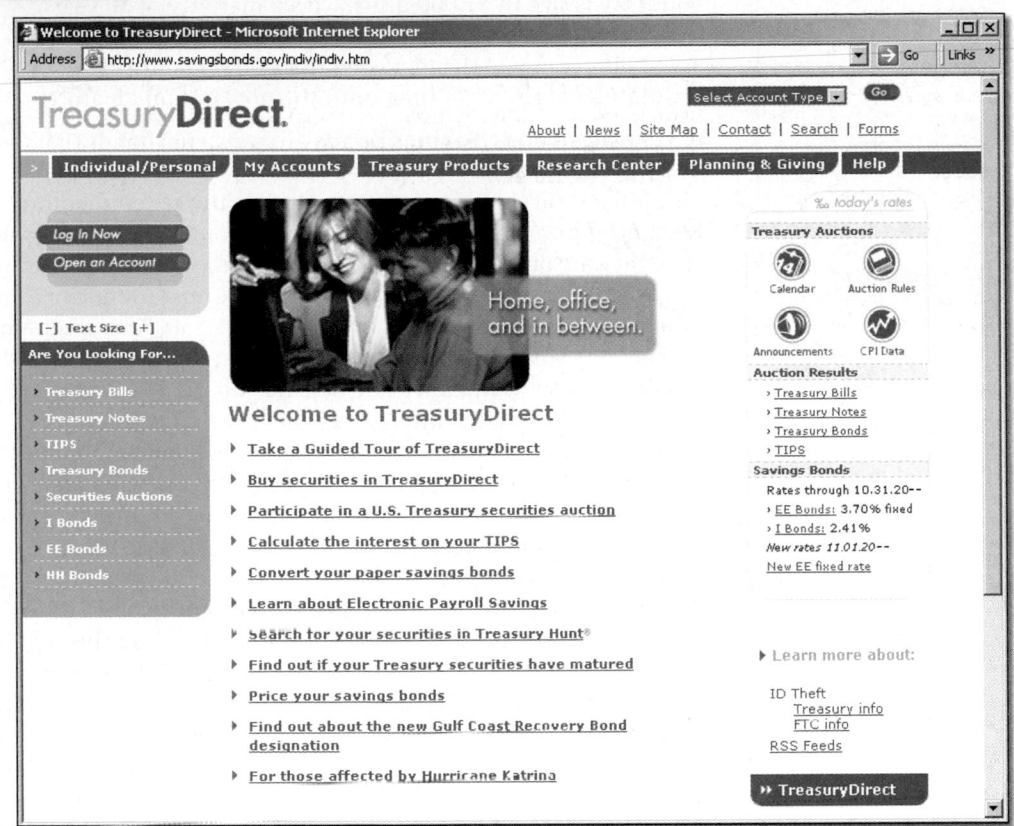

● **Direct from the Treasury Department** Individuals, institutions, and government agencies can buy U.S. bonds over the Internet. **Why might a government agency want to buy bonds?**

Treasury Bills Treasury bills are sold in units of $1,000. They may reach maturity in four, 13, or 26 weeks. T-bills are discounted securities, which means the purchase price that investors pay is less than the face value of the T-bill. On the maturity date, the investor receives the full face value of the T-bill.

To figure out the dollar amount of return on a T-bill, subtract the purchase price of the T-bill from the face value. For example, suppose you buy a 26-week T-bill for $950. On the day the bond matures, you receive the face value of $1,000. The dollar amount of your return is $50 ($1,000 − $950 = $50). To find the rate of return on your investment, divide the dollar amount of the return by the purchase price ($50 ÷ $950 = .0526 = 5.26%). The rate of return on your T-bill is 5.26 percent. A T-bill held until maturity can be reinvested in another bill or paid to the owner.

RETEACH

U Universal Access

Experiential Learners Encourage students who learn best by experience to explore the TreasuryDirect Web site and to take notes about the questions the site answers for consumers. Tell students that learning from the answers to other peoples' questions can be a fast way to gain expertise of their own.

R Reading Strategy

Identify Word Parts Tell students that Treasury bills are also known as T-bills. Ask students to explain the acronym. (The word "Treasury" is shortened to just the "T" and a dash.)

W Writing Support

Develop an Example

T-bill Yields Have students research current yields on 26-week T-bills. Ask students to develop an example that parallels the one in the book that they could use to explain how the rate of return on a T-bill is calculated. (Answers will vary but should use parallel structure to the example in the book.)

Figure 31.1

● **Direct from the Treasury Department** Answers will vary, but students should understand that government agencies primarily receive funds in large blocks of money that they will then have to use over the course of months or even years. Instead of putting the money in a bank, which may not be permissible by law, these agencies buy T-bills because they are such a secure, dependable investment.

RETEACH (cont.)

S Skill Practice

Research Ask students to find the most authoritative source on the Internet for current interest rates for I Bonds and EE Bonds. (the Treasury Direct Web site at www.treasurydirect.gov) **L1**

Determine Meaning by Context Ask students to explain the word "registered" as it relates to savings bonds. (Students should understand bonds have serial numbers that are recorded with the name of the bond owner to show ownership and protect the bond owner and the government.) **L2**

Investigate Invite students to visit a local bank and ask about the process for purchasing a Series EE savings bond. Remind students to inform the bank employee that they do not intend to actually purchase a bond. Ask students to report on the following: the minimum investment, the interest rate, and the maturity date based on the date of the visit. (Answers will vary but should be based on current rates.) **L3**

Diversification
Diversification is the process of spreading your assets among several different types of investments to lessen risk. You want to avoid "putting all your eggs into one basket." *Is there ever a time when you should not diversify?*

Treasury Notes and Bonds Treasury notes are issued in $1,000 units, with a maturity of between two and 10 years. Treasury bonds are issued in $1,000 units, with a maturity of 30 years. Generally, the interest rates on notes and bonds are higher than on T-bills because of the increased risk of the rates rising or falling during the length of time until the note or bond matures.

U.S. Savings Bonds Savings bonds are registered bonds that are sold in denominations of $50 to $10,000. They allow people to earn interest on the savings they entrust to the government in exchange for the bond. Savings bonds cannot be bought and sold once they are purchased. They can be redeemed after one year.

A *Series EE* savings certificate costs half the amount of its face value to buy. For example, a $100 bond costs $50. After a certain number of years, it becomes worth its full face value. The time it takes to reach its maturity rate depends on the rate of interest. On Series EE bonds, the interest rate stays the same throughout the life of the bond. If you cash in a Series EE bond within five years, you have to pay a penalty. However, if you keep an EE bond past its maturity date, it will continue to earn interest for up to 30 years and can become worth more than face value.

Another type of savings bond is the *Series I* bond. Investors pay the face value for Series I bonds. If you want to buy a $500 Series I bond, you must pay $500. The interest rate on this bond fluctuates with the rate of inflation over time. As inflation goes up, the interest rate on the bond increases. However, the interest does not fall if there is deflation during a period of time. You can lose interest if you cash it in, or *redeem* it before its maturity date. For example, if you redeem a Series I bond during the first five years of your investment, you will forfeit, or lose, three months of interest.

EE bonds and I bonds are attractive to people who want safe, guaranteed long-term investments. Both classes of bonds are often purchased to finance education, supplement retirement income, or give as gifts. Interest from savings bonds is not subject to state and local income taxes. Investors who buy them to pay for a college education, or whose income is below a certain level, pay reduced taxes or no taxes at all.

Bonds Issued by Federal Agencies Besides the securities issued by the Treasury Department, bonds are issued by other federal agencies as well. Agency bonds, such as the participation certificates issued by the Federal National Mortgage Association (sometimes referred to as Fannie Mae®) and the Government National Mortgage Association (sometimes referred to as Ginnie Mae®), are almost risk-free. However, they offer a slightly higher interest rate than treasury securities. Their maturities range from one to 30 years, with an average life of about 12 years. Generally, their minimum denomination is $25,000.

550   **Chapter 31**   Investing

Diversification Answers will vary. Students should understand that putting all your eggs in one basket is not wise. However, individuals who do not have the minimum amount of money to make certain investments that require high minimum investments cannot take advantage of the benefits of diversification among different types of investments. In such cases, investors must use other techniques to minimize risk.

Municipal Bonds

Local and state governments issue municipal bonds. **Municipal bonds** are sold to finance city, town, or regional projects such as schools, highways, and airports. You can buy them from a broker or directly from the government that issued them. The main advantage of municipal bonds is that the federal government generally does not tax the interest earned on them. As with Treasury bonds, you do not have to hold on to a municipal bond until it reaches its maturity date. If you sell it before it **matures**, however, you might receive less than the face value of the bond.

Corporate Bonds

Bonds issued by corporations are called **corporate bonds**. Corporate bonds can be bought and sold through brokerage firms. They are usually used to finance construction and equipment. Construction of buildings and purchases of equipment can increase productivity, which then helps society maintain and improve the standard of living. These are ways that savings and investments contribute to the economy.

The value of a corporate bond fluctuates according to the overall interest rates in the economy. If you buy a corporate bond with a high interest rate and interest rates fall, the corporation may be able to *call* your bond, or buy it back before the maturity date. This way the company does not have to continue paying the higher interest rate. Many issue new bonds at lower rates.

✔ **Reading Check** | **Explain** How do corporate bonds help the economy?

❓ETHICS in Business

Putting the Client First

- **Critical Reading** Life is full of important decisions. Think about the kinds of decisions that you make as you read the question below.

  You work as a stockbroker for a large brokerage firm, and a major portion of your salary comes from commissions. Every time someone buys or sells stocks or bonds, you receive a portion of the fee your firm charges for the trade. A client comes to you and wants to make a number of changes to his portfolio. In your opinion, these changes would decrease your client's wealth because they would cause him to incur brokerage fees that would exceed the value he would realize on the transactions. However, you would profit substantially from the commissions associated with the brokerage fees.

- **Decision Making** Would you tell your client about the financial impact of the brokerage fees? Explain your answer.

Section 31.1 Bonds **551**

❓ETHICS in Business

Decision Making Answers will vary. Some students will feel that it is important to point out the true cost of the investment decisions made for each and every transaction. Other students may think that it is enough for the investor to have been informed at one time (for instance, when the investor opened the account) that each trade will trigger a fee, so the investor should be able to make decisions for him- or herself.

RETEACH (cont.)

R Reading Strategy

Identify Ask students to identify the main advantage of municipal bonds. (The federal government generally does not tax the interest earned on municipal bonds.)

W Writing Practice

Enrichment

Corporate Bonds Ask students to use library or Internet resources to locate an article about investing in corporate bonds. For example, the Bond Market Association Web site, investinginbonds.com, features a Learn More link. Ask students to read an article and write a brief summary. Remind students to include a properly formatted reference citation. (Summaries will vary, depending on the article chosen.)

U Universal Access

Auditory Learners Taking notes while trying to listen to lectures or classroom discussion can be distracting for some learners. Asking a volunteer to recap what has been said in class allows all students the opportunity to add to their notes or identify areas that need clarification.

✔ **Reading Check**

Explain Corporate bonds help the economy by increasing productivity, which then helps society maintain and improve its standard of living.

Student Activity Workbook 📂 Assign the Section 31.1 Activities.

RETEACH (cont.)

 **Critical Thinking**

Consider the Consequences

Corporate Bonds Ask students why it might be bad for an investor if a corporation decides to call a bond. (The value of a corporate bond fluctuates. When the interest rate rises, a corporation might decide to call a bond rather than pay the higher rate, negatively affecting investor profits.)

ASSESS

● After You Read

Have students complete the Section 31.1 After You Read section review.

Online Study Tools

Have students go to the Online Learning Center through **glencoe.com** to:

- Take the Section 31.1 **Practice Test**.
- Download free **Study-to-Go** content to their PDAs or cell phones.

CLOSE

Culminating Activity
Create a Chart

Organize students into groups of four. Ask each group to create a chart showing the characteristics of the types of bonds mentioned in this section. Reconvene as a class and create a master chart that can be used as a study aid. (Charts should reflect the information on pages 548–551.)

552

Advantages and Disadvantages of Buying Bonds

Bonds have many of the same advantages and disadvantages as savings accounts. One advantage is that most bonds are secure, especially those from government and large, established businesses. In particular, bonds and other securities issued by the U.S. government enjoy the full faith and credit of the federal government. Bonds also pay interest.

C Although they are liquid, one disadvantage of bonds is that an investor can lose money if a bond is sold or redeemed before it matures. Most bonds are written for a minimum of $1,000, which may make them out of reach for some investors.

Like savings accounts, bonds may not keep up with inflation. For example, if there is 4 percent inflation over the year, you must have 4 percent more money at the end of the year than at the beginning of the year to buy the same amount of goods and services. That means your bond must pay at least 4 percent a year after taxes if you are to keep up the purchasing power of your investment.

 Activity correlates to Math standards.

Section 31.1

● After You Read

Review Key Concepts
1. What are the two goals you should consider before starting to invest?
2. Identify some characteristics of bonds.
3. Name the four types of securities issued by the U.S. Treasury Department.

Academic Skills
4. **Mathematics** The six members of the Canterbury Investment Club have pooled their money to invest in the stock market. They meet monthly to discuss stocks, do financial research, and choose purchases. Each club member pays an initial $200 to join, then $25 a month. All of the money is invested in the stock market. Write an expression showing how much money the club was able to collect by the end of the first year.

THEORY **Variables and Expressions** Use a symbol such as *x* to represent a variable or an unknown quantity in an expression.

 For math help, go to the Math Appendix.

@ Go to the *Introduction to Business* Online Learning Center through **glencoe.com** to check your answers.

Section 31.1

Review Key Concepts
1. Limit your credit card charges or reduce or eliminate credit card debt. Start an emergency fund and add to it as your income increases.
2. Bonds and savings accounts generate funds that can be used in business and personal loans and earn interest. With bonds, the interest usually is paid once or twice a year. Many bonds are sold at a discount.
3. Treasury bills, notes, bonds, and savings bonds

Academic Skills
4. **Mathematics**
$$x = 6(\$200 + (12 \times \$25))$$

Stocks

Reading Guide

● Before You Read

Think about why stocks are generally considered more risky than bonds and other types of investments.

Read to Learn

- Discuss stocks and stock markets.
- Identify the advantages and disadvantages of owning stocks.

The Main Idea

A stock is a share of ownership in a corporation. Stock prices may change continuously. Though stocks offer the possibility of high rates of return on investment, they also carry a greater degree of risk.

Key Concepts

- Investing in Stocks
- Advantages and Disadvantages of Stocks

Vocabulary

Key Terms
stock
dividends
capital gain
capital loss
common stock
preferred stock
stockbroker
stock exchange
mutual fund

Academic Vocabulary

You will find these words in your reading and on your tests. Make sure you know their meanings.
indicates
illustrates
initiated
order

Graphic Organizer

In a figure like the one below, write notes about the advantages of owning stocks.

Stock Ownership

Advantages	Disadvantages

 Go to the *Introduction to Business* Online Learning Center through **glencoe.com** for a printable graphic organizer.

Academic Standards

English Language Arts
NCTE 1 Read texts to acquire new information
NCTE 7 Conduct research and gather, evaluate, and synthesize data to communicate discoveries

Science
Content Standard G Students should develop understanding of historical perspectives

---

Reading Guide

● Before You Read

Students might point out that you have more risk of losing your investment and there is no guaranteed return on your investment.

D Develop Concepts

The Main Idea Ask students: Why do stock prices change continuously? (Some students might point out that the share price of stock is determined by what the market will bear.)

FOCUS

🔔 Bell Ringer Activity

Stocks
Locate a recent newspaper article on a market response to news about a particular company. Read the headline and key and ask students to explain what it means to investors when the price of a stock goes up or down. (Students should recognize that the value of the stock goes up or down with the price of the stock.)

Preteaching

Presentation Plus! 💿

The Presentation Plus! CD provides visual teaching aids for this section.

PuzzleMaker 💿

Use the Vocabulary PuzzleMaker to create a puzzle of the section's key terms. Students can complete the puzzle on paper or on a computer.

Graphic Organizer

Tell students to go to the Online Learning Center through **glencoe.com** for a printable graphic organizer. (Answers include: Advantages: larger return, does better over time, different levels of risk, liquid. Disadvantages: more risk, different levels of risk, may be speculative, no guarantee of getting all the money from investments.)

NCLB Connects academics to content.

553

Discussion Starter

Create a display of books and magazines that offer investing advice. Read the titles of some of the articles, chapters, or books that you consider thought provoking. For example, you might find magazine articles with titles such as, "Pay Yourself First," "It's Never Too Late to Start Investing," and "When to Dump a Loser." Point to the display and ask students where they plan to look for investment advice. (Students should realize that some sources of information are more reliable than others. They also should understand that being knowledgeable is a key to successful investing.)

R Reading Strategy

Apply Knowledge Ask students why sole proprietorships and partnerships do not sell stock. (Answers will vary, but students should understand that sole proprietorships and partnerships are forms of business ownership. If a business organized by one of these forms wanted to sell stock, it would have to change its form of business to that of a corporation first.)

● As You Read

Students might have invested money in a small after-school business that earned a profit. Others may have purchased savings bonds or stocks through their parents or guardians.

Investing in Stocks

A **stock** is a share of ownership in a corporation. When you buy stock, you receive a *stock certificate* that **indicates** ownership in a corporation. Stock prices may change throughout the day, every business day. There is no promise that a stockholder will get his or her money back or that he or she will receive income from owning stock. Therefore, stocks are generally more risky than bonds. Sole proprietorships and partnerships do not sell stock. **Figure 31.2 illustrates** types of investments and their levels of risk.

Companies that sell stock must follow rules set up by the Securities and Exchange Commission, or SEC. The SEC is a U.S. government agency that supervises the exchange of securities to protect investors from wrongdoing. The SEC also has strict guidelines that financial professionals must follow.

● As You Read

Think about the different types of investments. Have you ever had an investment? Did it make or lose money?

Return on Stocks

Just as bonds have specific characteristics, so do stocks. One is the return or yield on a stock. The amount of money the stock earns depends on its type of return and rate of return.

Figure 31.2 — *Possible Investments*

Investment Pyramid

High Risk

Low Risk

Level 4
Speculation

Level 3
Growth

Level 2
Safety and Income

Level 1
Financial Security

Options, commodities, precious metals and gems, speculative stocks, junk bonds, collectibles

Income and growth stocks, mutual funds, real estate, convertible bonds

U.S. Treasury securities, conservative corporate bonds, state and municipal government bonds, income and utility stocks

Cash, CDs, savings accounts, money market accounts, U.S. government bonds

● **Investment Pyramid** Building for your financial future takes a solid investment strategy. Without a solid foundation, you risk losing your investment. **What does this chart show about the possible risk and potential return for investing in stocks?**

554 **Chapter 31** Investing

Figure 31.2

● **Investment Pyramid** The chart shows that income and utility stocks are medium-low risk and offer a rate of return that is appropriate for safety and income. Income and growth stocks are moderately high risk and offer growth of income. Speculative stocks are high risk and are appropriate for speculation only.

Types of Returns on Stocks There are two ways that you can receive a return on stocks. One is through the payment of **dividends**, which is a share of profits given to stockholders. If a corporation makes a lot of money over a certain period of time, it can decide to distribute at least some of the profits in the form of dividends. Dividends are usually paid quarterly in cash or in more shares of stock.

Many stockholders receive a return on stock when they sell it. Selling stock for more than you paid for it results in a capital gain. A **capital gain** is a profit made from the sale of a financial asset such as stock or a bond. A **capital loss** is an amount lost when an asset is sold for less than its cost. As with other forms of income, the government taxes the amount received in dividends or capital gains.

The return on foreign stocks is a bit more difficult to determine since dividends are generally issued in the currency of the nation where the firm has its headquarters. For example, suppose you have stock in a firm based in England. The currency there is the pound. If a dividend of 2 pounds is announced and the exchange rate is 1 pound = $1.90, then the dividend would be 2 (pounds) × $1.90 = $3.80.

Rate of Return The rate of return on stocks is always expressed as a percentage of the original investment and figured on an annual basis. For example, suppose $1,000 earns $50 of interest in a savings account one year. The rate of return on the investment is 5 percent ($50/$1,000 = 0.05). A single share of stock whose value increases from $50 to $55 in a year and pays a $5 dividend during the year has a 20 percent rate of return ($10 return/$50 original investment = 0.20).

✔ Reading Check **Identify** What are the two ways you could receive a return on stocks?

● **Market Quotes** Every day that the market is open the stocks listed on an exchange are traded. The prices at which they are traded are broadcast to the public. **How would you find the names of the companies for the stocks shown here?**

Develop an Example
Capital Gain and Loss Ask students to use the current price of a stock and develop an example to explain capital gain and capital loss. (Examples should be based on current stock rates.)

C **Critical Thinking**

Rate of Return Ask students to calculate the rate of return for this example: Vera bought 256 shares of Mirtx Inc. for $75 per share. A single share of stock increases in value to $81 and pays a $3 dividend during the current year. What is the rate of return? (The rate of return is 12%. Calculate the return by adding the increase in the stock price and the dividend: $81 − $75 + $3 = $9. Calculate the rate of return by dividing the return by the original investment: $9 ÷ $75 = 0.12 or 12%. The number of shares purchased has no bearing on the calculation.)

✔ Reading Check

Identify when dividends are paid or when you sell the stock for more than you paid for it

Discuss the Photo
● **Market Quotes** Stock symbols and the names of the companies they represent are listed in print and online in financial news sections.

TEACH (cont.)

S Skill Practice

Guided Practice

Compare and Contrast Ask students to create a table to compare and contrast common and preferred stock. (Tables will vary slightly. Three areas of comparison should be included: ownership, dividends, and voting privileges.) **L1**

Create a Poster Ask students to work in pairs to create a poster explaining the different types of stock ownership. Suggest that they enlarge an actual listing and include callouts to explain the entries. (Posters will vary but should include descriptions of common and preferred stock.) **L2**

Investigate and Report

Ask students to visit the Web site for one of the companies mentioned in the textbook and report on the types of stock they have offered. If possible, have students create an electronic presentation with links to the actual Web site. (Reports will vary depending on the company chosen.) **L3**

ASSESS

Review Key Terms

Have students write sentences using each key term.

Study-to-Go Have students go to the Online Learning Center through **glencoe.com** to download free **Study-to-Go** content to their PDAs or cell phones.

Types of Stocks

When a company sells stock, it usually offers two different types. **Common stock** is stock that provides the most basic form of corporate ownership. It entitles the stockholder to voting privileges. All corporations must issue common stock. Many issue common stock only. For each share that is owned, the stockholder gets a vote in how to run the corporation.

Preferred stock is stock that gives the owner the advantage of receiving cash dividends before common stockholders receive any. This is important if a company is having financial problems. If the company pays dividends, preferred stockholders will receive their dividends before common stockholders. Preferred stockholders do not vote on company issues. Many preferred stocks stipulate the limit on what can be paid as far as a dividend. A dividend does not have to be paid each year.

Stocks carry different levels of risk. *Blue-chip stocks* are stocks in large, well-established companies that have a good track record of success and profitability. *Speculative stocks* are stocks in new firms without an established track record. They are often small firms that are developing new goods and services.

✔ Reading Check **Contrast** How do common stocks and preferred stocks differ?

> **● As You Read**
>
> Think about purchasing stock from a stockbroker compared to buying over the Internet. Which method would you choose? Why?

Stockbrokers

A **stockbroker** is a person who buys and sells stocks, bonds, and other securities for clients. Stockbrokers act as a link between buyers and sellers. They facilitate transactions. Many give financial advice. As a fee for their services, stockbrokers charge a *commission,* which is either a percentage of the value of the stock or a set amount for each transaction.

Many people lower their investment fees by buying and selling securities using the Internet. With online trading, the trade is **initiated** by the individual via a computer. The **order** is sent to a brokerage firm. Online brokerage houses, such as E*Trade® and TD AMERITRADE®, tend to charge less for each trade because there usually is no stockbroker involved. Some of the largest and more traditional brokerage firms also allow online trading. They include Merrill Lynch® and Charles Schwab®.

Stock Exchanges

Most stocks are bought and sold through a trading market known as a stock exchange. A **stock exchange** is an organized market for buying and selling financial securities. When people sell stocks or bonds through their stockbroker, their order is sent to the broker's representative on the stock exchange floor. An auction takes place at a booth where the stock is bought and sold.

✔ Reading Check

Contrast Common stock provides the most basic form of corporate ownership. It entitles the stockholder to voting privileges. Preferred stock gives the owner the advantage of receiving cash dividends before common stockholders receive any. Preferred stockholders do not have voting rights.

> **● As You Read**
>
> Some students may like the idea of cutting their fees and using the Internet whenever they want, while others may prefer the personal assistance of a stockbroker.

Some of the best-known exchanges are the New York Stock Exchange (NYSE®) and the American Stock Exchange (Amex®). There are also regional exchanges such as the Chicago Stock Exchange. Only companies listed on an exchange can have their stocks traded there. Companies are listed on exchanges with codes called *stock symbols,* or ticker symbols. These codes are used to identify the stock. For example, the stock symbol for Walt Disney Company® is DIS, and for FedEx® it is FDX. Stock symbols and closing prices are listed in print and online in financial news sections.

Over-the-Counter Markets

Over-the-counter securities are not listed or sold through stock exchanges. They are traded directly between buyers and sellers in person or via computer. The transactions may be facilitated by individual dealers. Many over-the-counter securities can be bought and sold through the National Association of Securities Dealers Automated Quotations (NASDAQ®) market. The NASDAQ is an electronic stock market system that quotes over-the-counter securities.

Mutual Funds

Mutual funds lessen the risk of investing in the stock market. A **mutual fund** is a fund created by an investment firm that raises money from many shareholders and invests it in a variety of stocks or other investments. A mutual fund has great buying power. If the investments owned by the mutual fund make a profit, then the mutual fund's shareholders are likely to earn a dividend.

Real World

Mock Portfolios
Before investing money in the stock market, practice first. Build a mock portfolio by choosing at least three companies that interest you. Write each company's ticker symbol next to its name and the date. Document their prices each day to track their performance. Read stories about them. *If you are a teen, how can you buy stock when you are ready?*

Science/TechTRENDS

Stock Tickers
Stock tickers were first used in the 1870s as a means of conveying stock prices over long distances. Before the ticker, information concerning stocks was delivered by hand in either written or spoken messages. Because the length of time individual stock information remains useful is short, it had not been sent over long distances. Instead, summaries of the day's trading were sent. Stock tickers are the ancestors of the modern computer printer allowing text to be transmitted over a wire to a printing device. Today, stock tickers are transmitted electronically and can be monitored on the Internet and on many news programs.

WebQuest

Go to the *Introduction to Business* Online Learning Center through **glencoe.com** for links to Web sites where you can research electronic stock tickers. Write a few sentences about your experiences viewing electronic stock tickers.

glencoe.com

RETEACH

W Writing Practice
Research and Report
Stock Symbols Ask students to look at the financial page of a local or national newspaper and write two paragraphs to describe the condition of a company's stock. (Reports will vary, depending on the business and the newspaper.)

U Universal Access
Hands-on Learners Many students can benefit from a hands-on, real-life experience. Invite interested students to pick a NASDAQ stock and follow its activity for several weeks and report on its progress.

R Reading Strategy
Draw a Conclusion Securities that make up a mutual fund are not stagnant—the same group of securities that is in a fund today will not necessarily be in the fund tomorrow, next week, or next month. Ask students to explain how mutual funds limit the risk of investing in the stock market. (Fund managers are likely to know more about the markets and make better choices than individual investors.)

Student Activity Workbook Assign the Section 31.2 Activities.

Activity correlates to Science standards.

Real World

Mock Portfolios Answers will vary. Some students might suggest opening a joint account with a parent or adult relative. Others might suggest an informal "purchase" of shares from a parent or relative.

Science/TechTRENDS

WebQuest

Stock Tickers Answers will vary depending on student experiences viewing stock tickers.

RETEACH (cont.)

 Writing Strategy

Develop an Argument

Investing over the Long Term Ask students to examine the statement, "Most people who are investing for retirement will own individual stocks or bonds for a number of years." Have students write a letter to the editor of a financial newspaper giving an opinion of whether this is a good or a bad thing. (Most students will feel that it is a good idea to have a long holding period. However, some students may point out that holding periods should vary depending on the investor's needs.)

R **Reading Strategy**

Determine Meaning by Context

Day Traders Have students read the sentence about day traders. Ask if they think the name *day trader* means that these people only make trades during the period from 9 a.m. to 5 p.m. (Answers will vary but students should not take a literal reading of the term. Day traders trade on exchanges around the world and around the clock.)

✔ Reading Check

Explain You can purchase such stocks through the National Association of Securities Dealers Automated Quotations (NASDAQ) market. The NASDAQ is an electronic stock market system that quotes over-the-counter securities.

Short- and Long-Term Investing

W Most people who are investing for retirement will own individual stocks or bonds for a number of years. Long holding periods are an excellent way to build wealth while minimizing risk. Other investors buy and sell more often in an attempt to benefit from day-to-day fluctuations in the value of a stock. *Day traders* **R** are people who buy and sell stock, usually on the Internet, based on minute-by-minute changes in the price of the stock. This is extremely risky. Day traders not only risk losing their original investment, but they also could face additional losses if they borrowed money to buy stocks whose prices fell.

✔ Reading Check **Explain** How can you purchase stocks that are not listed on a major exchange?

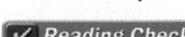 *Reader and Case Study*

Not Your Average Science Project

As high school students select topics for the annual Intel Science Talent Search, they typically gravitate toward math, biochemistry, and medicine. Chad Sandler chose mutual-fund managers.

Sandler, 17, a senior at North Shore Hebrew Academy High School in Great Neck, N.Y., wanted to develop a profile of an ideal fund manager. He focused on demographic data, including where fund managers lived, what schools they attended, and what academic degrees they held. His project, "The Highways and Byways of Fund Management: Selected Demographic Characteristics as Predictors of Mutual Fund Success," was a semifinalist among 120,000 submissions for the 2006 Intel competition.

Based on previous academic research, Sandler thought managers who graduated from top-tier universities and held MBAs would outperform their peers, and they did. But he also discovered some surprises. First, fund managers based in mountain time zone areas had better track records than those located in U.S. commercial centers. While a top-notch academic background is useful at the start of a

career, after six years in the business, managers from second-tier universities matched the performance of tier-one graduates. "New managers remain with the herd until they are more confident and established in their position," Sandler says.

 CASE STUDY Go to the *Introduction to Business* Online Learning Center through **glencoe.com** for the *BusinessWeek* Reader Case Study.

Active Learning

Like banks, mutual funds pool money from many investors. However, a mutual fund's specific purpose is to invest in securities like stocks and bonds. To learn more about investing, form an investment group with two classmates. Choose one person to be the "banker," another to be the "mutual-fund manager," and a third to be a "stock market investor." Create a presentation to convince your class that each team member would have been most successful in investing $1,000 over a two-week period.

BusinessWeek Reader and Case Study

Not Your Average Science Project

CASE STUDY Have students go to the *Introduction to Business* Online Learning Center through **glencoe.com** to download a Case Study activity that corresponds to the article. The activity and answer key are also available on the TeacherWorks Plus CD.

Active Learning

Students should give appropriate advice for the role they choose to play. For example, the mutual-fund manager should give advice about how mutual funds allow investors to diversify and thus decrease risk compared to stock investments, but would allow higher returns than a bank would pay.

Advantages and Disadvantages of Stocks

A general principle when investing is that the greater the risk, the greater the possibility of a larger return. A major disadvantage of stocks is that you have more risk of losing your investment when putting money into them rather than a savings account or bonds. You also are not guaranteed a return each year with a stock. However, a big advantage of stocks is that long-term comparisons of returns on stocks and returns from savings accounts or bonds show stocks do better over time. Common-stock ownership allows stockholders to help make decisions about the company in which they are investing.

C If a company declares bankruptcy, its stockholders may receive little or none of their investment back. Bondholders must be paid before stockholders. If anything is left, preferred stockholders are paid. Common stockholders are only paid if any money remains.

Liquidity refers to how easily an investment can be turned into cash. Most stocks can quickly be turned into cash by selling them. You are not guaranteed to get all the money out of your investment, however, because the value of the stock might have gone down since you bought it. Stock returns generally keep up with inflation, meaning that the value of an investment in them does not decrease when inflation rises.

 Activity correlates to English Language Arts standards.

Section 31.2

After You Read

Review Key Concepts
1. Discuss stocks and stock markets.
2. Identify an advantage and a disadvantage of stocks.
3. Why is it important to discuss your financial goals with a financial professional?

Academic Skills
4. **English Language Arts** Work with a group of students to research investment tips and guidelines for beginning investors. Create a poster display or bulletin board entitled "Top 10 Investment Tips for New Investors." When writing the ten tips, use parallel construction. For example, begin each tip with a verb.

5. **English Language Arts** Work with a group of three or four other students to search local newspapers for advertisements for investments such as stocks, bonds, mutual funds, CDs, and so on. Highlight or circle terms such as *rate of return, yield, fixed rate,* and *variable rate*.

 Go to the *Introduction to Business* Online Learning Center through **glencoe.com** to check your answers.

Section 31.2

Review Key Concepts
1. Stock is a share of ownership in a business. Return is the amount of money the stock earns. Stocks are traded on stock exchanges.
2. Advantage: possibility of receiving a higher rate of return. Disadvantage: riskier than savings accounts or bonds.
3. so you can reassess your investment strategies as your needs change

Academic Skills
4. **English Language Arts** Tips should reflect parallel construction.
5. **English Language Arts** Answers will depend on the advertisements chosen.

RETEACH (cont.)

C Critical Thinking

Compare and Contrast
Advantages and Disadvantages of Stocks Ask students to explain why investment in stocks may be part of a financial plan to help a 35-year-old achieve long-term financial goals for a secure retirement. (Comparisons with savings accounts and bonds show stocks do better over time.)

ASSESS

After You Read

Have students complete the Section 31.2 After You Read section review.

Online Study Tools

Have students go to the Online Learning Center through **glencoe.com** to:
- Take the Section 31.2 **Practice Test**.
- Download free **Study-to-Go** content to their PDAs or cell phones.

CLOSE

Culminating Activity
Your Investment Goals Over Time

Ask students to explore an investment broker's Web site and report on a feature that they find interesting. (Many banks, insurance companies, and brokerage companies have Web sites that include tips, calculators, and other tools that students might find interesting.)

Vocabulary Review

1. Students should write complete sentences using each term correctly.

Review Key Concepts

2. Limit your credit card charges and reduce or eliminate credit card debt. Start an emergency fund and add to it as your income increases.

3. See page 545.

4. The federal government sells T-bills, notes, and bonds in $1,000 denominations, each for a different time period. It also sells U.S. Savings Bonds. Municipal bonds are loans to local and state governments. Corporate bonds are generally used to pay for new construction or new equipment. These changes can lead to increased productivity at a company.

5. Advantages: security, earnings, and liquidity. Disadvantages: required minimum investment, lack of liquidity, inflation risk.

6. Stock is part ownership in a business. It can be common or preferred. The return on a stock is variable.

7. Stocks offer the possibility of receiving a higher rate of return than many bonds and savings plans but they are riskier.

Section 31.1 *Summary*

Bonds Investing is using money to participate in an enterprise that offers the possibility of profit, especially buying bonds and stock. A bond is a certificate issued by a government or company promising to pay back borrowed money at a fixed rate of interest on a specified date. Like savings accounts, bonds earn interest. Most bonds are considered a safe investment. Governments issue bonds to help raise the money to fund their regular activities. The federal government sells a variety of bonds and other securities. State and local governments sell municipal bonds. Corporations usually sell bonds to pay for construction and equipment.

Section 31.2 *Summary*

Stocks Stocks are shares of ownership in a business. Only corporations sell stock. When a company sells stock, it usually offers two different types: common stock and preferred stock. Brokers buy and sell stock through stock exchanges. Unlike stocks on organized exchanges, over-the-counter stocks are not traded in a specific place. They are traded directly between buyers and sellers. Mutual funds are created by investment firms by raising money from many shareholders and investing it in a variety of stocks. One major advantage of stocks is their potential for high returns on investment. A disadvantage is their higher rates of risk.

Vocabulary Review

1. On a sheet of paper, use each of these key terms and academic vocabulary terms in a sentence.

Key Terms			Academic Vocabulary	
investing	savings bonds	capital loss	participate	indicates
security	municipal bonds	common stock	eliminate	illustrates
yield	corporate bonds	preferred stock	commission	initiated
bond	stock	stockbroker	matures	order
coupon rate	dividends	stock exchange		
bond discount	capital gain	mutual fund		

Review Key Concepts

2. Discuss the two goals to set before you start making investments.

3. Name five characteristics of bonds.

4. Differentiate between types of federal, municipal government, and corporate bonds.

5. Describe the advantages and disadvantages of investing in bonds.

6. Discuss stocks and stock markets.

7. Identify the advantages and disadvantages of owning stocks.

560 **Chapter 31** Review and Activities

Critical Thinking

8. Series EE bonds continue to earn interest for up to 30 years.

9. Stocks offer the possibility of receiving a high rate of return. Bonds typically offer better returns than savings accounts and are less risky than stocks.

10. The federal government offers different types of investment options with various denominations and maturity dates in order to attract a variety of investors who have different amounts of money to invest and who want to invest for different periods of time.

11. The decision might depend on whether the money would not be needed for a while.

Critical Thinking

8. Why are Series EE savings bonds popular with the public?

9. Why do people invest in stocks and bonds?

10. Why do you think the federal government offers different types of investment options with various denominations and maturity dates?

11. If you have only a small amount of money, would you invest in a high-risk stock or a low-risk bond? Explain why?

12. Imagine you own 100 shares of common stock in a corporation. What will happen to your investment if the company declares bankruptcy?

13. Stocks that are not listed on exchanges or traded over the counter may be traded via the company's main office. The company will then try to sell them for the stockholder. Do you think this type of stock is more or less liquid than those on an exchange? Explain your answer.

14. Why do federal, state, and local governments not issue stocks?

Write About It

15. "Some bonds are riskier than some stocks." Write two or more paragraphs indicating how this might be true.

16. Contact a brokerage firm, or go online and research one. Find out about how various mutual funds are classified. Write an e-mail to your teacher on your findings.

17. Write at least two paragraphs either agreeing or disagreeing with the following statement: "As people grow older, they should put more of their money in bonds rather than stocks."

18. List the advantages and disadvantages of buying a corporate bond instead of putting savings in a CD. After reviewing the list, would you buy a corporate bond or a CD? Explain your answer.

19. Review Figure 31.2 on page 554, which discusses the investment pyramid. Then create your own investment pyramid showing how you would choose to invest money based on the levels of risk indicated in the chapter. Write a brief statement explaining your choices.

Technology Applications

Online Research

20. When considering an investment, it is important to make wise tactical decisions despite the hype you might hear in the media. Most technology stocks are traded on the NASDAQ. Find out more about the NASDAQ. What does the name mean? Where is it located? What is its history? How many different stocks are traded on it? Write a one-page report on your findings. Then discuss your report with your classmates.

Business Ethics

Help Your Clients—or Help Yourself?

21. Imagine that you are being interviewed for a job as a financial adviser for an investment firm. The interviewer says the company's average clients with the most savings are over the age of 55. However, this group includes the most conservative investors. Your job would be to encourage this group to invest in high-risk stocks, which would bring in more commissions but could possibly lead to major losses for the investors. Should you take the job?

Chapter 31 Review and Activities **561**

Technology Applications

20. According to its Web site, the NASDAQ is the largest U.S. electronic stock market. It lists about 3,300 companies. It trades more shares each day than any other U.S. stock market. When it began trading in 1971, it was the world's first electronic stock market.

Business Ethics

21. Answers will vary. As an advisor, your goal should be to find the best investment for your clients, given their individual situation.

Critical Thinking

12. The company's assets would be sold. After debts were paid, preferred stockholders would be paid before common stockholders if money were available.

13. Less liquid because it takes time to find a buyer. This is not the case with stocks traded on an exchange.

14. because they are not corporations

Write About It

15. Answers will vary, but the stock of a blue-chip company is usually less risky than the bond of a relatively new firm.

16. Many brokerage firms offer "no-load" mutual funds. Some focus on large-, mid-, or small-sized companies. Others focus on international stocks or specific sectors.

17. For most people, saving for retirement means making safe investments that will generate returns. Because stocks usually are more risky than bonds, it is safer to invest more of your money in bonds as you get older.

18. Advantages: more likely to earn higher rates of interest longer; may not incur a penalty if bond is sold before maturity. Disadvantages: usually needs more investment; not insured by the FDIC.

19. Each student's pyramid and choices will be different.

Applying Academics to Business

English Language Arts

22. Research one of the leading stock exchanges in the world. Examples include the NYSE, the London Stock Exchange, and the Nikkei Exchange in Tokyo. Write a two-page essay telling how the exchange was started and how it has changed over the years. Include such information as the volume of trading that occurs and the process used to buy and sell stocks.

Mathematics

23. Sarah buys 500 shares of stock at $18 and sells the holding for a capital gain of $3,000. What was the share price at the time of the sale?

> **THEORY** **Capital Gain or Loss** The difference between how much you invest initially and the current value of that investment is called a *capital gain* if the current value is greater than the initial investment. If the current value is less than the initial investment, the difference is called a *capital loss*.

English Language Arts

24. Explore at least three Web sites devoted to helping the young investor. Write a few paragraphs comparing and contrasting their features. Tell what you think about the graphics, the appropriateness and accuracy of the information they provide, and the ease of use of the sites. Rank the three sites in order listing the best site first.

Mathematics

25. Locate the financial section of the newspaper. Choose three different stocks and study the stock listings for the following information:

Which stock traded the most shares on this day? How many shares were traded?

If you buy 100 shares of each stock you selected, how much would it cost you today? How much would it have cost you yesterday?

> **THEORY** **Reading a Chart** Charts are generally organized into rows and columns. Read down the column and across the row to find specific information.

Active Learning

Conducting a Survey

26. Conduct a survey of your family and friends to find out if they have ever invested in bonds. If yes, what kind? How did they purchase the bonds? What do they think about savings bonds as an investment? If they have never purchased a bond, why not? Prepare a report on your findings.

Business in the Real World

Research a Local Brokerage Firm

27. Investigate a brokerage firm. Ask about the services it provides, the educational outreach it offers, and the fees it charges. If possible, invite a stockbroker to your classroom to discuss his or her job. Ask the stockbroker about the skills and other requirements needed to become a stockbroker.

ExamView Assessment Suite CD allows you to print out ready-made unit and chapter tests, complete with answer keys. You can also create customized tests.

TeacherWorks Plus provides complete teacher resources in one convenient package. It includes customizable lesson plans in calendar format, and instant access to many print program resources.

Real LIFE *skills*

WHICH BOND IS BETTER?

28. Maria has $10,000 to invest. She is considering purchasing a $10,000 corporate bond that offers 7% or a $10,000 municipal bond that offers 5%. Additional income from the corporate bond that she might receive would be taxed at 33%. Which of the investments will result in the greatest gain? Be sure to consider any taxes that might apply.

Business CAREERS

FIND YOUR DREAM JOB

29. Go to the *Introduction to Business* Online Learning Center through **glencoe.com** for a link to the Occupational Outlook Handbook Web site. Click on the "OOH Search/A-Z Index" link and enter the job category of "financial managers." Then write a one-page report about this type of occupation. Conclude your report with a list of things you could do now to prepare yourself to pursue the occupation.

Role Play

ADVISING AN INVESTOR

30. Situation Your 40-year-old aunt would like to invest part of the $300,000 she has saved in CDs. She has asked you and two of your friends to look at the various investment options that she could consider and help her to decide which would be best.

Activity Your presentation should focus on comparing the different types of bonds and stocks to CDs.

Evaluation You will be evaluated on how well you meet the following performance indicators:

- Discuss the investor's financial situation and goals.
- Describe the different types of government and corporate bonds.
- Describe the differences between common stock and preferred stock.
- Describe the various types of CDs.
- Choose the best investment.

Standardized Test Practice

Directions Choose the letter of the best answer. Write the letter for the answer on a separate piece of paper.

1. Which is NOT true about a non-terminating, non-repeating decimal?

A It is a rational number.
B It can be expressed using an exponent.
C It can be expressed using integers.
D It is part of the system of real numbers.

TEST-TAKING TIP Test anxiety can lower your test score. Talk with your family, teachers, and counselors about ways to manage and reduce test stress.

READING Go to the *Introduction to Business* Online Learning Center through **glencoe.com** for a list of outside reading suggestions.

glencoe.com

Real LIFE *skills*

28. Municipal bond: $10,000 × 0.05 = $500, interest per year. Corporate bond: $10,000 × 0.07 = $700, interest per year. $700 × 0.33 = $231, tax factored on corporate-bond gain. After taxes, $700 − $231 = $469, gain. The municipal bond would be the better choice.

Business CAREERS

29. Financial mangers oversee the preparation of financial reports, direct investment activities, and implement cash management strategies. A bachelor's degree is required for most positions. Experienced managers are often considered for promotions to top management positions. In preparation, develop basic computer skills, prepare for college admission, and develop decision-making and problem-solving skills.

Role Play

30. Presentations should address the competencies noted in the Role Play. Answers should reflect materials developed in the chapter and current conditions in the financial markets.

Standardized Test Practice
1. A

STRATEGIES FOR STANDARDIZED TEST PREP SUCCESS

Test Stress Anxiety over tests can result in students complaining of headaches, stomachaches, and other ailments. These complaints should be checked out medically, but if a pattern becomes obvious for a student with no medical explanation, encourage parents to try talking with their student to get at the root cause and find some new ways of coping. Explain that everyone experiences some stress over these situations, even teachers and parents.

Standards-Based Lesson Planning
Introduction to Business provides students with instruction and assessment in the following fundamental content areas:

Content Standards Correlations	
Summarize other types of investments.	pp. 567–570, 572–575, 576–579
Identify various ways in which money can be invested.	pp. 567–570, 572–575, 576–579
Compare and contrast various investment opportunities, both insured and uninsured.	pp. 567–570, 572–575, 576–579

NCLB
Activities, information, and skills practice will help your students attain No Child Left Behind proficiency. Students will improve their abilities in the following academic standards areas:

Academic Standards Correlations		
English Language Arts	Activities/Features	Page
NCTE 3 Apply strategies to interpret texts	After You Read Applying Academics to Business Standardized Test Practice	pp. 575, 578, 579
NCTE 4 Use written language to communicate effectively	Applying Academics to Business	p. 578
NCTE 12 Use language to accomplish individual purposes	After You Read	p. 575
Mathematics		
Data Analysis and Probability Select and use appropriate statistical methods to analyze data	Ask S&P	p. 564
Data Analysis and Probability Formulate questions that can be addressed with data and collect, organize, and display relevant data to answer them	Applying Academics to Business	p. 578
Problem Solving Apply and adapt a variety of appropriate strategies to solve problems	Applying Academics to Business	p. 578
Problem Solving Solve problems that arise in mathematics and in other contexts	After You Read	p. 570
Science		
Content Standard F Students should develop understanding of environmental quality and natural and human-induced hazards	Science/Tech Trends	p. 573

Correlations   This chart shows the 21st Century Skills, foundation skills, and workplace competencies that students develop as they work in this chapter.

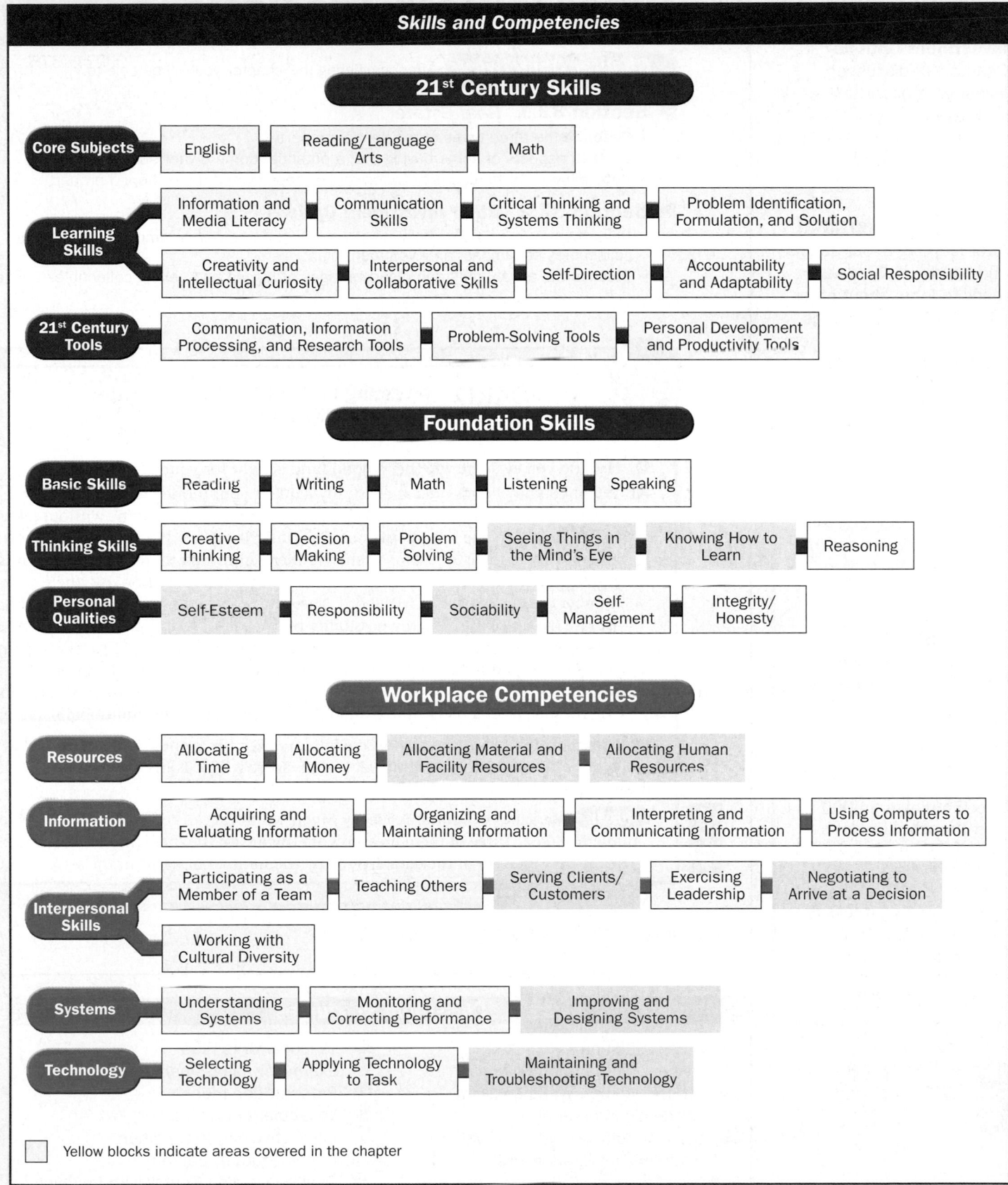

Skills and Competencies

21st Century Skills

Core Subjects
- English
- Reading/Language Arts
- Math

Learning Skills
- Information and Media Literacy
- Communication Skills
- Critical Thinking and Systems Thinking
- Problem Identification, Formulation, and Solution
- Creativity and Intellectual Curiosity
- Interpersonal and Collaborative Skills
- Self-Direction
- Accountability and Adaptability
- Social Responsibility

21st Century Tools
- Communication, Information Processing, and Research Tools
- Problem-Solving Tools
- Personal Development and Productivity Tools

Foundation Skills

Basic Skills
- Reading
- Writing
- Math
- Listening
- Speaking

Thinking Skills
- Creative Thinking
- Decision Making
- Problem Solving
- Seeing Things in the Mind's Eye
- Knowing How to Learn
- Reasoning

Personal Qualities
- Self-Esteem
- Responsibility
- Sociability
- Self-Management
- Integrity/Honesty

Workplace Competencies

Resources
- Allocating Time
- Allocating Money
- Allocating Material and Facility Resources
- Allocating Human Resources

Information
- Acquiring and Evaluating Information
- Organizing and Maintaining Information
- Interpreting and Communicating Information
- Using Computers to Process Information

Interpersonal Skills
- Participating as a Member of a Team
- Teaching Others
- Serving Clients/Customers
- Exercising Leadership
- Negotiating to Arrive at a Decision
- Working with Cultural Diversity

Systems
- Understanding Systems
- Monitoring and Correcting Performance
- Improving and Designing Systems

Technology
- Selecting Technology
- Applying Technology to Task
- Maintaining and Troubleshooting Technology

☐ Yellow blocks indicate areas covered in the chapter

Chapter 32

Chapter Overview

Introduce the Chapter

Real Estate and Other Investment Options
Chapter 32 discusses investment opportunities in real estate, precious metals and stones, and collectibles, as well as investment diversification.

Building Background
After learning about stocks and bonds, students are ready to learn about other investment opportunities. This chapter can help them consider their options.

Ask STANDARD &POOR'S

>> Math Answer
John's score of 661 is six points above the mean of his friends' scores. (723 + 591 + 645 + 614 + 702 = 3,275; (3,275 ÷ 5 = 655)

>> Extension Activity
Ask students to describe the annual earnings of the following group using all three measures of central tendency. Aaron earns $50,000 per year. Cecilia makes $4,000 per month. Lindsay's annual salary is $48,000. Mitchell earns $1,000 per week. Selma's gross pay every two weeks is $4,600. (The mean is $61,680, the mode is $48,000, and the median is $51,000)

N C L B Activity correlates to Math standards.

Real Estate and Other Investment Options

Chapter Objectives   After completing this chapter, you will be able to:

▶ **Section 32.1** *Real Estate*
- **Describe** the three types of residential property.
- **Discuss** aspects of home buying that a potential home owner should know.
- **Determine** the differences between rental property and undeveloped property.

▶ **Section 32.2** *Other Investment Options*
- **Describe** how precious metals, precious gems, and other commodities as well as collectibles can impact an investment plan.
- **Discuss** the advantages and disadvantages of buying and selling collectibles online.

Ask STANDARD &POOR'S   **Investing in Bonds and Real Estate: Credit Quality and Volatility**

Q: How do you evaluate whether a bond fund is right for your portfolio?

A: When you buy bonds, you are basically lending your money to the issuer of the bond. A bond fund is like a mutual fund that aims to earn income without taking on unreasonable risk by investing in bonds. Bond funds also pay out regular income dividend distributions to shareholders. Although there is a common misconception among investors that bonds and bond funds are low-risk, there are a number of risks associated with both. These include credit, prepayment, and interest rate risks. Credit risk is the possibility that the issuers of the bonds may default, or not pay back the debt. Prepayment risk is the chance that the issuers will prepay at a time when interest rates have declined. Interest rate risk involves the risk that the market value of the bonds owned by a fund will fluctuate as interest rates do. The prospectus of a bond fund should disclose these and any additional risks.

Mathematics John is comparing his credit score with his friends' scores. His friends' scores are 723, 591, 645, 614, and 702, and his score is 661. Is his above or below the mean average of his friends'?

N C L B

THEORY   **Measures of Central Tendency** Single numbers can represent a whole list of numerical data. Three of these measures are the mean, the median, and the mode. The mean is the sum of the data divided by the number of items in the set.

 Classroom Resources

- Student Edition
- Teacher Wraparound Edition
- Student Activity Workbook with Academic Integration
- Student Activity Workbook with Academic Integration TAE
- *Fast File*, Unit 10 Resources
- Inclusion in the Business Education Classroom

- TeacherWorks Plus
- *ExamView Assessment Suite*
- Presentation Plus!
- Vocabulary PuzzleMaker
- Interactive Student Edition
- Online Student Edition
- Online Learning Center with Podcasts

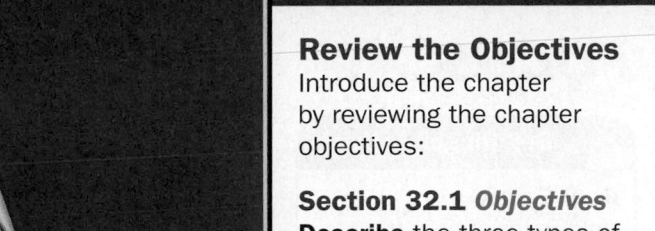

Review the Objectives
Introduce the chapter by reviewing the chapter objectives:

Section 32.1 *Objectives*
Describe the three types of residential property. (single-family homes, usually on their own lots; multi-unit housing, usually single buildings divided into units; manufactured homes, usually prefabricated or mobile homes)

Discuss aspects of home buying that a potential homeowner should know. (amounts of home mortgage loan and down payment, size, condition, quality, and location of home)

Determine the differences between rental property and undeveloped property. (Rental property is any type of dwelling unit or other property rented for a length of time for profit. Undeveloped property is unused land intended only for investment purposes.)

Section 32.2 *Objectives*
Describe how precious metals, precious gems, and other commodities as well as collectibles can impact an investment plan. (Precious metals and gems can act as hedges against inflation. Collectibles offer pleasure and an opportunity for profit.)

Discuss the advantages and disadvantages of online investing. (Advantages: convenience and efficiency of using the Internet and the ability to trade with people worldwide. Disadvantages: lack of income payments, difficulty in selling, possibility of fraud.)

● **The American Dream** Buying a home is the most expensive purchase most Americans will make. **Why do you think home ownership is so popular if it is so expensive?**

Chapter 32   Real Estate and Other Investment Options   **565**

Discuss the Photo
● **The American Dream** Read the caption on the photo to students: Buying a home is the most expensive purchase most Americans will make.

Ask students: Why do you think home ownership is so popular if it is so expensive? (Answers may include the advantage of not paying rent, the ability to build equity, security, tax advantages associated with payment of a mortgage, etc.)

FOCUS

 Bell Ringer Activity

Real Estate
Hold up or project the real estate pages of the newspaper. Point out the various sections and ask students what kinds of listing they would expect to find in each section.
(Answers will depend on the sections included in the specific newspaper.)

Preteaching

Presentation Plus!
The Presentation Plus! CD provides visual teaching aids for this section.

PuzzleMaker
Use the Vocabulary PuzzleMaker to create a puzzle of the section's key terms. Students can complete the puzzle on paper or on a computer.

Graphic Organizer
Tell students to go to the Online Learning Center through **glencoe.com** for a printable graphic organizer. (Advantages: security; freedom to do with the property as you want; tax deductions; value may rise. Disadvantages: financial risk; saving for down payment is often difficult; illiquidity; costs besides mortgage payments, such as insurance and property taxes, repairs and maintenance.)

N C L B Connects academics to content.

Real Estate

 **Reading Guide**

● Before You Read
Think about the different types of homes, commercial buildings, and other properties in which you could invest.

D

Read to Learn
- Describe the three types of residential property.
- Discuss aspects of home buying that a potential home owner should know.
- Determine the difference between rental property and undeveloped property.

The Main Idea
Real estate is an investment option. Residential property, such as single-family homes, is usually considered a good investment. Property can also generate income.

Key Concepts
- Investing in Real Estate
- Buying a Home
- Income Property

Vocabulary
Key Terms
real estate
residential property
real estate agent
equity

income property
rental property
undeveloped property

Academic Vocabulary
You will find these words in your reading and on your tests. Make sure you know their meanings.
attached
fluctuate
assembled
nevertheless

Graphic Organizer
List some types of real estate in a chart like the one below.

Types of Real Estate

Homes	Income Property

 Go to the *Introduction to Business* Online Learning Center through **glencoe.com** for a printable graphic organizer.

N C L B

Academic Standards
English Language Arts
NCTE 1 Read texts to acquire new information
NCTE 9 Develop an understanding of diversity in language use across cultures
Mathematics
Problem Solving Solve problems that arise in mathematics and in other contexts

---

Reading Guide

● Before You Read
Students might mention houses, condominiums, commercial property, farms, and undeveloped land.

D Develop Concepts
The Main Idea How do people make money by investing in real estate? (Real estate investors make money by collecting rent and selling property for a profit.)

Investing in Real Estate

Real estate has always been a favorite investment for Americans. **Real estate** is land and anything **attached** to it, such as buildings or natural resources. Unlike stocks and bonds, a piece of property is something you can use. You can take pride in owning it. However, if you are new to the real estate market, you may be confused by the different choices you face.

For most Americans, a home is their largest financial asset. A home is usually considered a good investment because, generally, home prices have risen steadily over the years. This does not necessarily mean that the return on home ownership is better than on other types of investments. It also does not mean that everyone finds it to be a good investment. For example, some people buy homes in unpopular locations, where home values are stagnant or do not rise much. In other cases, people buy when the price is extraordinarily high and sell when prices have fallen. Homes **fluctuate** in value, just like other investments.

Buying a house is the most expensive purchase and major investment most people make in their lives. Before buying a home, there are a number of factors to consider.

Types of Homes

Residential property is property in which an individual or family lives. Single-family homes, multi-unit housing, and manufactured homes are forms of residential property. The type of residential property that people pick depends on their income and needs.

> **✔ Reading Check** **Identify** What are the three types of residential properties?

International Business

International Real Estate
International real estate can be complicated and should not be purchased on impulse. As appealing as an Italian villa might be, there are risks and regulations to consider. Currencies can be unstable, the political climate might not be receptive to foreigners owning property, and ownership laws can be complex. Potential buyers need to put thought and research into their purchase.

Examples of Languages Across Cultures

Q: In Greek, how do you say "How do you do?"
A: χαίρω πολύ. (pronounced: 'khai-ro po-'lēē)

Research some of the precautions people need to be aware of when buying real estate in Italy. What are some of the laws and restrictions Italy has when it comes to foreigners buying property?

International Business

International Real Estate Students should be aware that, while every country has different rules, some of the things to consider are tax ramifications, ownership restrictions, development issues, as well as currency and political issues. People purchasing land in other countries need to be aware of the restrictions placed on owning property.

TEACH

Discussion Starter
Investing in Real Estate
Ask students how home ownership impacts a community. (It is generally believed that home ownership has a positive impact on a community because people tend to take care of their own homes.)

R Reading Strategy

Explain Ask students to explain why a home is generally considered a good investment. (A home is generally considered a good investment because home prices have risen steadily over the years. However, this does not necessarily mean that the return on home ownership is better than on other types of investments.)

> **✔ Reading Check**

Identify Some types of residential properties are single-family and multifamily homes, apartments, townhouses, condominiums, co-ops, and manufactured homes.

Tax Advantages Owning a home provides a sense of security and stability because you do not have to fear that the rent will be raised or that you will have to move if the landlord does not renew your lease. You also have the freedom to do almost anything you want to the property.

S Skill Practice

Guided Practice

Compare and Contrast Ask students to compare and contrast the various types of multi-unit housing described on this page using a table format. (Table should include the basic information presented on this page.) **L1**

Locate Listings Ask students to find a real estate listing in the classified section of the local newspaper and one on the Internet. Have students create a short report highlighting the differences. (Reports might note that Internet real estate listings provide more information, especially photos.) **L2**

Make a Poster Ask students to make a poster showing all of the home types described on this page, using labels to illustrate their unique features. Suggest that they use photos from free local real estate magazines. (Posters should creatively illustrate home types and features.) **L3**

ASSESS

Review Key Terms

Have students write sentences using each key term.

 **Study-to-Go** Have students go to the Online Learning Center through **glencoe.com** to download free **Study-to-Go** content to their PDAs or cell phones.

As You Read

Think about the different types of homes you have seen. What type would you like to own?

Building Equity As you pay down the principal of your home, your equity increases. For example, if you make a $30,000 down payment on a $150,000 house and pay $3,000 of principal over four years, your equity will increase from $30,000 to $33,000. Your equity also increases as the value of your home increases. *What would your equity be if the value of your home increased by $20,000 over those four years?*

Single-Family Homes The most popular residential property is the single-family house. It is usually on its own lot with its own yard. It is separate from other buildings and provides privacy. Single-family houses range from modest two-bedroom homes to huge mansions. **Figure 32.1** includes median home costs in different parts of the United States.

Multi-Unit Housing Multi-unit houses are usually single buildings divided into various units, with a separate person or family living in each unit. Multi-unit housing includes duplexes, townhouses, condominiums (or condos), and cooperatives (or co-ops). A *duplex* is a house that is divided into two halves and is inhabited by two families with separate entrances. A *townhouse* is usually a single-family house of two or three stories that shares a wall with a similar house. A *condominium* is a building or complex in which units of property, such as apartments, are owned by individuals. Each owner pays a monthly fee for maintenance and renovations of common areas. A *cooperative* is a jointly owned apartment building. Each co-op owner pays a monthly fee to pay for maintenance renovations of common areas, and, real estate taxes.

Manufactured Homes A manufactured home is usually one of two types. Prefabricated houses are partly **assembled** at a factory. The pieces are then transported to a building site and put together there. The other type is a mobile home. Mobile homes are usually fully assembled in factories. Generally small, they **nevertheless** contain many of the features of larger houses, such as fully equipped kitchens, bathrooms, and fireplaces. Mobile-home owners often do not own any land but rent space for the house. Because manufactured homes can be inexpensively mass-produced, they usually cost much less than other types of houses.

Buying a Home

Few people have enough money to pay for a house in full. Most have to finance it with a *home mortgage loan,* or a long-term property loan. To buy a house also requires a down payment, which is usually 20 percent. The down payment is money that a potential home buyer must provide to obtain the loan. That means if you want to buy a house for $100,000, you need $20,000 for the down payment. The higher the down payment, the lower the mortgage loan will be.

Homebuyers often obtain a real estate agent to help them find a home. A **real estate agent** is a person licensed to arrange the buying and selling of homes and other types of real estate. Real estate agents usually charge their fees to the seller and not the buyer. You must be at least 18 years old to buy real estate on your own.

As You Read

Some students may prefer a single-family home, while others might prefer a condo.

Building Equity The equity would be $53,000 ($30,000 + $3,000 + $20,000 = $53,000).

Figure 32.1 – Housing Costs

Location	Average Household Income	Median Home Price	Price-to-Income Ratio
Atlanta, GA	$95,146	$170,859	1.80
Baltimore, MD	102,474	230,681	2.25
Boston, MA	116,736	289,596	2.78
Chicago, IL	103,335	225,826	2.18
Dallas, TX	102,147	126,728	1.24
Detroit, MI	83,792	118,894	1.42
Houston, TX	102,129	107,041	1.05
Los Angeles, CA	101,088	405,668	4.01
Miami, FL	84,753	217,430	2.57
New York, NY	114,379	403,375	3.53
Philadelphia, PA	107,030	195,813	1.83
San Francisco, CA	150,877	678,082	4.49

Source: Housing Prices in America: Valuation Methodology & Findings, National City Corporation

● **The Cost of Living** The value of housing in different regions of the country can vary considerably. Review the average household income, median home price, and the price-to-income ratio for selected metropolitan areas. **In which three areas will the average person use the most income for housing? In which area will a person pay the least?**

Home Values

Several factors affect the value of a house, including its size, condition, quality, and location. Location is especially important. The distance between your home and work, available public transportation, and the quality of your local school system and public services also affect a home's value.

Home Equity The amount of equity you have in a home is very important. **Equity** is the value of a piece of property less the amount still owed on the money borrowed to purchase it. It is the amount on the house you actually own as opposed to how much you owe.

✔ **Reading Check** **Analyze** Would it be a good investment to buy a house at a very low price in an area where the major employer has moved away?

Figure 32.1

● **The Cost of Living** The three areas with the highest cost-to-income ratios are: San Francisco, CA; Los Angeles, CA; and New York, NY. The three areas with the lowest cost-to-income ratios are: Houston, TX; Dallas, TX; and Detroit, MI.

✔ **Reading Check**

Analyze It is likely that purchasing a home in this area would not be a good investment for two reasons: the value of the house is not likely to increase and it might be difficult to sell the house.

RETEACH

R **Reading Strategy**

Apply Knowledge Ask students to identify a residential area in your community and explain why the location is desirable. (Answers might point to a combination of factors such as light traffic, closeness to schools and parks.)

U **Universal Access**

English Language Learners Students whose native language is other than English often have difficulty formulating questions about newly learned material. Organize the class into small groups. Have groups write question starters, such as what, where, when, how, why, and who, at the top of separate pieces of paper. Have groups generate as many questions as they can about the information in this section. Lead a class discussion to answer a few questions from each group.

W **Writing Support**

Enrichment

Predatory Lending Have students use Internet or library resources to find information about predatory lending. Ask students to write a short description of this practice. (Descriptions will vary, but students should understand that predatory lending causes people to lose their homes and their investments.)

Student Activity Workbook ☞ Assign the Section 32.1 Activities.

RETEACH (cont.)

C Critical Thinking

Compare

Rental Property Ask students to create a list of the advantages and disadvantages of rental property. (Advantage: income from rent payments, increase in property value. Disadvantages: maintenance costs and risk of lost income if property is vacant or rents are not paid.)

ASSESS

● **After You Read**

Have students complete the Section 32.1 After You Read section review.

Online Study Tools

Have students go to the Online Learning Center through **glencoe.com** to:

- Take the Section 32.1 **Practice Test**.
- Download free **Study-to-Go** content to their PDAs or cell phones.

CLOSE

Culminating Activity

Real Estate Showcase

Organize the class into five groups. Ask each group to find and develop a presentation about a home within a 50-mile radius of your school. (Presentations should explain the unique features of each property.)

Income Property

Another reason for buying real estate is to obtain **income property**, or property used to generate income. With income property, the owner can produce income in two ways, depending on the property. They can collect rent or sell the property for a profit.

C **Rental property** is any type of dwelling unit or other property rented for a length of time. An apartment building is a common form of rental property. Commercial property is another type. Commercial properties are rented to businesses. They include buildings for warehouses, offices, and restaurants. Sometimes land is rented to produce crops, graze cattle or sheep, or harvest natural resources, such as timber.

Undeveloped property is unused land intended only for investment purposes. The land usually does not have utility services. It cannot be farmed because it has not been cleared. Most people who invest in undeveloped property hope that its value will increase over the years. In some cases, though, the land's value stays the same or decreases. For example, a planned highway might never be built, leaving the land along its proposed route undeveloped. With undeveloped land, there is no rent paid to the owner. The financial gain earned on undeveloped property comes through the sale of the property after it has risen in value.

NCLB Activity correlates to Math standards.

Section 32.1

● **After You Read**

Review Key Concepts

1. Describe different types of residential property.
2. What are some factors to consider before buying a home?
3. Discuss the two forms of income property.

Academic Skills

4. **Mathematics** Maria is thinking of investing $300,000 in bonds that would pay 7% interest annually or using the money to buy rental property. How much money would she have to receive in rent for the rental property to give her a higher return on her investment than on the bonds?

 THEORY **Problem Solving** When solving a word problem, carefully examine the knowns and the unknowns. Then determine how to write an equation that answers the question.

 For math help, go to the Math Appendix.

@ Go to the *Introduction to Business* Online Learning Center through **glencoe.com** to check your answers.

Section 32.1

Review Key Concepts

1. single-family homes, on their own lots; multi-unit housing, single buildings divided into units; manufactured homes, prefabricated or mobile homes
2. home mortgage loan and down payment, a real estate agent, size, condition, quality, and location
3. collecting rent from rental property or selling property for a profit

Academic Skills

4. **Mathematics** The bonds will pay $300,000 \times 0.07 = $21,000 interest. For the rental property to give her as good a source of income, she would need to earn more than $21,000 in rent.

Other Investment Options

FOCUS

Reading Guide

Before You Read

Think about the different types of items that you could collect that might make good investments.

Read to Learn

- Describe how precious metals, precious gems, and other commodities as well as collectibles can impact an investment plan.
- Discuss the advantages and disadvantages of buying and selling collectibles online.

The Main Idea

D Investment plans should include a variety of investments. Aside from real estate, stocks, and bonds, a diversified portfolio might include commodities, such as precious metals and precious gems, as well as collectibles.

Key Concepts

- Diversifying Your Investment Plan
- Investing in Collectibles

Vocabulary

Key Terms
diversify
precious metals
precious gems
commodities exchange
collectibles
fraud

Academic Vocabulary

You will find these words in your reading and on your tests. Make sure you know their meanings.

finally   sites
despite   schemes

Graphic Organizer

List four diversified investments you can investigate in a graphic like the one below.

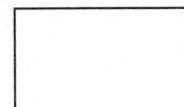

Diversified Investments

 Go to the *Introduction to Business* Online Learning Center through **glencoe.com** for a printable graphic organizer.

Academic Standards

English Language Arts

NCTE 1 Read texts to acquire new information

NCTE 3 Apply strategies to interpret texts

NCTE 12 Use language to accomplish individual purposes

Science

Content Standard F Students should develop understanding of environmental quality and natural and human-induced hazards

Reading Guide

Before You Read

Answers will vary and might include things that have no real investment value.

D Develop Concepts

The Main Idea Ask students: What should a diversified portfolio include? (A diversified portfolio should include real estate, stocks, and bonds, commodities such as precious metals and precious gems, and collectibles; students should realize that a portfolio does not need to contain all of these things to be diversified.)

Bell Ringer Activity

Other Investment Options

Hold up an old toy, tool, plate, or magazine that is of no particular value. Describe the item's history. For example it might be something that belonged to your mother or grandfather and it is 50 years old. Ask students if they think it is a collectible. (Answers will vary. Students should realize that just because something is old, it is not necessarily a collectible.)

Preteaching

Presentation Plus!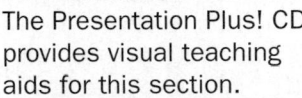

The Presentation Plus! CD provides visual teaching aids for this section.

PuzzleMaker

Use the Vocabulary PuzzleMaker to create a puzzle of the section's key terms. Students can complete the puzzle on paper or on a computer.

Graphic Organizer

Tell students to go to the Online Learning Center through **glencoe.com** for a printable graphic organizer. (Answers include: precious metals, precious gems, commodities, and collectibles.)

 Connects academics to content.

TEACH

Discussion Starter
Investing Basics
Ask students to discuss why it is particularly important for people to invest in what they know when considering investing in commodities and collectibles. (Answers will vary. Students might mention that the more you know about commodities and collectibles, the better your chances for making a good investment.)

R Reading Strategy

Explain Ask students to explain how diversifying your investment plan limits, but does not eliminate, your risk. (Students should understand that each type of investment has some risk, but the levels of risk vary. The circumstances that cause some investments to lose in value do not have the same effect on all investments.)

● As You Read

Both often are used to make jewelry. Precious metals also are used to make money, fixtures, silverware, dinnerware, and other items for the home. They also are used to make dental fillings. Precious gems are used to make crowns and tiaras, and special adornments for personal items, such as jewelry boxes. In industry, diamonds are often used for cutting.

Diversifying Your Investment Plan

R There are many different types of investments from which to choose, allowing people to diversify their plan. To **diversify** means to vary investments in order to spread risk or to expand. A diversified investment plan (or portfolio) might include real estate, stocks, bonds, and commodities. It could also include precious metals, gems, and collectibles.

● As You Read

Think about some different uses of precious metals and precious gems.

Investing in Precious Metals

Many people invest their money in precious metals as a hedge against inflation. A *hedge* is a means of protection or defense against loss. **Precious metals** include valuable ores such as silver, gold, and platinum. They are commodities that are usually valued by the ounce. The price of gold rises when people believe that war, political unrest, or inflation may be near. For example, in 1979, the price of gold was about $100 per ounce. As inflation and political tensions grew, the price of gold rose to an all-time high of more than $850 an ounce in 1980. As international tensions ease or the political situation stabilizes, the price of gold falls.

BusinessWeek *Reader and Case Study*

Copper's Golden Hue

The not-so-precious metal's price hits an all-time record, as gold and oil also soar. Here's why this may just be the beginning.

It's a familiar tale. World prices for an industrial commodity soar to record highs as growth in demand—particularly from rapidly industrializing giants like China and India—outstrips increases in output. Talk of nationalization by populist leaders in Third World countries roils the market, and speculators pile in hoping for outsize returns.

Thinking of oil? Not this time. The precious resource we're talking about is copper. Prices for the base metal hit an all-time high of $7,815 a metric ton on Tuesday, May 9, the same day that gold topped $700 an ounce, its highest level in 25 years.

And copper prices haven't peaked yet, in all likelihood, despite a nearly 80% run-up since the start of the year. Supplies are stretched tight. Industrialization and urbanization—the

twin forces reshaping the economies of China and India—are also stoking demand, as copper is needed for construction and the manufacture of everything from cars to microprocessors.

 CASE STUDY Go to the *Introduction to Business* Online Learning Center through **glencoe.com** for the *BusinessWeek* Reader Case Study.

Active Learning

Copper is widely used in electronics because it conducts electricity so readily. Research other metals that conduct electricity well and find out what they all have in common. Write an e-mail to your teacher explaining the reasons that increasing demand for these metals can be partially explained by increasing construction and manufacture in India and China.

572 **Chapter 32** Real Estate and Other Investment Options

glencoe.com

BusinessWeek *Reader and Case Study*

Copper's Golden Hue

 CASE STUDY Have students go to the *Introduction to Business* Online Learning Center through **glencoe.com** to download a Case Study activity that corresponds to the article. The activity and answer key are also available on the TeacherWorks Plus CD.

Active Learning

All forms of metals are likely to be subject to increasing demand (and therefore more expensive) as countries like India and China become more developed and add to their power and communications infrastructures and electronics become more extensively used.

Science/Tech TRENDS

Eco-Friendly Building

Eco-Friendly building is a term that is used when natural materials, rather than man-made materials, are used in the construction of buildings and homes. Differentiating between man-made and natural material can be difficult in today's world, where technology is present in almost every production process. Since it is tough to completely remove workers from the building process, it is more accurate to define eco-friendly building as construction that minimizes the use of materials that require large amounts of energy for their manufacture. It doesn't mean that you have to live in a log cabin to call your home eco-friendly. The goal of eco-friendly building is to use materials and techniques that don't add to pollution, waste fossil fuels, or misuse the resources of the environment.

Web Quest

Go to the *Introduction to Business* Online Learning Center through **glencoe.com** for links to Web sites where you can research how eco-friendly building can be used to lessen the environmental impact of construction. Look for information on different types of materials and how they are used. Write a few paragraphs about the materials and how structures can be designed to save energy.

Investing in Precious Gems

Throughout history people have prized the precious gems that lie embedded in rock below the earth's surface. **Precious gems** (or gemstones) are rough mineral deposits (usually crystals) that are dug from the earth by miners and then cut and shaped into brilliant jewels. These gems include diamonds, sapphires, rubies, and emeralds. They appeal to investors because of their small size, beauty, ease of storage, durability, and potential as a protection against inflation.

Whether you are buying precious gems to store in a safe-deposit box or to wear as jewelry, you will want to keep in mind the risks associated with this type of investment. First, you cannot easily convert diamonds and other precious gems into cash. Also, as a beginning investor, you may have difficulty determining whether the gems you are buying are of high quality. Political unrest in gem-producing countries can affect supply and prices. **Finally**, you will likely have to buy your gems at higher retail prices and sell them at lower wholesale prices. The difference is usually 10 percent to 15 percent and sometimes as high as 50 percent.

The best way to know exactly what you are getting in an expensive precious gem is to have the stone certified by an independent geological laboratory, such as the Gemological Institute

"Precious" Investments

Investing in precious metals and precious gems can be simple and fun. You can buy them as jewelry from a trusted company, and then wear your investment. You can also buy shares of stock in companies that mine, process, and sell them. The New York Mercantile Exchange is a trading forum for precious metals. Other exchanges trade stock in precious-gem and metal companies. *Which method of investing in precious metals and precious gems would you prefer? Why?*

S Skill Practice

Guided Practice

Explain Ask students to explain how you can earn money investing in precious gems. (selling them for more than you paid) **L1**

Investigate Ask students to use the Internet to investigate some common problems with investing in precious gems. (Students might report on the relatively closed market for uncut gems, the high cost of entering the market, or scams.) **L2**

Research and Report Ask students to research "conflict diamonds." Instruct them to write a short report, including an explanation of the term and how the situation affects their feelings about investing in precious gems. (Conflict diamonds are sold to finance wars, revolutions, and terrorist activities.) **L3**

ASSESS

Review Key Terms

Have students write sentences using each key term.

 Study-to-Go Have students go to the Online Learning Center through **glencoe.com** to download free **Study-to-Go** content to their PDAs or cell phones.

N C L B Activity correlates to Science standards.

"Precious" Investments

Some students might prefer the idea of investing in a tangible item and buying through merchants. Others might prefer a stockbroker to help them choose a good stock.

Science/Tech TRENDS

Web Quest

Eco-Friendly Building Paragraphs might describe things like Faswall (a material used for walls and foundations) or earth plaster, which is made from mud and used for interior wall surfaces.

RETEACH

R Reading Strategy

Provide Examples Ask students to provide some additional examples of agricultural commodities. (Answers will vary. Some examples are wheat, wool, cotton, cattle, sugar, soybeans, and oats.)

W Writing Support

Enrichment

Researching Collectibles
Have students use library resources to locate a magazine devoted to collecting. Ask students to select and read one article. Instruct students to write a review of the article, including a brief summary. (Summaries should include a topic sentence and supporting details.)

U Universal Access

Students with Visual Impairments Coping with the volume of printed material in class can be a challenge for students with visual impairments. To make lectures more helpful to students with visual impairments, think carefully about what you say in class. Use examples that are clear and specific. Sensitivity to student needs is the key.

Student Activity Workbook ✎ Assign the Section 32.2 Activities.

574

---

of America®. The certificate should list the stone's characteristics, including its weight, color, clarity, and quality of cut. The grading of gems, however, is not an exact science. Experiments have shown that the same stone submitted twice to the same laboratory may get two different ratings.

Despite the attraction of precious metals and gems, the investment risks are sizable, and metals and gems can fluctuate greatly in value.

✔ Reading Check **Explain** What are some risks to investing in precious gems?

Real World

Commodities Exchanges
Commodities are the raw materials that producers use to create goods and food. There are about 50 different commodities handled on more than a dozen exchanges in the United States and Europe alone. They include: live cattle and pigs, cocoa, cotton, eggs, frozen-concentrate orange juice, plywood and lumber, sugar, foreign money, and mortgage interest rates. *Why do you think people invest in commodities?*

Investing in Other Commodities

Some people like to "play the market" for commodities such as oil, corn, and coffee. Through a **commodities exchange**, investors can buy contracts for quantities of a given commodity for delivery at a future date. Most investors want to sell their contract before the delivery date. They hope that the price of the commodity will rise in the world market. If it does, they can make a significant return. However, if prices decrease, they can lose a great deal. Even when you think you know the market very well, an unexpected event—for example, a freeze during the time coffee beans are about to be picked—can spell the difference between rags and riches.

Investing in Collectibles

Collectibles are items that appeal to collectors and investors. They can include rare coins and books, works of art, antiques, and stamps. Each of these items offers the knowledgeable collector or investor both pleasure and an opportunity for profit. Many collectors have been surprised to discover that items they bought for their own enjoyment had increased greatly in value while they owned them.

Collectibles on the Internet

Before the Internet became popular, finding items to add to a collection could be time-consuming. Collectors had to pore over magazines for collectors to research the values of items they wished to buy. Then they had to go to shows, sometimes far away, where collectors met to buy and sell their items. That process has changed. The Internet has made buying and selling collectibles efficient and convenient, and the number of Web **sites** for collectors has exploded. Today, eBay is the biggest online auction site.

The Pros and Cons of Online Collecting It is easy to see why the Internet has such appeal. With a few keystrokes, buyers

---

✔ Reading Check

Explain Investing in precious gems is costly, gems are not easily converted into cash, and it is difficult to assess gems for quality or value. The investor may have to buy them at retail prices and sell them at wholesale prices.

Commodities Exchanges Investing in commodities can diversify a portfolio and provide a hedge against rising inflation. Also, most commodities are things that can have a global impact, as they are used all over the world.

can search for items to add to their collection. Sellers can reach people around the world. Prices are not necessarily lower on the Internet. Still, it is easier to do comparison shopping, and most Web sites do not charge a commission.

Collecting on the Internet has its drawbacks. Collectibles do not offer interest or dividends. You may have a hard time selling items in your collection at a good price on short notice. If your collection grows significantly in value, you will have to purchase insurance against damage and theft. As an online buyer, you cannot size up a dealer in person or easily examine objects for flaws or trademarks. Furthermore, fraud is an ever-present danger.

Staying Aware of Fraud

Collecting on or off the Internet can be a satisfying hobby and a good investment. Nevertheless, a wise collector must always be alert to **schemes** and scams. **Fraud** is the crime of obtaining money or some other benefit by deliberate deception. How do you know that the baseball glove you bought was actually signed by Mickey Mantle? Could your Civil War-era postage stamp be counterfeit? Is that old Barbie® doll, Lionel® train, or Darth Vader® action figure really authentic? The safest way to steer clear of fraud is to learn everything you can about the items you collect and to buy and sell only with reputable dealers

Collectibles Are you a collector? Almost everyone is at some time in his or her life. Have you seen or heard of Beanie Babies®, Cabbage Patch Kids®, and Pokémon® cards? They were popular toys that people scrambled to collect in the 1980s and 1990s. Supply and demand affects collecting. When compared with other investments, however, collectibles do not provide reliabe returns. *Why are collectibles not as safe as some other investments?*

Section 32.2

• After You Read

Review Key Concepts
1. How can precious metals, precious gems, and other commodities as well as collectibles impact an investment plan?
2. Describe the function of a commodities exchange.
3. What are some pros and cons of online investing?

Academic Skills

4. **English Language Arts** Unlike stocks, collectibles can be hard to valuate and research. Work with a partner to research some of the terms associated with collectibles. Write the definitions of the terms *new-in-box*, *mint condition*, and *fair condition*.

5. **English Language Arts** Create a poster of your dream house. Use magazines, the Internet, or your own drawings to depict the features it will have, where it will be located, and what it will look like. Write captions and callouts describing your home and its features. Then find a real home that looks like your design using a newspaper or the Internet.

@ Go to the *Introduction to Business* Online Learning Center through **glencoe.com** to check your answers.

RETEACH (cont.)

C Critical Thinking

Assess
Online Collecting Ask students to elaborate on the cons of online collecting. (Authenticity must be assured and flaws diminish the value of an item.)

Collectibles Collectibles can go out of fashion.

ASSESS

• After You Read

Have students complete thc Section 32.2 After You Read section review.

Online Study Tools
Have students go to the Online Learning Center through **glencoe.com** to:

- Take the Section 32.2 **Practice Test**.
- Download free **Study-to-Go** content to their PDAs or cell phones.

CLOSE

Culminating Activity
Consumer Tips
Ask students to create a tip sheet to help consumers avoid fraud related to collectibles. (Tip sheets should include suggestions for avoiding fraud.)

  Activity correlates to English Language Arts standards.

Section 32.2

Review Key Concepts
1. as hedges against inflation and possible sources of profit
2. They allow investors to buy contracts for quantities of a given commodity for delivery at a future date.
3. pros: convenience, ability to trade worldwide; cons: possibility of fraud, inability to see items

Academic Skills
4. **English Language Arts** New-in-box: never removed from packaging. Mint condition: still in same condition as when sold. Fair condition: some wear.
5. **English Language Arts** Answers will vary, depending on the design.

Vocabulary Review

1. Students should write complete sentences using each term correctly.

Review Key Concepts

2. single-family homes, multi-unit housing, manufactured homes

3. the amounts of the home mortgage loan and down payment, size, condition, quality, and location of home

4. Income property is property used to generate income, from rental property or selling property for a profit. Rental property is any type of dwelling unit or other property rented for a length of time for profit. Undeveloped property is unused land intended only for investment purposes.

5. They all offer ways to diversify an investment plan. Precious metals and precious gems can act as hedges against inflation. Collectibles offer investors pleasure and an opportunity for profit.

6. Advantages: convenience, ability to trade with people all over the world and compare prices. Disadvantages: lack of income payments, difficulty in selling, possibility of fraud, and an inability to see the buyer or seller and the item.

Section 32.1 *Summary*

Real Estate Real estate has always been a popular investment for many people in the United States. Unlike stocks and bonds, a piece of property is something that an investor can use. Real estate investments can be in your own home and in income property. With residential property, one can choose from single-family homes, multi-unit housing, and manufactured homes. Income property offers the opportunity to earn money by collecting rent from the property or by selling it for a profit. A major disadvantage of investing in real estate is the difficulty of converting it to cash quickly.

Section 32.2 *Summary*

Other Investment Options Investing in precious metals, gems, and other commodities, or collectibles can be another way to diversify your investment portfolio. With these types of investment, the only way an investor can profit is to sell the item for more than the purchase price. With any of these investments, there is considerable risk. Investors should be sure to develop an understanding of the market and the items in that market. Being aware of possible fraudulent practices in the areas of gems and collectibles is important. This is especially true for online collectors.

Vocabulary Review

1. On a sheet of paper, use each of these key terms and academic vocabulary terms in a sentence.

Key Terms		Academic Vocabulary	
real estate	diversify	attached	finally
residential property	precious metals	fluctuate	despite
real estate agent	precious gems	assembled	sites
equity	commodities exchange	nevertheless	schemes
income property	collectibles		
rental property	fraud		
undeveloped property			

Review Key Concepts

2. Describe the three types of residential property.

3. Discuss aspects of home buying that a potential home owner should know.

4. Determine the differences between rental property and undeveloped property.

5. Describe how precious metals, precious gems, and other commodities as well as collectibles can impact an investment plan.

6. Discuss the advantages and disadvantages of buying and selling collectibles online.

576 **Chapter 32** Review and Activities

Critical Thinking

7. Condos are usually less expensive, require less maintenance, and have amenities. Costs for maintenance and amenities are shared by all of the owners.

8. Usually, home prices will rise over time, and homeowners will see a return on their investment.

9. No, not always. While there is a finite amount of land, not all of the land is habitable or desirable.

10. Some people do not want to feel encumbered by owning a home. Many renters like not having to worry about maintenance or utility payments. Some do not want to worry about mortgage payments.

Critical Thinking

7. Why do you think some people prefer to buy a condominium instead of a single-family home?

8. Why do you think people are willing to go into debt to buy a home?

9. Some people think that land will always increase in value because there is a limited amount of it and an increasing number of people to use it. Do you think this is true? Why or why not?

10. Why might someone who has money to purchase a home opt to rent instead?

11. What warnings would you give a friend who is interested in putting most of his savings into baseball cards?

12. Why might it be better to sell a collectible through eBay than an antiques dealer?

13. Indicate whether investing in commodities is a low- or high-risk type of investment. Support your position.

Write About It

14. Research precious and semi-precious stones. Choose at least two each. In a one-page paper, discuss what makes them more valuable or less valuable than others.

15. Write at least two paragraphs indicating the advice you would give a friend who is thinking of buying a home.

16. In two or more paragraphs, discuss the risks associated with buying income property, precious gems, or other commodities.

17. Watch a TV program or go to an auction that focuses on collectibles. Write at least one page indicating what you have learned about collectibles.

18. What effect do anti-fraud laws have on the art market? Develop a paragraph supporting your answer.

19. In at least two paragraphs, explain what would happen to investments in precious gems and metals if the economy were strong. How would the results differ if the economy suffered a decline?

Technology Applications

Internet

20. Suppose you are a potential real estate buyer or seller. Go to the Web sites of at least three real estate firms in your area. Scan the listings that they have. What did you see at the Web sites that you think was helpful? Write at least 250 words about what you liked about the listings and what you think should be improved.

Business Ethics

Finding a Valuable Item

21. Imagine that you own a secondhand shop. One day, a man brings in a box of trinkets from his grandmother's attic. He says it is all junk and asks for $10. You glance through it and agree. After he leaves, you notice a pocket watch buried in the corner. You realize it is worth thousands of dollars. What should you do?

Technology Applications

20. Answers will depend on the Web sites that are reviewed.

Business Ethics

21. Some students will say that the owner should contact the individual who brought in the box and give him a fair amount for the watch. Other students may feel that it is up to the seller to know the value of items before he or she makes the deal.

Critical Thinking

11. Values for sports memorabilia can fluctuate. Baseball cards have low liquidity. Suggest that he or she research the market and consider diversifying.

12. The seller might make more profit.

13. They are high-risk investments, affected by weather conditions, and social and political events.

Write About It

14. Diamonds and sapphires are precious stones because their rarity makes them highly valuable. Turquoise and garnets are semi-precious stones because they are abundant.

15. Advantages include having an investment that can be seen and used. Another is that mortgage interest paid is tax deductible, which means owners can subtract it from their federal tax liability.

16. Answers should reflect the advantages and disadvantages of each type of investment.

17. Many shopping channels offer collectibles such as coins and figurines. Many auction houses showcase more expensive collectibles.

18. Anti-fraud laws mean that individuals and companies cannot copy a work of art and try to sell it as their own or as the original.

19. When the economy is strong, they usually lose value. During economic instability, their value rises.

Applying Academics to Business

22. Answers will vary depending on the character chosen.

23. Income from rents: $1,500 × 36 months = $54,000

Increase in value: $100,000 × 0.17 = $17,000

Total: $54,000 + $17,000 = $71,000

Expenses: $14,000 × 3 = $43,200

Net gain: $71,000 − $43,200 = $27,800

24. Possessions: belongings, goods, assets, chattels

Land: home, house, estate, acreage

Intellectual property: idea, literary work, invention, patent

25. A line graph would probably be best for displaying the type of data gathered here because line graphs are used to show change over time.

Active Learning

26. Answers will depend on the interviewees' individual experiences and responses.

Business in the Real World

27. Answers will depend on interviewees' job and responses.

Applying Academics to Business

English Language Arts

22. Choose a character from a novel or play you have read. Research homes in your region that are for sale, and choose one you think might be appropriate for your character. Think about whether your character would be likely to live in the country or in the city, in a modest cottage or in a mansion. Write a paragraph or two about why the house you have chosen fits the character.

Mathematics

23. Wanda purchased an income property for $100,000. Her annual expenses were about $14,400, and the monthly income from rent averaged $1,500. She sold the property after three years for 17% more than the amount she paid for it. What was her net gain?

> **THEORY** **Net Gain** Net gain is the difference between the original value of an asset, or what you paid for it, and the value of all cash generated from owning it.

English Language Arts

24. Property can refer to possessions, land, or products of the mind, called intellectual property. Find synonyms or examples for the word *property,* and list them under the three categories.

Mathematics

25. Imagine that you have $5,000 to invest and you decide to invest in three different precious metals. Using the Internet, you track the prices daily for a month and then display your data in a graph. Tell what type of graph would be best to display the data you have gathered. Explain why it is appropriate and other types are not.

> **THEORY** **Data Analysis** Different types of graphs are suitable for displaying different types of data. Types of graphs include pie or circle charts, line graphs, bar graphs, scatter plots, and histograms.

Active Learning

Selling a House

26. Identify a person in your family or neighborhood who has just sold a house. Interview that person, asking the following questions: What did you do to the house before putting it on the market? Did you use a real estate agent? Why or why not? What did you find most difficult about selling your home? Indicate your findings in a one- to two-page paper.

Business in the Real World

Profile a Career

27. Research the careers associated with the real-estate profession. Choose one of the following: sales agents, brokers, real-estate lawyers, appraisers, and urban planners. Interview someone in the profession. How did he or she prepare for it? What type of education or training is required to do the job? Write a one-page paper on your findings.

578 **Chapter 32** Review and Activities

ExamView Assessment Suite CD allows you to print out ready-made unit and chapter tests, complete with answer keys. You can also create customized tests.

TeacherWorks Plus provides complete teacher resources in one convenient package. It includes customizable lesson plans in calendar format, and instant access to many print program resources.

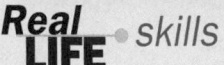 **Real LIFE** skills

DEVELOPING HOME-BUYING SKILLS

28. Interview someone who owns a house about what is involved in home ownership. Ask the following questions: What was the main reason you purchased a house? What are the difficulties that you had in purchasing a house? What are the costs of owning a home? If you sold it, would you buy another one? Write a report of at least one page on your findings. Discuss your report with your classmates.

 **Cool Business CAREERS**

FIND YOUR DREAM JOB

29. Go to the *Introduction to Business* Online Learning Center through **glencoe.com** for a link to the Occupational Outlook Handbook Web site. Click on the "OOH Search/A-Z Index" link and enter the job category "jewelers and precious stone and metal workers." Then write a one-page report about this area of occupation. Conclude your report with a list of things you could do now to prepare yourself to pursue the occupation.

Role Play

REASON FOR BUYING INCOME PROPERTY

30. Situation You are a real estate agent meeting with someone who has money to invest. This person would like to invest in real estate, stocks, or bonds.

Activity You are trying to encourage this investor to put his or her money into rental income property instead of stocks or bonds.

Evaluation You will be evaluated on how well you meet the following performance indicators:

- Discuss the advantages and disadvantages of owning income property.
- Identify the advantages and disadvantages of owning stocks and bonds.
- Develop your arguments in an organized way.
- Use correct English and project your voice.

Standardized Test Practice

Directions Choose the letter of the best answer. Write the letter for the answer on a separate piece of paper.

1. Which is the best synonym for the word *gem* as it is used in this chapter?

A delight
B dear
C jewel
D find

 **TEST-TAKING TIP** Eat well before taking a test. Have a good breakfast or lunch and avoid junk food. Studies show that you need good nutrition to concentrate and perform your best.

 READING Go to the *Introduction to Business* Online Learning Center through **glencoe.com** for a list of outside reading suggestions.

 **Real LIFE** skills

28. Answers will depend on interviewees' responses.

Cool Business CAREERS

29. Jewelers and precious stone and metal workers use tools to design, manufacture, and repair jewelry. Work requires concentration and attention to detail. Some workers attend vocational or technical schools or receive on-the-job training. Some colleges and art schools offer fine arts degrees. Opportunities for advancement depend on individual skill and initiative. As preparation, take art classes and develop interpersonal skills.

Role Play

30. Presentations should address the competencies noted in the Role Play. For instance, stocks and bonds offer the potential for interest and/or dividends to be earned. Stocks are more risky than bonds. The owner of rental income property generally cannot use it if the renter is using it, but it would provide a steady flow of income that would most likely be more than the return on a stock or bond.

Standardized Test Practice
1. C

 **STRATEGIES FOR STANDARDIZED TEST PREP SUCCESS**

Test Stress The ability to concentrate during a test is one of the keys to consistently getting high scores. Students will do better if they are rested, well fed, and comfortable on test day. Suggest that if they find their mind wandering or their attention straying, they say to themselves, "Be here now!" as a way to gently bring their attention back to the task at hand. Also encourage students not to judge their progress as they work through a test.

FOCUS

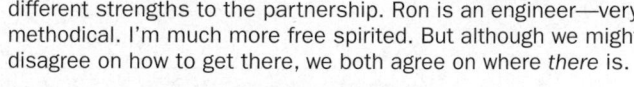

Bell Ringer Activity

Civil Engineering Equipment

Ask students what kinds of equipment they think a company that builds roads and bridges would need to buy. (Answers may include heavy equipment such as tractors, backhoes, etc.) Write a list of objects on the board. Ask students to brainstorm a list of local projects the company could help build. (Answers may include a variety of improvement projects, such as roads, bridges, and aqueducts.)

TEACH

Teaching Points
The Basics of Credit

Ask students to explain the steps involved in the financial planning process. (determine your financial situation, develop your financial goals, identify alternative courses of action, evaluate your alternatives, create and use your financial plan of action, and review and revise your plan) Ask students to identify reasons it might be important for companies like IMS Engineers, P.A., to have good financial planning processes. (Engineering projects can take a long time and can be very expensive. If the company doesn't manage money well, it could even go out of business.)

John Calhoun
Rod Hill

CEO & COO, Integrated Management Services Engineers
Based in Jackson, Mississippi, IMS offers civil engineering services. IMS is one of only a handful of minority-owned engineering firms in the United States. This interview is with John Calhoun. John Calhoun and Rod Hill founded the firm.

Q & A

Describe your job responsibilities.

John: As CEO, I am responsible for the success and failure of the company's operations, marketing, strategy, financing, and creation of company culture. My main duty as CEO is formulating a strategy and vision. The CEO ultimately sets the direction. The CEO's second duty is building culture. Work gets done through people, and people are profoundly affected by culture. Culture is built in dozens of ways, and the CEO sets the tone.

What skills are most important in your business?

John: Resourcefulness, good listening and communication skills, a sharp and inquisitive mind to probe for answers, and the ability and discipline to maintain a meaningful and healthy lifestyle.

What is your key to success?

John: A broad education, broad curiosity, boundless enthusiasm, belief in people and teamwork, willingness to take risks, devotion to long-term growth, rather than short-term profit, commitment to excellence, readiness, and vision.

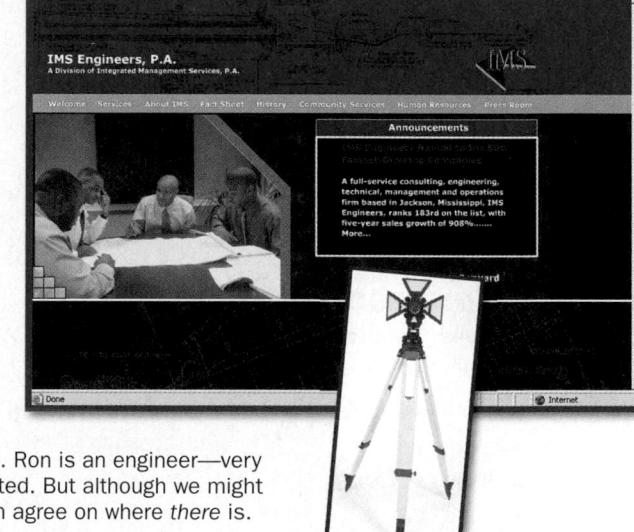

Some entrepreneurs start their companies alone. IMS was developed as a partnership. Do you see any challenges in partnerships verses going it alone?

John: Ron and I knew we wanted to create a quality engineering firm. Our partnership is based on mutual respect and friendship. We were best friends at college. We bring different strengths to the partnership. Ron is an engineer—very methodical. I'm much more free spirited. But although we might disagree on how to get there, we both agree on where *there* is.

What advice would you give students interested in starting a business?

John: Have big dreams and never stop dreaming of more. Know how to define success for yourself. Don't have someone define it for you. Establish excellent networks of people who support what you are doing. View obstacles as challenges and, at times, welcome them. Walk through fear and take calculated, or sometimes bold, risks.

Critical Thinking *What consequences might result from launching a niche company?*

580   **Unit 10**   Real-World Business and Career Profile

Critical Thinking

A niche market is a focused and narrowly defined group of potential customers for a specific product or service. Businesses that target niche markets often create custom-made goods or services for them. Niche markets can be very profitable when there is a lack of established vendors addressing the need for the product or service.

Some Qualifications Needed to Own a Civil Engineering Firm

Academic Skills and Abilities

Physics; engineering; mathematics (especially algebra, geometry, trigonometry, and calculus); interpersonal skills; general business management skills; verbal and written communication skills; multitasking, organizing, and planning skills

Academic Skills Required to Complete Tasks at Integrated Management Services Engineers			
Tasks	Math	Science	English Language Arts
Hold meetings			◆
Assign duties			◆
Design to meet customer needs	◆	◆	◆
Oversee construction	◆	◆	◆
Maintain safe work sites	◆	◆	◆
Schedule employees	◆		◆
Order supplies and equipment	◆		◆
Analyze financials	◆		◆

Education and Training

For a typical bachelor's degree in engineering, the first two years are spent studying mathematics, basic sciences, introductory engineering, humanities, and social sciences. In the last two years, most courses are in engineering, usually with a concentration in one specialty.

Career Path

The major civil engineering specialties are structural, water resources, construction, environmental, transportation, and geotechnical engineering. Many civil engineers hold supervisory or administrative positions, from supervisor of a construction site to city engineer. All 50 states and the District of Columbia require licensure for engineers who offer their service to the public. Independent of licensure, various certification programs are offered by professional organizations to demonstrate competency in specific fields of engineering.

Preparing for a Career
Self-Assessment Checklist
Use this self-assessment checklist to help determine ways you can build a successful career path.

✔ Keep your work area neat and organized to enhance safety and efficiency.

✔ Be professional. Limit personal phone calls, non-work-related e-mail, and distractions.

✔ Plan your day's schedule, keeping in mind any meetings and duties that require you to be considerate of other people's time.

✔ Complete the most important work first—don't get caught up in minor details.

✔ Avoid procrastinating—it may prevent you from producing top-quality work on schedule.

✔ Tackle one task at a time, and do not get side-tracked.

✔ Try to empathize with customers and co-workers to gain a better understanding of the situation.

✔ Pay attention to body language. Be alert to facial expressions, which often give clues to a person's inner feelings.

ASSESS

Write About It
Integrated Management Services Engineers
Ask students to write a summary of what they like about IMS Engineers, P.A.'s concept. (Students may say that they like the idea of being able to build long-term assests for the community that will be used by so many people.)

Academic Vocabulary
Career Planning
Ask students to read the Self-Assessment Checklist, then write one or more paragraphs about preparing for a career. Have students use some words from the Academic Vocabulary Glossary. (Example: Forming productive *relationships* with co-workers is an excellent way to enhance your job performance as well as your enjoyment of your work. Being able to rely on *team resources* makes everyone more productive.)

CLOSE

Cooperative Learning
Technology Applications
Ask students to work in pairs and develop an idea for a service business they can form. Have them work together to develop an advertisement for the business. Encourage students to use technology applications to design the advertisement. (Brochures should include marketing copy, visuals, and business information.)

Preparing for a Career
Investing in Yourself Getting a good education is a way for people to invest in themselves. Remind students that their educations will not end with high school or college, though. People should strive to learn a little bit more every day. Ask students: Why is it important to be committed to your education? (Answers will vary but may include because their education is an investment in their future.) Tell students they will have an opportunity to think about careers and the career-planning process as they read the Self-Assessment Checklists in this book.

FOCUS

Discussion Starter

Lead a discussion about how to ensure a healthy financial future. Ask students how they can make their financial futures secure.

Step 1

Brainstorm Skills

Have students go to the *Introduction to Business* Online Learning Center through **glencoe.com** for a graphic organizer they can use to brainstorm the skills needed to complete the project.

Step 2

Think About the Financial Future You Want

Students can use the Occupational Outlook Handbook Web site to explore occupations that will help them build a sound financial future.

TEACH

Step 3

Build Background

Technology Have students brainstorm ways they will use technology to build financial security in the future. (New technologies are being developed every day that can help people plan their finances and build wealth. Being technologically savvy will also help students perform basic tasks more productively.)

Building a Financial Future

You want to make your future as secure as possible. You want to plan for the future by building and managing your personal finances, making and living within a budget, and planning your financial future.

Thematic Project Assignment

In this project you will write a personal financial plan that describes how you want to plan for your financial future. Your plan might include a savings account, investments in bonds or stocks, or a retirement fund.

Step 1 Brainstorm Skills You Need to Complete This Activity

Your success in writing a personal financial plan will depend on your skills. Preview the activity, then brainstorm a list of the skills you will need to use to complete the activity and describe how you will use them. Skills you might use include:

Academic Skills	reading and writing
Basic Skills	speaking, listening, and thinking
Technology Skills	word processing and keyboarding

 SKILLS PREVIEW Go to the *Introduction to Business* Online Learning Center through **glencoe.com** for a graphic organizer you can use to brainstorm the skills you will use to complete the project.

Step 2 Think About the Financial Future You Want

Think about what you want your future to be like. Do you want to own a home someday? Would you like to have a family? Do you want to someday retire from your job? Would you like to travel? Think about how much money you will need to do some of the things you want in the future.

Step 3 Build Background Knowledge

Preview information on building a financial future.

Building a Financial Future

Dreaming about what the future holds for you is one thing. Being practical and building a financial future is quite another. Building a secure financial future takes research, careful planning, and discipline. First, you must research to be able to make wise choices about where to invest or to put your money. Second, you must plan how you are going to save and put money away for investments. Third, you must have the discipline to put money into a savings account or some other investment account.

Building a financial future is an important part of adulthood and should be an important part of everyone's life. No one knows what the future holds. The more secure you are financially, the better your future will be.

Globalization Ask students to write an essay about the impact of globalization on their financial futures. (Outsourcing of jobs may impact their career potential, but so will the growing markets for American goods and services. Globalization makes it even more important to be flexible and to have strong basic skills.)

Step 4

Connect with Your Community

Ask students to describe how their community will shape their financial futures. (Encourage students to recognize that their community helps them by providing them with education, and that education can lead to financial security.)

Step 4 Connect with Your Community

Interview two adults in your community about how they have planned for their financial future. Ask the adults how they learned about financial planning. Think about how important it is to plan for your financial future.

Step 5 Research How to Plan for Your Financial Future

Use library and Internet resources to research ways you can plan for your financial future. Use the project checklist as a guide to your research. Keep records of your sources of information.

Step 6 Develop a Plan for Your Financial Future

Use word-processing and spreadsheet software to develop a plan for your financial future that includes all of the information described in the project checklist.

Developing a Plan for Your Financial Future

✔ Make a list of two things you want for your future. These might include a new vehicle, a home, a vacation, a college education, or a family.

✔ Use library and Internet resources, phone calls, or personal interviews to research the cost of each of the things on your list. For example, contact a local college to learn what the cost is of a two-year or four-year degree. Write this amount next to "a college education" on your list.

✔ Visit local banks in your area to learn about savings accounts, CDs, special college savings accounts, and other ways to save money. Also, use the Internet to research other types of investments, such as stocks and U.S. savings bonds.

✔ Create a chart that illustrates the items you want for your future, the amount you predict you will need, how you plan to obtain the money (such as through a savings account or by buying U.S. savings bonds), and when you will need the money.

Self Connections

✔ Describe the results of your research with the adults you interviewed.

✔ Explain what the investigation and its results mean to you.

Step 7 Evaluate Your Presentation

RUBRIC Go to the *Introduction to Business* Online Learning Center through **glencoe.com** for a rubric you can use to evaluate your final report.

583

TEACH (cont.)

Step 6

Develop a Plan for Your Financial Future
Give students these tips on writing:

- Know your audience.
- Organize your report by developing an outline and using titles and subtitles.
- Write concisely (briefly but completely).
- Write in easy-to-read, simple language.

ASSESS

Step 7

Evaluate Your Financial Plan
Rubric Encourage students to use the rubric to evaluate their financial plans.

CLOSE

Culminating Activity
Financial Plan Interviews
Have students form pairs and interview each other about their financial planning research and how their opinions and perceptions of financial planning evolved during the course of the project. (Interviews will vary depending on students' reactions to their research.)

Step 5

Research How to Plan for Your Financial Future
Students can go to the *Introduction to Business* Online Learning Center through **glencoe.com** for a rubric they can use as a content checklist when researching their financial plans.

Chapter	Section	Unit Objectives
Chapter 33 *The Basics of Risk Management*	33.1	**Discuss** risk and risk management.
		Describe different types of risk.
	33.2	**Describe** four ways that individuals and businesses can handle risk.
		List types of insurance protection.
Chapter 34 *Vehicle and Property Insurance*	34.1	**Describe** types of vehicle insurance.
		Identify laws that make vehicle insurance protection a necessity.
		Give examples of factors that affect the cost of vehicle insurance.
	34.2	**List** some examples of insurance for real and personal property.
		Describe protection provided by homeowners insurance policies.
Chapter 35 *Life and Health Insurance*	35.1	**Identify** ways to protect your family financially.
		Describe the different types of life insurance.
		Discuss the costs of life insurance.
	35.2	**Analyze** reasons it is important to protect your health.
		Determine ways to pay for various health-care costs.

Understanding the Coding

Brackets Brackets on the reduced student edition page correspond to teaching strategies and activities in the Teacher Wraparound Edition. As you teach the lesson, the brackets show you exactly where to use the teaching strategies and activities.

Letters The letters on the reduced student edition page identify the type of strategy or activity. See the key below to learn about the different types of strategies and activities.

Ability Levels Leveled teaching strategies are identified by one of three codes to give you an idea of their suitability for students of varying learning styles and abilities.

Resources Key program resources are listed in each chapter. Icons indicate the format of resources.

KEY | to Letters

D **Develop Concepts** activities help teachers gauge and plan for students' concept development.

R **Reading Strategy** activities help you teach reading skills and vocabulary.

C **Critical Thinking** strategies help students apply and extend what they have learned.

U **Universal Access** activities provide differentiated instruction for English language learners and suggestions for teaching various types of learners.

S **Skill Practice** provides leveled instruction for meeting individual needs and learning styles.

W **Writing Support** activities provide writing opportunities to help students comprehend the text.

NCLB **No Child Left Behind** activities help students practice and improve their abilities in academic subjects.

KEY | to Ability Levels

L1 Strategies should be within the ability range of all students. Often full class participation is required.

L2 Strategies are for average to above-average students or for small groups. Some teacher direction is necessary.

L3 Strategies are designed for students able and willing to work independently. Minimal teacher direction is necessary.

KEY | to Resource Icons

📁 Print Material

💿 CD-ROM

🖥 Online Learning Center with Podcasts

BusinessWeek *Reader and Case Study*

In Unit 11, your students can learn more about business in the real world through the following *BusinessWeek* Readers and Case Studies:

Winning the Game of Risk
Some pros say investors aren't paying enough attention to risk. Some smart steps can help protect your investments. (page 594)

The Fixer-Upper Fixes Up
Ralph Kastner had both planning and luck on his side. When he started Tuff Equipment Rentals in 1999, he drew up a hurricane plan. He had flood insurance as well as coverage for the replacement value of his equipment. Now Kastner's particular service—renting small equipment—has become one very hot niche. (page 607)

Health Care: Benefits Surprise
Group coverage too pricey? Individual policies may be better than you think. (page 626)

Chapter Features and Activities

Chapter	Feature Title	Mathematics Activity	Page
33	The Basics of Risk Management: Credit Risk Assessment	Calculating Debt-to-Income Ratios	586
34	Vehicle and Property Insurance: Risk Management	Front-End Estimation of Insurance Costs	602
35	Life and Health Insurance: Whole Life vs. Term Insurance	Percent Savings on Health Insurance	618

BusinessWeek *Reader and Case Study*

Chapter	Feature Title	Active Learning	Page
33	Winning the Game of Risk	Develop a Poster Depicting Controllable Risk	594
34	The Fixer-Upper Fixes Up	Research Different Kinds of Insurance Policies and Fees	607
35	Health Care: Benefits Surprise	Research Health Savings Accounts for Tax Treatment	626

Science/Tech TRENDS

Chapter	Feature Title	WebQuest Activity	Page
33	Air Bags	The Technology of Air Bags	595
34	Autonomous Underwater Vehicles	Applications of AUVs	610
35	Medical Technology	Advances in Medical Technology and Communications	627

?ETHICS in Business

Chapter	Feature Title	Page
33	Conduct in the Workplace	590
35	Gambling on Self-Insurance	621

International Business

Chapter	Feature Title	Page
34	Lloyd's of London	605

Reading Strategies

Before You Read

Graphic Organizer

As You Read

✔ Reading Check

After You Read

Unit Overview

Introduce the Unit
Introduce the unit by describing the main concepts of each chapter in the unit.

Unit 11 is about risk management and how it affects everyday life.

Chapter 33 discusses risk and how to manage it. Different types of risks faced by individuals and businesses are identified, and strategies for handling risk are presented.

Chapter 34 discusses real and personal property insurance. It describes kinds of insurance with a focus on vehicle and homeowners insurance.

Chapter 35 is about life and health insurance. Types of insurance and their costs are discussed.

00:00 OUT OF TIME?

If class time is too short to cover all of the chapters in this unit, have students:

- Write down the vocabulary terms and their definitions.
- Read the chapter summaries at the beginning of each chapter review.
- Go to the *Introduction to Business* Online Learning Center through **glencoe.com** to download free Study-to-Go content to their PDAs or cell phones.

Risk Management

584

Real-World Business and Career Profile — Preview

Advanced Physical Therapy P.C. Tell students that at the end of this unit, they will learn about Advanced Physical Therapy founder JoAnne Jonathan and how she achieved her success. Advanced Physical Therapy was one of the first companies to offer outpatient physical therapy in Indiana. Today, the company is expanding and offers wellness and illness prevention programs for large industries. Ask students why offering wellness and illness prevention services to businesses might be a successful business concept. (Illness and injury cost businesses productivity, so these businesses might want to use a service that can reduce that risk.)

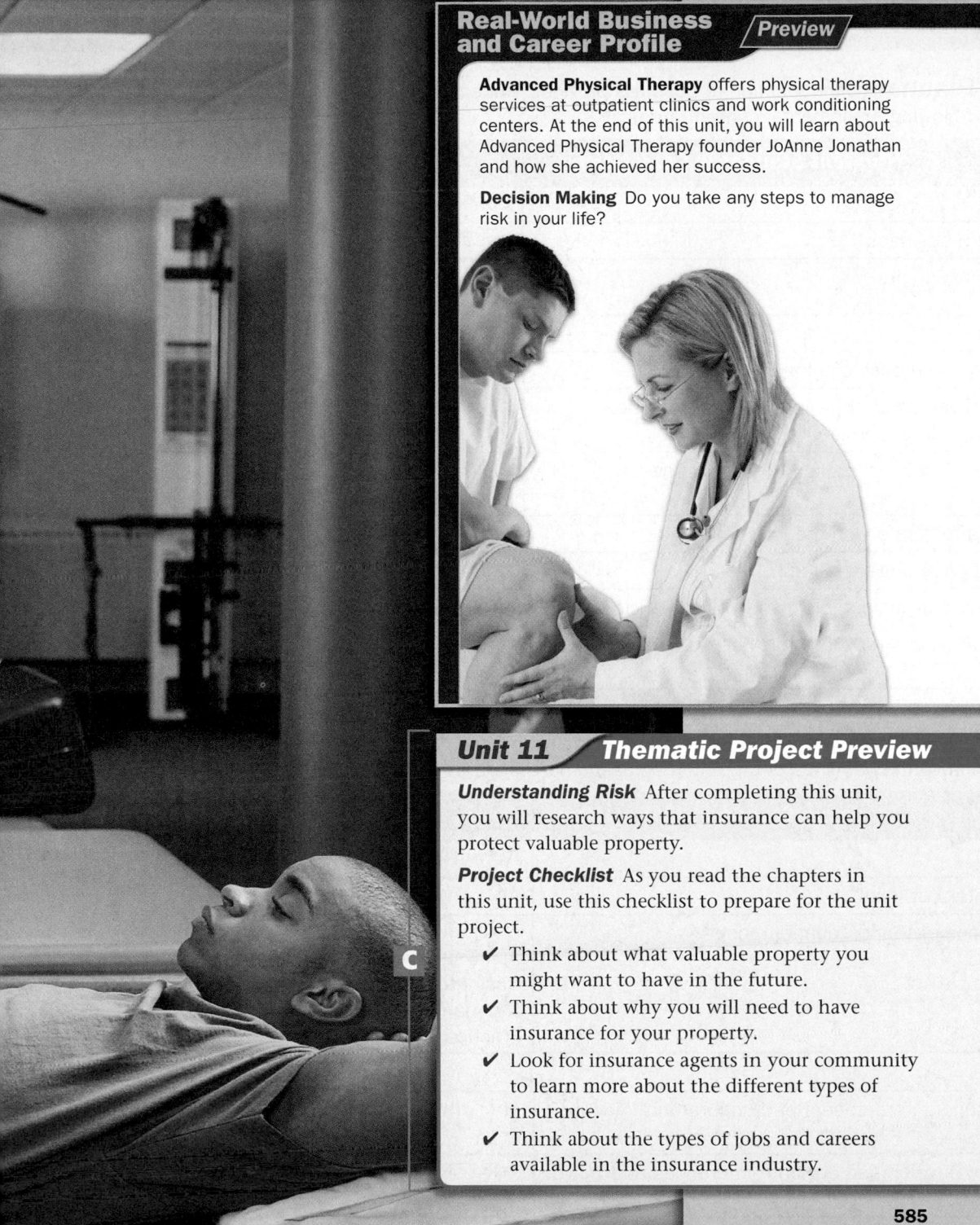

Real-World Business and Career Profile

Preview

Advanced Physical Therapy offers physical therapy services at outpatient clinics and work conditioning centers. At the end of this unit, you will learn about Advanced Physical Therapy founder JoAnne Jonathan and how she achieved her success.

Decision Making Do you take any steps to manage risk in your life?

Unit 11 — Thematic Project Preview

Understanding Risk After completing this unit, you will research ways that insurance can help you protect valuable property.

Project Checklist As you read the chapters in this unit, use this checklist to prepare for the unit project.

- ✔ Think about what valuable property you might want to have in the future.
- ✔ Think about why you will need to have insurance for your property.
- ✔ Look for insurance agents in your community to learn more about the different types of insurance.
- ✔ Think about the types of jobs and careers available in the insurance industry.

585

Build Background

Ask students these questions to activate prior knowledge:

Chapter 33
Why is it important to learn about risk management? (Risk is inevitable, but you can lessen the impact of risk by planning and implementing strategies to manage risk.)

Chapter 34
Why do you need to learn about vehicle and property insurance? (Young drivers and soon-to-be drivers generally are familiar with vehicle insurance. In some cases they are paying for insurance on their own car or truck. Although they might not be as familiar with homeowners insurance, the concept probably is not new. This chapter helps students put their limited knowledge into perspective and prepares them for the responsibility of protecting themselves and their property.)

Chapter 35
Why do you need to know about life and health insurance? (Students should not be surprised to learn that life and health insurance coverage costs vary dramatically. Knowing the basics will help them evaluate their choices as they become more independent, start careers, and think about protecting their loved ones.)

Unit — Thematic Project Preview

Understanding Risk
Tell students that when they complete this unit, they will understand what insurance is and what types are available. Students will be able to consider what types of insurance they will need. Encourage students to think about the types of jobs and careers they might choose within the insurance industry.

C Critical Thinking
Ask students why health and other insurance are important. (Unfortunately, everybody is subject to various risks during their lifetime. Insurance is a way of protecting yourself or your family or business financially against the consequences of these risks.)

Standards-Based Lesson Planning
Introduction to Business provides students with instruction and assessment in the following fundamental content areas:

Content Standards Correlations	
Analyze the various forms of risk.	pp. 589–592, 598, 599
Identify the risk factors in owning a business.	pp. 589–592, 595, 596, 599–601
Analyze various forms of risk management.	pp. 589, 592, 594, 595–597, 599–601
Examine the need for risk protection.	pp. 589–592, 594–597, 599–601
Identify reasons for buying personal and business insurance.	pp. 590, 596–597, 599, 600
Evaluate the advantages and disadvantages of having income protection through insurance policies and government programs.	pp. 590, 591, 596–597
Discuss accepted rules, regulations, policies, procedures, processes, and workplace safety.	pp. 591, 595–596, 599, 601
Identify good work attitudes that affect safety on the job.	pp. 591, 595, 599, 600
Discuss the importance of having an emergency plan.	pp. 592, 595, 599
Identify major causes of, and ways to avoid, common work-related accidents.	pp. 594, 595, 599
Explain the various types of insurance and how each provides protection against possible loss.	pp. 597, 600

NCLB
Activities, information, and skills practice will help your students attain No Child Left Behind proficiency. Students will improve their abilities in the following academic standards areas:

Academic Standards Correlations		
English Language Arts	Activities/Features	Page
NCTE 3 Apply strategies to interpret texts	After You Read	p. 597
NCTE 12 Use language to accomplish individual purposes	After You Read Applying Academics to Business Standardized Test Practice	pp. 597, 600, 601
Mathematics		
Algebra Use mathematical models to represent and understand quantitative relationships	After You Read	p. 592
Data Analysis and Probability Develop and evaluate inferences and predictions that are based on data	Ask S&P	p. 586
Problem Solving Monitor and reflect on the process of mathematical problem solving	Applying Academics to Business	p. 600
Problem Solving Solve problems that arise in mathematics and in other contexts	Applying Academics to Business	p. 600
Science		
Content Standard G Students should develop understanding of historical perspectives	Science/Tech Trends	p. 595

Correlations   This chart shows the 21st Century Skills, foundation skills, and workplace competencies that students develop as they work in this chapter.

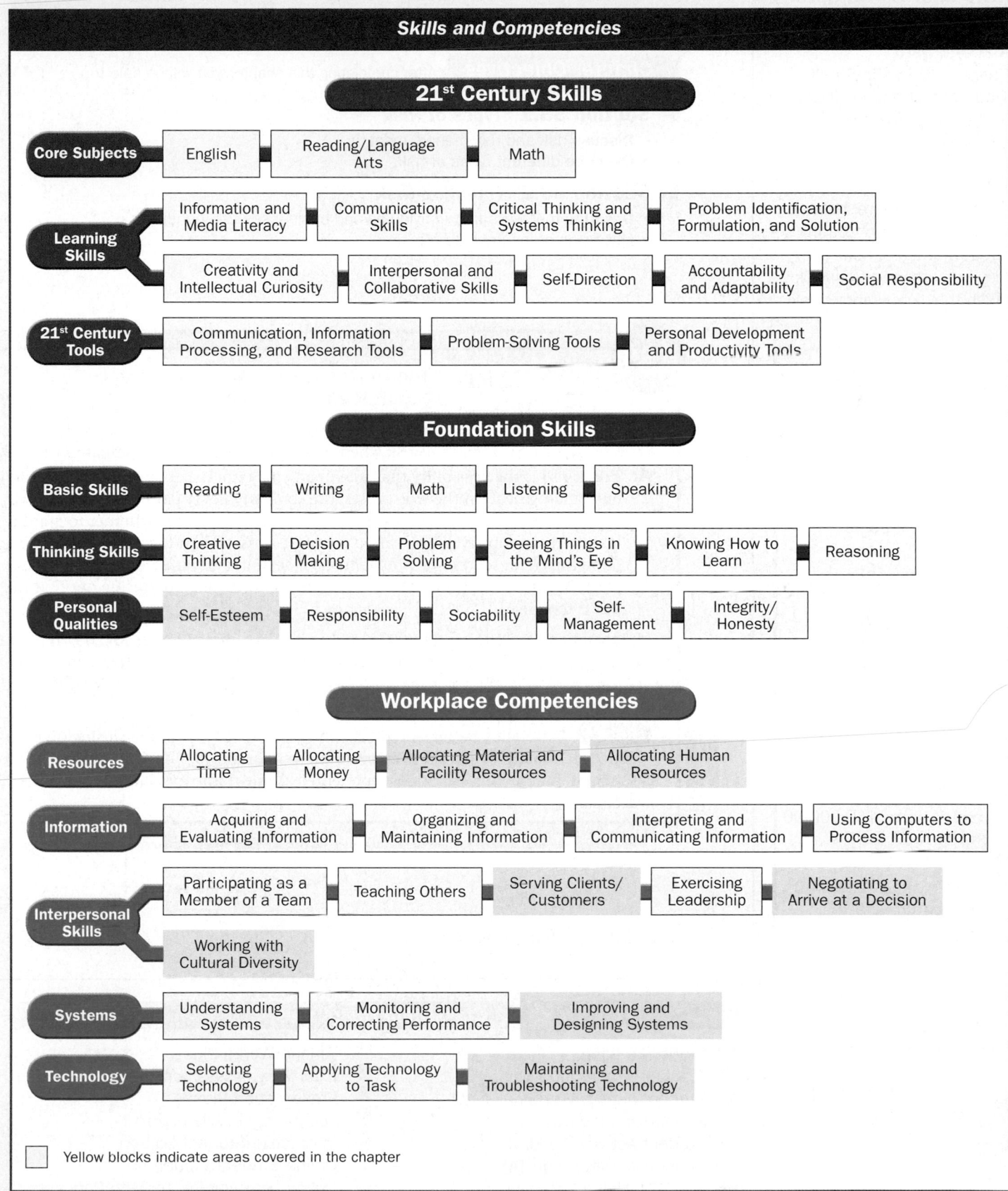

Skills and Competencies

21st Century Skills

Core Subjects
- English
- Reading/Language Arts
- Math

Learning Skills
- Information and Media Literacy
- Communication Skills
- Critical Thinking and Systems Thinking
- Problem Identification, Formulation, and Solution
- Creativity and Intellectual Curiosity
- Interpersonal and Collaborative Skills
- Self-Direction
- Accountability and Adaptability
- Social Responsibility

21st Century Tools
- Communication, Information Processing, and Research Tools
- Problem-Solving Tools
- Personal Development and Productivity Tools

Foundation Skills

Basic Skills
- Reading
- Writing
- Math
- Listening
- Speaking

Thinking Skills
- Creative Thinking
- Decision Making
- Problem Solving
- Seeing Things in the Mind's Eye
- Knowing How to Learn
- Reasoning

Personal Qualities
- Self-Esteem
- Responsibility
- Sociability
- Self-Management
- Integrity/Honesty

Workplace Competencies

Resources
- Allocating Time
- Allocating Money
- Allocating Material and Facility Resources
- Allocating Human Resources

Information
- Acquiring and Evaluating Information
- Organizing and Maintaining Information
- Interpreting and Communicating Information
- Using Computers to Process Information

Interpersonal Skills
- Participating as a Member of a Team
- Teaching Others
- Serving Clients/Customers
- Exercising Leadership
- Negotiating to Arrive at a Decision
- Working with Cultural Diversity

Systems
- Understanding Systems
- Monitoring and Correcting Performance
- Improving and Designing Systems

Technology
- Selecting Technology
- Applying Technology to Task
- Maintaining and Troubleshooting Technology

Yellow blocks indicate areas covered in the chapter

Introduce the Chapter

The Basics of Risk Management

Chapter 33 is about risk. Types of risk and strategies for handling risk are presented.

Building Background

Students are more inclined to take risks than to think about managing risk. They may be surprised to see how much they know about risk.

Ask STANDARD &POOR'S

》 Math Answer

Add up Danielle's debt: $1,800 + $6,200 = $8,000. Now divide her debt by her income: $8,000 ÷ $32,000 = 0.25. Since 0.25 < 0.31, she should be eligible.

》 Extension Activity

Provide the following information and ask students to calculate the debt-to-income ratio for each person listed. Which would qualify for a credit line if the bank's cutoff were 0.25?

Amanda earns $50,000.00 and her total debt is $1,000.00.

Declan earns $42,000.00 and his total debt is $16,800.00.

(The debt ratios are: Amanda, 0.020 and Declan, 0.400. Amanda would qualify.)

N C L B Activity correlates to Math standards.

The Basics of Risk Management

Chapter Objectives After completing this chapter, you will be able to:

▶ **Section 33.1** *Types of Risk*
- **Discuss** risk and risk management.
- **Describe** different types of risk.

▶ **Section 33.2** *Handling Risk*
- **Describe** four ways that individuals and businesses can handle risk.
- **List** types of insurance protection.

Ask STANDARD &POOR'S **The Basics of Risk Management: Credit Risk Assessment**

Q: How does a bank assess its risk when making a large loan to a company?

A: Credit risk is the possibility that a company may not make timely payments on its outstanding debt. In the worst cases, the company never pays back what it owes. Banks must assess a company's credit risk before they decide whether to grant a loan to the company. Using various credit risk assessment templates, banks determine the credit scores, the probabilities of default, and rating estimates of the company. Based on this information, they may grant the loan or decide not to if the risk is too great.

Mathematics Danielle has $1,800 in credit card debt and still owes $6,200 on her car. Her annual income is $32,000. She has requested a credit line from the bank. Before granting her the credit, the bank must calculate her debt-to-income ratio. If the bank's cutoff for granting credit is 0.35, will she be eligible?

N C L B **THEORY** **Calculating Ratios** A ratio is a comparison of two numbers using division. Ratios are usually written in simplest form, so the ratio "8 out of 10" is written 4 to 5, 4:5, or $\frac{4}{5}$. Sometimes a ratio is represented as one number as either a percent or a decimal.

Classroom Resources

- Student Edition
- Teacher Wraparound Edition
- Student Activity Workbook with Academic Integration
- Student Activity Workbook with Academic Integration TAE
- *Fast File*, Unit 11 Resources
- Inclusion in the Business Education Classroom

- TeacherWorks Plus
- *ExamView Assessment Suite*
- Presentation Plus!
- Vocabulary PuzzleMaker
- Interactive Student Edition
- Online Student Edition
- Online Learning Center with Podcasts

● **Managing Risk** Businesses face many different types of risk. **Why do you think it is important for people to know what risks a business might face?**

Chapter 33   The Basics of Risk Management   **587**

Review the Objectives
Introduce the chapter by reviewing the chapter objectives:

Section 33.1 *Objectives*
Discuss risk and risk management. (Because people and businesses cannot eliminate all risk, they must reduce and manage it. Risk management is the systematic process of managing risk to achieve objectives. It involves making choices that reduce opportunities for loss or injury.)

Describe different types of risk. (An insurable risk is a risk that can be insured. An uninsurable risk is risk that is not insurable because of the risk involved. A controllable risk can be controlled. An uncontrollable risk cannot be controlled.)

Section 33.2 *Objectives*
Describe four ways that individuals and businesses can handle risk. (Individuals and businesses can avoid risk, reduce risk, retain risk, and transfer risk.)

List types of insurance protection. (Life insurance offers protection for a family and relatives of a person after death. Property insurance covers damages or losses to property. Liability insurance covers damages that you can accidentally cause to someone else or to his or her property. Health insurance provides funds to pay bills in case of accident or sickness.)

Discuss the Photo
● **Managing Risk** Read the caption on the photo to students: Businesses face many different types of risk.

Ask students: Why do you think it is important for people to know what risks a business might face? (So that business owners can plan ways to manage risks.)

FOCUS

Types of Risk

Write the word *risk* on the board and ask students what kinds of risks businesses and individuals face. Ask a volunteer to record the responses on the board. Follow up by asking students how people and businesses deal with these risks. (Answers will vary. Students might mention car accidents, fire, and theft.)

Preteaching

Presentation Plus!

The Presentation Plus! CD provides visual teaching aids for this section.

PuzzleMaker

Use the Vocabulary PuzzleMaker to create a puzzle of the section's key terms. Students can complete the puzzle on paper or on a computer.

Graphic Organizer

Tell students to go to the Online Learning Center through **glencoe.com** for a printable graphic organizer. (Answers include—Insurable: auto accidents; Uninsurable: violent acts of nature; Controllable: polluting the environment; Uncontrollable: doing business in a foreign country.)

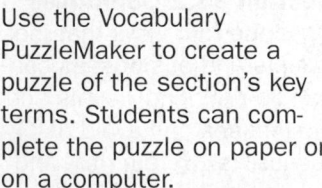 Connects academics to content.

Types of Risk

Reading Guide

● Before You Read

Think about the various types of risk that you face in your daily life.

D

Read to Learn
- Discuss risk and risk management.
- Describe different types of risk.

The Main Idea

Everybody faces risk that can lead to loss, injury, or even death. Individuals and businesses can use strategies to manage risk as ways to reduce or avoid loss.

Key Concepts
- Risk Management
- Types of Risk

Vocabulary

Key Terms
risk
risk management
insurable risk
insurance
uninsurable risk
controllable risk
uncontrollable risk
pure risk
economic risk
human risk
natural risk

Academic Vocabulary

You will find these words in your reading and on your tests. Make sure you know their meanings.
criteria
minimize
decade
occurences

Graphic Organizer

In a figure like the one below, give examples of each of the four types of risk.

Types of Risk	Examples
Insurable	
Uninsurable	
Controllable	
Uncontrollable	

 Go to the *Introduction to Business* Online Learning Center through **glencoe.com** for a printable graphic organizer.

Academic Standards

English Language Arts
   NCTE 1 Read texts to acquire new information

Mathematics
   Algebra Use mathematical models to represent and understand quantitative relationships

N C L B

Reading Guide

● Before You Read

Students might suggest driving or riding in a car, getting in an elevator, and darting across a street.

D Develop Concepts

The Main Idea Ask students: Why is it necessary to manage risk rather than to merely avoid it? (Answer will vary. Students should understand that some risk cannot be avoided.)

Risk Management

All people and businesses make decisions that create risk. A **risk** is the possibility of loss or injury. You face risk daily. Some types of risk may be easier for you to tolerate than others. For example, if you ride in a car, bus, train, or plane, you take the risk of having an accident. You can also fall down the stairs at home or at school. *Business risk* is risk that businesses specifically face, such as the potential for financial loss. You cannot eliminate all risk, but you can reduce and manage it. **Risk management** is the systemic process of managing risk to achieve your objectives.

✓ Reading Check **Define** What is risk?

Types of Risk

There are several different types of risk. Risk may be insurable or uninsurable, as well as controllable or uncontrollable. Risk can be further identified as pure, economic, human, or natural risk.

An **insurable risk** is a risk that meets an insurance company's **criteria** for insurance coverage. **Insurance** is paid protection against loss due to injury or property damage. Drivers who have vehicle insurance present insurable risk. **Uninsurable risk** is a risk that is unacceptable to insurance carriers because the likelihood of loss is too high. A store owner might have difficulty finding insurance for a shop that is located in a flood zone.

Figure 33.1 — *Planning to Manage Risk*

RISK

- Risk Planning
- Risk Identification
- Risk Assessment
- Risk Response
- Risk Reporting

● **Are You Prepared?** Being prepared to face risk is an important way for businesses to manage the possible consequences. **Which step do you think is most important?**

Figure 33.1

● **Are You Prepared?** Answers will vary, but planning is probably the most important step because it allows the other steps to proceed smoothly. Some students may feel that risk response is equally important because planning is useless without execution of those plans.

Discussion Starter
Managing Everyday Risks
Ask students what things they do every day to manage risk. (Answers will vary. Students might suggest locking their doors and windows, locking valuables in the trunk of a vehicle rather than leaving them on the seat of the car, and wearing seat belts.)

R Reading Strategy
List Types of Risk Ask students to make a list of types of risk. (Types of risk include insurable, uninsurable, controllable, uncontrollable, pure, economic, human, and natural risks.)

✓ Reading Check

Define Risk is the possibility of loss or injury.

Virtual Business
Introduce security to students using the Virtual Business Retailing Security activity. In this simulation, students learn why security is important to the success of a business.

TEACH (cont.)

S Skill Practice

Guided Practice

Define Ask students to define economic risk. (Economic risk occurs when there is likelihood of economic loss.) **L1**

Create a Table Ask students to create a two-column table with the three categories of economic risk in the left column and some examples in the right column. (The left column of the table should include personal risk, property risk, and liability risk.) **L2**

Create a Poster Ask students to create a poster related to economic risk. (Posters should expand on the concepts discussed in the text.) **L3**

ASSESS

Review Key Terms

Have students write sentences using each key term.

STUDY TO GO Study-to-Go

Have students go to the Online Learning Center through **glencoe.com** to download free **Study-to-Go** content to their PDAs or cell phones.

✔ Reading Check

Identify personal risks: illness, disability, unemployment; property risk: damage to or loss of property; and liability risk: potential losses to others that occur as a result of injury or damage you may have caused

---

? ETHICS in Business

Conduct in the Workplace

■ **Critical Reading** Life is full of important decisions. Think about the kinds of decisions that you make as you read the question below.

You are the head of the human resources department for a small company. Your company has experienced a rash of thefts. Several employees have mentioned their suspicions about one particular employee. However, no one has come forward with evidence against the employee.

■ **Decision Making** Should you confront this employee or conduct a search of his or her work area? What should you tell the police? Explain your answer.

● As You Read

Think about the losses businesses can incur from bad checks.

● As You Read

The business incurs a loss when the check is returned unpaid. The business also may be charged a service fee by its bank or incur other costs related to the pursuit of payment.

Controllable risk occurs when conditions can be controlled to **minimize** the chance of harm. Environmental damage is a controllable risk that, in many cases, can be prevented. An **uncontrollable risk** cannot be controlled. For example, risk involved in doing business in the global marketplace cannot be controlled.

Pure Risk

A **pure risk** is the threat of a loss with no opportunity for gain. If you drive a car, for example, you run the risk of being in an accident and suffering loss and/or injury. Your insurance company will not issue you funds for avoiding an accident. Therefore, if you avoid an accident, you do not have an opportunity for gain. Of course, you would still try to drive carefully and avoid accidents. Businesses run the risk of loss from employee theft, burglary, bad checks, and accidents involving customers and employees. Businesses do not receive insurance funds for avoiding financial losses due to these occurences. The purpose of insurance is to hedge against the risk of potential financial loss.

Economic Risk

Economic risk occurs when there is likelihood of economic loss. Even if you are very careful, you will not be able to avoid all risk. You can, however, protect yourself against economic loss. For businesses, economic risk results from changes in overall business conditions. If businesses fail to change their products when competitors offer more features, they may lose sales and face economic harm.

Economic risk can be related to property and to your own personal well-being. It can be placed in three categories: personal risk, property risk, and liability risk. *Personal risk* is risk associated with illness, disability, loss of income, unemployment, aging, and premature death. *Property risk* is the risk of damage to or loss of property due to theft, wind, fire, flood, or some other hazard. *Liability risk* is the potential for losses to others that occur as a result of injury or damage that you may have caused.

✔ Reading Check   **Identify** What are the categories of economic risk?

Human Risk

Human risk is the risk of harm caused by human mistakes, dishonesty, or another risk that is attributed to people. Risk may be caused by people who are careless or dishonest. A friend might

---

? ETHICS in Business

Decision Making False accusations can have a negative impact on a company. However, employing someone suspected of a crime might threaten everyone's safety and expose the company to legal risks. Investigation may be necessary, provided it is done discretely.

borrow something from you and damage or lose it. You might lose money to someone who snatches your wallet or purse. For businesses, human risk ranges from the financial impact of theft or embezzlement to job-related injury or illness.

Customer Dishonesty Human risk can be caused by customer theft, fraudulent payment, or nonpayment. Losses due to shoplifting are passed on to consumers through higher prices. Price increases are needed to pay for inventory shortages, security personnel, and the installation of theft prevention systems. Other examples of customer dishonesty include nonpayment of accounts or the use of stolen checks or credit cards.

Employee Risk Employees represent another human risk to businesses. Employees may cause loss. Companies depend on employees to do their job well. For example, commercial airlines prepare crews for emergencies caused not only by mechanical problems but also by human factors. If a flight attendant fails to keep an aisle clear, a passenger could trip and fall, break an arm, and sue the airline. Accidents like these can be financially devastating to a small business. The possibility of employee theft poses another risk to businesses.

Computer-Related Crime Over the past **decade**, computer-related crime has emerged as a significant new human risk to business. Malicious programs called computer worms or viruses can be inadvertently downloaded by employees and can wreak havoc on internal computer networks and communication systems. Hackers may break into computer systems to gain access or information for mischievous or criminal purposes.

● **Natural Disasters**
Damage from a tornado can be devastating. **What type of risk does a tornado represent?**

Types of Risk   **591**

Discuss the Photo
● **Natural Disasters** A tornado is a natural risk, over which people do not have control.

Section 33.1

RETEACH

U Universal Access
Learners with Dyslexia
Consider these tips on classroom management when a student has dyslexia:

1. Use instructional methods that provide structure, such as using lists to summarize, previews to pre-organize, and repetition to reinforce.

2. Use visuals and graphics to clarify the chapter content.

3. Provide frequent feedback.

4. Provide activities to enable students to put concepts and theory into practice.

W Writing Support
Enrichment
Employee Theft Ask students to locate and summarize a news article about employee theft. Consider asking students to include a copy or printout of the article. (Summaries will vary, depending on the article selected.)

R Reading Strategy
Summarize Ask students to summarize the content under the heading "Computer-Related Crime." (Summaries will vary but should include types of crimes, perpetrators, and ways to reduce computer-related crimes.)

Student Activity Workbook ☞ Assign the Section 33.1 Activities.

RETEACH (cont.)

C **Critical Thinking**

Explain
Natural Risk Ask students to explain why natural risk is often unavoidable. (Most natural risk is associated with weather, which is uncontrollable. People cause other forms of natural risk because their actions are also often uncontrollable.)

Weather Disasters
Answers include by implementing emergency evacuation procedures.

ASSESS

After You Read
Have students complete the Section 33.1 After You Read section review.

Online Study Tools
Have students go to the Online Learning Center through **glencoe.com** to:

- Take the Section 33.1 **Practice Test**.
- Download free **Study-to-Go** content to their PDAs or cell phones.

CLOSE

Culminating Activity
Discuss Risk
Organize students into small groups to discuss risks found in schools. Have students work as a class to consolidate their findings. (Students should understand that schools face most of the risk types.)

592

Computer crime is committed by many different kinds of people—from current or past employees to professional cyber thieves. Businesses can reduce computer crime by keeping computer networks secure and using passwords, encoded firewall programs, and virus detectors. Employees can be trained on privacy policies and proper handling of confidential information.

Crime Prevention People try to avoid risks associated with crime by taking precautions at home and in public. To protect against theft, many businesses install closed-circuit TV systems and point-of-service terminals that generate reports. They also thoroughly review job applicants. To protect against losses due to bad checks and credit cards, they use check-reader and credit-authorizer machines. Companies hire security guards and install high-quality locks, proper lighting, and alarm systems.

Natural Risk

A **natural risk** is the possibility of a catastrophe caused by a flood, tornado, hurricane, fire, lightning, drought, or earthquake. These natural **occurrences** can cause damage or loss of property. Some risk is caused by people and is also called natural risk. Power outages, oil spills, arson, terrorism, and even war are classified as natural risk.

Weather Disasters
The United States sustained 67 weather-related disasters between 1980 and 2005, in which overall damages and costs reached or exceeded $1 billion at the time of each event, according to the National Climactic Data Center. *How can businesses and people prepare for such disasters?*

N C L B Activity correlates to Math standards.

After You Read

Review Key Concepts
1. Why do businesses and individuals practice risk management?
2. What are the four main types of risk discussed in the chapter?
3. Describe some types of human risk.

Academic Skills
4. **Mathematics** Your auto insurance policy has a bodily injury ratio of 1:4. This ratio describes the relationship between the maximum coverage for individual bodily injury and all bodily injury. If the most the policy pays for individual bodily injury is $150,000, what is the most it will pay for all bodily injury?

THEORY **Ratios** A ratio is a comparison of two quantities. A ratio of 1:2 means one part of the first quantity to two parts of the other. If the first quantity is 10, find the second quantity by multiplying by 2 to get 20.

 For math help, go to the Math Appendix.

 Go to the *Introduction to Business* Online Learning Center through **glencoe.com** to check your answers.

Review Key Concepts
1. Both individuals and businesses face risk and use risk management strategies to prevent and reduce losses.
2. insurable, uninsurable, controllable, and uncontrollable
3. customer dishonesty such as theft, fraudulent payment, or nonpayment, employee dishonesty, and computer-related crimes

Academic Skills
4. **Mathematics** The ratio 1:4 as $150,000:x; x = $600,000. The total amount your insurance company would pay for bodily injury is $600,000.

Handling Risk

Reading Guide

D

● Before You Read

Think about what you do to handle the risk you face in your day-to-day life.

Read to Learn
- Describe four ways that individuals and businesses can handle risk.
- List types of insurance protection.

The Main Idea
Risk of loss be avoided, reduced, retained, or transferred. Insurance is a way to transfer the risk of loss to an insurance company, which agrees to cover you economically if certain types of risk result in a loss.

Key Concepts
- Handling Risk
- Insurance Protection

Vocabulary
Key Terms

premium   hazard
peril   insurance policy

Academic Vocabulary
You will find these words in your reading and on your tests. Make sure you know their meanings.

retain   undergo
mode   conversely

Graphic Organizer
In a figure like the one below, list and describe four ways individuals and businesses can handle risk.

Ways Businesses Handle Risk

 Go to the *Introduction to Business* Online Learning Center through **glencoe.com** for a printable graphic organizer.

Academic Standards
English Language Arts
NCTE 1 Read texts to acquire new information
NCTE 3 Apply strategies to interpret texts
NCTE 12 Use language to accomplish individual purposes
Science
Content Standard G Students should develop understanding of historical perspectives in science

N C L B

FOCUS

🔔 Bell Ringer Activity

Handling Risk
Write or project these words on the board: *avoid, reduce, retain,* and *transfer.* Ask students which of these is the best way to handle risk. (Answers will vary. Students should understand that there is no single way to handle all kinds of risk. Most people use a combination of these methods.)

Preteaching

Presentation Plus! 💿
The Presentation Plus! CD provides visual teaching aids for this section.

PuzzleMaker 💿
Use the Vocabulary PuzzleMaker to create a puzzle of the section's key terms. Students can complete the puzzle on paper or on a computer.

Graphic Organizer
Tell students to go to the Online Learning Center through **glencoe.com** for a printable graphic organizer. (Answers are to avoid risk, reduce risk, retain risk, or transfer risk.)

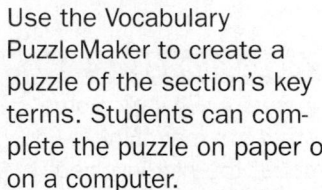

N C L B Connects academics to content.

Reading Guide

● Before You Read

Students might suggest wearing protective gear while playing sports and using virus protection software.

D Develop Concepts

The Main Idea Ask students: What are the four ways individuals and businesses can manage risk? (avoid, reduce, retain, and transfer risk) Follow up by asking how insurance helps manage risk. (Insurance is a way to transfer the risk of loss to an insurance company, which agrees to cover an insurance holder economically.)

Discussion Starter
Dealing with Risk
Ask students what life would be like if they avoided all types of risk. (Students should understand that it is impractical, and likely impossible, to avoid all risk. Even with precautions there is always the possibility of slipping in the shower, getting a paper cut, or being hit by lightning.)

R Reading Strategy

Provide Examples Ask students to provide some additional examples of risk avoidance from their personal life. (Examples related to individuals might include using anti-virus software, not giving personal information over the Internet, and not picking up hitchhikers.)

● As You Read

Answers will vary. Some students may think about the risk involved with driving or using public transportation. One way to lessen risk is to use seat belts. Some might think about other pure risks, such as crime. To avoid crime, they should mindful of their surroundings and protect themselves and their belongings.

● As You Read

Think about the ways that you can avoid risk.

Handling Risk

Since you cannot completely avoid all risk, you must learn to handle it. There are four ways to handle risk. You can avoid, reduce, **retain**, or transfer risk. Most people and businesses use a combination of all these methods.

Risk Avoidance

Avoiding risk involves thinking about the consequences of decisions. For example, you could avoid the risk of a train accident by never riding a train. However, this would eliminate a **mode** of transportation that is considered very safe. In many cases you can avoid risk, but sometimes it is not practical to do so. For a business, risk avoidance means refusing to engage in a particularly hazardous activity. For instance, market research can lead a business to conclude that investment in a product or service is not worth the risk. All business decisions should be made with consideration of the potential for benefit and for risk.

BusinessWeek *Reader and Case Study*

Winning the Game of Risk

Some pros say investors aren't paying enough attention to risk. Here are some smart steps to help protect your investments.

This may sound amazingly self-evident, but it's worth repeating: Investing is inherently risky. And too much risk may be hazardous to your financial health. Anyone who has ever watched a stock like Google® or General Motors execute a power-dive knows how much sudden downturns can hurt a portfolio.

But unless you wish to stash your assets in the Bank of Posturepedic, you will have to take on some risk as you put your money to work. The trick is to take on the right amount for your age and your financial circumstances.

It's not always easy, especially when financial market upswings can make investors complacent. Market veterans have increasingly warned against excessive risk. Most recently, bond-fund guru Bill Gross cited a possible downside in indexes he deems overvalued. "The crash of risk assets and their return to normalcy may be hard to time, but…these periods never end well," the PIMCO chief investment officer wrote in his latest monthly outlook.

How much risk is too much? "It's difficult to define," says Phil Edwards, managing director of Standard & Poor's Investor Services.

 CASE STUDY Go to the *Introduction to Business* Online Learning Center through **glencoe.com** for the *BusinessWeek* Reader Case Study.

Active Learning

Think about the risk you face every day—and the steps you take to minimize risk. Develop a poster about planning for a risk you think is controllable. Include five or more steps you take to control the risk.

BusinessWeek *Reader and Case Study*

Winning the Game of Risk

 CASE STUDY Have students go to the *Introduction to Business* Online Learning Center through **glencoe.com** to download a Case Study activity that corresponds to the article. The activity and answer key are also available on the TeacherWorks Plus CD.

Active Learning

Posters should demonstrate students' understanding of the way their choices can reduce risk in their lives.

Science/Tech**TRENDS**

Air Bags

Air bags are used for cushioning people or equipment. In automobiles, an air bag is known as a supplementary restraint system (SRS). Air bags distribute the force of a crash and reduce the chance that an occupant's upper body will strike the interior of the vehicle. There were air bags in airplanes as early as the 1940s. In the 1960s, U.S. inventor Allen Breed designed a "ball-in-tube" sensor for crash detection that would trigger the air bag. The first use of air bags in a production car was in 1973, but the majority of the market did not accept the technology. In 1984, the U.S. government required automakers to have air bags as standard equipment by 1989. The National Highway Traffic Safety Administration (NHTSA) mandated air bags in 1998.

Web*Quest*

Go to the *Introduction to Business* Online Learning Center through **glencoe.com** for links to Web sites where you can research how the technology of air bags has evolved over the years. Look for the pros and cons of air bags, and how technology is trying to eliminate the negative aspects of them. Write a paragraph about where air bag technology is headed.

Risk Reduction

Some risk cannot be avoided entirely. Instead you may need to practice risk reduction. For instance, your home should have smoke alarms and fire extinguishers. They can reduce the risk that a fire will cause damage. When you use equipment or tools, follow safety rules, wear protective glasses, and work in a properly designed work area to reduce the risk that you will be hurt.

Businesses practice risk reduction, too. For example, retail stores place electronic tags on expensive merchandise to discourage theft. This may not eliminate shoplifting, but it can reduce it. Business owners reduce risk by designing work areas to lower the chances of accidents or fire. They educate their employees about the safe use of equipment and keep safety equipment ready for use. Businesses also provide information about the correct use of products and warn customers about possible hazards.

Screening and Training Employees For most businesses, the best way to reduce risk from employee carelessness and incompetence is through effective employee screening, orientation, and training. Businesses screen applicants' backgrounds and check references. Some companies now require prospective employees to **undergo** drug testing before being hired. Drug abuse can increase human risk by making employees careless and more likely to ignore or forget safety rules.

Real World

Workplace Safety
The financial impact of workplace accidents is staggering. To manage this risk, businesses design work areas to avoid accidents. They also provide safety training. They try to address hazards before accidents occur. They comply with state and federal health and safety regulations and place first-aid kits throughout the workplace. *What are some things that companies can do to protect employees who work with hazardous materials?*

Section 33.2   Handling Risk   **595**

Real World

Workplace Safety Companies can protect employees who work with hazardous materials by providing protective clothing and equipment and training on the proper handling methods.

Science/Tech**TRENDS**

Web*Quest*

Air Bags Answers might describe how air bags are being tailored to the severity of the crash as well as the size and position of the occupant, or the use of multistage inflators that deploy with less force in moderate collisions.

RETEACH

R Reading Strategy

Define Ask students to use their own words to define shoplifting. (Shoplifting occurs when someone posing as a customer steals goods from a store during regular business hours.)

W Writing Support

Enrichment

Illustrate Risk Retention
Provide the following scenario: Marvin owns a lawn service and has three commercial mowers. He has decided not to insure the mowers against theft. Ask students to write a paragraph that illustrates risk retention in Marvin's case, using the textbook content as a guide. (Answers should indicate an understanding that Marvin has retained the risk and will pay the cost of replacing a mower if it is stolen.)

U Universal Access

Students with Hearing Impairments If you have students with hearing impairments, slow down your speech patterns, but do not use an unnatural, choppy style of pronunciation. Instead, use groups of words that make sense together. Then increase the length of pauses between groups of words and sentences. This will give students more time to process what they see and hear.

Student Activity Workbook ✎ Assign the Section 33.2 Activities.

596

R

Preventing Theft
Theft by employees and customers is one of the largest and most costly forms of human risk. *Shoplifting* is the act of stealing merchandise from a business. It is estimated that one-third of lost inventory is caused by shoplifting. Businesses often educate store employees about how to prevent it. They use adequate lighting and mirrors, and store expensive items in locked display cases to prevent theft. *What are some other ways that businesses can prevent theft?*

Risk Retention

W It may be impossible to avoid certain types of risk. Bearing financial responsibility for the consequences of loss is called *risk retention*. For instance, suppose that your watch is valuable, but you enjoy wearing it anyway. If you take your chances on losing or damaging it, you will have to pay to replace it if necessary. You have chosen to retain the risk of the economic loss that you will lose or damage the watch.

A business may retain the risk that customer tastes will change and merchandise will not sell. They can underestimate the risk and stock too much merchandise. If consumer demand for that merchandise changes, they may have a greater loss than planned.

✔ Reading Check **Define** What is risk retention?

Risk Transfer

Insurance provides a way to transfer a risk of loss to an insurance company. Insurance divides a possible loss among large numbers of people or companies. Economic risk is shared most effectively when many people or businesses are involved. Each individual or company then pays a fee for protection.

Insurance Protection

Insurance protection requires careful planning and decision making. Choosing the right insurance plan is an important step. Insurance companies provide almost any kind of insurance you might want. How do you make your insurance choices? You must look at your individual situation and then choose the protection that fits your needs.

With insurance protection, no one person or business has to bear a loss alone. A **premium** is the price an insured person or business pays for insurance protection for a specified period of time. Insurance works on the "principle of large numbers," which means many share a loss so that no one person or business carries all the risk.

U *Risk, peril,* and *hazard* are important terms in insurance. In everyday life, these terms have almost the same meanings. In the insurance business, however, each word has a distinct and special meaning. While risk is the chance of loss or injury, **peril** is anything that may possibly cause a loss. It is the reason someone takes out insurance. People buy insurance against a wide range of perils, including fire, windstorms, explosions, robbery, and accidents. **Hazard** is anything that increases the likelihood of loss through peril. For example, defective electrical wiring in a house is a hazard that increases the change that a fire will start.

✔ Reading Check

Define Risk retention is the act of retaining financial responsibility for the consequences of loss.

Preventing Theft Answers will vary. For example, businesses can prevent theft by using tamper-proof price tickets or electronic tags, and by hiring uniformed security guards to reduce losses from theft.

Individuals and businesses can insure property and people against potential loss by purchasing insurance policies. An **insurance policy** is a contract between a person and an insurance company to cover a specific risk. In return for the premium, or price for insurance coverage, the insurance company agrees to protect the policyholder against financial loss in case of an accident or loss that is covered in the policy.

C

Types of Insurance

There are several types of insurance for consumers. *Life insurance* offers protection for family members after someone dies. *Property insurance* covers damages or losses to your property. **Conversely,** *liability insurance* covers damages that you may have caused accidentally to someone else or to someone's property. *Health insurance* provides money to pay medical bills in case of accident or sickness.

Many businesses offer life and health insurance coverage to their employees. They also carry liability and property insurance to protect their property. Companies carry *workers' compensation insurance* to protect workers who are injured on the job. Workers' compensation insurance is required by the government and paid for by employees. It provides medical and income benefits to employees injured on the job. Job-related illnesses, such as carpal tunnel syndrome, are also covered.

Government Protection The federal government handles protection for some kinds of disasters or risk that private companies cannot cover. For example, lost crops or widespread destruction from floods or tornadoes can be costly. If necessary, the federal government can step in to declare a federal disaster area and provide financial aid. *What are some other ways that government helps people and businesses deal with financial risk?*

N C L B Activity correlates to English Language Arts standards.

Section 33.2

After You Read

Review Key Concepts
1. What are four ways to handle risk?
2. What is the difference between risk retention and risk transfer?
3. Identify some types of insurance.

Academic Skills

4. **English Language Arts** Look at the terms below. Cross out the one that does not belong with the others. Circle the term that could be used as the heading in a list with the others.

   liability   property damage
   bodily injury   safety

5. **English Language Arts** Write a letter to your state's commissioner of insurance asking for information on the minimum automobile insurance requirements for your state. Write a paragraph about the response you receive.

N C L B

 Go to the *Introduction to Business* Online Learning Center through **glencoe.com** to check your answers.

Section 33.2

Review Key Concepts
1. avoid, reduce, retain, or transfer risk
2. Risk retention: retaining financial responsibility for the consequences of loss. Risk transfer: transferring financial responsibility or a portion of it.
3. Life insurance protects a person's family. Property insurance covers property damage or loss.

Academic Skills
4. **English Language Arts** The term that does not belong is *safety*. The term that could be used as the heading is *liability*.
5. **English Language Arts** Paragraphs will vary but should explain what is required by law for automobile insurance as well as the consequences if the minimums are not met.

Section 33.2

RETEACH (cont.)

C **Critical Thinking**

Consider the Consequences

Insurance Protection Ask students to explain how insurers protect policyholders. (Students should understand that insurers cover all or part of the cost associated with a financial loss.)

Government Protection The federal government runs the Social Security and Medicare programs, which help older people.

ASSESS

After You Read

Have students complete the Section 33.2 After You Read section review.

Online Study Tools

Have students go to the Online Learning Center through **glencoe.com** to:
- Take the Section 33.2 **Practice Test**.
- Download free **Study-to-Go** content to their PDAs or cell phones.

CLOSE

Culminating Activity
Risk Management
Invite an insurance professional to speak to students about risk management. As a courtesy, provide a copy of your lesson plans relating to insurance to the speaker. (Answers will depend on the speakers' discussions.)

597

Vocabulary Review

1. Students should write complete sentences using each term correctly.

Review Key Concepts

2. Because people and businesses cannot eliminate all risk, they must reduce and manage it. Risk management is the systematic process of managing risk to achieve objectives. It involves making choices that reduce opportunities for loss or injury.

3. An insurable risk is a risk that can be insured. An uninsurable risk is risk that is not insurable because of the risk involved. A controllable risk can be controlled. An uncontrollable risk cannot be controlled.

4. Individuals and businesses can avoid risk, reduce risk, retain risk, and transfer risk.

5. Life insurance offers protection for the family and relatives of a person after death. Property insurance covers damages or losses to property. Liability insurance covers damages that you accidentally cause to someone else or to his or her property. Health insurance provides funds to pay bills in case of accident or sickness.

Section 33.1 Summary

Types of Risk Every person and business risks loss. Risk may be controllable or uncontrollable and insurable or uninsurable. Economic risk includes personal risk, property risk, and liability risk. Human risk caused by human mistakes or dishonesty is a particular problem for businesses. Natural risk caused by the weather can result in financial loss and damage.

Section 33.2 Summary

Handling Risk Risk can be avoided, reduced, retained, or transferred. Individuals and businesses try to avoid and reduce risk whenever they can, but some risk is inevitable. Both businesses and people can transfer risk. Insurance provides a way to transfer risk to an insurance company. Insurance enables a large number of people to share a possible loss.

Vocabulary Review

1. On a sheet of paper, use each of these key terms and academic vocabulary terms in a sentence.

Key Terms

risk
risk management
insurable risk
insurance
uninsurable risk
controllable risk
uncontrollable risk
pure risk

economic risk
human risk
natural risk
premium
peril
hazard
insurance policy

Academic Vocabulary

criteria
minimize
decade
occurrences

retain
mode
undergo
conversely

Review Key Concepts

2. Discuss risk and risk management.

3. Describe different types of risk.

4. Describe four ways that individuals and businesses can handle risk.

5. List types of insurance protection.

Critical Thinking

6. It is always best to consider possible risks and ways to avoid them.

7. Answers include using a buzzer to alert salespeople when someone enters a store, surveillance cameras, theft-deterrent packaging, electronic devices on items, and locked display cases.

8. Answers might include warning systems and disaster plans.

9. Economic risk is the chance of a financial loss because of an accident, fire, theft, unemployment, or other occurrence. Economic loss is financial loss because one of the risks is encountered.

10. Being careless will only drive up the cost of insurance. When losses increase, everybody pays larger insurance premiums.

Critical Thinking

6. Some people would rather take their chances than to try to avoid risk. Do you think this is a good or bad approach to risk?

7. What types of anti-shoplifting measures have you observed in stores?

8. Tornadoes, hurricanes, and floods have caused devastating losses in recent years. What do you think can be done to reduce losses from disasters?

9. Explain the difference between "economic risk" and "economic loss."

10. Some people do not take precautions to avoid risk because they think that their insurance company will reimburse them for any losses that they incur. What do you think?

11. How can businesses take precautions against customer dishonesty without offending their honest customers?

12. What advice would you give business owners to make their computer systems safer?

13. What problems can insurance companies face because of natural disasters?

Write About It

14. Research uninsurable risk. What types of risk are uninsurable? Why? Is there a way to avoid an uninsurable risk? In at least one page, discuss your answer.

15. In at least two paragraphs, discuss some of the safety measures that your school has in place to reduce the risk of loss or injury.

16. Many employees take company property for their personal use. Write a brief e-mail to your teacher about the impact this can have on a business.

17. One way to reduce risk is to increase safety. List guidelines for people to reduce their risk of property loss, injury, or death on the road.

18. Choose a business in your community. Research the risk that this type of business might encounter. Write at least two paragraphs on your findings.

19. An insurance agent helps people to identify the purposes of their insurance plan and develops a program for them. Research the job of insurance agent. Write a report on the qualities that a good insurance agent should have.

Technology Applications

Spreadsheet Software
20. Injuries and illnesses in the workplace can result in lost wages, increased medical expenses, and higher workers' compensation payments. Research the number of injuries and illnesses and their sources among U.S. workers. Prepare a spreadsheet and chart summarizing the information you obtain. Use the Internet or reference books in your library to find information.

Business Ethics

Should She Return the Check?
21. Imagine that someone broke into your friend Teresa's home and stole her jewelry box. Teresa files a police report as well as an insurance claim for the stolen items. In both reports, she lists several pieces of jewelry as stolen, including a diamond necklace insured for $1,000. In a few days, the insurance company issues her a check for $1,000. The following week, she finds the necklace hidden in a closet. What should she do?

Chapter 33 Review and Activities **599**

Critical Thinking

11. All customers should be treated respectfully. To customers who oppose the precautions, explain that they are observed with everyone as a way to keep track of inventory, which protects against higher prices.

12. Answers include anti-virus, firewall, and spyware-protection software, restricting access to the systems, and monitoring the systems.

13. Catastrophic losses from natural disasters can be so great that they can bankrupt some insurance companies. Some increase their policyholders' premiums to make up the costs.

Write About It

14. Almost every risk has a type of insurance to protect it. Costs escalate according to the degree of risk. Most insurance policies detail what is covered and what is not.

15. Answers will be based on your school's safety measures.

16. Students should understand that stealing costs companies money.

17. Answers should include safety guidelines.

18. Answers will depend on the business chosen.

19. Insurance agents must know about all types of insurance and know their customers well to make recommendations based on customers' needs and funds.

Technology Applications

20. In a recent year, the reported injuries were: sprains, 43.0%; bruises, 8.8%; cuts, 7.7%; fractures, 6.9%; heat burns, 1.5%; carpal tunnel syndrome, 1.6%; tendonitis, 0.6%; chemical burns, 0.6%; amputations, 0.6%; and traumatic injuries, 3.7%. Sources included chemicals, containers, furniture, fixtures, and machinery.

Business Ethics

21. Because the necklace has been returned, she will not incur economic losses. She should return the check.

599

Applying Academics to Business

English Language Arts

22. Work with a group of three or four students to research the different types of vehicle insurance coverage. Create an outline for a short presentation, and give it to the class.

Mathematics

23. You recently purchased a used car for $5,000 with help from a bank that loaned you the money with a 6% simple interest loan. If your insurance costs you $230 quarterly, how much will the insurance and interest cost you in the first year?

> **THEORY** **Problem Solving** Before solving a word problem, decide which operations you will use and how they relate to each other.

English Language Arts

24. Make a list of items you would want to have covered by insurance. Write a paragraph discussing why these items are important to you.

Mathematics

25. You are billed for insurance quarterly, or every three months. Your first bill gives you the option of paying the total or a lesser amount every month. If the total quarterly amount is $215 and the optional monthly amount is $79, what is the difference in the amount you would pay if you chose the monthly option?

> **THEORY** **Comparing Rates** In a problem such as this, you will need to choose whether to compare the cost on a monthly, quarterly, or yearly basis.

Active Learning

Attitudes About Risk

26. People have different ways of handling risk. Work in teams. Survey at least 10 people in your neighborhood or school about their attitudes toward risk. Which risk do they run each day at home, at school, or at work? What are some ways they avoid or reduce each risk? Compile your findings, and share the results with the class.

Business in the Real World

Sick-Leave Policies

27. Time off from work because of employee illnesses is a huge cost to businesses. Many companies have wellness policies in place to promote good health. Interview a local business owner about his or her sick-leave policy. Ask about the number of sick days each employee is granted. Does the business also offer exercise and fitness programs? Write a report of your findings, and share it with the class.

ExamView Assessment Suite **CD** allows you to print out ready-made unit and chapter tests, complete with answer keys. You can also create customized tests.

TeacherWorks Plus provides complete teacher resources in one convenient package. It includes customizable lesson plans in calendar format, and instant access to many print program resources.

Real LIFE skills

DEALING WITH UNCONTROLLABLE RISK

28. Suppose you have a retail store that sells imported furniture. Your main supplier is in a country that is undergoing major economic and political changes. These changes are being closely watched by your federal government, which may adjust its trade policies with the country. In one page or more, discuss the types of risk you might encounter and how to address them.

Business CAREERS

FIND YOUR DREAM JOB

29. Go to the *Introduction to Business* Online Learning Center through **glencoe.com** for a link to the Occupational Outlook Handbook Web site. Click on the "OOH Search/A-Z Index" link and enter the job title "insurance underwriter." Then write a one-page report about this type of occupation. Conclude your report with a list of things you could do now to prepare yourself to pursue the occupation.

Role Play

REDUCING RISK FROM HAZARDS IN THE SCHOOL

30. Situation You have been asked to present a plan for reducing risk at your school. With three of your classmates, prepare a list of risks and ways to reduce or eliminate them.

Activity As a group, create a presentation for your school administrators on risk and your suggestions for reducing or eliminating them.

Evaluation You will be evaluated on how well you meet the following performance indicators:

• Describe the process your group followed to identify risk in school.

• List the causes of various risks.

• Suggest ways to reduce or eliminate each risk.

• Prepare a written report using presentation software.

Standardized Test Practice

Directions Choose the letter of the best answer. Write the letter for the answer on a separate piece of paper.

1. Which best completes the sentence?

_____ insurance covers damage done to another person's vehicle or property.

  A   Collision
  B   Property damage liability
  C   Bodily injury liability
  D   Miscellaneous coverage

TEST-TAKING TIP When studying for a test, write important ideas, definitions, and formulas on flash cards. Make a tape of your notes. Use these tools to review and prepare for test day.

READING Go to the *Introduction to Business* Online Learning Center through **glencoe.com** for a list of outside reading suggestions.

glencoe.com

Real LIFE skills

28. The business owner would face the uncontrollable risks associated with doing business in the global marketplace. Either country may decide that it needs to reevaluate its trade policy. Your supplies could be affected. You should find other suppliers before your business is affected.

Business CAREERS

29. Insurance underwriters identify and calculate the risk of loss from policyholders, establish appropriate premium rates, and write insurance policies to cover the risk. A bachelor's degree is required for most positions and continuing education is necessary for advancement. Employment is expected to grow more slowly than average. As preparation, develop strong computer and communication skills.

Role Play

30. Presentations should address the competencies noted in the Role Play. Answers will vary. However, students should indicate an understanding of risk management.

Standardized Test Practice
   1. D

STRATEGIES FOR STANDARDIZED TEST PREP SUCCESS

Test Prep Encourage students to develop productive habits of mind when they study, such as comparing and contrasting ideas, looking for unusual connections between seemingly dissimilar concepts or events, and visualizing problems, idea, or relationships so that words and numbers do not get in the way. Thinking hypothetically (asking, "What if . . .?") and thinking metaphorically (saying, "This is like . . .") are also good techniques for learning and retaining challenging content.

Standards-Based Lesson Planning
Introduction to Business provides students with instruction and assessment in the following fundamental content areas:

Content Standards Correlations	
Examine the need for risk protection.	pp. 605–608, 610–613, 614–617
Compares and contrasts insurance policies.	pp. 605–608, 610–613, 614–617
Distinguish between the different forms of insurance.	pp. 605–608, 610–613, 614–617
Evaluate the major types of auto insurance available and the basis of costs.	pp. 605–608, 614–617
Evaluate property insurance costs and benefits to individuals and businesses.	pp. 605–608, 614–617
Calculates the monetary consequences of being uninsured.	pp. 610, 613, 615
Differentiates between coverage available on vehicle and property insurance.	pp. 605–608, 610–613, 614–617

NCLB
Activities, information, and skills practice will help your students attain No Child Left Behind proficiency. Students will improve their abilities in the following academic standards areas:

Academic Standards Correlations		
English Language Arts	Activities/Features	Page
NCTE 3 Apply strategies to interpret texts	Applying Academics to Business	p. 616
NCTE 8 Use information resources to gather information and create and communicate knowledge	Applying Academics to Business	p. 616
NCTE 11 Participate as members of literacy communities	After You Read	p. 613
Mathematics		
Data Analysis and Probability Formulate questions that can be addressed with data and collect, organize, and display relevant data to answer them	Applying Academics to Business	p. 616
Number and Operations Compute fluently and make reasonable estimates	Ask S & P After You Read Standardized Test Practice	pp. 602, 608, 617
Number and Operations Understand meanings of operations and how they relate to one another	Applying Academics to Business	p. 616
Science		
Content Standard E Students should develop understandings about science and technology	Science/Tech Trends	p. 610

Correlations   This chart shows the 21st Century Skills, foundation skills, and workplace competencies that students develop as they work in this chapter.

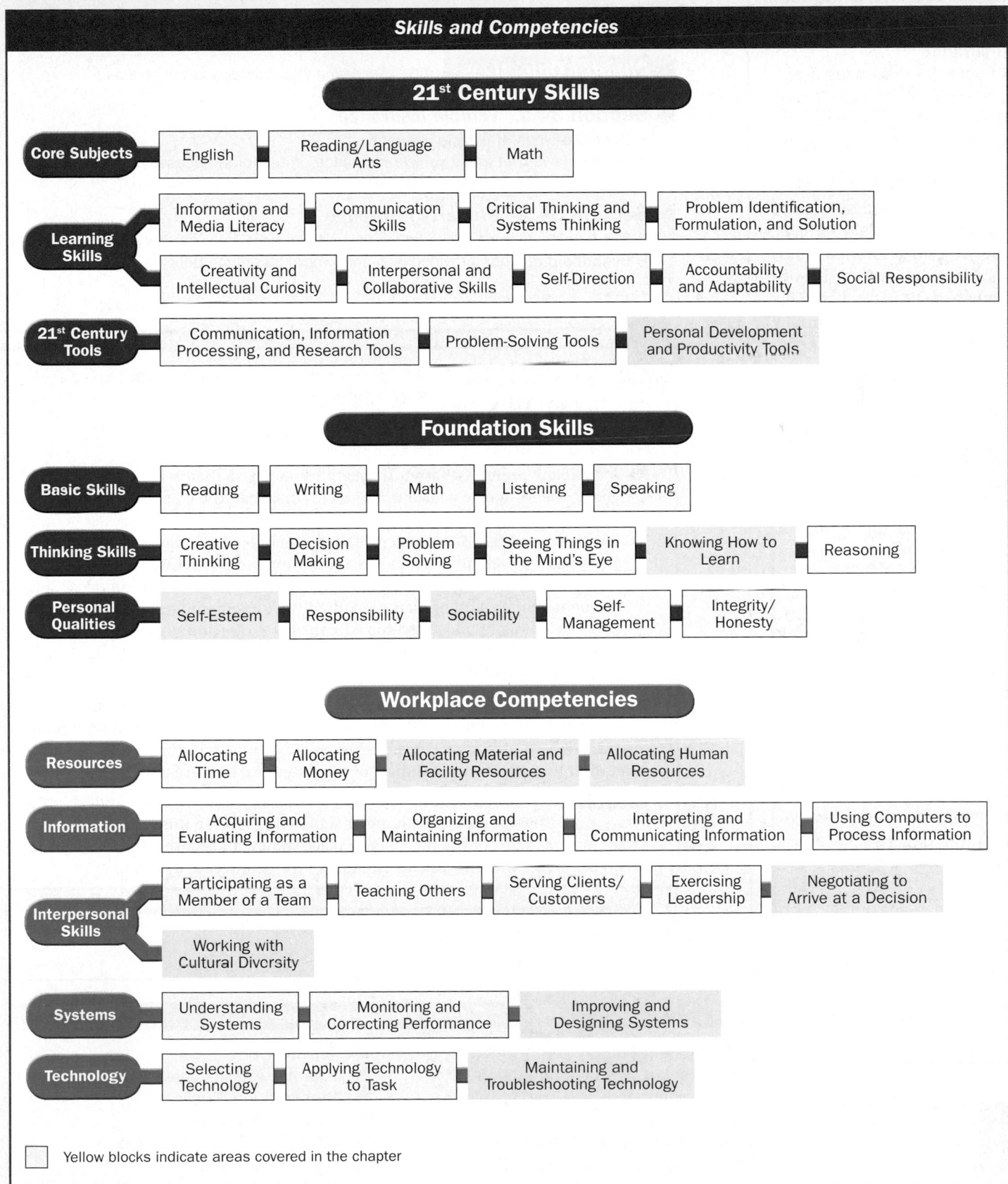

Skills and Competencies

21st Century Skills

Core Subjects
- English
- Reading/Language Arts
- Math

Learning Skills
- Information and Media Literacy
- Communication Skills
- Critical Thinking and Systems Thinking
- Problem Identification, Formulation, and Solution
- Creativity and Intellectual Curiosity
- Interpersonal and Collaborative Skills
- Self-Direction
- Accountability and Adaptability
- Social Responsibility

21st Century Tools
- Communication, Information Processing, and Research Tools
- Problem-Solving Tools
- Personal Development and Productivity Tools

Foundation Skills

Basic Skills
- Reading
- Writing
- Math
- Listening
- Speaking

Thinking Skills
- Creative Thinking
- Decision Making
- Problem Solving
- Seeing Things in the Mind's Eye
- Knowing How to Learn
- Reasoning

Personal Qualities
- Self-Esteem
- Responsibility
- Sociability
- Self-Management
- Integrity/Honesty

Workplace Competencies

Resources
- Allocating Time
- Allocating Money
- Allocating Material and Facility Resources
- Allocating Human Resources

Information
- Acquiring and Evaluating Information
- Organizing and Maintaining Information
- Interpreting and Communicating Information
- Using Computers to Process Information

Interpersonal Skills
- Participating as a Member of a Team
- Teaching Others
- Serving Clients/Customers
- Exercising Leadership
- Negotiating to Arrive at a Decision
- Working with Cultural Diversity

Systems
- Understanding Systems
- Monitoring and Correcting Performance
- Improving and Designing Systems

Technology
- Selecting Technology
- Applying Technology to Task
- Maintaining and Troubleshooting Technology

☐ Yellow blocks indicate areas covered in the chapter

Chapter 34

Chapter Overview

Introduce the Chapter

Vehicle and Property Insurance
Chapter 34 discusses real and personal property insurance with a focus on vehicle and homeowners insurance.

Building Background

Young drivers and soon-to-be drivers are generally familiar with vehicle insurance. They might not be as familiar with homeowners insurance. This chapter helps students put their knowledge in perspective and prepares them for the responsibility of protecting their property.

STANDARD &POOR'S

>> Math Answer
$1,300. To calculate using front-end estimation, change $2,348 to $2,300 and $3,652 to $3,600. Then subtract: $3,600 − $2,300 = $1,300.

>> Extension Activity
Ask students to use front-end estimation to estimate the total for the following sets of numbers

Set A: 2,968.18 + 4,341.73 + 3,720.53

Set B: 92,579.22 + 42,534.05

(Set A: 2,900.00 + 4,300.00 + 3,700.00 = 10,900.00)

(Set B: 92,000.00 + 42,000.00 = 134,000.00)

N C L B Activity correlates to Math standards.

Vehicle and Property Insurance

◄ Chapter Objectives After completing this chapter, you will be able to:

▶ **Section 34.1** *Vehicle Insurance*
- **Describe** types of vehicle insurance.
- **Identify** laws that make vehicle insurance protection a necessity.
- **Give** examples of factors that affect the cost of vehicle insurance.

▶ **Section 34.2** *Property Insurance*
- **List** some examples of insurance for real and personal property.
- **Describe** protection provided by homeowners insurance policies.

Ask

STANDARD &POOR'S **Vehicle and Property Insurance: Risk Management**

Q: How do companies protect themselves against risk?

A: A company protects its assets through insurance, so that in the event of an emergency, the insurance will cover the cost rather than the company. Depending on the function the company serves, different types of insurance are necessary or at least recommended for risk management and reduction. For example, environmental and pollution liability insurance is a necessity for contractors, wastewater treatment facilities, and the power industry. Other types such as worker's compensation, management liability, and primary casualty insurance are important to numerous companies. Companies must also consider the types of health insurance packages they will provide their employees. Of course, all of these insurance options carry heavy costs, but without them, a company could go under as a result of a single crisis.

Mathematics You are house shopping and are trying to choose between two different neighborhoods. Insurance for the house you looked at in the first neighborhood will cost $2,348, and for the one in the other neighborhood will cost $3,652. Use front-end estimation to make a quick estimate of the difference in these costs.

N C L B

THEORY **Front-End Estimation** Front-end estimation can be used to quickly estimate sums and differences before adding or subtracting. To use this technique, add or subtract just the digits of the two highest place values, and replace the other place values with zero. This will give you an estimate of the solution of a problem.

Classroom Resources

- Student Edition
- Teacher Wraparound Edition
- Student Activity Workbook with Academic Integration
- Student Activity Workbook with Academic Integration TAE
- *Fast File*, Unit 11 Resources
- Inclusion in the Business Education Classroom

- TeacherWorks Plus
- *ExamView Assessment Suite*
- Presentation Plus!
- Vocabulary PuzzleMaker
- Interactive Student Edition
- Online Student Edition
- Online Learning Center with Podcasts

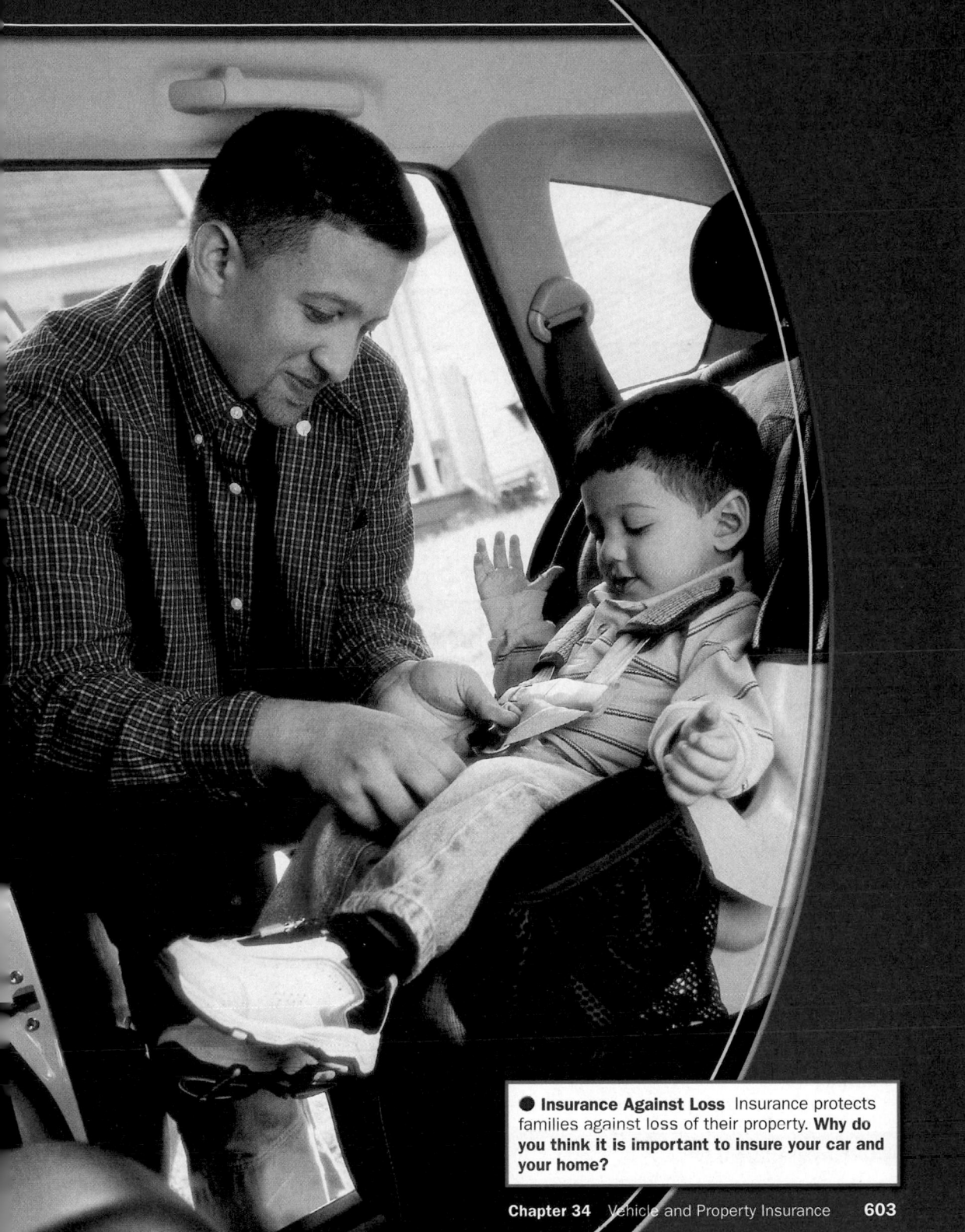

● **Insurance Against Loss** Insurance protects families against loss of their property. **Why do you think it is important to insure your car and your home?**

Chapter 34 Vehicle and Property Insurance **603**

Section 34.1 *Objectives*
Describe types of vehicle insurance. (The types of vehicle insurance that drivers can buy include personal liability, medical expense, uninsured/underinsured motorists, comprehensive, collision, and miscellaneous coverage.)

Identify laws that make vehicle insurance protection a necessity. (Most states have financial responsibility laws and compulsory insurance laws that make vehicle insurance protection mandatory.)

Give examples of factors that affect the cost of vehicle insurance. (Factors that affect the cost of vehicle insurance include the amount of money insurers pay each year in insurance claims; the type of vehicle; how the vehicle is used; where the vehicle is driven; age of the driver; and amounts of deductibles.)

Section 34.2 *Objectives*
List some examples of insurance for real and personal property. (Examples include renters insurance, standard fire policy, liability protection, additional living expenses coverage, and homeowners policies.)

Describe protection provided by homeowners insurance policies. (Homeowners policies combine four essential kinds of home protection into one, including protection for the structure of a home, personal belongings, liability, and additional living expenses coverage.)

Discuss the Photo
● **Insurance Against Loss** Read the caption on the photo to students: Insurance protects families against loss of their property.

Ask students: Why do you think it is important to insure your car and your home? (Answers will vary but students should understand that the loss of property can seriously endanger a family's financial stability. Insurance allows families the ability to protect themselves from this risk.)

FOCUS

Bell Ringer Activity

Vehicle Insurance
Ask: Why do drivers need vehicle insurance? (Even the safest drivers are sometimes involved in accidents.)

Preteaching

Presentation Plus!
The Presentation Plus! CD provides visual teaching aids for this section.

PuzzleMaker
Use the Vocabulary PuzzleMaker to create a puzzle of the section's key terms. Students can complete the puzzle on paper or on a computer.

Graphic Organizer
Tell students to go to the Online Learning Center through **glencoe.com** for a printable graphic organizer. (Answers include—bodily injury liability: injury to others; property damage liability: damage to another's vehicle or property; collision: damage to your vehicle; medical payments: medical costs for you and your passengers; comprehensive coverage: damage to your vehicle from sources other than auto accident; uninsured/underinsured motorist protection: protects you from damage from people who cannot pay; miscellaneous coverage: includes items like rental car insurance.)

N C L B Connects academics to content.

Vehicle Insurance

Reading Guide

Before You Read

Think about the reasons you would want to buy insurance for your vehicle.

Read to Learn
- Describe types of vehicle insurance.
- Identify laws that make vehicle insurance protection a necessity.
- Give examples of factors that affect the cost of vehicle insurance.

D

The Main Idea
With so many vehicles on our streets and highways, vehicle insurance is a necessity. Drivers must decide what types of coverage they need and can afford, and they have many decisions to make about their insurance needs.

Key Concepts
- Insuring Your Vehicle
- Laws on Vehicle Insurance
- The Costs of Insurance

Vocabulary
Key Terms

actual cash value	compulsory insurance law
depreciation	no-fault insurance
financial responsibility law	claim
	deductible

Academic Vocabulary
You will find these words in your reading and on your tests. Make sure you know their meanings.

issues	exceed
quote	vary

Graphic Organizer
In a figure like the one below, give reasons the following types of protection are important considerations in purchasing vehicle insurance.

Vehicle Insurance Protection	Reasons for Buying Coverage
Bodily Injury Liability	
Property Damage Liability	
Collision	
Medical Payments	
Comprehensive Coverage	
Uninsured/Underinsured Motorists Protection	
Miscellaneous Coverage	

 Go to the *Introduction to Business* Online Learning Center through **glencoe.com** for a printable graphic organizer.

Academic Standards
English Language Arts
> **NCTE 1** Read texts to acquire new information
> **NCTE 9** Develop an understanding of diversity in language use across cultures

Mathematics
> **Number and Operations** Compute fluently and make reasonable estimates

---

Reading Guide

Before You Read

to protect yourself and your passengers in the event of an accident

D Develop Concepts

The Main Idea Ask students: Why is vehicle insurance a necessity? (Most states require it. It is costly to repair a damaged vehicle or to cover medical costs resulting from an accident.)

Insuring Your Vehicle

Not only does being a safe driver benefit everyone on the road, but having vehicle insurance also provides protection in a number of situations.

There are several ways drivers can reduce the risk of financial losses that result from accidents. One way is to buy insurance, paid protection against losses due to injury or property damage. To get insurance, the driver purchases a policy from an insurance company. The policy explains how much and what kinds of protection he or she has. The company that **issues** the policy is the *insurer,* and the buyer of the policy is the *policyholder.*

Types of Vehicle Insurance

The type and amount of protection you have with an insurance policy depends on how much you are willing to pay. Vehicle insurance offers seven types of protection:

- bodily injury liability coverage
- property damage liability coverage
- collision insurance coverage
- medical payments coverage
- comprehensive coverage
- uninsured/underinsured motorists protection
- miscellaneous coverage

The most basic type of coverage (required by most states) is *liability insurance.* Liability insurance protects vehicle owners from claims of injury or property damage to others in case they are held responsible for an accident. A driver should at least have liability insurance and then add other types of coverage. An insurance agent can help you choose the protection you need.

✔ Reading Check **Identify** What are the seven types of vehicle protection?

Bodily Injury Liability Coverage Bodily injury liability insurance covers injuries to someone else. All drivers must have this type of coverage. The policy states the amount of protection in thousands of dollars. One figure applies to injuries to one person, and the second is a total for one accident. For 100/300 bodily injury coverage, the insurer pays up to $100,000 for injuries to one person. For one accident, insurance pays claims up to a total of $300,000. A good rule is to buy as much coverage as you can afford. Once you have basic insurance, it does not cost that much to increase protection.

International Business

Lloyd's of London

Lloyd's of London is one of the most recognizable names in the world of insurance. Lloyd's is known for its ability to insure almost anything including dancers' legs and pianists' hands. Lloyd's is actually a centuries-old insurance exchange. It began in Edward Lloyd's coffee house in 1688 in London. Today, Lloyd's provides insurance through a network of underwriting syndicates, a form of insurance company. Individuals who independently assume a portion of the losses fund these syndicates. This separates Lloyd's from most of its competitors because it is neither a company nor a corporation, but an insurance and reinsurance market.

Examples of Languages Across Cultures

Q: In French, how do you say: "That's too bad!"

A: C'est dommage! (pronounced: say dōmazhe)

What types of policies does Lloyd's issue? What are some of the more unusual policies they have written?

TEACH

Discussion Starter
Insuring Your Vehicle
Start a discussion by asking students why they might need vehicle insurance. (Answers will vary. Students might point out that it is required by law. They also might suggest that repairing damage to cars, other structures involved in accidents, and paying for medical costs due to injury can be expensive.)

R Reading Strategy

Paraphrase Ask students to use their own words to describe the terms *insurer* and *policyholder.* (Students should understand that the insurance company that issues the policy is the "insurer" and the person who buys the policy is the "policyholder.")

✔ Reading Check

Identify The seven types of vehicle insurance coverage are bodily injury liability; property damage liability; medical payments; collision coverage; comprehensive damage; uninsured and underinsured motorists protection; and miscellaneous coverage.

International Business

Lloyd's of London Students should indicate that Lloyd's syndicates write a wide range of policies. One of the more unusual ones included Tina Turner's legs, but the syndicate was also largely responsible for the rebuilding of San Francisco after the devastating 1906 earthquake and fire. They are reportedly considering ways to insure space travel.

TEACH (cont.)

S Skill Practice

Guided Practice

Create a Table Have students create a two-column table for the types of protection offered by vehicle insurance giving types and explanations. (Tables should include the basic information presented in the textbook.) **L1**

Identify Ask students to locate a newspaper article about a vehicle crash. Have them identify the types of protection offered by vehicle insurance that cover the accident costs. (Answers will depend on the article.) **L2**

Illustrate an Idea Have students create an illustration of types of vehicle insurance protection. Students should label their displays to illustrate the liability coverage concepts. (Displays should illustrate bodily injury and property damage liability, and collision insurance. Encourage students to use photos from the newspaper in their illustrations.) **L3**

ASSESS

Review Key Terms

Have students write sentences using each key term.

Study-to-Go Have students go to the Online Learning Center through **glencoe.com** to download free **Study-to-Go** content to their PDAs or cell phones.

● **Policies and Premiums** The amount of coverage and deductibles determines the cost of your premium. **If the policyholder has a claim under collision coverage, how much must the policyholder pay out of his or her own pocket before the insurance company pays?**

Figure 34.1 – **Vehicle Insurance**

Coverage	Limits
Personal Liability (per accident)	$500,000
Medical Expense	$5,000
Uninsured/Underinsured Motorists	$500,000
Comprehensive	$50 deductible
Collision	$500 deductible
Towing	$50
Rental Reimbursement	$26 a day/maximum of $900

Property Damage Liability Coverage Property damage liability insurance covers damage to another person's vehicle or other property caused by the insured. All drivers should have property damage liability insurance. A policy might **quote** all liability limits together. The figure 100/300/50 means the insurer will pay $100,000 for injuries to one person, a total of $300,000 for one accident, and $50,000 for property damage. **Figure 34.1** shows an example of types and amounts of coverage for a policyholder.

Collision Insurance Coverage While property damage liability insurance covers damage to someone else's vehicle, collision insurance covers damage to the policyholder's vehicle. The maximum amount covered is based on the **actual cash value** of the policyholder's vehicle, which is the value of the automobile when it was new minus depreciation. The actual cash value of a vehicle is the amount it is worth used. **Depreciation** is the decline in value of an asset, such as a house, equipment, or a vehicle, because of use.

S

Medical Payments Coverage Medical payments coverage is also called personal injury protection. It covers injuries to drivers and anyone else in their vehicle to pay medical bills.

Comprehensive Coverage Comprehensive insurance covers damage to a policyholder's vehicle caused by things other than an auto accident. It covers losses from falling objects, theft, flood damage, vandalism, and other causes. Comprehensive coverage cannot **exceed** the actual cash value of a policyholder's vehicle.

Uninsured/Underinsured Motorists Protection This coverage protects drivers from people who cause accidents but cannot pay for the damages. With this coverage, anyone riding with you is also protected. It also protects you if you are hit by a vehicle while walking or if you are in an accident caused by a hit-and-run driver. Most states require this coverage.

● **As You Read**

Think about why some states require drivers to buy coverage against people who have little or no vehicle insurance.

606   Chapter 34   Vehicle and Property Insurance

Figure 34.1

● **Policies and Premiums** The policyholder would pay a $500 deductible for collision coverage. Follow up with the following: After a crash, the policyholder rents a car for 15 days at a total cost of $600. How much will the insurance company pay to reimburse the policyholder for the car rental? ($390; it pays just $26 per day)

● **As You Read**

Before these laws were enacted, there were high rates of accidents involving uninsured and underinsured drivers, including hit-and-run accidents.

Miscellaneous Coverage Drivers can add other types of protection to their policies, such as coverage for a rental car. Vehicle owners must also add insurance to cover someone else who uses their car. People who are required to drive a vehicle for their job can add that vehicle to their policy. Those who ride motorcycles, motor scooters, or snowmobiles need insurance, too. Most policies will not cover damages caused as a result of racing.

Laws on Vehicle Insurance

Vehicle insurance laws **vary** from state to state. All states have some form of financial responsibility law. A **financial responsibility law** requires drivers to pay for any damages or injuries they cause in an accident. Most states also have some form of compulsory insurance law. A **compulsory insurance law** requires drivers to have a minimum amount of car insurance. With **no-fault insurance**, drivers involved in accidents collect damages from their own insurer no matter who is at fault.

BusinessWeek *Reader and Case Study*

The Fixer-Upper Fixes Up

Ralph Kastner had both planning and luck on his side. When he started Tuff Equipment Rentals in 1999, he drew up a hurricane plan. He had flood insurance as well as coverage for the replacement value of his equipment. Now Kastner's particular service—renting small equipment—has become one very hot niche.

Kastner wasn't feeling so lucky when, four days after Katrina, he returned to his 5,000-square-foot office and showroom in Slidell, Louisianna, near Lake Pontchartrain. Although he had moved much of his inventory to higher ground, more than half of his equipment, from backhoes to rental cars, was underwater. Thick sludge covered the floor. Kastner had $2.5 million in equipment and vehicle damage and $200,000 in building damage. "The main thing I was thinking was: 'How hard is it going to be to come back from this?'" says Kastner.

Kastner began a cleanup that would last eight weeks. But his customers wouldn't wait. He set up his 24-person, $3 million company in a 12-by-60-foot trailer and started filling out orders by hand because the computers weren't working. Kastner ordered replacement equipment and placed new orders for gear people would need to repair and rebuild their houses: power washers and boom lifts to raise people up so they can fix buildings or cut trees. To stay open, he took $200,000 from his company's cash flow and borrowed $175,000 from a home-equity line of credit. He spent $75,000 on computers and telephones—things he was surprised to find his insurance didn't cover.

 CASE STUDY Go to the *Introduction to Business* Online Learning Center through **glencoe.com** for the *BusinessWeek* Reader Case Study.

> **Active Learning**
>
> Research the extent of different kinds of insurance policies. Write an e-mail to your teacher explaining how the fees vary with differences in coverage and deductibles.

glencoe.com

Section 34.1 Vehicle Insurance **607**

RETEACH

W **Writing Support**
Enrichment
Insurance for Repairs Ask students to use library or Internet research to learn how "aftermarket parts" relate to vehicle insurance. Ask students to write a short report on their findings. (Aftermarket parts are parts that are not produced by the original equipment manufacturer. Most states have rules regarding the use of aftermarket parts when an insurance company is paying for the repair.)

R **Reading Strategy**
Explain Ask students to explain the concept of an "underinsured" motorist. (An underinsured motorist has vehicle insurance but the policy does not provide enough coverage to pay for all the costs resulting from a crash.)

Student Activity Workbook Assign the Section 34.1 Activities.

BusinessWeek *Reader and Case Study*

The Fixer-Upper Fixes Up

CASE STUDY Have students go to the *Introduction to Business* Online Learning Center through **glencoe.com** to download a Case Study activity that corresponds to the article. The activity and answer key are also available on the TeacherWorks Plus CD.

> **Active Learning**
>
> In their e-mails, students should incorporate an assessment of how different fees are associated with differences in coverage and deductibles.

RETEACH (cont.)

C Critical Thinking

Explain

Insurance Premiums Have students explain why insurance premiums vary. (Students should describe the many factors involved in determining premiums.)

Insurance Costs Lack of driving experience is one reason premiums are higher for teens.

ASSESS

● After You Read

Have students complete the Section 34.1 After You Read section review.

Online Study Tools

Have students go to the Online Learning Center through **glencoe.com** to:

- Take the Section 34.1 **Practice Test**.
- Download free **Study-to-Go** content to their PDAs or cell phones.

CLOSE

Culminating Activity

Insurance Laws

Organize students into small groups. Ask students to research vehicle insurance requirements in your state and prepare a guide to vehicle insurance. (Guides should incorporate current laws.)

 Activity correlates to Math standards.

608

Real World

Insurance Costs Several factors affect the cost of insurance, including the amount of insurance claims paid, coverage, and the deductible as well as the type of coverage. Other factors include the type of vehicle, uses of it, where it is driven, and the driver's age. For instance, premiums are higher for teen drivers than for older drivers. A driver with a safe driving record may qualify for a discount on premium costs. *Why do you think premium costs are higher for teens?*

The Costs of Insurance

A **claim** is a request for payment from an insurer for any damages covered by a policy. The more money insurance companies pay in claims, the more they charge for insurance to make up for it.

Insurance Premiums

The premium an insurance company charges a policyholder covers the policyholder for a limited period of time. The amount of a premium depends on characteristics of the driver and the vehicle, different policy provisions, and other factors. At the end of the period, the policy can usually be renewed. The insurance company may cancel a policy or refuse coverage for someone with a record of accidents.

Deductibles

Most collision insurance has a deductible. A **deductible** is an amount in damages a policyholder must pay before the insurance company pays a claim. For example, suppose you get into an accident and it costs $700 to repair the damage to your car. If your deductible is $200, you must pay $200 of the damages, and the insurer will pay the other $500. Deductibles make drivers responsible for small losses. Insurance helps pay for larger losses.

Section 34.1

● After You Read

Review Key Concepts

1. Identify seven types of vehicle insurance coverage.
2. List and describe three types of laws that affect vehicle insurance.
3. What factors affect the cost of vehicle insurance?

Academic Skills

4. **Mathematics** Several years ago, Stacy bought a home for $123,000. This year, she insured it for 150% of the purchase price. If the home is destroyed, how much will she receive from her insurance company?

THEORY **Percents Greater than 100**
Convert a percent greater than 100 to a decimal in the same way you convert any percent. Multiply the percent by 100 by moving the decimal point two places to the left.

 For math help, go to the Math Appendix.

 Go to the *Introduction to Business* Online Learning Center through **glencoe.com** to check your answers.

Section 34.1

Review Key Concepts

1. See page 605.
2. Financial responsibility: drivers pay for damages or injuries they cause. Compulsory insurance: drivers have a minimum amount of car insurance. No-fault insurance: drivers involved in accidents collect damages from their own insurance companies.

3. amounts and types of coverage, amount of deductible, type of vehicle, use of and where vehicle is driven, driver's age and driving record

Academic Skills

4. **Mathematics** 150% = 1.5
   1.5 * $123,000 = $184,500

Property Insurance

Reading Guide

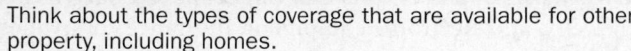

Before You Read

Think about the types of coverage that are available for other property, including homes.

Read to Learn

- List some examples of insurance for real and personal property.
- Describe protection provided by homeowners insurance policies.

The Main Idea

D Property owners can buy insurance to protect their real property, such as a house or business, and their personal property, such as furniture, jewelry, and equipment. Insurance companies write policies for homeowners, renters, and business owners to protect against many kinds of risk.

Key Concepts

- Insuring Your Property
- Homeowners Policies

Vocabulary

Key Terms

real property
personal property
renters insurance
standard fire policy
extended coverage
homeowners policy
rider
replacement value

Academic Vocabulary

You will find these words in your reading and on your tests. Make sure you know their meanings.

consists   civil
injured   nuclear

Graphic Organizer

In a figure like the one below, give reasons the following types of protection are important considerations in purchasing property insurance.

Property Insurance Protection	Reasons for Buying Coverage
Renters Insurance	
Standard Fire Policy	
Liability Protection	
Additional Living Expenses	
Business Insurance	
Homeowners Policy	

 Go to the *Introduction to Business* Online Learning Center through **glencoe.com** for a printable graphic organizer.

Academic Standards

English Language Arts
   NCTE 1 Read texts to acquire new information
   NCTE 11 Participate as members of literacy communities
Science
   Content Standard G Students should develop understanding of science as a human endeavor

---

Reading Guide

Before You Read

Students might mention coverage for real property and personal property. They might mention renters insurance, fire insurance, liability protection, and homeowners policies.

D Develop Concepts

The Main Idea Ask students: Who buys property insurance? (Property owners including homeowners, renters, and business owners buy property insurance.)

TEACH

Discussion Starter
Insuring Your Property
Start a discussion by asking why people buy insurance to protect their property. (Students might suggest that property insurance protects the property owner by paying some or all of the costs to replace or repair property that is lost or damaged by disasters, accidents, theft, and vandalism.)

R Reading Strategy

Distinguish Ask students to distinguish real property from personal property. (Real property is property attached to land, such as a house, business, garage, or other building. Personal property consists of possessions that can be moved, such as furniture, jewelry, and electronic equipment. Students might suggest that the contents found inside of a structure would be personal property.)

✔ Reading Check

Contrast Real property is property attached to land whereas personal property can be moved.

Real World

College Bound Renters should keep records for personal property such as a computer, jewelry, and clothing. They should list their personal property and assess the value of each item that they want to insure before contacting an insurance company.

610

Insuring Your Property

Each year property is destroyed by earthquakes, fires, and other disasters. Property is also destroyed or damaged by lesser causes, such as accidents, theft, and vandalism. Property insurance provides protection from financial loss on property.

Types of Property Insurance

R The two kinds of property you can insure are real property and personal property. **Real property** is property attached to land, such as a house, business, garage, or other building. **Personal property** consists of possessions that can be moved, such as furniture, jewelry, and electronic equipment. Insurance companies offer different kinds of protection for real and personal property.

✔ Reading Check **Contrast** What is the difference between real property and personal property?

Renters Insurance Suppose you live in an apartment. Your possessions inside the apartment are worth about $10,000. The owner of the building will probably have property insurance, but the owner's insurance will not pay for loss or damage to your personal property. Apartment renters can buy **renters insurance**, which covers loss or damage to a renter's personal possessions. Renters insurance covers items such as TVs, large appliances, and furniture. It can also include liability protection in case someone is **injured** in a renter's apartment. The cost of renters insurance depends on the amount of coverage, the type of the building, and the location of the apartment.

Real World

College Bound If your plans include college after high school and you will live off campus, you should consider renters insurance. *What steps do you need to take before getting renters insurance?*

Science/Tech TRENDS

Autonomous Underwater Vehicles
Autonomous underwater vehicles or AUVs are unmanned, robotic vehicles used to explore oceans. Around 200 AUVs have been built since the mid-1970s. The main purpose of AUVs is to carry a payload. The type of payload depends on the mission. However, it can include things such as instrumentation to map the sea floor or equipment needed by underwater pipelines. Scientists use cameras in conjunction with AUVs to discover evidence of ancient civilizations on the sea floor.

Web Quest

Go to the *Introduction to Business* Online Learning Center through **glencoe.com** for links to Web sites where you can research the applications of AUVs. Write a few paragraphs about other underwater vehicles and how they compare with AUVs. Then describe a business start-up idea using AUVs to provide a service.

Science/Tech TRENDS

Web Quest

Autonomous Underwater Vehicles
Paragraphs might describe such things as submersibles, remotely operated vehicles, and towfish. Business ideas might include underwater agriculture in freshwater lakes or the mining of valuable ores.

N C L B Activity correlates to Science standards.

● **Property Damage** Fires are the number one cause of property damage to homes. **How does property insurance protect homeowners?**

Standard Fire Policy Property owners can buy individual insurance policies to protect themselves against specific types of threats. Fires pose the greatest threat to property. They account for a large share of all property damage in the United States. Many people buy a **standard fire policy** to insure against damage due to fire or lightning. A policyholder can add other types of protection to this basic policy with **extended coverage**.

Liability Protection Liability insurance protects property owners from the costs of injuries to others on their property. It pays for two things: actual damages for which property owners are held liable, such as medical expenses, and legal expenses for the accident in case they are sued.

Coverage for Additional Living Expenses Additional living expenses insurance provides coverage for the cost of renting another place to live if a home is damaged. The amount of coverage might be limited to 10 percent or 20 percent of the coverage on your home. If the coverage on your home is $150,000, additional living expenses insurance may cover only up to $15,000 or $30,000 of your costs while you live somewhere else. The length of time you are covered might also be limited to six months or a year.

Business Insurance Business owners need property insurance just like renters and homeowners. Business owners can get insurance to cover the costs of property. They can also get liability insurance to protect themselves from claims by anyone injured on the premises. It is especially important for business owners to carry insurance because of the potential loss of income if they have to close for a while.

● **As You Read**

Think about liability protection for a business you may own one day. What other kind of liability protection might you consider other than insurance for injuries of employees or customers?

Section 34.2 Property Insurance **611**

Discuss the Photo
● **Property Damage** Property insurance covers losses to homes from such risks as fire.

● **As You Read**

Product liability insurance would protect your business against losses from injuries sustained by products you produce.

Section 34.2

TEACH (cont.)

S Skill Practice
Guided Practice
Explain Ask students to explain who is protected by liability insurance. (the policyholder from the costs of injuries to others on their property) **L1**

Describe Ask students to describe the two things that liability insurance covers. (the actual damages for which the property owner is held liable and legal expenses in case the injured person sues) **L2**

Investigate Have students use library or Internet resources to determine why a homeowner should consider calling his or her insurance agent before starting construction on an in-ground backyard swimming pool. Lead a classroom discussion related to liability insurance for swimming pools. (Calling the agent can help the homeowner determine if the insurance premium will go up and if the policy's coverage is adequate.) **L3**

ASSESS

Review Key Terms
Have students write sentences using each key term.

 **Study-to-Go**
Have students go to the Online Learning Center through **glencoe.com** to download free **Study-to-Go** content to their PDAs or cell phones.

611

RETEACH

U **Universal Access**

Students with Visual Impairments Students with visual impairments often have difficulty seeing text or images on the screen when using a computer. First, be sure the student's eyes are the correct distance from the monitor. Increasing the size of the font (type size) may help. Use the zoom feature to enlarge text and images. It may also be helpful to change the screen contrast and to choose color combinations that are distinct.

W **Writing Support**

Enrichment

Benefits of Insurance Ask students to write an example of a situation where a homeowner might benefit from having property insurance and the outcome of a scenario with and without property insurance. (Examples will vary but a specific situation should be described and alternative outcomes considered.)

R **Reading Strategy**

Create a Table Ask students to create a two-column table. Instruct them to list the four types of protection offered by a homeowners policy in the left column and a brief explanation in the right column. (Tables will vary, but should include the information discussed in this textbook.)

Student Activity Workbook 📄 Assign the Section 34.2 Activities.

612

● **Insurance When You Need It** When people need to file a claim, there are a number of steps they must take. **Why do you think this insurer's Web site tells claimants to take photos of the damage?**

U

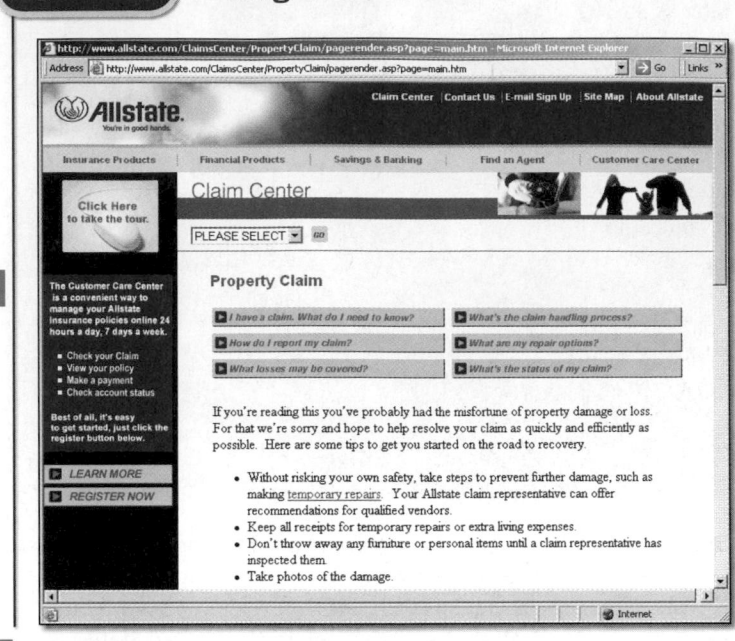

Figure 34.2 – **Filing a Claim**

Homeowners Policies

As You Read

Think about what you might need to prove to your insurance company that you sustained a loss. What types of proof would you need?

W

Many insurance companies offer a combination policy with essential protection called a homeowners policy. A **homeowners policy** covers damage to property and personal property, additional living expenses if a home is destroyed, and liability protection. Policies are fairly standard in all states and protect against loss from fire, windstorms, explosions, riot or **civil** commotion, and other perils. **Figure 34.2** shows an insurance company's Web page for policyholders to file a claim.

R

These policies offer four types of protection. Structural protection covers the cost to repair or rebuild the house if it is damaged or destroyed. Most standard policies also cover garages or sheds that are detached from the house. The policies offer protection for personal belongings, such as furniture and clothes. Items such as jewelry and silverware are covered, but usually for a limited amount. Liability protection in homeowners policies protects against costs of injury or property damage to other people. If a home is badly damaged, additional living expenses protection pays the costs to live elsewhere while it is being rebuilt.

Homeowners policies do not cover loss from floods, earthquakes, landslides, acts of war, or **nuclear** hazards. However, riders can be added for them. A **rider** is an addition to a policy that covers specific property or damages. Insurance for natural disasters costs more where they are known to occur regularly.

Figure 34.2

● **Insurance When You Need It**
so that the claimant will be able to prove the extent of the damage

As You Read

Answers may vary. For instance, some proof of ownership, preferably receipts, will detail the price you paid for the item that was lost as well as when it was purchased. Other proof would be pictures or engraved identifications on the items.

Amount of Insurance

Insurance companies usually recommend that homeowners insure their home for 80 percent of its market value. Even a large fire or flood does not destroy a building completely. The land and the building's foundation will not be destroyed and will hold their value.

You can also insure property for either its actual cash value or its replacement value. The actual cash value is the value of the property new minus devaluation from use. For example, suppose you bought a home for $100,000, but it has depreciated in value by $20,000. If the home is destroyed by a mudslide, the insurer will pay only $80,000. The **replacement value** is the full cost of repairing or replacing the property, regardless of the depreciation value. In this case, the insurer would give you the full amount to repair or replace the destroyed home. As in any situation that might involve insurance, it is important to remember that without it, you would have to pay the full cost to replace the house, which could be $100,000 or more.

Property insurance has many of the same costs as vehicle insurance. The number of claims insurers pay each year affects the overall cost of insurance. Premiums depend on the amount of coverage and the type of policy needed. The amount of a premium is also determined by specific factors, such as the amount of the deductible and the location of the property. The type of home, the building materials in it, and preventive measures that the property owner takes are also key factors.

Homeowners Coverage A homeowners policy usually offers basic coverage, which provides protection for a dwelling and personal property. Additional coverage can be added to basic protection. Special coverage can be added for special items, such as jewelry, for up to $500. A homeowner can also buy extra coverage with a rider. The extra cost is usually low. *What are some items that a homeowner might protect with a rider?*

N C L B Activity correlates to English Language Arts standards.

Section 34.2

After You Read

Review Key Concepts
1. In addition to vehicles, what types of property can be insured?
2. What types of coverage are included in homeowners policies?
3. What factors affect the cost of property insurance?

Academic Skills
4. **English Language Arts** Make a list of at least five different types of property insurance. Pair up with another student and discuss what the function of each type of insurance is and who would purchase it.

5. **English Language Arts** In groups of three, discuss and make a list of the things that might lower your homeowners insurance costs. Then make a poster using pictures and graphics from magazines illustrating those concepts.

@ Go to the *Introduction to Business* Online Learning Center through **glencoe.com** to check your answers.

Section 34.2

Review Key Concepts
1. real and personal property
2. protection against loss from fire, windstorm, explosion, riot or civil commotion, vandalism, and theft
3. the number of claims, amount of coverage, type of policy, deductible, location; type of home and materials in it; and preventive measures being taken.

Academic Skills
4. **English Language Arts** renters insurance, fire insurance, liability protection, additional living expenses, business and homeowners insurance
5. **English Language Arts** Posters might include such things as deadbolts, alarm systems, smoke detectors, and sprinkler systems.

RETEACH (cont.)

C Critical Thinking

Explain

Amount of Insurance Ask students to explain why a homeowner who recently paid $500,000 for a house should insure the home for $400,000. (because the land and foundation will hold their value)

Homeowners Coverage Items that would not be covered under the basic policy.

ASSESS

After You Read

Have students complete the Section 34.2 After You Read section review.

Online Study Tools

Have students go to the Online Learning Center through **glencoe.com** to:
- Take the Section 34.2 **Practice Test**.
- Download free **Study-to-Go** content to their PDAs or cell phones.

CLOSE

Culminating Activity

Inventory Checklist
Have students create an inventory checklist that could be used to document an insurance claim. (date of purchase, purchase price, replacement costs, serial numbers, photographs and video images)

Vocabulary Review

1. Students should write complete sentences using each term correctly.

Review Key Concepts

2. The types of vehicle insurance that drivers can buy include personal liability, medical expense, uninsured/underinsured motorists, comprehensive, collision, and miscellaneous coverage.

3. Most states have financial responsibility laws and compulsory insurance laws that make vehicle insurance protection a necessity.

4. Factors that affect the cost of vehicle insurance include the amount of money insurers pay each year in insurance claims; the type of vehicle; how the vehicle is used; where the vehicle is driven; age of the driver; and amounts of deductibles.

5. Examples include renters insurance, standard fire policy, liability protection, additional living expenses coverage, and homeowners policies.

6. Homeowners policies combine four essential kinds of home protection into one, including protection for the structure of a home, personal belongings, liability, and additional living expenses coverage.

Section 34.1 *Summary*

Vehicle Insurance Vehicle insurance is a necessity for drivers. Insurance companies offer protection from bodily injury and property damage liability, medical payments, and collision expenses. They also offer comprehensive coverage, uninsured/underinsured motorists coverage, and miscellaneous coverage. All states require drivers to prove their financial responsibility in case of an accident. Vehicle insurance is the best way to demonstrate financial responsibility. The costs of vehicle insurance depend on several factors, including characteristics of the policyholder and the vehicle, and the amount of the deductibles.

Section 34.2 *Summary*

Property Insurance Renters, homeowners, and business owners need property insurance. Many different kinds of property insurance protect both real property and personal property against threats such as earthquakes, fires, floods, and various other disasters. Property owners can buy individual insurance policies to cover specific types of threats. Property insurance protects against loss of property, liability for injuries on the property, and additional living expenses in case a home is damaged or destroyed. A homeowners policy is a standard policy that combines various types of protection into one policy. Homeowners can insure their home for either its actual cash value or its replacement value.

Vocabulary Review

1. On a sheet of paper, use each of these key terms and academic vocabulary terms in a sentence.

Key Terms

actual cash value
depreciation
financial responsibility law
compulsory insurance law
no-fault insurance
claim
deductible
real property

personal property
renters insurance
standard fire policy
extended coverage
homeowners policy
rider
replacement value

Academic Vocabulary

issues	consists
quote	injured
exceed	civil
vary	nuclear

Review Key Concepts

2. Describe types of vehicle insurance.

3. Identify laws that make vehicle insurance protection a necessity.

4. Give examples of factors that affect the cost of vehicle insurance.

5. List some examples of insurance for real and personal property.

6. Describe protection provided by homeowners insurance policies.

614   Chapter 34   Review and Activities

Critical Thinking

7. Teen drivers have more accidents than any other group of drivers.

8. Racing is too risky and injuries are too likely for coverage.

9. Insurance companies assume that the chances of loss are not greatly increased if the teen drivers drive their parents' cars.

10. The lender has a vested interest in the home because it holds the note on it.

11. Businesses usually operate with a small profit margin. Business interruption insurance provides protection to help them stay in business.

Critical Thinking

7. Why do teens pay more for vehicle insurance than most drivers?

8. Vehicle insurance will not cover a driver in a motorcycle-racing contest. Why do you think this is so?

9. Why can teen drivers be included on an adult's insurance policy?

10. Why would a bank of mortgage company insist that a new home owner buy homeowners insurance?

11. Why is it important for businesses to be able to buy insurance to cover profits that would have been earned if a disaster had not occurred?

12. What do you think is the purpose of a deductible in property insurance?

13. What are some examples of homeowners who should add special riders to their property insurance coverage?

14. Why do you think the number of claims that a property owner has over a period of time affects the cost of insurance and renewal?

Write About It

15. Write two or more paragraphs describing features of vehicles that help to reduce the cost of vehicle insurance.

16. In at least two paragraphs, describe ways that teen drivers can get the best rates for vehicle insurance.

17. Prepare a poster with a list of safe driving rules and a list of safe passenger rules that you can display in your school.

18. Insurance companies recommend that policyholders prepare an inventory of insured items they own and the replacement cost of each item. Make a list of your personal property and replacement costs. Summarize the type of insurance you need.

19. Research business insurance in the library or online. Write a short paper describing the types of insurance available for small-business owners. Include insurance policies related to buildings, vehicles, inventory, employees, and customers.

Technology Applications

Spreadsheet Software

20. Collect data from a family member, a neighbor, or a library or online source about the premiums charged by insurance companies for vehicle coverage. Prepare a spreadsheet that shows the types of coverage and the premium charged for each type. Create a chart that shows the percentage of the total premium for each type of coverage.

Business Ethics

Insurance Reimbursement

21. Imagine that your small business was burglarized, and expensive appliances and merchandise were stolen. The insurance company has asked you for an itemized list of stolen items. Your partner offered to help you "pad" the figures for the inventory. What could be the consequences of this unethical behavior?

Critical Thinking

12. to discourage small claims, which increase insurance costs

13. Homeowners who are collectors of valuable items or homeowners in a high-crime areas.

14. Insurance works on the "principle of large numbers," which means many share a loss so that no one person or business suffers the entire loss.

Write About It

15. Cars that have air bags and seat belts and those with security devices can sometimes be insured for less money than others. Sports cars and those that have a high theft rate usually cost more to insure.

16. Teens who attend an approved driving school, maintain at least a B average in school, have a spotless driving record, and who choose a high deductible and plan to pay some losses themselves can get a better rate.

17. Points to include: safe driving guidelines and tips for being a safe passenger.

18. Students may list CDs, CD players, MP3 players, computers, computer software, bicycles, and clothing.

19. Papers may include policies that cover losses similar to those covered in homeowners policies, business interruption insurance, casualty, and vehicle insurance.

Technology Applications

20. Data and charts will vary depending on the results of the student research.

Business Ethics

21. If the insurance company discovered the figures were padded, you could receive much less than you are entitled to for your losses. If you submit a false claim, the insurance company may refuse to pay and may bring legal action against you.

Applying Academics to Business

22. Students should recognize that the cost of insurance is dependent on a number of different factors.

23. Students should compute the value of each category, the total value of all items, and the percent of the total each category represents.

24. *Aircraft* should be crossed out. *Eleven Perils* could be used as a heading.

25. $810 \times \frac{1}{3} = $270 or $810 \div 3 = $270; She would pay $810 − $270 = $520.

Active Learning

26. Answers will depend on the state.

Business in the Real World

27. A graduated license system requires drivers to have a learner's permit followed by a special restricted license. During the learner's permit phase, they can drive only with a licensed adult driver with them. They can drive only during certain times and under certain conditions. For example, teens usually are not allowed to drive during nighttime hours until later in their driving experience. There are restrictions on the number of teen passengers they can carry. Graduated licensing programs substantially reduce teen accidents.

Applying Academics to Business

English Language Arts

22. Find two insurance companies that offer renters insurance and are located in different areas. Find out what the insurance costs and what it covers. Make note of how and why the prices might differ. Give a presentation summarizing what you have found.

Mathematics

23. Imagine you are going to buy insurance for the contents of your room. Take an inventory of the items. Make a list or chart categorizing the items under appropriate headings, such as furniture, clothing, electronics, and books. Estimate the total cost to replace each item. Figure a total replacement cost for each category. Make a pie chart showing the relative values of the categories of items.

> **THEORY** **Pie Charts** Pie charts are useful for showing how the parts of a whole relate to each other.

English Language Arts

24. Look at the list of terms below. Cross out the one that does not belong with the others. Circle the term that could be used as the heading in a list with the others.

> fire
> explosion
> eleven perils
> earthquake
> aircraft

Mathematics

25. Eva's insurance agent told her that if she installed an alarm system in her home, she could reduce her annual premium by $\frac{1}{3}$. If Eva pays $810 now, how much would she pay if she installed the alarm system?

> **THEORY** **Inverse Operations** Multiplication and division are inverse operations. Multiplying one number by another is the same as dividing the first number by the inverse of the second. $a \times \frac{1}{b} = a \div b$

Active Learning

State Requirements for Vehicle Insurance
26. Research the laws in your state about motor vehicle insurance. Find answers to questions such as: Are drivers required to carry insurance? What type of coverage is required? What are the penalties for drivers who do not carry vehicle insurance? What types of discounts do companies have available for drivers who qualify for discounts?

Business in the Real World

Graduated Driver Licensing Systems
27. Research whether your state has a graduated driver licensing system for teen drivers. Interview several 19- to 23-year-olds and parents about their experience with the program. If your state does not have this system, read about it in the library or online, and interview young adults and parents about their licensing experiences. Summarize the opinions of both groups.

ExamView Assessment Suite CD allows you to print out ready-made unit and chapter tests, complete with answer keys. You can also create customized tests.

TeacherWorks Plus provides complete teacher resources in one convenient package. It includes customizable lesson plans in calendar format, and instant access to many print program resources.

Real LIFE skills

PLANNING FOR THE FUTURE

28. Insurance cannot protect you from life's accidents, but it can help protect you financially. Proper insurance can help to put people back in the position they were in before an accident. The most common types of insurance are health, life, homeowners, and auto insurance. Write an e-mail to a family member or friend discussing the type of insurance that you think is most important.

Cool Business CAREERS

FIND YOUR DREAM JOB

29. Go to the *Introduction to Business* Online Learning Center through **glencoe.com** for a link to the Occupational Outlook Handbook Web site. Click on the "OOH Search/A-Z Index" link and enter the job category "real estate brokers and sales agents." Then write a one-page report about these types of occupations. Conclude your report with a list of things you could do now to prepare yourself to pursue the occupation.

Role Play

THE VALUE OF INSURANCE

30. **Situation** You have been asked to give a presentation on the value of vehicle insurance. Include information on the kinds of vehicle insurance available and recommendations for coverage for teen drivers.

Activity With a partner, create an outline of information on vehicle insurance for teens for your presentation.

Evaluation You will be evaluated on how well you meet the following performance indicators:

- Identify types of coverage available for vehicles.
- Explain amounts of coverage that teen drivers should consider.
- Prepare a list for recommended insurance coverage for teen drivers.
- Create a written outline of points for your presentation.
- Project your voice and use correct grammar.

Standardized Test Practice

Directions Choose the letter of the best answer. Write the letter for the answer on a separate piece of paper.

1. $\frac{11}{24} - \frac{5}{12} =$

A $\frac{5}{8}$ C $\frac{1}{4}$

B $\frac{6}{24}$ D $\frac{1}{24}$

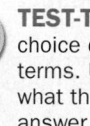 **TEST-TAKING TIP** Analyze multiple-choice questions very carefully. Note key terms. Use your knowledge and anticipate what the answer should be. Find an answer choice that looks like the one you predict.

 READING Go to the *Introduction to Business* Online Learning Center through **glencoe.com** for a list of outside reading suggestions.

Real LIFE skills

28. E-mail responses will be based on students' opinions.

Cool Business CAREERS

29. Real estate brokers and sales agents facilitate the sale of property from one entity to another. They spend part of their time in the field, some in an office or from home, frequently long hours including evenings and weekends. Every state requires licensing. Prospective agents must be at least 18 years old, have a high school diploma, and pass a written test. Advancement comes in form of higher commissions. As preparation, develop interpersonal, basic computer, and organizational skills.

Role Play

30. Presentations should address the competencies noted in the Role Play. Answers will be based on students' research.

Standardized Test Practice
   1. D

 STRATEGIES FOR STANDARDIZED TEST PREP SUCCESS

Test Savvy Explain to students that they should watch out for multiple-choice items with the words *not* or *always* in the question. *Which of the following is* NOT *true?* In cases like this, the task is to eliminate the true statements and choose the false statement. *Which of the following is* ALWAYS *true?* In cases like this, the task is to eliminate the statements that are either false or only sometimes true, and choose the statement that is true in all cases.

Standards-Based Lesson Planning   *Introduction to Business* provides students with
instruction and assessment in the following fundamental content areas:

Content Standards Correlations	
Compare and contrasts insurance policies.	pp. 621–624, 626–629, 630–633
Distinguish between the different forms of insurance.	pp. 621–624, 626–629, 630–633
Examine the need for risk protection.	pp. 621–624, 626–629, 630–633
Evaluate the various types of life insurance policies.	pp. 621–624, 630–631, 633
Determine the value of major types of health insurance.	pp. 626–629, 630–633
Calculate the monetary consequences of being uninsured.	pp. 626, 631
Differentiate between coverage available on life and health insurance.	pp. 621–624, 626–629, 630–633

NCLB   Activities, information, and skills practice will help your students attain No Child Left
Behind proficiency. Students will improve their abilities in the following academic standards areas:

Academic Standards Correlations		
English Language Arts	Activities/Features	Page
NCTE 3 Apply strategies to interpret texts	Applying Academics to Business	p. 632
NCTE 7 Conduct research and gather, evaluate, and synthesize data to communicate discoveries	After You Read Applying Academics to Business	pp. 629, 632
NCTE 12 Use language to accomplish individual purposes	After You Read	p. 629
Mathematics		
Algebra Represent and analyze mathematical situations and structures using algebraic symbols	Applying Academics to Business	p. 632
Number and Operations Compute fluently and make reasonable estimates	Ask S&P After You Read Applying Academics to Business Standardized Test Practice	pp. 618, 624, 632, 633
Science		
Content Standard F Students should develop understanding of science and technology in local, national, and global challenges	Science/Tech Trends	p. 627

Correlations   This chart shows the 21st Century Skills, foundation skills, and workplace competencies that students develop as they work in this chapter.

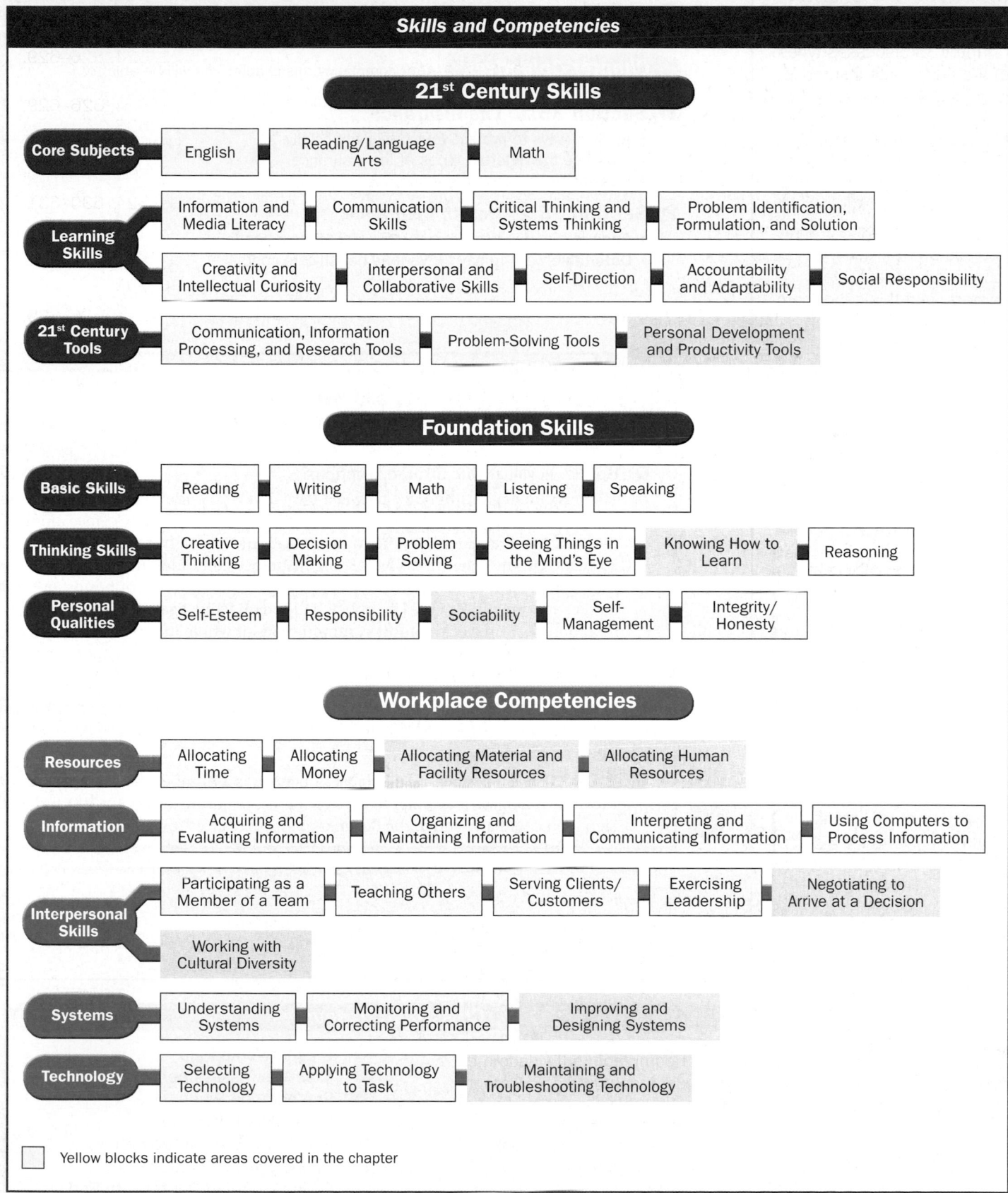

Skills and Competencies

21st Century Skills

Core Subjects
- English
- Reading/Language Arts
- Math

Learning Skills
- Information and Media Literacy
- Communication Skills
- Critical Thinking and Systems Thinking
- Problem Identification, Formulation, and Solution
- Creativity and Intellectual Curiosity
- Interpersonal and Collaborative Skills
- Self-Direction
- Accountability and Adaptability
- Social Responsibility

21st Century Tools
- Communication, Information Processing, and Research Tools
- Problem-Solving Tools
- Personal Development and Productivity Tools

Foundation Skills

Basic Skills
- Reading
- Writing
- Math
- Listening
- Speaking

Thinking Skills
- Creative Thinking
- Decision Making
- Problem Solving
- Seeing Things in the Mind's Eye
- Knowing How to Learn
- Reasoning

Personal Qualities
- Self-Esteem
- Responsibility
- Sociability
- Self-Management
- Integrity/Honesty

Workplace Competencies

Resources
- Allocating Time
- Allocating Money
- Allocating Material and Facility Resources
- Allocating Human Resources

Information
- Acquiring and Evaluating Information
- Organizing and Maintaining Information
- Interpreting and Communicating Information
- Using Computers to Process Information

Interpersonal Skills
- Participating as a Member of a Team
- Teaching Others
- Serving Clients/Customers
- Exercising Leadership
- Negotiating to Arrive at a Decision
- Working with Cultural Diversity

Systems
- Understanding Systems
- Monitoring and Correcting Performance
- Improving and Designing Systems

Technology
- Selecting Technology
- Applying Technology to Task
- Maintaining and Troubleshooting Technology

Yellow blocks indicate areas covered in the chapter

Chapter Overview

Introduce the Chapter

Life and Health Insurance
Chapter 35 discusses types of life and health insurance, including their costs.

Building Background

Life and health insurance coverage costs vary dramatically. Knowing the basics will help students evaluate their choices as they become more independent, start careers, and think about protecting their loved ones.

Ask STANDARD &POOR'S

>> Math Answer
Your percent savings is 15.5% ($154 × 12 = $1,848; $1,848 − $1,600 = $248; $248 ÷ $1,600 = 0.155; 0.155 × 100 = 15.5%).

>> Extension Activity
Ask students to calculate the asset allocation for the following portfolio, how each component relates to the entire portfolio as a decimal, and then convert decimals to percentages.

David: domestic stocks, $39,000; foreign stocks, $3,000; bonds, $8,000.

(David: domestic stocks, 0.7800 (78.00%); foreign stocks, 0.0600 (6.00%); bonds, 0.1600 (16.00%).

N C L B
Activity correlates to Math standards.

Life and Health Insurance

Chapter Objectives After completing this chapter, you will be able to:

▶ **Section 35.1** *Life Insurance*
- **Identify** ways to protect your family financially.
- **Describe** the different types of life insurance.
- **Discuss** the costs of life insurance.

▶ **Section 35.2** *Health Insurance*
- **Analyze** reasons it is important to protect your health.
- **Determine** ways to pay for various health-care costs.

Ask STANDARD &POOR'S

Life and Health Insurance: Whole Life vs. Term Insurance

Q: How do I evaluate life insurance options?

A: There is one major difference between term and whole life insurance: a term policy is just life coverage. When the insured dies, a term policy pays the face amount of the policy to the beneficiary. Term insurance can be bought for periods of one to 30 years. On the other hand, whole life insurance combines an investment component with a term policy. The investment could be in the form of bonds and money market accounts or stocks. The policy builds cash value against which you can then borrow. Three of the most common types of whole life insurance are traditional, universal, and variable. With both term and whole life insurance, you have the option of locking in the same monthly payment over the life of the policy.

Mathematics You have been offered two different health insurance options. You can pay either $154 a month or $1,600 for the year. What will be your percent savings if you chose the year-long option?

N C L B

THEORY **Change a Decimal to a Percent** A percent is a number that compares a number to 100. Changing a decimal to a percent is easy—just multiply by 100 and add a % sign. You could also move the decimal point two places to the right.

Classroom Resources

- Student Edition
- Teacher Wraparound Edition
- Student Activity Workbook with Academic Integration
- Student Activity Workbook with Academic Integration TAE
- *Fast File*, Unit 11 Resources
- Inclusion in the Business Education Classroom

- TeacherWorks Plus
- *ExamView Assessment Suite*
- Presentation Plus!
- Vocabulary PuzzleMaker
- Interactive Student Edition
- Online Student Edition
- Online Learning Center with Podcasts

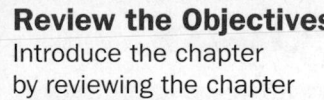

Review the Objectives
Introduce the chapter by reviewing the chapter objectives:

Section 35.1 *Objectives*
Identify ways to protect your family financially. (through investments and estate planning and health and life insurance)

Describe the different types of life insurance. (Cash-value insurance provides both savings and death benefits. Whole life insurance provides savings and pays benefits at death. Universal life insurance gives a policy-holder more flexibility in premium payments and benefits. With variable life insurance, the cash-value part of the premium is used for investments. Term insurance is for a specific period of time.)

Discuss the costs of life insurance. (The amount of the premium depends on the type of policy and the amount of coverage.)

Section 35.2 *Objectives*
Analyze reasons it is important to protect your health. (Protecting your health can help you to live longer. Health insurance provides protection against the costs of illness and accidents.)

Determine ways to pay for various health-care costs. (major medical insurance, hospital expense insurance, surgical expense insurance, medical expense insurance, and group health insurance)

● **Taking Care of Your Family** Life insurance and health insurance are available to help people of all ages take care of their families. **Why do you think life insurance and health insurance are important to your family?**

Chapter 35 Life and Health Insurance **619**

Discuss the Photo
● **Taking Care of Your Family** Read the caption on the photo to students: Life insurance and health insurance are available to help people of all ages take care of their families.

Ask students: Why do you think life insurance and health insurance are important to your family? (Life insurance protects families against the loss of income and other problems that follow the loss of a family member. Health insurance covers illnesses and injuries and is a way for people to stay healthy.)

Section 35.1

FOCUS

Bell Ringer Activity

Life Insurance
Ask students: How much is a life worth? (Encourage discussion, but remind students that it is impossible to put a price tag on human life.)

Preteaching

Presentation Plus!
The Presentation Plus! CD provides visual teaching aids for this section.

PuzzleMaker
Use the Vocabulary PuzzleMaker to create a puzzle of the section's key terms. Students can complete the puzzle on paper or on a computer.

Graphic Organizer
Tell students to go to the Online Learning Center through **glencoe.com** for a printable graphic organizer. (Answers include: Whole life: premium stays same, provides savings, and pays benefits at death. Universal: premium payments applied to insurance protection, expenses of insurance company for the policy, and interest-earning investments for policyholder. Investments earn interest and build savings. Variable life: the cash-value part of the premium is used for investments rather than savings; the remainder is used for guaranteed death benefits.)

N C L B Connects academics to content.

Life Insurance

Reading Guide

● Before You Read
Think about your family's expenses and the main person who makes sure that those expenses are paid.

Read to Learn
- Identify ways to protect your family financially.
- Describe the different types of life insurance.
- Discuss the costs of life insurance.

The Main Idea
Life insurance is a way to protect a family's standard of living after the person who is financially responsible for the family dies. There are several types of life insurance. Some of them also build savings.

Key Concepts
- Protecting Your Family
- Types of Life Insurance
- Costs of Life Insurance

Vocabulary
Key Terms
life insurance
proceeds
beneficiary
cash-value insurance
term insurance

Academic Vocabulary
You will find these words in your reading and on your tests. Make sure you know their meanings.
estate
purpose
survivor
features

Graphic Organizer
In a figure like the one below, list three types of cash-value life insurance in the left column and some notes about each type in the right column.

Life Insurance Type	Notes

 Go to the *Introduction to Business* Online Learning Center through **glencoe.com** for a printable graphic organizer.

Academic Standards
English Language Arts
   NCTE 1 Read texts to acquire new information
Mathematics
   Algebra Represent and analyze mathematical situations and structures using algebraic symbols

Reading Guide

● Before You Read
Answers will depend on family situations.

D Develop Concepts
The Main Idea Ask students: What is the main purpose of life insurance? (Answers will vary. Life insurance is a way to protect a family's standard of living.)

Protecting Your Family

People provide for their future by saving money and wisely investing their funds. They provide for their families with investments and **estate** planning. No matter how well they plan, investments and a well-written will may not be enough. Just as vehicle insurance and property insurance protect against losses to property, life insurance and health insurance protect people.

● **As You Read**

Think about your family's expenses and how they are paid.

Types of Life Insurance

Life insurance is insurance that is paid to a person or people designated to receive the funds when the insured person dies. The **purpose** of life insurance is to protect the standard of living of the survivors.

Buying life insurance can help you protect the people who depend upon you from financial losses caused by your death. Those people could include a spouse, children, an aging parent, or a business partner. Upon the policyholder's death, the insurance company pays the survivors the value of a life insurance policy, or the **proceeds**. A **beneficiary**, who is a **survivor**, is someone who receives part or all of the proceeds. The person who buys life insurance names one or more beneficiaries for the policy.

There are several types of life insurance to fit different needs. The cost of life insurance varies, depending on the type of coverage and characteristics of the policyholder.

✔ **Reading Check** **Define** Who is a beneficiary?

?ETHICS in Business

Gambling on Self-Insurance

■ **Critical Reading** Life is full of important decisions. Think about the kinds of decisions that you make as you read the question below.

Insurance contracts are often seen as a form of gambling. The insurance company is gambling that you will not suffer the kind of loss against which you are insured. In return for taking on this risk, the company receives your premium. There have been a number of proposals, however, to make health insurance mandatory, either at the federal or the state level. The people making these proposals say that when people without health insurance gamble that they will not get sick, society ends up paying the bill.

■ **Decision Making** Some people do provide for loss by a process called self-insurance. However, if people do not self-insure enough to cover their bills, the burden of their care might still have to be paid by society. Do you agree that people should be forced to buy health insurance? Explain your opinion.

Section 35.1 Life Insurance **621**

● **As You Read**

Most students probably will list housing, food, transportation, clothing, and medical expenses. Expenses likely are paid by parents, grandparents, or other guardians. Some students also may contribute.

?ETHICS in Business

Decision Making Students might suggest that requiring people to have health insurance places an unfair burden on healthy people and could undermine the health insurance system.

Section 35.1

TEACH

Discussion Starter
Start a discussion by asking students if they think that stay-at-home moms and dads need to be covered by life insurance. (Students should understand that anyone who makes a significant contribution to the family finances probably should be covered by life insurance. Although parents who do not work outside often do not contribute to the family income, their absence might increase family expenses. If the stay-at-home parent dies, the other parent might have to pay someone to provide some or all of these services.)

R Reading Strategy

Make a Distinction Ask students to make a distinction between a survivor and a beneficiary. (A survivor is usually a living person who is related to someone who has died. Survivors generally include spouses and children, but they also can include parents, other relatives, and other persons who have close relationships with the deceased. A beneficiary is a person who has been designated to receive all or part of the proceeds of a life insurance policy, not necessarily a relative.)

✔ **Reading Check**

Define A beneficiary is someone who receives part of the proceeds from a life insurance policy.

621

TEACH (cont.)

S **Skill Practice**

Guided Practice

Identify Ask students to identify another name for cash-value insurance. (Cash value insurance is also called permanent insurance.) **L1**

Explain Ask students to explain the benefits of cash-value insurance. (Cash-value insurance provides savings and death benefits.) **L2**

Draw a Conclusion Ask students to explain why a policyholder would choose to borrow against a cash-value insurance policy rather than canceling the policy and taking the current cash value with no repayment obligation. (Answers will vary. If the policyholder borrows against the policy, all or part of the death benefit is still available. If the policy is cancelled, there is no death benefit.) **L3**

ASSESS

Review Key Terms
Have students write sentences using each key term.

Study-to-Go
Have students go to the Online Learning Center through **glencoe.com** to download free **Study-to-Go** content to their PDAs or cell phones.

● **Life Expectancy** This chart shows life expectancy in the United States. **How many more years may a 15-year-old female expect to live compared to a 15-year-old male? What effect do these figures have on the cost of life insurance?**

Source: *The World Almanac and Book of Facts*

Figure 35.1 — *Length of Life*

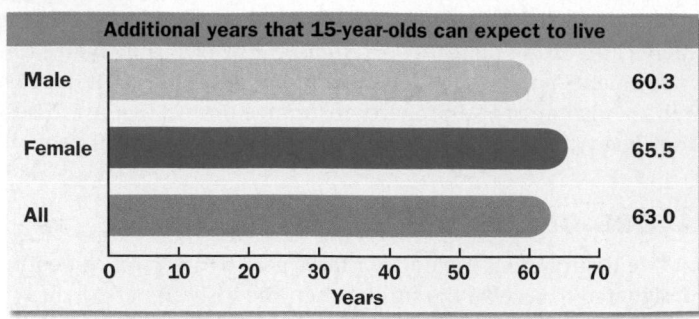

Additional years that 15-year-olds can expect to live

	Years
Male	60.3
Female	65.5
All	63.0

Cash-Value Insurance

Cash-value insurance, or permanent insurance, provides both savings and death benefits. Part of the premium pays for death benefits, and the rest builds up cash value like a savings account. The cash value increases throughout the life of the policy. If a policyholder cancels the policy, he or she can receive the amount of the cash value. In an emergency, this person can borrow part or all of the cash value, but must pay interest on it. Policyholders can buy different forms of cash-value insurance.

Whole Life Insurance

With whole life insurance, a premium that stays the same is paid throughout the policyholder's lifetime. The policy remains in force until the insured dies, as long as the premiums are paid. Whole life insurance provides savings during the policyholder's life and pays benefits at death. **Figure 35.1** shows the number of years a person in the United States can expect to live. One of the factors in the cost of life insurance is the number of years a person will pay premiums.

✔ **Reading Check** **Compare** How are cash-value insurance and whole life insurance similar?

Universal Life Insurance

With universal life insurance, a policyholder has more flexibility in premium payments and benefits once the policy has built cash value. Premium payments are applied to three areas: insurance protection, expenses of the insurance company for the policy, and interest-earning investments for the policyholder. The investments earn interest and build savings. A policyholder may be able to increase the death benefit after passing a physical examination or change premium payments. Policyholders purchase universal life insurance if they want flexibility in premium payments and death benefits as their financial situation changes.

622 **Chapter 35** Life and Health Insurance

Figure 35.1

● **Life Expectancy** The life expectancy of a 15-year-old female is 5.2 years longer than a 15-year-old male. Increased life expectancy means premiums are paid longer.

✔ **Reading Check**

Compare Both provide savings. With cash-value insurance, part of the premium pays for death benefits, and the rest builds up cash value. Whole life insurance provides savings during the policyholder's life and pays benefits at death.

Variable Life Insurance

W With variable life insurance, the cash-value part of the premium is used for investments such as stocks, bonds, and mutual funds, rather than savings. Like other types of cash-value insurance, the rest of the premium is used for guaranteed death benefits. The cash value is variable because it can increase or decrease in value, depending on how well the investments do. For example, if a portion of the premium is used to invest in stocks and the stocks double in value, the cash value may be doubled.

Policyholders can buy a policy that has **features** of both universal and variable life insurance. Variable-universal life insurance has the investment features of variable insurance as well as premium and death-benefit adjustments of universal life insurance.

Term Insurance

R **Term insurance** covers a person for a specific period of time. The length of the term might be five, 10, or 20 years. Term insurance pays benefits only if the insured dies during the term of the policy. If the insured person lives beyond the term of the policy, the policy has no value. It can be renewed, but usually with a higher premium. Term insurance is sometimes called "pure protection," since it is used only to pay death benefits and does not build cash value. The major advantage of term insurance is its low cost, compared to cash-value insurance.

How does term insurance work? If Gabriel buys a five-year, $10,000 policy, he has protection for five years. If he dies during the term of the policy, his beneficiary will receive $10,000. After five years, his coverage ends. Gabriel can then renew the policy. As he gets older, however, his premium will increase.

Policyholders often have term insurance as a part of group life insurance. An employer or organization might provide term insurance for employees or members. One master insurance policy covers everyone in the group. When a member of the group leaves, the coverage ends for that person. For example, if you work for a company that provides term insurance as a benefit, you lose that coverage if you leave the company.

● **High-Risk Occupations** Some occupations are riskier than others. **Why is insurance for a high-rise construction worker more expensive than for other workers?**

Real World

Shop Around There are companies known as "insurance consultants," who, for a fee (paid by the customer), will shop around for the best insurance policy among many companies. An "insurance broker" performs the same service, but the fee is usually paid in the form of a commission from the insurer that is selected rather than directly from the customer. *What would be the advantage of paying a consultant to find insurance for you or your family?*

Discuss the Photo
● **High-Risk Occupations** High-rise construction is a more dangerous occupation, and the chances of injury or death are higher than for safer occupations.

Real World

Shop Around The consultant may be able to evaluate many insurers and get the best deal that suits your needs. You probably could do the same research, but these professionals have special expertise in the field.

RETEACH

W Writing Support
Enrichment
Write an Essay Ask students to write a short essay explaining why some parents purchase life insurance for their minor children. (Students should understand that children need life insurance to cover possible funeral and burial expenses.)

R Reading Strategy
Paraphrase Ask students to use their own words to explain how term insurance works. (A term insurance policy has a death benefit of a specific amount. The policy has no cash value and provides no savings. The policy has a term and if the insured dies within the term, the death benefit is paid to the designated beneficiaries.)

U Universal Access
Students with Low Self-Esteem How can students begin to manage outcomes and predict their own success? Tell students that successful people often visualize success. They picture themselves succeeding in whatever they do. Once they "see" themselves succeeding, the path between where they are and where they want to be becomes clearer. Imagining themselves performing the steps needed to reach the goal makes the goal more attainable.

Student Activity Workbook 📂 Assign the Section 35.1 Activities.

RETEACH (cont.)

C Critical Thinking

Distinguish

Costs of Life Insurance Why are people charged different premiums for the same type of life insurance coverage? (Premiums are based on how long the policyholder is likely to live.)

● As You Read

It ensures that family members are financially secure after the insured passes away.

ASSESS

● After You Read

Have students complete the Section 35.1 After You Read section review.

Online Study Tools

Have students go to the Online Learning Center through **glencoe.com** to:

- Take the Section 35.1 **Practice Test**.
- Download free **Study-to-Go**  content to their PDAs or cell phones.

CLOSE

Culminating Activity
Study Guide

Assign the following topics to groups of students: (1) Types of Life Insurance, (2) Cash-Value and Whole Life Insurance, (3) Universal Life and Variable Life Insurance, (4) Term Insurance, and (5) Cost of Insurance. Ask the groups to prepare a two-minute presentation on their topic using presentation software.

624

Workers or their companies usually pay less for a group policy than for individual policies. If the company provides coverage as a benefit, the employee usually pays a small part of the cost for the coverage. The employer pays the rest of the cost of the insurance. Some companies may pay the entire cost as a benefit to their employees.

● As You Read

Think about the importance of life insurance as people age.

N C L B
Activity correlates to Math standards.

Costs of Life Insurance

As with any type of insurance, the amount of the premium on a life insurance policy depends on the type of policy and the amount of coverage. Term insurance costs less than cash-value insurance. A policy for $100,000 costs more than a policy for $50,000.

C Factors such as the policyholder's age, health, and occupation also affect the cost of the premium. Many people have to take a physical before they are sold an insurance policy to ensure that they are in good health. The older a person is, the higher the premium will be because of the likelihood the company will have to pay benefits sooner. Life insurance also costs more for people in dangerous occupations, such as a firefighter or a stunt pilot.

Section 35.1

● After You Read

Review Key Concepts
1. What are the different types of life insurance?
2. How is term insurance different from whole life insurance?
3. What are three factors that affect the cost of life insurance?

Academic Skills

N C L B

4. **Mathematics** Drew has a health insurance plan with a deductible of $750. The cost Drew paid for a doctor's appointment was $120, and the prescription he was given costs him $90 each time he gets it filled. After how many refills will he reach his deductible?

THEORY **The Deductible** The deductible in an insurance policy is the portion of any claim that is not covered by the insurance provider. It is usually a fixed amount that must be "met," or paid by the insured, before the full benefits of a policy can apply. Adding each out-of-pocket expense the insured makes will indicate how close he or she is to reaching the deductible.

 Math For math help, go to the Math Appendix.

@ Go to the *Introduction to Business* Online Learning Center through **glencoe.com** to check your answers.

Section 35.1

Review Key Concepts
1. cash-value insurance, or permanent insurance, whole life insurance, universal life insurance, variable life insurance, and term insurance
2. With term insurance, a policyholder pays premiums for a stated period of time. Term insurance does not build cash value. At the end of the term, the policy ends. It may be renewed. Whole life insurance builds cash value, and premiums are usually paid throughout the insured's lifetime.
3. the insured's age, health, and occupation

Academic Skills
4. **Mathematics**
   ($750 − $120) ÷ $90 = 7 refills

Health Insurance

Reading Guide

● Before You Read

Think about the steps you can take to protect yourself in case of illness or injury.

Read to Learn

- Analyze reasons it is important to protect your health.
- Determine ways to pay for various health-care costs.

The Main Idea

Health-care costs are often more than the average consumer can afford. Health insurance provides protection in case of illness or accident. Insurance companies and government health insurance programs are sources consumers turn to for help with their medical expenses.

Key Concepts

- Protecting Your Health
- Paying for Health-Care Costs

Vocabulary

Key Terms

coinsurance	preferred provider
copayment	organization (PPO)
pre-existing condition	Medicare
health maintenance	Medicaid
organization (HMO)	

Academic Vocabulary

You will find these words in your reading and on your tests. Make sure you know their meanings.

medical	percentage
mental	stress

Graphic Organizer

In a figure like the one below, note some types of health insurance.

Types of Health Insurance

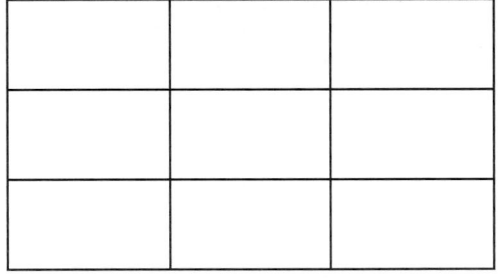

 Go to the *Introduction to Business* Online Learning Center through **glencoe.com** for a printable graphic organizer.

Academic Standards

English Language Arts

NCTE 1 Read texts to acquire new information

NCTE 7 Conduct research and gather, evaluate, and synthesize data to communicate discoveries

NCTE 12 Use language to accomplish individual purposes

Science

Content Standard F Students should develop understanding of science and technology in local, national, and global challenges

🔔 Bell Ringer Activity

Health Insurance
Project or write the following question on the board: Who should pay for health care? (Answers will vary. Students might feel that people should be responsible for their own health care. Others might point out that some people cannot pay for their own care.)

Preteaching

Presentation Plus! ◉
The Presentation Plus! CD provides visual teaching aids for this section.

PuzzleMaker ◉
Use the Vocabulary PuzzleMaker to create a puzzle of the section's key terms. Students can complete the puzzle on paper or on a computer.

Graphic Organizer
Tell students to go to the Online Learning Center through **glencoe.com** for a printable graphic organizer. (Health insurance types include: major medical, hospital, surgical, medical expense, group health, government health, Medicare, and Medicaid.)

N C L B Connects academics to content.

Reading Guide

● Before You Read

Students might mention purchasing health insurance, saving money to cover routine health-care costs, and other preventative measures.

D Develop Concepts

The Main Idea Ask students: Why don't people just pay for health care the same way they pay for other purchases? (Health-care costs are often more than the average consumer can afford.)

625

TEACH

Discussion Starter
Protecting Your Health
Discuss why businesses are willing to spend money on wellness and fitness programs for their employees. (Students should understand that it costs less to provide health insurance for people who are physically fit and take care of their health.)

R Reading Strategy

Draw a Conclusion Ask students why they think health insurance policies often require policyholders to pay deductibles, coinsurance, and copayments. (Students might suggest that these payments mean the insurance company pays less. Other students might point out that making policyholders responsible for some of the costs helps hold down costs.)

● As You Read

Most students will say that health insurance is important because it can help people to receive proper medical care. However, it is important to remember that some students may not have medical insurance.

✔ Reading Check

Explain People should try to obtain health insurance because it provides protection against the costs of illness and accidents.

● As You Read

Think about the importance of health insurance.

Protecting Your Health

Many people are concerned about what would happen to their families if they died. They also worry about what would happen if they became sick or disabled. Health care for a serious illness or accident is very expensive. Few people have enough savings to pay for **medical** costs on their own. A stay in the hospital may cost $5,000 or more *per day*. Health insurance provides protection against the costs of illness and accidents.

✔ Reading Check **Explain** Why is health insurance important?

Paying for Health-Care Costs

Many health insurance policies have **coinsurance**, a percentage of medical expenses that a policyholder must pay beyond the deductible. For example, you may have to pay 20 percent of the medical expenses for a serious illness. Many policies also require a **copayment**, or a fee paid each time a service is used. You might

---

BusinessWeek *Reader and Case Study*

Health Care: Benefits Surprise

Group coverage too pricey? Individual policies are better than you think.

Bryan Barnall has long prided himself on providing health insurance for the four employees of Printing Plus, his Lincoln, Nebraska, commercial printer. Then his carrier upped his premiums by 50% two years in a row, and Barnall had to dump his group plan. But he didn't leave his employees in the lurch.

Barnall's workers now buy individual policies through his agent. Each pays $50 a month toward premiums; Barnall pays the rest and gives each employee $75 a month to put into a health savings account (HSA). Barnall deducts his entire outlay from his taxes. And he has cut the annual health-care costs for his $350,000 company in half, to about $12,000. "The change initially made my employees a bit nervous, but they're all happy now," says Barnall.

That's because as soon as his workers came to grips with the high deductibles most individual

policies carry, they realized they were coming out just fine. A single worker typically pays about $70 a month for a policy with a $2,550 deductible. Because Barnall's staff are young and healthy, the money building up in their HSAs will likely cover their medical costs. What they don't use will earn interest.

ⓐ CASE STUDY Go to the *Introduction to Business* Online Learning Center through **glencoe.com** for the *BusinessWeek* Reader Case Study.

Active Learning

Research health savings accounts to find out the rules under which they are given favorable tax treatment. Write an e-mail to your teacher explaining the benefits and risks associated with HSAs.

626 **Chapter 35** Life and Health Insurance

BusinessWeek *Reader and Case Study*

Health Care: Benefits Surprise

ⓐ CASE STUDY Have students go to the *Introduction to Business* Online Learning Center through **glencoe.com** to download a Case Study activity that corresponds to the article. The activity and answer key are also available on the TeacherWorks Plus CD.

Active Learning

Answers will vary but e-mails should cover the basics of setup, deposits, and withdrawals as part of their discussion of benefits and drawbacks.

Science/Tech TRENDS

Medical Technology

Innovation and advancements in medical technology have brought new and effective ways of helping people with heart disease, cancer, diabetes, and other diseases. However, some claim that the cost of developing and using these technologies is driving health-care costs sky high. Still, certain technologies seem to offer a cost advantage. For example, a surgeon in Atlanta can perform a procedure on a patient in Tulsa using remote-controlled robotics and the Internet.

Web Quest

Go to the *Introduction to Business* Online Learning Center through **glencoe.com** for links to Web sites where you can research advances in medical technology and medical communications. Write a paragraph explaining what you find. Discuss how innovations and advancements in these areas might help people in developing nations or soldiers in battle.

---

pay between $5 and $15 every time you visit a doctor or have a prescription filled. Another factor is the number of people covered by a policy, such as a family with children. The more people covered by a policy, the higher the premium.

Some services, such as dental, vision, or **mental** health care, might not be covered by a health insurance policy. In those cases, people must pay themselves or pay for additional insurance. Many policies also will not cover a **pre-existing condition**, a serious health condition diagnosed before a person obtained health insurance. For example, someone with a heart condition may have difficulty obtaining coverage for it.

Major Medical Insurance

Major medical insurance, sometimes called catastrophic insurance, is the most important coverage for a serious illness or accident. It pays for most kinds of care in and out of a hospital, including hospital care, doctors' fees, tests, x-rays, and nursing care. Most policies have a deductible of several hundred dollars. With some plans, the insured also must pay coinsurance.

Major medical insurance is intended to cover health-care costs not covered by other types of insurance. The insurance company usually pays 75 percent or 80 percent of the costs and the policyholder pays the other 20 percent or 25 percent. For example, suppose your insurance has a $1,000 deductible and a coinsurance payment of 20 percent. If you are hospitalized and your medical bills come to $6,000, you will pay $2,000 ($1,000 deductible plus 20 percent of $5,000).

glencoe.com

Online Health Help
Health insurers have launched campaigns to get their members healthy. A recent survey of three large insurer sites, WellPoint®, UnitedHealth Group®, and Aetna®, evaluated their services to determine if these sites are helpful. The survey found that the information, health assessments, and personalized interactive tools help people fashion specific plans tailored to their needs. *Why do you think health insurers are making these tools available online?*

Real World

Online Health Help Online health services can help prevent diseases, which can affect an insurer's bottom line.

Science/Tech TRENDS

Web Quest

Medical Technology Researchers hope that remote-controlled robotics will be able to assist soldiers wounded in battle and to allow remote hospitals to perform medical procedures.

RETEACH

W Writing Support

Enrichment

Summarize Ask students to locate and summarize a recent news article that focuses on concerns about lack of health insurance. Remind students to include a properly formatted referenced citation. Consider asking students to turn in a printout or copy of their article. (Summaries will vary depending on the article selected.)

R Reading Strategy

List Ask students to list the two types of insurance that are often combined with hospital expense insurance to form basic health coverage plans. (The types of insurance that are often combined with hospital expense insurance to form basic health coverage plans are: surgical expense insurance and medical expense insurance.)

Student Activity Workbook ☞ Assign the Section 35.2 Activities.

● **Health Insurance**
This chart shows the percentages by age groups of the U.S. population not covered by health insurance. **What age group has the largest percentage without health insurance coverage?**

Figure 35.2 — **Who Is Covered?**

U.S. Health Insurance Coverage

Age	Percent Not Covered
Under 18 years of age	10.7%
18-44	22.5%
46-64	13.1%
All	15.7%

Source: *The World Almanac and Book of Facts*

Hospital Expense Insurance

W Hospital expense insurance pays for hospital care for a given period of time. It covers room and board, tests and x-rays, operating room costs, nursing care, and fees for medicine and treatments. Like major medical insurance, it might have a deductible. Some policies set a limit for each specific expense. Others set a maximum amount per day for a certain number of days. Hospital expense is the most popular type of health insurance because hospitalization is very expensive. **Figure 35.2** shows the **percentage** of the U.S. population that is not covered by any health insurance. Lack of health insurance is a concern for many people.

✔ **Reading Check** **Explain** Why is hospital expense insurance the most popular type?

Surgical Expense Insurance

R Surgical expense insurance pays part of a surgeon's fee for an operation. Most policies set a maximum payment for a particular surgical expense. A policy lists the surgical procedures and the costs allowed. In many cases, major medical insurance picks up where this coverage ends. Surgical expense insurance is usually bought with hospital expense insurance.

Medical Expense Insurance

Medical expense insurance covers the costs of a doctor's care *not* involving surgery. It might cover visits to a doctor's office or a doctor's calls at a hospital. This insurance is usually bought with hospital and surgical expense insurance. Insurance companies often combine all three types into basic health coverage plans.

Group Health Insurance

A group health insurance plan is the least expensive form of health insurance for most people. A company or organization may provide group insurance for its employees or members.

628 **Chapter 35** Life and Health Insurance

Figure 35.2

● **Health Insurance** The age group that has the largest percentage without health insurance coverage is 18–44.

✔ **Reading Check**

Explain Hospital expense insurance is the most popular type because hospitalization is very expensive.

The company pays for part or all of the cost for the plan, and employees may be able to add coverage at their own expense.

A **health maintenance organization (HMO)** provides health care at its own health center for a fixed fee per month. With an HMO, policyholders must go to a designated clinic. If they pick a doctor who is not part of the HMO, the patient must pay additional costs. HMO plans stress preventive health care to keep down medical costs.

A **preferred provider organization (PPO)** is a group of doctors and hospitals that agree to provide specified medical services to members at prearranged fees. With PPOs, members receive more coverage if they choose health-care providers approved by or affiliated with the plan. PPO health-care providers agree with the insurer to provide health care at reduced rates. While HMOs offer limited referrals to outside specialists, PPOs allow policyholders to choose their own physicians and hospitals within certain limits.

Government Health Insurance

Medicare is the U.S. government's major health insurance program for the elderly. With Medicare, the government partially pays for the health-care costs of people over age 65. **Medicaid** is a federally and state-funded health-care plan for people who are unable to pay for insurance or health care. It provides coverage for the aged, blind, and disabled, and for low-income families who qualify.

Medicare Part D
Medicare coverage Part D was introduced in 2006 to provide prescription drug coverage. Many insurance companies and organizations offer Part D plans. People covered by Medicare pay a deductible, copayment or coinsurance, and a monthly premium for their medical insurance. Some medical services are not covered by Medicare. Plan costs vary. *Do you think it is important for someone with Medicare to also have private medical insurance? Why or why not?*

 Activity correlates to English Language Arts standards.

Section 35.2

After You Read

Review Key Concepts
1. What are the different ways to provide insurance for health-care costs?
2. How might policyholders be required to pay for part of their health-care costs?
3. What types of health-care programs are available?

Academic Skills
4. **English Language Arts** Find and read an article about managed health care. Write a few paragraphs about it. Discuss what it means to consumers in terms of quality and accessibility of medical care.

5. **English Language Arts** In groups of three, identify and define three types of health insurance. Give a brief presentation on the one you feel would be the most beneficial.

@ Go to the *Introduction to Business* Online Learning Center through **glencoe.com** to check your answers.

Section 35.2

Review Key Concepts
1. major medical insurance, hospital expense insurance, surgical expense insurance, medical expense insurance, and group health insurance
2. with a deductible, a copayment, or a share of the cost through coinsurance
3. HMOs, PPOs, Medicare, and Medicaid

Academic Skills
4. **English Language Arts** Students' paragraphs will depend on the article chosen.
5. **English Language Arts** Some of the types include major medical, hospital expense, surgical expense, medical expense, group health and government health.

RETEACH (cont.)

C Critical Thinking

Explain
Preferred Provide Organizations Ask students to explain how a preferred provider organization differs from a health maintenance organization. (An HMO allows fewer choices about where a member can receive care and has a more limited group of physicians than a PPO.)

Medicare Part D Some students may feel that it is important to have both.

ASSESS

After You Read

Have students complete the Section 35.2 After You Read section review.

Online Study Tools
Have students go to the Online Learning Center through **glencoe.com** to:

• Take the Section 35.2 **Practice Test**.
• Download free **Study-to-Go** content to their PDAs or cell phones.

CLOSE

Culminating Activity
Other Insurance Topics
Organize students into small groups. Ask each group to prepare a two-minute presentation on one of the topics in the chapter.

629

Chapter 35 *Review and Activities*

1. Students should write complete sentences using each term correctly.

Review Key Concepts

2. through investments and estate planning and health and life insurance

3. See page 619.

4. It depends on the type of policy and the amount of coverage, policyholder's age, health, and occupation.

5. Health insurance provides protection against the costs of illness and accidents.

6. Major medical pays for care in and out of a hospital. Hospital expense insurance pays for hospital care for a given period of time. Surgical expense insurance pays part of a surgeon's fee. Medical expense insurance covers the costs of a doctor's care not involving surgery. A group health insurance plan covers employees or members of a company.

Critical Thinking

7. Some students may feel that a person who does not have dependents but has savings and investments to cover expenses and bills after death may not need life insurance.

Section 35.1 *Summary*

Life Insurance Just as vehicle insurance and property insurance protect against losses to property, life insurance and health insurance protect people. Life insurance provides protection for a policyholder and survivors. Cash-value insurance provides both protection and savings. A policyholder can borrow the cash value of a policy, if needed, and will pay interest on the loan against the policy. With whole life insurance, a premium that stays the same is paid throughout the policyholder's lifetime. Term insurance provides protection but does not build cash value. Since it does not build savings, term insurance is less expensive than cash-value insurance.

Section 35.2 *Summary*

Health Insurance Health-care costs for a serious illness or accident can be financially devastating to a family. Insurance companies provide various types of health insurance. Major medical insurance, sometimes called catastrophic insurance, is the most important coverage for a serious illness or accident. Hospital expense insurance, surgical expense insurance, medical expense insurance, and group health insurance are also available. Most policies offer a combination of protection. A policy may combine major medical, hospital expense, and surgical expense insurance. Federal and state governments also offer health-care insurance through Medicare and Medicaid.

Vocabulary Review

1. On a sheet of paper, use each of these key terms and academic vocabulary terms in a sentence.

Key Terms

life insurance
proceeds
beneficiary
cash-value insurance
term insurance
coinsurance
copayment

pre-existing condition
health maintenance
   organization (HMO)
preferred provider
   organization (PPO)
Medicare
Medicaid

Academic Vocabulary

estate   medical
purpose   mental
survivor   percentage
features   stress

Review Key Concepts

2. Identify ways to protect your family financially.

3. Describe the different types of life insurance.

4. Discuss the costs of life insurance.

5. Analyze reasons it is important to protect your health.

6. Determine ways to pay for various health-care costs.

---

8. It attracts workers to a company, and workers are more productive when they do not have to worry about bearing the total costs of serious illnesses and injuries.

9. Life insurance is less expensive for young people, who have a long life expectancy. If a young person buys term insurance, it will provide inexpensive protection. If a young person buys cash-value insurance, the policy can build cash value over a long time.

10. Some consumers want only protection, while others want to build savings and investments.

11. Answers may vary, but major medical insurance covers the most serious injuries and illnesses.

Critical Thinking

7. Describe a person for whom you think life insurance is not necessary.

8. Why are companies willing to provide health insurance plans for employees?

9. Should people consider buying some life insurance while they are young? Explain your answer.

10. Why do you think insurance companies offer a wide variety of life insurance policies?

11. Which type of health insurance do you think is most important? Why?

12. Is it fair that employees who hold term life insurance lose that coverage when they leave their company? Explain your answer.

13. Should the government provide health coverage for retired people? Why or why not?

14. If someone cannot afford all types of insurance, in what order of importance would you put the different types? Explain your thoughts.

Write About It

15. If you applied for life insurance, who would you list as beneficiaries? Explain your choices in at least two paragraphs.

16. Suppose the parents of two small children would like to buy life insurance for themselves. In at least two paragraphs, outline a plan for life insurance that you think would be suitable for them.

17. You are a health columnist for a newsletter aimed at people in the entertainment industry, such as dancers, actors, and writers. Write an article explaining why these artists should have adequate disability insurance coverage.

18. How might your lifestyle affect your life expectancy? In at least one page, discuss how your choices could affect your insurance rates.

19. Research the idea of national health-care coverage. Include information about the political, social, and economic issues involved. Then write a two-page paper on your findings.

Technology Applications

Presentation Software

20. Suppose your family would like to purchase health insurance. Research at least three insurance companies. Use the Internet, or contact the companies directly to obtain quotes. Find out if a deductible, copayment, and/or coinsurance are required. What are their policies regarding pre-existing conditions? Based on your findings, which (if any) plan would you choose? Prepare a slideshow of your information for the class.

Business Ethics

Should One Price Fit All?

21. Suppose you visit your doctor. In the waiting room, you overhear a conversation between an elderly patient and a medical assistant. The assistant tells the patient that his insurance will not cover an emergency procedure that cost $3,000. The patient says he cannot pay the whole amount. After discussing the situation with the doctor, the patient is told that the cost will be lowered to $1,500. With a partner, discuss the ethical issues involved.

Chapter 35 Review and Activities **631**

Critical Thinking

12. Because companies see many employees come and go, most cannot afford to provide all former employees with life insurance.

13. Many cannot pay without the help of the government.

14. Answers will vary depending on the needs of the insured.

Write About It

15. Someone who is dependent on a policyholder usually is named as a beneficiary. Family members or friends also can be named as beneficiaries. The choice of beneficiary is a policyholder's decision.

16. For instance, with young children who are still dependent on them, the parents may want to buy term insurance that offers pure protection.

17. Students should mention the possibility of an entertainer being unable to perform and the financial dangers of becoming disabled without insurance.

18. Answers will vary but should discuss various health problems and lifestyle choices.

19. A national health insurance plan would enroll all citizens in the plan. Part of the cost of all coverage would be paid by the federal government, with citizens contributing a share. The government would have much more control over medical facilities and the cost of health services.

Technology Applications

20. Presentations will vary based on each student's findings. Students should express their opinion regarding which plan they would choose.

Business Ethics

21. One major ethical issue involves the doctor's duty to alleviate suffering. On the other hand, lowering of the cost for one patient may not seem fair to others. Another ethical issue is who should bear the burden of medical care for elderly people. There also is the ethical issue of eavesdropping on a conversation.

Applying Academics to Business

English Language Arts

22. Look at the list of terms below. Cross out the one that does not belong with the others. Circle the term that could be used as the heading in a list with the others.

government health insurance
Medicaid
health maintenance organization
Medicare

Mathematics

23. Amber lost her job, but she could continue her health insurance through COBRA. Her monthly cost for the plan with COBRA is 23% higher than an insurance plan she could purchase herself. If the plan she could purchase on her own would cost $163 a month, what would the COBRA plan cost her?

> **THEORY** **Percents Greater than 100**
> Percents greater than 100 represent values greater than 1. If something is 23 percent greater than the original value, it equals 100 percent of the original value plus 23 percent of that value. Percents can be converted to decimals, as follows: $1.00 + 0.23 = 1.23$.

English Language Arts

24. In groups of four, choose one of the following insurance topics: cash-value life, term life, government health, or group health insurance. Research the topic and prepare a short presentation.

Mathematics

25. Jenn's medical bills total $11,000. Her insurance policy states that the policyholder has a $100 deductible and the insurance company will pay 75% of the remaining balance. Write and solve an equation to find how much of the $11,000 Jenn will have to pay.

> **THEORY** **Solving Equations** To solve an equation, use the correct order of operations. First, simplify within the parentheses, and then evaluate any exponents. Multiply and divide from left to right, then add and subtract from left to right.

Applying Academics to Business

22. Health maintenance organization should be crossed out.

23. $1.23 \times \$163 = \$200.49$

24. Student's answers will vary depending on the topic chosen.

25. $x = \$100 + 0.25$ ($\$11,000 - \$100$)
$x = \$2,825$

Active Learning

26. In a recent year, all U.S. life insurance companies as a group invested $481 billion in government bonds, $2 trillion in corporate securities (two-thirds of their investments), more than $285 billion in mortgages and real estate, $105 billion in policy loans, and $244 billion in other investments. In that year, life insurance companies collected about $135 billion in life insurance premiums and about $109 billion in health insurance premiums.

Business in the Real World

27. Answers will depend on interviewees' responses. Advantages of a PPO are that policyholders probably can choose their doctors and medical facilities. The plan may negotiate a lower cost with the health-care provider, which lowers the premium. One advantage of an HMO is that the premiums are likely to cost less.

Active Learning

Insurance Company Investments

26. Go to a library or check the Internet for information about how insurance companies invest the premiums they collect from policyholders. Prepare a chart or poster on your findings, and share it with your class.

Business in the Real World

Health-Care Plans

27. Interview someone you know who has health care through an HMO or a PPO. Ask for his or her opinion on the advantages and disadvantages of the plan. Share your findings through an oral report to your class.

ExamView Assessment Suite CD allows you to print out ready-made unit and chapter tests, complete with answer keys. You can also create customized tests.

TeacherWorks Plus provides complete teacher resources in one convenient package. It includes customizable lesson plans in calendar format, and instant access to many print program resources.

Real LIFE • skills

CONNECT WITH ECONOMICS AND LAW

28. Many companies that once sold just life insurance have "reinvented" themselves as financial services companies. Some promote themselves as "one-stop shops" for all your financial service needs. Access the Web site of your state's insurance regulatory agency. Find out what requirements insurance agents must meet to be able to sell other financial products, such as mutual funds. What are the pros and cons of buying financial products from an insurance company versus a stockbroker?

FIND YOUR DREAM JOB

29. Go to the *Introduction to Business* Online Learning Center through **glencoe.com** for a link to the Occupational Outlook Handbook Web site. Click on the "OOH Search/A-Z Index" link and enter the job title "actuaries." Then write a one-page report about this type of occupation. Conclude your report with a list of things you could do now to prepare yourself to pursue the occupation.

Role Play

RESEARCHING LIFE INSURANCE

30. **Situation** You have been asked to prepare a presentation on various types of life insurance, such as term, whole life, and variable life insurance. Research different types of insurance, and present your ideas to your classmates.

Activity Prepare an outline of your presentation on the different types of life insurance.

Evaluation You will be evaluated on how well you meet the following performance indicators:

- Prepare a written outline of your presentation.
- Contrast the types of life insurance you have researched.
- Describe the type of person for which each type might be suitable.
- Discuss the factors that a consumer should consider when choosing among types of life insurance.
- Answer questions about life insurance.
- Project your voice and use correct grammar.

Standardized Test Practice

Directions Choose the letter of the best answer. Write the letter for the answer on a separate piece of paper.

1. $2\frac{4}{9} \times \frac{3}{16} =$

   A $\frac{33}{67}$ C $\frac{1}{2}$

   B $1\frac{3}{8}$ D $\frac{11}{24}$

 **TEST-TAKING TIP** If you are allowed to use a calculator at a testing site, make sure it is one that is authorized. Turn off other electronic devices, such as phones, pagers, and alarms.

 READING Go to the *Introduction to Business* Online Learning Center through **glencoe.com** for a list of outside reading suggestions.

glencoe.com

Real-World Business and Career Profile

FOCUS

Bell Ringer Activity

Taking Risks
Ask volunteers to share experiences they have had that involved taking calculated risks. (Students are likely to have decided is take the risk of learning to do something fun like learning tricks on a skateboard or bicycle.) Write a list of risks on the board. Ask students to brainstorm companies in your area that help people recover after they take risks. (Students may mention hospitals, doctors' offices, physical therapy clinics, lawyers, and many more.)

TEACH

Teaching Points
Risk Management
Ask students to describe four ways that individuals and businesses can manage risk. (Individuals and businesses can avoid risk, reduce risk, retain risk, and transfer risk.)

Ask students to identify ways a business like Advanced Physical Therapy can help people manage risk. (Advanced Physical Therapy offers wellness and illness prevention services, which are ways for companies to avoid risk. The company also offers physical therapy, which helps people recover from injuries without long-term effect, which is a way to reduce long-term risks.)

JoAnne Jonathan
President and CEO, Advanced Physical Therapy, P.C.
Advanced Physical Therapy offers physical therapy services. The Indianapolis-based company's services are available at 10 outpatient clinics and three work conditioning centers.

Q & A

Describe your job responsibilities.
JoAnne: I meet with department heads throughout the company to include finance, marketing, billing, and regional directors of clinics. I review past business and future trends, solve current problems and create new opportunities for business growth.

What skills are most important in your business?
JoAnne: People like doing business with people they like. Being a problem solver is also important so you can anticipate problems with corrective action.

What is your key to success?
JoAnne: My success comes from the people I've hired and trained. Some of them have been with us for 17 or more years. They do a good job, and we provide ongoing training for all of the staff. Our goal is to make you feel better and to try to have fun while doing it, for both the patients and the staff.

What skills did you learn in high school that helped you become a successful entrepreneur?
JoAnne: I learned something from just about every subject, but especially math and statistics. School teaches you how to figure out problems. It also gives you discipline— you learn how to learn. I apply that to launching and running a business. You also learn communication at school, whether it's reading and writing skills that I use in understanding contracts or public speaking, doing conference calls, or interviews.

What advice would you give students interested in starting a business?
JoAnne: Read books and journals, take classes, and talk to mentors. Have financial backing for worse-case scenarios. Hire the best-qualified people. Partnerships may have their advantages, yet I chose to start my company alone. Prepare to put in a lot of time building, refining, and working in the business. You have to love and have a passion for your business. Maintain honesty and integrity in all that you do.

Critical Thinking *What might be the benefits and disadvantages to starting a company alone verses building a partnership?*

Critical Thinking
Starting a company alone means that you receive all of the profits of the business and take sole responsibility for the debts and actions of the business. A partnership brings added resources, but can also include differences of opinion about various issues, such as the direction the company should head in, managerial style, etc.

Some Qualifications Needed to Own a Physical Therapy Clinic

Academic Skills and Abilities

Biology; chemistry; interpersonal skills; general business management skills; verbal and written communication skills; multitasking, organizing, and planning skills

Academic Skills Required to Complete Tasks at Advanced Physical Therapy			
Tasks	Math	Science	English Language Arts
Hold meetings			◆
Assign duties			◆
Develop patient treatment plans		◆	◆
Assess patient progress		◆	
Customer service			◆
Schedule employees	◆		◆
Order supplies and equipment	◆		◆
Analyze financials	◆		◆

Education and Training

All states require physical therapists to pass a licensure exam before they can practice, after graduating from an accredited physical therapist educational program.

Career Path

Physical therapists are expected to continue their professional development by participating in continuing education courses and workshops. In fact, a number of states require continuing education as a condition of maintaining licensure.

Preparing for a Career
Self-Assessment Checklist

Use this self-assessment checklist to help determine ways you could make your workplace more healthful.

✔ Think about the factors that can ensure your health in your workplace.

✔ Recharge yourself by getting enough sleep, eating healthy food, and pursuing an active lifestyle.

✔ Think about ways to stay on guard to prevent injury or addictive behavior.

✔ Consider ways you can improve ergonomics and avoid repetitive stress injuries.

✔ Create a list of positive ways to cope with stress. Include ways of recognizing signs that stress has become a problem as well as ways to find solutions.

✔ Think about the ways that your attitude, abilities, and skills can enhance your ability to deal with stress.

✔ Consider ways that you can make the workplace more efficient and to ensure the kind of support that will help you recognize and avoid problems.

✔ Learn first aid so that you will be prepared to help others and to respond quickly to emergencies.

635

ASSESS

Write About It
Advanced Physical Therapy, P.C.
Ask students to write a summary of what they like about Advanced Physical Therapy's business concept. (Students may say that they like the idea of a business that makes people well, helps people to stay healthy, and reduces their risk of injury or ill health.)

Academic Vocabulary
Career Planning
Ask students to read the Self-Assessment Checklist, then write one or more paragraphs about preparing for a career. Have students use some words from the Academic Vocabulary Glossary. (Example: In order to prepare for risk, people need *adequate* time and training so that they can *anticipate potential* problems. If people *allocate* a bit of each day so that they can *assess* ergonomics and workplace hazards, workers can have happier, healthier careers.)

CLOSE

Cooperative Learning
Technology Applications
Ask students to work in pairs and develop an idea for a business that helps people improve their health. Have them work together to develop an advertisement for the program. (Brochures should include marketing copy, visuals, and program information.)

Preparing for a Career

Minimizing Career Risks No career choice is risk-free. Remind students that careers in fields that seem to offer little potential for advancement today may grow explosively 10 years from now because of changing technology, and vice versa. Ask students: Why is it important to know the risks that are particular to different careers? (If you know the risks, you can plan ways to manage them.) Tell students they will have an opportunity to think about careers and the career-planning process as they read the Self-Assessment Checklists in this book.

FOCUS

Discussion Starter
Lead a discussion about understanding risk. Ask students how they can learn to manage risk.

Step 1

Brainstorm Skills
Have students go to the *Introduction to Business* Online Learning Center through **glencoe.com** for a graphic organizer they can use to brainstorm the skills needed to complete the project.

Step 2

Think About the Type of Vehicle You Want
Students can use the Internet and car ads to explore options.

TEACH

Step 3

Build Background
Technology Have students brainstorm ways they can use technology to manage risk. (They can use the Internet to research companies that offer auto insurance and learn more about technologies intended to make cars safer so that they can learn to avoid or reduce risk. It is impossible to avoid all risks or to plan for every eventuality. However, learning about their options can make people better able to manage the most common risks.)

Understanding Risk
You will most likely own a vehicle someday. Your vehicle will be a valuable piece of property that you will want to insure. Vehicle insurance will help cover costs of the vehicle in case of an accident.

Thematic Project Assignment
In this project you will make a chart that compares vehicle insurance policies.

Step 1 Brainstorm Skills You Need to Complete This Activity

Your success in making a chart that compares vehicle insurance policies will depend on your skills. Preview the activity, then brainstorm a list of the skills you will need to use to complete the activity and describe how you will use them. Skills you might use include:

Academic Skills	reading and writing
Basic Skills	speaking, listening, and thinking
Technology Skills	word processing, keyboarding, and graphic software

 SKILLS PREVIEW Go to the *Introduction to Business* Online Learning Center through **glencoe.com** for a graphic organizer you can use to brainstorm the skills you will use to complete the project.

Step 2 Think About the Type of Vehicle You Want

Think about the type of vehicle you dream of having. You work hard for the money to pay for the vehicle, so you want to make sure you have insurance to cover the vehicle in case it is stolen or damaged in an accident.

Step 3 Build Background Knowledge

Preview information on comparing vehicle insurance policies.

Insurance *Is a* Must *for* Car Owners

Are you thinking of buying your first car? Before you sign your name on the dotted line, make sure you have already arranged for insurance coverage. An insurance agent can help you choose which kind of insurance is best for you. Check with more than one agent to make sure you are getting the right coverage for the best price.

What type of insurance should you consider? Your agent will know the minimum requirements for your state. Ask an adult to help you decide what you need to protect your property and yourself, your passengers, and other people in case you have an accident.

Step 4 Connect with Your Community

Interview two adults in your community. Ask them about the type of vehicle insurance coverage they have. Ask them who their agent is, the name of the company that insures them, and why they chose this company. Think about how important insurance is to help you manage risk.

Step 4

Connect with Your Community
Ask students to describe how their community shapes their response to risk.
(A strong community is also a strong guard against risk. For instance, communities hire police and fire fighters to avoid, reduce, and share risks in the community.)

Step 5 Research Vehicle Insurance

Use library and Internet resources, phone calls, or personal interviews to research vehicle insurance. Use the project checklist as a guide to your research. Keep records of your sources of information.

Step 6 Develop a Chart Comparing Vehicle Insurance

Use word-processing and spreadsheet software to develop a chart that compares vehicle insurance that includes all of the information described in the project checklist.

Developing a Chart Comparing Vehicle Insurance

✔ Make a list of five different vehicle insurance companies. Vehicle insurance may be listed as car insurance. Use the Internet, phone book, or personal interviews to find the names of insurance companies.

✔ Choose a vehicle that you would like to own someday.

✔ Use a computer spreadsheet program to keep track of the information you are going to gather.

✔ Use the Internet, or call or visit five insurance agents or insurance companies to ask what coverage is recommended for the vehicle of your choice. Also, ask the cost of each type of coverage. Take detailed notes. Ask about the following coverage: bodily injury liability, property damage liability, collision coverage, medical payments coverage, comprehensive coverage, uninsured and underinsured motorists protection, and miscellaneous coverage. Use this information as the base for comparisons with other insurance companies.

✔ Make a chart that shows the type of vehicle, the coverage, and the cost of the coverage for the five different insurance companies. Also, add a column that shows any recommendations for different coverage and the cost of that coverage.

Self Connections

✔ Describe the results of your research with the adults you interviewed.

✔ Describe the type of vehicle insurance they have.

✔ Explain what the investigation and its results mean to you.

Step 7 Evaluate Your Presentation

@ **RUBRIC** Go to the *Introduction to Business* Online Learning Center through **glencoe.com** for a rubric you can use to evaluate your final report.

637

TEACH (cont.)

Step 6

Develop a Chart Comparing Vehicle Insurance
Give students these tips on writing:

- Know your audience.
- Organize your plan by developing an outline and using titles and subtitles.
- Write concisely (briefly but completely).
- Write in easy-to-read, simple language.

ASSESS

Step 7

Evaluate Your Chart
Rubric Encourage students to use the rubric to evaluate their charts.

CLOSE

Culminating Activity Understanding Risk Interviews
Have students form pairs and interview each other about the insurance plans they researched and how their opinions and perceptions of auto insurance evolved during the course of the project. (Interviews will vary depending on students' reactions to their research.)

Step 5

Research Vehicle Insurance
Students can go to the *Introduction to Business* Online Learning Center through **glencoe.com** for a rubric they can use as a content checklist when researching their charts.

Number and Operations

▶ *Understand numbers, ways of representing numbers, relationships among numbers, and number systems*

Fraction, Decimal, and Percent

A percent is a ratio that compares a number to 100. To write a percent as a fraction, drop the percent sign, and use the number as the numerator in a fraction with a denominator of 100. Simplify, if possible. For example, $76\% = \frac{76}{100}$, or $\frac{19}{25}$. To write a fraction as a percent, convert it to an equivalent fraction with a denominator of 100. For example, $\frac{3}{4} = \frac{75}{100}$, or 75%. A fraction can be expressed as a percent by first converting the fraction to a decimal (divide the numerator by the denominator) and then converting the decimal to a percent by moving the decimal point two places to the right.

Comparing Numbers on a Number Line

In order to compare and understand the relationship between real numbers in various forms, it is helpful to use a number line. The zero point on a number line is called the origin; the points to the left of the origin are negative, and those to the right are positive. The number line below shows how numbers in percent, decimal, fraction, and integer form can be compared.

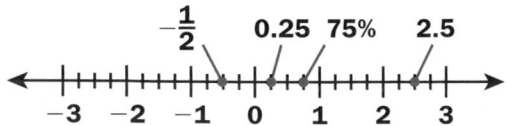

Percents Greater Than 100 and Less Than 1

Percents greater than 100% represent values greater than 1. For example, if the weight of an object is 250% of another, it is 2.5, or $2\frac{1}{2}$, times the weight.

Percents less than 1 represent values less than $\frac{1}{100}$. In other words, 0.1% is one tenth of one percent, which can also be represented in decimal form as 0.001, or in fraction form as $\frac{1}{1,000}$. Similarly, 0.01% is one hundredth of one percent or 0.0001 or $\frac{1}{10,000}$.

Ratio, Rate, and Proportion

A ratio is a comparison of two numbers using division. If a basketball player makes 8 out of 10 free throws, the ratio is written as 8 to 10, 8:10, or $\frac{8}{10}$. Ratios are usually written in simplest form. In simplest form, the ratio "8 out of 10" is 4 to 5, 4:5, or $\frac{4}{5}$. A rate is a ratio of two measurements having different kinds of units—cups per gallon, or miles per hour, for example. When a rate is simplified so that it has a denominator of 1, it is called a unit rate. An example of a unit rate is 9 miles per hour. A proportion is an equation stating that two ratios are equal. $\frac{3}{18} = \frac{13}{78}$ is an example of a proportion. The cross products of a proportion are also equal. $\frac{3}{18} = \frac{13}{78}$ and $3 \times 78 = 18 \times 13$.

Representing Large and Small Numbers

In order to represent large and small numbers, it is important to understand the number system. Our number system is based on 10, and the value of each place is 10 times the value of the place to its right.

The value of a digit is the product of a digit and its place value. For instance, in the number 6,400, the 6 has a value of six thousands and the 4 has a value of four hundreds. A place value chart can help you read numbers. In the chart, each group of three digits is called a period. Commas separate the periods: the ones period, the thousands period, the millions period, and so on. Values to the right of the ones period are decimals. By understanding place value you can write very large numbers like 5 billion and more, and very small numbers that are less than 1.

Scientific Notation
When dealing with very large numbers like 1,500,000, or very small numbers like 0.000015, it is helpful to keep track of their value by writing the numbers in scientific notation. Powers of 10 with positive exponents are used with a decimal between 1 and 10 to express large numbers. The exponent represents the number of places the decimal point is moved to the right. So, 528,000 is written in scientific notation as 5.28×10^5. Powers of 10 with negative exponents are used with a decimal between 1 and 10 to express small numbers. The exponent represents the number of places the decimal point is moved to the left. The number 0.00047 is expressed as 4.7×10^{-4}.

Factor, Multiple, and Prime Factorization
Two or more numbers that are multiplied to form a product are called factors. Divisibility rules can be used to determine whether 2, 3, 4, 5, 6, 8, 9, or 10 are factors of a given number. Multiples are the products of a given number and various integers.

For example, 8 is a multiple of 4 because $4 \times 2 = 8$. A prime number is a whole number that has exactly two factors: 1 and itself. A composite number is a whole number that has more than two factors. Zero and 1 are neither prime nor composite. A composite number can be expressed as the product of its prime factors. The prime factorization of 40 is $2 \times 2 \times 2 \times 5$, or $2^3 \times 5$. The numbers 2 and 5 are prime numbers.

Integers
A negative number is a number less than zero. Negative numbers like –8, positive numbers like +6, and zero are members of the set of integers. Integers can be represented as points on a number line. A set of integers can be written {..., –3, –2, –1, 0, 1, 2, 3, ...} where ... means "continues indefinitely."

Real, Rational, and Irrational Numbers
The real number system is made up of the sets of rational and irrational numbers. Rational numbers are numbers that can be written in the form a/b where a and b are integers and $b \neq 0$. Examples are 0.45, $\frac{1}{2}$, and $\sqrt{36}$. Irrational numbers are non-repeating, non-terminating decimals. Examples are $\sqrt{71}$, π, and 0.020020002….

Complex and Imaginary Numbers
A complex number is a mathematical expression with a real number element and an imaginary number element. Imaginary numbers are multiples of i, the "imaginary" square root of –1. Complex numbers are represented by $a + bi$, where a and b are real numbers and i represents the imaginary element. When a quadratic equation

does not have a real number solution, the solution can be represented by a complex number. Like real numbers, complex numbers can be added, subtracted, multiplied, and divided.

Vectors and Matrices

A matrix is a set of numbers or elements arranged in rows and columns to form a rectangle. The number of rows is represented by m and the number of columns is represented by n. To describe the number of rows and columns in a matrix, list the number of rows first using the format $m \times n$. Matrix A below is a 3×3 matrix because it has 3 rows and 3 columns. To name an element of a matrix, the letter i is used to denote the row and j is used to denote the column, and the element is labeled in the form $a_{i,j}$. In matrix A below, $a_{3,2}$ is 4.

$$\text{Matrix A} = \begin{pmatrix} 1 & 3 & 5 \\ 0 & 6 & 8 \\ 3 & 4 & 5 \end{pmatrix}$$

A vector is a matrix with only one column or row of elements. A transposed column vector, or a column vector turned on its side, is a row vector. In the example below, row vector b' is the transpose of column vector b.

$$b = \begin{pmatrix} 1 \\ 2 \\ 3 \\ 4 \end{pmatrix}$$

$$b' = \begin{pmatrix} 1 & 2 & 3 & 4 \end{pmatrix}$$

▶ Understand meanings of operations and how they relate to one another

Properties of Addition and Multiplication

Properties are statements that are true for any numbers. For example, $3 + 8$ is the same as $8 + 3$ because each expression equals 11. This illustrates the Commutative Property of Addition. Likewise, $3 \times 8 = 8 \times 3$ illustrates the Commutative Property of Multiplication.

When evaluating expressions, it is often helpful to group or associate the numbers. The Associative Property says that the way in which numbers are grouped when added or multiplied does not change the sum or product. The following properties are also true:

- **Additive Identity Property:** When 0 is added to any number, the sum is the number.

- **Multiplicative Identity Property:** When any number is multiplied by 1, the product is the number.

- **Multiplicative Property of Zero:** When any number is multiplied by 0, the product is 0.

Rational Numbers

A number that can be written as a fraction is called a rational number. Terminating and repeating decimals are rational numbers because both can be written as fractions.

Decimals that are neither terminating nor repeating are called irrational numbers because they cannot be written as fractions. Terminating decimals can be converted to fractions by placing the number (without the decimal point) in the numerator. Count the number of places to the right of the decimal point, and in the denominator, place a 1 followed by a number of zeros equal to the number of places that you counted. The fraction can then be reduced to simplest form.

Writing a Fraction as a Decimal
Any fraction $\frac{a}{b}$, where $b \neq 0$, can be written as a decimal by dividing the numerator by the denominator. So, $\frac{a}{b} = a \div b$. If the division ends, or terminates, when the remainder is zero, the decimal is a terminating decimal. Not all fractions can be written as terminating decimals. Some have a repeating decimal. A bar indicates that the decimal repeats forever. For example, the fraction $\frac{4}{9}$ can be converted to a repeating decimal, $0.\overline{4}$.

Adding and Subtracting Like Fractions
Fractions with the same denominator are called like fractions. To add like fractions, add the numerators and write the sum over the denominator. To add mixed numbers with like fractions, add the whole numbers and fractions separately, adding the numerators of the fractions, then simplifying if necessary. The rule for subtracting fractions with like

denominators is similar to the rule for adding. The numerators can be subtracted and the difference written over the denominator. Mixed numbers are written as improper fractions before subtracting. These same rules apply to adding or subtracting like algebraic fractions.

Adding and Subtracting Unlike Fractions
Fractions with different denominators are called unlike fractions. The least common multiple of the denominators is used to rename the fractions with a common denominator. After a common denominator is found, the numerators can then be added or subtracted. To add mixed numbers with unlike fractions, rename the mixed numbers as improper fractions. Then find a common denominator, add the numerators, and simplify the answer.

Multiplying Rational Numbers
To multiply fractions, multiply the numerators and multiply the denominators. If the numerators and denominators have common factors, they can be simplified before multiplication. If the fractions have different signs, then the product will be negative. Mixed numbers can be multiplied in the same manner, after first renaming them as improper fractions. A fraction that contains one or more variables in the numerator or denominator is called an algebraic fraction. Algebraic fractions may be multiplied using the same method described above.

Dividing Rational Numbers

To divide a number by a rational number (a fraction, for example), multiply the first number by the multiplicative inverse of the second. Two numbers whose product is 1 are called multiplicative inverses, or reciprocals. $\frac{7}{4} \times \frac{4}{7} = 1$. When dividing by a mixed number, first rename it as an improper fraction, and then multiply by its multiplicative inverse. This process of multiplying by a number's reciprocal can also be used when dividing algebraic fractions.

Adding Integers

To add integers with the same sign, add their absolute values. The sum then takes the same sign as the addends. The equation $-5 + (-2) = -7$ is an example of adding two integers with the same sign. To add integers with different signs, subtract their absolute values. The sum takes the same sign as the addend with the greater absolute value.

Subtracting Integers

The rules for adding integers are extended to the subtraction of integers. To subtract an integer, add its additive inverse. For example, to find the difference $2 - 5$, add the additive inverse of 5 to 2: $2 + (-5) = -3$. The rule for subtracting integers can be used to solve real-world problems and to evaluate algebraic expressions.

Additive Inverse Property

Two numbers with the same absolute value but different signs are called opposites. For example, -4 and 4 are opposites. An integer and its opposite are also called additive inverses. The Additive Inverse Property says that the sum of any number and its additive inverse is zero. The Commutative, Associative, and Identity Properties also apply to integers. These properties help when adding more than two integers.

Absolute Value

In mathematics, when two integers on a number line are on opposite sides of zero, and they are the same distance from zero, they have the same absolute value. The symbol for absolute value is two vertical bars on either side of the number. For example, $|-5| = 5$.

Multiplying Integers

Since multiplication is repeated addition, $3(-7)$ means that -7 is used as an addend 3 times. By the Commutative Property of Multiplication, $3(-7) = -7(3)$. The product of two integers with different signs is always negative. The product of two integers with the same sign is always positive.

Dividing Integers

The quotient of two integers can be found by dividing the numbers using their absolute values. The quotient of two integers with the same sign is positive, and the quotient of two integers with a different sign is negative. $-12 \div (-4) = 3$ and $12 \div (-4) = -3$. The division of integers is used in statistics to find the average, or mean, of a set of data. When finding the mean of a set of numbers, find the sum of the numbers, and then divide by the number in the set.

Adding and Multiplying Vectors and Matrices

In order to add two matrices together, they must have the same number of rows and columns. In matrix addition, the corresponding elements are added to each other. In other words $(a + b)_{ij} = a_{ij} + b_{ij}$. For example,

$$\begin{pmatrix} 1 & 2 \\ 2 & 1 \end{pmatrix} + \begin{pmatrix} 3 & 6 \\ 0 & 1 \end{pmatrix} = \begin{pmatrix} 1+3 & 2+6 \\ 2+0 & 1+1 \end{pmatrix} = \begin{pmatrix} 4 & 8 \\ 2 & 2 \end{pmatrix}$$

Matrix multiplication requires that the number of elements in each row in the first matrix is equal to the number of elements in each column in the second. The elements of the first row of the first matrix are multiplied by the corresponding elements of the first column of the second matrix and then added together to get the first element of the product matrix. To get the second element, the elements in the first row of the first matrix are multiplied by the corresponding elements in the second column of the second matrix then added, and so on, until every row of the first matrix is multiplied by every column of the second. See the example below.

$$\begin{pmatrix} 1 & 2 \\ 3 & 4 \end{pmatrix} \times \begin{pmatrix} 3 & 6 \\ 0 & 1 \end{pmatrix} = \begin{pmatrix} (1\times3)+(2\times0) & (1\times6)+(2\times1) \\ (3\times3)+(4\times0) & (3\times6)+(4\times1) \end{pmatrix} = \begin{pmatrix} 3 & 8 \\ 9 & 22 \end{pmatrix}$$

Vector addition and multiplication are performed in the same way, but there is only one column and one row.

Permutations and Combinations

Permutations and combinations are used to determine the number of possible outcomes in different situations. An arrangement, listing, or pattern in which order is important is called a permutation. The symbol P(6, 3) represents the number of permutations of 6 things taken 3 at a time. For P(6, 3), there are $6 \times 5 \times 4$ or 120 possible outcomes. An arrangement or listing where order is not important is called a combination. The symbol C(10, 5)

represents the number of combinations of 10 things taken 5 at a time. For C(10, 5), there are $(10 \times 9 \times 8 \times 7 \times 6) \div (5 \times 4 \times 3 \times 2 \times 1)$ or 252 possible outcomes.

Powers and Exponents

An expression such as $3 \times 3 \times 3 \times 3$ can be written as a power. A power has two parts, a base and an exponent. $3 \times 3 \times 3 \times 3 = 3^4$. The base is the number that is multiplied (3). The exponent tells how many times the base is used as a factor (4 times). Numbers and variables can be written using exponents. For example, $8 \times 8 \times 8 \times m \times m \times m \times m \times m$ can be expressed 8^3m^5. Exponents also can be used with place value to express numbers in expanded form. Using this method, 1,462 can be written as $(1 \times 10^3) + (4 \times 10^2) + (6 \times 10^1) + (2 \times 10^0)$.

Squares and Square Roots

The square root of a number is one of two equal factors of a number. Every positive number has both a positive and a negative square root. For example, since $8 \times 8 = 64$, 8 is a square root of 64. Since $(-8) + (-8) = 64$, -8 is also a square root of 64. The notation $\sqrt{}$ indicates the positive square root, $-\sqrt{}$ indicates the negative square root, and $\pm\sqrt{}$ indicates both square roots. For example, $\sqrt{81} = 9$, $-\sqrt{49} = -7$, and $\pm\sqrt{4} = \pm2$. The square root of a negative number is an imaginary number because any two factors of a negative number must have different signs, and are therefore not equivalent.

Logarithm

A logarithm is the inverse of exponentiation. The logarithm of a number x in base b is equal to the number n. Therefore, $b^n = x$ and $\log_b x = n$. For example, $\log_4(64) = 3$ because $4^3 = 64$.

The most commonly used bases for logarithms are 10, the common logarithm; 2, the binary logarithm; and the constant e, the natural logarithm (also called $ln(x)$ instead of $\log_e(x)$). Below is a list of some of the rules of logarithms that are important to understand if you are going to use them.

$$\log_b(xy) = \log_b(x) + \log_b(y)$$

$$\log_b(x/y) = \log_b(x) - \log_b(y)$$

$$\log_b(1/x) = -\log_b(x)$$

$$\log_b(x)y = y\log_b(x)$$

▶ Compute fluently and make reasonable estimates

Estimation by Rounding
When rounding numbers, look at the digit to the right of the place to which you are rounding. If the digit is 5 or greater, round up. If it is less than 5, round down. For example, to round 65,137 to the nearest hundred, look at the number in the tens place. Since 3 is less than 5, round down to 65,100. To round the same number to the nearest ten thousandth, look at the number in the thousandths place. Since it is 5, round up to 70,000.

Finding Equivalent Ratios
Equivalent ratios have the same meaning. Just like finding equivalent fractions, to find an equivalent ratio, multiply or divide both sides by the same number. For example, you can multiply 7 by both sides of the ratio 6:8 to get 42:56. Instead, you can also divide

both sides of the same ratio by 2 to get 3:4. Find the simplest form of a ratio by dividing to find equivalent ratios until you can't go any further without going into decimals. So, 160:240 in simplest form is 2:3. To write a ratio in the form 1:n, divide both sides by the left-hand number. In other words, to change 8:20 to 1:n, divide both sides by 8 to get 1:2.5.

Front-End Estimation
Front-end estimation can be used to quickly estimate sums and differences before adding or subtracting. To use this technique, add or subtract just the digits of the two highest place values, and replace the other place values with zero. This will give you an estimation of the solution of a problem. For example, 93,471 – 22,825 can be changed to 93,000 – 22,000 or 71,000. This estimate can be compared to your final answer to judge its correctness.

Judging Reasonableness
When solving an equation, it is important to check your work by considering how reasonable your answer is. For example, consider the equation $9\frac{3}{4} \times 4\frac{1}{3}$. Since $9\frac{3}{4}$ is between 9 and 10 and $4\frac{1}{3}$ is between 4 and 5, only values that are between 9×4 or 36 and 10×5 or 50 will be reasonable. You can also use front-end estimation, or you can round and estimate a reasonable answer. In the equation 73×25, you can round and solve to estimate a reasonable answer to be near 70×30 or 2,100.

Algebra

▶ *Understand patterns, relations, and functions*

Relation

A relation is a generalization comparing sets of ordered pairs for an equation or inequality such as $x = y + 1$ or $x > y$. The first element in each pair, the x values, form the domain. The second values in each pair, the y values, form the range.

Function

A function is a special relation in which each member of the domain is paired with exactly one member in the range. Functions may be represented using ordered pairs, tables, or graphs. One way to determine whether a relation is a function is to use the vertical line test. Using an object to represent a vertical line, move the object from left to right across the graph. If, for each value of x in the domain, the object passes through no more than one point on the graph, then the graph represents a function.

Linear and Nonlinear Functions

Linear functions have graphs that are straight lines. These graphs represent constant rates of change. In other words, the slope between any two pairs of points on the graph is the same. Nonlinear functions do not have constant rates of change. The slope changes along these graphs. Therefore, the graphs of nonlinear functions are *not* straight lines. Graphs of curves represent nonlinear functions. The equation for a linear function can be written in the form $y = mx + b$, where m represents the constant rate of change, or the slope. Therefore, you can determine whether a function is linear by looking at the equation. For example, the equation $y = \frac{3}{x}$ is nonlinear because x is in the denominator and the equation cannot be written in the form $y = mx + b$. A nonlinear function does not increase or decrease at a constant rate. You can check this by using a table and finding the increase or decrease in y for each regular increase in x. For example, if for each increase in x by 2, y does not increase or decrease the same amount each time, the function is nonlinear.

Linear Equations in Two Variables

In a linear equation with two variables, such as $y = x - 3$, the variables appear in separate terms and neither variable contains an exponent other than 1. The graphs of all linear equations are straight lines. All points on a line are solutions of the equation that is graphed.

Quadratic and Cubic Functions

A quadratic function is a polynomial equation of the second degree, generally expressed as $ax^2 + bx + c = 0$, where a, b, and c are real numbers and a is not equal to zero. Similarly, a cubic function is a polynomial equation of the third degree, usually expressed as $ax^3 + bx^2 + cx + d = 0$. Quadratic functions can be graphed using an equation or a table of values. For example, to graph $y = 3x^2 + 1$, substitute the values −1, −0.5, 0, 0.5, and 1 for x to yield the point coordinates (−1, 4), (−0.5, 1.75), (0, 1), (0.5, 1.75), and (1, 4). Plot these points on a coordinate grid and connect the points in the form of a parabola. Cubic functions also can be graphed by making a table of values. The points of a cubic function from a curve. There is one point at which the curve changes from opening upward to opening downward, or vice versa, called the point of inflection.

Slope

Slope is the ratio of the rise, or vertical change, to the run, or horizontal change of a line: slope = rise/run. Slope (m) is the same for any two points on a straight line and can be found by using the coordinates of any two points on the line:

$$m = \frac{y_2 - y_1}{x_2 - x_1}, \text{ where } x_2 \neq x_1.$$

Asymptotes

An asymptote is a straight line that a curve approaches but never actually meets or crosses. Theoretically, the asymptote meets the curve at infinity. For example, in the function $f(x) = \frac{1}{x}$, two asymptotes are being approached: the line $y = 0$ and $x = 0$. See the graph of the function below.

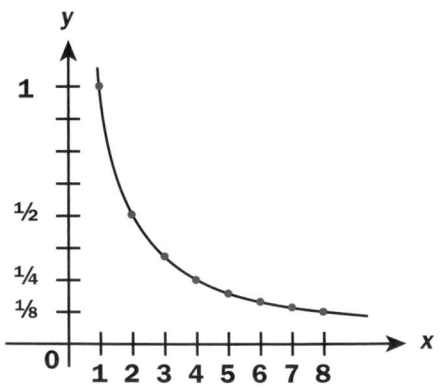

Represent and analyze mathematical situations and structures using algebraic symbols

Variables and Expressions

Algebra is a language of symbols. A variable is a placeholder for a changing value. Any letter, such as x, can be used as a variable. Expressions such as $x + 2$ and $4x$ are algebraic expressions because they represent sums and/or products of variables and numbers. Usually, mathematicians avoid the use of i and e for variables because they have other mathematical meanings ($i = \sqrt{-1}$ and e is used with natural logarithms). To evaluate an algebraic expression, replace the variable or variables with known values, and then solve using order of operations. Translate verbal phrases into algebraic expressions by first defining a variable: choose a variable and a quantity for the variable to represent. In this way, algebraic expressions can be used to represent real-world situations.

Constant and Coefficient

A constant is a fixed value unlike a variable, which can change. Constants are usually represented by numbers, but they can also be represented by symbols. For example, π is a symbolic representation of the value 3.1415…. A coefficient is a constant by which a variable or other object is multiplied. For example, in the expression $7x^2 + 5x + 9$, the coefficient of x^2 is 7 and the coefficient of x is 5. The number 9 is a constant and not a coefficient.

Monomial and Polynomial

A monomial is a number, a variable, or a product of numbers and/or variables such as 3×4. An algebraic expression that contains one or more monomials is called a polynomial. In a polynomial, there are no terms with variables in the denominator and no terms with variables under a radical sign. Polynomials can be classified by the number of terms contained in the expression. Therefore, a polynomial with two terms is called a binomial ($z^2 - 1$), and a polynomial with three terms is called a trinomial ($2y^3 + 4y^2 - y$). Polynomials also can be classified by their degrees. The degree of a monomial is the sum of the exponents of its variables. The degree of a nonzero constant such as 6 or 10 is 0. The constant 0 has no degree. For example, the monomial $4b^5c^2$ had a degree of 7. The degree of a polynomial is the same as that of the term with the greatest degree. For example, the polynomial $3x^4 - 2y^3 + 4y^2 - y$ has a degree of 4.

Equation

An equation is a mathematical sentence that states that two expressions are equal. The two expressions in an equation are always separated by an equal sign. When solving for a variable in an equation, you must perform the same operations on both sides of the equation in order for the mathematical sentence to remain true.

Solving Equations with Variables

To solve equations with variables on both sides, use the Addition or Subtraction Property of Equality to write an equivalent equation with the variables on the same side. For example, to solve $5x - 8 = 3x$, subtract $3x$ from each side to get $2x - 8 = 0$. Then add 8 to each side to get $2x = 8$. Finally, divide each side by 2 to find that $x = 4$.

Solving Equations with Grouping Symbols

Equations often contain grouping symbols such as parentheses or brackets. The first step in solving these equations is to use the Distributive Property to remove the grouping symbols. For example $5(x + 2) = 25$ can be changed to $5x + 10 = 25$, and then solved to find that $x = 3$.

Some equations have no solution. That is, there is no value of the variable that results in a true sentence. For such an equation, the solution set is called the null or empty set, and is represented by the symbol $\varnothing$ or {}. Other equations may have every number as the solution. An equation that is true for every value of the variable is called the identity.

Inequality

A mathematical sentence that contains the symbols < (less than), > (greater than), ≤ (less than or equal to), or ≥ (greater than or equal to) is called an inequality. For example, the statement that it is legal to drive 55 miles per hour or slower on a stretch of the highway can be shown by the sentence $s \leq 55$. Inequalities with variables are called open sentences. When a variable is replaced with a number, the inequality may be true or false.

Solving Inequalities

Solving an inequality means finding values for the variable that make the inequality true. Just as with equations, when you add or subtract the same number from each side of an inequality, the inequality remains true. For example, if you add 5 to each side of the inequality $3x < 6$, the resulting inequality $3x + 5 < 11$ is also true. Adding or subtracting the same number from each side of an inequality does not affect the inequality sign. When multiplying or dividing each side of an inequality by the same positive number, the inequality remains true. In such cases, the inequality symbol does not change. When multiplying or dividing each side of an inequality by a negative number, the inequality symbol must be reversed. For example, when dividing each side of the inequality $-4x \geq -8$ by -2, the inequality sign must be changed to $\leq$ for the resulting inequality, $2x \leq 4$, to be true. Since the solutions to an inequality include all rational numbers satisfying it, inequalities have an infinite number of solutions.

Representing Inequalities on a Number Line

The solutions of inequalities can be graphed on a number line. For example, if the solution of an inequality is $x < 5$, start an arrow at 5 on the number line, and continue the arrow to the left to show all values less than 5 as the solution. Put an open circle at 5 to show that the point 5 is *not* included in the graph. Use a closed circle when graphing solutions that are greater than or equal to, or less than or equal to, a number.

Order of Operations

Solving a problem may involve using more than one operation. The answer can depend on the order in which you do the operations. To make sure that there is just one answer to a series of computations, mathematicians have agreed upon an order in which to do the operations. First simplify within the parentheses, and then evaluate any exponents. Then multiply and divide from left to right, and finally add and subtract from left to right.

Parametric Equations

Given an equation with more than one unknown, a statistician can draw conclusions about those unknown quantities through the use of parameters, independent variables that the statistician already knows something about. For example, you can find the velocity of an object if you make some assumptions about distance and time parameters.

Recursive Equations

In recursive equations, every value is determined by the previous value. You must first plug an initial value into the equation to get the first value, and then you can use the first value to determine the next one, and so on. For example, in order to determine what the population of pigeons will be in New York City in three years, you can use an equation with the birth, death, immigration, and emigration rates of the birds. Input the current population size into the equation to determine next year's population size, then repeat until you have calculated the value for which you are looking.

▶ *Use mathematical models to represent and understand quantitative relationships*

Solving Systems of Equations

Two or more equations together are called a system of equations. A system of equations can have one solution, no solution, or infinitely many solutions. One method for solving a system of equations is to graph the equations on the same coordinate plane. The coordinates of the point where the graphs intersect is the solution. In other words, the solution of a system is the ordered pair that is a solution of all equations. A more accurate way to solve a system of two equations is by using a method called substitution. Write both equations in terms of y. Replace y in the first equation with the right side of the second equation. Check the solution by graphing. You can solve a system of three equations using matrix algebra.

Graphing Inequalities

To graph an inequality, first graph the related equation, which is the boundary. All points in the shaded region are solutions of the inequality. If an inequality contains the symbol $\leq$ or $\geq$, then use a solid line to indicate that the boundary is included in the graph. If an inequality contains the symbol $<$ or $>$, then use a dashed line to indicate that the boundary is not included in the graph.

▶ Analyze change in various contexts

Rate of Change

A change in one quantity with respect to another quantity is called the rate of change. Rates of change can be described using slope:

$$\text{slope} = \frac{\text{change in } y}{\text{change in } x}.$$

You can find rates of change from an equation, a table, or a graph. A special type of linear equation that describes rate of change is called a direct variation. The graph of a direct variation always passes through the origin and represents a proportional situation. In the equation $y = kx$, k is called the constant of variation. It is the slope, or rate of change. As x increases in value, y increases or decreases at a constant rate k, or y varies directly with x. Another way to say this is that y is directly proportional to x. The direct variation $y = kx$ also can be written as $k = \frac{y}{x}$. In this form, you can see that the ratio of y to x is the same for any corresponding values of y and x.

Slope-Intercept Form

Equations written as $y = mx + b$, where m is the slope and b is the y-intercept, are linear equations in slope-intercept form. For example, the graph of $y = 5x - 6$ is a line that has a slope of 5 and crosses the y-axis at $(0, -6)$. Sometimes you must first write an equation in slope-intercept form before finding the slope and y-intercept. For example, the equation $2x + 3y = 15$ can be expressed in slope-intercept form by subtracting $2x$ from each side and then dividing by 3: $y = -\frac{2}{3}x + 5$, revealing a slope of $-\frac{2}{3}$ and a y-intercept of 5. You can use the slope-intercept form of an equation to graph a line easily. Graph the y-intercept and use the slope to find another point on the line, then connect the two points with a line.

Geometry

▶ *Analyze characteristics and properties of two- and three-dimensional geometric shapes and develop mathematical arguments about geometric relationships*

Angles

Two rays that have the same endpoint form an angle. The common endpoint is called the vertex, and the two rays that make up the angle are called the sides of the angle. The most common unit of measure for angles is the degree. Protractors can be used to measure angles or to draw an angle of a given measure. Angles can be classified by their degree measure. Acute angles have measures less than 90° but greater than 0°. Obtuse angles have measures greater than 90° but less than 180°. Right angles have measures of 90°.

Triangles

A triangle is a figure formed by three line segments that intersect only at their endpoints. The sum of the measures of the angles of a triangle is 180°. Triangles can be classified by their angles. An acute triangle contains all acute angles. An obtuse triangle has one obtuse angle. A right triangle has one right angle. Triangles can also be classified by their sides. A scalene triangle has no congruent sides. An isosceles triangle has at least two congruent sides. In an equilateral triangle all sides are congruent.

Quadrilaterals

A quadrilateral is a closed figure with four sides and four vertices. The segments of a quadrilateral intersect only at their endpoints. Quadrilaterals can be separated into two triangles. Since the sum of the interior angles of all triangles totals 180°, the measures of the interior angles of a quadrilateral equal 360°. Quadrilaterals are classified according to their characteristics, and include trapezoids, parallelograms, rectangles, squares, and rhombuses.

Two-Dimensional Figures

A two-dimensional figure exists within a plane and has only the dimensions of length and width. Examples of two-dimensional figures include circles and polygons. Polygons are figures that have three or more angles, including triangles, quadrilaterals, pentagons, hexagons, and many more. The sum of the angles of any polygon totals at least 180° (triangle), and each additional side adds 180° to the measure of the first three angles. The sum of the angles of a quadrilateral, for example, is 360°. The sum of the angles of a pentagon is 540°.

Three-Dimensional Figures

A plane is a two-dimensional flat surface that extends in all directions. Intersecting planes can form the edges and vertices of three-dimensional figures or solids. A polyhedron is a solid with flat surfaces that are polygons. Polyhedrons are composed of faces, edges, and vertices and are differentiated by their shape and by their number of bases. Skew lines are lines that lie in different planes. They are neither intersecting nor parallel.

Congruence

Figures that have the same size and shape are congruent. The parts of congruent triangles that match are called corresponding parts. Congruence statements are used to identify corresponding parts of congruent triangles. When writing a congruence statement, the letters must be written so that corresponding vertices appear in the same order. Corresponding parts can be used to find the measures of angles and sides in a figure that is congruent to a figure with known measures.

Similarity

If two figures have the same shape but not the same size they are called similar figures. For example, the triangles below are similar, so angles A, B, and C have the same measurements as angles D, E, and F, respectively. However, segments AB, BC, and CA do not have the same measurements as segments DE, EF, and FD, but the measures of the sides are proportional.

For example, $\dfrac{\overline{AB}}{\overline{DE}} = \dfrac{\overline{BC}}{\overline{EF}} = \dfrac{\overline{CA}}{\overline{FD}}$.

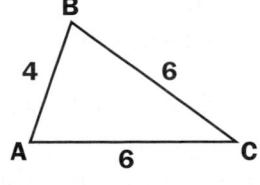
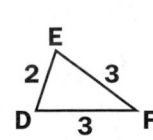

Solid figures are considered to be similar if they have the same shape and their corresponding linear measures are proportional. As with two-dimensional figures, they can be tested for similarity by comparing corresponding measures. If the compared ratios are proportional, then the figures are similar solids. Missing measures of similar solids can also be determined by using proportions.

The Pythagorean Theorem

In a right angle, the sides that are adjacent to the right angle are called legs. The side opposite the right angle is the hypotenuse.

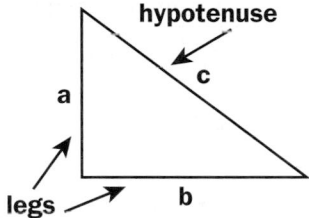

The Pythagorean Theorem describes the relationship between the lengths of the legs a and b and the hypotenuse c. It states that if a triangle is a right triangle, then the square of the length of the hypotenuse is equal to the sum of the squares of the lengths of the legs. In symbols, $c^2 = a^2 + b^2$.

Sine, Cosine, and Tangent Ratios

Trigonometry is the study of the properties of triangles. A trigonometric ratio is a ratio of the lengths of two sides of a right triangle. The most common trigonometric ratios are the sine, cosine, and tangent ratios. These ratios are abbreviated as *sin*, *cos*, and *tan*, respectively.

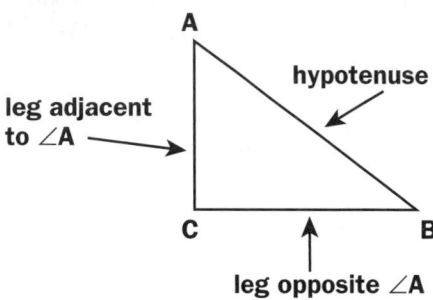

If ∠A is an acute angle of a right triangle, then

$$sin\ \angle A = \frac{\text{measure of leg opposite } \angle A}{\text{measure of hypotenuse}},$$

$$cos\ \angle A = \frac{\text{measure of leg adjacent to } \angle A}{\text{measure of leg opposite } \angle A},\ \text{and}$$

$$tan\ \angle A = \frac{\text{measure of hypotenuse}}{\text{measure of leg adjacent to } \angle A}.$$

▶ Specify locations and describe spatial relationships using coordinate geometry and other representational systems

Polygons
A polygon is a simple, closed figure formed by three or more line segments. The line segments meet only at their endpoints. The points of intersection are called vertices, and the line segments are called sides. Polygons are classified by the number if sides they have. The diagonals of a polygon divide the polygon into triangles. The number of triangles formed is two less than the number of sides. To find the sum of the measures of the interior angles of any polygon, multiply the number of triangles within the polygon

by 180. That is, if *n* equals the number of sides, then (*n* − 2) 180 gives the sum of the measures of the polygon's interior angles.

Cartesian Coordinates
In the Cartesian coordinate system, the *y*-axis extends above and below the origin and the *x*-axis extends to the right and left of the origin, which is the point at which the *x*- and *y*-axes intersect. Numbers below and to the left of the origin are negative. A point graphed on the coordinate grid is said to have an *x*-coordinate and a *y*-coordinate. For example, the point (1,−2) has as its *x*-coordinate the number 1, and has as its *y*-coordinate the number −2. This point is graphed by locating the position on the grid that is 1 unit to the right of the origin and 2 units below the origin.

The *x*-axis and the *y*-axis separate the coordinate plane into four regions, called quadrants. The axes and points located on the axes themselves are not located in any of the quadrants. The quadrants are labeled I to IV, starting in the upper right and proceeding counterclockwise. In quadrant I, both coordinates are positive. In quadrant II, the *x*-coordinate is negative and the *y*-coordinate is positive. In quadrant III, both coordinates are negative. In quadrant IV, the *x*-coordinate is positive and the *y*-coordinate is negative. A coordinate graph can be used to show algebraic relationships among numbers.

▶ Apply transformations and use symmetry to analyze mathematical situations

Similar Triangles and Indirect Measurement
Triangles that have the same shape but not necessarily the same dimensions are called similar triangles. Similar triangles have corresponding angles and corresponding

sides. Arcs are used to show congruent angles. If two triangles are similar, then the corresponding angles have the same measure, and the corresponding sides are proportional. Therefore, to determine the measures of the sides of similar triangles when some measures are known, proportions can be used.

Transformations

A transformation is a movement of a geometric figure. There are several types of transformations. In a translation, also called a slide, a figure is slid from one position to another without turning it. Every point of the original figure is moved the same distance and in the same direction. In a reflection, also called a flip, a figure is flipped over a line to form a mirror image. Every point of the original figure has a corresponding point on the other side of the line of symmetry. In a rotation, also called a turn, a figure is turned around a fixed point. A figure may be rotated 90° clockwise, 90° counterclockwise, or 180°. A dilation transforms each line to a parallel line whose length is a fixed multiple of the length of the original line to create a similar figure that will be either larger or smaller.

▶ *Use visualizations, spatial reasoning, and geometric modeling to solve problems*

Two-Dimensional Representations of Three-Dimensional Objects

Three-dimensional objects can be represented in a two-dimensional drawing in order to more easily determine properties such as surface area and volume. When you look at the rectangular prism below, you can see the orientation of its three dimensions, length, width, and height. Using the drawing and the formulas for surface area and volume, you can easily calculate these properties.

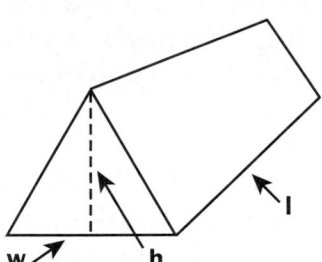

Another way to represent a three-dimensional object in a two-dimensional plane is by using a net, which is the unfolded representation. Imagine cutting the vertices of a box until it is flat then drawing an outline of it. That's a net. Most objects have more than one net, but any one can be measured to determine surface area. Below is a cube and one of its nets.

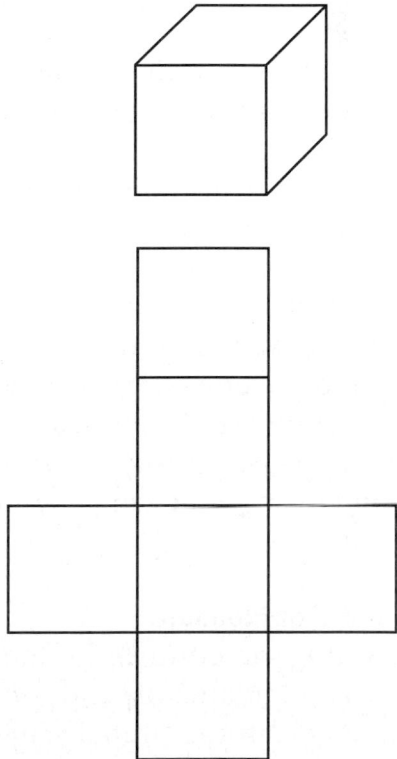

Measurement

▶ Understand measurable attributes of objects and the units, systems, and processes of measurement

Customary System
The customary system is the system of weights and measures used in the United States. The main units of weight are ounces, pounds (1 equal to 16 ounces), and tons (1 equal to 2,000 pounds). Length is typically measured in inches, feet (1 equal to 12 inches), yards (1 equal to 3 feet), and miles (1 equal to 5,280 feet), while area is measured in square feet and acres (1 equal to 43,560 square feet). Liquid is measured in cups, pints (1 equal to 2 cups), quarts (1 equal to 2 pints), and gallons (1 equal to 4 quarts). Finally, temperature is measured in degrees Fahrenheit.

Metric System
The metric system is a decimal system of weights and measurements in which the prefixes of the words for the units of measure indicate the relationships between the different measurements. In this system, the main units of weight, or mass, are grams and kilograms. Length is measured in millimeters, centimeters, meters, and kilometers, and the units of area are square millimeters, centimeters, meters, and kilometers. Liquid is typically measured in milliliters and liters, while temperature is in degrees Celsius.

Selecting Units of Measure
When measuring something, it is important to select the appropriate type and size of unit. For example, in the United States it would be appropriate when describing someone's height to use feet and inches. These units of height or length are good to use because they are in the customary system, and they are of appropriate size. In the customary system, use inches, feet, and miles for lengths and perimeters; square inches, feet, and miles for area and surface area; and cups, pints, quarts, gallons or cubic inches and feet (and less commonly miles) for volume. In the metric system use millimeters, centimeters, meters, and kilometers for lengths and perimeters; square units millimeters, centimeters, meters, and kilometers for area and surface area; and milliliters and liters for volume. Finally, always use degrees to measure angles.

▶ Apply appropriate techniques, tools, and formulas to determine measurements

Precision and Significant Digits
The precision of measurement is the exactness to which a measurement is made. Precision depends on the smallest unit of measure being used, or the precision unit. One way to record a measure is to estimate to the nearest precision unit. A more precise method is to include all of the digits that are actually measured, plus one estimated digit. The digits recorded, called significant digits, indicate the precision of the measurement. There are special rules for determining significant digits. If a number contains a decimal point, the number of significant digits is found by counting from left to right, starting with the first nonzero digit. If the number does not contain a decimal point, the number of significant digits is

found by counting the digits from left to right, starting with the first digit and ending with the last nonzero digit.

Surface Area

The amount of material needed to cover the surface of a figure is called the surface area. It can be calculated by finding the area of each face and adding them together. To find the surface area of a rectangular prism, for example, the formula $S = 2lw + 2lh + 2wh$ applies. A cylinder, on the other hand, may be unrolled to reveal two circles and a rectangle. Its surface area can be determined by finding the area of the two circles, $2\pi r^2$, and adding it to the area of the rectangle, $2\pi rh$ (the length of the rectangle is the circumference of one of the circles), or $S = 2\pi r^2 + 2\pi rh$. The surface area of a pyramid is measured in a slightly different way because the sides of a pyramid are triangles that intersect at the vertex. These sides are called lateral faces and the height of each is called the slant height. The sum of their areas is the lateral area of a pyramid. The surface area of a square pyramid is the lateral area $\frac{1}{2}bh$ (area of a lateral face) times 4 (number of lateral faces), plus the area of the base. The surface area of a cone is the area of its circular base (πr^2) plus its lateral area (πrl, where l is the slant height).

Volume

Volume is the measure of space occupied by a solid region. To find the volume of a prism, the area of the base is multiplied by the measure of the height, $V = bh$. A solid containing several prisms can be broken down into its component prisms. Then the volume of each component can be found and the volumes added. The volume of a cylinder can be determined by finding the area of its circular base, πr^2, and then multiplying by the height of the cylinder. A pyramid has one-third the volume of a prism with the same base and height. To find the volume of a pyramid, multiply the area of the base by the pyramid's height, and then divide by 3. Simply stated, the formula for the volume of a pyramid is $V = \frac{1}{3}bh$. A cone is a three-dimensional figure with one circular base and a curved surface connecting the base and the vertex. The volume of a cone is one-third the volume of a cylinder with the same base area and height. Like a pyramid, the formula for the volume of a cone is $V = \frac{1}{3}bh$. More specifically, the formula is $V = \frac{1}{3}\pi r^2 h$.

Upper and Lower Bounds

Upper and lower bounds have to do with the accuracy of a measurement. When a measurement is given, the degree of accuracy is also stated to tell you what the upper and lower bounds of the measurement are. The upper bound is the largest possible value that a measurement could have had before being rounded down, and the lower bound is the lowest possible value it could have had before being rounded up.

Data Analysis and Probability

▶ *Formulate questions that can be addressed with data and collect, organize, and display relevant data to answer them*

Histograms

A histogram displays numerical data that have been organized into equal intervals using bars that have the same width and no space between them. While a histogram does not give exact data points, its shape shows the distribution of the data. Histograms also can be used to compare data.

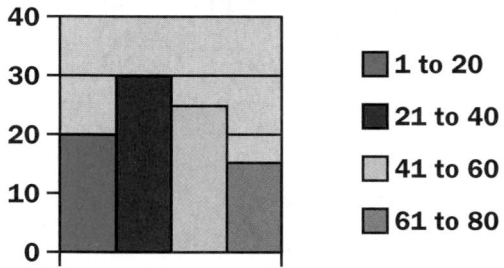

- ■ 1 to 20
- ■ 21 to 40
- ☐ 41 to 60
- ▨ 61 to 80

Box-and-Whisker Plot

A box-and-whisker plot displays the measures of central tendency and variation. A box is drawn around the quartile values, and whiskers extend from each quartile to the extreme data points. To make a box plot for a set of data, draw a number line that covers the range of data. Find the median, the extremes, and the upper and lower quartiles. Mark these points on the number line with bullets, then draw a box and the whiskers. The length of a whisker or box shows whether the values of the data in that part are concentrated or spread out.

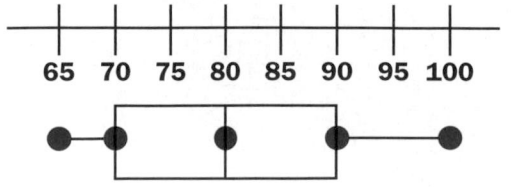

Scatter Plots

A scatter plot is a graph that shows the relationship between two sets of data. In a scatter plot, two sets of data are graphed as ordered pairs on a coordinate system. Two sets of data can have a positive correlation (as *x* increases, *y* increases), a negative correlation (as *x* increases, *y* decreases), or no correlation (no obvious pattern is shown). Scatter plots can be used to spot trends, draw conclusions, and make predictions about data.

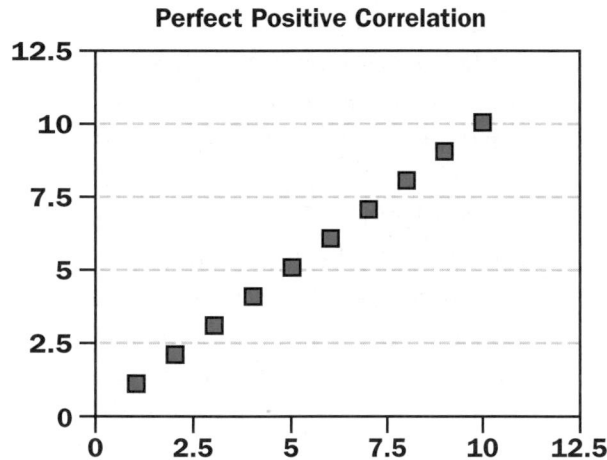

Perfect Positive Correlation

Randomization

The idea of randomization is a very important principle of statistics and the design of experiments. Data must be selected randomly to prevent bias from influencing the results. For example, you want to know the average income of people in your town but you can only use a sample of 100 individuals to make determinations about everyone. If you select 100 individuals who are all doctors, you will have a biased sample. However, if you chose a random sample of 100 people out of the phone book, you are much more likely to accurately represent average income in the town.

Statistics and Parameters

Statistics is a science that involves collecting, analyzing, and presenting data. The data can be collected in various ways—for example through a census or by making physical measurements. The data can then be analyzed by creating summary statistics, which have to do with the distribution of the data sample, including the mean, range, and standard error. They can also be illustrated in tables and graphs, like box-plots, scatter plots, and histograms. The presentation of the data typically involves describing the strength or validity of the data and what they show. For example, an analysis of ancestry of people in a city might tell you something about immigration patterns, unless the data set is very small or biased in some way, in which case it is not likely to be very accurate or useful.

Categorical and Measurement Data

When analyzing data, it is important to understand if the data is qualitative or quantitative. Categorical data is qualitative and measurement, or numerical, data is quantitative. Categorical data describes a quality of something and can be placed into different categories. For example, if you are analyzing the number of students in different grades in a school, each grade is a category. On the other hand, measurement data is continuous, like height, weight, or any other measurable variable. Measurement data can be converted into categorical data if you decide to group the data. Using height as an example, you can group the continuous data set into categories like under 5 feet, 5 feet to 5 feet 5 inches, over 5 feet five inches to 6 feet, and so on.

Univariate and Bivariate Data

In data analysis, a researcher can analyze one variable at a time or look at how multiple variables behave together. Univariate data involves only one variable, for example height in humans. You can measure the height in a population of people then plot the results in a histogram to look at how height is distributed in humans. To summarize univariate data, you can use statistics like the mean, mode, median, range, and standard deviation, which is a measure of variation. When looking at more than one variable at once, you use multivariate data. Bivariate data involves two variables. For example, you can look at height and age in humans together by gathering information on both variables from individuals in a population. You can then plot both variables in a scatter plot, look at how the variables behave in relation to each other, and create an equation that represents the relationship, also called a regression. These equations could help answer questions such as, for example, does height increase with age in humans?

▶ Select and use appropriate statistical methods to analyze data

Measures of Central Tendency

When you have a list of numerical data, it is often helpful to use one or more numbers to represent the whole set. These numbers are called measures of central tendency. Three measures of central tendency are mean, median, and mode. The mean is the sum of the data divided by the number of items in the data set. The median is the middle number of the ordered data (or the mean of the two middle numbers). The mode is the number or numbers that occur most often.

These measures of central tendency allow data to be analyzed and better understood.

Measures of Spread

In statistics, measures of spread or variation are used to describe how data are distributed. The range of a set of data is the difference between the greatest and the least values of the data set. The quartiles are the values that divide the data into four equal parts. The median of data separates the set in half. Similarly, the median of the lower half of a set of data is the lower quartile. The median of the upper half of a set of data is the upper quartile. The interquartile range is the difference between the upper quartile and the lower quartile.

Line of Best Fit

When real-life data are collected, the points graphed usually do not form a straight line, but they may approximate a linear relationship. A line of best fit is a line that lies very close to most of the data points. It can be used to predict data. You also can use the equation of the best-fit line to make predictions.

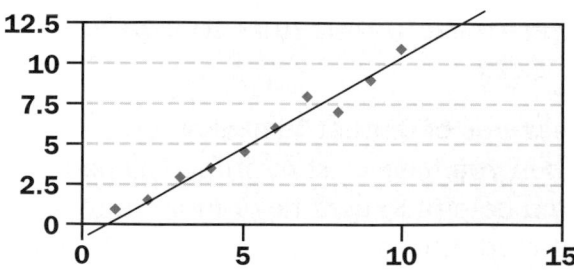

Stem and Leaf Plots

In a stem and leaf plot, numerical data are listed in ascending or descending order. The greatest place value of the data is used for the stems. The next greatest place value forms the leaves. For example, if the least

number in a set of data is 8 and the greatest number is 95, draw a vertical line and write the stems from 0 to 9 to the left of the line. Write the leaves from to the right of the line, with the corresponding stem. Next, rearrange the leaves so they are ordered from least to greatest. Then include a key or explanation, such as $1|3 = 13$. Notice that the stem-and-leaf plot below is like a histogram turned on its side.

0|8
1|3 6
2|5 6 9
3|0 2 7 8
4|0 1 4 7 9
5|1 4 5 8
6|1 3 7
7|5 8
8|2 6
9|5

Key: **1|3 = 13**

▶ *Develop and evaluate inferences and predictions that are based on data*

Sampling Distribution

The sampling distribution of a population is the distribution that would result if you could take an infinite number of samples from the population, average each, and then average the averages. The more normal the distribution of the population, that is, how closely the distribution follows a bell curve, the more likely the sampling distribution will also follow a normal distribution. Furthermore, the larger the sample, the more likely it will accurately represent the entire population. For instance, you are more likely to gain more representative results from a population of 1,000 with a sample of 100 than with a sample of 2.

Validity

In statistics, validity refers to acquiring results that accurately reflect that which is being measured. In other words, it is important when performing statistical analyses, to ensure that the data are valid in that the sample being analyzed represents the population to the best extent possible. Randomization of data and using appropriate sample sizes are two important aspects of making valid inferences about a population.

▶ *Understand and apply basic concepts of probability*

Complementary, Mutually Exclusive Events

To understand probability theory, it is important to know if two events are mutually exclusive, or complementary: the occurrence of one event automatically implies the non-occurrence of the other. That is, two complementary events cannot both occur. If you roll a pair of dice, the event of rolling 6 and rolling doubles have an outcome in common (3, 3), so they are not mutually exclusive. If you roll (3, 3), you also roll doubles. However, the events of rolling a 9 and rolling doubles are mutually exclusive because they have no outcomes in common. If you roll a 9, you will not also roll doubles.

Independent and Dependent Events

Determining the probability of a series of events requires that you know whether the events are independent or dependent. An independent event has no influence on the occurrence of subsequent events, whereas, a dependent event does influence subsequent events. The chances that a woman's first child will be a girl are $\frac{1}{2}$, and the chances that her second child will be a girl are also

$\frac{1}{2}$ because the two events are independent of each other. However, if there are 7 red marbles in a bag of 15 marbles, the chances that the first marble you pick will be red are $\frac{7}{15}$ and if you indeed pick a red marble and remove it, you have reduced the chances of picking another red marble to $\frac{6}{14}$.

Sample Space

The sample space is the group of all possible outcomes for an event. For example, if you are tossing a single six-sided die, the sample space is {1, 2, 3, 4, 5, 6}. Similarly, you can determine the sample space for the possible outcomes of two events. If you are going to toss a coin twice, the sample space is {(heads, heads), (heads, tails), (tails, heads), (tails, tails)}.

Computing the Probability of a Compound Event

If two events are independent, the outcome of one event does not influence the outcome of the second. For example, if a bag contains 2 blue and 3 red marbles, then the probability of selecting a blue marble, replacing it, and then selecting a red marble is $P(A) \times P(B) = \frac{2}{5} \times \frac{3}{5}$ or $\frac{6}{25}$.

If two events are dependent, the outcome of one event affects the outcome of the second. For example, if a bag contains 2 blue and 3 red marbles, then the probability of selecting a blue and then a red marble without replacing the first marble is $P(A) \times P(B$ following $A) = \frac{2}{5} \times \frac{3}{4}$ or $\frac{3}{10}$. Two events that cannot happen at the same time are mutually exclusive. For example, when you roll two number cubes, you cannot roll a sum that is both 5 and even. So, $P(A$ or $B) = \frac{4}{36} + \frac{18}{36}$ or $\frac{11}{18}$.

THE BUSINESS PLAN:
YOUR ROAD MAP TO ENTREPRENEURIAL SUCCESS

Developing a good business plan can put you on the track to success in a small business. A business plan summarizes an entrepreneur's proposed business venture. It provides an organized report of a company's goals and how management intends to achieve those goals. A business plan is a continuing work in progress that should evolve as your business evolves. Developing a business plan is like outlining a strategy for turning your business idea into a reality.

What Is a Business Plan?

- **A guide to the company's operations**
- **A document presenting your company's strategic vision**
- **A tool to persuade lenders and investors to finance your business**
- **A standard by which you can measure and improve business performance**
- **A plan to use as a basis for making sound business decisions**

BUSINESS PLAN ELEMENTS

The Business Plan Appendix explains the content requirements for the essential elements of a business plan.

BUSINESS PLAN TEMPLATE

 Go to the *Introduction to Business* Online Learning Center through **glencoe.com** for a document template in which you can write your own business plan.

ASSIGNMENT

Select a business that you are interested in starting. Then develop a business plan for the venture. When you are finished writing the business plan, package the business plan using the guidelines on pages 672–673. Then present it and defend it in an oral presentation.

 MANAGEMENT TEAM PLAN

In the Management Team section of the business plan, you will present your management team's qualifications for making the venture a success.

KEY MANAGEMENT
- Describe each management team member, including title, salary, abilities, duties, responsibilities, educational experience, previous industry and related work experience, and past successes. Describe the benefits that team members will provide to the company.
- Provide copies of the owners' tax returns, personal financial statements, and résumés.

ADVISORS AND PROFESSIONAL SERVICE PROVIDERS
- Describe the role, responsibilities, and members of the advisory board, if you have one.
- List the outside consultants the company will use. Include accountants, attorneys, bankers, insurance agents, technology advisors, Web developers, security contractors, and payroll specialists.

 COMPANY DESCRIPTION

The Company Description outlines the company's basic background information, business concept, and goals and objectives.

BUSINESS HISTORY AND DESCRIPTION
- Explain your reasons for starting a new business or expanding an existing business.
- Describe the entrepreneurial opportunity.
- Provide a history of the business with development milestones that have been completed to date and the current status of the business.
- Describe the legal structure of the business and why you chose it.
- Include details about prior funding, royalty, partnership, and joint venture agreements.

GOALS AND OBJECTIVES
- Establish the business's goals and objectives and relate them to the investment you seek.
- Explain why you think the venture will succeed.

PRODUCT AND SERVICE PLAN

The Product and Service Plan describes the features and benefits of the business's products and services.

OVERVIEW OF PRODUCTS AND SERVICES

- Describe the product or service, including purpose, size, shape, colors, features, benefits, cost, functionality, design, quality, capabilities, technology, protections, and unique selling points.
- Describe competing and similar technology.
- Describe the need the product or service addresses in the market and how it benefits customers.
- Explain briefly how the products and/or services will be produced, the materials required, and the type of labor needed.

PRODUCT DEVELOPMENT STATUS

- Discuss the history and current status of product development.
- Provide projected dates for achieving other stages of development.

 VISION AND MISSION STATEMENTS

The Vision and Mission Statements section of the business plan sets forth the guiding principles by which a company functions. These statements and vision statement should be clear and concise. They communicate what the business stands for, what its founders believe in, and what the company intends to achieve.

VISION STATEMENT

- Write a vision statement that establishes the scope and purpose of your company and reflects its values and beliefs.
- Express the company's vision in broad terms so that it will stand the test of time.
- Convey the future of the company as its founders see it.
- Develop strategies for achieving the vision of the business.
- Establish criteria for monitoring achievement of the vision.

MISSION STATEMENT

- Write a mission statement that expresses the specific aspirations of a company, the major goals for which it will strive.
- Define the direction in which the company will move.
- Convey a challenging yet achievable mission that the organization will be dedicated to accomplishing.
- Develop strategies for achieving the mission of the business.
- Establish criteria for monitoring achievement of the mission.

INDUSTRY OVERVIEW

Your business plan must address basic trends and growth within the industry. Think of your industry as those companies providing similar, complementary, or supplementary products and services.

INDUSTRY TRENDS AND GROWTH

- Describe the industry, including size by both revenue and number of firms.
- Describe how the industry functions, including a general explanation of the industry's distribution system.
- Describe the barriers of entry to the industry.
- Describe the positive and negative trends in the industry.
- Describe the past and future trends in the industry.
- Discuss growth trends and how many companies are expected to enter the industry in the future.
- Explain the factors that are influencing growth or decline in the industry.
- Include the failure rate in the industry.
- Describe the typical profitability in the industry.
- Describe the government regulations that affect the industry in general and your business in particular.
- Describe the local, national, or international industry standards with which your business will need to comply.
- Include current and historical industry employment data.
- Provide visualizations of industry data (charts, tables, graphs).

MARKET ANALYSIS

The Market Analysis section of the business plan is important because it presents your market research and features a customer demographic profile that defines the traits of the company's target market. Information about potential target markets should originate from primary and secondary research resources.

TARGET MARKET DEMOGRAPHIC PROFILE

- Write a demographic profile of the company's target market.
- Identify and explain market segments.
- Describe the market niche served.
- Describe the size of the target market.
- Explain if your market is domestic or international and describe the cultures and ethnicities within it.
- Describe the geographic statistics of your target market; where are your customers from and where do they live?
- Describe what members of the target market do for a living, their level of income, their social and economic status, and their level of education.
- Describe the ages, genders, family structures, lifestyle, and leisure activities of the target market.
- Explain what motivates the target market.

- Answer specific questions about your target market that are directly related to your products or services.
- If your product or service is marketed to businesses, describe the target market in terms of industry, product and/or service, geographic location, years in business, revenue, number of employees, and buying motivations.
- Describe how you analyzed your target market.
- Provide visualizations of demographic, geographic, and psychographic data (charts, graphs, tables).

TARGET MARKET PROJECTIONS

- Describe the proportion of the target market that has used a product or service like the company's product or service before.
- Project how much of the product or service the target market will buy (gross sales and/or unit sales).

MARKET TRENDS AND GROWTH

- Describe current trends and trends that have been forecast to occur within the target market.
- Describe the historical growth, current market size, and the growth potential of the market.
- Provide visualizations of market trend statistics (charts, graphs, tables).

CUSTOMER NEEDS ANALYSIS

- Conduct market research to uncover customers' wants and needs and to survey their impressions of the business and its promotions.
- Use the market research results to write a customer needs analysis that interprets and prioritizes the needs of the business's current and future customers.
- Prepare a visualization that presents highlights from the results of your customer needs analysis.
- Explain how the company will meet the target market's needs.

COMPETITIVE ANALYSIS

The Competitive Analysis section of the business plan should focus on demonstrating that the proposed business has an advantage over its competitors. You can gather information on competitors by viewing their Web sites; by talking to their customers, vendors, suppliers, and employees; by attending trade shows; and by searching newspaper and magazine databases.

COMPETITIVE OVERVIEW

- Identify, investigate, and analyze your top direct competitors, businesses that are offering identical or similar products or services as your business.
- Identify, investigate, and analyze your top indirect competitors, businesses that are offering products and services that are close substitutes.

- Identify, investigate, and analyze your top future competitors, existing companies that are not yet in the marketplace but could enter the marketplace at any time.
- Explain whether the business will have nonlocal competitors.
- State the locations of your top competitors.
- Describe how long your competitors have been in business.
- Describe the products and services your competitors sell and how much they sell (in units and sales dollars).
- Evaluate your competitors' product selection, product quality, and product availability.
- Describe the markets or market segments your competitors serve.
- Describe the benefits offered by the competition.
- Describe your competitors' images and their level of growth and success.
- Describe your competitors' advertising and promotion strategies and branding, packaging, and labeling strategies.
- Describe your competitors' pricing policies and pricing structures.
- Explain competitors' customer service and after sale service policies.
- Assess your competitors' financial condition and level of debt.
- Evaluate your competitors' equipment and production capacity.
- Outline the strengths and weaknesses of each of your competitors.
- Include charts or pie graphs showing the market share among your competitors as well as trends and changes over time.
- Prepare a grid or table that presents highlights from the results of your competitive analysis.

COMPETITIVE ADVANTAGE
- Describe the competitive advantage of your venture.
- Explain the key assets that your business has and its competitors do not have.
- Differentiate your company's products and services from your competitors' products and services.
- Describe how your business strategies and marketing mix strategies (product, place, price, promotion, and people decisions) will help you to attract and defend market share.
- Explain the percentage of the market the business intends to capture and how the business will achieve this market penetration.

MARKETING PLAN

A Marketing Plan describes a company's marketing mix strategies or how it plans to market, promote, and sell its products or services.

MARKETING MIX STRATEGIES
- Write a marketing plan, including an Internet marketing plan if appropriate, with product, place, price, promotion, and people strategies.
- Describe the marketing mix strategies and explain the message they are meant to convey.

- Describe the company's plan for finding the best market.
- Explain how the marketing mix strategies will be implemented and evaluated for effectiveness.

PRODUCT STRATEGY

- Describe your product, including how it functions, its design, image, appearance, packaging, labeling, warranties, service, and support.
- Describe the product's branding, including brand name(s), brand marks, trade names, trade characters, trademarks, logos, and corporate symbols.

PLACE STRATEGY

- Explain how your product will be made available to customers and where it will be sold.
- Describe channels of distribution and how they will help to foster market penetration.

PRICE STRATEGY

- State your company's pricing objectives and pricing strategy goals.
- Develop a pricing structure that takes into account fixed and variable costs, the competition, company objectives, proposed positioning strategies, the target market, and the consumer's willingness to pay.
- Describe the typical prices in the industry and how your business's prices compare.
- State whether you will accept checks, credit, debit cards, or other forms of payment.

PROMOTION STRATEGY

- Explain the company's promotional goals and promotional messages and how they will appeal to the target market.
- Develop a pre-opening promotional plan to establish a positive image and promote interest.
- Detail the promotions to be used, such as advertising, publicity and public relations, sales promotion, personal selling, direct mail, and e-mail.
- Describe the specific marketing mediums the company will use to deliver the promotional message to the target market. Include how often each will be used, what they will cost, why you chose them, and why they will appeal to the target market.
- Describe the marketing materials you will you need, who will design them, how much they will cost, and how they will be designed to appeal to the target market.
- Describe the sales team, the sales process, and the sales incentives the company will offer.
- Provide your media budget and detail the cost of marketing materials per prospect.
- Provide examples of marketing materials.
- Describe how you will evaluate the effectiveness of promotional strategies.

PEOPLE STRATEGY

- Explain how you will recruit, hire, and train the people and employees who will help you to achieve business success.

OPERATIONAL PLAN

The Operational Plan section of the business plan includes information about all the processes that take place in the business.

LOCATION

- Describe where your business will be located, the number of locations, the zoning, the square footage needed, the layout and type of space, and renovations needed.
- Explain why you chose the location.
- State the average traffic count in front of the outlet.
- Describe any factors that hinder or help accessibility to the business and visibility of the site.
- Describe the businesses near your business's site, including target markets.
- Describe any community sign laws and local parking laws.
- Identify tax rates and state how they compare to other sites you considered.
- Project costs associated with the location.
- Describe how much the business can expand before it will need to relocate.
- Provide a map of the business location and facility layout blueprints.

PROPERTY OWNERSHIP OR LEASE TERMS

- Detail the terms of the lease or purchase of the property.
- Provide a copy of the proposed lease or building space purchase agreement.

EQUIPMENT NEEDS

- Describe and provide blueprints and specifications for the machinery and equipment needed.
- Explain whether you will purchase or lease the equipment.

MANUFACTURING PROCESSES AND COSTS

- Describe the manufacturing process and the technology requirements.
- Assess the manufacturing process in terms of direct and indirect costs.

SUPPLIERS AND PURCHASING

- Outline your key suppliers and the purchasing process.
- Provide copies of purchase orders and letters of intent from suppliers.

STORAGE AND INVENTORY

- Analyze the inventory needed to open and operate the business.
- Describe storage needs, space required, and costs involved.
- Explain inventory control procedures, equipment, and technology.

CHANNELS OF DISTRIBUTION

- Describe the channels of distribution and the associated costs.
- Explain the degree of difficulty in gaining industry distribution access.

QUALITY MEASURES AND SAFETY
- Describe how quality will be measured, controlled, and improved.
- Explain security precautions and health and safety regulations.

ORGANIZATIONAL PLAN

The Organizational Plan offers information about the business's legal structure, methods of and responsibilities for record keeping, and legal and insurance issues. It also covers the people aspects of the business, including staffing and training of personnel, and the organizational structure of the planned business.

LEGAL STRUCTURE
- Describe your legal structure and why it is advantageous for your company.
- Describe any legal agreements governing how owners can exit the company, how the company can be dissolved, how profits will be distributed, and who will have financial responsibility for losses.
- Project future changes in the company's legal structure and how such changes would benefit the company.
- Provide a copy of your partnership agreement if you have formed a partnership.
- Provide a copy of the Articles of Incorporation if the company is formed as a corporation.
- Provide a copy of the franchise contract and supporting materials if the company is a franchise.

RECORD KEEPING
- Describe the accounting system that will be used and why it was chosen.
- Describe what record keeping will be done internally and who will be responsible for keeping internal records.
- Explain when the business will use an outside accountant, such as to finalize monthly/year-end statements.
- Describe who within the company has the expertise to read and analyze the financial statements provided by outside accountants.
- Describe how you will use your financial statements to implement changes to make your company more profitable.

LEGAL AND INSURANCE ISSUES
- Describe any legal considerations that will impact your business, such as legal liability issues, government regulations, environmental regulations, zoning matters, or licensing requirements.
- Identify the insurance company the business will use, the types of insurance the business will need, and the costs involved.

LABOR, STAFFING, AND TRAINING
- Outline human resource policies, including staffing and personnel management procedures.
- Diagram and describe the organizational structure of the business.

- Provide an organizational flowchart.
- Develop a job description for each position on the organizational flowchart, including skill sets needed and salaries offered.
- Describe how many employees the business will have and in what types of positions.
- Outline hours of operation, scheduling policies, and types of shifts worked by employees.
- Complete a work schedule for a typical work week.
- Develop charts or graphs that classify employees by function, skill set, hourly pay, and part-time or full-time status.
- Identify situations where outsourcing should be used for hiring needs.

 FINANCIAL PLAN

The Financial Plan presents past and current finances and financial forecasts and explains the assumptions made when calculating forecast figures. It includes the investment proposal and three key financial statements: a cash flow statement, income statement, and balance sheet.

INVESTMENT PROPOSAL

- Describe why you are applying for financing and how you plan to raise and use the money.
- Describe various investment structures and project when investors can expect to earn a profit.
- Identify, categorize, and analyze the start-up costs and fixed and variable operating expenses.
- Project the total cash needed to start the business.
- Include details about revenue streams and prior funding agreements.

EXIT STRATEGY

- Outline the business life cycle and explain your long-term plans for the business.
- Explain how your investors can expect to recoup their investment and earn a sufficient return.
- Define how investors can cash out their investment and achieve liquidity.

CASH FLOW PROJECTION

- Plan a cash budget that forecasts cash inflow (cash revenue from sales) and outflow (cash disbursements) projections for the first year and quarterly or yearly projections for the second and third years.

PROJECTED THREE-YEAR INCOME STATEMENT (PROFIT AND LOSS STATEMENTS)

- Prepare a three-year income projection that includes monthly projections for revenues, expenses, and profits (Revenues – Expenses = Profit or Loss) for the first year and quarterly or yearly projections for the second and third years.

PROJECTED BALANCE SHEET

- Prepare a projected balance sheet (assets, liabilities, and net worth) with quarterly projections for the first year and yearly projections for the second and third years.

BREAK-EVEN ANALYSIS

- Prepare a break-even analysis detailing when the company's expenses will match the income.
- Present the data in a graph format with sales on the X-axis and units sold on the Y-axis.

HISTORICAL FINANCIALS

- Provide cash flow statements, income statements, and balance sheets from the last three years if the company is an existing business.

FINANCIAL ASSUMPTIONS

- State the assumptions on which the financial projections are based.
- Explain how you derived forecasts for sales, costs of goods sold, operating expenses, accounts receivable, collections, accounts payable, inventory, taxes, and other items.
- Disclose whether the financial statements have been audited by a certified public accountant.

FINANCIAL RATIOS

- Calculate liquidity ratios to measure creditworthiness.
- Calculate profitability ratios to show operational performance.
- Calculate turnover ratios to measure changes in certain assets and to expose nonincome-producing assets.

GROWTH PLAN

Planned growth can be very rewarding, and unplanned growth can be chaotic. The Growth Plan looks at how the business will expand in the future. Investors and lenders like to know that a business has plans to deal with growth in a controlled way.

GROWTH STRATEGIES

- Describe how and when the business owners would like the business to grow.
- Describe the products or services the business will develop to achieve growth.
- Describe the planned growth cycle.
- Describe how the business's growth strategies focus on the business's areas of expertise.
- Describe whether market research will be used to support and justify growth strategy decisions.
- Identify the critical skills that are needed to effectively manage growth.
- Explain how you will evaluate and initiate revisions to growth strategies.

BUSINESS LOCATION ISSUES

- Assess the current business location and how it can accommodate growth.
- Explain if growing the business will mean having to relocate the business to a larger facility.
- Analyze the costs involved in expanding or upgrading current facilities and/or moving to new facilities.
- Evaluate whether the business's lease agreement allows for modifications to the building and facilities.
- Describe alternative affordable premises.
- Explain if and when warehousing and storage facilities will be expanded to accommodate growth.

EFFECTS OF GROWTH

- Explain how planned growth will affect human resource expenses and management and staffing needs.
- Describe how planned growth will affect company goals and objectives.
- Assess if the business's target market will be affected by the growth plan.
- Describe how planned growth will affect technology and equipment needs.
- Describe how planned growth will affect the manufacturing process and costs.
- Explain how planned growth will affect financial control procedures, record keeping policies, and legal and insurance issues.
- Evaluate how planned growth will affect the sales team and sales process.
- Describe how planned growth will affect promotional goals and messages and marketing mix strategies (product, place, price, promotion, and people decisions).

GROWTH FINANCING

- Examine how growth costs will affect the overall financial health of the business in the short term and the long term.
- Evaluate growth financing options and describe the best plan to finance growth.
- Provide visualizations of growth projections (charts, tables, graphs).

CONTINGENCY PLAN

The Contingency Plan examines the assumptions in the business plan and the greatest risks to the business and suggests plans to minimize the risk.

- List and examine the assumptions in the business plan.
- Examine risks that could cause the business to fail.
- Categorize business risks as human, natural, or economic; as speculative, controllable or uncontrollable; and as insurable or uninsurable.
- Identify the most significant risks that the new venture faces and describe plans the business owners have developed to deal with any of the situations should they arise.

- Describe how the company will respond to changes in market conditions caused by demographic shifts, socioeconomic trends, economic events, energy costs, and changes in government policies.
- Explain how the company will anticipate and respond to competitive threats from expected and unexpected sources, price cutting by competitors, and the introduction of new products by competitors.
- Explain how the company will handle cost overruns.
- Outline contingencies to meet staffing challenges and limit problems due to a dependence on key people.
- Describe how the company will respond if projected sales and revenue targets are not achieved.
- Describe the company's contingency plan in case of a major accident, event, or disaster that interrupts cash flow.
- Explain how the company will respond to product liability lawsuits.

EXECUTIVE SUMMARY

The Executive Summary recounts the key points in the business plan. It is written last because it summarizes the most important information from the business plan. Investors rely on it to decide if the business concept interests them. The executive summary should be just two pages long, and it should answer who, what, where, why, when, and how.

- Describe the company's mission, goals, objectives, current stage of development, owners, and key management team members.
- Describe the company, business model, legal structure, industry, product or service, target market, and the unique opportunity.
- Include evidence that justifies the soundness and future success of the opportunity.
- Describe the strategies the company will use to beat the competition.
- Include financial highlights such as:
  - The investment you are seeking
  - How much equity you would be willing to transfer
  - Collateral offered
  - How the funds will be used
  - How and when any loans will be repaid
  - Three-year projections of sales
  - Estimated annual after-tax profits

COVER PAGE

Every business plan should have a Cover Page. It is the first page the investor sees when he or she reads the business plan. Include this information:

- The company name, address, phone number, Web site address, e-mail address, and company logo

TITLE PAGE

The page following the cover page is the Title Page. It includes this basic information about the business and the business plan:

- The company name
- The names, titles, and addresses of the owners
- The date the business plan was issued
- The name of the person who prepared the business plan

TABLE OF CONTENTS

The Table of Contents details the components of the business plan and the page numbers where they can be found within the business plan. Include this information in the Table of Contents:

- The titles of the major sections and subsections of the business plan
- The page number where each section and subsection is located

SUPPORTING DOCUMENTS

The Supporting Documents section of the business plan includes items, exhibits, and documentation relevant to the business. Include these items:

- Copies of the owners' résumés, personal financial statements, and tax returns
- For franchised businesses, a copy of franchise contract
- For franchised businesses, all supporting documents provided by the franchisor
- For partnerships, a copy of the partnership agreement
- For corporations, a copy of the Articles of Incorporation
- Photos, blueprints, and detailed specifications of products
- An organizational blueprint
- Photos and blueprints of the layout of the business's facilities
- Photos, blueprints, and detailed specifications for all equipment and machinery
- A map of the business location
- Copy of proposed lease or purchase agreement for building space
- Copy of contracts, licenses, and other legal documents
- Copies of purchase orders and letters of intent from suppliers
- Business cards
- Market research highlights
- Marketing materials
- Press releases
- Visualizations of industry data, demographic data, and market trend statistics

Key Terms Glossary

A

ability Skill that an individual has already developed

accounting equation A concept that states that assets must always equal the sum of liabilities and owner's equity

accounting The function of business that involves maintaining and auditing records, sending out and paying bills, and preparing financial reports for a business

accounting The systematic process of recording and reporting the financial position of a person or an organization

accounts payable The total amount a business owes to creditors

accounts receivable The total amount of money owed to a business. It represents money to be received in payments after goods or services are sold on credit.

actual cash value Value of the automobile when it was new minus depreciation

ad campaign A series of ad messages that share a single idea and theme

advertising agency A business that specializes in developing ad campaigns and ads for its clients

advertising Paid, non-personal form of communication that businesses use to promote their products and services

ageism Discrimination based on age

annual percentage rate (APR) Cost of credit on a yearly basis

antitrust laws Laws that allow the federal government to break up monopolies, regulate them, or take over them

aptitude Potential for learning a skill

assets Property or other items of value owned by a business

audience The number of homes or people exposed to an ad

autocratic leadership A leadership style in which one person runs everything and makes all decisions without consulting others

B

baby boom generation Persons born in the United States between 1946 and 1964

background check The process of verifying certain information provided by a job applicant

bait and switch Sales tactic in which buyers are tempted by an advertised bargain but are then persuaded to buy a more expensive item instead

balance of trade The difference in value between a country's imports and exports over a period of time

balance sheet A report of the balances in all asset, liability, and owner's equity accounts at the end of an accounting period

bank account A record of how much money a customer has deposited into or withdrawn from a bank

bank reconciliation Process of seeing whether an account holder's records agree with a bank's records for an account

bank statement The bank's record of all the transactions in a bank account

bankruptcy Legal process in which a borrower is relieved of debts after showing an inability to pay

banner ads Ads displayed across the top or bottom of a computer screen and stay there

beneficiary Someone who receives all or part of the proceeds of an insurance policy, or a survivor of a deceased policyholder

benefits Extras that workers receive, such as health and life insurance, sick leave, retirement plans, and holiday pay

Better Business Bureau (BBB) Nonprofit organization that collects information on local businesses and handles consumers' complaints

body language Nonverbal communication that includes posture, eye contact, facial expressions, and gestures

bond discount Difference between the amount you pay for the bond and its face value

bond Certificate issued by a government or company promising to pay back borrowed money at a fixed rate of interest on a specified date

boycott A refusal to buy a company's goods or services

brand name Trade name for a product or service produced by a particular company

breach of contract The failure of one party to live up to the terms of a contract

break-even point The point at which total revenues, or sales, equal total costs and expenses of making and distributing a product or service

brick-and-mortar Actual buildings, such as stores and warehouses

brokerage firms Financial institutions that sell stocks and bonds and also may offer a wide range of financial services to clients

budget deficit When the government spends more on programs than it collects in taxes

budget surplus A situation in which a government's revenue exceeds its expenditures during a one-year period

budget variance Difference between the budgeted amount and the actual amount that is spent

budget A plan specifying how money will be issued or spent during a particular period

bureaucracy Formal organization with several levels of management

business Any commercial activity that seeks profit by providing goods and services to others in exchange for money

business cycle The rise and fall of economic activity over time

business ethics Rules based on moral principles about how businesses and employees ought to conduct themselves

business etiquette Conduct that is considered socially acceptable in business

business plan A written description of a new business venture that describes all aspects of the business

C

canceled checks Checks that have been cashed

capital gain Profit made from the sale of a financial asset such as stock or a house

capital loss Amount lost when an asset is sold for less than its cost

capital resources The things used to produce goods and services

capital Money supplied by investors, banks, or owners of a business. Start-up capital is the money used to pay for the various assets and expenses of a new venture or business.

career Work history of one or more jobs in the same or related fields of interest

cash advance Loan given in cash by a credit card company in anticipation of the borrower's being able to repay it

cash flows The amount of money that is available to a business at any given time

cash-value insurance Insurance that provides both savings and death benefits; also called permanent insurance.

centralized organization An organization that puts authority in one place—with top management

certificate of deposit (CD) Type of savings account that requires a specified amount of money be deposited for a set period of time

channel of distribution A pathway to direct products to consumers

charge account Credit provided by a store or company for customers to buy its products

check register Checkbook log in which an account holder records checking account transactions

check Written order directing a bank to pay money on demand to the person or company named on it

chronological résumé A list of your achievements in time order

claim Request for payment from an insurer for any damages covered by an insurance policy

Key Terms Glossary

clearance sale Sale to clear out goods that are going out of season or are no longer profitable

clicks-and-mortar The use of both the Internet and buildings, such as stores and warehouses, to conduct business

code of ethics A set of guidelines for maintaining ethics in the workplace

coinsurance Percentage of medical expenses that a policyholder must pay beyond the deductible

collateral Property or goods pledged by a borrower to use as security against a loan if the loan is not repaid

collectibles Items that appeal to collectors and investors

collection agent Person or business that collects payments for overdue bills

command economy An economic system in which a central authority makes the key economic decisions

commercial banks Banks that offer the entire range of banking services, such as checking and savings accounts, loans, and financial advice; also called full-service banks

commercial credit Credit used by businesses

commodities exchange Exchange where investors can buy contracts for quantities of a given commodity for delivery at a future date

commodities Items that are traded, especially unprocessed materials such as oil, food grains, and metals

common stock Stock that provides the most basic form of corporate ownership

comparative advantage The ability of a country or company to produce a particular good more efficiently than another country or company

comparison shopping Comparing the prices of competing brands or stores

compensation Pay and benefits

competition The contest between businesses to win customers

compound interest Interest earned on both the principal—the money deposited into a savings account—and any interest earned on it

compulsory insurance law Law that requires drivers to have a minimum amount of car insurance

computer An electronic device that accepts, processes, stores, and outputs data at high speeds, based on programmed instructions

computer-aided design (CAD) Software for designing products with a computer

conflict of interest Conflict between self-interest and professional obligation

conservation The process of preserving, protecting, and planning the management of resources

consolidation loan Loan that combines all your debts into one loan with lower payments

consumer Person who uses goods and services

consumer advocates Groups and individuals who work to protect, inform, and defend consumers

Consumer Credit Protection Act or Truth in Lending Act Federal law that requires creditors to inform consumers about the costs and terms of credit

consumer credit Credit used by people for personal reasons

consumer movement Movement to pass laws protecting consumers from unfair and unsafe business practices

consumer rights Protections included in the Consumer Bill of Rights. They are: the right to be informed, the right to choose, the right to safety, the right to be heard, the right to have problems corrected, the right to consumer education, and the right to service.

contract A legal agreement between two or more parties to do business

controllable risk Risk that can be controlled to minimize the chance of harm

controlling Keeping the company on track and making sure goals are met

cookies Bits of information about a computer user that are stored on the computer user's hard drive

cooperative Organization that is owned and operated by its members

copayment Fee paid each time a service is used

copyright The exclusive legal right given to artists to own their creations

corporate bonds Bonds issued by corporations to finance things such as construction and equipment

corporate culture A company's shared values, beliefs, and goals

corporation Company that is registered by a state and operates apart from its owners

cosigner Someone who agrees to be responsible for a debt if the main applicant does not pay it

cost per thousand (CPM) The media cost of exposing 1,000 readers or viewers to an advertising impression

coupon rate Rate of interest on a bond

cover letter Letter that accompanies a résumé and tells the employer about an applicant, explaining why the person is applying for a job

credit counselor Someone who helps consumers work out a plan for getting out of debt and managing their money

credit limit The maximum amount a card holder can charge on a credit card

credit rating A measure of a person's ability and willingness to pay debts on time

credit report Document showing a person's credit history, including a record of past borrowing and repaying

credit unions Not-for-profit banks set up by organizations for their customers to use

credit An agreement to get money, goods, or services now in exchange for a promise to pay in the future

creditor Person or organization that lends money or provides credit

culture The beliefs, customs, and attitudes of a distinct group of people

current assets Assets that are either used up or converted to cash during the normal cycle of the business

D

database management A computer program used to store data organized especially for rapid search and retrieval

debit card Bank card that immediately takes money from a checking account when it is used

debtor Person who borrows money or uses credit

decentralized organization An organization that gives authority to a number of different managers

deductible Amount in damages a policyholder must pay before the insurance company pays a claim

deductions Amounts that are taken from pay before a worker receives a paycheck

deficit Situation that occurs when more money is spent than is earned or received

deflation A general decrease in the cost of goods and services

delegating Giving managers and employees the power to run things and make decisions.

demand The amount or quantity of goods and services that consumers are willing to buy at various prices

democratic leadership A leadership style in which managers work with employees to make decisions

demographics Facts about the population

departmentalization Dividing responsibility among specific units, or departments

deposit The money put in a bank account

depreciation Decline in value of an asset

depression A deep recession that affects the entire economy and lasts for several years

Key Terms Glossary

desktop publishing Software used to produce publications such as reports, newsletters, and magazines

digital workflow Linking all the steps in a process digitally

direct deposit The electronic transfer of a payment directly from the payer's bank account to the account of the person being paid

direct distribution Distribution of goods or services from the producer directly to the customer

direct-mail advertising Ads sent by mail to people's homes

discrimination Unfair treatment of a person or group, usually because of prejudice about race, ethnicity, age, religion, or gender

diversify To vary investments in order to spread risk or expand

diversity A variety of employees with different backgrounds and identities

dividends A share of profits given to stockholders

down payment A portion of the total cost that is paid when a product or service is purchased

E

e-commerce Electronic commerce, or business conducted on the Internet

economic risk Risk that involves the likelihood of economic loss

economic system The method that a society chooses to use and distribute resources

economics The study of how individuals and groups of individuals strive to satisfy their wants and needs through making choices

e-learning Electronic learning; the process of learning online

electronic funds transfer (EFT) Allows money to be transferred from one bank account to another through a network of computers

embargo A ban on the import or export of a product

employability skills Basic skills that are needed to get, keep, and do well at a job

endorsement Signature of the payee on the back of the check

entrepreneur A person who recognizes a business opportunity and organizes, manages, and assumes the risks of starting and operating a business

entrepreneurial resources The people who recognize opportunities and start businesses

entrepreneurial Acting like an entrepreneur or having an entrepreneurial mindset

entrepreneurship The process of recognizing a business opportunity, testing it in the market, and gathering the resources necessary to start and run a business

entry-level job Job suitable for a worker who is new to a job, field, or subject

Environmental Protection Agency (EPA) A federal agency that enforces rules that protect the environment and control pollution

Equal Credit Opportunity Act Federal law stating that credit applications can be judged only on the basis of financial responsibility

Equal Pay Act Law passed in 1964 that requires men and women be paid the same wages for doing equal work

equilibrium price The point at which the quantity demanded and the quantity supplied meet

equity Value of a piece of property less the amount still owed on the money borrowed to purchase it

ergonomics Design factors for the workplace that are intended to maximize productivity by minimizing a worker's discomfort

e-tail Electronic retail

ethics Moral principles by which people conduct themselves personally, socially, or professionally

e-tickets Electronic tickets

e-workforce People who work with computers while doing business

exchange rate The price at which one currency can buy another currency

executive summary A brief recounting of the key points contained in a business plan

expense Amount of money used to buy or do something

exports Goods and services that one country sells to another country

express warranty Warranty that is explicitly stated, in writing or verbally

extended coverage Other types of protection added to a basic insurance policy

extracurricular activities Activities that students do besides schoolwork

extranet An extension of the intranet of a company or organization that gives authorized outsiders controlled access to the intranet

F

factors of production All the economic resources necessary to produce a society's goods and services

Fair Credit Billing Act Federal law that requires creditors to correct billing mistakes brought to their attention

Fair Credit Reporting Act Federal law that allows individuals to examine and correct information used by credit reporting agencies

Fair Debt Collection Practices Act (FDCPA) Federal law that serves to regulate collection agencies

Federal Deposit Insurance Corporation (FDIC) Government agency that insures bank accounts

Federal Reserve System The central bank of the United States

Federal Trade Commission (FTC) Agency that enforces antitrust laws and regulates interstate trade

finance The function of business that involves money management

finance charge The total amount it costs a borrower to have the lender finance the loan

finance companies Financial institutions that offer short-term loans to businesses and consumers, but at much higher interest rates than banks charge

financial forecast An estimate of a business's financial outlook for each of the next few years

financial institution A firm that manages money

financial plan A set of documents that outline the essential financial facts about a new firm or venture

financial responsibility law Law that requires drivers to pay for any damages or injuries they cause in an accident

financial statements Documents summarizing the changes resulting from business transactions that occur during an accounting period

fixed assets Items of value that are held for more than one year

fixed expenses Expenses that occur regularly and are regularly paid

fixed rate An interest rate that always remains the same

Food and Drug Administration (FDA) A federal government agency that protects consumers from dangerous or falsely advertised products

franchise Contractual agreement to use the name and sell the products or services of a company in a designated geographic area

fraud The crime of obtaining money or some other benefit by deliberate deception

free trade Few or no limits on trade between countries

free-rein leadership A leadership style that requires the leader to set goals for managers and employees and then leaves them alone to get the job done

frequency The number of times an audience sees or hears an ad

full warranty A guarantee about the quality of goods or services.

full-time job A job that requires at least 40 hours of work each week

Key Terms Glossary

G

garnishment of wages A court order to take all or part of a debtor's paycheck if he or she stops making payments

generally accepted accounting principles (GAAP) Rules that provide a way to communicate financial information to others

generic products Plainly labeled, unadvertised products that are sold at lower prices than brand-name goods

global economy The interconnected economies of the nations of the world

goals Things to be accomplished

goods Physical products

grace period Amount of time allowed to repay a debt without having to pay interest charges

grade labels Labels indicating the level of quality of foods

gross domestic product (GDP) The total value of the goods and services produced in a country in a given year

gross pay The total amount of money a worker earns for a specific time

group training Teaching several employees together

H

hacker A person who illegally gains access to and sometimes tampers with information in a computer system

hardware The physical components of a computer system

health maintenance organization (HMO) Organization that provides health care at its own health centers for a fixed fee

hierarchy A formal chain of command with one person at the top who makes all the decisions

homeowners policy Insurance that covers damage to property and personal property, additional living expenses if a home is destroyed, and liability protection

human relations The study of how people interact in the workplace and how communication can be improved

human resources The people employed in a business, commonly referred to as personnel

human resources management The process of finding, selecting, training, and evaluating employees

human risk The risk of harm caused by human mistakes, dishonesty, or another risk that is attributable to people

I

identity theft Theft of a person's financial information for the purpose of committing fraud under that person's identity

imports Goods and services that one country buys from another country

impression A single exposure to an advertising message

impulse buying The act of making unplanned purchases

income The actual amount of money earned or received during a given period

income property Property used to generate income

income statement A report of the revenue, expenses, and net income or net loss for an accounting period

indirect distribution Distribution involving one or more intermediaries

inflation A general increase in the cost of goods and services

inflation risk Risk that the rate of inflation will increase more than the rate of interest on savings

infomercial A 30-minute commercial

information technology (IT) Using computing, electronics, and telecommunications to process and distribute information in digital and other forms

initiative The ability to act and make decisions without the help or advice of others

installment loans Loans repaid in regular payments over a period of time

insurable risk Risk that meets an insurance company's criteria for insurance coverage

insurance Paid protection against loss due to injury or property damage

insurance companies Financial institutions that provide protection against problems such as fire and theft

insurance policy A contract between a person and an insurance company to cover a specific risk

integrity An adherence to a code of ethical values, such as honesty, loyalty, and fairness

interest A fee charged for the use of money

Interest-bearing account An account that pays earns interest on the balance for the depositor

interests An individual's favorite activities

Intermedlary A business that moves goods from one business to another

international trade The exchange of goods and services between nations

Internet A global computer network that connects many computer networks to allow information to flow freely around the world

internship A temporary paid or unpaid position that involves direct work experience in a career field

interstate commerce Business that takes place between states

intranet A computer network within an organization

intrastate commerce Business within each state

investing Committing money or capital in order to gain a financial return

J

job Work that people do for pay; also known as an occupation

job description A detailed outline of the duties, qualifications, and conditions required to do a specific job

job interview A formal face-to-face discussion between an employer and a potential employee

job objective A statement about the type of job a job applicant wants

job shadowing The act of following another worker for a few days on a job

L

labor resources Individuals who make the goods and services for which they are paid

leadership Taking a company and its employees in a direction based upon a vision

leading Providing direction and vision

legal monopoly A company that is allowed to operate without competition

liabilities Creditors' claims to the assets of a business

licenses Legal permits to conduct business

life insurance Insurance that is paid to a person or people designated to receive the funds when the insured person dies

limited liability A claim that holds a firm's owners responsible for no more than the capital that they have invested in it

limited warranty A warranty that covers only certain parts of a product or requires the customer to bear some of the expense when repairs are needed

line and staff authority An organizational structure with direct lines of authority as well as staff who advise line personnel

line authority An organizational structure in which managers at the top of the line are in charge of those beneath them, and so on

liquidity The ability to quickly turn an investment into cash

loss leaders Advertised products that sell at a loss to bring customers into a store

M

management The process of achieving company goals by planning, organizing, directing, controlling, and evaluating the effective use of resources

manufacturers Businesses that make finished products out of processed goods

market A group of customers who share common wants and needs

market economy An economic system in which economic decisions are made in the marketplace, where buyers and sellers meet to exchange goods and services, usually for money

market research The gathering and analysis of information on the size, location, and makeup of a product market

marketing concept The process of determining the wants and needs of customers and providing them more efficiently and effectively than competitors

marketing mix The four main elements of marketing, also called the four Ps: product, place, price, and promotion. It sometimes includes a fifth P, for people.

market segmentation The division of a market for a product into groups of customers who have the same needs and traits

marketing The process of planning, pricing, promoting, selling, and distributing ideas, goods, and services

mass media Means of communication, such as television, radio, and newspapers

maturity date The date when the money deposited into a certificate of deposit becomes available to the depositor

media planning The process of selecting advertising media and deciding the time and space in which the ads should appear

Medicaid Federally and state-funded health-care plan for people who are unable to pay for insurance or health care

Medicare U.S. government's major health insurance program for the elderly

middle managers Managers who carry out the decisions of top management

mission statement A statement that expresses the specific aspirations of a company, the major goals for which it will strive

mixed economy A combination of a market economy and a command economy

monetary system A system in which goods and services are directly exchanged using money

money A standard of value and a means of exchange or payment

money management A method of planning to get the most from one's money

money market deposit account A form of money market fund offered by banks, savings and loans, and credit unions

money market fund A type of mutual fund, or pool of money, put into a variety of short-term debt (less than one year) by businesses and governments

monopoly A company that controls an industry or is the only one to offer a product or service

mortgage An agreement in which a borrower gives a lender the right to take property if a loan is not repaid

mortgage companies Financial institutions that provide loans specifically for buying a home or business

multi-channel retailer A company that uses several means to sell products

multinational corporation A company that does business in many countries and has facilities and offices around the world

municipal bonds Bonds issued by local and state governments to finance city, town, or regional projects such as schools, highways, and airports

mutual fund A fund created by an investment firm that raises money from many shareholders and invests it in a variety of stocks or other investments

N

national debt The total amount of money a government owes

natural resources Raw materials from nature used to produce goods

natural risk The possibility of a catastrophe such as a flood, tornado, hurricane, fire, lightning, drought, or earthquake

needs Things that you must have in order to survive

net pay Gross pay minus deductions

networking The practice of building informal relationships with people whose friendship could bring advantages such as job or business opportunities

no-fault insurance Insurance that requires drivers involved in accidents to collect damages from their own insurance companies no matter who is at fault

nonprofit organization A type of business that focuses on providing a service rather than making a profit

O

occupation Activity in which one engages; also known as a job

Occupational Safety and Health Administration (OSHA) A division of the U.S. Department of Labor that sets and enforces work related health and safety rules

oligopoly A small number of companies that control an industry

on-the-job training Learning a new job by actually doing it

operating system Software that controls the operation of a computer and directs the processing of programs

operational managers Managers who are responsible for the daily operations of a business

opportunity cost What you give up when you make one choice instead of another, sometimes called a tradeoff

organizational chart A chart that shows how the firm is structured and who is in charge of whom

organizing Getting resources arranged in an orderly and functional way to accomplish goals and objectives

orientation The process of helping new employees adjust to a company

outsourcing Using outside sources to do tasks traditionally handled by internal staff

outstanding checks Checks that have been written but have not yet been cashed

overdraft protection A line of credit for overdrawn checks

overdrawing Writing checks for more money than the balance in the account

owner's equity An owner's claims to the assets of a business

P

partnership A business owned by two or more people who share its risks and rewards

patent A legal grant for the sole right to own an invention

performance appraisal An evaluation of how well an employee is doing a job

personal financial planning Spending, saving, and investing money to assure a certain kind of lifestyle as well as financial security

personal property Possessions that can be moved, such as furniture, jewelry, and electronic equipment

personality The sum total of a person's feelings, actions, habits, and thoughts; characteristics that make someone special

planning The act or process of creating goals and objectives as well as the strategies to meet those goals and objectives

pollution The contamination of air, water, and land

pop-up ads Ads that appear for a few seconds when a computer user first logs on to the Internet or clicks on to a Web site

Key Terms Glossary

precious gems Rough mineral deposits (usually crystals) that are dug from the earth by miners and then cut and shaped into brilliant jewels

precious metals Valuable ores such as silver, gold, and platinum

pre-existing condition Serious health condition diagnosed before a person obtained health insurance

preferred provider organization (PPO) Group of doctors and hospitals that agree to provide specified medical services to members at prearranged fees

preferred stock Stock that gives the owner the advantage of receiving cash dividends before common stockholders receive any

premium The price an insured person or business pays for insurance protection for a specified period of time

presentation program Software for creating slide shows for presentations

price discrimination Act of charging various prices for the same product or service in different markets or to different customers

price The amount of money given or asked for when goods and services are bought or sold

prime time The time period when the TV or radio audience is the largest

principal The amount of borrowed money that is still owed and on which interest is based

privatization Hiring a business to offer a public good or service

proceeds The face value of a life insurance policy

processors Businesses that change raw materials into more finished products

procurement The buying and reselling of goods that have already been produced

producer A business that gathers raw products in their natural state

product liability The legal responsibility that manufacturers have to make a safe product

production The process of creating, expanding, manufacturing, or improving goods and services

profit The money left over after a business has paid the cost of providing its goods and services

promotion A move to a higher-level job that has more authority, responsibility, and pay

promotional sale A sale that offers a special buy on a new product or product that is in season

property Anything of value that is owned or controlled

prosperity A peak of economic activity

protectionism The practice of the government putting limits on foreign trade to protect businesses at home

pure risk The threat of a loss with no opportunity for gain

Q

qualifications Education, skills, and work experience needed to do a particular job

quota A limit placed on the quantities of a product that can be imported

R

random access memory (RAM) A computer memory used to hold all of the data and instructions required during operations

rate of return The percentage of increase in the value of savings from earned interest

real estate Land and anything attached to it, such as buildings or natural resources

real estate agent A person licensed to arrange the buying and selling of homes and other types of real estate

real property Property attached to land, such as a house, business, garage, or other building

recall An order to take back and repair or replace a product that has defective parts

recession A slowdown of economic activity

recovery A rise in business activity after a recession or depression

Key Terms Glossary

recruitment Actively looking for qualified people to fill a job

recycling The collecting of products for processing so that they can be used again

reference Someone who comments on a job applicant's character and qualifications for a job

regular savings account A savings account that allows consumers to deposit or withdraw money at any time and to earn interest on deposited funds

relationship marketing A strategy to build customer relations

rental property Any type of dwelling unit or other property rented for a length of time

renters insurance Insurance that covers loss or damage to a renter's personal possessions

replacement value The full cost of repairing or replacing property, regardless of its depreciation value

repossess To take back

reserves Funds set aside for emergencies, such as a rush of withdrawals at a bank

residential property Property in which an individual or family lives

resources Items that people can use to make or obtain what they need or want

résumé A summary of an individual's skills, education, and work experience

retailer A business that purchases goods from a wholesaler and sells them to the consumer, the final buyer of the goods

revenue The income that governments get from all sources; the money that comes into a business from the sale of goods and services

rider An addition to an insurance policy that covers specific property or damages

risk The possibility of loss or injury

risk management The systemic process of managing risk to achieve your objectives

S

safe-deposit box A secure box in a bank's vault for the safe storage of a customer's valuables

salary A fixed amount of pay for each week, month, or year

saving Putting money aside for future use

savings and loan associations Financial institutions that hold customers' funds in interest-bearing accounts and invest mainly in mortgage loans

savings bonds Registered bonds that are sold in denominations of $50 to $10,000

scarcity A shortage of resources

search engine A computer program that searches for specific words on the Internet and returns a list of documents in which they were found

secured loan A loan backed by collateral

security A tradable document that shows evidence of debt or ownership

self-managed teams Work groups that supervise themselves. With these teams, the manager's role is replaced by the team leader's role.

separation Leaving a company for any reason

services Tasks that businesses perform for consumers

signature card A record of a bank customer's signature used by the bank to verify the customer's identity

simple interest Interest earned only on money deposited into a savings account, called the principal

skill The ability to perform a task based on training and experience

small business An independently owned business that usually has the owner as its manager

Small Business Administration (SBA) A U.S. agency that protects the interests of small businesses

social responsibility The duty to do what is best for the good of society

software A computer program that contains a set of instructions that tell a computer what to do

sole proprietorship A business owned by only one person

spreadsheet A computerized worksheet for entering and charting data

standard fire policy Insurance that covers damage due to fire or lightning

standard of living The level of material comfort as measured by the goods and services that are available

startup A newly formed business that usually is small

statement of cash flows A financial report that shows incoming and outgoing money during an accounting period (often monthly or quarterly)

stereotype To identify a person by a single trait or as a member of a certain group rather than as an individual

stock exchange An organized market for buying and selling financial securities

stock Share of ownership in a business

stockbroker A person who buys and sells stocks, bonds, and other securities for clients

stop payment An order for a bank not to cash a particular check

subsidies Grants given to lower costs

supply The amount of goods and services that producers will provide at various prices

surplus Extra money that can be spent or saved

sweatshop A shop or factory in which workers are employed for long hours at low wages and under unhealthy conditions

T

target marketing Marketing that helps companies focus on the people most likely to buy their goods or services.

tariff A tax placed on imports to increase their price in the domestic market

tax An amount of money people and businesses pay governments to help run a nation, state, county, city, or town

tax incentives Reductions in taxes that a government gives to a business or an individual to encourage a particular behavior

telecommunications The transmission of information over communication lines

telecommuting An arrangement that allows employees to work at home while communicating with the workplace by phone, fax, or modem

term insurance Insurance that covers a person for a specific period of time

test-market Offering a product in a limited market for a limited time

top-level managers Managers who are responsible for setting goals and planning for the future as well as leading and controlling the work of others

trade The activity of buying and selling goods and services in domestic or international markets

trademark A name, symbol, or characteristic that identifies a product

transfer A move to another job within a company at the same level and pay

transit advertising Posters placed on the sides of buses, in subway stations, inside trains, and at airports

trust A group of companies that band together to form a monopoly and cut out competition

turnover The number of employees who leave an organization and are replaced over a certain period

U

uncontrollable risk Risk that cannot be controlled to minimize the chance of harm

undeveloped property Unused land intended only for investment purposes

uninsurable risk Risk that is unacceptable to insurance carriers because the likelihood of loss is too high

unlimited liability A liability that holds the owner fully responsible for a company's debts

unsecured loan A loan that is not backed by collateral

usury law A law restricting the amount of interest that can be charged for credit

V

values Important beliefs and ideas that guide a person's decisions and life

variable expenses Expenses that change and can be controlled more easily than fixed expenses

variable rate An adjustable interest rate charged by financial institutions such as banks

virtual business or **dot-com company** A business that operates on the Internet

virtual reality An artificial, three-dimensional visual world created by a computer

virus A program that is part of another and inserts copies of itself, often damaging the stored data

vision statement A statement that establishes the scope and purpose of a company and reflects its values and beliefs

volunteerism Working without pay

W

wage An amount of money paid to an employee on an hourly basis

wants Things that a person does not have to have to survive, but would like to have

warranty A written guarantee from the manufacturer or distributor that states the conditions under which a product can be returned, replaced, or repaired

wearable computer A small portable computer that is designed to be worn on the body during use

Web browser A computer program used for displaying and viewing Web pages

webcast A broadcast made on the Internet

wholesaler A business that distributes goods; also known as a distributor

withdrawal The money taken out of a bank account

word processing Writing, editing, and producing documents, such as letters and reports, through the use of a computer program

World Wide Web A system for accessing, changing, and downloading a large set of hypertext-linked documents and other files located on computers connected through the Internet

Y

yield The amount of money an investment earns

Academic Vocabulary Glossary

A

access The act of approaching or entering; to get at

accommodation The provision of what is needed; adaptation or adjustment

accumulate To increase gradually in quantity or number

accurate Free from error, especially as the result of care

achieve To carry out successfully; accomplish

achievement A result gained by effort

acquire To get as one's own

adaptable Capable of changing

adequate Sufficient for a specific requirement

adjust To adapt or conform

administrator One who manages or supervises

affect To produce an effect upon

allocate To apportion for a specific purpose or to particular persons or things

alteration The act of making something different

alternative One of two or more things, courses, or propositions to be chosen

analyze To study or determine the nature and relationship of component parts

annual Occurring or happening every year or once a year

anticipate The act of looking forward

approach The taking of preliminary steps toward a particular purpose

area A geographic region

assemble To bring together for a particular purpose

assess To determine the importance, size, or value

assignment A specified task

associate To connect one thing with another in the mind

assurance A statement intended to inspire confidence

attitude A feeling or emotion toward a fact or state

author One who originates or creates

authority The power to influence or command thought, opinion, or behavior

authorize To invest with legal authority

automatic Done by machine; mechanical

available Present or ready for immediate use

aware Having or showing realization, perception, or knowledge

B

behalf In the interest of or to benefit someone else

benefit An advantage

bond An interest-bearing certificate of public or private indebtedness

bulk Not divided into parts or packaged in separate units

C

challenging Arousing competitive interest, thought, or action

civil Of or relating to citizens

comment To make an observation or remark expressing an opinion or attitude

commission A fee paid to an agent or employee for transacting a piece of business or performing a service

commit To pledge or assign

common Shared by two or more parties

communicate To transmit information, thought, or feeling so that it is satisfactorily received or understood

community A body of persons of common and especially professional interests scattered through a larger society

compare To examine and note the similarities or differences of

complement To fill out or complete

complex A whole structure (such as a building) made up of interconnected or related structures

comprehensive Covering completely or broadly

concept Something conceived in the mind

conduct A mode or standard of personal behavior

conflict Competitive or opposing action of incompatibles

consider To think about carefully

consist To be composed or made up—usually with *of*

constant Continually occurring or recurring

contact To get in communication with

contribute To play a significant part in bringing about an end or result

control To exercise power or influence over something

controversy A discussion marked especially by the expression of opposing views

conversely Reversed in order, relation, or action

convert To change from one form or function to another

convince To bring to belief, consent, or a course of action

cooperate To act or work with another or others

create To produce or bring about by a course of action or behavior

criteria Standards on which a judgment or decision may be based

crucial Of extreme importance

D

data Factual information used as a basis for reasoning, discussion, or calculation

decade A period of 10 years

decline The state of decreasing

demand An urgent request

demonstrate To illustrate and explain, especially with examples

design To devise for a specific function or end

despite In spite of

determine To settle or decide by choice of alternatives or possibilities

device A piece of equipment

display To put or spread before the viewer

dispose To get rid of

dispute A disagreement

distinct Distinguishable to the eye or mind as discrete; separate

distribute To divide among several or many

diverse Differing from one another

document A writing conveying information

duration Time during which something exists or lasts

E

edit To alter, adapt, or refine, especially to bring about conformity to a standard or to suit a particular purpose

element A constituent part

eliminate To put an end to; remove

emphasis Special importance or significance

enable To make possible, practical, or easy

encounter To come upon or experience, especially unexpectedly

enforce To carry out effectively

enormous Marked by extraordinarily great size, number, or degree

ensure To make sure, certain, or safe

error Something produced by mistake

establish To gain full recognition or acceptance

estate The assets and liabilities left by a person at death

estimate To determine roughly the size, extent, or nature of

ethnic Of or relating to large groups of people classed according to common racial, national, tribal, religious, linguistic, or cultural origin or background

evaluate To determine the significance, worth, or condition of, usually by careful appraisal and study

evident Capable of being seen or noticed

Academic Vocabulary Glossary

exceed To be greater than or superior to

expand To increase the extent, number, volume, or scope of

expert Someone with special knowledge or ability

F

facilitate To help bring about

factor One that actively contributes to the production of a result

feature A prominent part or characteristic

federal Of or relating to the central government or a federation as distinguished from the governments of the constituent units

fee A sum paid or charged for a service

final Last in a series, process, or progress

flexible Characterized by a ready capability to adapt to new, different, or changing requirements

fluctuate To shift back and forth uncertainly

focus To concentrate attention or effort

formula A group of symbols associated to express facts or data concisely

function The action for which a person or thing is specially fitted or used or for which a thing exists

fund A sum of money or other resources set apart for a specific purpose

G

gender A sex, or the behavioral, cultural, or psychological traits typically associated with one sex

generate To bring into existence, produce

goal The end toward which effort is directed

grant To give or transfer formally

guarantee An assurance for the fulfillment of a condition

guideline An indication of policy or conduct

H

hence Because of a preceding fact or premise

I

identify To establish the identity of

illustrate To show clearly

image A visual representation of something

impact A significant or major effect

incentive Something that incites or has a tendency to incite to determination or action

incline To lean, tend, or become drawn toward

income A gain or recurrent benefit usually measured in money that derives from capital or labor

incorporate Unite or work into something already existent so as to form an indistinguishable whole

indicate To point out or point to

individual A single human being

initiate To cause or facilitate the beginning of

injure To inflict bodily harm

insert To put into something

instance A step, stage, or situation viewed as part of a process or series of events

institution An established organization or corporation

integral Essential to completeness

integrity The quality of possessing firm moral principles and values

interact To act together, toward others, or with others

intermediate Being or occurring at the middle place, stage, or degree between extremes

internal Of, relating to, or occurring on the inside of an organized structure

involve To engage as a participant

issue To put forth or distribute, usually officially

item A distinct part in an enumeration, account, or series; an article

J

justify To prove or show to be just, right, or reasonable

L

label To describe or designate with or as if with a label

labor Human activity that provides goods or services in an economy

link To couple or connect

locate To determine or indicate the place, site, or limits of

M

maintain Keep in an existing state

major Greater in dignity, rank, importance, or interest

manual A book that is conveniently handled; a handbook

mature To become due

mean To indicate or signify

media A channel or system of communication, information, or entertainment

medical Of, relating to or concerned with physicians or the practice of medicine

medium Intermediate in quantity, quality, position, size, or degree

mental Of or relating to the mind

method A procedure or process for attaining an object

military Of or relating to soldiers, arms, or war

minimize To reduce or keep to a minimum

minimum The least quantity assignable, admissible, or possible

mode Particular form or variety of something

monitor To watch, keep track of, or check

mutual Shared in common

N

network A group of radio or television stations linked by wire or radio relay

nevertheless In spite of that; however

nuclear Produced by a nuclear reaction (as fission)

O

objective Something toward which effort is directed

observe To watch carefully

obtain Gain or attain, usually by planned action or effort

occurrence Something that occurs; an event

option An alternate course of action; a choice

order A request or demand

overall Including everything

overseas Situated, originating in, or relating to lands beyond the sea

P

panel A group of persons who discuss a topic of public interest

participate Have a part or share in something

partner A member of a partnership, especially in a business

percentage The result obtained by multiplying a number by a percent

perform To carry out a function

period A portion of time determined by some recurring phenomenon

physical Having material existence

plus In addition to

policy A definite course or method of action selected from among alternatives and in light of given conditions to guide and determine present and future decisions

portion A part or share of something

pose To pretend to be someone else

Academic Vocabulary Glossary

potential Existing in possibility

predict To declare or indicate in advance

primary Of first rank, importance, or value

prime Having the highest quality or value

principle A rule or code of conduct

priority Something given or meriting attention before competing alternatives

process A series of actions or operations leading to an end

professional One who engages in a pursuit or activity professionally

prohibit Forbidden by authority

project To plan, figure, or estimate for the future

publication A published work such as a magazine or journal

purchase To obtain by paying money or its equivalent

purpose The goal or intended outcome of something

pursue Employing measures to obtain or accomplish

Q

quote To state the current price of something

R

random Lacking a definite plan, purpose, or pattern

range A series of things in a line

region A broad geographic area distinguished by similar features

registered Enrolled formally

regulate To bring under the control of law or constituted authority

reject To refuse to accept or acknowledge

relationship The state of being related or interrelated

relaxed Easy of manner; informal

release To make available to the public

rely To be dependent

remove Get rid of; eliminate

require Demand as necessary or essential

research To collect information about a particular subject

resolved Cleared up, decided

resource A source of supply or support

respond To react in response

restore To bring back to or put back into a former or original state

restrict To confine within bounds

retain Keep in possession or use

reveal To make publicly or generally known

revise Look over again in order to correct or improve

role A function or part performed, especially in a particular operation or process

route An established or selected course, travel, or action

S

scenario An account or synopsis of a possible course of action or events

schedule A procedural plan that indicates the time and sequence of each operation

scheme An elaborate and systematic plan of action, especially a crafty or secret one

section A distinct part or portion of something written

sector A sociological, economic, or political subdivision of society

secure Free from risk or loss

seek Go in search of

series A number of things or events of the same class coming one after another in spatial or temporal succession

set Put into a position

shift To change the place, position, or direction of

significant Of a noticeably or measurably large amount

similar Having characteristics in common

simulate To give or assume the appearance or effect of

sole Having no sharer; being the only one

source One that provides information

specific Applying to, characterized by, or distinguishing something particular, special, or unique

stable Firmly established

strategy A careful plan or method

stress To emphasize

structure Coherent form or organization

submit Present or propose to another for review, consideration, or decision

sufficient Enough to meet the needs of a situation

suggest To mention or imply as a possibility

sum The result of adding numbers

summary An abstract, abridgment, or compendium

supplement Something that completes or makes an addition

survey A detailed critical inspection

survivor One who remains alive after the death of

sustain To give support or relief to

symbol Something that stands for or suggests something else by reason of relationship, association, convention, or accidental resemblance

T

task A usually assigned piece of work often to be finished within a certain time

team A number of persons associated together in work or an activity

technical Of or relating to proficiency in a practical skill

technique A method of accomplishing a desired aim

technology The practical application of knowledge, especially in a particular area

temporary Lasting for a limited time

theory A hypothesis assumed for the sake of argument or investigation

trace Discover signs, evidence, or remains of

tradition An inherited, established, or customary pattern of thought, action, or behavior

transferable The ability to be moved to a different place, region, or situation

transit The transportation of passengers by means of a local public transportation system

transmit To send or convey from one person or place to another

transport To transfer or convey from one place to another

trend A prevailing tendency or inclination

U

ultimate Last in a progression or series

undergo Submit to

unique Distinctively characteristic

utilize To make use of

V

valid Having legal efficacy or force

vary To make differences between items

vehicle A means of carrying or transporting something

version A form or variant of a type or original

via By way of

vision An image or concept in the imagination

visual Capable of being seen; visible

W

welfare The state of doing well, especially in respect to good fortune, happiness, well-being, or prosperity

Index

A

AARP. *See* American Association of Retired Persons (AARP)

ability, 353

Academic Skills and Abilities
  civil engineering, 581
  computer-aided design, 491
  computer hardware development, 287
  educational camp director, 383
  e-travel, 249
  food services, 69
  information technology consulting, 343
  manufacturing, 157
  paper manufacturing, 437
  physical therapy clinic, 635
  software development, 211

access cards, 207

accommodation, for persons with disabilities, 278, 280

accountant, 300

accounting
  balance sheet, 304
  for business, 300–301
  as business function, 102
  computerized, 305
  defined, 300
  electronic data interchange (EDI) and, 300
  financial claims in, 301–302
  financial reports and, 301
  financial statements, 302–305
  generally accepted accounting principles (GAAP), 301
  income statement, 303
  "language of business," 301
  property ownership and control, 301–302
  questionable, 301
  statement of cash flows, 304–305
  terms used in, 301–302
  See also financial plan

accounting equation, 302

accounting period, 302

accounting software, 143, 300, 303, 304, 336

accounts payable, 302

accounts receivable, 301

Ace Hardware, 393

ACORN. *See* Association of Community Organizations for Reform Now (ACORN)

action-orientation, of successful entrepreneurs, 77

action plan, for financial goals, 500

actual cash value
  collision insurance, 606
  homeowners insurance, 613

actual damages (insurance), 611

adaptation to change, 354

adaptive technologies, 278

ad campaigns, 240

additional living expenses insurance, 611, 612

addition, of multiple numbers, 512

Adecco (employment agency), 359

Adobe InDesign desktop publishing software, 336

Advanced Physical Therapy, P.C., 585, 634–635

advertising
  bait-and-switch tactic, 410
  as consumer information source, 429, 431
  for credit cards, 478
  cross-cultural, 237
  defined, 103, 235
  emotional, 396
  false, 182
  humor in, 236
  information in, 396
  out of state, 182
  rational, 396
  slogans, 235
  studying, by consumers, 396
  top 10 companies by dollars spent, 236

advertising agencies, 240

advertising media
  cross-cultural advertising, 237
  direct-mail, 237
  directory, 237
  infomercials, 236
  magazines, 236
  mass media, 235
  newspapers, 235
  online, 238
  outdoor, 238
  print media, 235
  radio, 237
  television, 236
  transit, 238
  webcasting, 238
  why companies advertise, 235
  See also media measurement; media rates; target markets

advertising rates. *See* media rates

Aetna, 627

African Americans, in management positions, 279

age
  Age Discrimination in Employment Act, 280
  baby boom generation, 279, 354
  of computer users, 314, 315
  of employees, work permits and, 367
  life expectancy chart, 622
  older workers, 259
  of people uninsured, 628
  of retirement, working past, 279
  retirement account balances by, 532
  of U.S. workers, 279

Age Discrimination in Employment Act, 280

ageism, 280

agency bonds, 550

aggressive portfolio, 162

Agora Partnerships, 100

agreements. *See* business agreements, protecting

agriculture
  gross domestic product (GDP) and, 50
  subsidies for, 187

agriculture-based economy, 39

air bags, 595

algebra
  equations, 18, 106, 122, 146, 154
  graphing, quantitative relationships, and, 34
  solving for the unknown, 380
  variables and expressions, 4

algebraic expressions, 4, 74

Alienware, 253, 286–287

alliances, in trade, 172–173

allocation of resources, by governments, 189

allowance (teen income), 500

Alternative Board, The (TAB), 118

American Association of Retired Persons (AARP), 259, 397

American City Business Journals, 78

American Express, 451

American Stock Exchange (Amex), 557

Americans with Disabilities Act (ADA), 62, 280

Amex. *See* American Stock Exchange (Amex)

Index

X

Y

Z

Credits

Photo Credits

Cover: Jeremy Woodhouse/Masterfile.

AFP/Getty Images **251**; age fotostock/SuperStock **55**, **365**, **483**, **555**; Courtesy of Alienware **252–253**, **286**(br), **286**(tl); Bartomeu Amengual/eStock Photography **342**(br); Artiga Photo/Corbis **255**; Artiga Photo/Masterfile **109**; BananaStock/SuperStock RF **xvii**, **443**; Paul Barton/Corbis **134**; Blend Images/Getty Images RF **458**; Brand X Pictures/Jupiter Images (RF) **214–215**; Rolf Bruderer/ Masterfile **565**; William Thomas Cain/Getty Images **217**; Courtesy of Calhoun & Hill **495**(tr); Yvette Cardozo/Index Stock **248**(tl); Ken Chernus/Getty Images **xiv**, **348**; Steve Chenn/Corbis **162**; Benjamin Clasen **2–3**, **68**(tl); Comstock/Jupiterimages RF **466**; Comstock/ SuperStock RF **125**; Gary Conner/Index Stock **311**; Corbis/Royalty Free **71**, **113**, **145**, **210**(tl) **446**, **463**, **529**, **584–585**, **634**(br), **634**(tl); Creartas/SuperStock RF **53**; David Kelly Crow/PhotoEdit **150**; Bob Daemmrich/PhotoEdit **263**; © Dell Inc. All rights reserved. Reprinted by permission. **429**; Dex images/Corbis **xix**, **603**; George B. Diebold/Corbis **xi**, **195**; Digital Vision Ltd./SuperStock RF **101**; Digital Vision/Getty Images (RF) **72–73**, **376**; DLILLC/Corbis **156**(br); Patrick Durand/Corbis Sygma **161**(tr); Courtesy of Enlightened Partners **291**(tr); Rachel Epstein/PhotoEdit **412**; Courtesy of Expeditiontrips.com **248**(br); Gaetano/Corbis **436**(tl); Courtesy of Geomagic **490**(br), **490**(tl); Getty Images/Royalty Free **159**, **583**, **637**; Michael Goldman/Masterfile **342**(tl); Rick Gomez/Masterfile **374**; Dale Guldan/Index Stock **611**; David P. Hall/Masterfile **389**; Toru Hanai/Reuters/Corbis **226**; Al Harvey/Masterfile **623**; Larry Hirshowitz/Corbis **7**; Jack Hollingsworth/Getty Images RF **viii**, **141**; Dave G. Houser/Post/Houserstock/Corbis **241**; Index Stock RF **580**(br); Chad Johnston/Masterfile **xii**, **293**; Joson/zefa/Corbis **5**; Jupiter Images/Royalty Free **345**; Jupiter Images/Superstock **213**; Catherine Karnow/Corbis **439**; Michael Keller/Corbis **497**, **499**, **513**, **585**(tr); Michael Keller/Index Stock **580**(tl); Rich La Salle/Index Stock **41**; Lester Lefkowitz/Getty Images **494–495**; Darryl Leniuk/Masterfile **386–387**; Wang Leng/Getty Images **396**; Chris Leslie Smith/PhotoEdit **320**; James Leynse/Corbis **167**; Lissette LeBon/SuperStock **46**; Robert Llewellyn/Imagestate **537**; R. Ian Lloyd/ Masterfile **62**; Tim Mantoani/Masterfile **75**; Don Mason/Corbis **289**; Masterfile/Royalty Free **156**(tl), **179**, **273**, **326**, **382**(tl), **421**, **619**; Joe McBride/Getty Images **vi**, **37**; Jim McGuire/Index Stock **183**; Media Bakery RF **160–161**; Roy Morsch/zefa/Corbis **475**; Courtesy of Rachel Muir **347**(tr); Jaro Munoz/epa/Corbis **440–441**; Eric Nguyen/Jim Reed Photography/Corbis **xx**, **587**; Owaki-Kulla/ Corbis **93**; Gabe Palmer/zefa/Corbis **13**; Courtesy of P.B.Loco **2–3**(r), **68**(br); Jose Luis Pelaez, Inc./Corbis **270**; Photodisc Green/ Getty Images (RF) **405**; Nicholas Prior/Getty Images **346–347**; Purestock/SuperStock RF **232**; Bryan Regan Photography/Raleigh NC **441**(tr); Reuters/Corbis **221**, **591**; Mark Richards/PhotoEdit **313**; Chris Rogers/Index Stock **436**(br); Rubberball/Jupiter Images RF **382**(br); Chuck Savage/Corbis **253**(tr); Courtesy of Seventh Generation **73**(tr); George Shelley/Masterfile **385**; Scott Sinklier/Corbis **452**; Scott Smith/Index Stock **25**; Ron Stroud/Masterfile **351**; Justin Sullivan/Getty Images **331**; SuperStock Royalty Free **493**; Tim Tadder/Corbis **290–291**; Mario Tama/Getty Images **545**; ThinkStock LLC/Index Stock RF **210**(br); ThinkStock/SuperStock **329**; Tim Davis/Getty Images **387**(tr); Ty Milford/Getty Images **215**(tr); Susan Van Etten/PhotoEdit **357**; Ron Wurzer/Getty Images **97**; David Young-Wolff/PhotoEdit **21**, **84**, **197**, **297**.

Extended Figure Sources

Figure 4.1: 2005 National Business Ethics Survey, Ethics Resource Center; **Figure 5.1:** *Entrepreneurship & Small Business Management, 2006;* **Figure 5.2:** *Entrepreneurship & Small Business Management, 2006;* **Figure 6.1:** BizStats.com, 2003; **Figure 9.1:** ComScore Media Metrix (reported online at www.infoplease.com); **Figure 10.1:** U.S. Census Bureau (2004 cumulative); **Figure 11.1:** Tax Foundation, http://www.taxfoundation.org; **Figure 14.1:** Advertising Age; **Figure 14.2:** *The World Almanac and Book of Facts 2005;* **Figure 15.1:** CareerBuilder.com, http://careerbuilder.com; **Figure 16.1:** Civilian Labor Force and Participation (projections by 2014). U.S. Bureau of Labor Statistics, Civilian Labor Force and Participation; **Figure 18.1:** "Computer Usage in the U.S." Time Almanac 2005; **Figure 19.1:** Microsoft Office Publisher; **Figure 20.1:** "What Work Requires of Schools: A SCANS Report for America 2000." U.S. Department of Labor, http://www.dol.gov; **Figure 21.1:** U.S. Census Bureau, Bureau of Labor Statistics, 2003; **Figure 22.2:** "How America Shops." Retail Traffic, http://retailtrafficmag.com/mag/retail_america_shops; **Figure 23.2:** J.D. Power and Associates, http://consumercenter.jdpower.com/cc/rd/cc/index.asp; **Figure 24.1:** Recalls.gov, http://www.recalls.gov; **Figure 27.1:** Federal Trade Commission, http://ftc.gov/ftc/consumer.htm; **Figure 27.2:** Federal Trade Commission, http://ftc.gov/ bcp/conline/edcams/credit/index.html; **Figure 28.1:** Consumer Expenditure Survey, 2004. U.S. Department of Labor, Bureau of Labor Statistics, http://www.bls.gov/cex/csxreprt.htm; **Figure 31.1:** TreasuryDirect, http://www.savingsbonds.gov/indiv/indiv.htm; **Figure 32.1:** DeKaser, Richard J., and John G. Charamonde. "Housing Prices in America: Valuation Methodology & Findings." National City Corporation, July 2005; **Figure 34.1:** Allstate Insurance Company, http://www.allstate.com/ClaimsCenter/PropertyClaim/ pagerender.asp?page=main.htm; **Figure 35.1:** *The World Almanac and Book of Facts 2006;* **Figure 35.2:** The World Almanac and Book of Facts 2006

***BusinessWeek* Sources**

From Adversity, Software Success, April 12, 2005, Newsmaker Q&A; *Graphing the Development Gap*, February 22, 2006, Andrew Blum; Net or Newspapers?, July 4, 2005, Jon Fine; *It's Getting Easier Being Green*, December 5, 2005, Taja di Leonardi; Get Creative! August 1, 2005, Bruce Nussbaum; *For the Poor, Help from MBAs*, August 17, 2005, Francesca DiMeglio; *Dig Before You Decide*, March 15, 2006, Keith McFarland; *Memo to Students: Writing Skills Matter*, April 26, 2006, Julie Gordon; *Technology's Impact on Business*, June 20, 2005, Cliff Edwards; *Going Global For An MBA*, March 2, 2006, Jack Ewing, Kerry Capell, Andrea Zammert; *How China Controls the Internet*, January 13, 2006, Bruce Einhorn; *Peter Kight's Excellent Adventure*, February 6, 2006; *The Art of Chinese Relationships*, January 6, 2006, Michelle Dammon Loyalka; *TV Eyeballs Close-Up*, March 27, 2006, Timothy J. Mullaney; *What Works: Eyes On The Prize*, December 5, 2005, Virginia Munger Kahn; *Fashion, with a Conscience*, November 1, 2004; *I Am My Own Accountant*, March 20, 2006, Larry Armstrong; *Math Will Rock Your World*, January 23, 2006, Stephen Barker, Bremen Leak; *Digital Books Start A New Chapter*, February 27, 2006, Burt Helm; *Picture Your Business with a Logo*, April 5, 2006, Stacy Perman; *These Technicians Are Better Than Robots*, December 26, 2005, Kenji Hall, Hiroko Tashiro; *All Together Now*, December 5, 2005, Rachael King; *HP Wants Your Old PCs Back*, April 10, 2006, Lorraine Woellert; *How to Stand Up to the Nickel-and-Dimers*, September 29, 2003, Toddi Gutner; *Big Plastic's Online Challenger*, December 30, 2005, Peter Burrows; *Personal Finance for Freshmen*, November 14, 2005, Lindsey Gerdes; *Stopping a Scam from Spreading*, April 3, 2006, Sonja Ryst; *Follow My Money*, March 6, 2006, Jessi Hempel; *Fiscal Fitness for Teens*, July 5, 2005, Isabelle Sender; *Not Your Average Science Project*, February 20, 2006, Lauren Young; *Copper's Golden Hue*, May 9, 2006, Mara DerHovanesian, Colin Barraclough; *Winning the Game of Risk*, April 6, 2006, Marc Hogan; *The Fixer-Upper Fixes Up*, December 5, 2005, Eve Tahmincioglu; *Health Care: Benefits Surprise*, December 5, 2005, Joshua Kendall.

Teacher Wraparound Edition